THE LETTERS OF
T. S. ELIOT
VOLUME 5

By T. S. Eliot

THE COMPLETE POEMS AND PLAYS

verse
COLLECTED POEMS 1909–1962
FOUR QUARTETS°
THE WASTE LAND AND OTHER POEMS
THE WASTE LAND:
A Facsimile and Transcript of the Original Drafts
edited by Valerie Eliot
INVENTIONS OF THE MARCH HARE:
POEMS 1909–1917
edited by Christopher Ricks
SELECTED POEMS

plays
MURDER IN THE CATHEDRAL
THE FAMILY REUNION
THE COCKTAIL PARTY
THE CONFIDENTIAL CLERK
THE ELDER STATESMAN

literary criticism
THE SACRED WOOD
SELECTED ESSAYS
THE USE OF POETRY AND THE USE OF CRITICISM
VARIETIES OF METAPHYSICAL POETRY
edited by Ronald Schuchard
TO CRITICIZE THE CRITIC
ON POETRY AND POETS
FOR LANCELOT ANDREWES
SELECTED PROSE OF T. S. ELIOT
edited by Frank Kermode

social criticism
THE IDEA OF A CHRISTIAN SOCIETY
edited by David Edwards
NOTES TOWARDS THE DEFINITION OF CULTURE

letters
THE LETTERS OF T. S. ELIOT
Volume 1: 1898–1922
Revised Edition
edited by Valerie Eliot and Hugh Haughton
THE LETTERS OF T. S. ELIOT
Volume 2: 1923–1925
edited by Valerie Eliot and Hugh Haughton
THE LETTERS OF T. S. ELIOT
Volume 3: 1926–1927
edited by Valerie Eliot and John Haffenden
THE LETTERS OF T. S. ELIOT
Volume 4: 1928–1929
edited by Valerie Eliot and John Haffenden

THE LETTERS OF
T. S. Eliot

EDITED BY
VALERIE ELIOT
AND
JOHN HAFFENDEN

VOLUME 5
1930–1931

Yale
UNIVERSITY PRESS
New Haven & London

First published in the
United States in 2015 by Yale University Press.
First published in
Great Britain in 2014 by Faber and Faber Limited.

Yale University Press books may be
purchased in quantity for educational, business, or
promotional use. For information, please e-mail sales.press@yale.edu
(U.S. office) or sales@yaleup.co.uk (U.K. office).

Typeset by Donald Sommerville.
Printed in the United States of America.

Library of Congress Control Number: 2014952943
ISBN 978-0-300-21179-5 (cloth: alk. paper)

A catalogue record for this book is available from the British Library.

This paper meets the requirements of
ANSI/NISO Z39.48-1992 (Permanence of Paper).

10 9 8 7 6 5 4 3 2 1

CONTENTS

ILLUSTRATIONS

ACKNOWLEDGEMENTS

For help and advice in many capacities, including copyright permissions, the publishers and editors would like to thank the following individuals and institutions. (Sadly, some of those named below are now deceased, but we wish still to put on record our gratitude to them.) Dr Donald Adamson; The American Jewish Archives, Cincinnati, Ohio; Dr Norma Aubertin-Potter, Librarian in Charge, Codrington Library, All Souls College, Oxford; Joan Bailey; Owen Barfield; Tansy Barton, Special Collections Administrator, Senate House Library, London; H. Baugh; T. O. Beachcroft; Anne Olivier Bell; Bibliothèque Nationale, Paris; Kenneth Blackwell, McMaster University; Michael Harry Blechner, McFarlin Library, University of Tulsa; Mary Boccaccio, McKeldin Library, University of Maryland; Maxwell Bodenheim; John Bodley; William H. Bond; University of Bonn Library; Ann Bowden; British Library; Valerie Brokenshire; Jewel Spears Brooker; Robert Brown, Archivist, Faber & Faber Ltd; Richard Buckle; Penelope Bulloch, Balliol College Library; Professor P. H. Butter; William R. Cagle and Saundra Taylor, Lilly Library; University of California, Los Angeles; Douglas Campbell; Humphrey Carpenter; François Chapon, Bibliothèque Littéraire Jacques Doucet; Mrs Charlton; Dr Joseph Chiari; David Chinitz; Alexander P. Clark, Firestone Library, Princeton University; Alan Clodd; Marguerite Cohn; John Constable; Joyce Crick; Arthur Crook; Tony Cuda; Dr Robin Darwall-Smith, Archivist, University College, Oxford; Roy Davids; Dr A. Deiss, General Secretariat, Swiss Medical Institutions; Giles de la Mare; the Literary Trustees of Walter de la Mare; Rodney G. Dennis; Valentine Dobrée; Kenneth W. Duckett, Southern Illinois University at Carbondale; Ellen S. Dunlap, Harry Ransom Humanities Research Center; Peter du Sautoy; Donald D. Eddy, Department of Rare Books, Cornell University Library; Professor Charles W. Eliot; Sarah Ethier, University of Wisconsin-Milwaukee Libraries; Matthew Evans; Sir Richard Faber, KCVO; Toby Faber; Elizabeth A. Falsey; Christopher Farley; David Farmer, Harry Ransom Humanities Research Center (and Warren Roberts, Mary Hirth, Mrs Sally Leach, and other members of staff); Anton Felton, Continuum Ltd; Mrs Harry Fine; Mrs Burnham Finney; Henri Fluchère; Fondren Library; Jennifer Formichelli; Galleria Nazionale d'Arte Moderna,

Rome; Donald Gallup; Special Collections, Isabella Stewart Gardner Museum, Boston, Mass.; K. C. Gay, Lockwood Memorial Library, State University of New York, Buffalo; Herbert Gerwing, University of Victoria; Mrs Ghika; Catherine Gide; Robert Giroux; Estate of Enid Goldsmith; Warwick Gould; Herbert T. Greene; J. C. Hall; Dr Michael Halls; Saskia Hamilton; Sir Rupert Hart-Davis; Professor E. N. Hartley, Institute Archives, MIT; Harvard University Archives; Michael Hastings; The Library, Haverford College; Nicky Hemingway; Cathy Henderson, Harry Ransom Humanities Research Center; Robert Henderson; David Higham Associates Ltd; Roger Highfield; Robert W. Hill, New York Public Library; Michael Hofmann; Michael Holroyd; Judith Hooper; Hornbake Library, University of Maryland; Lélia Howard; Penelope Hughes-Hallett; J. W. Hunt, Royal Military Academy, Sandhurst; Jeremy Hutchinson; Lord Hutchinson; Robin Jackson, The British Academy; Carolyn Jakeman; P. D. James; Dorothy O. Johansen, Reed College, Portland, Oregon; Gregory A. Johnson, Alderman Library, University of Virginia; William Jovanovich; William L. Joyce and Howard C. Rice, Jr., Princeton University; Paul Keegan; Professor John Kelly, St John's College, Oxford; Dr P. Kelly, National Library of Scotland; Mary Kiffer, Assistant Secretary, John Simon Guggenheim Memorial Foundation, New York; Modern Archives Centre, King's College, Cambridge; Monique Kuntz, Bibliothèque Municipale, Vichy; Major N. Aylward Leete; Mrs Dorothy Milburn Léger; Lockwood Memorial Library; Kenneth A. Lohf, Librarian for Rare Books and MSS, Butler Library, Columbia University; London Library; Pat Lowe; Richard Luckett; Richard M. Ludwig, and Howard C. Rice Jr., Princeton University Library; Jim McCue; Mary C. McGreenery, Harvard Alumni Records; Ed Maggs; Professor B. K. Matilal; Francis Mattson, Berg Collection, New York Public Library; R. Russell Maylone, Special Collections Department, Northwestern University Library; Bernard Meehan, Keeper of Manuscripts, Trinity College Dublin; Wim van Mierlo; Mrs Edward S. Mills; University Library, Missouri History Museum; Joe Mitchenson; Kate Mole, Librarian/ Archivist, The British Academy; Frank Vigor Morley; Leslie A. Morris, Houghton Library, Harvard University; Lewis Morris; Tim Munby; Mary Middleton Murry; The Bursar, New College, Oxford; Richard Ollard; James M. Osborn; Anne Owen; Martin Page; Stephen Page; Alasdair Paterson, University of Exeter Library; Fondation Saint-John Perse; Lord Quinton; Craig Raine; Benedict Read; Real Academia de la Historia; Dr R. T. H. Redpath; Joseph Regenstein Library, University of Chicago; Clare Reihill; Dorothy Richards; I. A. Richards; Canon Pierre Riches;

Helene Ritzerfeld; Alain Rivière; Sir Adam Roberts; Rosenbach Museum & Library; Anthony Rota; Carol Z. Rothkopf; Mme Agathe Rouart-Valéry; A. L. Rowse; Lord Russell; Mrs N. Ryan; Professor Alfred W. Satterthwaite; Marcia Satterthwaite; Schiller-Nationalmuseum, Marbach am Neckar; Gerd Schmidt; Susan Schreibman; Rev. Karl Schroeder, SJ; Ronald Schuchard; Grace Schulman; Timothy and Marian Seldes; Miranda Seymour; Christopher Sheppard, Brotherton Collection, Leeds University Library; Ethel C. Simpson, Trustee, John Gould Fletcher Literary Estate; Samuel A. Sizer, Special Collections, University Libraries, University of Arkansas; Janet Adam Smith; Theodora Eliot Smith; Natasha Spender; Sir Stephen Spender; Martha Sprackland; Tom Staley; Dom Julian Stead; Alix Strachey; James Strachey; Kendon L. Stubbs, University of Virginia Library; Barbara Sturtevant; University of Sussex Library; Lola L. Szladits, Berg Collection, New York Public Library; Allen Tate; Elizabeth Stege Teleky, The Joseph Regenstein Library, University of Chicago; David S. Thatcher, University of Victoria, British Columbia; Alan G. Thomas; Dr Michael J. Tilby; Kathleen Tillotson; Trinity College, Cambridge; Francois Valéry; Judith Robinson-Valéry; The Paul Valéry Collection, Bibliothèque Nationale, Paris; University of Virginia Library; Rebecca Volk, Archivist, Jesuits in Britain Archives; Graham Wallas and Angela Raspin, London School of Economics; Michael J. Walsh; Jemma Walton; J. Waterlow; Dr George Watson; John Weightman; John Wells, Cambridge University Library; James White, National Gallery of Ireland; Brooke Whiting, Department of Special Collections, University Research Library, University of California, Los Angeles; Widener Library, Harvard University; Helen Willard; David G. Williams; Dr Charlotte Williamson; George Williamson; Julia Ross Williamson; Patricia C. Willis, Beinecke Rare Book and Manuscript Library, Yale University; Harriet Harvey Wood; Woodson Research Center, Rice University; Dr Daniel H. Woodward, Huntington Library; Yale University Archives; Michael Yeats. For permission to quote from copyright material, we thank Alastair Kershaw (Richard Aldington); The Ezra Pound Literary Property Trust, and James Laughlin (Ezra Pound). Letters by W. H. Auden are copyright the Estate of W. H. Auden, and may not be reprinted without permission. Letters of Harold Raymond are from *Letters of Harold Raymond* by Harold Raymond, published by The Random House Group Limited and are reprinted by permission of The Random House Group Limited. Extracts from unpublished letters by Stephen Spender are courtesy of Matthew Spender. Letter by C. S. Lewis copyright © C. S. Lewis Pte Ltd.

Special thanks go to Matthew Hollis, my editor at Faber and Faber; to Donald Sommerville for his superb and patient copy-editing and typesetting; to Iman Javadi for swift and skilful help with translations; to David Wilson for proofreading; to Douglas Matthews for indexing; to Sara Ayad for researching the pictures; and to Mrs Valerie Eliot's assistant Debbie Whitfield for her steadfast commitment and long hard work. John Haffenden is most grateful to the Arts and Humanities Research Council for assistance with research expenses, and to the Institute of English Studies, University of London, for hosting the AHRC-funded T. S. Eliot Editorial Research Project.

PREFACE

Volume 5 of the *Letters of T. S. Eliot* documents a period of two years in which the poet, critic and editor endeavours, between the ages of forty-two and forty-four, to place his newly avowed faith in Christianity – 'the Catholic Church in England', as he knowingly styles it – at the centre of his life. He tries too to express in his poetry some of the deepest and harshest implications of his faith, including a struggle with renunciation and a reaching for transcendence.

It is a tough time for Eliot, morally and socially. Several of his friends and associates, including Virginia Woolf, Herbert Read and A. L. Rowse, are at odds with his religious commitment; some are even antagonistic or patronising. 'Anyone who has been moving among intellectual circles and comes to the Church, may experience an odd and rather exhilarating feeling of isolation,' he remarks, though the sense of alienation is probably more upsetting than he would admit. The strain is both social and personal. He finds in his religion not devotional delight and balm, but a locus of moral and spiritual struggle very like that of the 'dark night of the soul' of the Spanish mystic St John of the Cross. 'To me,' Eliot writes, 'religion has brought . . . not happiness, but the sense of something above happiness and therefore more terrifying than ordinary pain and misery: the very dark night and the desert.' And he tells his friend John Hayward: 'I know just enough . . . of "the peace of God" to know that it is an extraordinarily painful blessing.' Becoming a Christian means embracing a rigorous ascetic vocation: 'Thought, study, mortification, sacrifice.' The Church is for him fundamentally an institution of order and authority, with 'fixity of dogma'. To William Force Stead he writes: 'The man who disbelieves in any future life whatever is also a believer in Hell . . . People go to Hell, I take it, because they choose to; they cannot get out because they cannot change themselves.' Thus his demanding faith gives ultimate meaning and purpose to his life: now and again in his earlier years, he discloses at this time, he had felt 'on the verge of insanity or imbecility . . . If I had died even five years ago [that is to say, before he became a Christian in 1927], everything that I had suffered up to then would, so far as I can see, have been waste and muddle.'

Eliot becomes an active participant in Church counsels; joins the Literature Committee of the English Church Union, and undertakes to be a 'Departmental Editor' on a projected *Encyclopaedia of the Christian Religion*. In January 1931 he makes his first retreat at the Society of the Sacred Mission, at Kelham in Nottinghamshire. He becomes acquainted with the journalist and writer on mysticism Evelyn Underhill, and entertains at home in London the American journalist and like-minded philosopher Paul Elmer More, whom he considers 'extremely kind . . . loveable'. More momentously, he gains authority as a critical apologist for Church doctrine and deliberations, when he publishes in March 1931 an outspoken pamphlet in the 'Criterion Miscellany' series entitled, with deceptive mildness, *Thoughts After Lambeth*. This brief, sharp essay on the arguments and resolutions of the 300 bishops assembled at the Lambeth Palace Conference of 1930 is written with advice from senior clergy including William Temple, Archbishop of York (and future Archbishop of Canterbury), who approve the value of Eliot's strictures on Christian doctrine. 'The World is trying the experiment of attempting to form a civilised but non-Christian mentality,' writes Eliot at the outset of the 1930s:

> The experiment will fail; but we must be very patient in awaiting its collapse; meanwhile redeeming the time: so that the Faith may be preserved alive through the dark ages before us; to renew and rebuild civilization, and save the World from Suicide.

He composes during this period two of his most tantalising and admired poems. The first is the multilayered, hallucinatory, talismanic, prayerful and penitential set of six lyrics entitled *Ash-Wednesday* (1930) – initially dedicated 'To My Wife' – which he characterises as a 'deliberate modern *Vita Nuova*':

> Redeem
>
> The time. Redeem
> The unread vision in the higher dream
> While jewelled unicorns draw by the gilded hearse.
> [. . .]
> Redeem the time, redeem the dream
> The token of the word unheard, unspoken
>
> Till the wind shake a thousand whispers from the yew
>
> And after this our exile

While denying that this sequence is 'devotional', he humbly declares that 'it attempts to state a particular phase of the progress of one person' – that is to say, 'an intermediate phase' of his own spiritual development. It is about 'the experience of man in search of God, and trying to explain to himself his intenser human feelings in terms of the divine goal'. If it is obscure, he says, he hopes that it expresses a 'good' kind of obscurity – 'the obscurity of any flower: something simple and to be simply enjoyed, but merely incomprehensible as anything living is incomprehensible'.

The other great lyric of this period is the beautifully tactful, wondrous *Marina* (1930). 'The theme is paternity,' he explains: the poem functions as 'a comment on the Recognition Motive in Shakespeare's later plays'. In addition, the first part of the satirical–political and personal nightmare of *Coriolan*, entitled 'Triumphal March', is published in October 1931, with illustrations by the fine artist and designer E. McKnight Kauffer. 'Difficulties of a Statesman' (the second part of *Coriolan*) appears in the French periodical *Commerce*. Eliot publishes too his translation of *Anabase*, by St-John Perse (*nom de plume* of the French diplomat Alexis St Léger Léger).

Eliot's output as critic and lecturer remains as high as ever, despite – and perhaps because of – a home life that is perennially edgy and distressing. He writes an Introduction to Christopher Isherwood's 'bad' translation of Baudelaire's *Journaux Intimes*. He delivers a series of six radio talks on seventeenth-century poetry, covering aspects of the work of Donne, Herbert, Crashaw, Vaughan, Traherne, Marvell, Milton, Cowley and Dryden. He writes an introduction to G. Wilson Knight's study of Shakespeare, *The Wheel of Fire*; an introduction to Johnson's *London: A Poem* and *The Vanity of Human Wishes*; and an introduction to Pascal's *Pensées*, for the Everyman Library. He admires what he terms Pascal's 'unique combination and balance of qualities'. He also contributes three BBC talks to mark the tercentenary of the birth of John Dryden. And he publishes in an American anthology the influential essay 'Donne in Our Time'. Eliot pronounces there: 'Donne was, I insist, no sceptic.'

In his professional career, as a director of Faber & Faber and editor of the small-circulation but influential periodical *The Criterion*, he remarks, with ironic asperity: 'I am not really interested in contemporary literature to begin with, and it frequently happens that what I do like is, by a natural coincidence, published by my own firm.' Despite affecting occasional jadedness – 'Qua publisher I always take a depressed attitude about verse' – he continues to prove himself one of the greatest talent-spotters of the century. In the period covered by this volume of letters, he promptly recognises the talents of the new generation of poets headed by W. H. Auden ('I have been struck from the beginning, not only by his remarkable literary abilities, but by his general activity and curiosity of mind and variety of intellectual interests'), Stephen Spender ('I have hopes, but he is a mere nurseling'), and Louis MacNeice (whose poetry he finds 'very interesting', although he will wait until 1935 to publish MacNeice's collection *Poems*). He prints Auden's *Paid on Both Sides* in the *Criterion*, and brings out Auden's first collection *Poems* from Faber & Faber later the same year. 'Publishing is more venturesome than banking,' he tells an old colleague at Lloyds; and as if to prove the point, he encourages his fellow directors at Faber & Faber to put out James Joyce's *Haveth Childers Everywhere* (the complete work, *Finnegans Wake*, lies some years in the future). But perhaps the one slip of the period occurs when Eliot and his fellow directors turn down a proposal by Eric Blair (George Orwell) to translate from the French a Zolaesque fiction about a Parisian prostitute by Jacques Roberti entitled *À la Belle de Nuit*. (Blair says he is quite familiar with the milieu and the slang made use of in the novel, but that does not avail him.)

In his capacity as mentor and fosterer of upcoming writers, Eliot meets and likes Hugh MacDiarmid (pseudonym of C. M. Grieve). He invites Marianne Moore to contribute to the *Criterion*. He delights in making friends with the curious, charismatic poet Ralph Hodgson. He writes introductions for Seán Ó'Faoláin (among others), with a view to securing for him a foothold in literary journalism and publishing. In addition, he inaugurates regular meetings of the 'Criterion Club' – some of them held at Harold Monro's famous 'Poetry Bookshop' opposite the British Museum – for getting together with regular contributors to the *Criterion* including Bonamy Dobrée and Herbert Read, and with the guests whom they wish to cultivate (they include William Empson).

The domestic background to all this successful professional enterprise remains disrupted and distressing. Virginia Woolf, one of the witnesses to the continuing torment of the Eliots' marriage, relates in her diary that 'Poor Tom is all suspicion, hesitation and reserve . . . There is a leaden sinister look about him. But oh – Vivienne! Was there ever such a torture since life began! . . . This bag of ferrets is what Tom wears round his neck.' According to another friend, Vivien is 'positively hostile' to Eliot's involvement in religious affairs, deriding them as 'monastic'. It is perhaps symptomatic of the mutual discontent of Eliot and his wife that they cannot settle on a place to live in peace: they move house every few months, from 177 Clarence Gate Gardens (near Regent's Park) to

43 Chester Terrace (close to Eaton Square), and then back to 68 Clarence Gate Gardens. After dining with the couple, Eliot's old friend Conrad Aiken gossips that he found Vivien 'shivering, shuddering, a scarecrow of a woman' who 'directed at T[om] a cold stream of hatred'. Vivien reports feeling a 'fearful shock' when her brother Maurice suddenly marries, without notice, a young American named Ahmé Hoagland. Eliot confirms that this event has 'desolated' her. (Perhaps her brother's rush to marry a young American revives in her sorry feelings about her own rushed and secretive marriage to Eliot in 1915.) Eliot seeks to encourage her to develop independence and her own circle of acquaintance, and strives to ensure that friends including Ottoline Morrell, Mary Hutchinson and Alida Monro see as much as possible of Vivien by herself: 'the more people she can see without me the more people I might be able to see without her!' Having said so much, he promptly rephrases the observation more positively: 'If she can be persuaded to believe that people she likes want to see her, the more self-confidence and independence she might acquire.' The American academic Willard Thorp, who visits the Eliots at home in London at this time, notes that Eliot is obliged to deal with Vivien 'like a patient father with a fractious child'.

A respite from the developing moral void of his home life is held out by an irresistible offer from Harvard University that he become Charles Eliot Norton Lecturer for the academic year 1932–3. Eliot promptly resolves to go there alone. Whether or not he sees this development as a chance to leave Vivien for good cannot be known at this stage. For the time being, as another friend, Robert Sencourt, remarks, Eliot strives diligently to 'establish serenity between them'.

JOHN HAFFENDEN
2014

VALERIE ELIOT
EDITING THE LETTERS

The Letters of T. S. Eliot owes everything to Valerie Eliot (1926–2012). She had been Eliot's greatest fan ever since, aged fourteen, she listened to a recording of 'Journey of the Magi' played to the class by her English teacher at St Anne's School, Reading. From that moment Valerie Fletcher (as she then was) felt a spiritual connection. 'I was overwhelmed by it,' she wrote. 'I remember intense excitement, as though a bomb had exploded under me. I knew something had happened, I knew this was different.' One of the first things she read by Eliot was his self-revealing introduction to the *Collected Poems of Harold Monro* (1933): 'There is no way out. There never is. The compensations for being a poet are grossly exaggerated; and they dwindle as one becomes older, and the shadows lengthen and the solitude becomes harder to endure.' It moved her profoundly. 'It was extraordinary that I felt I just *had* to get to Tom, to work with him. That introduction to Monro's poems haunted me.' Later, she sought out ways of working for him, and she hoped to become his secretary. For a year after leaving school, 1945–6, she worked in the Rare Manuscript Library of the Brotherton Library at Leeds University; and in 1948–9 she was secretary to the author Charles Morgan. However, her passion for all things Eliotic persisted, and became something of a family joke; and even Dylan Thomas – for whom she did occasional secretarial work in the late 1940s – knew her open secret. He was going to see Eliot at his office, Thomas told Valerie one day. 'What is it worth to you if I push his secretary down the stairs?' In time, astonishingly, a tip-off from a family friend meant that she did secure the position as Eliot's secretary, in 1949, and she acquitted herself admirably in the job. She revered the man and his work, and she came to love him – though she did not tell her love. Eliot considered her the best secretary he had ever had, and favoured her so far as to give her an introduction to Max Beerbohm one summer when she was holidaying in Rapallo. However, after seven years of working with Valerie, his admiration grew into deep love, and the 68-year-old Eliot found the courage to propose to her by letter – 'Dear Miss Fletcher'– in November 1956. They were married at St Barnabas Church, Addison Road, London, on 10 January 1957 (when Valerie was just thirty). The marriage lasted for eight years – 'minus four days', as Valerie would poignantly say – and it brought them both the most intense happiness.

T. S. Eliot enjoyed reading the letters of many writers from Samuel Taylor Coleridge and Baron von Hügel to James Joyce, and he shared his enjoyment with Valerie: they would often read aloud to one another. She it was who kept on pleasantly pestering him about his own letters, and her enthusiasm for having them published at some point. Taking the hint, the uxorious Eliot came to agree that she might in due time make a selection – posthumously. In a memo to his executors, signed in December 1960 – indeed, it was set down earlier than one might imagine – he stipulated: 'I do not wish my Executors to facilitate or countenance the writing of any biography of me.' However, he went directly on to authorise an edition of his selected letters – 'if the selection is made by my wife'. (In June 1970 Valerie would tell T. S. Matthews: 'It was with the greatest difficulty that I persuaded him not to ban the publication of his letters.') In the same memo, Eliot expressed his loving faith in his wife, though not without mentioning the hope, or the heavy hint, that she would safeguard his interests exactly as he saw them. 'I wish my wife Esmé Valerie Eliot to have sole control over my correspondence, to preserve or destroy letters written to me, and copies of letters written by me, at her discretion.'

Widowed at thirty-eight, Valerie dedicated the best part of the remainder of her life – nigh on fifty years – to recovering as many of her husband's letters as possible. 'I suppose it's an emotional outlet, if I'm honest,' she once said. 'I've put everything into it.'

Originally, long before he met Valerie, the very thought that anyone might publish his letters went wholly against the poet's wishes. He dreaded in particular the likelihood that the story of his unremittingly unhappy private life with Vivien Haigh-Wood Eliot (1888–1947) – from whom he formally separated in 1933, but from whom he was not to be divorced – might one day be played out for a curious public.

So too, when he learned, late in life, that his intimate friend Emily Hale had placed all of the letters he had written to her – more than a thousand, covering thirty years of their relationship – in the Firestone Library of Princeton University, so ensuring that they would be preserved for the interest and instruction of posterity, he reproached her with some vehemence:

> I have the greatest dislike to revealing my private affairs to the public now or at any time merely because of my importance in the world

of letters whatever that may be. I have indeed no desire to give information about my private life to the scholars and biographers who have nothing better to do than pry into the biographies of men of letters, and I am afraid that in the same spirit I have destroyed your letters to myself. The thought that posterity may be interested in my work naturally gives me some pleasure but not the thought of posterity being interested in my private life.

It did not seem to occur to Eliot that what he thought a selfish and tasteless decision on her part might well have been meant as a generous tribute to him. It was an unusually ill-tempered letter, begotten by shock. Those letters were to be embargoed until fifty years after Emily's death; but Eliot could scarcely countenance even the idea that an archivist, in a professional capacity, might read his private letters and keep the confidence.

To Ann Bowden, at the Harry Ransom Humanities Research Center at the University of Texas, Eliot wrote in August 1961 in more measured vein on a related subject: 'As for the Aldington correspondence, I appreciate your interest in these letters but I cannot at present adjust my mind to the publication of any volume of my correspondence during my lifetime. It seems to me that this is a matter better left to my executors, and perhaps even better to a remote posterity, if that remote posterity is still interested in my correspondence . . .' With the writer Richard Aldington he had enjoyed a close but at times warily ambivalent relationship through the 1920s, only for the friendship to be betrayed by the publication of Aldington's spiteful lampoon *Stepping Heavenward* (the present volume details that particular falling-out, and the enmity that ensued). At least in his dealings with third parties, therefore, Eliot was realistic enough to appreciate that a selection of his letters was bound to be published at some time.

We know that Eliot himself destroyed some batches of letters written by himself, and indeed some written to him (including perhaps most of Emily Hale's: a few have survived); and we must suppose he destroyed, or arranged to destroy, others. It seems possible, for example, that a box of papers faithfully burned by his editorial colleague Peter du Sautoy at Eliot's direction included some letters from Eliot's first wife Vivien. In addition, Eliot's bibliographer Donald Gallup informed Valerie on 9 November 1987, 'I remember Theresa telling me that she and Tom burned most of Tom's letters to Henry.' (Theresa Eliot was T. S. Eliot's sister-in-law: the wife of his older brother Henry.) Similarly, following the death of Eliot's mother Charlotte in 1929, Henry returned to his brother a number of the letters he had written to her; and Eliot told Henry on 25 May 1930: 'I am glad to have the letters to make ashes of. I should never have wanted to read them again, with all the folly and selfishness; and I don't want anyone else ever to read them and possibly print them; and if I could destroy every letter I have ever written in my life I would do so before I die. I should like to leave as little biography as possible.'

However, since Eliot made his firm decision to allow his wife to edit the letters as early as 1960, it seems likely that he grew much warmer towards the project during his declining years as he came to appreciate Valerie's passion for it. Her joy was his greatest gratification. The journalist Michael Davie, in a profile of Valerie Eliot published in the *Observer* on 15 May 1983, reported: 'Mrs Eliot told me a moving thing. "Tom did destroy a lot of letters. He told me, 'If I had known I was going to marry you, I wouldn't have done it.'"'

Notwithstanding Eliot's gentle promptings in the memo to his executors quoted above, I have come across no evidence to suggest that Valerie destroyed any letter written by Eliot. Everything in her temperament and conduct points to her wish to conserve everything written by her late husband. Morally, she was incapable of junking any piece of paper on which he had written anything. My conviction in this regard is supported by Karen Christensen, who worked as Mrs Eliot's assistant in the 1980s – and who is in certain respects critical of her ways and means – in an article entitled 'Dear Mrs Eliot . . .' (*The Guardian*, 29 Jan. 2005): 'it would have been impossible for her to destroy anything of Eliot's'. And Valerie offered her own testimony, which I believe to be reliable, in March 1969: 'I was . . . to destroy papers at my discretion, but this I have not done.'

Innumerable carbon copies of the letters Eliot posted from Faber & Faber, following his appointment as director in 1925, are kept in the Faber Archive. The archive, then, was Valerie's first recourse – and at Faber's, in the days before the firm took on a full-time archivist, the tactful editor John Bodley would be tasked to help her hunt down obscure items in neglected corners. But Valerie quickly realised that the carbons did not always tell the full story, since Eliot often 'had the blithe habit' (as she put it to Frederick Tomlin in 1977) of making holograph additions and emendations to the top copies which were not routinely recorded on the carbon copies. Thus her necessary objective was to track down the signed originals wherever possible.

Further problems came to daunt her: 'up to 1925, when my husband went to Faber's,' she wrote in a letter, 'he was casual about keeping copies of letters and many of them were written by hand, too. So a good deal of time has to be spent in seeking the whereabouts of the early ones. Many of the correspondents, too, are now dead, and they were not necessarily writers of importance whose papers have been preserved, or are easily available.' She was referring in particular to the early years when Eliot edited the *Criterion* – before the periodical was adopted by Messrs Faber & Gwyer Ltd – and when he wrote many letters by hand. (He had a very legible hand, but in later years he would always prefer to write a letter on the typewriter, blaming writer's cramp.) Consequently, before the age of the computer and the internet, Valerie had to write hundreds of blind letters of enquiry to widows, children or associates, and even to remote possible connections, and to hunt down wills at Somerset House. In the beginning she had little idea as to which libraries in the UK and elsewhere held major and minor collections; she knew of the foremost Eliot holdings at King's College, Cambridge, and at Harvard and Texas (which she had visited with her husband), but not much else. Richard Ellmann (who had once hoped to be able to write a biography of Eliot's early life, up to the period of *The Waste Land*) obliged her by typing out a comprehensive but not exhaustive list of US research libraries. Thus the track of her work for years to come was immediately laid down; as she told an American friend in May 1966:

> I am kept busy answering a large correspondence about Tom and his work and I foresee that I shall be trampled under foot and vituperation (when permission is withheld!) by the increasing number of would-be PhDs who want access to Tom's unpublished papers. And I chase round the world (metaphorically speaking) after his letters. Some were sold in a New York saleroom recently and have gone to earth in the University of Texas who have kindly supplied me with copies. There is a fair amount of detective work involved as I look up wills in order to trace the estate of deceased friends and writers to whom Tom wrote. I find it satisfying and moving to see the picture of him that emerges in his own words over the years but one cries too over his anguish at certain periods.

As that last phrase indicates, the pursuit of the letters was by no means a disinterested academic exercise. It was emotionally taxing, often exhausting, as she lived with him, in all the troubles and triumphs of his earlier life, through all the months of her grieving widowhood. Her work on the letters, she told another correspondent, was 'occasionally rather desolating, when Tom is describing his current troubles'. Yet she never failed to find her vocation invaluable and fulfilling. 'It's fun,' she would say. 'It's very exciting to recover him in this way.' She became addicted to the research; it was all-consuming, and she relished in particular that 'detective element'. As Michael Davie reported in 1983, 'Mrs Eliot is not being dilatory. She works seven days a week, absorbed by the chase.'

The editing and annotating were demanding work, too: she told her intimate friend Mary Lascelles on one occasion: 'It is a Ulalume sort of day, wet too, and . . . this morning was spent grappling with an article on "A Method of Rearranging the Positive Integers in a Series of Ordinal Numbers Greater than That of Any Given Fundamental Sequence of Ω", in order to annotate a letter from Tom to Norbert Wiener, the "father" of cybernetics. This editorial work is an excellent discipline but how my imagination longs to have its way!' However, at other times – since she had a great sense of humour, and a love of gossip and anecdote – she thoroughly enjoyed the chase after teasing references that might never be solved. For example, she told her friend Carol Rothkopf in 1975: 'I am thinking of offering a prize for the solution of the following: the carbon of a letter to a Dr Moore: "I return herewith with my humblest apologies something which I discovered on my coat collar some time after I left you."' (Her co-editor would still like to receive answers to that one, though a prize is not guaranteed.)

The very largest part of her time was to be spent on her top priority, garnering the primary materials: the letters. 'Apart from my editing work,' she told another correspondent, William D. Quillian, on 8 March 1977, 'collecting, sorting and checking absorb my time.' The scale of the work was huge: it was like assembling a gigantic jigsaw puzzle of hundreds of thousands of pieces, with no template to start out from – a fair number of letters (several to Ezra Pound, for instance) are undated – and there were in the case of many of the principal correspondents, including Pound, literally hundreds of letters to track down and put in order, with outgoing and incoming letters in correct sequence.

At every turn there were setbacks to be negotiated, obstacles to be overcome, puzzles to be revolved and solved, as well as some surprises and unexpected bonuses. Indeed, there can be no doubt that she became an astute researcher and editor. In 1972, for example, she told Lascelles: 'In a note to *The Waste Land* Tom gave a passage from *Blick ins Chaos* by the German novelist and Nobel Prize winner, Hermann Hesse, whom he had visited in Switzerland in 1922 as a result of his admiration for his critical work. There was no correspondence in the files but I had a hunch that Tom had written a "fan" letter and I finally traced a son living in

Frankfurt who has not only produced it – written in French – but also two others in German and one in English for good measure. A success of this kind makes up for many disappointments.' But she was disappointed to have to tell T. S. Eliot's American publisher Robert Giroux on 19 July 1968, apropos Michael Holroyd's biography of Lytton Strachey: 'In it he quotes, with my permission, part of an important letter from Tom dated 1st June, 1919. Tom kept none of his correspondence with Lytton (whom he disliked) so I asked for a photostat of this particular letter and was told by Holroyd . . . that it had disappeared. So down I went to Marlow where the Strachey papers are kept and spent hours searching through them in case this item had been misfiled, but I eventually returned home cross-eyed and disappointed.'

She benefited from a wealth of willing co-operation; and on 7 October 1966 she was happy to tell Rupert Hart-Davis that she had received only one refusal so far:

> That was from Mrs Vinogradoff [Julian Morrell] who said she might want to sell the letters and would get more for them if they were unpublished. Fortunately Tom did not write anything of importance to her mother [Lady Ottoline Morrell]. Bertrand Russell has promised to force a trunk to which he has lost the key and I only hope he does not get distracted by his present well-publicised activities . . .

And she went on, in the same letter:

> As usual the Pounds are causing a headache! Mary [de Rachewilz, Pound's daughter] sent all Ezra's private papers to Yale recently without consulting Dorothy [Pound] who has control in her role of legal guardian. Dorothy turned up here in a fury and said she would not allow the crates to be unsealed for many years after Ezra's death. I hope that when she has calmed down a little she will change her mind. She is perfectly willing in principle that I should have access . . .

Such ups and downs were almost a daily occurrence. With respect to the first item – Eliot's letters to Ottoline Morrell – it was fortunate that Valerie was mentally prepared for the long haul, as she was able to report to Lascelles only nine years later: 'After months of enquiry throughout America I have at last traced 111 letters from Tom to Ottoline Morrell of which I had copies of only 26. Mrs Vinogradoff sold them some years ago without learning their destination.' There were in fact 126 letters to Morrell housed at Texas University, and some were of importance. (Valerie's remark that 'Tom did not write anything of importance' to

Morrell was of course written in a miffy moment – it is perfectly natural to sniff at what one can't have.) The problem of the Pound papers too was solved only after a lapse of seven years, as Valerie wrote to T. S. Eliot's beloved cousin Eleanor Hinkley: 'Yale have bought the Pound crates for $292,000 and Ezra's daughter, Mary, is being appointed Curator of the collection. I am hoping to have access to Tom's letters to his friend, because much of their correspondence (written in the style of Uncle Remus) is undated, and I understand that Ezra often kept envelopes.'

However, as with all research, it was the outstanding 10 per cent of the ached-for and angled-for materials that proved the most exhaustingly elusive – and all the more desirable for being elusive. In the summer of 1975 she suffered from a prolonged illness, requiring hospitalisation; and she told Gallup on 14 October that year about some of the missing links, including the French connection – specifically, Eliot's early dealings with certain prominent writers associated with the periodical *Nouvelle Revue Française*:

> Through my illness, I have lost three months' work on Tom's letters, and I doubt if I shall be able to deliver the manuscript by the end of December. Some time ago I was in touch with Jacques Rivière's son in the hope that he might have some of Tom's letters to his father, of which I have a number of carbons. He replied that he had none, but that he would go through the *NRF* material in Mme [Jacques] Paulhan's possession and write to me again. That was a year ago, and I have heard nothing, but recently I learnt that a French bookseller has been offering three of Tom's letters to Rivière, and I am trying to trace his name. Due to the kindness of an American university librarian, I was sent a note about a comprehensive collection being sold by International Bookfinders of Pacific Palisades, California. It mentioned that there were eighteen letters, of which ten were typed, written between 1922 and 1954, but gave no details of date or recipient. I have written to them, asking for information, but fear the collection may have been bought by someone who wishes to keep it private . . .

It was frustrating too when a few other parties did not respond as readily as Valerie would have wished. It was not that she expected others to jump at her command, although admittedly to some correspondents Valerie's approach felt like a royal command. Her ever-developing authority as a scholar brought her confidence and *savoir faire*, and her increasing wealth in later years brought her the patina of power; she was also a glamorous woman, and she had the glamour of being T. S. Eliot's widow. But she found it difficult to comprehend how others seemed on occasion reluctant to return her offer of quid pro quo. She was always willing to reciprocate, despatching letters to other literary estates in return for copies of their original Eliot letters, and supplying letters to scholars authorised by other estates to edit their letters. On 6 March 1973, for example, she advised John Kelly, editor of the letters of W. B. Yeats: 'I have already extracted a number of letters from Yeats to TSE, and when I am sure that I have found them all, I will send you photostats.'

Similarly, she wrote on 14 October 1977 to Michael and Edna Longley:

> As I am preparing my husband's correspondence for publication, I wrote to Mrs MacNeice earlier this year to enquire whether any of his letters to her husband had been preserved, but received no reply. I understand from Professor [E. R.] Dodds that she was abroad at the time, and he thinks that you may have taken copies of the letters in the course of your work.
>
> If, being on the spot, you could obtain Mrs MacNeice's approval, I should be grateful if you would kindly let me have photostats at my expense of any TSE letters, or, if they are lent to me, I will have them copied and returned by registered post on the same day. I have carbon copies of 116 letters, but would of course prefer to have sight of the originals in case of holograph additions. It would seem from my files that the two men did not correspond in 1955 or from 1959 to 1962, which is odd, especially as Louis came to one of TSE's birthday parties in the later period.

The Longleys correctly responded that they had not yet reviewed the MacNeice letters; and of course they were not authorised to transmit to another scholar letters which were owned by Mrs MacNeice. Four months later, on 1 March 1978, Valerie consulted Charles Monteith (then Chairman of Faber & Faber) apropos the problem, as she saw it, of Mrs MacNeice:

> I approached her in February last year about Tom's letters, but received no reply. I then wrote to Dodds, who sent me copies of four letters and said he would send her a reminder. Still no reply. I have also been in touch with the Longleys who are preparing a biography of Louis, but 'have not yet gone through the vast bulk of correspondence which Hedli possesses'. I have carbon copies of 116 TSE letters and feel sure more than four originals must have been

preserved. The Longleys are planning to examine Louis' letters to Tom which I have extracted from the files and put into a folder, and I wonder whether I might bargain a little? In other words say that Mrs MacNeice must play her part by producing Tom's side of the correspondence at the same time. Please allow some blackmail!

In time, of course, the problem was civilly resolved, without recourse to 'blackmail' or any other form of bargaining.

In such ways she made herself into an expert, assiduous and determined (not to say hard-nosed) scholar – the scholar-editors she aspired to emulate, she once remarked, were Gordon Haight, Gordon Ray, 'the Dickens trio', and Richard Ellmann – and she was not prepared to let go of any of her literary quarries once she had got it by the tail. Just how exact, and exacting, she was in her record-keeping can be gathered from a letter to Clive Driver at the Rosenbach Foundation, dated 13 January 1976:

At present I am working to 1930, so I cannot say how many of [TSE's] letters to Marianne [Moore] I shall be using. I enclose a list of my carbons and photostats, which total 75 letters, 2 postcards, and one cable. On a letter from Marianne dated 30th March 1954 TSE had written 'answered 10. 4. 54'; so I should appreciate a copy of his reply at your convenience. Would you like me to check your list of Marianne's letters to TSE when it is ready?

At the end of those first ten years, when she was pressed by Faber & Faber to notify them when they might expect to receive the first part of what was initially projected to be a three-volume set of letters, she proclaimed with justifiable pride in her achievement, in a letter of 5 February 1977 to Peter du Sautoy (Monteith's predecessor as Chairman):

I have assembled from several countries Tom's correspondence relating to the first four years of the [*Criterion*'s] existence, the period before he joined the firm, and I am enriching our holding of the later years by tracing letters which Tom either wrote by hand or typed himself without retaining a copy – and as you know a number of carbons lack the bottom lines. Furthermore, many of the contributors were or became personal friends as well as Faber authors – Ezra [Pound], [Herbert] Read, [Bonamy] Dobrée, [Wyndham] Lewis, Aldington, Joyce, to name a few – and I have prepared complete collections of each which means that they no longer have a separate existence in the Criterion boxes. When I have completed my task I must re-plan the storing of Tom's correspondence because there is over-lapping and muddle at Harlow [where the Faber & Faber archive was then housed] and I have accumulated at least twice as much fresh material.

Our three volumes will reflect Tom's work as editor, though it is in his role as publisher that he advises authors in a similar way to the help he received from Ezra.

In a speech given at the Faber & Faber offices in Queen Square in February 1987, she stressed likewise: 'Publishing suited TSE's temperament and I think it is true to say that some of his finest criticism will be found in his letters to correspondents known and unknown and in marginal comments on returned texts.' The grand topic of TSE's marginal notes on returned texts still awaits the right PhD candidate.

It was a magnificent feat of research and retrieval on her part, the bringing back together of probably the overwhelming majority of the letters of the lifetime of the foremost man of letters of the twentieth century. 'Searching for early material is the hardest but rewarding task,' she wrote on 1 June 1977 to Ellen Dunlap at Texas, 'and I could write a book about it.'

She had determined too, she said in letters to other enquirers, that the first of the three volumes would comprise 750 letters by Eliot and about forty by other people. And she made known in a letter of 8 March 1977 to William D. Quillian this additional pertinent information: 'After I have completed my selection, the entire correspondence will have to be reorganised to include later garnerings (which have doubled the size since 1965) before it can be made available to scholars.'

There was one outstanding problem which Valerie never quite got to grips with in the earliest years of her research. So intent was she on amassing the letters that – for understandable reasons – she did not fully face the necessity to figure out just how many of the letters might fit into the three-volume selection that she envisaged. On 20 April 1967 she told Mary M. Hirth, of the Harry Ransom Humanities Research Center, Texas: 'I dare not begin to make a selection just yet.' Five years later, she told Robert Giroux, on 21 June 1972: 'I hope a natural break will occur in 1932, but again this will be influenced by the amount of correspondence that ought to be included.' It was natural for her to apprehend a break in the narrative in 1932, for that was the year when a major break had actually occurred: Eliot had broken away from his first wife in order to spend a year at Harvard, and he was to seek a legal separation on his return home in 1933. The couple would never again live together, and

Eliot would see Vivien on only a couple of occasions thereafter. (One might speculate also that Valerie would therefore have hoped for a second break at about the end of the Second World War; and the third and final volume would carry the story through to T. S. Eliot's death in January 1965.) However, just a year later, in July 1973, she advised Hinkley, 'The first volume of Tom's correspondence will probably go up to 1935.' But then, on 11 November 1975, in a letter to Mario Praz, she reported: 'The (generously) selected correspondence will appear in three volumes, the initial one ending about 1927.'

The reason for bringing the date forward is not far to seek: additional caches of letters were still coming to light, notably including letters to Ezra Pound. 'I doubt if the first volume of the correspondence will appear until the spring of 1977,' she advised her friend Professor L. C. Knights, 'as the Pound situation I mentioned is unlikely to be settled by September when I should have to go to press . . . It is galling, but I must include all Tom's epistles to Ezra.' (Valerie recognised that Pound had been the prime figure in Eliot's career, so she wanted to print every one of Eliot's letters to him.) She wrote too, in the same month (May 1975), to Carol Rothkopf: 'I am determined to wait until I have access to [James] Laughlin's Pound letters.' After just another year, she explained to Giroux in New York on 1 June 1976:

> Another Pound setback. Some more letters from Tom have turned up in the possession of the heir of William Bird . . . with whom Ezra left papers on his departure from Paris in 1924. The executors now claim them as their property, to be sold to the Lilly Library, but the Pound estate disputes this and a court case may follow. Whatever the outcome it is obvious that this cache will not be available for my first volume goes to 1926 – and should be ready for you and Peter [du Sautoy] next month. I suppose this material will have to be an appendix to volume two. O dear.'

In truth, she could not bear the idea of having to introduce an appendix of earlier letters into a later volume: after toiling for so many years at her appointed task, she anticipated volumes of formal perfection, with every letter in its proper place. This latest 'Pound setback', as she called it, was to be overcome over a year later, as she told Giroux on 27 October 1977: 'William Cagle of the Lilly Library says that the dispute with Yale over the Bird papers has been settled and Indiana University is to get Tom's twenty letters and one postcard written to Ezra before 1924, and will be sending me photostats. I am delighted that we shall be able to include them in their proper place in volume one instead of as an appendix to a later volume.'

But no sooner was that obstacle overcome than another precious bunch of letters came to light, as Valerie told Lascelles on 27 July 1977:

> Owing to a recent death 207 TSE letters, 25 postcards and 4 telegrams are to be made available to me by the University of Texas. There was a further twenty years' ban on their release before I told a piteous story to the recipient's Q.C. son [Jeremy Hutchinson, son of Mary Hutchinson]. Until the photostats arrive I do not know what number fall within the compass of the first volume or how many I shall want to use, but I expect footnotes will have to be adjusted at a time when I am suffering from footnote-it-is – that is a compulsion to annotate everything I read, a condition exacerbated by the recollection of Johnson's remark about it being impossible for an expositor . . .

She received copies of those long-embargoed letters to Mary Hutchinson by the turn of the year, as she informed Edward Mendelson (W. H. Auden's literary executor and sympathetic fellow editor) on 14 February 1978: 'I have been busy adjusting footnotes in the first volume as I have had to include a further twenty letters from Ezra which have now become available after the legal argument between Yale and Indiana; and 207 letters from another recipient who died recently.'

This was to become a frustrating and in fact self-hampering problem. Since Valerie was aiming to shape each volume in terms of a single continuous run of footnotes, any infiltration of additional letters meant that all the succeeding notes would be dislocated, requiring retyping (this was still some time before the advent of the computer in the 1980s). Yet the bulk of her text was expanding exponentially with almost every day's delivery of mail; and there were few rare book and manuscript dealers or specialist librarians throughout the world who were unaware of her interest in buying, or begging to borrow, every new find. At times she would feel almost harassed by news of new letters, for all the practical difficulties they raised, while unequivocally welcoming them in her heart. But how to squeeze the whole into a manageable volume, without leaving out countless plums: that was the problem.

'You may recall', wrote William R. Cagle, Lilly Librarian, on 9 December 1981, 'that a few years ago we acquired a small number of Mr Eliot's letters to Ezra Pound in the papers of William Bird. Now, by good fortune, we have added some 12,000 letters written to Ezra and Dorothy Pound from the estate of Mrs Pound and among them are approximately another hundred letters from Mr Eliot.' The level of anxiety Valerie felt at that moment is apparent in her response of 22 December to Cagle's courteous notice: 'I feel stunned at the thought of another 100 letters from TSE to Ezra Pound, but assume that the majority of them were typed and that I have the carbon copies. I have in fact prepared a number of letters in this way, not knowing whether the originals existed or not. My four volumes are laid out and the first must go to the printer soon.'

The number of volumes had been revised upward to four by 1980. By 1983 Michael Davie reported, 'There will be four volumes, possibly five.' Karen Christensen has likewise testified that by the mid-1980s, 'There had been plans to publish five volumes.' And in a letter to Valerie in February 1991 John Bodley referred to 'II, III, IV, V and so on'.

In the event, Volume I of the Letters appeared in 1988; it covered the period ending in 1922 with the publication of *The Waste Land* and the founding of *The Criterion*. (The volume sold 10,187 copies in its first year.) Interestingly, Volume II – spanning 1923–7 – was advertised in the Spring and Autumn 1990 catalogues of both Faber & Faber Ltd and Harcourt, Brace, Jovanovich, complete with a compelling blurb and jacket design. But Volume II was not to be published in that form, and the reason may be deduced from the fact that the period 1923–7 had ultimately to be packaged into two volumes of the *Letters* – II, 1923–5; and III, 1926–7.

This is not to find fault with Valerie's policy. Her ambitious strategy was to determine the total quantity of the letters, and then to divide the whole into portions. However, given Eliot's prolificness as letter-writer, the letters themselves would have to dictate the ultimate number of volumes, since among other considerations the scale of annotation required could not be predetermined.

Just as she could never bring herself to abolish a letter, so too Valerie saw that while letters are documents to edit, they are not documents in a case. All the same, she herself loved biographies, and in particular she loved the life of her husband. She had many years of training, beginning as his secretary for eight years, then for the further eight years as his wife, in deciphering his handwriting, gathering his memories, learning his mind. She had read and reread his works, along with numerous critical commentaries. She had heard Eliot comment on details of background and reference in his works. In addition, over the course of her research career, she made herself into the indisputable world expert on Eliot's life and texts. And so for Valerie, the business of editing the letters was to some extent a mode of simultaneously bowing to his directive that there should be no biography and bypassing it by laying down all the very best building blocks of a biography.

She told Aurelia Hodgson in January 1966 – almost a year to the day after Eliot's death – 'Although Tom has forbidden a biography I hope to incorporate interesting biographical facts which seem relevant.' And just a few months later again, in August 1966, she advised Giroux: '[Tom] has made a definite ruling [against a biography] and I cannot go against his wishes. However, the letters will make a most marvellous autobiography, and be a valuable quarry for biographers fifty years hence!' Similarly, on Easter Day 1972 she wrote to Elizabeth Wilson: 'I shall treasure your letter, and leave it with my husband's papers, so that a future biographer may have a correct perspective.' Ironically, such declarations came close to disobedience: if letters are an essential part of the materials of biography – indeed, Valerie sometimes referred to the letters she was accumulating as 'material' – she took infinite pains to be the helpmeet of a future biographer: gathering the raw materials whilst she may. (Even Eliot himself was occasionally given to remarking in later years – as in a letter to Wilder Penfield dated 1 May 1964 – 'I don't think I produced any memorable verse during my undergraduate days. This [his Class Day Ode, 1910] and the various poems which appeared in the Harvard Advocate are now only of biographical interest.') But I do not mean to tease this point too far: there is no doubt whatever that Valerie worked consistently to honour the letter of Eliot's will. As she told Thomas Dozier of *Time-Life* on 3 March 1970, 'As the sole literary executrix, I must carry out his instructions, and refuse any would-be biographer access to private papers and unpublished material.' So she took her professional stand where her husband had drawn his absolute line.

All the same, a further irony arises from the fact that Valerie invariably delighted in sharing her husband with friends, visiting scholars, casual enquirers – she would excitedly chat about him well into the night – and now and then she showed visitors some of Eliot's letters to herself. Commentators who have criticised her for being protective of his reputation and guarding his letters have rather missed the point, albeit often understandably. She did seem to sit on the letters for such a tiresome age, though she never meant to take so long over it all. There was a widespread feeling that Valerie was simply holding back the letters and so impeding other scholars in their legitimate enquiries; whereas the truth was, as I have tried to explain, she was just as much of a researcher as they were, spending years in doing the primary research. She saw little reason why other scholars thought they had a right to carve out for their own purposes parts of the research she was frantically engaged upon, and she was anxious to retain copyright control. From the outsider's point of view, she seemed overprotective and obstructive. In truth, she was simply adhering as best she could to her brief as literary executor.

While it was easy for her to spot the more transparently disingenuous approaches vis-à-vis Eliot's letters – as when the playwright Michael Hastings wrote to ask her for help with the biographical research for his play *Tom & Viv* – on the basis, as he told her, that his text specifically dealt with the story of Vivienne, 'to the exclusion of all others' – she saw too, without cynicism, that several other researchers sometimes sought permission to make use of unpublished letters by Eliot, or extracts from them, in the context of critical studies or collateral biographies of all sorts. She tried to be consistent in her response to enquirers, though of course she sometimes got it wrong. She was often very willing to assist petitioners with one-off quotations from the letters, so long as she felt the request did not trespass into Eliot-biography – at that point, the drawbridge was raised again. However, there is no doubt whatever that she was ready to engage with what she termed 'the PhD industry': to talk with scholars; to hearken to what they told her; and to help where she felt she could help. My first encounter with her occurred in 1976, after I wrote to her about my own work and received in reply a friendly letter dated 12 December 1975: 'I am interested to hear that you are writing a biography of John Berryman, and wonder if you would care to come for drinks when you next have occasion to be in London. We could discuss our respective ploys . . .' Our meeting went well, or at least I felt so. Truth to tell, I could not recall much of what we had said, because on the morrow I was in no condition to remember very much at all. I remember I was not allowed to approach the study, but she did show me the dozens of box files stacked on and under the dining room table, and labelled with all the dates of Eliot's lifetime. 'I can never have anyone to dinner now,' she said with a smile. She told me too of the day when as a schoolgirl in Reading she had seen a German fighter plane swoop down on a bridge she was crossing and fire off some rounds. 'I could see his face distinctly,' she said, looking up with her mind's eye. More to the point, she asked me about my relations with John Berryman's widow Kate, and she pointed me knowingly in the direction of Henry James's story 'The Real Right Thing' (not to be confused with 'The Real Thing'). A year or two later, when I thought to write a study of Eliot's friend John Hayward, I asked Valerie for permission to see the Hayward–Eliot correspondence at King's College Cambridge, and she declined. She must have suspected that my interest in Hayward masked an approach to Eliot biography. But there was nothing personal in that particular ban: we carried on meeting now and again for drinks, and she continued to be as helpful as I could wish with my work on W. H. Auden and William Empson. Over the years, quite a few scholars approached her in the hope of being appointed official biographer. The list included, in addition to Ellmann ('Although I think he will do a competent job in assessing Tom's achievement, he lacks empathy. Tom eludes him as a person.'), several of the foremost biographers of the day including Leon Edel, R. W. B. Lewis, Graham Hough, Frank Kermode, L. C. Knights, Park Honan and Andrew Motion. All were turned down. The bottom line was Tom's will: her sworn duty was 'not to facilitate or countenance a biography'.

In addition, her duties as executor extended to the administration of an exceptionally complex literary estate: it necessitated a massive correspondence of her own, which ate into the time she had available for editing. She wrote in June 1977, 'Though I began compiling my husband's correspondence in 1965 I had to break off to edit the manuscript of "The Waste Land", and I do all my own research and most of the typing, as I have a secretary only one day a week and we spend the time meeting the demands of the PhD industry.' The editing of *The Waste Land: A facsimile and transcript of the original drafts*, which took her over three years of full-time research and travel – it involved visits to the USA, and to Ezra Pound in Italy – was a major accomplishment by any standards. She also undertook, in the years following her husband's death, to collect all of his essays, reviews, introductions, prefaces and other prose writings, some of them unknown even to Eliot's bibliographer. As Ronald Bush reported of Eliot's Clark Lectures, delivered at Cambridge University in 1926, in his book *T. S. Eliot: A Study in Character and Style* (1984): 'At the time of this writing, Mrs Eliot is preparing the entire series for publication.' (That great project is being carried forward by Ronald Schuchard and his team of co-editors in *The Complete Prose of T. S. Eliot: The Critical Edition*.) She was vigilant too in seeking to ensure that fresh editions of Eliot's works met the highest standards of scholarly scrupulousness and textual exactitude. Late in the 1970s, for instance, she was told by Faber & Faber that the time had come for a new edition of *Four Quartets* – 'but,' she responded in a letter to Charles Monteith on 7 March 1978,

> there is little point in publishing a facsimile of the first edition. The first collected edition was published in America in 1943 but was so poorly done, due to unskilled labour, that out of 4,165 copies 3,377

had to be destroyed . . . The first Faber edition the following year also carried Tom's error in *The Dry Salvages* of 'hermit' for 'horseshoe' crab. In addition there are fresh printing errors . . . If you approve I will prepare a completely accurate text very quickly.'

And so she did, in less than a month: she wrote to Monteith again on 4 April 1978,

> I attach a copy of *Four Quartets* which is accurate in layout and text. As an additional precaution I have checked all the words against Tom's recording of the poems . . . I am surprised at the way the printers of the *Collected Poems and Plays* and the paperback edition of the *Collected Poems* have altered the indentation of Tom's lines. When these volumes are next reprinted can the Quartets be restored to their original state? . . . I think I had better see a proof.

She was nothing if not exacting.

But she did feel the strain of all the manifold work she had embarked upon, and the weight of expectation. 'I am in disgrace at Fabers for not delivering my manuscript,' she said on more than one occasion, and she was not joking. But her sense of duty to Eliot, his works and his letters, was paramount, no matter the pressure. She wrote on 1 March 1969: 'I live in terror of failing Tom. It is not arrogance that makes me undertake this task, but instructions in his Will. He made me his sole executrix and said I was to edit his letters and any unpublished material worth preserving.' She knew full well too that some academics considered her an amateur in a world of professionals, and that she should stand aside and leave Eliot to them. However, when the British Academy awarded her in 1972 the Rose Mary Crawshay Prize for her editorial work on the facsimile edition of *The Waste Land*, she was surely justified in writing to another friend, Sheila Pellegrini: 'I feel overwhelmed and grateful – grateful because it gives me a standing of my own; it is no longer a case of the poet's relict tinkering with the works!' She won the Rose Mary Crawshay Prize for an unprecedented second time for her work on the *Letters*.

This is the first volume in the series to be put through the production process since the death of Valerie Eliot in November 2012, so this seems an obvious necessary opportunity for her co-editor to offer grateful thanks to her.

The world of literary scholarship owes her an enormous debt, since the scope of the work she undertook with such energy – combing the research libraries of the world, contacting the poet's surviving friends, family, colleagues and associates, and of those who were deceased, their descendants, heirs and assigns – has yielded a culturally priceless trove of tens of thousands of letters. The scale of Valerie's success in reconstituting the story of T. S. Eliot's life through his letters, which is in so many ways the history of modern literature and modern times, is seriously impressive. With almost every passing month, further letters emerge in salerooms and in the hands of private individuals or collectors, and this will go on well into the future; but it is no exaggeration to say that the overwhelming majority, from all stages of the poet's life, have now been gathered up and put in place by Valerie Eliot. Accordingly, her name will rightly stand as co-editor of the *Letters* on all succeeding volumes in this series.

Incidentally, and surprisingly – yet somehow not in the least surprisingly – it is clear from Eliot's 1960 memo that he was happy for all of the letters he had written to Valerie herself to be published at some stage. He wished the world to know the details of how he had adored her.[1] It was almost certainly with that thought in mind that Valerie came to make a preliminary selection, in 1977, of a passage of prose by her husband that she thought might form a suitable epigraph to the *Letters*; it was a fragment from an otherwise unpreserved lecture on 'Poets as Letter Writers' delivered at Yale in 1932:

> The desire to write a letter, to put down what you don't want anybody else to see but the person you are writing to, but which you do not want to be destroyed, but perhaps hope may be preserved for complete strangers to read, is ineradicable. We want to confess ourselves in writing to a few friends, and we do not always want to feel that no one but those friends will ever read what we have written.

JOHN HAFFENDEN

---

1 – However, Valerie requested in her will, dated 20 December 2007, that TSE's letters to her should not be published until at least ten years after her death.

BIOGRAPHICAL COMMENTARY
1930–1931

1930   JANUARY – TSE and Vivien are living at 177 Clarence Gate
Gardens, London, NW1. 'We have not found moving into a flat
beneficial either in health or in any other way, and are on the point
of taking another house – a "decayed house" but I believe a good
one, with a potential garden, and in the favourite vicinity of Eaton
Square.' TSE is elected a Corresponding Member of the Colonial
Society of Massachusetts. He contributes 'The Place of Pater' to
The Eighteen-Nineties, ed. Walter de la Mare (1930); this essay is
also to appear as 'Arnold and Pater', *The Bookman* (Sept. 1930).
He is invited to be Turnbull Lecturer at Johns Hopkins University,
Baltimore, 'either in this academic year or the next': the six
lectures, which are to be spread over two weeks, carry an honorarium of $1,500. He writes an Introduction for Christopher Isher-
wood's translation of Baudelaire's *Journaux Intimes*, though he
considers Isherwood's work 'bad'; TSE's introduction is to be
reprinted, as 'Baudelaire', in *Selected Essays* (1932). His essay
'Poetry and Philosophy' is sold to *The Bookman* (Feb. 1930) for
$150, and will appear with a title made up by the editor, 'Poetry
and Propaganda'. TSE publishes W. H. Auden's 'Paid on Both
Sides: A Charade' in *Criterion* 9; and writes of Auden, in June
1932: 'He has always struck me as a man of great promise and
ability, and there are few young men in whose future I am so much
interested. I have also a great liking for him personally and believe
him to have both high principles and commonsense.' 21 FEBRUARY
– publishes 'Religion without Humanism', in *Humanism and
America*, ed. Norman Foerster. 22 FEBRUARY – TSE's brother-in-
law Maurice Haigh-Wood marries Emily ('Ahmé') Cleveland
Hoagland, an American dancer. Vivien writes on 25 March: 'I had
a fearful shock, my brother . . . suddenly got married, in Italy. He
arrived back, with a sick wife. An American. Very young.' TSE
joins the Literature Committee of the English Church Union, and
undertakes to be a 'Departmental Editor' on a projected

Encyclopaedia of the Christian Religion. 14 MARCH – TSE gives
the first of a series of six BBC talks on seventeenth-century poetry
which are published in the *Listener*, in order: 'Thinking in Verse: a
Survey of Early Seventeenth-century Poetry', 12 Mar.; 'Rhyme and
Reason: The Poetry of John Donne', 19 Mar.; 'The Devotional
Poets of the Seventeenth Century: Donne, Herbert, Crashaw',
26 Mar.; 'Mystic and Politician as Poet: Vaughan, Traherne,
Marvell, Milton', 2 Apr.; 'The Minor Metaphysicals: From Cowley
to Dryden', 9 Apr.; 'John Dryden', 16 Apr. 25 MARCH – Vivien
writes to Mary Hutchinson: 'we have had a most terrible time in
trying (unsuccessfully) to find another little house as nice as 57
Chester Terrace. It has been a great rush at the last, for us to get
out of here by Quarter Day [5 April].' END OF MARCH – TSE and
Vivien drive to the south coast, to pass two weeks at the Lansdowne
Hotel, Eastbourne. APRIL – the Eliots move to 43 Chester Terrace,
near Eaton Square, SW1. TSE is elected a Fellow of the Royal
Society of Literature. 27 APRIL – TSE writes to John Hayward: 'it
has taken me nearly forty-two years to acquire a faint perception
of the meaning of Humility – the first of the virtues – and to see
that I am not a person of any great importance. It is exactly as if
one had been living on drugs and stimulants all one's life and had
suddenly been taken off them. I know just enough – and no more
– of "the peace of God" to know that it is an extraordinarily
painful blessing.' 29 APRIL – TSE publishes *Ash-Wednesday*
(begun in December 1927) – dedicated 'To My Wife' – with a
design by Edward Bawden. TSE calls his poem 'a deliberate
modern *Vita Nuova*'. Another correspondent is advised, 'Do not
worry at being unsure of the meaning, when the author cannot be
sure of it either. The *Vita Nuova* might give you some help; but on
the other hand it is much more obscure than I have the talent to
be.' To Algar Thorold he writes, 19 May: 'Who am I, to know
what I mean?' To Charles Williams, 22 May: 'Can't I sometimes
invent nonsense, instead of always being supposed to borrow it?'
To M. C. D'Arcy, 24 May: 'I don't consider it any more "religious"
verse than anything else I have written: I mean that it attempts to
state a particular phase of the progress of one person. If that
progress is in the direction of "religion", I can't help that; it is I
suppose the only direction in which progress is possible.' To
Geoffrey Curtis, 17 June: 'As for obscurity, I like to think that
there is a good and a bad kind: the bad, which merely puzzles or

leads astray; the good, that which is the obscurity of any flower: something simple and to be simply enjoyed, but merely incomprehensible as anything living is incomprehensible.' To Bishop George Bell, 20 July: 'you would be shocked yourself to learn how much of the poem I can't explain myself. Certain imagery – the yew trees, the nun, the garden god – come direct out of recurrent dreams, so I shall abandon them to the ghoulish activities of some prowling analyst. The three leopards are deliberately, however, the World, the Flesh and the Devil; and the whole thing aims to be a modern *Vita Nuova*, on the same plane of hallucination, and treating a similar problem of "sublimation" (horrid word). However pathetically it falls below that amazing book, the comparison is useful, in making clear that this is not "devotional" verse. That can only be written by men who have gone far ahead of me in spiritual development; I have only tried to express a certain intermediate phase.' MAY – TSE lectures on 'Poetry and Philosophy' at the Children's Theatre, London. 10 MAY – TSE writes of the *Criterion*: 'The purpose of the review is to provide a small salary for the editor and to give publicity to the authors whom the editor and his colleagues consider worthy.' 13 MAY – seeks a remedy for an infringement of his copyright: *Prize Poems 1913–1939*, ed. Charles Wagner, with introduction by Mark van Doren (published by Charles Boni, New York), includes, without permission, the text of *The Waste Land*. 17 MAY – TSE writes to Stephen Spender, a student at Oxford, 'I think the time will come when you will have to choose between writing verse and writing novels; because I do not believe that any human organism can be stored with enough energy to cultivate two such different modes of speech . . . Residence in a University, enforced for three or four years, is unpleasant to anyone who is eager for artistic expression; but my belief is that it is best to put up with it. It may take you a year or two to recover; but the experience, and even the holding-back is useful in the long run.' (TSE's secretary will say on 1 January 1932: 'he is very much assured of the merit of Mr Spender as a poet'.) 22 MAY – TSE publishes his translation of *Anabase*, a poem by St-John Perse (pseudonym of the diplomat Alexis St Léger Léger). 23 MAY – TSE writes to Frederic Manning, author of *Our Privates We*, about 'the question, which will haunt men like myself of my generation till we die – "how would I have behaved?" And that question will be a tormenting nuisance to me for the rest of life.' JUNE – TSE writes to Paul Elmer More, 'To me, religion has brought at least the perception of something above morals, and therefore extremely terrifying . . . I had far rather walk, as I do, in daily terror of eternity, than feel that this was only a children's game in which all the contestants would get equally worthless prizes in the end.' 11 JUNE – the Eliots take a lease on 68 Clarence Gate Gardens, which Vivien describes as 'a large flat, of five rooms, bathroom and kitchen, and a long corridor. It is absolutely full of furniture, and thick carpets, and lots of everything, and it takes immense energy to keep it clean. We have enough belongings to fill a fair sized house, and it will be a pity if we cannot move into a decent house within the next few years.' TSE begins work on *Marina*, and thinks too of translating two plays by Hugo von Hofmannsthal: *Der Kaiser und die Hexe* and *Das Salzburger Grosse Welttheater*. He starts up regular meetings, held at the Poetry Bookshop opposite the British Museum, of the 'Criterion Club' – bringing together associates of the *Criterion* including Bonamy Dobrée and Herbert Read and guests. 22 JULY – TSE rejects poems by Ronald Bottrall submitted at the suggestion of F. R. Leavis. 25 JULY –contributes what he calls 'a somewhat prophylactic introduction' to G. Wilson Knight's *The Wheel of Fire* (Oxford University Press). Enrique Munguía Jr. publishes a Spanish translation of *The Waste Land* – *El Páramo* – in *Contemporáneos* (Mexico City). 8 AUGUST – TSE writes, 'I find that as one gets on in middle life the strength of early associations, and the intensity of early impressions, becomes more evident; and many little things, long forgotten, recur . . . And I feel that there is something in having passed one's childhood beside the big river, which is incommunicable to those who have not. Of course my people were Northerners and New Englanders, and of course I have spent many years out of America altogether; but Missouri and the Mississippi have made a deeper impression on me than any other part of the world.' 10 AUGUST – he tells William Force Stead: 'in this life one makes, now and then, important decisions; or at least allows circumstance to decide; and some of these decisions are such as have consequences for all the rest of our mortal life. Some people find themselves consequently in circumstances such that the whole of their mortal life must be a torment to them. And if there is no future life then Hell is, for such people, here and now; and I can see nothing worse in a Hell which endures to eternity and a Hell which endures until mere annihilation; the mere stretch of endless time, which is the only way in which we can ordinarily apprehend "immortal life", seem to me to make no difference.' 23 AUGUST – TSE agrees to publish James Joyce's *Haveth Childers Everywhere*. September – he is visited in London by relations from the USA, including the historian Samuel Eliot Morison. 2 SEPTEMBER – TSE informs his brother: 'I don't think I ever told you that Vivienne has acquired a small car . . . It has been a great inducement to her to get out of doors, and I think has done her good. I have learned to drive fairly well. The chief interest in driving, to me, is that the ability to drive removes an inferiority complex which I believe many men suffer from nowadays until they learn. I always had the feeling, though recognising its absurdity, of being the one human being incapable. I think that the satisfaction of finding that you can do what every blockhead is doing, as well as he does it, is almost greater than the satisfaction of doing something which nobody else can do as well. Perhaps it is partly that literary or artistic or philosophic eminence is never certain . . . Anyhow, I drive fairly well, though handicapped by a feeling of odious conspicuousness (which men seem to suffer from more than women). And Vivienne, who I thought at first would never learn, is driving better and better, and I really think at last will be able to drive like anyone else.' 18 SEPTEMBER – publishes Auden's *Poems*, and tells him: 'I shall look forward with great interest to your new play as I feel sure that poetic drama is the line you ought to follow.' Writes to an old colleague at Lloyds Bank: 'Publishing is more venturesome than banking, and involves even a greater amount of time spent in interviewing Bores. The only thing in its favour is that one is not called upon to hang about the Offices of the Mighty – only to be rebuked for one's ignorance of Hungarian or Czech or something equally recondite.' 25 SEPTEMBER – *Marina*, with drawings by E. McKnight Kauffer, is published as 'Ariel Poems no. 29'. OCTOBER – Robert Sencourt reports, after staying for a while with the Eliots, that Vivien 'was developing a tendency to find fault with everything, both in herself and in those around her.' 5 OCTOBER – Conrad Aiken gossips that he has had lunch with TSE and Gordon George (Sencourt): 'After the first course Vivian [*sic*] appeared, shivering, shuddering, a scarecrow of a woman with legs like jackstraws, sallow as to face. She examined me with furtive intensity through the whole meal:

flung gobs of food here and there on the floor; eyed me to see if I had seen this: picked them up: stacked the dishes, scraping the food off each in turn; and during everything constantly directed at T a cold stream of hatred, as he did (so it seemed to me) toward her. George said something about pure intellect. Tom, giving his best pontifical frown, said there was no such thing. Vivian at this looked at me, then at Tom, and gave a peacock's laugh. Why what do you mean, she said. You argue with me every night in your life about pure intellect, don't you. — I don't know what you mean, says Tom. — Why don't be absurd—you know perfectly well that every night you tell me that there is such a thing: and what's more, that you have it, and that nobody else has it. — To which Tom's lame reply was You don't know what you're saying.' 14 OCTOBER – TSE writes to his cousin Eleanor Hinkley, 'It is odd that when you produce a certain form of literary composition yourself, such as verse, you feel that every aspirant in the same form has some claim upon you; and somehow it works out, that the more incompetent the aspirant, the greater the claim.' MID-OCTOBER – TSE publishes 'Introductory Essay' to an edition of Samuel Johnson's *London: A Poem* and *The Vanity of Human Wishes*. 16 OCTOBER – 'my wife is in bed with laryngitis of indefinite duration'. At the suggestion of Dean Inge, Ernest Rhys invites TSE to write an introduction to Pascal's *Pensées* for the Everyman Library published by Dent. 17 OCTOBER – TSE remarks to Mary Hutchinson, 'Fundamentally I am sure [Vivien] wants to see old friends, and likes to be badgered by them (though this is a good deal to ask of the friends) as it stimulates her self-esteem, which is always in need of support and sustenance. She was . . . desolated by her brother's marriage . . . and it is still a very sensitive point.' 28 OCTOBER – TSE asserts to Elmer More: 'I am quite aware that I am a minor romantic poet of about the stature of Cyril Tourneur, that I have little knowledge and no gift for abstract thought; but if there is one thing I do know, it is how to punctuate poetry.' 29 OCTOBER – TSE is elected Hon. Vice-President of the Glasgow University Distributist Club (President, G. K. Chesterton). 30 OCTOBER – TSE portends his next work, to Wilson Knight: 'I have been rereading *Coriolanus*. I wonder if you will agree with me – it is rather important – I feel now that the political criticism, so much mentioned, is a very surface pattern; and that the real motive of the play is the astonishing study of the mother–son relation: "he did it to please his mother . . ." I think of writing a poem on this and on Beethoven's version Coriolan.' 7 NOVEMBER – TSE writes to Bonamy Dobrée, 'I think we are in agreement that "Order" and "Authority" are more dangerous catchwords now, than "Liberty" and "Reform" were fifty or seventy-five years ago. Order and Authority may point more directly to the yellow press and the crook capitalists than Liberty and Reform pointed to Socialism. I am terrified of the modern contempt of "democracy". I am also inclined slightly to resent (with mild amusement) being regarded by some as a Romaniser; whenas I believe that when the Vatican put it over the Action Française I was one of only two or three persons in this country to protest against this political thimblerigging. I am as scared of Order as of Disorder. The great thing seems to me to be to simplify issues into such as any man will be ready to put his fists up for.' 8 NOVEMBER – Virginia Woolf writes in her diary, 'But oh – Vivienne! Was there ever such a torture since life began! – to bear her on ones shoulders, biting, wriggling, raving, scratching, unwholesome, powdered, insane, yet sane to the point of insanity, reading his letters, thrusting herself on us, coming in wavering trembling – Does your dog do that to frighten me? Have you visitors? Yes we have moved again. Tell me, Mrs Woolf, why do we move so often? Is it accident? Thats what I want to know (all this suspiciously, cryptically, taking hidden meanings). Have some honey, made by our bees, I say. Have you any bees? (& as I say it, I know I am awaking suspicion). Not bees. Hornets. But where? Under the bed.' 13 NOVEMBER – TSE publishes a review-essay 'Cyril Tourneur' in the *TLS*. 19 November – he resolves to write a pamphlet about the Lambeth Conference, feeling that a pamphlet just published by F&F, entitled *The Lambeth Conference*, by George Malcolm Thomson (Criterion Miscellany 24), is inadequate and in parts vulgar. 'Personally, I am apprehensive lest this pamphlet, being produced by my own firm, might be taken to represent my own views; impersonally, the chairman agrees with me that it is desirable to produce as soon as possible another pamphlet, covering more or less the same ground from a different point of view.' MID-DECEMBER – TSE visits George Bell, Bishop of Chichester, who expresses the hope that TSE will write something for the Canterbury Festival for religious drama. TSE also meets E. Martin Browne, director of religious drama for the diocese. Max Rychner publishes a German translation of *Ash-Wednesday* I – 'Perch' Io non Spero' – in *Die Neue Schweizer Rundschau*. Angel Flores publishes a Spanish translation of *The Waste Land*: *Tierra Baldía* (Barcelona). 30 DECEMBER – Vivien writes: 'I am very lame at present.'

1931 JANUARY – the Eliots move to 68 Clarence Gate Gardens. TSE joins the Oxford & Cambridge Club. 3 JANUARY – Vivien tells Mary Hutchinson she has had 'a sort of breakdown'. (She will report further on 27 January, 'I have been in bed for nearly 3 weeks, with gastric influenza & bronchitis. So all my hardly acquired fat has disappeared. Thank God. Never get fat. It is the most horrible experience.') The first part of *Coriolan* (Ariel Poems) is published, with the title 'Triumphal March'; and 'Difficulties of a Statesman'. 17 JANUARY – TSE makes his first retreat at the Society of the Sacred Mission, Kelham Theological College, Nottinghamshire. 20 JANUARY – TSE is elected Hon. Fellow of the Mark Twain Society. FEBRUARY – TSE gets his own office at F&F, having hitherto shared a room with his American colleague Frank Morley. 2 FEBRUARY – TSE writes to Hayward: 'As for suffering, it is very queer indeed. Of course, I admit that I know little, perhaps less than most, of physical suffering, and I am sure that you know much of both. But I have had considerable mental agony at one time or another ... And I never found that I could make any conscious deliberate use of suffering – for one always feels that one must turn it to account in some way, and can't ... Then a pattern suddenly emerges from it, without one's seeming to have done anything about it oneself. And I don't suppose it is ever the same pattern for any two people. And I don't want to "convert" anyone: it's an impertinence ... Another thing is that faith is not a substitute for anything: it does not give the things that life has refused, but something else; and in the ordinary sense, it does not make one "happier". Perhaps it makes it more possible to dispense with "happiness". I suppose that whatever I have, that I count of positive goods in my life, are what most men would hold to be merely shadows and deceptions.' 6 FEBRUARY – TSE writes to his brother: 'Vivienne still has her car, or rather traded it in for this year's model of the same make; and it has helped her to get out and about very much more than she had done for several years. Only she has now been in bed with influenza for nearly a month; she is beginning to get up.' 14 FEBRUARY – Chatto & Windus publishes *Thomas Stearns Eliot* by Thomas McGreevy, to whom TSE writes:

'Your *explication de texte* of *The Waste Land* interested me very much. I can say without irony that it is extremely acute; but I must add that the author was not nearly so acute or learned as the critic. You have told me, in fact, much that I did not know; and I feel that I understand the poem much better after reading your explanation of it. Well! I supposed that I was merely working off a grouch against life while passing the time in a Swiss sanatorium; but apparently I meant something by it.' 5 MARCH – TSE publishes *Thoughts After Lambeth*, as Criterion Miscellany 30. (Criterion Miscellany pamphlets, as TSE tells Clive Bell, are intended 'to defend some cause, or to strike at some iniquity or folly of the day'.) In his response to the Church of England Conference 1930, TSE stresses the necessity for teaching Christianity to young people, and expresses conservative views on birth control. (Of *The Waste Land*, he incidentally points out, it was a 'nonsense' for any critic to have suggested – as I. A. Richards did – that the poem expressed 'the disillusionment of a generation'.) TSE writes later: 'my theological pamphlet ... took a terrible length of time, and involved a great deal of correspondence too – I could hardly have done it without the help of the Archbishop of York, but that is not for publication, as my views are not supposed to have any official sanction, and as a whole, they are solely my own.' (He will later say, in July 1932: 'I am quite convinced that beyond a point it is intolerable to apply one's own views of conduct to people who do not accept the beliefs which alone justify them.') MID-MARCH – TSE joins 'a sort of small editorial committee' to help run *The English Review*. 18 MARCH – William Empson is TSE's guest at a *Criterion* evening. 20 MARCH – TSE delivers his address 'Charles Whibley: a literary memoir' at the English Association, London. APRIL – TSE contributes three talks to the BBC – 'solely from mercenary motives' – to mark the tercentenary of the birth of Dryden, which are subsequently published in the *Listener*: 'John Dryden – I: The Poet Who Gave the English Speech', 15 Apr.; 'John Dryden – II: Dryden as a Dramatist', 22 Apr.; 'John Dryden – III: Dryden the Critic, Defender of Sanity', 20 Apr. TSE publishes in the *Criterion* Thomas Mann's attack on Nazism, 'An Appeal to Reason'. 4 MAY – he hopes that F. S. Flint will become the regular poetry critic for the *Criterion*: 'we ought not to have a young man, but someone of mature enough years not to be poisoned by the stuff he would have to review.' TSE completes his introduction to

Pascal's *Pensées*. 5 MAY – Caresse Crosby (Black Sun Press, Paris) invites TSE to write a preface to her husband Harry Crosby's posthumous volume of poetry entitled *Transit of Venus*. 8 MAY – publishes *Haveth Childers Everywhere*, by James Joyce (Criterion Miscellany 26). 11 MAY – Auden submits *The Orators*, on which TSE initially comments: 'My chief objection to [the second part] is that it seems to me to have lumps of undigested St. Jean Perse embedded in it . . . And the third part is apparently perfectly lucid, but I must confess that so far I cannot make head or tail of it.' 12 MAY – TSE lunches at Liddon House with the journalist and writer on mysticism Evelyn Underhill, in company with the American critic Austin Warren who subsequently observes: 'Eliot . . . no longer was the handsome, elegant young man familiar from his earlier photographs: he now was spectacled and his teeth had become carious. His intonation was distinctly British. He looked the man of affairs, not my image of a poet or literary man.' TSE finds Warren 'an eccentric young man'. MID-MAY – TSE entertains Paul Elmer More – 'an extremely kind man and loveable personality' – at home in Clarence Gate Gardens. 28 MAY – the Eliots' dog is injured in a fall. 30 MAY – TSE spends a weekend at Corpus Christi College, Cambridge. 2/3 JUNE – Vivien tells Mary Hutchinson, following a dinner at home: 'I am dreadfully sorry and shocked at what happened last night and this morning. I had so much looked forward to you all 3 [Mary and St John Hutchinson, and Jim Barnes] coming. Something seemed to upset Tom very much indeed yesterday . . . At any rate he was quite beside himself for most of the night.' JULY – TSE's brother Henry loses his job in advertising (a casualty of the Depression); he is anxious to get into publishing, and TSE does what he can to help. The Eliots are visited by American nieces. TSE reviews John Middleton Murry's *Son of Woman: The Story of D. H. Lawrence*, in *Criterion* 10; and Hilaire Belloc's *Essays of a Catholic Layman in England*, in the *English Review* (July). He questions, in the *Criterion*, the Unitarianism of his childhood: 'things were either black or white.' 14 JULY – TSE lunches again with Evelyn Underhill. The Hutchinsons dine with the Eliots. In her biography of Vivienne, Carole Seymour-Jones relates: 'July 1931 found Vivienne sitting next to Ottoline at a Gower Street tea-party with Virginia Woolf, David Cecil, Elizabeth Bowen, Alida Monro, Leslie Hartley, Juliette Huxley and Dorothy and Simon Bussy among others.

Diplomatically, Ottoline decided to look after Vivienne, whom she feared might make a scene, and left Virginia and Elizabeth Bowen to talk to each other, while L. P. Hartley discussed with Vivienne a detective story she was planning to write. It was, decided an exhausted Ottoline afterwards, rather like conducting an orchestra, trying to induce harmony among her disparate guests.' Seymour-Jones remarks further: 'But Vivienne did not forget Ottoline's kindness: in her 1934 diary she recalled how, "ill, late, flustered", she used to motor to fetch Tom to take him to 10 Gower Street. "Inconspicuous [and] as inoffensive as possible", she would sit in the shadows of the garden: "Ottoline used to keep me by her which was kind of her," while the literary ladies and gentlemen talked".' 15 JULY – TSE accepts two poems by Louis MacNeice for publication in the *Criterion*. 16 JULY – TSE is invited to become a member of the Committee of the Royal Society of Literature; but he declines: 'I do not feel that a director of any publishing firm . . . should take part in any such committee of selection.' MID-JULY – William Force Stead and Evelyn Underhill dine chez Eliot. 18 JULY – TSE writes of Vivien, 'We hope that my absence for a time may have the effect of strengthening her nerves (and nerve), after she has been to some extent on her own feet.' Vivien tells Hutchinson that 'I really do wish to move to 51 Gordon Square, & shall do that – & that I cannot endure my present servants much longer.' 20 JULY – James and Nora Joyce, and Ottoline Morrell, take tea with the Eliots. According to Carole Seymour-Jones (whose source is the diary of Ottoline Morrell): 'Tom and Vivienne greeted Joyce like a king . . . and this time it was Ottoline who felt left out as the two writers fell into deep conversation . . . The company listened to a gramophone recording of Joyce reading "Anna Livia Plurabelle", followed by Tom reading "Ash Wednesday"; it was, thought Ottoline, greatly inferior to Joyce's work.' 12 AUGUST – TSE writes to Lilian Donaghy about her husband, the Irish poet Lyle Donaghy, who has suffered a breakdown: 'You will, I hope, excuse me for writing about the matter as if I knew you, but it is only because I happen to have more knowledge of this type of nervous illness than most people. Such cases are very difficult to handle, because they rarely want to stay in a sanatorium voluntarily, and no one wants to go so far as certification . . . All the symptoms you describe are known to me. I am quite certain that people in such a state ought not, as much for their own sakes as for that of others, be with their family and friends. The manifestations of mania are always more pronounced with the persons they know best than with others. Furthermore, those near can do no good but only harm; and it is a heartrending business to wear oneself to shreds for anyone when one knows all the time that he or she only becomes the worst for it ... Professional outsiders are the only people to deal with such cases, and the only people whose nerves can stand the strain of dealing with them.' 10 SEPTEMBER – TSE belatedly submits his preface to Harry Crosby's posthumous collection *Transit of Venus*: 'I have to put it down to indifferent health and fatigue' – 'I am far from asserting ... that I understand in the least what Crosby was up to, or that I am sure I should like it if I did. I doubt whether anyone himself engaged in the pursuit of poetry can "like", any more than he can "understand", the work of his contemporaries ... What I do like, in a serious sense, is the fact that Crosby was definitely going his own way, whether I like the way or not.' 18 SEPTEMBER – he is invited to deliver a talk on Dryden to be broadcast to the USA by the Columbia Broadcasting System. 19 SEPTEMBER – contributes 'Introduction' to Pascal's *Pensées*, translated by W. F. Trotter (Everyman's Library), praising Pascal's 'unique combination and balance of qualities'. 23 SEPTEMBER – asks for first refusal on Auden's play *The Fronny*. LATE SEPTEMBER – lunches with the American critics Willard Thorp and George Williamson. 8 OCTOBER – TSE publishes 'Triumphal March', with two illustrations by E. McKnight Kauffer (Ariel Poem 35). 'Difficultés d'un homme d'état' ('Difficulties of a Statesman') appears in *Commerce* 29 (Winter 1931/32): English text with facing-page translation by Georges Limbour. Publishes Auden's 'Speech for a Prize-Day' in the *Criterion*. Introduces the Irish writer Seán Ó'Faoláin to various literary editors. MID-OCTOBER – entertains at home Willard Thorp and his wife. 19 OCTOBER – TSE tells his brother-in-law, 'The situation is that Vivienne is extremely hard up at present, owing to the fall in the dividends of securities and not having yet reduced her expenditure to fit. (Her chief expenses are of a kind difficult to reduce).' 28 OCTOBER – TSE writes to Hutchinson: 'No, Vivienne is not more ill ... I mean there is no particular acute problem at the moment, only the permanent one ... I should be grateful if you could occasionally see her without me: the more people she can see without me ... And also, I wish that you might some time induce her to go out of doors with you. She can't drive without me or a driver; but I see no physical reason why she should not walk a little, or go out in somebody's else conveyance.' NOVEMBER – TSE publishes 'Preface' in *Transit of Venus: Poems by Harry Crosby*. 4 NOVEMBER – Eric Blair (George Orwell) wishes to translate for F&F *À la Belle de Nuit*; but TSE turns down the proposal. 11 NOVEMBER – TSE lunches with C. M. Grieve (Hugh Mac-Diarmid) and Major C. H. Douglas, theorist of Social Credit. 17 NOVEMBER – TSE accepts appointment as Charles Eliot Norton Lecturer at Harvard, 1932–3. 18 NOVEMBER – TSE meets the Vicomte Léon de Poncins. 1 DECEMBER – TSE publishes an influential essay 'Donne in Our Time' in *A Garland for John Donne 1631–1931*, ed. Theodore Spencer – 'Donne was, I insist, no sceptic' – expressing confidence in the conviction that Donne's reputation would soon be on the rise. 2 DECEMBER – TSE delivers a paper on John Marston to the Elizabethan Society, King's College, London. 9 DECEMBER – has lunch with Osbert Sitwell. 10 DECEMBER – invites Marianne Moore to contribute (a poem or a review) to the *Criterion*. 11 DECEMBER – TSE meets Ralph Hodgson at a soirée at Ottoline Morrell's house at 10 Gower Street, London, in company with Lord David Cecil, L. P. Hartley and S. S. Koteliansky (Ukrainian émigré translator)). According to John Harding, '"Kot" . . . berated Eliot loudly for not joining in the struggle for a Lawrentian "new world order". Hodgson's quiet aside that "the future is a mystery and man's only obligation is to find the courage to face it" appeared to strike a chord with Eliot. At the end of the evening, as the coats were being handed out, Eliot said to Hodgson, "Must I wait another 43 years before we meet again?"' Vivien writes to Morrell: 'I was so happy at your house today. I feel so "family" with you, & among yr. friends, always, & always did. Particularly today did it strike me, for I had just been through such a fearful time, with T. All of a sudden. We had 4 people to dinner last night, & they did not seem to have at all a good effect, anyhow, not in combination. I was really horrified, for it is now so long that anything like it had happened. I find now, more & more, that Tom is happier, & his best self with you, & with the people you have about you . . . Do please realise how enchanted I was to meet . . . Ralph Hodgson. The latter is truly delightful . . .' (On 4 July 1932 Vivien will tell Morrell: 'You have given us so many beautiful afternoons during this whole year, no-one could be grateful enough, whatever they might feel. I feel that the part of my life which is around you is the only part I can endure to contemplate. You know that it is entirely due to you that I have been able to keep up.') 12 DECEMBER – TSE gives his transatlantic talk on Dryden: 'I was so fidgety, from abstinence from tobacco and indulgence in throat lozenges, having had a heavy cold for days past.' 22 DECEMBER – 'Vivienne is worn out by Christmas and other things & is in bed with a bronchial cough & bad headache.' 25 DECEMBER – Vivien writes to a friend, 'I am glad your Christmas Day was nice & calm. Ours was rather terrible.' 28 DECEMBER – 'Vivienne is really in very poor health, and I want to get her to bed – She is in bed, but I mean, to settle down.'

ABBREVIATIONS AND SOURCES

PUBLISHED WORKS BY T. S. ELIOT

ASG	*After Strange Gods* (London: Faber & Faber, 1934)
AVP	*Ara Vos Prec* (London: The Ovid Press, 1920)
CP	*The Cocktail Party* (London: Faber & Faber, 1930)
CPP	*The Complete Poems and Plays of T. S. Eliot* (London: Faber & Faber, 1969)
EE	*Elizabethan Essays* (London: Faber & Faber, 1934)
FLA	*For Lancelot Andrewes: Essays on Style and Order* (London: Faber & Gwyer, 1928)
FR	*The Family Reunion* (London: Faber & Faber, 1939)
Gallup	Donald Gallup, *T. S. Eliot: A Bibliography* (London: Faber & Faber, 1969)
HJD	*Homage to John Dryden: Three Essays on Poetry of the Seventeenth Century* (London: The Hogarth Press, 1924)
IMH	*Inventions of the March Hare: Poems 1909–1917,* ed. Christopher Ricks (London: Faber & Faber, 1996)
KEPB	*Knowledge and Experience in the Philosophy of F. H. Bradley* (London: Faber & Faber, 1964; New York: Farrar, Straus & Company, 1964)
L	*Letters of T. S. Eliot* (London: Faber & Faber, Vol. 1 [rev. edn], 2009; Vol. 2, 2009; Vol. 3, 2012; Vol. 4, 2013)
MiC	*Murder in the Cathedral* (London: Faber & Faber, 1935)
OPP	*On Poetry and Poets* (London: Faber & Faber, 1957; New York: Farrar, Straus & Cudahy, 1957)
P	*Poems* (London: The Hogarth Press, 1919)
P 1909–1925	*Poems 1909–1925* (London: Faber & Gwyer, 1925)

POO	*Prufrock and Other Observations* (London: The Egoist Press, 1917)
SA	*Sweeney Agonistes: Fragments of an Aristophanic Melodrama* (London: Faber & Faber, 1932)
SE	*Selected Essays: 1917–1932* (London: Faber & Faber, 1932; 3rd English edn, London and Boston: Faber & Faber, 1951)
SW	*The Sacred Wood: Essays on Poetry and Criticism* (London: Methuen & Co., 1920)
TCC	*To Criticise the Critic* (London: Faber & Faber, 1965; New York: Farrar, Straus & Giroux, 1965)
TUPUC	*The Use of Poetry and the Use of Criticism: Studies in the Relation of Criticism to Poetry in England* (London: Faber & Faber, 1933)
TWL	*The Waste Land* (1922, 1923)
TWL: Facs	*The Waste Land: A Facsimile and Transcript of the Original Drafts*, ed. Valerie Eliot (London: Faber & Faber, 1971; New York: Harcourt, Brace Jovanovich, 1971)
VMP	*The Varieties of Metaphysical Poetry*, ed. Ronald Schuchard (London: Faber & Faber, 1993; New York: Harcourt Brace, 1994)

PERIODICALS AND PUBLISHERS

A.	*The Athenaeum* (see also *N&A*)
C.	*The Criterion*
F&F	Faber & Faber (publishers)
F&G	Faber & Gwyer (publishers)
MC	*The Monthly Criterion*
N.	*The Nation*
N&A	*The Nation & The Athenaeum*
NC	*New Criterion*
NRF	*La Nouvelle Revue Française*
NS	*New Statesman*
TLS	*Times Literary Supplement*

PERSONS

CA	Conrad Aiken
RA	Richard Aldington
RC-S	Richard Cobden-Sanderson

BD	Bonamy Dobrée
CWE	Charlotte Ware Eliot, TSE's mother
EVE	(Esmé) Valerie Eliot
HWE	Henry Ware Eliot (TSE's brother)
TSE	T. S. Eliot
VHE	Vivien (Haigh-Wood) Eliot
GCF	Geoffrey (Cust) Faber
MHW	Maurice Haigh-Wood
JDH	John Davy Hayward
MH	Mary Hutchinson
AH	Aldous Huxley
JJ	James Joyce
GWK	G. Wilson Knight
DHL	D. H. Lawrence
FRL	F. R. Leavis
WL	Wyndham Lewis
FVM	Frank (Vigor) Morley
OM	Ottoline Morrell
JMM	John Middleton Murry
EP	Ezra Pound
HR	Herbert Read
IAR	I. A. Richards
BLR	Bruce Richmond
ALR	A. L. Rowse
BR	Bertrand Russell
ES	Edith Sitwell
WFS	William Force Stead
CW	Charles Whibley
OW	Orlo Williams
LW	Leonard Woolf
VW	Virginia Woolf
WBY	W. B. Yeats

ARCHIVE COLLECTIONS

Arkansas	Special Collections, University Libraries, University of Arkansas
BBC	BBC Written Archives, Caversham
Beinecke	The Beinecke Rare Book and Manuscript Library, Yale University

Berg	Henry W. and Albert A. Berg Collection of English and American Literature, the New York Public Library
Bodleian	The Bodleian Library, Oxford University
BL	The British Library
Brotherton	The Brotherton Collection, Leeds University Library
Buffalo	Poetry Collection, Lockwood Memorial Library, State University of New York, Buffalo
Butler	Rare Books and Manuscripts Division, Butler Library, Columbia University, New York
Caetani	Fondazione Camillo Caetani
Cambridge	Cambridge University Library
Cornell	Department of Rare Books, Olin Library, Cornell University
Bib Jacques Doucet	Bibliothèque littéraire Jacques Doucet, Paris
Edinburgh	Edinburgh University Library
Exeter	Exeter University Library
Faber	Faber & Faber Archive, London
Harcourt Brace	Harcourt Brace & Company
Harvard	University Archives, Harvard University
Houghton	The Houghton Library, Harvard University
House of Books	House of Books, New York
Howard	Lelia Howard
Huntington	Huntington Library, San Marino, California
King's	Modern Archive Centre, King's College, Cambridge
Lambeth	Lambeth Palace Library
Lilly	Lilly Library, Indiana University, Bloomington
Magdalene	Old Library, Magdalene College, Cambridge
Marshall	Marshall Library, University of Cambridge
Morgan	Pierpont Morgan Library, New York
National Gallery of Ireland	National Gallery of Ireland, Dublin
NHM	Natural History Museum Archives
Northwestern	Special Collections Department, Northwestern University Library, Evanston, Illinois
Princeton	Department of Rare Books and Special Collections, Princeton University Library
Reading	Reading University Library

Renishaw	Sitwell Papers, Renishaw Hall, Derbyshire
Rosenbach	Rosenbach Museum and Library, Philadelphia, PA
Southern Illinois	Southern Illinois University Library, Carbondale
Sussex	Manuscript Collections, University of Sussex Library
Syracuse	Syracuse University Library, Syracuse, New York
TCD	The Library, Trinity College, Dublin
Templeman	Templeman Library, University of Kent at Canterbury
Texas	The Harry Ransom Humanities Research Center, University of Texas at Austin
UCLA	University of California at Los Angeles
VE Papers	Vivien Eliot Papers, Bodleian Library, Oxford
Victoria	Special Collections, McPherson Library, University of Victoria, British Columbia
Wellesley	Wellesley College Library
Williamson	Mrs M. H. Williamson (Dr Charlotte Williamson)
Wyoming	University of Wyoming

CHRONOLOGY OF *THE CRITERION*

The Criterion

Vol. 1. No. 1. 1–103, Oct. 1922; No. 2. 105–201, Jan. 1923;
No. 3. 203–313, Apr. 1923; No. 4. 315–427, July 1923.

Vol. 2. No. 5. 1–113, Oct. 1923; No. 6. 115–229, Feb. 1924;
No. 7 231–369, Apr. 1924; No. 8 371–503, July 1924.

Vol. 3. No. 9. 1–159, Oct. 1924; No. 10. 161–340, Jan. 1925;
No. 11 341–483, Apr. 1925; No. 12. 485–606, July 1925.

The New Criterion

Vol. 4. No. 1. 1–220, Jan. 1926; No. 2. 221–415, Apr. 1926;
No. 3. 417–626, June 1926; No. 4. 627–814, Oct. 1926.

Vol. 5. No. 1. 1–186, Jan. 1927.

The Monthly Criterion

Vol. 5. No. 2. 187–282, May 1927; No. 3. 283–374, June 1927.

Vol. 6. No. 1. 1–96, July 1927; No. 2. 97–192, Aug. 1927; No. 3.
193–288, Sept. 1927; No. 4. 289–384, Oct. 1927; No. 5. 385–480,
Nov. 1927; No. 6. 481–584, Dec. 1927.

Vol. 7. No. 1. 1–96, Jan. 1928; No. 2. 97–192, Feb. 1928;
No. 3. 193–288, Mar. 1928.

The Criterion

Vol. 7. No. 4. 289–464, June 1928

Vol. 8. No. 30. 1–183, Sept. 1928; No. 31. 185–376, Dec. 1928;
No. 32. 377–573, Apr. 1929; No. 33. 575–772, July 1929.

Vol. 9. No. 34. 1–178, Oct. 1929; No. 35, 181–380, Jan. 1930;
No. 36, 381–585, Apr. 1930; No. 37, 587–787, July 1930.

Vol. 10. No. 38. 1–209, Oct. 1930; No. 39. 211–391, Jan. 1931;
No. 40. 393–592, Apr. 1931; No. 41. 593–792, July 1931.

Vol. 11. No. 42. 1–182, Oct. 1931; No. 43. 183–374, Jan 1932;
No. 44. 375–579, Apr. 1932; No. 45. 581–775, July 1932.

EDITORIAL NOTES

The source of each letter is indicated at the top right. CC indicates a carbon copy. Where no other source is shown it may be assumed that the original or carbon copy is in the Valerie Eliot collection or at the Faber Archive.

del.   deleted

MS   manuscript

n. d.   no date

PC   postcard

sc.   *scilicet*: namely

ts   typescript

<   >   indicates a word or words brought in from another part of the letter.

Place of publication is London, unless otherwise stated.

Some obvious typing or manuscript errors, and slips of grammar and spelling, have been silently corrected.

Dates have been standardised.

Some words and figures which were abbreviated have been expanded.

Punctuation has been occasionally adjusted.

Editorial insertions are indicated by square brackets.

Words both italicised and underlined signify double underlining in the original copy.

Where possible a biographical note accompanies the first letter to or from a correspondent. Where appropriate this brief initial note will also refer the reader to the Biographical Register at the end of the text.

Vivienne Eliot liked her husband and friends to spell her name Vivien; but as there is no consistency it is printed as written.

'Not in Gallup' means that the item in question is not recorded in Donald Gallup, *T. S. Eliot: A Bibliography* (1969).

THE LETTERS
1930–1931

Criterion Club[1]

Your attendance is required at a meeting of the Club on Wednesday next, the 10th September, at 6 p.m. precisely, at the Poetry Bookshop.[2]

Guests to be invited for 8 p.m. precisely.

Your attention is called to the following bye-laws.

I. Each member is allowed to invite two Guests at his own expense. The expenses for each member and his guests are to be paid to Mr Monro at the beginning of the meeting.

II. It is understood that the Guests are to be persons of the male sex, either already useful or potentially useful to THE CRITERION. If, at the following meeting, a majority of the members agree that any Guest introduced was for any reason unsuitable, the Member introducing that guest may be reprimanded. A repetition of the offense may debar the member from enjoyment of the privilege.

TO   Morley
      Read
      Dobrée
      Flint
      Monro.

1 – W. H. Auden said in 1932, 'A modern satirist in search of a subject would be far more likely to select a *Criterion* dinner than a Newspaper peer' (cited in 'Auden, Us and Them', *TLS*, 6 Oct. 1966).
2 – See Joy Grant, *Harold Monro and the Poetry Bookshop*; J. Howard Woolmer, *The Poetry Bookshop 1912–1935: A Bibliography* (1988).

1930

1 January 1930   [*The Criterion*,
                                  24 Russell Square, London]

Dear Miss Malnick,

I am sending you a copy of the *Criterion* containing notices of Russian Periodicals which I hope will interest you. I must at the same time thank you for your kindness in having sent to me the Periodicals from Moscow.

I am extremely anxious to keep up as full as possible a review of Russian Periodicals in the *Criterion*, and indeed, attach more importance to it than to any other of our reviews of Foreign Periodicals. Would you be so kind as to let me know to what address I should send a copy or copies of the *Criterion* in return; or had I best merely send a couple of copies of each issue to you?

Please remember also that I shall always be interested to have my attention called to any Russian literature suitable for translation, either for the *Criterion*, or for my publishing house.

With all best wishes for The New Year,

                                  Yours sincerely,
                                  [T. S. Eliot]

1–Dr Bertha Malnick, scholar and translator, was to become Reader in Russian Studies in the School of Slavonic and East European Studies, University College London, 1946–66. Her PhD thesis was entitled 'The origin and the early history of the theatre in Russia, 1672–1756' (1935).

1 January 1930   [Faber & Faber Ltd,
                                            24 Russell Square, London]

Dear Professor Taylor,

Thank you very much for your kind letter.[2] I have had the Singer *Platon der Gründer* sent to you.[3] In so important a matter, we are prepared to wait your convenience, and are prepared to ask the German publishers to wait your convenience, in order to have the benefit of your opinion.

I understand that Dr Singer is more or less one of the Stephan [*sic*] George[4] group, and has a good deal in common with such writers as Ernst Bertram[5] (whose *Nietzsche* was a remarkable book), Scheler[6] and Worringer.[7]

As for the book itself, if you are cordially in favour of its publication, and if we then decide to publish a translation, I do not suppose that we shall want the copy back. But if the decision is unfavourable, I suppose that we ought to return it to the publishers.

I had been for a long time, intending to get into communication [*typing runs off the page*] consider contributing an essay to the *Criterion*. Your attitude on theological matters is so close to my own that it would be also a personal pleasure to me. I wondered if the Desclée edition of S. Thomas

---

1–Alfred Edward Taylor (1869–1945): Professor of Moral Philosophy in the University of Edinburgh, 1924–41; President of the Aristotelian Society, 1928–9. His publications include *St Thomas Aquinas as a Philosopher* (1924); *Plato, the Man and his Work* (1927).

2–Taylor agreed on 24 Dec. 1929 to offer an opinion on Dr Kurt Singer's *Platon der Gründer* (1927); but he might not be able to read the book until late January – 'is there any great hurry?'

3–Kurt Singer (1886–1962), German economist and philosopher, taught in Hamburg, 1924–33, then at Tokyo Imperial University, 1931–35; author of *Platon der Gründer* (1927).

4–Stefan George (1868–1933): German lyric poet and translator associated with Stéphane Mallarmé and Paul Verlaine. Classicist and élitist (his disciples called him 'Master'), his works include *Hymnen, Pilgerfahrten, and Algabal* (1900), *Der Krieg* (1917), *Das neue Reich* (1928).

5–Ernst Bertram (1884–1957), poet and scholar, was a lecturer at the University of Bonn until 1922, when he was appointed Professor of German Literature at Cologne University; author of *Nietzsche: An Attempt at Mythology* (1918), and essays on literary figures including Hugo von Hofmannsthal, Stefan George, and Thomas Mann (who became his friend and correspondent).

6–Max Scheler (1874–1928): German philosopher specialising in ethics, value theory, phenomenology, philosophical anthropology; Professor of Philosophy and Sociology at Cologne, 1919–28; a notable influence on Karol Wojtyla, the future Pope John Paul II, who wrote his *Habilitation* (1954) on Christian ethics in the light of Scheler. His works, including *Nation und Weltanschauung*, are gathered in *Gesammelte Werke* (Bern, 1963).

7–Wilhelm Worringer (1881–1965), German art historian.

(to which I am a subscriber, and of which some sixteen volumes have appeared) might make the pretext for an essay, if I could get them to send a set. Have you seen this edition? But indeed almost anything by you would be an honour to my review.

Yours faithfully,
[T. S. Eliot]

TO *Stephen Spender*[1]   CC

1 January 1930   [Faber & Faber Ltd]

Dear Spender,

I am very glad to know that you are back in London and look forward to seeing you.[2] Could you perhaps lunch with me on Thursday, the 8th, say at 1.15, at The Royal Societies Club?[3]

Yours sincerely,
[T. S. Eliot]

TO *J. L. Donaghy*[4]   CC

2 January 1930   *The Criterion*

Dear Mr Donaghy,

I owe you many apologies for the delay, due to pressure of all sorts of business at this time of year. Here is a line to Mr Leonard Woolf, whom I hope you will soon see. If you care to look in on me one morning next week I shall be very pleased to see you.

I have not yet read your new poems, for the reason that I could not use more myself in the immediate future in any case; but I will study them at leisure and write to you again.

---

1 – Stephen Spender (1909–95), poet and critic: see Biographical Register.
2 – Spender had written on 29 Dec. 1929 that he was back in London until 1 Feb.
3 – Spender was to recall, in his autobiography *World within World* (1951): 'At our first luncheon [TSE] asked me what I wanted to do. I said: "Be a poet." "I can understand you wanting to write poems, but I don't quite know what you mean by 'being a poet'," he objected.'
4 – John Lyle Donaghy (1902–49), Irish poet and teacher, was educated at Larne Grammar School, County Antrim, and Trinity College, Dublin. His early poetry was published by the Yeats family's Cuala Press; and he was a friend of Samuel Beckett. His works include *At Dawn over Aherlow* (1926), *The Flute over the Valley* (1931), *Into the Light, and Other Poems* (1934).

With all best wishes for the New Year,

Yours sincerely,

[T. S. Eliot]

TO C. A. Siepmann[1] TS BBC

2 January 1930 *The Criterion*

Dear Mr Siepmann,

I ought perhaps to have answered your letter of the 17th December, to say that the dates mentioned suit me.[2] But I waited in the expectation of the formal contract, which has not yet arrived. Am I to expect it?

By the way, if you ever have time to answer this question: I have an Irish poet about, named Donaghy – rather a good poet – who is a friend of George (A.E.) Russell,[3] and says he has given Broadcast talks from Dublin. He wants to get any sort of literary work. Is it any use my sending him to anyone in the B.B.C., or would it be better for him to get an introduction from the Broadcast people in Dublin?

With best wishes for the New Year,

Yours very truly,

T. S. Eliot

TO Leonard Woolf[4] CC

2 January 1930 [*The Criterion*]

Dear Leonard,

This is to introduce to you Mr John Lyle Donaghy of Dublin. Mr Donaghy is primarily a poet, and I published a long poem by him in a

1–Charles Arthur Siepmann (1899–1985), radio producer and educationalist: see Biographical Register.
2–Siepmann had confirmed arrangements for a series of broadcast talks on 'Seventeenth Century Poetry': 'The dates of your six talks will be (1) Friday, 7th March, (2) Thursday, March 13th, and (3), (4), (5) and (6), Fridays, March 21st, 28th, April 4th and 11th respectively . . . and the fee for each talk, twelve guineas . . . A formal contract letter for your signature will be sent . . .'
3 – Æ: pseud. of George William Russell (1867–1935), Irish poet, painter, nationalist, mystic; friend of WBY and JJ; worked for some years as Assistant Secretary of the Irish Agricultural Organization Society; editor of the *Irish Homestead*, 1905–23; *Irish Statesman*, 1923–30. His works include *Collected Poems* (1913, 1926). He was known for his generosity towards younger writers. See Nicholas Allen, *George Russell (Æ) and the New Ireland 1905–30* (2003).
4–Leonard Woolf (1880–1969), writer and publisher: see Biographical Register.

recent number of the *Criterion*.[1] I have advised him to try to see you, because he has a collection of poems ready which I think ought to be published, and I should be glad if you could consider them. Also, he is desirous of getting reviewing to do. I have promised him some reviewing for the *Criterion*.

Mr Donaghy has worked on the *Irish Statesman*, and knows A.E. quite well. He has also, I understand, given talks from the Dublin Broadcast Station.

Yours ever,
[Tom]

TO *Julian Bell*[2]   CC King's

2 January 1930   *The Criterion*

Dear Bell,

This is a very belated acknowledgement of your letter of November.[3] You have a very good lot of poets – Empson and White and Bronowski [I] have already had an eye upon – and I like your birds very much. They are real birds, to begin with; and I have spent a great deal of time myself in bird study – though in another country. I will see that the series is reviewed, and look forward to more of them.

Yours sincerely
[T. S. Eliot]

1 – 'The Pit', *C.* 9 (Oct. 1929), 89–95.
2 – Julian Bell (1908–37), poet, scion of Bloomsbury: son of Clive and Vanessa Bell; nephew of LW and VW. Educated at King's College, Cambridge – where he became acquainted with William Empson and John Lehmann and disapproved of their modernistic tendencies: see his article 'The Prospect of Poetry', *Cambridge Review*, 7 Mar. 1930 – he wrote two volumes of minor verse, *Winter Movement* (1930) and *Works for Winter* (1936). After teaching English for some months at Wuhan University, China, 1935–7, he volunteered as an ambulance driver during the Spanish Civil War and was killed near Madrid in July 1937.

See Julian Bell, *Essays, Poems and Letters*, ed. Quentin Bell (1938); Hong Ying, *K: The Art of Love*, trans. Nicky Harman and Henry Zhao (2002); and Peter Stansky and William Abrahams, *Journey to the Frontier* (1966), as well as Stansky and Abrahams, *Julian Bell: From Bloomsbury to the Spanish Civil War* (Stanford, 2012), who correctly remark: 'Eliot's connections and affiliations with Bloomsbury were social and literary, rather than spiritual and philosophical' (42).

3 – Bell had sent (16 Nov. 1929) 'the accompanying works': the first six titles in a series of single new poems by young Cambridge poets – William Empson, T. H. White, John Davenport, Michael Redgrave, Jacob Bronowski, and 'Chaffinches' by Bell himself – entitled *Songs for Sixpence*, ed. J. Bronowski and J. M. Reeves (1929).

TO *Erich Alport*[1]

TS BL

2 January 1930   Faber & Faber Ltd

Dear Alport,

Many thanks for your letter of the 19th December.[2] I have meanwhile written fully to Clauss, after lengthy consultation with my directors, to explain that we felt sure that his treatment of the subject would be more suitable for a longer book than for a short pamphlet; that we were not at the moment able to undertake the longer book; but that we should like to keep it in mind and probably raise the question again later.[3]

Gundolf[4] is now in the hands of Grierson, a first rate authority, who will give his opinion as soon as he can; and Singer's Plato has gone to the greatest Plato scholar in Britain. We hope that the publishers of both will be patient; because with such big and expensive (and probably unprofitable) books as these, we really must take the best opinions before deciding.

With all best wishes for the New Year,

Yours sincerely
T. S. Eliot

1 – Dr Erich Alport (b. 1903), educated in Germany and at Oxford, was author of *Nation und Reich in der politischen Willenbildung des britischen Weltreiches* (1933). In the early 1930s GCF often sought his advice about German books suitable for translation into English.
2 – Alport reported that Max Clauss had written to TSE 'a fortnight ago', and had written again. He considered Clauss '*the* man to write' a study of German nationalism '& of new conservative tendencies': 'he has a reliable judgement, by instinct & knowledge, of politics & social forces.' For Clauss see TSE letter to him 3 Jan. 1930, below.
3 – Clauss had submitted in Dec. 1929 a synopsis of a proposed study of German nationalism: a portrait of political Germany at the present time, with all its currents and cross-currents.
4 – Friedrich Gundolf, né Gundelfinger (1880–1931), *Shakespeare: sein Wesen und Werk* (1928).

TO *E. M. Forster*[1]   CC

2 January 1930   [London]

Dear Forster,

  This is a very belated reply to your letter of the 17th ultimo.[2] I am very
sorry that I was unable to hear Mauron,[3] but it is too late to repine about
that now. As to Cavafy, I remember that I have two poems of his, which
I thought rather good; and I think that I should like to print them. I put
them aside, because I had no prospect of having room for more verse for
some time ahead. But I will look them out, and write to him direct.[4]

                                         Yours always sincerely,
                                         [T. S. Eliot]

TO *David Higham*[5]   CC

3 January 1930   [London]

Dear Higham,

  I find I failed to answer your letter of the 7th December![6] Anyway, I
am glad that some American publisher is enquiring about something for a

---

1–E. M. Forster (1879–1970), novelist and essayist: see Biographical Register.

2–Forster had seen his friend, the Greek poet Constantine P. Cavafy (1863–1933), who
lived in Alexandria, Egypt (where he worked as journalist and civil servant), and conveyed
to TSE 'a friendly and vague' message from him. (See Forster's account of Cavafy in his
Alexandria [1922]). Cavafy wished to know whether TSE was going to publish the two
poems he had sent. Mauron was due to arrive on 18 Nov.: 'I expect to go to the first of his
lectures,' wrote Forster.

3–Charles Mauron (1899–1966) trained as a chemist but suffered from increasingly
impaired eyesight. Author of *The Nature of Beauty in Art and Literature*, trans. Roger
Fry (Hogarth, 1927), he translated into French VW's *To the Lighthouse* and *Orlando*, and
collaborated with Fry on translations from Mallarmé. His later works include *Aesthetics
and Psychology* (1935) and *Des métaphores obsédantes au mythe personnel* (1962).

4–TSE may have forgotten that he had already published Cavafy's 'Two Poems. For
Ammones. If He Did Die', trans. G. Valassopoulo, in *C.* 8 (Sept. 1928), 33–4.

5–David Higham (1896–1978) worked for Curtis Brown Ltd, 1925–35; then for David
Higham Associates; author of *Literary Gent* (memoir, 1978). FVM told Helen Jacobs, 20
May 1935, of Higham: 'He is an ebullient young man with a curly moustache, and an
eager but not very accurate tennis player'; and he wrote to Joseph Chiari on 7 Feb. 1953
(when Higham was a director of Pearn, Pollinger, & Higham): 'Higham is a very active and
pushing agent.'

6–'We now have an enquiry from an American publisher of limited editions for something
of yours. I thought at once of that material that was in question with the Holliday Book
Shop. Did that ever go over? But if there is anything else that you might think more suitable,
do let me have it and we will see what we can fix up. One thing that does strike me as

limited edition. I feel however that it would be more prudent for me not to float any more limited editions in America until the end of the year at the soonest – for the reason that we are disposing of *two* (one a translation, the other some original poems) for next spring; and I don't want to dump too much at once. I may however have another essay to send along to you in a month or two.

With many thanks and best wishes for the New Year,

Yours sincerely,

[T. S. Eliot]

TO *Max Clauss*[1]   CC

3 January 1930   [London]

My dear Clauss,

I have been hoping to hear from you, but meanwhile I am writing to ask two questions. (1) should our payment for 'Der Hauptmann von Kapernaum' which amounts to £5:10:– be sent to you or direct to the author (care of you).[2] (2) I should like to hear from you very soon about the next year's competition, so that we can announce it in the next issue. I think that the notoriety of simultaneous publication in five languages, together with the collective payments, is sufficient inducement for young or little known writers; but I should be glad to hear from you whether you approve the association of an American periodical[3] or not. If yes, I

---

possible is that essay on POETRY AND PHILOSOPHY [*sic*] which we sent over to New York, after the serial side has been dealt with.' See 'Poetry and Propaganda', *Bookman* 70: 6 (Feb. 1930), 595–602.

1–Max Clauss (1901–88), German journalist and writer; editor of *Europäische Revue* (Berlin).

2–In 1929, a prize, 'The Five Reviews' Award', had been launched by five European literary reviews – C., *Europäische Revue* (Berlin), *NRF* (Paris), *Revista de Occidente* (Madrid), *Nuova Antologia* (Milan) – with the first of five annual awards going to the best short story written in German; subsequently for stories in English, French, Italian and Spanish; with the winning fiction being printed in all of the five reviews. The first award was adjudged by Clauss, E. R. Curtius and Thomas Mann (replacing the late Hugo von Hofmannsthal). TSE hailed this development in his 'Commentary', in C. 9 (Jan. 1930): 'It is not merely a means of bringing to notice new prose writers in five languages . . . We remark upon it still more as visible evidence of a community of interest, and a desire of co-operation, between literary and general reviews of different nations . . . All of these reviews, and others, have endeavoured to keep the intellectual blood of Europe circulating throughout the whole of Europe.' Ernst Wiechert, 'The Centurion' ('*Der Hauptmann von Kapernaum*'), C. 9 (Jan. 1930), was the first winner.

3–*Hound and Horn*.

suggest that there should be at the end an American award, distinct from the English award, which would be followed by the French, Italian and Spanish *before* the American.[1]

With most cordial wishes for the New Year,

Yours sincerely,
[T. S. Eliot]

TO *Hugh Macdonald*[2]

TS Williamson

3 January 1930   *The Criterion*

Dear Macdonald,

This is a very tardy reply to your letter of the 11th November. I really did not want to reply until I could give you such a reply as you would like to have. For the next three months, I have got involved in (1) a set of B.B.C. talks on 17th century poetry (2) an essay for a book on the 1880s which Walter de la Mare is editing[3] and (3) a book of some kind for my own firm. The last of these is becoming more and more and more unreal: but the first two will have to be done. Supposing I can do that introduction for you some time during April, is that any use to you or not?[4] I hope so, because I should like to do it. And by the way, is there any modern edition of Johnson's poems – or of those two poems – which is of any use?

I will write again in a week or two and suggest a meeting. Meanwhile, I hope I may hear from you.

1–Clauss replied on 14 Jan. that TSE should send payment for 'Der Hauptmann von Kapernaum' to the account of the *Europäische Revue*, but that copies of the Jan. issue should be sent to the author. As to the 'Five Reviews' prize, he was in agreement with TSE's proposals ('*je suis d'accord avec toutes vos suggestions pour l'avenir*' ['I agree with all your suggestions for the future']). He was writing a new circular for the five magazines, and a correspondence with the American review should follow.

2–Hugh Macdonald (1885–1958), who trained as a solicitor, went into partnership with Frederick Etchells to produce fine editions under the imprint of The Haslewood Books, 1924–31. His own works include *England's Helicon* (1925), *The Phoenix Nest* (1926), *John Dryden: A Bibliography of Early Editions and of Drydenianae* (1939), and *Portraits in Prose* (1946).

3–TSE, 'The Place of Pater', in *The Eighteen-Eighties*, ed. Walter de la Mare (1930); first published as 'Arnold and Pater', *The Bookman* 72: 1 (Sept. 1930), 1–7.

4–Macdonald enquired on 11 Nov. 1929, 'Our American agents keep asking us when the Johnson poems with your introduction will be ready . . . We should very much like to get the book out in the Spring of next year . . .' *London: A Poem and The Vanity of Human Wishes by Samuel Johnson, LL.D, with an Introductory Essay by T. S. Eliot*, came out in Autumn 1930.

With all New Year wishes,

Yours ever,
T. S. Eliot

TO *Bruce Richmond*[1]

3 January 1930   [Faber & Faber Ltd]

Dear Richmond,

I send herewith at last my belated review of *A Game at Chesse*.[2] When I finally got down to the job, I discovered that it is really a book for Pollard or Wilson or one of the bigwigs of text criticism, and not for me. The editor is not in the least interested in the literary or dramatic merits of the play! and his textual ingenuities are too deep for me. However, I thought I owed you a review of it anyway. If you prefer, scrap it and I will return the book to send to someone else. All that I can say (as you will see) is that here is a good text at last of a fine play. And it makes me want to scrap my essay on Middleton and write another, longer and better one. Meanwhile I want to write an essay to show the extent to which literary criticism must depend upon the researches of scholars (i.e. we know a lot more about Chapman than Swinburne did).

I want to review for you the Southwell next. (I regret now having lent my text of Southwell to Gordon George two years ago). I doubt whether vol. III of *The History of the Novel* is worth more than half a column.

Yours ever,
[T. S. E.]

---

1 – Bruce Richmond, editor of the *Times Literary Supplement*: see Biographical Register.
2 – 'A Game at Chesse' – on Thomas Middleton, *A Game at Chesse*, ed. R. C. Bald (1929) – *TLS*, 1460 (23 Jan. 1930), 56. '[T]he work of Middleton is more various than that of any other Elizabethan except Shakespeare himself . . . [O]ne of the few conjectures which we may safely make about this personage named Middleton is that he must have been a chess player, and that he was a poet who was fascinated by the dramatic element in the game; and we feel safe in asserting that the brilliant and ironic chess game in *Women Beware Women* is by the same hand as *A Game of Chesse*. And that it was the interest in, and the constraint of, the same game that produced the particularly orderly play by this exceedingly disorderly and even slovenly dramatist . . . [Mr Bald's] introduction is the best introduction to the play from the point of view of the historian . . . And the interest of the Jacobean public in *A Game at Chesse* was comparable to that of the modern public in any book or play which is expected, from hour to hour, to be "withdrawn" from circulation or from the stage under pressure from public authorities . . . But though the textual theories are for experts, the historical attributions are for everybody.'

TO *Charles Lavell*[1]   cc

5 January 1930   [Faber & Faber Ltd]

Dear Sir,

I am returning to you with thanks the two novels by Mr Douglas Goldring which accompanied your letter of the 18th ultimo.[2] I remember reading *The Fortune* with considerable interest at the time of its appearance.[3] We do not feel inclined however to take over at the present moment any novels of Mr Goldring which have already been published. If however Mr Goldring should send us a new novel which we liked well enough to publish the situation would be altered. But in general I cannot recommend my firm to add a new name to their list except by something hitherto unpublished.

> With many thanks,
> Yours faithfully,
> [T. S. Eliot]

FROM *TSE's Secretary* TO *Frank Slater*[4]   TS copy

5 January 1930   [Faber & Faber Ltd]

Dear Sir,

Mr Eliot has asked me to thank you for your kind letter of the 3rd, and to explain to you that he has found the giving of sittings for portrait sketches consumes so much time and has had heretofore such unsatisfactory results that, as he is very busy, he must regretfully decline any further invitations, however flattering.

> Yours faithfully,
> [Laura Maude Hill]
> Secretary.

1–Charles Lavell, Authors' and Playwrights' Representative, 13 Serjeants' Inn, Fleet Street, London: Douglas Goldring's agent.
2–Lavell had sent *The Fortune* (first published in Dublin in 1917) and *Façade* (Oct. 1917).
3–TSE reviewed *The Fortune* in *The Egoist* 5: 1 (Jan. 1918), 10. EVE wrote to Donald Gallup on 8 Jan. 1976: 'I can confirm that C54a, a review of Goldring's "The Fortune", is by Tom.'
4–Frank Slater (1902–65), artist, had been commissioned by the *Saturday Review* to do a portrait of TSE.

TO *T. O. Beachcroft*[1]

CC

6 January 1930   [*The Criterion*]

Dear Beachcroft,

I feel that it is time that I let you have these poems back.[2] I think that they are very skilful and that it is quite worth your while to have written them, but candidly I do not see what can be done with them at the moment. I don't think it desirable to pick out one or two for publication in the *Criterion*, because I think that the whole point of such a tour de force is its being kept up through a number of poems. On the other hand I cannot see any sale for a book of them. I[t] seems to me that they will have to wait until you have got a name in other ways. But this is only one man's opinion and you had better take others.

Meanwhile your Traherne has won much applause and I should like always to see anything that you write, either prose or verse, and would like to send you things for review.[3]

Do you know Donne well enough to review Hayward's text and Grierson's cheaper edition together?[4]

Yours sincerely,
[T. S. Eliot]

---

1 – T. O. Beachcroft (1902–88), author and critic. A graduate of Balliol College, Oxford, he joined the BBC in 1924 but then worked for the Unilevers Advertising Service until 1941. He was Chief Overseas Publicity Officer, BBC, 1941–61; General Editor of the British Council series 'Writers and Their Work', 1949–54. His works include *A Young Man in a Hurry* (novel, 1934) and *Collected Stories* (1946).

2 – Unidentified.

3 – 'Traherne, and the Doctrine of Felicity', C. 9 (Jan. 1930), 291–307. (He further published 'Traherne and the Cambridge Platonists', *The Dublin Review* 186 (Apr. 1930), 278–90.)

4 – Review of *John Donne: Complete Poems and Selected Prose*, ed. JDH; *Poems*, ed. H. J. C. Grierson, C. 9 (July 1930), 747–50.

TO C. C. Martindale[1]

CC

6 January 1930   [Faber & Faber Ltd]

Dear Sir,

I must apologise for not having answered your postcards immediately. I am writing to say that we are delighted to hear that you will be able to write the pamphlet for us.[2]

It would suit us to perfection if we could have your manuscript (of 5000 to 10,000 words) by the end of this month. If this date is possible for you I will send you a contract with that date; if not, I should be glad to know by what date you could let us have it. But I hope that the end of January will not be inconvenient. We arrange to produce these pamphlets very quickly upon receipt of manuscript: but you will of course receive proof.

Yours faithfully,
[T. S. Eliot]
Director.

TO *Walter de la Mare*[3]

TS De la Mare Estate

6 January 1930   *The Criterion*

My dear De la Mare,

Many thanks both for your letter about the 80s, and for the honour which you have, I suspect, inveigled others into agreeing to bestow upon

1 – Cyril Charlie Martindale, SJ (1879–1963), scholar, preacher, lecturer and broadcaster, became a Catholic convert in 1897 and entered the Jesuit noviciate. A prize-winning essayist at Pope's Hall (later Campion Hall), Oxford, he was ordained in 1911 and taught classics at Oxford, 1916–27. He then joined the staff of the Farm Street Church in Mayfair, London, where he was energetic in social causes. Celebrated for his lucid, forceful sermons and broadcasts, he gained worldwide renown for his involvement in the Roman Catholic international university movement and as a member of the central committee for the planning of the Eucharist Congresses. A prolific author, he was to publish over eighty books including *Faith of the Roman Church*; *What are Saints?*; *Broadcast Sermons*; *The Message of Fatima*; sixty pamphlets, and numerous articles. See Philip Caraman, *C. C. Martindale* (1967).

2 – *The Index*, a pamphlet in the Criterion Miscellany series (1930) defending the restrictions and defining the licence allowed to Roman Catholic readers.

3 – Walter de la Mare (1873–1956), poet, novelist, short-story writer, worked for the Statistics Department of the Anglo-American Oil Company, 1890–1908, before being freed to become a freelance writer by a £200 royal bounty negotiated by Henry Newbolt. He wrote many popular works: poetry including *The Listeners* (1912) and *Peacock Pie* (1913); novels including *Henry Brocken* (1904) and *Memoirs of a Midget* (1921); anthologies

me.[1] I must confess that the Royal Society of Literature, like the British Academy, is terra incognita on my map; and it is an honour I had never dreamed of – it is not so very many years since I was called a literary bolshevik (in the *Morning Post*, to be sure).[2] But I am highly pleased at being elected to the fellowship of a society to which you and several other writers whom I honour belong. I should be grateful if you would lighten my darkness by telling me what are the obligations and responsibilities of such a distinction.

The story, by the way, has gone to the printers, and you will receive proof duly.[3]

With most grateful thanks,
Yours sincerely,
T. S. Eliot

---

including *Come Hither* (1923). He was appointed OM, 1953; CH, 1948. See Theresa Whistler, *Imagination of the Heart: The Life of Walter de la Mare* (1993).

1 – De la Mare wrote (Dec. 1929) on behalf of the Royal Society of Literature: 'I have the honour to inform you that at the last meeting of Council a wish was expressed that you should accept the Fellowship of this Society, and I was asked to convey to you an invitation to join.' (The other new Fellows included Edith Wharton.) De la Mare sought to reassure TSE on 7 Jan.: 'I was merely asked to be the channel of communication, and a real happiness that was.'

2 – See TSE's 'London Letter' (Apr. 1927), *The Dial* 72: 5 (May 1927), 511: 'We have, then, a large number of writers giving the public what it likes . . . and the *Morning Post* to tell it that everything new is a symptom of Bolshevism.' See the notice of Alfred Noyes's recent paper on 'Some characteristics of Modern Literature': 'He set up a valiant and vigorous defence of the Victorian poets, and lashed with scorn the teachings of certain modern and middle-aged critics. The white light of vision, he declared, had been shattered, and we were in danger of intellectual disintegration . . . An obscene book, actually barred by the police, had received columns of attention in literary journals. The *Ulysses* of James Joyce was praised for its foulness. One writer said that its very obscenity was beautiful. Yet, in the view of Mr Noyes, the book was unspeakably degraded, a disgusting blot on our national heritage of literature . . . Nowadays a negative and despairing philosophy was advanced in a new and startling way . . . Could not the critics realise that poetry, in its deepest and broadest sense, is religion' ('The Victorian Poets: Mr Noyes' Criticism of Some Modern Critics', *Morning Post*, 26 Oct. 1922, 5). See too Alfred Noyes, 'Rottenness in Literature', *Sunday Chronicle*, 29 Oct. 1922, 2.

3 – 'The Picnic'.

6 January 1930   [Faber & Faber Ltd]

Dear Sir Frederick Pollock,

I am very much obliged to you for your kind letter. I knew your name first as an authority upon Spinoza; but it is evident that you also know a great deal more about Dante than I do; and I value your approval very highly.

I agree that the Temple is often unsatisfactory, either as graceful English or as exact translation. Yet for the passage you mention I still feel that 'vanity' is right. The word may convey a greater range of meaning to me than to others; but I should have thought that the reader who was ignorant of the original meaning of 'vanitas' might be ignored! The word – with the allusion to Ecclesiastes – is so much richer than 'emptiness' is.[2]

I only know Benvenuto da Imola by name; I wish I knew him face to face; but I am sure you are right about him.[3]

My remark about the quotation from Keats ought perhaps to be read in connexion with Richards's *Practical Criticism*: you might be justified in blaming me for writing a note comprehensible only to readers of that book. I still feel that my distinction between the quotation from Dante, the quotation from Shakespeare, and the quotation from Keats is valid. And I am not even sure that I accept the whole of your interpretation.[4] I believe

---

1 – Sir Frederick Pollock, 3rd Baronet (1845–1937), Barrister-at-Law; Fellow of Trinity College, Cambridge; Corpus Professor of Jurisprudence, University of Oxford, 1883–1903; Professor of Common Law at the Inns of Court, 1884–90. Editor of the Law Reports, 1895–1935, he was also the first editor of the *Law Quarterly Review*; Chairman of the Society of Authors from 1894. He was admitted to the Privy Council in 1911. Publications include *The Principles of Contract at Law and in Equity* (1876), *Spinoza: His Life and Philosophy* (1880), and *History of English Law before the time of Edward I* (with F. W. Maitland, 1895). Pollock was the father-in-law of Orlo Williams.

2 – Pollock wrote on 5 Jan., of TSE's *Dante* (1929); repr. *SE* (1932). 'It seems to me just the right thing to help and encourage beginners . . . The "Temple" Dante is quite as useful as you say, wonderfully good in its compass: but the English not always happy in detail. When Statius says *nostra vanitate* he does not mean vanity in any accepted English sense, but "the fact that we are shades" – emptiness (so my old friend A. J. Butler and probably others) is the nearest one word.'

3 – '[Y]ou would enjoy Benvenuto da Imola's commentary, being as I note free from vulgar prejudice against medieval Latin . . . B. d. I. was a man of excellent sense . . .'

4 – 'I am puzzled by your censure of Keats's aphorism. Obviously Beauty = Truth is nonsense, taken as a literal equation. But aphorisms are not equations even in prose: they are cryptic hints to be expanded. My expansion is something like this – the notion of Beauty, when you get beyond the mere fact of pleasurable experience, involves a certain order & harmony, and the more so the higher you go (music, architecture). Now order & harmony are of the essence of Truth as soon as you get beyond the correctness of this or that particular

that a 'work of art' (of course I am not referring to Keats's poetry) may be evil as well as good; that at least a very close simulation of 'order and harmony' may exist in works of art which are evil; and that the ultimate identity of the True, the Good and the Beautiful is only in the Absolute, where all cows are the same colour. Wd. you say that the proposition Beauty is Goodness, Goodness is Beauty is as valid as that of Keats?

If you are interested, I should be glad to send you a curious book which we have recently published, which aims to prove that Dante was a disciple of the *Cathari*, and a cryptic heretic. It is called *New Light on the Youth of Dante*.[1]

Yours sincerely,
[T. S. Eliot]

TO *Edith Sitwell*[2]   CC

6 January 1930   [Faber & Faber Ltd]

Dear Edith,

Thank you very much for your letter. It is a very great pleasure to me to think that you like the poem.[3]

I am venturing to write to ask you about Sachie.[4] Several months ago I wrote to ask him whether he would contribute a volume to 'The Poets

---

assertion. And the ordered harmony of intellectual construction brings with it a sense of beauty (as in pure mathematics – or a comprehensive legal doctrine – or in more complex matter Dante's scheme of the universe however little you accept it as corresponding to the facts now verifiable). So the conceptions of truth and beauty both bear witness to the same universal order.'

1 – Gertrude Leigh, *New Light on the Youth of Dante* (1929).

2 – Edith Sitwell (1887–1964): poet, biographer, anthologist, novelist; editor of *Wheels* 1916–21. Her collection, *The Mother and Other Poems* (1915), was followed by *Clown's Houses* (1918) and *The Wooden Pegasus* (1920). In 1923, her performance at the Aeolian Hall in London of her cycle of poems, *Façade* (1922), with music by William Walton, placed her briefly at the centre of modernistic experimentation. Other writings include *Collected Poems* (1930), *Fanfare for Elizabeth* (1946), *The Queens and the Hive* (1962), *Taken Care Of* (memoirs, 1965). She was appointed DBE in 1954. See John Pearson, *Façades: Edith, Osbert and Sacheverell Sitwell* (1978); *Selected Letters of Edith Sitwell*, ed. Richard Greene (1997); Richard Greene, *Edith Sitwell: Avant-Garde Poet, English Genius* (2011). TSE remarked to Mary Trevelyan on 16 Oct. 1949: 'Edith and Osbert [Sitwell] are 70% humbug – but kind – and cruel' (Trevelyan, 'The Pope of Russell Square', unpub. MS, 19).

3 – Sitwell wrote on 1 Jan.: 'I cannot tell you what a happiness and pride it was to me, on my return from the country, (where I was spending Christmas), to find the beautiful "Animula" waiting for me. How lovely it is, and what a great priviledge [*sic*] it is to possess it with an inscription from you. I do not need to tell you how deeply I value it.'

4 – Sacheverell Sitwell (1897–1988): writer, poet, art critic; youngest of the Sitwell trio. TSE thought him the 'most important and difficult poet' in *Wheels* (1918). Reviewing *The*

on the Poets'; I suggested Shelley as the subject. He replied that he would like to do it, if he need not be pressed for time. I sent him a contract dated for May 31st next, but said that if that was not enough time for him we would make it six months later. Since then I have written twice but have had no answer. I did not want to write again, thinking that he might be abroad or fearing that he was ill. Could you give me any news of him?

I am looking forward to your Pope.[1] And Vivienne and I both hope that we may see you soon.

Yours ever sincerely,
[T. S. E.]

TO *E. McKnight Kauffer*[2]   TS Morgan

6 January 1930   Faber & Faber Ltd.

My dear Kauffer,

Many thanks for your New Year letter. I hope that the year will be a successful and happy one for yourself.

People's Palace, he praised its 'distinguished aridity', and said he 'attributed more' to Sacheverell Sitwell than to any poet of his generation (*Egoist* 5: 6, June/July 1918). But 'Sachie' was best known for idiosyncratic books on travel, art and literature, including *Southern Baroque Art* (1924).

1 – *Alexander Pope* (F&F, 1930).

2 – E. McKnight Kauffer (1890–1954) – christened Edward Kauffer, he took the middle name McKnight in tribute to Professor Joseph McKnight (University of Utah) who had sponsored him to study in Paris – was an American artist who became renowned for his graphic designs, book illustrations and posters. He lived from 1914 to 1940 in England, gaining fame for his London Underground posters; he also illustrated books and book covers. On his return to New York in 1940, his chief client was American Airlines. His wife Marion Dorn (1896–1964) was a distinguished textile, rug and carpet designer. See Mark Haworth-Booth, *E. McKnight Kauffer: A Designer and His Public* (1979).

Asked in 1949 to contribute to a 'profile' of Kauffer, TSE wrote these words: 'I almost never succeed in remembering the first occasion of meeting anybody, especially after they have been friends of mine for a long time. I think it was at the end, or shortly after the end of the first World War that I met McKnight Kauffer, who was already, I think, better known and remarked among the younger artists than I was amongst the men of letters. He was in appearance very much the same figure that he is today: tall, slender and elegantly dressed, and wearing whatever he wore with a grace that would make the best of the best efforts of the best tailor. (I cannot venture to say much about his appearance, because there is said to be a facial resemblance between Kauffer and myself – at any rate, when I have asked for him at the building in which he lives, several successive porters have taken for granted that I was his brother).'

I am afraid that my play is still no further forward than those two fragments published in the *Criterion*.¹ When there is more, you shall know of it.² Meanwhile I have sent you the new *Criterion*, to ask you to read a verse play *Paid on Both Sides*, by a young man I know, which seems to me quite a brilliant piece of work.³ I should like to know whether you think the Gate Theatre would consider it – and first whether you like it yourself. This fellow is about the best poet that I have discovered in several years.⁴

With most cordial wishes,

Yours ever,

T. S. Eliot

то *Ada Leverson*⁵

ts Berg

7 January 1930   *The Criterion*

My dear Mrs Leverson,

Your letter did eventually arrive at our present address, 177 Clarence Gate Gardens, N.W.1 and gave us much pleasure.⁶ Vivienne and I had both been meaning to reply but have neither of us been very well. It was a great pleasure to hear from you although disappointing to learn as usual that you are just going abroad. We hope we may see you in the spring when you return. We read with great amusement your parody of Osbert and I am very grateful to you for letting me see it. I wish that it were

1 – TSE, 'Fragment of a Prologue', NC 4 (Oct. 1926), 713–18; 'Fragment of an Agon', NC 5 (Jan. 1927), 74–80; reprinted together as the unfinished *Sweeney Agonistes* (1932).

2 – Kauffer urged on 29 Dec. 1929: 'I hope so much that you will finish your play – and that I may have the privilege of doing something for it – does the "Fragment of an Agon" come into it – is it a part? . . . Is there any of it that I can see to start off with?' He responded to this letter from TSE on 14 Jan.: 'I shall study the two fragments I have of your own play with the idea that sometime we shall do it together both in book form and on the stage.'

3 – W. H. Auden, 'Paid on Both Sides', C. 9 (Jan. 1930).

4 – 'You are very right,' replied Kauffer (14 Jan.), '*Paid on Both Sides* is excellent and I have sent it to the Gate [Theatre, Notting Hill, London] for their decision which I hope to hear soon.'

5 – Ada Leverson, née Beddington (1862–1933): salonière (her friends included Aubrey Beardsley and Max Beerbohm); novelist and contributor to the *Yellow Book* and *Punch*. She was an intimate friend of Oscar Wilde, who dubbed her 'The Sphinx' and saluted her as 'the wittiest woman in the world', and she was loyal to him in his trials. TSE's friend Sydney Schiff was her brother-in-law. See Violet Wyndham, *The Sphinx and her Circle: A Biographical Sketch of Ada Leverson 1862–1933* (1963); Julie Speedie, *Wonderful Sphinx: The Biography of Ada Leverson* (1993).

6 – Leverson's undated letter, sent to 57 Chester Terrace, enclosed a parody of Osbert Sitwell under the title 'The Man who helped Himself', along with a parody of Viola Tree entitled 'Answers to Correspondents'. Leverson was about to leave for Florence 'until about April'.

suitable for the *Criterion* but that review has now become very middle-aged and I feel that it would be more suitable elsewhere.

With all good wishes from both of us and hoping to see you on your return.

Yours every sincerely,
T. S. Eliot

TO *Edward Meryon Wilson*[1]   CC

7 January 1930   [Faber & Faber Ltd]

Dear Sir,

Some considerable time ago you sent me some translations which you had made from Góngora.[2] I am not myself competent to criticise any translation from Góngora but I was able to obtain an expert opinion which I may say is very favourable to you. We do not feel however that this would be suitable for our list; but I am writing to encourage you to find some other publisher. If neither of the University Presses would publish it, I would be very glad to recommend it to the Hogarth Press.

As I have had your typescript so long I am holding it until you let me know to what address it should be sent.

I should be very glad to publish one or two of the poems in the *Criterion* if I find it possible to do so before your book appears. I should be glad if

1–Edward Meryon Wilson (1906–77) read Modern Languages at Trinity College, Cambridge; held the Esmé Howard Studentship at the Residencia de Estudiantes, Madrid, 1929–30; the Rouse Ball Studentship at Trinity College, Cambridge, 1930–1; Jane Eliza Proctor Visiting Fellowship at Princeton University, 1932–3; gained his PhD at Cambridge in 1934. He taught at Cambridge from 1933, and was appointed Cervantes Professor of Spanish, University of London, 1945–53; Professor of Spanish, Cambridge University (in succession to J. B. Trend), 1953–73; and Vice-Master of Emmanuel College, 1961–5. He was President of the Association of Hispanists of Great Britain and Ireland, 1971–3; President of the International Association of Hispanists, 1971–4. His publications include *The Solitudes of Don Luis de Góngora* (1931; 2nd edn, 1965), and *Poesías liricas en las obras dramáticas de Calderón* (with Jack Sage, 1964).

2–Wilson had submitted on 19 May 1929 passages from his translation from the 'Soledades'. 'Part of what I enclose will appear in the next number of *Experiment*. I should also like to know if I was to continue, if a publisher would take the risk of publishing it.'

you would suggest any that seem to you specially suitable and which have not appeared in other periodicals.[1]

Yours faithfully,
[T. S. Eliot]

TO *Howard Baker*[2]

CC

7 January 1930   [*The Criterion*]

Dear Mr Baker,

I find your essay very interesting indeed and should like to publish it. I do not think, however, that I shall be able to use it for six months or more and if in the meantime you wish to publish it elsewhere I should be glad if you would let me know. But if you allow me to publish this essay in the *Criterion*, I hope you will not mind removing from it the references to myself. I am afraid that you will find this difficult as they are rather interwoven in your article. But you will understand that I prefer, so far as possible, not to be mentioned in essays which I publish. Until I hear from you I retain the typescript.[3]

Yours truly,
[T. S. Eliot]

TO *Vivyan Eyles*[4]

CC

7 January 1930   [*The Criterion*]

Dear Miss Eyles,

I was very interested in your story and of course have a great respect

---

1–Wilson wrote on 3 Feb., 'I enclose the portions which you selected, with a few notes; I hope that they are satisfactory. Before sending my typescript to the Hogarth, I intend to revise it thoroughly and add to it.' Wilson's translation of lines from *Las Soledades* (1614), by Luis de Góngora y Argote (1561–1627), appeared in C. 9 (July 1930), 604–5.

2–Howard Baker (1905–90): American poet, playwright, critic. Born in Philadelphia and educated at Stanford University and at the Sorbonne (where he was assisted by Ernest Hemingway and Ford Madox Ford), he taught at Berkeley University, 1931–7, and at Harvard, 1937–43. Works include *Orange Valley* (novel, 1931), poetry including *Letter from the Country* (1941), and *Persephone's Cave: Cultural Accumulations of the Early Greeks* (1979).

3–Baker sent from Paris on 28 Jan. a revised version of his essay, having taken out references to TSE. (Allen Tate had prompted him to send it.) 'Belief and Dogma', C. 12 (July 1933), 608–20.

4–Vivyan Leonora Eyles (1909–1984), daughter of the novelist M. Leonora Eyles and stepdaughter of D. L. Murray, was to become a Lecturer in English Literature, University of

for Mr Stead's opinion.[1] I feel however after reading it several times that I concur with Mr Middleton Murry. The story is indeed intensely painful and I cannot feel that it has quite the significance which alone justifies harrowing people's feelings to that extent. I find in it however very considerable ability and should be very glad to see more of your work.

Yours sincerely,

[T. S. Eliot]

TO *Walter Lowenfels*[2]   cc

7 January 1930   [*The Criterion*]

Dear Mr Lowenfels,

I am returning 'Reality Prime' which interests me very much but I feel it would probably be better policy not to publish it apart from the whole book of which it is a part. The form being original I think that it needs a complete book in which to establish itself.

I congratulate you on *The Finale of Seem*[3] which I have enjoyed very much and thank you for sending me a copy.

Yours sincerely,

[T. S. Eliot]

Liverpool. In 1934 she married Mario Praz (separated 1942, divorced 1947); and in 1948 she married Wolfgang Fritz Volbach, art historian. She had one daughter, Lucia Praz (born 1938).

1 – The nineteen-year-old Eyles (in her first year at St Hugh's College, Oxford) confessed on 2 Dec. 1929 that JMM had rejected her story – 'one of the grounds for so doing, being that it is too harrassing' – but that WFS recommended her to send it to TSE (even though WFS had not actually read it).

2 – Walter Lowenfels (1897–1976): American poet, journalist, author, activist; member of the Communist Party; editor of the *Daily Worker* from the late 1930s until 1953. After working for his father (a butter manufacturer), 1914–26, he lived in Paris (1926–34), where he came to know expatriates including Ford Madox Ford and Henry Miller, and where he co-founded in 1930 the Carrefour Press. In 1953 he was arrested by the FBI and charged with conspiracy to overthrow the US government: his conviction in 1954 was overturned for lack of evidence. His works include *Episodes & Epistles* (1925) and *Steel, 1937* (1937). See too Hugh Ford, *Published in Paris: American and British Writers, Printers, and Publishers in Paris, 1920–1939* (1975).

3 – *Finale of Seem: a lyrical narrative* (1929)

TO *A. L. Rowse*[1]   TS Exeter

9 January 1930   Faber & Faber Ltd

Dear Rowse,

1. I have not forgotten Hancock and the pious Pitcairn Islanders. I will have decided shortly and write to you. I apologise for the delay, which has been due to searching for other ways of publication.[2]

2. As for your own article.[3] I did and do want something from you for the next number, which is otherwise rather a dull one. The last date is *February 7th*. I was counting on your essay on communism. As for your suggestion about Newman and Marx, that is capital: if you can't do it by Feb. 7th will you fix it for 6 months later? (when I wrote 'capital' I was unaware of a pun).[4] But meanwhile: can you do anything, can you write an essay around Clark, in time for the next number?[5] I had worked out the next number depending on a political-historical essay from you, you see. So please let me know whether you can carry out any of your suggestions by then or not.

I agree about Collingwood: I felt the same way.[6] I am delighted that you admire Auden; I am very enthusiastic about his work, and want it to be

1 – A. L. Rowse (1903–1997), historian; Fellow of All Souls, Oxford: see Biographical Register.

2 – Rowse wrote on 6 Jan., 'Do you still intend to use W. K. Hancock's manuscript about the mutiny of the Bounty sometime?' The essay did not appear in C. See 'Politics in Pitcairn', *Nineteenth Century and After* 109 (1931), 575–87; *Politics in Pitcairn and Other Essays* (1947). W. K. (later Sir Keith) Hancock was Australia's foremost historian; author of *Ricasoli and the Risorgimento in Tuscany* (F&G, 1926) and *Australia* (1930); accounts of British mobilisation on the home front during WW2; a Survey of British Commonwealth Affairs; and a biography of the South African statesman Jan Smuts. He was a founder of the Australian National University. See Jim Davidson, *A Three-Cornered Life: The Historian W. K. Hancock* (2010).

3 – '[A]bout the Communism article: I do shrink from it! I feel I haven't anything like command of such a vast subject. However I am prepared if you expect it, to write a straightforward article . . .' See 'The Theory and Practice of Communism', C. 9 (Apr. 1930), 451–69.

4 – 'I've been reading Newman's "Essay on the Development of Christian Doctrine' very carefully; and sometime soon I wd like to write on Newman + Marxism! I expect you know how closely Newman's "theory of developments" – as he called it – is an anticipation of Darwin + Marx, only in the sphere of ideas.' For Newman, see TSE to Smyth, 24 Jan. 1930, below.

5 – 'I want to write a little article – or a long review – a propos of G. N. Clark's *The Seventeenth Century*. It's an extremely good & important book, and for some years I have been following his historical writing. May I write a short article on "Historical Materialism & Mr G. N. Clark" or some such title?' See Rowse, 'G. N. Clark's Conception of History', C. 10 (Jan. 1931), 222–32.

6 – 'I was disappointed by Collingwood on "Value" in the current number of the *Criterion* – that's like him, he can be very airy & light weight at times, as very suggestive at others.'

forwarded in every way possible. He is my best poetic discovery in some years' time.[1]

Have you seen a book called *Politics* published by Daniels and written sympostically by some of the *New Age* people? It is pretty feeble; yet it does show some effort to restate the problems; and I think that if we could find three or four people with nothing necessarily in common except a perception that all political problems need to be restated, we might use it as a peg for a discussion. I[f] you have not seen the book, may I show you my copy? The difficulty is to find people who can think up to date about politics, and who think enough to be free of labels.

By the way, I wish you would tell David Cecil that I should like to have him writing in the *Criterion*.[2] I understand that his book on Cowper is very good: at any rate the man who has reviewed it for the *Criterion* thinks so.[3]

Don't expect much of my new poems.[4] They are very few. I think more of a translation I have made of *Anabase* by St Léger Léger, which will also be published in the spring.[5]

Please write as soon as you can.

Yours ever,
T. S. Eliot

———

R. G. Collingwood (1889–1943), philosopher and historian, was Fellow of Pembroke College, Oxford; later Waynflete Professor of Metaphysical Philosophy, Magdalen College, 1935–41. His works include *The Principles of Art* (1938) and *The Idea of History* (1945). See further Fred Inglis, *History Man: The Life of R. G. Collingwood* (2009).

1–'Auden's charade ["Paid on Both Sides: A Charade", C. 9 (Jan. 1930), 268–90] I was delighted by: he is a real discovery for you: some of the verse in it was of great beauty I thought. Do you know a young friend of his & mine, whom I'd like to introduce to you, Stephen Spender by name? I haven't seen much of his verse, but I've great belief in him.'

2–Lord David Cecil (1902–86): historian, biographer; Fellow of Wadham College, Oxford, 1924–30; Fellow of New College, 1939–69; Professor, Oxford University, 1948–70; author of *Early Victorian Novelists: Essays in Revaluation* (1934), *Jane Austen* (1936), and studies of various writers including Jane Austen, Hardy, Shakespeare, Walter Scott.

3–David Cecil's *The Stricken Deer, or The Life of Cowper* (1929) was reviewed by Richard Church, C. 9 (Apr. 1930), 545–48. Rowse responded on 11 Jan.: 'I'll certainly let Cecil know: yes, his book is exceedingly well written.'

4–'I can't tell you how much I look forward to your later poems coming out this spring.'

5–*Anabasis* (by Alexis St Léger Léger [pseud. St-John Perse, 1887–1995], poet and diplomat) was publicised by F&F as having been translated 'in collaboration with the author . . . Here, the French text appears side by side with Mr Eliot's English version, so that readers may judge for themselves of the merit and accuracy of the translation, and of the beauty of the original' (*Faber & Faber Spring Announcements 1930* and jacket copy).

TO *P. T. R. Gillett*   CC

9 January 1930   [Faber & Faber Ltd]

Dear Mr Gillett,

It is very pleasant to hear from you again, and I wish indeed, for old time's sake, that I could help in the way you suggest.[1] But I have discussed the matter with the Chairman, and I find that it is a definite rule that no discount advantages may be given to private individuals, even to near relatives of the Board and the Staff; the only exceptions occasionally made are in favour of authors whose works we publish.

But in cases where there is a rush on a first edition I may be sometimes able to see that you get a copy at the ordinary price when booksellers might tell you that it was unobtainable; and I will send you a complimentary copy of a small thing of my own as a partial amends for being unable to accede to your request.

Publishing has some advantages over banking, certainly; but not all the advantages. It is much more precarious.

Yours sincerely,
[T. S. Eliot]

TO *Montgomery Belgion*[2]   CC

9 January 1930   [*The Criterion*]

Dear Belgion,

Yours of the 6th. With diffidence, I think it is much more important, in the *Criterion*, to get a book reviewed by the right man than to get it reviewed timely. People don't go to the *Criterion* for stop-press notices of new work. I am, however, asking Fernandez if he would care to do it; but I don't want anyone of less size than Richards or Fernandez.[3]

---

1 – P. T. R. Gillett, who had been a colleague at Lloyds Bank, asked on 6 Jan.: 'I want to know if you would be good enough to let me have some books published by your house at special terms – you know BCs [bank clerks] have not too much money to spare – & since you left & took up your rightful occupation, your list contains books I covet – I should like if possible to have a signed Sassoon – the sequel to the memoirs of a F.H.M. [*Fox-Hunting Man* (1928)] – that was a fine book.

'I trust you are doing well – I know you must be happier away from "Bankdom".'
2 – Montgomery ('Monty') Belgion (1892–1973), author: see Biographical Register.
3 – MB proposed 'with all diffidence' that if IAR did not write on his *Our Present Philosophy of Life* in good time, it should be offered to someone else who would definitely produce a review for the April issue. His book was reviewed by Ramon Fernandez in C. 9 (July 1930), 759–63.

Process and Reality: date, February 6th the last possible.[1] If you can't do it to your satisfaction in the time let me know and we will put it into June.

(3). I quite agree that 'the effects of imaginative literature' is a subject for study.[2] But I think an historical study would show that these effects have differed at different epochs, and that the element of propaganda has grown since the middle of the 18th century. I would tie this tin-can to the tail of your 'something that has been going on *all the time*'. One point: people are perhaps more affected by propaganda since the word itself was discovered. I feel that a contemporary poem may have more 'propaganda' effect merely because people now *want* to find propaganda in poetry. There are many cross-currents to be taken account of.

Your (b) and (c) do not seem to me to touch my objection. That is, that you seem to abolish (which you can't do) the ordinary distinction between 'artist' and 'artisan'.[3] If you call musicians and painters and sculptors merely 'artisans', you are really merging the 'artist' in the 'artisan'; because the only thing you have to set against the artisan is the worker in words, who, you say, is always a propagandist. But you would not say that it is propaganda that makes the difference between the artist and the artisan?

I have bothered a good deal about 'classic' and romantic. The trouble there is that the terms change their meaning for every decade you are talking about. And I suspect that your word propaganda, which is fairly

---

1 – MB asked for a deadline for his review of A. N. Whitehead's *Process and Reality: An Essay in Cosmology*, which HR had passed to him. See his untitled review in C. 9 (Apr. 1930), 557–63.

2 – MB wrote on 6 Jan.: '(3) (a) I don't think that there is any doubt about our being able to observe the people around us being influenced by the propaganda in contemporary works of imaginative literature, just as they are influenced by propaganda in the popular press. I also think it must be admitted that we do not necessarily fully understand yet what are the effects of imaginative literature: I mean, it surely remains possible for someone to point out something new, i.e. something that has been going on all the time, but that has not been insisted upon.'

3 – '(b) As to Epstein, or Michelangelo, or Donatello, the question is not, as I see it, whether a work of sculpture contains any "intelligible" propaganda, or not, but whether it can possibly contain any propaganda, intelligible or not, which is not dependent for its effectiveness on the spectator's having heard or read certain things . . . (c) I do not think you impale me on the horns of your dilemmas, because I was not intending any distinction between poets and other artists as regards their being on a level with all artisans. It seems to me, or at least I suspect, that all artists, poets included, cannot be other than artisans, although the poet, or rather the writer of imaginative literature, does employ theories of life as part of his working material.'

new, has the same trouble. I should be glad if you would explicate the propaganda in the *Odyssey*, or even in *Phèdre*.

Yours
[T. S. Eliot]

TO *Christopher Dawson*[1]

cc

10 January 1930   [Faber & Faber Ltd]

Dear Mr Dawson,

I enclose our contract, which I hope you will be able to return signed quickly, so that we may send you the counterpart. As I believe I told you, our contracts with all contributors to the *Criterion Miscellany* are identical.[2]

Did I tell you that the end of January would suit us very well indeed?

You will shortly receive proofs of your essay, which will occupy an important place in the March number.[3] It is possible that I may have to hold over the Dante review.[4]

Yours sincerely,
[T. S. Eliot]
Editor.
Director, Faber & Faber Ltd

TO *C. C. Martindale*

TS Valerie Eliot

10 January 1930   *The Criterion*

Dear Sir,

Following my letter of a few days ago, I enclose our contract. I hope that you will find it satisfactory, so that you can return it to us immediately and receive the counterpart.

---

1 – Christopher Dawson (1889–1970), cultural historian: see Biographical Register.
2 – The contract for Dawson's pamphlet *Christianity and Sex* (Criterion Miscellany 13, 1930).
3 – 'The End of An Age', C. 9 (Apr. 1930), 386–401.
4 – Untitled review of Gertrude Leigh, *New Light on the Youth of Dante*, and Carl Vossler, *Mediæval Culture: An Introduction to Dante and His Times*, in C. 9 (July 1930), 718–22.

I enclose a cutting from today's *Nation*, which will illustrate the sort of misunderstanding that I had in mind, and which will I hope aid to convince you of the desirability of your essay.[1]

Yours faithfully,
T. S. Eliot
Director, Faber & Faber Ltd.

TO *A. E. Taylor*   CC

10 January 1930   [Faber & Faber Ltd]

Dear Professor Taylor,

I thank you very warmly for the very great trouble and care that you have given to the Singer book.[2] We regard your opinion as final. The small fee which we have sent is very inadequate compensation for so conscientious (and I may say, monumental!) a report.

---

1 – The enclosure was a letter, dated 4 Jan., from T. D. Lowe of the Glasgow Literary Club on 'Catholics and Literature': 'After reading Mr Leonard Woolf's interesting article on Messrs. Chesterton and Belloc, one cannot but reflect upon the limitations of that world as evidenced by the recent issue of a revised version of the Catholic "Index of Banned Books". No sincere Catholic can say "Securus Orbis Librorum Judicat", nor can Mr Woolf's interesting prediction that Mr Belloc will one day attribute *Candide* to the Catholic Church be fulfilled, since *Candide* is one among many books that Mr Belloc is forbidden to read. One suspects, however, that Mr Belloc has peeped several times into Voltaire, and also that he has done more than peep into the *Decline and Fall of the Roman Empire*, another banned book. An "apologia" of the Index from the pen of either Mr Chesterton or Mr Belloc would make excellent reading; it would probably prove to be a best seller. True, we have an official defence from Cardinal Merry del Val, but his advocacy would convince no one who retains any vestige of individual intelligence.

'I suppose it is too much to hope that either "G. K. C." or Mr Belloc will break a lance in support of the Index. That is a topic on which clever Catholics wisely prefer to maintain silence.'

2 – Taylor wrote on 2 Jan., after reading about 40 pp. of Dr Kurt Singer's *Platon der Gründer* – 'The Germans are at last finding out what we have known all along in this country' – and on 6 Jan.: 'I do not recommend publishing an English version of Dr Singer's book, unless it were explicitly published not as an interpretation of Plato, but as a study in the pathology of the Teutonic mind. To my mind a book which goes from first to last on the assumption that Plato was a "superman", like the heroes of Wagner's *Ring* . . . merely calls for the comment that no one is entitled to make it his postulate that Plato was the same sort of person as Nietzsche without giving convincing justification . . . It is funny that Dr Singer should take Nietzsche in this way for gospel, since his name could seem to show that he is certainly a "bourgeois" and perhaps a Jew . . .' His two-page reader's report (6 Jan.) deplored Dr Singer for caricaturing 'Plato's real meaning.' GCF wrote to Erich Alport on 9 Jan. 1930: 'I am sorry to begin by saying that we have turned down Singer's Plato. We had a very long report on it from A. E. Taylor, who is the leading English Platonist, which made it impossible for us to come to any other decision. He regarded the book as too essentially German in character to bear translation into English . . .'

It may interest you to know that I sent another book by one of the same German group – a book on quite a different subject – to my friend and your colleague Grierson; and that his opinion of that book is very similar to your opinion of Singer. It is a disappointment to me, because I should like to be able to think that the Germans were more European than they are.

I have to speak of two matters. (1) My Board was very much interested in your suggestions, and particularly Jaeger's *Aristotèles*.[1] If you consider that this book really needs trans- [*runs off the page*] (1) on the size of the book (2) on the public to be reached apart from students of Greek philosophy who know German – and I take for granted that anyone who at all specialises in Greek philosophy does and must know German (my own attainments you would consider very low, but I possess Diels, Siebeck and Heinrich Meier). We should like now and then to publish a translation of some important work of German scholarship. But qualified translators are few, and must be well paid; the work is not worth doing unless it can be done thoroughly; and a young firm cannot afford it unless there is likely to be considerable success of esteem, and a steady, even if small demand.

(2). I will try to persuade Desclée to send a set of their Aquinas for you.[2] It is a handy popular edition, each volume done by some eminent French O.P. such as Garrigou-Lagrange.[3] But French publishers are stupid and covetous, and they may not see how well worth their while it would be.

Yours sincerely,
[T. S. Eliot]

---

1 – Taylor recommended (2 Jan.) Werner Jaeger's *Aristotèles: Grundlegung einer Geschichte seiner Entwicklung* (1923) as 'the most important book written' on Greek philosophy; see *Aristotle: Fundamentals of the History of His Development*, trans. Richard Robinson (1934). Jaeger (1888–1961) was Professor of Classics, Berlin University, 1921–36; Professor of Classics, Chicago, 1936–9; Harvard, 1939–61. His other works include editions of the Church father Gregory of Nyssa; Aristotle's *Metaphysics* (ed., 1957); and *Paideia: die Formung des griechischen Menschen* (3 vols, 1933–47: *Paideia: The Ideals of Greek Culture*, trans. Gilbert Highet, 1939–44); and he founded the journals *Die Antike*, 1925–55, and *Gnomon* (est. 1925).

2 – Taylor hinted on 2 Jan., 'It would be tempting, if one got the chance, to try an article about St Thomas in connection with the Desclée ed. which I regret not to have seen . . . [I]f I attempted anything of the kind, I should want to discuss Thomas as a philosopher, not as a theologian . . .'

3 – Réginald Marie Garrigou-Lagrange, OP (1877–1964): Dominican priest; leading Catholic Thomist theologian; author of *Le sens commun: La Philosophie de l'etre et les Formules Dogmatiques* (3rd edn, 1922), and *Les Trois Conversions et les Trois Voies* (1933): both in TSE library.

TO *Douglas Goldring*[1]   CC

10 January 1930   [Faber & Faber Ltd]

Dear Goldring,

Thank you for your letter of the 5th instant.[2] Your agent had already sent me the two books, and I had discussed them with some of my Board. Indeed I remember *The Fortune* very well, and my opinion about it has not changed. But I have now acquired the publisher's point of view, and that is, *particularly* for a young firm: it does not do for us to take over books which have already been published, unless we have first obviously taken on the author's new works. If, that is, we publish a new book or two, so as to be recognised as the publishers of that author, we can afford to republish his earlier works. In other words, can you offer us one or two new novels first? and if we went in for these, we should certainly want to collect your previous work.

Hoping to hear from you,

                        With all best wishes,
                        [T. S. Eliot]
                        Director.

TO *Hugh Macdonald*   TS Williamson

10 January 1930   *The Criterion*

Dear Macdonald,

Very many thanks for your letter.[3] And it is extremely generous of you to send me a box of cigars. Punch, too. My first cigar, smoked in New York in 1906, was a Punch. I acquired a taste for good cigars – one of the few branches of knowledge that I did pursue successfully – in America;

1–Douglas Goldring (1887–1960), novelist, dramatist, publisher, editor, travel writer, was assistant editor of *The English Review* (under Ford Madox Ford), 1908–9. His works include the novel *The Fortune* (1917), as well as *South Lodge* (1943).
2–Goldring invited F&F to reissue his pacifist novel *The Fortune*, which had been published in Ireland: 100 copies had been sent out for review in the UK, but there had been no significant sale in 1917–18. TSE had reviewed the work with approval in *The Egoist* 5: 1 (Jan. 1918), 10.
3–Macdonald wrote on 8 Jan.: 'April will do very well for the Introduction to the Johnson poems. We can then publish the book in June . . . Can you give me any notion of the number of words it will run to? . . . I will get you a modern edition of the poems if I can find one that is of any use . . . Last year you sent us *A Song for Simeon* which we much value. I am sending you a few cigars . . . I wish you could find time to see me as we must settle outstanding points . . .'

but this is the first time in my life that I have ever had a whole box of them. Thank you again. I want you to know that the quality is not lost on me!

My wireless talks run through April, but I hope to have them all *written* by the middle of March, and I think a fortnight's intensive work should do the Introduction, though I ought to be rereading Johnson at once. I will get him out of the London Library, but I thought you might know of some modern edition which I might buy. And I should like to borrow your text to look at.

I think about 4000 words will be my length. I don't want to review the whole of satire from Juvenal: but I ought to try to define the characteristic merits of the late Augustan poetry of England, and fix the place of Johnson among the innumerable small but competent coupleteers of his time. I have a set of Poets, including the Phillipses, Shenstone and Churchill, which is useful.

I am glad that it has now become really necessary that we should meet; and I will ring you up at the Law Courts on Monday or Tuesday to try to fix a day for lunch.

As you have *Simeon* I will send you his successor, such as it is.

With best wishes for the New Year to Mrs Macdonald and yourself,

yours ever,

T. S. Eliot

It was Walter Scott who originally awoke me to the merit of Johnson's poetry. Have you ever considered what a mine of information, and what learning and good taste, is to be found in Scott's chapter heading quotations? An essay might be written on the subject.

I hope you will be able to price the Johnson fairly low.

TO *John Middleton Murry*[1]   TS Northwestern

15 January 1930   *The Criterion*

My dear John,

I am very sorry to find that I did not reply to your question about the essay on Values.[2] I thought I had done so. I have just been going through the material which I had promised to publish in the March number and

1 – John Middleton Murry (1889–1957), writer, critic, editor: see Biographical Register.
2 – JMM reminded TSE on 10 Jan. that he had said he would let him know whether he had enough room in his next number for 'the essay on Values, of which I spoke'. JMM, 'The Detachment of Naturalism', C. 9 (July 1930), 642–60.

I [am] more than doubtful of being able to find room for it, although I should like to produce it immediately after Fernandez. Now could you let me have the article and if I cannot get it into March I will put it certainly into the June number. I should be very sorry not to have it because this is a problem which I should like to follow up from various points of view.

I want to send you a big book on Saint John of the Cross which has been sent to me by a French Carmelite named Father Bruno.[1] I don't know who he is but he seems to be acquainted with the work of Baruzi which I believe you have read.[2] I should like to read the book myself but as I shall not be able to find time for a long while I will send it on to you if you have not already had a copy. If it is a good book I should be glad to have a note of it for the *Criterion*.[3]

Yours ever affectionately,
Tom

TO *Stuart Gilbert*[4]

CC

15 January 1930   [Faber & Faber Ltd]

Dear Mr Gilbert,

Thank you for your letter of January 12th.[5] I am glad to hear from you that the matter is not so serious as it sounded from what Mr Schwartz

1 – Père Bruno de Jesus Marie, OP, *S. Jean de la Croix* (1929).
2 – A copy of Jean Baruzi, *Saint Jean de la Croix et la problème de l'expérience mystique*, 2nd edn rev. (1931), inscribed by the author, is in TSE's library. JMM responded (17 Jan.): 'Yes, I studied Baruzi's fine book very closely. Père Bruno's will have to be very good to stand comparison: but quite likely it *is* very good.'
3 – The work was not reviewed in *C*.
4 – Stuart Gilbert (1883–1969), English literary scholar and translator, was educated at Hertford College, Oxford (taking a first-class degree in Classics), and worked in the Indian Civil Service; and then, following military service, as a judge on the Court of Assizes in Burma. It was only after his retirement in 1925 that he undertook work on Joyce, having admired *Ulysses* while in Burma. After befriending Joyce and others in his Paris circle (including Sylvia Beach and Valery Larbaud), he wrote *James Joyce's 'Ulysses': A Study* (F&F, 1930). He helped JJ with the French translation of *Ulysses;* and in 1957 edited *Letters of James Joyce* (with advice from TSE). In addition, he translated works by Antoine de Saint-Exupéry, Roger Martin du Gard, Paul Valéry, André Malraux, Jean Cocteau, Albert Camus, Jean-Paul Sartre and Georges Simenon.
5 – Jacob Schwartz – proprietor of Ulysses Bookshop, 187 High Holborn – had reported to TSE Gilbert's complaint that Edmund Wilson, in his essay 'James Joyce', *The New Republic* 61: 785 (18 Dec. 1929), 84–93, had cheekily quoted from the manuscript of Gilbert's yet unpublished book on JJ. But Gilbert reassured TSE on 12 Jan.: 'I fear that Schwartz may have exaggerated my feelings in the matter; he happened to be present at Mr Joyce's when I was reading the article, and, as a matter of fact, I was more amused than indignant. I wish

said. I am still unable to find out whether, or if so how, Mr Edmund Wilson[1] could have seen your Ms. It had not been sent to America by us I find and we have so far only discussed it with representatives of American firms in London.

Also I do not believe that the publication of Mr Wilson's article will affect the sale of the book unfavourably. We have [e]very hope that it will be taken by an American publisher and that if so it will have a good sale in America.

With all best wishes,
Yours sincerely,
[T. S. Eliot]

TO *René Taupin*[2]

MS Valerie Eliot

17 January 1930   *The Criterion*

Dear Sir,

I have to thank you for sending me so graciously your *Influence du Symbolisme français*. Of course I read the book because I read with avidity anything which mentions myself; but having read from vanity, I remained to admire.

I would say that yours is the 'best' book on the subject, except that I know no other to which to compare it. It is indeed the only book on the subject. I do not know which more to admire, your address in informing yourself fully and accurately, or the just criticism issuing from your exact information.

---

he (Mr Wilson) had mentioned that Messrs Faber and Faber are publishing my book – otherwise no harm is done.'

1–Edmund Wilson (1895–1972), highly influential literary critic, social commentator and cultural historian; worked in the 1920s as managing editor of *Vanity Fair*; later as associate editor of *The New Republic* and as a prolific book reviewer. Major publications include *Axel's Castle: A Study in the Imaginative Literature of 1870–1930* (1931) – which includes a chapter on TSE's work, sources and influence – *The Triple Thinkers: Ten Essays on Literature* (1938), and *The Wound and the Bow: Seven Studies in Literature* (1941). TSE was to write to Geoffrey Curtis on 20 Oct. 1943: 'Edmund Wilson is a very good critic except that, like most of his generation in America, he has mixed his literary criticism with too much political ideology of a Trotskyite variety and perhaps he is also too psychological, but I have a great respect for him as a writer and like him as a man.'

2–René Taupin (1905–1981): French translator and critic who lectured in Romance Languages at Columbia University, New York. A friend of Louis Zukofsky, and correspondent of EP, he was author of *L'Influence du Symbolisme Français sur la Poésie Américaine (de 1910 à 1920)* (1929): *The Influence of French Symbolism on Modern American Poetry* (rev. edn 1981).

The points on which I can correct you are very few. I did *not*, I regret to say, ever know Apollinaire or Salmon whilst in Paris. My acquaintance with their works dates from a moment – say 1921 – when my own style was already formed. On the other hand, I knew the work of Laforgue long before I knew the work of Pound or Hulme or Gourmont or any of the American poets you discuss. My first poems are almost pure Laforgue, with a little Baudelaire. Gautier I should never have studied but for the suggestion of Pound; and to Gautier *and* Pound I owe the series of poems which you rightly put in the Gautier tradition. And – a very small correction – the influence of the Elizabethan dramatists was much stronger upon me than that of Donne.[1]

I wonder if it would interest you to write for the *Criterion* at some time (1) a paper on the influence of Gourmont in England and America, or (2) a paper on the influence of Hulme?[2] The influence of Hulme is more difficult to define, because it has not ended. For instance, I believe that it was myself who brought Hulme to the notice of Ramon Fernandez.

With very many thanks,

I am
Your Obedient Servant,
T. S. Eliot

1 – See ch. VI: 'Deuxième phrase de l'Imagisme: T. S. Eliot', 220: 'Eliot a connu pendant son séjour à Paris Apollinaire et [André] Salmon, et . . . ses théories étaient assez voisines de celles de ces poètes.' Detecting in some of TSE's *Sweeney* poems the influence of Apollinaire and Salmon, he declared (221–2): 'La poésie d'Eliot est de leur tradition: c'est une habile groupement d'impressions sensorielles imaginés; et l'art de ce groupement, Eliot l'a en partie reçu de l'école d'Apollinaire, des Elizabéthains, de Laforgue, de même qu'il a reçu de Baudelaire et de Corbière certains procédés de diction ou certain art dans le choix des images.' ('While he was in Paris, Eliot knew both Guillaume Apollinaire and André Salmon, and . . . their influence is audible in certain of his poems. . . . The poetry of Eliot belongs to the same tradition: it is a skilful grouping of highly imaginative sense impressions. The art is one which Eliot learned partly from the school of Apollinaire, partly from the Elizabethans, and partly from Laforgue, just as he learned from Baudelaire and from Corbière certain practices of diction and the choice of images' [*The Influence of French Symbolism on Modern American Poetry*, trans. William Pratt and Anne Rich Pratt, revised and ed. William Pratt, 1985, 190–1].)
2 – Taupin, 'The Example of Rémy de Gourmont', C. 10 (July 1931), 614–25.

TO *Samuel Eliot Morison*[1]   CC

17 January 1930   [Faber & Faber Ltd]

My dear Morison,

I was very glad to get your letter of December 19th,[2] as it clears up two problems. The volume of Winthrop papers[3] reached me, but no letter about it; so I admired it and put it away wondering why I was treated to so handsome a book. Now I understand, I am very doubtful whether I am the competent person to review it: I have no special knowledge of the period, and no connexion with the Winthrop family. If I don't review it, I ought to return it. Can you allege any excuse for my reviewing it?[4]

The other mystery was my election as a member of the Colonial Society. I was much pleased by this, although I could not understand how it happened; I now believe it to be due to your good offices.

I am sorry to suspect that I never thanked you for your little history of the U.S.A. which I read with great interest, not the [*typing runs off the page*] your comments on contemporary figures. I can only reciprocate by sending you my *Dante*, a small book which has a similar 'one hour' function which I hope it fulfils.

With many thanks, and hoping to see you again before a long time has passed,

Yours sincerely,
[T. S. Eliot]

1–Samuel Eliot Morison (1887–1976), American historian and a cousin of TSE, was for thirty years from 1925 Professor of History at Harvard. In 1922 he became the first Harmsworth Professor of American History at Oxford. His works include *The Maritime History of Massachusetts* (1921), the history of Harvard University (5 vols, 1930–6), *History of U.S. Naval Operations* (15 vols), the *Oxford History of the American People* (1965), and *The European Discovery of America* (1972). A Fellow of the Society of Antiquaries and of the American Philosophical Association, he served too as President of the American Historical Association. His awards included the Bancroft Prize (twice); the Pulitzer Prize (twice); the Alfred Thayer Mahan Award of the Navy League; the Gold Medal for History, National Institute of Arts and Letters; and the President's Medal for Freedom. See also Morison, 'The Dry Salvages and the Thacher Shipwreck', *The American Neptune* 25: 4 (1965), 233–47.
2–'I write to give you a word of welcome to the Colonial Society of Massachusetts, of which you were elected a corresponding member today. Membership involves no dues or obligations . . .
'Did you receive the volume of Winthrop Papers sent to you for review for the *New England Quarterly*?'
3–*The Winthrop Papers*, vol. I (1929).
4–Morison replied on 3 Feb.: 'Winthrop's writings have little literary merit, but contain much human interest. His Experientia and letters to his wife give one the clue to the workings of a puritan mind. For this reason I thought the volume might interest you . . . [Y]our position is unique in that you have gone around the world to get to him!'

TO *A. E. Taylor* CC

17 January 1930   [Faber & Faber Ltd]

Dear Professor Taylor,

I have shown your last letter to my Board, and after what you say, we feel unanimously that we should see Jaeger's book – not to form our own opinion of its value, for your opinion is final – but merely to reckon what it would cost us to publish it.[1] Could you let me know the name of the publisher, so that I may send for a copy?

I am also authorised to ask you whether, in the event of our deciding to venture on a translation, you could (1) recommend a translator (2) give the book the very great advantage of an Introduction, or at least a Preface, by yourself? Such a book would not be a money-maker; we should publish it for its distinction; and the mere evidence of your imprimatur would make a great difference.

And as for a translator, you will realise the advantage of finding a person not only competent, but already familiar with and believing in the particular book: and I thought you [may] know of such an one, perhaps among your own pupils.

Yours very sincerely,
[T. S. Eliot]
Director.

TO *E. Gordon Selwyn*[2] CC

17 January 1930   [Faber & Faber Ltd]

Dear Dr Selwyn,

I will repeat the apologies and regrets which I expressed to you feebly over a feeble telephone. I was very sorry not to be able to lunch with

---

1–Taylor had urged, on 13 Jan.: 'Werner Jaeger is the big man in Greek philosophy, now at the University of Berlin.' His *Aristoteles* 'lays the foundations on which serious further study of the great Greek tradition in philosophy will have to build . . . Jaeger has shown on a big scale [438 pp.] the right method to follow in getting at Aristotle's mind . . . [It is] *the* outstanding book.'

2–The Revd Edward Gordon Selwyn (1885–1959): editor of *Theology: A Monthly Journal of Historic Christianity*, 1920–33. Educated at Eton and King's College, Cambridge (Newcastle Scholar; Porson Scholar and Prizeman; Waddington Scholar; Browne's Medallist; 2nd Chancellor's Medallist), he was Rector of Redhill, Havant, 1919–30; Provost in Convocation, 1921–31. He was to become Dean of Winchester, 1931–58. His writings include *The Approach to Christianity* (1925); *Essays Catholic & Critical by Members of the Anglican Communion* (ed., 1926).

you, but remind you of your promise to forewarn me of your next visit to London in February, and to lunch with me on one of those days at the Royal Societies'.

I am very glad to hear that my paper on 'Lives of Jesus' will still be acceptable, because I look forward to writing.[1] At the moment I am worrying over some B.B.C. talks and over an essay for an omnium Clarendon Press volume on the '80s; but as soon as I can find that I shall be able to write these, I will set to work on the essay for you.

I still wish that *Theology* could exchange with the *Criterion*. After all, there is a good deal of theological matter in the *Criterion* – some people murmur, too much – and I think that the *Church Times* and such papers ought to take more notice of us.

By the way, my firm is publishing early in the spring, on my recommendation, a very remarkable book on the Trial and the Resurrection.[2] The author is a man, unknown to me, who was convinced by an ingenious examination of the records, to believe in the Resurrection. It is amazingly matter of fact, and the way the man works out the events from the moment of Gethsemane according to the *time* that must have elapsed, is very brilliant. I shall see that a copy is sent to you, or even an advance proof copy. If I was wrong about this book, I ought not to be publishing in a firm at all! At the same time, we are publishing a small book of verse of my own, entitled 'Ash Wednesday'.[3]

Yours sincerely,

[T. S. Eliot]

1 – Selwyn had written on 8 Jan.: Your article . . . on Lives of Jesus will be welcome any time.'
2 – *Who Moved the Stone?* by Frank Morison – pseud. of A. H. Ross (1881–1950), advertising agent and writer – was to become a perennial bestseller. TSE's Reader's Report (18 Dec. 1929) reads:

'I began reading this book with every prejudice against it, but was very quickly interested. I should like us to publish this book. I suggest of course no advance and modest royalties.

'I have not come across any book at all like this. It is not dogmatic theology or on the other hand sloppy modernism, and it is not biblical criticism in the ordinary sense. It is unsectarian but not "non-sectarian". It is well written, and as absorbing as a detective story. I am impressed by the author's sincerity.

'I admit that from a popular point of view the first part of the book is the most exciting. The reconstruction of the night and day after Gethsamene [*sic*] is very remarkable; the portraits of Pilate and his wife Claudia are done with great discretion. I expected at every moment that the author would indulge in the extreme Maurois-Ludwig-Fleg imagination, e.g. at this point Pilate took another sip of wine, scratched his nose, and spoke as follows etc. but there is none of that at all.

'I think however that the book should be read and approved by at least three directors before we accept it.'
3 – Described in the blurb: 'A sequence of six poems with certain recurrent themes. They are further developments of a style used by the author in at least one of his recent "Ariel Poems".'

19 January 1930[2]   [Faber & Faber Ltd]

Dear Lord Brentford,

I have found the *Ladies' Home Journal* rather tiresome. Although my first letter was perfectly clear, the Editor wrote merely to thank me for having sent me [*sc.* him] the pamphlet.[3] I replied quoting my previous letter, and pointing out that my purpose had not been only to enrich the archives of his paper. I now hear from him that he cannot use the essay.

I do not know directly any reviews in America which are likely to pay better than the *Forum*. There is the *Bookman*, which pays me thirty pounds for an essay, apparently irrespective of length. But I feel that it would have been better to have consigned your essay to some professional agency, such as the New York house of Curtis Brown Ltd., rather than to have proffered the clumsy services of an amateur like myself. Perhaps you will consider doing so now.

The pamphlet has been very successful from our point of view. You may have seen last week a long article by E. M. Forster in the *Nation*.[4]

Please let me know what further you would care to have me do.

I am,

Yours very truly,

[T. S. Eliot]

1 – William Joynson-Hicks (1865–1932), solicitor and Conservative politician. As Stanley Baldwin's Home Secretary, 1924–9, 'Jix' (as he was known) earned a reputation as a reactionary on account of his commitment in the banning of Radclyffe Hall's *The Well of Loneliness* – though he would redeem himself in part with his support for the Equal Franchise Act (1928); and he was in favour of penal reform. He was created Viscount Brentford in 1929. GCF wrote to H. W. Yoxall on 19 Oct. 1928: 'There is one good point about "Jix" at any rate, and that is the handle which he gives to people who, like myself, thoroughly dislike him.'
2 – Misdated 1929.
3 – Brentford, *Do We Need a Censor?* (Criterion Miscellany 6, 1930).
4 – 'Mr D. H. Lawrence and Lord Brentford' – on D. H. Lawrence, *Pornography and Obscenity*; Viscount Brentford, *Do We Need a Censor?* – *N&A* 46: 15 (11 Jan. 1930), 508–9. 'Lord Brentford wants to suppress everything except marriage, and Mr Lawrence to suppress nothing except suppression; that the one sounds the trumpet of duty, the other the trumpet of passion . . . Is not the solution to be found . . . in the dull drone of tolerance, tolerance, tolerance? I hope so . . . Unlike Mr Lawrence, I would tolerate everybody, even Nosey Parker and Peeping Tom.'

TO *Christopher Dawson* CC

19 January 1930   [Faber & Faber Ltd]

Dear Mr Dawson,

I am sending you herewith the counterpart of the agreement about your essay. I shall be glad to hear from you that you have received it.

The question of the title does not of course affect the agreement in any way. But from what you say about the title, I feel that you have perhaps misunderstood us.[1] What we want is less a dialectical rejoinder to Russell[2] etc. than a *positive statement* from a point of view which shall clearly be that of a Roman Catholic layman. We wish less a *refutation* on general grounds, than a positive statement of the Catholic point of view and principles, as they appear to a layman; incidentally, as far as you like, bringing in reference to the views of Russell and Judge Lindsay etc. After all, the only philosophy of the matter which can stand against theirs is the Catholic, and that is considerably the senior of theirs.

I hope that these hints will not make it necessary for you to 'scrap' anything you have written. We find that we can, if need be, give you several weeks longer; though of course the earlier we get the manuscript the better for us.

Yours sincerely,
[T. S. Eliot]

I read your paper in *Order* with great interest, also your essay in the new *Dublin Review*.[3]

TO *Ramon Fernandez*[4] CC

19 January 1930   [*The Criterion*]

My dear Fernandez,

I am writing rather precipitately, to ask whether you would be willing to review either Herbert Read's book of essays *The Sense of Glory*, or

---

1–Dawson wrote on 12 Jan.: 'I gathered that you wanted a reply to the Bertrand Russell school from a Catholic point of view, & consequently what I have written is rather a criticism of the new moral theories than a positive statement of Catholic principles. In fact I have approached the subject from the sociological rather than the theological point of view.'
2–Bertrand Russell (1872–1970), British philosopher: see Biographical Register in *L* 3.
3–Dawson had published an essay on Catholicism and Sex in the Catholic journal *Order*; and 'Islamic Mysticism', *The Dublin Review* 186: 372 (Jan. 1930), 34–61.
4–Ramon Fernandez (1894–1944), philosopher, essayist, novelist, was Mexican by birth but educated in France, where he contributed to *NRF*, 1923–43. Works include *Messages*

Belgion's book *Our Present Philosophy of Life*, of which I understand Belgion has sent you a copy. I don't want to bother you, but I have to arrange for review of both of these books quickly; and if you do me the favour of reviewing one, I must quickly find someone else to review the other; so I do hope that you are in Paris and can let me have a line at once.[1]

Your essay has impressed a good many people,[2] and Murry is now writing an essay which I understand will claim you as an ally. Some day I hope to arrange a meeting at which you, Murry, Richards, Belgion, Read and myself may all be present!

Yours ever,
[T. S. Eliot]

TO *Bernard Bandler*[3]

19 January 1930   Faber & Faber Ltd

Dear Mr Bandler,

Thank you for your letter of the 9th instant, and at the same time I must apologise for not answering your previous letter. There are several matters to deal with.

First, I had already anticipated your suggestion about your participation in the 'Five Reviews' Prize, and had made the proposal to Clauss that the *Hound & Horn* should make a sixth, without waiting to consult you. I am all the more pleased that it should have occurred to you independently. I hear from Clauss that he is favourable, and that you may be hearing from him direct about it. I only wish that I had thought of it sooner: but I suggested to him that you might be willing to print the Wiechert story as soon as possible, and then to print the following prize-winners simultaneously.

I am sorry that so far we have not managed to collaborate, and the Fernandez essay would have been an excellent instance.[4] The difficulty

---

(1926) – which included an essay on 'Le classicisme de T. S. Eliot' – and *De la personnalité* (1928).

1 – Fernandez reviewed Belgion, *Our Present Philosophy of Life*, C. 9 (July 1930), 759–63.
2 – 'A Humanist Theory of Value', trans. TSE, C. 9 (Jan. 1930), 228–45.
3 – Bernard Bandler II (1905–93), co-editor of *Hound & Horn*. Born in New York, he gained an MA in philosophy from Harvard University, where he taught for two years before enrolling in the College of Physicians and Surgeons at Columbia University: he was in practice for many years as psychiatrist and Boston University professor.
4 – Bandler hoped for an exchange of articles such as Fernandez's on 'A Humanist's Theory of Value'. 'Obviously, *The Hound & Horn* in proportion as *The Criterion* is superior to it,

41

is one of time. That is, I have never stipulated for any but first British serial rights, so that the author's approval would have to be obtained by you. I might, I think, in instances where I believe the essay is one which you would like, obtain the consent of the author beforehand, but making plain that I cannot commit you to publication.

I think that it would be inadvisable, from either your point of view or ours, that we should duplicate more than *one* article or story or poem in each issue; and I shall be glad if you will agree to this condition.

My March–April list will contain an essay on the theories of Berdiaeff [*sc.* Berdyaev][1] and Toffanin[2] by Christopher Dawson, a story by Walter de la Mare, a paper on War Books by Tomlinson, another essay on Italian art by Adrian Stokes,[3] an essay on Communism by Rowse, and some other matter. Possibly the Dawson essay might be the most useful to you, Toffanin's and Berdiaeff's theories are just as unknown in England as in America. I will send you a galley proof. Dawson is a coming man here.

You shall hear from me again before long.

Yours ever sincerely,
T. S. Eliot

Middleton Murry is writing an essay on the same subject as Fernandez, for me. I think I might get him to let you print it.[4]

TO *Henry Eliot*[5]

TS Houghton

19 January 1930   Faber & Faber Ltd

My dear Henry,

A separate point which I omitted from yesterday's letter.[6] I had lunch a few days ago with a man named Leslie Hotson[7] and his wife. Hotson

---

will be the magazine more benefited by the exchange; but we hoped that our similarities of purpose, your interest in us, and your generosity, might bring about an exchange. As for payment, we thought that each magazine might pay for every article at its usual rates, or exchange simple and without further recompense, as you thought fit.'

1 – Nikolai Berdyaev (1874–1948), religious and political philosopher; Russian Orthodox nonconformist; exiled in 1922, he subsequently worked in Berlin and Paris.

2 – Giuseppe Toffanin (1891–1980), scholar of humanism, taught from 1928 at the University of Naples. His works include *La fine dell'umanesimo* (1920) and *Che cosa fu l'umanesimo* (1929).

3 – Stokes, 'Painting, Giorgione and Barbaro', *C.* 9 (Apr. 1930), 482–500.

4 – JMM, 'The Detachment of Naturalism', *C.* 9 (July 1930), 642–60.

5 – Henry Ware Eliot, Jr (1879–1947), TSE's brother: see Biographical Register.

6 – TSE's letter of 18 Jan. 1930 has not been found.

7 – Leslie Hotson (1897–1992), Canadian-born Shakespearean researcher and controversialist. Educated at Harvard, he taught at Harvard and at New York University before

seems to be a literary scholar of distinction: he has made discoveries about Marlowe[1] and we are publishing a book of his with new letters of Shelley.[2] His wife is a cousin of ours: I should like to know who she was; I believe that she is a daughter of Will Comstock.[3] Anyway, Hotson had heard that Aunt Rose[4] has a lot of old family letters; I suppose the boxes and boxes that mother ransacked when she wrote the life of grandpa;[5] but going back to the 18th century and including letters of the Adamses, Jefferson, and presumably Lincoln, Sumner etc. etc. He understands that Aunt Rose intends to burn them all. Now a good many of these must be

---

joining Haverford College in 1931. Works include *Shakespeare versus Shallow* (1931), *Shakespeare's Sonnets Dated* (1949), *The First Night of Twelfth Night* (1954), and *Mr. W. H.* (1964).

In a later year, when he applied for a visiting fellowship at King's College, Cambridge, TSE wrote of him on 1 Nov. 1953: 'I . . . have known him for a good many years, and like him. I was of course unaware what qualifications, other than those of scholarly achievement, would be sought for in making the appointment to this Special Fellowship.

'Dr Hotson's eminence in the special field of literary-historical research is indisputable, though his conclusions have sometimes been disputed. Cambridge scholars in English Literature will be well acquainted with the nature of his studies and the results he has obtained; and King's will decide for itself whether this is the sort of work it wishes to advance. Dr Hotson is a man of immense industry; and I have no doubt that this appointment would be highly advantageous for labours that he pursues with the greatest zeal; nor do I doubt that the results of his investigations, during the tenure of the Fellowship, would be as remarkable as his previous discoveries.

'Dr Hotson's character is above reproach: he is a man of great integrity. I believe that the reason for his resignation from a Professorship at Haverford College, Pennsylvania, during the war, was due to a conflict between his outspoken pro-British sympathies and the views of the President (at that time) of the College, who was a somewhat authoritarian Isolationist. This is what I have been told. He has spent much time in England, for as long as two years at a stretch, carrying on his research in the Record Office and elsewhere. He is a member, I believe, of the Unitarian branch of the Society of Friends in America, and a member of the Athenaeum.

'Dr Hotson is also a person of considerable charm: talkative, a good raconteur and excellent mimic, and [has] some proficiency on several minor musical instruments. His wife is a member of the well-known and very numerous Boston family of Peabody, and is herself a person of great activity . . .

'I can only add, that I feel sure that, within his own province and according to the standards of that province of scholarship, he would in the course of his tenure produce a really important piece of work.'

1 – *The Death of Christopher Marlowe* (1925) argued that Marlowe was deliberately murdered.

2 – *Shelley's Lost Letters to Harriet* (1930) was based on Hotson's discovery in the Public Record Office London of nine letters from the poet to his pregnant first wife (including the news that he was in love with Mary Godwin), who subsequently drowned herself in the Serpentine.

3 – Mrs Hotson was TSE's cousin Mary Peabody.

4 – Rose Greenleaf Eliot (1862–1936), daughter of William G. and Abby A. Eliot.

5 – Charlotte Eliot, *William Greenleaf Eliot: Minister, Educator, Philanthropist* (1904).

of considerable historical interest, and could not possibly offend living members. I wondered if there was any chance of retrieving them, of somebody – not necessarily myself, you for instance or even Sam Morison – editing the really valuable ones as a book? It ought to be a good book not only for America but for England. Andrew Eliot's war diaries, which have already been printed, I believe, might be included. Anyway, it would be a crime if all this stuff were destroyed without some scholar going through them with a view to publication; and I doubt whether Aunt Rose has any more right to them than any other member of the family.

If such a book were possible I could get my firm to publish it here, and I am sure I could get Morison (who is Professor of American History at Harvard, and whom I know) to take an interest in it.

What do you think?

yours affectionately in haste,
Tom

TO *Bonamy Dobrée*[1]   TS Brotherton

20 January 1930   *The Criterion*

Dear Bungamy,

I shall be happy to lunch with you on Wednesday the 29th (by the way, 2 days before (Eric) Partridge[2] shooting ends). The only Out about your Club is the lack of privacy, i.e. we won't lunch unless Belgion is certain to be in Paris. Not that I am not on the Best of Terms with Belgion, but I really have more opportunities of seeing him than I require; and I don't see you very often nowadays. So why not some privy place like the Ritz or the Cosmoo or the Low Societies Club (no not the latter perhaps, of the 2 Gummerys Belgion[3] is preferable to Summers).[4]

1 – Bonamy Dobrée (1891–1974), scholar, editor and critic: see Biographical Register.
2 – TSE puns on the name of Eric Partridge (1894–1979), New Zealand-born lexicographer, etymologist, philologist, who lectured in English Literature at East London College; author of *Slang Today and Yesterday* (1933), *Shakespeare's Bawdy* (1947), *Usage and Abusage* (1942).
3 – Montgomery Belgion is often referred to, in peculiarly English fashion, as 'Gummers'.
4 – Montague Summers (1880–1948), scholar of Restoration theatre, occultist, demonologist, graduated in theology from Trinity College, Oxford, and attended Lichfield Theological College, whereafter he was ordained and practised as a deacon. However, in 1909 he migrated to the Roman Catholic Church and thereafter posed as a religious (researchers have found no record of an ordination). An industrious researcher, he published editions of works by writers including Aphra Behn, Congreve, Wycherley and Otway; and he was

I am all agog for your impersonation of Chesterfield: I have laid in a new Battery, and expect to hear you at double strength.[1]

Yours ever
(etc. vide The Times)
T. S. E.

I have just started my catalogue raisonné of the Games played at the Bolovian Court.[2] I believe it will revolutionise Bolovian scholarship. I distinguish sharply, mind you, between the Games and the Sports.

P.S. The point is, what no other scholars, not even Kunz or Krapp or the indefatigable Professor Wilbur C. Prossew of Siwash University has ferreted out, that the Games were played according to the Kalander, e.g.

Betweeen Christmas and Candlemas –
   Musical Arse
   Blind Man's Bum
   Clap In Clap Out
Between Candlemas and Septuagesima –
   Postman's Cock
   Piss in the Ring
   Crap as Crap Can
Between Septuagesima and Sexagesima –
   Drop the Handkerchief
   Rum Tum Tidy
   etc.

––––

instrumental in setting up the Phoenix Theatre, 1919–25, to be followed by the Renaissance Theatre, 1925–8.

1 – 'Lord Chesterfield (A Conversation between The Hon. Horace Walpole and Dr Matthew Maty [Principal Librarian at the British Museum] in Strawberry Hill. 1766)', C. 11 (Jan. 1932), 198–208.

2 – TSE was to inscribe (undated) a copy of *Thoughts after Lambeth* (1931): 'to Bonamy Dobrée, my pupil in Bolovian theology, T. S. E.' (courtesy of Paul Rassam: Cat. 27). BD would write to EVE, 'Easter Sunday '65': 'I was very interested in what Conrad Aiken said about King Bolo and his Queen. Have you anything about them? Tom once sent me a drawing of them, which I have, but didn't tell me much about them. I do, however, know something of the Bolovians and their religion. Tom loved elaborating a fancy, and all this is extremely amusing.'

20 January 1930   *The Criterion*

Dear Alport,

Thank you for your letter of the 7th.[1] It is interesting to learn that it may be several years before Scheler's work is ready. So I think we will drop that subject for the present; and I will meanwhile consider the possibilities of the small book, and write to you when I have read it. I notice that one or two things are not included, e.g. Mensch und Geschichte, which I admired particularly; but I suppose that would be available too.[2]

Now I have had recommended to me in the very strongest terms by one of our greatest scholars the following:

Aristotèles, Grundlegung einer Geschichte seiner Entwicklung. Berlin: Weidmannsche Buchhandlung, 1923.

Could you please find out for us from the publishers whether this is free and get them to send us a copy? Of course we should want to have world rights in English.

Meanwhile I shall not write to Frau Scheler; but if you write, will you kindly say that we are considering the smaller book.

Yours sincerely,
T. S. Eliot

TO *A. E. Taylor*   CC

20 January 1930   [Faber & Faber Ltd]

Dear Professor Taylor,

Thank you for your letter of the 18th.[3] I am sending for a copy of Jaeger's book; and you shall hear from us again about it.

---

1 – Alport had just heard from Scheler's widow. (Märit Furtwängler, who became Scheler's second wife in 1912, was a sister of the conductor Wilhelm Furtwängler.) 'It is impossible, she says, to estimate even roughly when the editors of the Anthropologie and the – very important – rest of Scheler's unfinished work will have finished with their task; it may be still some years.'

2 – Scheler's posthumous *Philosophische Weltanschauung* (collected essays and lectures) comprised the title essay, 'Mensch in Geschichte', 'Der Mensch im Seitalter des Auggleichs', 'Die Formen des Wissens in die Bildung', and a lecture on Spinoza. TSE had printed Scheler's 'Future of Man' in *MC* 7 (Feb. 1928), 100–19.

3 – 'Certainly I should feel honoured by being allowed to write a brief Preface to an English version [of Werner Jaeger's *Aristotèles*]. As for an *Introduction*, I feel (1) that there is a suggestion of patronage towards the author about such a thing which would be a little arrogant when the author is a scholar of Jaeger's eminence, and (2) that in any case an

I appreciate your modesty about the 'Introduction'; but I believe that a short preface by yourself would be as suitable as a preface or an Introduction by anyone else. An Introduction would only I feel be desirable if the book required any advance explication to the reader. Of course I know Joachim's attainments, and to my shame indeed he knows mine, as he was my tutor;[1] and I should be interested to find out whether he knows the book – I suppose he does. But for even that small public which would read such a book, the difference of qualification between Joachim, Ross and yourself would be an imperceptible refinement; and we should be happy to have your name, even in this small way, on our list.

I thank you for your remarks about translation, which I shall make use of when the time comes.[2]

With many thanks,
Yours very sincerely,
[T. S. Eliot]

———

Introduction would come better from someone who has done more considerable work on Aristotle than myself.' He recommended as more suitable W. D. Ross, Provost of Oriel College, Oxford, editor of *Metaphysics*; and Prof. H. H. Joachim of Oxford, editor of Aristotle's *De generatione*.

1–Harold H. Joachim (1868–1938): Fellow and Tutor in Philosophy at Merton College, Oxford, 1897–1919; British Idealist philosopher and disciple of F. H. Bradley; author of *The Nature of Truth* (1906), an influential account of the 'coherence theory' of truth. TSE recalled buying *The Nature of Truth* at Harvard, and taking it with him in 1914 to Oxford. According to Brand Blanshard, it was said that 'if you started any sentence in the *Nichomachean Ethics* of Aristotle, Joachim could complete it for you, of course in Greek' ('Eliot at Oxford', *T. S. Eliot: Essays from the Southern Review*, ed. James Olney, 1988).

On 6 July 1915 Joachim had penned this testimonial: 'Mr T. S. Eliot spent last year (Oct. 1914–June 1915) in working at Philosophy at Merton College, Oxford. During that time, he was my pupil, & brought me Essays (partly on modern Logic & Metaphysics, but mainly on the philosophy of Plato & Aristotle) every week. I was greatly impressed with his ability & enthusiasm for the subject, & also with his conscientiousness & patient endeavour to master the details in every piece of work. From what I have seen of him & of his work, I am quite sure that he would make a most successful teacher: & that he would deserve & win the affection, as well as the respect, of his pupils' (copy with EVE).

TSE wrote an obituary letter in *The Times* (4 Aug. 1938), and paid tribute to Joachim in the introduction to *Knowledge and Experience in the Philosophy of F. H. Bradley* (1964). In a late letter, he said 'he taught me more about how to write good prose than any other teacher I have ever had' as well as revealing 'the importance of punctuation in the interpretation of a text such as that of the *Posterior Analytics*' (24 June 1963: Merton). TSE's notes on Joachim's lectures on Aristotle's *Nichomachean Ethics*, 1914–15, are at Houghton: MS AM1691.14 (17).

2–Taylor recommended, as promising translators, F. Hardie, Corpus Christi College, Oxford; and Allan K. Stone, University College, Bangor.

TO *John Middleton Murry*   TS Northwestern

20 January 1930   *The Criterion*

My dear John,

I am very distressed by your letter.[1] Apart from personal feelings, I feel exactly as you do about the disappearance of any quarterly review, or of any review of our type. The decease of the *Adelphi* will certainly make stiffer going for the *Criterion*. I should have thought that it might be possible to find a few guarantors, to make an editorial salary possible. But I know quite well that that is not easy. Yet I wish I could talk to you about it. I was quite certain at one time that the *Criterion* was at an end; and indeed started sending contributions back; but the determination of others revived it. I wish that I could talk to you about it, before it is too late. If in town, wouldn't you look in at the office for a few minutes on Wednesday afternoon?

                                        Yours affectionately
                                        Tom

TO *John Middleton Murry*   TS Northwestern

21 January 1930   *The Criterion*

Dear John,

About two years ago, when the *Criterion* was on the point of foundering, I heard that Jonathan Cape was interested and would have been glad to take it over. It occurs to me that *a fortiori* Cape should be glad to run the *Adelphi*. Of course you know Cape and I don't; and this might not meet with your approval anyway; but I have reason to believe that I could set things in motion to induce Cape to make overtures towards you.

                                        Yours in haste
                                        Tom

1–JMM wrote on 17 Jan. that he was 'in a rather bad way just now. I am finding it hard to earn a living. (Living is, of course, unduly heavy with me owing to incessant illness.) And I have had to decide to give up *The New Adelphi* at the end of the present volume simply because it demands too much unremunerated labour.'

21 January 1930   [London]

Dear Marguerite,

I was very glad to get your letter of the 14th. We cordially reciprocate your wishes for the New Year. We are and shall be in greater confusion than you have been.[2] We have not found moving into a flat beneficial either in health or in any other way, and are on the point of taking another house – a 'decayed house'[3] but I believe a good one, with a potential garden, and in the favourite vicinity of Eaton Square. So if you could run over to London by Eastertide, we might be able to furbish it up just enough to be worthy to receive you there.

I listened this morning to the yarnings of various eminent delegates to the Naval Conference, after the King's inauguration of it; but I hope that I shall hear something from Léger. If I don't hear in a week or so, I suppose I shall write to him care of the French Embassy.

I should like to leave over the question of *Eloges* until we see how *Anabase* goes.[4] Also an able young French Jew named Edouard Roditi[5] (whose health endured the Oxford climate for only half a term) has already translated half of it – he came to me, poor devil, with a complete translation he had made of *Anabase*, and took his disappointment very bravely. In any case, I have a fancy to try to translate some Hofmannsthal next, if I can get permission;[6] so it would be a year or two before we need consider *Eloges*. I don't expect *Anabase* to go very rapidly; but I have a notion that in three or four years Léger's method will show an influence on the younger American and English writers. (I shall then say *e cio lui fece Romeo persona umile e peregrina*).[7]

---

1 – Marguerite Caetani, née Chapin (1880–1963) – Princesse di Bassiano – literary patron and editor: see Biographical Register.
2 – 'I passed the holidays in the usual confusion of last days before a journey when one is to be away for three months . . .'
3 – 'Gerontion', 7: 'My house is a decayed house'.
4 – 'I do hope you will see Léger. He desires it very much. Would you consider translating "Eloges" or will you wait to see the reception accorded to "Anabase" before thinking of it?'
5 – Edouard Roditi (1910–92), poet, critic, biographer, translator: see Biographical Register.
6 – TSE had conceived the notion, in Dec. 1929 – as he told HR – to translate what he called 'one or two [of the] Jacobean verse plays' of Hugo von Hofmannsthal (1874–1929) 'back into Jacobean': namely, *Die Hochzeit der Sobeide* and *Die Frau im Fenster*. TSE was to write: 'Hofmannsthal is worthy to stand with Yeats and with Claudel as one of the three men who did most, in the same age, to maintain and re-animate verse drama . . .' ('Preface', Hofmannsthal, *Poems and Verse Plays*, ed. and introd. Michael Hamburger [1961], xi–xii).
7 – Dante, *Paradiso*, Canto 6, 134–35: '*e cio li fece / Romeo, persona umile e peregrina*'.

I have some volumes of Kassner by me and will look through them.[1] I hope he may get the Nobel Prize, though I don't think that makes very much impression on Anglo-Saxon readers: it has gone too often to obscure Scandinavians. I don't believe that a volume of essays could be safely put out here: I mean that it would probably be ignored, and one failure makes it more difficult to establish an author later. The best thing I could do for him would be to find an essay to publish in the *Criterion*, and later find someone to write an article about him.

Have you heard anything of *La Vigile* (?) [*sic*], a review which I am told Du Bos is going to start in opposition to the *N.R.F.* or rather in opposition to Gide. I cannot help feeling sympathetic to anything which is anti-Gide, but I wonder what Paulhan[2] has to say about it.[3]

I was Angry about the spelling of my name, but it is a Venial rather than a Deadly Sin: Elyot, Eliott or Aliot have been used at various periods; the only real insult is to spell it Elliot or Elliott, which is Scotch.[4] I will send you a proof of the complete set when I have one.

Affectionately,

[Tom]

P.S. It is possible that Vivienne's brother, Maurice Haigh-Wood, may be in Rome on business some time in February. If you are to be there after the 15th I will ask him to call on you. He knows Rome very well, and speaks Italian fluently.

---

1 – 'Kassner is being proposed for the Nobel prize by a group of German friends . . . I would so like to have a collection of his essays published in England.' Rudolf Kassner (1873–1959), Swiss cultural philosopher. Works include *Die Grundlagen der Physiognomik* (1922); *Das inwendige Reich: Versuch einer Physiognomik der Ideen* (1952).

2 – Jean Paulhan (1884–1968), editor of *Nouvelle Revue Française* (in succession to Jacques Rivière), 1925–40, 1946–68. He was active in the French Resistance during WW2. His works include *Entretiens sur des fait-divers* (1930); *Les Fleurs de Tarbes, ou, La Terreur dans les lettres* (1936); *On Poetry and Politics*, ed. Jennifer Bajorek *et al.* (2010). See William Marx, 'Two Modernisms: T. S. Eliot and *La Nouvelle Revue Française*', in *The International Reception of T. S. Eliot*, ed. Elisabeth Däumer and Shyamal Bagchee (2007), 25–33

3 – Cf. Harvey Breit, *New York Times Book Review*, 21 Nov. 1948: 'Mr Eliot feels that André Gide, last year's winner of the Nobel Prize for Literature, deserved the award. "However one feels about Gide's content," he said, "for forty years he has been an immense figure ('figger,' Mr Eliot says). There is no question about his style. *Si le grain ne meurt* is a remarkable book. I read Gide as long ago as 1910. He makes an impression on you. There is good evidence of it in Charles DuBos [*sic*], who was a fine writer and a close friend of Gide's and who fundamentally disagrees with him as much as I do. But you have to cope with Gide. *Travels in the Congo* is a wonderful book. So is the Russian book"' (*The Writer Observed*, 1956).

4 – 'I am in despair over the mistake in the spelling of your name! I can't imagine how it happened. Can you ever forgive "Commerce" and me? – It is really despairing.'

22 January 1930   *The Criterion*

Dear Rowse,

Your article on Communism[1] has gone at once to the printer; I don't worry about its quality or suitability, and I shall read it comfortably in proof. As for the review, and the projected review of Clark, I *may* have to hold them both over to the following number; but shall use them then in any case.

I think your present title is quite satisfactory.

I send the Daniels book in order to get your opinion as to whether it might be made the peg for a symposium on politics, and if so whether you would be one and suggest others? It is hardly good enough for a review, as it gets you nowhere; it refers portentously here and there to the Douglas scheme,[2] as if quoting the Bible; but it might just make the excuse for several people with something to say, saying it.

I am writing to Spender.[3] As for Jacob, I can only say that I have met him, and that I should very much like to have him as a contributor on some other occasion; but as I have turned down your own review, I am not going to revise my decision for anybody else.[4]

I will write to Cecil, and try to keep him up to it.[5] Many thanks.

Yours always,
T. S. Eliot

1 – 'The Theory and Practice of Communism', C. 9 (Apr. 1930), 451–69.
2 – The theory of 'social credit' set out by the economic theorist C. H. Douglas (1879–1952).
3 – Rowse had urged on 11 Jan.: 'After Auden, I'd like to commend a young Stephen Spender to your attention: he's rather a follower of the former, but also most interesting to watch.' He wrote again on 21 Jan., 'The young man Stephen Spender asked me to ask Faber about a mss of his you have: I hope you don't mind my becoming a missioner for them all & sundry. There's Jacob too: I know you're not wanting to be reviewed [*Dante*], but he's been very anxious to . . .'
4 – '[A] friend of mine Dr. E. F. Jacob . . . he's now Professor of Medieval History at Manchester, has been for some time very anxious to review your Dante. He knows Dante very well, and would do a good article.' E. F. Jacob (1894–1971) was a Fellow of All Souls College, Oxford, and taught too at Christ Church, Oxford (Rowse had been a pupil); Professor of History, Manchester University, 1929–44; Chichele Professor of Modern History, Oxford, 1950–61.
5 – Rowse (21 Jan.): 'I gave David [Cecil] your message, & he said he'd love to write for the *Criterion* & might on "Wuthering Heights": only he'd have to be kept up to it.'

TO *Geoffrey Rossetti*   TS Mary Rossetti Rutterford

23 January 1930   *The Criterion*

Dear Mr Rossetti,

Excuse me for not answering your letter of the 2nd instant immediately. I hope you will let me know of the fortunes of Toffanin.[1] If the Press should not want to do it I know another publisher who would be interested.

I should like positively to encourage you to write the essay on your great-aunt – for whom I have a strong admiration – not for *Goblin Market* much, but other things – I wish any of my great-aunts had written *Goblin Market* however. Of course I do not yet know your original work, but I should like to, and if your essay was at all good I would print it in the *Criterion*.[2]

By the way, are Rossettis Roman Catholics or not? It would be frivolous to ask whether they are fascists.

Yours sincerely,
T. S. Eliot

TO *Henry Allen Moe*[3]   CC

23 January 1930   [Faber & Faber Ltd]

Dear Mr Moe,

Two or three weeks ago I replied to your request for an opinion of Edward Dahlberg.[4] Since then I have read his *Bottom Dogs* which has considerably improved my opinion. The book is no work of art, but has

---

1 – 'I have written to Professor Foligno at Oxford about Toffanin's book. He wrote . . . to say he will see the University Press about the matter as soon as he returns to England.'
2 – Rossetti asked if it might write 'a shortish critical account of my Great-Aunt Christina Rossetti, whose centenary is next December'. See 'Christina Rossetti', C. 10 (Oct. 1930), 95–117.
3 – Henry Allen Moe (1894–1975) worked from about 1925 until his retirement in 1963 as the first Secretary, then Administrator, and ultimately President of the National Endowment for the Humanities. He was also President of the American Philosophical Society, 1959–70.
4 – Edward Dahlberg (1900–77), novelist and essayist, was born in Boston to a single mother, and spent most of his teenage years in the Jewish Orphan Asylum in Cleveland. He went on to the University of California at Berkeley and to Columbia University. In the late 1920s he lived in Paris and in London, where his autobiographical novel *Bottom Dogs* (1930) was published with an introduction by D. H. Lawrence. After visiting Germany in 1933, he was for a while a member of the Communist Party, and in later years was a writer and college teacher. Other works include *Do These Bones Live* (essays, 1941) and *The Confessions of Edward Dahlberg* (1971).

the same sincerity I found in the work he showed me, and some parts are really good writing. Anyway I read it through with great interest, and I very rarely can read anything that looks like a novel. The book has been well received here, considering especially how strange the natives must find it. I think the boy is worth the Foundation taking a gamble in, especially if he is wisely looked after by his wellwishers in Europe.

Yours sincerely,
[T. S. Eliot]

TO *Jack Isaacs*[1]　　　　　　　　　　　　　　　　　CC

23 January 1930　　　　　　　　*[The Criterion]*

Dear Isaacs,

Aaronson's book I have just given to a young Irishman who is interested. The review will probably not appear till June; the 'body' of our January number (by the way I commend Auden) was so fat that the reviews had to be cut down, with the result that I shall be a quarter behind (not hind quartered) for a sixmonth. What sort of Bloom will sprout from Aaronson plus Donaghy I don't know; but it will bear some fruit.[2]

Donaghy, I told him of Rosenberg, and he accepted my suggestion that he should do a retrospective review of Rosenberg at the same time. Now could you help him to get a copy of the Rosenberg volume? I haven't one, and I have forgotten who published it; but cd. you get us a review copy

1–Jacob (Jack) Isaacs (1896–1973), English scholar, educator and film critic, served in France in WW1 in the Royal Garrison Artillery before going up to Exeter College, Oxford. In 1924 he became Assistant Lecturer in English at King's College, London; Lecturer from 1928. A founding member of the Film Society (1925–38), he performed in Eisenstein's *Lost*. He was the first Montefiore Professor of English at the Hebrew University of Jerusalem in Palestine, 1942–5; and Professor of English Language and Literature, Queen Mary College, London, 1952–64. Famed for his lectures, and skilled as bibliographer, theatre historian and broadcaster, he was author of *Coleridge's Critical Terminology* (1936) and *An Assessment of Twentieth-Century Literature* (1951). He edited, with William Rose, *Contemporary Movements in European Literature* (1928). TSE wrote of him, 20 Mar. 1939: 'I regard him as one of the most intelligent men of my acquaintance, quite able to hold his own and to command attention in any social or intellectual gathering. He is also a person of charm and urbanity, and I should think must be a very stimulating and fructifying influence upon his pupils.' In another reference (3 July 1951), TSE said: 'I understand that he is a brilliant and stimulating lecturer.'

2–Isaacs had given TSE L. Aaronson's *Christ in the Synagogue*: 'Aaaronson was a friend of Isaac Rosenberg, and you may see some at any rate racial affinities . . . I really do think he ought to be read . . .' J. L. Donaghy reviewed Aaronson's volume in C. 11 (Apr. 1932), 420–1.

now? You may remember that I had expressed admiration for Rosenberg, and printed a few of his poems, a good many years ago.

I should certainly like to get in touch with the newer Russian writers, and if you get Shklovsky (?) to send something (preferably in some language that I could read myself) I should be very grateful.[1] The difficulty is that I can't commission in the dark and anything like that would have to be subject to our opinion.

As for our not meeting, it is chiefly because you are so lazy. I see very few people except those who are or may be useful to the *Criterion*; and I have found that you will never write for it, or so far as I know, for anything else; so naturally I put business before pleasure. But perhaps when Richards returns from China you might be enticed to a discussion.

Yours sincerely,
[T. S. Eliot]

TO *Ezra Pound*[2]   TS Beinecke

23 January 1930   [London]

Dear EP,

If your poem by Macleod[3] is one about the Signs of the Zodiac, dont send it along, as it has come in.[4] He sent me a kind of play once that was always I mean almost good, and has written an enthusiastic kind of prose work. The Zodiac looks interesting & I will look him up if he is about.

If you have not seen *Bottom Dogs* by Ed. Dahlberg I have a spare copy for you. This is not a work of Art, but the Orphan Asylum in Cleveland O. is very good of its kind. Ed. is a crude sort of cuss and a jeweranian americum, geranium not too diaphane, but I sort of took to him and am backing him with Moe, so that he may visit Rapallo.

Other problems will be tackled as the vitality seizes me. I shall be sending you *Death in the Dark*, a detective novel of New York life by

1–Isaacs recommended Viktor Shklovsky (1893–1984), of the 'Formalist' school of criticism.
2–Ezra Pound (1885–1972), American poet and critic: see Biographical Register.
3–Joseph Todd Gordon Macleod: see TSE to Macleod, 10 Feb. 1930, below.
4–This remark presumes a letter from EP which has not been found. However, EP did publish 'Libra, or, The Scales', one of the twelve zodiacal cantos that comprise *The Ecliptic*, in his anthology *Profile* (1932); while TSE printed 'Leo, or, The Lion', in C. (July 1930), 671–4.

Stacey Bishop,[1] which may amuse you. The title I wanted is 'Who Pulled that Fire Alarm?'.

Yours couerteouesly.

T.

want yr. opinion of Auden. You should have received comp. copy of CRITERIUM inc. Horace as well as Cheque.[2]

TO *F. S. Oliver*[3]   cc

24 January 1930   [*The Criterion*]

Dear Oliver,

I want to write a few lines to tell you that Macmillan sent a copy of your book, and that I withheld it from reviewers long enough to read it

---

1 – Stacey Bishop was a pseudonym of George Antheil (1900–1959), American avant-garde composer, pianist and author. TSE wrote a reader's report on *Death in the Dark* – or 'The Denny Murder Case' as it was called in draft – on 21 July 1929:

'This is a very good detective story. It has two faults. There are a good many improvements to be made in the style – to remove, *not* the more striking Americans, but grammatical slips, prolixity and general crudities. Second, it is too closely patterned on Van Dine. This would not matter quite so much if the author did not here and there sneer at the methods of his model: the latter passages should be removed. And it would have been better if the hero made more of his knowledge of music, which is great, and less of his knowledge of literature and plastic art, which is superficial.

'There are several practical points to be considered. 1. What is the state of the detective market, and can we capture any of what exists? 2. This book is a by-product of an important coming musical composer: is that fact of any use to us, even were it not for the anonymity? 3. It is [Is it] of any use, in the detective market, publishing *amateur* writers ("Midnight" was a specimen of amateur work)? Is not the proper game in this line to get a man who can turn out one good book a year, and back him for a long period? so that we should like to know whether the author of this story has any others in him, and is likely to get them out.

'These are questions I cannot answer myself. I should like [A. J. B.] Paterson to read the book, and it is worth a third opinion too.

'I think that the scientific patter is rather overdone, and should be reduced.'

GCF wrote by hand at the foot of TSE's screed, 'I agree.'

Death in the Dark was to be published by F&F later in 1930, with this blurb: '"A shot in the dark" . . . "A shot in a room crowded with witnesses" . . . "A shot in an empty police cell" . . . "Each time in the forehead." . . . These were some of the headlines in the New York papers during the investigation of the notorious Denny Murders. No one connected with the crimes escaped suspicion, yet how and by whom they were planned and executed is the central mystery of this quick and thrilling narrative. It is a first novel by a New York criminologist of Red Indian ancestry.'

2 – C. 9 (Jan. 1930) included EP's essay 'Horace', 217–27, and WHA's 'Paid on Both Sides: A Charade', 268–90.

3 – F. S. Oliver (1864–1934), businessman, author, polemicist: see Biographical Register.

myself; and that I enjoyed it immensely.[1] So many books pass through my hands in one way or another that it is rare for my jaded appetite to read any book purely for pleasure, except the simplest detective story (to say nothing of time); but I read and enjoyed yours (and only one other in the last three months) without any professional excuse. Of course I have only a distant acquaintance with the period, and it is a period which I never knew intimately even in literature. Still I *can* enjoy a good prose style, & yours seemed to me a good deal better than Lytton Strachey's, and a great deal more life in it.

I observe some Machiavellian traces on your theory of politics, which I thoroughly enjoyed. It seems to me that the reviewers have not taken quite enough notice of the place of Carteret[2] in your political drama. The character of Bolingbroke I already knew something of for literary and theoretical motives; but Carteret was to me a most interesting revelation; and his place in the book, as the second foil to Walpole (after Bolingbroke) is most effective.

You suggested that the book was not suitable for review in the *Criterion*. I should certainly disagree myself; but my opinion is confirmed by the fact that two of my regular reviewers have sued for it, and so I have given it to one of them.[3]

Yours sincerely,
[T. S. Eliot]

TO *Stephen Spender*

CC

24 January 1930   [*The Criterion*]

Dear Mr Spender,

You may remember that we had some correspondence about an unhappily deferred visit of mine to Oxford. That is one reason why it is I who am writing to you about your story.[4] We think it very promising; it begins well; but [is] not quite sustained throughout. As for the Miscellany, remember that we want so far as possible only to publish stories that

---

1 – *The Endless Adventure*, vol. I: *1710–1727* comprises the first part of a trilogy surveying English politics – 'the endless adventure' – through the lifetime of Sir Robert Walpole (1676– 1745).
2 – John Carteret, 2nd Earl Granville (1690–1763); Lord President of the Council, 1751–63.
3 – Review by William King, *C.* 9 (July 1930), 722–4.
4 – Spender had submitted a story, 'The Haymaking', on 18 Dec. 1929. FVM, whom TSE asked for an opinion, wrote on Spender's letter on 12 Jan. 1930: 'This is too unsure & tentative: doesn't seem to me to come off. But the lad needs & deserves encouragement.'

have some obvious reason for being more suitable in that form than in a magazine; and the *Criterion* can only use four or five pieces of fiction in a year.

But I wish particularly to urge you to send me more of your work from time to time; I liked this enough to have a great curiosity in your future writing.

Yours sincerely,
[T. S. Eliot]

TO *Mario Praz*[1]   cc

24 January 1930   [*The Criterion*]

My dear Praz,

I have not yet answered your kind letter of the 25th December. I take it that you did not stop over in London, as I heard nothing from you, and that you are again in Liverpool. I think you are very lenient with my Dante essay, and am pleased if in any way it supports your own views. I have not seen the *Corriere*, but look forward to your *Cultura*.[2]

I am glad you met Pound; I have heard from him about your meeting; and the pleasure was evidently mutual.[3]

I also liked Montale's translation.[4]

---

1 – Mario Praz (1896–1982), scholar and critic of English literature: see Biographical Register.

2 – 'I read yr *Dante* with great interest, and, considering the purpose for wch the book was written, I must say that the work could not have been done better . . . I approached your book more with a view to knowing more about you than about Dante (not because I cannot learn more about Dante, of course!) but because I think that it is very hard to say something novel . . . Still, you have contrived to find this new way, and what you say about Dante's frame of mind, and his (more or less generally medieval) peculiar angle for looking at the world (allegory) confirms me in certain opinions of mine about the changes of viewpoints and methods of approach wch form the backbone of the history of culture . . . I am going to write a notice of your book for the *Cultura*. Pelligri spoke of it very highly in the *Corriere della Sera* for Dec 9th . . .'

3 – 'I met Ezra Pound here the other day: he showed me some proofs of his Cavalcanti. I had no means of testing whether the critical text is really going to be a safe one . . . On the whole, his work looks a little of a farrago; but this is only a very superficial impression. The man, of course, is charming.'

4 – 'I like Montale's rendering of yr *Song for Simeon* [in *Solaria*]. I should be rather interested to see a translation of it in *terza rima*.' Eugenio Montale (1896–1981) was a poet, prose writer, translator, editor; winner of the Nobel Prize for Literature, 1975. TSE told the Italian Consul, Liverpool, on 11 Dec. 1959: 'I have a very high respect for the poetry of Eugenio Montale and, though my knowledge of Italian is imperfect, feel a spiritual kinship with him. I know also that he has made what seemed to me very successful translations

My reference to Our Lady and Cleopatra was a slip (to be corrected in any future edition; I was referring to *La Maddalena ai piedi di Christo,* where the Magdalen and Cleopatra are rather jumbled.[1] I think that the point is just as good, however.

Hoping to hear from you soon,

Yours ever,

[T. S. Eliot]

TO *C. K. Scott Moncrieff*[2]   CC

24 January 1930   [The Criterion]

Dear Scott Moncrieff,

I passed your letter to the proper department, with the cheque, and hope you have now received the books you graciously ordered.[3] I agree with you about Crashaw and Shelley. I fear I was more controversial than just; but it is very difficult in criticism not to respond to prejudice by prejudice.[4]

---

of several of my own poems into Italian. There is no Italian poet whom I would rank higher . . .' See too Montale, 'Eliot and Ourselves', in *T. S. Eliot: A Symposium*, ed. Richard March and Tambimuttu (1948), 190–5.

1 – 'It is a pity that the editing of the Italian text [in TSE's *Dante*] has not been properly looked into (there are many misprints). On p. 55 you wrote Marino's comparison between the beauty of Our Lady and the opulence of Cleopatra. I miss the allusion, unless you meant Marino's madrigal on St Mary Magdalen, translated by Sherburne (Grierson, Metaphys. Poets, p. 157).' (Apropos the *Paradiso*, TSE delights in 'the power of association' Dante exercises when, in 'speaking of the Divine vision', he yet introduces 'the Argo passing over the head of wondering Neptune.' TSE continues: 'Such association is utterly different from that of Marino speaking in one breath of the beauty of the Magdalen and the opulence of Cleopatra (so that you are not quite sure which adjectives apply to which). It is the real right thing, the power of establishing relations between beauty of the most diverse sorts; it is the utmost power of the poet.')

2 – C. K. Scott Moncrieff (1889–1930), translator, was educated at Edinburgh (first-class honours in English Language and Literature), and received the Military Cross for gallantry in WWI, having been lamed in 1917. From 1923 he worked full-time as a freelance translator, after publishing translations of the *Chanson de Roland* (1919) and *Beowulf* (1921); he gained lasting fame as translator of Marcel Proust's *A la recherche du temps perdu*: *Remembrance of Things Past*. His version of Proust's 'The Death of Albertine' appeared in C. 2 (July 1924), 376–94.

3 – Scott Moncrieff had ordered copies of *Dante, For Lancelot Andrewes* and *Poems 1909–25*.

4 – Scott Moncrieff wrote on 26 Dec. 1929: 'I should like to discuss Shelley and the *New Statesman* . . . with you. What roused my anger (I have not yet seen your essay) was the reviewer's impudent assumption that you were too stupid to regard for a moment (and dismiss) the popular IV form assumption that the sphere is the moon. – I suppose most

I was amused by your account of the difficulty with Sharp, whom I don't know personally at all.[1] The number of 'rightful heirs' must outnumber the whole House of Lords. Nevertheless, Henry Mond will be a Peer,[2] and Clifford Sharp[3] won't.

Do write again when you feel better. And I wish you would send me something you have written, when you have written it. 'Cousin Fanny and Cousin Annie' is too good to stand alone.[4]

Yours very sincerely,
[T. S. Eliot]

---

people if asked point blank would say so, but a thoughtful person, reading the lines over, would hesitate, as you did.

'As to Crashaw and Shelley, Crashaw wrote in a formal language of great beauty which lay ready to his hand. Shelley lived in a jazz age like our own, when everything had been upset by 20 years of war, the language worst of all. It always seemed to me . . . that Shelley's poetry is a translation into rather crude and careless English of something which we may perhaps be able to read and understand later on.'

1 – 'I have had a breach with the *New Statesman* . . . It began with a correspondence on House of Lords reform, in which Clifford Sharp made a misstatement in an editorial note. I pointed this out, and he said it was a slip of his pen, and proceeded to make several more. I wrote him a cogent letter, beginning "Slips of the pen should as a rule be avoided in written controversy". This letter returned to me in surprisingly few days with a long holograph endorsement saying that it had arrived too late for publication; that he was sorry; and that if the truth were known, he was the rightful heir to the de Clifford peerage!!! I wrote back pointing out that owing to a change in the arrangement by which I received the *New Statesman*, my letter had reached him a day *earlier* than any of the letters he had previously printed (with a week's delay) in the *N.S.*, and pointed out that his peerage claim still further vitiated his argument . . .

So my last word was as follows:
This Editor and I have differed:
He thinks he should be Lord de Clifford;
While I, though disinclined to carp,
Must write him down as still d – – Sharp – '

2 – Henry Mond (1898–1949), politician, industrialist, financier, succeeded his father as 2nd Baron Melchett in 1930.

3 – Clifford Sharp (1883–1935), journalist; first editor of the *New Statesman*, 1913–30. See further Adrian Smith, *The 'New Statesman': Portrait of a Political Weekly, 1913–1931* (1996).

4 – 'Cousin Fanny and Cousin Annie', *NC* 4 (April & July 1926), 262–75, 508–18.

24 January 1930   [Faber & Faber Ltd]

Dear Smyth,

The dates are even more difficult than I feared.[2] March 6th is no good at all, because I am giving my first B.B.C. talk of the series either that night or the next; I think I can just manage Feb. 27th; but cannot let you know definitely until Friday morning. But I believe it will be possible. If I can, I will give your people something fresh and suitable; at the worst, I must give them my paper on Newman, Arnold and Pater.[3]

Another vexation is that I have just been made aware that I had already promised Oliver's book to some one else; it is my own fault for not making a note of the fact. But I hope you can let me have the review you promised, by the 6th February?[4]

Yours ever,
[T. S. Eliot]

---

1 – Charles Smyth (1903–87): ecclesiastical historian and preacher in the Anglican communion. In 1925 he gained a double first in the History Tripos at Corpus Christi College, Cambridge, winning the Thirlwell Medal and the Gladstone Prize, and was elected to a Fellowship of Corpus (R. A. Butler was elected a Fellow on the same day). He edited the *Cambridge Review* in 1925, and again in 1940–1. He was ordained deacon in 1929, priest in 1930; and in 1946 he was appointed rector of St Margaret's, Westminster, and canon of Westminster Abbey. (On 28 Apr. 1952 TSE expressed the view, in a letter to Janet Adam Smith, that Smyth should be 'moved up to where he so eminently belongs, an episcopal see'.) Smyth's works include *Cranmer and the Reformation under Edward VI* (1926); *The Art of Preaching (747–1939)* (1940); and a biography of Archbishop Cyril Garbett (1959).

2 – It had been proposed that TSE give a talk to the Historical Society at Corpus Christi.

3 – John Henry Newman (1801–90): priest, theologian; leader of the Oxford Movement; convert to Roman Catholicism, 1845; appointed cardinal, 1879; beatified, 2010. Works include *Essay on the Development of Christian Doctrine* (1845); *The Idea of a University* (1852, 1857); *Apologia Pro Vita Sua* (1864, 1865); *The Dream of Gerontius* (1865). Matthew Arnold (1822–88): poet, cultural critic; Oxford Professor of Poetry from 1857; author of *Empedocles on Etna, and Other Poems* (1852); *On Translating Homer* (1861); *Literature and Dogma* (1861); *Culture and Anarchy* (1869). Walter Pater (1839–94): essayist and literary and art critic; author of *The Renaissance: Studies in Art and Poetry* (1873); *Marius the Epicurean* (1885); *Appreciations, with an Essay on Style* (1889).

4 – Review of E. L. Woodward, *Three Studies in European Conservatism*; Christopher Hollis, *The Monstrous Regiment*; Bede Jarrett, OP, *A History of Europe*, in *C.* 9 (Apr. 1930), 553–5.

TO *The Superintendent, Town Department,*
   Royal Insurance Co.   CC

24 January 1930   [177 Clarence Gate Gardens,
                                   London]

Dear Sir,
              T/BA: Policy No. H.93527: Household Goods.
I have not yet replied to your letter of the 30th November for the reason
that I have been expecting to move again. For the present, however, I
should have advised you that all my property is located either at this
address or at Shoolbred's Warehouses. I no longer have any property at 38
Burleigh Mansions or at 9 Clarence Gate Gardens or at any other address.
    All personal effects, jewellery etc. are at this address, 177 Clarence
Gate Gardens. The property stored with Shoolbred's is wholly household
furniture and bedding: and its insured value may be taken as one-fifth that
of the total insured value of the furniture.
                                   Yours faithfully,
                                   [T. S. Eliot]

TO *Edward Meryon Wilson*   CC

24 January 1930   [Faber & Faber Ltd,
                                   24 Russell Square, London]

Dear Mr Wilson,
    Thank you for your letter of the 15th January. I am sending back the
translation from Góngora as request[ed] by registered post, to the above
address. I should be glad if you would let [me] have a fresh copy of the first
selection you suggest (The Traveller) and of The Invocation to Hymen.[1]
I will use the longer of these if possible. You can send the poems either
direct to Leonard Woolf Esq., the Hogarth Press, 52 Tavistock Square,
W.C.2., mentioning my name, or if you prefer you can return them to me
to send on to him. Meanwhile I hope that you will enjoy thoroughly your
stay in Madrid.[2]
                                   Yours sincerely,
                                   [T. S. Eliot]

1 – Wilson suggested a few passages from his work for TSE to print in *C.*, including 'the
river description "The traveller, grateful for his one night stay . . ."' and the 'invocation to
Hymen'.
2 – Wilson was enjoying his Esmé Howard Studentship at Residencia de Estudiantes, Madrid.

TO *Ralph K. Brown*

24 January 1930   [Faber & Faber Ltd]

Dear Mr Brown,

I do indeed remember, and hope that at some time I may fulfil the hope;[1] but I am afraid that I cannot undertake anything this term. I have one such engagement, which I am doing my best to get out of, because I have so much work to do here that I ought not to attempt anything else. I am very sorry that none of the dates you mention is the least possible. So I hope that you will pass me on as a liability to your successor.

By the way, I should like to know what has become of Butler Hallahan – I have never heard of him.[2]

With sincere regrets and all best wishes,

Yours sincerely,

[T. S. Eliot]

TO *Edward Dahlberg*

24 January 1930   [Faber & Faber Ltd]

Dear Dahlberg,

I believe I have not answered your letter of the 17th October,[3] but I have been very rushed for months past. This is not an adequate reply, but is merely an acknowledgement and an expression of good wishes for 1930. Meanwhile I have had an enquiry from the Guggenheim Foundation which I have answered. That was before *Bottom Dogs* arrived; so I have written again to tell them that I like the book. I don't think it's a masterpiece yet; but it is a genuine document; there is some very good writing in it; and the chapters about the Orphanage are about as well done as the thing can be done; they gave me great pleasure; so I congratulate you on the book. Putnams [*sc.* Putnam's] seems to think the book is well received here; though what an Englishman, or even many eastern Americans, can make of it I don't know. There is a peculiarity about names like Walnut and

---

1 – Ralph K. Brown (Hon. Secretary of the Hesperides, Trinity Hall, Cambridge) wrote on 7 Jan.: 'I wonder if you remember visiting the "Hesperides" at their dinner in May, 1928, when you expressed a willingness to speak to the society at a meeting if you could find the time.'
2 – Brown answered ('Feb.'): 'Butler Hallahan is with the American Embassy at Buenos Ayres, I am almost certain.' Hallahan (d. 1974), who came in 1927 from Princeton University to Trinity Hall, Cambridge, had been Secretary of the Hesperides in 1928.
3 – Not found.

Chestnut Street which only a middle westerner can perceive; and I was born close enough to the St Louis levee to get that.[1]

Yours every sincerely,
[T. S. Eliot]

TO *The Corresponding Secretary, Colonial Society of Massachusetts*

cc

24 January 1930   [Faber & Faber Ltd]

Sir,

I have your notification of the 19th December, stating that I have been elected a Corresponding Member of the Colonial Society of Massachusetts; and I beg you to convey to the Society my deep sense of the honour which has been conferred upon me.

I am, Sir,
Your obedient servant,
[T. S. Eliot]

TO *John Cournos*[2]

cc

24 January 1930   [Faber & Faber Ltd]

Dear Cournos,

I was glad to hear from you again, and to hear that Mrs Cournos is really convalescent. I don't know how you have managed to get through this time.[3] I was also glad to get the Russian notes, which have gone to press, and I think I have a short note on your collection of Soviet short stories. I am wondering how long the present British government will succeed in getting on with the Soviets; there seems to be a little friction already.

I have not been to the Grove[4] for a long time; the assembly still meets, but I believe at a certain Swiss restaurant somewhere in Kensington. I hope to see you there in the spring.

1–Dahlberg replied on 15 Mar.: 'Your letter gave me very much pleasure . . . Then too, I want to thank you a great deal for the two letters you wrote about me to the Guggenheim Foundation . . . But it did not come off . . . perhaps, I will try again next year.'
2–John Cournos (1881–1966): US poet, novelist, essayist, translator: see Biographical Register.
3–Cournos wrote on 14 Jan., from Gstaad, Switzerland, 'where, at the doctor's orders, I have brought Mrs Cournos for convalescence. We hope to remain here for about three weeks, after which I haven't the least idea where we will go.'
4–The Grove Tavern, Beauchamp Place, where contributors to C. would gather for drinks.

With all best wishes to you and Mrs Cournos,

Yours sincerely,

[T. S. Eliot]

TO *Edward Sackville-West*[1]   CC

24 January 1930   *The Criterion*

Dear Sackville-West,

You must be aware of, if not reconciled to, the dilatory habits of the editor of the *Criterion*.[2] I have read over your Rilke a good many times. Unfortunately, I do not know Rilke in German; but here is my opinion for what it is worth. This seems to me a very efficient and successful translation; but I cannot feel that Rilke is a writer who carries over well into English. For a whole book of translated Rilke I think this would go well; but I don't think it makes an immediate enough impression for a selection in the *Criterion*. That, I suspect, is wholly due to the gap between the English and the German temperament.

I wonder if you have ever thought of trying a translation from George – I don't know his work well, but Du Bos is very enthusiastic about it – or from Hofmannsthal, who I believe might carry over into English better than most? I hope you will go on with translations.

Yours sincerely,

[T. S. Eliot]

1–Edward ('Eddy') Sackville-West, fifth Baron Sackville (1901–65): novelist and music critic; patron of the arts; heir to Knole House, Sevenoaks, Kent. Educated at Eton and Christ Church, Oxford (which he left without taking a degree), he wrote novels including *The Ruin* (1926) and *Simpson* (1931, winner of the Femina Vie Heureuse Prize); and *A Flame in Sunlight: The Life and Work of Thomas de Quincey* (1936, winner of the James Tait Black Memorial Prize) and *The Rescue: A Melodrama for Broadcasting*, set to music by Benjamin Britten (performed in 1943, and published, with illustrations by Henry Moore, 1945). For twenty years from 1935 he wrote 'Gramophone Notes' for *NS*; and in 1950–5 he was a director of Covent Garden (arranging among other things for the first performance of Michael Tippett's *The Midsummer Marriage*). In 1949 he was received into the Roman Catholic Church; and in 1962 he acceded as Lord Sackville. See Michael De-la-Noy, *Eddie: The Life of Edward Sackville-West* (1988).

2–Sackville-West submitted his translations from Rilke's *Duiner Elegien* on 12 May 1929.

TO *David Higham*   CC

24 January 1930   [Faber & Faber Ltd]

Dear Higham,

Thank you for your letter of the 13th. I had also heard from the *Bookman* direct. I hope they will send the cheque soon. It is quite satisfactory; the same amount that they paid me for a previous article.[1]

I am afraid that the essay I [am] engaged upon will not do for Random House, but only for serial publication. It is for a Milford book of essays by the Royal Society of Literature; and I think they want the book rights for America as well.[2] So it will have to go to the *Forum*, or some such paper. But I shall have completed my next series of B.B.C. talks by the middle of April. I can't make any engagements about that yet; because if it makes anything like a book F.&F. would do it; but it is a notion; and otherwise I should be willing to do an essay exclusively for first publication by Random House, if they pay better than a periodical. On the whole, I think that it is the best idea.

> Yours sincerely,
> [T. S. Eliot]

TO *Robert Shafer*[3]   CC

28 January 1930   *The Criterion*

Dear Mr Shafer,

I believe that I wrote to you to explain why it was impossible to use another Humanism essay at present and to express my regret.[4] I wanted

---

1 – 'Poetry and Philosophy' had been sold to *The Bookman* for $150.

2 – 'The Place of Pater', *The Eighteen-Nineties*, ed. Walter de la Mare (1930), 93–106. H. S. Milford (1877–1957) was publisher to Oxford University Press.

3 – Robert Shafer (1899–1956): Professor of English at the University of Cincinnati, 1927–55; author of *Christianity and Naturalism* (1926); *Humanism and America* (co-ed., 1930); *Paul Elmer More and American Criticism* (1935).

4 – Shafer wrote on 20 Jan., apropos his reply to Allen Tate's essay 'The Fallacy of Humanism' which TSE had not accepted for C.: 'It does seem to me that when an editor publishes such a piece as Mr Tate's, he can't escape a certain responsibility to the other side . . . The essay you printed was not Mr Tate's first attack upon the so-called humanists, and I felt that someone was bound to try to check him in his grossly unfair and reckless methods. I was not eager to take the job – did so in fact with extreme reluctance – and I hope I'll never have occasion for a similar effort. The result is dubious. I've already had a number of letters expressing the conviction that my reply was needed and is sound; but Mr Tate himself thus far has only been angered unmeasurably. I've received from him an insulting and threatening

Middleton Murry to use this in the *Adelphi*. But he declined probably correctly on the grounds that it referred too closely to work in the *Criterion*. I was very glad to see it in the *Bookman*, and enjoyed it very much.[1] I will send my copy of the *Bookman* to Tate and shall be interested to know whether he can find any reply.[2] Though of course as I have not been able to publish your article I should not be able to publish one from him.

Yours sincerely,
[T. S. Eliot]

TO C. C. *Martindale*

Charles King & Martyr 1930   [Faber & Faber Ltd]
[30 January]

Dear Father Martindale,

I am glad to know that you stand by the cockatoos, as the picture of that favorite bird cutting the wires is one which I would unwillingly relinquish. But I had always thought of the wombat as arboreal, a sort of teddy bear, and having been nourished in my childhood on the *Natural History* of the Revd Mr Wood, I remember that when young it is a 'pretty and affectionate pet', but that after maturity it is 'apt to fly into uncontrollable passions'.[3]

---

letter demanding an apology, and I've been credibly informed that if he doesn't receive one immediately he intends to force one from me by physical violence. I don't know how this may strike you, but it is very interesting to me as Mr Tate's notion of a "gentlemanly" reaction.'

1 – Robert Shafer's 'Humanism and Impudence', *The Bookman* (NY), 70: 5 (Jan. 1930), 489–98, replied to Allen Tate's 'The Fallacy of Humanism', which came out in *C.* and *Hound and Horn*.

2 – Allen Tate, 'The Same Fallacy of Humanism: A Reply to Mr Robert Shafer', *The Bookman* 71: 1 (Mar. 1930), 31–6; Shafer, 'In Wandering Mazes Lost: A Final Note', ibid., 37–9.

3 – John G. Wood observed of the wombat, or Australian badger: 'In its temper the Wombat is tolerably placid, and will permit itself to be captured without venting any display of indignation. Sometimes, however, it is liable to violent gusts of rage, and then becomes a dangerous antagonist, as it can scratch most fiercely with its heavy claws, and can inflict tolerably severe wounds with its chisel-like teeth. Easily tamed, it displays some amount of affection for those who treat it kindly, and will come voluntarily to its friends in hopes of receiving the accustomed caress' (*The Illustrated Natural History*, I: *Mammalia* [1862], 481). TSE may otherwise have been recollecting Wood's account of the koala, or Australian bear. Martindale insisted, in a PC (20 Jan.): 'I believe you thought the wombat *nested* arboreally: some silly encyclopedia I looked [into] says it Emerges Nocturnally from its Eastern Crannies. All I can say is that MY wombat was on a high road, had been run over by a car (which doubtless it had attacked in one of those hours of uncontrollable rage, having

To descend to graver matters, I take it that we may hope for your essay by the beginning of February, or at least before you leave London, I trust not for the Antipodes again. When you return, I hope that my friendship with Father D'Arcy may be sufficient credentials to make me bold to ask you to lunch with me.

I am looking forward most hungrily to your pamphlet. But, by the way, is it not true that some of the works of my friend Maurras[1] are on the *Index*?

Yours sincerely,
[T. S. Eliot]

---

wished to TROT innocuously down to a lake whose beauty had lured it from tree cranny or other lair den or domicile) & was a cross between a pig & a dachshund.'

1–Charles Maurras (1868–1952): French poet, critic, political philosopher and polemical journalist; founding editor and moving spirit of the monarchist paper, *L'Action Française* (1908–44) – which was ultimately to support Pétain and Vichy during WW2. TSE was to write of Maurras, in a letter to Vernon Watkins dated 10 Apr. 1946: 'He was condemned as a collaborator and is in prison for the rest of his life unless he is later released on compassionate grounds. Maurras was one of those whose collaboration, if it can be called that, was the result of mistaken judgement and certainly not unpatriotic or self-interested motives.' Building on 'three traditions' – classicism, Catholicism, monarchism – Maurras's ideology was to become increasingly, intransigently, right-wing, authoritarian and anti-democratic. In 1925 TSE had planned to write a book about Maurras; and he later wrote 'The *Action Française*, M. Maurras and Mr. Ward', *MC*. 7 (March 1928). TSE said he had been 'a reader of the work of M. Maurras for eighteen years', and, far from 'drawing him away from' Christianity – during 1926 Maurras was even condemned by the Pope, with five of his books being placed on the *Index* – it had had the opposite effect. (Paul Elmer More wrote to Austin Warren on 11 Aug. 1929, of Eliot: 'some time between *The Waste Land* and *For Lancelot Andrewes* he underwent a kind of conversion, due largely I believe to the influence of Maurras and the Action Française' – quoted in Arthur Hazard Dakin, *Paul Elmer More* [1960], 269. However, Eliot would write this comment in the margin of his copy of Dakin's book on More: 'Hardly possible. But Maurras convinced me, as he convinced my friend Massis, of the social importance of the *Church*. But there is a gap here which Maurras could not bridge.') In a later essay, TSE cited Léon Daudet, Whibley and Maurras as the 'three best writers of invective of their time' (*SE*, 499). Eliot would ultimately write of Maurras to William Force Stead, on 19 Mar. 1954: 'I am a disciple of Charles Maurras only in certain respects and with critical selection. I do owe Maurras a good deal, and retain my admiration for him, but I think he had serious errors of political judgment – in fact, he should have confined himself, I think, to the philosophy of politics, and never have engaged in political agitation at all. In that, however, I may be wrong – one never knows what things would have been like, had they been different.' See further James Torrens, SJ, 'Charles Maurras and Eliot's "New Life"', *PMLA* 89: 2 (Mar. 1974), 312–22.

Charles King & Martyr 1930   [*The Criterion*]

Dear Sir,

I am very grateful to you for your letter and your most useful information.[1]
I wonder if you would do me a further kindness by suggesting which of
the people you have mentioned would be most suitable to review Vol. VI
of the *Cambridge Mediaeval History* – a volume dealing chiefly with the
Papacy?[2]

I should also be grateful if you would keep in mind that I am looking
not only for churchmen to write on church subjects, but for Anglican
'intellectuals' (to use a word which I detest) of wide enough interests to be
able to review more general works from an (implicit) Anglican position?
I include laymen. This is to offset a balance of very able R.C.'s whom I
have admitted.

If you should be in London at any time I should be very much honoured
if you could find the time to lunch with me.

With many thanks,
[T. S. Eliot]

1 – The Revd H. D. A. Major, DD (1871–1961) – New Zealand-born Principal of Ripon
Hall, Oxford, 1919–48; founder and editor of the *Modern Churchman*, 1911 – had advised
on 25 Jan., 'I always think that J. C. Hardwick, Partington Vicarage, Manchester, is excellent
in reviewing theological & philosophical & ethical books where they take modern science
into account.

'The Rev. J. S. Boys-Smith, Fellow & Dean of St John's Coll. Camb. is excellent for
philosophy & theology & Church History.

'Mr Michael Oakeshott, Fellow of Gonville & Caius College Cambridge is a good
reviewer of religious books which have relations with political and social history . . . The
Revd. Dr. Martin, of St John's Vicarage, Rastrick Yorks. is excellent for mediaeval Church
History.'

2 – Major replied (30 Jan.) that Dr [E. J.] Martin would be the best; also perhaps Dr Norman
Sykes, King's College, London, who had written *Edmund Gibson* (Clarendon Press). See
Martin's untitled review of *The Cambridge Medieval History*, vol. VI: *The Victory of the
Papacy*, ed. J. R. Tanner, C. W. Previté-Orton and Z. N. Brooke, in C. 9 (July 1930), 742–4.

TO *Charles Harris*[1]   CC

Charles King & Martyr 1930   [Faber & Faber Ltd]

Dear Sir,

My friend the Revd William Force Stead has I understand mentioned me to you. He also gives me to understand that you will be in London for the Assembly. I am on the strength of his introduction writing to ask you if you would do me the favour of lunching with me on Wednesday, February 5th, when I expect you will be in London, at the Royal Societies Club, 63 St. James's Street, at one o'clock. I shall be very much gratified if you will.

Yours very truly,
[T. S. Eliot]

TO *Carrol Romer*[2]   CC

30 January 1930   [*The Criterion*]

Dear Mr Romer,

Very many thanks for writing to me and for letting me see the story by Mrs Romer.[3] It interested me very much and it seems to me a very good piece of work. I must explain however that the *Criterion* can only publish four or five pieces of fiction during the year and that my policy is, so far as possible, not to compete with other magazines or to publish things which might be equally acceptable elsewhere. I try to make a special place for the *Criterion* by publishing stories which are good of their kind but of a kind which other periodicals would probably refuse on the ground of lack of popular interest. If the *Criterion* is not to do this sort of pioneer work there is really no justification for its existence when there are so many other well established reviews.

1–The Revd Charles Harris, DD (1865–1936): Prebendary of Hereford Cathedral from 1925; Vicar of South Leigh, Witney, Oxfordshire, 1929–34; Chairman of the Book Committee of the (English) Church Union since 1923; Assistant Editor of *Literature and Worship*, 1932. His works include *Creeds or No Creeds?* (1922); *First Steps in the Philosophy of Religion* (1927).
2–Carrol Romer (1883–1951): editor of *The Nineteenth Century and After*, 1925–30; Assistant Registrar, 1931–3; King's Coroner and Attorney, Master of the Crown Office and Registrar of the Court of Criminal Appeal, 1933–46.
3–Submitted on 17 Jan.

I have heard much of you from my friends Professor Babbitt and Dr. More, and I hope that we may at some time have the opportunity to talk.

Yours sincerely,

[T. S. Eliot]

TO *Max Clauss*

CC

30 January 1930   *The Criterion*

My dear Clauss,

Please remember that I am anxiously waiting to get from you some more detailed information of your procedure with the German side so that we may arrange the English competition. I would like to know everything you can tell me as to how you managed the competition, as I am rather terrified by the flood of bad fiction which I expect to come in.

Did I write to tell you that since I wrote to suggest engaging the *Hound & Horn* in the Competition I heard from one of the Editors of that periodical to whom the idea had occurred simultaneously. He begged me to put him in touch with you and to use my good offices to persuade you and the other editors to accept their collaboration. I suggested, if you are in accord, that the *Hound and Horn* ought to publish our translation of 'The Centurion' in the meanwhile.

Yours always sincerely,

[T. S. Eliot]

TO *Marguerite Caetani*

CC

Charles King & Martyr 1930   [Faber & Faber Ltd]

Dear Marguerite,

About Traherne, I think Herbert Read is the best man for you.[1] I could put you onto period specialists, Grierson or Mario Praz, who are friends of mine; but Read knows Traherne well and as a man of letters is more suitable. I have mentioned it to him, and he would like to do it; but for the next month is busy giving the Clark Lectures at Cambridge, which

---

1—Caetani wrote on 23 Jan.: 'In the near future I would like very much to give in *Commerce* a selection of Traherne . . . accompanied by a preface and the same for Sidney. Of course my highest ambition would be if you could write one of these prefaces or both . . .

'I thought vaguely of Herbert Read having just been reading *The Sense of Glory* [1929] and seen how enthusiastic he is about those two.'

I gave a few years ago; so he could not tackle it for at least a month. I only suggest that if he writes the introduction he ought also to *make the selections* himself. I suggest your writing to him,

> Herbert Read,
> Broom House,
> Seer Green, near Beaconsfield, Bucks.

and tell him about how much preface and how much selection you want. Your having no fixed scale of payment is a nuisance to me, in such negotiations, but I suggest from £15 to £20 according to the amount you want; £15 probably quite adequate.[1]

Can you tell me any address to which I might write to Léger from whom I have not heard, except the Embassy?

[*Incomplete: typing runs off the carbon copy*]

TO *E. R. Curtius*[2]   CC

30 January 1930   [Faber & Faber Ltd]

My dear Curtius,

I have been hoping to hear further from you about the projected volume on English Wegerieter.[3] I am pretty sure I could get for you, if you wanted, the new collected edition of Virginia Woolf, as the volumes appear.

Meanwhile I am wondering whether you would have time to write for the *Criterion* a review of Herbert Read's recent book *The Sense of Glory*. It contains nine essays on the following writers: Froissart, Malory, Descartes, Swift, Sterne, Vauvenargues, Hawthorne, Henry James, Bagehot, and is I think a book of some importance. I do not know how many of his previous books you have in your possession, but if you will let me know I will see that you get the others. I am sending you herewith a copy of his short pamphlet *In Retreat* which we have just republished.[4] I think that

---

1–HR wrote to TSE ('Tuesday'): 'The Traherne job would rather amuse me, but how long have I to do it in? Wordsworth [i.e. his Clark Lectures] is simmering down, but I couldn't turn to it for 3 or 4 weeks. It need not take me long once I begin on it. £15 would be very suitable.'
2–Ernst Robert Curtius (1886–1956), German scholar of philology and Romance literature: see Biographical Register.
3–Curtius (5 Dec. 1929) was 'not unfavourably disposed towards' TSE's idea: he had in mind essays on DHL, E. M. Forster, Robert Graves, AH, JJ and TSE – 'but I ask you to complete the list'.
4–Curtius said he was willing (1 Feb.) to review HR's book of essays, but in the event he did not do so. TSE wrote later that he considered HR's *In Retreat* (Criterion Miscellany 8)

you will find it a very interesting piece of writing and personally I should very much like to see it in a German translation if you thought that there might be any interest in it. Of course I have not mentioned this point yet to Read himself.

Cordially yours,
[T. S. Eliot]

TO *Ramon Fernandez*   CC

30 January 1930   [*The Criterion*]

My dear Fernandez,

Thank you very much for your letter of the 23rd.[1] I am extremely pleased that you are satisfied with my translation, and shall be very much interested to hear what you think of Murry's book; and if you thought it worth while at any time to write out some statement of the relation of your philosophy to his I should be delighted to publish it. I have sent you a copy of Belgion's book.[2] I don't suppose you will have time to write a review of it by the 6th of February, when the March number goes to press. But that number will be rather crowded in any case and the review would be equally welcome for the June number.

When your Molière came in I was up to the eyes in work and other reading and I lent it to Herbert Read who has not yet returned it to me. I shall read it as soon as I can get it back from him and write to you about it.[3]

'in its kind one of the few prose masterpieces that our period will leave behind' ('Views and Reviews', *The New English Weekly*, 20 June 1935). The blurb (Spring 1930) – perhaps by TSE – reads: 'The narrative, by an infantry officer and writer of assured position, of the retreat of the British Fifth Army from St Quentin in March, 1918. *In Retreat* was written in 1919, and originally issued in the *Hogarth Essays* in 1925. Though championed by a few, it remained a noble fragment overlooked by many, and *The Times Literary Supplement* of November 29, 1929, mentioned it as "that neglected little masterpiece". It is now available for the first time at a shilling.'

1 – 'I think your translation [of 'A Humanist Theory of Value'] is wonderful, and it was a pleasure to see my own thoughts so well handled. I think it is indeed the vocabulary that makes the main difference between Mr Middleton Murry's ideas and mine. But the vocabulary may be a sign of some deeper variance.'

2 – Fernandez agreed to review Belgion's *Our Present Philosophy of Life*, which he said 'seems to be interesting enough'.

3 – 'I should very much like to know your opinion of my *Molière* [*La vie de Molière* (1929)], as it is a new form of criticism I have tried to realise.' See C. 9 (July 1930), 759–63.

I should not think of visiting Paris, even for a few days, without trying to see you.

Yours very sincerely,

[T. S. Eliot]

P.S. Will you review Belgion's book at any length you like up to 1500 words.

TO *John Dover Wilson*[1] TS National Library of Scotland

30 January 1930 *The Criterion*

Dear Dover Wilson,

I am very glad that you wrote to me about Robertson's article, because I had been under the delusion that I had already written to suggest your writing a rejoinder and that you had not replied.[2] As a matter of fact the idea occurred to me from the moment when Robertson told me what he wanted to write; and he appeared to be quite glad if I could get a reply from you. My first idea had been to ask you to reply in the same number; but Robertson's article was so long that it would have completely swamped the issue if I had published a reply from you simultaneously.

Anyway I should be very glad if you could let me have an article on this subject in time for the June number; and especially if you could let me have it by the middle of April. Robertson's article is decidedly on the long side and I should prefer to have something of not over 5000 words. Also I should be glad to know as soon as possible what title you will give the essay.[3]

With many thanks,

Yours sincerely,

T. S. Eliot

1–John Dover Wilson (1881–1969): literary and textual scholar; Professor of Education, King's College, London, 1924–35; Regius Professor of Rhetoric and English Literature, Edinburgh University, 1935–45. Renowned as editor of the New Cambridge Shakespeare, 1921–66. His writings include *Shakespeare's Hand in the Play of 'Sir Thomas More'* (1923); *The Essential Shakespeare* (1932); *The Fortunes of Falstaff* (1943); *Shakespeare's Happy Comedies* (1962).
2–Dover Wilson wrote on 23 Jan., 'I have been reading Robertson's "Shakespearean Idolatry" in the January *Criterion* [246–67]. He constantly invites a rejoinder . . .'
3–Dover Wilson replied (25 Feb.), 'Have begun an article . . . entitled "Idolatry and Scepticism in Shakespearian Studies: a reply to Mr J. M Robertson". I shall try to "rag" him a bit . . .'

TO *Desmond Morse-Boycott*[1]

cc

31 January 1930[2]   [*The Criterion*]

Dear Father Morse-Boycott,

I owe you many apologies for the delay in reporting on your essay 'The Religion of the School-Boy' which has been due to numerous distractions. While I found it very interesting myself and felt very sympathetic to your views, I finally came to the conclusion that the *Criterion* was not quite the proper place for it. Specific problems of education and particularly the early education of children hardly fall within our province. Nevertheless I hope that some day you will be able to let me have something else which may be more obviously within the *Criterion*'s range.[3]

In the hope also of meeting you at some future date,

I remain,
Yours sincerely,
[T. S. Eliot]

TO *Messrs. Farrar & Rinehart*[4]

cc

31 January 1930   [Faber & Faber Ltd]

Dear Sirs,

I must apologise for the delay in acknowledging the galley proofs of *Humanism*.[5] I have myself read the book and one of my fellow directors has also read it with the greatest interest. It seems to me that Mr Foerster has managed his task with very great ability and it is a book which you must be proud to publish.

I am rather at a loss to know what to suggest about placing the book in England. So far as our firm is concerned we feel that the book would be well worth publishing as a distinction for the list of any firm, but that it

---

1 – The Revd Desmond Morse-Boycott (1892–1979): Assistant Curate of St Mary the Virgin, Somers Town, London, 1919–35, and journalist. Writings include *Ten Years in a London Slum* (1929) and *The Secret Story of the Oxford Movement* (1933).
2 – TSE typed '1929'.
3 – Morse-Boycott replied (17 Feb.) that his article – which he had called (letter to TSE, 16 Sept. 1929) 'my comic tract for Church of England people (and others), and [which] is designed to be a small antidote to prevalent melancholy' – had been accepted by *The Review of the Churches*.
4 – This was the first year of Farrar & Rinehart's existence.
5 – Proofs of *Humanism and America: Essays on the Outlook of Modern Civilisation*, ed. Norman Foerster (1930), had been sent to TSE by John Farrar on 10 Dec. 1929.

would certainly sell very few copies. The subject is of course one of world-wide importance, but so far the interest in it is very largely confined to America and to a very small number of intellectuals in Europe and I fear that the appearance of the book might defeat its purpose with any wider British public – that is to say a superficial examination might confirm instead of dispelling the impression that Humanism is a subject of local interest for America. I am holding the proofs in case you want me to send them on to some other publisher or possibly to one of the literary agencies.

With very many thanks,

I remain,
Yours very truly,
[T. S. Eliot]

TO *William Force Stead*[1]   TS Beinecke

3 February 1930   *The Criterion*

My dear Stead,

I am answering now your letter of the 24th.[2] I am not answering your two previous letters with enclosures, because if I am to be of any use to you in that matter it will take time and I have not yet had time to give concentrated attention to the MS.[3] But I am looking forward to doing so. Many thanks for your kindness and the trouble you have taken. I have written to Harris to ask him to see me when he is in London next week and I return his letter to you herewith. His handwriting suggests complete illiteracy, but what you say about him makes me anxious to meet him. I have already got into touch with A. E. Taylor on account of a German book on which I wanted his opinion with a view to publication. I have not yet seen him but found him extremely amicable in correspondence

1 – Willliam Force Stead (1884–1967), poet, critic, diplomat, clergyman: see Biographical Register.
2 – 'Harris looks like his letter, scrambling and untidy. He has a short bulky figure and the squat head and sharp nose – also the untidy clothes – of an old French Abbé. But it's the mind that is the man and his mind is well versed in philosophy theology and psychology . . . Harris by the way holds a retreat at his Vicarage 3 or 4 times a year and specialises in curing nervous disorders by modern psychology plus orthodox religion.'
3 – Stead sent TSE on 4 Jan. a poem – 'a continuation of *Uriel*, the long poem at the end of my last book "Festival in Tuscany" . . . an attempt to suggest the gigantic mystery of change, creation, or "Becoming".'

and I have suggested a piece of work which he may be willing to do at some time.

I have meanwhile heard from Major who has given me several names and I have written to him. Also I am lunching this week with Selwyn who is coming up for the Assembly.

For your kindness and solicitude I am more than grateful. I will not touch on more personal matters in a letter but hope that you may be able to come up and lunch with me in a few weeks.

But referring to the last paragraph of your letter it is only fair to say that I see Francis Underhill[1] pretty regularly from time to time, that I like him very much and have found him helpful to me personally. I am very grateful to you for the introduction.

Yours affectionately,

T. S. E.

TO *H. Carrington Lancaster*[2]   CC

3 February 1930   [Faber & Faber Ltd]

Dear Sir,

I apologise for my delay in answering your kind letter of the 19th December; the delay has not been neglect.[3] Indeed I feel very much honoured by the invitation, and very deeply regret that I cannot accept it. This year is quite impossible for me, and next year I cannot yet foresee; but if circumstances permitted, be sure that I would accept 'in principle'; I only hope that the opportunity may be offered me at some future time.

1–See TSE to Underhill, 16 Oct. 1930, below.
2–Henry Carrington Lancaster (1882–1954): Professor of French Literature, Chair of the Department of Romance Languages, Johns Hopkins University, 1918–47; editor-in-chief of *Modern Language Notes*, 1928–54; author of *History of Dramatic French Literature in the Seventeenth Century* (9 vols, 1929–42).
3–Lancaster (Chairman, Committee on Lectures) invited TSE to be Turnbull Lecturer at Johns Hopkins University, Baltimore, 'either in this academic year or the next'. The six lectures, to be spread over two weeks, carried an honorarium of $1,500. 'While we should prefer to have you come in the spring of 1930, we should be glad to have you, if that time does not suit you, in the fall of 1930, or the winter or spring of 1931.' The Turnbull Foundation, he explained, 'was created by Mr and Mrs Lawrence Turnbull in memory of their son. Both have since died, so that we are obliged to abide by the conditions laid down in the will, in accordance with which the lecturer is asked to comply with the following condition: "In each course of lectures delivered on this Foundation, there shall be an explicit and reverent recognition of God as the Infinite Source of all Love and Truth and Beauty and of the principle that all true and enduring art must be permeated with the purest morality."' TSE was to give the Turnbull Lectures in 1933: see *VMP*.

I may add that the terms laid down by the founders of the Turnbull Foundation would not be likely to be infringed by anything that I might say.

With my sincere recognition of the honour that your Committee and University have thought fit to do me, and with equally sincere regrets,

I remain,
Yours very sincerely,
[T. S. Eliot]

TO *A. L. Rowse*   TS Exeter

3 February 1930   *The Criterion*

My dear Rowse,

Many thanks for your letter of the 2nd which I answer with uncommon promptitude.[1] I am glad that you think Daniels' book is good enough to hang a symposium on. You evidently have not been a reader of the *New Age* (quite a lively little paper sometimes) or you would have been familiar with these names; they are all Douglas-schemers.

I have heard well of Walter Elliott[2] but fear he is a difficult bird to catch. (By the way I am not sure whether you mean *longo intervallo* to apply to

---

1 – Rowse wrote, apropos the Daniels volume on politics: 'I am agreeably surprised, for it is from a group I have never heard of, and is really quite interesting. It should provide a very good occasion for a symposium on politics, and I should be delighted to contribute, though I shall be very jealous of its luck for I shall finish my own postponed book on "politics and the younger generation" by then. However, here are my suggestions.

'Far and away the best would be Walter Elliot for Conservatism, if you could get him. (If not either Oliver Stanley or Boothby, longo intervallo).

'For an academic view, [R. H.] Tawney wd be very good, esp. on ethical side of politics. For liberalism, Lionel Robbins, the new Professor at London School of Economics: he's a live young man and I can't think of anybody such on Liberalism unless there's a young man at Cambridge. (Oh, Kingsley Martin of *Manchester Guardian* might do as second string.)

'It would be attractive perhaps to elicit some definite statement of ends from Maxton, and failing him, John Strachey might do. He's younger & has a new line.

'Then I would strongly suggest Maurice Dobb, Pembroke Coll. Cambridge, who is a Communist [author of *On Marxism To-Day*] and a very original thinker.

'I do hope these suggestions will be useful. I have on the whole kept to young people with an attitude of their own and not those like Belloc, Cole, Russell etc . . .'

2 – Rt. Hon. Walter Elliot (1888–1958): Scottish Unionist Party politician; Parliamentary Under-Secretary of State for Scotland, 1926–9; Financial Secretary to the Treasury, 1931–2; Secretary of State for Scotland, 1936–8; author of *Toryism and the Twentieth Century* (1927).

Elliott vs. Stanley[1] & Boothby;[2] or to Elliott & Stanley vs. Boothby – the difference is of some importance).

But I should like you to consider once again whether we had better try to get a few active politicians, such as Elliott and Maxton,[3] or rather people who think about these matters without having any constituency axes to grind? Also, I should have thought that Tawney[4] (about whom I know very little really) was almost as stale – not as Belloc,[5] nor even as Russell, but say as stale as Cole.[6] I want something fresher from Laski.[7] The other names are interesting: Robbins,[8] Martin,[9] and anyone so new to practical politics as John Strachey.[10]

1–Oliver Stanley (1896–1950): Conservative Member of Parliament for Westmorland, 1924–45.

2–Robert Boothby (1900–86): Conservative politician; author and broadcaster.

3–James Maxton (1885–1946): Scottish Labour MP; chair of the Independent Labour Party, 1926–31, 1934–9; proponent of Home Rule for Scotland. His writings include *Lenin* (1932).

4–R. H. Tawney (1880–1962) – economic historian, social critic, ethical socialist, Christian socialist; President of the Workers' Educational Association, 1928–44 – was Professor of Economic History at the London School of Economics, 1931–49. His works include *The Acquisitive Society* (1920) and *Religion and the Rise of Capitalism* (1926).

5–Hilaire Belloc (1870–1953): prolific author, poet, journalist and wit; apologist for Roman Catholicism; anti-Semite; advocate of the Distributist movement. His publications include *The Path to Rome* (1902); *The Servile State* (1912); *The House of Commons and Monarchy* (1920); *Europe and the Faith* (1920); and *The Jews* (1922). See A. N. Wilson, *Hilaire Belloc* (1984).

6–G. D. H. Cole (1889–1959): political theorist, economist, historian, libertarian socialist, Fabian; writer, with his wife Margaret, of detective fiction; Reader in Economics, University College, Oxford, 1925–44; Chichele Professor of Social and Political Theory, 1944–57. Works include *The Life of William Cobbett* (1925), *The Intelligent Man's Guide through World Chaos* (1932). See Margaret Cole, *The Life of G. D. H. Cole* (1971); L. P. Carpenter, *G. D. H. Cole: An Intellectual Biography* (1974); A. W. Wright, *G. D. H. Cole and Socialist Democracy* (1979).

7–Harold J. Laski (1893–1950): Professor of Political Science, London School of Economics, 1926–50; editor of the Left Book Club; chairman of the Labour Party, 1945–6.

8–Lionel Robbins, later Lord Robbins (1898–1984): economist; Head of the London School of Economics from 1929; Chair of the Committee on Higher Education which produced the Robbins Report, 1963, advocating a massive expansion of higher education provision in the UK.

9–Kingsley Martin (1897–1969): journalist; editor of the *New Statesman*, 1930–60.

10–John Strachey (1901–63) – son of John Strachey, editor of *The Spectator* – was educated at Magdalen College, Oxford, and went on to edit the *Socialist Review*, having joined the Labour Party in 1923. He was MP for Birmingham Aston, 1929–31, and was for a while a member of Sir Oswald Mosley's New Party before joining the Communist Party for the later 1930s. He was Labour MP for Dundee, 1945–50, serving as Minister for Food in 1946 (when he was made a Privy Counsellor) and Secretary of State for War, 1950–1. A Marxist-Leninist theorist of repute in the 1930s, he wrote *The Coming Struggle for Power* (1932), *The Menace of Fascism* (1933).

I mean, I don't want just to get good-selling names for this group discussion, but coming thoughtful people each of whom has something to contribute, quite apart from whatever party label he may have. I agree firmly about keeping to young people. The *Criterion* doesn't want to know what Kipling[1] thinks of Stalin, or what Lansbury[2] thinks of Mussolini etc. etc.

There is no hurry about it; I want to get the right men, and keep them afterwards.

I should like to write a long letter about your Communism, which I thoroughly enjoyed. There are two or three points I may raise, when [the] time comes. But an editor's existence is very ascetic – i.e. one's business is to excite other people to write, and [not] to have time to read, write or think oneself.

As most of my letters to you seem to be trying to cover several subjects very rapidly, I may have omitted to reply to your suggestion about Jacob. I should [like] very much to have him; I met him once at All Souls, and found that he really knew something about the Middle Ages; but as I veto'd a review of my *Dante* by you, I was not going to remove it for anyone else.

Yours ever,
T. S. Eliot

P.S. I had already thought of Maxton (this is a secret) and had written to ask him to do something for us: No reply.

Don't return the book.

---

1 – Rudyard Kipling (1865–1936): immensely popular poet and writer. Much travelled (in his early years he pursued a successful career as a journalist in India, 1882–8, and was thereafter, in TSE's phrase, an 'imperial patriot'), his many works include *Departmental Ditties* (1886), *Plain Tales from the Hills* (1888), *The Light that Failed* (1890), *Barrack-Room Ballads* (1892), *The Jungle Book* (1895), *Kim* (1901), and *Puck of Pook's Hill* (1906). He was awarded the Nobel Prize in 1907. See further TSE's introductory essay in *A Choice of Kipling's Verse* (1941) – extolling the great ballad-writer and verse writer, and observing in passing: 'He might almost be called the first citizen of India. And his relation to India determines that about him which is the most important thing about a man, his religious attitude. It is an attitude of comprehensive tolerance ... No attentive reader of Kipling can maintain, however, that he was unaware of the faults of British rule: it is simply that he believed the British Empire to be a good thing ... I cannot find any justification for the charge that he held a doctrine of race superiority ... Kipling is not a doctrinaire or a man with a programme' – and 'The Unfading Genius of Rudyard Kipling', *Kipling Journal* 26: 129 (Mar. 1959), 9–12. TSE told Eleanor Hinkley, 30 July 1955: 'In an introduction, you can't be as critical as you would be in an independent essay. There are aspects of Kipling that I don't like – one might summarize by saying "the vulgar streak" ...'
2 – George Lansbury (1859–1940): politician and reformer; leader of the Labour Party, 1932–5.

TO *Charles Harris*   CC

3 February 1930   [Faber & Faber Ltd]

Dear Sir,

I shall expect you with pleasure at the Royal Societies' Club, 63, St James's Street, on Wednesday by 1:30.[1] I have invited my friend and colleague, Mr Herbert Read, to join us at lunch, but he is obliged to leave immediately after, so we shall have half an hour or so for a talk by ourselves, if you are not too rushed. Many thanks for your letter. I will return the E.C.U.[2] pamphlet, which I had never seen, and which interested me very much, when we meet.

Yours sincerely,
[T. S. Eliot]

TO *M. C. D'Arcy*[3]   CC

4 February 1930   [*The Criterion*]

My dear D'Arcy,

Very many thanks for your painstaking letter. I have looked the matter up, and the facts are as More says. So I shall print the short excerpt from his letter (which was mostly about unrelated and partly personal matters) and your rejoinder; and I hope that will close the matter.[4]

1–Harris (E.C.U. Literature Committee) welcomed the opportunity (30 Jan.) to meet TSE for lunch.

'As you are now "one of us", I enclose a battered copy of our confidential "Report" . . .

'We have now in hand a great international and interdenominational venture, under Catholic leadership and control, some of the details of which (if you are interested) I will disclose to you next Wednesday. I desire your advice and assistance . . . In my pastoral work, I have specialized in the spiritual treatment of nervous and moral diseases, mainly upon the lines of the New Psychology.'

The object of the E.C.U. Literature Committee was: 'To promote study and research, and the dissemination of literature, in all branches of theology and ethics; and in those departments of philosophy, psychology, and natural science, which are closely related to religion.'

2–English Church Union.

3–Martin D'Arcy (1888–1976), Jesuit priest and theologian: see Biographical Register.

4–Paul Elmer More's 'An Absolute and an Authoritative Church' appeared in C. 8 (July 1929), 616–34; D'Arcy's reply in C. 9 (Oct. 1929), 117. More complained: 'I wrote as follows (page 629): "The dogma of *original sin* . . . corresponds with an indisputable trait of human nature . . . But the dogma of *original guilt* is a pure fabrication of occidental theology." Father D'Arcy accuses me of charging at windmills, and to prove his point quotes me thus: "The dogma of *original sin* is a pure fabrication etc."' D'Arcy wrote to TSE on 25 Jan. 1930: 'I willingly rely on his word & that being the case I am very sorry to have done

As a matter of fact, I felt at the time that his subject was not quite suitable for the *Criterion*, but I was anxious to get something from him and that was all he had to give. It had to be considerably mutilated to be squeezed in. But in general I prefer articles which tend to bring men of right tendencies together, rather than those which may provoke what I may call internecine conflict. That is why I hope this particular affair is closed.

With many thanks,
Yours sincerely,
[T. S. Eliot]

The Morgan review will do for June. I will notify you in due course.[1]

TO *James Joyce*[2]   CC

4 February 1930   [Faber & Faber Ltd]

My dear Joyce,

I am writing to you because Gilbert has suggested, and I understand is keen to have, a small *signed* edition of his *Ulysses*. We are none of us, I must say, very enthusiastic; because we do not think that Gilbert's signature is enough (as he is still unknown) to justify even a small edition; but one of my fellow-directors has suggested the following way out, which I put to you very tentatively:

We would do as Gilbert wishes and publish a small limited signed edition, *if it were signed also by you*. The only way to do this would be a jocular one; that is for us to print NIHIL OBSTAT (IMPRIMATUR[3] might be too strong) with a space for you to sign under it. Gilbert could sign elsewhere.

---

what I hate doing, misquote, & thereby appear to him to do him an injustice. It is for him therefore, – or for you as interpreting what you think he would wish, – to decide whether a formal & public expression of my regret should be made . . . I must have lapsed into the ordinary habit of taking original sin to include peccatum originatum as well as peccatum originans, – to include guilt as well as sin . . . [However,] I think the distinction Mr More makes is at its best unimportant, & my comment on original *guilt* would be just the same as on original *sin*. I send you however a letter of regret for publication, if Mr More wishes for it. I have tried to write it so that the matter will be ended.'
1 – Not done.
2 – James Joyce (1882–1941): Irish novelist, playwright, poet; author of *A Portrait of the Artist as a Young Man* (1916), *Ulysses* (1922), *Finnegans Wake* (1939).
3 – '*Nihil obstat*' – 'nothing forbids'; '*imprimatur*' – 'let it be printed'.

This is not my idea; and I am very doubtful, even with your recommendation (without which we should certainly not have taken the book) whether you wish to express so much approval. I merely say that if you did this we could sell a good many at once of a limited edition; otherwise there seems no point in a limited edition.

I am of opinion that the book is a good book; but a limited signed edition of a book by a new author is hopeless.

I hope that you are in better health than when Schwartz saw you. But if you prefer *not* to sign a small edition of Gilbert's book, you need not answer this at all; if on the other hand you would do it, perhaps Mrs Joyce (to whom I wish to be remembered most cordially in any case) could send me a post card to that effect?

Yours always sincerely,
[T. S. Eliot]

TO *Leonard Woolf*

CC

4 February 1930 [Faber & Faber Ltd]

Dear Leonard,

I am writing to ask whether the Hogarth Press would be willing to send to my friend Professor Dr E. R. Curtius, Bonn a/Rh., Joachimstrasse 14, the collected edition of Virginia's works as and when they appear? It is not a commercial proposition, because it will only mean in the first place, an article in one of the better German literary periodicals. Why I am interested is as follows. Curtius is one of the most influential critics in Germany, and has written several books which are the established German criticism of contemporary French literature. At my suggestion, he is going to do a book on contemporary English literature; he has already done long studies of Joyce[1] and myself. But he can't afford to buy many English books; so I said I would try to help him to get what he needed; primarily Virginia, secondly Forster, and one or two others. Finally, there will be a book which we shall publish in England.[2]

1 – 'James Joyce und Sein Ulysses', *Neue Schweizer Rundschau*, 1929. (Curtius's essays on JJ were to be offered to F&F, in a translation by Martin Turnell, in Oct. 1933, but FVM turned them down on 17 Nov. 1933.)
2 – LW replied (undated: Feb. 1930) that he would send the 'uniform edition' to Curtius.

Another point. I have a young man named Morton (Exeter College)[1] who has done some fairly good reviewing for me. He specialises on the French Revolution and Napoleon, with folklore and witchcraft as a sideline, and general literature in the background. He writes verse also, about as well as three or four dozen others; but that should not count against him. I may say in his favour that he was not passed to me and did not come begging to me; I got in touch with him first through reading a review of my own verse by him in some local magazine, and being struck by one or two intelligent observations which no one else had made; and so I wrote to him.[2]

This time, I shan't send the man to you unless you think it worthwhile for reviewing purposes. I enclose a specimen from the next *Criterion*.

We never meet nowadays; but we have not been very well here; and have seen very few people; and are on the point of moving again, into a house.[3] I hope you are both well.

Yours ever,
[Tom]

1 – A. L. Morton (1903–87), Marxist historian; in the 1930s he worked for the *Daily Worker* and contributed to other magazines; from 1946 he chaired the Historians Group of the Communist Party of Great Britain. *A People's History of England* (1938) is a modern classic. Later works include *The Everlasting Gospel: A Study in the Sources of William Blake* (1958) and *The World of the Ranters: Religious Radicalism in the English Revolution* (1970). See *Rebels & Their Causes: Essays in Honour of A. L. Morton*, ed. Maurice Cornforth (1978); *History and the Imagination: Selected Writings of A. L. Morton*, ed. Margot Heinemann (1990).

Morton sent TSE his CV: 'I went from Westbourne College to Peterhouse, Cambridge [not Exeter Coll. – in Oxford – as TSE says]. While at Cambridge I read for an Honours degree in History and English. I contributed reviews, etc. to the *Cambridge Mercury*, the *New Cambridge*, and other magazines.

'More recently I have been reviewing books on historical subjects and on witchcraft in the *Criterion*. I have also published critical articles in the *Decachord*, and poems in the *Decachord* and the *London Aphrodite*.

'The periods of history in which I am specially interested are those of the French Revolution and the Nineteenth Century. More generally, I have specialised on economics and social history. I have made a special study of witchcraft, and, as a logical extension of that, of folk-lore and anthropology. I have also a good general knowledge of modern literature, and a more detailed knowledge of modern poetry.'

2 – 'As regards Morton, I am giving up the Literary Editorship of the *Nation* next week so that it is not much use my doing anything in the matter. What I suggest is that he should apply to Blunden who succeeds me on the *Nation*.'

3 – VW would write to Clive Bell on 6 Feb., 'Tom by the way writes today that he is just moving to a house, from a flat, – the 5th move in 6 months; which means I suppose that the worm in Vivien turns and turns, and not a nice worm at that' (*The Letters of Virginia Woolf IV: A Reflection of the Other Person*, ed. Nigel Nicolson [1978], 133).

TO *A. L. Rowse*   TS Exeter

4 February 1930   *The Criterion*

Dear Rowse,

As you took such an interest in my Politics suggestion, I wonder if you could help me with the following. I want to get some competent person to round up in an article the considerable literature (or some of it) of the last year or so on Disarmament, Peace Pacts etc. I have some stuff – Murray, Sturzo, Madariaga, Zimmern; and I should like to get a good essay for the June number, which could probably take in the Naval Conference in retrospect.

It is difficult to think of anyone with whom the *Criterion* could associate itself. I don't need necessarily an expert – perhaps better not; and certainly not anyone with preconceived or already expressed views, and neither a humanitarian nor a militarist. It is much easier to say who not than to say who! It might be any highly intelligent detached person who could take the trouble to read the books etc. Later on, I want (apart from the Politics discussion) to get several views on the subject of Nationalism – a word much used for years, but the meaning not very often analysed.

Yours ever,
T. S. Eliot

TO *John Cournos*   CC

5 February 1930   [Faber & Faber Ltd]

Dear Cournos,

This is a line in great haste, having just had your letter of the 2nd.[1] I am terribly sorry to hear of your new difficulties. I expect this is the best you

---

1 – Cournos wrote from Paris, from where he was hoping to travel with his wife and children to the USA. 'The fact is, I can't give Mrs Cournos the after-care she needs; and she needs a great deal after such an operation as she's had. Physically, she's improving, but her nerves are in a bad way; and as it is a matter of many months there's nothing to do but take her over to her mother, who can look after her better than I can . . . I am trying to raise the money so I can sail by the 13th – 20th at the latest. Some friends in England and elsewhere are trying to help me, and I myself am raising heaven and earth. In the meantime, I must have money to see me through my daily needs, and wonder if, in the circumstances, you can once more break the rule and send me whatever is due for my Russian article. I have an idea it is Six Pounds at least . . . I am sure you will understand that only the most desperate straits force me to ask you this favour.' Cournos and his family eventually sailed in Mar.; he told TSE (14 Mar.): 'It's been a perfect nightmare.'

can do. Please give me an address in America, and let me know how soon you may be back in Europe again.

I am sending you my personal cheque for ten pounds (which I hope you can cash! I happen to know that it is still good) merely in order to save time. I shall recoup myself from the firm; and we will put the excess of what is owed you (I will let you know how much it comes to) against your future contributions, upon which I confidently depend in any case. Your Russian periodicals are invaluable. One or two have arrived since; I will hold them till further notice.

With best wishes and all sympathy,

Yours ever,
[T. S. Eliot]

TO *Geoffrey Faber*[1]   TS Valerie Eliot

6 February 1930   177 Clarence Gate Gardens, N.W.1

My dear Geoffrey,

I must explain that my behaviour this afternoon was expressive more of surprise than appreciation.[2] That is itself partly due to your tactful way of introducing a matter which had been arranged. I merely want to let you know that I am immensely pleased – apart from the fact that my present financial worries make it very important to me – to feel that what I have done, although it falls far short of my ambitions – for the firm, has been not only recognised but overrated.

Yours ever affectionately,
T. S. E.

TO *C. C. Martindale*   CC

7 February 1930   [Faber & Faber Ltd]

Dear Father Martindale,

I have read your essay on the Index with great enjoyment.[3] It only occurs to me, as a humble onlooker and sympathiser, that there are a few minor ways in which it could be fortified. For instance, I send you the note

---

1 – Geoffrey Faber (1889–1961), publisher and poet: see Biographical Register.
2 – The occasion of this letter is not known, but presumably GCF had raised TSE's salary.
3 – Martindale wrote on 3 Feb., 'A line to tell you that I finished the article y'day; it isn't at all good. Perhaps you will prefer not to use it. Anyway, I have to live up to its doctrine and

by Leonard Woolf in the latest *Nation*, which seems to me to represent exactly the point of view which your essay has to confute.[1] I think, that is, that Woolf's points ought to be met squarely.

May I suggest tentatively that my own view is that the Index is superior to the British Censorship precisely because it is undemocratic? I mean that it does in practice recognise the real fact that there are a great many books which the ordinary man should not read, but which the superior man ought to read; and as I understand, your Church makes it quite easy for the man who is entitled to read the books to read them. Whereas the British Censorship says, through the lips of Brentford, that if a book is

---

submit it to Censura Praevia (the first time in my life I've used that word!) as, being in the SJ, I can't and don't wish to publish anything without someone's giving it the Once Over.' He submitted a fifteen-page, single-spaced typescript entitled 'The Censorship of Books and the Roman "Index"'.

1–LW, in 'A Censorship at Work', *N&A* 46: 19 (8 Feb. 1930), 642, discussed the nature of papal censorship (instituted in the mid-sixteenth century) as manifested by a new edition of the *Indice dei Libri Proibiti, riveduto e pubblicato per ordine di Sua Santità Pio Papa XI* (1929), which he characterised as 'a thoroughly amusing and interesting volume':

'A book is placed upon the Index by decree of the Pope, who, since the time of Pope Sixtus V, acts on the advice of the Congregation of Cardinals of the Index. If a book has been placed upon the Index, no Roman Catholic may read it without special dispensation from a priest. Apparently a book which has once been prohibited may be silently omitted from a subsequent edition of the Index . . . It is an amusing fact that the writings of Copernicus and Galileo, which had been prohibited for centuries, quietly disappeared out of the Index published in 1835 – which seems to indicate that His Holiness is of opinion that it is safe for Roman Catholics to learn astronomical facts only three hundred years after their discovery. But though Catholics may not read a book on the Index, that does not mean that they may read all books which are not on it. The Church forbids them to read whole categories of books, the most important of which are those defending "heresy" or undermining religion, those written by non-Catholics which treat of religion, and books defending such things as suicide and divorce. The penalties against those who read prohibited books are very severe and involve excommunication.

'The Index . . . contains 563 pages, and I reckon that it condemns between five thousand and six thousand books. I find that the names of about one hundred really well-known, and in most cases great, writers, thinkers, or scientists, are included . . . A study of this list of names and of the books condemned by the Index might perhaps cause even the most convinced upholder of censorship of books and opinions some doubts. I do not know whether the Pope when condemning a book is infallible, but he and the Congregation of Cardinals would probably claim a certain amount of divine authority for their work in compiling the Index. The late Home Secretary [Viscount Brentford] and other lay and Government censors would hardly claim as much. But even though the Papal censors had the advantage of divine assistance, what a sorry spectacle this Index presents! Everything new contributed by the greatest thinkers during the last three hundred years has been condemned by them on its first appearance, and even today no Roman Catholic may read any of the great English philosophers or any of the great eighteenth century thinkers . . . What are we to think of a censorship with this object which includes Erasmus but omits Charles Darwin, which condemns *Zoonomia* and misses *The Origin of Species*?'

such that a small child should not have access to it, then nobody at all shall see it![1]

I wonder if you could call at my office one morning towards the latter part of next week, and have a few words with me and my colleague Mr F. V. Morley, who with myself has the responsibility of [*typing runs off the page*] could settle very quickly the few points in question in a very admirable essay which we shall be proud to publish.[2]

1 – Lord Brentford, *Do We Need a Censor?* (Criterion Miscellany 6, 1930).

2 – Frank Vigor Morley (1899–1980), son of a distinguished mathematician – his brothers were the writer Christopher, and Felix (who was to become editor of *The Washington Post*) – was brought up in the USA before travelling as a Rhodes Scholar to New College, Oxford, where he earned a doctorate in mathematics. After working for a while at the *Times Literary Supplement*, he became London Manager of The Century Company (Publishers) of New York. In 1929 he became a founding director of Faber & Faber, where he would be a close friend of TSE: for some time they shared a top-floor office at Russell Square. On 4 January 1932 Morley wrote of himself to F. Gilchrist Thompson of Jonathan Cape Ltd, which was to publish his book *Lamb before Elia* (1932): 'As to career it is, alas, not so much chequered as check-mated. I was born at Haverford, Penn., the seat of a Quaker College in which in due course I was entered, but the war intervened and caused a kind of tussle with Quakerism in which I am sorry to say Quakerism was worsted. After a completely undistinguished period with the American Army I returned, supposedly to study mathematics, to a good place called Johns Hopkins University. Actually I played at mathematics but worked at a subject called lacrosse, which seems to be played by women in this country [UK] but which is still a serious blood-letting, Red Indian pursuit in my native black blocks. I was successively a seaman on the Pacific, a member of the United State [words missing,] temporary manufacturer of air-cooled motor cars, and then a Rhodes Scholar at New College, which paved the way for becoming a stoker in SS. *Antwerp* on the Harwich–Antwerp run across the North Sea. The only item in this which has any bearing on literary criticism is my brief yet glorious career in the [words missing.] After coming to England I always intended to go home but never quite got round to doing so – so here I still am inventing Brothers' Clubs to take the place of legitimate adventures.'

In 1933 when TSE separated from Vivien, Morley arranged convivial temporary accommodation for him near his farmhouse at Pike's Farm, Lingfield, Surrey. In 1939 Morley moved to the USA, where he became Vice-President of Harcourt Brace and Company (and during the war he served on the National War Labor Board in Washington, DC). In 1947 he returned with his family to England to take up the post of Director at Eyre & Spottiswoode. A large, learned, ebullient figure, he earned the sobriquet 'Whale' – though not merely on account of his corpulence: in his youth he had spent time aboard a whaling ship (he was revolted by the slaughter), and subsequently wrote (with J. S. Hodgson) *Whaling North and South* (1927) – which was reviewed in the *Monthly Criterion* by his friend Herbert Read. His other publications include *Travels in East Anglia* (1923), *River Thames* (1926), *Inversive Geometry* (1933), *My One Contribution to Chess* (1947), *The Great North Road* (1961), *The Long Road West: A Journey in History* (1971), and *Literary Britain* (1980); and contributions in verse (along with verses by Eliot, Geoffrey Faber and John Hayward) to *Noctes Binanianae* (1939).

Morley Kennerley told *The Times* (25 Oct. 1980) that 'one of his hobbies was to work out complicated problems for his friends, and for those baffled there were amazing practical jokes. Convivial lunches with interesting people were a joy to him . . . He found jobs for

One other point: should your imprimi potest etc. be given after the title page, or is that unnecessary?

> Yours sincerely,
> [T. S. Eliot]

I suggest Thursday or Friday morning about 11:30 or 12; but could of course arrange some other time.

---

many and squeezed me into Fabers where he generously put up with my sharing a corner of his room for some years. I was present all day during his interviews, dictation, visitors and often lunch. How he put up with all this I do not know. His correspondence with Ezra Pound was quite something, and I think he out-Pounded Pound. As his family say, he was a compulsive letter writer and was rarely without a pencil in his hand or pocket.'

In 1939, when Morley was on the point of returning to the USA, Geoffrey Faber wrote of him to the editor of *The Times*: 'Morley is a quite outstanding person . . . [His] first obvious quality is that he is a born "mixer", with an extraordinary range of friends in different walks of life. He is a very good talker, though rather fond – like many Americans – of spinning the yarn out. But he never spins without a purpose. As a negotiator he is in a class by himself. His judgment of men and situations is first rate. He knows the personnel of both the English and American publishing and journalistic worlds. As for his mental equipment, he took a doctorate at Oxford with a mathematical thesis. The story is that nobody in Oxford could understand it, and help had to be got from Cambridge. But he is at least as good a man of letters as he is a mathematician' (Faber Archive).

FVM supplied TSE with a handwritten memo about Martindale's typescript: 'Simply won't do in present form. Facetiousness is the worst way to deal with a critical & hostile audience. I think he should start with part II, explain the Index (however awkward) as an institution analogous to state censorship – thus putting on his side all who vote for state censorship [the history here, paralleling state cen.]. Then palliate awkwardness (as Belloc turning his back on Gibbon) by the doctrine of private sanction, or whatever it is that lets good Catholics eat jugged hare on Friday when they feel fish is one too many in a day of trubbles. Then examine just how objectionable it is; what the procedure is . . . As it stands he is knocked out before starting.'

TO *J. Gordon Macleod*[1]   CC

10 February 1930   [Faber & Faber Ltd]

Dear Sir,

I have at last got your address.[2] I am very much interested by your poem. I should like to publish some part of it in the *Criterion*; and I have hopes that we may be able to make you an offer to publish it as a book.[3] Do you ever come up to London? if so, I wish you would suggest one or two mornings in the near future on either of which it would be possible for you to call here and talk it over.

Yours sincerely,
[T. S. Eliot]

TO *T. H. White*[4]   CC

10 February 1930   [*The Criterion*]

Dear Mr White,

I rather liked your poem, and I hope confidently to have something of yours in the *Criterion* before long; but the *Criterion* grinds very slowly indeed. So I return this with best wishes for the anthology.[5]

1–Joseph Todd Gordon Macleod (1903–1984), poet, playwright, actor, theatre director, historian and BBC newsreader, was educated at Balliol College, Oxford (where he was friends with Graham Greene), and in 1929 joined the experimental Cambridge Festival Theatre, of which he became director, 1933–5 (his productions included Chekhov's *The Seagull* and Ezra Pound's Noh plays, and five of his own plays). In 1938 he joined the BBC as announcer and newsreader, retiring to Florence in 1955: it was during the BBC period that the poetry he produced under the pseudonym 'Adam Drinan' became sought-after in Britain and the USA: he was much admired by writers including Basil Bunting and Edwin Muir. His first book of poems, *The Ecliptic* (1930), was published by TSE at F&F. His plays included *Overture to Cambridge* (1933) and *A Woman Turned to Stone* (1934). See *Selected Poems: Cyclic Serial Zeniths from the Flux*, ed. Andrew Duncan (2009); and James Fountain, 'To a group of nurses: The newsreading and documentary poems of Joseph Macleod', *TLS*, 12 Feb. 2010, 14–15.
2–Macleod, who lived in Sussex, had sent his poem (which had long been buried at the Hogarth Press) on 10 Jan. 1930, with a letter on headed notepaper.
3–'Leo: Sign from *The Ecliptic*', *C.* 9 (July 1930), 671–4. *The Ecliptic* (F&F, 1930).
4–T. H. White (1906–64) read English at Queens' College, Cambridge (where he was a friend of Ian Parsons). His works include the bestselling Arthurian trilogy *The Once and Future King* (1958) – made over into the popular musical *Camelot* (1959).
5–White wrote on 29 Jan., 'I have been asked to contribute unpublished poems to an Anthology which the Hogarth Press is bringing out. As the only unpublished poem I possess is the one I sent you yesterday, may I ask you to decide about it rather soon, so that I can send it on to them if you don't want it.' White's poem (unidentified) did not appear in *C*.

And do please send me new things as produced (I mean as written, not as published).

Yours sincerely,
[T. S. Eliot]

TO *The Editor,* The Reader CC

10 February 1930 [Faber & Faber Ltd]

Dear Sir,

I apologise for the delay in answering your letter of the 31st January.[1] Your previous letter has not reached me.

I am afraid that the subject you suggest is impossible, for the following reason: I have to give some Broadcast talks on that subject in March, and according to the contract the *Listener* has the serial rights, and it would be obviously impossible for me to provide two sets of articles on the same subject at the same time.[2] Perhaps at some later date you will care to suggest some other subject.

With many regrets,
Yours faithfully,
[T. S. Eliot]

1 – The editor wrote on 20 Jan. asking 'if you would be good enough to consider writing a series of articles on Seventeenth Century Poets for THE READER [National Home-Reading Union]'.

2 – TSE's series of six broadcasts on seventeenth-century poetry were to be published in *The Listener* (1930): 'Thinking in Verse: a Survey of Early Seventeenth-century Poetry', 12 Mar., 441–3; 'Rhyme and Reason: The Poetry of John Donne', 19 Mar., 502–3; 'The Devotional Poets of the Seventeenth Century: Donne, Herbert, Crashaw', 26 Mar., 552–3; 'Mystic and Politician as Poet: Vaughan, Traherne, Marvell, Milton', 2 Apr., 590–1; 'The Minor Metaphysicals: From Cowley to Dryden', 9 Apr., 641–2; 'John Dryden', 16 Apr., 688–9.

The talks as published were shorter than the broadcast versions, as R. S. Lambert (editor of *The Listener*) advised TSE on 25 Feb.: 'we are hoping to be able to print these talks in *The Listener* after delivery. The talks, however, being half-an-hour in length, will make articles of some 3,600 words each, which are too long for our columns. As we are anxious not to run any risk of unsuitable editing of your MSS., I should like to know whether you would be willing to indicate by pencil marks upon your MSS., or in any other place that you think fit, places where cuts might be made so as to reduce the length of the printed version to about 2,500 words.

'This is the course which we generally pursue in regard to the publication of half-hour talks, and it would help us very much to achieve satisfactory results if you would agree to this course.'

TO *J. E. Pouterman*[1]   CC

10 February 1930   [Faber & Faber Ltd]

Dear Mr Pouterman,

I return herewith the corrected proof of my introduction to the *Journaux Intimes*.[2] I agree that the quotations ought to be set in similar type.

In Mr Isherwood's version I have taken the liberty of reinstating 'incendiaries'. I cannot find 'arsonaries' in the large English dictionary which I have consulted.

I should be very glad to see the remainder of the translation galleys when ready.

Yours sincerely,
[T. S. Eliot]

TO *Ruth M. Harrison*[3]   CC

10 February 1930   [Faber & Faber Ltd]

Dear Madam,

I remember my correspondence with you quite well, and if you care to give me as a reference, I shall be glad to give a favourable testimonial – though I fear that it will, to university authorities, appear but slender evidence.[4]

1 – The Blackamore Press, London: publisher of Baudelaire's *Intimate Journals* (1930), trans. Christopher Isherwood; with intro by TSE.
2 – Pouterman (1 Feb.) sent galleys of TSE's 'Introduction', plus the first portion of the text; he hoped TSE would review the galleys of the rest of the translation when they became available.
3 – Following six years at the École Supérieure, Vevey, Switzerland, Ruth Harrison won a scholarship to Westfield College, London, where she gained a first class degree in French (with English subsidiary); she then took a six-month secretarial training course at Mrs Hoster's College. After a year of working in temporary posts at Girton College, Cambridge, she spent five years as Secretary to the Headmistress, Roedean School, Brighton. 'I have subscribed to the *Nouvelle Revue Française* and the *Criterion* ever since I discovered them,' she added to her CV.
4 – Harrison asked (8 Feb.) for a reference: 'I read French at the University (London) and since then I have (for family and financial reasons) been secretary here [Roedean School]. But always my chief interest has been modern literature, as understood by the *Nouvelle Revue Française*, and by your paper and Mr Middleton Murry's. I am now advised to put in for a Fellowship at Oxford. There are very few fellowships open to women, and the competition will be high. Also, I have . . . taken no research degree and produced no written evidence of my work, and for that reason I am a weak candidate. I am most anxious to have this opportunity of coordinating a few ideas, and particularly of doing some consecutive reading. As far as I can see, I should make Bergson's philosophy of time and free will my

As for your dissertation, my chief fear, from your brief outline, is that you may cast your net too wide, and attempt to coordinate more than can be coordinated. Bergson with or contra Thomism (via Maritain, who began under Bergson) is one good subject; the relation of both to humanism is a possible subject (Fernandez also is a good part Bergsonian); but the notion of bringing in symbolist poetry (itself a large subject and a vague term) rather frightens me. And I believe that as a rule university authorities are more impressed by intensive study than by extensive synthesis.

Yours very truly,
[T. S. Eliot]

TO *Christopher Dawson*   CC

10 February 1930   [Faber & Faber Ltd]

Dear Mr Dawson,

Many thanks both for your proof and for the ms. of your pamphlet.[1] The latter I have not read, but one of my colleagues has read it and tells me it is excellent; and has taken it to be typed; after which I look forward to reading it myself.[2] I do not think that you [will] have to wait very long for proof.

With many thanks,
Yours sincerely,
[T. S. Eliot]

TO *C. K. Scott Moncrieff*   CC

10 February 1930   [Faber & Faber Ltd]

Dear Scott Moncrieff,

At the moment, I have hardly the right to answer letters except on business, so many are there; but one point you mention is a point that excuses a letter to you.[3] We have come to the conclusion that the

---

centre-piece and study it in relation with symboliste and later poetry and with modern humanism, and possibly the Thomist movement.'

1 – *Christianity and Sex* (Criterion Miscellany, 1930).

2 – Dawson submitted his essay on 30 Jan. '"Catholicism & Sex" is in itself the best title, but it does not quite cover my subject which is that of the conflict between Catholicism & the new moral theory . . . I have named it provisionally "Catholicism & Modern Theories of Sex" . . .'

3 – Scott Moncrieff wrote on 29 Jan., 'as you refer to Cousin Fanny & Cousin Annie, may I now ask as I meant to ask when the series was first announced whether you will put it

Miscellany is not really the place for fiction or verse, unless it be there as a document of a peculiar kind, such as a specimen of Joyce's latest work. But we have the notion of starting another series of small cheap paper-bound books, to include solely verse and fiction; and if this matures, I will write to you about it. But meanwhile is there no prospect of another story for the *Criterion* itself?

I hope your next report of yourself will be more encouraging.[1]

> Meanwhile,
> Yours ever sincerely,
> [T. S. Eliot]

TO *K. de B. Codrington*[2]   CC

10 February 1930   [Faber & Faber Ltd]

Dear Codrington,

I can't think of any precise parallels, nor do I quite know what a precise parallel to this would be; but your Islamic heresies seem to follow the general lines of heresy everywhere: i.e. pushing one subject as far as it will go; and they have the universal characteristic of heresies in being much more 'reasonable' or intelligible than orthodoxy, and on the other hand quite uninteresting.[3] Two of the great and permanent possibilities of heresy in Christianity have always been: Tritheism vs. Unitarianism, and the Arian controversy ended (so to speak) by Athanasius. There is also the Manichaean heresy, of course (Albigensianism). My great point is that heresy is always with us, and must always be a variation of a few possible forms.

---

in your Criterion Miscellany. I have never yet published any volume of original work, and should like to have a little keepsake to scatter among the friends who are bewildering me with their kindness.'

1–Scott Moncrieff, who told TSE that he was suffering from gastric ulcers, was being cared for by the Little Company of Mary, Calvary Hospital, Rome, where he was admitted in Nov. 1929. In fact, he was suffering from cancer, and died on 28 Feb. 1930.

2–Kenneth de Burgh Codrington (1899–1986) worked in the India Section, Victoria & Albert Museum; later a professor of Indian Archaeology. His writings include *An Introduction to the Study of Mediaeval Indian Sculpture* (1929), and *Cricket in the Grass* (reminiscences, 1959).

3–Codrington asked TSE about heresy in 'more-or-less Vedantic eclecticism': 'In my ignorance I wonder if there are any Christian parallels to the acceptance of such limits or extremes in theology. The Indian acceptance of the alternatives is not theological but personal, an acknowledgement of the necessary in personality born in the flesh and of its opposite, the necessary process inherent in the experience of life – whether it is considered a delusion or not.'

Would you care to look at Paul More's *Christ the Word*, for a useful and lucid account of Christian heresy up to Athanasius? I believe I could lend it to you. Of course you can find similar difficulties in pure metaphysics and in mysticism too.[1]

I shd. imagine that Islam veered widely between Jehovah and *tat tvam asi*.[2]

Yours ever
[T. S. Eliot]

That book on ju-ju I sent you looked to me rather interesting.

TO *A. L. Rowse*   TS Exeter

10 February 1930   *The Criterion*

Dear Rowse,

Thank you for your letter.[3] I think I will try Ayerst.[4] But I don't want the sort of article that might fitly appear in the *Contemporary Review*. You're quite sure he has a mind of his own?

---

1 – Codrington reported on 8 Mar. that he had found Elmer More's work 'interesting and instructive': 'He seems to jib at the historical side of the revelation and to seek stability on grounds of the traditional integrity of the various streams of thought which go to make up Christianity as the world knows it.'

2 – *Tat tvam asi* (Sanskrit: 'Thou art that'): one of the grand pronouncements (*Mahavakyas*) deriving from chapter 6 of the Chandogya Upanishad (*c.* 600 BC). In Hinduism, the Atman, the immanent eternal Self, is held to be identical with the Ultimate Reality, the Absolute, the Divine Ground. See Aldous Huxley's remarks, in *The Perennial Philosophy* (1945), ch. I – 'That Art Thou' – on 'the universal immanence of the transcendent spiritual Ground of all existence'.

3 – 'For your Disarmament article, I should suggest either Kingsley Martin or D. G. O. Ayerst: but the latter a good deal more than the former . . .

'I should think it a good thing to include two young politicians in the discussion on politics: & Elliot wd certainly be the best for Toryism if one can get him: one might. Stanley or possibly John Buchan (who is at any rate new as a politician & a reader of the *Criterion*) would do very well in his place. I don't think much of [Robert] Boothby. For somebody outside of politics, what about Keith Feiling? Not that I think much of him either: but where to look for anything in Toryism in these days which gives any lead to thought? . . . John Strachey, anyhow, would in fact produce something better qua thought . . .

'You surprise me in not knowing Tawney's work, for I should have thought his point of view very close to yours. And he's a superb historian: have you read *Religion and the Rise of Capitalism*. He's got a book coming this season on "Equality as a Social Policy". It's bound to be good, and I should very much like to hear your views on it.'

4 – David George Ogilvy Ayerst (1904–1992), educated at Christ Church, Oxford (where he chaired the University Labour Club), worked from 1927 in Berlin, as part-time correspondent for the *Manchester Guardian*, and in 1934 he changed course to become a schoolmaster.

I am not very enthusiastic about the 'young Tories'. Elliot I shan't try, for the reason that we have already tried him on a pamphlet, and drawn a blank. I am considering tackling Stanley. Feiling has always struck me as a dull dog.[1] In my opinion, the only sort of Toryism worth reading would be something that every loyal member of that party would immediately disown. I prefer my Socialism straight rather than dissolved into up-to-date Conservatism.

John Strachey is a good suggestion, and I will try him.

As for Tawney, I always dislike hearing of anything that I *ought* to read; but from what you say, I shall have to.[2]

I have sometimes wished that there might exist an informally political club of few members (in which I might be allowed to buzz irresponsibly) consisting not of people attached to any existing allegiance, but rather of a cross-section of opinion, youngish men of divers backgrounds and sympathies, having chiefly in common the desire to look at politics present and future, and each individual inspired by a critical dislike of his own party (if he has one). The obvious difficulty is that a few people like yourself are never in London. Otherwise, does it seem to you a silly fancy?[3]

Yours ever,
T. S. Eliot

I'll see about returning Pitcairn; I have retained it in the hope that it might fit into the Miscellany, and perhaps it still may; but I will return it in any case.

By the way, if you ever want to see any of the Miscellany, drop me a line and you shall have one.[4]

1–Keith Feiling (1884–1977) taught modern history at Christ Church, Oxford, before becoming Chichele Professor of Modern History at All Souls, 1946–50. Works include *A History of the Tory Party, 1640–1714* (1924), *What is Conservatism? An interpretation* (Criterion Miscellany 14, 1930), and *Warren Hastings* (1954; James Tait Black Award).

2–Rowse (25 Feb.): 'I am sure – in spite of the "ought" – you won't be disappointed in Tawney: he's the very best, – of that particular kind.'

3–Rowse (25 Feb.): 'I really can't tell about the political club, for I am never in London. When I do come, I should certainly like to have some means of meeting you and of discussing things.'

4–Rowse replied that he liked F&F's series of pamphlets, in particular *Obscenity and Pornography* (Criterion Miscellany 5) by D. H. Lawrence (1929): 'I don't know if you know how much it expressed the minds of young men, say, here. I hate the world of the old.'

TO *Marguerite Caetani*   CC

10 February 1930   [Faber & Faber Ltd]

Dear Marguerite,

Very many thanks for your letter of the 5th. I wrote to Léger (care of the French Embassy) some ten days ago,[1] but have had no reply. So I can only wait.

John Hayward is a great friend of mine, and I am sure that he could find you the texts you want if anyone could.[2] This is, if they exist. You might write to him, using my name, at 23, The Grange, Wimbledon Common, S.W. But I suggest giving him a wider range than merely texts of Traherne! It might keep him occupied for the rest of his life.

At any rate, we have now secured a house – one to which we shall not be ashamed to ask you. I expect we shall be in it by the end of March.

Affectionately,

[Tom]

TO *The Editor,* The Times Literary Supplement   CC

14 February 1930   [*The Criterion*]

Sir,

In reply to your memorandum,[3] I should be very glad indeed if you would let me wait for the fourth volume of Baker's *History of the English Novel* and review the two volumes together. To tell the truth I have not found a great deal of meat in Vol 3 and should not feel satisfied to give it more than half a column. But I think that a column or a column and a half is quite possible for the two volumes together, with a retrospective glance at Volume 2. So that the publishers ought to be satisfied.[4]

Yours faithfully,

[T. S. Eliot]

1 – Not found.
2 – 'Mirsky told me that he thought John Hayward editor of the Nonesuch Donne would be able to find us texts of the 17th & 18th Cent, unpublished. I am now wondering if one might not ask him if it would be possible to find something of Traherne to add to our Selection.'
3 – E. St John Brooks, writing on behalf of the editor of the *TLS* (12 Feb. 1930), asked whether it would suit TSE to write about the third volume of E. A. Baker's *History of the English Novel* along with vol. 4: *Intellectual realism from Richardson to Sterne*, to be published in April.
4 – See front-page review, 'The Growth of the English Novel', *TLS*, 17 July 1930. Not in Gallup.

TO *Edmund Blunden*[1]   TS Texas

14 February 1930   *The Criterion*

Dear Blunden,

I only heard from Leonard Woolf the other day that you were succeeding him on the *Nation*. As Woolf is leaving I am very glad to hear that you are to be his successor. I am writing now to pass on two matters which I had previously put to Woolf. One is whether you could make any use as a reviewer of a young man named A. L. Morton who has done a certain amount of reviewing for me. I enclose a galley proof of a review of some Napoleonic literature which he has done for the next *Criterion*.[2] Morton comes from Eastbourne College and took his degree at Peterhouse Cambridge. His speciality is the French Revolution and the Napoleonic Period, but he seems to be pretty widely read in economic and social history and in witchcraft and folklore. If you think he might be of any use to you his address is, 53 Hornsey Rise Gardens, N.19. I may say that I first made his acquaintance not through his seeking me out, but through reading a very intelligent review by him in some local paper about which I wrote to him. The other man I am recommending is a man who has already been in touch with Woolf and who actually has some books in hand which he is reviewing for the *Nation*. He is also, I think, a good man: J. L. Donaghy, a Dublin Protestant. He is rather a good poet and is also reviewing for the *Observer*. For some reason he thinks that he needs a new introduction to you although he is, as I say, already working for the *Nation*. But I think that a line of recommendation like this is better than another formal introduction.[3]

Yours sincerely,
T. S. Eliot

1–Edmund Blunden (1896–1974), who won the Military Cross for valour in Flanders in 1916, entered literary journalism in 1920 when he took up a part-time editorial post at *A*. He was Professor of English at the Imperial University, Tokyo, 1924–7; and in 1930–1 (as TSE notes here) literary editor of *N*. He was Fellow and Tutor in English 1931–44 at Merton College, Oxford (where his students included the poet Keith Douglas and the Canadian critic Northrop Frye); and for a year after WW2 he was assistant editor of the *TLS*. In 1947 he returned to Japan with the United Kingdom Liaison Mission; and he was Professor of English, Hong Kong, from 1953 until retirement in 1964. He was made CBE in 1964, and in 1956 received the Queen's Gold Medal for Poetry. In 1966 he accepted election as Oxford Professor of Poetry (the other candidate being Robert Lowell), but stood down before the completion of his tenure. See further Barry Webb, *Edmund Blunden: A Biography* (1990).
2–*C*. 9 (Apr. 1930), 513–15.
3–Blunden replied (n. d.): 'I like the specimen of A. L. Morton's reviewing wh. you send & will remember it (there's a New Army of reviewers on my tablets!) when some books afford occasion. Donaghy came to see me. I gave him what space I could to illustrate his Talents.'

TO C. C. *Martindale*   CC

14 February 1930   [Faber & Faber Ltd]

Dear Father Martindale,

Thank you for your charming letter (undated) and for your postcard dated the 11th, by the postman.[1] I am glad to have your note but I still think, if I may say so, that a little re-organisation in form might improve the essay immensely.[2] I am quite sure that you know a great deal more about bargees and Australians than I do; but my point is that I have had peculiar opportunities for learning about the minds of people like Leonard Woolf who are, I fear, the people who are going to review the essay, and I am anxious that your case should be put at its full strength. So as there is now no immediate hurry, I suggest that we should leave the matter over until you return in a fortnight; which will give me an excuse for the additional pleasure of meeting you.

I will write again to Mount Street by the 26th.[3]

Yours sincerely,
[T. S. Eliot]

TO *Sidney Dark*[4]   CC

14 February 1930   [Faber & Faber Ltd]

Dear Mr Dark,

You may remember meeting me once last year at lunch at the University Club with Will Spens.[5] I am presuming on this acquaintance to send you personally a copy of the book the Ms. of which came in to our office and which I myself was the first to read and recommend warmly for publication, it is *Who Moved the Stone?* by Frank Morison and we are

1 – Martindale wrote, 'the nihil obstat & the imprimatur are both given, and, leave *not* to have them printed should you wish that they be not . . .'
2 – Martindale had written, 'I . . . enclose a sort of paragraph which I think can actually be inserted into the text or anyway appended as a note to some place where I say that critics don't know how the Index works, or, that students can at once get leave for what they want.' In fact, his 'paragraph' ran to three single-spaced TS pages rebutting Leonard Woolf's article.
3 – Martindale was working in Cardiff, and would return to 114 Mount Street on 26 Feb.
4 – Sidney Dark (1872–1947), editor of the Anglo-Catholic *Church Times*, 1924–41. Works include *Archbishop Davidson and the English Church* (1929), *The Lambeth Conferences, their History and their Significance* (1930), and *The Church Impotent or Triumphant* (1941).
5 – William (Will) Spens was Master of Corpus Christi College, Cambridge, 1927–52. See TSE to Spens, 25 July 1930, below.

publishing it on March 5th. It is a very brilliant account of the Passion by a man who started with every possible prejudice against the authenticity of the Resurrection and who was convinced by his study of the text. I am all the more anxious that you should read the book yourself because it is a book which might easily at this season of the flood of popular theology, be lost among the dozens of second rate books of Lenten literature. I do hope that you will read it and let me know what you think of it.

Yours sincerely,
[T. S. Eliot]

TO *Raffaello Piccoli*[1]   CC

15 February 1930   [Faber & Faber Ltd]

Dear Mr Piccoli,

I seem to have very bad luck in attempts at meeting you.[2] I misread your letter for Friday, tomorrow, when I do not expect to be available in the afternoon. I only discovered my mistake this afternoon but still hoped as I was here that you might look in or ring up on chance. It is my own fault and I am very sorry indeed, but I hope that we may meet at least at the end of term.

Yours sincerely,
[T. S. Eliot]

TO *Henry Eliot*   TS Houghton

16 February 1930   177 Clarence Gate Gardens, N.W.1

My dear Henry,

Thank you for your letter of the 6th and especially for sending me the typescript of mother's reminiscences and father's essay, which I am

1–Raffaello Piccoli (1886–1933): Professor of Italian, Cambridge University. His works include *Astrologia Dantesca* (1909) and *Benedetto Croce: An Introduction to His Philosophy* (1922). He translated plays by Shakespeare; poems by Shelley; plays by Robert Greene, George Peele, Christopher Marlowe; and he was a Dante scholar. In the 1920s he contributed some 'Letters from Italy' to *The Dial*. He translated *Ash-Wednesday* I, which he sent to TSE on 13 June 1930; his translation of 'Perch' Io non Spero', entitled 'Le Ceneri', appeared in *Cambridge Review*, vol. 51 (week of 9 June 1930), 492. Geoffrey Rossetti told TSE on 9 June: 'The Professor has translated all the poems in *Ash-Wednesday* it may interest you to hear.' TSE referred to Piccoli in 1939 as 'my regretted friend . . . whose death a few years ago was a great loss to Cambridge'.
2–Piccoli wrote on 10 Feb.: 'I am coming to London on Thursday for a lecture . . .'

delighted to have.[1] They do throw light on the characters of two very wonderful people. Much, most indeed, of what mother wrote about her life was unknown to me, and I regret very much that she did not bring it up to the time of her marriage, or later.

Would you in return like to have a copy of her manuscript account of her visit to England with you, or have you a copy? If not, I should like to make you one.

Thank you for your trouble about the family letters. In any case, it would be a job for someone on the spot. The cost of having copied out all those letters would be too great; and I should want manuscript letters posted to me here. And the publication of many of them would require the assent of other families such as the Adamses. If worth doing, it is a task for a future historian. As I said, my letter was inspired by an alarmist rumour from Leslie Hotson that Aunt Rose had a large number of letters of historical value, which she proposed to burn.

I will write more fully about other matters soon.

With much love,
Tom

TO *Owen Barfield*[2]   TS Bodleian

17 February 1930   *The Criterion*

Dear Mr Barfield,

I write to say that I like your essay on The Psychology of Reason very much, and it has the advantage over many contributions submitted of not

1–Charlotte Eliot's 'reminiscences', an eight-page essay on her childhood and schooldays – 'I was born in Baltimore, Md., where my father was in the shoe business, but when he failed on account of uncollectible [*sic*] southern debts, we moved from there to Boston when I was about five years old . . .' – came with a covering note by HWE: 'These reminiscences of Mother's were written in the summer of 1925, at Nantucket, Mass., doubtless for her children, though she was too unassuming ever to let us see them. They were found in going through her desk, December, 1929. This is the copy she typed herself; her pencil draft she must have destroyed.' HWE Sr's 'essay' is a four-page Graduation Address on 'Philosophy: The Science of Truth', read at Washington University, 18 June 1863 ('Sanctus Ludovicus, Mo.'). HWE's letter not found.
2–Owen Barfield (1898–1997), writer, philosopher, anthroposophist, studied at Wadham College, Oxford, where he took a first in English Language and Literature, 1921. (At Oxford he and C. S. Lewis – whom he later called 'the most unforgettable friend – part of the furniture of my existence' – became founder members, with J. R. R. Tolkien, Charles Williams and Lord David Cecil, of the Inklings: see *Owen Barfield on C. S. Lewis*, ed. G. B. Tennyson, (1989). From 1929 to 1959 he worked as a solicitor in his father's law firm. His publications include *History in English Words* (1926) and *Poetic Diction: A Study in Meaning* (1928).

being too long to publish. There is only one point which I should like to ask you to consider. I feel that whereas it is all right to use people like Wells, Shaw, Inge etc., merely as specimens or indexes of extensively maintained points of view, but it is a little unwise to deal with a man like Richards in the way you do. Although I am in general sympathy with what seems to me your attitude towards Richards, I feel that it does not strengthen your case to refer to him *in passing*; and that if one is going to bring in Richards at all one ought to go into the question pretty thoroughly. It is not with Richards a case of a point of view that can be summed up and dismissed quickly, but a work still in process of development which has not had a great many various possibilities. I feel[,] that is, that one cannot attack Richards in general but only particular statements by Richards. This is only a minor point in your essay and some time I should like to see you write a thorough discussion of Richards but, as I say, I feel that your present mention of Richards weakens rather than strengthens your position.[1]

Yours sincerely,
T. S. Eliot

P.S. Perhaps you would come up and have a talk with me?

TO *Erich Alport*   TS BL

17 February 1930   [Faber & Faber Ltd]

Dear Alport,

Thank you for your letter of the 6th.[2] I am very glad to hear that you also know and have a high opinion of Werner Jaeger and look forward to the copy which you are procuring. From everything I hear about the book it seems to me that it is probably a book that we ought to consider very seriously.

TSE told Barfield, 25 Mar. 1960: 'I must take this opportunity of telling you my very high opinion of your last book that we published, *Saving the Appearances*. It is one of those books which make me proud to be a director of the firm which publishes them. It seemed to me too profound for our feeble generation of critics nowadays. I seem to remember that at the time when some of our critics ought to have been tackling it, they were exciting themselves about Colin Wilson's *Outsider*. Such is the decay of literary journalism in this generation.' He advised Richard de la Mare on 15 July 1962: 'I feel very strongly that Barfield is an author too valuable to let go. Of course he is difficult to sell but I think he will make his mark in the long run. I myself have a high regard for his work and I think you have also.'
1 – Barfield's 'Psychology and Reason' – *C.* 9 (July 1930), 606–17 – does not mention Richards.
2 – Alport reported on *Aristotèles* by Werner Jaeger – 'a very famous & first rate savant . . . He is very willing to see his book translated into English & asks for an offer.'

If you are in London for a week from the 20th I certainly look forward to seeing you and hope that we may be able to have lunch together.

Yours sincerely,

T. S. Eliot

TO *D. L. Murray*[1]   CC

17 February 1930   [Faber & Faber Ltd]

Dear Mr Murray,

I am taking the liberty of sending you a copy of a book which we are publishing on March 5th called *Who Moved the Stone?* I have no personal knowledge of the author and the apparent subject is one which I always avoid – that is to say popular theology. But I have read the book as one of the readers here and was immediately excited by it and my excitement was sustained to the end. It is a study of the Passion from the Last Supper to the Resurrection and is written by a man who was convinced of the essential authenticity of the Gospel narrative in the course of his writing. It is, I think, really one of those rare books which can handle such a subject in a way to interest and to hold the respect of every class of reader.

I have given copies to Gordon Selwyn and a few other people and I should be more than interested to know what you think of the book also.

Yours sincerely,

[T. S. Eliot]

1–D. L. Murray (1888–1962) worked for the *TLS* from 1920 and became editor, 1937–45, in succession to Bruce Richmond. From the late 1920s he was also a popular historical novelist.

TO *Darsie Gillie*[1]   CC

18 February 1930   [Faber & Faber Ltd]

My dear Gillie,

I was glad to get your letter of the 10th of February enclosing the contract signed by Pilsudski.[2] As you recognise the signature yourself I don't think we need to bother about having it attested.

I enclose herewith the counterpart of the agreement and should be very much obliged if you would forward it to Pilsudski for us.

As for the agreement between Pilsudski and yourself about which you should have 25% of the royalties. The simplest and most satisfactory arrangement seems to be that he should sign a letter address[ed] to us on the strength of which we would ourselves disburse the royalties in that way. I therefore enclose three copies of a letter which we have drawn up for him to sign; one copy for him to keep, one copy for you, and one copy, the most important, to be returned to us.

---

1 – Darsie R. Gillie (1903–72): Berlin correspondent of *The Morning Post*; later in the 1930s he reported from Warsaw, and as Paris correspondent of the *Manchester Guardian*. During WW2 he worked for the BBC as French News Editor; and in 1944 he returned to the *Guardian;* ultimately, he would be the BBC's representative in Paris.

2 – Jósef Pilsudski (1867–1935), Polish nationalist, born in Lithuania, educated at Kharkov University, joined in 1892 the Polish Socialist Party and built up a private revolutionary army of 10,000 men, then the Polish Legions, which during WW1 fought against Russia alongside the Austro-Hungarians and Germans. Having secured Poland's independence (after 123 years of ever-varying partitions), Pilsudski became Chief of State, 1919–22, representing Poland at the Versailles Treaty, and Commander of the Polish Forces in the Polish–Soviet War. In 1923 he gave up his leadership of the army, but three years later he staged a coup and became the virtual dictator of the Second Republic of Poland, 1926–35.

F&F advertised Pilsudski's memoirs (published as *The Memories of a Polish Revolutionary and Soldier,* 1931) in 1930: 'These memoirs of the great Field Marshal, one of the most powerful and remarkable figures of post-war Europe, have an interest beyond that of most memoirs of notable people. They have not been written since the Marshal has become famous; they are the events of his full and adventurous life put down as they occurred, some of them long before his name was known. The Marshal has been a revolutionary, a warrior, and a governor of a great people. Here is his analysis of various periods in his career, written not for notoriety, but for the interest of discovering what, in a man of action, have proved the mainsprings of action. Such memoirs, covering his career from the beginning, have a unique directness and documentary value; they have also the dramatic quality which belongs to great events as they are seen "from the inside".

'Thus the *Memoirs of Marshal Pilsudski* is not one of those books which are published only because they bear a world-famous name. It is the more thrilling because it is not a mere "looking backwards" over past adventures, or a mere narrative of political intrigue. It is an important document in the history of the liberation of Poland; and yielding insight into the mind of their leader, it yields insight also into the character of the Polish people.

'The memoirs have been translated and carefully knit together by Mr D. R. Gillie, Foreign Correspondent of the *Morning Post*.'

It has never been quite clear to me what legal authority Stachiewicz[1] has to act or to sign on behalf of Pilsudski. If he has full Power of Attorney, no doubt he will sign this letter on behalf of the Marshal. But I wish you would make quite sure of this point and let me know the exact legal situation.

I have taken note of your new address to which all future correspondence should be sent.

Yours very sincerely,
[T. S. Eliot]

TO *The Editor,* The Forum   CC

18 February 1930   [Faber & Faber Ltd]

Dear Sir,

I wrote to you some weeks ago asking if you would care to consider Lord Brentford's essay entitled *Do We Need a Censor?* for publication in the *Forum* and you kindly replied by cable offering 200 dollars. Since then Lord Brentford appeared to have [lost] interest in the matter or perhaps was merely too busy in other ways. But I have just heard from his Secretary saying that that offer would be accepted if you still care to use the essay. I enclose a copy of the essay in the pamphlet form in which we have issued it here. In this form we have found it very successful but I do not believe that many copies have left England.[2]

1 – Brigadier General Julian Stachiewicz (1890–1934), Polish military officer, historian and writer, was the director from 1923 of the Biuro Historyczne Wojskowe (Military Bureau of History) in Warsaw. Gillie described Stachiewicz, in his 'Translator's Preface', as 'the administrator of the Marshal's literary interests and joint editor of the complete edition of his writings, now in process of publication by the "Instytut Najnowszej Historji Polskiej"' (Pilsudski, *The Memories of a Polish Revolutionary and Soldier* [1931], ix).
2 – TSE wrote a little later, in a reader's report dated 28 May 1930, on a proposed pamphlet on the Cinema in the Criterion Miscellany series entitled 'Celluloid', by David Ockham:
'I have read this essay with sustained interest and considerable sympathy.

'I feel that the subject is too large for treatment in the Miscellany. I mean that a Miscellany pamphlet, of the militant type, should go straight for one simple point, and aim at concentration not diffusion. It is either too soon or too late, to consider the whole subject of Films. It is too early to have much material on which to base a discussion of mass-production Art vs. individual Art. My own feeling, whenever I read any general observations on the Cinema, is that the subject has just got out of control, and has not yet reached a point at which it may again come under the control of intelligence. At present, the Film just is, that's all; and one feels that so far what is going to happen will happen according to the fatality of Industry operating upon Helplessness.

Will you in any case be so kind as to reply direct to Viscount Brentford, 70 Queen's Gate, London S.W.7.

Yours very truly,
[T. S. Eliot]

TO *M. C. D'Arcy*   CC

19 February 1930   [Faber & Faber Ltd]

My dear D'Arcy,

I am sending you a book called *Who Moved the Stone?* by Frank Morison, which my firm is publishing on Ash Wednesday. I am very keen about this book myself and am very curious to know what people will think of it who are better qualified to judge of its merits or defects than I am. If you can find time to read it I should be very grateful to know however briefly, what opinion you form.[1]

Yours ever sincerely,
[T. S. Eliot]

TO *George Bell*[2]   TS Lambeth

19 February 1930   Faber & Faber Ltd

My dear Lord Bishop,

I am presuming on the strength of having made your acquaintance at dinner at Lambeth Palace to send you an advance copy of a book called *Who Moved the Stone?* by Frank Morison, which we are publishing

---

'The best part of this essay, and the most *pamphletaire*, is the part about censorship. If he could expand this into a whole pamphlet with the same animation, I should think twice about it. In fact, I believe that the only possible excuse for another Censorship Pamphlet is the Film censorship, which is the most flagrant iniquity of all.

'But I think that a general pamphlet about films would merely give the impression that we were looking for subjects. The Miscellany wants to have subjects forced onto it, rather than to seek for them.'

1–D'Arcy (undated) was 'fascinated' by Morison's book: 'could not lay it down & like you think it an extremely valuable study . . . The reconstruction seems to me on the whole masterly.'

2–Rt Revd George Bell, DD (1883–1958): Dean of Canterbury, 1924–9; Bishop of Chichester, 1929–58; President of the Religious Drama Society of Great Britain from 1929; chairman of Universal Christian Council for Life and Work, 1934–6. His works include *Randall Davidson, Archbishop of Canterbury* (1935) and *Christianity and World Order* (1940). In 1935 he commissioned TSE to write *MiC* for the Canterbury Festival.

on Ash Wednesday. I know almost nothing about the author, but the manuscript was first submitted to me for a reading and I recommended it enthusiastically. It is, I think, an unusual type of book; it does not belong in the ordinary category of popular theology which for the most part I thoroughly dislike; and for that reason I am anxious that it should not be submerged in the flood of popular Lenten literature. It is an examination of the facts of the Trial and the Passion based on rather an acute examination of the time which the various scenes in the drama must have taken. I have no motive in sending it to you except that of curiosity to know your opinion of it; and the hope that if you approve the book you may recommend it to others.

> I am, my dear Lord Bishop,
> Yours very sincerely,
> T. S. Eliot

TO *G. K. Chesterton*[1]   TS Dorothy Collins

19 February 1930   Faber & Faber Ltd

My dear Chesterton,

I am taking the liberty of sending you a book called *Who Moved the Stone?* by Frank Morison, which my firm is publishing on Ash Wednesday, in the hope that you may find time to read it and tell me what you think of it and, of course, if you like it, in the hope that you may mention it or

---

1–G. K. Chesterton (1874–1936): author and journalist; an Anglican who converted in 1922 to Roman Catholicism; author of novels including *The Napoleon of Notting Hill* (1904) and *The Man who was Thursday* (1908), and shorter fictions including the popular Father Brown stories. His non-fiction includes studies of Chaucer (1932) and St Thomas Aquinas (1933); and collections of essays including *Heretics* (1905) and *Orthodoxy* (1908). See *The Autobiography of G. K. Chesterton* (1936); Joseph Pearce, *Wisdom and Innocence: A Life of G. K. Chesterton* (1996).

TSE wrote of him, in a memorial note in C. 16 (Oct. 1936), 69: 'It is not for his attainments in pure letters that he should be celebrated here: though it may be said that if he did nothing to develop the sensibility of the language, he did nothing to obstruct it. Nor are his religious convictions precisely our affair. What matters here is his lonely moral battle against his age, and his courage, and his bold combination of genuine conservatism, genuine liberalism, and genuine radicalism.' When asked by Cyril Clemens for his recollections of Chesterton, TSE wrote on 9 Sept. 1937: 'I am afraid that I cannot be of very much help to you in your biography of G. K. Chesterton because, although I had a little correspondence with him, I never actually met and talked to him. I certainly admired his work with the obvious reservations and expressed my general opinion very briefly in an Editorial Note in the *Criterion* after his death; and the impression given by his letters was of a man of great charm, generosity and unpretentiousness.'

recommend it. It is a study of the Passion and the Resurrection by a man personally unknown to me, who started from a frankly modernist or free thinking position and ended by conviction of the essential authenticity of the Gospel story. It is not by any means an ordinary popular book of liberal Lenten devotion.

Yours sincerely,
T. S. Eliot

TO *John Middleton Murry*   TS Northwestern
19 February 1930   Faber & Faber Ltd

My dear John,

I have delayed answering your last letter hoping that I might have something further to suggest.[1] But nothing very material has occurred to me. I am sincerely troubled about the matter and should feel better if we might have an opportunity of meeting, even if only for a short time. Is there any chance of your coming up to London one day in the near future?

I enclose a copy of a book which Faber & Faber are publishing on March 5th called *Who Moved the Stone?* by Frank Morison; this is merely for your personal interest. I was very much excited by my reading of the book and I should particularly like you to read it and tell me what you think of it.

Yours affectionately,
Tom

---

1 – JMM had written on 23 Jan.: 'I appreciate very much your kind suggestions . . . Personally, I should be downright *glad* if the A[*delphi*] comes to an end. Of late, it has been a fearful burden. Whenever I have given my mind to it for several days I have felt that I ought not to be doing this: that I ought to be earning money, keeping pace with my responsibilities which seem to grow heavier instead of lighter. Since the chances of anyone in his senses paying me a sufficient salary for editing the A. to make me feel guiltless in this respect (it would have to be £200 a year) are remote, I prefer an abrupt ending . . . So you see how difficult it is for me to make a response to your kind suggestion that Cape should be approached.'

19 February 1930   [Faber & Faber Ltd]

My dear Thorold,

A review copy of this book *Who Moved the Stone?* by Frank Morison will doubtless reach the *Dublin Review* before the date of publication, March 5th. But so many popular theological works are appearing at this moment that this one may be overlooked. I am therefore sending you an advance copy with my personal recommendation to you. I know but little about the author. The manuscript came in to my office and I was the first of the firm to read it and recommend it with enthusiasm. If you do have time to read I shall be very curious to know what you think of it.

Yours always sincerely,
[T. S. Eliot]

P.S. I should like to know how you are getting on with Humanism? I have a new book entitled *Humanism and America* which I do not altogether like but which I think you ought to see, and I will lend you my copy as soon as I can spare it.

1–Algar Thorold (1866–1936), diplomat, author, journalist, son of Bishop Anthony Wilson Thorold of Winchester, was editor of *The Dublin Review*, 1926–34. TSE wrote in a memorial note in C. (Oct. 1936, 68) that Thorold 'had been a frequent contributor since very early in our history: his knowledge, especially of modern French philosophy and theology, was invaluable. Having written very few books – his [Six] *Masters of Disillusion* has been out of print for many years – he was not known to a very wide public, and another generation will not be aware that *The Dublin Review,* under his editorship, was one of the most distinguished periodicals of its time. Being half-French by birth [his mother was Emily Labouchère], and at the same time thoroughly English, with the culture of the past and the curiosity of the present, he held a position as a man of letters such that we could say of him, that he was the sort of man whom we could ill afford to lose.' On 24 Nov. 1954, when Dom Michael Hanbury, OSB (St Michael's Abbey, Farnborough), asked TSE to recall Thorold for the *Dublin Review,* TSE responded (1 Dec.): 'I certainly remember the man himself not only with regard and respect, but affection.'

20 February 1930   *The Criterion*

Dear Mr Rendall,

In reply to your letter of the 19th² (I am sorry that you failed to catch me on the telephone), I should suggest that the reading was confined to the metaphysicals; I think that the introduction of Dryden and Milton in a half hour would be rather confusing, especially to the listeners who knew something about them and nothing about the metaphysicals. Donne, Herbert (particularly for his lucidity), a little Vaughan and one Traherne, one Crashaw (St Theresa?), Marvell's Coy Mistress and possibly King's Exequy, would be my prescription, sticking mostly to the well known things, but including Donne's sonnet 'At the round world's etc' as a specimen of his devotional verse.

But these are mere suggestions.

Sincerely yours,
T. S. Eliot

I don't think Cowley, or any of the minor people, are good for the purpose: they need explanatory patter.

P.P.S. I should like to rehearse my first talk one morning a couple of days before delivery. Half an hour is different from twenty minutes, and I like to get things right. I should start with more of a swing if I had tried it over first. Will you get me a studio half hour between 11:30 and 1 one morning, and be present to criticise?

I think Dobrée has improved his delivery considerably. I criticised his Chesterfield severely, & I think he has simplified his later talks.³

---

1 – Richard A. Rendall (1907–1957), educated at Winchester and Trinity College, Cambridge, joined the BBC as an announcer, progressing in 1929 to the Talks Department. In later years he was Assistant Director of Television; Director of Empire Services from 1940; Acting Controller, Overseas Services; and Controller of the Talks Division, 1945–50. He was made CBE in 1951.
2 – 'I have discovered that we have a blank in our programme for eight o'clock on Monday, 3 March . . . [W]e are thinking of putting in a reading from 17th century poetry by way of a prelude to your series . . . I do not know whether it would be best to confine the reading entirely to the metaphysicals or to go on to Dryden and Milton.'
3 – BD and John Bailey were giving a series of broadcast talks on eighteenth-century personalities.

TO *Hugh Macdonald*   TS Williamson

20 February 1930   *The Criterion*

Dear Macdonald,

Samuel Johnson's Satires

I have your letter of the 20th instant and accept the terms therein proposed for me to provide an introductory essay of about 4000 words.[1] It is understood that if I fail to keep my part of the engagement, viz. to provide an essay of that length during the month of April, the agreement becomes void, but that such default on my part shall not be the subject of legal action against me.

I should like to have the £30 on delivery of satisfactory manuscript, but if it suits you better to make payment on the date of publication I make no objection, provided that the book is published within three months of delivery of my manuscript.

That's that. I enjoyed our lunch and hope to see you again soon. It is good of you to provide me with all the material I need.[2] So far as I can see, I can devote the first fortnight in April to cleaning it up and should let you have my copy by April 15th at the latest.

We must continue our radio discussions.

Yours ever
T. S. Eliot

TO *Messrs. James & James*   CC

21 February 1930   [Faber & Faber Ltd]

Dear Sirs,

Income Tax.

I make my returns to the Collector, 40 Russell Square, for the Covent Garden District Inspector.

1–Macdonald wrote: 'We agree to pay you £30 for an introductory essay of about 4000 words. It is important that we should receive the manuscript in April if possible. If we do we will publish the book in May. We agree to the copyright returning to you at the end of two years . . .'

2–'I am sending you a copy of Johnson's Poems. On Saturday I will, if possible, send you a text showing the alterations Johnson made after the first edition had been published.' After spending time collating editions in the British Museum, Macdonald wrote again on 4 Mar.: 'However there is very little in it from the point of view of the literary critic. Please take it that the texts in the edition I sent you are substantially correct. They embody Johnson's alterations.'

My assessments of applications for the last 3 years (27–28, 28–29, 29–30) are numbered 4149, 4227 and 4227 respectively. I take it that the correct number for all of them is 4227?

The situation is rather curious: I made my return for 27–29 [*sc.* 27–28] in due course, but have never had an application for payment. I have not yet completed my return for 28–29; and as for 29–30, it has been my practice for several years to wait until April to make up my accounts, which is more satisfactory to me, as my income though moderate is very complicated, fluctuating, and unpredictable, and which seems to satisfy the authorities, who apparently are still more unbusinesslike than I am.

Yours faithfully,
[T. S. Eliot]

TO *Aldous Huxley*[1]

CC

24 February 1930   [Faber & Faber Ltd]

My dear Aldous,

When I saw you several weeks ago I suggested your doing that article on The Modern English Language in the pamphlet in the *Criterion Miscellany* and I thought that you seemed not indisposed to agree. So I now want to bring the question nearer to the point and ask you when, if ever, you think you could let us have such an essay? The length would be really whatever you like, the ordinary length of these pamphlets has between 5,000 and 10,000 words. If it is above that length we usually have to raise the price and we are anxious to keep as many of the pamphlets as possible at the price of 1/-. Alternatively another idea has occurred to us that may or may not appeal to you. We thought that a pamphlet by you on the problem of Good and Evil in the modern world would have a great success and be extremely valuable as a document of our time. I mean a general statement of the problem of conduct, individual and social from a modern point of view such as yours. It would really be a concise statement of the point of view and the preoccupation with moral problems which is so strong in all your work but which a great many people are inclined to misunderstand. I mean that your name is being used every day as a symbol of a point of view and I am sure that half the time it is used quite mistakenly.

I have put this very vaguely because if it suggests to you anything worth doing it is better to leave to you all the precisions which will suggest

---

1–Aldous Huxley (1894–1963), novelist, poet, essayist: see Biographical Register.

themselves. If you cared to do this I should still like to have a line on the Language article for the *Criterion* itself.

Anyway I wish you would write to say 'yes' or 'no' to these two suggestions.[1]

Mary showed us an admirable photograph of you and Maria in the *Sketch* the other day. I hope you are both in good health, though I fear that the winter climate of Paris is not as good a climate as you ought to have.

With best wishes to both of you from Vivienne and myself.

Yours ever,
[Tom]

TO *Joseph Needham*[2]   CC

24 February 1930   [*The Criterion*]

Dear Mr Needham,

Thank you for your letter.[3] I have always been rather averse to splitting up essays into two numbers of the *Criterion* and it is certainly not desirable for a quarterly if it can be avoided. Especially in the case of anything at all abstract or philosophical it is a great pity; after three months the reader will not have the first part of the essay very clearly in his head and it is only a small number of very serious readers who will take the trouble to re-read the first part before reading the second. But if you think that the essay would be too seriously mutilated by such abbreviations as I have suggested I will go through it again and see if I think this is a possible form of publication.[4]

Yours very truly,
[T. S. Eliot]

1 – See further TSE's letter to Huxley, 10 Apr. 1930, below.
2 – Joseph Needham (1900–95), biochemist, historian of science and civilisation in China, and Christian socialist, was educated at Gonville and Caius College, Cambridge (a Fellow for life, he served as Master for ten years from 1966). His early writings included *The Sceptical Biologist* (1929) and *Chemical Embryology* (3 vols, 1931); but his major project – conceived during WW2 when he established the Sino-British scientific cooperation office and served as scientific counsellor at the British Embassy in Chongqing – was a comprehensive history of Chinese science, technology and medicine. A polymath and a pro-Chinese witness (he was for some years declared *persona non grata* by the USA), he was ultimately regaled with honours. In 1992 he was made a Companion of Honour; and in 1994 he received the Einstein Medal from UNESCO.
3 – Needham suggested (20 Feb.) splitting his essay 'Religion and the Scientific Mind' (forty-four typescript pages) into two parts.
4 – 'Religion and the Scientific Mind', C. 10 (Jan. 1931), 233–63.

TO *Charles Harris*   CC

24 February 1930   [Faber & Faber Ltd]

Dear Harris,

It would be a great help to me in preparing my scheme of arrangement
for you if I could have some idea of how much space you will be able
to allocate to these subjects. Perhaps it is too early for you to say; but I
should like to have some suggestion to work upon.[1]

I shall be very busy for the next two or three weeks but hope to find
time to return your circular with comments.

Yours sincerely,
[T. S. Eliot]

TO *Roy Campbell*[2]   CC

24 February 1930   [Faber & Faber Ltd]

My dear Campbell,

When I spoke to you about a pamphlet on Bullfighting you seemed
rather disinclined to attempt it. But I put the matter to one side with

---

1–Harris had written on 20 Feb., about the planning by the E.C.U. Literature Committee of
the *Encyclopaedia of the Christian Religion* of which TSE was to become a 'Departmental
Editor': 'Perhaps you can give me some hints on the way in which you could personally help.
We want to do *Religion and Morals in Modern Literature* (the Drama, the Novel, Poetry,
Films etc.). This will give you the general idea. As to the way of carrying it out in detail, I
desire enlightenment.'

2–Roy Campbell (1901–57), South-African-born poet, satirist and translator, arrived in
England in 1918 and was taken up by the composer William Walton and the Sitwells, and by
WL. He made his name with the long poem *Flaming Terrapin* (1924). Later poetry includes
Adamastor (1930) and *Talking Bronco* (1946). See Peter F. Alexander, *Roy Campbell: A
Critical Biography* (1982).

TSE wrote to G. J. B. Allport, BBC, on 6 Sept. 1945: 'I have a great respect for Mr Roy
Campbell and an admiration for his work. I like him personally and have no hesitation
in expressing my gratification that you should take him on your staff. I hope that Mr
Campbell's knowledge of foreign languages and literature and of South Africa and the East
will also be useful. He is a distinguished poet and should need no recommendation.'

To the publisher Henry Regnery (26 Dec. 1953), he volunteered this support: 'I am
astonished that no collection of Roy Campbell's poems should have hitherto been published
in the United States, since he has been for many years one of the most conspicuous figures
in English poetry in my time. His work is unclassifiable: it cannot be defined in terms of any
movement. But the best of his work will surely be included in whatever assemblage of the
poetical remains of our time, later generations will consider of permanent worth.' And again
to Regnery, on 1 June 1960: 'I am myself less keen on his original poems than on some of
his translations. Those from *Saint John of the Cross* seem to me quite remarkable and there

the determination to approach you about it again. The objections you made do not seem to us of any importance. The mere fact that in your opinion Hemingway is a more accomplished bullfighter than yourself carries no weight with us and would carry no weight with the reading public. We have more confidence, in fact, that you would give us what we want than Hemingway would. And after all, you are still in the midst of the bullfighting world and Hemingway has been out of it now for some considerable time.

It is merely therefore a question of whether you are willing to do this or whether you absolutely don't want to do it at all. As for your modesty in the matter, please leave that in our hands.

Alternatively if there is some other subject that would really interest you more, I wish you would suggest it; but I should be very disappointed indeed not to get the Bullfighting pamphlet out of you.[1]

With all best wishes to Mrs Campbell and yourself,

Yours sincerely,

[T. S. Eliot]

TO *H. J. C. Marshall*[2]　　　　　　　　　　TS Royal Literary Fund

25 February 1930　　　　　　　　[*The Criterion*]

Sir,

I understand that the P.E.N. Club has proposed the name of Mr John Cournos for a grant from the Royal Literary Fund. Mr Cournos has told me this; so if any word of mine can possibly make such a grant more likely, I shall be very glad.[3]

---

are also several first-rate translations from Rimbaud and, I think, other French poets . . . For some reason which was never quite clear to me, he gave his *Collected Poems* to another publisher.'

1–In 1929 Campbell had written an article on bullfighting; in 1932 he would put out a volume called *Taurine Provence*, a study of the 'Philosophy, Technique and Religion of the Bullfighter'.

2–H. J. C. Marshall (1873–1947): Secretary of the Royal Literary Fund, 1919–45.

3–Cournos said (20 Feb.) he had been nominated by the P.E.N. Club for a grant from the Royal Literary Fund. The Secretary, H. J. C. Marshall, had advised him that 'some additional letters from friends might be useful, also brief letters from the doctors'. As Cournos commented in his letter to TSE, 'They want to be satisfied as to the authenticity and deservingness of my claims.'

I have known Mr Cournos, off and on, for many years. For several years past he has contributed to the *Criterion* summary reviews of Russian periodicals; reviews of which I have thought very highly, and which other persons have told me that they found very interesting and profitable. Mr Cournos has also done excellent work in translation from the Russian; and has been associated for many years with the same group of writers as myself.

I am quite sure that his position at present is a very difficult one, and has been for several years past, owing to family illnesses; and I am sure that a grant from the Fund would be well bestowed upon him.

I shall be very glad to answer any questions about him that you may care to put.

> I am, Sir,
> Your Obedient Servant,
> T. S. Eliot
> Editor, *The Criterion*
> Director, Faber & Faber Ltd.

TO *John Cournos*   cc

25 February 1930   [Faber & Faber Ltd]

Dear Cournos,

This is only a line in haste to say that I have written to Marshall, and hope that my letter may help. I am appalled by your troubles.[1]

> Yours ever,
> [T. S. Eliot]

---

1 – 'Now listen to the incredible!' wrote Cournos (20 Feb.). 'A week ago my young daughter (who had the reputation for being sturdy) went to the hospital with acute sinusitis. There was fear at first of her losing her eyesight, but luckily she has escaped with an inch-and-a-half cut over the left eye-brow. The incision was made today, and she will remain another fortnight in the hospital.

'Item No. 2. My wife, suffering with a cold and sinusitis of another order and the after-effects of her operation and with fretting over the little girl, became nervously exhausted. She too is in the hospital to obtain rest and care. Nothing terribly serious, I think . . .

'What next? I ask myself. I wish I knew how to exorcise the devils.'

TO *Montgomery Belgion* CC

25 February 1930 [Faber & Faber Ltd]

Dear Belgion,

Many thanks for your suggestion. I will order the book and offer it to Empson; I have been anxious to find something to try him out on.[1]

I'll make the suggestion to Curtius; I take it that you are quite sure that a copy *was* sent to him.[2] Only, if I can fix it up through the assistance of Curtius, don't you think it would be reasonable to constitute Faber & Faber (*quorum pars minima sum*) your agents for the German rights? on usual agency terms. After all, my acquaintance with Curtius, as my acquaintance with you, are at the disposal of the firm!

Incidentally, I have other correspondents – Holland, Italy, Spain and Esthonia (a rising market that, they have just translated Macbeth and some of my juvenile verses). If you like.

I am delighted to hear that you are improving, in spite of your doctors. Can you shave yet?[3]

Yours ever,
[T. S. E.]

TO *Bonamy Dobrée* TS Brotherton

25 February 1930 *The Criterion*

Dear Bonamy,

I must apologise for not answering sooner, but I have been very very busy – not Prossew this time but that infamous charlatan Freidegger of Zurich. More about him later. So will you lunch with *me* at the Low Society Club on Wednesday March 5th, which, you observe, is Ash Wednesday?

Yours for all honest service,
Tom

1 – Belgion suggested (24 Feb.) 'a young mathematician such as Empson' to write on E. A. Burtt's *The Metaphysical Foundations of Modern Science*. See C. 10 (Oct. 1930), 167–71.
2 – Belgion hoped that E. R. Curtius might be able to arrange for a translation of his *Our Present Philosophy of Life*.
3 – Belgion had been suffering from a skin complaint.

TO *C. C. Martindale*

3 March 1930   [Faber & Faber Ltd]

Dear Father Martindale,

Thank you for your note.¹ I was on the point of writing to ask you to lunch with me and my fellow director Mr F. V. Morley on Thursday. If you could do that, and come to the Royal Societies' Club (63 St James's Street) at 1, or whatever time suited you, I should be highly pleased. I find I am engaged tomorrow afternoon, and Wednesday all day; so I cannot ask you to share a dried haddock with me on Wednesday. If you cannot lunch on Thursday I think Thursday or Friday morning here, would be possible; but I should much prefer the more hospitable suggestion; and even a Lenten lunch is a good preparation for talk.

Yours sincerely,
[T. S. Eliot]

P.S. I have just seen your portrait in the *Radio Times*, in a row of Famous Broadcast Preachers: the selection is certainly catholic with a small c.²

TO *Bonamy Dobrée*

3 March 1930   *The Criterion*

Dear Bonamy,

The Low Society Islanders' Club is 63 St. James's St., and as I find I have a fixture at 12, could you make it one thirty. I will reserve a table first.

I dont know anything about the 18th century – eggers, all I know about that period I have learned from your own Voice (if you drank less gin it wouldnt be so husky); but I know that Freidegger is half-Scotch and half-vermouth; his mother was I believe a Hammond; his name being Franz Hammond Freidegger.

Yrs etc.
T.

---

1 – Not found.
2 – The paragraphs accompanied an article, 'Religion and the B.B.C by Philemon', *Radio Times*, 26: 335 (28 Feb. 1930), 495.

TO *Henry Crofton*[1]   CC

3 March 1930   [Faber & Faber Ltd]

My dear Crofton,

At the moment I am buried in business – the firm's business, my personal business, preparing some B.B.C. talks, and my own most grievous business – negotiating for a small house again – I tremble to think of my solicitors' bill at the end. So for a week or two I can probably do no more than turn the matter over and over in my mind.[2]

1–H. C. Crofton had been a colleague at the Colonial and Foreign Department, Lloyds Bank.

2–Crofton wrote on 28 Feb.:

'I don't think you have ever met my old friend Platonoff. He was, in his youth, a Classical as well as a Science double first at Petrograd University. His father was Grand Chamberlain to the Tsar, but he being, even at that time, very liberal minded was nauseated by the corruption of the aristocratic Russia of those days, broke away from his people and came to London, became, however, reconciled to his father before his death just before the outbreak of the war, and was for five years my colleague at the Russian Commercial Bank before I joined Lloyds.

'At the outbreak of the war he immediately went back to Petrograd with a view to serving in his own Guards regiment where he had done his military training. Knowing his sterling worth and whiteness through and through the authorities would not let him go to the front but sent him back to London to control the Russian munition buying Commission. Here he found several old gentlemen, contemporaries of his father, who were piling up fortunes. In spite of this he succeeded through tact and personality, without alienating any of the old gentlemen, in cleaning up the Aegean [*sc.* Augean] stable.

'Then came the Russian revolution and he tried for a commission in our army and did a course at Grantham. Things going from bad to worse in Russia a commission became out of the question for some time in our army, but eventually he took out a Labour Battalion recruited from the East End, and swept up Vimy Ridge in the last 18 months of the war.

'Meanwhile, his two brothers, officers in the Russian Navy, had been murdered by their men, one of his sisters had been shot in Petrograd while hospital nursing, the old family place, about one hundred miles from Petrograd, had been sacked and burnt to the ground, and his wonderful old mother eventually succeeded, after appalling privations, in getting through to him [in] England. He was married to one of his own class years before in Petrograd and has one child of thirteen.

'On his return from France he was left absolutely destitute with two women and a child on his hands. The only thing at the moment seemed to be to start as a foreign exchange broker, which he did and he succeeded in making a decent living until about a year ago, in spite of being too clean to take advantage of all the corruption that existed in the boom days in the Foreign Exchange market.

'Two years ago he got his British nationalization papers through (I think probably a solitary case) which alone speaks for his record.

'You know as well as I do that there is nothing left now in the way of foreign exchange business for brokers, and though he has retained his friends in various Banks he is now literally on his last legs.

'Forgive me for writing you this long and somewhat rambling letter, but Platonoff is a very dear friend of mine, and, I think, the finest character I know.

There are, first, various odd jobs and small pickings I can help with: such as 'reading' – reporting on a book now and then for a small fee of a few guineas; or translating books and articles. I can also get people reviewing on certain journals; but I do not stand in with any daily newspaper except *The Times*; I could always get in touch with Garvin of the *Observer*.[1] Most of the literary work going for Russians falls to my friend (or rather acquaintance) Prince Mirski, also I believe the son of a Court Official; (I wonder if Mr Platonoff knows him? I do not know Mirski quite well enough to be able to gauge his kindness of heart; but he also, I imagine, was on his beam ends after the revolution, and was lucky to get a lectureship at London University. Mirski seems that odd composition of aristocrat and savage for which only Russia had the recipe). Mirski has the merit of writing excellent English prose. But your friend's qualifications are staggering, and I feel that there must be not merely a pittance, but some well paid niche into which he should fit.

He might tutor some wealthy child. For this, and schoolmasterships, Gabbitas & Thring are the best agents. I got a job through them, when I was trying to be a schoolmaster.

I should like to know

1. How much difference does it make to him whether he lives in London or in the country or provinces?

2. How perfectly does he know English? Can he write as good English, say, as the average honours man from Oxford or Cambridge?

3. Could he be pushed as an authority on Russian literature? by stretching a few points, just as I stretched several when I entered Lloyds Bank as a linguist?

4. Could he qualify for a private-secretaryship? Does he know shorthand (extremely unlikely, I suppose)?

5. This is really reverting to 3, and also to 1. (q.v.) I thought I might (after meeting him) enquire about the possibilities of a Lectureship at Oxford, Cambridge or some provincial or Scottish university, such as Mirski holds at London.

6. And finally: what is the minimum amount of money that he needs per annum?

'All this leads up to ask you whether it ever lies in your way to have an opportunity of getting him some coaching in the evenings. Apart from his classical attainments he is a master of Russian, French, German and English, and it would be a very great gratification to me if I could manage to find him some work which would enable him to keep his home together.'

1–Viola Garvin (1898–1969): poet; literary editor of the *Observer*.

The odd pickings, such as I mentioned first, are only worthwhile to supplement some regular income, however small; and that is the first thing to find.

I think that in about a fortnight I can suggest a day or two and accept your invitation to meet him at lunch. But even if I could have proposed a day at once, I should have put these questions first to you.

About coaching (which you suggested) I cannot at the moment [think] what there may be for anyone to do resident in London; I imagine that it takes time for a university coach to build up a practice.

Let me know meanwhile anything more about him along the lines I have suggested. First I will arrange with you to lunch with you and him. I should like a private hobnob with you; but another stile to take first is that I have it on my conscience to ask you and Aylward together to lunch with me. He was so touchingly disappointed at your nonappearance that day, that I owe it to him to get you both to lunch as soon as I can.

I mentioned shorthand, and the size of income needed, because there is one, and only one, very small post going in my firm. It is for a secretary to myself and one other director. The chief qualifications are: shorthand typing, ability to file etc., to be able to deal with visitors and correspondents, and to arrange interviews, and (as my fellow director said plaintively) still more to arrange (tactfully) that we should *not* have interviews. My own demands are an ability to take down letters in French, if possible to take down my letters in bad German and put them into good German, and (also if possible) an ability at least to read Italian. The pay would not be more than £150 p.a. to begin with; and we had not even envisaged the possibility of getting an intelligent *male* for that price. Only, I think that a highly capable person – especially as the firm is slowly becoming more prosperous, might depend on gradual improvements of salary; because a really efficient, cultivated and interested person would in effect become my assistant editor. My first secretary, a young woman, was that in fact if not in name; and I was very seriously crippled in my work by her death.[1]

> Ever yours,
> [T. S. Eliot]

1 – Irene Pearl Fassett was TSE's secretary 1923–8.

TO *C. C. Martindale*

8 March 1930   [Faber & Faber Ltd]

Dear Father Martindale,

Thank you for your letter. I think I may say with conviction that our lunch was at least as pleasant for Mr Morley and myself as it was for you; and for us it was very instructive about matters in which we are both much interested.

I am very rushed at the moment with broadcasting and other matters; but I will return the ms. with pencilled comments as soon as I possibly can; and we shall see what can be done.

In any case, I think we were animated half by the desire to have your name on our list; so if we cannot get this right we shall undoubtedly try something else! And of course if we could aid your mission as well as ourselves, it would be very gratifying. I should like to hear more about that. And I am very glad that [I] have made your acquaintance.

By the way, I have liked Father Steuart's book, which Thorold mentioned to me, very much and should like to tell him so.[1]

Sincerely yours,
[T. S. Eliot]

TO *Bruce Richmond*

18 March 1930   [Faber & Faber Ltd]

Dear Richmond,

In suggesting that I should write about Tourneur you are exposing me to serious temptation: I want to write about Tourneur more than about any other Elizabethan, and the occasion may never occur again.[2] But at present (1) I am giving weekly Broadcasting for the next month, and three talks are still unwritten. (2) I have promised Walter de la Mare an essay on Pater for some R.S.L. collection, by the end of March. (3) I have promised

1–See TSE's (anon.) notice of R. H. J. Steuart, SJ, *The Inward Vision*, C. 9 (Apr. 1930), 577: 'This book is superficially a collection of Lenten meditations like any other; but it really summarizes a good deal of serious philosophic thought and understanding, misleadingly simple in expression. We mention it in the hope of bringing it to the notice of a few readers who might otherwise overlook it.' Not in Gallup.

2–Richmond advised (13 Mar.): 'there has arrived an edition of Tourneur [*The Works of Cyril Tourneur*] by Allardyce Nicoll (a worthy but uninspiring pundit). I should like to send this to you, if you have a reasonable expectation of being able to do it within a month or six weeks?' 'Cyril Tourneur', *TLS*, 13 Nov. 1930, 925–6; repr. in *SE*.

Macdonald an essay on Johnson's Satires by the middle of April. (4) I have promised Milford a short introduction to some Shakespeare essays by one Wilson Knight, by the end of April.[1] (5) I have been house hunting and must be moving by the 5th April. Judge therefore the extent of the pain you cause me. I don't want to do Tourneur and Ford together: one would have to spend all the essay in pointing antitheses, as they are so different. So I think the only thing for me to do is to resign the commission [*typing runs off the page*] and do it there at leisure, and without payment. Besides, I have sundry books of yours on hand, you know; Southwell, and Thorndyke, and Baker.

Is anyone writing about Whibley for the *T.L.S.*?[2]

1 – TSE wrote an 'Introduction' to GWK, *The Wheel of Fire* (1930).
2 – Charles Whibley (1859–1930) took a first in Classics in 1883 from Jesus College, Cambridge, and embarked on a career as journalist, author and editor, and as a well-connected social figure (his intimates were to include Lord Northcliffe and Lady Cynthia Asquith). After working briefly for the publishers Cassell & Co., he wrote for the *Scots Observer* and the *Pall Mall Gazette* (for a while in the 1890s he was Paris correspondent, a posting which enabled him to become acquainted with Stéphane Mallarmé and Paul Valéry), for the *Daily Mail*, and above all for *Blackwood's Magazine* – where he produced for over twenty-five years a commentary, 'Musings without Method', comprised of sharp High-Tory substance and style. TSE hailed his column as 'the best sustained piece of literary journalism that I know of in recent times'. Richard Aldington jealously thought Whibley 'a pernicious influence' on Eliot: 'Eliot was already too much influenced by Irving Babbitt's pedantic and carping analysis of Rousseau – indeed to some extent he founded his prose style on Babbitt – and in Whibley he found a British counterpart to his old Harvard professor. Whibley was . . . a good scholar, but a hopeless crank about politics. He was the very embodiment of the English Tory don, completely out of touch with the realities of his time. "Whig" and "Whiggism" were his terms of contempt and insult to everybody he disliked, and anybody can see how Eliot picked them up. But Whibley took Eliot to Cambridge, where his conversation enchanted the dons and procured him friends and allies, vastly more important and valuable than the Grub Street hacks who had rejected him.' His friend F. S. Oliver wrote (17 April 1930), in some personal reminiscences put down at TSE's request, of 'the apparently impulsive and prejudiced character of C. W. that when he came to deal with the craft of writing he had no favour, or fear, or anger for friends or enemies. I never knew him once to praise good-naturedly a book because it was written by a very close friend; nor have I ever known him to disparage a book with real merits, but which happened to be written by someone whose character and opinions he held in detestation. Contrary to the general idea of him he was one of the most *tolerant* people (as regards literature) that I have ever known . . . [I]t is this quality of truthful, courageous, penetrating, sympathetic literary criticism which I should put first among all his brilliant capacities . . . [H]e was I think the best critic who lived in my time.' Whibley's books included *William Pitt* (1906), *Political Portraits* (1917, 1923), and *Lord John Manners and his Friends* (1925). See TSE, *Charles Whibley: A Memoir* (The English Association Pamphlet no. 80, Dec. 1931).
 Whibley had died on 4 Mar. 1930.

Having mentioned the subject, would you mind my giving you as a reference (social not financial) to a house agent? I have forgotten when I last imposed upon you in this way; but having moved twice in the last year, and recently having gone as far with three houses as giving references, I have pretty well gone the round of my friends; and I now write a note of apology to my bank every time.

I should very much like to see you; but tea this week is impossible. Are Wednesday or Thursday ever possible for you to lunch with me? I do owe you a lunch and should like to have you accept it.

Yours ever,

[T. S. Eliot]

TO *H. J. C. Grierson*[1]   TS James Fergusson Books & MSS, 2010

18 March 1930   [Faber & Faber Ltd]

Dear Grierson,

It could not have been my voice, but only the ingenuity of the electrical engineers, that caused the thunder.[2] It is quite true that I was referring to the note on The Ecstasie in your big edition; and I will apologise on Friday for not having collated it with the Introduction to the Metaphysical Poets.

If my talks are really successful, then the sale of the latter volume ought to go up by leaps & bounds – but I have the depressing feeling that I am merely talking down without exciting enthusiasm.

1–H. J. C. Grierson (1866–1960), Regius Professor of Rhetoric and English Literature, University of Edinburgh, 1915–35: see Biographical Register.

2–Grierson had been listening to TSE's broadcasts on metaphysical poetry. In his remarks on Donne TSE quoted two 'very difficult stanzas' from 'The Ecstasie': 'This poem has been taken as a statement of a mystical philosophy of love; and even Professor Grierson, whose opinion I must respect, speaks of it as important because of being Donne's "metaphysic of love", referring quite rightly to obvious origins in neo-Platonic philosophy. Well, it is perhaps a little reckless of me to ask you to take Donne's philosophy less seriously than Professor Grierson does, but I cannot see that Donne held this philosophy except for the purpose of this particular poem.'

Grierson wrote on 16 Mar.: 'I heard, or rather my wife did . . . a statement that I took the philosophy of Donne too seriously. Perhaps I did in my not too happy Introduction in 1912 [*The Poems of John Donne*, II, 41–5] written under great stress, and even there I meant more to suggest that the different phases of Donne's love-poetry had in them a latent philosophy. But in my Metaphysical Poets [*Metaphysical Lyrics & Poems of the Seventeenth Century* (1921)] p. xxviii I pretty expressly disclaimed this in words that Praz endorsed.'

I ought to have written to say how much we are obliged for your very careful report on Gundolf.[1] I think you are very fair to him, but I am pretty certain that we should lose money on him.[2]

Yours sincerely,

T. S. Eliot

TO *H. H. Joachim*   CC

19 March 1930   [Faber & Faber Ltd]

Dear Professor Joachim,

I hope you remember an old pupil who suddenly writes to you about once very five years. I am now writing to you on a matter of business for the firm with which I am connected.

Some weeks ago I was in touch with A. E. Taylor about a German work on Plato which had been suggested to us, and on which he gave us very kindly his opinion; in the course of correspondence he mentioned the *Aristotèles* of Werner Jaeger as a valuable book worth translation; but said modestly that you or Ross probably knew much more about the book than he did. Therefore I am writing to you to ask (1) how good a book you find it to be (2) whether you think that it is a book to justify a translation – I mean, is it a book which undergraduates and other students of Aristotle who know a little German would use, or is it one which would probably be read only by those who can read it in German anyway?

I have got a copy of the book here; but my busy if futile life has left me no time to keep up Aristotle!

I may add that we should not expect such a book to be really profitable; but if it is a really first rate work of scholarship which should go on with small sales for some years, we should be glad to publish it for the honour of the firm.

---

1 – Grierson wrote on 16 Mar.: 'The more I read the more I feel doubtful. It is not critical but entirely interpretative in the tradition of Goethe in *Wilhelm Meister*.'
2 – Grierson replied to this letter on 20 Mar.: 'Whatever the significance of that poem ['The Ecstasy'], probably a seducer's plea, it does develop a thought, which is perversely used in the poem, that Donne took seriously and returned to in his sermons – the noted interdependence of body & soul, their inseparability in Love and even in eternal Life. He was not a systematic philosopher but he had some thoughts to which he again & again recurs. But I accept your distinction between "metaphysical" & philosophical poets . . . No, I suppose Donne was not a mystic but occasionally in the sermons he approaches an adumbration of the mood of ecstasy which is the condition of the mystics' realisation of the divine.'

With all best wishes to Mrs Joachim and yourself,

I am,

Yours very sincerely,

[T. S. Eliot]

TO *J. M. Barrie*[1]   cc

19 March 1930   [*The Criterion*]

Sir,

I am taking the liberty of writing to you as a friend of the late Charles
Whibley. He was not only one of the first contributors to the *Criterion*
over seven years ago, but was a consistent supporter of the review in every
way, as well as being so kind a friend to me that I feel his loss very deeply.

I am anxious to have some memorial notice of him in a review for which
he did so much. Although I saw much of him and corresponded with him
regularly, my friendship with him is only of seven years standing; and I
feel that it would be more worthy of him to have a notice by someone who
had known him intimately throughout his career, as well as by someone
much more eminent than myself. I should be more than grateful to you,
both as Editor and because I personally want to do adequate honour to
Whibley's memory, if you would consent to write something – anything,
from four hundred to any number of words that you would write.

Incidentally, I should like to establish some communication with you;
for as you probably know, there will be [the] question of aiding his
executors in the publication both of his own works and those of Henley.

I am, Sir,

Yours very truly,

[T. S. Eliot]

FROM *TSE's Secretary* TO *J. E. Pouterman*   cc

21 March 1930   [*The Criterion*]

Dear Sir,

Referring to your letter of the 1st Mr Eliot has asked me to return
herewith the proofs of Mr Isherwood's translation which he has gone

1–Sir James Barrie, Bt (1860–1937): playwright and novelist; author of *The Admirable
Crichton* (1902) and *Peter Pan* (1904); appointed OM, 1922; President of the Society of
Authors, 1928.

through. He wishes me to call your attention to the necessity for checking errors in several Greek quotations.

Referring to the third paragraph of your letter, Mr Eliot has no objection to your title page except that he does not wish to appear as the Editor.[1] If you will delete the word 'edited' leaving merely 'with an introduction by T. S. Eliot' it will be quite satisfactory.

As to the matter of signing fifty limited copies. Mr Eliot is quite willing to do this provided that he be paid a sum based on the additional profit of the limited edition; this sum to be arranged between you and himself as soon as the exact number of signed copies and the price of the signed edition has been decided. He wishes to point out that in his opinion the future value of his signature to limited editions is in direct ratio to the rarity of the signature, and that therefore he cannot afford to sign editions, apart from the time required, without extra payment.

Yours faithfully,

[Secretary]

FROM *Vivien Eliot*[2] TO *Mary Hutchinson*[3]   MS Texas

Tuesday, 25 March 1930   177 Clarence Gate Gardens, N.W.1

My dear Mary

I am very sorry indeed that we were not able to come to dinner tonight. I nearly rang you up, but telephoning is so hateful.

I hope Tom explained that we are moving (again) next Monday & Tuesday – & that we have had a most terrible time in trying (unsuccessfully) to find another little house as nice as 57 Chester Terrace. It has been a great rush at the last, for us to get out of here by Quarter Day. I personally

---

1 – Pouterman had asked, 'Will you kindly let me know whether you have no objections to the title-page of the volume consisting of the following text:

Charles Baudelaire

INTIMATE JOURNALS

Squibs & Crackers

My Heart Laid Bare

Selection of Consoling Maxims upon Love.

For the first time translated into English by Ch. Isherwood,

Edited with an Introduction by T. S. Eliot.

and also whether I may announce that the de luxe copies (40 or 50) on special paper will be signed by you.'

2 – Vivien Eliot, née Haigh-Wood (1888–1947): see Biographical Register.

3 – Mary Hutchinson (1889–1977), a half-cousin of Lytton Strachey; prominent hostess, author: see Biographical Register.

have felt very sick & ill for the last few weeks. I had a fearful shock, my brother (who you know) suddenly got married, in Italy.[1] He arrived back, with a sick wife. An American. Very young. All done without our knowledge. My Mother has been terribly upset over it, & it has aged her very much. What has made it all so much worse, is that he had to go back to Italy almost at once, *with* the wife, & with only a *temporary* job. Heaven knows what will happen to them. So now we are moving again, but not with much *hope*, this time.

Good-night, Mary.

Yours ever
Vivienne

You *must* come and see our new house almost at once. Perhaps we cld. come round & see you next Sunday for a minute.

TO *Walter de la Mare*   CC

27 March 1930   [Faber & Faber Ltd]

Dear de la Mare,

I do not know quite what to say, because I ought to have written to you ten days ago, and have been too busy and distracted to do even that.[2] I have been engaged, and shall be for another fortnight, in an inferno of private difficulties and embarrassments, largely concerned with moving into a house (which is to take place on Tuesday next); and the plain fact is that unless some extension is possible I must simply default, about my essay for your 80s volume, in the most humiliating and inexcusable fashion. One of the complications is that I had already embarked upon a set of six B.B.C. talks, of which I have given three; and once having started, I cannot drop them and must go on, however feebly, to some sort of end. If an extension is possible, I may still redeem my reputation: if not, I can only accept the contumely, and what matters more, the burden on my conscience [*typing runs off the page*]

1–In fact, MHW (as VHE knew) had not 'suddenly got married, in Italy'. VHE and TSE had been given some notice: a ledger of expenditure kept by TSE and VHE includes the information that on 15 Feb. 1930 they spent 2/6d on 'flowers for Maurice's wife' (Bod MS Eng. Misc. c. 62). Furthermore, *The Times* had announced, on 22 Feb. 1930, 1, that MHW had married Emily Cleveland Hoagland, 'younger daughter of Mr Herbert CLEVELAND HOAGLAND, of Westport, Connecticut, and New York City, and the late Mrs Hoagland', on 15 Feb. 1930.
2–Walter de la Mare would sometime remark: 'Eliot has a little way, with which I cordially sympathise, of leaving his correspondence to mature' (cited in S. C. Roberts, *Adventures with Authors* [1966], 137).

. . . Society of Literature, because if I write the essay it is one sum and if I don't it is another; and chiefly because I have had no time to write any letters at all.[1]

> Yours very sincerely,
> [T. S. Eliot]

TO *Eliot C. Lodge, Principal, Westfield College* CC

27 March 1930   [Faber & Faber Ltd]

Dear Madam,

I must apologise for the delay in answering your enquiry of the 10th instant concerning Miss Ruth Harrison. It has been wholly [due] to pressure of other business.

I have never actually seen Miss Harrison. I knew her first as a subscriber to the *Criterion*, who wrote once or twice to make extremely intelligent suggestions for the review. Since then she has written to me about one or two matters, and consulted me about a dissertation she was preparing. My knowledge of her, you see, is slight; I can only say that such as it is it gives me considerable faith in her intelligence, width of information, and standards of scholarship. I have reason to believe that she is very well acquainted with contemporary France and French thought.[2]

> Yours faithfully,
> [T. S. Eliot]

1–De la Mare responded to this letter on 29 Mar.: 'I am awfully sorry to hear of all your troubles, and still more sorry that I am adding to them. If you could let me have your paper latest by the end of April I think that would be time enough for the C.U.P. I wish it weren't going to be such a burden and hope the additional time will make it all right.'
2–Harrison was offered a Postgraduate Research Studentship at Westfield College, University of London, by 29 Mar.

TO *F. Boillot*[1]   TS copy

27 March 1930   [Faber & Faber Ltd]

Dear Sir,

I have to apologise for not answering your letter of the 26th February, and to express my regrets for any inconvenience I may have caused you.[2] I have been extremely busy with both business and private affairs, or I would not have failed at least to signify my appreciation of the honour done me by the University in inviting me to deliver the Skemp Memorial Lecture. It would be a gratification to me in every way; but I feel that as I am not able at present to predict my position in January 1931, I ought not to accept an honour which I might not be able to justify; or an undertaking which I might find myself carrying out very badly, or even not at all. So I can only repeat my appreciation of the honour, and my expression of regret that I cannot distinguish myself by receiving it.

I am, Sir,
Your obedient servant,
[T. S. Eliot]

TO *Huw Menai*[3]   CC

28 March 1930   [Faber & Faber Ltd]

Dear Mr Menai,

I am extremely sorry for the delay in coming to a decision about your manuscript – not however a long delay as ordinary publishers' decisions go.[4] The reason for the delay is not directly any indecision about the

---

1–Félix Boillot (1880–1961): Professor of French Language and Literature, University of Bristol. A distinguished veteran of WW1 – Officier de la Légion d'Honneur; Croix de Guerre with two bars; Polish Cross for Valour; Médaille d'or de l'Académie Française – he was later to serve as a major on the staff of the Allied Military Committee, 1939–40.

2–'As Chairman of the Arthur Skemp Memorial Fund Committee, I have been entrusted with the task of suggesting a suitable lecturer to give the biennial Skemp Memorial Lecture next session. The fee is twenty pounds and the lecture is to be delivered preferably in January of 1931. The University wishes to keep the manuscript after the lecture has been delivered and reserves the right of publication . . .'

3–Huw Owen Williams (1886–1961) – 'Huw Menai' – went to work at the age of sixteen in the pits at Gilfach Goch, Glamorgan. He published poems in local newspapers including *Merthyr Express* and *Western Mail*; and his first book was *Through the Upcast Shaft* (1920).

4–Menai had written (27 Mar.) to ask after the progress of a manuscript entitled 'Back in the Return' which he had submitted six weeks earlier. TSE's secretary wrote on 31 Mar. to recommend that Menai contact 'a very good literary agent' such as A. D. Peters: 'If you care to use Mr Eliot's name in writing to either publishers or agents, he would be very willing.'

quality of your work. It has been a question of deciding our policy for the immediate future about the publication of poetry, and we have come to the conclusion that we do not intend to publish at present any collections of verse of considerable size. There is in our minds the question of publishing within a season or two a few very small books of verse to be priced very cheaply. In that event, and if you do not decide upon another publisher in the mean time, we should like to consider the question of making a selection out of this book to form a small volume of the right size.

I dare say however that this would not meet your wishes in any case and that you would quite naturally prefer to arrange to publish this volume as it stands. In that case I will hold the manuscript at your disposal until I hear from you. I should suggest Chatto & Windus or perhaps Gollancz as possible publishers unless you prefer to put the matter into the hands of one of the recognised agents.

With all best wishes.
Yours sincerely,
[T. S. Eliot]

TO *Editor,* The Nation & Athenaeum CC

30 March 1930[1]   [Faber & Faber Ltd]

Sir,

Mr E. M. Forster, in a letter in your issue of March 29, says 'straight out' that the late D. H. Lawrence was 'the greatest imaginative novelist of our time'.[2]

1–Published *N&A* 47: 1 (4 Apr. 1930), 11.
2–'D. H. Lawrence', *N & A* 46: 26 (29 Mar. 1930), 888:
    'Sir, – I never knew D. H. Lawrence well, but my memories, such as they are, date from the period so sympathetically and beautifully described in O. M.'s article ['D. H. Lawrence, 1885–1930 by One of His Friends', *N&A* 46: 25 [22 Mar. 1930], 859–60]. I, too, was shown the woods in spring and taken a walk near Arundel. Perhaps my character did not pass the test of the Sussex downs, anyhow I heard little from him in after years – only an occasional postcard.
    'The war tortured him but never paralyzed him; the tremendous nightmare chapter in *Kangaroo* is sufficient proof of that, and all through his later work the vitality continues. Now he is dead, and the low-brows whom he scandalized have united with the high-brows whom he bored to ignore his greatness. This cannot be helped; no one who alienates both Mrs Grundy and Aspatia can hope for a good obituary Press. All that we can do – those of us who agree, as I do, with your correspondent Mr Hellyar [*N&A* 46: 25 (22 Mar. 1930), 858] – is to say straight out that he was the greatest imaginative novelist of our generation. The rest must be left where he would have wished it to be left – in the hands of the young. Yours, &c., E. M. Forster.'

I am the last person to wish to disparage the genius of Lawrence, or to disapprove when a writer of the eminence of Mr Forster speaks 'straight out'. But the virtue of speaking straight out is somewhat diminished if what one speaks is not sense. And unless we know exactly what Mr Forster means by *greatest*, *imaginative*, and *novelist*, I submit that this judgment is meaningless. For there are at least three 'novelists' of 'our generation' – two of whom are living – for whom a similar claim might be made.

I am Sir,
Your obedient servant,
[T. S. Eliot]

TO *John Heywood Thomas*[1]   CC

31 March 1930   [*The Criterion*]

Dear Sir,

I like your essay on D. H. Lawrence and should be glad to print it. I cannot however say at the moment whether I can use it in the next (June) number, because I may be having a note of the late Mr Charles Whibley and I feel that two obituary articles would be too dismal. In that case I should like to use it in December. But if you wish to place it elsewhere more quickly I will not stand in your way.

If however you elect to leave the essay with us, may I suggest that as in any case over two months will elapse before publication, the post script

---

Forster replied in *N&A* 47: 2 (12 Apr. 1930), 45: 'Mr T. S. Eliot entangles me in his web. He asks what exactly I mean by "greatest", "imaginative", and "novelist", and I cannot say. Worse still, I cannot even say what "exactly" means – only that there are occasions when I would rather feel like a fly than a spider, and that the death of D. H. Lawrence is one of these.'

1 – John Heywood Thomas (1902–1969), a miner's son from Llwynhendy, Llanelli, was at the time of this letter a teacher of French at the Junior School of Cardiff Technical College. He was subsequently awarded a Fellowship at University College, Cardiff – partly on the strength of his MA thesis, *The Socialistic Theories of Anatole France* (1928), and partly on the strength of the article on D. H. Lawrence published in *C.* – which was followed by *L'Angleterre dans l'oeuvre de Victor Hugo* (1934). Appointed lecturer in 1932, he worked for thirty-four years at Cardiff, where from 1943 he was Head of the Department of French and Romance Philology. Colleagues included P. M. Mansell Jones (then Senior Lecturer in French), also known to TSE.

which you have added might well be incorporated into the essay itself. At the beginning or at the beginning and end.[1]

Yours faithfully,
[T. S. Eliot]

TO *The Editor,* The Bookman[2]   cc Princeton

31 March 1930   [Faber & Faber Ltd]

Sir,

It is not often that I feel obliged to reply to criticism of my own work. If one tried to correct every misunderstanding, one would have no time for anything else. But in reading your 'Chronicle and Comment' for March 1930, I find what is to me a more serious matter: a travesty, as I take it, of my attitude to one of the greatest men of our time; so I ask you, as an act of justice, to print my own comments. The matter is all the more serious because your 'Chronicle and Comment' is unsigned, and therefore bears, at least, editorial approval.[3]

---

1 – 'The Perversity of D. H. Lawrence', C. 10 (Oct. 1930), 5–22.
2 – Not published. Quoted (in part) in Roger Kojecky, *T. S. Eliot's Social Criticism* (1971), 75.
3 – Seward Collins, in an unsigned critique of *Humanism and America*, commented on TSE's brief contribution 'Religion Without Humanism' that it was 'written with all his usual brightness . . .; also with his customary cryptic hints and grave jests. But it has absolutely nothing to do with humanism as understood elsewhere in the book and as currently used in both England and this country. Eliot identifies the American humanistic movement with *cultivated skepticism* – which must surprise such openly avowed Christians as Paul E. More . . . and will puzzle . . . all those critics who condemn humanism for being near-Christian . . . [T]he mark of Babbitt's principal work plainly shows in Eliot's criticism, with its hostility towards excessive or perverted romanticism, its emphasis on classicism, its power of definition, its respect for the great traditions. In fact much of Eliot's influence has derived from the fact that he has served as a channel for Babbitt's ideas . . .'
    Pointing out that TSE wrote on Babbitt and More even in *SW* (1920) – in a way at once 'cryptic' and 'on the whole respectful' – Collins went on: 'After an interval of ten years Eliot returned to the subject of Babbitt and devoted three of his infrequent essays largely to casting scorn on a man from [*sc.* for] whom he professes the highest admiration and to whom he acknowledges a large debt . . . He still agrees with most that Babbitt says . . . and yet . . .besides the ridicule, he seeks to reduce Babbitt's work to a mere plea for culture and to a statement of a philosophical and religious stand which Eliot does not share – thereby denying the very parts of his work on which he himself had fed. Eliot's acceptance of Christianity seems to enter into his attitude, but it is hardly a sufficient explanation, in the circumstances, for his writing about Babbitt considerably more sharply than he has ever written about anyone toward whom he feels open enmity.
    'Eliot's attitude is all the more surprising in view of the manner in which he has written about Charles Maurras, another agnostic who has, like Babbitt, done supremely important work in the attack on modernistic errors . . . It is doubtful if Eliot agrees with as many of

There is much in this commentary with which I agree; and so far as you criticise or censure my own writings I am indifferent. What I resent is your suggestion that I 'cast scorn' on a man for whom I 'profess the highest admiration'. I overlook the suggestion of insincerity. Again it is suggested that my purpose is to 'ridicule' Mr Babbitt; and again that my intention may be to do him what damage I can. This is, I submit, a grave misrepresentation.

Again, your critic says that I write about Babbitt 'considerably more sharply' than I have written about anyone towards whom I feel 'open enmity'. I take exception to the suggestion that I feel open enmity towards anybody. I do not expect your critic to have read all of my hurried journalistic writing. But he should not generalise as if he had. Towards whom have I professed 'open enmity'? Not even towards Mr Shaw or Mr Wells, whom I regard merely as objects for the paleontologist. If towards anybody, towards such men as Mr Bertrand Russell and Mr Middleton Murry, about whose various doctrines I have written far more 'sharply' than about those of Mr Babbitt; but for whom, nevertheless, I have a warm personal feeling.

Your critic also makes capital out of the fact that I display for Charles Maurras 'nothing but the greatest respect and affection', whereas I treat Babbitt with 'patronising admiration and easy ridicule'. My personal acquaintance with M. Maurras is but slight; my acquaintance with Mr Babbitt is of many years. Your critic quite overlooks the circumstances: that when I have spoken of Maurras it has been to defend him against what I believed to be injustice, whilst Mr Babbitt, I am very glad to say, needs no such defence. I do not consider that any parallel can be drawn between my attitude towards Maurras and my attitude towards Babbitt;

Maurras's secular opinions as of Babbitt's; it is certain that Maurras has expressed a more contemptuous attitude toward orthodox Christianity than has Babbitt; yet for the one Eliot displays nothing but the greatest respect and affection, for the other patronizing admiration and easy ridicule.'

Collins asserted further that TSE fails 'to use the term humanism in its contemporary sense. (If he is being misled by the late T. E. Hulme's use of the word, as Mr Shafer has suggested, he should note that the word is being used in the present discussions in a sense directly counter to Hulme's. Hulme identified humanism with the Renaissance and the modern consequences (which is nearer to the general and historical use). But the present humanistic movement is largely opposed to the final results of the Renaissance.' Collins asserted in conclusion: 'Eliot remains a good humanist, and should properly be included in any humanist symposium. But his present paper, like the two that preceded it, is mainly irrelevant, because of his cramped use of the term humanism. This in turn seems to rise from some quirk in his attitude toward Babbitt' ('Chronicle and Comment', *The Bookman* 71: 1 [Mar. 1930], 76–9).

and I should be the first to admit that there are far grosser positive errors and far greater dangers in the doctrine of Maurras than in that of Babbitt.[1] If indeed there is any patronage about, your critic is responsible for some: he refers to my 'usual brightness' and 'grave jests' et cetera.

May I state that for the teaching of Babbitt himself I have the greatest admiration; and to Mr Babbitt the deepest gratitude. My own position seems to me to be very close indeed to that of Mr More; for example as put in his admirable essay in your same number.[2] What differences there are between Mr More and myself are all on our own side of the fence, do not concern the general issues of humanism, and would appear to most humanists to be trivial theological details.

My chief apprehension about 'humanism' has been lest the teaching of Mr Babbitt should be transformed, by a host of zealous disciples, into the hard and fast dogma of a new ethical church, or something between

1 – TSE delivered what was perhaps his final reckoning of Maurras in a 'message' written at the behest of Henri Boergner in Jan. 1953:

'There have been famous writers, men whose thought and whose gift of language have affected the attitude towards life of innumerable readers during their lifetime, and whose influence has declined from the moment of their death. I can think of such in my own language: writers of such eminence that their every pronouncement, in their lifetime, seemed to their admirers – and perhaps to themselves – assured of enduring fame; yet whose reputation, after the journalistic feux d'artifice of the obituary moment, has begun to sink into oblivion. Maurras is not one of these.

'On the contrary. His reputation and influence, during his lifetime, were paradoxical and ambiguous. During that stormy life his name represented a party, a movement. There were many who adhered, not to Maurras, but to the movement, the party, he chose to represent. In the eyes of those who feel only political emotions, and judge only in political terms, he represented no more. The experience of more discerning admirers was paradoxical. He was not a believer, yet there are those whom he strengthened in their allegiance to the Church; and, through their allegiance to the Church, in their submission to God. I speak as an Englishman: I found Maurras unjust to Britain, failing in understanding of the meaning of the British Empire – yet his writings helped me to appreciate better the merits of the British political tradition. Besides the minority who subscribe to the integral political programme of Maurrasism, there was a smaller minority who are grateful for having learned something from Maurras.

'Death, I believe, can only reveal his permanent importance. When opinion is purified from the passions of the time, he will prove, I believe – tel qu'un lui-même enfin l'éternité le change – to belong not to a party but to his whole people, as a great prose writer in the language which has the greatest prose tradition of any modern language. And such works as *Reflexions sur l'Intelligence* and *Anthinéa* will become part of the heritage of all European people.'

TSE quotes a line from *L'Avenir de l'intelligence* at the close of *Triumphal March*. EVE wrote to Prof. Walter Langlois, Dept. of French, Univ. of Kentucky, 15 July 1968: 'the study of the influence of Maurras on my husband would make a fascinating subject for a Ph.D. student.'

2 – More, 'A Revival of Humanism', *The Bookman* 71: 1 (Mar. 1930), 1–11.

a church and a political party. If that is to happen, I confess that I prefer the subtle psychologising of Mr Ramon Fernandez, a study of which I recommend to all American humanists, to the vague moralising of some of Mr Babbitt's disciples.

On one point however I must say that your critic is near the truth. I do certainly associate the contemporary use of the word 'humanism' with that of T. E. Hulme. Hulme's use of the term is traditional and just; and if our new humanists mean something entirely different then they should call it by some other name.

I am, Sir,
Your obedient servant,
[T. S. Eliot]

TO *Paul Elmer More*[1]   TS Princeton

5 April 1930   Faber & Faber Ltd

My dear More,

Considering the enormous amount of unanswered correspondence that I have on hand, I am replying to your letter very promptly.[2] But I must confess that I should have been writing to you at once even had I not heard from you: though your letter gave me much pleasure and I should have tried to write to you promptly.

At almost the same time of receipt of your letter, I received a copy of the *Bookman*: I was pretty well incensed by the editorial commentary in that number, which you must have seen, as it contains your essay:[3] and I enclose [for] you the (only) copy of a letter which I have addressed to the Editor. If they choose not to print it, I should at least like some friend to know how I feel about the matter.

I liked your essay in the same review extremely. It may be of course that I wished to find that your views were similar to mine; but it seemed to me that you said what I should have liked to have said myself. My small paper in the volume was written hastily and under difficulties: I was unable to revise it; and I fear [it] looks rather frivolous and Chestertonian among so much serious matter.

1 – Paul Elmer More (1864–1937), critic, scholar and writer: see Biographical Register.
2 – More asked on 6 Mar. whether TSE had seen Shafer's reply to Allen Tate in *The Bookman*. 'I thought the article rather ill-advised and not much clearer in its argument than Tate's . . . I myself have an article in the March *Bookman* on Humanism amd Religion . . .'
3 – More, 'A Revival of Humanism', *The Bookman* 71: 1 (Mar. 1930), 1–11.

I find the book better than it seemed to me on reading the proof. And G. R. Elliott's paper is very good indeed.[1] My only fear is lest Humanism may become a popular parlour game – 'Are you a humanist?' – whereas I should like to internationalise it, and bring the best minds of each country to bear on common problems – Foerster's book is too local – one should at this point try to open more communications instead of closing them up by establishing creeds and party professions – some of the men are almost as dogmatic as I. A. Richards.

This is not really a reply to your letter, for the good reason that we have been moving again, are still in great confusion, and your letter is buried away somewhere with a mass of correspondence.

I will write again when I have found it.

Yours always sincerely,
T. S. Eliot

TO *E. Gordon Selwyn*   CC

9 April 1930   43 Chester Terrace,
                                                    Eaton Square, S.W.1.

Dear Selwyn,

I must apologise for delaying the reply to your kind letter;[2] but the reason is that I have waited to see how I should be placed on Friday myself. The fact is that we have only just moved to this new address; I must be at home on Friday afternoon and have to rush off to broadcast afterwards. I shall be at 24, Russell Square all the morning; that is rather out of the way for you; but if you could have an *early* lunch with me at the club before your meeting I should be very glad indeed. Say 12 or 12:30? Or we might at least meet there for a few minutes in the morning? If you can, please send me a wire; if not, don't trouble, and we must wait for your next visit. We have just moved to a house many sizes too small, and the place is still in such confusion that we cannot ask anyone here.

Yours ever,
[T. S. Eliot]

1 – G. R. Elliott, 'The Pride of Modernity', *Humanism and America*, ed. Norman Foerster, 75–104. TSE later referred to Elliott as 'one of the most interesting literary critics amongst American scholars' (letter to the editor of the *Review of English Studies*, 14 Aug. 1936). See also TSE to Elliott, 21 July 1931, below.

2 – Selwyn wrote (7 Apr.), 'I have enjoyed *Who moved the Stone?* & written a long review for my May number [*Theology*]. Are you going to send me *Ash Wednesday*? And what about your article on Gore's *Jesus of Nazareth*? I want to see you some time about a plan in my head . . .'

Ash Wednesday – an advance copy, shall reach you next week. It does not appear (to my vexation) till April 29.

TO *Kenneth Ingram*[1]   CC

10 April 1930   [Faber & Faber Ltd]

Dear Mr Ingram,

Certainly, I feel honoured by being asked to send a message to the Congress, to which I look forward.[2] But as I have felt, after an occasion on which I addressed the Literature Association, that I struck rather the wrong note; so I should like to be sure this time that I strike the right one! Could you show me please any samples of 'messages'? I think I can give you what you want, if I know what you want. But I am rather a bungler at such matters.[3]

I should be pleased, incidentally, if you would occasionally review for the *Criterion*? And I should be much pleased if you would now and then indicate some book or books which you would be willing to treat.

Yours sincerely,
[T. S. Eliot]

TO *James Houghton Woods*[4]   CC

10 April 1930   [Faber & Faber Ltd]

Dear Professor Woods,

You will be surprised to hear from an old pupil and faithful student of Patanjali on the following subject. You must be surprised, first, that since

1–Kenneth Ingram (1882–1965), author and barrister, founded and edited *Green Quarterly* (The Society of SS Peter & Paul, Westminster House, London) in 1924. He wrote too for the *Anglo-Catholic Chronicle*. At a later date he was Vice-Chairman of the National Peace Council. His works include *Why I Believe* (1928) and *Has the Church Failed?* (1929).

2–Ingram asked on 9 Apr. whether TSE would 'be so kind as to send a message of greeting [to the Fourth Anglo-Catholic Congress, Royal Albert Hall, 29 June–6 July 1930.] Your message would appear in the Congress Daily Chronicle, which I have been asked to edit . . . Please say exactly what you think best, as I would much prefer that these messages were personal rather than formal. Your message should not exceed 500 words . . .'

3–Ingram thanked TSE for his 'Message' on 30 Apr.: 'It will do excellently and could not, I think, be improved.'

4–James Houghton Woods (1864–1935): Professor of Philosophy at Harvard, 1913–34; Chair of the Department of Philosophy and Psychology, 1914–16. He introduced courses in Indian philosophy, and his *Yoga System of Patanjali* (1914) was the first American scholarly

you lost sight of me I have become a director of a publishing firm (see above). Now, I have lately been in communication with a co-religionist of mine, A. E. Taylor, about a German book on Plato; in the course of which correspondence he recommended very strongly a book by one Prof. Werner Jaeger on Aristotle. I thereupon wrote to my old tutor Harold Joachim, who confirmed Taylor's opinion.

Now with men like Taylor and Joachim extolling this book (which I have myself only glanced at) I feel that my firm – which aims at respectability – the chairman being a fellow of All Souls – ought to publish an English translation if possible. What I want to ask you is (1) do you know the book (remember that I treasure in my library a copy of Meyer's Aristotle which you presented me) and (2) could you persuade the Harvard University Press to go into the publication with Faber & Faber Ltd.? If you do know the book (and you know most things) what do you think of it? And if you don't, do you still think that the Harvard Press would consider going in with us on a book which certainly, from the English end, is going to be a financial loss, but a gain in prestige. I could send you copies of Taylor's and Joachim's letters, which are extremely enthusiastic. I am sure that it is a great book. Also, if you wish, I can send you the book itself; but my belief in your omniscience is so strong that I am sure you must know the book already.

With most cordial wishes to Mrs Woods and yourself, and kind memories from my wife, and the tribute of your old pupil in the mysteries of Patanjali and Vachaspati Michra and Vijnana Bikshu[1] –

---

study of Indian philosophy. TSE studied Greek Philosophy with him in 1911–12, and 'Philosophical Sanskrit' in 1912–13. After TSE submitted his thesis, Woods told him he wanted to create a 'berth' for him in the Department. TSE recorded later that 'a year in the mazes of Patanjali's metaphysics under the guidance of James Woods left me in a state of enlightened mystification' (*ASG*, 40). TSE's notes on Woods's lectures in 1911–12 are in the Houghton Library.

1–TSE told M. S. S. Iyengar, 6 Mar. 1952: 'I only took up the study of Indian philosophy *seriously* during the period 1911–14, when at Harvard University. I worked on the elements of Sanskrit and Pali for two years with Professor C. R. Lanman, and on Sankhya philosophy with Professor J. H. Woods. Since that period I have never had the leisure to pursue these studies seriously, and have, indeed, lost all my slight proficiency in the languages. It was during this period that I read with Professor Lanman, the *Bhagavad-Gita*, some selected Upanishads in Sanskrit, as well as some of the Nikayas in Pali. I also read the *Sankhya-Bhasya-Karika* and commentary in Palanjali with Professor Woods. I have never written anything specifically about these studies.' And to Bandana Lahiri, 5 Sept. 1963: 'There are obviously certain Indian influences on my writing, at least on some of my poetry. I spent two years when in the Graduate School at Harvard studying Sanskrit and one year studying Pali. I read in Sanskrit the Maha Bharata, several of the Upanishads, especially I think those two short ones, the Katha and the Isha. I also read, and was thoroughly confused by, the

Bo Brahmana[1]
Yours sincerely,
[T. S. Eliot]

TO *Roy Campbell*   cc

10 April 1930   [Faber & Faber Ltd]

My dear Campbell,

This is to say that we still rely upon you to provide us with a pamphlet upon bullfighting sooner or later; we only fear that what your conscience will bring forth will be too highly technical and accomplished – for God's sake don't rely upon your local colleague too much, but say whatever comes into your head. I shall remind you of this from time to time.[2]

I congratulate you upon the 'advance' success of *Adamastor,* which promises well. If the book sells, I shall be more sanguine of the future of Britain. I never read modern verse, except when I put on my editorial mask to read what is 99% rubbish. I happened to read your 'Tristan da Cunha' out of curiosity because I had read a German poem on the same subject.[3] I am glad I did: I know that you are a poet; and I urged my firm to publish your book on the strength of that.[4] I am sure that you will

---

commentary of Patanjali on the Sankhya Bashya Kharika. I read these works with Professor Charles Rockwell Lanman, except the Patanjali which I read with Professor James Horton [*sic*] Woods. I also read several of the Buddhist scriptures, but only in the transliteration into the Latin alphabet.'

1 – Salutation to a Brahman or priest.

2 – Campbell had written (undated): 'I have neither the experience nor the material to write an interesting essay on the bullfights.' However, his wife had suggested he ask a friend, a retired toreador, to collaborate with him. In a further letter (n.d.) he wrote: 'I have only been in a public arena five times. This year I hope to get more experience . . . But I shall certainly try to do it.'

3 – Johannes Theodor Kuhlemann (1891–1939), 'Tristan da Cunha', *Der Strom* (1919), 23–6.

4 – Campbell replied: 'Few things have given me more pleasure and confidence than your last letter. A word of encouragement from you is worth far more to me than any other sort of notice I could get . . . [*Adamastor*] seems to have had many commercially-useful notices . . . My chief anxiety was about its worth as poetry and I could have wished for no greater reward for the work I have put into it for the last five years than that it should be favourably regarded by such a poet as you' (quoted, in part, in Alexander, *Roy Campbell*, 117). He wrote too: 'Your note to the *New Statesman* gave me more ambition than I had had previously, I think. (I was very depressed at that time about my work.)' He was referring to TSE's letter about Campbell's poem 'Tristan da Cunha', in *NS*, 22 Oct. 1927: see *L* 3. See too Jim McCue, 'Roy Campbell and The Dry Salvages', *Notes & Queries* 61: 1 (Mar. 2014), 121–3.

agree with me that if one wants to write verse oneself one should not read contemporary poetry. I should advise all beginners to avoid my own.[1]

With most cordial wishes to Mrs Campbell and yourself,

Yours ever sincerely,

[T. S. Eliot]

TO *Aldous Huxley*   cc

10 April 1930   [Faber & Faber Ltd]

My dear Aldous,

Many thanks for your letter, which was very disappointing.[2] I feel, and Morley, with whom I discussed the matter, that you have perhaps taken our Miscellany (in one sense) more seriously than it is meant. We mean it to be serious, to be primarily a vehicle for people to express their moral, political and even theological views *immediately*: that is to say, we should like you to write out your opinions and views of the moment without any reading or documentation. The ideal Miscellany Pamphlet would be written straight off in one afternoon without consulting any authorities. Do you understand? and will it make any difference?[3]

---

1 – Campbell replied: 'Few English poets have ever impressed their personality and genius on their generation as strongly as you have. I don't know if I would advise beginners *not* to read your work: they have to be pretty sturdy and independent intellectually not to be completely swallowed up by it for the time being.'

2 – Huxley, who had been 'living in a whirl of spirit-expending activity', said (22 Mar.) he found TSE's idea for a pamphlet on the Modern English Language 'a very interesting one. My only objection is that it's so interesting that it would involve me in an enormous amount of reading and writing – more than I could permit myself with all that I have to do and want to do and have embarked on doing at the moment' (*Letters of Aldous Huxley*, ed. Grover Smith [1969], 333).

3 – FVM told Francis P. Miller on 8 May 1936, of the Criterion Miscellany venture:

'When I joined Faber seven years ago, we were faced with the task of starting a new publisher's imprint, to rise out of the ashes of an older one (Faber & Gwyer). We had a first rate editorial equipment, but very little else; none too much capital, and a few, but not many, valuable authors and titles. We wanted to begin publishing in the Spring 1929, but due to protracted negotiations about the transformation from Faber & Gwyer, we had nothing particularly with which to make our bow. What we wanted to do was to impress upon an apathetic world that ours was going to be an intelligent and lively imprint; and to that end, primarily for the publicity and not for profit, I suggested pamphlets. There was great merit in the suggestion for us at that particular time. We could get out pamphlets quickly; they were cheap to give away and provided good advertisement; and many well known authors, who would have been beyond our reach for their regular books, were pleased to champion various causes in pamphlet form. Because we had a number of very good names on the pamphlets, booksellers backed us up fairly well. Our means of distribution was

It will make a difference to the opinion of me held by my directors, if I cannot entice you –

Alternatively, I have a suggestion which is entirely my own, but which was acclaimed. It is that you should write – in the same spongetaneous [*sic*] way – an essay of 10,000 words or so on Lawrence qua Poet, for the Poets on the Poets Series. I believe I gave you a copy of my *Dante* in that series. I wrote that very rapidly, only verifying my quotations; and I believe that what [*line missing*] suggest treating Lawrence's verse and ignoring his prose; but one could treat Lawrence as a *poet*, through all his work. Cape have already published a biography of Lawrence, but I believe inferior and hurried. An essay by you would do his memory more benefit than anything I can think of.[1]

I believe I gave you a copy of my *Dante*? If not, I will send you one.[2] But in this series, the whole point is that the author should care about his subject and deal with it exactly as he pleases. I really am most keen about this; even more than about getting you to write a pamphlet; so I do hope you will consider it and write to me as soon as ever you can.

With best wishes to you and Maria from Vivienne and me,

Yours ever,

[Tom]

---

almost entirely the bookshops, which was what we wanted. We were, as you see, really more concerned with attracting attention and goodwill in the Book Trade than with looking for other means of distribution.

'Now we soon found out that names count more with the Book Trade than anything else; and that topical subjects, even if handled exceptionally well, didn't sell unless the author's name was known; and that of topical subjects anything in the field of economics was apt to come out worst. That was round about 1929 and 1930 . . . But by and large, a pamphlet by D. H. Lawrence would sell very well, and a pamphlet on economics would be a plug.

'We made our impact, and we stopped when the going was good; that's to say, when we had skimmed the cream of available authors. We had the benefit of being imitated by other publishers, some of whom went on flogging the idea after booksellers were bored with it. We never made any dramatic statement that our series was ended, for some time we may wish to revive or add to it; but having achieved the contacts and made the impression we wanted, we went on to our more general object of book publishing. There is no more editorial work about full size books than there is about pamphlets. I didn't regard pamphlets as being a lasting or lucrative field. I did regard them as having novelty at that time and as being very convenient for us; for, as I say, we had editorial power to burn, and had a jump in that way on rivals who, in every other way, were much better off than we were.'

1–Huxley regretted (24 Apr.) he could not write on DHL's poetry for two reasons: (i) he was 'contracted exclusively' to Chatto (UK) and Doran (USA); (ii) 'I don't really like a great deal of D.H.L.'s poetry, which seems to me insufficiently organized artistically – rather the raw material of poetry (the most astonishing raw material very often) than poetry itself' (*Letters*, 334).

2–Huxley said (24 Apr.) he 'liked' TSE's *Dante* 'for being so much to the point & saying such a lot in so small a compass'.

TO *C. K. Ogden*[1]   [Berg]/cc

11 April 1930   [Faber & Faber Ltd]

Dear Ogden,

You will remember when we last met I made the suggestion that if Joyce's records were marketed in time we might insert a slip advertising them in *Anna Livia Plurabelle*.[2] Since then I have a letter from Stuart Gilbert proposing that we should announce that these records can be obtained from you, so I am writing to you now to ask what the situation is.[3]

First, are you dealing with these records yourself or does H.M.V. take any responsibility for them. The point is that I feel that H.M.V. ought to pay us for the printing and insertion of such a slip. In this case you will understand that there is no reciprocal advertisement to be gained: the slip may help to sell the record but unless H.M.V. do some advertising on their own, the record will not help to sell the pamphlet.

Furthermore I have no particulars about the number or the price.[4]

Yours ever,

[T. S. Eliot]

1–C. K. Ogden (1889–1957), psychologist, linguist, polymath, was educated at Magdalene College, Cambridge, where in 1912 he founded *Cambridge Magazine* and co-founded (1911) the Heretics. He went on to devise 'Basic English' – 'an auxiliary international language' based on a vocabulary of just 850 English words – 'BASIC' being an acronym for British American Scientific International Commercial; and in 1927 he established in London the Orthological (Basic English) Institute. Works include *The Foundations of Aesthetics* (with IAR and James Wood, 1921), *The Meaning of Meaning* (with IAR, 1923), *Basic English* (1930); and with F. P. Ramsey he translated the *Logisch-Philosophische Abhandlung* of Ludwig Wittgenstein (*Tractatus Logico-Philosophicus*, 1922). He was editor of the psychological journal *Psyche*, and he edited the series 'The International Library of Psychology, Philosophy and Scientific Method'. See W. Terrence Gordon, *C. K. Ogden: a bio-bibliographical study* (1990); *C. K. Ogden: A Collective Memoir*, ed. P. Sargant Florence and J. R. L. Anderson (1977)
2–*Anna Livia Plurabelle* was to be published as Criterion Miscellany 15 (1930). See also Gordon Bowker, 'Joyce in England', *James Joyce Quarterly* 48: 4 (Summer 2011), 667–81.
3–In due course, a note was printed, at Ogden's expense, to be slipped into each copy of *ALP*:
'Mr Joyce's own reading of the last four pages of *Anna Livia Plurabelle* has been recorded on a 12 inch double-sided Gramophone Record, which is obtainable (price Two Guineas) from
'The Orthological Institute, 10 King's Parade, Cambridge.'
4–Ogden replied on 22 Apr., 'The Joyce record is a private one & nothing to do with H.M.V. (except that one of their studios was used for the recording).
'If there are ever any profits Joyce gets 50% & the Orthological Institute the rest . . .
'I should be very glad to pay for the printing of the slip.
'As to advertising – the hearing of the record will create a certain demand for the book presumably.'

TO *J. M. Barrie*   CC

11 April 1930   [Faber & Faber Ltd]

Dear Sir James Barrie,

Thank you for your letter of the 21st March which I ought to have answered before. I am really very deeply disappointed that you cannot write a notice and am sorry to learn the reason for your inability. I hope that your health is improving.[1]

I have not yet heard anything further from Mrs Whibley, about either her husband's work or Henley's but when I do I will take the liberty of consulting you.

Yours sincerely,
[T. S. Eliot]

TO *Gerard Hopkins*[2]   CC

11 April 1930   [Faber & Faber Ltd]

Dear Mr Hopkins,

I must apologise for having been so busy that I have not yet answered your letter of 31st March. However I have seen Wilson Knight a day or two ago and I think that the matter is settled. I do not propose to use the Hamlet article in the next number for the reason that I have had to keep space for a Shakespeare article by Dover Wilson; and I have explained this to Knight.[3]

---

1 – Barrie had replied to TSE's approach of 19 Mar.: 'Thank you for your letter about Charles Whibley who was indeed one of my most loved friends. I am not able unfortunately to write the article you kindly suggest to me, as I am not in a condition to do anything of the kind at present, but I trust you will get a better hand and indeed unless you do it in Blackwood's I wish you would do it yourself. I am going off to the sea on Monday and will not be in London except once for an hour or two for a fortnight, but any time thereafter that you care to see me to discuss such affairs as you mention I shall be much at your service.'

2 – Gerard Hopkins (1892–1961): publisher and translator. A nephew of Gerard Manley Hopkins – whose poetry, letters and diaries he would put into print – he was educated at Balliol College, Oxford (where he was president of OUDS), and won the Military Cross during WW1. In 1919 he joined Oxford University Press, serving as publicity manager and later editorial adviser. He became well known for his prodigious feats of translation: his output included vols 7–27 of Jules Romain's *Men of Good Will*; biographies by André Maurois; Proust's *Jean Santeuil*; memoirs, broadcasts, plays. He was made Chevalier de la Légion d'Honneur, 1951.

3 – Hopkins wrote (31 Mar.): 'I have just heard from Mr G. Wilson Knight on a matter about which he is shy of approaching you himself. He tells me that his Hamlet article is not in the current *Criterion*, and rather wants to know whether you propose to use it in the next number.'

I have another matter I should like to bother you about. An Irishman named Seán Ó'Faoláin[1] has been working for several years on a collection of old Irish verse which I believe (but am not sure) he would like to publish with text and parallel translation.[2] I have not seen this work and should not be competent to judge it; but I have seen a very interesting essay which he has written on early Irish Poetry. I believe that he knows Robin Flower, the Celtic expert at the Museum,[3] who is probably as good a man as anyone to advise about the value of the book. When he mentioned the book to me it struck me that it was more a University Press book than one for a private publisher, and so I volunteered to give him an introduction to you. His address is 51 Queen's Road, Richmond, Surrey, and you will probably hear from him.[4]

Sincerely yours,
[T. S. Eliot]

TO *W. H. Wagstaff*   CC

11 April 1930   [Faber & Faber Ltd]

Dear Sir,

I must apologise for my rudeness in not answering immediately your kind letter of the 2nd of March and the following letter which I have unfortunately mislaid. I have been extremely busy with private affairs the last few weeks and I am afraid have neglected everything else. I must

1 – Seán Ó'Faoláin (1900–91): Irish novelist and short story writer: see TSE to Ó'Faoláin, 31 Dec. 1930, below.
2 – Ó'Faoláin told TSE on 3 Feb. 1929 that he was gathering up the 'only corpus of material in Irish that is beautiful enough in itself to be worth study': 'I have collected from learned and semi-learned journals and from published volumes all the noteworthy lyrics written in Irish between *c.* 700 and 1400 AD . . . I have put the Gaelic on one side and the English on the other, and prepared notes where necessary. It is hoped that Irish students of the older language will find here, collected for the first time, material for sane judgement on the product of the traditions we so belaud.'
3 – Robin Flower, 'Bláithin' (1881–1946), was Deputy Keeper of Manuscripts, British Museum, 1929–44; Hon. Lecturer in Celtic, University College, London; Chairman of Council, Irish Texts Society; Hon. Acting Director, Early English Text Society. A poet and translator, his works include *Ireland and Medieval Europe* (1927), *Catalogue of Irish Manuscripts in the British Museum*, vol. 2 (1928), and a translation of *The Islandman*, by Tomás Ó Criomthain (1934).
4 – *Old Irish Lyrics* was rejected by OUP on 12 Aug. 1930: letter from Charles Williams to TSE.

express my regret at having been unable to attend my admission on the 9th instant and add my apologies.[1]

I remember the tenor of the letter but not the exact contents. Would you be so kind as to let me know what the fee due from me is as I have forgotten.

With many apologies,

> I am,
> Yours very truly,
> [T. S. Eliot]

TO *Norman Foerster*[2]   CC

14 April 1930   [Faber & Faber Ltd]

Dear Mr Foerster,

I have to apologise to you under so many different headings that I really cannot remember them all. First you asked me to revise my manuscript

---

1–On 7 Mar. 1930, W. H. Wagstaff, Hon. Secretary of The Royal Society of Literature, advised TSE: 'I have the honour to inform you that you have been elected a Fellow of this Society. I shall be pleased to receive a cheque for £5. 5. o (being Two Guineas annual subscription and three Guineas Entrance fee) at your convenience . . . The next "admission" of Fellows will take place on April 9th . . .' Three days later, having recalled that TSE was to be a contributor to *The Eighteen-Eighties* (ed. de la Mare), he wrote: 'It would be in accordance with the Council's practice for the entrance fee to be waived in this case.'

TSE explained, in a note of 7 Nov. 1960 penned in his copy of *The Eighteen-Eighties*: 'Walter de la Mare invited me to contribute to this book. Then he discovered that the contributors were expected to be F.R.S.L. so I became an F.R.S.L. for the occasion. I read this paper at a meeting of the R.S.L. with Dean Inge in the chair (a good chairman, nearly stone deaf). I received £7. 7. o in payment. The annual dues to the R.S.L. were one guinea, so after 7 years I resigned' (TSE Library).

2–Norman Foerster (1887–1972) – he was a contemporary of TSE's at Harvard, though they did not meet there – taught at the University of North Carolina, Chapel Hill; then as Director of the School of Letters, University of Iowa, 1930–44. See Robert Falk and Robert E. Lee, 'In Memoriam: Norman Foerster 1887–1972', *American Literature* 44 (Jan. 1972), 679–80; J. David Hoeveler Jr., *The New Humanism: A Critique of Modern America, 1900–1940* (1977).

TSE wrote in 'American Critics', *TLS*, 10 Jan. 1929 – a review of *The Reinterpretation of American Literature,* ed. Foerster – 'Mr Norman Foerster is one of the most brilliant of Mr Babbitt's disciples, and one of those nearest to the master. His recent work, *American Criticism* . . . contains, besides much sound criticism, an authoritative exposition of the "New Humanism".' He would characterise Foerster, in *Thoughts after Lambeth* (1931), as 'the fugleman of Humanism. Mr Foerster, who has the honest simplicity to admit that he has very little acquaintance with Christianity beyond a narrow Protestantism which he repudiates, offers Humanism because it appeals to those "who can find in themselves no vocation for spiritual humility"! without perceiving at all that this is an exact parallel to

which I should very much like to have done as I thought that your and Elliott's criticisms were quite valid.[1] Secondly you asked me to supply a photograph which I failed to do having none. Third you send me your essay which I should have liked to print but did not have room for within the time limit, so I am returning it with apologies.

I like the book much better than I expected. If I may say so I think you have managed very well both as introducer and chooser. I was particularly struck by Elliott's essay.[2] I am having the copy reviewed by P. S. Richards[3] who is an English friend of More's.

I was very much incensed, by the way, by the *Bookman*'s recent editorial interpretation of my attitude towards Babbitt.

I like my own essay in the book not at all, but it was written under great difficulties and should have been both revised and expanded.

Hoping to hear from you again.

Yours sincerely,
[T. S. Eliot]

saying that Companionate Marriage "appeals to those who can find in themselves no vocation for spiritual continence" . . . One can now be a distinguished professor, and a professional moralist to boot, without understanding the devotional sense of the word *vocation* or the theological sense of the virtue *humility;* a virtue, indeed, not conspicuous among modern men of letters' (*SE*, 359–60).

1–Foerster had cited G. R. Elliott's comments on TSE's essay 'Humanism without Religion' in a letter of 31 Aug. 1929, as follows: 'I think Eliot's spritely skit is very valuable for our book, for purposes of comparison and contrast with the others. I agree with about 51 per cent of what he says; that is about the average of agreement we may expect among contributors. I should be glad if you could induce him to clarify and enlarge it a bit in passages; see my pencillings. I should like Philistines-of-intelligence to understand more easily his points. If only he would say soon and plainly that what HE means by humanism is Balance, that would make the piece easier reading. – You may pass on to him the foregoing, as from a fellow (semi?) anglo-catholic.'

Foerster went on in his letter of 31 Aug.: 'I agree with Elliott in his pencillings. Page 2, the paragraph beginning "For there is no doubt" is marked "Connection of ideas not clear enough." Page 4, paragraph beginning "I have already said" is marked "This sentence [last of the paragraph] should either be omitted or made coherent with what precedes." Page 4, next paragraph, sentence beginning "Yet in surrendering" is marked "Can you not *expand* this sentence? The reader does not find its point self-sufficient." These are the only comments of moment, but I agree that revision and clarification for the plain reader (say the reader of the *Forum* rather than the *Criterion*) would be desirable throughout.' Foerster hoped that TSE might 'get up a revised and somewhat amplified copy', and forego any reading of the proof.

2–G. R. Elliott, 'The Pride of Modernity', *Humanism and America*, 75–104.

3–Philip S. Richards, review of *Humanism and America*, C. 9 (July 1930), 744–7.

15 April 1930   [Faber & Faber Ltd]

My dear Thorold,

Thank you for your letter.[1] I should certainly be pleased to leave myself in Hague's hands.[2] I will see that he is sent review copies of *Anabasis* and of my new poems as soon as they appear. I was very much interested by the note on *Who Moved the Stone?* in the *Dublin* and wondered who had written it.[3] I like your new number. I was particularly struck by Alfred Noyes who seems to me much better as a theological controversialist than as a poet.[4] The article by Sir James Marchant is extremely interesting, but if he is not a Roman Catholic himself I wholly fail to appreciate his point of view.[5]

I shall be very much interested to know that the success of reducing your price is maintained; as if so it will be an example for us to ponder.[6]

1–Thorold wrote on 11 Apr.: 'I am meditating an article on your Poetry . . . and I think of letting René Hague try to do his best. He is a very sincere admirer; I think, and would be disciple.'

2–See review by René Hague of *Dante*, in *Dublin Review* 186: 372 (Jan.–June 1930), 173–5: 'Mr Eliot's essay is an exhibition of that pelican-like digestion which assimilates the beautiful and disgorges it again for the delight of his readers. So does he at once feed his own mind and produce poetry at the same time. This is what the book *shows* throughout, but particularly in one striking passage, where Mr Eliot quotes and translates that passage from the *Purgatorio* ("*esce di mano a lui, che la vagheggia Prima die sia . . . l'anima semplicetta*") which was presumably the inspiration of, and regurgitated in, his own *Animula*. Such points are the most exciting parts in his book, as they are a considerable aid to the appreciation of his poetry.'

3–H. J. C., 'Some Recent Books', *Dublin Review*, 373 (Apr. 1930), 347–50. 'The usual arguments for the truth of the Resurrection – the empty tomb, the early history in Acts, the witness of St Paul – are urged with particular freshness and strength, and the author insists forcibly on the point that the first preaching and conversions were not in Galilee, but at Jerusalem where the evidence was at hand if the Apostles' story was false. There is a great deal to learn from this very lively and confident study, and it ought to help dry-as-dust critics to a vivid realization of the Gospel records as straightforward and unharmonised witnesses' (350).

4–Noyes, 'The Unguarded Statement', ibid., 199–216.

5–James Marchant, 'The Spiritual Pilgrim', 177–98 – on the Anglican Church as the 'Bridge Church' ('A bridge is not an abiding place. To some Anglicans, and their numbers increase, the Canterbury bridge has borne them across disturbed waters to secure safety and peace at the last in the holy city of their souls') – on Vernon Johnson, *One Lord, One Faith*; Eric Milner-White and Wilfred L. Knox, *One God and Father of All*; Ronald A. Knox, *A Spiritual Æneid*; Robert Hugh Benson, *Confessions of a Convert*; and *The Future of the Church of England*, by various writers.

6–'I know you will be glad to know that the Jan. no at the reduced price [3/6d] sold as never before in the memory of man. If we can only keep this up, we shall turn the corner.'

I expect to go away for a few weeks after Easter but if you are at home in May do come up to town and lunch with me one Wednesday.

Yours ever,

[T. S. Eliot]

P.S. I think the simplest way is for us to send review copies of these two books to the *Dublin Review* for you to give to Hague. One appears on the 29th of this month and the other on the 20th May. If that is too late please let me know.

TO *Marguerite Caetani*   CC

15 April 1930   [Faber & Faber Ltd]

Dear Marguerite,

Please forgive me for not answering your letter of March 5th and thereby causing you to write again. I have been extremely busy and confused myself. We have been moving again but we move so often that it is not safe to write to me at any other address than 24 Russell Square. I hope you are now well settled. My brother-in-law who has just married an American girl is supposed to be settling in Rome but I do not know when he will be there as his wife is ill with appendicitis in Genoa at the moment. You did promise yourself to come to England this Easter but I suppose that you will have to remain in Rome at least until the hot weather. I wish you would send me a photograph of your new Villa.[1]

I was very glad to see Léger although it was a very brief and hurried visit and I do not suppose that he will be in London any more as his conference appears to have faded out.[2] He looked extremely tired when I saw him. About the two points that you ask me.[3] I think it would be better to stick to Read for the whole of the Traherne arrangement. After all that is not a question of digging out any rare or unpublished material but merely of making a selection from the Century's and writing a short explanatory preface.

1–The Caetani family moved on 6 Mar. into Palazzo Caetani, 32 Via Botteghe Oscure, Rome.
2–'Léger told me he was so happy to have seen you,' said Caetani (27 Mar.).
3–Caetani asked on 5 Mar., 'Now for Traherne and Read and Hayward. Wouldn't it be rather queer to ask Hayward to look up texts and not ask him also to make the short preface and the choice? Thinking this I have written neither to one nor the other. Please advise me. You see I don't want an important essay, but a short introduction for French readers to make them understand the rare and exquisite quality of Traherne, of his life and the poetry of his prose.' On 27 Mar. she asked again 'what to do in regard to Read once we ask Hayward to look up texts[?]'

As for Hayward if you have anything else in mind, or even if you have not, you could write to him and find out if he had any suggestions himself of things in which he is interested. He would really be a very good man for the work you had in mind. I believe I gave you the address of both of these men. I will write to you again as soon as I can. We shall probably go away to the seaside for a few weeks after Easter. Perhaps I shall have some time then.

Yours ever affectionately,

[Tom]

TO *John Gould Fletcher*[1]   CC

15 April 1930   [The Criterion]

Dear Fletcher,

Many thanks for the notice of Ludwig's *Lincoln*.[2] I am particularly glad to have it as I have seen one or two really favourable reviews of that abominable charlatan. I should have explained that all I wanted from you about the Maritain book was a short note; all that is really necessary is to mention its existence and say that the translation is better than that of the other text – if it is better.[3] I sent the only copy of *Humanism in America* that I had to P. S. Richards to try him out on and that is why I had only a set of galley proofs to send you. I am not particularly keen that the book should have any notoriety because I think that my own contribution is a very poor one.

I am probably going away for a few weeks after Easter and until then I am very rushed, but I hope you will be in town during May and can come and lunch with me.

Yours ever,

[T. S. Eliot]

1 – John Gould Fletcher (1886–1950), American poet and critic: see Biographical Register.
2 – Untitled review of Emil Ludwig, *Lincoln*, in C. 9 (July 1930), 737–9.
3 – Fletcher noted (10 Apr.) that he had reviewed Maritain's *Scholasticism and Art* 'some time ago', so it did 'not require more than a few lines to point out the merits of the new translation'.

16 April 1930   [Faber & Faber Ltd]

My dear Curtius,

This is to remind you that I hope very much indeed that you will be able to let me have some reviews [*sic*] of Read's book *The Sense of Glory* in time for our next number. We really ought to have it by May 1st., because if you write it in German, we shall need a few days for the translation. But rather than not have it at all, I would keep the reviews back for a few days longer. Please do send me a line to let me know to expect.[1]

I have had sent to you a copy of *Our Present Philosophy of Life*, because I thought that the book might interest you. If you have time to read it, I shall be very glad if you will let me know whether you think it possible that some German Publisher might be interested in arranging for a translation.

I must apologise for the fact that for some time the *Criterion* was sent to your old address, and hope that you are now receiving the *Criterion* regularly.[2] I am sending you under separate cover a copy of my very small book of Verse in *hommage* to the translator of one of these pieces.[3]

> Yours ever,
> [T. S. Eliot]

TO *H. P. Collins*[4]   CC

16 April 1930   [Faber & Faber Ltd]

Dear Mr Collins,

It is now several years that we have been trying vainly to meet.[5] I am very glad to hear from you yourself and to learn that you are improving.

---

1 – Curtius did not review HR's book. 'I ask you to be patient,' he wrote on 1 May.
2 – Curtius had recently moved to Bonn.
3 – *Ash-Wednesday* (published 24 Apr. 1930). Curtius had translated 'Perch' Io non Spero'.
4 – Harold Poulton Collins (1899–1985): English editor and critic; TSE recommended Collins on 16 Jan. 1953 (for an unknown opening): 'Mr H. P. Collins was for some years a valued contributor to the *Criterion* under my editorship, and not only offered articles for my use, but was extremely helpful in reviewing books. I always had the most satisfactory relations with him and can recommend him warmly for careful and conscientious work. I think that he would be very efficient also in other kinds of editorial assistance.'
5 – Collins had written on 11 Apr. that he was still quite unwell: he 'had in fact nearly three months successively in bed', and was still 'not equal to any work'. He went on: 'I had written part of a little book on contemporary criticism and could easily finish it if I was a little better.'

I hope that when you are able to get about one of your first attempts will be to let me see you.

I am delighted to know that you are interested in the questions you mention. May I express the hope that you will succeed in finishing your book and that you will let Faber & Faber see it before you show it to any other publisher.

With all best wishes for your recovery.

Yours sincerely,
[T. S. Eliot]

TO *Douglas Goldring* CC

16 April 1930   [Faber & Faber Ltd]

Dear Goldring,

We have talked over the question of your Memoirs;[1] and while we feel that there are extremely interesting possibilities in your outline, we cannot say that this is enough to justify our making any arrangements or suggestions. Is it likely that you will be working upon the book in the near future, because if you are, we should be very much interested to see any parts of it that you like.

I have been very much occupied lately, and am trying to get away for a brief holiday after Easter. When I return I will write to you again and fix up for lunch.

Yours sincerely,
[T. S. Eliot]

1 – Goldring had enquired on 27 Mar. about his memoirs, to be called *Odd Man Out*. The volume was ultimately to be published by Chapman and Hall, 1935.

TO *Alfred Kreymborg*[1]   CC

17 April 1930[2]   [Faber & Faber Ltd]

Dear Kreymborg,

It is indeed a very long time since we have had any correspondence, and your letter was very welcome.[3] I am too busy to write about all things thereof, and I hope that you may possibly take another Marionnette tour through Europe, but I am afraid that there is small chance of my coming over to New York in the near future.

Certainly use the Poems you mention. My only possible objection is that all date from what I now call my youth, and I should be rather pleased if you agree to put in something that I have written more recently.[4] My only general prohibition is that I never allow Anthology use of THE WASTE LAND either in whole or in part.

I usually say a guinea or five dollars per poem, but if this is too much for the funds at your disposal, please let me know, and I will try to be accommodating.

Yours very cordially,
[T. S. Eliot]

TO *Charles Harris*   CC

17 April 1930   [Faber & Faber Ltd]

Dear Harris,

I have kept your confidential memorandum so long that I feel I ought to return it although my suggestions are by no means exhausted. I enclose

---

1 – Alfred Kreymborg (1883–1966): poet, playwright, puppeteer (who also supported himself for some years as a professional chess-player). His works include *Puppet Plays* (1923) – which TSE found fascinating – and *Lima Beans* (1925); and *Troubador* (1925), which includes an account of his meetings with TSE in London. In 1915–19 he edited *Others* (which published TSE's 'Portrait of a Lady') – see Suzanne Churchill, *The Little Magazine Others and the Renovation of American Poetry* (2006) – and he would become co-editor, with Van Wyck Brooks, Lewis Munford and Paul Rosenfeld, of *American Caravan*, an annual anthology of new writing.
2 – There are two letters to Kreymborg dated 17 April. They differ slightly but only in one or two words.
3 – Kreymborg wrote on 2 Mar. to request permission to print in a 'supplementary anthology' (no title given) – 'to be used as a cross-reference' to a recent survey of American poetry that he had also edited, entitled *Our Singing Strength* (which included an 'inadequate chapter' on TSE himself) – these poems: 'Portrait of a Lady', 'The Hippopotamus', 'Preludes' and 'Gerontion'.
4 – Kreymborg agreed (6 Aug.) to use 'Salutation'.

also one page of notes, but I should not like you to accept any of my suggestions without confirming their value in other quarters. I shall have other suggestions to make about America. I think that a cousin of mine, S. E. Morison, who is Professor of American History at Harvard, and I think a high Churchman, might be very helpful about the early history of Puritanism in America. In fact, I am sure that he will be very valuable.

Paul Elmer More is an American of great authority, and with strong sympathies. I should like to see John Dewey[1] as a contributor. I think I can certainly put you in touch with the best Unitarians. I am extremely sceptical about Vida Scudder; she is a sentimental old lay preacher in the guise of a Professor of English Literature.[2] E. K. Rand,[3] Chandler Post,[4] and Ralph Cran[5] are all first class. I am not sure that there is not some better authority on Buddhism than Burlingame.[6] Sylvain Levi of the Sorbonne,[7] if he is still living, is the greatest authority but Irving Babbitt is also very good.

This is all I have to write at the moment, but I hope that we can meet early in the summer and discuss the matter further.

Yours very sincerely,
[T. S. Eliot]

---

1 – John Dewey (1859–1952): philosopher, psychologist, educator, pragmatist.
2 – Vida Scudder (1861–1954), writer, professor, Christian socialist and activist, joined in 1888 the Companions of the Holy Cross, a group of Episcopalian women dedicated to prayer and intercession (many of her writings seek to reconcile the ideals of St Francis of Assisi and Marx). She taught from 1887 at Wellesley College, and was promoted to full professor in 1910. Her works include *Saint Catherine of Siena as Seen in Her Letters* (1905) and *The Franciscan Adventure: A Study in the First Hundred Years of the Order of St Francis of Assisi* (1931).
3 – E. K. Rand (1871–1945): classicist and medievalist; Professor of Latin, Harvard University, from 1909; Pope Professor of Latin, 1931–42; founder of the Mediaeval Academy of America, 1925; author of *Ovid and His Influence* (1925); *Studies in the Script of Tours* (2 vols, 1929–34); *The Building of Eternal Rome* (Lowell Lectures, 1943)
4 – Chandler Post (1881–1959): Professor of Greek and Fine Arts, Harvard, 1922–34; Boardman Professor of Fine Arts, 1934–50. Works include *A History of European and American Sculpture* (1921) and *A History of Spanish Painting* (12 vols, 1930–47).
5 – Unidentified, possibly Ronald Crane (1886–1967) of the University of Chicago.
6 – Eugene Watson Burlingame (1876–1932): author of *Buddhist Parables* (1922).
7 – Sylvain Lévi (1863–1935), orientalist and indologist, taught Sanskrit at the Sorbonne, 1889–94, and was Professor at the Collège de France, 1894–1935; President of the Société asiatique, 1929; author of *La Doctrine du sacrifice dans les Brâhmanas* (1898), *Hôbôgirin: Dictionnaire du Bouddhisme d'après les sources chinoises and japonaises* (with Takakusu Junjiro, 1929).

TO *W. H. Wagstaff*   CC

21 April 1930   [Faber & Faber Ltd]

Dear Sir,

Thank you for your letter of the 15th instant.[1] I was uncertain until now which sum I should pay, as I was uncertain whether I should be able to complete my essay in time.

I now send my cheque for two guineas, with apologies for the delay.

Yours very truly,
[T. S. Eliot]

TO *Walter de la Mare*   CC

21 April 1930   [Faber & Faber Ltd]

Dear De la Mare,

Here is my contribution. I fear that it is too short, also that everything I have said has been said before; and am thoroughly dissatisfied with it. Also, if you use it, you may prefer to change the title, if you can think of a more attractive one.

But if you do use it will you let me know; and also please say again *before* what date I may publish it in America?

I hope you like the production of *Desert Islands*.[2] It seems to me admirable.

Yours sincerely,
[T. S. Eliot]

TO *Hugh Macdonald*   MS Williamson

22 April 1930   *The Criterion*

Dear Macdonald,

The enclosed is much shorter than I expected it to be, but I have been short of wit lately. If it won't do at this length, let me know, but if it will,

1 – Wagstaff explained that new Fellows of the Royal Society of Literature normally paid an entrance fee of three guineas in addition to the annual subscription of two guineas; but in the case of contributors to the forthcoming volume on the 1880s, the entrance fee was waived.

Wagstaff later asked (1 July) whether TSE would be able to read his paper on Pater at 5.15 on 22 Oct. The proof of 'The Place of Pater' was sent out to TSE on 24 June 1930.

2 – De la Mare's *Desert Islands and Robinson Crusoe*, with decorations by Rex Whistler (F&F, 1930).

then I think we should revise the price, as what I had in mind when we settled the price was about 15 of these pages.[1]

I shall be going away for a fortnight at the beginning of next week, so if you can let me hear from you before then.

Yours always sincerely,
T. S. Eliot

TO *Arnold Pinchard*[2]   CC

22 April 1930   [Faber & Faber Ltd]

Dear Sir,

I send you the enclosed application form, (together with my cheque for five guineas) at the instance of Prebendary Harris. He told me that you would be so good as to second the nomination (possibly he has explained the matter to you); but if you do not feel disposed to do so, as you do not know me, I am sure that Fr. Underhill, or Fr. Whitby would be quite willing to give their names.

Yours faithfully,
[T. S. Eliot]

TO *A. L. Rowse*   TS Exeter

23 April 1930   *The Criterion*

Dear Rowse,

Thank you very much for your letter.[3] This is not a proper answer to it as I am in a great hurry and am going away for a fortnight at the end of

---

1 – TSE's typescript ran to just over eight pages, and it broke off abruptly. Macdonald responded the next day: 'I like it very much . . . I don't suggest that you shall add to it, but as the poems are also short we shall have to bring out the book at a smaller price than we had anticipated. This does, from your point of view, affect the question of the payment to you. The last thing we wish is to be mean but if you will accept less than the arranged amount it will make matters easier for us.'

2 – The Revd Arnold Pinchard (d. 1934), who was ordained in 1886, had been Secretary since 1920 of the English Church Union; editor of *The Religious Life* (1934).

3 – ALR wrote on Good Friday that he expected to finish off his book *Politics and the Younger Generation* in a month's time. 'It is proletarian, socialist, in some ways puritan, in other ways amoral and of course, without religious belief. I don't suppose you will care for the mixture. But I want to send it to you all the same: if Faber would care to publish it, I'd like him to, if he could manage it at once. If he doesn't, there is another publisher who asked me about it, who probably would.' The catalogue blurb for *Politics and the Younger*

the week. This is merely to say that we should very much like to have a chance to publish *Politics of [sic] the Younger Generation*. Unfortunately there is only one other director on hand at the moment, so that we cannot discuss it properly. But I will leave your letter to be brought up at the next week's Book Committee and will ask that in my absence one of the directors should write to you. I cannot say myself, as that is not my department, how soon we would publish such a book on receipt of the manuscript. But *a priori* I cannot see any particular reason why a book of this sort should have to be squeezed in to the usual publishing season. But please give us a chance to write to you about it before you make any engagement elsewhere. I am afraid that your article will be too late for the June *Criterion*, so may I have it for the September number, and the earlier the better so far as I am concerned. I shall write to your other matters later.

> In haste,
> Yours ever,
> T. S. Eliot

TO *Hugh Macdonald*   TS Williamson

23 April 1930   *The Criterion*

Dear Macdonald,

Thank you for your letter. Personally, I should prefer to see a cheaper book, though of course it will be much less profitable. As you probably expected (as I did) that my preface would run to 15 or 18 pages, shall we halve the fee and call it fifteen guineas instead of thirty? With my right to republish at the end of two years or when your edition is sold out, whichever date be the earlier.[1]

Generation (F&F, 1931) reads: 'This book is a re-statement of Socialistic principles and policy. Mr Rowse believes that the Labour movement in this country is in need of fresh constructive thinking.' ALR wrote later: 'Youthful books on politics are not much good, and mine was no exception. Eliot was encouraging, took it seriously and published it – I can't think now why he did. Pushing me into literature would have been better, though it may have been that, from the publisher's point of view, there were plenty of promising young writers; few enough to write intelligently about politics – certainly not from a Marxist point of view' (*A Man of the Thirties* [1979], 39).

1 – Macdonald responded to this letter on 24 Apr.: 'I enclose a cheque for 15 guineas. I think you have been too generous now. If we find we make any real profit on the book we will pay you, say, another £5 . . . We agree to your right to republish the essay at the end of two years or when our edition is sold out whichever date be the earlier.'

Yours in haste,
T. S. Eliot.

P.S. I am inclined to think that the Killigrew Ode was rather a reversion; but I cannot remember at the moment in what year it was supposed to be written.[1]

TO *Caroline Gordon*[2]   cc

23 April 1930   [*The Criterion*]

Dear Mrs Tate,

I must apologise for having kept your story so long.[3] I found it very interesting myself but am doubtful whether the ordinary *Criterion* reader would be able to make much of it. But I should very much like to see more of your work.

Yours sincerely,
[T. S. Eliot]

TO *C. A. Siepmann*   ts BBC

24 April 1930   Faber & Faber Ltd

Dear Mr Siepmann,

Thank you very much for your letter of the 17th April.[4] It is very kind of you to express such appreciation. I cannot help wishing that you had heard all of my talks so that you could give me a candid opinion of the delivery as well as the matter.

It seems to me that you do everything possible to help your speakers and I have not the slightest suggestion to make.

1–Macdonald liked TSE's talks on Dryden (23 Apr.). 'I suppose Dryden's Ode to the Memory of Anne Killigrew is in parts metaphysical? . . . I haven't the date of the poem in my memory. But if it was late it must have been a return by him to a style he had thrown over early.'

2–Caroline Gordon (1895–1961), American novelist, first wife of the poet and critic Allen Tate.

3–Gordon pointed out on 29 Jan. that she had had no word about her story 'Funeral in Town', submitted 'several months ago'.

4–'I think I know what time and trouble their preparation must have caused you, and I should like you to have our thanks for all you have done and for your patience at our importunate requests for more and more rehearsals . . . I wish I had had an opportunity of hearing more of your talks, but I read them in the *Listener*, and I should like you to know how much I, personally, enjoyed them.'

With very many thanks,

Yours sincerely
T. S. Eliot

TO *John Middleton Murry*   CC

24 April 1930   [*The Criterion*]

My dear John,

This morning has arrived a copy of *The Escaped Cock* by D. H. Lawrence, published by the Black Sun Press in Paris. So far as I know this has never been published before and I should be very glad if you would care to review it for the *Criterion* with any other of Lawrence's posthumous work that you think fit.

Affectionately,
[Tom]

TO *Theodor Haecker*[1]   CC

24 April 1930   [*The Criterion*]

Dear Mr Haecker,

It has taken me a long time to report to you on your essay.[2] I have read it with very great interest and have shown it to a colleague who was equally interested. The great difficulty is that it is very much too long for the *Criterion* and for a quarterly review I dislike printing essays in two parts. Therefore I am returning it to you with the hope that you may either be able to reduce it to a length suitable for us or else that you will send me something else. 6000 words is about the limit for the *Criterion*.

1–Theodor Haecker (1879–1945): German author and cultural critic; translator into German of Kierkegaard and Newman. A Catholic convert from 1921, he became a prominent opponent of the Nazi regime, and his journals are witness to his keen resistance to National Socialism: see *Journal in the Night*, trans. Alexander Dru (1950).
2–TSE referred Haecker's essay to Arthur Wheen, who on 24 Feb. 1930 sent him a seven-page summary, adding: 'If you don't feel equal to reading all this, my opinion is that the essay is worth doing, though verbose.' (Wheen would later translate Haecker's *Virgil, Father of the West* [1934].) See 'Theodicy and Tragedy', trans. Alexander Dru, C. 13 (Apr. 1934), 371–81.

I very much hope that you will let me have something to publish as I have read one of your books of essays with very great interest and sympathy.[1]

> Yours very truly,
> [T. S. Eliot]

TO *Seward Collins*[2]   CC

24 April 1930   [Faber & Faber Ltd]

Dear Mr Collins,

Thank you for your letter of the 10th instant.[3] I am sorry if I misunderstood your comments in the *Bookman* but perhaps it is as well from my point of view if you will publish my letter, as possibly other people may have come to the same conclusion that I came to myself. I daresay that there is an ambiguity in my writings about Mr Babbitt; but after all my position I feel is very close to that of Mr More in the same number in which you wrote your comment.

With many thanks for your courtesy.

> Yours sincerely,
> [T. S. Eliot]

1–This remark may refer to *Soren Kierkegaard und die Philosophie der Innherlichkeit* (1913), which is in TSE's library.

2–Seward Collins (1889–1952): editor of *The Bookman*, 1927–33; *The American Review*, 1933–7. A wealthy graduate of Princeton, during the 1930s he shifted his interest from humanism (he had been a devotee of Paul Elmer More and Irving Babbitt) towards anti-communism and a fascist ideal (he said in 1936 that he admired Hitler and Mussolini). See too Michael Jay Tucker, *And Then They Loved Him: Seward Collins & the Chimera of an American Fascism* (2005).

3 – 'This is to acknowledge receiving today your letter of March 31 about "Chronicle and Comment" in the March *Bookman*. [See TSE's letter to the Editor of *The Bookman* above.] While unsigned, the department was not intended to be anonymous, and was in fact written by myself. I naturally regret that you resent some of my opinions and that you feel I have misrepresented you. I shall be very glad to publish your letter in the next available issue, and in a note, if not to make amends, at least to attempt to clear up some of the misunderstanding.

'In the meantime I hasten to assure you that there was no imputation of insincerity in my describing you as casting scorn and at the same time professing the highest admiration. I was using "profess" not in the sense of "pretend" but in the sense in which you have yourself used it in the third paragraph of your letter. I find a puzzling ambiguity in your writings about Mr Babbitt, but insincerity would be the last explanation that would occur to me.'

TO *David Higham*

24 April 1930   [Faber & Faber Ltd]

Dear Higham,

I am sending you herewith a copy of an essay which I have written for Walter de la Mare who is editing a volume of essays on the Eighties by Fellows of the Royal Society of Literature, to be published in October by the Cambridge University Press.[1] De la Mare tells me that there is no objection to my publishing this in a periodical in America provided it appears before October; but of course the sooner the better. Do you think that anything can be done with it? I doubt whether the *Bookman* would take it because they have recently published a long essay on 'Pater' by Cuthbert Wright, but I should be glad to have it appear in any review that would pay anything for it.[2]

I have been very rushed lately and am rather confused about the other projects we were discussing. I expect to be going away for a fortnight next Monday but if you are to be in town I should be glad if you would lunch with me as soon as we can arrange it after my return.

Yours sincerely,

[T. S. Eliot]

TO *Walter de la Mare*

24 April 1930   [Faber & Faber Ltd]

Dear De la Mare,

Thank you for your letter.[3] I am glad to hear that my paper just qualifies in length for your book. I should, if it is not too much trouble, like to have one copy of it as I shall send the only copy I have to America in the hope of getting it published there before the end of September.

I should be quite willing to read my paper in the autumn. I suppose that you mean some time in September as the book is coming out in October. It is difficult to say at the moment whether it will then be convenient, but

1 – 'The Place of Pater', *The Eighteen-Nineties*, ed. Walter de la Mare (1930), 93–106
2 – Higham replied on 28 Apr. that he would be glad to pursue American serial rights for TSE's essay on Pater: it was printed as 'Arnold and Pater', *The Bookman* 72: 1 (Sept. 1930), 1–7.
3 – De la Mare wrote on 23 Apr., of 'The Place of Pater': 'It *is* rather short by comparison with the other papers, but it is very far indeed from short if measured by the quantity of meaning . . . And would you feel inclined to read it in the early autumn at 2 Bloomsbury Square?'

if you could give me some idea of the date which would suit you I could probably tell you more definitely.

I should have liked to hear Martindale's lecture[1] as he is a friend of mine, but I am expecting to go to the seaside for about a fortnight at the beginning of the week.

With many thanks,
Yours sincerely,
[T. S. Eliot]

TO *Charles Harris*

CC

25 April 1930   [*The Criterion*]

Dear Harris,

This is merely to thank you for your letter of the 18th and to say that I will keep your memorandum until we meet. So far as I know I shall be in town between the 16th and the 20th of June and shall hope for a word from you before then so that we can arrange to meet. I will also keep the 17th of July, as in all probability I shall be in London during most of that month.[2]

I wonder if you could have your publishers send the *Criterion* a copy of the new edition of your book.[3] I think that I could find an intelligent reviewer for it.

With all best wishes,

Yours sincerely,
[T. S. Eliot]

---

1 – De la Mare told TSE (23 Apr.) that Fr C. C. Martindale was to give a lecture on Cardinals Newman and Manning on 30 Apr.
2 – 'I write to acknowledge your welcome paper of notes and suggestions [not found] . . . I had thought of Etienne Gilson . . . I shall be in London for the Assembly June 16–20 . . . The vitally important plenary meeting of *the Editorial Board* [of the *Encyclopaedia*] (at which the Americans will be present) will be held on July 17 . . . at 31 Russell Sq. W.C.1. I want you to be present as literary adviser . . . Last week the E.C.U. Council voted me the £10,000 guarantee, I asked for (amid loud applause), similarly the S.P.C.K. So we are in funds . . .'
3 – See M. C. D'Arcy's review of the 4th edn of Harris's *Pro Fide*, C. 10 (Oct. 1931), 181–3.

TO *Marguerite Caetani*

CC

25 April 1930   [Faber & Faber Ltd]

Dear Marguerite,

I am writing in great haste as we are on the point of leaving for a fortnight at the seaside. I hope that by now you have received my previous letter which I sent to Versailles in reply to your questions about Read and Hayward. Read, by the way, is taking a holiday at Vence at the moment and I am sending him a line to ask him if he should stop in Paris on his way back to try to see you.[1]

I have passed on the list of books that you want to the proper department. I can't think of any other of our books that you would care for at the moment, unless Ruffredo were interested in Villari's *Expansion of Italy* which I consider an excellent book on the contemporary colonial policy.

If Lélia is going in for English literature I am not sure that she might not be better off at Cambridge than at Oxford.[2] But it all depends on what professors and dons happen to be at either place at the moment when she goes up. I will write to you more fully on my return. I am in such a rush at the moment that I must ask my Secretary to sign this letter for me.

Yours ever affectionately,
[Tom]

P.S. The date of publication of *Anabasis* is the 22nd May.

TO *E. McKnight Kauffer*

CC

25 April 1930   [Faber & Faber Ltd]

My dear Kauffer,

Thank you very much for your letter of the 24th. I am writing at once to return your Sweedish [*sic*] friend's letter, as I am going away almost at once and I want to be sure that you get it back. I should be quite ready to sign a book for the young man.[3]

---

1 – 'Herbert Read has never turned up,' wrote Caetani in a later letter. 'I was very disappointed.'

2 – Marguerite wrote on 13 Apr., 'Lélia and I go back to Versailles next week . . . Camillo stays to take his exams and Ruffredo stays with him. He will go to the Lycée here for two or three years and then Oxford *I hope* for both he and Lélia. Lélia to go in for English Literature.'

3 – Kauffer, who enclosed a letter from 'our joint admirer', wrote: 'I count this day one for which I am grateful for I believe it is publishing day for "Ash Wednesday". I am moved

When I come back I will let you know and I should be very glad indeed
to sit to you. We must meet first; and I hope that we may all four meet
before very long.

With many thanks for your praise.

Sincerely yours,
[T. S. Eliot]

TO *John Hayward*[1]   TS King's

27 April 1930   *The Criterion*

Dear Hayward,

Thank you very much for your letter.[2] I do not expect to receive many
like it; not many people will really like that sort of verses.

I know very well that sort of discouragement and almost panic. I don't
think I have so much of it now; but then it has taken me nearly forty-two
years to acquire a faint perception of the meaning of Humility – the first
of the virtues – and to see that I am not a person of any great importance.
It is exactly as if one had been living on drugs and stimulants all one's
life and had suddenly been taken off them. I know just enough – and no
more – of 'the peace of God' to know that it is an extraordinarily painful
blessing.

Perhaps the yew does not mean so much as you suppose. It happened
to occur in two or three dreams – one was a dream of 'the boarhound
between the yewtrees'; and that's all I know about it.

We are probably going to the seaside for a fortnight. I will write on my
return and ask you to lunch with me.

Affectionately yours,
T. S. Eliot

The address at present is 43, Chester Terrace, Eaton Square S.W.1. But 24
Russell Square is always safest.

---

profoundly by the power of those magnificent poems. And I thank you for an experience
that will become an influence. I shall have a copy of those poems to send to Sweden. Will
you sign it for the young man?' The young man was Erik Mesterton, poet and translator:
see letter 16 May 1930, below.

1 – John Hayward (1905–65), editor, critic, anthologist: see Biographical Register.
2 – Not found.

TO *Dorothy Pound*[1]

6 May 1930   [Faber & Faber Ltd]

My dear Dorothy,

Thank you for your letter of the 4th which I received because we returned from the sea-side earlier than we expected.[2] I am sending you a copy of the *Criterion* you want also a small book inscribed for E. P. which I think you had better look over first to decide whether it is suitable reading for him.

As we have returned to London, may we hope to see you before you leave for Frankfurt? Our address is 43 Chester Terrace, Eaton Square, S.W.1. If you can find the time do drop a line to Vivienne or ring up *Sloane 9043*.

Ever affectionately,
[Tom]

TO *Colin Still*[3]   CC

6 May 1930   [Faber & Faber Ltd]

Dear Mr Still,

I am very glad to hear from you.[4] I am sorry however to know that your book is out of print and I should be very grateful if you would lend me a copy which I shall return in due course. Perhaps the book could be

---

1–Dorothy Shakespear Pound (1886–1973), artist and book illustrator, married EP (whom she had met in 1908) in 1914. See David A. Lewis and Dorothy Pound, *Dorothy Shakespear (1886–1973): an exhibition of dreamscapes and alphabets* (1997).

2–Dorothy Pound wrote from 34 Abingdon Court, Kensington, London:

'Dearest Thomas . . . I will forward the *Criterion* to Ezra as soon as it comes.

'I shall surely come to see you later on. Meanwhile I hope to be going to Frankfurt on May 21st for the first performance of "Transatlantique, or The People's Choice" by one Geo. Antheil – where I shall meet Ezra who is in Paris at present . . . My love to Vivienne.'

3–Colin Still was author of *Shakespeare's Mystery Play: A Study of 'The Tempest'* (1921) and *The Timeless Theme: A Critical Theory Formulated and Applied* (1936).

4–Still, who wrote on 30 Apr. (at the suggestion of GWK), offered to show TSE his out-of-print book *Shakespeare's Mystery Play*. 'Please believe that in making this suggestion I am moved only by the desire to give any help I can to Mr Knight's work.' TSE remarked in his Introduction to Knight's *The Wheel of Fire*, 'that in a work of art, as truly as anywhere, reality only exists in and through appearances. I do not think that Mr Wilson Knight himself, or Mr Colin Still in his interesting book on *The Tempest* called *Shakespeare's Mystery Play*, has fallen into the error of presenting the work of Shakespeare as a series of mystical treatises in cryptogram, to be filed away once the cipher is read; poetry is poetry, and the surface is as marvellous as the core' (xx).

revived. At any rate I know that Mr Knight is very enthusiastic about it and as I overlooked it when it was published it is quite likely that many other people who would be interested have overlooked it as well.

I should be very glad to see you if you could look in at my office any day except Saturday either this week or next week at about 12 o'clock.

Yours faithfully,
[T. S. Eliot]

TO *Walter de la Mare*   TS De La Mare Estate

8 May 1930   Faber & Faber Ltd

My dear De la Mare,

I am very much pleased and honoured by your inscribing a copy of *Desert Islands* to me (and I shall be able to give my own copy to someone who would like it and cannot afford it – and even Directors get only one free copy!)[1] The 'gratitude', I think, should be the other way about; as I feel proud of your having cared to include a poem of mine among your – notes, shall I call them? Therefore I have sent you a copy; and I only pray that you may like *any* of the other parts as well as the one you took.

I have read the first part of *Desert Islands* with great delight; it is written in a siren style that might charm even the dullest of subjects into animation; but who does not like this subject? Only I feel much more tenderly, in retrospect, towards the Swiss Family Robinson, especially the giddy Jack, and the slothful Ernest (who seemed to me as a child to resemble myself the most nearly): I doubt however whether any child has had much patience for the angelic Francis.[2]

With very grateful thanks,

Yours sincerely,
T. S. Eliot

I shall read the 'notes' gradually.

---

1 – *Desert Islands and Robinson Crusoe*, inscribed: 'To T. S. Eliot with gratitude & all good wishes from Walter de la Mare April 30 1930.'
2 – De la Mare thanked TSE on 2 June for sending him a copy of *Ash-Wednesday* – 'a delight of a very particular and personal kind'. 'As for the *Swiss Family Robinson*, I believe that it was the general aspect of Mr Robinson that rather blinded me to giddy Jack and slothful Ernest.'

TO *Michael Sadler*[1]   cc

9 May 1930   [Faber & Faber Ltd]

My dear Master,

I have not forgotten that I promised to fake for you a manuscript copy of *Ash Wednesday*. So, as earnest, and as something which I think has relatively more interest, I am sending you herewith, meanwhile, the *genuine* manuscript, (2) my own altered typescript (3) final typescript, of my 'Ariel' poem for next autumn ('Marina'). If I make alterations in the proof (and I have an uneasy feeling that the poem is still only half baked) I will send you that too to complete the document.[2]

Sincerely yours,

[T. S. Eliot]

I intend a crisscross between Pericles finding alive, and Hercules finding dead – the two extremes of the recognition scene – but I thought that if I labelled the quotation it might lead readers astray rather than direct them. It is only an accident that I know Seneca better than I know Euripides.

TO *James Nixon*   cc

10 May 1930   [*The Criterion*]

Dear Sir,

I have to acknowledge yours of the 24th ult.[3] I am sorry for you: first for being a senior in high school, which is a painful moment in life; and second for having elected to write a term report about me. But I should like to see that report.

Re queries. I am still the editor of the *Criterion*, and until the words 'edited by T. S. Eliot' are removed from the cover you may take it (if

1 – Sir Michael Sadler (1861–1943): Master of University College, Oxford, 1923–34.
2 – Sadler responded on 12 May: 'Please accept our grateful thanks for your gift . . . We are happy that The Friends will be able, through your kindness, to make this gift to the Bodleian.' Sadler acknowledged the gift of the sheets of *Marina* on 18 Oct. 1930. (He acknowledged TSE's gift of 'the corrected typescript' of *Anabasis* on 17 Jan. 1931.) TSE's benefaction was announced in 'The Friends of the Bodleian: Gifts to library this year', *The Times*, 22 Oct. 1930, 13.
3 – James Nixon wrote from 'United States of America, Rochester, Indiana': 'I am a senior in high school. For a term report I chose you as the author about whom I would write. I have read a great many of your poems and have found them to be very inspiring.

'May I ask a question or two? First, are you still the editor of the *Criterion*? If so, what is the purpose of the magazine? And do you ever intend to make a lecture tour of the United States?'

you ever see that periodical) that I am still the editor. The purpose of the review is to provide a small salary for the editor and to give publicity to the authors whom the editor and his colleagues consider worthy. And I should very much like to give some lectures in America.

Yours faithfully,
[T. S. Eliot]

TO *I. A. Richards*[1]   TS Magdalene

12 May 1930   Faber & Faber Ltd

My dear Richards,

Your *undated* letter from Peking (why does your letterhead read *Peiping*?) was very welcome today.[2] I think I have neglected, or rather postponed, writing to you for the same reason; that I have nothing more as yet to say about belief, and probably shan't until you are more accessible for discussions.

I have sent you the new poems, such as they are; also you shall have a copy of *Anabasis*, as soon as it is available. If I did not send you the Belgion book I will send a copy at once; he wanted you to see it; and is himself very much concerned with you. Fernandez has reviewed the book for the next *Criterion*.[3]

1 – I. A. Richards (1893–1979), theorist of literature, education and communication studies: see Biographical Register.

2 – IAR wrote from Tsing Hua University, Peking, in response to a (now lost) letter from TSE:
'I've been putting off writing until I had something solid to say about Belief. Realising now that this may be equivalent to Doomsday, here at last is an acknowledgment of your letter and of the *Dante* which I think is going to be very useful to me. You did mention a book by Belgion as on the way, but it hasn't come. Meanwhile a Chinese here has given me *Animula* copied out by him, and I like it extremely . . . The *Bookman* article came my way. I feel you are quite right about the number of individual and other disturbing influences on the problem. All I shall try to do is to make a kind of chart of the possibilities of differences and of the number of types of belief theories which might be held . . . – Apparently my "poetry without any belief" which you find so difficult to conceive, is just Chinese Poetry. On the other hand it is comparatively (to our poetries) a trivial, hopscotch literature . . . We are lingering on here from June till December before going to Harvard to give a Practical Criticism course there for the spring. We may rather enjoy America after China's improvisations amid the ruins. A people now without hope, or any sort of confidence in themselves inside their dress of pride. I confess I miss what we are accustomed to call morality . . . It would be odd if I became a Christian out here . . .' (*Selected Letters*, 54–5)
IAR explained on 19 Oct. 1930 that 'Peiping' was a southern Nationalist name for Peking, introduced because Nan king ('South Capital') was capital at the time. 'Pe king North Capital seemed to them no longer as suitable since Peiping means, I think, city in the plain.'

3 – Ramon Fernandez, review of Montgomery Belgion, *Our Present Philosophy of Life*, in C. 9 (July 1930), 759–63.

The undergraduates of Cambridge are, some of them, in a great state of distress at your prolonged absence, and complain that Lucas[1] is now lording it, swoln with pride and rank mists,[2] over the intellectual life of the university.

I am sorry to hear that your absence is to be for another year; but no doubt you will find Harvard, for a season, interesting. You probably know that your name is already one to conjure with, in fact is being employed for conjuring tricks, in America. Have you seen a book by one Geoffrey West, who finds that you and Murry are brothers?[3] Murry, on the other hand, has just come out for Fernandez as the truly inspired.[4]

What you say about the Chinese is extremely interesting; and I hope to hear more about them, at least when you return.

Fernandez is waiting to know what you think about him, but I am afraid he must wait. If you are to be in Pekin till December I shall have several things to send you. If you write out your paper for the Chinese Literary Society will you let me print it?

I have half expected to hear that you and Mrs Richards had joined the Dyhrenfurths on their Kangchenjunga climb.[5]

1 – F. L. ('Peter') Lucas (1894–1967): poet, novelist, playwright, scholar; Fellow and Librarian, King's College, Cambridge. Author of *Seneca and Elizabethan Tragedy* (1922), he was praised for his edition of the *Complete Works of John Webster* (4 vols, 1927) – TSE said he considered him 'the perfect annotator'. Lucas published an unfavourable review of *The Waste Land* in *NS* (3 Nov. 1923); and he attacked TSE in *The Decline and Fall of the Romantic Ideal* (1936). Later, as E. M. W. Tillyard related, Lucas was to become 'openly hostile' to TSE (*The Muse Unchained: An Intimate Account of the Revolution in English Studies at Cambridge* [1958], 98). T. E. B. Howarth gossiped that matters were to become so rancorous that Lucas 'would not even allow Eliot's work to be bought for the library' (*Cambridge Between Two Wars* [1978], 166).
2 – Agamemnon is called 'O tumide': 'O thou swollen with pride' (Seneca, *Troades*, 301); 'spiritus tumidos': '[swollen] pride' (*Agam.*, 248). Milton, *Lycidas*: 125: 'the hungry sheep look up, and are not fed, / But swoln with wind, and the rank mists they draw, / Rot inwardly . . .'
3 – Geoffrey West concludes *Deucalion or the Future of Literary Criticism* by seeking to reconcile the theories of IAR and JMM. John Gould Fletcher remarked in his review of the work that IAR's 'scientific investigation into the stimuli evolved by art leads, or is meant to lead, to the "harmonious individual", the man who has achieved an equilibrium permitting "free play to all his faculties" . . . Mr Murry starts from the opposite side, from the individual himself, and attempts to relate the individual's intuition of poetic value to the universe at large . . . Mr West bravely attempts to reconcile these positions' (*C.* 9 [Apr. 1930], 576).
4 – JMM, 'The Detachment of Naturalism', *C.* 9 (July 1930), 642–60: 'The recent essay of M. Ramon Fernandez on *A Humanist Theory of Value* [*C.* 9 (Jan. 1930), 228–45] is a tonic influence to a discussion which was previously in danger of becoming a sectarian polemic . . . M. Fernandez' theory of value stands firm on its own legs.'
5 – In 1930 Günther Dyhrenfurth (1886–1975), Professor of Geology at Zurich and a seasoned mountaineer, led an expedition to conquer Kangchenjunga, the third-highest mountain in

My *Bookman* paper[1] was a poor attempt, a paper written in a hurry to fulfil a promise connected with the collection of funds for repairing the organ of a Bloomsbury church: so don't take it seriously. Some American named Williamson has just covered exactly the ground of my Clark lectures,[2] so I am wondering what to write next.

My wife joins me in best wishes to both of you,

Yours ever,

T. S. Eliot

TO *Mark Van Doren*[3]   TS Butler

13 May 1930   Faber & Faber Ltd

Dear Mr Van Doren,

I have just received from the publishers a copy of *Prize Poems: 1913–1929*,[4] and as it is dignified by your name as introducer, I take the liberty of laying before you certain facts about the inclusion of *The Waste Land* of which I am sure you are wholly ignorant.

I have not had the slightest previous intimation from anybody that it was desired to use *The Waste Land* in this way. No letter accompanied the book. The publishers make acknowledgement to me, but I have no cognisance of them, and have never granted permission to anyone to use *The Waste Land* or any part of it. MacVeagh could not have given permission, as the *Dial* had only ordinary periodical rights, and the prize carried no conditions with it.[5] Liveright could not have given permission, because his period of publication expired in 1927, and he had not anthology rights anyway.

Charles Boni[6] appears simply to have lifted my best poem and my best financial asset; though even without a Boni, the money I have had out

the world. The assault failed in the face of poor weather and snow conditions. One of the climbing team, an Englishman named Frank Smythe, published *The Kangchenjunga Adventure* (1930).

1 – 'Poetry and Propaganda', *The Bookman* 70: 6 (Feb. 1930), 595–602.

2 – George Williamson, *The Donne Tradition* (1930).

3 – Mark Van Doren (1894–1972), who was literary editor of N., 1924–8, taught English for many years at Columbia University. His pupils included John Berryman and Allen Ginsberg.

4 – *Prize Poems 1913–1929*, ed. Charles Wagner; intro. Van Doren (Boni & Liveright, 1930).

5 – Lincoln Macveagh (1890–1972): publisher and diplomat; President, Dial Press, 1923–33.

6 – Charles Boni (1894–1969), a graduate of Harvard, co-founded in 1923 – with his brother Albert Boni (1892–1981) – the major modernist publishing house of Albert and Charles Boni. TSE was mistaken in blaming Charles Boni: the offending anthology was in fact put out by the firm of Boni & Liveright, established in 1917 by Albert Boni and Horace

of *The Waste Land* is small recompense for the years of sweat, hell and technical study.

I am sure that neither you nor Kallen,[1] Colum[2] and Untermeyer,[3] whose names appear as general advisers on the Series, know anything of the circumstances. I am writing to my brother in New York, to ask him to obtain advice of counsel on this matter. This letter is merely to lay the situation before you.

Yours sincerely,
T. S. Eliot

TO *Colin Still*   cc

13 May 1930   [Faber & Faber Ltd]

Dear Mr Still,

I read your book through the same day, so shall have it returned to you tomorrow, as you said you would like it back quickly.[4]

I enjoyed it immensely, and am I think mostly in agreement. What immensely strengthens your case is leaving open the question of Shakespeare's 'consciousness'.[5] And in this connexion, I venture to suggest

---

Liveright, which had published the first US book edition of *The Waste Land*, complete with notes, in Dec. 1922.

1–Horace Kallen (1882–1974), German-born philosopher, co-founded the New School for Social Research, New York. Fellow of the Jewish Academy of Arts and Sciences, he was a leader of the American Jewish Congress; a member of the executive board of the World Jewish Congress; Chair of the YIVO Institute for Jewish Research. His works include *Cultural Pluralism and the American Idea* (1956). See Ranen Omer, '"It Is I Who Have Been Defending a Religion Called Judaism": The T. S. Eliot and Horace M. Kallen Correspondence', *Texas Studies in Literature and Language* 39: 4 (Winter 1997), 321–56.

2–Padraic Colum (1881–1972) was associated with WBY and Lady Gregory at the beginning of the Irish Theatre movement in 1902. Following periods in the USA and Hawaii (where he surveyed myths and folklore), he wrote poetry, novels, books for children and essays. Works include *Collected Poems* (1932) and *Our Friend James Joyce* (with Mary Colum, 1959).

3–Louis Untermeyer (1885–1977): poet, editor, translator, parodist, anthologist; co-founder and contributing editor of *Seven Arts* magazine; Poet Laureate Consultant to the Library of Congress, 1961–3; author of *Collected Parodies* (1926); *Long Feud: Selected Poems* (1962).

4–Still sent his *Shakespeare's Mystery Play: A Study of 'The Tempest'* (1921) on 10 May: 'If I were issuing a new edition . . . the whole work would be revised and amplified to make clearer my main contention that all great imaginative art has ultimately the same mystical quality as the myths and mysteries of antiquity and must of necessity resemble them to some extent in outward form.' *The Tempest* deals allegorically with the same ideas as those upon which the ancient rites of initiation were based – 'conceived as a reversal of the Fall of Man' (204) – and Prospero stands in such a schema for the pagan 'hierophant' (75): 'it is an allegorical account of those psychological experiences which constitute what mystics call Initiation' (8).

5–Still maintains: 'many, if not all, of the resemblances now in question would result autoto you an experiment. If you have not my poems I shall be very glad to send them to you. I only offer mine, not out of vanity, but because there is a good deal of symbolism in them, and because I know how much of it is conscious; but I think that a test of the 'consciousness' of a living versifier who can respond for his own knowledge and awareness might throw some light on the general problem. Some of the symbolism I have used was of course intentional; some was unintentional; and some symbolism is used (as of 'red rock') which has been called to my attention by critics, which so far as I know was wholly spontaneous. And although my recently published poem (*Ash-Wednesday*) is a deliberate modern *Vita Nuova*, I was not fully aware of the significance of the 'veiled lady' until I read your book.[1] My 'veiled lady' was, as a matter of fact, a direct employment of a dream I had, together with the yew trees and the garden god.

I think that there is some permanent basis for the mother-sister-daughter complex.[2]

What I should like to see you do (as you make suggestions) is a book in which your conclusions about *The Tempest* should be fortified by conclusions about other of Shakespeare's later plays.

Do you know Cornford's book on Attic Comedy?[3] If not, you ought to, because he has a good deal to say about the ritual marriage.

I shall drop you a line in a week or so and ask you to lunch with me and discuss these matters in which we are both interested. Meanwhile, I thank

---

matically and of necessity – *without any conscious effort whatever on Shakespeare's part* – from the development of this theme through the only allegorical medium which would command the approval of a sound æsthetic judgment' (13); 'my main theory does not necessarily require the reader to believe that Shakespeare deliberately contrived the resemblances which have been noted, or, indeed, to presume even that he knew anything whatever about the mystic rites of the pagan world' (59). Elsewhere, however, he argues that it is difficult to credit the possibility that the similarity between play and pagan rites was wholly fortuitous: 'every authentic initiation ritual is based upon certain permanent realities' (84).
1 – Still finds 'occasion to mention the passage in *Ecclesiasticus* (iv. 17–19) wherein Wisdom is represented as the beloved of the aspirant, whom she encourages in his trials, and to whom she finally unveils herself, revealing her secrets. The same allegory occurs in the *Zohar* . . . This Veiled Lady is evidently a personification of Truth, in its particular aspect as a Secret Doctrine which the tradition of Jewish mysticism postulates for the Bible . . . [I]f every phase of the relation between the aspirant and the Hidden Truth (or Wisdom) be expressed in these allegorical terms of a lover and his beloved, then the last stage of initiation – which involves the fulfillment of the aspirant's desire – must necessarily be represented as involving a consummated marriage, figurative of the complete union of the aspirant with Truth' (76–7). It is 'the Lady herself who takes the initiative and makes the overtures leading to a full and consummated union' (78). The Veiled Lady 'is the Bride of the initiate' (101); 'Miranda is an allegorical figure. She is the Veiled Lady who is Wisdom, the Lady who unveils herself' (174).
2 – Not specifically discussed by Still.
3 – See Francis M. Cornford, *The Origin of Attic Comedy* (1914), ch. ii: 'The Exodus'.

you most cordially for the sight of your book: I found it very exciting throughout. The parallel with Virgil was quite new to me.[1]

Yours sincerely,

[T. S. Eliot]

TO *J. S. Barnes*[2]

TS Mrs Buona Barnes

13 May 1930

Faber & Faber Ltd

Dear Jim,

I was surprised to hear that you were back in London.[3] You don't say how long you are to be here, but when you know, perhaps you will tell

1–Still seeks to highlight parallels: 'If *The Tempest* describes (as I contend it does) a pilgrimage through Purgatory to Paradise, its essential theme is precisely the same as that of Dante's *Divina Commedia*; and these recurrent resemblances to *Aeneid VI* suggest the interesting possibility that Shakespeare followed, in a sense, the example of Dante in *taking Virgil as his guide*' (33).

2–James Strachey Barnes (1890–1955): son of Sir Hugh Barnes. Brought up in Florence by his grandparents, Sir John and Lady Strachey, he went on to Eton and King's College, Cambridge. During WW1 he served in the Guards and Royal Flying Corps. Enamoured by Italy, he came in time to forge a friendship with Mussolini; and as a Roman Catholic he sought to credit the notion that Fascism and Catholicism were compatible.

TSE was to write to HWE on 7 Jan. 1937: 'There is a man whom I have known for some years named Jim Barnes, otherwise Major James Strachey Barnes . . . Jim is rather a queer bird. He is a cousin of the Stracheys and I think his father is a head of the Anglo-Persian Oil Company or something of the sort. He is very correct, having been to Eton, Cambridge, in the Blues and ended the War in the Air Force. He is a violent Italophile, a pal of Mussolini, and wrote a couple of books about Fascism in its early stages. He is also some kind of honorary valet to the Pope, being a R. C. convert.'

To Sir Robert Vansittart on 12 Jan. 1939 (when Barnes was applying for the post of Assistant Director of the British Institute in Florence): 'James Strachey Barnes is the younger brother of an old friend of mine, Mrs St John Hutchinson, and I have known him, in this way, off and on for a good many years. He wrote two books on Fascism . . . and was one of its earliest champions in this country. He was brought up in Italy (before going to Eton: he was subsequently in the Blues, then a Major in the Air Force, and at King's after the War), has an Italian wife, and is the most convinced pro-Italian and pro-Fascist that I know. He is a Roman Catholic convert, and has or had some honorary appointment at the Vatican; but manages to combine this with a warm admiration for Mussolini, from which it follows that he has disapproved of British policy whenever that policy did not favour Italian policy. He was for a time a correspondent of Reuter, and in that capacity was with the Italians in Abyssinia. He has since lectured in America on international politics, and I believe took the opportunity of defending Italy. In private life he is rather a bore, and talks more than he listens, somewhat failing to appreciate that the person to whom he is talking may have other interests and other engagements . . . but that my conscience is uneasy if I give a recommendation in which I do not say all that I know which may be relevant . . .'

See also David Bradshaw and James Smith, 'Ezra Pound, James Strachey Barnes ("the Italian Lord Haw-Haw") and Italian Fascism', *Review of English Studies* 64 (2013), 672–93.

3–Barnes asked (8 May): 'My dear Tom Eliot, Excuse me for bothering you; but I should so

me, so that we may meet before you leave. I am so glad to hear that you are really settled in a job which sounds interesting in itself, and which should incidentally give you the opportunity and experience for learning and writing about central and Levantine Europe. I have always hankered to learn modern Greek, and you will do so.

The aesthetic essay will appear in September.[1] June is rather a muddled number: more of some kinds of contribution than I wanted have had to go in; and on the other hand some regular parts of the review have this time failed me.

What has happened to Mary? I sent her a copy of my new book, but there has been complete silence.[2]

Yours ever,
T. S. Eliot

TO *Henry Eliot*   TS Houghton

13 May 1930   Faber & Faber Ltd

My dear Brother,

I have been storing up a letter to write you for a long time, but it is a long letter, and as time goes on it becomes longer and longer, so it is not yet written. And meanwhile, I am obliged to consult you on a matter of business. I don't want you to take a great deal of labour; but it is a case for getting the opinion of a good New York lawyer used to copyrights, and

---

like to know if my "art" article is to appear, as you rather foreshadowed, in the next number of the *Criterion*? Or, if not, when? I have now got a very satisfactory job & shall be shortly going to live in Budapest for two years, travelling there on behalf of Vickers Aviation Ltd. all over Eastern Europe & Turkey, from Poland to Greece. It ought to be great fun.' (He had written to TSE with the same news on 31 Mar., but TSE appears not to have responded to that letter.)

1 – 'The Nature of Art and the Function of Art Criticism', C. 10 (Apr. 1931), 462–79.

2 – Barnes responded by postcard (15 May): '[MH] is getting worse & worse about answering letters; but always remains the best of friends of her friends.'

now that Quinn[1] is dead I have no legal representative in New York; and a London solicitor would be of little use in the following matter.

I have just received a paper-bound book issued by Charles Boni: *Prize Poems 1913–1939* edited by Charles Wagner with an introduction by Mark van Doren. It is stated to be one of a series under the direction of several people, among whom I know Horace Kallen, Padraic Colum, and Louis Untermeyer. In this book *The Waste Land* is printed entire (but without the notes).

I knew nothing whatever of this until receiving the book, and have had no correspondence either from the firm of Boni, whom I do not know, or from anyone else. So far as I am concerned the poem has simply been lifted from me for Boni's profit.

I shall ask you to get a copy of the book in New York if you can. You will observe that 'acknowledgement' is made to me in a preface; also to Lincoln MacVeagh (whom I know) for general 'permission to reprint the *Dial* poems'; and to Horace Liveright, for 'permission by special arrangement to reprint the *Waste Land*'.

The Waste Land was printed in the *Dial* merely as a contribution. The *Dial* therefore had merely first American serial rights. No conditions were attached to the Prize, which furthermore was never for any single work but was a general tribute to the author thus honoured. Lincoln MacVeagh accordingly could have had no rights to assign.

As for Liveright, I send herewith a copy of the contract, which was drawn up by John Quinn. There is no mention of anthology rights, and in any case Liveright's right to publish the *Waste Land* expired in 1927.

My point is that *The Waste Land* is my longest and most profitable poem; it is a considerable asset to me; I should never have given my consent to its publication in this form had I been asked; and I object to being robbed in this way.

1–John Quinn (1870–1924): Irish-American corporate lawyer in New York; patron of modernist writers and artists; collector of manuscripts. He gave generous support, both financial and legal, to writers including Conrad, WBY, JJ and EP. TSE began corresponding with him at the urgent prompting of EP, who had read about him as a patron in the *New Age* in Jan. 1915: the correspondence ran until Quinn's death. EP urged TSE's importance upon Quinn ('I have more or less discovered him,' he claimed). Quinn bought from TSE (for a fair price) the drafts of *The Waste Land*, which were ultimately deposited in the New York Public Library. Though a supporter of the Irish nationalist cause, he worked for the British intelligence services, helping to report upon *agents provocateurs* who were working in the USA to mobilise anti-British groups of Irish and Germans. See Harvey Simmonds, *John Quinn: An Exhibition to Mark the Gift of The John Quinn Memorial Collection* (1968); B. L. Reid, *The Man from New York: John Quinn and His Friends* (1969).

I shall not allow you to incur any personal expenses in the matter: the more so because Faber & Faber Ltd. as the publishers of my collected poems (which have not been published in America) are also interested, and would participate in any legal expenses, if I have any case to pursue.[1]

I enclose a copy of a letter which I am writing to Mark van Doren. If you ever see Kallen, he might have some suggestion to offer.

In haste your loving brother
Tom.

TO *Richard Aldington*[2]   cc

13 May 1930   [Faber & Faber Ltd]

My dear Richard,

It is very long since I have heard from you or you from me; but we were friends when we last communicated; and I hope that your feelings towards me have not changed since then; as certainly my feelings towards you are always those of affection and gratitude.

I am writing now because Harriet Weaver[3] came to see me today and told me that you wanted the copies in stock of the Poets' Translation Series, Nos. 1 and 6, destroyed except 25 copies each which you wanted sent to you.[4] I told her that we would do whatever you wished, because in the matter of the Egoist Press books taken over Faber & Faber consider themselves merely agents; but that I would for the firm write to you and ask you to give me – or preferably, write a letter to Faber & Faber Ltd. for my attention – your exact instruction, which shall be carried out. Will you do this?

This raises the question of the eventual disposal of the remnants of the Egoist Press publications which we hold. It would be a shame to

1–HWE replied on 14 Aug. that Stern (presumably a legal adviser) told him over the telephone 'that Boni apparently conceded your claim without raising any point of law, which will simplify the matter. He said that Boni was willing to pay, but would not make a definite offer until he had seen Liveright, who seems to be elusive. Stern said that he thought Boni was trying to buy out Liveright.'

2–Richard Aldington (1892–1962), poet, critic, translator, biographer, novelist: see Biographical Register.

3–Harriet Shaw Weaver (1876–1961), editor and publisher: see Biographical Register.

4–The Egoist Press Poets' Translation Series comprised: (no. 1) Greek Songs (900 copies); (no. 2) 'Anyte and Sappho' (900 copies); (no. 3) Choruses from Euripides (1,000); (no. 4) Latin Poets (1,000); (no. 5) Poseidippos and Asklepiades (500); (no. 6) Meleager of Gadara (750).

remainder books and booklets which have an historical interest and will eventually have considerable money value; there are just too many of each to dump on the second hand market as first editions. I should like your advice. Is there any bookseller who could dispose advantageously of, for instance, the stock of 235 copies of Marianne Moore's first edition?[1] Our position is that we only want one [sc. out] of any receipts from sales our proper due in overhead expenses; Harriet wants nothing; so the rest would be for the author.

I am afraid it is hopeless to revive the Poets' Translation Series at present; an admirable idea; and if I could set half of the young verse writers of today onto translating instead of loading the world with imitations of everybody, I should feel virtuous.

Ever affectionately,
[T. S. Eliot]

TO *A. L. Rowse*

13 May 1930   Faber & Faber Ltd

My dear Rowse,

This is to introduce to you Mr Montgomery Belgion, the author of a book called *Our Present Philosophy of Life* which we published and which I believe you have seen, and of various articles and reviews in the *Criterion* which you will have seen (if you read the *Criterion*). Mr Belgion is to be in Oxford shortly, and would like to meet you. I should be very glad if you might meet. I don't think he accepts your philosophy of life any more than he accepts mine: but I think that if you meet the consequences may be interesting. He is a friend of Ramon Fernandez, who I want you to know, and also in a sense (that sense was well fished for[2]) of Gide.

Yours ever,
T. S. Eliot

---

1 – The stock of books handed over to C. in Aug. 1924 had included 268 copies of Marianne Moore's *Poems* (out of a printing of 500).
2 – 'That sort was well fish'd for' (*The Tempest*, II. i, 100).

TO *Ezra Pound*

13 May 1930   [Faber & Faber Ltd]

Dear Ezzum,[1]

We have on hand 236 copies ord. edition of *Quia*, having sold 4.[2] We have on hand NO copies of limited edition, having sold 6.

What remain may be considered rather as first editions for 2nd hand bookseller; and I feel that a firm of general publishers like F&F are not the people to dispose of such stock to best advantage. Question remains whether such works could be filtered adroitly through 1 or more sellers (like J. Schwarz[3]) for profit of authors? I disapprove strongly of remaindering, unless author strongly wishes it. Your suggestions invited. Will write again about other matters, when you have some address. Understand from D. by post that you are just going to Frankfurt.

etc.

[T. S. E.]

TO *Harold Monro*[4]

14 May 1930   Faber and Faber Ltd

My dear Harold,

I am sorry that after such a long interval your first news should be so gloomy.[5] I hope that your fragments are gradually reassembling now. I should be glad if we could lunch together in the middle of any week in the near future.

I have done nothing about *Adamastor*, so will send you a copy, if you can let me have a review of it for the September number; that is, towards the end of July.[6]

1–The top copy of this letter – the first paragraph, and part of the first sentence of the second paragraph – is in Beinecke.
2–The stock of the Egoist Press edition of EP's *Quia Pauper Amavi* handed over to F&G in Aug. 1924 was 271 (of 500 copies printed), plus 47 of the signed limited edition of 100 copies.
3–Ulysses Book Shop, 20 Bury Street, W.C.1.
4–Harold Monro (1879–1932), poet, editor, publisher, bookseller: see Biographical Register.
5–Monro wrote on 6 May, 'I've just been released from a Nursing Home having had my head nearly knocked off by a surgeon, from which operation it took me over 3 weeks to recover.'
6–Monro wished to review Roy Campbell's *Adamastor* – 'an important book'. Untitled review, C. 10 (Jan. 1931), 349–56.

I will keep Gribble in mind.[1]
Did you get a copy of *Ash-Wednesday* which I sent to you?
Let me know about lunch when you are well enough and not at Selsea.

yours ever,
Tom

TO *Vivyan Eyles*   CC

14 May 1930   [Faber & Faber Ltd]

Dear Miss Eyles,

Thank you very much for your kind invitation of the 30th.[2] I must apologise for the delay (partly due to the fact that I had changed my address). Meanwhile, a letter similar to yours had come from the President, Father Gray O.P., to which my secretary replied for me.

There are two reasons for my declining: first, that there can be no member of the Italian Club who does not know more about Italian literature than I do; and second, that I cannot possibly afford the time at present either to visit the Club or to prepare an address for it. I should very much like to come, but prudence and cowardice rather than modesty suggest to me that I should prefer to be present rather as an auditor than as a speaker.

I remember your story very well; and I hope you will send me another, and I hope that it will be a little less grim than the last.

I have heard nothing from my friend Stead, and wonder whether he is still in Washington.

With very grateful thanks,

Yours sincerely,
[T. S. Eliot]

---

1 – 'Gribble, whom you know, a good translator I believe . . . is very anxious to obtain some work – from the German, French, or Italian. Your firm might be glad of his services . . .' Possibly Leonard Gribble (1908–85), who was to become renowned as a prolific crime writer.
2 – An invitation to address the Oxford University Italian Club, in May.

14 May 1930   Faber & Faber Ltd

My dear Rowse,

Thank you for your letter of last Saturday.[1] I feel that you are disappointed in *Ash Wednesday*; and I am disappointed too; because I fancy that parts IV and V of it are much better than II ('Salutation'). But please wait for a 'Promised Land' as merely a remote possibility after another ten or fifteen years. The always present struggle is to be honest about the stage one has got to and really knows; and not to write about anything until you know what it is you are writing about.

I object to the suggestion that 'creation' is the justification of 'faith'. Creation may possibly be some evidence of faith, but what has it to do with justification? The only justification of faith is that that is what one believes to be true and that is all there is to be said about it.

'D'un jeune homme qui est venu me voir'. You may remember a parable about the sowing of seed. There is certainly the difference that one is possibly sowing bad seed as well as good; and the horrid possibility that it is all tare-seed: nevertheless, the point holds good, that one must scatter it anywhere in the hope that some of it will sprout and come to maturity [*typing possibly runs off carbon page here*] What is thy servant to know what sort of soil lies in the mind of that facile Spanish-French-Jewish youth of such precocity?[2] If one out of a hundred is sheltered or assisted, what does it matter about the ninety-nine who turn into businessmen, civil servants and golf players?

I am using your review of Lindsay.[3]

I should like the Clark or some other *article* for September.[4]

Cecil seems to have let me down on a review he promised.[5]

---

1 – Rowse wrote, of *Ash-Wednesday*: 'It was a great joy to find "Salutation" in its place, for it is my favourite among the later poems. But what we expect someday of you, have I said it before?, is a new and other Waste Land . . . These things are just what I'd like to discuss with you, but you must be tired of being a kind of lay confessor to young men. There was one waiting for you the day I was in the office, that was disillusioning: a not very hopeful type I thought: intelligent, charming, aesthetic, cosmopolitan, but with his mind & character all over the place.'

2 – Probably Ramon Fernandez. Or possibly E. F. Jacob.

3 – ALR's review of A. D. Lindsay's *The Essentials of Democracy*, in C. 10 (Oct. 1930), 179.

4 – 'G. N. Clark's Conception of History', C. 10 (Jan. 1931), 222–32.

5 – Possibly Lord David Cecil had undertaken to review Edith Sitwell's *Alexander Pope*.

I agree with you that Feiling's pamphlet is invertebrate.[1] I think a better pamphlet could have been written, and a more unorthodox. But before you think about pamphlets yourself – and I hope you will – please finish *Politics and the Younger Generation*. We want to see that soon.

New Age: wait till further notice.[2]

Ever yours,
T. S. Eliot

TO *Orlo Williams*[3]

CC

15 May 1930   [*The Criterion*]

Dear Williams,

I must apologise for not having communicated with you before, and I will now answer your questions.[4]

1. It is too late for any copy for the next number and the next date is therefore August 1st.

2. I think that we might as well ignore Lucas's book especially in view of the fact that you have already had to review it twice. As you will remember we agreed that single novels ought not to be reviewed in the *Criterion* unless there is some special reason. The *Marizius Case* was rather different because it seemed to me time that we said something about Wasserman's work so I was very glad to have that from you.[5] But

---

1 – 'Feiling's *Conservatism* is such an extraordinarily invertebrate work. I'd like to write a pamphlet in reply. "What Conservatism is not" might be the title.' GCF was to write to Feiling on 21 Nov. 1930, regretting that *Conservatism* had sold only 1,736 copies: 'in spite of all our efforts, we have not been able to remove the prejudice against political pamphlets. None of the political or quasi-political pamphlets in the Miscellany have sold anything like as well as the other titles in the series . . . The other factor is that CONSERVATISM is in a perfectly real sense too good. There are not enough people (so it would appear) who want to think out seriously the back-ground of their political creed.'

2 – 'Oh! and what am I to do with the *New Age* book on Politics . . .' (*The New Age*, edited from 1922 by A. R. Orage – whose interests included Fabian Socialism, the Social Credit theories of C. H. Douglas, and all manifestations of modernism – was struggling for survival.)

3 – Orlando (Orlo) Williams (1883–1967), Clerk to the House of Commons, scholar, critic: see Biographical Register.

4 – OW asked on 13 May: '(1) Do you want any more copy for next number? . . . (2) Do you want me to review F. L. Lucas' novel *Cécile*, in view of the fact that I have just written 2 reviews of it in *Times* & *Literary Suppt*? (3) What about Italian periodicals? . . . (4) Linati asks me if I can tell him of any exhaustive book on modern American literary criticism . . .'

5 – *Der Fall Maurizius* ('The Maurizius Case', 1928), by the German-Jewish author Jakob Wasserman (1873–1934), was reviewed by OW in *C.* 9 (July 1930), 778–9.

please remember that in the case of single novels which I send on to you it is entirely a matter for your discretion whether we notice them or not.

3. It is entirely an oversight of mine that I did not give you due warning that I should have liked to have a review of Italian Periodicals this number. It is now too late. As a matter of fact I had been depending on Flint who has failed so that this number will be unfortunate in having no such review at all. I should be very grateful if I could have something for the September number.

4. I cannot think at the moment of any good treatise on Modern American literary criticism. There is a good deal of it but I have not yet seen it summed up. If I can think of one I will let you know.

Yours ever,
[T. S. Eliot]

TO *Laurence Binyon*[1]   TS Mrs Gray

16 May 1930   Faber & Faber Ltd

Dear Mr Binyon,

Who am I to criticise translations of Dante? The only attempts at any translation that I have made, suggest to me that it is quite impossible to translate anything; and I feel that in my small essay on Dante, I may lead readers to the erroneous impression that Dante is translatable.[2]

---

1 – Laurence Binyon (1869–1943), poet and art historian, worked for the British Museum from 1893, becoming Assistant Keeper of the Department of Prints and Drawings, 1909, Keeper, 1932; art critic of the *Saturday Review*, 1906–11; friend of WBY and T. Sturge Moore. His works include the catalogue of the BM's British Drawings (4 vols, 1898–1907); *English Watercolours* (1933); *Painting in the Far East* (1908); *Landscape in English Art and Poetry* (1930); collections of poetry including *London Visions* (1896, 1899), *The Sirens* (1924–5), *Collected Poems* (2 vols, 1931); and verse-dramas including *Attila* (1909), *Arthur* (staged with music by Edward Elgar, 1923), and *Boadicea* (1927). His Charles Eliot Norton Lectures – he was TSE's successor – were published as *The Spirit of Man in Asian Art* (1935).
2 – Binyon wrote on 14 May: 'Will you accept the enclosed little book of versions from Dante? [*Dante: Episodes from the Divine Comedy rendered in verse by Laurence Binyon* (1928).] You will probably not approve of them, & Heaven knows how well I know that the attempt is really impossible & that anyone familiar with the original must find them poor enough. But I have been reading your pamphlet with so much interest because I approached Dante in the same way, through the Temple Classics (being no Italian scholar) & still more because I agree with you that Dante is the best of all poets to train oneself by: indeed I have made my translations with that object, for discipline & exercise; there is nothing like it for getting to know something of Dante's art & mind – though I am really only a beginner – and I shouldn't have published these versions had not Mario Praz been rather enthusiastic about them, & wanted me to do more. I have done more, but I doubt if I shall go on – unless just for my own private discipline.'

But I do like your translations, and I cannot believe that you are as ignorant of Dante as I am. I like your metric, and I think you are right to stress (as it seems to me you do) the Teutonic element in English: I believe that we can only approach the divine informality of Dante's Latin speech through our own origins.

If I may make a few unimportant criticisms:

Will 'Galahalt' do for 'Galeotto': the implications of 'Galahad' are so strong for us.[1]

I am not quite satisfied with

'As if of Hell asserting great disdain'[2]

because 'asserting' seems to me to weaken the contempt: possibly I am affected by 'despitto' sounding like 'spit'.[3]

'Ancestors' seems to me a weak word in English for family Pride: I wish that it might have been 'Forbears'.[4]

Ulysses: the Italian gives me somehow the notion of a *licking* tongue, i.e. the metaphor seems in the Italian more closely welded to the image.[5]

'Sweet son':[6] is it not rather The sweetness of having a son?

'Old honoured father':[7] should one not give more the allusion to the *pietas* of Aeneas? I confess that 'honoured' has to me the devilish suggestion of a K.B.E. or something of that sort.

'Debito amore' does not suggest to me 'overdue':[8] I may be quite irrelevant, but I think of it as being merely 'due' to Penelope who was a boring person.

'Tardi', I can't think of the right word, but it suggests to me that the physical reflexes were not as immediate as they had been.[9]

Isn't 'bruti' enough, without 'of the field'. 'You weren't made to lie down with the animals'.[10]

1–In the second circle of Hell: 'The book I say / Was a Galahalt to us, and he beside / That wrote the book' (*Episodes*, p. 8). Cf. *Inf.* V, 137: 'Galeotto fu il libro, e chi lo scrisse.'
2–Ibid., p. 10.
3–*Inf.* x, 36: 'come avesse lo inferno in gran dispitto'.
4–Virgil 'looked at me a little, and with a kind / Of scorn he asked: "Who were thy ancestors?"' (ibid.). *Inf.* x, 42: 'mi dimandò: "Chi fur li maggior tui?"'
5–Binyon, *Episodes*, p. 13. *Inf.* xxvi, 85–90: 'Lo maggior corno della fiamma antica / cominciò a crollarsi mormorando, / pur come quella cui vento affatica. / Indi la cima qua a là menando, / comme fosse la lingua che parlasse, / gittò voce di fuori e disse . . .'
6–Ibid., p. 13. *Inf.* xxvi, 94: 'nè dolcezza di figlio . . .'
7–Ibid. *Inf.* xxvi, 94–5: 'nè la pieta / del vecchio padre . . .'
8–TSE misquotes Binyon's 'long-due love' (ibid., 13). *Inf.* xxvi, 95: 'nè il debito amore'.
9–'I and my crew were old and stiff of thew' (ibid., 13). *Inf.* xxvi, 106: 'Io e i compagni eravam vecchi e tardi'.
10–'". . . Ye were made / Not to live life of brute beasts of the field / But follow virtue and knowledge unafraid"' (ibid., 14). *Inf.* xxvi, 119: 'viver come bruti'.

'Them' (Ugolino) rather suggests to me that there were more children, but these were all that were with him.[1]

P. 24. Is 'Flame' within 'my veins' right? Isn't 'veins' suggested to you by the preceding? and isn't the collocation of the metaphor and the physiology a little violent?[2]

I hope you will not consider this sort of comment impertinent. It is the sort that I should like to have myself; and I shall send you my *Ash Wednesday*, which is merely an attempt to do the verse of the *Vita Nuova* in English, so that you may have me at your mercy. Anyway, I am sure that Praz is right, and I do hope you will some time complete the translation. Carey [*sic*] is painful; Longfellow is weary; and my cousin Norton is dull.[3] And I do not know of anyone living who could translate Dante as well as that. Ezra could do parts, but he will never understand the whole pattern.[4]

With many thanks,

yours sincerely,
T. S. Eliot

1 – 'When I awoke dark on my stony bed / I heard my children weeping in their sleep, / Them who were with me . . .' (ibid., 14). Cf. *Inf*. xxxiii, 38–9: 'pianger senti' fra il sonno i miei figliuoli, / ch' eran con mecco . . .'

2 – Beatrice appears like 'a living flame', so that Dante feels his spirit 'trembling' and 'broken'; his 'old love . . . smote' his 'sight', and 'pierced' his heart 'like to a spear'. He says to Virgil: 'Scarce one drop remains / Of blood in me that trembles not: by this / I recognize the old flame in my veins' (ibid., 24).

3 – Henry Francis Cary (1772–1844), British author and translator, published his blank-verse translation of the *Divina Commedia* in full in 1814; it was praised by Samuel Taylor Coleridge. Henry Wadsworth Longfellow (1807–1882), American poet and teacher, published his version in 1867. Charles Eliot Norton (1827–1908) – cousin of Charles William Eliot, president of Harvard; author, translator of Dante; editor of *North American Review*; friend of James Russell Lowell, Longfellow, Thomas Carlyle, Edward FitzGerald, Leslie Stephen and John Ruskin (for whom he was literary executor); first Professor of the History of Art at Harvard, 1875–98 – is commemorated by the Charles Eliot Norton Lectures, which TSE was to deliver in 1933. TSE's secretary to David R. Clark, 19 Aug. 1963: 'He believes that the prose translation made many years ago by Charles Elliot [*sic*] Norton has a very scholarly standing, but he has not read it.'

4 – Binyon replied on 28 May: 'Thank you so much for your letter. The criticisms are welcome, though I fear for me too often a counsel of perfection: I mean I should like to carry out your suggestions but can't manipulate the phrasing to get the wanted effect. However I am not persuaded by all of your criticisms, because evidently you have different associations from mine in the matter of certain words. "Forbears", for instance, is rather a dim word to me, "ancestors" much more vivid. Nor has "honoured" the flavour it has for you, though I admit it is not the right word. I wanted to suggest *pietas*, but haven't found the word. I agree also that "asserting great disdain" is not quite right, but again am at fault.'

16 May 1930   [Faber & Faber Ltd]

My dear Leonard,

Thank you very much for your letter[1] which I did not bother to answer immediately as I gathered that you might not be back in London for some little time. It was very comforting to me as it arrived simultaneously with a letter from a young man in Chelsea unknown to me who told me that my new book was so bad that it was no better than Edith Sitwell's.[2]

1–LW wrote on 5 May: 'You are the only living poet I can read twice; only in your case, I cannot stop at twice & go on rereading until something from outside intervenes to stop me. The usual thing happened to me the other evening with *Ash Wednesday*. It is amazingly beautiful. I dislike the doctrine, as you probably know, but the poetry remains & shows how unimportant belief or unbelief may be' (*Letters of Leonard Woolf*, ed. Frederic Spotts [1989], 238).

2–The 'young man from Chelsea' was named Peter Foy, who wrote on 12 May:

'Please read this, even if it seems over-rude.

'I was disappointed with "Ash Wednesday", not because I was expecting a rare pleasure, but because it seemed to shew that you have run short of that essential element in poetic composition – sensuous imagery. You have almost descended to the level of E. Sitwell at her most rampant.

'After forcibly feeding myself with such lines as

    And place is always and only place
    And what is actual is actual only for one time
    And only for one place
and
    The one veritable transitory power
and
    Both in the day time and in the night time
    The right time and the right place are not here
    No place of grace for those who avoid the face

such overwhelming homesickness assailed me that relief was only obtained by a hurried rush to the Waste Land.

'The technique of "Ash Wednesday" is marvellous, excellent, just what I have been expecting from you. But now that it has come I am disappointed. It reminds me too vividly of those times when I have nothing to do, and sit down, and say "What shall I do – Oh, yes, I'll write some verse – and bring in that new idea I thought of yesterday." Such uninspired pieces are usually interesting but seldom poetry.

'You must not think I am objecting to isolated lines, or to the poem as a whole. III is excellent, II and IV very beautiful, but I – well, please forgive me if I say that it reminds me of water in a ditch; and the rest of the sequence is below your level.

'I suppose you were working up to a climax of imagination and then retreating again. But I wish you hadn't. It is unkind of you to embarrass me and others by shewing feet of clay.

'I hope some rotten secretary doesn't read this and chuck it into the waste basket. I am very keen that you should understand what I am trying to say. I want to see you write an inspired poem using the technique which you have been developing (a sort of Cubism, isn't it) and what has now reached perfection in "Ash Wednesday".'

TSE telephoned Foy and invited him to meet late in May.

I don't know the country you have been visiting at all.[1] If we can scrape up the money to exchange our small car for a better one I may be tempted to visit it, but taking it down to Eastbourne and back a few days ago I discovered that neither the engine nor the brakes could be trusted on a very steep hill and but for finding a steep bank to back it into at one place it might have ended in disaster.

If or when you are back in London there is a young man I am meaning to trouble you with; not in person as he is at present living in Spain. His name is Edward Meryon Wilson and he went down from Cambridge about a year ago, he has done a volume of translations from Góngora which he would like to get printed. I have shewn them to J. B. Trend[2] who considers them highly competent – I may still have Trend's report which he made on the book. It didn't seem to me quite a book for Faber & Faber and I am not at all sure it is not more suitable for the Hogarth Press; but I promised him to bring it to your notice; so if you are willing to look at the translations I will have them sent round and also called for if you do not want them. Possibly it would do better for one of the University Presses; and if you do not want it I will tackle Madariaga.[3]

With love to Virginia and yourself.

Yours ever,
[T. S. E.]

1 – The Woolfs were touring the West Country.
2 – J. B. Trend (1887–1958), journalist, musicologist, literary critic, wrote music chronicles for C. See Margaret Joan Anstee, *JB – An Unlikely Spanish Don: The Life and Times of Professor John Brande Trend* (2013). See also TSE to Trend, 4 Sept. 1931, below.
3 – Salvador de Madariaga (1886–1978): Spanish diplomat, writer, and historian; author of *Englishmen, Frenchmen, Spaniards: An Essay in Comparative Psychology* (1929). TSE's idea was that Madariaga might be able to find a publisher for Wilson's translations of Góngora.

TO *Erik Mesterton*[1]   TS Erik Mesterton

16 May 1930   Faber & Faber Ltd

Dear Sir,

I am replying personally to part of your kind letter of the 22nd ultimo.[2] I am complimented by your wish to look up my earlier and not reprinted periodical writings. But I am afraid that will be a matter of some difficulty; I am myself very careless, and could not find many of my occasional notes without considerable research. For the *Egoist*, you might write to

Miss Harriet Shaw Weaver,
74, Gloucester Place,
London W. 1.

the former editor and proprietor, who would be able to furnish you with copies if anyone could. There is a good deal of my writing, largely unsigned, in the files of the *Egoist* 1917–1919. As for *Art and Letters* I have no idea to whom to apply about that defunct periodical: but the only thing of mine that I remember, which has never been reprinted, is an essay on Marivaux.[3] I will try to find out the address of Miss Anderson, who edited the *Little Review*.[4]

But I don't think that anything of mine in these deceased periodicals will help you very much. The history of 'classicism' (so far as I am concerned) is the history of my association with Irving Babbitt in America, with Maurras, and Maritain in France, and with Charles Whibley in England. Also with Curtius, and perhaps with Hofmannsthal.

Yours sincerely,
T. S. Eliot

1 – Erik Mesterton (1903–2004): Swedish author, critic, translator; editor during the 1930s of the poetry magazine *Spektrum*, founded in 1931. With the poet and novelist Karin Boye (1900–41), he translated *TWL*. See *The Waste Land: Some Commentaries*, trans. Llewellyn Jones (1943: from a prefatory essay to *Dikter i Urval* (1942)); and Mesterton, *Speglingar: Essäer, brev, översättningar* (1985).

2 – Mesterton wrote to F&F: 'I hope to introduce the ideas and writings of Mr Eliot to the Swedish public . . . [T]he conditions for studying the preparations and earlier development of "Classicism" in contemporary English literature are very hard in Sweden. It is unfortunate not to be able to get a clear conception of the genesis of the movement represented by the *Criterion*.' To that end, Mesterton wished to read TSE's earlier essays. 'Do you happen to know whether, and if so from whom, such numbers of various periodicals (*Egoist*, *Art and Letters*, the *Little Review* etc.) as contain contributions by him not reprinted in book form, may still be had?'

3 – 'Marivaux', *Art and Letters* 2: 2 (Spring 1919), 80–5.

4 – Margaret Anderson (1886–1973): American co-editor, with her lover Jane Heap (1883–1964), of *The Little Review*, 1914–29. TSE would describe Anderson, in a F&F reader's

17 May 1930   [Faber & Faber Ltd]

Dear Mr Parker,

I am sorry that I cannot help you very much; but really in these matters an author cannot be expected to know more than his readers.[1] That is, what I know about the poems that you don't is mostly irrelevant for your purpose; and the 'metaphor' is no good unless it can mean things for the reader that it didn't mean consciously for me. Do not worry at being unsure of the meaning, when the author cannot be sure of it either. The *Vita Nuova* might give you some help; but on the other hand it is much more obscure than I have the talent to be. If you call the three leopards the World, the Flesh and the Devil you will get as near as one can, but even that is uncertain.

Yours very truly,

[T. S. Eliot]

---

report on her autobiography 'My Thirty Years War', as 'an egotistical and interesting character'. Jane Heap he considered 'a most agreeable person' (letter to Desmond Hawkins, 22 May 1936).

1–Philip Parker (St John's College, Oxford) asked on 2 May for help with 'the metaphor' of *Ash-Wednesday*: 'I think my briefest course will be to note the particular phrases in question. In the first poem –

> Because I cannot drink
> There where trees flower . . .

(Is this – inability to derive complete appeasement from objective phenomena?)

> I renounce the blessed face.

Poem II   three white leopards
     "   III   the "ancient rhyme" and the "gilded hearse"
     "   IV   "deny between the rocks"

I have made III analogous to Keats'"chambers of thought", though not sharply. Have I stumbled there?'

TO *Nevill Coghill*[1]

17 May 1930   [Faber & Faber Ltd]

Dear Mr Coghill,

It is very thoughtful of you to offer me tickets for your production of *Samson Agonistes*[2] – a play which I admire immensely, and which – if there ever has been a performance before – I have never had the opportunity of seeing – and I wish indeed that I could come; but the latter part of May and the beginning of June finds me very rushed indeed. I have one engagement in Oxford during that time, which I hope to be able to keep; but I cannot allow myself any further indulgence. I shall have to content myself with reading any accounts of the performances afterwards.

With many thanks and regrets,

Yours sincerely,
[T. S. Eliot]

TO *Maurice Leahy*[3]

17 May 1930   [Faber & Faber Ltd]

Dear Mr Leahy,

I am greatly honoured by your invitation to meet the Catholic Poetry Society, and also by Father D'Arcy's giving a reading from my writings;

1–Nevill Coghill (1899–1980), born in Castletownshend, Co. Cork, studied at Exeter College, Oxford, and taught at the Royal Naval College, Dartmouth, before being elected in 1924 to a Research Fellowship at Exeter College and then a full Fellowship. From 1957 he was Merton Professor of English. A passionate member of the Oxford University Dramatic Society, he put on many plays (including *Measure for Measure*, starring Richard Burton, in 1944); and he was friends with C. S. Lewis and J. R. R. Tolkien, and with his pupil W. H. Auden. His primary interest was Chaucer: he translated *The Canterbury Tales* (1956) and *Troilus and Criseyde* (1971), and he wrote *The Poet Chaucer* (1949), *Geoffrey Chaucer* (1956) and *Shakespeare's Professional Skills* (1964). He later edited the Faber Educational editions of *MiC*, *FR* and *CP*.

When Coghill asked FVM, 18 May 1936, 'I enclose a satirical verse-play which I would like you to read with a view to publishing it if it appeals to you. My hopes are that it might make an item in the Criterion Miscellany', TSE wrote on his letter: 'NO. Certainly not. T.S.E.'

2–Coghill wrote on 5 May, 'On the strength of our mutual acquaintance with Wystan Auden I am venturing to offer you two tickets for any performance of *Samson Agonistes*, which I hope to produce in the Fellows' Garden, Exeter College, on May 22, 23, 24, 26, 28, at 2:15 pm.'

3–Maurice Leahy, author, editor; Hon. Sec. and Editor of the Catholic Poetry Society (founded in London in 1926, in association with G. K. Chesterton, Hilaire Belloc, Sheila Kaye-Smith and Ronald Knox); author of *An Anthology of Contemporary Poetry* and *The*

and I wish that I could accept; but as I am moving house very shortly, I dare not, with my ordinary work, make any engagements at all before midsummer.[1] Such an occasion deserves some preparation, for which I have not the time. I confess that your other suggestion rather frightens me, as I am no Dante scholar and not even a good Italian scholar.[2] But I hope that I may be given another opportunity to meet the Society later; though a discussion with Father D'Arcy is particularly tempting.

With many thanks and cordial regrets,

Yours sincerely,

[T. S. Eliot]

TO *H. P. J. Marshall*   CC

17 May 1930   [Faber & Faber Ltd]

Dear Mr Marshall,

May you flourish in Moscow,[3] and get enough to eat, and return filled with cinematographic knowledge and a dislike of barbarians. I cannot see my way to giving any commission; and as you know I have a good man already who reviews Russian periodicals; but I am sure that after you have been there a time you will have more definite suggestions to make. By all means send and recommend any books that you think worth translating – if we accepted any, it would be of course with a commission to yourself. And certainly send on any writings of your own.

I gave the editors of *Transition* your address and asked them to write direct. I have asked my secretary to give you their names and address; and if you travel via Paris, suggest that you should look them up.

Yours sincerely,

[T. S. Eliot]

Insight of the Curé of Ars; taught at Fordham University; Boston College; Seton Hall University, New York.

1–Leahy wrote on 10 May: 'Father Martin D'Arcy recently told me that he was going to read some of your Works at one of our Meetings. Incidentally, when Father D'Arcy is reading some selections from your Works would you oblige me very much by attending on that occasion, and taking part in a discussion with Father D'Arcy on any points of Modern Poetry that you care to suggest? We shall greatly welcome you. Would Friday, May 23rd suit you at 5.45?'

2–Leahy suggested as an alternative: 'Miss [Barbara] Barclay-Carter, who has translated many Works from the Italian, is going to speak on Dante. In view of your admirable little book on Dante, which I am reviewing in our Periodical, I wonder if you would care to take part in a very general discussion on Dante with Miss Barclay-Carter.'

3–H. P. J. Marshall (The Film Guild of London) had secured a scholarship to study at the Cinema Institute in Moscow. He wrote on 8 May that he was going there in three weeks.

17 May 1930   [Faber & Faber Ltd]

Dear Mr Spender,

Thank you for your letter and for sending me your poems.[1] I like them, and I hope you will let me keep them for a time to show to one or two friends. I think that Lewis has chosen the best; but I may be able to use some of the others.[2] I think the time will come when you will have to choose between writing verse and writing novels; because I do not believe that any human organism can be stored with enough energy to cultivate two such different modes of speech; but meanwhile you are right to try both forms and time will tell you which is yours.

Of course being at Oxford is paralysing to you. Residence in a University, enforced for three or four years, is unpleasant to anyone who is eager for artistic expression; but my belief is that it is best to put up with it. It may take you a year or two to recover; but the experience, and even the holding-back is useful in the long run. But forgive me for being sententious. Please [*typing runs off the page*][3]

---

1 – Spender wrote from University College, Oxford (2 May), that he was sending 'all the poems I have written . . . so that you can get some sort of survey of the whole, if you want it.

'I have never sent you poems before, because it is only now that I have felt I could really be helped by disinterested criticism. Please say what you really think about them. I have shown them to friends; and a few well-known people have been very keen on them, but I have never felt very much assisted by their praise. E. R. Curtius liked them very much, for example, but I think what appealed to him most may have been the point of view they expressed . . .

'If you could say just very shortly what you felt, soon, I should know where I stand. I want very much to know this now, because being at Oxford has a most paralyzing effect on me I find; and now I feel sometimes that it has deprived me of all the freshness and vitality I had when I came here and given me nothing instead. I do not think that is true . . .

'Before coming here, & in my first two years, I wrote the sketch of a novel, which I hope to revise in 1931. The characters in the 1st poem are from that book. Marston is a person both in the book and existing in real life as a friend of mine whom I hero-worshipped at one time. He is referred to constantly in the poems, and was the first impulse of my poetry.

'In July of last year I went to Germany and wrote some poems there, two of which I send. After that I tried to leave Oxford, but in vain . . .

'The poems marked W. L. are "reserved" by Wyndham Lewis for the "Enemy" No 4.'
2 – 'Four poems' – dedicated to W. H. Auden – 'The Port', 'The Swan', 'Lines written when walking down the Rhine', 'Not to you I sighed', *C.* 10 (Oct. 1930), 32–4.
3 – Spender replied on 20 May: 'I am very happy and proud that you should like my poems.

'I expect that you are right about Oxford; only I have revolted so much from it that I feel I have neither learnt anything nor done my own work. However, I expect that is nonsense, and anyhow I should not complain of such things . . . Please do not bother to reply.'

Spender's biographer John Sutherland writes that 'an unnamed "friend" sent his poems to Eliot, which led to four of them being published in the *Criterion* in October 1930 . . . In his jubilant letter to Carritt, Stephen recalled that Eliot said "that he liked the poems very much"' (*Stephen Spender: The Authorized Biography* [2004], 98).

TO *G. Wilson Knight*[1]

17 May 1930   [Faber & Faber Ltd]

Dear Mr Wilson Knight,

Thank you very much for your letter of the 15th. I was glad to meet Mr Still, and hope to see him again to discuss matters more fully. I read his book with great interest and some speed, as I felt that I ought to see it before sending in my introduction. It did not, as a matter of fact, make any difference to what I wrote; but I am glad to have read it. Will you please ask Milford to send you a galley or page of what I have written, as I should like to feel sure that it satisfied you before it was published.

I am very much pleased that you like my new poems. I don't consider myself that they are any better as poetry than 'The Hollow Men', and there is no reason why they should be – no reason, I mean, inherent in the content. All one can ask of oneself (or of anyone else) is that one's expression at each phase shall be adequate to that phase, and that the phase itself shall have some general human significance. To return to our great exemplar, I like *King Lear* as well at least as any play of

---

(Gabriel Carritt – 'Tristan' in Spender's autobiography *World Within World* – was an Oxford friend of SS; later a member of the Communist Party and journalist on the *Daily Worker*.)

1–G. Wilson Knight (1897–1985) served in WW1 and took a degree in English at St Edmund Hall, Oxford, in 1923. He held teaching posts before being appointed Chancellors' Professor of English, Toronto University, 1931–40. In 1946 he was made Reader in English Literature at the University of Leeds, where he became Professor, 1955–62. Works include *The Wheel of Fire: Five Essays on the Interpretation of Shakespeare's Sombre Tragedies* (1930) – for which TSE wrote the introduction, having recommended the work to OUP – and *The Imperial Theme: Further Interpretations of Shakespeare's Tragedies including the Roman Plays* (1931).

TSE wrote, in a reference addressed to the Universities Bureau of the British Empire, 31 May 1937: 'I have known Mr Wilson Knight in connexion with his essays on Shakespeare's plays, which have attained a considerable reputation. My opinion of these essays is sufficiently indicated by my having committed myself in writing the introduction to the first of the volumes, which was published by the Oxford University Press ... Although I think Mr Wilson Knight sometimes presses a point too far, I have a very high opinion of his Shakespeare scholarship.'

On 29 Oct. 1956, TSE wrote of him to Helen Gardner: 'I found his first book about Shakespeare's imagery very stimulating indeed – in fact, I wrote a preface to it, but by the time the third volume came out, I began to feel that it was enough to submit a few of Shakespeare's plays to such analysis, but I did not want to read any more.'

GWK was to situate himself in relation to TSE in 'My Romantic Tendencies', *Studies in Romanticism* 9: 1 (Winter 1967), 556–7. See also Wilson Knight, 'J. C. Powys and T. S. Eliot', *Contemporary Review* 228: 1321 (Feb. 1976), 78–85; 'Thoughts on *The Waste Land*', *The Denver Quarterly* 7: 2 (Summer 1972), 1–13.

Shakespeare's. I should like to know which line worried you; otherwise your criticism gives me much pleasure.[1]

I wish indeed that I could accept your very tempting invitation; but alas, I fear that I must not make any engagements for this summer, even one of pure pleasure.[2] I hope another time; and I also hope that you may some day have the opportunity of presenting a play in London. Have you heard for instance of the Grafton Theatre (enclosed).[3] I cannot tell what they will do; but they are enlightened people; and the sort whom one might approach with suggestions.

With many thanks and best wishes,

Sincerely yours,
[T. S. Eliot]

TO *Ursula Roberts*[4]   TS copy

19 May 1930   Faber & Faber Ltd

Dear Mrs Roberts,

Thank you very much for the copy of *The Shield* with your article which I found extremely interesting, as did another Director to whom I shewed it.[5] There are two reasons however why we do not think that we could publish it in the Miscellany. One is that we feel that so far as this firm is concerned enough has been said on the subject for the moment and that

---

1 – Knight had been studying *Ash-Wednesday*: 'They have given me great delight . . . Their peculiar serenity contrasts very strongly with The Hollow Men. Yet I do not know that that necessarily makes me like them better . . . One line, in Ash-Wednesday, I found difficult – but perhaps it is my fault. I felt that a slight alteration was more in keeping with your rhythm & meaning & that there may have been a mistake – but I may have missed the point.' The line was: 'Distraction, music of the flute, stops and steps of the mind over the third stair . . .'
2 – Knight was putting on a production of *A Midsummer Night's Dream* for the School Speech Day on 5 July, and hoped TSE might find the time to come down to Cheltenham to see it.
3 – The Grafton Theatre was a former cinema in Tottenham Court Road, London.
4 – Ursula Roberts (1887–1975): poet, novelist and spiritualist, who sometimes wrote as 'Susan Miles'; wife of William Corbett Roberts (1873–1953), Rector of St George's Church, Bloomsbury, 1917–38.
5 – Roberts sent (3 May) a copy of *The Shield* with an article by herself called 'Pornography and Art'. 'It is very sketchy and inadequate, and in places, I think, confused; but I should rather like to work out the ideas more thoroughly. Would there be any chance of your considering something on the same lines, but less hastily written, for your Criterion Miscellany series?' She added: 'May I take this opportunity of saying how very much interested I was in your reading at the Poetry Bookshop? I was surprised to hear you say that the "You'd be bored" . . . "I'd be bored" poem [from *Sweeney Agonistes*] couldn't easily be read aloud. I had delighted in reading it to various friends. Its rhythms seemed to me to call for reading aloud.'

it would be inadvisable to revive it at the present time; the other reason is that articles in this series have to be of a very popular character: pamphlets at the price of 1/- have to sell in very large numbers to justify publication and I think that your article is unsuitable in a sense for the very reasons for which it interested me. It is rather a philosophical discussion on the subject and I think it would be decidedly over the heads of most of the people who can be expected [to] buy these pamphlets. Even one, of which I am sending you a copy herewith and which you may have read, rather suffers in this respect.

I hope however that you may have other suggestions later either for the Miscellany or for the *Criterion* itself .

I did not know until you sent me *The Shield* that you were Susan Miles whose small book of verse called *Dunch* I read and reviewed in the *Egoist* a great many years ago.[1] I enjoyed those poems very much. Have you published any verse since then?

Yours sincerely
T. S. Eliot

TO *Algar Thorold* CC

Monday, 19 May 1930   [*The Criterion*]

My dear Thorold,

Thanks for your letter and card.[2] *Anabase* will arrive soon, and also Jan. 1927.[3] And I have had Dawson's pamphlet sent to the *Tablet*.

I am much impressed by Dawson's note.[4] I do not know enough of the literature of the subject, and dare not offer my own opinion therefore. I wonder if it is one that the Church prefers not to be gone into, or not? For it is difficult to do so, it seems to me, without skating on very thin eggs: the dilemma of keeping everybody out, or of letting everybody in. I think Dawson ought to expand the thesis very considerably. His danger seems to me that of insufficient cases. The suggestion that the gap is at the bottom rather than at the top does not quite satisfy me, because it is still more at the bottom that we have to consider what 'lack of opportunity of knowledge' means: the inferior nature has, has it not, less 'opportunity' than the higher; of three peasants, an Irish, a north German,

---

1 – 'Short Notices', *Egoist* 5: 5 (May 1918), 75.
2 – Not found.
3 – The Jan. 1927 issue of C. which René Hague had requested.
4 – Not found.

and an Egyptian fellah, can we say from ordinary human observation that one has not merely had better luck than the others? The question of 'opportunity' becomes more acute as one gets nearer home. If I for instance had spent my life in Boston instead of London, the mere weight of ancestral tradition, of atmosphere and surroundings, might very likely have operated to keep me an Unitarian, though possibly a more and more devout one. Just as the influence of England probably operates on me who was born in the heart of New England Unitarianism, as not upon you who were born the son of (or who were born the son of one who became) an English Bishop? I mean that if we go into the matter truly, do we not have to confess that what *must appear to us* as accidents have been largely operant: so is it expedient to raise the question at all? I do not doubt, any more than you do, that these matters are ordered justly – but can we hope to penetrate that order ourselves? I should like to have a long evening, with say, you and Dawson and Maritain and possibly Rawlinson,[1] over this subject. For you, the question applies (amongst other) to me; for me, it applies to all of those whom I have loved most dearly. So I only say – though I like the line of Dawson's thought, which in its subtlety is worthy of him – is it expedient to print?[2]

I want you to read *Ash Wednesday* and will have another copy sent. But I have had so many letters asking me to explain what it means, that I almost wish I had not published it. Who am I, to know what I mean?

The address of *Lady* (sic) Gwyer (her husband is Sir Maurice Gwyer K.C.B.[3] the King's Proctor and a good Protestant – I once reminded him

1 – The Ven. Canon A. E. J. Rawlinson, DD, The College, Durham.
2 – Thorold responded to this paragraph in a separate letter (22 May):
'There was never any question of printing. D. & I had a conversation once on the subject & we noted points as we went along . . . The Vatican Council defined that all men without exception receive sufficient grace for salvation & this is in consequence an article of Faith for R[oman Catholic]s. The point is, how this dogma can be reconciled with facts of observation. Not only do non-moral causes like education & heredity play or seem to play a large part, but the psychic variability of individuals – to certain minds "Faith" seems to be really impossible – seems to effectually disprove a "flat rate" of spiritual opportunity. This has always distressed me very much & at a certain time made my own faith very shaky . . .
'I think we must admit that there exists no possible experimental verification of that article of Faith. This should not disturb our confidence in God whose methods of action on the creature are as infinite as his nature & also as impenetrable to created intelligence . . .
'And given all this, I cant help feeling that Dawson is right in principle. Does not the *salvific* quality of the Church lie in her sacramental system rather than in the formal acceptance of her teaching? . . . Now all the theologians teach that although we are bound to approach the sacraments if we know about them, God is not bound to confine grace to the sacraments.'
3 – Maurice Gwyer (1878–1952) – knighted in 1928 – and his wife Alsina (daughter of the philanthropist Sir Henry Burdett) were co-proprietors of the company that had run the joint enterprise of the Scientific Press (launched by Burdett, who had died in 1920), the *Nursing*

that but for Protestantism there would be no King's Proctor – is 16, Young Street, Kensington W.8. I am sorry to hear about her brother;[1] I knew his health had been very bad for some years.

If you are in town early in June shall we try to lunch on that Wednesday? I will tell you more about More. Perhaps some people want to postpone Armageddon – at any rate not 'implement' it!

Yours ever
[T. S. Eliot]

In Confidence: I may be needing a man to review French periodicals regularly, as my present colleague, I regret to say, may find himself too busy. Is Hague[2] up to that? is he in touch and does he know enough? A certain sense of humour and even a capacity for levity is needed in such a reviewer, as well as love of reading French periodicals, time to do so also: for I can only keep the Periodicals Reviews up to standard by using people who like to receive and read them anyway – otherwise the pay is quite inadequate. It should also be someone of wide interests and considerable tolerance.

TO *Gordon Fraser*[3]   CC

19 May 1930   [Faber & Faber Ltd]

Dear Mr Fraser,

Thank you for your letter of May 17th.[4] I should be interested to hear some more about your project if you would let me know; but I am afraid

---

Mirror, and the general publishing house of Faber & Gwyer. Although the Gwyers were co-owners – Mrs Gwyer understandably felt it her duty to be the vigilant trustee of her late father's interests – Maurice Gwyer was a major shareholder but did not serve as a director of the company, and was otherwise fully employed in public service, as Treasury Solicitor.

1 – Francis Burdett was about to undergo an operation in Hampstead Hospital.

2 – René Hague (1905–81): printer and scholar. Born in London of Irish parents, he was schooled at Ampleforth College, Yorkshire. In 1924–5 he met the craftsman Eric Gill (he would marry Gill's daughter Joan), and the artist and writer David Jones; and with Gill he founded the Pigotts Press, which they ran until 1956. Hague's works include *A Commentary on 'The Anathemata' of David Jones* (1977) and *Dai Greatcoat: A Self-Portrait of David Jones in His Letters* (1980). See Barbara Wall, *René Hague – A Personal Memoir* (1989).

3 – Gordon Fraser (1911–81), book and greetings card publisher, established in 1930 an imprint called The Minority Press while a student at St John's College, Cambridge, issuing several pamphlets by FRL and others; and from 1935 he ran a bookshop in Portugal Place. He would later become world-renowned as a publisher of greetings cards.

4 – Fraser wished to reprint, at his Minority Press, TSE's introduction to the Etchelle & Macdonald (Haslewood Books) edition of Dryden's *Of Dramatick Poesie* (1928). 'In Cambridge there is a particular demand for it and only a few can afford 31/6 . . . [T]here are people here who want it and can't get it and [we] are willing to remedy this by publishing at 1/6 or 2/6.'

that for the present I cannot allow my dialogue on Dramatic Poetry to be published. I believe that the edition is not yet sold out, partly on account of the high price which everyone agrees was a mistake; but I feel an obligation to the publishers not to reproduce it in any way for some time to come and in any case I should have to give my own firm the option of republishing it first because that is part of my contract with the firm as a Director.

With many thanks,
Yours sincerely,
[T. S. Eliot]

TO *Charles Williams*[1]

CC

22 May 1930   [Faber & Faber Ltd]

Dear Mr Williams,

Thank you for your letter of the 17th.[2] I like Knight's essays myself, but it was no doubt a feeling similar to yours which made me attempt a somewhat prophylactic introduction. I hope it succeeds.

Many thanks for your remarks about *Ash Wednesday*; though I should be happier if you and Milford and Hopkins had been able to project yourselves into the skulls of these hypothetical great grandchildren.[3] I

1–Charles Williams (1886–1945), novelist and writer on theology, worked as a reader for Oxford University Press. After removing in 1939 from London to Oxford (where he lectured and tutored), he became a member, with C. S. Lewis and J. R. R. Tolkien, of the 'Inklings'. TSE admired Williams's 'spiritual shockers': the later novels including *War in Heaven* (1930), *The Greater Trumps* (1932) and *All Hallows' Eve* (1945).
2–Williams had read TSE's introduction to *The Wheel of Fire* (1930) – 'and am content to admire it. To be absolutely truthful, I am a little nervous of W. K.'s work, though I like it, and your own supplied the judicious touch I think the book needed.'
    TSE observed in his piece: 'It is . . . the prejudice or preference of any one who practises, though humbly, the art of verse, to be sceptical of all "interpretations" of poetry, even his own interpretations . . .' Guardedly glossing 'interpretation' as seeking 'to pounce upon the secret, to elucidate the pattern and pluck out of the mystery, of a poet's work', he noted further: 'I believe that there is a good deal in the interpretation of Shakespeare by Mr Wilson Knight which can stand indefinitely for other people . . . I confess that reading his essays seems to me to have enlarged my understanding of the Shakespeare pattern, which, after all, is quite the main thing . . . More particularly, I think that Mr Wilson Knight has shown insight in pursuing his search for the pattern below the level of "plot" and "character" . . .' (xvi–xx).
3–Williams noted, of *Ash-Wednesday*: 'It will not perhaps displease you to know that Mr Milford and [Gerard] Hopkins and I all, separately and together, agreed that it seemed to suggest to us that our great-grandchildren would find it great poetry . . . Without asking for meaning or interpretation or anything, it did just occur to us to wonder whether there

am still wondering whether it would have been more of a compliment if you had made it a generation less, – or a generation more? Anyway, no bibliography is going to help you, and I'm damned if I will – or rather if I would-if-I-could. Perhaps in another *janma*, as the Orientals are supposed to say. But if one can explain *obscurus* by *obscurior*, and the less by the greater, the *Vita Nuova* may help. But if the three leopards or the unicorn contain any allusions literary, I don't know what they are. Can't I sometimes invent nonsense, instead of always being supposed to borrow it?

Yours ever sincerely,
[T. S. Eliot]

TO *Algar Thorold* CC

23 May 1930   [*The Criterion*]

My dear Thorold,

Many thanks for your letter.[1] I find your report on Hague about what I should expect. I doubted whether he had either experience or knowledge enough.

As for what you say further, it gives me both pleasure and pain.[2] I am very doubtful about it from your point of view. We pay for the reviews of foreign periodicals at the same rate as the body articles: £2 per 1000 words; but it only means as a rule two reviews of two to three thousand words each per annum; and particularly with French (and American) periodicals, of which there are so many, it means looking through a vast mass of printed matter; so the game is far from the value of the candle for anyone except an amateur who enjoys reading the periodicals anyway. Let us both think it over. I mean that the reason you give for doing seems to me a reason for not doing it. Articles for American magazines is the only writing I know of that is well paid.

---

were any –, well, say, allusion – in the "three leopards" or the "unicorns dragging a gilded hearse" that one would perhaps be happier for recognizing . . . We have looked at Dante, but unachievingly.'

1 – Thorold doubted (20 May) whether René Hague was up to the job of producing a French chronicle. 'I do not think he would have either the technical experience, nor the experience of life necessary to do what you want.'

2 – Thorold had offered to become the reviewer of French periodicals: 'The fact is I need to earn a little more . . . I am of course half-French, though that does not carry any real qualification!'

I think it would be a better employment of time if you did two long reviews for the *Criterion* a year. That is not well paid either; but better pay in relation to the time expended; and also I think your name would give us more prestige that way, than merely as initials at the end of the number. Can you suggest anything you would care to do for September?[1]

About reading French books.[2] The trouble is that very few get as far as that. We have got shyer and shyer of French books; novels almost never do well; it is only an occasional learned work that I think might be acceptable; in such rare events we might ask you not only for an opinion, but perhaps to translate if you would. In fact, most of those that interest me personally are more suitable for Sheed[3] than for us.

I have given instructions that the 'Miscellany' should be sent to the *Dublin* as published. There is no general subscription.

I return herewith the review by Gill.[4] I cannot agree with you that the review is so good, when it comes to Mitchison, – as you find it.[5] However, it is very interesting, and will do the sales good. And I can reassure you about the risks. Of course I cannot guarantee Mrs Mitchison,[6] whom I do not know, but I have taken the liberty of showing the review to another director who does know her, and he could see nothing libellous in it at all. So I don't think you need worry. But the use of the word 'homosexuality' seems to me a mistake; I think that Gill instead of reviewing is chasing a notion of his own which is interesting and I dare say valuable, but irrelevant and weakens his opinion of the pamphlet.

I hear from Lady Gwyer that her brother Francis is at

    83, Cornwall Gardens,

    S.W.7. Telephone Western 0818.

She asks me to tell you this. But she does not write as if the operation were a really dangerous one.

Yes. Gill is right about 'concupiscence', and the point is well taken.[7]

---

1 – Thorold asked to review, in Oct., 'Lawrence & Sex, if you agree'.

2 – Thorold asked too if he could be of service in reading 'any French books . . . with a view to translation – I don't mean translation by me . . .'

3 – Sheed & Ward, London, publishers.

4 – Eric Gill (1882–1940): sculptor, stonecutter, printmaker; designer of typefaces including Gill Sans and Perpetua.

5 – 'I enclose a review (in confidence) by Eric Gill on Dawson & Mitchison. Do you think that in the latter case he is really too rude – or even possibly libellous? There is the word "indecent" that lawyers might not like . . .' The books were Naomi Mitchison, *Comments on Birth Control* (Criterion Miscellany 12); Christopher Dawson, *Christianity and Sex* (Criterion Miscellany 13).

6 – Naomi Mitchison (1897–1999): novelist, journalist; commentator on African affairs.

7 – 'Gill's theological criticism of Dawson's use of "concupiscence" is correct.'

Incidentally, I happen to know that when one is the *victim* of libel it is difficult to get anything. I was once libelled and was assured by the lawyers that I ought to be satisfied with a note of apology in very small type in an obscure part of the newspaper some days after!

I hope you have received Jan. 1927 *Criterion* for Hague. Note that the play of which this is a fragment is to be called *Sweeney Agonistes*. And I hope Hague will not call *Ash Wednesday* religious or devotional verse[1] – it is merely an attempt to put down in words a certain *stage* of the journey, a journey of which I insist that all my previous verse represents previous stages. I am sure you will appreciate the distinction.

Yours ever,
[T. S. Eliot]

TO *Frederic Manning*[2]   CC

23 May 1930   [Faber & Faber Ltd]

Dear Manning,

I have been waiting in the hope of hearing from you at some address or other; but I have given up hope, and so send this letter in duplicate, one to the Commonwealth Bank, the other care of Mrs Fowler.

First to thank you for *Her Privates We*.[3] I should not have said much about it before in any case, as I have only had the time to begin it in the last two days; and am still only half through. I am liking it very much indeed. I don't know what a book like this means to a man who has been through it. To one who has not, there is some consolation in perceiving what one has in common with those who did: but we are left always the question, which will haunt men like myself of my generation till we die – 'how would I have behaved?' And that question will be a tormenting nuisance to me for the rest of life.[4]

---

1 – The anonymous author of *The Listener*'s Book Chronicle said of the 'six new poems' that make up *Ash-Wednesday*: 'If he would only be willing to let down the barriers a little, to catch some part of the unconsciousness and the abandon of [Francis] Thompson, we should have in him a religious poet who would be worthy to rank with Crashaw' (*Listener*, 14 May 1930, 864).

2 – Frederic Manning (1882–1935), Australian writer: see Biographical Register.

3 – Manning inscribed a copy of the fifth impression of *Her Privates We* by Private 19022 (1930): 'T. S. Eliot from Private 19022'.

4 – Manning responded on 27 May: 'I am glad that you like the book, or as much of it as you have read, but you must tell me what you think of it as a whole, as I tried to show a single and indivisible experience. And don't reproach yourself: in some rude fashion fate

I have not sent you a copy of my last verse pamphlet, not knowing where to send it.

If you get this, please let me have news of you. And when you can, will you answer two questions. (1) Is there any chance of getting a political essay for the *Criterion*, or a political pamphlet for the Miscellany, out of you? You said, you know, that you wanted now to do some political writing. (2) Would Private 19022 consider translating for us, for a suitable remuneration, a German war book very highly recommended to us – a book dealing with the war from the experience of an artilleryman? I have enough faith in the man who recommended it to believe that it is a good book.[1]

Yours ever,
[T. S. Eliot]

TO *Veronica Wynne*[2]   CC

24 May 1930   [Faber & Faber Ltd]

Dear Madam,

In reply to your letter of the 19th instant, I shall be honoured by 'serving' for another year on the Council of the League; but I am not aware of having been of any service whatever. This I regret.

Yours truly,
[T. S. Eliot]

---

allots us our appropriate parts – and there is always the present emergency to provide a sufficient test.'

1 – Manning affirmed that he would like to write a political study, but not yet. In answer to TSE's second question, he said he did not know German well enough to translate the book. The book was probably *Partenau* (1929), by the doctor and writer Max René Hesse (1877–1952), which was ultimately translated by GCF (anon.) and published as *The White Flame* (F&F, 1932).

2 – Veronica Wynne was Secretary of the Arts League of Service.

TO *Gerald Barry*[1]   CC

24 May 1930   [Faber & Faber Ltd]

Dear Sir,

In reply to your kind letter of the 23d instant, I hope that you will excuse me from sitting for a portrait.[2] There is nothing that I find more painful, except inspecting the consequences. I mean no disrespect to Mr Oppfer, of whom I know nothing. And I feel as kindly towards the *Week End Review* as towards any periodical; but I prefer my obscurity.

Yours very truly,

[T. S. Eliot]

TO *M. C. D'Arcy*   CC

24 May 1930   [Faber & Faber Ltd]

My dear D'Arcy,

I leave *Ash Wednesday* in your hands with confidence, to interpret to Oxford. But *please* don't let the young men call it 'religious' verse. I had a shock on reading *The Granta* to see stated categorically that it was 'the finest religious poem in English since Crashaw'.[3] If it was, it wouldn't be; and anyhow it was I who told them of a poet named Crashaw; and such assertions can only do me harm. I don't consider it any more 'religious' verse than anything else I have written: I mean that it attempts to state a particular phase of the progress of one person. If that progress is in the direction of 'religion', I can't help that; it is I suppose the only direction in which progress is possible.

I look forward to seeing you in July. I hope you found Belgion endurable.

Yours sincerely,

[T. S. Eliot]

1–Gerald Barry (1898–1968), journalist, was educated at Corpus Christi College, Cambridge, became founder-editor of *The Week-end Review*, 1930–4; editor of the *News Chronicle*, 1936–47; and Director-General of the Festival of Britain, 1948–51. He was to be knighted in 1951. Later roles included being in charge of educational programmes at Granada Television; Chairman of International Literary Management; Director, New Statesman and Nation; Chairman of the New Barbican Committee.
2–'I am arranging for the publication of a short series of portraits in the WEEK-END REVIEW by the Danish artist, Mr Oppfer. I am very anxious to include your portrait in this series . . .'
3–J. D. [probably John Davenport], 'Eagle's Wings', *The Granta* 39: 887 (16 May 1930), 419: 'The six poems in this volume constitute the finest religious poetry written in English since Crashaw . . . They are impeccable.'

to *Bonamy Dobrée*

ts Brotherton

24 May 1930   Faber & Faber Ltd

Dear Bungamy,

A copy of *Ash Wednesday* (of which copies only reach me occasionally and in small quantities) should have come to the Priory.[1]

Want Americana[2] by July 25th. I am delighted to send you H. & H.[3] with Gummers, and wish that Gummers himself was with you. Gummers is worse and worse, and has taken to limericks, since his (triumphal) visit to Oxford.[4]

Have you no ink eraser?

I shd. be glad if you would come to lunch one day to discuss the demerits of Sir. W. Morris Bt.'s handbrakes.

Yours etc.
T. S. E.

to *Henry Eliot*

ts Houghton

25 May 1930   Faber & Faber Ltd

My dear brother,

This is only to be a fragment of a letter after all; but at least it will not be devoted to my grievances against New York publishers. Except to tell you that I have a cheque from Horace Liveright Inc. some of the amount being itemised as '½ permission $37.50'. I have written to Liveright to ask what this 'permission' is; meanwhile I do not cash the cheque, in the probable event of it being for the robbery I wrote about. Thirty-seven fifty is a beggarly sum for lifting my best known piece.

This letter is really merely to thank you for sending me the Apostles' Bell. I could have asked for nothing better; and it is more to me than many more costly things. And also the little old Bible I shall cherish. I cannot remember whether it is the one we read from on Sunday mornings, in turn; that may have been another one of Father's. I am glad that Theodora[5]

---

1 – BD was living at Mendham Priory, Harleston, Norfolk.
2 – BD's 'American Chronicle' for C.
3 – *The Hound & Horn*.
4 – BD asked on 10 May: 'When do you want Americana by? I won't start till I get the last *Hound and Horn*, which I suspect you of keeping so as to get Gummers's article by heart.' The reference is to Montgomery Belgion's article 'God is Mammon', *Hound & Horn*, Spring 1930.
5 – Theodora Eliot Smith (1904–92) – 'Dodo' – daughter of George Lawrence and Charlotte E. Smith (TSE's sister). A graduate of Vassar College (AB, 1926), she studied too at Radcliffe

should have Charlotte's portrait of me. And I am glad to have the letters to make ashes of. I should never have wanted to read them again, with all the folly and selfishness; and I don't want anyone else ever to read them and possibly print them; and if I could destroy every letter I have ever written in my life I would do so before I die. I should like to leave as little biography as possible. So that's done and done with.

Do send more news of you. I wish either for a slump in steamship ticket prices or a great elevation of your income, and that you might come. Even a fortnight would be a wonderful treat. I wonder when and whether I shall see you again.

The picture frame reached Vivienne safely. She will write when she can; but is far from well at present and we are moving on June 11th. Future address: 68, Clarence Gate Gardens N.W.1.

Ever affectionately,
Tom

Don't bother about the Adams letters. I did not want those *particularly*: I had merely imagined that there might be a great number of historically valuable letters altogether.

I am glad to hear about Mill Creek. I hope it goes through, more particularly if it meant enough addition to your own income to make that trip to Europe possible.

TO *G. Wilson Knight*   CC

25 May 1930   [Faber & Faber Ltd]

Dear Mr Wilson Knight

Thank you for your letter of the 20th May, to which I have not time to reply [as] fully as it deserves. I disagree on one point.[1] I do not think that the 'core of metaphysics' in Shakespeare is at all exactly equivalent to the Thomism etc. in Dante. There is an indefinite overlapping, of course.

College, 1926–7. She taught at Bryn Mawr School, Baltimore, from 1931, and attended summer school sessions at Cambridge University (1929, 1931, 1936, 1939); Oxford University (1937); London Speech Institute (1938); and Harvard (1940, 1941, 1942). TSE delighted in her company on each visit.

1 – Wilson Knight wrote: 'My own feeling is that if we may postulate a "philosophic core" to a great work of poetry, then in Dante we have it – by chance, as it were – ready to hand in the Aquinas system, & need not search for it. In Shakespeare <I refer to the latter half of his plays (1600–1612)> there is exactly *the same core* of metaphysics, but it has to be very carefully abstracted. When you have it, you have what bears to Shakespeare's work the relation Dante's philosophy bears to his poem.'

What is important in both is something which is a fusion of thought and feeling, and which is never quite translateable into abstract language. The existence of an impressive scholastic philosophy behind Dante, and of only Renaissance stoicism etc. behind Shakespeare, does not mean either that the one poet is greater or less great than the other.

The line you like so much is not absolutely original.[1] Somewhere or another Donne makes a pun on the world being so called because it is 'whirled'.[2] But I think without modesty that I have improved upon the hint, and any rhythmical value the line has is mine.

The theory that the poet should do without adjectives is I think merely an exaggeration of the truth, obvious in either verse or prose (and the writing of verse or prose has much the same difficulties), that the adjective is the part of speech most easily abused.[3] If one uses too many, then the value of each is debased; but the right adjective in the right place has tremendous capacities. It may be a very humble one in itself; too many poets nowadays seem to think that an extensive and recondite vocabulary is a good thing in itself: I hesitate three times before using a word in verse that I should shrink from using in speech.

Sincerely yours,
[T. S. Eliot]

I hope that my preface is as suitable as you seem to believe.

TO *Erich Alport*

TS BL

25 May 1930   Faber & Faber Ltd

Dear Alport,

I must apologise for my delay in answering your letter of the 4th instant;[4] but I hope that you received the copy of *Ash Wednesday* which was sent to you directly.

---

1 – Wilson Knight admired the line, in *Ash-Wednesday*: 'Against the Word the unstilled world still whirled': 'By a quite unprecedented technique it gets a quite unique effect – that of movement which is stationary, stillness in motion; which is, of course, the peculiarity of a whirling object, with a stationary axis.'

2 – John Donne, 'Good Friday, 1613: Riding Westward' ('Let man's Soul be a sphere'), 8: 'so our souls admit / For their first mover, and are whirled by it'.

3 – 'I find, too, that you use adjectives with unusually great effect . . .'

4 – Alport wrote, 'I hear from Professor Gundolf that you have rejected his "Shakespeare". He is rather upset about it for Prof. Hartmann in New York has stopped translating the work & has broken off negotiations with an American publisher after you had written that you "should wish to entrust the work of translation to a scholar resident in England".'

I am very sorry indeed to have given disappointment about Professor Gundolf. We took a long time over it, and I consulted two distinguished Shakespeare scholars, one of whom took a long time himself over reading and reporting. He was so much interested that he bought the book; but he could not encourage us to publish, for the reason that the public would be very small, and the expense of translation and publication of such a massive book would be very heavy; and we felt that we simply could not afford it.

I think that the time may come later, and meanwhile I want to arouse interest in Gundolf. I have asked an intelligent scholar who is very keen on Gundolf to write an article on him for the *Criterion*.[1] Would you mind telling Professor Gundolf this? I should also very much like Professor Gundolf to let me have something suitable, and of suitable length, to translate in the *Criterion* (about 5000 or 6000 words). Would you ask him, and could you give me his address so that I may write myself?

As for the Jaeger book.[2] I cannot say anything definite yet. We definitely want to do the book, on which I have had strongly favourable reports from two of the greatest scholars in the country; but we are anxious to secure American cooperation, which is what has delayed matters. I am hopeful, however.

Incidentally, I should be very glad if you would occasionally drop me suggestions about German writers to be represented in the *Criterion*. Curtius never has time; Scheler is dead and Hofmannsthal is dead; and I need new material. I had a very interesting essay from one Theodor Haecker, but it was much too long for my review – I hope he will send me something else. Essays of course are the most useful contributions. I want men of the trempe[3] of Gundolf, Scheler, Worringer etc. Bertrand perhaps – I say perhaps because I once tried to get something from him. I wish there was anyone competent to translate George. I have rather run out of continental writers lately, and I want more.

Yours ever sincerely,

T. S. Eliot

---

1 – Max Rychner was to write an obituary: 'German Chronicle', *C.* 11 (Oct. 1931), 96–104.
2 – 'Have you heard from Prof. [Werner] Jaeger about his *Aristotèles?*'
3 – *Trempe* (Fr.): temper.

TO *F. S. Oliver*   CC

30 May 1930   [Faber & Faber Ltd]

My dear Oliver,

Thank you very much for your letter of the 29th.[1] I was tempted by the possibility of adding to my regular income; but I anticipated that if the position was of enough importance to be worth taking on, its implications would conflict with my present engagements. I suspect that your friend was unaware of my integral association with Faber & Faber. I am grateful to you for your part in the matter, in spite of your disclaimer.

I hoped that you would like Thomson's pamphlet.[2] There is no reason why I should not tell you that the Porpoise Press is a very small Edinburgh venture which is now being backed by Faber & Faber. It is actually run chiefly by Thomson himself and a fellow Scot named George Blake.[3] In

---

1 – Not found.

2 – *Will the Scottish Church Survive?* (1930). George Malcolm Thomson (1899–1996) worked for the *Evening Standard* and *Daily Express*, and served during WW2 as Principal Private Secretary to the 1st Lord Beaverbrook. Works include *A Short History of Scotland* (1930); *The Lambeth Conference* (1930). He was awarded the OBE in 1990. See further George McKechnie, *The Best-Hated Man: Intellectuals and the Condition of Scotland between the Wars* (2013).

3 – See Alistair McCleery, *The Porpoise Press 1922–39* (1988). George Blake (1893–1961), novelist, journalist, publisher – author of *The Shipbuilders* (1935) – co-founded the Porpoise Press in hopes of refashioning a national publishing industry in Scotland. The Press was taken over by F&F in the 1930s.

GCF wrote to H. M. Cohen, 14 Oct. 1930: 'We recently acquired the stock and good will of a small private business in Edinburgh called The Porpoise Press. The Porpoise Press exists for the purpose of publishing pamphlets, books and poems of Scottish national interest. It has hitherto been run in a very haphazard way by a single individual, and has just about paid its way. There are, however, considerable possibilities in it; and we are now working it up, with the assistance of two Scotchmen, named Blake and Thomson. Blake is one of our directors. Thomson is not. The arrangement with them is that they each take 25% of any net profits there may be arising from the Porpoise Press; and the management of the Press is entrusted to a sort of joint Committee consisting of Blake, Thomson and three of our own people. The whole of the business organisation is provided by us, and we put up all the money and collect all the income.'

Blake had been editor for four years of *John O' London's Weekly*, and for two years of *Strand Magazine*. On 20 June 1930 GCF wrote to offer him a Principal Directorship at F&F, starting on 1 Jan. 1931; but in the event he worked for F&F from 1 Aug. 1930. On 10 Oct. 1930 FVM told Henry S. Canby (editor of the *Saturday Review of Literature*) that 'my very good friend' was 'the recently appointed Fiction Editor to Faber and Faber . . . The fact that we have been able to snaffle him for Faber and Faber, shows the happy reputation which we have been establishing . . . There is a very interesting Scottish nationalist movement; and it is really producing some brilliant writers.' FVM, in a letter to John Livingston Lowes, 12 Dec. 1930, wrote of the Porpoise Press as 'our new and lively subsidiary'. Blake was to take leave of F&F in 1932. On 22 Dec. 1951 TSE wrote to Harry Levin, of 'my old friend':

the past, it has produced little but meagre volumes of mediocre verse, some of it no more Scottish than the man who joined a Scots regiment because he had his clothes cleaned at the Perth Dyeworks; but these young men are really ambitious to do something for their country, ardent nationalists – I share the views of my friends of *Action Française* about local self-government – and if they can get together other writers as good as Thomson himself I think they may do something interesting. If they do anything as good as this pamphlet I will let you know.

I am pleased that you have read my poem; had I thought that you would do so I should have sent you a copy. The reviews have been rather stupid, and I gather that no reviewer has the faintest knowledge of the Catholic liturgy – even well known Old Testament lines are quoted as if I had invented them myself – but the *Nation* today is not so bad.[1]

I still hope to see you after Whitsun, and before you leave. As for troubles, my experience is that they are 'but nails to drive each other out'.[2]

Yours ever sincerely,
[T. S. Eliot]

TO *Charles du Bos*[3] CC

Sunday after Ascension [1 June] 1930   [Faber & Faber Ltd]

My dear Du Bos,

I cannot tell you how immensely touched and flattered I am by receiving *Approximations III* with an inscription which is a letter in itself.[4] First,

---

'George Blake's great-grandfather emigrated from Somerset to Scotland, and the Blakes have married Scotch [*sic*] wives ever since; and George Blake is about as Lowland-Scots as anyone can be.'

1 – Francis Birrell, 'Mr T. S. Eliot', *N&A* 47 (31 May 1930), 292–3; repr. *T. S. Eliot: The Critical Heritage*, ed. Michael Grant (1982), I, 251–3.

2 – Proverbial – as in Shakespeare's *Two Gentlemen of Verona*, II. 4. 189: 'As one nail by strength drives out another . . .' – and derived ultimately from Aristotle's *Politics* 1314a.

3 – Charles du Bos (1882–1939), French critic of French and English literature (his mother was English, and he studied for a year at Oxford), contributed one review to *C.*, in 1935. He wrote essays on Shakespeare, Shelley, Byron, Flaubert, Goethe, Mérimée and Mauriac, and was admired for his posthumously published journals (6 vols, 1946–55).

4 – In fact, the fourth series of *Approximations* (1930), inscribed: 'To T. S. Eliot, to whom I intend to write a long letter as soon as I have done with the "service" of this book, – / thanking him for his excellent *Dante*, and still more grateful to him since I have purchased and read *Ash Wednesday* which I scarcely dare to praise as poetry (though I consider that as much as it is the finest contemporary poetry I know of) on account of the depth of emotion the book awakens in me, / from his friend Charles du Bos / Sunday May 20th 1930 / I will be delighted to let Faber and Faber have my book on Pater: you will find here a foretaste of it.'

your appreciation of *Ash Wednesday* gives me the greatest satisfaction. The reviews of the poem that I have so far received incline me to believe that no English journalist has the slightest acquaintance with the Catholic liturgy, or even with the Old Testament: my quotations have been quoted as if original; and my original images have been referred to the liturgy – but no appreciation has given me greater pleasure than yours.

I also appreciate the fact that you are known to be the worst correspondent in Europe – you have an international reputation for never answering letters; and I am honoured by receiving occasional letters from you inscribed on the fly-leaves of your books. Recognise, then, that if you ever do write me 'a long letter' I shall estimate it at its real worth.

As you have now read *Ash Wednesday* I shall not send you a copy: but I will send you a copy of my translation of Léger's *Anabase*: knowing that if anyone is competent to weigh its merits against its faults [you are].

It is a great pleasure to know that your *Pater – when* you finish it! – may come to Faber & Faber – I look forward to it with the keenest interest. In the autumn I shall send you a volume of essays by Fellows of the Royal Society of Literature, edited by de la Mare, to which I have contributed a superficial essay on *Marius*[1] in relation to *Literature and Dogma*. You may not like it: but if I am wrong, I look to you to correct me.

Also – I want something by you for the *Criterion*. Do you think that I might use your essay on [Stefan] George – who is quite unknown in England? It would be necessary, I think, to print the quotations in the original German with translations into English – if there is anyone who *can* translate George into English. If you ever *do* write me that letter you promise, I hope you will not overlook this suggestion.

Yours always cordially,
[T. S. Eliot]

TO *Paul Elmer More*

TS Princeton

2 June 1930   *The Criterion*

My dear More,

Many thanks for your letter of the 20th May.[2] I am very much pleased that you should think so well of the small *Dante*. It really pretends no

---

1 – TSE wrote (*c.* 1960) in his copy of Walter Pater's *Greek Studies* (1895), for EVE's benefit: 'I had this, & Marius, & Imaginary Portraits, when I was at Milton' (TSE Library).
2 – Letter not found.

more than it professes: to be a simple account of my own experience; it is not literary criticism; but I have some reason to believe that it has performed its function and re-started some of that large number of people who once tackled Dante (with a translation) and gave up after a few cantos. My only original contribution is possibly a few hints about the *Vita Nuova,* which seems to me a work of capital importance for the discipline of the emotions; and my last short poem *Ash Wednesday* is really a first attempt at a sketchy application of the philosophy of the *Vita Nuova* to modern life.

I confess myself surprised by your confession about Dante. I have to confess myself (1) that I have always *enjoyed* Virgil far more than Homer. Is that not shocking? Indeed, I feel very much more at ease in the company of Latin writers than of Greek – in verse. I feel at ease (in that sense) certainly with Plato and Aristotle, and to a less degree with Thucydides; but among poets, I feel nearer to Virgil, and Ovid and Catullus and Propertius – even, if you like, Ausonius and Statius and Claudian, certainly with Adam of St Victor – than even with Sophocles, to me the profoundest of the Greek poets. I never look at Euripides if there is a play on the same subject by Seneca. But why not admit these failings? And (2) I am completely blind to the poetry of Goethe, except a few lyrics. The only Goethe whom I cherish and have found useful is the Goethe of Eckermann.[1] There is another confession for you.

But, equally seriously, I am perturbed by your comments on Hell. To me it *is giustizia, sapienza, amore.*[2] And I cannot help saying, with all due respect of a (somewhat) younger and (much) more ignorant man, that I am really shocked by your assertion that God did not make Hell. It seems to me that you have lapsed into Humanitarianism. The Buddhist eliminates Hell – for I remember the yarn of the Hellpot Prayer,[3] and I know that even Channa shall be saved[4] – only by eliminating everything positive

---

1 – Johann Peter Eckermann, *Conversations with Goethe.*
2 – Dante, *Inf.* III (inscription at Hell Gate): '*Giustizia mosse il mio Fattore; / fecemi la divina Potestate, / la somma Sapienza e il primo Amore.*': 'Justice moved my high Maker; what made me were the divine Power, the supreme Wisdom, and the primal Love.' See 'Dante', *SE,* 244–5.
3 – 'In times gone by, when men lived twenty thousand years . . . there were living at Benares four sons of wealthy merchants.' This rich foursome spent their lives bribing beautiful women to commit adultery with them, with the consequence that when they died they were 'reborn in the Hell of the Iron Cauldron, sixty leagues in measure . . . and there endured torment for sixty thousand years. Even so the time of their release from suffering has not yet come' (*Buddhist Legends Translated from the original Pali text of the Dhammapada,* with commentary by Eugene Watson Burlingame, Part 2: Books 3 to 12 [1921], 106–7).
4 – The Elder Channa thrice reviled the two Chief Disciples. 'The Teacher said, "Monks, so long as I remain alive, you will not be able to teach Channa. After my decease, however,

about Heaven (*uttama paranibbana* being obviously not heaven).[1] Is your God Santa Claus? It seems to me that there is even some logical fallacy there: you expect the Cause of morality to be itself moral and subdued to the Laws it has created (see *Principia Mathematica* on the Cretan Liar[2]). To me, religion has brought at least the perception of something above morals, and therefore extremely terrifying; it has brought me not happiness, but the sense of something above happiness and therefore more terrifying than ordinary pain and misery; the very dark night and the desert. To me, the phrase 'to be damned for the glory of God' is sense not paradox; I had far rather walk, as I do, in daily terror of eternity, than feel that this was only a children's game in which all the contestants would get equally worthless prizes in the end.

And I don't know whether this is to be labelled 'Classicism' or 'Romanticism'; I only think that I have hold of the tip of the tail of something quite real, more real than morals, or than sweetness and light and culture.

Your citation of Norton and Mather[3] (the former, I may say as a kinsman, a great prig) does not worry me. I may mention that my poor poem *Ash Wednesday* has I observe pleased certain Orthodox and is also

---

you will succeed." When the Great Decease was at hand, the Venerable Ananda asked the Teacher, "Reverend Sir, how shall we deal with the Elder Channa?" Then the Teacher directed Ananda to inflict upon Channa the publishment known as "brahmadanda." After the decease of the Teacher . . . Ananda pronounced sentence. Hearing the sentence, Channa was overwhelmed with sorrow and sadness at the thought of having fallen after being freed three times. He cried out, "Do not ruin me, Reverend Sir," and thereafter performed his duties faithfully, in no long time becoming an Arahat endowed with the Supernatural Faculties' (ibid., 166).

1 – The Buddha teaches that 'rebirth and the sufferings of repeated existences would come to an end only when Craving had been . . . utterly destroyed . . . [T]he seeker after Salvation, which is of course Escape from the Round of Existences, Nibbana, must first accept the Four Noble Truths; and he must so meditate upon the Three Characteristics of all existing things, Impermanence, Suffering, and Unreality, as to eradicate utterly the cause of rebirth and suffering, namely, Craving. By so doing he becomes what is called an Arahat, obtains Supernatural Knowledge and the Supernatural Powers, and attains the Nibbana of the Living. At death the Five Elements of Being of which he is composed are utterly destroyed . . . He has at last attained the Summum Bonum, Deliverance from the Round of Existences, Supreme Nibbana' (*Buddhist Legends*, Part I . . . trans. of Books 1 and 2 [1921], 17–18).

2 – The statement 'All Cretans are Liars' is said to have been made by the Cretan philosopher Epimenides. Thus the paradox is one of self-reference, since his claim may in fact be false. See Bertrand Russell, 'Mathematical Logic as Based on the Theory of Types', *American Journal of Mathematics* 30: 3 (July 1908), 222–62; Douglas Hofstadter, *Gödel, Escher, Bach* (1979).

3 – Charles Eliot Norton. Cotton Mather (1663–1728), Puritan minister, author and pamphleteer.

accepted by my atheist friends. This is the same thing on a very small scale. The half-Christians hate anything thoroughgoing; the whole-pagans need not be bothered by it, and can perhaps appreciate the 'poetry' better than the less emancipated. But, on the other hand, how to apply any of this to you, who are infinitely more learned in theology than I (and in every other subject) passes my ability. So please accept these comments as merely the irreverences of an humble disciple. I please to think that in the present juncture we are one on certain essentials.

Yours sincerely,
T. S. Eliot

P.S. I have never seen Shafer, but having met the mild blond garrulous and frail stripling Tate, your news made me explode with laughter. It seems to me that an exhibition match (fly-weight) between these two bantams might bring in money for the Cause.

TO *Bruce Richmond*   cc

2 June 1930   [Faber & Faber Ltd]

Dear Richmond,

I have your letter of the 30th ultimo with enclosure.[1] In fact, Colhoun came to see me last week. It was quite clear that he had not done very much work for you, but I gathered that the *Taine* was satisfactory (I did not read it myself). Anyway, he impressed both Morley and myself quite favourably; and, as Trend never has time, and never wanted to do it, I am going to give [him] the Spanish Periodicals to review regularly for the *Criterion*, and possibly further small pickings; so he departed well pleased.[2]

---

1 – The enclosure was a letter to BLR from Charles K. Colhoun, dated 24 May: 'If you happen to know Mr Eliot personally, would it, I wonder, be trespassing too much on your kindness to me to ask him if the firm would really consider me quite seriously for regular work with them – that is with a view to accepting me eventually as a member after probation with them . . . As you have kindly accepted the "Taine" from me, would you care to entrust me with any more work?' BLR wrote that Colhoun could do translations from French or Spanish. 'I was quite favourably impressed with [Colhoun], and the only small review that he has done for us was quite well done.'

2 – GCF wrote to B. E. Nicolls, BBC, on 13 Nov. 1930, about a young man who might be suitable for work on *The Listener*: 'His name is Charles K. Colhoun . . . He came to us last April with a letter of introduction from Bruce Richmond, who had been favourably impressed by him. He has fluent French and Spanish (both acquired abroad) and a sound paper-knowledge of German. He took his degree from Oxford in 1928 and taught at Durham School for a year. Since then he has been looking out for work. Eliot has used

In two or three weeks I may venture to suggest another meeting. Could we not undertake another City Pilgrimage this summer? I hear that Lancelot Andrewes' tomb has been furbished up, and I want to look into the matter.[1]

> Yours ever,
> [T. S. E.]

TO *J. E. Pouterman* CC

2 June 1930   [Faber & Faber Ltd]

Dear Mr Pouterman,

Thank you for your letter of the 30th ultimo. I must apologise for not having written to you sooner. I should think that early September would be as good a time for publishing the Baudelaire *Intimate Journals* as any. As for my fee for signing a limited edition, of not more than 60 copies, I think, after consideration and discussion with fellow directors, that twenty-five pounds is a suitable figure. Will you let me hear that you agree?[2]

> Yours sincerely,
> [T. S. Eliot]

TO *H. B. Lathrop* CC

2 June 1930   [Faber & Faber Ltd]

My dear Sir,

In reply to your letter of the 22nd ultimo, I will gladly tell you what I know about Mr Louis Zukofsky.[3] I must say first that I have never met him, and therefore cannot speak at all about his 'personal characteristics'.

---

him to some extent for the *Criterion* . . . Eliot and Morley speak well of him, and say he is intelligent and has character.'

1 – The tomb of Bishop Lancelot Andrewes is in Southwark Cathedral, London.

2 – The sheets of the fifty copies of *Intimate Journals*, plus one copy for Pouterman's private library, were delivered to him by the binders on 28 Aug.

3 – Zukofsky had applied for a position as assistant in the Department of English, University of Wisconsin, Madison. Prof. Lathrop wrote: 'I am most interested in knowing whether he has a good mind, a significant and interesting personality, a loyal spirit, and adequate knowledge.' See also TSE to Zukofsky, 20 June 1930, below.

Mr Zukofsky first attracted my notice by various poems which he sent me. I have published two of his poems. A good deal of verse is submitted to me as Editor of the *Criterion*, and we only publish two or three poets in a year in that periodical; so that this means that I thought well of his verse.

He also sent me a long essay on Henry Adams, which was too long, and in its actual form unsuitable for the *Criterion*, but which struck me as a valuable piece of work.[1] I have in hand an essay by him on Ezra Pound's Cantos, which I intend to use.[2]

This is all that I know about Mr Zukofsky, but I may say in confidence that it was enough to make me feel justified in recommending him for a Guggenheim Fellowship.

In short, if his qualities of personality, about which I am wholly ignorant, are suitable, I can recommend his mind as wholly worthy; and I should imagine that his knowledge is quite adequate.

Yours very truly,

[T. S. Eliot]

TO *Kenneth Ingram*   CC

2 June 1930   [Faber & Faber Ltd]

Dear Ingram,

This is in haste, and also confidential. I have just had a letter from Fr Morse-Boycott to say that he is arranging a special Anglo-Catholic edition of the *Sunday Referee*, and asking me to send 100 words on 'where are we going?' Do you know anything about this?[3]

I know nothing about Fr. Morse-Boycott except that I believe he is doing good work in a slum parish – and, in my few communications with him, I have somehow the impression that he may be indiscreet and over-zealous. So I want to know: is this *Referee* business approved or is he doing it quite on his own? and should I contribute?

Personally, I have no objection, except that I feel that if the same people write messages in various organs, the effect may be rather diminished.

1 – 'Henry Adams: A Criticism in Autobiography', Parts I, II, III, in *Hound and Horn*, May, July, Oct., 1930; repr. in *Prepositions: The Collected Critical Essays of Louis Zukofsky*, 80–124.

2 – 'The Cantos of Ezra Pound', C. 10 (Apr. 1931), 424–40.

3 – Morse-Boycott, a staff member of *The Referee*, had approached TSE on 27 May: 'I want to have a symposium entitled "Where are we going?" by prominent clergy and laymen . . . Will you let us have 100 words? . . . May I beg of you to keep this special edition a secret?'

By the way, my letter was marked *strictly private*. I feel quite justified in consulting you: either you know about the scheme already; or if you don't, then there is something dubious about it. Do please let me know at once.[1]

Yours sincerely,
[T. S. Eliot]

TO *Rose Esther Haigh-Wood*[2]

12 June 1930   68 Clarence Gate Gardens, N.W.1

Dear M.I.L.,[3]

This is purely a business letter. I am writing to ask first whether you have received notice from The Eagle Oil Transport Co. Ltd. about the 50 shares belonging to the Estate. These Preference Shares are being (all the preference shares of the Company, I mean) purchased by another company under an 'option', and so we have to sell them. They are giving £6 for every £5 share, so the sum due the estate is £300. There should be certain forms to be signed in order to get the money by July 1st. Will you let me know whether you have had them? I expect that your signature and mine will suffice. The money will of course have to be reinvested. Vivienne has a few herself, and I shall be writing to Birks & Co to ask for suggestions for reinvestment; and I therefore suggest that I should at the same time ask them to suggest a new investment for the Estate.

Another point. I have just received a business letter from Maurice – with no personal news at all – in which he says that the Income Tax Adjustment Agency have let him know that James & James say they sent to Maurice the Rent Accounts and Tax Receipts. Maurice has not received them. Are they among those papers which were returned to you? You will remember that you showed me some envelopes containing business papers sent to Maurice in Italy at the wrong address and returned to you. Were they among these, and if so what have you done with them?

I am writing a line to James to ask if he has heard anything from Coall[4] about the annual accounts.

1–Ingram responded (6 June) that Morse-Boycott was 'the regular type of modern journalist, keen, virile, and often vulgar in his methods. But I do not think any harm can come of this effort, in which he is editor rather than author, and I feel that *The Referee* deserves support.'
2–Rose Esther Haigh-Wood (1860–1941), wife of Charles Haigh-Wood (1854–1927), artist.
3–Mother-in-law.
4–Talbot Coall & Son (Estate Agents, Receivers, Auctioneers & Valuers).

As I like to keep business files separate, I will say no more in this letter, but hope to write again soon.[1]

Affectionately your son in law
[Tom]

TO *Raymond W. Postgate*[2]   CC

12 June 1930   [Faber & Faber Ltd]

Dear Sir,

I must apologise for not answering at once your first letter, but have been so engaged with private matters that I have had to neglect business.[3] I was quite aware that my agreement with Knopf had lapsed, and had been intending to take up the matter, so I am glad that you have written. Could you suggest one morning next week when it would be convenient for you to come in to discuss these questions with me?

I am not inclined to renew the agreement for the original volume which Knopf published, but possibly we might discuss the publication of something more inclusive.[4]

Yours very truly,
[T. S. Eliot]

1 – Mrs Haigh-Wood responded on 13 June that she had sent the Income Tax papers to James & James 'about a week ago', and the Eagle Oil Transport Company papers to Maurice.
2 – Raymond Postgate (1896–1971), journalist and author, was European representative of Alfred A. Knopf, 1930–49. A rebel and left-winger in his youth – in 1920 he had been a founder-member of the Communist Party of Great Britain, though his affiliation lasted only for a few months – he gained a reputation as a writer of labour and radical history: early works included *The International (Socialist Bureau) during the War* (1918), *The Bolshevik Theory* (1920), and *Robert Emmet* (1931). Later he worked for the Board of Trade, 1942–50. But his claim to fame came about when he launched in 1951 the annual volumes of the *Good Food Guide*, which he would edit until 1968. Other publications include *The Plain Man's Guide to Wine* (1951). See J. Postgate and M. Postgate, *A Stomach for Dissent: The Life of Raymond Postgate* (1994).
3 – Postgate had written briefly on 28 May; then again on 11 June: 'this is to call your attention to the fact that your agreement with us for the publication of your poems has lapsed without either of us observing the fact. You will remember it was to run for ten years, and this term expired some little while ago. We propose to renew it as it stands if this is agreeable to you.'
   (Postgate had earlier [24 Mar.] told Richard de la Mare that Knopf was not interested in taking TSE's translation of *Anabase* unless it came with 'any of Mr Eliot's own stuff'.)
4 – Postgate wrote again on 24 July: 'We have just imported [into the USA] 500 copies of *The Sacred Wood* from Methuen in sheets, and so a collected edition of your prose works would not be, at the moment, profitable. On the other hand, we should very much wish to

13 June 1930   [68 Clarence Gate Gardens]

My dear Maurice,

In reply to your letter of the 9th instant.[2] I have stirred up James & James about Coall and hope to get some action soon, of which I shall advise you. Coall is certainly a scoundrelly boy to delay things like this. I shall keep my foot on it.

I have written to James & James, and also to your mother, about the Rent Accounts. I know that some business papers sent to you in Italy were returned to Compayne [Gardens], and I have asked your mother (who you know is in Anglesey) what they were and what she has done with them.

I have also asked her whether she has received papers from the Eagle Oil Transport about the Estate 50 pref. Shares which are called in (£5 shares called at £6). There is £300 coming to the Estate on July 1st, and I have asked your mother's consent to my asking Birks's advice about immediate reinvestment.

Re the Talbot. We have tried it out a couple of times. It seems to me a good car, and I find the gear change easier than the Morris Minor, though I have just got the hang of the latter. But I consider it too heavy for Vivienne, and also she is used to left hand gear and brake, which has the advantage that the person sitting beside her can give a hand; it would be some months before she was up to driving this car, and even then it would be hard work for her. I should like her to have a rather larger car, but I think that a Morris Cowley, which has the same controls as her present car, would be the best.

So we are trying to get the C.M.I. to find a purchaser. It appears that if the car was sold to them or to any other dealer, you would only realise about £75 for it, whereas a private purchaser might give £110 or £120; so it seems best to keep it garaged for a time, in the hope of a purchaser turning up. If your friend is really interested, will you refer him to the

---

do this eventually . . .' He reported too that Knopf had only eighty copies left of TSE's poems, 'so that a collected edition could quite easily be arranged for right away. We find that the Faber & Faber edition has had but little sale in America and should not interfere very greatly. We could offer at the beginning only a 10% royalty, unless you are prepared to give us anthology rights on the customary fifty fifty basis, when we could pay a straight 12½%.' TSE sought FVM's opinion.

1 – Maurice Haigh-Wood (1896–1980), brother of VHE: see Biographical Register.

2 – 'I have had a note from the Income Tax Adjustment Agency saying that they have heard from James & James that the Rent Accounts & Tax Receipts were forwarded to me, but I have not received them, so I have written a line to James to enquire.'

C.M.I. mentioning our name. At present, the C.M.I. say they have not room to garage it, so we have left it at the Belgravia Garage, Caroline St., S.W.1., where we kept our car when we were at Chester Terrace. I suppose it is insured? You know that the licence has expired, so that it can only be driven under a 'trade number' plate, which means that not more than two people can ride in it at once. We want to do all we can about it, and Vivienne has taken no end of trouble, but if you hear of a possible buyer, steer him to me. It is a great nuisance and burden to you to have this car on your hands, but after all, any car can be sold for *some* price; which is more than can be said for the house we have just left. I would pay anybody £150 to take it off my hands, and still profit by the bargain.[1]

This is really a hurried note. We are both worn out, having only just got into our new flat (68 Clarence Gate Gardens, telephone Ambassador 1518), and I have many arrears. I do hope you and Ahmé are both fairly well, in spite of the heat.

Ever affectionately,
[Tom]

TO *Allanah Harper*[2]   CC

16 June 1930   [Faber & Faber Ltd]

Dear Miss Harper,

Thank you for your letter of June 10th, enclosing the essay on my verse for *Echanges*.[3] It is as difficult to judge criticism of one's own work, as it is to judge the fidelity of one's own portrait; but at any rate I can say that I found this essay extremely interesting, and that it did not worry or annoy me at all. The only regret I have is that it takes no account of ASH WEDNESDAY, or of the fragment of my unfinished play, SWEEENY [*sic*]

1–Maurice authorised TSE on 20 June to sell the car to the 'Trade'. He wrote too: 'I am awfully sorry indeed to hear that the house in Chester Terrace was such a disappointment. It really is too bad the filthy luck you have had!'

2–Allanah Harper (1904–92), socialite and editor, edited the Anglo-French review *Échanges*, 1929–31, publishing writers including TSE, WHA, Stein, VW, Léon-Paul Fargue and André Gide. See Harper, 'A Magazine and Some People in Paris', *Partisan Review* (July–Aug. 1942).

3–D. S. Mirsky, 'T. S. Eliot et la fin de la poésie bourgeoise', *Échanges* 5 (Oct. 1931/Dec. 1931), 44–58; an abridged translation appeared as 'The End of Bourgeois Poetry', *New Masses*, 13 Nov. 1934, 17–19. Harper wrote, 'I fear you will think it most amateurish . . . I shall be only too pleased to add or correct anything in it that you may mention.'

AGONISTES. I am sending you a copy of the number of the *Criterion* which contained that fragment.

> Yours sincerely,
> [T. S. Eliot]

TO *Harold Monro*   CC

16 June 1930   [*The Criterion*]

My dear Harold,

Re yours of the 2nd and 10th instants.[1]

I agree cordially on most points. I do not think it necessary to add Trend, partly because Trend would mean Williams, who is not persona grata to everybody. About Fletcher, I think further discussion is necessary; for the present, as I believe Fletcher is abroad, let us keep the committee to the persons named. The fewer the better anyway.

I should like to share the expense whether I am present or not, but (1) is it fair to ask Bonamy, who is seldom in London, to do so when absent (2) can Frank afford it? There ought perhaps to be some conditions about the entertainment to be afforded; else you will find it left to you to select and purchase the cheer and collect the expenses afterwards, which is not very satisfactory for you.

---

1 – Monro had discussed with HR the plan that TSE and Monro had put up together to hold at the Poetry Bookshop regular monthly evenings of the Criterion Club.

'Herbert was very keen that we should pursue the matter. Our joint recommendations amounted to the following:-

'That a Committee of eight should be established consisting of yourself, him, myself, Bonamy, Frank Flint and Morley. The other two tentative suggestions were Fletcher and Trend. There seemed to be two further obvious people, not necessarily them, but somehow we could not bring them to mind and I also cannot now, although we then, and I at any time, were able to decide against certain other people.

'That the arrangement must be regular and official and that we should fix it for the last Wednesday in each month, notices in the form of reminders being sent out to those eight one fortnight before the last Wednesday in each month.

'That the eight (or six?) be entitled to bring one or two guests each time, but that the guests be not entitled to come again on their own initiative without one of the Committee.

'That the first occasion be Wednesday 25th June and we much hoped that your being occupied with other matters up to the end of June would not interfere with this one day . . .

'We hoped that this time the thing could be kept going. Of course the plan would be for the Committee to subscribe to pay for refreshments, probably on a rough average, or by some other method to be decided. The intention is to use the rooms as convenient for the purpose and to ignore as far as possible the idea of any particular form of hospitality being offered, i.e., that there is any particular host. But we felt it important that it should be official in the sense that it should be definitely associated with THE CRITERION.'

I am sorry that I am not yet sure whether I can turn up on the 25th – else I should have written to you before – and I don't expect to be able to say before next Monday. But I hope that the first meeting will take place then in any case. I will let you know at the first moment about myself. In future, I shall try to support every meeting.

yours ever,
[T. S. E.]

TO *Ezra Pound*

16 June 1930   Faber & Faber Ltd

Right Honorable Rabbit:[1]

Your undated communication to our accountant[2] has been passed on to me to deal with. Without animadverting on the tone which you thought fit to adopt toward an accountant who is young and unmarried and has never heard such words as you have introduced into your invective, I pass on to remark that it was supposed that the volumes in question were the property of The Egoist Press, by which firm they were handed over to this firm. The arrangement between us was that the profits of the sale of copies should be handed over to the authors, with the mere deduction of a reasonable sum for the firm's expenses.

Your statement that the volumes are your property puts a new complexion on the matter. I am writing to Harriet for confirmation, but meanwhile I am sending you a new invoice of storage charges for your property, which you may hang on your wall in place of the one you have returned.

I am,
Respected Sir,
Your Obedient Servant,
T. S. Eliot

---

1 – EVE told Harry M. Meacham (author of *The Caged Panther: Ezra Pound at St Elizabeths*, [1967]), 14 Feb. 1967: 'my husband and Pound liked talking *Uncle Remus* together, and in fact my husband used to recite extracts to me. He called Pound "Rabbit" and he became "Possum".'
2 – Not found.

TO *G. W. S. Curtis*[1]   TS Houghton

17 June 1930   Faber & Faber Ltd

My dear Curtis,

(If I don't call you 'father' you shall not call me 'Mr'). I shall be in London, and glad to see you, but the weekend is a bad time for me.[2] If you can stay over, could you lunch on the following Tuesday after the 29th – the 1st July? If not, could you look in on the Monday? But surely you will want to be in London during part at least of that week.

I am pleased that you like the verses.[3] As for obscurity, I like to think that there is a good and a bad kind: the bad, which merely puzzles or leads astray; the good, that which is the obscurity of any flower: something simple and to be simply enjoyed, but merely incomprehensible as anything living is incomprehensible. Why should people treat verse as if it were a conundrum with an answer? when you find the answer to a conundrum it is no longer interesting. 'Understanding' poetry seems to me largely to consist of coming to see that it is not necessary to 'understand'.

As for 'eschate ora' (I am too lazy to leave a blank and pen it in properly) isn't the real meaning that it is always the end of the world?[4] Or at least, one's own death is the end of the world, and is always at hand. I live, so far as I live at all, in that sense of imminent peril.

Yours ever,
T. S. Eliot

TO *Desmond Morse-Boycott*   CC

17 June 1930   [Faber & Faber Ltd]

Dear Father Morse-Boycott,

As I said on the telephone, it is difficult to write one 'message' after another, but here is something which you can use or not as you think fit:

There is no doubt a large public which is indifferent, there is a much smaller public which is hostile, and there is another public

---

1 – The Revd Geoffrey Curtis was Vice-Principal of Dorchester Missionary College, Burcote, Abingdon.

2 – Curtis was to be in London for the weekend of 29 June, and hoped for a meeting.

3 – 'I love so the inscription in my copy of Ash Wednesday: and its contents also have magic for me, great magic. But they are very obscure.'

4 – 'I am comforted you do not hope to turn again. With me too it is ἐσχάτη ὥρα – a last hour.' (*Eschate ora*: 'the last hour'. See 1 John 2: 18.)

which is rejoiced, when the Anglo-Catholic Congress takes place. To my mind the value of these congresses will prove to be, in time, still more for the first two categories than for the third: the first will learn that there is something to think about, the second that there is something which it has thought mistakenly about. The third, we need to remember, consists not only of those who take part in the worship and in the instruction, but of a great many others, scattered about the country, who cannot take part, but who must be helped and encouraged in their missionary work of example and steadfastness, by knowing that such a congress is taking place.

There. Edit it or revise it if you think fit. Or write and say that you want something else.[1]

I hope that I may take advantage of your hospitable sausages at 4d. per lb. before very long.

Yours sincerely,
[T. S. Eliot]

TO *T. F. Burns*[2]   CC

17 June 1930   [*The Criterion*]

My dear Burns,

Very many thanks for sending me the Huegel Petrine notes.[3] You have lost a sale by doing so, as I should certainly have bought it: I have been a Huegel enthusiast for some years now; I keep the various volumes of letters near and dip into them every now and then – I particularly like

---

1 – See TSE in *Sunday Referee*, 29 June 1930 (as advertised in *The Times*, 28 June 1930, 14). (The *Sunday Referee* published a box on p. 3: 'Anglo-Catholic Congress: To-day, in addition to all usual editions, a special issue of the "Sunday Referee" has been published, dealing with the Anglo-Catholic Congress. Readers who require copies of this special issue should order direct from the Manager, "Sunday Referee", 17 Tudor-street, E.C.4., enclosing 3d. in stamps.')

2 – Tom Burns (1906–95), publisher and journalist, was educated at Stonyhurst (where he was taught by Fr Martin D'Arcy) and worked with the publishers Sheed & Ward, 1926–35. From 1935 he worked for Longmans Green – where among other undertakings he arranged to finance Graham Greene's mission to enquire into the persecution of the Catholic Church in Mexico – and he became in addition a director of the Tablet Publishing Company, 1935–85. During WW2 he was press attaché to Sir Samuel Hoare, British Ambassador to Spain. He was chairman of Burns & Oates, the premier Catholic publishing house, 1948–67; editor of *The Tablet*, 1967–82.

3 – Friedrich von Huegel, *Some Notes on the Petrine Claims* (1930).

reading the letters to Miss Greene.[1] In fact, I hope to write an essay on him one of these days: I reviewed one of his books for the *Dial* a few years ago, but it by no means represents my present opinions.[2]

All the more grateful because this book is wholly unsuitable for *Criterion* review. You will understand that, I think.

Perhaps Morley was a little 'previous' about Malta.[3] I do want to call attention to an important controversy; but I have a feeling that both sides have more to say than has been said. Still, my views on the Blue Book will differ from yours.

What about the Unicorn?[4]

I shall read *No Popery* with interest.

Yours ever,
[T. S. Eliot]

TO *William Force Stead*   TS Beinecke

20 June 1930[5]   Faber & Faber Ltd

My dear Stead,

I must apologise for not having answered immediately your delightful letter, but I think that a note from me must have gone astray.[6] Some time ago I wrote to you at Worcester and said, would you please let me know as soon as you returned from Washington, but I rather inferred from your letter that you had been back for some time.

Of course I am more than delighted that you like my book as you are one of the few people whom I am expecting to have some notion of what it is about. Some damned fool of a Cambridge paper referred to it as devotional poetry, which rather misses the point.

1–In C. 8 (Apr. 1929), TSE noted that *Letters from Baron Friedrich von Hügel to a Niece*, ed. Gwendolen Greene, was a 'book of great value' (568). Hügel (1852–1925) was born in Florence but lived in England from the age of fifteen; a leading Roman Catholic and scholar, he was venerated as a religious teacher.
2–'An Emotional Unity' – on *Selected Letters of Baron Friedrich von Hügel (1896–1924)*, ed. Bernard Holland – *The Dial* 84: 2 (Feb. 1928), 109–12.
3–'Morley tells me you have much to say on Malta in the *Criterion* . . .'
4–Burns was planning a club to be called The Unicorn.
5–Carole Seymour-Jones, *Painted Shadow: The Life of Vivienne Eliot* (2001: 586, n. 37), misdates this letter 30 June 1930.
6–Stead wrote from Worcester College, Oxford, on Ascension Day (29 Apr.) 1930, 'Listen, sweet Sir, you have written a beautiful book of poems. I am in love with it . . .' Stead had spent the Easter vacation visiting family and friends, and his old haunts, in Baltimore and Maryland, and enthused at length about the world supremacy of Washington, DC.

The America that you revisited is, alas, the part of America that I do not know. I envy you in having such enduring ties. As for me, I was a nomad even in America. You see, my real ancestral habitat is Massachusetts and my branch of my family only lived in the South for about fifteen years. Everything I remember about Missouri is now swept away in modern improvements; but, on the other hand, I was enough of a southerner to be something of an alien in Massachusetts; and even in my youth the New England of my associations existed more in Maine than in Massachusetts.

I doubt whether a visit to America would produce the same effect on me as you say it has on yourself, but I think I should be quite open to conviction. But for me it would have to mean New York or Boston and not the country you describe. Anyway I am delighted to hear that you are now a Fellow of Worcester and that you are destined so far as we can see to remain in England.

I have not very much news but would like a long talk with you as soon as you can come up to London. I am always here.

Ever affectionately,
T. S. E.

TO *Friedrich Gundolf*[1]   CC

20 June 1930   [*The Criterion*]

Sir,

Having read with the greatest interest a considerable part of your *Shakespeare* and having heard also a great deal about your work from various friends, I am venturing to ask if you would do me the honour of contributing an essay, or a part of some unpublished work, to the *Criterion*. I am sending you a copy of this review for your information.

If you should be willing to do me this kindness, and Dr Alport tells me that you may not be unfavourable, the suitable length is between 5000–6500 words. Our payment is the same to all contributors, £2 for 1000 words, and for contributions which have to be translated, the translation fee of 15/- for 1000 words has to be deducted from the author's fee. The

1–Friedrich Gundolf: pseud. of Friedrich Gundelfinger (1880–1931), German-Jewish literary scholar and poet; Professor at Heidelberg University (where Joseph Goebbels was one of his students); works include *Shakespeare und der deutsche Geist* ('Shakespeare and the German Spirit', 1911); *Goethe* (1916); *Stefan George* (1920); and translations of Shakespeare (1908–14).

Criterion is a review of small circulation, but among the most cultivated public of England and America, and we cannot afford to pay higher fees.

I should like to leave the subject to you. I would only suggest that for early publication I should prefer some other subject than Shakespeare, merely for the reason that the *Criterion* has had a good deal of Shakespearian matter from Mr J. M. Robertson and Professor Dover Wilson, and Mr W. J. Lawrence. Possibly the work of Stefan Georg would be a suitable subject, but you would have to keep in mind that his work is still known to only a very small public in England – a much smaller public, in fact, than the work of Rilke.

I first attempted to read Georg's poems after hearing my friend Du Bos talk about him. It might be very difficult to convey anything about Georg to an uninstructed English public and possibly you may have some other suggestion to make.

In asking you to contribute to the *Criterion*, I am actuated not only by consideration of the interests of the *Criterion*, but also by the desire to get your name before the public with a view to the publication of one or more of your books at some future date. I have suggested to Dr Stewart of the University of Aberdeen that he should write an article about you.

I not only admired your *Shakespeare* myself, but received expressions of admiration for it from my friend Professor Grierson of Edinburgh. We were very much tempted to publish the book but felt that at the present time such a venture would be too costly for a young firm like Faber and Faber.

> I am, Sir,
> Your obedient servant,
> [T. S. Eliot]

TO *Louis Zukofsky*[1]   TS Beinecke

20 June 1930   *The Criterion*

Dear Mr Zukofsky,

In reply to your letter of the 27th of May,[2] I want to publish your essay on Pound, though I fear it may require a good deal of cutting to be short enough for the *Criterion*. If I had it set up and sent to you in Galley-proof, would you be willing to abbreviate it as much as is necessary? I have been rather dilatory about this. I rather want to get from Pound an unpublished canto to print in the *Criterion* first. I should be glad if you would let me know if the delay matters and if you are publishing your article in America first.

I am afraid that I can't use your poems for some time to come; but I should very much like to keep them. Perhaps, in that case also, you would be so good as to let me know if you are publishing them elsewhere.[3]

Yours sincerely,
T. S. Eliot

TO *Charles Mauron*   CC

23 June 1930   [*The Criterion*]

Cher Monsieur Mauron,

Je vous dois mille excuses.[4] Pendant l'année passée j'ai été toujours à quatre chemins, ayant déménagé quatre fois, et, tenant a faire moi-même la traduction de votre article, j'ai dû remettre la besogne de mois en mois. Maintenant, désirant me mettre à l'oeuvre, je ne puis plus trouver le

1–Louis Zukofsky (1904–78), son of Lithuanian Jewish parents, grew up speaking Yiddish and was educated at Columbia University (he was taught by Mark Van Doren and John Dewey). In 1927 he sent to EP 'Poem Beginning "The"' – a parody of *TWL* – which EP put out in his review *The Exile*, no. 3 (Spring 1928), 7–27. He worked for the Works Projects Administration, 1934–42, and in the English Department of the Polytechnic Institute of Brooklyn, 1947–66. A leader of the 'Objectivist' group (associates included William Carlos Williams), his works include '*A*' (published in full in 1978); *All: The Collected Short Poems, 1923–1964* (1971); and *Autobiography* (1970). See *Selected Letters of Ezra Pound and Louis Zukofsky*, ed. Barry Ahearn (1987); Mark Scroggins, *The Poem of a Life: A Biography of Louis Zukofsky* (2007).
2–Zukofsky (27 May): 'May I know what you intend doing with my essay on Pound's Cantos, and "A" 1 and 2 ?'
3–Zukofsky responded on 27 June: 'my essay on Pound and A 1–2 are not going to be published in America first, and I am willing to cede the complete rights to the *Criterion*.'
4–Mauron asked (20 May) after the fate of his essay 'En lisant Bergson'.

manuscrit, qui m'avait accompagné de maison à maison. Pendant que je fais continuer la recherché, pourriez-vous m'envoyer une copie, afin que je puisse compléter la traduction (je vous le jure) à temps pour le numéro de septembre? Je tiens beaucoup à publier cet article; et je serai tout navré si j'aurai perdu le seul exemplaire.[1]

Toujours avec mes amitiés sincères,

Votre

[T. S. Eliot][2]

TO *Hamish Miles*[3]   cc

23 June 1930   [*The Criterion*]

Dear Miles,

I should be very glad if you would care to review for the September *Criterion* Gilbert's *Ulysses*, together with our *Anna Livia Plurabelle* and the other fragments obtainable. Would you do it?[4]

Also: some time ago I saw an excellent article by you in *Bifur*[5] on contemporary British politics. I have been wondering if you would consider writing something about politics for the *Criterion*. I do not want real professionals like Laski or the abler younger men of any party, so much as more detached articles by people like yourself, who have no

1 – On 4 July Mauron sent a further copy of his essay but it did not appear in C.

2 – *Translation*: Dear Mr Mauron, I owe you a thousand apologies. During the past year, I've always been on the move, having moved four times, and, being keen to translate your article myself, I've had to postpone the job month after month. And now that I'd like to get down to it, I can no longer find the manuscript which I had taken with me from house to house. While I continue my search, could you send me a copy so that I can complete the translation (I swear to you) in time for the September number? I am very keen to publish this article, and I would be very sorry if I had lost the only copy. Yours sincerely, T. S. Eliot

3 – Hamish Miles (1894–1937): writer; translator of George Sand and André Maurois; for many years an editor at Jonathan Cape.

4 – Miles reviewed Stuart Gilbert's study, plus three 'fragments' – *Anna Livia Plurabelle*, *Tales Told of Shem and Shaun* (Paris: Black Sun Press), *Haveth Childers Everywhere* – in C. 10 (Oct. 1930), 188–92. As for *Anna Livia Plurabelle*, Gilbert had told TSE on 25 Mar. 1930, Joyce 'would very much like, if it can be managed, that the covers should be "turf-brown" with gold lettering'. Later, after a sample design had been inspected by JJ, Gilbert wrote on 8 May: 'As for the cover of A L P, he now leaves it to you: the lettering can be any colour you like – except blue. The idea of the gold lettering was, I think, an allusion to the "peeld gold of waxwork her jellybelly" (p 33, Gaige Edition). Thus brown and gold are A L P's colours.' *Anna Livia Plurabelle* – 'bound . . . in the nearest we can get to Liffey colour,' as FVM told Caradoc Evans – was published as Criterion Miscellany 15 on 12 June; Gilbert's study of *Ulysses* on 29 May.

5 – The Paris-based literary periodical *Bifur* brought out just eight issues (1929–31).

political axe to grind, and are primarily students of literature, the arts and philosophy. Such a person might for instance, do a good essay on such a subject as Disarmament, or on the more general political conclusions to be drawn from the Simon report.[1]

Yours ever,
[T. S. Eliot]

TO *Erich Alport* TS BL

23 June 1930   Faber & Faber Ltd

Dear Alport,

Thank you very much for your interesting letter of the 10th.[2] I am writing to Gundolf as you suggest.

I should be very grateful if you would be so kind as to have a copy of the February number of *Die Neue Rundschau* sent to me. Of course the name of Cassirer is well known to me and I think that many years ago I read one of his books. I thought of him as a very old man and one of the post-Kantians of Marburg.[3]

I should be very grateful also if you would have a copy of Westphal's book sent to me at my expense. And that reminds me to ask you if you could put me in touch with some good bookseller whom you know, in Hamburg or elsewhere, from whom I could order from time to time any German books that I want. The simplest way for me is to buy ten or twenty mark notes and send them over as a deposit; money orders are such a complicated business and I don't suppose they want to be bothered

1 – The Indian Statutory Commission, led from 1927 by Sir John Simon (and including Clement Attlee), which addressed the issues of constitutional reform, published its 17-vol. report in 1930.

2 – Not found.

3 – Ernest Cassirer (1874–1945), trained in the Neo-Kantian Marburg School, was later a proponent of philosophical idealism. Alport wrote: 'In the February number of *Die Neue Rundschau* . . . there was an extremely interesting essay by Ernst Cassirer on the subject of "Leben und Geist in der neueren Philosophie", therefore chiefly on Scheler. Cassirer is the Professor of Philosophy at the University of Hamburg, and one of the most distinguished & best known scholars of this country. I should think that he would gladly write something for the *Criterion*. A younger member of this University has just published a book that is arousing great attention: Dr Otto Westphal, *Feinde Bismarcks* [*Enemies of Bismarck*]. But the book does not contain political history, as the title might suggest, but purely *Geistesgeschichte*, a history of the thought & cultured opinion in Germany of the last 50 or 70 years. Dr Westphal is really a professor of History at Hamburg; the solid historical foundation of his reasoning is just what makes the book so valuable. It is *Geistes-Soziologie* of the very best kind . . . Westphal is strongly influenced by humanism, of course.'

with my London cheques. I should be very grateful if you would do this for me and have the Westphal book ordered in this way.

I should very much like also to read something of Heidegger. During the month of August 1914, I sat in Marburg, smoking cigars and reading the works of Husserl, and I still know just enough about the subject to be extremely interested in the work of a disciple.[1]

I have had sent to you the *Anabasis* and the two pamphlets you asked for.

> With many thanks,
> Yours very sincerely,
> T. S. Eliot

P.S. If you are so kind as to give my name and address to some German bookseller, would you kindly ask him to send me the following of Hofmannsthal's: *Der Kaiser und die Hexe* and *Das Salzburger Grosse Welttheater*.[2] And please give my kindest regards to Curtius.

TO *Virginia Woolf*[3]   CC

24 June 1930   [68 Clarence Gate Gardens]

My dear Virginia,

I was very happy to have a charming letter from you, but was more than shocked by the news which you communicate, with such appalling

---

1 – 'The greatest philosophical scholar in Germany – many think him the greatest living philosopher – is Heidegger, as you probably know. He lives in Marburg, is comparatively young & has just refused a call to the chair of philosophy (Hegel's chair) at Berlin. He is a disciple of Husserl (of Freiburg) & has developed the latter's Phaenomenologie on quite original lines.' For TSE on Husserl, see *L* 1, 49.

Alport wrote again on 11 July: 'Cassirer is not such a *very* old man, though one of the "post-Kantians of Marburg". He is very much alive & has taken quite an individual development for himself in the later years of his life.

'Gundolf was most willing to contribute to the *Criterion* when I saw him at Heidelberg. He suggested an essay on Moericke which he read as a paper last winter. I heard it, it is one of the best he has written. But perhaps you could make him write about Kleist (he has published a book on Kleist some years ago) who, of course, is more important, & of more general interest today, than Moericke; or make him write about George of whom he is, and always was, *the* interpreter.'

2 – *Der Kaiser und die Hexe* ('The Emperor and the Witch', 1897); *Das Salzburger große Welttheater* ('The Salzburg Great World Theatre', 1922: an adaptation of *The Great World Theatre* by Pedro Calderón de la Barca, 1875). They were recommended by Curtius on 7 June.

3 – Virginia Woolf (1882–1941), novelist, essayist and critic: see Biographical Register.

stoicism.[1] I have been so long out of any world that I was quite unaware that you had had, or were about to have, or even were in danger of having to have a very serious operation. I wonder, are you well enough to go out? We should love to have you to tea at our new flat – 68 Clarence Gate Gardens – one day this week. Incidentally, we shall have staying with us, off and on, a niece of mine who is a great admirer of yours and has come to London at the wrong time of year, three years running, in the hope of being able to gaze upon you. Would you come?

But in any case, I should like to come in to see you if I may, one day soon, if you are fit for my tedious company.

I saw you once several months ago on the opposite side of Southampton Row, but the sundering traffic flowed between and I was unable to dash across in time to catch you.

As for *Ash Wednesday* and even *Anabasis,* I do not consider that you are in a position to gibe at my obscurity. Are you not aware that there are many people in the world who consider your own works the depths of obscurity, as well as the height of prose writing? After all, I think that perhaps the chief result and reason for re-reading a thing many times is not that one gets to understand it better, but merely that one gets used to it – that is, understanding a thing chiefly means that one no longer bothers about the supposed need for understanding it.

Vivienne sends love; she has not been at all well herself.

Ever affectionately,

[T. S. E.]

TO *Jacob Bronowski*[2]   CC

24 June 1930   [Faber & Faber Ltd]

Dear Mr Bronowski,

I have no objection to your using GERONTION, A SONG FOR SIMEON, and THE JOURNEY OF THE MAGI, if you like, in an

1–VW wrote on 9 June: 'I am a wretch not to have thanked you before for *Anabasis*. I have a feeling that I shall in the end admire it very much – but I get slower & slower & slower with poetry. Your six readings will be 12 with me. I don't yet fathom *Ash Wednesday*. I like to roll it round in my mind when I am walking over the downs. Up till this moment, far from reading *Anabasis* 12 times over, I've been utterly dissipated by a bad operation on the kidneys of my book. It is a known fact that an event like that can destroy a fortnight of one's life so that one wishes one has never been born. I can't read, write, or think . . . still your affectionate Virginia.'

2–Jacob Bronowski (1908–74) – Polish-born scientist, humanist, writer and broadcaster, whose family came to the UK in 1920 – read mathematics at Jesus College, Cambridge. After

Anthology to be published in America, but not in England.[1] (I mean neither to be set up in England or to be published in imported sheets). I always insist, when giving anthology rights, on a small fee and await an offer from you.

At the same time, I should have thought that the supply of anthologies of verse in America must already have exceeded any possible demand, and before accepting finally, I should be glad to know what other authors you propose to include.

I have much enjoyed the series of sixpenny Cambridge Poems which I believe you are editing.

Yours sincerely,
[T. S. Eliot]

TO *Jacob Bronowski*   CC

27 June 1930   [Faber & Faber Ltd]

Dear Mr Bronowski,

I have your letter of the 26th instant. In reply to your first paragraph, I do not feel that I can accept less than a guinea for each poem, and that seems to me a very slender emolument.[2] I am giving the authority simply to oblige yourself because I have seen some of your work and like it; but my point is that neither Brewer and Warren nor any other publisher should undertake the publication of Anthologies unless they are in the position to pay reasonable fees.

---

gaining his doctorate in 1933, he taught at the University College of Hull, 1934–42; and after WW2 he became scientific deputy to the British Joint Chiefs of Staff mission to Japan (where he wrote a report on the effects of the atomic bombs on Hiroshima and Nagasaki). For thirteen years from 1950 he was Director of the Coal Research Establishment of the National Coal Board, working on the development of smokeless fuel; and in 1964 he became Senior Fellow at the Salk Institute for Biological Studies in San Diego, California. Works include a critical study of William Blake (1944). In later years he won acclaim for his thirteen-part TV series *The Ascent of Man* (1973).

1–Bronowski asked permission (23 May) to reprint three poems, 'Gerontion' and 'A Song for Simeon' – 'and another which you may like to suggest?' – in an anthology of modern English poetry to be published by Brewer and Warren, New York. 'Of course if you were prepared to give me any unpublished work – or not previously published in book form – I would be very grateful, and have no doubt that I could arrange suitable terms for you.'

2–'May I, before offering you an exact fee, consult my publishers? They will of course pay for particular authority [*sc.* anthology] rights at my recommendation: but you will understand that in a book of this size such payments can only be exceptional and at best nominal. I would therefore be very grateful to you if you would be prepared to accept a purely nominal fee, say of one or two guineas.' (The phrase 'authority rights' was borrowed from TSE's own mistyped letter.)

Commenting on your second paragraph,[1] it seems to me that the majority of your contributors are very much junior to the minority; and my first criticism is that you need a few more names to fill the gap between age and youth (myself being among the aged) as well as a few name[s] worth having for their own sake, such as Harold Monro and F. S. Flint. Whatever you may think of the Sitwells' poetry, I think that something by Edith and Sacheverell ought to be included.

I have discussed with my fellow directors your request to publish in this anthology *Paid on Both Sides* by W. H. Auden. We are about to publish a volume of Auden's poems in which we have world rights and *Paid on Both Sides* is the longest, and to my mind the finest, thing in it. We are publishing the book at a low price so that the right people buy it and we do not expect any profit as this is his first book. I am afraid that we cannot afford to surrender such a valuable part of his work, particularly at the moment when the book is in the press.

As for D. H. Lawrence, the *Criterion* has no further claims on its contents after publication.[2] I should suggest that you apply to Curtis Brown Ltd who have always been Mr Lawrence's agents and who know as much about the rights as anybody.

Yours sincerely,
[T. S. Eliot]

TO *C. K. Ogden*   TS Valerie Eliot

30 June 1930   *The Criterion*

Dear Ogden,

Not having come across you at the Club[3] for some time, I am writing to claim my copy of the Joyce gramophone record.[4] Can you let me know how it can be sent to me here, and I will send my cheque forthwith.

---

1 – 'The book is a "European Caravan" containing French, Italian, German and Russian sections in translation; and this English section is my province. There will be verse and prose in each section: among the contributors to my section I expect to have Waley, Lawrence (D. H. – my efforts to find where T. E. is have failed), Empson, Aldington, Auden, Boyle, Paul, Power, Rootham, Beckett, Joyce, McGreevey, Read, O'Flaherty, Woolf, Gilbert, H.D., Hudson and others. Briefly, I want to show the *movement* and *direction* of modern English writing . . .'
2 – Bronowski wanted to reprint from C. Lawrence's story 'Mother and Daughter'.
3 – Royal Societies Club, 63 St James's Street, London S.W.1.
4 – The record of Joyce reading *Anna Livia Plurabelle* was made by the Orthological Institute in Aug. 1929. TSE later said of *Finnegans Wake*: 'Joyce's last book has to be read aloud;

Hamish Miles is reviewing our *Anna Livia Plurabelle*, together with *Shem and Shaun*, and *Haveth Childers Everywhere*, and Gilbert's *Ulysses* in the September *Criterion* and he would like very much to review the gramophone [record] at the same time. Would it be possible, in consideration of the fact that we are advertising the record with *Anna Livia* (which, I may mention, is now in its third impression) to provide a review copy of the record? Miles has a gramophone. But if you can't give away a copy, I will lend him mine when it comes.[1]

By the way, I had intended to send you a complimentary copy of Gilbert's book when it was published, and by an oversight this wasn't done. If you have not got a copy I should be delighted to send you one now.

Yours sincerely
[T. S. Eliot]

TO *Dorothy Pound*

TS Lilly

30 June 1930   Faber & Faber Ltd

Dear Dorothy,

I have just had a line from Ezra strongly recommending Obermer.[2] I gathered from you when you came to tea, and also from Ezra's note, that you are seeing Obermer at present. Would you be so kind as to let me have a confidential line to 24 Russell Square, either now or perhaps just before you leave, to tell me what you think of him?

Ever affectionately,
T. S. E.

P.S. Will you come again soon? I know you hate telephoning so I don't expect that, but do, please, suggest yourself.

---

preferably by an Irish voice; and as the one gramophone record which he made attests, no other voice could read it, not even another Irish voice, as well as Joyce could read it himself. This is a limitation which has made the appreciation and enjoyment of his last book so very slow.' JJ's reading from *ALP* is available on the *Irish Poets and Writers* CD (British Library, 2013). James Campbell, in 'Out of darkness' ('NB', *TLS*, 29 Mar. 2013, 32), has called it 'one of the strangest recitations in English . . . Only when Joyce breaks into Latin – "Hircus Civis Eblanensis" – does it briefly make sense.'

1 – Hamish Miles's review of the three fragments from JJ's *Work in Progress*, and of Gilbert's *James Joyce's 'Ulysses'*, in C. 10 (Oct. 1930), 188–92, does not mention the famous recording.

2 – Letter from EP not found. Dr Edgar Obermer, London, was author of *Health and a Changing Civilization* (1935) – a work preoccupied with the 'neuro-endocrine-circulatory system'.

TO *F. R. Leavis*[1]

1 July 1930   [*The Criterion*]

Dear Mr Leavis,

I was very much interested by your article on 'Modern Poetry',[2] but for purely personal reasons it is very difficult for me to judge it and it would also be unsuitable for me, as Editor, to publish an essay which deals at such length and so kindly with my own work.

I hope very much that you will be able to send me something before long, against which this reason will not intervene.

Yours very truly,
[T. S. Eliot]

TO *James Houghton Woods*

1 July 1930   [Faber & Faber Ltd]

Dear Professor Woods,

Thank you very much indeed for your very kind letter.[3] As for the Jaeger book, we have written to the publishers to explain that we cannot afford to produce such a book without additional American support and that the matter cannot be settled until the Autumn. I do not think anyone else is likely to snap the book up and it is really a labour of love to produce it

---

1–F. R. Leavis (1895–1978): literary critic; Fellow of Downing College, Cambridge, 1927–62, Reader from 1959; founding editor of *Scrutiny*, 1932–53. His works include *New Bearings in English Poetry* (1932), *The Great Tradition* (1948), *The Common Pursuit* (1952), and *D. H. Lawrence: Novelist* (1955). See further Ian MacKillop, *F. R. Leavis: A Life in Criticism* (1995); Christopher Hilliard, *English as a Vocation: The 'Scrutiny' Movement* (2012).

On 23 July 1942, TSE was to write to Sir Malcolm Robertson, British Council, to recommend a subsidy for *Scrutiny*: 'Some of us are privately not very happy when we see so many emigré periodicals cropping up mostly of dubious ephemeral value – copies are sent to me and I wonder who reads them – while it is such a struggle to keep any serious indigenous magazines alive.'

2–Unidentified; presumably a draft portion of the forthcoming *New Bearings in English Poetry*.

3–Woods had replied on 7 June to TSE's letter of 10 Apr.: 'I have never forgotten that we worked together on Patanjali; but lately I have learned much more from you than you ever acquired from me . . . With regard to Werner Jaeger we have been dealing with him here for the last four or five years in classes . . . In fact, the old prejudice against the Platonic metaphysics which has previously existed in England is, I think, being dispelled by the new Platonic studies in Germany.

'With regard to the book, I have not yet succeeded in getting an opinion from the syndics of the [Harvard University] press . . . In the autumn I will try to get a definite decision.'

at all. If I don't hear from you in October, I will write again. Meanwhile I look forward very keenly to your visit to Cambridge, and to seeing you and Mrs Woods in your new house. I am keenly disappointed to hear that you were here several years ago, and failed to find me. It is true that I have been extraordinarily nomadic in domestic residences, but 24 Russell Square will always reach me.

With all best wishes,

Yours always gratefully,
[T. S. Eliot]

TO *F. McEachran*[1]   CC

2 July 1930   [Faber & Faber Ltd]

Dear Mr McEachran,

I must apologise for my delay in answering your letter of the 5th of June, and also for my letters of introduction never reaching you.[2] As a matter of fact, I confess that I find that they were never sent, and the reason they were never sent is that they were never completed. I had been under the delusion that they had gone to you and I am glad that I shall have another opportunity, and will certainly let you have these letters and any others you wish when you go to Paris, so please let me have [*sc.* know] in good time whether you are going this summer. I fear, however, that in August most of my friends will be in the country.

I am sorry that I did not spot your mistake in the title of Cornford's book and that your letter arrived when it was too late to make the alteration.[3] But it is a very small point, after all, and a very natural mistake. I was thankful that your Greek quotation was not completely disordered.

Sincerely yours,
[T. S. Eliot]

1 – Frank McEachran (1900–75), schoolmaster, classicist, author, was to become a friend of TSE and contributor to C. In the 1920s he taught at Gresham's School, Holt, Norfolk (where W. H. Auden was a pupil); then at Shrewsbury School (where Richard Ingrams, later editor of *Private Eye*, was a student). Alan Bennett has acknowledged that the eccentric, charismatic Hector, in *The History Boys* (2004), is based on McEachran (Dave Calhoun, 'Alan Bennett: interview', *Time Out*, 2 Oct. 2006). On TSE's recommendation, F&F brought out McEachran's first books, *The Civilised Man* (1930) and *The Destiny of Europe* (1932). Other works include a study of J. G. Herder (1939). See John Bridgen, 'Sometime Schoolmasters All: Frank McEachran and T. S. Eliot . . . and a few others', *Journal of the T. S. Eliot Society (UK)* 2010, 21–40.
2 – McEachran asked TSE to send some letters of introduction to him in Paris at Eastertime.
3 – McEachran had failed to correct, in the proofs of his article 'Tragedy and Philosophy', the title of F. M. Cornford's book *Myth-Historicus* (which he had given as *Mythico-Historicus*).

3 July 1930   [Faber & Faber Ltd]

Dear Mrs Whibley,

Thank you for your letter of the 2nd. I am very glad to hear that everything is right about the copyright with *Blackwood's*, and also I await your typescript of the Henley manuscript.[1]

I have been meaning to write to you about your Urquhart Manuscript.[2] If you think that a youngish man, not academic, is the most suitable, the name of Hamish Miles occurs to me immediately. He is a young man of letters, a Scot from Edinburgh, a reader for Jonathan Cape, and is at present writing a book on Dr Jowett which we shall publish.[3] One reason why I thought of him is that he edited, or at least wrote an excellent introduction to Urquhart's *Admirable Crichton,* which was published by the Pleiad Press.[4] My books are in such disorder that it takes me a week to find any book that I want, but I will send you my copy as soon as I can disinter it. I think that he would like the job; he is a warm admirer of his compatriot Urquhart, and I believe him to be a thoroughly conscientious worker. He is an Oxford man and I imagine somewhere between thirty and thirty-five.

But if you wanted someone of established reputation, I daresay that my friend Professor Grierson of Edinburgh would relish the work. He is an extremely busy man, however, and might not have the time to do it. But if you like the idea I would ask.

I am rather in the dark in making these suggestions, because I have not read the manuscript. I mean I do not yet know whether these epigrams are an important contribution to literature, or merely amusing fire-crackers. Nor do I know the amount of expurgation that such a person

1 – TSE had undertaken to compile a collection of CW's articles from *Blackwood's Magazine.*
2 – George Blackwood stated that the copyright in CW's column 'Musings Without Method' (*Blackwood's Magazine*) was the property of the author. Mrs Whibley had mentioned (20 June) that she had 'a manuscript of Urquhart's Epigrams': 'I spoke airily of editing it myself – well, this plan is quite out of the question, and I wonder whether you would know of any man who would be able, willing & eager to edit it. It needs a good scholar – and *not* a greybeard.' (Thomas Urquhart [1611–60], Scottish writer; translator of Rabelais.)
3 – *Benjamin Jowett* was announced in F&F's Autumn catalogue: 'Few men have ever exercised so great an influence, or lived so long after their death in the lives of other men, as Benjamin Jowett, the famous Master of Balliol College, Oxford (from 1870 to 1893).' But Miles did not finish his work; the biography was ultimately to be written by GCF.
4 – Sir Thomas Urquhart, *The Life and Death of the Admirable Crichton ... From the original text of The Discovery of a most Exquisite Jewel, 1652*; with introduction by Hamish Miles (1927).

as Lord Brentford might think desirable. Certainly, if the latter point was important, a man like Miles might have a much freer hand than Grierson.

For Grierson, I know, would have no personal prudishness, but his important academic position might necessarily affect his attitude.

I will wait until I hear from you again, before taking any further steps.

One other point. I feel, and I gather that you feel, that perhaps Frederick Macmillan[1] ought to have the refusal of the *Musings*; but if the Urquhart manuscript is not already pledged, or if Charles did not, to your knowledge, promise it to any publisher, my firm would be very much interested in it. From what you say about the book, I should think that it might be most suitable for a limited edition, though I dislike limited editions myself. But in either case, I think we have the proper means for handling it.[2]

I was much disappointed that you did not see my wife the other day, but she was, in fact, in bed; but I hope we shall have better luck next time you are in London. Thank you very much for coming.

Yours very sincerely,

[T. S. Eliot]

TO *Charles R. Walker*   CC

3 July 1930   *The Criterion*

Dear Mr Walker,

I have your letter of the 6th of June and can only repeat my renewed apologies for the delay in returning your manuscript.[3] I frequently do mislay manuscripts, and occasionally lose them altogether. In the case of yours, I found it, after a long search, and mislaid it again before I had had time to write to you. I am appalled at the inventory you have drawn

---

1 – Mrs Whibley wrote (20 June), 'old Frederick Macmillan was such a friend of Charles's, that I think he would be the only consideration'. Sir Frederick Macmillan (1851–1936): Chairman of Macmillan & Co.

2 – Mrs Whibley answered on 5 July that the Urquhart had been promised to Peter Davies.

3 – Walker (Concord, New Hampshire) submitted 'The Mental Climate, A Study in the Deluge of Words' – attacking 'one of the problems of the intellect in the contemporary scene' – in the summer of 1929, and he had written several times to chase it up. TSE's secretary told him on 9 May 1930 that the MS had been 'mislaid'. Since his essay had been out of circulation for ten months, he challenged TSE on 6 June: 'Having for ten years or more been an editor on a number of magazines, including the *Atlantic Monthly*, the *Bookman* etc., I appreciate the difficulties of a busy office, and have myself on occasion used the words *"for the moment mislaid your manuscript"*. You, having been for some years a writer can likewise appreciate *my* position.'

up of my iniquities. I am quite sure that you would never have done such yourself, but I am sure that you were a good editor, and it is quite plain that I am a very bad one.

With renewed regrets, and hoping to see you again in London.

Yours sincerely,
[T. S. Eliot]

TO *K. F. Summers*   CC

4 July 1930   [Faber & Faber Ltd]

Dear Miss Summers,

I am greatly honoured and pleased by the invitation which you have conveyed to me to join your committee.[1] I was very much tempted to accept, but the truth is that I have so many irons in the fire at present that I could not give the time necessary; and I very much dislike being a merely nominal member of anything. So I hope that you will express to your committee my regret and cordial sympathy.

With very many thanks,
Yours truly,
[T. S. Eliot]

TO *Marguerite Caetani*   TS Howard

4 July 1930   Faber & Faber Ltd

Dear Marguerite,

I must apologise for not having answered your last letter. I don't know whether you knew that we were moving again and have not yet got at all settled, and we have had a niece of mine staying with us until yesterday, which added to the confusion. She has now made off to Prague, so I have a little more freedom. Our address is, by the way, 68 Clarence Gate Gardens, N.W.1.

I wonder if you have yet communicated with either Read or Hayward? I haven't seen either of them lately. Nor have I yet made my enquiries about Richard Hughes, whom I do not know.[2] I wonder if you know

1–K. F. Summers (Anglo-Catholic Congress, Catholic Literature Association) invited TSE (30 June) to become a member of the Executive Committee of the Association.
2–'Do you think,' wrote Caetani (undated), 'you could get something from the author [Hughes] of "High Wind over [sic] Jamaica" for "C[ommerce]"?'

The Stricken Deer; it occurred to me that possibly David Cecil might be able to give you some interesting prose for *Commerce*, but I speak with diffidence since he recently let me down over a review which he promised for the *Criterion*.

About the essay of Kassner which you mention; how could I get hold of a copy?[1] I want to publish something by him, but feel that the 'Sterne' is now a little out of date.

I recommend to your notice part of a poem in the last *Criterion*, by Gordon Macleod, the whole of which we are intending to publish as a book.[2]

Friedrich Gundulf has promised me an essay for the next *Criterion*. Have you ever thought of him for *Commerce*? Du Bos or Curtius could tell you all about him.

I trust you will let me know your address in Brittany. Do you return to Rome in the Autumn?

Yours ever affectionately,
Tom

TO *Olivia Shakespear*[3]   TS Beinecke

7 July 1930   Faber & Faber Ltd

Dear Mrs Shakespear,

I enclose copies of correspondence which I have had with Ezra regarding the stock of *Quia Pauper Amavi*, which we hold. You will observe that

---

1 – 'Concerning Vanity', trans. M. Gabain, *C.* 10 (Oct. 1930), 35–54.
2 – Macleod, *The Ecliptic* (1930). FVM wrote an undated F&F memo on *The Ecliptic*: 'I am personally in favour of doing this long poem as well as Auden's book . . . I'm inclined to rank this lad above Auden: more staying power?; but Auden's not to be sneezed at; he *may* not go off; & the two are very different.' Auden's *Poems* was published on 9 Oct. 1930; so were *The Ecliptic* and also *The Pursuit*, by Philip Graves of *The Times*. 'It seemed pretty good to me,' wrote GCF of *The Pursuit* in a letter to his friend 'A/C 388171 T. E. Shaw [Lawrence]', on 24 Jan. 1930.

GCF wrote to Philip Graves on 30 Jan. 1930: 'It would help enormously if Lawrence would give it a preface. That isn't a suggestion made for the sake of selling-power which anything known to be from his pen would have. The difficulty about "Pursuit" is to "place" it. It belongs to the Seven Pillars Constellation; an authentic member, I think.

'If Lawrence could be persuaded to nail it where it belongs, its significance would not be missed – as otherwise, it very well may be.'
3 – Olivia Shakespear (?1864–?1938), novelist and playwright, had a brief love affair with WBY, 1895–6. See *Ezra Pound and Dorothy Shakespear: Their Letters 1909–1914*, ed. Omar S. Pound and A. Walton Litz (1984), 356–7.

he requests us to send the stock to you.¹ Knowing what it means to store quantities of books in a flat, I think it more prudent to write and ask for your approval before sending the parcel. Are you prepared to take in these books, or would you like me to give you the exact dimensions of the parcel, before it is sent. The tone of the correspondence suggests to me that Ezra may have given his instructions precipitately, without first asking your permission.

Yours always sincerely,
T. S. Eliot

TO *Philippa Whibley*   TS copy

7 July 1930   [Faber & Faber Ltd]

Dear Mrs Whibley,

This is merely to acknowledge your last letter and to mention the Urquhart.² I have heard a good deal lately, in other connexions, about John Sparrow;³ and all I have heard is to the good. I believe that he would be an excellent editor; even if he does not know the subject already, I understand he can be trusted to make himself a master of any subject he takes up. So I must leave it at that. I am not a near friend of Miles; so that I have no reason for pushing either one or the other; let us be clear on that

---

1 – EP had suggested (undated letter) that Mrs Shakespear (his mother-in-law), 34 Abingdon Court, Kensington, should be sent the remaining stock: 251 copies of *Quia Pauper Amavi* and 293 copies of 'Dialoges of Fontanelle' were despatched to her on 14 July 1930.

2 – Mrs Whibley thanked TSE on 5 July for his offer to publish the Urquhart MS. Prof. George Stuart Gordon [1881–1942], President of Magdalen College, Oxford, had recommended John Sparrow – 'a young Fellow of All Souls, & a scholar . . . I think your Mr Hamish Miles sounds a good man . . . One of the chief points in favour of Mr Miles, is, I think, the fact that he knows something of Urquhart, & that he likes him. Sparrow knows little or nothing – although this is not altogether a disqualification.' Of the MS, she wrote, 'I should say that it is an important work – certainly [more] than mere fire-crackers . . . Of course a large number of the epigrams are, I suppose, obscene – or rather, Lord Brentford would insist that they are – but I know that Charles wished to edit the book more or less unexpurgated . . . It would be a fairly expensive book to buy, which would naturally save it from the ravening jaws of policemen & frumps. Rather than see the book mutilated by expurgation, I would place it upon the fire.'

3 – John Sparrow (1906–92) was so precocious as a scholar at Winchester College that at the age of sixteen he published an edition of John Donne's *Devotions upon Emergent Occasions* (1923). Educated after school at New College, Oxford, he was called to the Bar at the Middle Temple, 1931. From 1929 he was a Fellow of All Souls College, becoming Warden, 1952–77. Works include *Sense and Poetry: Essays on the Place of Meaning in Contemporary Verse* (1934), *Controversial Essays* (1966). See John Lowe, *The Warden: A Portrait of John Sparrow* (1998).

point. If it were merely the question of an introductory essay, I believe that Miles would write a more lively one; but perhaps the question of an introduction can be left open; and in that case I have no doubt Sparrow would be as good as Miles. I know however that Sparrow has taken on some heavy work for the Clarendon Press; so with him, it would be a question how soon he could do this job.

I have read the Henley manuscript once, and shall be writing about that quite soon.

Yours sincerely,
[T. S. Eliot]

TO *Ezra Pound* TS Beinecke

7 July 1930   Faber & Faber Ltd

Dear Rabbit,

I have been in treaty with Mr Louis Zukofsky (like everybody whom I have endorsed for a Guggenheimer he has failed) about publication of an Essay on yr. Cantoes & have agreed with him amicably to publish as much of same as will fit in comforamably to a No. of the *criterion;* but I think & he thinks too in that kase it wd. be decent of you to let appear one (1) cantoe either simulataneousley prior or subsequent or compline; I think pertikerly (pronunciation of H. M. Goereg Vth) as you have given cantoes to *Hound & Horn* (Hornhound) which cant pay *very* much more than I do (I know Kirstein & Bandler) you might consider this carefu lley even privately printed cantoe might serve. please reply by return of Poste.

yrs. etc.
T. S. E

TO *Antonio Marichalar*[1]   TS Real Academia de la Historia

7 July 1930   *The Criterion*

Cher Monsieur et ami,

Depuis longtemps je n'ai plus de nouvelles de vous. Avez-vous tout-à-fait oublié votre chronique que nous estimons tant, et êtes-vous trop affairé de m'en envoyer pour le prochain numéro? J'y attaché beaucoup d'importance. Nous sommes en retard avec tous nos chroniques, c'est Rychner qui avait dû attarder, suite d'une grippe. En tout cas, j'attendrais avec impatience un mot de vous, et j'espère vivement que vous pouvez reprendre votre position dans le *Criterion*. (Le recevez-vous reguliérement?)

Recevez, cher monsieur et ami, l'assurance de mes sentiments cordials.
[T. S. Eliot][2]

TO *F. S. Oliver*   CC

7 July 1930   [Faber & Faber Ltd]

Dear Oliver,

Thank you for your letter of the 4th.[3] It is at least as much my fate [fault] as yours, that we have not met. We have had to move again – did I tell you? – and are now at 68, Clarence Gate Gardens N.W.1. In consequence, though I have had to see many people at my office on business, I have seen few of my friends for a long time; my wife is in very poor health; and we have not even had time to think of a summer holiday. I hope you have got off to Scotland, as I imagine that Scotland is the best place for a Scot's convalescence – I shall telephone to Kenry House to ask where to send this note.

---

1 – Antonio Marichalar, Marquis of Montesa (1893–1973): author, critic, biographer, journalist; contributor to the newspaper *El Sol* and the periodical *Revista de Occidente* (on subjects including Claudel, JJ, Valéry, and VW). Works include *Mentira desnuda:* 'The Naked Lie' (essays on European and American culture, 1933); *Riesgo y ventura del duque de Osuna* (1932): *The Perils and Fortune of the Duke of Osuna*, trans. H. de Onís; *Julián Romero* (1952).
2 – *Translation*: Dear Sir and Friend, It is a long time since I had any news of you. Have you completely forgotten your Letter from Spain, which we so greatly appreciate, and are you too busy to send me a letter for the next number? I consider it very important. All our Letters from Abroad are late. Rychner missed the deadline because of 'flu. In any event I shall look forward impatiently to hearing from you, and I greatly hope that you will be able to take your place again in the *Criterion*. (Do you get it regularly?) / With my warmest good wishes, [T. S. Eliot].
3 – Oliver regretted that he had not seen TSE for a year: 'I have been rather so-so just lately . . .'

King will, I am sure, be pleased to know that his review pleased you.[1] Without flattery, I found it rather inadequate myself. I almost wrote a letter to the *Nation* about their review;[2] but decided that perhaps it was not my place; and every week I am tempted to write a letter to the *Nation* about something they have said.

I wonder whether the 'trust' even will escape the Vulture Snowden?[3] I hope so.

I have (in confidence) taken upon myself the task of trying to make a volume (possibly more, but I doubt it) of selections from 'Musings without Method'. It is proving rather difficult.

I am very sorry indeed that I have not seen you before you go to Jedburgh. But I hope that you will return in the autumn in good health, and that we may meet then.

Yours always sincerely,
[T. S. Eliot]

1 – 'I am very glad my book gave pleasure to Mr King. That is the kind of review an author likes.' *The Endless Adventure* I: *1710–1727*: review by William King, C. 9 (July 1930), 722–4.

2 – R. R. Sedgwick, 'Eighteenth-Century Politics', *N&A* 46 (15 Feb. 1930), 675, cited Oliver's declaration that he had used 'no books that are not familiar to every reader who has interested himself in the first half of the eighteenth century', to decry the book in hand: 'it would not get an undergraduate a first-class in the subject in a reputable history school'.

3 – 'Partly owing to Mr [Philip] Snowden [Labour Chancellor of the Exchequer] and partly to the natural process of attrition, I have been induced to make a settlement out of which my obligations – such as those to Messrs. Faber & Faber – will be discharged in future. "The Kenry Trust", as it is called, will pay the remaining instalments of my guarantee.' TSE was to write in his 'Commentary', C. 10 (Oct. 1930), 1–3: 'Mr Snowden becomes more unpopular, and his policies more obviously ruinous; yet one shudders at the disturbance and expense of an Election which might merely instate Mr Churchill in his place . . . It is true that the present Government has acquitted itself moderately well in Foreign Affairs. That is to say . . . in foreign affairs the Labour Government has not deviated from the Liberal policy of the previous Conservative Government . . . The rot in Parliament is only a symptom of the rot without . . .'

TO *Shane Leslie*[1]   CC

7 July 1930   [Faber & Faber Ltd]

Dear Mr Leslie,

Thank you for your letter of the 11th instant.[2] I shall look forward to
seeing your book on Bodley.[3] I do not think that there is much likelihood
of my wanting to publish a translation of that small book of Maurras in
the near future; but I thank you for letting me know. I am still doubtful
as to what is the best book of Maurras to try in translation first; and I am
more than doubtful whether the book you mention, which as you know
is on the *Index*, would be tactically a good book to introduce him by. I
still incline to the *Avenir de l'Intelligence* as the book for beginners. But
perhaps we might meet some day to discuss such questions.[4]

Yours very truly,

[T. S. Eliot]

1 – Sir Shane Leslie (1885–1971): diplomat and author. Born into the Anglo-Irish Protestant
Ascendancy – first cousin on his mother's side to Winston Churchill – he read classics at
King's College, Cambridge, where he became a Roman Catholic for life as well as an Irish
Nationalist (though christened John Randolph, he styled himself 'Shane' – the Irish form of
his name). He also resigned the Irish estates entailed upon him and was for several years
actively committed to Irish Nationalist affairs (he stood for Parliament as a Nationalist in
the 1910 election, unsuccessfully). In 1907 he went to Russia and visited Leo Tolstoy, and
for a while he studied Scholastic Philosophy at Louvain University. He edited the *Dublin
Review*, 1916–26, and published works including *The End of a Chapter* (1916); *Henry
Edward Manning: His Life and Labours* (1921); *Mark Sykes: His Life and Letters* (1923);
The Skull of Swift (1928). He succeeded as third baronet on the death of his father in 1944.
2 – 'We corresponded about a translation of Ch Maurras – *L'anglais qui a connu la France*
– You very kindly forewent yours while I translated it for my Life of Bodley, whom it
concerned. It proved very unwieldy in English and would have swamped my book. I kept
only paragraphs; so the way is still open for a separate version. If Maurras is to appear in
English I believe *La chemin de Paradis* would reveal his genius & subtlety and philosophy
best . . .'
3 – *Memoir of John Edward Courtenay Bodley* (1930).
4 – TSE was to write, in his reader's report on a translation by A. Chisholm of *The Illusion*
by Charles Maurras, on 16 Oct. 1936: 'If I had thought that there was any money to be
made by a translation of *L'Avenir de l'intelligence* I would have suggested it years ago; and
I think we could find a better translator. The author is in error in thinking that nothing of
Maurras has been translated: Shawn [*sic*] Leslie did his little book on J. C. Bodley, to say
nothing of my translation of an essay on criticism in the *Criterion*.'

TO *J. F. Scanlan*[1]

7 July 1930   *The Criterion*

Dear Mr Scanlan,

I hope you will remember having met me at the Savile Club at lunch one day. Belgion did give me your address, but I have lost it and your Club tell me that they will forward it.

I am writing to ask – if you are in town – whether you could help me out by translating an essay by Julien Benda[2] for the *Criterion*. Casting about in my mind, I concluded that I knew of no one who could translate abstract French – which as I know from experience is a particularly delicate matter to translate – as well as you; so I hope you can do it. I have only received the essay today; and I want to use it in the September *Criterion*; could you and would you care to – translate it, say within two weeks? I have only glanced at it; it looks heretical (for me as well as for you): it is on The Idea of Order and the Idea of God;[3] but if it worries your conscience, I may say that I shall try to get someone like D'Arcy to reply to it; so that all will be for the Faith. I hope you will get this and can [*typing runs off the page*]

[T. S. Eliot][4]

1 – J. F. Scanlan was translator of works by Jacques Maritain including *Art and Scholasticism* (1930) and *Saint Thomas Aquinas: Angel of the Schools* (1931).
2 – Julien Benda (1867–1956): journalist, political-social philosopher, critic. Born into a Jewish family in Paris, he studied history at the Sorbonne, and was recognised as a noted essayist and '*intellectuel*', writing for periodicals including *Revue Blanche, Nouvelle Revue Française, Mercure de France, Divan* and *Le Figaro*. A passionate upholder of the Graeco-Roman ideal of rational order and disinterestedness — Eliot said Benda's 'brand of classicism is just as romantic as anyone else's' — his works include *Dialogues à Byzance* (1900), complete with pro-Dreyfus pieces; *Le Bergsonisme: ou, Une Philosophie de la mobilité* (1912); *Belphégor: Essai sur l'esthétique de la présente société française* (1918); *Le trahison des clercs* (1927): The Treason of the Intellectuals, trans. RA (1928). See further Ray Nichols, *Treason, Tradition, and the Intellectual: Julien Benda and Political Discourse* (1978).
3 – 'Of the Idea of Order and the Idea of God: study for a system of metaphysics', trans. J. F. Scanlan, C. 10 (Oct. 1930), 75–94
4 – Scanlan replied (9 July): 'I don't think any cas de conscience need arise. What wd puzzle me is why the *Criterion* shd bother about such a silly cerebralist as Julien Benda, who has not even the merit of being a Frenchman:– but that is neither nor here.'

TO *Gordon Fraser*   CC

7 July 1930   [Faber & Faber Ltd]

Dear Mr Fraser,

Thank you for your letter of the 5th instant, to which I must reply very briefly.[1] Your announcement that you intend to publish an English edition of Van Doren's book comes as a surprise, because I did not suppose that you were going in for general publishing. However, it is a good book, and deserves an English edition. I should suggest that you should first try my friend Mr Bonamy Dobrée (with my support) as he could write as good a preface as I could, and just possibly has more time to do so; also, he has not I think written so many 'introductions' or 'prefaces' as I have; and therefore his might really carry more weight. His address is Mendham Priory, Harleston, Norfolk. But if you can eventually get nothing better, I might be able to do a *short* preface for a very worthy book.

Yours in haste,
[T. S. Eliot]

TO *Desmond Morse-Boycott*   CC

8 July 1930   [Faber & Faber Ltd]

Dear Father Morse-Boycott,

I have thought over the case of your young poet, which is, alas, like many that I have had to deal with.[2] (I usually advise them to get a steady job in a bank or insurance company, and once or twice have helped to that end). I agree that it was most ill-advised of the parent to have his son's 18-year verse 'published', especially as this is a delusive form of publication: it is not publication but merely *printing*. It is bad for a boy

---

1–Fraser wrote that he had received permission to reprint Mark Van Doren's book on Dryden; he wondered whether TSE might write an introduction to it: 'This book is by far our most largest undertaking; and if it had only a short foreword by you would stand a greater chance of recognition.' See *The Poetry of John Dryden* (1931).

2–Morse-Boycott wrote (undated): 'I crave a thousand pardons . . . as I am about to do a dastardly thing . . . A lady came and begged me to do something journalistically for a young man who is going to pieces. He seems to have great ability but no niche in life . . . She has left me this book of poems, which the boy's father foolishly published for him when he was 18. It turned his head. I can't judge poetry, any more than I can judge wine . . . Will you glance at a few, and return me the book with just a note . . . saying whether the boy has possibilities in him, and if so, what market there is for poetry? I should say *verse*. Poetry is left to the few great ones . . .'

if he cannot write, and worse if he can. I believe in retarding these young ambitions as long as possible.

In my experience, it is quite impossible to judge of the future of anyone from what he writes at 18. At 20 or 21, perhaps; never at 18. I can't say that this boy will be a poet; only that there is enough in his verse to show that he might be and ought to be, a useful human being in *some* capacity. He has ability; but I doubt whether it is for poetry. Numbers of ardent youths must express themselves in verse to begin with. In the majority of cases, it means that they are good for something; in the minority, for some form of paper and ink; in one in a million, for verse. But poetry should be discouraged: those who can bear that burden will assume it in spite of everybody and everything and in spite of what they themselves, in lucid moments, recognise as best for them.

If now you could give me a little more information (confidential) about this youth – his present age, his state of decay, his background etc. – I could consider whether I ought to see him or not. But if you are not in a position to tell me more about him, a good deal about him, then I can only say, let him be put into a position where he can earn his own living, first.

Sincerely yours,
[T. S. Eliot]

TO *Geoffrey Faber* MS Valerie Eliot

8 July 1930 [Plain paper]

G. C. F.

Would you please glance at this as it concerns an acquaintance of yours.[1]

1–Hoffman Nickerson (1888–1965) – a friend of TSE at Harvard (see obituary in *New York Times*, 25 March 1965, 37) – had submitted his article 'Oman's Muret' (on the battle of Muret, 1213) on 28 June 1930. 'With all due modesty, I believe that this article will make a sensation in its field. [Sir Charles] Oman has a considerable reputation and although I long ago heard rumors of how flimsy and bad he is I would have hardly believed it myself unless I had gone deeply into the thing. The old fraud!'

Sir Charles Oman (1860–1946): military historian; Prize Fellow of All Souls; Chichele Professor of Modern History at Oxford University from 1905; President of the Royal Historical Society, 1917–21; Conservative Member of Parliament for Oxford, 1919–35; knighted in 1920. His numerous narratives include *The Art of War in the Middle Ages* (1885); *A History of the Art of War in the Middle Ages* (2 vols, 1898); and *History of the Peninsular War* (7 vols, 1902–30).

I have not yet read it. The author is another friend of mine and has written a good book on American Revolutionary History which the *T.L.S.* reviewed I believe very favourably.[1]

T. S. E.

TO *Basil Willey*[2]   CC

10 July 1930   *The Criterion*

Dear Sir,

I must apologise for the delay in deciding about your interesting essay,[3] to which I have devoted a good deal of consideration. I think, in the whole, that it is not suitable for fitting in with the contents of the *Criterion* already arranged for the immediate future, but I should be very much interested to see some other essay from you.

Yours faithfully,
[T. S. Eliot]

TO *J. A. H. Ogden*   CC

10 July 1930   *The Criterion*

Dear Sir,

I have your letter of the 15th inst. enclosing your poem 'The Camp'. As a matter of fact, manuscripts offered to the Criterion Miscellany are primarily dealt with by another director,[4] and very often are not

1–GCF replied (undated memo): 'I should be rather sorry if this was published in the *Crit.*, because it would look (to Oman) as though I had gone out of my way to embrace an opportunity of attacking him. I haven't any doubt that he deserves all he gets from Nickerson! (tho' I had always supposed – on hearsay – that his one merit was in military history!) But the subject is technical – of a technicality outside the usual *Criterion* field; & the place for the attack is surely in one of the historical journals. Oman is something other than a mere acquaintance; he is, in All Souls, an opponent (not of course personally, so far as I am concerned), & I should hate to have him thinking that I chose this method of getting my own back. And he *would* think so!'
2–Basil Willey (1897–1978): Lecturer in English, Cambridge University, from 1923; King Edward VII Professor of English Literature, 1946–64; works include *The Seventeenth Century Background* (1934) and *The English Moralists* (1964).
3–'Cosmic Toryism and the Religious Attitude' was submitted on 3 Apr.: 'The enclosed essay (about 3500 words) is an outcome of some lectures I have given recently for the English Tripos in this University. The actual point of departure was a discussion of eighteenth-century deism.'
4–FVM.

seen by me at all. But in this case, your manuscript was, as a matter of fact, shown to me and I agree that although very interesting in itself it was positively unsuitable for the purposes of the Miscellany. We have so far published only one pamphlet of verses, those of the late D. H. Lawrence,[1] and we are not likely to publish any more verse in the series. The series is not really suitable for either verse or fiction and is intended for exactly what is implied by the word 'pamphleteering' – a spirited essay on some controversial topic of the day, by a writer who has knowledge and convictions. You must therefore understand that it is no criticism whatever, but merely a definition of the scope of the Miscellany, that has led us to return your manuscript.

Yours very truly,
[T. S. Eliot]

TO *Algar Thorold*

CC

11 July 1930   [*The Criterion*]

My dear Thorold,

I am writing again to ask if you would care to look at a MS. I have. It is an account by a learned American friend and contemporary of mine of the battle of Muret at which Simon de Montfort smashed the Albigensians. My friend is distinctly an authority on military strategy, and his Essay in itself is extremely interesting reading. He is also wholly orthodox in his attitude towards the Albigensians.

I confess that I am rather in a quandary about this article, because I myself encouraged him to write it. Now that it is written I find it contains extremely damaging criticism of Sir Charles Oman as a Medieval Historian; and for purely private reasons which I could explain to you in conversation, I am not in a position to publish an article so destructive of Oman's reputation, so I thought that it might suit the *Dublin Review*, and it seems to me an Essay which on its own merits deserves publication and would perhaps make something of a sensation.

Yours ever,
[T. S. Eliot]

P.S. Jacques Maritain has just sent me a copy of his new book on S. Thomas, called *Le Docteur Angélique*. I have not had a review copy

1 – DHL's collection of twenty-three satirical poems, *Nettles*, was published as Criterion Miscellany 11 on 13 Mar. 1930.

but if you have received a copy yourself, would you consider whether it is suitable to review [with] D'Arcy's book which you have.[1]

TO *Covici, Friede Inc.*   CC

11 July 1930   [Faber & Faber Ltd]

Dear Sirs,

I have today received from you a copy of *Circumference: Varieties of Metaphysical Verse*, edited by Genevieve Taggard.[2]

I thank you for sending me a presentation copy of a handsome book, particularly as this is a courtesy of which many publishers of anthologies are ignorant; and I am all the more sorry to remark that the book appears to have had no proof-reading at all. I have not yet had time to compare other texts, but if the text of other authors is as badly mutilated as mine, I can only condemn the book altogether; and as the name of one English poet appears on the flap as *Vaughn*, I suspect that there may [be] other errors which I have not detected.

Of the four poems of mine which you have taken, there is not one without some error. Most are errors of punctuation but three are more serious.

My line	'But every week we hear rejoice'[3] appears as 'But every week we *here* rejoice'.
My line	'I shall not want Capital in Heaven'[4] appears as 'I shall not *meet* Capital in Heaven'.
My line	'The Father and the Paraclete'[5] appears as 'The Father *of* the Paraclete'.

[*typing runs off the page*]

above makes their respective stanzas utter gibberish, and the last makes me responsible for a really original and remarkable heresy. I deeply resent such gross mutilation of my work, and I write to ask what you are prepared to do about the matter.

Yours faithfully,
[T. S. Eliot]

1 – *Le Docteur Angélique* (1930), inscribed 'à T. S. Eliot avec l'admiration et le profonde sympathie de Jq Maritain'. Thorold did not review Maritain. See his review of M. C. D'Arcy's *Thomas Aquinas*, C. 10 (Apr. 1931), 568–71.
2 – *Circumference: Varieties of Metaphysical Verse 1456–1928*, ed. Genevieve Taggard (1929).
3 – 'The Hippopotamus', l. 19.
4 – 'A Cooking Egg', l. 13.
5 – 'Mr Eliot's Sunday Morning Service', l. 16.

13 July 1930   [Faber & Faber Ltd]

Dear Mr Sayers,

It is some time since I promised to write to you, but I am always very busy and have many things to attend to.[2]

I have read your poems several times and I think it quite worth your while to go on writing. I never like to encourage anyone to write verse; but you have fortunately, a definite and excellent occupation of a very different kind, so that there should be no danger of your trying to live by journalism. The Law will help you to write good verse, far more than it will interfere with you. One cannot write poetry all the time; and the rest of the time it is far better to be in a solicitor's office than scribbling reviews of books or writing columns for newspapers.

As for your letter.[3] Don't hang about worrying over your disposition, but just accept it. And for God's sake don't worry about the lack of academic learning. If it comes one's way it is a good thing; if not, one must do with what one has. I have seen good poets ruined because they were too conscious of being uneducated; and by the time they had more or less educated themselves they had lost all impulse to write poetry. Read as much as you can on any subjects outside of poetry, that interest you, but don't try to work your reading into your verse until it comes in naturally of itself. Read Ezra Pound (I will send you a copy) and Gerard Hopkins

1–Michael Sayers (1911–2010), Dublin-born writer of Jewish Lithuanian ancestry, had been taught French at Trinity College, Dublin, by Samuel Beckett. In the 1930s he was drama critic of the *New English Weekly*, and for a while shared a flat in Kilburn, London, with George Orwell and Rayner Heppenstall. Some of his early stories were included in *Best British Short Stories*, ed. Edward O'Brien; but in 1936 he left London for New York, where he worked as dramaturge for the designer and producer Norman Bel Geddes. During WW2 his interests and writings pursued a pro-communist direction, for which he was later blacklisted by the House Un-American Activities Committee (having until that time enjoyed much success as a writer for NBC Television). In later years he wrote plays for the BBC, and he contributed episodes to TV series including *Robin Hood* and *Ivanhoe*. He worked too on the screenplay of *Casino Royale* (1967).

2–Sayers had submitted (5 Apr. 1930) what he called 'a volume of – for want of a better adjective – impressionist poems, written during my seventeenth year. I am now just 18.'

3–Sayers lamented on 1 May, 'there is much regarding my work, and artistic activity in general, that either puzzles or awes me. Like Edgar Poe I am of a melancholy disposition, a "funeral mind" . . . I am aware of my total lack of academic learning . . . [E]ither I begin where you have left off at the "Hollow Men" (that is all of your work I really know) or savagely, it must be savagely, repudiate you and Joyce and Proust – as Lawrence did, or tried to do . . . I cannot thank you sufficiently in words for your kindness towards me.'

for verse *technique*,[1] but as for content, read anything you like. (There will be a cheap edition of Hopkins I believe in the autumn).

Don't bother whether to 'accept' or to 'reject' me and Joyce and Proust. We are all utterly different anyway, and probably quite different from what you think we are. Don't bother about your 'direction'. You say that if you follow me you must 'discard sound'. That is bosh; I have taken as much trouble over 'sound' as anybody, and you are not to worry about following or not following anyway. If there is anything in you it will come out of itself, and nothing is more difficult than to know when one is original and when one is imitative; so one simply must not care.

Get all the fun out of life you decently and morally can, in your own particular circumstances; send me some more verses in six months time, and then come and see me and have a talk about it.

Sincerely yours,
[T. S. Eliot]

TO *D. S. Mirsky*[2]   CC

14 July 1930   [Faber & Faber Ltd]

My dear Mirsky,

I have not seen you for a long time, except once when I passed you in Piccadilly Circus in a taxi. I wish that we might meet again before long, especially if you are about to leave London for the summer.

---

1 – TSE wrote of Gerard Manley Hopkins in an undelivered lecture, 'The Last Twenty-Five Years of English Poetry' (1939), for an Italian audience: 'He is a Victorian, certainly, but such a highly individual one that I should place him among the "eccentrics". He was aloof from the popular currents of his time; and he was a Jesuit priest leading a religious life. The originality and the beauty of his verse, and often the greatness of the poetry, are incontestable; though it has a certain resemblance to that of his contemporary George Meredith. Hopkins is I think the greater poet of the two. His vocabulary, and his metric are both very original. His influence has been that which one might expect of a powerful eccentric poet suddenly appearing complete: it was immediate, it was very patent, taking the form of imitation of his metres and his verbal ingenuities such as the fabrication of new compound words. I think it may be transient, but it cannot be overlooked in considering the writing of some of the younger poets.'

After quoting the first eight lines of 'The Windhover', the lecture picks up: 'It appears to be a kind of fusion of the image of a hawk seen in the air, and the thought of Our Lord. You will recognise that Hopkins is highly idiosyncratic; that although he is not traditional, his speech is his own peculiar speech, and not the common speech of his own or any period. In this respect, I should call him, in the French sense, a less *classic* poet than the later Yeats.'

2 – Dmitri S. Mirsky (1890–1939): son of Prince P. D. Svyatopolk-Mirsky, army officer and civil servant (on his mother's side he was descended from an illegitimate son of Catherine

A Mrs Bertha Malnick, who says that she knows you, has sent me a book, a critical work on Tolstoy by R. Eichenbaum, who, she says, is a critic with a very high reputation in Russia now, and which she would like to see translated into English.[1] Now, I can't read a word of Russian, and so, before doing anything further about the book, I am writing to you first to ask if you know it and what you think of it. I should be very grateful for any information you can give me.

Yours ever,
[T. S. Eliot]

TO *John Gould Fletcher*   CC

15 July 1930   [Faber & Faber Ltd]

Dear Fletcher,

Thank you for your letter. It is a bit awkward about the Essay you suggest.[2] I should be glad to have from you such an article but the majority of the books you have mentioned have already been given for review to various people who asked for them – Harold Monro is supposed to be doing a long review of Campbell – and I have not intended *Ash Wednesday* or *Anabasis* to be reviewed at all. Perhaps you could enlarge the scope of your Essay and lay rather less stress on the books you mentioned.

---

the Great). Educated at the University of St Petersburg, where he read Oriental languages and classics, he served as an army officer and was wounded during WW1 while fighting on the German front; later he served in the White Army. In 1921, he was appointed lecturer in Russian at the School of Slavonic Studies, London (under Sir Bernard Pares), where his cultivation and command of languages brought him to the attention of a wide literary circle. His works include *Contemporary Russian Literature* (2 vols, 1926) and *A History of Russian Literature from the Earliest Times to the Death of Dostoevsky, 1881* (1927). In 1931 he joined the Communist Party of Great Britain (see 'Why I became a Marxist', *Daily Worker*, 30 June 1931), and in 1932 returned to Russia where he worked as a Soviet literary critic (and met Edmund Wilson and Malcolm Muggeridge). In 1937 he was arrested in the Stalinist purge, found guilty of 'suspected espionage', and sentenced to eight years of correctional labour: he died in a labour camp in Siberia. See G. S. Smith, *D. S. Mirsky: A Russian–English Life, 1980–1939* (2000).

Mirsky later did TSE this crude disservice: 'The classicists led by T. S. Eliot, came forward as conscious supporters of the re-establishment of classical discipline, of a hierarchy, and as open enemies of democracy and liberalism – in short, as the organized vanguard of theoreticians of a capitalist class going fascist' (*The Intelligentsia of Great Britain*, trans. Alec Brown [1935], 123).

1 – Boris Mikhailovich Eikhenbaum (1886–1959) wrote a number of books on Tolstoy.
2 – Fletcher wished to write on 'Some Recent Tendencies in Poetry', covering volumes by Hart Crane, Archibald MacLeish, Roy Campbell and Laura Riding, as well as *Anabasis*, by St-John Perse (in TSE's translation), and *Ash-Wednesday*.

Could [you] lunch with [me] on Thursday and we could talk it over? Would it suit you to call for me here about 1.15? It is possible that I may be a little late as I have a meeting elsewhere at a quarter to twelve.

Yours ever,

[T. S. Eliot]

TO *Nancy Cunard*[1] CC

16 July 1930 *The Criterion*

Dear Nancy,

I have ordered a copy of Ezra's *Cantos*,[2] when it comes out, but I am writing now to ask if you would be so good as to let me know about when publication may be expected, as I have a long essay on him by Louis Zukofsky which I want to publish in the *Criterion*.[3]

With all best wishes,

Yours ever,

[T. S. Eliot]

1 – Nancy Cunard (1896–1965): writer, journalist, publisher, political activist; daughter of Sir Bache Cunard, heir to the Cunard Line shipping business, and of an American heiress named Maud Alice Burke, who flourished as a London hostess under the name of 'Emerald' Lady Cunard (1871–1945). Nancy cultivated lovers and friends including Michael Arlen, AH and Louis Aragon. In 1920 she moved to Normandy where she ran the Hours Press (successor to Three Mountains Press), 1928–34: her productions included works by EP and Beckett. Her own works include *Black Man and White Ladyship* (1931); *Negro: An Anthology* (1934); *Authors Take Sides on the Spanish War* (1937) – a pamphlet sponsored by *Left Review* – *Poems for France* (1944); memoirs of Norman Douglas (1954) and George Moore (1956); and *These Were the Hours: Memories of My Hours Press, Réanville and Paris, 1928–1932* (1969). See *Nancy Cunard: Brave Poet, Indomitable Rebel*, ed. Hugh Ford (1968); Anne Chisholm, *Nancy Cunard* (1981); Shari Benstock, *Women of the Left Bank: Paris, 1900–1940* (1986); François Buot, *Nancy Cunard* (2008). Lois G. Gordon, in *Nancy Cunard: Heiress, Muse, Political Activist* (2007), surmises an affair with TSE.

2 – *A Draft of XXX Cantos* (1930), with alphabet designs created by Dorothy Pound, was published by Cunard.

3 – Cunard replied (20 July) that she would send him *XXX Cantos*, and send a copy also to Zukofsky. She added, 'Mother disappointed at not hearing from you about dinner tomorrow night' – but her mother must have been trying to reach TSE at his former address in Clarence Gate Gardens.

16 July 1930   *The Criterion*

My dear Du Bos,

I was overwhelmed by your letter.[1] Some day far ahead when my library and private papers are looked through for anything of value, I imagine your letter to me as being put up to auction at Hodgson's as one of the longest letters you have ever been known to write, at least to anyone in England.

What you say gives me much pleasure. I am enclosing, with considerable apprehension, a copy of the essay on Pater which I mentioned.[2] I am sure that you will disagree with every word of it, but I am all the more anxious that you should see it at once, rather than come across it by chance later.

I am really sorry about Kassner.[3] He has been on my mind and conscience for a long time and I have wanted to do anything I could for him in England. As a matter of fact, I wrote a few days ago to Madame de Bassiano and asked her to convey to him, as I did not know where he was at the moment, my regrets and to ask him whether he had anything more recent than the essay on 'Laurence Sterne', which he might prefer me to see. If by any chance you should be seeing him, I should be grateful if you would give him the same message.

About your essay on Stefan George.[4] I am rather at a loss to think of anyone in England who could translate your quotations properly. I think that Edward Sackville-West would do it as well as anybody, if he would. I know that he knows the work of Rilke and has made some translations from him, but I do not know how well he knows George,

---

1–Du Bos, in his letter of 11 July, praised *Ash-Wednesday* as 'deeply moving' (he had read passages to friends including E. R. Curtius, 'who already loved them'); *Anabasis* he had not yet read 'closely enough', but he admired the 'patience and courage' of 'serious translation work'.

2–Du Bos would read 'with interest' TSE on Walter Pater. '*Marius* is a subject on which . . . I could not keep back my frank opinion, but, precisely on account of the degree of my allegiance, I am myself in need of a corrective and will therefore read you with the utmost impartiality.'

3–'Kassner was a little put out at your not bringing out in the *Criterion* his essay on Sterne . . . [P]ersonally I find the essay full of truth and subtlety, with the most delicate lightness of touch, and yet going far: Kassner suffers a little, I think, of not meeting with more appreciation . . .'

4–Du Bos accepted 'with joy' TSE's offer to publish his essay on George. 'Of course, as you say, the text of the poems should be given in German, with the translation following. I suppose you can secure a translator, though here again he will have a hard task: I took a good deal of pain in bringing out in my translations all the shades of the meaning . . .'

and it would be necessary for me to have from you all the references to the texts from which you quote. There is plenty of time for this because I could not publish your essay until December. Failing a good translator, I should have to give your French translation in foot-notes; but I should still want the German text. I should also like to know whether you would translate your essay yourself or would prefer to have it done here. All this importunity requires another communication from you, and that I despair of getting.

I am glad that you have seen something of Gordon George.[1] He has peculiarities that irritate many people, perhaps more here than abroad; but he has a very sincere interest in literature and ideas and what is more, a real interest in saintliness.

It is good to hear that you may be spending part of next year in England.[2] I look forward to seeing something of you then. I was sorry to see so little of Maritain when he was here, as I have a strong admiration and affection for him.[3]

I wonder if you have seen anything of Jean de Menasce[4] of late? I have heard nothing of him for a long time and so have been rather anxious about him.

Yours ever sincerely,
[T. S. Eliot]

1 – Gordon George (Robert Sencourt) – 'whose sincerity and seriousness I much appreciate' – had given Du Bos a copy of the last number of C.
2 – 'Will my book on Pater ever be written? It all turns upon a year of quiet concentration spent, if possible, half in England and half in Italy . . . My intention would be to pass next summer and next autumn in Oxford and in London.'
3 – '[Jacques] Maritain came back from England much pleased with his stay and particularly with his intercourse with you.' Maritain had visited England in March.
4 – Jean de Menasce (1902–73), theologian and orientalist (his writings include studies in Judaism, Zionism and Hasidism), was born in Alexandria into an aristocratic Jewish Egyptian family and educated in Alexandria, at Balliol College, Oxford (where he was contemporary with Graham Greene and took his BA in 1924), and at the Sorbonne (Licence es-Lettres). In Paris, he was associated with the magazines *Commerce* and *L'Esprit*, and he translated several of TSE's poems for French publication: his translation of *TWL* was marked '*revue et approuvée par l'auteur*'. He became a Catholic convert in 1926, was ordained in 1935 a Dominican priest—Father Pierre de Menasce—and went on to be Professor of the History of Religion at the University of Fribourg, 1938–48; Professor and Director of Studies, specialising in Ancient Iranian religions, at the École Pratique des Hautes Études, Paris. TSE came to consider him 'the only really first-rate French translator I have ever had' (letter to Kathleen Raine, 17 May 1944).

18 July 1930   Faber & Faber Ltd

Dear Clive,

It is a long time since I have seen you – except once out of a taxi window in Gordon Square – I waved an umbrella at you, but without succeeding in being noticed – but I now have the excuse of writing to you, to put forward a suggestion which may be called, Business.

You may be aware that my firm has taken up Pamphleteering, with shilling books of five to twelve thousand words called the Criterion Miscellany. I am sending you separately a few to glance at. Ever since the regretted end of the Hogarth Essays particularly, I have had in mind to ask you if you would at any time honour us with a pamphlet.

They are meant to be real pamphlets – to defend some cause, or to strike at some iniquity or folly of the day.

Why I have chosen this moment to write to you – not even knowing where you are – is that the phrase 'the standard of living' is now always hovering on the lip of every politician of every stripe. It occurred to us that the author of *Civilisation* might be inclined to dissociate the elements of this muddled parrotery [*sic*] or shibboleth. Does the English workman really hold a higher standard of living than his continental equal, or is it merely cinema, wireless and motorcycles and more wasteful housekeeping and cooking. It could be considered, of course, by comparing the good old British Slum with conditions in any German town – but what I am suggesting to you is rather the question of the Briton's notion of Values in life compared with the Values of continental civilisations. But of course this is merely a suggestion. You may be more exasperated by some other parrotcall, or may be cherishing some cause or public grievance which is ready to burst into flame.

---

1 – Clive Bell (1881–1964), author and critic of art who was contemporary at Cambridge with Lytton Strachey and LW, was at the centre of both the domestic interminglings and the aesthetic ideals and the artistic endeavours of the Bloomsbury circle. He married in 1907 the artist Vanessa Stephen; and while she went on to share her life and work from 1915 with the artist Duncan Grant, Bell enjoyed a relationship with his acknowledged mistress, MH. With Roger Fry, Bell mounted the first Post-Impressionist exhibition at the Grafton Galleries, London; and in later years, with an independent income, he resided for much of the time in his beloved France, where he cultivated friendships with Picasso and other artists. He was influential as an art and exhibition critic for *N.* and *NS*; and his notable books include *Art* (1914), *Since Cézanne* (1922), *Civilization: An Essay* (1928), *Proust* (1928), and *Old Friends* (1956), which includes a kind account of TSE. See too *Bloomsbury* (1968), by his son Quentin Bell; Frances Spalding, *Vanessa Bell* (1983); James Beechey, *Clive Bell* (2000).

Anyway, forgive my impertinence, and please let me hear from you. I wish you would find [time] to dine with us when if ever in London. We have moved I believe four times since I last saw you.

Yours ever,
T. S. Eliot

TO *George Bell* TS Lambeth

20 July 1930   *The Criterion*

My dear Lord Bishop,

It is really disgraceful of me to have kept your kind letter so long unanswered.[1] Part of the delay is due to a slight illness, and the rest is really a compliment: it was difficult for us to bring ourselves to decline so charming an invitation. Besides, one always has peculiar pleasure in an invitation renewed. But the fact is that my wife has been in poor health for some time past, and has accordingly been very timid of visiting country houses, to say nothing of a Palace. This is our only reason for declining. But, if you and Mrs Bell are to be in Chichester during August and September, we should not be afraid of running down to Chichester for a day or two in our small car – I suppose the Anchor is still in existence, an excellent hotel – and if we had the inducement of believing that we might call upon you, we should be much more likely to revisit a country which we know and love. So, whenever you have the time, I should be grateful for a line to let me know during what part of the summer we might be sure of finding you there.

I am very much pleased by what you say of *Ash Wednesday*. Most of the people who have written to say that they couldn't understand it seemed to be uncertain at any point whether I was referring to the Old Testament or to the New; and the reviewers took refuge in the comprehensive word 'liturgy'.[2] It appears that almost none of the people who review books in England have ever read any of these things! But you would be shocked yourself to learn how much of the poem I can't explain myself. Certain imagery – the yew trees, the nun, the garden god – come direct out of recurrent dreams, so I shall abandon them to the ghoulish activities of

1 – Bell had written on 4 July on behalf of his wife and himself to invite the Eliots to visit them at Chichester for the weekend of either 16–18 Aug. or 23–25 Aug.

2 – Bell had been 'deeply moved' by *Ash-Wednesday*: 'I won't pretend that I understand it all, but even what I don't understand haunts me and I like the whole atmosphere of the poem . . .'

some prowling analyst. The three leopards are deliberately, however, the World, the Flesh and the Devil; and the whole thing aims to be a modern *Vita Nuova*, on the same plane of hallucination, and treating a similar problem of 'sublimation' (horrid word). However pathetically it falls below that amazing book, the comparison is useful, in making clear that this is not 'devotional' verse. That can only be written by men who have gone far ahead of me in spiritual development; I have only tried to express a certain intermediate phase.

With many thanks to you and Mrs Bell,

I am,
Yours very sincerely,
T. S. Eliot

TO *James B. Pinker & Sons*[1]

21 July 1930   [Faber & Faber Ltd]

Dear Sirs,

We shall shortly be paying over to you, as agent for Mr James Joyce, the royalties on *Anna Livia Plurabelle* up to June 30th of this year.[2]

I have just head from Mr Joyce, giving me his address until the end of August: Grand Hotel, Llandudno. He has instructed me to ask you to deduct your fee and send the balance to him at that address, by registered post, in an open cheque. He is particularly anxious that the cheque which you send him should *not* be *crossed*.[3] I should be obliged if you would let me have your confirmation, so that I may inform Mr Joyce that the matter will be in order.

Yours faithfully,
[T. S. Eliot]

1 – Literary, Dramatic and Film Agents.
2 – FVM wrote to Critchell Rimington (The John Day Co.) on 18 July: 'The Joyce item in our Miscellany . . . we are making a very decent little profit on doing this book at a shilling.'
3 – JJ wrote to TSE with these instructions on 17 July.

TO *Desmond Morse-Boycott*

22 July 1930   [Faber & Faber Ltd]

Dear Father Morse-Boycott,

I have the letter which you enclose, giving information about your young man: I will keep this letter unless you wish it returned.[1] I think that the best thing to do now is for you to give him an introduction to me, and suggest that he should write and ask for an appointment to come and see me. If preferable, he need not know that we have had any previous correspondence about him.

I am doubtful, however, whether there is anything I can do for him. I am afraid that he is just too young and probably too uneducated to be of any use at present. I think that he really ought to try to get a job, however small, and stick to it for a few years, while he is reading and developing himself, but if there is any chance of my being able to give him good advice, I am quite ready to see him.

Yours sincerely,
[T. S. Eliot]

TO *W. J. Lawrence*[2]

22 July 1930   [*The Criterion*]

Dear Mr Lawrence,

I must apologise for my delay in writing to you, but I have been extremely busy. I shall have to say what I always do say to you: that I shall be very glad to publish this study 'The Secret of the Bad Quartos', but cannot promise to do so before March next. Of course, if I found room before then, I would publish it; but I have had rather a good deal of Shakespeare matter lately, and as I have much other material waiting, I should like to give it a rest. But, of course, if you find it convenient to publish the Essay elsewhere in the meantime, you are perfectly at liberty

---

1 – Morse-Boycott had been informed by the Revd W. H. Moore on 11 July that the young man in question, Fred Peel Yates, twenty-one, was the son of a sixty-year-old country vicar from Essex who had done well at the County High School, securing the School Medal, but had failed thereafter to gain a scholarship to Cambridge. For a while he worked in a bank, but he had been dismissed because of being 'intemperate' and 'slack'. He was in need of spiritual advice and guidance.

2 – W. J. Lawrence (1862–1940): theatre and textual historian; author of *The Elizabethan Playhouse and Other Studies* (2 vols, 1912–13).

to do so.[1] I hope that when you are in London again we may have the opportunity of a longer interview.

Yours very sincerely,

[T. S. Eliot]

TO *J. B. Pouterman*   CC

22 July 1930   [Faber & Faber Ltd]

Dear Mr Pouterman,

I have thought over your letter of the 15th inst. and as I gave you my assurance that I would sign a certain number of copies, I do not wish to embarrass you at the last moment.[2] I am ready to accept £18 (eighteen pounds) for signing an edition of not more than fifty copies.

I am pretty closely in touch with the situation of the Limited Edition Market in New York, and am not in the least surprised at the attitude of Random House. I know that the slump in the Stock Market has affected considerably the trade in Limited Editions, which I never considered to be more than a transient success.

Yours sincerely,

[T. S. Eliot]

TO *Erich Alport*   TS BL

22 July 1930   Faber & Faber Ltd

Dear Alport,

Many thanks for your letter of the 11th and for your kind offices with Gustav Braun,[3] who has written very amiably and immediately sent two of the books I asked for. I must explain that we do exchange with *Der Neue Rundschau*, but the German and Swiss periodicals have always gone directly to my friend Randall who is Secretary of the Legation in Bucarest,[4] so that I never see the ordinary exchange copies at all. If I were

---

1–'The Secret of "The Bad Quartos"', *C.* 10 (Apr. 1931), 447–61.
2–'I find the fee of £25 for signing the 60 copies almost prohibitive . . . and feel greatly embarrassed . . . Could you not possibly reduce the fee to £18?' Pouterman was due to print only 650 copies, including signed copies, when he had planned for a print run of 1,000: Random House had decided to import into the USA just 250 copies, and not 650 as he had anticipated.
3–A Heidelberg bookseller.
4–Alec (later Sir Alec) Randall (1892–1977), diplomat and writer, entered the Foreign Office in 1920. In the early 1920s he was Second Secretary to the Holy See. He ended his career as

the perfect Editor, I should, of course, try to look at all the best foreign periodicals myself, with a view to spotting new writers; but unfortunately I have no time for that.

Gundolf has just sent his Essay on Mörike,[1] which I have not yet had time to read, but hope to publish in the *Criterion* either in September or December.

With many thanks for your kindness,

Yours sincerely,
T. S. Eliot

TO *Isaiah Berlin*[2]   MS Bodleian

22 July 1930   Faber & Faber Ltd

Dear Mr Berlin,

I was neglectful in not thanking you for your letter of the 27th May and copy of the *Oxford Outlook*, which I have read with much interest.[3] If you would care to do so, I should be very glad to arrange an exchange of the *Criterion*, particularly as I like to keep my eye on all periodicals such as yours, for the success of which I send my best wishes.

Yours sincerely,
T. S. Eliot

Ambassador to Denmark (where he was awarded the Grand Cross, Order of Dannebrog), 1947–52. He wrote on German literature for *The Criterion* and *TLS*. Later works include *Vatican Assignment* (1956) and *The Pope, the Jews and the Nazis* (1963).

1 – 'Eduard Mörike', trans. Wilhelmine E. Delp, *C.* 10 (July 1931), 682–708.

2 – Isaiah Berlin (1909–97), philosopher and historian of ideas, was born in Riga, Latvia, and brought to England with his family in 1920. Educated at St Paul's School, London, and at Corpus Christi College, Oxford, he gained a first in Greats and a second first in Philosophy, Politics and Economics; thereafter he won a prize fellowship at All Souls, 1932. He taught philosophy at New College until 1950. In 1957 he was appointed Chichele Professor of Social and Political Theory at Oxford; and in the same year he was elected to the British Academy, which he served in the capacity of Vice-President, 1959–61, and President, 1974–8. He was appointed CBE in 1946, knighted in 1957; and in 1971 he was appointed to the Order of Merit. From 1966 to 1975 he was founding President of Wolfson College, Oxford. His works include *Karl Marx* (1939) and *The Hedgehog and the Fox* (1953).

3 – 'A copy of *Oxford Outlook* has been sent to you because it was thought that you might feel some interest in the kind of thing that is now being written, and possibly believed, in Oxford; the most notable characteristic of this journal is its almost entirely critical content – three years ago it was full of poetry and short stories only. I hope that you will not think me importunate . . .' (*Letters 1928–1946*, ed. Henry Hardy [2004], 22).

TO *J. Griffin*

22 July 1930   [Faber & Faber Ltd]

Dear Sir,

I thank you for your letter of the 9th inst. and particularly for the honour which your Society desires to confer upon me.[1] Before answering your invitation, however, I shall be very grateful for a little more information. I know Mr Chesterton, of course, and am in general sympathy with his views; but I should be glad to have any statement of the principles of the League, so that I could be quite sure whether I was justified in associating myself with it or not.

> With many thanks,
> Yours very truly,
> [T. S. Eliot]

TO *Ronald Bottrall*[2]

22 July 1930   Faber & Faber Ltd

Dear Sir,

I must apologise for having kept so long your poems, which interested me very much.[3] On mature consideration, however, we have decided that

---

1 – J. Griffin, Hon. Secretary, The Distributist League, Glasgow University Branch, wrote: 'It has been suggested, in connection with the newly formed Glasgow University Distributist Club, that you will have sympathy with those political principles and aims for which the club stands. We therefore wish to ask you to do us the honour of accepting nomination for the position of Honorary Vice-President of the club.' (The President was G. K. Chesterton.)

2 – Ronald Bottrall (1906–89), poet, critic, teacher and administrator, studied at Pembroke College, Cambridge, and taught in Helsinki, 1929–31, before spending two years at Princeton. He was Johore Professor of English at Raffles University, Singapore, 1933–7, and taught for a year at the English Institute, Florence, before serving as British Council Representative in Sweden, 1941–5; Rome, 1945–54; Brazil, 1954–7; Greece, 1957–9; Japan, 1959–61. At the close of his career he was Head of the Fellowships and Training Branch of the Food and Agricultural Organization of the United Nations in Rome. His poetry includes *The Loosening* (1931) and *Festivals of Fire* (1934).

3 – Bottrall had written an undated letter:

'Several months ago I sent you four poems on which I asked your judgement. I greatly regret that I was then so precipitate, for I have since written a considerable number of poems and have decided to scrap three of the four which I sent you.

'I am sending this collection to you on the advice of Dr F. R. Leavis of Cambridge, who has been very interested in it; Mr I. A. Richards also, though he has not seen these poems, has commented favourably on prose work which I have done . . .'

In a letter to the *TLS* ('Reflections on the Nile', 24 Oct. 1980), Bottrall declared that he wished to make 'a deposition about my early relations with Leavis . . . During the four years

---

we cannot make any proposal to you for publishing them at present, as we have several volumes of verse about to appear, and we are not inclined at the moment to commit ourselves to anything further.

I should, however, very much like to see more of your work from time to time.

Yours very truly,
T. S. Eliot

TO *J. D. Aylward*[1]   CC

22 July 1930   [Faber & Faber Ltd]

Private and Personal

My dear Aylward,

I was touched and pleased by your ringing up and hope that it was not a shock to you to hear that I was not knocked down and killed by a motor bus. On the contrary, your report of the news has brought me to life, and I am writing to suggest that you should have a return lunch with me before long.

I am writing to Crofton to whom I have owed a letter for a long time, but I am not suggesting that he should lunch as well at the moment, because when I last heard from him, he wanted me to meet a friend of his, who has been anxious to get literary work of any kind; so I thought that I ought to give Crofton an opportunity of arranging a meeting with that

---

I was at Cambridge, 1925–29, I met Leavis once, at a breakfast party given by Mansfield Duval Forbes, when we spoke for about three minutes. I did not even attend his lectures, which began, I think, in 1928 . . . In December 1929, I began to write poetry seriously. When I had managed half a dozen poems or so, I wrote and asked a friend if he knew anyone who might be interested in having a look at them. He replied: "Send them to Leavis." I did and Leavis and his wife got quite excited about them. Queenie said: "Matthew Arnold as a modern." I sent them some more poems and Leavis suggested I should read Pound's *Hugh Selwyn Mauberley*. I met Leavis at his home in June 1930 and we talked in general terms about contemporary poetry, with little reference to mine . . . I never had what could be called a friendship with Leavis and saw him rarely. He had no influence whatever on my poetry. He helped me to find a publisher for *The Loosening* (1931) and I contributed several poems to *Scrutiny* at his request. I also published in *Scrutiny*, in 1933, an essay on *XXX Cantos of Ezra Pound*. That is all . . . I feel that I ought, in my old age, to record these things.'

The Times noted in Bottrall's obituary (27 June 1989) that in 1934 'T. S. Eliot, asked whom he believed to be the most promising young British poet, mentioned his name along with that of Louis MacNeice. Previously he had been tipped by F. R. Leavis as the most intelligent of the new young poets. Unfairly and irrationally his reputation suffered from this, since Leavis was so thoroughly disliked.'

1–James de Vine Aylward was a colleague and friend at Lloyds Bank.

man before we two lunched together. Hoping that you are getting a little week-end sea-faring,

I am, as always,
Sincerely your friend,
[T. S. Eliot]

TO *W. H. Auden*[1]

22 July 1930   [Faber & Faber Ltd]

My dear Auden,

In reply to your undated note, of course we wish the deleted phrases to be restored to their original form.[2] As soon as we have a revised page proof of the book, including *Paid on Both Sides*, you shall have a copy and I will ask you to make the restitution yourself while correcting the second proof.[3]

Yours ever,
[T. S. Eliot]

P.S. You have not let me know whether I am to return the typescript of *The Enemies of a Bishop*.

1–W. H. Auden (1907–73), poet, playwright, librettist, translator, essayist, editor: see Biographical Register. Auden wrote to Louise Bolgan on 13 Apr. 1945, of TSE: 'I shall never be as great and good a man if I live to be a hundred' (Amherst College Library).

2–'I hope you will be able to restore the banned line in "Paid on Both Sides" when it is published in book form.' WHA's short play, subtitled 'A Charade', was first published (slightly bowdlerised) in C. 9 (Jan. 1930), 268–90. The 'banned line', spoken by Boy to Doctor – 'Tickle your arse with a feather, sir' (p. 279) – was replaced with a conspicuous row of dots. See textual note by Edward Mendelson, who remarks that the play had 'suffered minor censorship and misreading when it appeared in *The Criterion*' (W. H. Auden and Christopher Isherwood, *Plays and other Dramatic Writings by W. H. Auden 1928–1938* [1989], 525–9).

3–On 6 May 1930 WHA wrote to FVM (who had posted him on 13 May 'the draft agreement for your *Poems*'): 'I have considerable alterations that I wish to make in the poems you have, some corrections, omissions, and additions. I will send the revised manuscript as quickly as possible. I hope that this will not interfere with your plans, as it may make the book slightly larger. Otherwise I am perfectly satisfied with the arrangement.' The proofs of *Poems* were sent to WHA on 4 July (he had submitted 'the new, and I hope final, manuscript' by 15 May). Messrs Trend & Co. were sent 'some extra copy' by the Publications Manager on 14 July. 'This is a charade entitled PAID ON BOTH SIDES which recently appeared in THE CRITERION. It is to come at the beginning of the book, so the page numbers will have to be altered. Please let us have proofs of this new matter as soon as you can.' The proofs of *Paid on Both Sides* were sent to Auden on 30 July; and he returned them, with corrections, on 9 Aug.: 'Dear Mr De la Mare . . . You will see that I want to cut a passage on p. 27. I know it is very late in the day and will upset the pagination. If it is impossible to do anything now I shall quite understand. I hope the other suggestions are clear.'

TO *Marguerite Caetani*   CC

23 July 1930   [Faber & Faber Ltd]

Dear Marguerite,

Thank you for your letter of July 15th which arrived a few days ago, also for the copy of Kassner's typescript, which arrived on Monday. I shall read it as soon as I can, with a view to publishing it, if suitable, in the December number.[1] If I decide to do so, I will write to you at once, and will ask you for Kassner's present address.

I don't quite understand what you mean by saying that it is you who think of the honoraire of the translator.[2]

Anabasis is proceeding very slowly. As a matter of fact, even with a translation, it appears to be almost unintelligible to the English reviewer. Most of the papers seem to have shirked the task of reviewing it altogether, and those which have reviewed it have been rather supercilious. It is really largely a matter of habit. The English Press has begun to get used to James Joyce, and even the *Times Literary Supplement* has taken *Anna Livia Plurabelle* much as a matter of course.[3] But Léger is quite unknown to them, and the English reviewer, faced with something he has never heard of before, is apt to take refuge in silence. As a matter of fact, *Ash Wednesday* has not had at all what is called a 'good press' either, and has sold rather in spite of the reviewers' opinions than because of them. Still I am not really dissatisfied with the sale of *Anabasis*, though I am disappointed not to have seen a single intelligent review. As you take the *Observer* you will have seen a review of both books in yesterday's issue, which is fairly typical.[4]

1 – Rudolph Kassner, 'Concerning Vanity', trans. M. Gabain, C. 10 (Oct. 1930), 35–54.
2 – 'Remember that it is I who think of the honoraire of the translator!' said Caetani (15 July).
3 – See 'Mr Joyce's Experiments' – a review of Anna *Livia Plurabelle* and *Haveth Childers Everywhere* – TLS, 17 July 1930, 588: 'In the light of recent research it is possible to demonstrate that the prodigious difficulties of Mr Joyce's latest work, provisionally entitled "Work in Progress", are at least the outcome of a logical and definite plan, even if it is impossible to follow with full understanding the details of its execution . . .'
4 – Anon, 'Logic of Imagination', *The Observer*, 20 July 1930, 5: 'In his preface to the translation of Mr Perse's *Anabasis*, Mr Eliot . . . explains that the apparent obscurity of Mr Perse's work is due "to the suppression of links in the chain of explanatory and connecting matter . . . The reader has to allow the images to fall into his memory successively without questioning the reasonableness of each at the moment; so that at the end a total effect is produced . . . There is a logic of the imagination as well as a logic of concepts." Like many of Mr Eliot's sayings, this is both pregnant and dark. It is dark because it appears to claim for the imagination the right to dispense with the rules of thought at the very moment when it is, apparently, adopting them. It is pregnant because it goes to the root of the new theory

The only new poem which I could give to *Commerce* is my Ariel poem for this autumn. The out about it is that I could not allow the English text to appear and I don't suppose you would care to publish a translation by itself. – Which reminds me to ask – Have you heard any news of Jean de Menasce lately? I have not heard from him for a very long time, but, on the other hand, I have had lately a charming, unexpected and surprisingly long letter from Du Bos.

Yours ever affectionately,
[Tom]

P.S. I don't think that we shall be going away until September.

TO *Arthur O. Lovejoy*[1]   CC

23 July 1930   [Faber & Faber Ltd]

Dear Dr Lovejoy,

I find that Herbert Read, whom I hoped would join us at lunch, cannot manage Friday, but would be delighted to come on Monday. Would Monday be equally convenient to you? If so, perhaps the easiest way to meet would be for you to pick us up at 24 Russell Square at one o'clock.

I very much hope that the change of date to Monday will not be awkward for you; the alteration is only due to the desire to include Read.

Sincerely yours,
[T. S. Eliot]

---

of verse . . . Mr Eliot does not advance on *Waste Land* [*sic*]. He is still desert-bound, but he has still the power to make us see the beauty that he refuses to overtake . . . But, though he is less a pontiff, he is more of a priest. He withdraws deeper into the shade of the altar, and his voice comes always more quietly – till at the end it is merged into the silence that he worships . . .

'It is the odder when he gives this indication of a change of spirit that he should simultaneously be offering an oblation to *Anabasis* – a poem in which . . . silence is completely out of control and creeps slowly over the spirit like a palpable advancing mist . . . Mr Perse pours out his images of some pilgrimage through a greater desert than that trodden by the Jews, and of the foundations of cities and civilisations richer than Judea and Babylon. But the images insult the intelligence because, like the ghosts that they are, they have no cause and no relation.'

TSE told Robert Hazel on 27 June 1952: 'what makes Perse's imagery possible, difficult as it often is, is a consistency of landscape, a setting in which every image finds its place . . .'

1–Arthur O. Lovejoy (1873–1962): Berlin-born philosopher; Professor of Philosophy, Washington University, St Louis, 1901–8 – where he became acquainted with the Eliot family – and Professor of Philosophy at Johns Hopkins University, 1910–38; editor of the *Journal of the History of Ideas*; author of *The Great Chain of Being* (1936). He lectured at the University of London in 1931.

TO *J. F. Scanlan*   CC

24 July 1930   *The Criterion*

Dear Scanlan,

Thank you for your admirable translation of Benda – of course I very nearly agree with you about Benda's work and about this essay particularly. He is a pedantic Sophist with a highly pretentious manner. As for a counterblast to Benda, however, I am not sure that a layman would not be more suitable than a cleric. I have thought of asking Maritain whether he would tackle it. I don't think that Massis would be quite up to the job.[1]

1 – Scanlan (19 July) suggested that the Revd Fulton Sheen might be able to assist Benda.

Henri Massis (1886–1970): right-wing Roman Catholic critic: contributor to *L'Action Française*; co-founder and editor of *La Revue Universelle*. Closely associated with Charles Maurras, his writings include *Jugements* (2 vols, 1924), *Jacques Rivière* (1925) and *La Défense de l'Occident* (1928). A defender of Mussolini and Salazar, his later works include *Chefs: Les Dictateurs et nous* (1939) and *Maurras et notre temps* (2 vols, 1951).

On 1 Nov. 1945 TSE wrote the following testimony: 'I, Thomas Stearns Eliot, British subject, of 24 Russell Square, London, WC1, England, doctor honoris causa of the Universities of Cambridge, Edinburgh, Leeds, Bristol, Columbia, Honorary Fellow of Magdalene College, Cambridge, a member of the board of directors of the publishing house of Faber & Faber, Ltd., London, testify that I have known Monsieur Henri Massis for over twenty years. The firm of publishers of which I am a director published an English translation of his *Défense de l'Occident*; and M. Massis was a contributor to a quarterly review, *The Criterion*, of which I was the editor. I saw M. Massis whenever I visited Paris, and when he visited London. I also received regularly *La Revue Universelle* of which on the death of Jacques Bainville he became the editor.

'The intellectual bond between myself and M. Massis was the common concern for the civilisation of Western Europe, the apprehension of the Germanic danger, and a similar diagnosis of its nature. Germany owed her highest achievement of culture to her allegiance to western civilisation; the future of Europe depended on whether Germany affirmed this allegiance, or whether she abandoned herself to her primitive instincts, seeking barbaric dominion in cultural isolation. After the rise of Hitler it was evident that Germany had taken the wrong course; that Germany was no longer one of the western peoples and that she had become a menace against which Europe should prepare herself. Such were my views, and such, I am sure, were the views of M. Massis, as his writings show. We were also in accord in attaching great importance to the development of the closest possible relations in every way, between France and England.

'My conversations with M. Massis, as well as his writings, left me with the strongest impression that he was not only a man of clear vision in these matters, but also a patriot of integrity and probity, who would never hesitate to sacrifice his own interests to those of his country. I should always have said that the love of France was one of his most conspicuous characteristics. And I cannot believe that so passionate a nationalist can be suspected seriously of having used his editorship of *La Revue Universelle* in order to ensure anything but the consolidation of an intellectual resistance to the plans of Germany for the subordination of his country.'

But your suggestion of Fulton Sheen[1] reminds me that I should very much like to meet him, if he is in London. Do you think that it could be managed? I would be very grateful if you would put me in touch with him. I have not read any of his work, but have heard it very highly spoken of. I am under the impression that he is a Jesuit, but perhaps I am wrong.[2]

Yours sincerely,
[T. S. Eliot]

TO *Philippa Whibley*   CC

24 July 1930   [Faber & Faber Ltd]

Dear Mrs Whibley,

I should have written to you before. I am getting on slowly with the Musings and find the work very interesting; and the distinction between what is reprintable and what is not, is for the most part more obvious than I had expected.

The question of the Henley is certainly very difficult; all the more difficult because it is Henley and not another; one does want to know something about Henley's influence upon and encouragement of other writers, and his formation of a political and imperial point of view largely through his contact with other men; and I imagine that the written records cannot altogether show this. But if you will let me keep the copy for a time, I shall be glad; and I hope to hear from you about it again when you have been able to assess the material you have in your hands.

I am sorry to have given you the pains of copying it all out yourself; I should not have asked you to give so much time as that.[3] And thank you for the list of Charles's other and earlier contributions to *Blackwood's*: I shall go through all these when I have finished the Musings themselves.[4]

1–The Revd Fulton Sheen (1895–1979) – educated at the Catholic University of America; the University of Louvain, Belgium; the Sorbonne; the Collegio Angelico, Rome – was ordained in 1919, won the Cardinal Mercier International Prize for Philosophy, 1925, and by 1934 was Papal Chamberlain. He was to be Auxiliary Bishop of New York (RC), 1951–66; National Director of the Society for the Propagation of the Faith, 1950–66; and Bishop of Rochester, New York, 1966–9. He was admired for his broadcasts and publications including *Freedom under God* (1940), *Philosophies at War* (1943) and *Communism and Conscience of the West* (1948).

2–Scanlan replied (undated) that Sheen was not a Jesuit but 'an ordinary secular'.

3–Mrs Whibley (20 June) had been copying out CW's unfinished life of W. E. Henley.

4–Mrs Whibley had sent on 3 July a list of the contributions that CW had made to *Blackwood's Magazine* before he started on his regular 'Musings' column in 1900.

I went to the Sale: I was not able to stay on that day to the moment when the French books came up, but I commissioned a shrewd Jewish bookseller whom I know, whom I found there, for several lots: but it appeared that in each case the prices soared far beyond what we could offer. Anyway, I am glad they did so well.[1]

Your visit, by the way, was a great success, and I hope you will let us know again when you are in London.

Sincerely yours,
[T. S. Eliot]

TO *D. S. Mirsky*   CC

24 July 1930   [Faber & Faber Ltd]

Dear Mirsky,

Many thanks for your kind letter of the 20th instant.[2] I was afraid, on the whole, that this was not a particularly propitious moment for a book on Tolstoy, however good; and I think that we had better decline this one. Your advice is very helpful.

I shall be in London during the first part of August, and very glad indeed to see you if we can arrange it.

Of course we should be delighted to have your services as translator when we do anything Russian; and I am glad to know that you would entertain such work. We are also glad of hints from time to time about anything worth translating.

Yours ever,
[T. S. Eliot]

---

1 – The sale of CW's library was organised by John Hodgson. Mrs Whibley had made a gift to TSE of CW's copy of Taylor's *Holy Living* – 'Charles had always kept it among his most treasured books.'

2 – 'Miss Malnick is a student of mine, & the book by Eichenbaum on Tolstoy is undoubtedly one of the most remarkable literary studies recently published in Russian. Of course it would be a good thing to have it translated, but I am not sure it would be a paying proposition. It is not so much a critical study as a very detailed *literary* biography of Tolstoy between 1850 & 1867 . . .'

TO E. McKnight Kauffer[1] TS Grace Schulman[2]

24 July 1930 *The Criterion*

My dear Kauffer,

I was relieved to hear from De la Mare that he had confided my *Marina* to you. I had meant to ask him to do so, before he went away, and was afraid that it had gone elsewhere. Yours is the only kind of decoration that I can endure.[3]

I hope you like it: I don't know whether it is any good at all. The theme is paternity; with a crisscross between the text and the quotation. The theme is a comment on the Recognition Motive[4] in Shakespeare's later plays, and particularly of course the recognition of Pericles. The quotation is from *Hercules Furens*, where Hercules, having killed his children in a fit of madness induced by an angry god, comes to without remembering what he has done.[5] (I didn't give the reference for fear it might be more distracting than helpful to the reader who did not grasp the exact point: the contrast of death and life in Hercules and Pericles.)[6]

I wonder whether this sort of explanation is useful or rather a bother to the artist? The scenery in which it is dressed up is Casco Bay, Maine. I am

1 – This letter was first printed in full in Grace Schulman's essay 'Notes on the Theme of "Marina" by T. S. Eliot', *Essays from the 'Southern Review'*, ed. James Olney (1988), 205–11.

2 – Schulman notes, 'Kauffer, who became a friend of my parents, Bernard and Marcella Waldman, when he returned to America (1939–55), gave the letter to me with a copy of the Ariel edition of "Marina"' ('Notes on the Theme of "Marina" by T. S. Eliot', 205).

3 – Kauffer wrote a marginal note here: 'this rattled me at first E. McKK.' (Richard de la Mare had just got married to Amy Catherine – daughter of the Revd S. A. Donaldson, DD, Master of Magdalene College, Cambridge – and was away on honeymoon.)

4 – See TSE on 'the Recognition Scene', in 'John Ford' (1932): 'In Shakespeare's plays, this is primarily the recognition of a long-lost daughter, secondarily of a wife; and we can hardly read the later plays attentively without admitting that the father and daughter theme was one of a very symbolic value to him in his last productive years: Perdita, Marina and Miranda share some beauty of which his earlier heroines do not possess the secret.'

5 – *Quis hic locus, quae regio, quae mundi plaga?* (*Hercules Furens*, Act V, 1, 1138).

6 – Kauffer repied on 29 July: 'What you tell me of "Marina" confirms a vague sense that I had already felt about it – but of course not anything like so clear as it is now. "Marina" is I think one of your best shorter poems. I wonder if you will like the drawing I did – which I regret that you have not yet seen . . . Mary Hutchinson has the first drawing for it – I did three or four.'

Richard de la Mare (F&F) wrote to Kauffer on the same day: 'First of all I must tell you how delighted I am with your drawings for Eliot's poem. In many ways I think them the most successful you have done for the series. Indeed, I am so excited by them that I dearly want to possess them. If you feel inclined to part with them, would you let me know what their price would be? I hasten to get in first, just in case someone else may feel as I do about them!'

afraid no scenery except the Mississippi, the prairie and the North East Coast has ever made much impression on me.

I wish we may meet soon.

Yours ever,
T. S. Eliot

TO *Clive Bell*

TS King's

25 July 1930   Faber & Faber Ltd

My dear Clive,

It was a surprise to hear from you at all and almost a shock to hear so quickly.[1] Indeed, I knew very well that you are now an expatriate – who in London does not know that fact to his regret? For indeed, you gave the most delightful lunch parties of all London. I will not say that there were never minor points of detail which Léon Daudet[2] might not have criticised, but perfection can not be expected in this country, and a lunch depends on the happy combination of host, guests, cooking, wine, brandy and cigars; and in this synthesis you had no superior.

But really your reasons for rejecting my highly flattering suggestion are quite inadequate. Even the laziest man in London – which is yourself – hardly needs two years of intensive application to write a book about French Art, without any literary diversion whatever. Even if you were as ignorant as you shamelessly pretend to be. You hint, of course, that your prices are high, as it was necessary for a whole syndicate of publishers to purchase you for this task. Nevertheless, I am not deterred: and I beg you again to release some impulse of honourable indignation for the benefit of King and Country, and indite some brilliant piece of criticism or invective over a week-end. And this is not the last that you will hear about this from me, either.

Your son is a sturdy sprout and I have read his verse with warm approval. He seems to be almost the only one at Cambridge who has

1–Bell, who wrote on 21 July from Charleston, Sussex (where he spent a month each summer), said he was really 'expatriated'. In Jan. 1932 there was to be 'a grand show of French painting at Burlington House. A syndicate of publishers have bribed me to write a little ad hoc treatise, which I am doing with extraordinary pleasure – for I know nothing about French painting before 1800, and learning is what I really enjoy. All the same, learning is long and it will take me all the time I am allowed – to the end of next July – to get the essay written and tidied up.'

2–Léon Daudet (1868–1942): right-wing journalist and novelist; critic of the Third Republic; co-founder, with Charles Maurras, of the royalist *L'Action Française*.

escaped the Chicago Semite¹ taint and who is uncontaminated by either Joyce, Lewis, Pound, Léger or myself.²

Ever yours,

T. S. E.

TO *G. H. Lane Fox Pitt-Rivers*³   CC

25 July 1930   [Faber & Faber Ltd]

Dear Mr Pitt-Rivers,

I daresay you will not remember meeting me, so I will remind you that I am a friend of Force-Stead and that I fully appreciated some very fine Napoleon which you generously dispensed one evening, about two years ago, at Worcester College.

My firm have had it in mind for some time to suggest to you to do something for us, or alternatively to suggest ourselves for anything that you had in mind to publish. Both Faber and myself are, for instance, very keen to induce you to write a pamphlet in our Criterion Miscellany series, of which I am sending you a few specimens. Malinowski, for example, has definitely promised us a pamphlet on 'Taboo in Modern Life'.⁴ Our pamphlets are primarily intended to be genuine pamphleteering, that is

---

1 – *Cf.* TSE, 'Burbank with a Baedeker: Bleistein with a Cigar' (1920), l. 16: 'A saggy bending of the knees / And elbows, with the palms turned out, Chicago Semite Viennese' (*CPP*, 40).
2 – Bell wrote: 'I am glad to notice that my child, who seems to spend a good part of his time inveighing against the Tomists, always speaks of the master with becoming respect.' Julian Bell (1908–37), poet, was to be killed in the Spanish Civil War.
3 – George Henry Lane Fox Pitt-Rivers (1890–1966): landowner, anthropologist and author. He was Private Secretary (1920–1) and ADC (1920–4) to the Governor-General of Australia; Secretary-General and Hon. Treasurer, International Union for the Scientific Investigation of Population Problems, 1928–37; Member of the Council of the Eugenics Society (of which he was a Life Member and Fellow). Works include *The Clash of Culture and the Contact of Races* (1927) and *Problems of Population* (ed., 1932). As years went on, he became involved with quasi-fascist and racialist groups, and he was interned as a political prisoner by order of the Home Secretary, 1940–2. Writing on *The Clash of Culture*, Geoffrey Tandy noted his 'less palatable observations': 'The gravamen of the charge against him is "clerkly treason". The time is still not yet and the anthropologist should stick to his anthropology' (*C*. 7 [June 1928], 440).
4 – See GCF to Bronislaw Malinowski, 31 Mar. 1931: 'We (i.e. self and Eliot and de la Mare) have read [the lecture] Aping the Ape. I liked it more than they did. They both felt that from the point of view of the lazy reader it didn't quite "ring the bell" quite hard enough. They may be right over that; but I agree with them that there's no possible form of publication outside the "Miscellany": and inside it there really isn't any possibility of exceeding the normal ten per cent royalty. So I suppose I must let you have it back.
'But how we should like to have a pukka book from you!'

to say, the definite expression of a point of view by someone who has knowledge and convictions, rather than merely informative booklets of the Home University type. But I think that you will see this quite clearly from the specimens I am sending. Would you, for instance, be inclined to write about 'Contemporary Religion' and possibly making use of your first-hand knowledge of savage races? Any suggestion I make is quite tentative and really intended to induce you to think about the question and perhaps make a counter-suggestion.

Yours sincerely,
[T. S. Eliot]

TO *Will Spens*[1]   CC

25 July 1930   [Faber & Faber Ltd]

Dear Spens,

It is a long time since I have had any communication with you and you may be surprised by the subject of this letter. To put it briefly, my directors have been discussing lately the fact that there is no available modern edition of the other works of Sir Isaac Newton than the Principia, and not even any selections from the other works. We are interested in exploring the possibilities of a[n] edition, either complete or selected, but in point of fact, none of us have enough knowledge about Newton's Works to be able to do more than ask someone who might know. We naturally turn to Cambridge for light, and as you are both a physicist and a theologian, and something of a Latin scholar as well, I naturally suggested that I should write to you about it. I am writing primarily to ask whether such a work is feasible and whether it is worth doing; secondly, if you are interested by the suggestion, we thought of you as Editor, if it were possible from your point of view. I should be very grateful for any observations you are willing to make.

Another point is that there seems to be no biography of Newton – do you think that such a biography is desirable and if so, is there anyone in England who could write it?

---

1 – Will Spens (1882–1962), educator and scientist, was Master of Corpus Christi College, Cambridge, 1927–52. Early in his career he gave a course of lectures on *Belief and Practice* (1915); he wrote on the Eucharist in *Essays Catholic and Critical by Members of the Anglican Communion*, ed. E. Gordon Selwyn (1926), and on birth control in *Theology* (1931). He was a member of the commission on Christian doctrine appointed by the Archbishops of Canterbury and York, 1922–38. He was knighted in 1939.

I have seen Dr Harris several times lately, and he told me that you had been in London; I hope that on some future occasion you will lunch with me.

Yours sincerely,
[T. S. Eliot]

TO *John Maynard Keynes*[1]   CC

26 July 1930   [Faber & Faber Ltd]

My dear Keynes,

I have been asked by my board to approach you with the suggestion that some printed word by you on the subject of Unemployment would be extremely timely and important; and if we can take any merit for such an obvious suggestion, we should very much like an opportunity of publishing it. I suggest 'it' because we had in mind, first a book like *The Economic Consequences of the Peace* or, if you were too busy for that, but had time for five or ten thousand words, we should very much like to have you in the *Criterion Miscellany*, of which I send you a few specimens. I know that such an appeal to you is almost hopeless as you are one of the busiest men in England, but it is so valuable in itself that I hope you will pardon my importunity.

I imagine that you are now at Firle,[2] but it seems safest to send this to Gordon Square.

Yours ever,
[T. S. Eliot][3]

1 – John Maynard Keynes (1883–1946): economist and theorist of money (expert on macro-economics); pamphleteer; patron of the arts (begetter and financier of the Arts Theatre, Cambridge), government adviser and negotiator; editor of *The Economic Journal*, 1912–45; columnist for *N&A* (of which he was chairman from 1923); intimate of the Bloomsbury circle; Trustee of the National Gallery; author of *A Treatise on Probability* (1921), *A Treatise on Money* (2 vols, 1930) and *The General Theory of Employment, Interest and Money* (1936). He married in 1925 the ballet dancer Lydia Lopokova (1892–1981). TSE declared in an obituary notice that *The Economic Consequences of the Peace* (1919) was 'the only one of his books which I have ever read: I was at that time occupied, in a humble capacity, with the application of some of the minor financial clauses of that treaty' ('John Maynard Keynes', *The New English Weekly*, 16 May 1946, 47).
2 – Keynes's country retreat was Tilton House, Firle, Sussex.
3 – Keynes replied (29 July), 'I am sorry to say that I cannot manage it. I am at present in the last stages of a book which has occupied seven years, and after that is finished my programme is full up for some little time to come.'

TO *Bonamy Dobrée*   TS Brotherton

28 July 1930   68 Clarence Gate Gardens

Dear Jujubhy,[1]

Yours of the 24th received. Four days by post chaise from Norflok to London; well well I wonder whether Cowper receipted his mother's Picture out of Norfolk (got it right that time) in the same duration.[2]

Powys excellent, none too strong;[3] Americana can be prun'd a bit, or the foam removed, by editor, or what is editor for?[4]

I have only heard from 'Literary Sub Editor' of *Spectator* saying, there will be a grand rally on Nov. 22nd to this effect, How can the World be Made more Tolerable? and wd. I contribute on the Future of Poetry? I have Replied: The Future of Poetry cannot be expected to make the world more Tolerable in the Future than the Past of Poetry has done in the Past; but I do not Wish my Name to Appear.[5]

Damn you for worrying me about *Anabasis*.[6] Léger ought to know enough English to distinguish between dung and saddle; but there you

---

1 – BD explained in his letter that the Managing Editor of *The Spectator* had recently addressed him as 'Jouamy Jobree' when asking for his opinion of a weekly column signed 'Orion'.

2 – William Cowper, 'On Receipt of My Mother's Picture Out of Norfolk' (1798).

3 – BD, review of John Cowper Powys, *The Meaning of Culture*, C. 10 (Oct. 1930), 178–9.

4 – 'I didn't know how to compete with Americana, so I just played the fool: I hope it'll do. I have also spat with fervour upon Powys the Cultured; may he find his hell passing eternity in the company of decayed ladies of a Cathedral Close.' BD, 'American Periodicals', *C.* 10 (Oct. 1930), 198–202.

5 – See below (31 July) for TSE's letter to Celia Simpson, Literary Sub-Editor of *The Spectator*.

6 – 'I have read *Anabase* . . . twice, and in bits, which is enough to make me believe it a very fine poem. I have also read *Anabasis*, which is very like it indeed. Some parts of the translation fill me with envy as a potential translator, and are brilliant.' But, he went on, 'Nothing will persuade me that *Anabasis* does not contain two undeniable *mistakes*. "They burnt the saddle of the malingerer" (I quote from memory) should be "They burnt the dung of the weakling". "They dressed the wounds of the animals" should be "They groomed the animals." If you don't like dung for *selle*, you could use the similar word stool. *Panser* is the ordinary word for to groom. I do not think that sex for *sexe* (meaning cock, prick or tool) is English, though I see from one of the American magazines that it is American. I do not think that in English I can wash my sex any more than I can wash my nationality. What I wash is my parts. Those are the only objections of fact I can make: there are others of opinion I would wish to put forward some time if it would amuse you to discuss them. This one may interest you to ponder:

'Part VII. Chamelles douces sous la tonte . . . I do not think means that the camels didn't mind being clipped: I should say rather: As camels smoothed by the shears, stitched with mauve scars . . . douces being opposed to the shagginess of unclipped camels: clipped camels do look as though they were consues de mauves cicatrices. I think that the whole paragraph may be right. I am quite aware that *panser* means *groom*, but it also means *dress*. As for *sex*, that was deliberate on my part, an innovation if you like. I admit that you know more about camels than I do; but then why did he put she-camels instead of he- or he-and-she camels. You are quite right about the camels and the hills, but I found that out in discussion with Léger.

One other point: *mille feux de villes avivés par l'aboiement des chiens* – the *Manchester Guardian* says I have made the towns, not the fires, 'awakened'.[1] Error. However, I owe you a glass of sherry about *selle*. Léger certainly overlooked that? But why should the stool of the weakling (malingerer) [be burnt] rather than his saddle? Answer me that. If he belonged to a race of horsemen it wd. be more significant to burn his saddle than his stool. Can you cite any authorities for burning the stool of the malingerer? Anyway, it's not so bad as the German translator who turned *Fétus de paille* into 'foetuses made of straw'.

August 16th then.[2]

Yrs etc.,
T. S. E.

---

is simply comparing a line of hills to a trail of camels, which finally barrack in the distant mist. I don't feel that your paragraph quite gives this idea. But you will take no notice of these ignorant vapourings.'

1 – B. S., 'Calculated Refinements', *The Manchester Guardian*, 10 July 1930, 7: 'The effect of *Anabasis* on the unsuspecting reader is much like that of the obscurer books of the Old Testament. This is vivid, pointed language, but what is pointed at he does not know. There are conspicuous or concealed refrains, but their connection with what surrounds them is ambiguous ... M. Perse has certainly produced a piece of masterly artifice, and purists and intellectuals will have fine times cracking their brains over it. Mr Eliot's admirable translation is printed with the original poem, page by page, and the merest tyro will be led to appreciate the nerve and precision of the French by recognising his occasional lapses – e.g.

cent feux de villes avivés par l'aboiement des chiens
for which he gives
a hundred fires in towns wakened by the barking of dogs,
and everyone would suppose it was the towns that were wakened, whereas the whole forms part of one subjective impression: "town fires vivified by the barking of dogs." That is the worst of putting so much store on calculated refinements; the object of the calculation is, after all, not very significant, and the small point, which all depends on your hitting, is sometimes missed.'

2 – They were to meet for lunch.

TO *A. L. Rowse*   TS Exeter

29 July 1930   *The Criterion*

My dear Rowse,

I am very glad to hear from you after this long time, and your letter gave me much pleasure. I don't want you to think, however, that I am indifferent to justification by good works. It is all a question of a nice statement in the abstract; I think that when it comes to reviewing the life of a human individual we should probably be pretty closely in agreement in valuation. I should only try to maintain distinction between works which spring from natural goodness, such that the being of its nature could not do otherwise, and those works which are good, or which at least are better because they are illuminated and directed by faith.[1]

Don't bother about the September number now. I think that I have enough material to make it up. I should always prefer with you to know some time in advance what you are going to do and plan for it, than to try to squeeze anything in at the last moment. I am not quite clear on one point; you say you have not yet written 'Historical Materialism and G. N. Clark', but you say you have written an article on Clark's conception of history. I think it would be over-doing Clark to have an article on him, and a review of him in the *Criterion*. So I should like to know which you prefer.

I shall be glad at any time to have an essay by you on 'Value', only provided that you do not employ the word 'humanism' too many times![2] There is always a risk of the *Criterion* appearing to outside observers to consist of a small number of philosophers chasing each other round and round in a circle. As to the book you mention that you would like to review, you forgot to mention the name of the publisher.[3]

Yours ever affectionately,

T. S. E.

1 – Rowse wrote (25 July): 'I am deeply in your debt by your giving me your last poems: I have read them over and over . . . Only I want to say on the subject of creation as the "justification" of faith, that we are both right: you in thinking that faith doesn't need justifying, it just is, but there are others who have thought that faith needed the justification of good works. I am surprised by the depth of Protestantism in you. As for me, it is perhaps because faith is impossible, that the idea of justification of oneself in creation is so essential. I have always felt it . . . it just *is*.'

2 – Rowse (25 July): 'I might send a section of a chapter I have been writing on "Society and Values" – it [is] all about culture & its relation to a leisure-class. It isn't my original contribution to the discussion on *Value* . . .'

3 – Max Weber's *Protestant Ethics and the Spirit of Capitalism*, introd. by R. H. Tawney.

TO *Kenneth Ingram*   CC

29 July 1930   [*The Criterion*]

Dear Ingram,

I have your letter of the 24th, suggesting that you might like to review
H. G. Wells' latest.[1] If we review it at all, I should be as glad to have
you review it as anybody. But as a matter of fact, I doubt whether it
is worthwhile for the *Criterion* to try to keep up with Wells. We have
reviewed him from time to time, and jeered at him and others; our attitude
towards Wells is pretty well defined; and I think that we might well leave
him alone for a few years. The book has not, as it happens, come in for
review, so I don't know whether it marks a new stage in the perpetual
evolution of Wells or not. But I think I would rather leave it alone.

I was glad to get your review of *The Drift of Civilisation*, which has
gone to press.[2] Are you particularly interested in Pascal or in Martin
Luther? I have two new books in, both translations from the French – the
latter translated very badly.

Yours sincerely,
[T. S. Eliot]

TO *The Literary Sub-Editor,* The Spectator   CC

31 July 1930   [Faber & Faber Ltd]

Dear Madam,

Thank you for your letter of the 21st instant, inviting me to contribute
to a special number of the *Spectator*.[3] I am sorry to say that I shall not
have time to accept your kind invitation within the time limits you
propose. And even if I did have time, I doubt if I could think of anything
to say. I can't see any hope that the tendencies of modern poetry are likely
to make the world a more tolerable place to live in, than the tendencies of
ancient poetry have made it in the past.

Yours faithfully,
[T. S. Eliot]

1 – *The Autocracy of Mr Parham* (1930).
2 – The review in question did not ultimately appear.
3 – Celia Simpson asked TSE to contribute to a special number of *The Spectator*, scheduled
for 22 Nov., 'to which we hope that many distinguished writers will contribute articles on
how the world can be made a more tolerable place to live in'; with that in view, she asked
TSE to write 'on tendencies in modern poetry, or on any other aspect of modern poetry
which interests you'.

TO *Hoffman Nickerson*   CC

8 August 1930   [Faber & Faber Ltd]

Dear Hoffman,

I have delayed writing to you, but when you read this letter, you will see that its excogitation took some time.

When you broached the suggestion of an analysis of one of Oman's historical blunders, I greeted the idea with enthusiasm and I am equally enthusiastic about your essay. I found it very much more damaging than anything I expected, knowing little myself of Oman's work. It was only on reading it that it occurred to me that I ought in fairness to shew it to my chairman, for the reason that he is a Fellow of All Souls' and knows Oman pretty well. The chairman also liked your essay, but asked me as a favour not to publish it. The reason is not quite what you might expect, but rather the reverse. It is, he has allowed me to tell you in confidence, that he is not on the very best of terms with Oman, that he is quite sure that if this essay were published in the *Criterion*, Oman is the sort of man who would be convinced that the chairman had had the article published out of personal spite, and as owing to his official position he is obliged to maintain civil relationships with Oman, the affair would be very embarrassing to him in this way.

Now I feel that I have a strong personal responsibility to you about this essay. What adds to the difficulty of publication in the *Criterion* and would strengthen Oman's suspicions is the fact that it is a type of article which is a new departure for the *Criterion* to publish; I have shewn it to a friend of mine who edits the *Dublin Review* – a really excellent Roman Catholic quarterly – but he finds it outside the scope of that paper. So I must put the matter up to you and ask you to suggest any periodical here to which you would like me to send it; and in particular, any of the more technical historical reviews. I should like to see the essay published, but if not, I feel definitely that we must at least make partial amends by paying for it.[1]

> With very many apologies,
> Yours ever,
> [T. S. Eliot]

1 – Nickerson (1 Sept.) accepted TSE's offer to pay for the article. 'Oman's Muret' was ultimately published in *Speculum* 6: 4 (Oct. 1931), 550–72.

TO *Allen Tate*[1]   TS Princeton

8 August 1930   Faber & Faber Ltd

Dear Tate,

Thank you very much for your letter of the 17th July. The *Hound and Horn* is usually sent to me, but the number you mention has not arrived. I appreciate fully your chivalry in defending me against Robert Shafer's insinuations, particularly as I have been so bored with the whole matter that I should probably not have bothered to do so myself.[2] I know very well the tactics you describe; they are similar to those used by Seward Collins in an editorial in the *Bookman*.[3] It seemed to me that Collins was virtually accusing me of dishonest behaviour towards Babbitt. I wrote a long and angry letter to which Collins replied very civilly promising to print; but so far he does not seem to have done so.

I am afraid that, rather like yourself, I am too much of an individualist and too little of a gang-fighter, to win the approval of any of these contending groups; and I am so sickened by the kind of publicity which these philosophical discussions have obtained in America, and by the reciprocal violence of vituperation, that I never want to hear the word *humanism* again.

By the way, I had a very interesting story from Mrs Tate, which I was sure, however, would be completely unintelligible to an English audience. I hope I may see some more of her writing.

1–Allen Tate (1899–1979), American poet, critic and editor: see Biographical Register.
2–'I have just read an essay by Robert Shafer in the current *Hound and Horn* which mostly concerns you. He makes a statement that I know from actual facts to be untrue – besides other statements that I am morally certain are false. He says that you "used extensively" my Fallacy of Humanism [*C*. 8 (July 1929), 661–81] in the writing of your "Second Thoughts" ['Second Thoughts on Humanism', *New Adelphi* 2: 4 (June/Aug. 1929, 304–10; repr. as 'Second Thoughts about Humanism', *Hound and Horn* 2: 4 (July/Sept. 1929), 339–50]. I have some letters that you wrote me at that time, and it is plain from several of these that your essay was finished when mine reached you, and that your allusion to my essay was a piece of generosity that you were not in the least obligated [to] show. I have therefore written a letter to the Editors of the *Hound and Horn*, stating the facts as I have stated them to you. Under ordinary circumstances, the incident would be trivial. Shafer, however, has recently laid about in all directions with wholesale charges of ignorance and dishonesty – in fact, all of us who have been presumed to disagree with Babbitt and More have been subjected to the worst kind of vilification. His tactics in the essay on you are typical – he disclaims any belief that his opponent is deliberately dishonest, which is contemptible and much worse.'
3–Anon (Seward Collins), 'Chronicle and Comment', *The Bookman* 71: 1 (Mar. 1930), 65–80.

And when shall I see another essay of yours?
With many thanks,

Yours ever,
T. S. Eliot

TO *Marquis W. Childs* Missouri Historical Society

8 August 1930 Faber & Faber Ltd

Dear Sir,

I have your letter of August [*sic*] 22nd 1930; and am very happy to comply as well as I can with your request. But it is very puzzling to try to condense a biography, an 'attitude', and an estimate of how St Louis affected me, into a paragraph.[1]

As I spent the first 16 years of my life in St Louis, with the exception of summer holidays in Maine and Massachusetts, and a visit to Louisiana which I do not remember, it is self-evident that St Louis affected me more deeply than any other environment has done. These 16 years were spent in a house at 2635 Locust Street, since demolished. This house stood on part of a large piece of land which had belonged to my grandfather, on which there had been negro quarters also in his time; in my childhood my grandmother still lived at a house [at] 2660 Washington Avenue, round the corner. The earliest personal influence I remember, besides that of my parents, was an Irish nursemaid named Annie Dunne, to whom I was greatly attached; she used to take me to my first school, a Mrs Lockwood's, which was a little way out beyond Vandeventer Place. The River also made a deep impression on me; and it *was* a great treat to be taken down to the Eades Bridge in flood time.

Then I was sent naturally to the now defunct Smith Academy, which was then somewhere at the lower end of Washington Avenue; I graduated from there with some distinction, having produced the Class Poem, which

---

1–Childs (*St Louis Post-Dispatch*) wrote: 'I contemplate an article on the St Louis background of various authors, most of whom are now distinguished. I wonder if you would give me, briefly, something about your early years here. Factually, a mere chronology would suffice . . .'

Childs used TSE's letter as the basis of an article 'From a Distinguished Former St Louisan' (*St Louis Post-Dispatch*, 15 Oct. 1930), prefacing it with three brief paragraphs opening: 'Of the recent authors who have left St Louis to achieve subsequent reputations of varying degrees of significance, none is more interesting, in many respects, than T. S. Eliot. While his audience has always been comparatively small, his influence has been very great. He has been a poets' poet and a critics' critic. Several controversies have raged about his work.'

even now seems to me not bad. I remember with particular regard Mme Jouvet-Kaufmann, the French mistress, who gave me my first taste for that language, Mr Roger Hatch, the English master, who encouraged my first attempts at verse, and Dr Jackson, the Latin master – the third and last subject in which I attained any proficiency.[1] I left St Louis in 1905, to go to Milton Academy in Massachusetts;[2] and apart from a few Christmas holidays, I have never seen St Louis again.

I do not quite know what else to say. But I find that as one gets on in middle life the strength of early associations, and the intensity of early impressions, becomes more evident; and many little things, long forgotten, recur. The occasions on which my nurse took me with her to the little Catholic Church which then stood on the corner of Locust Street and Jefferson Avenue, when she went to make her devotions: spring violets, and the rather mangy buffalo which I photographed in Forest Park; the steamboats blowing in New Year's day; and so on. And I feel that there is something in having passed one's childhood beside the big river, which is incommunicable to those who have not. Of course my people were Northerners and New Englanders, and of course I have spent many years out of America altogether; but Missouri and the Mississippi have made a deeper impression on me than any other part of the world. Besides, my father gave a good part of his life, and my grandfather the greater part, to the service of St Louis and the State; and my mother took a leading part in Juvenile Court reform there; and they all lie in Bellefontaine now.[3]

Yours very truly,
T. S. Eliot

1 – TSE was to write in a letter on 31 Oct. 1957, in answer to a question from a high school teacher in California: 'I regard . . . my education at Smith Academy in St Louis where the greater number of my school days were spent, as of the utmost importance. It was important because I was well-taught in what I consider the essential subjects: that is to say Latin and Greek, Elementary Algebra and Geometry, French and German, English and American History, and English which then consisted of a rigorous study of the rules of grammar and rhetoric.'
2 – Theresa Eliot was to write to EVE on 30 Apr. 1977: 'No one ever speaks of Tom's going to Milton Academy. He was 16 and ready for Harvard, but Henry insisted on Tom's going to Milton, as much to have some friends in Harvard, as he had had to go there from the Middle West with no Eastern boys' (EVE).
3 – Bellefontaine Cemetery, St Louis, Missouri.

TO *E. McKnight Kauffer*   TS Morgan

8 August 1930   Faber & Faber Ltd

My dear Kauffer,

Thank you very much for your letter of the 29th – I have been very behindhand lately. Since I wrote to you I have seen your illustrations, which I like very much, except for the one point about which I spoke to de la Mare. It seems to me a pity that de la Mare did not shew me the drawing when he received it, as it might have saved you considerable trouble. My criticism was not of the drawing at all, but merely meant that I don't want what I write now to have *The Waste Land* stamped upon it. But I think you will appreciate my point without my saying anything more.[1]

We are delighted to hear that you have become neighbours of ours, and I hope that you like your flat.[2] We shall probably be there through the whole of August and unless you are going away very soon we hope to see something of you in a week or so. Meanwhile, with best wishes to Marion[3] and yourself.

Yours ever,
T. S. Eliot

TO *I. A. Richards*   TS Magdalene

9 August 1930   *The Criterion*

Dear Richards,

I was very glad to get your letter of July 13th, but vexed that you have not had *Ash Wednesday* and *Anabasis*.[4] The first should have reached you

---

1 – Kauffer wrote (29 July) of his illustration for *Marina*: 'In the last – final [–] one I introduced the words give, sympathise, control as you have them in the "Waste Land" and indeed is there not in these three words the whole of equilibrium? . . . My admiration for what you do is one of the important things in my life.' Grace Schulman comments: 'He later rejected that design, not wanting to allude to the earlier poem' ('Notes on the Theme of "Marina" by Eliot', *Essays from the 'Southern Review'*, 206). Gallup notes: 'A few proof copies, in slightly variant blue paper wrappers, were made up for the publishers before publication. Six of these were distributed by E. McKnight Kauffer, at least one of them signed and inscribed to the effect that the words "Datta Dayadhvam Damyata" incorporated in the illustration . . . were deleted at T. S. Eliot's request' (Gallup, 42–3).
2 – The Kauffers had moved into 49 Chiltern Court, Clarence Gate, London NW1.
3 – Marion Dorn.
4 – IAR had written on 13 July, 'I've been reading *Ash Wednesday* with deep satisfaction and content. I read in a borrowed copy which alas! someone has again borrowed from me – and

at the same time as *Adamastor* (which latter was sent because the firm has decided to send you any books that might interest you, as and when (by the way, what does 'as and when' mean, if anything more than 'as') they appear). I particularly am curious to have your opinion of *Anabasis* of the original still more than of the translation.

I shall be very much interested in any results of your study of Chinese abstractions.[1] I dare say it is likely to be more profitable than my attempt, so many years ago, at studying Indian metaphysics in Sanskrit. The conclusion I came to then (after it is true only a couple of years' struggle with the language) was that it seemed impossible to be on both sides of the looking-glass at once.[2] That is, it made me think how much more dependent one was than one had suspected, upon a *particular* tradition of thought from Thales[3] down, so that I came to wonder how much *understanding* anything (a term, a system, etc.) meant merely *being used* to it. (Similarly I have observed with anything new in art, that when people say either that they cannot understand it or that they have come to understand it, that seems to mean largely either that they are not habituated to it or that they are). And it seemed to me that all I was trying to do, and all that any of the pundits had succeeded in doing, was to attempt to translate one terminology with a long tradition into another; and that however cleverly one did it, one would never produce anything better than an ingenious difformation (just as Deussen, who I suppose to be the very best interpreter of the Upanishads, has merely transformed Indian thought into Schopenhauerian – and the orientalism

---

your promised copy (with *Anabasis*) has not arrived' (*Letters of I. A. Richards*, 55–7).

1–IAR reported that he and his wife were sailing to Japan for six weeks, and would then be going back to China 'for 4 months to do something if possible with Chinese meanings. They don't seem to have developed many of our most important schemas e.g. Thought Will & Feeling : Truth : Subjective Objective : Substance – Attribute. These don't come into Classical Chinese "thinking" (Mentality? what is one to call it?) and are very doubtfully present in later literature . . . The problem is to invent some framework of reference by which to describe these differences . . .'

'All this has taken me back to Belief problems & I've been fairly busy intermittently . . . [I] propose to do an article in semi controversy with you for the *Bookman* on Belief – if you don't raise an objection . . .'

2–IAR was to open his essay 'Mencius through the Looking-Glass' (*So Much Nearer*, 1968): 'The odd title of this essay comes from T. S. Eliot. When I was working in Peking on *Mencius on the Mind* about 1930 he wrote to me . . . that reading in a remote text is like trying to be on both sides of the mirror at once. A vivid and bewildering image' (*Letters of I. A. Richards*, 59).

3–Thales of Miletus (*c.* 620 BC – *c.* 546 BC), pre-Socratic Greek philosopher: founder of the school of natural philosophy, eschewing mythological explanations of the universe.

of Schopenhauer is as superficial as superficial can be.[1]) In other words, I thought that the only way I could ever come to understand Indian thought would be to erase not only my own education in European philosophy, but the traditions and mental habits of Europe for two thousand years – and if one did that, one would be no better off for 'translating', and even if such a feat could be accomplished, it didn't seem worth the trouble. However, some such study (as far as one can) is I believe profitable, as getting outside of one's own skin, or jumping down one's throat.

By the way, as a minor problem, possibly susceptible of some experiment, I should like to discuss with you that question of *understanding* of poetry (in popular psychology) as *habituation*.[2]

Another useful piece of scavenging would be to elucidate the whole pseudo-controversy of Humanism, and Romanticism and Classicism. You ought to be ready for that after a few months at Harvard.

I like your comments on Campbell. You have put it much better than one would put it by saying that he is 'romantic'.[3]

I shall look forward to meeting your Mr Wu.[4]

With kindest regards from both of us to you and Mrs Richards,

> Yours ever,
> T. S. Eliot

I hope you can let me see some of your notes soon.

> T. S. E.

1 – See *Die Philosophie der Upanishads* (1898; English translation, 1906), by Paul Deussen (1845–1919), who founded in 1911 the Schopenhauer Society (Schopenhauer-Gesellschaft).
2 – See IAR's response to these comments (19 Oct. 1930), in *Letters of I. A. Richards*, 57–9.
3 – IAR had been reading Roy Campbell's *Adamastor*, 'very carefully (for me) . . . and have come to the conclusion that Campbell has plenty of quality & energy but only one theme – his personality versus the world – which after all was well dealt with by Shelley and Byron . . .'
4 – IAR had given a Chinese scholar an introduction to TSE. 'He is young, naïve, simple as a Huron, very scholarly in the old style, the leader of the movement *against* a vernacular literary Chinese & in favour of the old classic language. He also lectures on Romantic Poetry! at Tsing Hua University. (Heaven knows what he says about it!) . . . And his name is Mr *Wu*. (Chinese Wu Mi) I'm sure he could do you something interesting on the literary problem (or tangle) of modern China – where they have quite as difficult a job on as the West had in passing from Latin to vernaculars as literary languages.'

TO *E. Gordon Selwyn*   CC

9 August 1930   [Faber & Faber Ltd]

Dear Selwyn,

I wonder if you would be so kind as to tell me, in confidence, what you think of the work of a Revd Thomas J. Hardy of Torquay, who mentions that he has contributed to *Theology*? I know nothing about him; but he has sent us the script of a book on 'The Christianity of Christ' which I cannot make up my mind about.[1]

As I think I suggested to you, I should like my firm to go in for good popular theological books which for any of several possible and obvious reasons would appear better under the imprint of a general publisher than under that of the S.P.C.K. or any of the minor theological presses. What I doubt is, whether this is a powerful enough book to begin building up a theological side of the business with.[2]

Yours ever sincerely,

[T. S. Eliot]

1 – TSE wrote in his reader's report, dated 8 Aug. 1930: 'The first chapters of this book I found to be meritorious, but I suspect that the whole would not be striking enough to be distinguishable from thousands of other such books. However, it seems to gather point and persuasiveness as it goes on, and at the end I had a favourable impression. In other words, I think that the author has a point to make, but it takes him a good many pages even to lead one to hope that there will be a point.

'It is a thoughtful sincere book, I think; not showy or exciting. I am rather disposed in its favour; it has the advantage of not being controversial in the sense of supporting one ecclesiastical party rather than another. I do not think that it would be worthwhile, however, unless we considered building up a popular theological side; I should think that as we are at present it might, by itself, be not too easy to market.

'I notice (1) that the author published a book in 1907 (2) that he says he has contributed to "Theology". If he seems worth further enquiry, I can ask Canon Selwyn, the editor of that review, what he knows about him.'

2 – Selwyn replied (12 Aug.), 'Hardy is quite good. He is not an exact scholar, but is always glad to be corrected on such points: otherwise I think he has something to say & says it well. He was for some months a Roman Catholic; but came back to us again . . . He had written one or two quite good devotional books . . . The shells he shoots are better than the guns he carries, I fancy.'

TO *William Force Stead*   TS Beinecke

9 August 1930[1]   *The Criterion*

My dear Stead,

I was able to give a fairly satisfactory reading to your book[2] about a week ago; and now (I believe, but even in the middle of a letter an apparently more urgent letter may require to be written) am able to write you a line or two about them. Two general impressions first: though I don't much like the method of naming a book after one poem 'and other poems' (having done it myself) I think your arrangement, whether deliberate, chronological or fortuitous, is very good; for the transitions between the Umbrian and the Oxfordshire background enhance the effect. This leads to the second point: my admiration, as a fellowcountryman, at the degree to which you have absorbed these two landscapes. I do not think I am wholly deficient in the 'feeling for nature'; it is either that I have lived for many years almost exclusively in towns, or else that I only have it in association with strong human emotions – I don't think the latter – however that may be, I know I have to go back to Missouri and New England for natural imagery.

I think 'Instant of Creation' is extraordinarily good in technique; a little too like Bridges I think for me to appreciate fully; for Bridges' *Testament* is really and truly a blind spot in my eye. When I tell you which poems I like best, it is not necessarily saying that I think they are the best; I am not a 'pure' enough poet not sometimes to like something I know is not quite so good better than the other. But it may on the other hand be true that the title poem, less interesting technically than 'Instant of Creation', is as good as I think it is; or it may be simply that it expresses feelings that I know but have never seen so well expressed. This sense of dispossession by the dead I have known twice, at Marlow and at Perigueux.[3] And I

---

1 – Seymour-Jones, *Painted Shadow*, 586, n. 37, misdates this letter as 20 June 1930.
2 – *The House on the Wold and other Poems* (1930).
3 – The speaker of 'The House on the Wold' meditates in a fashion reminiscent of Robert Frost upon the meaning of the presences, revenants, in a very old cottage in the Gloucestershire Wolds: the dead are the true abiding proprietors of the house.

> Beside the tarn, he paused and saw the wood
> Rolling up and shrouding a thousand lives,
> Quick and instinctive, while he knew himself
> One solitary rational being, watched
> By soul-without-mind in eagerly living things.
> At times he felt himself submerged, going down
> Into an ocean of unthinking life,

particularly like 'At Bethel'. It stands for me for a theory I have nourished for a long time, that between the usual subjects of poetry and 'devotional' verse there is a very important field still very unexplored by modern poets – the experience of man in search of God, and trying to explain to himself his intenser human feelings in terms of the divine goal. I have tried to do something of that in *Ash Wednesday*.

———

> Exploring abysmal fears; and then, again,
> Coming gratefully back to conscious mind.
> And yet, returned, he knew that other life
> Watched him with mutual fear
> . . .
> His voyaging thought explored the wide-extending
> Far dim cathedral of forest creatures,
> Wondering if the tidal power that moved
> And swayed his home's confident foundation,
> Might be obscure wisdom of the mind's control,
> Or the woodland's own unhallowed emanation.

Cf. the final chorus of Act I of *FR*:

> In an old house there is always listening, and more is heard than is spoken.
> And what is spoken remains in the room, waiting for the future to hear it.
> And whatever happens began in the past, and presses hard on the future.
> The agony in the curtained bedroom, whether of birth or of dying,
> Gathers in to itself all the voices of the past, and projects them into the future.

Stead responded to this letter on 14 Aug.: 'I am surprised and delighted to find that you like the title poem. It is a plain honest statement of what seemed significant during my very uncomfortable 18 mo[nth]s at Finstock House, truthful both as to my internal experiences – (my feeling about the house, furniture, Wychwood and the natives) also external events which troubled nearly every one in the house . . .'

John Worthen, in *T. S. Eliot: A Short Biography* (2009), 92–3, remarks that the two occasions on which TSE experienced 'dispossession by the dead' came about 'when a vivid experience of the past (and of the hordes of unknown dead) became overwhelming: it led to a feeling of utter isolation. He had undergone such an experience at Périgeux in France in August 1919 – he suddenly announced to Pound a few days later, at Excideuil, "I am afraid of the life after death" [cited in canto xxix (1930)] – and another such experience had come earlier, at Marlow. Together with BR, the Eliots had rented 31 West Street, Marlow from December 1917, and though attempts have been made to link the experience of dispossession with Eliot's discovery (probably early in 1918 [Schuchard, *Eliot's Dark Angel*, 123–4]) of Vivien's adultery with BR, there is nothing to support that explanation and a good deal against. An experience of "dispossession by the dead" has very little to do with anger over a wife's adultery.

'Eliot subsequently wrote about the experience of dispossession on a number of occasions. In *The Family Reunion*, Harry describes "that sense of separation, / Of isolation unredeemable, irrevocable"; in "East Coker", Eliot imagined the "fear of possession" of old men. "Of belonging to another, or to others, or to God". Being "possessed" – taken over, completely, so that you are dispossessed of your old self and attachments – is terrifying but (for Eliot after 1927) would have been the only real solution to life's problems. In 1940, he would go so far as to announce that "You must go the way of dispossession". That "way" involved Christian conversion.'

Well, a letter is an unsatisfactory substitute for a conversation, a long unhurried evening talk (preferably in the country, but possible even in London). When shall we meet?

Affectionately,

T. S. E.

TO *Will Spens* CC

9 August 1930   [Faber & Faber Ltd]

Dear Spens,

Very many thanks for your helpful letter, though I learn with much regret that you cannot consider such a work yourself.[1] I do know about Andrade, and I believe one or two other directors know him; but I did not know that he was so particularly interested in Newton. If you should happen to think of anyone suitable for the theological side I should be grateful for a suggestion.

I expect to be in London throughout August and should very much like to see you.

This untidy typing is done by my own hand.

Sincerely yours,

[T. S. Eliot]

---

1 – Spens had replied (30 July): 'There is a man who is extraordinarily well qualified to do what you want on the scientific side – Professor Andrade of University College, Gower Street. He is not only a first rate modern physicist, but he is interested in, and I think is almost certainly the best English authority on, the history of physics in the 17th and 18th centuries. Further, I believe he has a particular interest in Newton, and has a collection of first editions of Newton's works . . .

'I do not suppose Andrade could do the theological stuff so far as annotations were concerned but I do not believe that is worth doing. In your place I should be inclined to publish a complete edition of the scientific work other than the Principia and to have an appended note or an introduction on the theological work . . . As regards the biography there again Andrade would be admirable with a certain amount of collaboration over Newton's theological interests.'

Edward Andrade (1887–1971) was Quain Professor of Physics, University College, London, 1928–50.

TO *Ezra Pound*   TS Beinecke

9 August 1930   *The Criterion*

Hon. Rabbit,

Re yours of the 11th ultimo from Venice, I would remind you that the reason I have never enquired for cantoes for publication in *Criterion* is that I believed that your price would be too high. We have one price only: £2 per 1000 words for prose and £1: 1:– (one guinea) per page for verse, high and low being treated alike.

I should like a contoe for December (i.e. by the middle of September) either to accompany or to precede the Zukofsky, preferably the former.

No objection to synchronisation with Hornhound,[1] but I wish they would stop printing articles on Humanism.

Respectfully and ergebenst[2]
T. S. E.

TO *Kenneth Ingram*   CC

9 August 1930   [Faber & Faber Ltd]

Dear Ingram,

I should like very much to join your Temple Bar Club,[3] and will send my five shillings as soon as possible after the first occasion on which, being in a post-office, I can remember to purchase an order therefor; laziness and bad memory struggling with thrift, I almost wish it had been ten shillings, so that I could have sent a cheque.

I suppose that a reminder of the meeting will be sent before October?

Reciprocally, have you heard anything of a club, started by Tom Burns of Sheed & Ward, to be called the Unicorn, and to have a house (with kitchen) in the Adelphi? It was to be mainly R. C. laymen, with an infusion of sympathetic others: Burns, Dawson and Thorold are the people from whom I heard about it, and I put myself down as a charter member. If it

1–*Hound & Horn.*
2–*ergebenst*: sincerely, faithfully (Ger.)
3–Ingram wrote on 1 Aug., 'I am forming a small society which will meet once a month near the Temple and discuss religious and philosophical questions: we want to include every point of view, as far as possible.' He explained further on 2 Aug. that the Club already included some Roman Catholics, Anglicans (Anglo-Catholic, Evangelical, Modernist and Central), Free Churchmen, Agnostics and others. At present we propose to limit the membership to 35.'

materialises I should like you to join (I believe it was to be five guineas a year). [*runs off the page*]

[T. S. Eliot]

TO *G. H. Lane Fox Pitt-Rivers* CC

9 August 1930   [Faber & Faber Ltd]

Dear Mr Pitt-Rivers,

I did not get your letter of the 31st [July] until Tuesday;[1] I trust that you got my telephone message to that effect, expressing my regret that I could not dine on either of those nights. I inferred, perhaps mistakenly, that you were in town only for a few days.

I was delighted that you should take an interest in my suggestion. I hope that we may meet soon to talk it over; and I think also that it would be more satisfactory if we could do so. The disadvantage of 'Sex Phobia and Marriage' is that the two pamphlets, of Christopher Dawson and Naomi Mitchison, in the series, are fairly recent;[2] I feel, and my directors feel, that it would not be the best policy to pursue the subject further at present, as we want the miscellany to cover as wide a ground as possible. The lecture to the Royal Institution I should very much like to see; the title, however, strikes me as probably more suitable for the *Criterion* itself than for the Miscellany. Actually, the subjects for the Miscellany should be much more topical – raising some question, or answering one, of the moment, or striking at some folly or abuse or iniquity of the day – than is needful for the *Criterion*. Anyway (1) may I see that paper? and (2) let us meet as soon as we can arrange it: I expect to be in town throughout August. I should be delighted to meet your friend, if he is to be in London at any time.

With many regrets at having missed seeing you,

Sincerely yours,

[T. S. Eliot]

1–'[T]he frankly polemical intentions of your pamphlet series . . . I should enjoy . . . Last year . . . I read a paper for the "World League for Sexual Reform" at the Wigmore Hall . . . My title was "Sex Phobia and Marriage" . . . Also I thought of finding a publisher for one of my lectures a year ago at the Royal Institution on "Race and Culture".' He added, 'I am meeting on August 4th my friend Georges Batault in London . . . I should like you to meet him. He writes for the "Mercure". He has done a monograph on Francois d'Assissi which should be translated. Could you perhaps dine with me & meet him on August the 4th or August the 5th . . .'

2–Christopher Dawson, *Christianity and Sex*; Naomi Mitchison, *Comments on Birth Control*.

TO *Paul Elmer More*   TS Princeton

10 August 1930   *The Criterion*

My dear More,

I have received your letter of the 9th July,[1] read, perpended, and trembled under your excommunication.

'And they that have done good shall go into life everlasting; and they that have done evil into everlasting fire.'[2]

So I am a Mohammedan? and/or a Calvinist? and the champion of Athanasius is a whole-Catholic?

Well, we might wrangle over this for ages. But having refused this, how much else of orthodox theology do you refuse? What about the Angels and Archangels and the Saints and Patriarchs? and devotions of Our Lady? and I do not forget that an eminent friend of ours has called you a *binitarian contra mundum.* No, sir, I call upon you to demonstrate your orthodoxy; or alternatively, to demonstrate that you are the *only* Catholic living. What are your views now on the Marriage at Cana, and the Loaves and Fishes?

I admit freely that I am a Bradleian; and that my thought and my belief may be more deeply influenced by Bradley than I know.[3] And that between different doctrines, I choose that which seems to me the 'less false', inasmuch as there are degrees of untruth.

I consider that one must be a whole-hogger or nothing; and doubtless you will raise the familiar cry of Why do I not go to Rome? I should not care to match my ignorance against your learning; I shall be far less educated at 80 than you were at 30; but have you considered this: The man who disbelieves in any future life whatever is also a believer in Hell. For in this life one makes, now and then, important decisions; or at least

---

1 – Not found.
2 – John 5: 28–9.
3 – F. H. Bradley (1846–1924): English Hegelian philosopher; Fellow of Merton College, Oxford, from 1870; author of *Ethical Studies* (1876), *Appearance and Reality* (1893), *Principles of Logic* (1922). TSE never met him – Bradley suffered from poor health and led a secluded life – but he completed in 1916 a doctoral dissertation later published as *Knowledge and Experience in the Philosophy of F. H. Bradley* (1964). TSE, who considered him 'the last survivor of the academic race of metaphysicians', would say to Leonardo Ariosto, 19 May 1961: 'one thing of which I am certain is that I was emotively deeply affected by F. H. Bradley's literary style, which I still admire very deeply. I think that the effect of style on the acceptance or rejection of a philosophy is a subject in itself, and I myself would put very high amongst influences on my life for this reason Plato, Spinoza in his Latin text, and Bradley. Aristotle also in flashes, but as so much of Aristotle is, I believe, simply lecture notes we have to make allowances.'

allows circumstance to decide; and some of these decisions are such as have consequences for all the rest of our mortal life. Some people find themselves consequently in circumstances such that the whole of their mortal life *must* be a torment to them. And if there is no future life then Hell is, for such people, here and now; and I can see nothing worse in a Hell which endures to eternity and a Hell which endures until mere annihilation; the mere stretch of endless time, which is the only way in which we can ordinarily apprehend 'immortal life', seem to me to make no difference.

People go to Hell, I take it, because they choose to; they cannot get out because they cannot change themselves. I am quite ready to concede that if they could change themselves they would be out of Hell. I admit the mystery as much as you do.

P.S. Why expect comfort from Bishops? Most of them (in this country at least) are chosen (I think) if well chosen, because they are able administrators and mediators; and are too occupied in smoothing over difficulties to be able to afford definite opinions of their own; and they have no time, poor things, to read anyhow.

Nothing will give me more pleasure than to continue this debate; for theology is the one most exciting and adventurous subject left for a jaded mind. But it would be *much* more satisfactory to do so over a cup of coffee and a glass of wine, than by correspondence chess.

And there are however other subjects to write about, but I shall try to put them into another letter.

Always with admiration and friendship,

Yours
T. S. Eliot

TO *Bonamy Dobrée*   TS Brotherton

10 August 1930   *The Criterion*

Dear Bonamy,

I never can make out whether you have a retinue of couriers like the Lord Lansdowne who has sometimes been accused of being the author of Junius' letters[1] (overrated compositions in *my* opinion, tho' I wish

1 – *Junius' Letters* was a compilation of private and open letters by the anonymous Junius, along with a number of replies, 1769–72. The collection was first published in two volumes in 1772 by Henry Sampson Woodfall, owner-editor of a London newspaper, the *Public Advertiser*.

Winston Churchill could write half as well); or whether you keep dashing up to Town surreptitiously or incognito: but your letters are *frequently* postmarked W.1 or W.2 whilst purporting to come from the Priory. I make no attempt to unveil the mystery; I merely mention it.

Now, I am afraid that the 12th is impossible.[1] It is not that I must be on the Moors (as King Bolo said to the Queen in presenting Columbo, 'he hunts with the Quorn and shoots over his own coverts') but I *did* think you said the 16th – which I did think at that moment was the Thursday, which I see it is not. Would the Wednesday do? Especially as I trust you will appear at the Poetry Bookshop at six of the clock precisely that evening, (if Harold is returned from his nursing home and well enough to do the honours). Guests at 8: I have asked Hayward and Vines.[2]

Yours &&fully,
T. S. E.

No: it is not my business to protect Gummers against you; I only wish you wd. join another Club.[3]

TO *Osbert Sitwell*[4]   TS Renishaw

11 August 1930   *The Criterion*

My dear Osbert,

It is indeed a long time since we have met,[5] but I am not aware of that being due to any unwillingness on my part. On the contrary, I have thought of you often and wondered whether I should ever have a chance to see you again. And I am always in London, and you apparently are

---

1 – BD had asked, in a letter of 2 Aug., whether TSE could manage lunch on Tues., 12 Aug.
2 – Sherard Vines (1890–1974), poet and academic, taught at Keio University, Tokyo, 1923–8; and was G. F. Grant Professor of English at University College, Hull, 1929–52. Works include *The Kaleidoscope* (1921), *Triforium* (1928), *Tofuku: or Japan in Trousers* (1931).
3 – BD wrote of the 'Americana' column he had submitted: 'Americaca. (It was the typewriter made that joke, but as it's rather a good one, I shall leave it . . .). Of course prune as you see fit . . . I suppose you'll cut my little gibe or jibe at Gummers [Montgomery Belgion]. I shall crave your permission to deal with him some time. He is an agreeable chap, but he stands for all that I hate, loathe, believe to be destructive and evil, and I would wish altogether to conspue [*sic*] him.'
4 – Osbert Sitwell (1892–1969): poet, novelist and man of letters. Early in his career, he published collections of poems, including *Argonaut and Juggernaut* (1919), and a volume of stories *Triple Fugue* (1924), but he is now celebrated for his remarkable memoirs, *Left Hand, Right Hand* (5 vols, 1945–50), which include a fine portrayal of TSE. TSE published one sketch by him in C. See further Philip Zeigler, *Osbert Sitwell* (1998).
5 – Letter from Sitwell not found.

never here; at any rate, whenever I have heard of you the report has come from Italy.

It would be delightful to come down to Renishaw; but Vivienne has not been at all well lately, and I am afraid that there is no possibility of getting away during this month. If she is better, we shall try to get away during September. In any case, if you should be passing through London about that time – or any time, for you can hardly help being in London occasionally – will you not, please, let us know, and give me an opportunity of seeing you.

Ever yours,
T. S. Eliot

TO *Israel Cohen*[1] CC

13 August 1930   *The Criterion*

Dear Mr Cohen,

I remember very well the meeting to which you refer and it is a pleasure to me to hear from you again.[2]

I have read with interest Mr Feldman's article on TCHERNICHOVSKY, but I don't feel, on thoughtful consideration, that it is very well adapted for a public which is largely unable to read the author himself. I feel that it would be much more to the point for us to have, now and then, some good piece of fiction or critical writing translated from Hebrew.

Sincerely yours,
[T. S. Eliot]

1–Israel Cohen (1879–1961): author and lecturer; General Secretary of the World Zionist Organisation, London; member of the Foreign Affairs Committee of the Board of Deputies of British Jews from 1931; works include *Jewish Life in Modern Times* (1914), *The Ruhleben Prison Camp* (1917), *A Ghetto Gallery* (1931), and pamphlets on Jewish and Zionist questions.

2–Cohen (who met TSE at a dinner at the Authors' Club, at the invitation of a mutual friend, Dr Giordani) submitted an article by R. V. Feldman on the Hebrew poet Shaul Tchernichovsky. 'As, so far as I know, no article on any subject connected with Hebrew literature has yet appeared in your review, you may perhaps see your way to using the enclosed.'

TO *The Manager, District Bank*   CC

14 August 1930   [68 Clarence Gate Gardens]

Dear Sir,

                    Exors. of C. H. Haigh-Wood Decd.

I have your letter L.M/GH of the 11th instant and regret that I cannot agree your figures.

According to your letter A/MB of the 31st ult. to Messrs. James & James, you transferred on that date the sum of £218:9:9d. from Exors.' Account to Mrs Haigh-Wood's account. This sum represented accrued dividends (detailed by you in that letter) credited to Exors.' Account in error, which had been paid in to you before the 30th ult. on which date you received £300:1:1d. from the Eagle Oil Transport Co. Ltd.

This last sum represents *capital repayment* and must therefore be reinvested whole by the executors. It is therefore incorrect if you have withdrawn any part of it to Mrs Haigh-Wood's private account.

I shall be obliged if you will confirm that you have *at least* £300:1:1d. on the Executors' Account.

                    Yours faithfully,
                    [T. S. Eliot]
                    Joint Executor.

TO *Elbridge L. Adams*   CC

14 August 1930   [Faber & Faber Ltd]

My dear Mr Adams,

I beg to acknowledge with thanks your letter of the 31st ultimo, enclosing a cheque for $437.40.[1]

1–The sum represented Fountain Press (NY) royalties on *Ash-Wednesday*: the first and signed edition, printed at the Curwen Press and published on 24 Apr. 1930, was limited to 600 numbered copies, of which 200 were reserved for sale in the UK by F&F and 400 for sale by the Fountain Press in the USA. Adams wrote: 'I did not realize when I wrote you that you had given us this work to publish at some loss to yourself. Indeed, my understanding of the genesis of this book as gleaned from the early correspondence and conversations with Mr Wells seems to be quite at variance with Mr Faber's and Mr de la Mare's. I can only say that I am sorry that there should have been the slightest misunderstanding, and hope you will forgive me for thinking that you perhaps would mitigate our loss by accepting royalties based upon the selling price.'

GCF had written to Adams on 3 July 1930: 'As regards the cost of *Ash Wednesday*, that was of course stated in the agreement, and was (I understood) arrived at by discussion between you and [Richard] de la Mare . . . We had an alternative offer from another firm of American publishers which would have given us a far larger profit than we made out of our

I am sorry about the misunderstanding, which was perhaps due to so many people having been concerned with the book at once. It is unfortunate that I happen to be in need of the money myself.

I am afraid that both the English and American market for expensive limited editions is going to be very dull for a long time to come; and I am sorry that the Fountain Press should be one of those to suffer. With very many thanks, and best wishes, I am,

Yours sincerely,
[T. S. Eliot]

TO *H. M. Tomlinson*[1]   CC

14 August 1930   [*The Criterion*]

Dear Tomlinson,

Thank you for yours of the 12th, and for the final draft of typescript which has reached me. It will be set up shortly for the December number.[2] Meanwhile I must tell you that I am in rather a stew over your review of Norman Douglas. You may remember that I got it just too late for the July number and was going to use it in September. Now whether it has been mislaid by me, or in the office, or by the printers, I do not know, but whatever it is we cannot lay our hands upon it. I am frightfully sorry about this, for my own sake as I was very anxious to use it. So if by chance you have another copy I should be very grateful if you could let me have it at once.[3]

With many apologies,
Yours ever sincerely,
[T. S. Eliot]

---

agreement with the Fountain Press . . . But . . . we did not wish to act in a way which you would have thought unfriendly.' GCF wrote again on 16 July: 'Eliot has consulted us about your letter to him of July 1st, to which he asks me to reply. He does not at all wish to forgo the royalties agreed on; and for our part we do not think that he should do so. As you know, we had a better offer for *Ash Wednesday* from another New York firm than yours; better both from Eliot's and from our point of view. We reluctantly refused this offer, because you were particularly keen to have the book; and because you considered that you had the prior claim to it. In these circumstances we feel, somewhat strongly, that neither Eliot nor we can be expected to make any further concessions.'

1 – H. M. Tomlinson (1873–1958): author and journalist; literary editor of *N&A*, 1917–23; author of *London River* (1921); *Gallions Reach* (Femina-Vie Heureuse Prize, 1927); *Norman Douglas* (1931).

2 – 'A Lost Wood', *C.* 10 (Jan. 1931), 211–21.

3 – Untitled review of Norman Douglas, *Three of Them*, *C.* 10 (Oct. 1930), 148–50.

TO *Herbert Read*[1]   CC

16 August 1930   [*The Criterion*]

Dear Herbert

Yes. I thought the evening most satisfactory, both profitable and jolly: though I did not find a diet of sandwiches and white wine very digestable [*sic*] in connexion with the mental strain which such a gathering entails. But we have made a good start.[2]

I have not seen the *N.R.F.* lately: could you lend me one of those you mention?[3]

I had ordered Santayana and do not know why it has not yet arrived. I shall be delighted if you can do an article on him for December.[4] So will he, I imagine. What, by the way, do you think of him as a possible contributor of a quarterly 'feature'? It would not take the place of the causerie we had in mind, but in addition? I have not the slightest notion whether he would do it or not.[5]

I agree with you that Cole would not do for that purpose; though he would be a good contributor, and I shall ask him to contribute.[6] I can't think of any outsider who could be relied upon. And everybody inside is too busy. I suppose, except myself. (Perhaps you could do it once in a while?) But, if I do it myself, I think the Commentary must be reconstructed, and I shall need help there. It would be literally a commentary on petits faits divers of the quarter; and the collaboration which was once so unanimously agreed upon, which never came to anything more than a note by Bone on the New City Architecture, and the (useless) note of Morley's which I showed you, would be almost essential. Such topics as one on which I would write a note myself – on the useless and insane multiplication of branches of banks – the Midland have in my neighbourhood two branches within two blocks of each other, to say nothing of the others – would be commentary

1–Herbert Read (1893–1968), English poet and literary critic: see Biographical Register.
2–HR had written (14 Aug.): 'Everybody was very pleased with our evening [a meeting of the Criterion Club] yesterday: it was very gemütlich & maintained its interest to the end.'
3–HR drew TSE's attention (14 Aug.) to some articles 'Sur l'Inde' by Jean Grenier, in the *NRF*: he thought they might make a book for F&F.
4–HR requested a copy of the new volume by Santayana: no article ensued.
5–HR responded (in letter mistakenly dated '4:8:30'), 'I think your suggestion of Santayana as a feature writer is a good one; the "Soliloquies" he contributed to Murry's *Athenaeum* were very attractive. He has written a good deal for the *Adelphi*, and may not be available (he must be about 70) . . .'
6–HR wrote (14 Aug.): 'On second thoughts I don't think so much of my suggestion of [G. D. H. Cole] for the causerie. Like Woolf, he is too prejudiced, & not philosophically minded enough. It would be far the best thing if you could do it.'

not causerie. Both are rather difficult arts, and it is still more difficult to practise both at once.[1]

We couldn't come down tomorrow – I have the admirable map, the result I suppose of military training – and next week you are away; so we must wait and see how things are before tomorrow fortnight.[2] I trust I shall see you before then.

Yours ever,
[Tom]

TO *Geoffrey Faber* CC

23 August 1930 [Faber & Faber Ltd]

Dear Geoffrey,

I don't want to bother you with unnecessary business, but there are two matters I ought to mention.

I have agreed verbally with James Joyce to publish another fragment in the Miscellany next spring on the same terms as *Anna Livia*.[3] This only after discussion with Morley, Paterson[4] and De la Mare; but I wanted to let you know before the contract was drawn up. Joyce professed himself very pleased with the form, the price and results of the previous. The chief point in my mind – for I doubt whether a second fragment will go *quite* as well as the first – is that if Joyce's operation in October is successful, he expects to finish the book in about a year; he will want to make a profitable contract, and I dare say a big advance, from some American publisher; but said that he would be very glad to have us take part in this. There is also some question as to whether Sylvia Beach should be recognised in some way – I mean, perhaps by having charge of continental distribution, and even printing. I told him that it was not essential for us that the book should be printed here, rather than on the continent, but that we should insist that our edition should be published over our name, and from London, else we could not handle it successfully. When the time comes, however, I think that we should not be so eager as to agree to excessive terms, such as certain American publishers might offer.

1–HR ('4:8:30'): 'Causerie and commentary need more discussion, perhaps at the next meeting, but everything points your way. But then, as you say, the commentary would have to be reconstructed.'
2–HR had invited TSE down to his Arts and Crafts home at Seer Green, Beaconsfield, for lunch 'on the first fine Sunday'. He was going to Brussels for up to two weeks from 18 Aug.
3–*Haveth Childers Everywhere* (Criterion Miscellany 26) was to be published on 8 May 1931.
4–A. J. B. Paterson (b. 1900) was Sales Manager of F&F; from Oct. 1930, Sales Director.

The point at the moment is that if you have any doubt about publishing a second fragment in the same way you should let me know before the contract is drawn up. It would be 'Haveth Childers Everywhere', and that leads to my second point.[1]

In the course of conversation with Joyce turning on the point of the amount of unnecessary trouble which New York publishers gave us, he mentioned, without my having brought in the name or any of my or our dealings with the person, that there was one New York publisher against whom he wished particularly to warn me – i.e. Elbridge Adams.[2] When I told this to de la Mare he replied characteristically that it was probably Wells's fault, but the detail appears to be this: The Fountain Press refused *Haveth Childers Everywhere* when it was first shown them in mss. Then it was brought out in Paris by one Henri Babou. Apparently Adams came to Paris and bought up half of Babou's edition of 600 copies. These copies are still in the New York custom house as Adams will not pay the duties; meanwhile Adams owes Babou the payment for them, out of which Babou owes Joyce fc. 25,000; and Babou cannot pay Joyce till Adams pays him.

There is also a tale from the same source, that Adams offered to assist the cause of an operatic tenor named Sullivan[3] in whom J.J. is philanthropically and patriotically interested, if Joyce would sign *all* of the 300 copies without additional emolument to himself. These 300 copies in the N.Y. Custom house, you may remember, are one of the 'assets' of the Fountain Press which Adams offered us. It occurs to me that we shall probably do better by publishing a shilling edition by direct arrangement with Joyce, than trying to market 300 extremely expensive copies.

I give you this information or gossip in confidence as I received it, primarily in relation to our consideration of the Fountain Press. The next piece of news also throws light on that, though it is primarily a nuisance to myself alone.

A few days ago I had a letter from Wells, saying that he has resigned from the Fountain Press (De la Mare tells me that Wells has found a

1 – GCF replied on 28 Aug. from Wales (he and his family were on holiday, establishing a vacation home at Ty Glyn Aeron) that he agreed 'entirely' about *Haveth Childers Everywhere*.
2 – Elbridge L. Adams and James R. Wells were directors of The Fountain Press, NYC.
3 – John Francis O'Sullivan (1878–1955), a leading tenor of the Paris Opera. Richard Ellmann notes: 'Stanislaus Joyce met him in Trieste and was pleased to find him reading *A Portrait of the Artist*. He wrote his brother and Joyce arranged to meet Sullivan in Paris. When he heard Sullivan sing in *Tannhäuser*, he became a violent partisan and spent much time during the next three years in trying to win for his friend the fame he deserved' (*Letters of James Joyce* III).

motor-car manufacturer willing to spend more money than Adams), and reminding me (what I had quite overlooked) that *Ash Wednesday* must be set up in America by October to preserve the copyright. He adds gently that if Adams is not inclined to do this (which Adams for the Press contracted to do in his agreement with me) he would be happy to publish on the same terms. Not feeling disposed to fall into Wells's hands merely from pressure of time, I wired to Adams to ask what he was doing. He replies that he has tried Macmillan without success and is now trying other publishers. I am about to wire back to suggest that Faber & Faber might arrange it in America themselves.[1]

That is enough for one letter, and I will put no more into this.

Yours ever,

[Tom]

TO *Herbert Read*

CC

23 August 1930   [*The Criterion*]

Dear Herbert,

I got your proof copy and letter last night, and hasten to reply to your three specific questions.[2] I think that your acknowledgement will do admirably. I take it that you are not putting anything more in the way of a preface, acknowledgements etc., in which case I should incorporate this with it; but it can stand very well by itself.

PP. 31–33. The distinction in my mind is not nearly so clear cut as you put it, but I think your remarks are quite justified by the words I used,

---

1 – GCF replied: 'Adams seems to be a variety difficult to classify – neither the shrewd businessman of Morley's & my diagnosis nor the simple-hearted fellow of de la Mare's! But what you tell me is certainly fuel for his pyre. I am more concerned about Ash Wednesday – copyright must not be lost on any account; & if Adams does not take immediate steps, you must get de la Mare or Morley to make arrangements on behalf of F & F.'

2 – HR asked TSE (22 Aug.) 'to glance at the enclosed proofs [of his *William Wordsworth*]. Don't bother to read it all: some of it is pretty dreary. But I would like you particularly to look at pp. 31–3, where I take your name in vain, & perhaps don't adequately represent your point of view; and pp. 196–8, where my dealings with humanism might strike you as being altogether too summary.' He asked TSE about the best way to express acknowledgements to Trinity College, Cambridge (where the book had begun as his Clark Lectures). His draft preface read: 'This book repeats, with only slight variations, a course of lectures which I gave at Trinity College, Cambridge, during Trinity Term of this year. I would like to express my deep obligation to the Master and Fellows of Trinity College for the honour they did me in electing me to the Clark Lectureship, and to thank them for their memorable hospitality during its continuance.'

and for the present purpose no harm is done. What you put is so to speak the Richards side of my view; I should say that in practice a complete analysis, in any case, of belief from assent, is impossible; and that probably beyond a certain (I mean an uncertain) degree assent becomes undistinguishable from belief. But without elaborating a whole treatise on *Gegenstandstheorie*[1] I don't see how one could put it differently without making hopeless confusion; so I should leave this just as it stands, as it seems illuminating for the explication of Wordsworth at this point.

PP. 196–7. I am not so certain about the advisability of bringing in Babbitt. The people (and that is nearly everybody in England) who know nothing about Humanism will find it irrelevant; and those who do will find it insufficient. I of course agree with your statement 'My objection to humanism . . . which inspired Wordsworth'; but I incline to think that this is too important a statement to be wasted in a place where it cannot be amplified. However, I may be wrong in making this criticism before I have read the whole book. I am interested to see whether your statement at the foot of the page leads to anything further.

I should like to keep the book as long as you can let me, as I have so far only had time to read the passages you indicated. On glancing over pages, I noticed several possible minor alterations – in one place you used 'to' where it seemed to me you meant 'toward' etc.

Yes, I hope the 31st will be possible, but I will communicate with you during the week.

> Yours ever,
> [Tom]

TO *E. R. Curtius* CC

27 August 1930 [Faber & Faber Ltd]

My dear Curtius,

I am writing to let you know that we have recently been given the opportunity of considering the *Frankreich* of yourself and Herr Bergstresser [*sic*].[2] I had already received your own volume from your publisher, by your kindness, for which I thank you; and was actually in the process of reading it.

---

1 – TSE adverts to *Über Gegenstandstheorie* ('Theory of Objects', 1914), by the Austrian philosopher Alexius Meinong (1853–1920).
2 – E. R. Curtius and Arnold Bergsträsser, *Frankreich* (2 vols, 1930).

First of all, we felt definitely that we could only consider your part of the work. Not only is Herr Bergstresser unknown in England, but the part of the subject with which he dealt would certainly interest only a small public. And as it appeared that your publishers were desirous of placing the complete work in England, we did not wish to stand in the way, and hope that they will succeed in doing so. Personally, however, I should much prefer to start publication of your work in England with something of a more general interest here; for example, either such a book as I have long been urging you to write, dealing with contemporary English literature, or one dealing with Germany or German literature. And I hope that, even if you do not care to complete the book which I suggest, that you have something else in hand which might be suitable. I shall be very much disappointed if your name is not added to the list of Faber and Faber, while I am one of the directors.[1]

With best wishes for yourself and Mrs Curtius,[2] and hoping to hear from you when you have time to write,

I am,
Yours sincerely,
[T. S. Eliot]

FROM *TSE's Secretary* TO *Brian Howard*[3]   CC

28 August 1930   *The Criterion*

Dear Mr Howard,

Here are such answers as Mr Eliot is able to give to your questions.[4] In a good many cases, he really cannot tell you much about the people in question, I am afraid, but I hope this will be of use:

1 – Curtius responded on 30 Aug.: 'I also want to start working on English literature again. But I wonder if I'll ever write about it. I don't find anything in it of the highest quality – with the only exception of T. S. E. (I don't regard Joyce as part of English literature). What I have read of Virginia Woolf is delightful, but nothing more. I am disturbed by a certain ladylike vagueness in *Orlando* as well as *Mrs Dalloway*. Huxley is an intellectual describer of his time, but he doesn't come up to the standard of Proust or Larbaud. Lawrence is an inverted Ruskin with the primitive seriousness of a prophet. Please forgive these disrespectful remarks. They may at least explain my reservations towards contemporary English literature.'
2 – William Stewart had told TSE on 19 Mar. that Curtius had recently got married.
3 – Brian Howard (1905–58), educated at Eton and Oxford: see Marie-Jacqueline Lancaster, *Brian Howard: Portrait of a Failure* (1968); reissued with intro. by D. J. Taylor (2005). LW gave Howard an introduction to TSE on 11 Feb 1930, since Howard was proposing to compile an anthology of modern poetry which LW was interested in publishing.
4 – Questions not found.

R. N. D. Wilson:	American, well over thirty – probably over forty – reputation during and post-war.
Richard Church:	English, well over thirty, post-war reputation.
Dudley Fitts:	American, round about thirty, or probably younger. Post-war reputation.
Archibald Macleish:	American, probably not much over thirty, post-war.
Louis Zukofsky:	American, probably not over thirty, post-war.

Is this the sort of thing you want?

Yours sincerely,
[Laura Maude Hill, Secretary]

TO *Basil Bunting*[1]   CC

29 August 1930   [Faber & Faber Ltd]

Dear Bunting,

I find that I have left your letter of the 15th of May unanswered[2] and that I never thanked you for the copy of the little book which you sent me.[3] If you are still in England and can ever come to see me, I should be very glad; I hope you will forgive my unpardonable carelessness.[4]

1–Basil Bunting (1900–85), Northumberland-born poet, lived in Paris in the early 1920s, working for Ford Madox Ford at the *Transatlantic Review*. From 1923 he was mentored by EP, whom he followed to Rapallo; and it was through EP that he became acquainted with JJ, Zukofsky and WBY. EP published his work in *Active Anthology* (1933); but his enduring fame came about after WW2 with the publication of *Briggflatts* (1966). *Collected Poems* appeared in 1968.

TSE wrote of him to J. R. Ackerley, 17 Aug. 1936: 'He is a good poet and an intelligent man'; and in a reference to the John Simon Guggenheim Memorial Foundation, 30 Dec. 1938: 'Bunting . . . is a very intelligent man and an able poet. I say "able", because I am still doubtful whether he will ever accomplish anything of great importance as an original author. I think he has just the qualities to qualify him as a translator of poetry . . . I back him strongly for the sort of work that he proposes to do [translation from Persian] – work, also, which is in itself worth doing.' See further R. Caddel and A. Flowers, *Basil Bunting: A Northern Life* (1997), and Richard Burton, *A Strong Song Tows Us: The Life of Basil Bunting* (2013).

2–Not found.

3–Presumably *Redimiculum Matellarum* (1930), Bunting's first collection of poems.

4–According to Carroll F. Terrell, in 'Basil Bunting: An Eccentric Biography', Bunting declared in a late interview that he had first met TSE in 1925: 'So far as I remember that conversation, he spent a long time urging upon me the necessity to read Dante.' (Bunting said he found the advice *de trop*, since he had already studied a great deal of Dante.) Terrell

We considered the possibility of publishing your small book in England but unfortunately had already taken on two or three booklets of about the same size and we did not feel that we could venture on this one at present. I liked your Villon[1] very much.

Yours sincerely,
[T. S. Eliot]

P.S. Do send me those remarks on Milton of which you spoke.

TO *G. Wilson Knight* CC

29 August 1930 [Faber & Faber Ltd]

Dear Mr Wilson Knight,

Thank you very much for your letter of the 21st and for the two reviews which I had not seen and which I return.[2] I hope that the book is doing well; and I must say that it was a great pleasure to me to write the introduction.

Your paper on 'The Transcendental Consciousness' interested me very much but seems to me a little inchoate and requires, I think, a good deal longer development to make the idea clear.[3] So I am returning it herewith hoping to see a good deal more of it later.

With best wishes,
Yours sincerely,
[T. S. Eliot]

---

relates this story as well: 'Later this same year, Bunting saw Eliot at a party wearing an enormous cape lined with red and eyebrows painted green. He responded to Bunting's expression of amazement with these words: "thought the party needed hotting up"' (*Basil Bunting: Man and Poet*, ed. Carroll F. Terrell [1981], 45).

Bunting claimed in 1976: 'I pointed out to [Eliot] – he hadn't noticed it himself – in 1922 or 1923, that the form "The Wasteland" [*sic*] took, if you omitted the fourth movement, is exactly that of a classical sonata. This seems to have stuck in his mind, so that when he wrote the "Four Quartets", each of them an exact copy of the shape of "The Wasteland", he calls them quartets – quartets being normally a sonata form. He takes it a rather different way than I would have done, but it is making use of what you can derive from the musical form, and doing it with great skill' (Jonathan Williams and Tom Meyer, 'A conversation with Basil Bunting', *Poetry Information* [London] no. 19, Autumn 1978, 38).

On 24 July 1935 Wishart Books Ltd submitted to F&F the MS of Bunting's 'Caveat Emptor', at the author's request. TSE jotted on Wishart's covering letter: 'Derives from Pound, with a certain pleasing neatness. Worth recommending elsewhere – try Dent. TSE.'

1 – *Villon* (1925), Bunting's first major poem.

2 – Reviews of GWK's book on Shakespeare; he mentioned too Blunden's review in *N.*, 12 July 1930.

3 – GWK had submitted one section from a four-part paper on *Pericles*. 'The rest is, in its way, satisfactory to me, but it can hardly, I suppose, be quite clear in so short a treatment.'

P.S. Before signing this, I received your second letter and manuscript, about which I will write as soon as I have had time to read it through.[1]

TO *Henry Eliot*[2]

TS Houghton

[late August 1930]   [68 Clarence Gate Gardens]

I should like the *Spectator*, because I read that set (there was also I think the *Bee* of Goldsmith if not the *Rambler* of Johnson):[3] it was I believe the first American edition, and mother did once promise it to me.[4] I should be very happy to have the photograph of father (it is shown in a photograph of mother's room which you took). I think you should keep the photograph album of mother's (which I don't remember) and you should certainly have the famous album with clasps: it has two photographs of father holding me in his arms, I suppose at about ten months, and that charming one of you and me (heads) together when you were about nine and I two.

I am glad that you have kept the bound volumes of the *Criterion* – Richard Scott is welcome to the unbound copies.[5] Some are quite out of print; anyway I think a complete file will have value in time.

There was a little tray cloth, embroidered in blue, which Vivienne made for mother. If that can be found, we should like Marion[6] to have it.

I have one (wooden) set of father's chessmen (tournament size) as well as the pocket chessboard he used in correspondence chess with me during

1 – GWK sent on 28 Aug. a paper which (he said) 'seems to me a correct way of unifying the two modes – art & morality – but you may disagree'.
2 – The first two pages of this letter (responding to HWE's letter of 14 Aug. 1930) are missing.
3 – *The Spectator*: weekly periodical ed. Joseph Addison and Richard Steele (1711–12), collected in seven volumes; briefly revived, ed. Steele, in 1714. *The Bee*: periodical ed. Oliver Goldsmith (1759). *The Rambler*, ed. Samuel Johnson (1750–2), amounted to 208 articles.
4 – HWE would write on 3 Sept.: 'I am sending you shortly the following books: *The Spectator* (this is not the first American edition, though it may be; but it is the Boswell which has that notation in pencil on the fly leaf. *The Spectator* however belonged to Thomas Heywood Blood, who, I think, was Mother's great grandfather . . . I am going to try to unravel the Blood genealogy . . . It has Thomas H. Blood's signature on the fly leaf of vol. II.)'
5 – 'I have taken the three bound volumes of the *Criterion*; the system of enumeration changes, but I have 37 issues, including the last one (July 1930). I have duplicates making an almost complete second set. As young Richard Scott, Grace's son, who is at Harvard, put in a request for the *Criterions*, I think I shall give him the duplicate set, though I fancy No. 1, containing the *Waste Land*, may have a collector's value.' (Scott, born 1910, son of Richard Gordon and Grace E. Scott, gained his AB in 1932 and became manager of Lederic Laboratories, Los Angeles.)
6 – TSE's sister.

the war; so if the set you mention is the ivory set (one or two men were broken and mended from time to time with red sealing wax) I wish you would keep it yourself.

I shall write you shortly more about myself; partly as an inducement to you to write more about *yourself*. Including such things as your *ears* and teeth. I wish you could come over to London and have a talk.

I am sorry that you have the additional worry of Mrs Garrett's health.[1] Mrs Haigh-Wood has not been at all well lately, so that we are glad to be nearer to her, so that Vivienne can motor from here in about fifteen minutes. She worries more about her mother, because of Maurice being so far away in Rome.

I will write further shortly.

Ever affectionately,
Tom

TO *Henry Eliot*

TS Houghton

2 September 1930   Faber & Faber Ltd

My dear brother,

This is first to thank you very much for sending me the Symonds, the Burritt, the Flaxman, the Palazzo Vecchio and the little photograph of me.[2] I also appreciate the beautiful care with which all your parcels are made up: I have never seen such well made parcels, except father's. I have the Apostles' Bell on the desk in front of me.

When Christmas comes I wish you would give me another Autopoint pencil,[3] if they are to be had! I lost one you gave me, the other I still use, but it is broken: they suit me better than any pencil I can find here.

I sent you lately a letter from Liveright, acknowledging his fault, and offering imperfect reparation. Since then I have received from him the cheque for $37.50; but have neither acknowledged it nor collected it, and

---

1 – 'As I think I told you, we have been in Haddam for somewhat over a month, owing to Mrs Garrett's [his mother-in-law] illness. She is much better . . .'
2 – John Addington Symonds, *The Renaissance in Italy* (7 vols, 1875–86), had been used by CWE when writing her *Savonarola: a dramatic poem* (1926). The 'Burritt' was a chart of the heavens. The English neoclassical sculptor and designer John Flaxman (1755–1826) produced illustrations for the *Iliad* and the *Odyssey* (1793), Aeschylus (1795), and Dante's *Divine Comedy* (1802); but it is not known to what TSE was referring. The photograph of the Palazzo Vecchio (Florence) had hung for years in an oak frame on CWE's wall, and she had kept on her bureau the 'little photograph' of TSE.
3 – Mechanical pencil made by the Autopoint Company, Chicago.

shall not do so until I hear from you or Stern. I also wrote to you about Adams. Since then we have wired him to offer *Ash Wednesday* to the John Day Company, but have had no reply yet.

We have not been away at all this summer, and I do not know when or whether we shall go. Being in London has at least enabled us to see a number of transient Americans: Uncle Chris and Abbey [*sc.* Abby],[1] both of whom were very charming: Uncle Chris strikes me as a particularly nice uncle. We have seen yesterday Lawrence Smith and his wife,[2] whom we saw last year. Lawrence always used to be a standing joke in the family, I think, but he has certainly improved with the years, and is not at all a bore. I imagine that his wife, whom we like particularly, has done him much good. By the way, Katherine spoke very appreciatively of lunching with you, and liked Theresa immensely.[3] I lunched yesterday with Sam Morison – a distant cousin whom I believe you have never met, and Professor of American History at Harvard – whom I find very agreeable and intelligent.

I don't think I ever told you that Vivienne has acquired a small car, though she has had it for many months now. When I say 'small', I mean something much smaller than anything you can imagine in America. It has been a great inducement to her to get out of doors, and I think has done her good. I have learned to drive fairly well. The chief interest in driving, to me, is that the ability to drive removes an inferiority complex which I believe many men suffer from nowadays until they learn. I always had the feeling, though recognising its absurdity, of being the one human being incapable. I think that the satisfaction of finding that you can do what every blockhead is doing, as well as he does it, is almost greater than the satisfaction of doing something which nobody else can do as well. Perhaps it is partly that literary or artistic or philosophic eminence is never certain. It is always possible that the whole thing is a delusion on one's own part and that of the public, to be discovered later on. Whereas the accomplishment of Lindbergh[4] or Amy Johnson[5] is definite, unique, and indestructible, and must be admitted by all. Perhaps that is why people scale mountains, hang about the North Pole, fly round the earth, and

1–Christopher Rhodes Smith (1856–1945): Unitarian minister; minister-at-large of the Benevolent Fraternity of Churches, Boston; and his daughter Abigail Adams Eliot (b. 1892).
2–George Lawrence Smith (1873–1962) had been married to TSE's sister Charlotte (1874–1926); his second wife was Mary Smoot (Mrs Robert Parkman Blake).
3–Katherine cannot be identified. Theresa Eliot was HWE's wife.
4–Charles Lindbergh (1902–74): American aviator; famous at this time for his Orteig Prize-winning non-stop solo flight from New York to Paris, May 1927.
5–Amy Johnson (1903–41): pioneering English aviator; famous for being the first woman to fly solo (in a secondhand de Havilland Gipsy Moth) from England to Australia, May 1930.

attempt records in general. The greatness of the person to circumnavigate the globe without descending to earth will be incontestable.

Anyhow, I drive fairly well, though handicapped by a feeling of odious conspicuousness (which men seem to suffer from more than women).[1] And Vivienne, who I thought at first would never learn, is driving better and better, and I really think at last will be able to drive like anyone else. If anything, she is too cautious (to my relief). And the English 'small car' (7 h.p.) is the most difficult of all to drive; it skids, it bounces; the handbrake goes back on you at awkward moments; it falls into a swoon in the middle of a steep hill, and has to be coaxed up like a donkey; and no one but a genius can change gears without making it scream frightfully. Its only merit, in short, is cheapness.

We are fairly comfortable here (68, Clarence Gate Gardens), and are certain to remain for some time, as I still have on my hands a perfectly unsaleable small house – which has all the disadvantages, and many more, of a 'small car', without the compensation of cheapness – which I cannot get rid of legally, unless some fool takes it off me, till 1932. But *Ash Wednesday* has helped out this year, and I must try to have some other book out in the spring.

I left off this letter at this point, and since then have just received a letter from Elbridge Adams (who appears to be on his way to London) saying that he has fixed up with Putnam to publish a trade edition of *Ash Wednesday* and will see that copies are printed and one sent to the Congressional Library in time to keep the copyright for me. So I think that matter is settled satisfactorily enough.[2]

I think I will stop this letter, as I have had it on the machine for three days, and write another soon.

Ever affectionately,
Tom

1 – Cf. Violet in *FR*: 'I think an open car / Is so undignified: you're blown about so, / And you feel so conspicuous, lolling back / And so near the street, and everyone staring.'
2 – Adams (The Fountain Press) reported to TSE on 27 Aug. that he had arranged with Putnam's to handle a trade edition of *Ash-Wednesday* (Macmillan and Farrar and Rinehart had turned it down 'on the ground that the special edition probably had absorbed the demand'): their contract gave them the right so to assign a trade edition to another publisher approved by the author. Adams added, 'I have arranged to protect your copyright by having the book produced and copies filed in the Library of Congress by the fifth of October . . . I have assigned this right without any remuneration to The Fountain Press, and it may interest you to know the total result of the contract with you so far as The Fountain Press is concerned is a loss of £36.83 [*sic*].'

5 September 1930   [*The Criterion*]

Dear Mr Sykes Davies,

I have read your essay on Lucretius with great interest and should very much like to publish it although I cannot at the moment assign a date.[2] I am afraid that I have been one of those people whom you justly reprimand who have only read the purple passages of Lucretius in Latin and who have relied upon Monro for the duller tracts of the work. But even had I not done so, my scholarship would be quite inadequate to reveal to me what you have pointed out.

At any rate, I have always wondered what classical Latin verse would have been had there been no Greek influence. I have sometimes thought that Mediaeval Latin verse, both sacred and profane, gave me a suggestion of what old Latin poetry would have been without the Greeks. But perhaps you will say that this is going too far.

Yours sincerely,

[T. S. Eliot]

1–Hugh Sykes Davies (1909–84): author and critic. Educated at St John's College, Cambridge – where he edited, with William Empson, the magazine *Experiment,* and where he took the Jebb Studentship and the Le Bas Prize, 1931 – he became University Lecturer and Fellow of St John's. In the 1930s he was a Communist and Surrealist, and co-created the London Surrealist Exhibition, 1936. Novels include *Full Fathom Five* (1956) and *The Papers of Andrew Melmoth* (1960); other writings include *Wordsworth and The Worth of Words* (1986).

TSE would write of him on 13 Mar. 1936, when he put in for a post at the University of Liverpool: 'I have known him pretty well for some years, and I regard his qualifications as exceptional. He has the advantage, not too common in these days, of a sound classical foundation, and I remember an essay of his on the earliest Latin versification which impressed me very much. For the study of criticism he has, I believe, much curious and out-of-the-way learning in Renaissance criticism and philosophy, both in Latin and in Italian, and I regard this as of great importance. He has very wide curiosity and acquaintance with a variety of subjects, as well as a solid knowledge of those which he professes. He is, I believe, something of an authority on the philosophy of Vico, but of this I am not qualified to speak. He has a brilliant mind, and I think also has the temperament which makes it possible for a teacher to acquire the friendship of his pupils. I have great pleasure in supporting his application.'

See George Watson, 'Remembering Prufrock: Hugh Sykes Davies 1909–1984', *The Sewanee Review* 109: 4 (Fall 2001), 573–80; repr. in Watson, *Heresies and Heretics: Memories of the Twentieth Century* (2013).

2–Sykes Davies submitted his essay with an undated note: 'The subject is one on which I feel quite strongly – Lucretius is being very much ill-treated. The new translation is no good, and the one that Robert Trevelyan is doing for the Nonesuch [Press] is just as bad.' See 'Notes on Lucretius', C. 11 (Oct. 1931), 25–42.

5 September 1930   [*The Criterion*]

Dear Cournos,

Yours of the 25th ult. received. I am very glad to have news of you, particularly as your news sounds not too dolorous; but you embarrass me with your cheque.[1] In fact, I think I owe you something on the cheque you sent me for *Ash Wednesday*. But I will work out, or ask the accountant, exactly how your *Criterion* account stands. And I do want if possible a Russian Chronicle from you for the December, which means by the middle of October, it will soon be settled.[2]

I have been in touch with a Miss Malnick, who seems to be some kind of Soviet agent in London, and exercised all my powers of charm upon her, to get her to persuade Moscow to send the *Criterion* to let the *Criterion* [*sic*] have all its literary and general periodicals, assuring her blandly that the *Criterion* was the only periodical in Britain which would appreciate them and give them a fair showing. Two have arrived (I can't read the names) and have been sent to you. I hope you have received them; because I am really very keen to have the *Criterion* have a scoop on Russian affairs; and there is almost nothing except your review of periodicals to indicate that there is anything in Russia except the tragic farce of communism. I confess that I detest bolshevism, not so much because it is communism, but because I feel that your ex- or rather ancestral compatriots are incompetent to make a success of anything. But I may be wrong.

I hope then that I may see you in the autumn.[3] Aiken is here, but has, surprisingly and I feel mistakenly, returned to his old habitat of Rye. I cannot conceive facing one's ghosts so voluntarily as that.[4]

---

1 – 'You generously sent me Ten Pounds when I needed it; of this I owe whatever balance there is after the fee for my last Russian chronicle in the *Criterion* is deducted . . . I enclose a cheque for Twenty Dollars which I hope will cover it . . .

'I have not come into a fortune, but since coming here I've been working like one sentenced to hard labour; and I am glad to begin the paying of my debts, by no means small!'

2 – 'Russian Periodicals', C. 10 (Jan. 1931), 382–91.

3 – 'I may get over to France at the end of September. The charitable North German Lloyd Line has offered mine and my wife's fare in exchange for a few articles in their magazine.'

4 – The following month, Conrad Aiken would gossip in a letter to Theodore Spencer (5 Oct. 1930): 'I lunched with Eliot, and Gordon George. Vivian, said Tom, had been much disappointed at being unable to join us, but as she was having a massage at four thought it easier to stay in bed. Gordon George was a kind of high church or catholic fairy who had written an article on T and was submitting it to him: Tom said that when revised he would himself send it to the *Bookman*. ['The Return of the Native', *The Bookman* 75 (Sept. 1932), 423–31.] – After the first course Vivian appeared, shivering, shuddering, a scarecrow of a

With regards to Mrs Cournos, and best wishes for your family and yourself,

Ever sincerely,
[T. S. Eliot]

P.S. Please let me have your address as soon as you get this.

TO *Brian Coffey*[1]   CC

9 September 1930   [*The Criterion*]

Dear Mr Coffey,[2]

I am interested in your poem, but here and there it reminds me of myself, so that I think that you will do better. I should like to see more of

---

woman with legs like jackstraws, sallow as to face. She examined me with furtive intensity through the whole meal: flung gobs of food here and there on the floor; eyed me to see if I had seen this: picked them up: stacked the dishes, scraping the food off each in turn; and during everything constantly directed at T a cold stream of hatred, as he did (so it seemed to me) toward her. George said something about pure intellect. Tom, giving his best pontifical frown, said there was no such thing. Vivian at this looked at me, then at Tom, and gave a peacock's laugh. Why what do you mean, she said. You argue with me every night in your life about pure intellect, don't you. – I don't know what you mean, says Tom. – Why don't be absurd – you know perfectly well that *every* night you tell me that there *is* such a thing: and what's more, that *you* have it, and that nobody *else* has it. – To which Tom's lame reply was You don't know what you're saying. – And thereupon I banged my fists on the table and said Hear hear and more more, and the hate subsided. – Now isn't this a dainty dish?' (*Selected Letters of Conrad Aiken*, ed. Joseph Killorin [New Haven and London, 1978], 162; according to Lyndall Gordon, the letter is misdated in Killorin's volume.)

1–Brian Coffey (1905–95), Irish poet, academic, teacher and translator (Mallarmé, Eluard, Pablo Neruda, Gérard de Nerval) – a son of Denis Coffey, President of University College, Dublin (UCD) – was educated at Clongowes Wood College, Co. Kildare, 1919–22, and at UCD, where he studied medicine before switching to mathematics, physics and chemistry; and he passed several years in France, studying classics at the Institution St Vincent in Oise; physical chemistry (under the Nobel Prize-winning physicist Jean Baptiste Perrin); and philosophy at the Institut Catholique, Paris (under Jacques Maritain). In Paris, he became friends with Thomas MacGreevy and Samuel Beckett, who – writing as 'Andrew Belis' – praised his work in 'Recent Irish Poetry', *Bookman* 86 (Aug. 1934), 235–6. During WW2 he was a teacher in England; he was then appointed Assistant Professor in Philosophy at St Louis University, Missouri, 1947–52; and he taught sixth-form maths in London, 1952–72. Works include *Poems* (with his friend Denis Devlin, 1930); *Three Poems* (1933), *Third Person* (1938). See *Irish University Review* V: 1: *Brian Coffey Special Issue* (Spring 1975); Donal Moriarty, *The Art of Brian Coffey* (2000).

2–Coffey wrote on 8 July to ask after a poem entitled 'Prayer' that he had submitted two months earlier. He enclosed a new poem, 'Wednesday Night', which TSE did not accept for C. But a poem by Coffey 'Plain Speech for Two' was to appear in C. 18 (Oct. 1938), 37–8.

your work. By the way, do you know what the word Modernist means? I do not.[1]

> Yours very truly,
> [T. S. Eliot]

TO *R. Ellsworth Larsson*[2]   cc

9 September 1930   [Faber & Faber Ltd]

Dear Larsson,

Many thanks for your letter of the 21st.[3] I am very glad to have news of you and I am sorry that I have not had time to write to you before. Of course I have no objection to your mentioning my name to the Guggenheim Trustees, though I warn you that no one recommended by me has ever received a fellowship yet, but I hope you will break the run of bad luck. I look forward to your next poem.

> Yours sincerely,
> [T. S. Eliot]

---

1 – Coffey replied on 15 Sept.: 'About the word Modernist. I used the word in the subtitle to "Wednesday Night" as a hasty and lazy afterthought . . . But I did this thoughtlessly, being tired. About that time I had been reading the cited poems in "A survey of modernist poetry" [by Laura Riding and Robert Graves, 1927]. I can find only this meaning in my head for the word – "that which is obviously the product of its particular age", and that does not look very well as a definition. And in any case every poem is included in it, and a poem needs no qualification.'

2 – Raymond Ellsworth Larsson (b. 1901), poet and journalist, grew up in Wisconsin and worked in newspapers until journeying in 1926 to Europe, where he visited France (his poetry appeared in *transition* in 1927), England and Belgium. After returning to the USA in 1929, he worked for a while as an advertising manager. He entered the Roman Catholic Church in 1932. In Jan. 1939 TSE was to write to Henry Allen Moe, The Guggenheim Foundation: 'Mr Larsson is . . . rather a minor imitator of myself, on the devotional side.'

3 – Larsson, who published in 1929 *O City Cities* (Payson and Clarke), wished to apply for a Guggenheim Fellowship, nominating TSE as a referee. He had meant to apply in 1929 but felt he had not achieved for himself 'any but a very temporary stability of affairs . . . Since then I have had a job writing advertisements for a chocolate manufacturer, have taken a flat of my own, and now, with the dissolution of the chocolate firm and the instability of Wall Street . . . I find myself determined now to apply.' He was proposing to write a long poem and a novel.

TO *Herbert Read*   CC

9 September 1930   [*The Criterion*]

Dear Herbert,

I have now read the whole of your book,[1] and find it extremely interesting. I am returning the proofs sooner than I should like to, because you wanted me to call attention to any errors that I spotted, and it is quicker to send you back the book than to make a list of them.

You will find a number of pages turned down. Some of these are for quite other reasons than textual errors, but you will immediately see for yourself which they are. I am not a very good proof reader myself, but there were two errors which you will find that I have marked, which are important, because they make nonsense of the phrases in which they occur. But I daresay that you or Bonamy have already spotted them.

I have a good deal to say about the book, but that can wait for a bit. Meanwhile I hope to see you at Harold's on Wednesday evening.

                                        Yours ever,
                                        [T. S. E.]

TO *Edwin Muir*[2]   CC

9 September 1930   [*The Criterion*]

Dear Muir,

Thank you for your letter of the 31st July. I like your poem, 'After the Fall', and should like to publish it, but cannot say definitely at what date; so if you would meanwhile prefer to use it elsewhere, please let me know.[3]

I look forward to your Essay on Kafka,[4] and should also look forward to seeing you in London if you ever came this way.

                                        Yours sincerely,
                                        [T. S. Eliot]

---

1 – *William Wordsworth*.
2 – Edwin Muir (1887–1959), Scottish poet, novelist, critic, translator: see Biographical Register.
3 – 'After the Fall', C. 10 (Apr. 1931), 421–3. TSE had consulted HR about Muir's submission (among others); and HR responded on 4 Aug.: 'There is nothing really good enough. Muir's is perhaps the best and I feel he deserves some encouragement: I don't know him, but there's something honest about his work.'
4 – 'I should have apologised . . . for not writing [to] you further about my proposed essay on Franz Kafka: but first illness and then other work kept me from getting at it. I still intend to write it . . .'

9 September 1930   [Faber & Faber Ltd]

Dear Joyce,

Many thanks for your card. It was a great pleasure to see your hand-writing, which I was able to read, even if you could not. I am sorry for the restrictions imposed on the Nursery Rhyme, but, if we can make use of it in the way we [*sc.* you] suggest, we will.[1]

I am enclosing the contract for *Haveth Childers Everywhere*, which you will find, I think, to be identical with the contract for *Anna Livia Plurabelle*. I also enclose a Form of Authority, addressed to ourselves, instructing us to pay royalties to Pinker[2] as before. That is to say, if those are your intentions, please sign and return it with the contract.

I hope you are finding the weather at Etretat more satisfactory than that of Llandudno and that you are making progress, as your card seems to

1 – While staying at the Euston Hotel, London, NW1, JJ had written a 'nursery rhyme' that he posted to TSE with a covering letter dated 18 Aug. 1930:

'To T. S. Eliot from James Joyce:
    A. L. P.
Buy a book in brown paper
From Faber and Faber
To see Annie Liffey trip, tumble and caper.
Sevensinus in her ringthings,
Plurabells on her prose,
Sheashell ebb music wayriver she flows.
    J.J.
Euston August 1930'

For *Haveth Childers Everywhere* JJ wrote the following verses:

Humptydump Dublin squeaks through his norse,
Humptydump Dublin hath a horrible vorse
And with all his kinks English
Plus his irismanx brogues
Humptydump Dublin's grandada of all rogues.

JJ sent TSE a PC (date illegible) stating, 'I forgot to say that if you ever use that nursery rhyme it should not be signed or initialled but seem to come from your advt writer'; and he would later complain that F&F had 'made no use of my advt rhyme' (*Letters* III, 247). Ellmann explained: 'The sales manager, W. J. Crawley, was hesitant. In the end the verses were used only on a mimeographed publicity release, to which was prefixed a note: "The sales department, puzzled as such departments are wont to be, have sought some light on the two James Joyce contributions to Criterion Miscellany. Below the explanations offered are passed on that you may be able to derive similar enlightenment." Joyce was annoyed' (ibid.).
2 – James B. Pinker & Sons, Literary, Dramatic and Film Agents.

indicate. My wife was very sorry indeed not to have seen Mrs Joyce while you were here, but hopes that you may both return next summer.

Sincerely Yours,
[T. S. Eliot]

TO *James Joyce*   CC

13 September 1930   [Faber & Faber Ltd]

Dear Joyce,

I return herewith the letter from Pinker which you sent me. I have also spoken to him on the telephone. We have no part in any arrangement for American publication of *Anna Livia* or any other fragment – though we hope we may have a part in the publication of the complete work. So go ahead and make your arrangements independently of us.

I hope that you will be able to go ahead this winter as you intend. I trust that you have received my previous letter enclosing the contract for *Haveth Childers Everywhere*.

With all best wishes,
Yours sincerely
[T. S. Eliot]

TO *Bonamy Dobrée*   TS Brotherton

13 September 1930   Faber & Faber Ltd

Dear Bonamy,

Thanks for your letter of the 8th.[1] We were very sorry you were absent; but very careful Herbert who was elected secretary took full notes which will be open to your inspection as minutes as soon as we buy a minute book to put them into.[2] The meeting, which was conducted in a violent storm, lionesses whelping etc.[3] was not so successful as the last: partly depressed by your absence, partly suffering from a paucity of guests. I was rather uncomfortable in a pair of dry trousers borrowed from Harold, and found sandwiches and white wine rather unsettling: next time (when you shall be present), I intend to have two eggs to my tea beforehand.

1 – BD had said he would not be able to 'get up to the Symposium on Wednesday'.
2 – Neither notes nor minute book has been found.
3 – TSE is alluding to *Julius Caesar*.

I have not had a chance to talk to Herbert yet, but hope to get him for an evening before he goes to Brussels.[1] I do feel the presence of desiccation; but from my point of view it will take the form, not of worrying about his style, but about his subject matter. The book is excellent, the views just; but I did not feel that he was deeply enough moved by the subject to justify it. His remark that criticism should be written like philosophy does not worry me, because it does not seem to me to mean much: there are so many ways in which *good* philosophical works have been written. The danger is chiefly of writing criticism like second rate philosophy. I doubt myself whether good philosophy any more than good criticism or any more than good poetry can be written without strong feeling. But one only argues from oneself: I am sure that any prose I have written that is good prose, is good because I had strong feelings (more than adequate knowledge) – my essay on Machiavelli, for instance, is not good, not because I did not know enough (which I didn't) but because I had not soaked deep enough in Machiavelli to feel intensely – therefore, in so far as there is any good in it, that is because it is not about Machiavelli at all.

Herbert's danger I think is industry, just as mine is torpor. The line I shall take is to try to suggest that he should write about something with passionate conviction – whether he is right or wrong won't matter so much!

Yours ever
T. S. E.

Incidentally, everyone is to produce a specimen causerie before next time.

---

1 – 'I am a little worried about Herbert's prose in Wordsworth [*William Wordsworth*]. It is in danger of going dead. I have tried to suggest this to him delicately . . . It is apparently deliberate. He says he wants his criticism to read like philosophy . . . but the only philosophy that people interested in poetry usually read, is philosophy that reads like poetry.'

TO *Charles Harris*

13 September 1930   [Faber & Faber Ltd]

Dear Harris,

Thank you for your letter of the 9th. I have heard nothing of Fr Underhill since he went abroad; but I had my secretary ring up Liddon House, and she was informed that he has returned.

Certainly, I will write to Chandler Post; but I am not clear how much, if anything, Post already knows of the matter.[1] May I trouble you to drop me a line to let me know whether he has already heard of the Encyclopaedia,[2] whether he has already been approached informally; or whether I should explain it all as if he had never heard of it?

I will try to put a few notes together before October, and look forward to seeing you.[3]

> Yours ever sincerely,
> [T. S. Eliot]

TO *G. W. S. Curtis*

13 September 1930   [Faber & Faber Ltd]

My dear Fr Curtis,

I was very glad to hear from you; and am not surprised that your new duties are worrying and unnumerable.[4] I should be delighted to lunch with you on Thursday next, if that is convenient for you, and I should like to see your church. (I have recently made a pilgrimage to [the] tomb of

---

1 – Harris wrote on behalf of the E.C.U. Literature Committee: '[P]lease write in my name to Prof Chandler Post of Harvard, asking him to be your American assessor and advisor. As you know him personally that is the best course.'

2 – The E.C.U. Literature Committee was planning an *Encyclopaedia of the Christian Religion*.

3 – 'Do not do anything much beyond devising a rough scheme, and thinking about contributors, before the first Thursday in October, when the Editorial Board meets . . .'

4 – Curtis, who had recently been appointed to the Charterhouse Mission, 40 Tabard Street, London SE1., and who felt 'so overwhelmed with a mass of apparently meaningless jobs and duties and distresses', wrote on 9 Sept. to ask TSE if he could find a day to lunch 'next week'.

Andrewes).[1] If not Thursday will you suggest one or two other possible days?

Yours ever,
[T. S. Eliot]

TO *J. Gordon Macleod*   cc

15 September 1930   [Faber & Faber Ltd]

Dear Mr Macleod,

I ought, in fact, to have written to you about that without waiting to be asked.[2] Mr Bronowski is a young Jew who has been very active in Cambridge literary and poetical circles in the last two or three years. I do not know how good an anthology he will make; but having given him permission to use a few of my own poems, I have gone further and given him some good advice; and it is naturally to my interest that the anthology should be as good as possible, and, I believe, that he should accept my recommendations. He seems quite intelligent and alert; but is handicapped by the time limit imposed by his publishers.

But I thought that the anthology would do your book good and no harm; by bringing your work before a larger public and making them ask for more. This was the primary motive.

I have noted your postscript. I hope that we may meet again before long, and will in any case write within a month.

Yours sincerely,
[T. S. Eliot]

---

1 – Curtis wished to show TSE St Hugh's Church and the tomb of Lancelot Andrewes in Southwark Cathedral, London.
2 – Macleod wrote on 8 Sept. to say that Bronowski had invited him (at TSE's suggestion) to contribute a poem to an anthology. Macleod had suggested that he use 'Virgo'.

TO *Lennox Robinson*[1]   CC

17 September 1930   [Faber & Faber Ltd]

Dear Mr Robinson,[2]

I am returning herewith the copies of my letters to John Quinn. I have corrected a few slips and have expunged only two short passages. I have no objection to any of the rest.

I wish most cordially that I could contribute some memories. But I never had the pleasure of meeting Quinn; the letters themselves show I think the kind and extent of my relations with him; though these letters are far from covering the whole of his benefactions to me. If there should be any question of publishing letters *by* Quinn, I think I have preserved all I received from him; some are concerned entirely with my own difficulties with New York publishers; and perhaps only interesting as showing the lengths to which he was prepared to go in the interests of any man of whose work he approved, even when the man was personally unknown to him.

Yours very truly,

T. S. Eliot

I find I have an introduction to you, from Padraic Colum, which I have never been able to present. If I come to Dublin this winter, as I hope, I shall take the liberty.

1–Lennox Robinson (1886–1958): playwright and director; Manager of the Abbey Theatre, Dublin, 1910–14, 1919–23; Director from 1923. His output featured plays including *The Whiteheaded Boy* (1916), *The Far-Off Hills* (1928), *Speed the Plough* (1954); *The Golden Treasury of Irish Verse* (1925), *Lady Gregory's Journals* (1946), and *The Oxford Book of Irish Verse* (with D. McDonagh, 1958). When asked in a later year to support the nomination of Lennox Robinson for the Nobel Prize, TSE wrote to the Secretary of the Royal Swedish Academy, 19 Feb. 1957: 'I am . . . writing to say that I know of no other Irish dramatist, with the exception of Mr Sean O'Casey, who is so well qualified as Mr Robinson for this great honour.'

2–Robinson wrote on 9 Sept. 1930: 'I am preparing for publication two volumes of letters addressed to John Quinn and I am anxious to use some of yours. I enclose a selection in order that you may have the opportunity of correcting them, or deleting passages – but I hope you will not be too cautious. I may not have room for all that I send. If you have any personal memory of Quinn it would be a help for me to have it; I do not want to write a formal biographical sketch but many of his correspondents are writing for me about him – a few hundred words, and this is valuable material and if you would do something of the sort I shall be very much obliged.'

TO *George Boyle*   cc

18 September 1930   [Faber & Faber Ltd]

My dear Boyle,

This is the first opportunity I have had of thanking you for sending me the truly magnificent volume which you have brought out.[1] Even had it reached me otherwise than direct from you, I should have recognised your hand in it – both in the text, and in the very tasteful reminiscences of the Book of Kells. It also makes me reflect that if many of us did not have to bury our talent in banks – and publishing houses – what a lot of art would be released! We want to write poetry, and paint, and make good furniture and architecture (possibly the Staff might have done better to Lloyds Bank than Sir Somebody).

Just as I once knew no scenery but that of E.C.3. with excursions into E.C.2, E.C.4, and S.E.1) so now I know none but that of W.C.1. I am not sure that it is any more pleasing, and the environment is rather less lucrative. Publishing is more venturesome than banking, and involves even a greater amount of time spent in interviewing Bores. The only thing in its favour is that one is not called upon to hang about the Offices of the Mighty – only to be rebuked for one's ignorance of Hungarian or Czech or something equally recondite.

I am reminded that it is a long time since I have seen a copy of *The Dark Horse*.[2] Would that periodical accept me as Subscriber again – even if not as a Contributor – the subscription to be sent to me here, and the copies either here by post, or to 45, New Oxford Street, to be called for?

After all, I have not expressed my pleasure in the fact that you remembered me and sent me a copy of your beautiful book. I am delighted that I am not forgotten.

Yours sincerely,
[T. S. Eliot]

1–Boyle – a quondam colleague at Lloyds Bank, 71 Lombard Street, EC3 – sent on 5 Sept. 'the little book I have written & produced with the aid of some of my colleagues': *'Twixt Lombard Street and Cornhill: Designed, Written and Illustrated by the Staff of Lloyds Bank Limited* (1930). The volume was issued as a souvenir marking the opening of Lloyds' new premises at 71 Lombard Street, EC3.
2–*The Dark Horse*, a monthly magazine for Lloyds Bank staff, was launched in Oct. 1919.

18 September 1930   [68 Clarence Gate Gardens]

Dear Sirs,

C. H. Haigh-Wood Estate.

The Trustees, after consultation with Messrs. H. W. Birks & Co. and with the consent of the beneficiaries, have agreed to reinvest a sum of £300 capital, representing the re-purchase of £250 pref. shares 6% by the Eagle Oil Transport Co. Ltd., into shares (£1 fully paid) of the Alliance Insurance Co. Ltd. These yield at present only £4:12:–, and the inducement to purchase (apart from the high standing of the company) is the prospect of capital appreciation.

As this investment is not Trustee Stock, I presume that the Beneficiaries should sign some form of approval of the purchase. I am not sure whether Mr Maurice Haigh-Wood, being Trustee as well as Beneficiary, needs to sign such a form; but no doubt my wife ought to do so to make the ceremony legal.

I should be obliged if you would prepare and send me a statement to be signed by my wife, and by her brother if necessary; and I suggest that the form when signed should be held by you. I should be glad to hear from you expressly, before Messrs. Birks are instructed to make the purchase, that the transaction is quite correct and proper.

Messrs. Birks & Co (all three partners) have considered a list of Estate Securities which I gave them. They suggest that certain Trustee Stocks which are at a premium, but which are due for repayment within a few years, should be sold – as the premium on them is of course declining steadily. There does not appear to my mind to be any advantage in this, *unless* the money is re-invested in *non*-Trustee Stock (of the best quality of course, such as the best industrial debentures). But (as Trustee solely) I am myself rather doubtful of the advisability of diminishing the proportion of Trustee Stock in the Estate, considering that that proportion is fairly small as things are.

Yours faithfully,
[T. S. Eliot]

TO *H. W. Birks & Co.*   cc

Dear Sirs

in re Haigh-Wood Estate.

I thank you for your letter of the 17th instant, which I have considered carefully.

The question of the re-investment of the Trustee Stock which you advise selling is on a slightly different footing from the re-investment of the proceeds of the Eagle Oil Transport re-purchase. That not being itself a Trustee Stock, I was quite ready to approve the reinvestment in something (Alliance Assurance £1 f. p. shares) which is actually a sounder investment than that from which the money derives. But when gilt-edged stock is sold, I have to consider whether I can recommend investing the proceeds in anything not equally secure. Especially in view of the fact that only a moderate proportion of the Estate is invested in Trustee Stock already.

Now, if the securities you recommend selling are sold, and re-invested in Trustee Securities such as those you quote, I am not quite clear in my mind as to what the advantage will be. There will be (if my figures are correct) £1024 capital against the present £1000 value; but the present gross income appears to be £60 p.a. (all being 6% stock); whereas the re-investment of 5% would reduce the gross income to £51:4:–. Do I understand that the premium on the securities you suggest for reinvestment is likely to increase to such an extent as to override the loss of income to the present beneficiary, or that we can re-invest now in probability of better terms than if we waited until the present securities are paid off at par? I should be grateful for a little more light on this point.

As for the purchase of Alliance Assurance shares, agreed upon at our interview, I have written to the Solicitors to the Estate, to have their approval of the legality, and to ask them to prepare forms for the beneficiaries to sign. As soon as this is in order, I will let you have instructions for the purchase, and as Mr Maurice Haigh-Wood and myself were in agreement about it at our interview, I presume that my sole instructions will suffice.

Thanking you cordially for your trouble,

I am,
Yours faithfully
[T. S. Eliot]

19 September 1930   Faber & Faber Ltd

My dear Alport,

We gave a great deal of consideration to *Feinde Bismarcks*,[1] and also obtained a very long report upon it, before we decided to reject it. Personally I am very sorry that we cannot see our way to publishing it. I myself was the first reader, and although I had time only to read sections here and there, I found myself immensely interested and recommended it strongly. The only objection I had to make was that the first section on Ludwig seemed to me unnecessarily thorough.[2]

Our only grounds for rejecting the book were that we felt that the public in England for such a work would be very small, apart from those persons who are already interested in the subject and know German. I wish that we could have published it.

Jaeger's *Aristotle* is still hanging fire until next month, when we hope that the Syndics of Harvard University Press will entertain favourably our suggestion that they should participate in the publication.

With all best wishes,
Yours ever,
T. S. Eliot

---

1 – Alport wrote (1 Aug.): '[Otto] Westphal's publishers [R. Oldenbourg] have sent his book *Feinde Bismarcks* ['Bismarck's Enemies', 1930] to F. & F. at my request . . .'
2 – TSE wrote in his undated reader's report: 'The name of this book is pleasing but does not really give a fair idea of its purpose or content. The first section is a real, thorough-going attack on the charlatanism of Emil Ludwig as an historical biographer, which does the heart good. But that does not quite give the key to the work which is much more comprehensive. It is really a synthetic study of Germany in the Nineteenth Century, with particular relation to the place and standpoint of Bismarck as a representative of the German political idea. It deals not only with the attitudes of various people toward Bismarck, but with the previous history of the attitude which opposed Bismarck.

'Dr Westphal has in a very high degree that synthetic faculty at which German philosophers aim, but which few arrive at. The book is written in a clear and translatable style and I have actually read everywhere, with great interest, the pages which I have cut. I was very much impressed by the author's ability, and found myself really enthusiastic about it. Whether it would find any sale in England I do not know, but if it could be obtained cheaply I would be very much in favour of its publication. I think it is well worth getting a considered outside opinion upon it.'

TO *T. F. Burns*   CC

22 September 1930   [Faber & Faber Ltd]

Dear Burns,

Thank you for your letter of the 12th instant.[1] I am interested to hear of the venture of Gill and Hague, and am obliged to you for suggesting me as a contributor. There is no objection *a priori*; but I have nothing whatever to offer anybody at present; and when I do have anything, it will be a question to put to my own firm, whether they wish to publish it themselves. In the case of a short poem, for instance, which was suitable for publication as a pamphlet by itself, it might be more desirable for them than for us.

As for the other matter, I should be very grateful if you would put to Gill and Hague the following suggestion. Ezra Pound has been at work for a long time on a definitive edition of the poems of Guido Cavalcanti, which does not exist in Italy. Some great scholar or other in Italy has collaborated with him in the textual criticism. Translations of the poems, including some of Rossetti's, will be included. This book had already been taken and partly set up by the Aquila Press. I understand that, for financial reasons, the Aquila Press is unable to continue, and it is necessary to find some other publisher to take it on.

It is a fine limited edition and is not in the line of Faber & Faber. Of course I don't know what capital Gill and Hague have for publication, or whether they would consider anything of this scope, but, at a venture, I should like them to know of the existence of this book.[2]

With many thanks,

Yours ever,
[T. S. Eliot]

1 – René Hague and Eric Gill were starting up a private press, Pigotts Press, to be distributed by Sheed & Ward. Burns approached TSE with a view to issuing a limited print run of a poem by him, adding: 'I would dislike a publisher who went about seeking whom he might wrest from the hold of another . . . I hope you won't think this sudden question impertinent.' In 1937 Pigotts Press was to print *In Parenthesis*, by David Jones (1895–1974). See further Thomas Dilworth, 'T. S. Eliot and David Jones', *Sewanee Review* CII (Winter 1994), 70: TSE met Jones for the first time at lunch at Tom Burns's flat in Chelsea in 1930.

2 – See *Guido Cavalcanti Rime* (Genoa, 1932), reviewed by Étienne Gilson, C. 12 (Oct. 1932), 106–12.

TO *Donald Friede*[1]   CC

22 September 1930   [Faber & Faber Ltd]

Dear Mr Friede,

Thank you for your letter of September 12th.[2] I am ashamed to be unable to enlighten you at the moment on my bibliography, as I don't collect my own first editions or anybody else's. And I have no copy of that Hogarth Press edition in question. I can only tell you this, that the first copies bound and those which I saw were bound in the wallpaper, described by Fry. I think that there were seven short poems in the volume, and I am sure that THE HIPPOPOTOMOS [*sic*] was in the first edition. To the best of my knowledge and belief only one edition was printed by the Hogarth Press, but it is quite possible that later copies of the same edition were bound in a different paper. I seem to remember that objections were raised by some purchaser to the wallpaper cover, which might account for it. The whole edition has been out of print for over six years, I believe. I will, however, ask Leonard Woolf when he returns to town, and let you know if he has any further information.

                                        Yours sincerely,
                                        [T. S. Eliot]

TO *Charles K. Colhoun*   CC

22 September 1930   [Faber & Faber Ltd]

Dear Mr Colhoun,

It has taken me a little time to answer your letter because I had naturally to discuss the matter with the other directors.[3] I am afraid first of all that there is no direct relation between regular work for the *Criterion* and an opening in the publishing firm; except that the regular work and

---

1 – Of Covici Friede Inc.
2 – Friede owned a copy of the first edition of TSE's *Poems* (Hogarth Press, 1919) bound in a blue marbled paper, with a label printed in red. But he had seen that a New York bookseller was selling an edition printed in a wallpaper design of mottled yellow, terra cotta, and 'dirty yellow'. To complicate matters, Varian Fry, in his bibliography of TSE (*The Hound & Horn*, 1928), described the first edition as bound in 'grey figured wall-paper with outer surface turned in and the reverse marbled with red, yellow, green and black water-colours', and with the label printed in red. Did Friede have a first edition or not? See Gallup, 24–5.
3 – Colhoun asked on 12 Sept. whether there might be a chance for him to join F&F; he had the opportunity of employment in America, but would prefer to stay in London and work for F&F.

occasional meetings have prejudiced us in your favour. However, I am obliged to say categorically that at present and so far ahead as we can see, there is no prospect of our being able to make any additions to the firm, even if new capital were introduced. I am afraid that the same conditions obtain in all London publishing firms at present, and, indeed, so far as I know, in many other lines of business. A publishing house, however pleased it may be with its relative success, is just as sensitive to the general state of business and political depression as any other enterprise.

I shall be very sorry indeed if my reply causes your precipitation to America, but it is only fair to tell you exactly how things are, and not to raise false hopes. I suppose that you have gone into the question of the difficulty of getting into America and surmounting the present labour legislation in that country.

I hope that you will come in again soon, if you care to talk things over with me.

Yours sincerely,
[T. S. Eliot]

TO *Leonard Woolf*   TS Sussex

22 September 1930   Faber & Faber Ltd

Dear Leonard,

I have not attempted to communicate with you or Virginia for a long time, because I felt certain that you were in the country. But as the time approaches when your return to London may be expected, I am writing to ask when that may be, as I should very much like to see you both as soon as you have time. I hope you have both been well; but I have seen no one this summer except business connections and American visitors. It is a long time since I even had news of you.[1]

On the matter of business: I have promised a young man from Cambridge, named Edward Meryon Wilson, to submit to you a number of translations from Góngora, which he has made, sufficient for a book. The translations seemed to me very accomplished, when he first offered them, but, not knowing enough Spanish to make head or tail of an author like Góngora, I showed them to J. B. Trend, and have a highly favourable report from him which I can give you. To tell the truth I am not sure that

1–See VW, 24 Sept. 1930: 'Our friends work us very hard. Heres Tom Eliot: when are you back?' (*Diary* III, 320).

it is the sort of thing you would care to do: I first thought of the Oxford Press; but it is by request of Wilson himself that I am approaching you.[1]

With love to Virginia from both of us.

Yours ever,
Tom Eliot

TO *M. C. D'Arcy*   CC

25 September 1930   [Faber & Faber Ltd]

My dear D'Arcy,

Many thanks for your letter of the 23d. I am greatly flattered that you should want me to contribute to the volume you are to edit.[2] I cannot at the moment quite see how any attainments of mine qualify me to fill a place in it; but I should be very happy to be there, provided the undertaking will fit in with other things I have to do, and provided that you can convince me that there is something for me to write.

I should like to talk to you about it, and I am sorry that you are leaving town so soon. Now, I believe that Gordon George is coming to stay with us over Monday and Tuesday. I should be delighted if you cared to look in either Monday or Tuesday evening for coffee; *or*, alternatively, if it were better to discuss this matter quite by ourselves, would you lunch with me on Monday at the 'Royal Societies'? So could you please let me have word here by Saturday what time and place suits you best? In any case I should be very annoyed to have let one more vacation go by without seeing you.

With kind regards from my wife and myself,

Yours sincerely,
[T. S. Eliot]

1–'I shall be interested to see the Góngora,' replied LW (25 Sept.; *Letters*, 239).
2–D'Arcy was planning a volume of essays by various hands on the topic of Authority, financed by a wealthy man named Edward Eyre. 'I am hoping that I might persuade you to write the first chapter, which would be just a statement according to your own ideas of the present position of society . . . I do think you are the ideal person for this as you have represented the ideas of the modern generation.' As for payment, he added, it would be 'exceptionally high'.

TO *J. D. Aylward*   Photocopy of TS

25 September 1930   68 Clarence Gate Gardens

Dear Jas. De Vine Aylward,

This is to ask you, Sir, whether you are to be in London during the next two or three weeks; to ask you whether you would be prepared to consider lunching with me say the 2nd week in October at 63, St. James's (your own), whether you would signify the week-day of your preference; and generally to offer you my respects and the good wishes of my consort; and to express my regret that you were not chosen to skipper the *Shamrock V*; and to condole with you on the universal degeneracy of human nature, and the lack of respect shewn by the Public to artists & philosophers.[1]

> I am, Sir,
> Yrs. for all Honble. Service
> T. S. Eliot

TO *George Boyle*   CC

25 September 1930   *The Criterion*

My dear Boyle,

Many thanks for sending me the last numbers – and for spurning my offered Capital.[2] The least I can do in return is to place the *Dark Horse* on the Exchange List of the *Criterion* – a much less readable publication, and which no living human being, including the Editor himself, has ever been known to read entire. But perhaps you might review our pamphlets on Unemployment & Protection, by Comyns Carr, Ernest Benn, and L. S. Amery?[3]

I am glad to hear that our friend is still flourishing, but equally glad to hear that your partnership is dissolved. As soon as I can find the time, and you are not too busy, I want to come down and get you to show me the new building.

---

1 – *Shamrock V*, a J-class yacht built in the UK in 1929 for Sir Thomas Lipton, competed unsuccessfully in the *America*'s Cup in 1930. One of Aylward's catchphrases was Figaro's '*Se hâtant de se moquer de tout, par crainte de devoir pleurer*' – 'hastening to laugh at everything, for fear of being compelled to weep'.

2 – Boyle thanked TSE (24 Sept.) for his 'charming letter re my book'; he would be delighted to put TSE on the mailing list for the periodical *The Dark Horse*, and would not expect payment.

3 – A. S. Comyns Carr, *Escape from the Dole* (Criterion Miscellany 19); Sir Ernest Benn, MP, *Unemployment and Work* (22); Rt. Hon. L. S. Amery, MP, *Empire and Prosperity* (23).

I am pleased to see the *Dark Horse* is flourishing; you have developed it a great deal since the early days.

> Sincerely yours,
> [T. S. Eliot]

TO *E. McKnight Kauffer*   MS Morgan

[end September 1930]   68 Clarence Gate Gardens, N.W.1[1]

Dear Ted,

I am delighted to have the beautiful drawing, with the inscription,[2] and shall have it framed to match the other (Simeon) which I appropriated.

I had not seen the original when in de la Mare's hands and was surprised by the difference. I must say that I like the colouring of the drawing you have given me very much better than that of the printed *Marina*. I wish that the poem had been printed according to this one.[3]

Until Marion called the other night we knew nothing of your illness. I do hope you are getting on: let me know when you would care to have me come to see you.

> Yours ever
> T. S. Eliot

The Hutchinsons showed us your *Don Quixote,* which we much admired. I should not have thought anything possible after Doré, but you have done it.[4]

1 – Written on notepaper headed 177, Clarence Gate Gardens, with '177' cancelled by hand.
2 – The McKnight Kauffer illustration to *Marina*.
3 – 'Kauffer's illustration for the Ariel edition of "Marina" shows neither a daughter nor any feminine image. It is a woodcut, predominantly blue and black, figuring forth a starlit sea in the background, and a double image of man in the foreground. A modern man, seen in profile and gazing at the sea, is joined to Hercules, who is one of the allusions in "Marina", and appears to be rising from him' (Schulman, 'Notes on the Theme of "Marina" by Eliot', 206).
4 – Miguel de Cervantes Saavedra, *Don Quixote de la Mancha*, with 21 colour plates by E. McKnight Kauffer (2 vols, London: Nonesuch Press, 1930). Kauffer replied on 6 Jan. 1931: 'I am encouraged to know that you like the Don Quixote. Now that I know you like it – I would like you to accept a copy from me. It will be here waiting for you.' When Pat Gilmour (Assistant Keeper, Modern Collection, The Tate Gallery) approached EVE in connection with a McKnight Kauffer exhibition she was planning, EVE replied: 'I wish I had McKnight Kauffer's original illustrations for the Ariel poems to lend you, but unfortunately they disappeared in the 'Thirties and I do not know what became of them, alas.' However, she went on, she still had the inscribed set of *Don Quixote* – 'the covers of which are water-stained, presumably as a result of wartime storing. There is also, framed, McKnight Kauffer's striking "portrait" of the knight which was so admired by TSE and was given to him by the artist or his wife' (EVE carbon).

TO *Henry Eliot*   TS Houghton

2 October 1930   68, Clarence Gate Gardens

My dear brother,

This is just to acknowledge receipt of a package containing Goldsmith, Addison, Antigone, and the Stearns Virgil. Also Paul & Virginia.[1] Also two of father's chess-problem books, which I prize particularly. Also another package received later, containing a copy of the Stearns coat-of-arms (identical with the coat displayed in *The Sentimental Journey*) presumably blazoned by Father, and certain early photographs. Of the latter, most I am delighted to have; but some I am returning to you, either because (1) I don't know who they are (2) I don't know why they have a family interest (e.g. Prof. Allen) or (3) because you have sent two copies of the same (one family group, before my arrival).

I have also your letter of Sept. 20, but not the parcel or parcels you mention therein. And I shall write presently in reply to the letter itself.

                                        Affectionately,
                                        Tom.

TO *G. H. Lane Fox Pitt-Rivers*   CC

2 October 1930   [Faber & Faber Ltd]

Dear Pitt-Rivers,

This is primarily to apologise for not having been able to let you know anything further beyond our meeting. It happens to be a moment when important decisions have to be delayed a little; our Chairman is also Estates Bursar of All Souls and the heaviest part of his work in that capacity falls in early October; so that I fear I cannot write to you at all definitely until a week hence. If you should have left for France, I suppose that letters will be forwarded from Hinton St Mary[2] – or alternatively,

---

1 – HWE had itemised, in a letter of 3 Sept.: '*Two volumes of Goldsmith*, containing The Bee and The Citizen of the World. I do not think Father ever had the other volumes. He loved the books, though, and they are full of his pencil marks. *The Virgil. Paul and Virginia*, which belonged to Father, and an *Antigone* of his, but I do not know whether that is the one you read or not; it has no sketches in it that I can find.' TSE's library holds Oliver Goldsmith, *The Miscellaneous Works*, new edn in six volumes: vols 3, 4, 5 and 6 in two (New York: William Durrell and Co., 1809), and *The Vicar of Wakefield*, illustrated by Rowlandson (London: R. Ackerman, 1823).
2 – Pitt-Rivers lived at the Manor House, Hinton St Mary, Dorset.

that you do not want to be bothered with correspondence at all while you are away.

I should be very glad to meet your friend Professor Mayo;[1] but I very rarely go out in the evenings, as, being a poor sleeper, I am instructed not to use my mind in the evening and to go to bed at ten. If a lunch were possible, it would be possible for me; if not, I should be glad, as a poor substitute, if Mr Mayo would communicate with me and lunch with me, under your absent auspices.

And if my old friend C. C. Little[2] should be in London, I should be very grateful if you would intimate to him that I should like very much to see him. He knows where to find me.

I hope, however, to be able to write to you before you have left England.

Yours sincerely,
[T. S. Eliot]

TO *James Houghton Woods*   CC

2 October 1930   [Faber & Faber Ltd]

Dear Woods,

I am writing to remind you that Faber & Faber are still waiting anxiously to know whether the Syndics of the Harvard University Press will, with your encouragement, consider favourably collaborating with me in an English translation of Jaeger's *Aristotle*. I need not remind you that both A. E. Taylor and H. H. Joachim wrote to me with enthusiasm about it.

Even if your reply is adverse, remember that it is always a pleasure to hear from you.

With kindest regards to Mrs Wood and yourself,

Yours sincerely,
[T. S. Eliot]

1–Elton Mayo (Cambridge, Mass.), whom Pitt-Rivers hoped to introduce to TSE.
2–Clarence C. Little (1888–1971): known to his Harvard friends as 'Pete'; scion of an upper-class Boston family; science researcher specialising in mammalian genetics and cancer; President of the University of Maine, 1922–5; of the University of Michigan, 1925–9; founding director of the Roscoe B. Jackson Memorial Laboratory at Bar Harbor; managing director of the American Society for the Control of Cancer (later the American Cancer Society); twice President of the American Society for Cancer Research, President of the American Eugenics Society; and, most controversially, Scientific Director of the Scientific Advisory Board of the Tobacco Industry Research Committee (later the Council for Tobacco Research), 1954–69.

TO *Rose Esther Haigh-Wood*   CC

6 October 1930   [68 Clarence Gate Gardens]

Dear M.I.L.,

I have a letter from Birks & Co. enclosing purchase note for 15 Alliance
Assurance Co. Ltd. £1 fully paid shares, which was the investment we
agreed upon to replace the 50 Eagle Transport Shares for which £300
was received. It only remains therefore to draw a cheque on the Trustees'
Account at the District Bank for £295:6:– to the order to Messrs. H. W.
Birks & Co., so if you will draw the cheque from the Trustees' Cheque
book which you have, and send it to me to sign also, I will forward it to
Birks. You will remember that this investment was Maurice's suggestion,
and that he and I discussed it with all the partners of Birks & Co., and
that Vivienne after consulting Mr James signed and left with him the form
of approval which he drew up for her as beneficiary. It is certainly a much
more reliable investment than the Eagle Oil which it replaces.

                                        Affectionately,
                                        [Tom]

TO *Director of Programmes, Copyright Section, BBC*
                                                            TS BBC

7 October 1930   Faber & Faber Ltd

Dear Sir,

In reply to your letter P/RJFH, of the 3rd instant, may I point out first
that, as my name is in the telephone book, you have, in sending the letter
to Liverpool, adopted an unnecessarily circuitous procedure.[1]

In reply to the first paragraph of your letter, I have no objection to your
broadcasting *The Hollow Men* and *Journey of the Magi*. I must point
out, however, that *Death by Water* is not a poem, but merely *one section*
of a poem, and I have the strongest objection, therefore, to allowing it
to be used by itself. If, on the other hand, you cared to have your reader
rehearse the two poems above mentioned, <and/or some other approved
poem>, I should be ready to assist him.

As for the second paragraph of your letter, I should be grateful if you
could give me more details about the forthcoming production of the

---

1–The letter had been addressed to TSE 'c/o Editorial Department, Literary Year Books
Press, Ltd., Liverpool'.

Hogarth Press; the authors included, and the terms which will be offered them.[1]

Yours faithfully,
T. S. Eliot

TO *E. Munguía Jnr.*[2]   CC

8 October 1930   [Faber & Faber Ltd]

Dear Sir,

In reply to your undated letter, I am greatly honoured by your design.[3] I have already heard of you from Mr Fletcher.

I must let you know, however, that THE WASTE LAND has already been translated into Spanish by Mr Angel Flores, and published in Madrid by the Edicion Cervantes.[4] If, however, you are still interested in attempting a translation yourself, I can see no reason why there should not be a fair field; and would only ask you, as a necessary condition, to let me see a copy of it for suggestions, before publication.[5]

With many thanks,
Yours sincerely,
[T. S. Eliot]

TO *C. Platonoff*   CC

8 October 1930   [Faber & Faber Ltd]

Dear Mr Platonoff,

You may remember lunching with me and Harry Crofton some time ago at my club, and my suggesting that it would be a great pleasure if you could come and have tea with me here, and a quiet talk one day.[6] I do not

---

1 – 'We are asking the Hogarth Press to write to you direct on the subject of reprinting.'
2 – Enrique Munguía (1903–40), Secretaría de Relaciones, Mexico, was a regular contributor to the monthly review *Contemporáneos* (he had translated essays by John Gould Fletcher and others).
3 – Munguía asked permission to publish a Spanish prose translation of *The Waste Land*, under the title *El Páramo*.
4 – *Tierra Baldía*, trans. Angel Flores (Barcelona: Editorial Cervantes, 1930).
5 – *El Páramo*, trans. Munguía, *Contemporáneos* 26/27 (July/Aug. 1930), 15–32.
6 – Crofton told TSE (28 Sept.), 'Platonoff's condition is unfortunately unchanged . . . I know he would love to have a talk. It is very good of you to remember him, but it is a very sad case.'

know what is most convenient for you, but any Wednesday or Thursday after this week would suit me very well, and it would be a great pleasure to renew your acquaintance.

Yours sincerely,
[T. S. Eliot]

TO *Marguerite Caetani*   CC

8 October 1930   [68 Clarence Gate Gardens]

Dear Marguerite,

I have been meaning to write to you for a long time in reply to your previous kind letter – and, by the way, our present address at 68 Clarence Gate Gardens, Regent's Park, N.W.1. is really valid, because I have so impoverished myself by moving, that we must now stay where we are, whether we like it or not.

About detective stories for Camillo;[1] I should unhesitatingly recommend all the stories of Freeman Wills Croft, most of which are now published at a shilling by Collins. Another good lot are those of Austin Freeman, which are obtainable also at a shilling or two. When so many good detective stories are obtainable at a shilling, I see no point in paying seven-and-six merely to read a book six months ahead of other people. I am not in favour of the stories of J. J. Connington and Lynn Brock (the Colonel Gore stories), because the first is sometimes, and the second usually, concerned with extremely nasty people, and I do not consider them suitable for either young or old. I am glad that Camillo is getting on so well with his examination. I have lost count of the years and do not remember how soon he is coming up to Oxford. I hope that event, at least, will induce you to visit England.

[*Unfinished.*]

---

1 – Caetani wrote (undated): 'I have had an awful fright with Camillo who seemed to be in for typhoid, but it is apparently liver. Anyhow we would be very grateful for the titles of 3 or 4 of the best detective stories you know.' (Camillo [1915–1940], last male heir of the Caetanis, was to be killed on the Albanian front in WW2.)

8 October 1930   [Faber & Faber Ltd]

Dear MacCarthy,

Many thanks for your letter and for sending me the two copies of *Life and Letters*. I have arranged for the *Criterion* to be sent regularly as an exchange.[2]

I think I agree almost entirely with your views on Huxley and Lawrence.[3] The only point I have to make about Huxley is that this sort of intellectual curiosity without any serious effort to decide what is worthwhile being curious about fails altogether to interest me; and the Huxley point of view seems to me in the end to be merely callow. I feel that Aldous is lacking in some element essential to a mature mind. I enjoyed your essay

---

1 – Desmond MacCarthy (1877–1952), literary and drama critic, was closely associated with the Bloomsbury Group. Literary editor of *NS*, 1920–7, editor of *Life and Letters*, 1928–33, he was from 1928 principal literary reviewer of the *Sunday Times*. See Hugh and Mirabel Cecil, *Clever Hearts: Desmond and Molly MacCarthy* (1990).

2 – MacCarthy wrote on 3 Oct. with two back numbers of *Life & Letters* – he was interested in TSE's views of what he had said about DHL and AH – and to arrange an exchange of his magazine with C.

3 – MacCarthy noted, in 'Notes on Aldous Huxley', *Life and Letters* 5 (July–Dec. 1930), 198–209, that Huxley is 'a writer not "deep" but "wide"'. Critics must accept the fact that, 'since his supreme merit lies in width of reference, in putting facts in juxtaposition which his omnivorous reading and perpetual reflection have assembled, his novels and stories must perforce be discquisitions illustrated by characters' (207–8). 'Mr Aldous Huxley's loyalty is committed to "a cool indifferent flux of intellectual curiosity". It is his point; it makes him unique among English writers of fiction. He is an Anatole France, only far more learned, who has not attained to the suavity of indifference. He is therefore more interesting, but less successful as an artist' (209).

MacCarthy remarked, in 'Notes on D. H. Lawrence', *Life and Letters* 4 (Jan.–June 1930), 384–95: 'Lawrence's intellect and heart (his responses to what he loved and hated) did not always work together. His intellect was apt to run theorizing ahead of his perceptions and responses, or, turning back, to over-emphasize them or add a gloss with a view to propaganda' (389). 'His peculiarity as a writer is that he succeeds so extraordinarily in responding with his whole body to what is before him . . . Only of the judgements of the mind as to the nature of things was he distrustful, and he distrusted them because analytical observation and reason interrupted and destroyed that deep vascular response to them which he most valued. It is certainly a very serious limitation in one who set out to respond to life as a complete man that he should have omitted to use, as far as was consistent with sanity, the human reason' (391). 'The young are interested in personal, not in social problems. Lawrence has, therefore, something to say to them on two questions crucial to them: how to preserve an inner integrity and hold themselves together in spite of rejecting all rules of thumb on conduct, and how to prevent sexual life degenerating into squalor though belief in prohibitions is going. The main drift of Lawrence's work, the strongest infection from it, is reverence for sex' (392). 'What he did . . . has made it easier for those who follow to take into poetry and literature the whole of life' (395).

on Lawrence more for the reason that I am much more interested in the subject. With a great deal of what you

[*lines missing*]

did not arise from my having a lower opinion of Lawrence than Forster has, but from a feeling of impatience with a worthless generalisation.[1] What is wanted for Lawrence now is not praise or blame, but patient analysis. Concerning the two men together, it is interesting to remark that Lawrence was a man who could say the same thing over and over without once becoming boring, whereas a feeling of tedium began to creep over me after one or two Huxley books.

But it would be pleasanter to weave theories over a lunch table and I hope you will suggest a day or two before very long when we might lunch together.

Yours sincerely,
[T. S. Eliot]

TO *William Force Stead*   TS Beinecke

9 October 1930   Faber & Faber Ltd

Dear Stead,

I tried to telephone to you this evening at 16, Bedford Place, but Enquiry could not find the number. This is to say that Gordon George is staying with us at present,[2] and he would like you to lunch with us at the English Speaking Union, 37, Charles Street, Berkeley Sq., at 1:15 tomorrow (Thursday). I shall be bringing Kenneth Ingram also. I do hope you can

---

1 – MacCarthy picked up E. M. Forster's undemonstrated claim that DHL was the greatest imaginative novelist of the generation, and TSE's complaint that Forster's statement was meaningless unless the words 'great' and 'imaginative' were defined. 'Now all assertive terms of praise are apt to be vague. Unfortunately, I missed Mr Forster's reply . . . but since I agree with him and might easily have used those vague terms myself, let me explain what I would have meant by them. By "great" when applied to a novelist, I would have meant to suggest that the writer in question was chiefly concerned with some of the most important things in life and had a power of conveying his preoccupation with them adequate to their importance; by "imaginative" that the merit of his work at its best was akin to poetry, and that the world which he had created was subjective and every detail of it saturated with emotion. Both these statements hold true of Lawrence' (390).

2 – Sencourt related, after his visit to Clarence Gate Gardens, that VHE 'seems to have been positively hostile to [TSE's] new-found church affiliations, deriding them as "monastic" . . . She was developing a tendency to find fault with everything, both in herself and in those around her. She did not join in his worship' (*T. S. Eliot: A Memoir*, ed. Donald Adamson [1971], 112, 120).

come. Could you please ring up Ambassador 1518 in the morning when you get this? I wish very much to see you. (But I wish I could see you privately for a few minutes some time too, for there is so much between us that is strictly private, and we have not met for a long time. Perhaps we could have a word after lunch to arrange some other, even brief, meeting).

> Ever affectionately
> T. S. E.

TO *Gertrude W. Page*

9 October 1930   [*The Criterion*]

Dear Madam,

I have your letter of the 10th ultimo, and the complaint you make about duplication of articles is serious enough to require a reply.[1] You say that you are not standing in judgment upon the ethical question involved. So far as there is any ethical question for the English editor, it is simply that he never has sufficient funds at his disposal to be able to pay any contributors for the world rights, nor to my mind would he be morally justified in doing so, even if he had the money. It is only right that an author should be able not only to secure as high payment as he can get, but, particularly, as wide a circulation as he can get.

And I doubt very much whether any serious American periodical is either wealthy enough or unscrupulous enough to bribe its contributors not to appear in London periodicals.

If, however, the only type of magazine matter which interests you consists of the fiction and articles which appear on both sides of the water, then I can only say that you do not appear to be interested in the *viewpoint* of one periodical rather than another, and accordingly there is no reason why you should take in any English periodical at all. I am not setting up the pretension that the *Criterion* is superior to the best American literary reviews, when I assert that it does not coincide with, or duplicate, any of them.

> Yours faithfully,
> [T. S. Eliot]

1 – Gertrude Page (Los Angeles, California) said that she saw no good reason to subscribe to *C.* (she already subscribed to fifteen or more other magazines) when so many of the English articles appeared in periodicals on both sides of the Atlantic.

TO *Edward Thompson*[1]   TS Bodleian

11 October 1930   68, Clarence Gate Gardens

Dear Mr Thompson,

I have taken the liberty – assuming that you remember me as a director of Faber & Faber who happens to be particularly interested in India, who had a few words with you, or rather who listened greedily to a few words from you, the other day – of directing towards you one Sir George Curtis, K.C.S.I. who admires your work, who is equally and earnestly interested in India (he is a retired Indian Civil now living in France); and who is anxious to get published either in England or New York a translation of a French book on India (by one André Philip [*sic*]).[2] I met Sir G. Curtis because he is the father of a young friend of mine who is a slum priest in South London, and for whom I have a warm affection. But I was much impressed, on one meeting, with the generous interest of his father, who is really and unselfishly concerned with the well-being of India, and who I think you will find knows India well: a few words about a mutual acquaintance, George Lloyd,[3] convinced me of his impartiality; so I hope you will be able to see Curtis either in Oxford or London.

May I take the opportunity of saying that I very much wish to induce you to lunch with me on any visit to London; not because I am one of the publishers of your last book, but because what you said to me about India was so congenial to my own prejudices or intuitions: after all, I have had Indian friends, and my interest in India was enough to make me spend two or three years, at one more leisured period, in the study of Sanskrit and Pali.

Sincerely yours,
T. S. Eliot

1–Edward Thompson (1886–1946), historian, novelist, translator, taught English literature in Bengal from 1910, becoming friends with Rabindranath Tagore, and later with Indian politicians and others. From 1923 he taught Bengali to Indian Civil Service probationers in Oxford, translated works from Bengali into English, and was celebrated as an expert on India; he was a Leverhulme Research Fellow, 1934–5; Hon. Fellow and Research Fellow in Indian History at Oriel College, Oxford, 1936–40. Works include *Rabindranath Tagore: Poet and Dramatist* (1926); *A History of India* (1927); *The Reconstruction of India* (F&F, 1930); *A Letter from India* (1932).
2–*L'Inde moderne*.
3–George Lloyd, first Baron Lloyd of Dolobran (1879–1941): Tory politician and colonial administrator; High Commissioner for Egypt and the Sudan, 1924–9; director of Lloyds Bank; Anglo-Catholic. See J. Charmley, *Lord Lloyd and the Decline of the British Empire* (1987).

TO *George Malcolm Thomson*   CC

13 October 1930   [Faber & Faber Ltd]

Dear Thomson,

I must apologise for not giving you the enclosed when I saw you. I found it in the envelope with your typescript.

Don't forget that we are going to lunch together on Thursday next, by which time I look forward to the revised *Lambeth Conference*.[1]

Sincerely yours,

[T. S. Eliot]

1–GCF had written to Thomson on 10 Oct. 1930:

'Reading through the proofs of *The Lambeth Conference* [Criterion Miscellany 23] I could not help feeling that you were in real danger of spoiling the effectiveness of your attack by allowing yourself too many and too easy gibes at the unfortunate Bishops. I am writing to ask you if you will not alter some of these references. I do this, with the less hesitation, because I am myself largely of your way of thinking. I am bound to say that, in spite of my disposition to enjoy an attack on the Lambeth Conference and its report, I found myself so much irritated by these references that I began to take up cudgels, mentally, on the other side. But I suppose you don't want your pamphlet to produce a hostile reaction in favour of the Bishops!

'I have marked in blue pencil on the proof you have already corrected the passages which most affected me in this way.

'Page 6. "consecrated". Whether they are consecrated or not has nothing to do with their thinking; the epithet only exhibits the pamphleteer's contempt for consecreation. Couldn't you find another?

Page 7. The reference to white slavery is rather uncalled for, don't you think? The supposition that they *could* approve is too ludicrous, even to be suggested by way of ironic denial. It only weakens your case, and may very easily be quoted as an example of needless offensiveness. Wouldn't you be content to substitute something like the following? "Incidentally, if the Bishops needed to condemn the drug traffic, why do they ignore the white slave traffic? When they etc." This makes the point you are after, and avoids any objection. The substitution I suggest is approximately the same length as the original, and therefore means the minimum of resetting.

Page 8. One says: "It's a weak case that needs to use this kind of sneer." Why not say, instead: "Nothing of the kind! The Bishops are well aware etc."

Page 10. Top line. "Their Lordships" again. Might I suggest "The question would seem to be settled. But the Bishops have not quite done with it."

"Criminal" seems a rather hyperbolic epithet. Why not "an absurd"?

Line 14 & 15. My objection here is not that the parenthesis is rude, but that it seems to me pointless. Perhaps I am dense; but the irony escapes me. I wouldn't press for its alteration; but I do think the passage would gain by being differently expressed. e.g. "It seems to refer – but the inhibitions of the Bishops prevent them from telling us what they are actually talking about – to the etc."

Page 15. I don't think the "episcopal pack" metaphor is a very happy one. Do you think you could end the paragraph differently?

'I expect you will think me absurdly squeamish. But I'm not alone in thinking that the pamphlet would gain in force by the alteration of the passages I have marked. So, if you can bring yourself to do so, I hope very much you will accept these comments, even if you privately think them unnecessary!'

TO *Edward Thompson*

MS Bodleian

14 October 1930   Faber & Faber Ltd

Dear Mr Thompson,

This morning I have simultaneously your letters of the 12th and 13th. I quite agree with you about the impossibility of your taking over Sir Geoffrey [*sc.* George] Curtis's responsibility.[1] I could see no reason myself why he should not allow his name to appear, and I daresay that it was merely because of Lloyd's views. I pointed out to him that if we could not use his own name or Lloyd's or anybody's else, the book would be of little use to us; and I merely sent him on to you because he admired your book and I thought you might give him some sensible advice. And he was very anxious to meet you.

As for the 27th, I should be delighted if we could lunch together on that day, and incidentally it might prevent you from circulating rumours that the weekends of publishers are longer than those of stockbrokers.[2]

Yours sincerely,
T. S. Eliot

TO *Leonard Woolf*

TS Reading

14 October 1930   Faber & Faber Ltd

Dear Leonard,

Very many thanks for your letter of the 10th.[3] The B.B.C. wrote to me first, as I told you, but were so vague about the matter of publication, that I thought it best to apply for information to you. They asked also for permission, both for broadcasting and for your anthology, to use *Death by Water*; but I told them that I objected strongly to have *The Waste Land*

---

1 – Sir George Curtis had suggested that his translation of the book might be published as by Thompson, who responded decisively in the negative. Thompson replied on 12 Oct.: 'And I want to be soon emeritus as regards this whole Indian controversy . . . And my name seems to be mud in such American papers as reach me . . . and in India it is being suggested that I was paid out of Indian revenues to conduct what is called my "mischievous anti-Indian propaganda".'

2 – Thompson had teased TSE by saying that 'a publisher's weekend extends from Thursday to Tuesday' – so that the day he suggested for lunch, a Monday, might prove difficult for TSE.

3 – 'It was suggested to us that we might publish an anthology of poems now being broadcast in the British Broadcasting Corporation's series of modern poetry. We should very much like to include "The Hollow Men" and "Journey of the Magi" for which I believe you have given permission to read in the series. We would pay a fee of two guineas per poem' (EVE).

mutilated by any fragment appearing in this way. But in the circumstances I have no objection to your using *The Hollow Men* and *Journey of the Magi*.

I gather from your postmark that you have now returned to London, and will write soon to suggest a day or two next week when I should like to come to tea. We are also anxious to get you to come and see us in our new flat.

With love to Virginia,
Yours ever,
T. S. E.

P.S. You remember my writing to you when you were at Rodmell about some translations from Góngora by a young man named Meryon Wilson, which were very well reported on by J. B. Trend? I am now sending them. If you can't do anything with them, will you let me know, as I have promised in that event to recommend him to one of the University Presses?[1]

T. S.E.

TO *Herbert Gorman*[2]   TS Southern Illinois

14 October 1930   Faber & Faber Ltd

Dear Mr Gorman,

In reply to your letter of the 6th: I must really say seriously that your 'congenital shyness' is either a blind for a desire for privacy (which I respect) or if not has reached the point of morbidity at which it ought to be controlled. But if you are not Fleeing (rather than Flying) until the 27th, will you not ring up and suggest coming in to see me one morning?[3]

1–LW replied on 23 Oct. 1930: 'I am afraid I must return The Solitudes of Góngora, translated by Wilson. I do not think we could do anything with it. It is, of course, interesting, but the English verse seems to me rather poor quality' (EVE). Wilson wrote again to TSE on 11 Dec., 'I wonder if you could tell me what the Hogarth Press are thinking about my poems.'

2–Herbert Gorman (1893–1954): American author and journalist. In 1926 he met JJ, who authorised him to write a study which ultimately appeared as *James Joyce: A Biography* (1940).

3–Gorman claimed 'a congenital shyness' had prevented him from seeing TSE throughout the summer. He was in London until 27 Oct. – 'when I fly to Paris (figuratively – not by air) . . .'

The matter of the Joyce record is one which I have discussed with Joyce himself, and a few days ago with Ogden.[1] I find that Ogden (who promised me a record many months ago, which I have not received) is perfectly willing that somebody else should do something about it. What I proposed to him, and what I shall propose to my board, is this: that the existing Joyce records should be deposited at Faber & Faber's, instead of in Cambridge; but first of all I wish to circularise all the people who might be interested, in England and America, to say that the record can be provided. I believe that it can be imported in France also, but am not sure. We should have to arrange with Ogden a distribution of receipts, because I could not ask my firm to store the records, and deal with the subscribers, postage, etc. at a loss. Where you could help this is in providing a list of probable American subscribers to the record.

Furthermore, I should like to see the work continue. Ogden says that it could be carried on if – as I suggested to him – a Society could be formed of even 25 people who would be willing to take a record by some distinguished author, at regular intervals, at an agreed price. It seems to me, that if we could get a respectable Editorial Board, that there should be at least 50 persons in England and America who would gladly subscribe – for it is much more interesting than any Book of the Month Club – to say four records a year – maximum subscription say seven or eight guineas – by noted authors – probably it would be impossible to turn out more than four a year: I feel sure that there *must* be an affluent public for gramophone readings by other authors than Joyce: even with *my* small means, I should like to possess gramophone records by Yeats, Virginia Woolf, etc.

I should like to discuss this project with you. Will you come to see me before you leave England?

Sincerely yours,
T. S. Eliot

1 – JJ had approached Gorman about the recording of *A.L.P.* arranged by Ogden, who had apparently gone off the idea. The consequence was that JJ could not even get hold of a copy of the record for himself. 'I wonder if you have any suggestions about this matter . . .?'

14 October 1930   Faber & Faber Ltd

My dear Eleanor,

I sit in sackcloth & ashes, but hope that you will shrive me. It is not that I did not read the play.² It is that whenever I have gone to my desk with the intention of writing to you, I have seen on the top of my tray, and also at the bottom, the Works of various poets and other writers who have written to me, and whom indeed I have weakly encouraged, to ask for Opinions and Advice; I have thought, these Hungry Sheep³ need my attention first, so conscience has deferred my writing to you – I must add that laziness has usually deferred my writing to them. It is odd that when you produce a certain form of literary composition yourself, such as verse, you feel that every aspirant in the same form has some claim upon you; and somehow it works out, that the more incompetent the aspirant, the greater the claim. One of the most definitely unpromising of my young incubusses (so to speak) has given me the most trouble: I got him a job in a bank in Paris; he got fired from that job; got work in a steamship agency; and now writes to say that he really *must* throw off this intolerable drudgery and devote himself seriously to poetry, and will I comment upon his latest manuscripts? Then there is a 'medical student' who wrote severely to tell me that lately my verse had become 'even worse than the worst that Edith Sitwell has written', but who nevertheless wants my opinion on his own, which appears to me to be nothing but the immediate effervescence of some 'companionate marriage'.⁴ Then there

---

1–Eleanor Holmes Hinkley (1891–1971): TSE's first cousin, second daughter of Susan Heywood Stearns (1860–1948) – TSE's maternal aunt – and Holmes Hinkley (1853–91), a scholar 'of rare modesty and delicacy of temperament'. Eleanor studied at Radcliffe College in Cambridge, Mass. – among the advanced courses she took was Professor George Baker's '47 Workshop' – and went on to act with Baker's group and to write plays for it (see *Plays of 47 Workshop*, 1920). Her other productions included *A Flitch of Bacon* (1919) and *Mrs Aphra Behn* (1933). *Dear Jane*, a comedy in three acts about Jane Austen written in 1919, was to be produced by Eva Le Gallienne at the Civic Repertory Theater, New York, for eleven performances in Nov. 1932. It was through amateur theatricals held at her family home, 1 Berkeley Place, Cambridge, Mass., that TSE met and fell in love with Emily Hale (Biographical Register, *L* 1) in 1912. EVE remarked, in an interview in 1971 with Timothy Wilson: 'His Stearns cousin who wrote plays, is a mixture of a Jane Austen and a Henry James character. I think she had the most understanding of Tom's work – sadly she died this year.'
2–*White Violets*, a murder mystery.
3–'the hungry sheep look up, and are not fed, / But swoln with wind, and the rank mists they draw, / Rot inwardly, and foul contagion spread' ('Lycidas', 125).
4–See letter to LW, 16 May 1930 above.

---

is the lonely schoolmaster in Trinidad, who writes stories which are the weakest possible imitation of Joseph Conrad, who is so humble (the really humble ones give the most trouble) that he will welcome *any* suggestions for improvement, as he has no one to talk to etc. Why any of these should disturb me, instead of half a dozen more prominent editors, I cannot make out; but I find that the really prominent editors are more attacked than I am. Anyway, this is merely a sketch of my reasons for not writing sooner.

Well: I have never *seen* any detective play, even one by the eminent Edgar Wallace; so I have no criterion; and a play is a play, and cannot be judged by a reading. But I really did find yours very exciting. I thought that the setting on an island – in Casco Bay or where? – extremely clever, the siren from the penal settlement very effective – reminded me of *Great Expectations* and the grand scene on the marsh. Also the surprises very effective, no delay about the movement, dramatically I thought perfect. I can see no reason, as a layman, why the play should not go with a bang. *My* only difficulty was with some of the characters themselves. They don't seem to belong to Beacon or Brattle St, or to any world that I know; and I am never sure, in such cases, how far it is that America has changed, and how far it is merely that I never knew America. They seem (some of them) extremely vulgar: I have become accustomed to the vulgarity of England – and it takes one years to perceive how profoundly vulgar can be that society in England which has the most glittering superficies of culture – and disaccustomed to the vulgarity of America – not, from this point of view, quite so corrupt. So I say it is not the structure but the characters that bother me; and I should be very grateful if you could give me a little light. Anyway, I enjoyed the play very much. May I keep the text?[1]

I have just sent you one or two things of mine. I infer that you did not like *Ash Wednesday*, as you never acknowledged it?[2]

We saw Penelope[3] several times, and Emily[4] once, this summer; so you will have had some reports of us. We are in a new flat, which is not a bad

1 – Eleanor replied (26 Oct.): 'By all means keep White Violets till I come over.'
2 – 'It wasn't because I didn't like *Ash Wednesday* (which I liked, in fact, the very best of anything you have done) but because my heart always sinks at the thought of writing anything that will be critically intelligent enough to interest you . . . – I liked it *immensely* (though I shall always have lurking tenderness for Animula over anything you may ever write).'
3 – Penelope Noyes, 1 Highland Street, Cambridge, Mass.
4 – Emily Hale (1891–1969): intimate friend of TSE; daughter of a Unitarian minister, the Revd Edward and Emily (Milliken) Hale, with lifelong Unitarian affiliations of her own. Brought up in Chestnut Hill and Cambridge, Mass., she taught at this time at Scripps College, California; later at Milwaukee Downer; Smith College; Concord Academy; Abbott Academy.

one. Vivienne joins with me in regret that you did not come over again this year: may it be next year?

With love to Aunt Susie,

Ever affectionately (and repentently [*sic*])

Tom

TO *Edward Dahlberg* CC

14 October 1930   [Faber & Faber Ltd]

Dear Dahlberg,

I seem to have been a very long time in writing to you about *Chelsea Rooming-House*; the delay has been due partly to the summer holidays, and collecting the necessary opinions.[1] Of course, for all I know, other arrangements may now have been made; nevertheless, we are prepared to publish them on agreed terms and I am writing first to ask whether the volume is still free, and if so, whether arrangements about the English rights are in the author's hands, or in those of Covici Friede.

Our proposal generally would be as follows; we should set up the book here, in a format and size similar to that of the two volumes of poems which I am sending you under another cover and which, by the way, I recommend. We should wish to be allowed permission to omit some poems at our discretion, and to publish a book at about the size and price

---

Lyndall Gordon, *T. S. Eliot: An Imperfect Life* (1998): 'Emily Hale returned to England in the summer of 1930, attending a Shaw Festival at Great Malvern . . . and lecturing for the Art Poetry Circle of the Lyceum Club and the American Women's Club in London. She stayed, at least some of the time, at Burford in the Cotswolds. Eliot wrote to her there in September, and once again on 6 October at an unknown address . . . Emily Hale . . . later told an ex-pupil: "A very dear friend of mine was involved, early in life, with a weak and selfish and seriously unstable partner. For many years I observed the blighting effect of this marriage on my friend"' (239). (The letter to an ex-pupil is quoted from T. S. Matthews, *Great Tom* [1973], 148.) Gordon notes: 'TSE wrote to her c/o Mrs R. H. Gretton, "Calendars", Burford, in Sept., and again on 6 Oct. to an unknown address. Princeton.' TSE's letters at Princeton are embargoed.

1–Dahlberg had first mentioned the 32-year-old Horace Gregory (1898–1982) to TSE – with reference to his forthcoming volume of poems, *Chelsea Rooming House* – on 25 June 1930: 'I feel he has discovered new pictorial and dramatic effects and that he is using the American language with vigorous originality and pliancy.' He wrote again on 21 July: 'I am sending you the proofs of *Chelsea Rooming-House* . . . I think [Gregory] has a big talent . . . What he is doing seems to me extremely significant, and on rereading them, I find myself very impressed by the poet's strange sense of deterioration . . .' Gregory's poems, he went on, were better than his own – 'have more impersonality and power, than mine. Besides, they are far superior in form.'

of one of these volumes (personally, I think that Gregory's book would be improved by some excision). And we should want to alter the title because of the different connotations of the word 'Chelsea' in New York, Boston and London. I think myself that the title simply *Rooming-House* would be good; the word 'rooming-house' is not familiar in English of course, but Gregory's poems are so positively local that this might be an advantage.

This is really a formal publisher's letter, so I am saying nothing about my own opinion of the poems, which you may for the moment take for granted, and I am deferring again, for a little while, a personal letter to yourself about your own work. If we published Gregory's book, I think we should want to do so early in the Spring, so I should be very grateful if you would let me know about it, or else put me in touch with Gregory and shew him the two books I am sending you.[1]

With all best wishes,
Yours sincerely,
[T. S. Eliot]

TO *D. S. Mirsky*   CC

14 October 1930   [Faber & Faber Ltd]

Dear Mirsky,

I have brought up the question of your essays[2] with my directors and while we are, from experience, very hesitant to publish volumes of collected essays by anyone whomsoever, I should still be very interested to see as much of the projected volume as you could let me have, and would promise to give you a quick decision about them. If you could let me have some or all of the material at once – the Tchehov [Chekhov] I very much admired – I should like to suggest your lunching with me soon after.

1–Dahlberg replied to this letter on 15 Nov. 1930: 'I am very grateful to you for the time and attention you gave to Gregory's book of poems. He is extremely pleased that the publication of his book should come through your hands . . . The title, *Rooming House* is very good.' However, Dahlberg was to write to Isabella Gardner on 7 Nov. 1958: 'I never cared much for Eliot as a poet, but liked him as a man. I persuaded him, being very wily, the meek Saint John the Baptist, to print *Chelsea Rooming House* in England. This was an enormity, for I did not ever like the book very much, but at that time I was very fond of Horace Gregory' (*Epitaphs of Our Times: The Letters of Edward Dahlberg* [1967], 225).
2–Mirsky raised the question of his 'collected literary essays' in a letter to TSE of 5 Oct. 1930.

By the way, would you be willing to review for the *Criterion* John Gould Fletcher's *Europe's Two Frontiers*? I am sure that Fletcher would not expect your review to be particularly favourable, but that he also would be very interested in your opinion.[1]

Yours sincerely,
[T. S. Eliot]

TO *Hugh Macdonald*

MS Williamson

15 October 1930   Faber & Faber Ltd

Dear Macdonald,

Thank you for your letter and for the cheque for five guineas.[2] I have received my seven copies today and quite agree with the praise given by the *Observer* to the production.[3] Certainly you could not have done it in any way which could have pleased me better.

It is very kind and tactful of you to say that you like the essay so much; all the more as the prospects for the book do not seem very bright. As soon as I can find a clear time I shall ask you to come and lunch with me.

With many thanks,
Yours ever,
T. S. Eliot

---

1 – Review of *Europe's Two Frontiers*, C. 10 (Apr. 1931), 534–6.

2 – Macdonald wrote on 13 Oct.: 'The *Johnson* was published on Friday. I am sending you six copies of the ordinary edition and one of the special. Let me know if you want more . . . The book has not been subscribed very well, but times are hard for this sort of book . . . [T]hank you very much indeed for the essay. I think it among the very best of your critical writings & it has given us great pleasure to publish the book.' (150 signed copies at £1. 1/–, and 300 at 10/6.)

3 – 'This is a tall folio containing Dr Johnson's two satires, with an introductory essay by Mr T. S. Eliot. Mr Eliot thinks nobly of "London" and "The Vanity of Human Wishes", and praises the Doctor, above all, for the admirable, precise placing of his rapier in satiric fence . . . And the format of the book could hardly be bettered in its plain, spacious, and proportioned style. Mr Etchells and Mr Macdonald have surpassed even themselves in this production' ('Books and Authors', *The Observer*, 12 Oct. 1930, 8).

TO *Francis Underhill*[1]   CC

16 October 1930   [Faber & Faber Ltd]

Dear Father Underhill,

Thank you for your letter of the 15th.[2] I am very sorry to have to choose the later date, but this coming week is an extraordinarily busy one for me, and I shall have very little time for meditation. Incidentally, I have to read a paper on Wednesday and it may amuse you to hear that Dean Inge is in the chair.[3]

So I shall accept gladly for Friday, the 31st, at twelve-forty-five. Thank you very much.

> Yours sincerely,
> [T. S. Eliot]

TO *Kenneth Ingram*   CC

16 October 1930   [Faber & Faber Ltd]

My dear Ingram,

I am writing to tell you that I am not sure that I shall be able to come to the first meeting of the Grecian Club.[4] This is a very busy week for me, and furthermore, my wife is in bed with laryngitis of indefinite duration.

1–Revd Francis Underhill, DD (1878–1943) – TSE's spiritual counsellor – Anglican priest and author; Warden of Liddon House and priest in charge of Grosvenor Chapel, Mayfair, London, 1925–32; later Dean of Rochester, 1932–7; Bishop of Bath and Wells from 1937. His publications include *The Catholic Faith in Practice* (1918) and *Prayer in Modern Life* (1928). TSE would notify the Revd D. V. Reed on 30 Mar. 1961 that he 'continued to be a penitent of Father Underhill during his period as Dean of the Cathedral' – i.e. Rochester Cathedral, 1932–7.

2–'What about . . . luncheon next Wednesday the 22nd . . . Or the same thing on Friday the 31st?'

3–TSE read 'The Place of Pater' at the Royal Society of Literature, Dr Inge presiding, on 22 Oct. The Very Revd W. R. Inge (1869–1954), 'the gloomy Dean', Dean of St Paul's, 1911–34, wrote on theology, politics and society – his works include *Lay Thoughts of a Dean* (1926) and *Wit and Wisdom of Dean Inge* (1927) – and wrote a column for the *Evening Standard*, 1921–46.

4–The Grecian Club was established to provide an opportunity for the discussion of philosophical, ethical, scientific, aesthetic and other problems, and to ensure that a wide diversity of views was represented. The Club came to include in its ranks legal, literary, scientific, ecclesiastical and other interests, and its membership embraced Christians of various schools, Jews, agnostics, and 'those whose religious opinions could not perhaps be exactly labelled'. Meeting on the third Tuesday of each month, the Club took its name from the meetings conducted in the eighteenth century at the Grecian Coffee House, outside the Temple.

In any case, I shall certainly come on Tuesday, November 18th. I saw the Master of the Temple[1] the other day, and he expressed great interest in the project.

Our lunch last week was very pleasant and I was glad to be able to introduce three people with strongly similar interests, but it will be more satisfactory still if you come to lunch with me one day, as we originally intended, privately, before November 18th. Would Tuesday the 21st, at one o'clock at 63 St James' Street be a possible date?[2]

Yours sincerely,
[T. S. Eliot]

TO *Algar Thorold*   CC

16 October 1930   [*The Criterion*]

My dear Thorold,

Thank you for your card. I am glad to hear that I may expect your review for the December number. Don't, I pray, try to be too safe.

I am afraid that I blundered stupidly about Bedoyère.[3] I really forgot, after you brought him to tea, how soon he was leaving London; when I was able to write and suggest a lunch, I suppose they had already left as I have had no reply. Will you please tell him that I was very sorry not to see him again and will you please remind him to write to me if there is any prospect of his visiting Boston, so that I may provide introductions to a few people whom I should like him to meet. By the way, Gordon George has left us and is now staying at the Mascot Hotel, York Street, W.1, where I have been visiting him as he is in bed with a bad cold. I enjoyed his stay very much.

---

1 – S. C. Carpenter, MA, DD (1877–1959): Master of the Temple, 1930–5; Chaplain to the King, 1929–35; Dean of Exeter, 1935–50. His works include *The Anglican Tradition* (1928).
2 – Ingram and TSE lunched together on that day.
3 – Thorold wrote on 10 Aug. of Michael de la Bedoyère (1900–73), his nephew and son-in-law, that TSE would find him 'very bright & receptive – at the moment rather in reaction against Scholastic thought, but I think this is merely a matter of necessary readjustment . . .' Educated as a scholastic and philosopher – he had entered the Society of Jesus, and gained first-class honours in philosophy, politics and economics at Campion Hall, Oxford, before a crisis of faith caused him to relinquish his noviciate – de la Bedoyère (who was by birth a count in the French nobility) worked for a time as assistant editor to Thorold on the *Dublin Review* before becoming editor of the *Catholic Herald*, 1934–62. Works include *The Drift of Democracy* (1931), *Lafayette* (1933), *Christian Crisis* (1940), and a study of Baron von Hügel.

My private address you now know and the telephone number is Ambassador 1518, so that if we can put in a lunch I hope you will let me know.

Yours,
[T. S. Eliot]

TO *Ernest Rhys*[1]

TS Texas

16 October 1930   Faber & Faber Ltd

Dear Mr Rhys,

Thank you for your letter of the 14th.[2] I am not so surprised to find you associating Pascal with London Bridge as I am to find you associating Pascal with myself. I am surprised also to learn that Pascal's *Pensées* are not yet included in the 'Everyman Library'. Also I feel that there are many other people available who could do the job much better than I; for instance, Bishop Gore, and Algar Thorold, and indeed a number of other people. On the other hand, it is a great temptation to me, especially in view of Aldous Huxley's obnoxious essay on Pascal which, no doubt, has had many readers. And I might be able to handle the subject more effectively in opposition to Huxley than many other people otherwise far better qualified.[3] The chief difficulty for me is that of time; I should have

---

1–Ernest Rhys (1859–1946): author and editor; friend of WBY and Madame Blavatsky, and participant from 1890 in the Rhymers' Club. From 1906 he was editor of Everyman's Library (J. M. Dent & Sons), which brought 983 volumes into print by the date of his death.

2–'You will be surprised to find me associating Pascal with London Bridge. But the other day as I was trying to deal with the simulacra of London in Art, I copied down some lines of your "Unreal City" ['A crowd flowed over London Bridge', etc.] These lines had been running in my head and somehow or other they give me a clue as I am casting about for a likely man to write a preamble to Pascal's *Pensées* for Everyman's Library. I wonder if you could be persuaded to . . .'

3 – 'As for Aldous Huxley,' Rhys replied (21 Oct.), 'one feels inclined to say to him as Pascal once said: "O présumptueux, voici un trait délicat . . ." but of course one must not promote him to be a true Pascal antagonist.'

On 26 Feb. 1936 Rhys asked to publish this letter by TSE in his forthcoming Letter Book. TSE replied, 27 Feb. 1936: 'I am not quite happy about the letter as it stands. I feel that the adjective obnoxious is rather strong without being supported by any account of my objections to Aldous Huxley's essay, which furthermore I have not read for a long time. Huxley is a friend of mine, and I therefore have no objection to lambasting him at length when the occasion arises, but I don't like to say anything in print which might appear merely captious or offensive in passing. My other objection is that I think the next sentence rather unfortunate in view of the essay which I actually wrote for you. In this essay I (quite rightly as I think) made no reference to Huxley at all, and therefore it looks rather weak to speak of handling the subject in opposition to him.

351

to go through the *Pensées* very carefully, and also, again, the *Provinciales*; refresh myself on *Port Royal,* and otherwise acquire knowledge. So if you want to bring the volume out very quickly, I think you would be well advised to go elsewhere. If you do not need the introduction for six or eight months, I should rather like to undertake it.

With many thanks,

Yours sincerely,
T. S. Eliot

TO *Arthur Wheen*[1]

[?17] October [1930]   [Faber & Faber Ltd]

Dear Wheen,

Many thanks for your letter of the 16th. I am very glad that you do like *Anabase*. It did not receive a single review that pleased me and I imagine that most reviewers found it too obscure to be able to say anything about it at all.[2]

'If you think that the letter would still be of sufficient interest with such mutilation I have no objection to your publishing it with the omission of the word "obnoxious", and of the following sentence, beginning "And I might be able to handle the subject more effectively . . .".'

The letter was so printed, cut in accordance with TSE's wishes, in Ernest Rhys, *Letters from Limbo* (1936), 248. In a brief commentary Rhys included these remarks: 'When Pascal's *Pensées* fell due to Everyman's Library, I wrote to Dean Inge and asked him if he would write a critical preface to the book. But he declined the task, saying that Pascal had never appealed to him. Then it was suggested that Mr Eliot would be a congenial critic, and luckily he agreed and wrote the Introduction, a brilliant essay in which the relation between Montaigne and Pascal is put into a critical consign with excellent effect' (249).

1 – Arthur Wheen (1897–1971), librarian and translator, grew up in Sydney, Australia, and came to Europe with the Australian Expeditionary Force in WW1 (he received the Military Cross for bravery in action). A Rhodes Scholar at New College, Oxford, 1920–3, he worked for the rest of his career in the Library of the Victoria & Albert Museum, becoming Keeper, 1939–62. He translated novels relating to WW1 and won great praise in particular for his translation of Erich Maria Remarque's *All Quiet on the Western Front* (1929); and he wrote one novella, *Two Masters* (1924, 1929). FVM considered his modest friend Wheen 'the best critic I know, bar none' (letter to Morley Kennerley, 5 July 1933). See further *We talked of other things: The life and letters of Arthur Wheen 1897–1971,* ed. Tanya Crothers (2011).

2 – Wheen had read *Anabasis* four times: 'It is very beautiful. I wish I understood it . . . In the introduction you explain that it has to do with Oriental peoples, and you also speak of a "logic of imagination" different from that of concepts. There is a note in Coleridge's Table Talk of January 6, 1823, as follows: "St John's logic is Oriental, and consists chiefly in position and parallel; whilst St Paul displays all the intricacies of the Greek system." I do not understand what he means, nor whether he refers to the Gospel or to the Revelation. But you will know. And if he has in mind the first chapter of the Gospel and the whole of

That is an interesting point you raise. I don't think I understand any better than you do what Coleridge meant, but I should think certainly that he was referring to the Gospel rather than to the Apocalypse. Nor do I understand what Coleridge meant there by 'oriental logic'. The contrast between Oriental and Greek could hardly be applied to the difference between Greek and Arabic metaphysics, as the Arabic is apparently largely a development of the Greek. Nor am I quite sure, to tell the truth, what I meant myself; and it is rather on my conscience that I must find the time to enquire.

Yours ever,
[T. S. Eliot]

TO *Mary Hutchinson*   TS Texas

17 October [1930]   Faber & Faber Ltd

Dear Mary,

Thank you very much for your letter.[1] You have been often on my mind during the summer, partly because I did not answer the last note I had from you, and I felt that I rather failed you, as there was a hint of pain in what you wrote which you do not often allow to appear; and when one has troubles of one's own I feel that one should be all the more responsive to those of others.

I had a card for Jim's reception,[2] but never can bring myself to attend such ceremonies, where there are many people. It seems that he met Vivienne's brother Maurice Haigh-Wood. I wish indeed that you would ring up V. <Preferably while I am *out*! – best time just before lunch, Mondays to Fridays.>[3] (Ambassador 1518 in the telephone book). We are not far away. Fundamentally I am sure she wants to see old friends, and likes to be *badgered* by them (though this is a good deal to ask of the friends) as it stimulates her self-esteem, which is always in need of support and sustenance. She was by the way desolated by her brother's marriage, coinciding with his settling in Rome, and it is still a very sensitive point.

---

the Revelation, then I thought it might have some bearing on that logic of the imagination to which you refer; but on second thought it seems to me now that the same formula is at the bottom of the historical narrative also – As in the arts, the significance is conveyed by the arrangement of images, Yes? No.'

1 – Not found.
2 – J. S. Barnes, her brother.
3 – Added by hand.

I am not sure that I like the Lady myself, but that is not quite the point in her mind.

With many thanks for your kindness, and with love to Jack,[1]

Ever affectionately,

Tom.

P.S. One reason for my being a bad correspondence [*sc.* correspondent] is that I find it preferable to write various of my private letters, including to my brother, at this office; typing them myself.

TO *Clere Parsons*[2]   CC

17 October 1930   [*The Criterion*]

Dear Mr Parsons,

You will by this time have received proof of your review of Rodker's book, and have seen that your letter of enquiry was unnecessary.[3] I have only glanced at the book, but your review struck me as very just as well as interesting, so it will appear in the December number. I had not expected it to be in time for September, in any case. I owe you an apology about Namier.[4] The book was ordered for you but by the time it came I had forgotten for whom it was ordered, and offered it to a man in America who is a specialist in that period. If he does not reply affirmatively within a reasonable time, I shall merely send it to you, and in the meantime ask you to accept my apologies for my unbusinesslike methods.

1 – St John ('Jack') Hutchinson – 'a brilliant barrister, with a rubicund appearance . . . a mind stocked with recondite information on a wide variety of subjects, and a gift for mimicry' (Daphne Fielding, *Emerald and Nancy: Lady Cunard and her daughter* [1968], 62).

2 – Clere Parsons (1908–31), poet – he knew WHA at Christ Church, Oxford, and succeeded him as editor of *Oxford Poetry*; he also edited *Oxford Outlook* – was to die of diabetes and pneumonia. TSE published his posthumous collection *Poems* (1932). See also *The Air Between: Poems of Clere Parsons (1908–1931)*, with introduction by T. W. Sutherland and afterword by Edouard Roditi (1989); Andrew McCulloch, '"Opulent lovely tongue": The poetry of Clere Parsons', *TLS*, 16 Dec. 2011, 14–15.

3 – Parsons feared (8 Oct.) his review of John Rodker's novel *Adolphe 1920*, posted on 11 Sept., had been thought unsatisfactory, since it had not appeared. See *C.* 10 (Jan. 1931), 333–6.

4 – Parsons had asked to review L. B. Namier, *England in the Age of the American Revolution*.

I am delighted to hear that you have got your appointment in Oxford,[1] and am only sorry that it must mean that you will be less in London. But please let me know the next time you are up in town.

Yours sincerely,
[T. S. Eliot]

TO *Rudolf Kassner*   cc

17 October 1930   [*The Criterion*]

Dear Dr Kassner,

Thank you very much for your letter of October 11th.[2] I owe you an apology for having printed the essay which Madame de Bassiano kindly sent me, without taking the trouble to ask first for your permission. But I relied upon her in the matter and also, not having been in communication with you for a long time, did not know where you were. I have written to explain to her, and as a matter of fact, asked her for your address. I liked the essay exceedingly and it happened, from my point of view, to fit in very well to that particular number. A cheque in payment will follow in due course.

I hope indeed that you may be able to come to London,[3] particularly because I see no prospect for myself of getting as far as Vienna, much as I should like to.

With many thanks,
Yours sincerely,
[T. S. Eliot]

1 – Parsons had got a job as secretary to Dr Herbert Craster (1879–1959), Keeper of Western Manuscripts, Bodleian Library, starting in Oct. 1930. Craster was Bodley's Librarian, 1931–45.

2 – Kassner was pleased that 'Concerning Vanity' had appeared in C. 10 (Oct. 1930), 35–54; but disappointed not to have seen a proof of the translation by M. Gabain, since there were 'some mistakes in it, which do me wrong'.

3 – Kassner had last visited London in 1912.

TO *W. K. Lowther Clarke*[1]   CC

17 October 1930   [Faber & Faber Ltd]

Dear Dr Lowther Clarke,

I have your letter of the 16th, enclosing the draft of editorial conditions.[2] So far as I can see, there can be no reasonable objections to those conditions, which I accept. There is only one suggestion I have to make. I don't know if there are cogent reasons for leaving the point indefinite, but it would be a convenience to me personally if a definite flat rate for translators could be given. I suppose that the rate of translation should always be in the same proportion to the rate of authors' payment. For the *Criterion*, for instance, we pay £2 per 1000 words, for articles, and for translation work, 15/- which, of course, is deducted from the author's fee. I fixed 15/- in the beginning because, on enquiry, I was informed that that was the usual Fleet Street rate. Now in the case of the Encyclopedia, I shall obviously have to offer a distinctly lower rate than that.

Yours sincerely,
[T. S. Eliot]

TO *Secretaire de la Direction, Action Française*   CC

Le 20 octobre 1930   [Faber & Faber Ltd]

Monsieur,

Désirant renouveler mon abonnement à *l'Action Française* quotidienne, échu depuis quelque temps, je vous envois ci-inclus 200 (deux cents) francs en espèces pour m'abonner pendant une année depuis aujourd'hui et pour couvrir les frais d'expédition.

1–The Revd William Kemp Lowther Clarke, DD (1879–1968): Editorial Secretary of the Society for Promoting Christian Knowledge, 1915–44; Canon Residentiary of Chichester Cathedral, 1945–65; Prebendary of Chichester Cathedral from 1943. Works include *New Testament Problems* (1929) and *Liturgy and Worship* (1932).

2–Clarke wrote (16 Oct.), with reference to the proposed Encyclopedia: 'I am sending you a copy of the Regulations for the procedure of the Board and Editors, as they emerged from our last meeting. I should be obliged if you would tell me by the end of the month whether you would be willing to accept these conditions.

'I would not suggest a watertight agreement providing for all possible emergencies. I think a simple acceptance of the proposed terms would be enough, leaving it to common sense to settle difficulties such as might arise from undue slowness on the part of the Editor, or from the problem of apportioning payments between an Editor who retired and his successor.'

Je vous prie, Monsieur, de recevoir l'assurance de ma haute considération.
[T. S. Eliot]¹

TO *Edmund Blunden*   CC

20 October 1930   [Faber & Faber Ltd]

Dear Blunden,

I have a young man named C. K. Colhoun, introduced to me by Bruce Richmond, as he has done some work for the *T.L.S.* His specialities are Spanish and French literature, particularly more or less modern. He is anxious to get more work in reviewing. He seems to me well informed and intelligent, and I have handed over to him the Spanish and French for notice in the *Criterion*.

I thought of giving him an introduction to you, but before bothering you with a probable interview, I thought it more considerate of your time to write first and find out from you whether you might have any use for such a person.²

I wish that we might meet from time to time.

Yours sincerely,
[T. S. Eliot]

TO *Stephen Spender*   TS Northwestern

20 October 1930   Faber & Faber Ltd

Dear Spender,

It is now a long time that I have not answered your letter, which I was very glad to get from Hamburg.³ I was glad to hear that Germany was agreeing with you. I suppose you are now in Berlin. Thank you for

1–*Translation*: Sir, As I would like to renew my subscription to the newspaper *L'Action Française*, which expired some time ago, I am enclosing 200 (two hundred) francs in cash to subscribe for a year from today and to cover postage costs. Yours faithfully, T. S. Eliot
2–Blunden replied (22 Oct.): 'Though I shd much like to include anyone of whom you give a good report on the reviewing staff here, the position is such as hardly to make it worth while Mr Colhoun's calling on me. So many reviewers already have some claim . . .'
3–Spender said (1 Sept.) he was leaving Hamburg for Berlin on 10 Sept. He enclosed a poem, adding: 'I have done 3 more chapters of a novel [*The Temple*] whilst being here, so that I hope to finish the whole of the first draft of it by Christmas.' He went on: 'Many people are starving here, but there is nothing to compare with that choking gloom of London: or I trust not.'

sending the poems; I hope you will find the time and the inclination to
write more; I confess that personally I take so little interest in novels that
I am inclined to deplore your devoting so much time to prose, instead of
poetry. However, we all have to find out by experience what we can do
best.

I am sending – under another cover – two volumes of verse which may
interest you – I am sure that Auden's will – in the hope that some day we
may have you appearing in same form, if you like it.[1]

Yours sincerely,
T. S. Eliot

TO *F. McEachran*   CC

27 October 1930   [Faber & Faber Ltd]

Dear McEachran,

I am returning herewith Robert Shafer's letter to you of the 4th instant,
enclosed with yours to me of the 18th. I see no harm in your contributing
to the symposium, although personally I am beginning to get very tired
of all this fuss the Humanist gangsters are kicking up in America; and
Shafer particularly uses rather rough methods. I think that either the essay
you mention[2] or a chapter of THE CIVILIZED MAN[3] would do nicely,
and Shafer ought to be very grateful to you. I don't think that it is worth

1–Spender replied to this letter on 5 Nov. 1930: 'I progress very slowly with the novel,
and I am putting it aside now in order to write a long poem, which I have never felt the
desire to do before . . . Whenever I have enough poems, I will offer them to you for your
consideration . . . All my work that I have done is very scrappy and inadequate, so I would
rather wait. I have so great an admiration for Auden and his work that I would like my
poems to be produced in the same edition as his are, when the time has come.' He enclosed
three poems (one being 'Souvenir de Londres', another a translation of a poem by Stefan
George opening 'My child came home').
2–McEachran asked TSE if he could offer Shafer his 'Tragedy and History', C. July 1930.
3–The F&F blurb of *The Civilized Man* (1930) – probably by TSE – reads: 'The author
of this book, whose essays in *The Criterion*, *The Nineteenth Century and After*, and other
periodicals, have already attracted a great deal of notice, has here attacked a problem which
has proved to be the great problem of the modern world. What is civilization? How has it
been founded during the course of history and how maintained? With great control of his
material Mr McEachran has put forward a view which is, we believe, more representative
of the best thought of the present generation than that found in any previous book on the
subject. The book is not a long one, nor, for all its erudition, is it difficult to read. It is the
author's ability to present suggestive and not inaccurate generalizations, which gives his
work particular freshness and interest.'
    In C. (Jan. 1931), TSE noted that 'we are now offered so many different prescriptions for
the individual Good Life. One of the most satisfactory (to me) of recent formulae is that of

your while to write a fresh essay merely for this book unless you have something on hand that you want to do anyway. I agree that a chapter from the book might be a good advertisement and I will assure you of the consent of this firm.

I have not been asked to contribute myself, but do not think me splenetic: I am only too thankful to have been excommunicated from the Humanist fold.

I am writing to P. S. Richards, so that you need not bother.

Yours sincerely,
[T. S. Eliot]

TO *René Hague*   CC

27 October 1930   [Faber & Faber Ltd]

Dear Hague,

The manuscript arrived and has been handed to Gordon George.[1] Thank you for sending me the specimen of your type, which is admirable.[2] I have already explained, some time ago, to Tom Burns that I should be delighted to help in any way I can, but that I fear it is unlikely that I shall write anything which would be suitable for you and at the same time unsuitable for my own firm, which has an option on all of my work. But we shall see.

I am expecting to see Thorold today and hope to see you before very long.

Yours sincerely,
[T. S. Eliot]

Mr F. McEachran (*The Civilized Man*), but perhaps it is satisfactory to me because it does not point to anything novel, but to something highly traditional.'

1 – Hague had posted to TSE on 20 Oct. a manuscript by Gordon George.

2 – 'I hope you liked our type. I asked Tom Burns to ask you whether we couldn't print an edition of the *Waste Land* with engravings by David [Jones] . . .'

TO *Allen Tate*   TS Princeton

28 October 1930   Faber & Faber Ltd

Dear Tate,

Thank you very much for your letter of September 28th, and for the extraordinarily interesting and provoking essay.[1] Personally I should very much like to print it, as indeed almost anything by you, but I am afraid that it is too local and that English readers would not have enough 'apperceptionsmass' to appreciate it.

Incidentally it seems to me that you succeed in refuting yourself by exhibiting that gift for abstractions which you rather deprecate when employed by a Northerner. Being a Yankee myself and perhaps also because of an hereditary entanglement with the Adams family, I could not help wishing that you could be here for an extemporary rough-and-tumble with me.[2] Still we do not want to relieve our passions on each other instead of on Seward Collins. By the way, I wish that Collins would stop employing English female novelists to write his essays for him.[3]

> Yours ever,
> T. S. Eliot

TO *Paul Elmer More*   TS Princeton

28 October 1930   Faber & Faber Ltd

My dear More,

Thank you very much for your letter of the 21st ultimo. I had not answered it before because I have been waiting for an opportunity to write at some length, and that opportunity is still lacking. So I will merely say: don't worry about the Macdonald book in connexion with the

---

1 – Tate's essay in the symposium *I'll Take My Stand: The South and the Agrarian Tradition.*
2 – John Adams, second President of the USA (and father of John Quincy Adams, sixth President), was an ancestor of TSE; TSE's paternal grandmother was Abigail Adams Cranch (1817–1908). Richard Cranch, who emigrated from the village of Kingsbridge, Devon, in 1746, at the age of twenty, became brother-in-law of the second President and uncle of the fourth. Tate replied on 8 Nov.: 'quite seriously, because you are related to the Adamses, I am mighty sorry to have said anything uncomplimentary in an essay that I sent to you. I admire Henry Adams [grandson of John Quincy] extremely; only I can't fathom his kind of mind. The best apology I can make is this – and I hope you will accept it: abusing New England is too precious a pastime in my part of the country to be given up lightly.'
3 – Storm Jameson, Vita Sackville-West and Rebecca West were contributors to *The Bookman.*

Criterion. I am quite satisfied if the book has been of interest to you and has provoked you to writing.[1]

Now I will leave out the whole body of your letter and reply to it in a week or two, and meanwhile I will merely retort to your last taunt.[2] Why, my dear More, are you so foolish as to discuss seriously with a mere ignoramous [*sic*] like myself questions of philosophy and theology, and then go for me on the one subject on which I know more than almost anyone living. I am quite aware that I am a minor romantic poet of about the stature of Cyril Tourneur, that I have little knowledge and no gift for abstract thought; but if there is one thing I do know, it is how to punctuate poetry.[3]

Yours ever,
T. S. Eliot

TO *James Joyce*   TS Buffalo
29 October 1930[4]   Faber & Faber Ltd

My dear Joyce,

I have just had today a letter from Herbert Gorman enclosing a letter to you from Ogden which I enclose back to you herewith, according to your instructions as passed on to me by Gorman. I hope that this will reach you before you leave for Zurich – where I trust that everything will pass

---

1 – More wanted to write a review of Macdonald, but it had turned into an essay that he thought would be more suitable for publication in the concluding volume of his *Greek Tradition*.

2 – More remarked on 21 Sept. that he had been reading *Ash-Wednesday* 'already several times': 'Parts of it I understand and certain passages give me the true thrill; but a fair portion of it just misses my poor brain altogether. I think I am sluggish in my intellectual comprehension of poetry; for I am often bewildered where men with not half my training seem to find no difficulties . . . And, confound it, you are too big a man to play tricks with punctuation.'

3 – More returned to his charge on 19 Feb. 1931, after having just read Thomas McGreevy's little book on TSE: 'It is a curious mixture of eulogy and disapproval. But evidently it is your *Waste Land* that got the lads. Have you seen "Bunny" Wilson's new volume of essays in which he gives you resounding praise? And this, despite that pernickety punctuation of yours, over which you gloat so horribly, and for which you are willing to admit any theological deficiencies! I admire you as a good theologian; I admire you, with some perturbation of spirit, as a poet; I admire you, despite your Baudelairianism, as a critic, – but confound your punctuation.'

4 – Published in 'Matters Journalistic: Five Unpublished Letters', *Areté* I (Winter 1999), 16–17.

satisfactorily – I shall mention you meanwhile in my prayers, if you do not consider that an impertinence.[1]

The scheme was not Faber & Faber's but mine, and is by no means dropped. I have just had time to speak to Ogden at the club, and ascertain from him that he would be glad of any cooperation that we can give. My idea is merely to have the records, or some of them, stored at Faber & Faber's, circulate a list of likely purchasers, and have a percentage on each sale to F. & F. just to cover cost of storage, packing and posting or local delivery. The first thing however is to compile a list of people who ought to want the record.

This is really only part of a larger scheme which I have put to Gorman, and should have put to Ogden if I had had time to see him or write. Ogden tells me that if he could be assured of a sale of 25 copies of any record, new records could be made indefinitely; I want to form a small society of at least that number of persons, who would undertake to buy at a fixed price say four records a year made by living authors from their own writings, relying on the discretion of a Selection Committee to be formed. This seems to me to be perfectly practical, and distinctly superior to the publications of limited signed editions. I agree with Ogden that there should be at least one, and in time preferably several records of different parts of *Ulysses*; and I should certainly like to have one out of *Haveth Childers*. I shall discuss this with Ogden again as soon as I can; meanwhile I think this is enough to enable you to reply to him. I must find out of course the customs regulations – especially in America – about import of records.

Anna Livia has sold up to date over 4,600 copies – 57 last week – I think it will go on indefinitely, even after the publication of the complete work; and I think it will help the sale of the work, as will *Haveth*. We are more than satisfied.

Yours ever,
T. S. Eliot

1 – 'The enclosed letter from TSE should not be shown to anybody,' Joyce wrote when sending it on to Sylvia Beach, some time in Oct./Nov. 'People will only laugh at it while as for me I need all the prayers that were ever breathed.'

Gorman had written (undated): 'I received a letter from Mr Joyce this morning enclosing the note from Ogden which, at his (Mr Joyce's) request, I turn over to you. Mr Joyce writes me: "The enclosed has just come from Ogden. Will you read it quickly and send it on to T.S.E. asking him to return it to me at once. I wish to know whether F. and F's scheme has dropped (as seems to be the case) before replying to C.K.O." Will you, therefore, post the Ogden letter back to Mr Joyce and inform him regarding the status of Faber and Faber and the record? Mr Joyce . . . goes to Zurich early next week, according to the latest plans, for another operation.' Joyce was due to see Professor Alfred Vogt on 23 Nov.

TO *W. H. Auden*

29 October 1930   [Faber & Faber Ltd]

Dear Auden,

I am glad that you like the way we produced your book;[1] we are very glad that we have done it.

I shall look forward with great interest to your new play as I feel sure that poetic drama is the line you ought to follow.

I will try to find a book for you, but it would be a great help if from time to time you would yourself suggest anything you wish to review.

Yours sincerely
[T. S. Eliot]

TO *Ottoline Morrell*[2]   TS Texas

29 October 1930   Faber & Faber Ltd

My dear Ottoline,

Thank you for your letter. I should very much like to see you, and I hope that by this time Vivienne has made some arrangement with you.[3]

1–*Poems* (3/6d) was published on 9 Oct. Auden had written, from Larchfield School, Helensburgh, 6 Oct.: 'I have just received the copies of my poems, for which many thanks. I think the format very attractive.

'May I take this occasion to say how I have appreciated your encouragement during the past two years and to thank you for it. It has meant much to me.

'I hope to have a new play [*The Fronny*] ready for you to read by Xmas if the intervals between teaching English grammar and Rugby football are sufficient.

'If you have any books you would care to let me review for the *Criterion* I should be grateful as I am very hard up.'

2–Lady Ottoline Morrell (1873–1938), hostess and patron: see Biographical Register.

3–Carole Seymour-Jones writes: 'Visiting Vivienne on 15 November 1930, [OM] walked into marital war. Vivienne was restless, constantly leaving the room and returning smelling more and more strongly of ether. She spoke to Tom as if he were a dog; he "grim . . . fat . . . horrid" remained formally polite to her until Vivienne went to sit sulking in a corner of the sofa where she was ignored by Ottoline and Desmond MacCarthy. After ten minutes' absence she made a dramatic re-entrance, demanding that someone come to talk to her. Ottoline spent a moment or two alone with Vivienne in her room, and then fled, vowing never to return. Vivienne's teeth had, she recorded in her journal, filled the air with ether and she was "half-crazed". Ottoline felt an almost equal measure of repulsion for Tom, who tried as usual to hold her hand. She sensed in him an hypocrisy and humbug, which demonstrated itself in his poetry, and which Ottoline now found a meaningless form without faith, and also in his attitude towards Vivienne, towards whom he still claimed to feel affection' (*Painted Shadow*, 464; citing Journal of OM, 15 Nov. 1930: the Goodman Papers). OM wrote to TSE on 20 Nov.: 'I don't think Vivienne looked very well, poor dear. But she said she enjoyed the motoring very much. I am sure it is good for her.'

About the books you have sent; I should naturally like to sign them all, both to please you and in the cause of charity, but I am only able to sign the two copies of *Journey of the Magi*. Of this poem no signed edition was issued and I am therefore free to sign them. But as to the others, I have discussed the matter with the chairman and he agrees with me that to sign copies of these – except of course such as I inscribe personally to friends – would be a definite breach of faith with the persons who have bought signed editions at a higher price on the clear understanding that the number of signed copies was limited. I hope you will appreciate this point of view, as it is one which naturally does not occur to the mind of anyone but author and publisher.

Yours ever affectionately,
Tom

TO *Gordon Fraser*   CC

29 October 1930   [Faber & Faber Ltd]

Dear Mr Fraser,

Thank you for your unsigned letter of the 17th instant, and for sending me the first set of Minority Pamphlets, of which I will try to include a note in the *Criterion*. My only criticism is that the cover design seems to me likely to limit unnecessarily the public for the pamphlets. I was particularly pleased with Leavis's MASS CIVILISATION[1] and should be glad if you would send me four copies with invoice. I suppose it has already been sent to Virginia Woolf and Arnold Bennett.[2]

1 – *Mass Civilization and Minority Culture*, by FRL: no. 1 of the Minority Pamphlets. On 7 Nov. 1930 FVM approached FRL about his pamphlet, which he said he had read 'with great interest. It ought to have a wide public – wider, if I may so without impertinence, than that at which the other titles in your series aim . . . The whole scheme of pamphleteering is nowadays a good one. More power to your elbow!' No response from FRL has been found.
2 – Arnold Bennett (1867–1931): author and journalist. His best-selling novels include *Anna of the Five Towns* (1902) and *The Old Wives' Tale* (1908). His plays, including *The Great Adventure* (1913), were just as successful, with naturalistic and effective dialogue; and it was in his capacity as a capable dramatist that TSE consulted him in the early 1920s – ironically when Eliot was attempting to write a determinedly (and ultimately uncompleted) experimental play, *Sweeney Agonistes*. It says much for Bennett that he took TSE seriously and gave him advice that was valued – though Bennett was not keen on *The Criterion*. See *The Journals of Arnold Bennett*, ed. N. Flowers (3 vols, 1932–5); and Margaret Drabble, *Arnold Bennett: A Biography* (1974).

Now about the Van Doren reprint.[1] I should very much like to help the book in every way as it is one of the best things about Dryden that I have ever read. But I feel that I have been writing rather too many introductions and prefaces lately, and one's value as an introducer is very easily exhausted by multiplying this work of chairmanship. Chesterton, for instance, is now about zero and Hugh Walpole, of course, considerably below that degree, so I should be very much obliged if you would write to Bonamy Dobrée, and I will back you up with a personal appeal.

Yours sincerely,
[T. S. Eliot]

TO *A. J. Montague*[2]   CC

29 October 1930   [Faber & Faber Ltd]

Dear Sir,

I must apologise for not having answered your informative letter of the 23rd ultimo.[3] On full consideration of this letter I am happy to accept the honour which you do me of being Honorary Vice-President.

1 – Having resolved to reprint Mark Van Doren's book on Dryden, Fraser wished TSE to write a preface – 'however short'. Failing that, he hoped TSE would encourage Dobrée to write an introduction.
2 – President of the Glasgow University Distributist Club.
3 – Montague had quoted to TSE the constitution: 'The object of the League shall be the restoration of liberty, especially by a more equitable distribution of ownership in the materials and instruments of subsistence and production.' Montague went on: 'Accepting Mr Belloc's thesis of the Servile State, we work against the establishment of that state under Capitalism or Socialism, which both take from the mass of men liberty, with property, and self-responsibility. At present our position is largely of (a) opposition to monopolism, and to bureaucratic encroachment on personal liberty; (2) support of private and especially individual enterprise.

'We do not set up against the political parties, but claim to have sympathisers and even avowed Distributists in all three.

'If you do us the honour of becoming an Honorary Vice-President of our Club you will, of course, express definite sympathy, as you have already done elsewhere, with Distributism, but you will not become an Ordinary member of the League . . . I may be permitted to remind you that in reviewing Mr Belloc's "Servile State" you raised no objection to his argument as far as it went but asked for more indication of a "way" . . . [W]e intend to make it our particular object in the University Club to apply the Distributist idea, and to try and work out piece by piece a "way". It is for this work that we ask your encouragement by accepting Honorary office, following the example of University clubs in seeking distinguished patronage.'

With much appreciation and sympathy,

I am, Sir,

Yours faithfully,

[T. S. Eliot]

TO *John Livingston Lowes*[1]   CC

29 October 1930   [Faber & Faber Ltd]

Dear Professor Lowes,

Thank you very much for your kind letter. I had been hoping to hear from you and should have written myself, had I known your address.[2]

As for your very kind and generous suggestion, nothing would give me more pleasure than to accept, but I fear there are insuperable obstacles and I could explain the situation much more satisfactorily to you in a few minutes talk than in correspondence. So is there any chance of your being up in London even for a day in the immediate future? Incidentally, I should be very happy, and so would everyone else, if I could get you to come as my guest to one of the occasional evening re-unions of men interested in the *Criterion*; the next occasion is, I think, November 10th; is there any possibility of your being able to come?

Yours very sincerely,

[T. S. Eliot]

TO *M. C. D'Arcy*   CC

30 October 1930   [Faber & Faber Ltd]

My dear D'Arcy,

Thank you very much for your letter of the 24th. I am so glad that you like 'Marina', and that you like the later work better than the earlier.[3]

---

1 – John Livingston Lowes (1867–1945), American scholar of English literature – author of the seminal study of Coleridge's sources, *The Road to Xanadu: A Study in the Ways of the Imagination* (1927) – had taught for some years, 1909–18, at Washington University, St Louis, where he had become known to TSE's family. He later taught at Harvard, 1918–39.

2 – Lowes, who was visiting Oxford, wrote on 25 Oct.: 'We of the department of English at Harvard still cherish the hope that you may be able at some time to come to us for a year, & I am writing now to ask if there is any possibility of your being able to do so for the year 1931–32. If that should be so, I shall write at once to Professor Murray, the chairman . . .'

3 – 'I have read it [*Marina*] again & again & think it extremely beautiful. My judgment is one of no account, but, if I may dare say so, your poetry seems to pass from strength to strength. I appreciated your older poems, I enjoy greatly your more recent ones.'

Now about your book.[1] It is, as you must know, a project which seems to me wholly admirable, and which has my warm sympathy. I still have two reasons for hesitating to accept your flattering offer: first, that I have no authority to write on the subject of Authority, and second, that candidly I am not sure that from my point of view it would be wise, as a public step. On the second point, therefore, I will, with your permission, take spiritual advice *sub sigillo* and write to you again as soon as I can.

Yours ever sincerely
[T. S. Eliot]

TO *Walter de la Mare*   TS De la Mare Estate

30 October 1930   Faber & Faber Ltd

My dear de la Mare,

Thank you very much for your kind letter[2] and for inscribing a copy of *On the Edge* to me[3] – an honour which I prize very highly. May I say, without impertinence, that I have enjoyed these stories immensely, and that I have here, as always, a warm admiration for your style.

I should, of course, have been pleased had you been able to sponsor me at the Royal Society of Literature meeting; except for that one defect it passed off as well as could be expected, except that the heat of the room was more than tropical.[4]

With many thanks for your kindness,

Yours ever,
T. S. Eliot

1–D'Arcy wrote of his proposed volume, 'Authority and Chaos': 'The idea is to produce a book dealing with the place of authority in culture, morals, Church & State & Church. The contributors are to be handsomely paid . . . My first thought was to get an introductory essay from you of a general character, – to present, if I may say so, the thought of the Desert Land [*sic*] & Hollow Men – to suggest that in the present condition of civilisation the souls of men are parched & disintegrating because of the loss of a spiritual control . . . [N]o writer commits himself to the views of other contributors, but I should want people who are at one in admitting the principle of authority in politics, morals & religion.'
2–De la Mare wrote on 21 Oct.: 'I shall treasure the copy of *Marina* you sent me, both for its own lovely sake and for yours.'
3–Not found in TSE's library.
4–De la Mare wrote that he was unable to get to TSE's lecture at the Royal Society of Literature on 22 Oct.; it was his 'wretched fate' that he had to give a lecture of his own on the same day.

TO *G. Wilson Knight*   CC

30 October 1930   [Faber & Faber Ltd]

Dear Wilson Knight,

Thank you very much for your letter: few people would take the trouble
to analyse a little poem like *Marina* so carefully, and few, I dare say, will
care for it.[1] I rather wanted you to like it, as you know the reference so
well; I suspect that few persons in my acquaintance can remember *Pericles*
at all clearly. I do not know whether you understood that the quotation
is from Seneca's *Hercules Furens*; and that I wanted a crisscross between
Hercules waking up to find that he had slain his children, and Pericles
waking up to find his child alive. I did not add the reference *Hercules
Furens* for fear of misleading people who had not read the play itself.

I have been rereading *Coriolanus*. I wonder if you will agree with me
– it is rather important – I feel now that the political criticism, so much
mentioned, is a very surface pattern; and that the real motive of the play
is the astonishing study of the mother–son relation: 'he did it to please his
mother. . .' I think of writing a poem on this and on Beethoven's version
Coriolan.

Being a member of the Council, I believe that you may shortly be invited
by the Shakespeare Association to address them. I hope you will; I think
it would be worth your while, if a date can be found which will suit you.

Yours sincerely,

[T. S. Eliot]

1–GWK wrote on 17 Oct., of *Marina*: '[T]he whole poem plays on that territory explored
in *Pericles* . . . I notice that you aim at a serene austerity of diction always now – &, though
I always liked the resonance & colour of large words & proud Satanic phrases in your
earlier work, I appreciate this kind also. It is the same movement which is clear enough in
Shakespeare. Even *Antony & Cleopatra* – though its theme is sensuous & charged high with
"glitter" & "glory" – is, as it were, all presented through a desensualising medium, a filter,
so that it results in something rarefied, almost ascetic . . . I am referring to sound rather than
imagery: & in your later poems it is rather the aural effect, not the visual, which I find to
possess this same austerity . . .'

TO *John Hayward*   TS King's

30 October 1930   Faber & Faber Ltd

My dear John Hayward,

Thank you for your letter.[1] It is always a particular pleasure to send
you the little things I write, because your acknowledgements are so
particularly satisfying.

I wonder if the reference at the head of the poem to the Hercules Furens
(Hercules coming to and finding that he has killed his children) gets over
to the few people who have read *either* Euripides or Seneca.

Can you lunch with me on Wednesday next?

                              Yours etc.,
                              T. S. E.

TO *Ottoline Morrell*   TS Texas

30 October 1930   Faber & Faber Ltd

My dear Ottoline,

I am so sorry about the books.[2] Had I understood that any of them were
to be inscribed for your own keeping I should have done so, and shall be
glad to do so at any time. As for the rest, let us not say that I set myself
up as an ethical authority against the formidable list of more eminent
authors which you give; but merely that I alone am also a publisher – in a
far less proprietary way than Virginia – and that when my Chairman has
convictions which my own conscience accepts, I have no choice?

I have no doubt that it is quite a usual thing, for everyone but myself.

I look forward to seeing you, if not on Monday, some day next week.[3]

                              Affectionately yours,
                              Tom

1 – Not found.
2 – OM wrote on 29 Oct.: 'I did not of course know that there could be any difficulty in
signing the books (except of course the boredom of doing it!) as De la Mare, W B Yeats,
J Stephens & Sassoon had done them for me . . . You are the first person who has refused
. . . I really thought it was quite a usual thing especially as it was not for commerce or Profit.'
3 – 'I wrote to Vivienne suggesting tea on Monday, but I haven't heard if that suits her.'

30 October 1930   [Faber & Faber Ltd]

Yes, my dear Virginia, you are a wretch; but it is possible that I am tainted with wretchedness myself, so who am I to judge.[1] I reject, however, your sophistical suggestion that if you remain silent you may receive more books from me: this is tainted with the more serious sin of insincerity; for you know as well as I do that when I have more Books to lay so to speak at your Feet they will arrive, whether you acknowledge receipt or no. What I dread more than being ignored, is your ability, which seems to grow like F. H. Bradley's, to profess, in published periods, your inability to comprehend, and thereby to avoid the obligation to criticise. I wonder if you treat all your typing and printing friends to the same maze of deceptively modest ambiguities as you treat me. I sometimes wish that Mrs Woolf would sometimes emerge from her smoke screen of prose-reserve, and say to me 'I think that the last thing you sent me is Rubbish!' Which I often suspect to be at the back of her mind.

May I come to tea on Wednesday or Thursday next?[2]

> Affectionately
> (and respectfully)
> [Tom]

1 – VW had written in late Oct.: 'What a wretch I am, never to have thanked you for anything! I have a feeling that if I don't thank you perhaps you'll send another book. I've been ruminating very slowly among those already sent. I think I get slower & slower, & more & more incapable of criticism as I get older. But I've been enjoying Johnson, whom I have read, thanks to you, & Baudelaire whom I have never read, & in time your poem will embed itself in me, as your poems do – I'm sure it's a lasting-possession but here again I am floored by my own incapacity not to feel but to say what I feel. But perhaps that's not expected of a mere prose writer. How I envy you poets – able to make these enduring monuments, instead of mere frivolity that one laps up in a second with one's tongue. And thanks to you I'm attempting Dante again – but then, I ask myself, why should anyone else write; I mean it all seems a little futile after that – What do you think? – in spite of spelling out the words, I can grasp that – other people's futility, I mean.

'But this abominable pen wont write – still less my abominable typewriter. & all I have to say really is wont you somehow come & see me? Tea or dinner next week? Only suggest . . .'
2 – VW responded to this letter on 2 Nov.: 'Yes, my dear Tom, come to tea on Thursday next, at four thirty, and you will find your ancient and attached Wolves very glad to see you. No, I'm not generally held to be ambiguous by the clients of the Hogarth Press – I give much pain and receive much abuse. But then Mr Eliot is not a candidate for publication – far from it; and I cant (no false modesty intended) suspect him of any very great concern about Mrs Woolf's opinion; and Mrs Woolf would have to dig among the roots of what it pleases her to call her mind were she to give it; and she is lazy; and catch Mr Eliot committing himself about Mrs Woolf in the same circumstances. But my smoke screen isnt made of doubts of

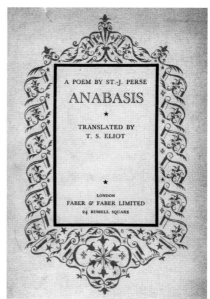

Ash Wednesday and *Anabasis* (both 1930). Dust jackets, with designs in red and black on green paper, by Edward Bawden.

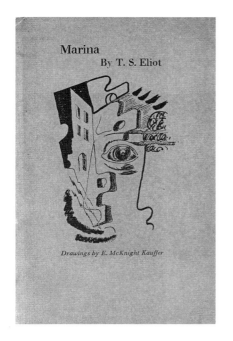

Ariel Poems: 'Marina' (September 1930), cover design in black on blue paper, and 'Triumphal March' (October 1931), in black on buff paper, both illustrated by Edward McKnight Kauffer.

Ezra Pound, photographed by Olga Rudge in 1931.

The 'admirable' photograph of
Aldous and Maria Huxley, in *The
Sketch*, 12 February 1930.

Herbert Read, by Jacob Kramer in
the Christmas Supplement to *The
Bookman*, December 1930.

The young Roy Campbell, the
'fishing and bullfighting' poet, in
the early to mid 1920s.

George Wilson Knight in character
as Buckingham in *Henry VIII*,
c.1930.

Francis Lees Underhill, Bishop of
Bath and Wells, 1930s.

Martin Cyril D'Arcy,
photographed by Vandyk,
*c.*1931–2.

Cyril Charles Martindale,
Jesuit scholar, photographed by
Lafayette in 1927.

William Temple, Archbishop
of York (later Archbishop of
Canterbury), 1930.

Vivien Eliot with their dog Polly, by Vandyk. Vivien sent the photograph
to her sister-in-law in December 1930.

T. S. Eliot, by Vandyk,
sent by Eliot to his brother in
December 1930.

Richard Aldington, photographed
in Sicily or the South of France by
Hilda Doolittle, 1929–30.

James Joyce (with cane), photographed with Moune Gilbert, Lucia Joyce
and Stuart Gilbert, in Strasbourg in 1928; Gilbert was working on his
translation of *Ulysses* at the time. Nora Joyce's hat is partially visible
over her husband's right shoulder.

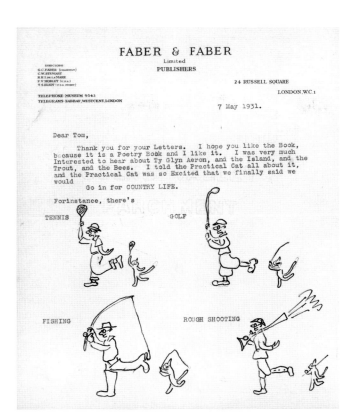

FABER & FABER
Limited
PUBLISHERS

DIRECTORS:
G.C.FABER (CHAIRMAN)
C.W.STEWART
R.H.I.DE LA MARE
F.V.MORLEY (U.S.A.)
T.S.ELIOT (U.S.A.ONLY)

TELEPHONE: MUSEUM 9543
TELEGRAMS: FABBAF,WESTCENT,LONDON

24 RUSSELL SQUARE

LONDON,W.C.1

7 May 1931.

Dear Tom,

    Thank you for your Letters. I hope you like the Book, because it is a Poetry Book and I like it. I was very much Interested to hear about Ty Glyn Aeron, and the Island, and the Trout, and the Bees. I told the Practical Cat all about it, and the Practical Cat was so Excited that we finally said we would

        Go in for COUNTRY LIFE.

Forinstance, there's

TENNIS   GOLF

FISHING   ROUGH SHOOTING

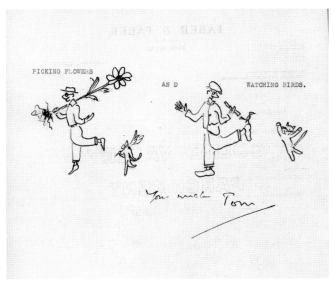

PICKING FLOWERS   AN D   WATCHING BIRDS.

Your uncle Tom

Letter from Eliot to his godson Tom Faber, 7 May
1931, containing one of the first mentions of his
eponymous 'Practical Cat'.

From left, W. H. Auden, with Stephen Spender and Christopher
Isherwood, Rügen, Germany, 1931.

From left, Vivien, Lord David Cecil, Elizabeth Bowen and Eliot,
photographed by Lady Ottoline Morrell in her garden at
Gower Street, 1931.

5 November 1930   Faber & Faber Ltd

Dear Marguerite,

Thank you so much for your kind letter of the 30th and for your cheque for £30 for the *Criterion* which I have transferred to the proper quarter and hereby officially acknowledge. Meanwhile I have heard from Kassner, who appears to be pleased that his essay was published;[1] it was spoken of very approvingly by *The Times Literary Supplement.* I shall be very

---

you, but doubts of myself rather, and of the whole business of criticising prose or poetry. Perhaps in talk – but then we never meet. Not for a whole year I think – except visions in streets which though aspiring arent substantial. Such is life. But one of these days we may somehow contrive to say something in spite of the smoke – who knows? And anyhow I have the honour to sign myself with sincerity your devoted and humble admirer / Virginia.' (*Letters* IV, 246). (TSE was to give VW's letter to Emily Hale, who taught theatre and diction at Scripps College, Claremont, California, 1932–4; and Hale was to give it to Ruth George [1880–1959], a teacher of English at Scripps, who would in time gift it to the Ella Strong Denison Library at Scripps.)

TSE visited VW on 6 Nov., as VW apprehended in a letter written that day to Vita Sackville-West: 'And Tom Eliot is bringing his wife – raving mad, seeing insults if I say China or India or do you like more water' (*Letters* IV: *1929–1931*, 248). On Sat., 8 Nov., VW put down in her diary this entry, beginning by comparing TSE with WBY, with whom she had chatted at OM's house on the 7th: '[Yeats] seemed very cordial, very generous . . . Compare him with Tom for instance, who came to tea the day before, & may be, for anything I know, as good a poet. Poor Tom is all suspicion, hesitation & reserve. His face has grown heavier fatter & whiter. There is a leaden sinister look about him. But oh – Vivienne! Was there ever such a torture since life began! – to bear her on ones shoulders, biting, wriggling, raving, scratching, unwholesome, powdered, insane, yet sane to the point of insanity, reading his letters, thrusting herself on us, coming in wavering trembling – Does your dog do that to frighten me? Have you visitors? Yes we have moved again. Tell me, Mrs Woolf, why do we move so often? Is it accident? Thats what I want to know (all this suspiciously, cryptically, taking hidden meanings). Have some honey, made by our bees, I say. Have you any bees? (& as I say it, I know I am awaking suspicion). Not bees. Hornets. But where? Under the bed. And so on, until worn out with half an hour of it, we gladly see them go. Vivienne remarked that I had made a signal that they should go. This bag of ferrets is what Tom wears round his neck' (*Diary* III, 331).

VW wrote to Vanessa Bell on 8 Nov.: 'My most horrid experience was a visit from Tom Eliot. This had been arranged for weeks. At the last moment he rang up to say that Vivien wanted to come too, and would we pretend that we had asked her. This sounded ominous, but was nothing to the reality. She is insane. She suspects every word one says. "Do you keep bees?" I asked, handing her the honey. "Hornets" she replied. "Where?" I asked. "Under the bed." Thats the style, and one has to go on talking, and Tom tries, I suppose, to cover it up with longwinded and facetious stories. And she smells; and she throws cheap powder over the bread; and she opens his letters, suspects me of being his mistress, so far as we could gather; and finally said that I had made a signal which meant that they were to go. So they did go, in about half an hour, and now he writes that he wants to come and see me alone, to explain I suppose; but I expect Vivien will appear too' (*Letters* IV, 250).

1 – Rudolph Kassner, 'Concerning Vanity', trans. M. Gabain, C. 10 (Oct. 1930), 35–54.

glad to see the other essay and I should like to have the book of French translations to consider, although I dare say I shall find most of the same essays amongst the books of his which you sent me some time ago.[1]

I am sorry that? you have had such a bad time of anxiety about Lélia. I suppose it is merely one of the incidents of adolescent growth to have such nervous ailments.[2] I suppose it has delayed your going to Rome; I wondered at the time whether you were present at Assisi.

As for myself, I have something in view which I want to write, and will let you have a part of it as soon as there is anything which satisfies me. I am seeing Mrs Woolf tomorrow, and will try to extract something for you from that elusive person, and I will write to Campbell as soon as I can.[3] He may be too busy fishing and bull-fighting to provide anything. If you care to write to him direct, his address is,

> Tour de Vallier,
> Martigues,
> Bouches du Rhone,
> France.

I take it from the slip of paper you enclosed that you wish to be sent a number of books, and have given instructions accordingly. I should like you to look attentively at the poems of Auden and Macleod. We should be quite glad, and I am sure the authors also would be glad, if you cared to use any parts for *Commerce*. I have another young man named Stephen Spender of whom I have hopes, but he is a mere nurseling, and I think it is very bad for children to be pushed ahead too fast.

I think it would be an excellent thing if you could have translations made of some of Wilfred (not Winifred) Owen, and Gerard Hopkins.[4]

---

1 – Caetani wrote on 30 Oct.: 'I am sending you a fine essay of his already translated in English to see if perhaps you could do anything about having it published. His book of French translations is coming out any moment . . .'

2 – 'I have had a nasty month of October worrying about Lélia – quite uselessly as it has turned out thank God. She began coughing and coughing and my doctor was away and I was only able to see him a week ago and be quite reassured. It turned out to be almost entirely nervous and probably I had made it much worse by fussing.' Lélia Caetani (1913–1977), sole daughter, was to marry Hubert Howard (1908–1987), a scion of the English Catholic house of Howard, who worked to preserve the Caetani heritage at Rome and at the castle of Sermoneta.

3 – 'Try to give me something soon of yours. As to other English authors – I would like again Mrs Woolf, Roy Campbell and who do you think we ought to have?'

4 – 'Would you approve of our translating certain poems of Winifred Owen and Gerald Manly Hopkins [*sic*]?' Wilfred Owen (1893–1918), soldier and war poet, was killed in France one week before the end of WWI. See Jon Stallworthy, *Wilfred Owen: A Biography* (1974). Gerard Manley Hopkins (1844–99), poet, Catholic convert and Jesuit priest; Professor of Greek and Latin, University College Dublin, from 1884.

You would, of course, have to write to the publishers for permission, as they are both dead. I expect to get into the country for a week early in December. As for your last question,[1] I cannot give you the title of Julian Huxley's best books, until he has written a good one.[2] The best books of Bertrand Russell are *The Philosophy of Leibnitz, The Principles of Mathematics*, the first volume of the *Principia Mathematica,* and an excellent volume on PHILOSOPHY in the 'Home University Library'. All the other books of his that I have read are bad books. The best books of Whitehead[3] are the remaining volumes of the *Principia Mathematica* (which I have not read and which I do not recommend for the reason that they are very expensive and composed entirely of mathematical formulae); but a book you should read if you are interested in such things is *Science and the Modern World* which is a very brilliant piece of work. If you are interested in Whitehead, I should think you would also be interested in Professor Eddington's book, and possibly in a book by Sir James Jeans, which has just come out, entitled *The Mysterious Universe*.[4] This is all I have time to write now. I hope Camillo is getting on well.

With love from Vivienne,

Yours affectionately,
Tom.

TO *Ahmé Haigh-Wood*[5]   CC

6 November 1930   [68 Clarence Gate Gardens]

Dear Ahmé,

I am very pleased to have your letter[6] and although I find your questions very difficult to answer, it is not because I am too surprised and

---

1 – 'When you write to me you would be an angel to give me the titles of the 2 or 3 best books of Bertrand Russell of Prof. Whitehead and of Julian Huxley.'

2 – Julian Huxley (1887–1975): zoologist and philosopher; brother of AH.

3 – A. N. Whitehead (1861–1947): mathematical logician and speculative philosopher; Fellow and Senior Mathematical Lecturer, Trinity College, Cambridge; Professor of Philosophy, Harvard University; Gifford Lecturer, Edinburgh University, 1927–8.

4 – Arthur Eddington (1882–1944): astrophysicist, philosopher, populariser of science; Fellow of Trinity College, Cambridge; Plumian Professor of Astronomy and Experimental Philosophy (1913). Works include *Space, Time and Gravitation* (1920), *Stars and Atoms* (1926), *The Nature of the Physical World* (1928). James H. Jeans (1877–1948): physicist, astronomer, mathematician; knighted in 1928. Works include *The Mysterious Universe* (1930), *The Stars in Their Courses* (1931).

5 – Wife of MHW; née Emily Cleveland Hoagland.

6 – Not found.

I am certainly not upset by it. I must say at once, however disagreeable it may sound, that I don't consider Dr Eliot's five-foot shelf of books to be a suitable present for Maurice. I have inspected this dismal collection, which is certainly a disgrace to the family of which we are all ashamed and I can say without hesitation that it would do Maurice no good; it would certainly induce melancholia and possibly develop a craving for alcohol. I thoroughly sympathize with your loyal desire to see him possess a larger library – I am not sure whether to gather from your letter that you do not wholly approve his present collection. I think it would be better to try to think of a few books at a time to give him, instead of an overpowering compendium, and if I can be of any further use to you I shall be delighted, and if you like, will make suggestions from time to time.

I hope you are both well and flourishing.

With love to Maurice,

Yours affectionately,

[Tom][1]

1 – No immediate reply has been found; but Ahmé wrote again from 96 Via Vittorio Veneto, Rome, on 12 Feb. 1931:

'It has been ages since you sent those lists of books to us Tom dear, and I feel ashamed for not having written to you before to thank you. It was very sweet of you. I am at loose ends as to which one I want . . . However one never gets anywhere without a decision so I will look over them all again and let you know which one Haighie and I think is the best for a start and let you know as soon as Haighie gets back to Rome. He is in Naples at the moment.

'There is a part I would like to discuss with you about your Sacred Wood sometime when I see you again. I won't discuss it here as it is much too complicated and will entail some argument. But I loved the book and will read it a number of times no doubt until I get its full depth. I think that I will walk in on you one day when I am in London and get you to take me out to luncheon. I want to know you better. Your books can be read so many times and now that I have a Dante's "la Divina Comedia" in Italian I must go back to the Poet on the Poets and reabsorb all that you said about Dante. Not reabsorb but just absorb, I don't flatter myself that I gathered it all at first at all. This letter sounds like a letter to my hero but it isn't at all anything like that as you would know if you knew me at all well. I merely am interested in the things that you write and want to know more about them, to understand them perfectly. Or is anyone incapable of doing that who did not write the works he or she wrote. What a complicated sentence that was. I think that you would be an awfully interesting companion to talk over a meal with. I don't mean that you are not at other times but that meals in an attractive place and a pleasing atmosphere are restful, and conducive to intelligent conversation provided that there is no one to rush you or to warn you of the time.

'If you have had time in the rush of things that you have to do at the office to read this, let me know if some day you will be willing to take an ignoramus and confide all you know and how and why you know it. Be good, be cheerful, be happy and be gay, you are too young to wear such a solemn face always. Love Ahmé.' (EVE)

When TSE sent her a copy of Contract Bridge at a Glance (F&F), Ahmé responded on 18 Sept. 1931: 'do tell me the exact date of your birthday – not just the fact that it is this month – Be good and keep smiling Tom – you are a different person when you do.'

TO *Bonamy Dobrée*   TS Brotherton

7 November 1930   Faber & Faber Ltd

Dear Bonamy,

Being an extremely disorderly person, I never answer letters when I should, and sometimes have fits of writing a long letter when I shouldn't. It is probably the sight of the Gas, Telephone, and Electricity third-time-of-asking Bills on my desk which impels me to answer your letter of 28th Sept. now. You remember I trust that we are to lunch on the 12th inst. Having been asked to lunch to meet Shane Leslie on that date, I was happy to say that I was engaged with you. Will you call at Russell Sq. before 1?

I think I agree with most of your letter. Except that when you say you 'see no prospect of religion becoming a live issue' I must say again: *distinguo*.[1] For from my point of view, it is primarily not of the slightest importance whether religion is a 'live issue' or not. From one point of view, it always has been, is and always will be the livest of issues; from another point of view, it never has been an issue at all except by accident for the majority of people. And on another hand, my dear Bonamy, it might at any time become what even you would call a 'live issue': the world is in a fluid state, and even 'national and racial characteristics' are in the 'meltingpot'; it may still happen that people may be stoned or brickbatted to death in London streets for religious convictions – for my part, I should not be altogether sorry: we need a few martyrs.

I think we are in agreement that 'Order' and 'Authority' are more dangerous catchwords now, than 'Liberty' and 'Reform' were fifty or seventy-five years ago. Order and Authority may point more directly to the yellow press and the crook capitalists than Liberty and Reform pointed to Socialism. I am terrified of the modern contempt of 'democracy'. I am also

1 – In a four-page TS letter, BD tried to set out 'the causerie' that TSE expected from those attending the next Criterion Club dinner. 'As far as I can see, we are at the edge of a revolution such as we went through in 1640–1660 . . . namely the transference of power from one set of people to another. I see even the possibility of a series of civil wars, in which Germany will give the lead. The depressing thing about the present revolution is that though the earlier one was at bottom a commercial one, it had at least two good cries which were not merely materialistic, namely that of religious reform and political freedom . . . I see no prospect whatever of religion becoming a live issue . . . In short, there is, as you say in your admirable Commentary of this number, no cause for which sacrifices can be made . . . Perhaps, however, the struggle, whether armed or not, may take the form of a party of order as against a party of democratic formlessness. Authority seems to have met with at least a temporary welcome in Italy . . . We should try to keep out of European politics as much as we can. We should try to become another America. We should simply shrug our shoulders if Germany turns nasty about war reparations.'

inclined slightly to resent (with mild amusement) being regarded by some as a Romaniser; whenas I believe that when the Vatican put it over the Action Française I was one of only two or three persons in this country to protest against this political thimblerigging. I am as scared of Order as of Disorder. The great thing seems to me to be to simplify issues into such as any man will be ready to put his fists up for.

I believe that I am working off on you a little preliminary bile before vomiting my complete commentary. I hope that is what it means.

About the American Civil War,[1] I can add two anecdotes provided originally by my grandfather who was a friend of both generals: that General Sherman detested more than all others one song, 'Marching through Georgia'; and that General Sheridan, the most brilliant of Northern American cavalry leaders (this should appeal to you as a cavalryman) was so frightened that he had always violent diarrhoea before every action.

I expect you then on Wednesday at 1/.

Yours ever,
T. S. E.

TO *A. E. Taylor*   CC

7 November 1930   [Faber & Faber Ltd]

Dear Professor Taylor,

My friend Martin D'Arcy S.J. has asked me to contribute an essay to a volume which he is editing on the subject of Authority. This seems to be a matter that craves worthy walking[2] and as he told me that he was asking you also to write, I am venturing to trouble you to let me know, if you will, whether you have been approached and whether you are inclined to accept or not. My own instinct is to keep out of it altogether. With many apologies.[3]

Yours sincerely,
[T. S. Eliot]

1 – BD ended his letter of 28 Sept., 'Since you want a causerie, I enclose one on the American Civil War. Do with it what you like . . .' The enclosure has not been found.
2 – 'It is the bright day that brings forth the adder, / And that craves worthy walking' (*Julius Caesar*, II: i, 14–15.
3 – Taylor replied (10 Nov.) that he was 'terrified' to hear that D'Arcy was about to approach him on such a subject – 'which I shall certainly not be able to write'.

TO *Clive Bell*

TS King's

7 November 1930   Faber & Faber Ltd

My dear Clive,

I saw Virginia yesterday and she told me, to my great distress, that you had just returned to London in a state of temporary eclipse. Please accept my expressions of sympathy; at the same time I regard it as possibly an unique opportunity to enjoy a little of your conversation: so may I come in to see you for an hour or two one afternoon? I say afternoon because my occasions for going out in the evenings are few, and it would be two or three weeks before I could come in for an evening.

Yours ever,
T. S. Eliot

TO *J. M. Robertson*[1]

CC

10 November 1930   *[The Criterion]*

My dear Robertson,

Thank you very much for your letter.[2] I have been hoping against hope that you would reply to Dover Wilson's reply and I think that Dover Wilson, whom I saw a week or two ago, hoped the same. However, although that must be abandoned, by all means print your article in the book, for which, when received, I will find another reviewer rather than Dover Wilson.

I was going to ask you to review for us Sir Edmund Chambers' new book. I am not sure whether it is yet out. At any rate, I have not yet received it. Possibly the publishers suspect that I might send it to you, but if the book does arrive, may I send it on to you?[3]

1–J. M. Robertson (1856–1933), author, journalist, politician: see Biographical Register.
2–Robertson wrote on 6 Nov. that he would not 'burden' C. with a reply to Dover Wilson's 'Reply' (C. 9 [July 1930], 631–41; concerning Robertson's 'Shakespearean idolatry'). 'But I am going gunning against the *Camorra* in a new book on "The State of Shakespeare Study" (dedicated to the British Academy), and I feel that Wilson should be pinned down to his fiasco – with a number of other Mandarins.' In his next letter (14 Nov.), Robertson pronounced that he thought Wilson 'had sunk to crookeries and *personalities*'.
3–Review of E. K. Chambers, *William Shakespeare: A Study of Facts and Problems*, C. 10 (Apr. 1931), 520–9.

I had also in mind to send you for review a book published in Edinburgh, called *Whisky*, by Aeneas Macdonald,[1] and the word suggests that I should like you to come and lunch with me again when you can.

Yours sincerely,

[T. S. Eliot]

TO *Charles Harris*

10 November 1930   [Faber & Faber Ltd]

Dear Harris,

I think that I ought to thank you in writing also for taking the trouble to write at such length about the Lambeth Conference.[2] The chairman is away until Wednesday but I am sure that he will regard this seriously and we will then see what can be done. It is an oversight on my part to have allowed this to go through without severe revision; due partly to the haste with which it is necessary to get some of the pamphlets done.

The great question on which I wish you could help me further is to decide who would be the best person to write another pamphlet. I would be prepared to put other work aside and write one myself if I felt that

1 – *Whisky* (1930), by Aeneas MacDonald, pseud. of George Malcolm Thomson. No review appeared in *C*.

2 – Harris wrote on 6 Nov., of G. M. Thomson's pamphlet on the Lambeth Conference: 'I suppose this kind of stuff appeals to a certain class of minds, and has a sale; but on its intrinsic merits it is not worth publishing. The author's arrogant and "superior" attitude, and his cheap and sometimes blasphemous gibes, are irritating and (to me at least) repulsive. His principal aim is to be "smart" . . . As your firm has actually published this cheap stuff, I think the best thing would be to publish another pamphlet dealing with the subject seriously.

'In my opinion, the Lambeth Conference is *epoch-making* – nothing less. Among its results are the following:

(1) It renders it *quite certain* that the future development of Anglicanism will be Catholic (in the ecumenical sense), not Protestant;

(2) The conference has all but achieved Reunion with the Orthodox East – an immense achievement;

(3) It has come to terms with modern philosophy, criticism and science (a thing which neither Rome nor the East has done or can do), and made it possible for thinking our modern outlook to be both Christians and Catholics. "Liberal Catholicism", which is now the official creed of the Anglican Communion, has before it an *immense future*.

'Personally, I have at times been very critical of the C. of E., but since Lausanne and Lambeth, *I am proud to be an Anglican* . . .

'I recommend you not to associate yourself prominently with the Roman book of Essays [ed. D'Arcy] which you have mentioned to me, but to throw your whole weight into the Liberal Catholic movement for which not only our Literature Committee, but also the whole Anglican Communion now (officially) stands.'

I was quite competent; furthermore, it does not seem quite correct to encourage a man to write an essay, publish it, and then turn round and censure it. The obvious suggestion, to my mind, is Kenneth Ingram, but I am not sure that Ingram is quite sound enough on some points which take a very important place to be quite trustworthy. I should like to know in confidence what you think of this.

Yours in haste,
[T. S. Eliot]

TO *Charles Harris*   CC

10 November 1930   [Faber & Faber Ltd]

Dear Harris,

I dictated to you today a letter which, as I was not returning to my office this afternoon, I asked my confidential secretary to sign for me. It was done in haste; and in fairness to Thomson, the author of the pamphlet,[1] I ought to add that I am myself more dissatisfied with the manner than the matter of his essay. It is more the unnecessary cheapness of his style than the content that raises my objections. Part of his own unfairness is that natural to an outsider, that he considers the matter absolutely and without any responsibility of his own; and is not concerned to mark any advance of episcopal opinion. On the question of 'Youth' I am much in sympathy with him; and on sexual matters he expresses in his own way some of my own dissatisfaction. On this point I find Ingram (*vide* his correspondence in the *Church Times*) very unsatisfactory.[2] The question in my mind is

---

1 – *The Lambeth Conference* (1930).

2 – A run of correspondence in the *Church Times*, Oct.–Nov. 1930, debated the implications of Resolution 15 of the Lambeth Conference, which provided: 'Where there is a clearly felt moral obligation to limit or avoid parenthood, the method must be decided on Christian principles. The primary and obvious method is complete abstinence from intercourse . . . nevertheless, in those cases where there is such a clearly felt moral obligation, and where there is a morally sound reason for avoiding complete abstinence, the Conference agrees that other methods may be used, provided that it is done in the light of the same Christian principles.'

Ingram argued in the *Church Times* 104 (24 Oct. 1930), 488: 'Because a practice may be abused or is liable to incite abuse, it is not proved bad.' He opposed the theory 'that the sex-act is a sin whenever it is potentially dissociated from the purpose of procreation. If this is so, we are led to the *reductio ad absurdum* that intercourse, after the woman has reached a certain age, is immoral . . . Some of your correspondents imply that because they show abstinence to be a higher ideal, they thereby prove contraception to be wrong. Actually they only prove it to be second-best. Lastly there is the argument that contraception involves excessive indulgence. I confess my inability to understand why self-control is incompatible

not whether there are not special cases, but, what none of the *Church Times* correspondents seems to me to have fastened on, what is to be the authority for these special cases? I feel that the Bishops, by virtually leaving the question to individual conscience to answer, have on this point surrendered the Catholic principle. Would it not have been better, if, in admitting the possibility of exceptions, they had counselled the public to consult properly ordained spiritual advisers when any person felt that the situation was exceptional? Even though, as would obviously happen at present, there would be the greatest diversity of judgement among the advisers themselves, and any astute enquiring layman or woman could certainly get the answer required by careful choice of adviser, still the principle of ecclesiastical authority could be preserved, while work was done to forward a greater uniformity of view among the clergy themselves. When the Roman Church intrudes too far – as it often does, and that is one reason for my own opposition to it – into the political field, the conscientious faithful can often arrange matters for themselves by choosing a confessor who will not ask inconvenient questions: this was admitted to me by a French friend during the excommunication of a certain political party several years ago. It would be a lesser scandal for Anglicans to choose pastors whom they know to be of their own views, than for them to receive a benediction upon their own desires and decisions.

It has occurred to me that possibly a joint pamphlet by Ingram and myself might do what is needed; we should have of course to indicate frankly our disagreements.

Sincerely yours,
[T. S. Eliot]

---

with contraceptive methods, and I am bound to emphasize that the non-use of contraceptives very frequently fails to avoid excess, with disastrous results.' Further, on 7 Nov. 1930, 556: 'I have no desire to engage in this correspondence for controversial purposes. I merely ask for information, i.e., for a rational explanation as to why contraception, within marriage, in moderation, and where procreation is undesirable, is an evil. So far, in my opinion, none of your correspondents have advanced such an explanation. Until they do so, I must retain my belief that Resolution 15 was justified.'

TO *The Director, House of the Sacred Mission*   CC

10 November 1930   [Faber & Faber Ltd]

Dear Sir,

Thank you very much for your kind letter of the 6th.[1] I had previously heard from Canon Underhill that the arrangement was not impossible, and I am happy to have your confirmation. Would the week from the 8th to the 15th December be convenient for you? That would, I think, suit me very well, but I should like to be assured, as I shall have many arrangements to make, as long in advance as possible.

> With grateful thanks, I am
> Yours very truly,
> [T. S. Eliot]

TO *Harold Monro*   CC

10 November 1930   [*The Criterion*]

Dear Monro,

I have asked a young man named Colhoun and Morley has asked J. G. MacLeod and Geoffrey Tandy.[2] Read has asked Grant Watson[3] and Jacob Kramer.[4] And I understand from John Hayward that he has been asked by Bonamy. That is all I know.

> Yours,
> [T. S. E.]

1 – Reginald Tribe, SSM, wrote from the Society of the Sacred Mission, Kelham Theological College: 'Yes, we are most glad to welcome visitors; and the kind of visit you propose fits in very well, for we have no separate retreat house here. Any time after Nov 25th would suit us.' It was eventually arranged that TSE would visit from 17 Jan.
2 – See TSE to Tandy, 23 Apr. 1931, below.
3 – E. L. Grant Watson (1885–1970): writer. After graduating from Trinity College, Cambridge (Natural Sciences, 1st class), he joined an ethnological expedition to Western Australia and came to love the country. A vagabond – he spent time in Fiji, Canada, Ceylon, Florence, London, New York and Paris, and cultivated Joseph Conrad, Gertrude Stein, DHL, Edward Thomas and Havelock Ellis – he produced works of fiction (including six 'Australian' novels) and short stories, as well as scientific-philosophical works. See *But to What Purpose: The Autobiography of a Contemporary* (1946); *Descent of Spirit: Writings of E. L. Grant Watson*, ed. Dorothy Green (1990); Suzanne Falkiner, *E. L. Grant Watson and Australia* (2001).
4 – Jacob Kramer (1892–1962): Ukrainian-born artist, whose Jewish family left Russia for England in 1900. He was brought up in Leeds, and went on to study at Leeds School of Art, 1907–13 – it was through his membership of the modernist Leeds Arts Club that he befriended HR – and at the Slade School of Art in London, 1913–14. Though briefly

TO M. C. D'Arcy   CC

11 November 1930   [Faber & Faber Ltd]

My dear D'Arcy,

I have been thinking over your kind offer carefully, and have come to
the conclusion, not so much for the reasons I suggested, but for others,
that I ought not to accept. The strongest reason is this: that my time is very
restricted, and I feel that my own people have the first claim upon me; and
I have undertaken certain work in connexion with the E.C.U. which will
give me plenty to do for several years. It has always been a temptation to
me to undertake more than I could fulfil, and then suffer vexatiously from
conscience. I do hope that you will understand and forgive: it would have
been a great pleasure to associate myself with you.

> Sincerely yours,
> [T. S. Eliot]

TO Bruce Richmond   CC

11 November 1930   [Faber & Faber Ltd]

Dear Richmond,

Montgomery Belgion has been pestering me about either an introduction
to you or perhaps he knows you already, and means that he would like me
to press his merits afresh on your attention. In any case, I do think he is
a capital man for certain types of book, and I can genuinely recommend
him. I think you know enough about his work to know what sort of book
he can best review. Incidentally, I think it would be good for him to do a
little anonymous reviewing.

I hope that you like the Tourneur, when you [have] finished reading it.[1]

> Yours ever,
> [T. S. Eliot]

---

associated with the Vorticist movement (he knew WL and William Roberts, and contributed
woodcuts to the magazine *BLAST*), he became best known as an English expressionist
painter: his work is well represented in the collections at Leeds City Art Gallery and Leeds
University Art Gallery. See further David Manson, *Jacob Kramer: Creativity and Loss*
(2006).
1 – TSE, 'Cyril Tourneur' – on *The Works of Cyril Tourneur*, ed. Allardyce Nicoll – *TLS*, 13
Nov. 1930, 925–6.

11 November 1930   [Faber & Faber Ltd]

Dear Mrs Crosby,

Thank you for your letter of the 5th. I was so sorry not to see you when you were in London, but your visit was quite unexpected.

I shall certainly have a notice of Proust's *Letters to Walter Berry* in the *Criterion* as soon as possible.² I found the letters very interesting and hope that when your edition is exhausted it may be possible to put them within the reach of a larger public. If so, I should be glad to suggest it to my own firm and should be grateful if you would let me hear from you on this point. Incidentally, I think that the book, like all your books, is beautifully produced.

I have received the three volumes of your husband's diary.³ So far I have had time only to dip into it, but it looks very interesting and I intend to read it through as soon as I can, and will then write to you fully.

About Rimbaud:⁴ I still think that the most successful thing as a business venture would be to have a translation, either complete, or properly selected, by Edith Sitwell, with a preface or introduction by her.⁵

---

1 – Caresse Crosby (1892–1970), née Jacob (her parents were wealthy New Yorkers), married in 1922 the poet Harry Crosby, with whom she set up in Paris an imprint called Editions Narcisse, which became the Black Sun Press: they published writers including JJ, DHL, Hart Crane and EP. Following Harry Crosby's suicide in Dec. 1929, she continued to expand the Black Sun Press – publishing works including Hart Crane's *The Bridge* (1930) and editions of her husband's writings – before returning to the USA. In later years she took initiatives in various fields: she opened the Crosby Gallery of Modern Art, Washington, DC; she launched a quarterly journal, *Portfolio: An Intercontinental Review*; and she became active in the international peace movement, co-founding both Citizens of the World and Women Against War. Writings include *Poems for Harry Crosby* (1931); *The Passionate Years* (memoir, 1953).

2 – 47 *Unpublished Letters from Marcel Proust to Walter Berry* (Black Sun Press, 1930). No review appeared in *C*.

3 – Harry Crosby, *Shadows of the Sun* (1928, 1929, 1930). Caresse Crosby wrote again on 16 Nov., apropos 'Harry's diary': 'Your criticism will guide me very much as to its publication.'

4 – Crosby hoped that TSE would write an introduction or foreword to an edition of Rimbaud.

5 – See *Prose Poems from 'Les Illuminations'*: put into English by Helen Rootham, With an Introductory Essay by Edith Sitwell (F&F, 1932). In the F&F catalogue: 'Jean Arthur Rimbaud is not merely one of the most romantic and unaccountable figures in the whole history of French literature, but a poet whose ultimate significance may prove to be greater than is yet understood, and whose influence upon the present generation of poets, in France, in England and elsewhere, has been enormous. Miss Helen Rootham is well qualified for the work of translation by many years devoted to the study of Rimbaud's writings.

'There is no one better qualified than Miss Edith Sitwell, whose own poetry is strongly affected by that of Rimbaud, to interpret him to English readers. A poet who has hitherto

My experience is that with anything of this sort, which requires really brilliant translation, it is better to have both Introduction and translation by the same person. I do not know whether you approached Miss Sitwell, as I suggested, but if you like, I should be very glad to take the matter up with her myself.

Yours very sincerely,
[T. S. Eliot]

TO *Sydney Schiff*[1]   CC

12 November 1930   [Faber & Faber Ltd]

My dear Sydney,

I do not know any way of apologising to you for my neglect of your kind and generous letter of the 1st of May,[2] or your equally kind and generous inscription of *A True Story* in April,[3] about which I hope to

---

been known to the great majority of poetry readers only as a mysterious influence upon other poets, is now made accessible and comprehensible by a happy collaboration of translator and interpreter.'

1–Sydney Schiff (1868–1944), British novelist and translator (illegitimate child of a stockbroker), patron of the arts and friend of WL, JMM, Proust, Osbert Sitwell, published fiction under the name Stephen Hudson. Works include *Richard, Myrtle and I* (1926); and he translated Proust's *Time Regained* (1931). In 1911 he married Violet Beddington (1874–1962), sister of the novelist Ada Leverson (Oscar Wilde's 'Sphinx'). See AH, *Exhumations: correspondence inédite avec Sydney Schiff, 1925–1937*, ed. Robert Clémentine (1976); Richard Davenport-Hines, *A Night at the Majestic: Proust and the Great Modernist Dinner Party of 1922* (2006); Stephen Klaidman, *Sydney and Violet: their life with T. S. Eliot, Proust, Joyce, and the excruciatingly irascible Wyndham Lewis* (2013).

2–Schiff wrote of *Ash-Wednesday*: 'My feeling about these six poems is intensely personal & close. They seem to be speaking aloud my own inmost thoughts about life, about my own spiritual life, thoughts unformed which shake the foundations of my being . . . There must be, I have always thought so, a strange affinity between us in our capacity for suffering . . . If only, at least, you will believe that your poetry means to me something infinitely precious and if you will be indulgent & forgiving towards me for my lame & halting fashion of telling you so, I shall feel comforted though nothing can compensate me for the loss of your affection which I have coveted always though denied all opportunity of kindling or regaining it . . .'

3–Schiff inscribed a copy of *A True Story* (1930), by Stephen Hudson: 'My dear Tom / Please accept this book, a part of which you early befriended, as a messenger of admiration, good-will & affection to Vivienne & yourself. Though we never see you, we constantly talk & think of you & any stray, rare bit of news is eagerly received. Couldn't we meet one day when we return after Easter (we're going to Devon on Saturday) for a few weeks before going abroad for the summer? / With our love to you both / Yours always / S. / April 2. '30' (TSE Library). (TSE had published 'Céleste' by Stephen Hudson, an early version of part of *A True Story*, in C. in 1924.)

have, at some future time, a talk with you. All I can do in reparation is to send you a copy of my latest Christmas card, and all I can say is that when one lives this way, one behaves this way.

If you are, or when you are in London, I should like to renew contact with you which has never, in my mind, been completely broken. And perhaps Violet would be so kind as to drop a line to Vivienne. Our present address, by the way, is

> 68 Clarence Gate Gardens
> Regent's Park
> N.W.1

and we are in the telephone book.

Affectionately yours,
[Tom]

TO *Ants Oras*[1]   TS COPY

12 November 1930   [Faber & Faber Ltd]

Dear Dr Oras,

I must apologise to you for my culpable negligence in not thanking you for your letter of the 30th of August, and for sending me a copy of *Looming*.[2] I am very proud and pleased to have some of my verses translated into Esthonian, and should, of course, be delighted if you cared to do any more. I am sending you a copy of my latest poem herewith.[3]

Yours very sincerely,
[T. S. Eliot]

---

1 – Ants Oras (1900–82): Estonian writer and translator; studied at Tartu University and at Oxford; taught at Tartu from 1928 (as Professor from 1934); and in his later years settled in Gainesville, Florida, where from 1972 he became Professor of English at Florida University. His writings include *The Critical Ideas of T. S. Eliot* (1932); a study of Milton; and many translations from English into Estonian (including Shakespeare, Goethe, Pushkin and Molière) as well as translations of Estonian works into English, German and other languages.

2 – The fifth issue of the magazine *Looming* (May 1929) contained 'Preludes', 'Portrait of a Lady', 'The Hippopotamus' and 'The Hollow Men'.

3 – 'Marina' appeared in *Mana* 3: 4 (1960), 188.

TO *W. H. Auden*   CC

12 November 1930   [Faber & Faber Ltd]

Dear Auden,

Many thanks for your interesting note on Baudelaire.[1] I do not really want to have this book reviewed in the *Criterion* and I think that the subject lends itself rather to a longer article. I do not think that the review form is really suitable for what you have to say. Does the subject interest you sufficiently to study it at greater length, and more generally, bringing in Baudelaire incidentally.[2]

Sincerely yours
[T. S. Eliot]

TO *Butler Hallahan*   CC

14 November 1930   [Faber & Faber Ltd]

My dear Hallihan [*sic*],[3]

I should have answered your kind letter long ago.[4] Meanwhile I hope that you have had your operation and are recuperating comfortably in the pleasant neighbourhood of Bryn Mawr.

My remark about Henry James was intended as a distinction rather than a suggestion of limitation, and there is, of course, something to be said for not having to earn one's living, especially if you make use of the time so profitably as James did. But I think that except where there is a strong passion for some particular kind of work, or an hereditary impulse in some serious direction, that the man of means will find it more difficult to concentrate his energies than the man who has only a few hours in the day.

---

1 – WHA wrote on 4 Nov.: 'I don't know if you already have a reviewer for Baudelaire's "*Journals Intimes*". If you haven't and you think the enclosed would be of any interest, please use it. In any case, if you have the time, I should be grateful to hear your opinion on it.'

2 – Edward Mendelson notes, 'Auden took up Eliot's suggestion, but abandoned it a few days later. He told his brother . . . on 15 November 1930: "I have been trying to write an article for the *Criterion* on Puritanism but I shall chuck it. I can't say things that way. Context and contact are everything. Or else joking verse." No trace of the manuscript survives' (WHA, *Prose and Travel Books in Prose and Verse* I: *1926–1938* (1996), App. v: 'Lost and Unwritten Work', 735).

3 – This letter survives in draft carbon copy: some words in the third paragraph are illegible because of being typed over.

4 – Letter not found.

I feel that in that unfinished book *The Sense of the Past*, James was beginning to see something new – which is certainly an [*several illegible words*] examination of certain types of English vulgarity, which is a much more subtle thing than American vulgarity, compare it with a crude fairy-story like 'The Great Good Place', where his conception of Heaven seems to be an endless weekend at a very large and substantial English country-house. Let me hear from you when you feel fit for it.

> Yours very sincerely,
> [T. S. Eliot]

TO *Edward Sackville-West*   CC

14 November 1930   *The Criterion*

Dear Sackville-West,

I am sorry to hear that you have had to retire to a nursing-home and that you are reduced to such austere fare.[1] Condole yourself with your prune by remembering that the blessed Gautama Buddha is said to have died from eating too many prunes at once. Somehow I feel that there is the ring of truth about this story.

Don't bother to return the bad book, but let me hear from you when you return, refreshed, to London.

> Yours ever,
> [T. S. Eliot]

TO *Frederick Macmillan*   CC

14 November 1930   [Faber & Faber Ltd]

Mr T. S. Eliot desires to thank Sir Frederick Macmillan for sending him the fine copy of the admirable portrait of Mr Charles Whibley, which he is very happy to have.[2]

---

1 – Sackville-West wrote on 1 Nov.: 'About that horrid little volume you sent me – German Lyric Poetry: it isn't worth a review, it's hopeless (scarcely a page to Holderlin!) & in any case I can't do one, because I'm in bed for a month in a nursing-home, receiving a glass of milk & a single prune each hour . . .'
2 – An engraving of a portrait of CW by Sir Gerald Festus Kelly.

TO *G. Wilson Knight* cc

14 November 1930 [Faber & Faber Ltd]

Dear Mr Wilson Knight,

Thank you very much for your letter of the 2nd November, and for the extraordinarily interesting enclosure. I am not quite sure, but I think that, in the case of this play, I can go with you almost the whole way. Indeed, I was astonished to find the conclusions which you arrived at by analysis so close to those suggested to me by personal experience.[1]

I am sending you a small pamphlet, written by an unknown Indian on *The Phoenix and the Turtle*. I wish you would look at it and let me know whether it interests you enough to write a review of it for me?[2]

Yours sincerely,
[T. S. Eliot]

TO *Enrique Fernandez Ledesma*[3] cc

15 November 1930 [Faber & Faber Ltd]

Sir,

I am honoured by your letter of the 11th of October, and beg to inform you that I have a photograph in preparation, of which I will send you a copy to deposit in the archives of the National Library.[4]

May I at the same time take the liberty of expressing the hope that you will secure a photograph of one of the most distinguished sons of your country – my friend Senor Ramon Fernandez, of Paris.

I am, Sir,
Yours faithfully,
[T. S. Eliot]

1 – Wilson Knight was about to write a full essay on *Coriolanus*; in the meantime, he sent TSE 'a couple of pages on the mother–son relation as I see it at present . . . I fear it is very crude . . . If I were asked to say in one sentence what the play stands for I think I should put it like this: *A conflict in the soul between a supreme but self-contained value and love* . . . I think, too, that both this play & *Antony & Cleopatra* are more easily understood by recognising that War-mobility is a competitor in the Shakespearean universe with Love as a "positive" value.'
2 – Wilson Knight reviewed Ranji's *Towards the Stars: being an appreciation of The Phoenix and the Turtle*, in *C.* 10 (Apr. 1931), 571–4.
3 – Enrique Fernandez Ledesma (1888–1939): Deputy Director (later Director) of the National Library of Mexico, 1929–36.
4 – The National Library of Mexico wished to collect photographs ('*con la firma al frente*') and autographs of world-famous cultural figures, and asked TSE to send '*su autógrafo y fotografía*'.

15 November 1930[1]   [Faber & Faber Ltd]

Sir,

I have just read Mr Brian Howard's interesting remarks about myself in your last issue but one.[2] I was glad also to read Mr Brooks's historical corrections, which are entirely justified, except that instead of Mr Huxley, a later arrival, he might have added one or two more eminent names.[3]

It is not however on this subject, whereon I am hardly qualified, that I wish to take up your space. I write as an amateur ornithologist, to protest

---

1 – Published under the title 'Mocking-Birds', *NS* 36: 917 (22 Nov. 1930), 203–4.
2 – 'Mr Eliot's Poetry', *NS* 36: 915 (8 Nov. 1930), 146, argued: 'It is now some ten years since *The Waste Land* appeared, like some austere and unfamiliar flower, in that blown-up cottage garden which was English poetry immediately after the war. The Georgian poets were busy planting hardy perennials . . . Suddenly – *The Waste Land*, and it may be said, with small exaggeration, that English poetry of the first half of the twentieth century began . . . The newest among Mr Eliot's longer poems has . . . a certain flamelessness . . . *Ash Wednesday* is . . . an important and beautiful poem. That it is grave, that it is what is termed "intellectual", is true. But it is this very quietness, this very severity, which imparts to it that particular quality of beauty so gratefully devoured by the sensitive modern mind. The courage for fine frenzies is already, let us hope, returning. It is being given to us, a trifle savagely, by Mr Roy Campbell. But it is Mr Eliot . . . who will have made these future frenzies possible and valuable again, if valuable they prove to be. Because, upon reflection, it was not the guns that had silenced the nightingale. It was the mocking-bird.'
3 – Benjamin Gilbert Brooks, 'Mr T. S. Eliot' (Correspondence), *NS* 36: 916 (15 Nov. 1930), 174: 'I feel I cannot allow the pretentious inaccuracy of Mr Brian Howard's article on T. S. Eliot to go unchallenged. He presents a wholly false summary of the history of recent poetical fashion, so as to give prominence to the influence of his author, and particularly to exaggerate the historical importance of one specific poem – *The Waste Land.*

'Eliot's real value, to my mind, is not in the "fearless" message, which is after all a private matter that concerns himself and God (and only non-poetically those whom the same problem confronts), but in his austere, determined and (if Mr Howard will pardon the phrase) his flame-like pursuit of the unity of technique with poetic idea . . .

'Again, the statement that *The Waste Land* appeared in the midst of Georgian "hardy perennials" is simply untrue. From 1910, at least, no one who counted wrote "cottage-garden" poetry . . . The poem of Eliot's that most influenced his own generation was *Prufrock* – which appeared about 1917 or (in magazine form) slightly earlier. Mr Howard can start his new epoch here, if he really must have Mr Eliot. But Yeats, Pound, Hueffer (Ford), Aldington, Huxley and Graves were equally important figures between 1912 and 1922: definitely *not* of the "cottage-garden" tradition, most emphatically dating from before *The Waste Land* . . .

'Finally, why distort the facts relating to Roy Campbell? He is alluded to in the concluding paragraph as one who "*is*" giving us "a courage for fine frenzies". I am not certain of the dates, but I know that *The Flaming Terrapin* is so near in time to *The Waste Land* (if it does not actually precede it) that to treat it as a salutary reaction reflecting value on Eliot is to be unfair to both poets. Surely, Mr Eliot's later work is important enough to need no such bush.'

against Mr Howard's use of the mocking-bird as an illustration. Mr Howard, no doubt deluded by the name of this unfortunate bird (who is also doubly maligned by his scientific style of *mimus polyglottos*), seems to think that the mocking-bird does nothing but mock. I dare say I have listened to more mocking-birds than he has; and my own observation is supported by the great authority of Dr Frank Chapman, who writes 'in my experience many mocking-birds have no notes besides their own, and good mockers are exceptional'. I have less knowledge of nightingales, except for their literary associations, which are useful; but I am ready to affirm that a fine mocking-bird in his own pure song is at least the nightingale's equal. Dr Chapman also says that the mocking-bird 'is a good citizen, and courting rather than shunning public life, shows an evident interest in the affairs of the day.'[1]

I will add only a few words by another authority, Dr R. W. Shufeldt, which I do not however quote as a specimen of prose style:

'I believe, were he successfully introduced into those countries where the Nightingale flourishes, that princely performer might some day wince as he was obliged to listen to his own most powerful strains poured with all their native purity by the [*sc.* this] king of feathered mockers.'[2]

> I am, Sir,
> Your obliged servant,
> T. S. Eliot

1–Frank M. Chapman, *Handbook of Birds of Eastern North America* (1895), 408. TSE cited Chapman's *Handbook* (a favourite of his childhood) in his note to l. 357 of *TWL*, with reference to the song of the hermit thrush.
2–Robert W. Shufeldt, MD, entry on 'Mocking-bird', in Alfred Newton, *A Dictionary of Birds* (1899), 585.

TO *George Williamson*[1]   TS Williamson

15 November 1930   Faber & Faber Ltd

Dear Mr Williamson,

Thank you very much for your kind letter of the 25th ultimo.[2] It makes me feel rather ashamed of myself, because I certainly ought to have written to you as soon as I had read your book.

I think that your book is an excellent piece of work, as also thinks my friend Mr Mario Praz, who is certainly more of an authority on the facts than am I. In truth, your book renders a good part of my projected work superfluous, and I have had to reconstruct its design. But that is perhaps a good thing; since I gave the Clark lectures, I think that the Metaphysical poets are much better known – I do not mean at all through my influence, but because it was something which was bound to happen. I should now, for instance, assume that the reader knows more than he did in 1925, and that he has access to your book. I shall, in fact, devote much more space to more general discussions, such as the nature of the theory of Belief. It may turn out to be something quite as rambling and inconsequential as *Biographia Literaria*.[3]

I am writing this at my office, and your book is at home. The next time I have occasion to consult it I will make note of any criticisms. At any rate you have succeeded in obliterating the more obvious traces of the

1–George Williamson (1898–1968) taught at Pomona College, Claremont, California, 1925–7; then in the Department of English, Stanford University, and later at the University of Chicago, 1936–68, where he was Professor of English from 1940. His publications include *The Talent of T. S. Eliot* (1929), *The Donne Tradition* (1930), and *A Reader's Guide to T. S. Eliot* (1953).

2–'Now that *The Donne Tradition* [1930] is published I hope that it may not fall too far short of the debt which it owes to you, and that I may soon have the pleasure of reading your "School of Donne" . . . In one or two reviews of my book mention has been made of your Clark Lectures, which I learned of only last December in a review by Mario Praz in *English Studies* . . . Will it be out soon? . . . The character of my book is somewhat limited by the fact that it was written for the doctorate in English at Stanford University . . .'

3–Earlier, TSE had mentioned to HR (in a now lost letter) his apprehension that Williamson's book had eclipsed his own work on Metaphysical Poetry (the expected publication, revised, of his Clark Lectures, 1926); and HR responded on 17 May 1930: 'The situation created by Williamson's book is awkward. I should very much regret not seeing your Clark lectures in print, and I don't think from a publisher's point of view your book would be affected . . . I believe your idea was to *expand* the lectures as given, making them more explicit. It would be worthwhile considering if they would not condense a little, into something rather like, in bulk & treatment, Coleridge's *Lectures on Shakespeare*. My general feeling is, that there was far too much of interesting general observation in the lectures, for them to be lightly scrapped.'

university dissertation, and I must add that I was greatly flattered by your references to myself.

Yours sincerely,
T. S. Eliot

TO *Bonamy Dobrée*

17 November 1930   Faber & Faber Ltd

Dear Bonamy,

I am obliged to you for calling my attention.[1] It's ALL wrong: please read COMMA after *sense*, SEMICOLON after *penetrate*; and COMMA after *experience*. That's better. I shall expect everyone but yourself to PURCHASE a new edition; as for you, please paste this into your copy if you have one.

Yr. remarks about duplication are a bit awkward for me, & I may cut them out. The fact is that I have recently written to an American lady (unknown) an angry lady,[2] who felt swindled by finding the same articles etc. in American and English periodicals, and it is a little humiliating to have to print a complaint to the same effect from you.

Yrs in haste,
Thomas S.

I have just composed *such* an informative letter in the *New Statesman*. I wonder if they will print it.

I have just got some ˆ ¨ ´ ' put on and have not learned the controls yet.

1 – BD's letter about TSE's poem 'Whispers of Immortality' has not been found.
2 – Gertrude W. Page: see 9 Oct. 1930, above.

TO *William Temple*[1]   CC

19 November 1930   [Faber & Faber Ltd]

Your Grace,

I am taking the liberty of sending you a pamphlet, which you probably will not have time to read, on The Lambeth Conference.[2] It is written by a young Scot of some journalistic ability and was done really at my instigation as I thought it would be interesting to have a comment on that conference by an outsider. There is much in the pamphlet with which I agree as well as a good deal which I find offensive. I am told by the chairman that I had better write another pamphlet myself, which I am not in the least anxious to do, but if no one else can be found, I suppose I must.

> I am,
> Your Grace's obedient servant,
> [T. S. Eliot]

TO *Charles Harris*   CC

19 November 1930   [Faber & Faber Ltd]

Dear Harris,

Private and Confidential

Replying to yours of the 11th,[3] it is arranged that I must try to tackle this pamphlet myself, though it is difficult to put aside enough other work to be able to get it done quickly. Meanwhile I should be grateful for any further suggestions. Ought I to read the Report (if obtainable) of the 1920 Conference?

I am sending you herewith, for inspection and return, the outline of a project put forward for a book to be published by my firm.[4] It is not a

---

1–William Temple (1881–1944) – son of Frederick Temple (1821–1902), Archbishop of Canterbury – taught Classics at Oxford University; was ordained in 1908; served as Headmaster of Repton School, Derbyshire, 1910–14; and was Bishop of Manchester until translated in 1929 to the Archbishopric of York. In 1942 he became Archbishop of Canterbury. Writings include *Christus Veritas* (1924), *Nature, Man and God* (1934), *Christianity and Social Order* (1942). In the 1920s he won authority as a leader of the movement for international ecumenism – 'this world-wide Christian fellowship', as he proclaimed it.
2–George Malcolm Thomson, *The Lambeth Conference* (F&F, 1930).
3–Not found.
4–Presumably the anthology of essays on Jesus Christ mentioned to Harris on 25 Nov. 1930.

type of symposium which interests me personally; but if it can be done without vulgarity, and is likely to be profitable, I have no objections to raise. I should be grateful for any comment that suggests itself to you; whether you think there would be a considerable public for such a book; and how best it could be ordered so as to be useful.

Yours sincerely,
[T. S. Eliot]

I have forgotten how many hundred thousand words was estimated for the Encyclopaedia in all – so that at the moment my percentage leaves me still in the dark. Would it be possible to say roughly how many words my section might have altogether? I could work on that.

TO *George Bell*   TS Lambeth

19 November 1930   Faber & Faber Ltd

My dear Lord Bishop,

I am sending you, with some diffidence, a pamphlet written by a young friend of mine on the Lambeth Conference.[1] It was written at my instigation because, having read other writings by the same man, I thought that it would be interesting to have a criticism of the Conference by someone quite outside the Anglican Communion; and as Thomson takes such a lively interest in the affairs of his own Church in Scotland, I thought that he would be a suitable selection. I am, I confess, a little perturbed by the result. Personally, I am apprehensive lest this pamphlet, being produced by my own firm, might be taken to represent my own views; impersonally, the chairman agrees with me that it is desirable to produce as soon as possible another pamphlet, covering more or less the same ground from a different point of view.[2] I have gone into the matter in some detail with the chairman, and with Prebendary Harris, and the upshot is that I am expected to write the pamphlet myself. As a peace-loving person I dislike thrusting my head into a beehive, and if anyone can suggest anybody more suitable I should be very grateful; but for the moment I am left struggling with the problem myself. If I do it, I may ask Kenneth Ingram to help me; there again the points of view are not exactly

1–Thomson, *The Lambeth Conference*.
2–Thomson, after reading TSE's pamphlet *Thoughts after Lambeth*, wrote on 8 Mar. 1931: 'I have read it with intense interest and great admiration. It has been a somewhat humbling experience for me and I am not at all sure that I can afford to be humbled. You have let me down very gently. Only one sentence made me squirm – and in that case I asked for it.'

the same, but perhaps the differences might be instructive. Meanwhile, if you can find time to read the pamphlet, and to reply to this letter, I should be extremely grateful for any suggestions.

There is another point on which I should be grateful for your advice. I have undertaken the editorial department of Literature and Art in a projected Christian Encyclopedia of some dimensions. I must, of course, have contributions on the subject of religious drama. The medieval period presents no particular difficulty: I should apply to someone like Sir Edmund Chambers,[1] or Miss Welsford.[2] But I think we should have also an essay on both the modern revivals of medieval religious plays, and original modern plays. If you could make any suggestions to me of possible authors, I should be very grateful; if not, I am afraid that I must eat my words, and apply to the Poet Laureate.[3]

I am, my Lord,
Yours sincerely.
T. S. Eliot

TO *Ottoline Morrell*   CC

19 November 1930   [Faber & Faber Ltd]

My dear Ottoline,

I am sorry I could not answer your letter of the 14th at once.[4] About Italian translators, the only person I know personally who likes to translate from the Italian is Orlo Williams, 16 Aubrey Walk, W.8: but he is a clerk of the House of Commons and only translates as a pleasant avocation. Please do not confound him with Iolo Williams.[5] I am, however, asking my secretary kindly to look up the names of persons who have [been] considered, or who have applied to the firm for this use.

1–Sir Edmund Chambers (1866–1954), theatre historian and editor, worked as a civil servant for the Board of Education, 1892–1926. He was the first president of the Malone Society, 1906–39; and his many distinguished publications include *The Medieval Stage* (2 vols, 1903); *The Elizabethan Stage* (4 vols, 1923); and *Shakespeare* (2 vols, 1930).
2–Enid Welsford (1892–1981): Fellow of Newnham College, Cambridge; Director of Studies in English, 1929–52; University Lecturer, 1928–59. Works include *The Court Masque* (1927) and *The Fool: His Social and Literary History* (1935).
3–John Masefield.
4–'I quite forgot today to ask you if you could recommend anyone to translate an Italian Novel. It is a good one called "L'Indifferente" by Alberto Maravia [*sc.* Moravia]. He is in London now – a *nice* & intelligent young man.'
5–Iolo Williams (1890–1962): journalist, author and art historian; bibliographical correspondent for the *London Mercury*, 1920–39.

I have signed the books for you, but I have left them at home. I will try to remember to bring them tomorrow to be sent round to you. I should be glad to do the same for Julian[1] if she would like it. But I wonder whether some Ariel Poems have gone astray as I am almost certain that I have sent a copy of each one as it appeared.[2]

Affectionately yours,
[Tom]

P.S. If Signor Maradici [*sc.* Moravia][3] returns to London, will you let me know? I see from your letter that he is just leaving, so it is no use my writing to him now.

TO *Austin Warren*[4]   TS Antonia J. Warren

19 November 1930   Faber & Faber Ltd

Dear Sir,

Thank you for your kind letter.[5] The interests which you have certainly seem to make it desirable that we should meet. I suggest that you should

---

1 – Julian Morrell (1906–90): only surviving child of Philip and Ottoline Morrell.

2 – 'Also thank you . . . for putting yr name in my books. They make them more precious somehow I don't know why. I will tell Julian of your offer. I shall see her next week.

'The vol. you gave me was *Ash Wednesday* & I have looked through all my Ariel Poems & I find you *did* send me *Simeon*. I had overlooked it as you put your name at the end.'

3 – TSE's misspelling reflected OM's eccentric handwriting of the name. OM replied on 20 Nov., 'Thank you very much for the names of Italian Translators. I will forward them to Signor *Moravia* (28 Oakley St.). I think he returns to London in a few days.'

4 – Austin Warren (1899–1986), American literary critic and author, taught for some years at the College of Practical Arts and Letters, Boston University; at the University of Iowa, 1939–48; and at the University of Michigan for twenty years from 1948; he was a Fellow of the Kenyon School of English in the summers of 1948–50; Senior Fellow of the School of Letters, Indiana University, 1950–64. Publications include *Richard Crashaw: A Study in the Baroque Sensibility* (1939) and *A Theory of Literature* (co-authored with René Wellek, 1949). See further *Teacher and Critic: Essays by and about Austin Warren*, ed. Myron Simon and Harvey Gross (1976).

5 – Warren wrote on 17 Nov. that he was working for a year at the British Museum on a study of Richard Crashaw, funded by a Rockefeller Fellowship. At Harvard Graduate School in 1921 he had studied Romanticism with Irving Babbitt; he was known too to Paul Elmer More and Norman Foerster; and he felt close to TSE's 'position' in *For Lancelot Andrewes*. He had published his doctoral dissertation, *Alexander Pope as Critic and Humanist* (1929), and he wrote for *Sewanee Review* and *The Bookman* (New York). He was keen to meet TSE.

ring up my secretary at this address and make an appointment. Twelve
o'clock on any day except Saturday would be convenient.[1]

Yours very truly,

T. S. Eliot

TO *Erich Alport*

TS BL

20 November 1930   Faber & Faber Ltd

My dear Alport,

I am glad to hear from you further about Curtius's book.[2] You must
understand that no reflection was made on the quality of Bergstrasser's
part of the work; the question was entirely one of saleability. Now that
I have heard from you so definitely, we are going into the question again
more thoroughly, and I will write both to you and to Curtius when we
have made up our minds.

The book you mentioned, by Zweig, sounds not only extremely
interesting, but quite possible for a London publisher.[3] I should like very

---

1 – Warren recalled, in 'A Survivor's Tribute to T. S. Eliot' (1985), 'I wrote Eliot . . . telling
him of the Crashaw project and asking him if I might meet him. He replied immediately,
with that generosity to younger writers for which he has justly been renowned, inviting me
to call at his office . . . The subject of our talk was chiefly the late, or later, Henry James;
after all these years I recognize that Eliot's talk during the meal about *The Sense of the Past*
and *The Ivory Tower* was apropos of what Eliot, confusing father and son, thought I was
writing about.

'When we met Eliot, who was about ten years older than I, that is about forty, no longer
was the handsome, elegant young man familiar from his earlier photographs: he now
was spectacled and his teeth had become carious. His intonation was distinctly British.
He looked the man of affairs, not my image of a poet or literary man' (*Essays from the
'Southern Review'* [1988], 287–8).

2 – Alport reported on 6 Nov.: 'I hear from Curtius that his part of the work on France, *Die
französiche Kultur*, is going to be translated & published by the firm of Grasset (who will
also translate & publish his *Balzac*). Now . . . the question of an English edition might be
approached from a different point of view. The first (Curtius) volume, as you may remember,
contains only 196 pages while the second numbers 324; it is also much easier to translate
and, of course, much easier and more entertaining to read than the economic & political
part. I need hardly to add that the reviews in the German as well as the French papers &
periodicals have been splendid; they all dwell on the excellence of the first volume which
is regarded as a masterpiece of sound judgement, connoisseurship & literary achievement,
while the great value & merit of the second volume are recognized. After all, the comparison
is not quite fair, for Dr [Arnold] Bergstraesse is a young man, & this is his first real book,
while Curtius is an experienced writer . . .'

3 – 'Stephan Zweig is shortly going to publish a book which promises to be very interesting.
It will contain three long essays on three persons with a particular power & influence on
people's minds: Mesmer, Mary Baker-Eddy and Sigmund Freud. The first two have already

much to see a copy of it the moment it appears and if possible to secure a limited option on it at once. If the book is not appearing immediately, would it be possible to get hold of the parts which have appeared in the newspapers?

You don't say how long you are staying at your hotel with the delightful name[1] in Saint-Tropez. If you are as fond of garlic as I am you may remain there eating the ayoli indefinitely. Saint-Tropez usually has one or two of my friends there in the winter, and I dare say you may see Roger Fry or Duncan Grant.

Yours ever,
T. S. Eliot

TO *Kenneth Ingram* cc

20 November 1930   [Faber & Faber Ltd]

Dear Ingram,

I must apologise about the other evening. About 6 o'clock I tried to ring you up at home to ask for more precise directions to the Prince's Room.[2] Your housekeeper said that you had not yet come in and that therefore she did not expect you. Later I started to try to find my way with a taxi, but as none of the men on the rank had the faintest idea where the Prince's Room was, and as the evening was very wet, I returned home. I hope that I may have exact bearings for the next occasion. I ought to have assured myself in good time.

Meanwhile, there is quite another matter I am anxious to talk to you about as soon as possible. Would you be free for lunch any day next week, or otherwise would it be convenient for you to call here when you are in this neighbourhood?

Yours sincerely,
[T. S. Eliot]

---

appeared . . . the third is probably going to be the longest & most interesting, for Zweig, as he told me, is a friend of Freud's and so has all the genuine information at his disposal. – If you think it worthwhile I might try and get an option (although it is most likely that Secker's have one already).'

1 – Hostellerie de l'Ayoli.

2 – Ingram responded on 21 Nov.: 'I am most awfully sorry about the meeting [of the Grecian Club] last Tuesday. I thought that *every* notice had typed on it "Prince Henry's Room" – Fleet Street – *opposite* Chancery Lane.' Future meetings would be held at the 'Cheshire Cheese' pub on Fleet Street.

TO *Richard Ellis Roberts*[1]   CC

20 November 1930   [Faber & Faber Ltd]

Dear Mr Roberts,

Thank you for your letter of the 11th and for your kind invitation to contribute to the *New Statesman*.[2] I should of course be very pleased to do so whenever possible. As for reviews, I feel that I have long since reached an age at which reviewing should be passed on to the younger generation, except of course in very special cases. If you think that the book you mention is a special case, I should be very glad to look at it and would tell you at once whether I thought it was something I could deal with or not.

Yes, I do know your brother, and your sister-in-law.[3] And I had hoped to meet you on Tuesday night, for which reason I had put off writing; but unfortunately I could not find a taxi-driver who knew where the Grecian Club was.

                                        Yours sincerely,
                                        [T. S. Eliot]

TO *G. Wilson Knight*   CC

21 November 1930   [Faber & Faber Ltd]

Dear Wilson Knight,

Thank you for your letter of the 15th, and for your remarks about my paper.[4] From what you say I cannot make out whatever may be the essence of Middleton Murry's criticism of your work. If I see him, I will raise the point. Now-a-days I only see him once a quarter.[5]

---

1 – R. Ellis Roberts (1879–1953): author, poet, journalist; translator of Ibsen; literary editor of *NS*, 1930–2, *Time and Tide*, 1933–4; editor of *Life and Letters*, 1934–5.
2 – Roberts offered H. F. B. Mackay's *Adventure of Paul of Tarsus* – 'a book whose literary merit is almost certain to get neglected because of its religious complexion'.
3 – William C. Roberts was Rector of St George's, Bloomsbury.
4 – 'I was very much interested in your article in the last *T.L.S.* ['Cyril Tourneur', 13 Nov. 1930] I think I am right in supposing it yours – both on grounds of style and subject matter. You will understand that some of the remarks in it – notably those on *Cymbeline* and the part on Shakespeare's development – gave me much pleasure, being so closely in harmony with my findings. I am glad to feel you agree, on grounds of pure style, with my idea that the final plays are progressive, not retrograde.'
5 – GWK noted that JMM had written. 'My work appears to trouble him, and he finds his outlook "fundamentally" different from mine.'

About the pamphlet, on *The Phoenix and the Turtle*,[1] I should have said about 800 words, but if you think it requires more space, let me know. It is a type of publication which is apt to be overlooked, and therefore, if good, we ought to be generous with space. I agree with you about Fletcher.

I am glad to hear that you have accepted the invitation of the Shakespeare Association.[2]

Yours sincerely,
[T. S. Eliot]

TO *J. M. Robertson*   CC

21 November 1930   [*The Criterion*]

My dear Robertson,

Thank you for your letter of the 14th and for your review of the Burdett book.[3] I believe that the Chambers book is coming, and if so, it will be passed on to you. You will have ample time, I hope, because the December number is in press, and I should therefore want it for March.[4]

Don't bother about *Whisky*; but I shall send you a complimentary copy for your private opinion.[5] And do I understand that you can make no appointment for lunch until after Hogmanay?

Yours sincerely,
[T. S. Eliot]

---

1 – Ranji, *Towards the Stars*.
2 – GWK was to read a paper to the Shakespeare Association – 'The Shakespearean Tempest', tracing the development in the plays of the symbol and image of 'tempests' – on 20 Mar. 1931.
3 – Robertson reviewed Osbert Burdett's *The Two Carlyles*: C. 10 (Jan. 1931), 363.
4 – 'I have so often "dotted him one" that I could handle this contraption with impressive calm – our accounts being already well balanced.' Untitled review of E. K. Chambers, *William Shakespeare: A Study of Facts and Problems*, C. 10 (Apr. 1931), 520–9.
5 – 'As to Whiskey, I am dubious of the utility of reviewing that booklet.'

TO *Richard & Sally Cobden-Sanderson*[1]   TS Texas

21 November 1930   68 Clarence Gate Gardens

Dear Sir and Madam,

I mean dear Madam and Sir. Touching your undated communication, I have given the matter my fullest consideration; and regret that I cannot give the countenance of my countenance to the soirée in question, nor allow my wife to do so. My reasons are as follows:

Cocktails are not ENGLISH.

Although I am aware of the tolerance recently granted to the word *coquetel*, they are not FRENCH.

Cocktails are not SCANDINAVIAN.

No connaisseur [*sic*] of Gin can approve the cocktail.

Let me consider these points in order.

The proper English potion at that time of day is a glass or more of light dry SHERRY. I do not think that even Sherry & Bitters can be tolerated: it is only a disguise for bad Sherry.

Of proper French potions there are several, as is well known; but my own fancy is ANIS DEL OSO, failing which a PICON CURACAO.

The proper Scandinavian potion is a glass of more of SCHNAPPS. I consider Swedish preferable to Norwegian, but that is a matter of taste.

The Cocktail or more is commonly drunk by persons who have not the slightest discrimination between one kind of GIN and another. Now GIN is the foundation of the Cocktail, every schoolgirl knows that; but not every Adult knows that the cocktail is the *ruin* of GIN. (See my forthcoming monograph entitled "The Palace of Gin"). Everything you add to GIN injures it; though in special circumstances a little water may be infused.

Of GIN there are several kinds: from Geneva, Hollands, and Booth, down through Nicholson's and Cremorne. Of these the most deteriorate, and therefore the least humiliated by the Cocktail, is Cremorne.

There is more that I could say about the Cocktail, but this verges upon social criticism, and I do not wish to enter upon disputatious or invidious subjects. What I have said above is incontrovertible.

1–Richard Cobden-Sanderson (1884–1964), printer and publisher, son of the bookbinder and printer T. J. Cobden Sanderson (1840–1922); grandson of the politician and economist Richard Cobden (1804–65). He launched his business in 1919 and was publisher of C. from its first number in Oct. 1922 until it was taken over by F&G in 1925. He also published three books with introductions by TSE: *Le Serpent* by Paul Valéry (1924); Charlotte Eliot's *Savonarola* (1926); Harold Monro's *Collected Poems* (1933). His wife was Gwladys (Sally).

Hoping therefore to have the pleasure of visiting you when none of the ingredients of the Cocktail except the Gin is in your house, I am, your faithful wellwisher & friend,

T. S. Eliot

TO *I. A. Richards*   TS Magdalene

21 November 1930   Faber & Faber Ltd

My dear Richards,

Very many thanks for your letter, which was more than welcome after such a long silence. Certainly I will prepare new copies of *Ash Wednesday*, *Anabasis*, and the poems which have gone astray. They shall not, however, be put down to your account.[1]

As I feel very uncertain from your letter to what address I ought to write, I shall not attempt to discuss any of the interesting points you raise until I know that you are solidly settled in Cambridge.[2] So this note is merely a forerunner, and I shall wait to hear from you from Cambridge. You don't even seem certain of your address at Harvard. There is a Dunster Hall, or was; I once lived there myself, sharing rooms with an eccentric French count, who eventually died of alcoholic psychosis. But I am rather doubtful if Mrs Richards is with you whether that is your address, because it was in my time purely an undergraduate dormitory. So I am addressing this letter as you see.

With kindest regards to Mrs Richards and yourself, from both of us,

Yours ever,

T. S. Eliot

1–IAR wrote on 19 Oct. that neither *Ash-Wednesday* nor *Anabasis* – signed copies posted by TSE – had reached him; and someone had taken the copy of *Ash-Wednesday* that he already possessed. 'Do . . . ask the Publishers to send me *Ash Wednesday*, *Anabasis* and *Animula* and open an account against me. *Only* do intercept them and inscribe.' TSE inscribed *Ash-Wednesday* 'for I. A. Richards / with the homage of T. S. Eliot.'

2–IAR was 'trying hard to practice being on both sides of the mirror' in preparation for writing *Mencius on the Mind*. 'At the least it gives me the best exercise I have ever had in multiple definition and imagining possible meanings . . . I'm realizing every week that your "understanding = familiarity" equation (suggested in your last letter [9 Aug. 1930]) is not *very* far wrong' (*Letters*, 57–9).

TO *Sylvia Beach*[1]   TS National Gallery of Ireland

Telegram 24 November 1930   [Faber & Faber Ltd]

IS JOYCE PARIS OR ZURICH PLEASE WIRE ADDRESS WRITING
ELIOT

FROM *Sylvia Beach*

Telegram [Undated]

JOYCE ZURICH HOTEL ELITE CARLTON PROBABLY RETURNING PARIS
THURSDAY
    SYLVIA BEACH

TO *Charles Harris*   CC

25 November 1930   [Faber & Faber Ltd]

Dear Harris,
                          Confidential
    Very many thanks for your letter of the 22nd. I have just obtained
the 1920 report: I wanted to observe the progress of ten years. Though
I wish my pamphlet (which is under weigh) to appear as a personal and

---

1–Sylvia Beach (1887–1962), American expatriate who in Nov. 1919 opened (with
Adrienne Monnier) Shakespeare & Company, a bookshop and lending library, at 8 rue
Dupuytren, Paris, moving two years later to 12 rue de l'Odéon. Her customers included
JJ (she published *Ulysses*), Gide, Maurois, Valéry, EP, Hemingway and Stein. Beach wrote
of TSE in 1923: 'He is such a charming fellow and so interesting, the old fashioned sort
of American and very good looking. I only wish he lived in Paris. He is our only modern
writer I like after Joyce . . . Everyone that he was exhibited to was carried away by Eliot'
(Noel Riley Fitch, *Sylvia Beach and the Lost Generation: A History of Literary Paris in the
Twenties and Thirties* [1984], 158). Beach and Monnier published their translation of 'The
Love Song of J. Alfred Prufrock' in the first issue of their magazine *Le Navire d'Argent*, June
1925 – 'we never heard any reproaches from our victim,' said Beach. TSE wrote in tribute
('Miss Sylvia Beach', *The Times*, 13 Oct. 1962): 'I made the acquaintance of Sylvia Beach,
and . . . Adrienne Monnier, on a visit to Paris early in the 1920s, and thereafter saw them
frequently during that decade. Only the scattered survivors of the Franco-Anglo-American
world of Paris of that period, and a few others like myself who made frequent excursions
across the Channel, know how important a part these two women played in the artistic
and intellectual life of those years.' See further *The Letters of Sylvia Beach*, ed. Keri Walsh
(2010); *James Joyce's Letters to Sylvia Beach 1921–1940*, ed. Melissa Banta and Oscar A.
Silverman (1987).

independent expression of view, and not as a perfunctory or 'framed' rejoinder to Thomson (whom I shall only mention in passing), I shall want to ask you and one or two others – I think Underhill and the Bp. of Chichester – to look it over before it goes to press. I hope to finish it about the middle of the month.

About the first part of your letter, I think we are in accord.[1] I regret the fuss raised by Romanisers on the one hand, and World-Leaguers-for-Sexual-Reform on the other; I approve the independence of the view expressed in the Report: but I must deplore the exhortation to exercise private judgement on one of the last matters on which it seems to me safe for the laity to exercise such private judgement. I shall put that down in my essay. Of course my view implies the necessity of educating the parish clergy, as well as more specialised directors, to the point at which they can exercise their responsibility properly – a very difficult responsibility in any case. I agree with you about the actual odiousness both of idea and methods: it is one reason (among others) why in my younger and unregenerate time I found (without any sense of sin) adultery to be quite unsatisfactory.[2]

II. About the Jesus-compilation.[3] I find that my view is not at all shared by everyone, and I shall not stand in the way of my firm's publishing such

1 – 'I consider the 1930s pronouncement obscure, lacking in clear principle, and likely to lead to serious abuse. I think that there are a few exceptional cases in which, after consultation between a skilful spiritual adviser and well-qualified medical man, contraceptives might be allowed for fear of worse evils . . . Their use concentrates attention upon physical sexual pleasure, and dissociates the sexual life, which in the normal man or woman is bound up with the parental instinct, and spiritual love. Any procedure which "splits off" physical pleasure and makes it an end in itself, is unhealthy and dangerous. The manipulation of contraceptives is repulsive, and lowers the tone of marriage, which is a most holy and beautiful relation.'

2 – TSE sent a draft by mid-Dec., along with a (now lost) letter. Harris responded on 20 Dec.:
  'It is miles better than the pamphlet it supplements and supersedes.
  'I am *quite* in agreement with what you say about spiritual guidance in connection with birth control.
  'On the other hand, I am inclined to agree with the bishops that "there is much (they do not say more than this) in the scientific and philosophic thinking of our time which provides a climate more favourable to faith in God than has existed for generations." . . .
  'Modern science allows spiritual views of the world (orthodox and heretical) to be held without coming into conflict with itself. This being the case, orthodoxy can easily overcome heresy, it being more coherent, complete, and satisfying.
  '[Sir James] Jeans is not a Christian. He regards God as a perfect *mathematician*. But this is an advance on the worship of blind physical energy . . . If God is a mathematician, he must be a great deal more, otherwise he would not have created the human mind – the greatest known thing in the universe.'

3 – Harris wrote on 22 Nov.: 'As to your proposed book, it does not appeal to me at all, and (I should say), it would not sell widely in England. But I understand the religious better than the secular public.'

a book if the majority think best; but I shall decline to have anything to do with it myself, as I find the idea too offensive. I shall if the book is approved, confine myself to trying to exercise censorship, but without any other responsibility.

I ought to say again that I write in confidence – personal confidences don't matter – but confidences about the internal affairs of my publishing house do matter.

Sincerely yours,
[T. S. Eliot]

P.S. I am delighted to hear about Temple.[1]

TO *George Bell*   TS Lambeth

25 November 1930   Faber & Faber Ltd

My dear Lord Bishop,

I am more than grateful to you for your kind and helpful letter.[2] About Thomson – I was more worried myself by his rather vulgar smartness of manner (and abominable abuse of metaphor) than by his matter. Certainly he is ignorant: evidently he knows very little of the history of the English Church – yet I believe that the impression of an alert journalist who has read the report and knows nothing else, is not wholly without value. I was particularly relieved to have your comment on the Youth section; because on this point I almost primed him, though I take no responsibility for the way in which he said it. As for the Sex Resolution, my own view is very simple: I welcome the independence of the Bishops in not slavishly following Rome, and I only regret the insertion of the clause allowing private judgement: it seems to me to be distinctly the place for insisting that the laity should take spiritual counsel and direction – and incidentally

---

1 – Harris wrote (22 Nov.), 'I have landed Leviathan. The Archbishop of York will edit the section *Social and Political Science*.'

2 – Bell wrote on 23 Nov.: 'I read Thomson's *Will the Scottish Church Survive*[?] with much interest. Indeed I even quoted one of its more pungent phrases when making a speech on Reunion at the Lambeth Conference . . . The pamphlet on *The Lambeth Conference* is both spicy and unfair: but it's ignorant . . . I don't think such a pamphlet can do much harm, I confess! Its temper is so curious. But nothing would please me more than a pamphlet by yourself on the same theme from your point of view – more giving TSE than replying to GMT . . .

'Thomson is thoroughly justified in what he says about the Youth section, which was very bad. He is too cheap by half on the Six Resolutions (you should read Spens in the December issue of *Theology*). He misses the point altogether in what he says about Reunion . . .'

for gradually making the parish clergy prepare themselves for being able to give (perhaps with the collaboration of medical men) wise direction. You may find such suggestions impertinent from me, but these are among the matters which I should like to discuss with you.[1] I will take care to read what Spens says.

Thank you very much indeed for your suggestions of names.[2] I rather dread Pollard,[3] because I find him so embarrassing to talk to, and cannot understand a word he says: but he is certainly a first rate scholar. I shall certainly try one from among your number however. Mine is an amazingly vague and difficult department to organise: but the thing I am sure must be avoided is the inclusion of articles which, for the matter, might as well be in any other encyclopaedia, but varnished over with the surface of piety. The reader I have in mind is the parish priest who is inclined to draw upon literature for embellishment or illustration, and who needs to be told how far particular authors – e.g. Wordsworth *can* correctly be drawn upon for Christian sentiment and how far they are suspect. I do not know whether my hypothetical curate or vicar exists; but this again is a subject on which I should like to have your views and knowledge.

It is very kind of you to ask us for the weekend of the 14th proximo: may I leave it and write to you in two days time? I was to have been at Kelham for a week then; but various circumstances, including the pressure of this pamphlet, now make it desirable to postpone my visit till the beginning of January; and apart from the pleasure of a visit, I think that the middle of December would fit in with the completion of my pamphlet, so that I could go through it with you, if you will. (Certainly I should not pass it for press without a few informal *nihil obstats* – I may show it to Underhill, Selwyn and Harris). So if I can arrange to come to Chichester I shall. I am not sure whether my wife can accompany me or not – she would very much like to come, it is a question of health – but

1 – Bell responded to this paragraph on 26 Nov.: 'I am very much interested in what you say about Thomson and also about the Lambeth Conference. I welcome your suggestions . . .'
2 – 'I am very glad to hear you are Editing Literature and Art in the new Christian Encyclopaedia, of which I know something. On Religious Drama you may think of A. W. Pollard also for the medieval side. For the revivals and the modern side I should recommend E. Martin Browne Director of Religious Drama in the Dio. of Chichester: just appointed by me – a practical man, *and* a scholar.' Other names he suggested included Lascelles Abercrombie; Sir Barry Jackson; Geoffrey Whitworth (Secretary of the British Drama League); Granville Barker.
3 – A. W. Pollard (1859–1944): Shakespearean scholar, 'new bibliographer', textual critic. Works include *Shakespeare Folios and Quartos: A Study in the Bibliography of Shakespeare's Plays, 1594–1685* (1909) and *Shakespeare's Hand in the Play of 'Sir Thomas More'* (ed., 1923).

possibly, if I can say definitely that I will come, her coming with me might be left open?[1]

With many thanks, and kind regards to Mrs Bell,

I am,

Yours very sincerely

T. S. Eliot

P.S. About the Report: I do not think that I am quite the only layman who feels that the mind of the Editor of the *Church Times* is neither supple, philosophic nor representative. I came in conflict with it a couple of years ago, when he seemed to me to present unfairly the case of some French friends of mine, because he started with the assumption that the Vatican must be right. (He was not, I must say, so unreasonable about Malta; but that may have been more patriotism than intelligence).[2]

TO *Joan Bennett*[3]   CC

26 November 1930   [*The Criterion*]

Dear Madam,

I have your letter of the 18th instant, which arrived too late for publication in the forthcoming number of the *Criterion*.[4] I am quite

1 – In the event, TSE alone went to Chichester for the weekend of 13–15 Dec. See Ronald C. D. Jasper, *George Bell: Bishop of Chichester* (1967), 125: '[Eliot] had just written *Ash Wednesday*; and on the Sunday evening he read it to a party which, though impressed, was none the less a little bewildered. Friendship between bishop and poet dated from that weekend, and, many years later, Eliot himself paid tribute to its influence in his future work.

'"I remember that Dr Bell travelled up to London with me on the following Monday. Not having consorted with bishops in those days, I found it strange to be journeying with a bishop in a third class railway carriage. On that journey the bishop spoke to me about Dr J. H. Oldham and his work for the Church and the world; and so that weekend brought about my acquaintance with two men, Mr [E. Martin] Browne and Dr Oldham, with whom I was later to be closely associated in quite different activities. Out of that meeting came the invitation in 1933 to write the church pageant which became *The Rock*."'

See too: 'one of his fellow-guests [at Chichester] recalled that "Mr Eliot did not join much in the conversation among the ten people who made up the party"' (Peter Ackroyd, *T. S. Eliot* (1984), 181; citing E. Martin Browne, *The Making of T. S. Eliot's Plays* (1969).

2 – Bell wrote in reply to this paragraph (26 Nov.): 'I like your postscript much.'

3 – Joan Bennett (1896–1986): Fellow of Girton College, Cambridge; Lecturer in English, Cambridge University, 1936–64; Warton Lecturer, British Academy, 1958, winner of the Rose Mary Crawshay Prize, 1963. Works include *Four Metaphysical Poets* (1934); *Virginia Woolf: Her Art as a Novelist* (1945); *George Eliot: Her Mind and her Art* (1948).

4 – 'In an article called "What is Criticism?" [*C.* 10 (Oct. 1930), 118–39] your contributor complains that Mr I. A. Richards "seems to have misunderstood the nature of aesthetic emotion". Perhaps he does not know that Mr Richards has more than once, in his printed

aware that Mr Belgion's interpretation of Mr Richards[1] is one which Mr Richards could hardly accept and as soon as Mr Richards has left China, where communication with him is difficult, I shall invite him to make his own statement. Mr Richards expects to go to Harvard within a few weeks, and it is possible that we may have a statement from him which will render your letter unnecessary. Meanwhile I will hold it as a possibility for publication in the March number.

Thanking you for your interest and trouble,

I am,
Yours truly,
[T. S. Eliot]
Editor.

TO *Rose Esther Haigh-Wood*   CC

26 November 1930   [68 Clarence Gate Gardens]

Dear M.,

This is a matter about which I should have written to you some days ago. I think that I have mentioned it to you. When Maurice was here and we called together upon Birks, we came to the conclusion that certain Corporation Stock held by the Estate (Birkenhead and Croydon Stock, amounting to £500 in all) ought to be sold, as it is nearing redemption date and will therefore decline in value until it reaches par. On the question of reinvestment, Mr James was inclined to recommend Industrial Debentures, which are strictly outside the scope of Trustees, and which can only be bought with the written assent of all beneficiaries. My own view was however that, as the Estate is already too large in variety and contains very few Trustee Debentures, that I could not approve exchanging these very sound Trustee Stocks for anything more speculative; and in this Maurice concurred with me and also did Mr Dunne, one of the partners of Birks's.

It is therefore proposed that the Stock above mentioned should be sold and reinvested in the new issue of Ayr Corporation Stock, a stock of precisely the same standing, but longer dated, so that it will not depreciate.

I have a letter from Maurice approving this step, and should be glad to

---

works, denied that such a thing exists. In chapter II of the *Principles of Criticism* [sic] called "The Phantom Aesthetic State" Mr Richards discusses the arguments for the existence of aesthetic emotion and concludes that "psychology has no place for such an entity."

1–IAR replied in C. 10 (Apr. 1931), 412–20; Belgion responded in C. 10 (Apr. 1931), 507.

know that you approve, and then will issue the instructions; but if you first want further explanation, please let me know.

Affectionately,
[Tom]

TO *M. C. D'Arcy*

27 November 1930   [Faber & Faber Ltd]

My dear D'Arcy,

Many thanks for your letter.[1] I do not know Coghill personally, but happen to have received from him recently a rather interesting poem which I am studying. I should like very much to meet him with you during the vacation, if you will arrange it. And I hope that if you are in town during the first half of January you will come as my guest to a meeting of a new club (inter-denominational and including atheists) for the study of religious problems – mostly laymen – I believe that Iddesleigh, whom you probably know and I don't, is a member. And who is Fr Lahey, who seems to me to have missed a great opportunity of saying something interesting about Hopkins?[2] For Hopkins himself, my admiration is almost unbounded.

Yours ever sincerely,
[T. S. Eliot]

TO *Allen Tate*

27 November 1930   Faber & Faber Ltd

Dear Tate,

Many thanks for your letter of November 8th.[3] I am delighted to have your book and intend to read it as soon as I can, but I am afraid that I

---

1 – D'Arcy wrote ('Nov.'): 'There is a very charming youngish Don here whom you may know by name, Coghill of Exeter. He is an Anglo-Catholic very attached to you & very desirous of meeting you.'

2 – D'Arcy replied on 20 Dec.: 'Lahey is a young Canadian S.J. – not yet a priest – who was over here for a year. I do agree with you that he has missed a grand opportunity.' G. F. Lahey's *Gerard Manley Hopkins* was reviewed by HR in *C.* 10 (Apr. 1931), 552–9.

3 – Tate wished TSE to review *I'll Take My Stand: The South and the Agrarian Tradition* (by a group of twelve authors, including Tate himself and John Gould Fletcher) in the Nashville *Tennessean*: 'We are trying to concentrate in that sheet a series of reviews whose position, even in the most general sense, is similar to ours – which is ultimately political as well as

shall have no time to read anything until after Christmas. I believe that I should be very glad indeed to write about the book for a Tennessee newspaper, if you nominated the newspaper. The only trouble is that of time. What with other things I have to do, I certainly could not complete anything before the end of January. Will you let me know whether a very late essay on the subject would be of any use?

You may be sure that I should not write in the spirit of 1860. In fact it seems to me that the importance of your thesis is not only for the South but for all local life in America. New England may have survived, or appeared to survive, for a few decades after 1865, but it seems to me to be today just as degraded as the South. Its servitude is perhaps disguised by the survival of a number of fortunes precariously established on wool and cotton, but as my people lost all their money in 1814 owing to the interference of the British Navy with the whaling industry, the prosperity of the Lowells does not interest me.

So far as I am concerned, you may say what you like about the Adams or anyone else, though I persist in believing that if they had not been turned out in 1829 by your abominable compatriot, Andrew Jackson,[1] the American democracy might have been preserved, and the Civil War averted.

Meanwhile I am sending you a pamphlet by a young friend of mine whose name indicates the same Pictish extraction as your own, which I think bears on the same problem of regionalism. I am wholly in sympathy with this movement, if only to relieve the kingdom of England from the dominion of Northern adventurers. I shall be very glad to have your opinion about it.[2]

Yours ever,
T. S. Eliot

---

philosophical and literary . . . [W]e hope to show that there is a widespread impulse back to tradition . . .'
1 – Andrew Jackson (1767–1845): seventh President of the United States of America, 1828–37.
2 – George Malcolm Thomson, *Will The Scottish Church Survive?* (1930). TSE was to write, in his opening address to the Anglo-Catholic Summer School of Sociology, 'Catholicism and International Order', of 'the yearning towards regionalism which we have observed springing up spontaneously in various parts of the world; in America, in Scotland, and even I have been told in North Germany. With such movements, after we have deducted the political nonsense and the sentimental-retrospective-literary nonsense, I am instinctively in sympathy . . . I have little hope for the future of America until that country falls apart into its natural components, divisions which would not be simply those of the old North and South and still less those of the forty-eight states' (*Christendom: A Journal of Christian Sociology* 3, 11 [Sept. 1933], 179–80).

28 November 1930   [Faber & Faber Ltd]

Your Grace,

I am very much obliged for your Grace's letter and for the pages of comment which you have added, which I shall find extremely useful.[1]

TSE would write in his 'Commentary' (*C.* 10, Apr. 1931, 483–5), apropos *I'll Take My Stand*: 'there is a general problem which concerns the whole world . . . The question of the Good Life is raised; and how far it is possible for mankind to accept industrialization without spiritual harm. The complaint is not merely that the South was ruined and subjected by the Civil War, but that it is now well on the way towards being northernized; that coal, oil, iron and factories have altered the relation of man to his world, and that the Good and Happy Life is becoming less possible. The old Southern society, with all its defects, vices and limitations, was still in its way a spiritual entity; and now the organization of society is wholly materialistic . . . [I]t is a sound and right reaction which impelled Mr Allen Tate and his eleven Southerners to write their book; and which impels Mr George Malcolm Thomson and his Scottish friends to affirm that Scotland ought to be something more than a Suburb of Greater London, or a confined industrial district populated by lower class Irish immigrants. And it is something of which politicians ought to take thought, if they are capable of thinking in any terms except "emergencies".'

1 – Letter not found. Temple wrote these comments:

'Page 7. It is easy to represent any re-affirmation of traditional beliefs as futile platitude. After all, B. Russell has been denying that there is any harm in "sexual intercourse between persons not married". It is worthwhile to re-affirm the old conviction.

'Again, there are two sets of people, one lax the other ascetic, who talk as if there is not "more in love than pleasure".

'The author has all the advantage of being one mind addressing one group. The Conference consisted of 300 minds addressing various groups. What is said to one group may be addressed to one level of morality, what is said to another to a different one.

'Pp. 8–13. No doubt the sections on Birth Control cannot [but] lack definiteness. I am not sure that this is a misfortune. I do not believe in the Roman attempt to give precise directions for conduct. I think this is both unscientific and unchristian. It is unscientific, because it contravenes Aristotle's rule not to demand more precision in the theory than there is in the facts. And it is unchristian because it is exactly what Christ refused to do. No doubt the Pharisees found His teaching (e.g. about the Sabbath) dreadfully indefinite.

'The chief new "facts and conditions" (p. 9) are the new estimate of the rights & functions of women, and the increasing pressure of industrial conditions. Our grandfathers didn't use contraceptives but neither did they practise abstention. They killed their wives.

'If it is recognized that procreation ought to be avoided in any case, the question of method arises. For some abstention is the only possible one to them, because contraceptives are (aesthetically) abhorrent, so that to use them is a sin against love.

'But there are others for whom this is not so, and for whom complete abstention involves the omission of much that fosters and maintains love. For them abstention itself is a sin against love.

'In either case, they should rely on the Holy Spirit. Why should He not "operate through science"? If He does not, a great deal has gone on in complete independence of Him, which appears to be contrary to John 1: 3 (see Greek) – unless indeed the author [? shows] so sharp a distinction between the Spirit & the Logos as to involve him in sheer Tritheism.

I think that apart from the question of good and bad taste, Thomson's unfairness is chiefly due to ignorance; he had read the letter of the Report, but was unacquainted with the background of Church History which is necessary to explain and justify it. I think that my own attempt at rectification will take the form of pointing out that the Anglican Church, gradually ceasing to be a National Church either in the good sense of Laud, or the bad sense of the eighteenth century and Headly, has been slowly establishing a much better position as a part of the whole Catholic Church.

There are, of course, details on which I also disagree. My personal point of view about Resolution 15 is certainly not that of the *Church Times*, and I do not want to say much about this over-discussed section. I do feel very glad that the Conference courageously took a different view from that of the Roman Church, and the only sentence I deplore is the recommendation to the exercise of private judgment. It seems to me to be one of the matters in which ordinary lay people may easily deceive [themselves] into fancying that they are being guided by the Holy Spirit, when they are guided by their own inclinations; and I could have wished that they were recommended more strongly to seek spiritual counsel. I am quite aware that in the present state of things anyone could get more or less the sort of counsel that he desired, if he knew where to go for it. But

---

'P. 14. It is curious to designate as a Hymn Fitzgerald's version of Omar's odd mixture of Muslim mysticism and Arab sensuality.

'P. 15. I give Thomson the Youth report!

'Pp. 23–26. It is notoriously difficult to settle the proper limits of variation. Everyone agrees to the principle "In essentials, unity; in non-essentials, diversity." But they differ about what is essential.

'The Church has never had a theory of what is inherent in the episcopate. There have always been maximisers, like S. Cyprian, and minimisers, like S. Jerome. But there has been agreement about the committal to them of certain functions. Of these the chief is Ordination. Thomson makes the importance of the rule of episcopal ordination turn on a special theory – that the Bishop confers a power of inducing the Presence of Christ in the Eucharist. But there are many traditions about this. One, no doubt, is the crisp, simple doctrine implied by Thomson. But the word in the Roman Ordinal is "potestas" (Accipe potestatem) which ought to mean not power but authority. Another view (which I myself hold) is this: the Sacraments belong to the Church and have their meaning only with the corporate life of the Church. Therefore they may only be celebrated and administered by those who have the Church's authority for this; that requires that only one commissioned to do so should celebrate; but the commission can only be given by one who was commissioned to give it. The historic Episcopate safeguards this continuity for authoritative commission – whatever may be the further theory held with regard to the effect of commission so given. Accordingly to insist on the Historic Episcopate, with its historic functions, but without insisting on any one particular interpretation of these, seems to me quite good sense, and in no way open to the comparison with the Khu Klan on p. 25.'

surely that would be far better (and would, even if the counsel were bad, exonerate the individual who sought it with full sincerity) than leaving the decision entirely with the persons most interested. The Youth Section did, I confess, seem to me senile and I am sorry that even indirect approval should be given to such well-meaning but dangerous people as Eddington and Jeans.

I shall send you a script of whatever I write, before it goes to press, and would be grateful then for any further comments, or corrections, you might have time to make.

With very many thanks,

I am,
Your Grace's obedient servant,
[T. S. Eliot]

TO *William Force Stead*   MS Beinecke

2 December 1930   *The Criterion*

My dear Stead,

I am shamed by your kind letter, as I have another letter of yours on my conscience. But my reason for delay is just that I *cannot* think of anything to do for your printer – he has haunted my mind ever since – curse you![1] The days are evil, and one has often to sit helplessly watching the unfortunate.

Re Merton – is this the Bodley Club or the High Table? In any case, in spite of the claim which I recognise gladly, I wd rather spend a quiet night with you at Worcester. *But* – you know, my dear fellow, how difficult it is for me to get away at all, & I am going to stay a night with the Bp. of Chichester about a pamphlet I have to write, & early in January I *must* get away for a week's rest at Kelham – so I can make no such engagements for a long time.

Could you come up and lunch with me soon? I want to talk to you – as for your suggestion – my dear – it has been put *strongly* by my wife's R.C. doctor – by Underhill – and by others less qualified. But I shd like to talk to *you* because *you* know how difficult it is. I will say that I have now a

1–Stead had requested help from TSE on 15 Oct. for 'this unfortunate . . . a bankrupt printer . . . Owing to a dispute with his mother the business failed when she withdrew her capital. He is literally walking the streets and is willing to do anything – even manual labour.'

certain happiness which makes celibacy easy for me for the first time.
I think you will know what I am speaking of.[1]

> Affectionately
> T. S. E.

TO *Margaret C. Deas*   CC

3 December 1930   [Faber & Faber Ltd]

Dear Madam,

    We have considered very carefully your suggestion for a new edition of
the *Poems of Lord Dorset*, and as the Board was in the case influenced by
my opinion, it devolves upon me to write to you.[2] We feel that your project
is thoroughly worth doing, but that it is not an undertaking for a young
firm of general publishers who have not specialised in modern editions of
neglected literature. There are, apart from the Oxford University Press –
which, in view of its excellently produced series of Jacobean and Caroline
poets, ought to undertake the work – several firms, smaller than our
own, which specialize more in this type of book, and could probably sell
it better than we could. I should suggest the Haslewood Press, among
others. Personally, I should like to see it done by the Oxford Press. If
either of these suggestions appeal to you, I should be very glad to write
personally on your behalf.

> Yours faithfully,
> [T. S. Eliot]

TO *Ernest Rhys*   CC

3 December 1930   [Faber & Faber Ltd]

Dear Mr Rhys,

    I find I did not answer your letter of the 21st October, and apologise
for the oversight.[3] If you have taken it for granted that I am ready to

---

1–Gordon, *T. S. Eliot*, 294, construes this letter thus: 'Father Underhill took it upon himself
to advise separation.' Seymour-Jones, 465, concurs.
2–Deas, who was just finishing her Cambridge PhD on the life and poems of Edmund
Waller, proposed (26 Nov. 1930) an edition of the poems of Charles Sackville, 6th Earl of
Dorset.
3–Rhys had written: 'Clearly you are the predestined Pascal man, and we will wait on your
pleasure and inspiration. Could you let me have the preamble in March or April?'

undertake the *Pascal*, you are quite right, but I feel also that circumstances compel me to be practical, and ask you for approximately the number of words expected, and the fee offered. I suppose that a preface in the *Everyman Library* is something bought outright, which the author has no right to reprint in any form, or at any time. Will you tell me also, whether I should be expected to compile the bibliography, as this is the part of the work which I most dread?

Yours sincerely,

[T. S. Eliot]

TO *D. S. Mirsky* CC

3 December 1930   [Faber & Faber Ltd]

Dear Mirsky,

I must apologise for not having written to you sooner, but my routine has been rather thrown out of joint lately by an extra piece of work I have taken on which will take most of my attention until the end of the year. I have received your review of Fletcher's book, and although it is severe, I like it, and shall use it. I shall not, however, be able to get it in until the March number. I know that Fletcher was prepared to be treated with severity by you, but nevertheless he said that he would be much more interested in a review from you than in one from anybody else.[1]

I should particularly have written to you sooner about your essays, and I hope that nothing has been lost by the delay. We considered the question very carefully. As I told you, there is very little to be done, ever, with a volume of collected essays. I do not mean that they do not sell at all, but that they only sell with a very slow acceleration throughout the years, as the author's reputation, made by other work, advances. With much regret, we did not feel that it was the type of book which a young firm could afford to take on in the present depression.

Please let me know if you are going abroad for the Christmas holidays. If so, will you lunch with me as soon as you return? If not, will you lunch with me during the Vacation?

Yours always sincerely,

[T. S. Eliot]

1–Review of John Gould Fletcher, *Europe's Two Frontiers: A Study of the historical forces at work in Russia and America as they will increasingly affect European Civilization*, in C. 10 (Apr. 1931), 534–6. Mirsky wrote on 16 Nov. 1930: 'I hope he will not be offended by it, but it is a singularly bad book.'

TO *Bonamy Dobrée*   TS Brotherton

4 December 1930   Faber & Faber Ltd

Dear Bonamy,

Many thanks for your two letters, with enclosures. As you know, I never read the *Criterion* but I am reading your encyclical letter on Detective Stories with interest. May I however take exception to your phrase 'in a mild way'. I object to the insinuation that mildness is one of my qualities.[1]

I had some talk with Herbert last night about the Anthology; hence it follows that I am sending you the reprint of Frederic Manning's first book. Would you care, first to review it for the *Criterion*,[2] and second, to look at it for a specimen of some type of prose. I've always thought it an extremely fine book of its kind, although, as you will see, the spirit of the work dates it clearly to Walter Pater, Anatole France and Loisy.[3] I hope to see you on the 10th.

                                        Ever,
                                        T. S.E.

TO *Michael Redgrave*[4]   cc

5 December 1930   [Faber & Faber Ltd]

Dear Mr Redgrave,[5]

Referring to section five of *The Hollow Men*, the first and last quatrains should be spoken very rapidly, without punctuation in a flat monotonous

1 – BD sent a galley proof of his article 'Thrillers and "Teccers"', from the *National Review*. 'Whereas romances and adventures, or for that matter the grimmest naturalistic novels, offer us a life into which we can enter, true thrillers or 'teccers are . . . a complete escape from life, and that is why they are read, not only by the empty-headed, but also by those subjected to the severest intellectual strain . . . Mr T. S. Eliot, the most difficult of modern poets and the most austere of critics, is in a mild way an authority on 'teccers.'

2 – BD reviewed Frederic Manning's *Scenes and Portraits*: *C.* 10 (July 1931), 733–6.

3 – Anatole France: pseud. of Jacques Anatole Thibault (1844–1924), poet, journalist, novelist, playwright; elected to the Académie Française, 1896; Nobel Laureate, 1921. In 1922 his oeuvre was placed on the Catholic *Index Librorum Prohibitorum*. Works include *La Rôtisserie de la Reine Pédauque* (1893) and *La Révolte des Anges* (1914). Alfred Loisy (1857–1940), controversial Roman Catholic priest and theologian, excommunicated in 1908. Professor of the History of Religions, Collège de France, 1908–31.

4 – Michael Redgrave (1908–85): stage and film actor, director, manager, author. He was to play the part of Harry, Lord Monchensey, in TSE's verse play *The Family Reunion* (Mar. 1939).

5 – Redgrave wrote from Magdalene College, 3 Dec.: 'The B.B.C. have honoured me by asking me to read some of your poetry next Monday (from an anthology of poetry meant for

voice, rather like children chanting a counting-out game. The intermediate part, on the other hand, should be spoken slowly although also without too much expression, but more like the recitation of a litany.[1]

Yours truly,
[T. S. Eliot]

TO *Gerard Hopkins* CC

5 December 1930   [Faber & Faber Ltd]

Dear Hopkins,

I have your letter of the 2nd of December, and although the copy of your uncle's poems which you are sending me has not yet arrived, I am writing at once to thank you.[2] As a matter of fact, I had been waiting impatiently for the appearance of the book for a long time, and have just bought two copies of the ordinary edition, one for myself, and one to give away. I shall now be able to give away the other. I have never before had the opportunity of studying them closely and may I now tell you how very warmly I admire almost everything he wrote.[3]

---

broadcasting, which includes *The Journey of the Magi* and part of *The Hollow Men* – as I suppose you know).

'Rehearsing *The Hollow Men*, I am at a loss when I come to the "Prickly-pear" verse. Reading it to myself I have never before found it out of keeping with the rest of the poem (as, indeed, it obviously is not) but when I try to speak it I find that whatever tone of voice I adopt is unsuitable.

'I am very sorry to have wasted even this amount of your time, but if you spend a little more of it in telling me in what sort of voice you would like this verse to read, I should be extremely grateful.'

1 – TSE would later remark to Robert I. Henkin (30 Nov. 1956): 'It is curious that one of the poems which has most attracted composers, should be "The Hollow Men", which never seemed to me suitable for musical setting at all.'

2 – 'We have just reprinted my uncle's *Poems* in a new edition, and I am having sent to you today a copy of the limited edition, which I hope you will accept with our compliments. In case you should think that we are committing the publisher's pet sin of accumulating money, where money can be found, I should like you to know that there is a cheaper edition at 7/6 . . .'

3 – TSE responded to a written question about the influence upon his work of the poetry of Gerard Manley Hopkins: 'Nothing at all. Remember that Pound and I had both written a great deal before we ever heard of Hopkins. I remember glancing at the first edition of Hopkins on the table of Roger Fry the art critic, who was interested. I did not read Hopkins until the edition came out which was prefaced by Charles Williams. I don't know whether Pound has ever read him at all. Hopkins became known just in time to influence poets like Auden, Spender and Day Lewis. Anybody who was young enough could hardly escape his influence. Day Lewis most, I think; but he seems to me closer to Thomas Hardy.'

I must confess that I was disappointed by Father Lahey; apart from the biographical facts and the appendix, the book seems to me valueless as criticism. Herbert Read, by the way, will be writing about both books in the March *Criterion*.[1]

With grateful thanks,
Yours sincerely,
[T. S. Eliot]

TO *Bonamy Dobrée*   TS Brotherton

9 December 1930   Faber & Faber Ltd

Dear Bonamy,

Thank you very much for your note of apology which is more insulting than the offence itself.[2] The only thing I can do at the moment to retaliate, that is, until tomorrow night, is to ask you to review *Nineteenth Century Drama, 1800–1850*, in two volumes, by Allardyce Nicoll, the master from whom you have learnt your scholarship and, no doubt, your literary taste.

Yours,
p.p. T. S. Eliot
[Secretary]

TO *Francis Underhill*   cc

9 December 1930   [Faber & Faber Ltd]

Dear Father Underhill,

I am all the more pleased at hearing from you, because I should have been writing to you in a day or two about other matters, in any case; and they are not unconnected.[3]

1–Review of G. F. Lahey, SJ, *Gerard Manley Hopkins*, and *Poems of Gerard Manley Hopkins*, ed. Robert Bridges (2nd edn with additional poems and an introduction by Charles Williams), C. 10 (Apr. 1931), 552–9.
2–BD wrote on 7 Dec., in response to TSE's of 4 Dec.: 'I'm sorry about "mild". I ought to have remembered that there is nothing people hate more than having their most salient characteristics mentioned. As a matter of fact, it was an insertion. Having said at the end that only those who gave their whole lives to 'teccers could pretend to be authorities, I felt impelled by my sense of truth to modify a balder statement about you.'
3–Underhill wrote on 1 Nov., 'I have written to the Director S.S.M. at Kelham . . . that you would like to spend a little time of quiet there, and that you might like to talk a little to him or some understanding member of the Community.'

I had made a tentative arrangement to go to Kelham either this week or the next; but suddenly found myself committed to a piece of work which must be finished as quickly; so I have since written to Fr Tribe[1] to ask if they can have me at the beginning of January. I believe he is away at the moment, as I have had no reply; but I very much hope that it will be possible. An additional reason for postponement was that I have the opportunity of discussing the matter I have in hand with the Bishop of Chichester over the weekend.

First of all, however, as I shall now not go away for a week till the New Year, will you please give me a 12:30 appointment some day next week or any day before Christmas? If possible, I should be grateful for a half hour one day beforehand, for a brief talk.

About the piece of work I mentioned: some time ago I commissioned on behalf of my firm a young Scot who had written an able, if somewhat superficial pamphlet on the condition of his own church, to write one for us on the Lambeth Conference.[2] The result is not altogether satisfactory (I will send it to you) and it was decided that we ought as quickly as possible to rectify matters by publishing another on more or less the same subject. As I was responsible for the first I had to be responsible for the second: and in short I have had to write one myself, putting other things aside.

It is not a job that I undertake at all gladly, or for which I feel myself in the least qualified. I therefore am asking several authorities to overlook it. I shall have a copy of my first *rough draft* ready to send to you by the end of this week. If you will read it and make any comments that occur to you, I shall be more than grateful.

To save misunderstanding, I must explain that what I have put down is admittedly quite in disorder; in fact it is badly written, has no structure, and is quite topsy turvy. It must be completely reconstructed and rewritten. What I want to know is whether I am saying the right sort of thing; what ought to be erased, and what ought to be said that I have not said – or errors of taste etc. I think that I can recast what I have written much more effectively; but while keeping it a personal expression of opinion, to make it sound.

Yours very sincerely,
[T. S. Eliot]

1 – Reginald Tribe, SSM, Director of Kelham Theological College, Newark, Notts.
2 – George Malcolm Thomson, *The Lambeth Conference* (1930).

TO *Angel Flores*[1]   CC

9 December 1930   [Faber & Faber Ltd]

Dear Mr Flores,

I have your letter of the 20th of November, and am sorry to find that you are disturbed by the appearance of another translation of my poem in Mexico City.[2] My chief apology however is for having failed through overwork to thank you for your kindness in sending me the copies of your translation and expressing my pleasure in it. It has also been approved by several friends who are much better Spanish scholars than I. I have only found one error myself: 'City Directors' are not political representatives like aldermen, but are directors of public limited companies, registered in the City.

The author of the Mexican translation had some claim upon me, being introduced by a mutual friend. I could see no reason why another translation should not be made, especially as it was for a Mexican periodical, or why it should compete with yours. I agree that there are a number of mistranslations. As a matter of fact, I had stipulated that the translation should be submitted to me before publication, and this was not done. I shall be writing to protest.

In Germany, for instance, two translations of one of my other poems were made, one by Dr Curtius and one by Dr Rychner.

I am very sorry, however, that this has been an annoyance to you.

                                    Yours very truly,
                                    [T. S. Eliot]

P.S. May I point out also that if I received even very slender royalties on any translation I should naturally consider that the only authorised translation. As a matter of fact, I have never had a penny for any writing of mine published in translation, except from France, where my authorised translator is, or was, Mr Jean de Menasce.

1–Angel Flores (b. 1900), Lecturer in Spanish Literature, Rutgers University, New Brunswick, New Jersey; author of *Spanish Literature in English Translation* (1926); English adviser for Editorial Cervantes of Barcelona.

2–'A few months ago I sent to you a dozen copies of my Spanish translation of "The Waste Land" [*Tierra Baldía*, Barcelona, 1930]. I have just learned about another *authorized* (?) translation (?) printed in the Mexican magazine *Contemporaneos* . . . [T]his so-called prose translation will harm you and the circulation of the Spanish edition which, incidentally, has been warmly received in Spain.'

9 December 1930   [Faber & Faber Ltd]

Dear Selwyn,

I shall send you, by the end of the week, the rough draft of a pamphlet which I have let myself in for writing, marginal to the Lambeth Conference. I shall be very much obliged if you can find the time to read it through and let me have any comments that occur to you – particularly because I think my point of view is nearer to that expressed in *Theology* – both editorially and elsewhere, except for Dr Williams – than to that, let us say, of the *Church Times*.

I want to explain why I undertook something for which I feel quite unfitted, and which I was loath to do. I instigated a young Scot who had written rather an able pamphlet upon his own church, to write one on the Lambeth Conference for us; as I thought that the point of view of an outsider might be interesting. I am not sorry that I did; although there is occasionally a slightly offensive and smart cheapness in his pamphlet and of course considerable misunderstanding. But it became immediately apparent that we could not afford to let it stand without some other pamphlet on the same subject; as I was responsible for the one, I had to be responsible for the other; and there seemed to be no one to write it but myself.

I will send you Thomson's pamphlet at the same time as my own draft. If you can read the latter, will you please keep in mind that I am aware that the arrangement and structure are all wrong; it must be completely rewritten. And I am not bothering about style until other doubts are settled; the whole thing is upside down and inside out; some points must be expanded and some contracted etc. What I need is criticism (1) on right or wrong interpretations (2) on omissions, and on commissions both of error and of bad taste. The notes are provisional; the one on the Episcopate is based on some notes given me by the Archbishop of York, but as I was unable quite to agree so far as I could understand him, I feel very uncertain about it. My point of view is naturally much more difficult to express nicely than is that of an irresponsible outsider. I must make the thing a little personal, both for persuasiveness, and partly to talk about some matters on which I feel confidence and partly to deal a few blows to my pet enemies and partly not to appear merely to be defending the Church to order. But I don't want to overdo this aspect. Much of what I have actually written is frankly tentative and subject to more learned opinion. I shall try to get several opinions, and Kenneth Ingram may add a few notes of his own.

Yours sincerely,
[T. S. Eliot]

TO C. M. Grieve[1]

10 December 1930   *The Criterion*

Dear Mr Grieve,

I should be very glad indeed if you would let me see the essay which you

---

1–Christopher Murray Grieve (1892–1978): pseud. Hugh MacDiarmid – poet, journalist, critic, cultural activist, self-styled 'Anglophobe', by turns Scottish Nationalist and Communist; founder member of the Scottish National Party, 1928; founder of the Scottish Centre of PEN. His works include *A Drunk Man Looks at the Thistle* (1926), *To Circumjack Cencrastus* (1930), 'First Hymn to Lenin' and Other Poems (1931), *In Memoriam James Joyce* (1955), *Hugh MacDiarmid: Complete Poems, 1920–1976* (2 vols, 1978). See further Alan Bold, *MacDiarmid, Christopher Murray Grieve: A Critical Biography* (1988); *The Letters of Hugh MacDiarmid*, ed. A. Bold (1984); and *Dear Grieve: Letters to Hugh MacDiarmid (C. M. Grieve)*, sel. and ed. John Manson (2011).

Grieve remarked to the novelist Neil M. Gunn (1891–1973) on 3 May 1928: 'Now as to Eliot, I believe (vide *Drunk Man*) he's a Scotsman by descent – but it's a damned long descent: and mentally he certainly fills the role you seem to have cast him for in your papers. He is pure Boston – ultra-English classicist in criticism: that's what makes him so unintelligible to mere English conventionalists – they can't follow their own ideas to their logical conclusions well enough to recognise their own supporters' (MacDiarmid, *Letters*, 222).

When invited by Albert Mackie of the *Edinburgh Evening Despatch* to a celebration in Edinburgh of MacDiarmid, TSE responded with this tribute (15 Aug. 1948): 'As I cannot be present, I should like to send my greetings to Hugh MacDiarmid and to the Makars assembled to do him honour. There are two reasons why I should have wished to be present on this occasion. The first is my respect for the great contribution of the Poet to Poetry – in general – in my time; the second is my respect for his contribution to Scottish Poetry – in particular. I value the latter also for two reasons. While I must admit that Lallands is a language which I read with difficulty – rather less fluently, in fact, than German – and a language the subtleties of which I shall never master, I can nevertheless enjoy it, and I am convinced that many things can be said, in poetry, in the language, which cannot be expressed at all in English. The second reason follows from the first: I think that Scots poetry is, like that of other Western European languages, a potentially fertilising influence upon English poetry; and – speaking as an English regionalist – I hold that it is to the interest of English poetry that Scots poetry should flourish. It is uncontested, and now everywhere recognised, that Hugh MacDiarmid's refusal to become merely another successful English poet, and his pursuing a course which at first some of his admirers deplored and some of his detractors derided, has had important consequences and has justified itself. It will eventually be admitted that he has done more for English poetry, by committing some of his finest verse to Scots, than if he had elected to write exclusively in the Southern dialect.'

TSE wrote to Richard Church, 21 Aug. 1963: 'I am delighted to know that you and I see eye to eye about C. M. Grieve, otherwise Hugh MacDiarmid. My own feeling about the

describe in your letter of the 9th instant.[1] As a matter of fact I had been meaning to get in touch with you in any case.

I do not know your poetry well, but I have a review of your last book from Edwin Muir, [which] arrived too late for the December number, but to be published in March, which is so enthusiastic that I mean to get a copy of your book for myself.[2]

If you are to be in London I should be very glad if you would come to lunch with me one day in January.

I do not know the other poets whom you mention, but I have great admiration for Dunbar, and should like to see a new edition.[3]

Yours sincerely
T. S. Eliot
Editor.

---

modern synthetic Lallans is that it has produced a group of second-rate versifiers.' Joseph Chiari noted, in *T. S. Eliot: A Memoir* (1982): 'Strange as it will appear to some, [Eliot], the self-proclaimed royalist and conservative, liked and respected the rebellious, ever explosive anti-monarchist Hugh MacDiarmid, whose poetry he admired and whose efforts to raise the Scots language to the level of a mature medium for all aspects of literature he applauded.'

1 – See full letter in *The Letters of Hugh MacDiarmid*, 434. Grieve offered an article on 'English Ascendancy in British Literature' – 'discussing the way in which . . . Irish, Scottish Gaelic, Welsh, and, to a lesser extent, Scottish Vernacular, and even English dialect literature and a case like the late Charles Doughty have been practically excluded from the knowledge of most British people – and consequently have had their potentialities inhibited – by the English ascendancy tendency . . . Apart from anything else it is absurd that English readers who would be ashamed to be found unfamiliar with what any significant writer in European literature "stood for", if not with his works, should know nothing of such great poets of our own islands as Aodhagan O'Rahaille in Ireland, Alasdair MacMhaighstir Alasdair in Scottish Gaelic, and William Dunbar in the Scots Vernacular.

'You may know of my own work as Scots poet over the pseudonym of Hugh M'Diarmid; and, over my own name I have written a considerable number of books on Scottish and allied cultural and political topics, while, as the former literary critic of the "New Age" I have a very wide knowledge of most European literatures, and more particularly of modern movements in thought, arts, and letters.'

See Grieve, 'English Ascendancy in British Literature', C. 10 (July 1931), 593–613; collected in *At the Sign of the Thistle* (1934).

2 – Muir, review of MacDiarmid's *To Circumjack Cencrastus*, C. 10 (Apr. 1931), 516–20.

3 – TSE told the Right Hon. W. S. Morrison, 19 Mar. 1958: 'it has always been a gratification to me that the Standard Edition of Dunbar [*The Poems of William Dunbar*, ed. W. Mackay Mackenzie, 1932] should be published by Faber and Faber.'

TO *William Empson*[1]

11 December 1930   [*The Criterion*]

Dear Empson,

I don't think your review is too long at all; but it did arrive too late for the December number.[2] I shall try to use it in March.

My chief complaint against you is not so much that you ought to buy a new typewriter ribbon which should be legible (e.g. this one which is quite new) but that you fail to tell us the name, author, price and publisher of the book you are reviewing. This is, I consider, the 8th type of ambiguity.[3]

I am having difficulty in finding anyone with *both* the leisure *and* the intelligence to review your book properly. I haven't the leisure, and am not quite certain that I have the intelligence; and so far I have enquired among the intelligent rather than the leisured.[4]

I believe that W. H. Auden and John Hayward are lunching with me on December the 18th. If so, would you care to join us?[5]

Yours sincerely,

[T. S. Eliot]

1 – William Empson (1906–84): poet and critic; author of *Seven Types of Ambiguity* (1930), *Some Versions of Pastoral* (1935), *The Structure of Complex Words* (1951), and *Milton's God* (1961). TSE took pains at F&F to publish *The Gathering Storm* (poems, 1940), and to raise interest in Empson's work in the USA. See further *Complete Poems*, ed. John Haffenden (2001); Haffenden, *William Empson: Among the Mandarins* (2005).
2 – Empson wrote ('Friday'): 'I am afraid this rather pompous review is already between 1,500 and 2000 words, so I have done nothing about the book on prose rhythm. Perhaps you would return this to me if it wants cutting, and let me know how many words you want.' See review of Katherine M. Wilson, *Sound and Meaning in English Poetry*, C. 10 (Apr. 1931), 529–34.
3 – Empson was to write to EVE on 6 Mar. 1978: 'Probably the first [letter] I received, when just down from Cambridge and allowed to do some reviewing for the *Criterion*, said that the review was all right but I should get a new typewriter ribbon and leave a double space after a full stop. Ever since I have done this when I remember, but my typing has remained amateurish. I thought it showed a fatherly attitude towards his contributors.'
4 – IAR encouraged TSE from China on 30 Nov.: 'Empson's book has just arrived, and, looking hastily through it, I am more than ever convinced that, in spite of all his youthful exuberance (overdoing it), he has the goods and the pen with which to deliver them. Do look into it yourself' (*Letters*, 60). See James Smith's review of *Seven Types of Ambiguity*, C. 10 (July 1931), 738–42.
5 – WHA had written to TSE (enclosing his play *The Fronny*) on 8 Dec.: 'I shall be in London on Thursday Dec 18th. Will it be possible for us to meet?' Empson wrote after the encounter ('Tuesday'): 'Thank you for making me meet Auden; he is very different from what I expected.'

TO *Edwin Muir*   CC

11 December 1930   [*The Criterion*]

Dear Muir,

Many thanks for the review of M'Diarmid, which interests me very much. It is not in the least too long; when one has to perform surgical operations on reviews of seventeen pages, a review of five pages is nothing. The only pity is that it arrives too late for the next number and must wait until March.

I am a little worried about *Kafka*. The trouble is that I have a long essay by Gundolf on Mörike – that is to say, an essay by a German whom no one in England has heard of about another German, equally unknown here; I have already held it up three months and it must go into the March number.[1] I don't quite like to follow it up with an essay, however interesting, on an Austrian whom no one has heard of; so that it may mean waiting longer than you would like.[2] If so, please make any other use of it you wish. I could, of course, use an essay on Wasserman if you cared to do that, three months sooner, that is, I could use the Wasserman in June.

Oddly enough I heard from Grieve only yesterday morning, and hope to make his acquaintance.

                            Yours ever sincerely,
                            [T. S. Eliot]

TO *James Joyce*   CC

11 December 1930   [Faber & Faber Ltd]

My dear Joyce,

I was extremely glad to receive a letter from you, perfectly legible, in your own script. Of course it is disappointing that Vogt[3] cannot finish up

---

1 – Friedrich Gundolf, 'Eduard Mörike', trans. W. E. Delp, C. 10 (July 1931), 682–708.

2 – Muir had finally submitted his essay on Kafka on 28 Sept.: 'I feel that I have been able to say only a few words about Kafka, whose work, besides, is so closely knit, that it calls for a commentary more than for anything else. And it is a handicap that he is virtually unknown.' Edwin and Willa Muir translated *The Castle* (1930), *The Trial* (1935) and *America* (1938).

3 – Professor Alfred Vogt (1879–1943): ophthalmologist. TSE wrote, in 'James Joyce': 'Throughout his life he had suffered from a very serious ailment of the eyes: an affliction which gave him periods of the most intense pain, and at times rendered him almost totally blind; one for which he had several operations, under a distinguished ophthalmic surgeon in Zurich.'

with you at once, and it is very trying for you to have to sit and wait, and not be able to get on with the book as you expected; yet I feel that things will turn out well in time and that the book will be finished; and a year or so does not matter for a grand thing like this.

By the way, Clive Bell has suddenly gone blind; he asked me about oculists; I told him about Vogt; and he learned elsewhere that Vogt and somebody in Baltimore were the only oculists in the world; so he has hastened off to Zurich; I don't know whether his case is in Vogt's way or not.

I am very sorry about *H.C.E.*[1] I had a letter explaining the situation from a man in Paris (Léon)[2] who I take to be your solicitor. We had promised the *H.C.E.* to the booksellers in this month, and it was being well subscribed; and of course it is all ready and the sooner we can bring it out the better. *A.L.P.*[3] is just on the point of reaching 5000 sale; and there is much interest in *H.C.E.* However, it is not an absolutely vital matter. What matters more is whether Kahane[4] is to have any say about *H.C.E.* when the whole book comes to be published. I shall raise this point with your solicitor.

I have by no means dropped the problem of the gramophone record. I am trying to get the British Broadcasting Corporation interested; nothing more can be done about that till after Christmas; but I shall plod ahead in January.

---

1 – *Haveth Childers Everywhere.*
2 – Paul Léon (1893–1942): cultured multilingual Jewish émigré from the Bolshevik revolution who had settled in Paris; he met JJ in 1928, when JJ was forty-seven and Léon thirty-five. He became JJ's unpaid assistant and amanuensis. See *The James Joyce – Paul Léon Papers in the National Gallery of Ireland: A Catalogue*, compiled by Catherine Fahy (1992); John Naughton, 'Arm in arm with a literary legend' (interview with Alexis Léon), *The Observer*, 13 Jan. 1991.
3 – *Anna Livia Plurabelle.*
4 – Jack Kahane (1887–1939), Manchester-born novelist and publisher, founded in 1929 – with his partner Henri Babou of the Vendôme Press (which had published Norah James's *Sleeveless Errand*, a novel that had been prosecuted in England in 1929; and which in 1930 issued JJ's fragment *Haveth Childers Everywhere*) – the Obelisk Press, to publish in Paris books that were either banned or deemed to be unprintable in the UK and USA. Obelisk Press productions ran to novels by Henry Miller including *Tropic of Cancer* (1934), *Black Spring* (1936), *Tropic of Capricorn* (1939), JJ's *Pomes Penyeach* (1932), and works by DHL, Anaïs Nin, Lawrence Durrell, Cyril Connolly, RA and Frank Harris. Kahane's son was Maurice Girodias, founder of the Olympia Press. See Neil Pearson, *Obelisk: A History of Jack Kahane and the Obelisk Press* (2007); James Armstrong, *Checklist of the publications of Henry Babou and Jack Kahane of the Obelisk Press* (2002); Gary Miers and James Armstrong, *Of Obelisks and Daffodils: The Publishing History of the Obelisk Press (1929–1939)* (2011).

With kindest regards from my wife and myself to you and Mrs Joyce,
Yours sincerely,
[T. S. Eliot]

TO *Herbert Read*   TS Victoria

11 December 1930   Faber & Faber Ltd

Dear Herbert,

I enclose a letter from a young friend of mine[1] who should have
had, some years ago, a Fellowship of Trinity Cambridge; then went to
Princeton; didn't like it; and has returned. I think he would do quite well
if there should be any vacancy; and I would certainly be prepared to
recommend him. What shall I say to him?

---

1 – James Smith (1904–72), critic and educator, won a double first in English and Modern
Languages (French and German) from Trinity College, Cambridge. According to a profile
in *Granta* (which he edited, 1925–6), he revived the Cam Literary Club, 'and even presided
over it for a year, in order to introduce Cambridge to T. S. Eliot' (cited in John Haffenden,
William Empson: Among the Mandarins [2005], 603). He was Vice-President of the Club
(the President being Professor Sir Arthur Quiller-Couch). Empson was to recall having
his weekly supervisions with I. A. Richards and then treacherously 'listening to the James
Smith group, who favoured T. S. Eliot and Original Sin' (195). Smith was to become an
occasional contributor to *The Criterion* and to *Scrutiny*: he wrote on Empson's *Seven Types
of Ambiguity* and on metaphysical poetry; and his other essays included studies of Croce,
Wordsworth, Marlowe, Chapman, Webster and Shakespeare (collected in the posthumous
Shakespearean and Other Essays, 1974). In the 1930s he taught at King Edward VII School
in Sheffield before becoming an HMI. During WW2 he was Director of the British Institute
at Caracas; and after the war he became Professor of English at Fribourg. FRL petitioned
TSE on 19 Nov 1946 to support Smith's application: 'He is, in my opinion, an incomparably
well-equipped man, but, by a series of accidents, he didn't start a university career when he
ought to have done, & so has never held a university post before. He is not long back from
Venezuela, where he spent five years establishing a British Institute – which (I have reason to
know) he did magnificently . . . He is a man for whom I would do anything that lay in my
power. It has always seemed to me a scandal that such pre-eminent qualifications shouldn't be
used in a university. And I'm worried about him generally: it's absurd that he should have to
go on living by hackwork. I've found his assistance in Downing-teaching very valuable, both
before the war, & since he has been back, but there's no post for him. I can't imagine a better
representative of English culture abroad. He's a classic & a philosopher, & can talk with
authority about almost any aspect of England in French & German that to my ear are perfect.
And he's a charming man, of complete integrity. (He's a Catholic, so would fit in at Freiburg,
which is Dominican, I'm told.)' TSE replied to Leavis on 21 Nov. 1946, 'I have hardly been
in touch with [Smith] for a number of years but I have enough confidence in him from my
knowledge in the past to be very glad to give him this support', and he enclosed a testimonial:
'I have known Mr. Smith ever since he was an undergraduate at Cambridge where I formed
a high opinion of his abilities. A little later I was a referee in connection with a dissertation
which he submitted and was to report very favourably thereon. I regard Mr. Smith as a man
of quite first rate abilities, and of exceptionally wide knowledge and interests.'

He is a Scot. Why he should be living at 19 Byron Street, Batley, Yorks (I mention the address so as to have it on my carbon of this letter, in case the enclosure gets lost) I don't know.

I will convey Auden's new Morality[1] to you as soon as possible. I think it is rather good, though I don't see that anything can be done with it at the moment. I chiefly worry about Auden's ethical principles and convictions, not about his technical ability; or rather, I think that if a man's ethical and religious views and convictions are feeble or limited and incapable of development, then his technical development is restricted. (Ezra seems to me to have made the utmost technical progress possible consistent with a juvenile ethics religion and economics. I am rather uncertain about Macleod too; he is duller than Auden; but seems to me also less flashy and to have more character: and character, not wits, seems to me the staying power for a poet. What do you think?

I thought the evening went off rather well. But do you share at all an odd feeling that I have, that somehow or other we are taking all this trouble in order to help Harold in some way? I don't mean that it isn't worth doing in itself; but that Harold's yearnings seem to take a front seat.

Yrs. in haste
T. S. E.

TO *G. Franklin Ludington*

CC

11 December 1930   [Faber & Faber Ltd]

Dear Sir,

I have your letter of the 17th ultimo.[2] The line about which you desire information is definitely and consciously and intentionally an echo of the line of the Shakespeare sonnet. I did not verify the quotation and it is perhaps accident, but I think an happy accident, that I altered slightly the line.

There was a good review of the poem in the *New York Sun*.[3] It is

---

1 – *The Fronny*.
2 – G. Franklin Ludington, a New York lawyer, had noted that l. 4 of *Ash-Wednesday*, 'Desiring this man's gift and that man's scope' (taken from Shakespeare's sonnet 29, 'Desiring this man's art and that man's scope') had been cited by E. K. Chambers in his recent study of Shakespeare, vol. i., p. 73. 'What I am eager to know,' he asked obscurely, 'is whether your line is an echo of a Shakespearian source, which I have not been able to discover, or whether it is illuminating but not illuminated by the Shakespearian connotation which Professor Chambers gives to it.'
3 – P. M. Jack, 'Eliot the Poet', *The New York Sun*, 15 Nov. 1930, 8; see letter to Jack, 16 Dec. 1930, below.

interesting to think that Sir Edmund Chambers can throw light on any line of mine; I wish I could reciprocate.

Yours very truly,
[T. S. Eliot]

TO *Michael Sayers* CC

11 December 1930   [Faber & Faber Ltd]

Dear Mr Sayers,

I am sorry not to have answered your letter sooner, but I have been and shall be very busy until after Christmas. I think that your question can best be considered verbally. If it has become very urgent, please ring up my secretary and see if we could make a morning appointment one day next week; but if not quite so urgent, I could give more time after Christmas.

I am not so firm about counters as you are; as I have served behind a counter myself.[1]

With best wishes,
Yours sincerely,
[T. S. Eliot]

TO *J. M. Scott Moncrieff*[2] CC

12 December 1930   [Faber & Faber Ltd]

Dear Madam,

Since seeing your letter in *The Times Literary Supplement* asking for letters from your son, I have had the *Criterion* files ransacked.[3] I enclose

---

1 – Sayers wrote (undated): 'When I last spoke to you I was studying Law, but my term at the School is at an end, and my father can no longer afford to keep me. I must either go into business or find a job more suitable to my temperament. As you were kind enough to take an interest in my writings, I wonder if you would advise me now; or, better still, give me a job . . . P.S. I'll take any job sooner than stand behind a counter.'

2 – Jessie Margaret Scott Moncrieff (1858–1936).

3 – Mrs Scott Moncrieff announced, in 'Mr C. K. Scott Moncrieff' (*TLS*, 30 Oct. 1930, 890), that a short memoir of her son was in preparation – 'with which it is desired to include some of his poems and extracts from his letters. I shall be indebted to those of his friends who may care to lend me material from which such extracts may be made. All letters would be carefully considered and returned at any early date to their owners.' See *C. K. Scott Moncrieff: Memories and Letters* (1931), ed. J. M. Scott Moncrieff and L. W. Lunn.

three which, I think, are the only ones of any interest: anything else is merely short notes about manuscripts, etc.

So far as I am concerned, there is, of course, no objection to the publication of the whole or any parts. I should be grateful if they might be returned to me at some time.

May I take the liberty of saying that although I did not know your son very well, for my part the only reason was that since I first made his acquaintance he was so seldom in England, and I never saw him in Italy. Had there been the opportunity, he was certainly one whose friendship I should have sought and prized.[1]

I am, Madam,
Your obedient servant,
[T. S. Eliot]

TO *Francis Underhill*

CC

15 December 1930   [Faber & Faber Ltd]

Dear Father Underhill,

Monday the 22nd would suit me very well, but I am not quite sure, as you say 12.30, whether you expect me first at Liddon House or directly in the Chapel? In view of my first letter I hope that you mean me to call at Liddon House but that must be according to your convenience. I should be grateful if you would let me know.

I am sending you tomorrow my first rough draft for comment. Please bear in mind that these are only disorderly notes and that I am quite aware that the whole thing must be re-written and given some structure. I am anxious to get it out, if possible, in good time before the Church Assembly (whatever that is) assembles.

With many thanks,

Yours sincerely,
[T. S. Eliot]

1 – Scott Moncrieff lived in Italy from 1923 until his death on 28 Jan. 1930.

TO *Paul Léon*   TS National Gallery of Ireland

15 December 1930   Faber & Faber Ltd

Dear Sir,

I should have answered your letter of the 4th instant on receipt, except that I thought that there *was some* possibility of my hearing from you again shortly.

The position is certainly very vexing, particularly *as we* had hoped to produce *Haveth Childers Everywhere* before Christmas, and the copies are actually quite ready for distribution. However, we quite understand that there is nothing to be done except to await Mr Kahane's written permission to produce the pamphlet by May 1st, 1931. I presume that you are obtaining this necessary document shortly, and of course I must emphasise the point that if, later on, Mr Kahane can see his way to releasing the Copyright before that date, that will be very much to our interest and to that of Mr Joyce.[1]

I am sorry that Mr Joyce has had this additional anxiety at this time.

> I am,
> Yours sincerely
> T. S. Eliot

TO *John Rodgers*   CC

15 December 1930   [*The Criterion*]

Dear Mr Rodgers,

I must apologise for the delay. It has been difficult for me to find the time to read *L'Homme contre l'histoire*,[2] but when I did read it, I found it extremely interesting. I fear, however, that it would be an impossible venture as a book, and even for the great majority of the readers of the *Criterion* I think that it assumes and requires too intimate a knowledge of the work and influence of Maurras and Barrès, to say nothing of Mistral, to be effective. In other words, I think that the idea is an extremely interesting and suggestive one, and that if it were possible to develop such an idea with English illustrations instead of French, it would make a most valuable essay.

---

1 – Babou and Kahane brought out their 'exclusive' edition of *Haveth Childers Everywhere* at the Fountain Press, Paris, in June 1930. F&F was to publish the work on 8 May 1931.
2 – *L'Homme contre l'histoire*, by André Chamson, was suggested by Rodgers (The University, Hull) on 30 Apr. 1930.

I am always grateful for suggestions of this sort, and thank you for letting me see the book.

Yours very truly,
[T. S. Eliot]
Editor.

TO *S. C. Roberts*[1]   CC

16 December 1930   [Faber & Faber Ltd]

Dear Sir,

Although I am not known to you personally, I am taking advantage of the fact that I belong to the firm which is about to publish your monograph on *Dr Watson* to approach you about two matters entirely unconnected with Faber and Faber. The two matters are two books for publication, in both of which I have taken a certain interest, and which seem to me more suitable for a University Press than for any general publishing firm.

The first author is an Irishman named Sean O'Faolain who has been working for some years in Celtic Literature, partly at Harvard and more recently at the British Museum. I know nothing whatever about Celtic literature and I know Mr O'Faolain only slightly; but he shewed me some time ago an essay which he had written on that subject, which seemed to me very sound sense and to be very upsetting to the ordinary Irish fantasies about their own medieval literature. I liked this essay very much. Mr O'Faolain is anxious to bring out a book of translations from what he considers the really good early Irish poetry, as distinct from the rubbish (I don't think there will be much about Deidre) with the Irish text on opposite pages. This seems to me an estimable undertaking, but it is obviously not a venture for any commercial publisher.

The other matter is rather the same, in as much as it is also one of translation. A young man from your University named Edward M. Wilson has been specialising in Spanish Literature and has just returned from a prolonged stay in Spain. He has been working for a long time on

---

1–Sydney Castle Roberts (1887–1966): author, publisher, biographer; Secretary of Cambridge University Press, 1922–48; Master of Pembroke College, 1948–58; Vice-Chancellor, Cambridge University, 1949–51; Chairman of the British Film Institute, 1952–6. He was knighted in 1958. His works include *A History of the Cambridge University Press 1521–1921* (1921); *Lord Macaulay: The Pre-eminent Victorian* (1927); *Doctor Watson: Prolegomena to the study of a biographical problem* (F&F, 1931); *Adventures with Authors* (1966).

the poetry of Góngora. I know nothing of Góngora but the translations seemed to me to be made into quite accomplished English verse. He has given me a considerable part of the manuscript, and I shewed it to J. B. Trend, whom I dare say you know, as the highest literary authority on Spanish Literature that I know and he spoke extremely well of it. This again does not seem to me a project for ordinary publishers.

If either of these notions appears to you, possible, I shall be very glad and will see that the manuscripts are sent to you at once. If not, I should be very grateful to have the bad news as quickly as possible.[1]

Yours sincerely,
[T. S. Eliot]

TO *Tom Faber*[2]

16 December 1930   Faber & Faber Ltd

My dear Tom!

Thank you very much for your photograph. You look very handsome, and you will be framed for my mantel-piece. Here is a photograph of your Uncle Tom when he was *smaller* [than] you are (it must have been very cold weather, mustn't it) and with his dog Toby. I hope *soon* to have *another* photograph of you when you will be *bigger* than

Your affectionate
Uncle Tom.[3]

1 – 'Frankly,' replied Roberts (17 Dec.), 'the Syndics never look very kindly on proposals for translations as such, but I will at least see that your inquiry receives careful consideration.' TSE's secretary told Wilson on 21 Jan. 1931: 'Mr Eliot has asked me to write and let you know that he has now heard from the Cambridge University Press that they do not feel that they can undertake to do your translation of Góngora. Mr Eliot is extremely sorry that his efforts have met with so little success, but the only suggestion he can think of at the moment is that you should try the Nonesuch Press.' S. C. Roberts wrote back to TSE on 24 Dec. 1930 to say that the Syndics of the Press had decided against the two books mentioned by TSE; he suggested the Irish Texts Society. In time, Wilson's Góngora was taken up by OUP.

2 – Tom Faber (1927–2004), physicist, publisher – TSE's first godchild – was to take a double first in physics at Trinity College, Cambridge; thereafter he became a Fellow of Corpus Christi College, Cambridge, 1953–2004; Lecturer in Physics, 1959–93, specialising in super-conductivity, liquid metals and liquid crystals; he wrote *Introduction to the Theory of Liquid Metals* (1972) and *Fluid Dynamics for Physicists* (1995). From 1969 he was a director of Faber & Faber, and served as Chairman of Geoffrey Faber Holdings, 1977–2004. TSE paid tribute to the young Tom in his preface to *Old Possum's Book of Practical Cats* (1939).

3 – Tom Faber replied from Ty Glyn Aeron, Ciliau Aeron, Cardiganshire, 5 Jan. 1931: 'I like your photograph very much. & I think your dog Toby looks very nice, but you don't look as grand as me because my suit has got a proper tie, & you have got a girls bonnet on: at least it looks like that to me.

TO *Peter Monro Jack*[1]   CC

16 December 1930   [Faber & Faber Ltd]

Dear Jack,

Thank you very much for sending me your review of *Ash Wednesday* in the *New York Sun*, which I should not otherwise have seen. I am writing to tell you that it is, on the whole, by far the most accurate interpretation of the poem that I have seen, and shews great insight. You are the only person who has, so to speak, spotted the White Leopards as The World, The Flesh and The Devil, except Arthur Waley who had come across something similar in Sudanese folklore. Wilson's review I did not like at all. I do not think I have seen Larsson's.[2]

'Why dont you come down here & see me. The sun is out, & I've never seen such lovely frost before. love from TOM

'I'm sorry this is so late my secretary has been busy & lazy.'

1–Peter Monro Jack (1896–1944), born in Scotland, graduated from Aberdeen University before becoming a doctoral research student at Trinity Hall, Cambridge, where E. M. W. Tillyard supervised his (uncompleted) thesis on the 'Aesthetic teaching of Walter Pater' – and where TSE was retained as his adviser (see *L* 3). He edited *The Gownsman*, and in 1926–7 was 'Skipper' (Literary Editor) of *The Granta*. In the late 1920s he taught at Michigan University before moving in 1930 to New York, where he became a lecturer and freelance writer. He was a regular reviewer for the *New York Times Book Review*.

2–P. M. Jack, 'Eliot the Poet', *New York Sun*, 15 Nov. 1930, 8:

'It is one of the few religious poems of this age, and I dare to say the greatest, for two reasons. It is an exact and necessary description of a peculiar devotional intensity that has somehow (not without difficulty) succeeded spiritual desolation; by its communication the reader is convinced that this attitude is the inevitable outcome of the hard discipline of living imaginatively in other ages as well as our own.

'The first part is in effect a renunciation of individualism, rationalism, critical realism – of any sort of positivism. What is renounced, however, is belief in these as the fullest expression of the human spirit. They are not; and if any one pretends to a more lasting faith he must first give up these inadequacies. The second part, sensuously very attractive, develops through imagery, and is more difficult to abstract. The imagery used is from the allegory of the scattered bones in Ezekiel xxxvii, but the poem is addressed to a lady, as Dante addressed his to Beatrice, and it is indirectly a poem for the Virgin Mary. It continues the disvaluing of personality. Three white leopards (worldly desire) have consumed the flesh – shall anything live? Shall these bones live? Possibly they may live through the lady's intercession. But "life" is an ambiguous and scarcely applicable word; so also is "love". Love that is satisfied is an even greater torment than love unsatisfied. There is presumably a state beyond life where flesh and bones are forgotten, personality and individuality are alike unimportant, love and not-love are indistinguishable; even the concern of Ezekiel with division and unity has no meaning. This is a state of forgetfulness and absoluteness beyond the reality principle, and this is the inheritance of man.

'The third part is a kind of allegory of one climbing the stairs beyond the reach of despair and hope to a strength which, however worthy (*Domine, non sum dignus*), he may share with the Centurion, through faith – but speak the word only . . . One notes here the dexterity with which Eliot has interlaced characteristically Dantesque imagery with the meaningful music of phrases from the Catholic service. The general feel of the Easter season – the life-

What are you doing in New York? Must I infer that you like our friend
Little have left Michigan as a victim of religious persecution?

With many thanks,

Yours sincerely,

[T. S. Eliot]

TO *Kenneth Ingram*   CC

17 December 1930   [Faber & Faber Ltd]

My dear Ingram,

Very many thanks for your very useful comment, and for its promptness.
I will delete Royden; also the Bradford Diocesan Conference (which I only
put in because it appealed to my sense of farce). I may add something
about the Ministry of Women, in your sense (by the way, I am thankful
that you dissuaded Williams from taking a stand upon such very slippery
ground – it would only inflame the passions of the other side); but I think
that this question is allied to the unmentioned question of celibate clergy.
Personally, I am in favour of a married clergy (except of course when
priests feel called to celibacy) and no women. I thought that the distinction
between the President of C.C.C. (Oxford) and the Master in Cambridge,
was clear enough. I have just learned from the Bp. of Chichester what
was intended by the mixed communion, but I still think that the language
is not precise enough to avoid misunderstanding. Furthermore, a new

---

death-resurrection cycle that had obsessed the poet when he began *The Waste Land* with the
lines, "April is the cruellest month" – the sense of humility that comes with the anointing of
the ashes (Remember, man, thou art dust, unto dust thou shalt return) on Ash Wednesday;
the prophetic voice of Ezekiel; the designs and symbols of Dante; all these form an intricate
contrapuntal development, unmistakable in the modern manner, on the theme of penitence.

'The fourth part calls on Mary, or Mary's advocate, to have mercy on our exile here, to
redeem the time, and the fifth part, continuing the intercessional, expands the Word of St
John with astonishing virtuosity. The last movement recapitulates the theme – because I do
not hope – recalls the waste land, reiterates the feeling of the Easter renewal, and ends on
the note of Dante's humility – in *la sua voluntade e nostra pace* – finally, "And let my cry
come to thee."

'Much more remains to be said about this memorable poem. But let us briefly say that
Eliot's theory of poetry is completely justified. The strong personal emotion from which
the poem no doubt originated has been deliberately simplified, disciplined and in a way
depersonalized; it has been purified and ennobled in its participation with similar experiences
in other literatures; its style makes it abundantly clear that Mr Eliot is rivaled only by Mr
Yeats in the poetical use of the English language.'

Jack wrote in his letter (undated): 'I've been annoyed with the reviews that appeared
during spring – like [Edmund] Wilson's, though I like him, and [R. Ellsworth] Larsson's in
the Commonwealth . . .'

doctrine of degrees of reception of the Eucharist seems to be called for; I think that there might be a great deal to be said for such a doctrine; but without such formulation of theory I distrust recommendation of the practice. The only two points on which I think I disagree from you (on those unmentioned here you may assume concurrence) are on Resolution 15 and on the Sacrament of Penance. On these two points, if I persist in my darkness, would you care to append notes of dissent?[1]

With very many thanks,

Yours

[T. S. Eliot]

TO *E. M. W. Tillyard*[2]

18 December 1930   Faber & Faber Ltd

Dear Mr Tillyard,

I am writing to you in the faint hope that you might have the time and might be willing to review for the *Criterion* William Empson's *Seven Types of Ambiguity*. It seems to me a book that the *Criterion* ought to review at some length, but it is very difficult to find a reviewer who knows enough about, or has enough sympathy with this sort of investigation to do it justice. If you would be willing to review it for our March number, we should be more than delighted.[3]

Yours sincerely

T. S. Eliot

1 – Ingram – to whom TSE sent 'a rough draft' of *Lambeth* on 15 Dec. – replied (18 Dec.): 'I think, with you, that there is a lot to be said for a doctrine of degrees of reception of the Eucharist. As to Resolution 15 and my point about the Sacrament of Penance, I don't feel that they are important enough to warrant a note of dissent in your essay. Certainly as regards Penance, I don't feel able to take so dogmatic an attitude as a note of dissent suggests; it was merely a query which I raised in regard to your argument, and on which my theory may not be legitimate.'

2 – E. M. W. Tillyard (1889–1962): Fellow in English of Jesus College, Cambridge, 1926–59; Master, 1945–59. Works include *The Personal Heresy: A Controversy* (with C. S. Lewis, 1939), *The Elizabethan World Picture: A Study of the Idea of Order in the Age of Shakespeare, Donne and Milton* (1942), *Shakespeare's History Plays* (1944), and *The Muse Unchained: An Intimate Account of the Revolution in English Studies at Cambridge* (1958). See obituary essay by Basil Willey, 'Eustace Mandeville Wetenhall Tillyard 1889–1962', *Proceedings of the British Academy* 49 (1963), 387–405.

3 – Tillyard replied on 22 Dec. 1930: 'I should have liked greatly to do it. As it is, I am getting leave of absence next term and shall be indulging in a little foreign travel. What time remains before I leave will, I fear, be more than comfortably occupied with other necessary undertakings.'

TO *Henrietta Bell*[1]   MS

18 December 1930   68 Clarence Gate Gardens

Dear Mrs Bell,

Enough time has passed for me to be able to say with conviction that I did not return with a cold. Even had this happened, I should have had no reason to repine, after such a very delightful and happy weekend. (I was about to add the adjective '*profitable*', but that it sounds cold, calculating, or designing.) Anyway, I shall not forget your hospitality; and I look forward to the possibility of another invitation at a more clement time of year, when my wife would be able to come too.

Yours very sincerely,
T. S. Eliot

TO *George Bell*   TS Lambeth

19 December 1930   Faber & Faber Ltd

My dear Lord Bishop,

I feared afterwards that I had given rather a lame response to your question about Devotions – a matter to which, to tell the truth, I had never given much thought – and have since turned the matter over in my mind. I think I hold substantially the view I attempted to put; but I should like to see how it looks on paper.

I want at least to make clear that I have never discussed the matter with anyone, and I have only personal feelings which cannot be altogether justified by reason. It is perhaps unreasonable to wish to see maintained integrally the offices of the Mass of the Pre-Sanctified and Holy Saturday, and yet to admit dislike of Exposition and the Corpus Christi evening procession. I suppose it represents the limit to which my own mind and sensibility can go in the direction of the realism of the Roman ritual. I can approve of the Host being borne from a chapel to the High Altar; but I do not enjoy seeing It carried in a mere perambulation of the aisles. Still less, naturally, would I like street processions.

I suppose that the justification for evening Devotions is the emotional necessity of providing an evening service, on Sundays, which should

---

1–Henrietta (née Livingstone), wife of Bishop George Bell. Donald Adamson (editor of Sencourt, *T. S. Eliot: A Memoir*, 114 n. 6) notes that the only copy of this letter is in his own collection. 'The original of this letter, as of two other letters from Eliot to the Bells, was lost in February 1968.'

not fall very flat after the solemnity of High Mass. This does seem to me a very real necessity, and particularly for the humbler people (who, as I said, seemed to take great pleasure in the Adoration office at St Mary's, and seemed to sing the Litany of our Lady with the greatest gusto). I am not sufficiently informed to know what is the antiquity of this office, or whether anything similar was practised in England before the Reformation. But I should think that it might be possible to devise a service which should include a recognition of the Host – a moment of particular intensity – without Exposition.

So far as my own feelings are concerned, I should be more than willing to sacrifice the extra-liturgical evening ceremonies altogether, against assurance of Reservation and the essential Lenten offices. The only valid argument from the point of view of parish clergy seems to me to be the effect upon the minds of their flocks; and with goodwill on the part of the clergy (that, I dare say, is expecting a good deal) and some alternative service which should be not merely [in] conformity with Low Church usage, I should have thought that they would be able to put the parishioners' minds at rest.

Mr Oldham[1] lunched with my wife and myself today; and I very much enjoyed meeting him, particularly before his leaving for America.

With many thanks for the weekend and for your help,

> I am,
> Yours very sincerely,
> T. S. Eliot

TO *Seward Collins*

CC

19 December 1930   [*The Criterion*]

Dear Mr Collins,

My friend Mr R. E. Gordon George who has frequently written for the *Criterion* as well as for *The Times* and other periodicals, under the pseudonym of 'R. E. Sencourt', has asked me to send you the enclosed essay in the hope that you will give it serious consideration for the *Bookman*. I do not know whether it is suitable material for the *Bookman*; and I am in great difficulty in judging its merit; first because it is partly about myself, and I can never exercise any critical discrimination over anything written about myself, and second, because the work of other

---

1 – See TSE to Oldham, 24 Feb. 1931, below.

poets mentioned in the article is, with the exception of my friend Force Stead's, wholly unknown to me. But I should be personally grateful if you would consider the manuscript, and I should be grateful, in the event of your finding the essay unsuitable for the *Bookman*, if you could suggest any other American periodical for which it might be more suitable.[1]

Yours sincerely,

[T. S. Eliot]

TO *The Editor,* The Times Literary Supplement   cc

19 December 1930   [Faber & Faber Ltd]

Sir,

I am gratified that so distinguished an author as Mr Oliphant should express approval of my article on Cyril Tourneur in your issue of November 13th.[2] To the points he raises I should like to reply as briefly as possible.

I am sorry if Mr Oliphant thinks that I attach excessive importance to the chronology of the Stationers' Register. I am by no means one of those who consider those records decisive. My point is really this: in the absence of any really cogent evidence to the contrary, I submit that the evidence of the Stationers' Register must be treated with respect. As I made clear in the article, I was once convinced that *The Atheist's Tragedy* was earlier than *The Revenger's Tragedy*; and I tried to present the considerations which now leave me with an open mind. Mr Oliphant does not himself offer any strong reasons for believing that *The Revenger's Tragedy* is the later play, and indeed, as he does not believe they are by the same author, he is not in a position to do so.

But I confess I cannot see why Mr Oliphant should raise this point at all or why he should question the Stationers' Register in this context in as much as he maintains his faith that *The Revenger's Tragedy* was written by Middleton. He says,

1–R. E. Gordon George, 'The Return of the Native', *The Bookman* 75 (Sept. 1932), 423–31.
2–E. H. C. Oliphant (Sarah Lawrence College, Bronxville, New York) questioned, in a letter headed 'Tourneur and *The Revenger's Tragedy*' (*TLS*, 18 Dec. 1930, 1087), TSE's support – in his anonymous article 'Cyril Tourneur' (*TLS*, 13 Nov. 1930, 925–6) – for the proposition that Tourneur wrote *The Revenger's Tragedy*. 'Nothing finer on the subject [than TSE's leading essay] has been written – at least nothing that has come under my notice,' opened Oliphant. All the same, the author's support for Tourneur's authorship was mistaken, he insisted. See further E. H. C. Oliphant, 'Tourneur and Mr T. S. Eliot', *Studies in Philology* 32 (Oct. 1935), 546–52.

'. . . would anyone dream for a moment of connecting the play with Tourneur but for the slight shred of external evidence [that exists] in his favour'.

If there were any considerable body of dramatic work definitely agreed upon to be Tourneur's, and if this body of work was closely similar to *The Atheist's Tragedy* and equally diverse from *The Revenger's Tragedy*, the shred of evidence would be very slight indeed. But, as things are, I cannot help feeling that Mr Oliphant has concentrated his attention more on the difference between the two plays attributed to Tourneur, than on the difference between *The Revenger's Tragedy* and those tragedies which we are sure were written by Middleton. We know more about Middleton than we do about Tourneur, and I submit that the differences between *The Revenger's Tragedy* and the whole of Middleton's work in tragedy are more significant than the differences between the two plays attributed to Tourneur.

> I am, Sir,
> Yours, etc.
> Your reviewer.

TO *The Editor,* The Nation & Athenaeum   TS Valerie Eliot

19 December 1930   Faber & Faber Ltd

THE BOOK OF BEAUTY

Sir,

I intervene in this matter with some diffidence and at the risk of being told to mind my own business, but as Mr Beaton and Mrs McLaren have so completely distorted what I take to be the point of Mrs Woolf's letter,[1] I feel that it is not impertinent for an outsider to draw attention to the real issue. And the fact that Mr Beaton is a very insignificant, though malodorous, insect, does not affect the general vermifugitive principle. I make no doubt that Mr Beaton is entirely within his legal rights and as,

---

1 – Virginia Woolf wrote, in *N&A* 47 (29 Nov. 1930), 291: 'I hope you will acquit me of any desire to ventilate a merely personal grievance if I ask you to publish the following facts. A book [*The Book of Beauty*] has just been issued of drawings and photographs by Cecil Beaton. To my surprise, I find that two sketches of myself are included. My permission was not asked. I have never had the honour of meeting Mr Beaton. He has twice kindly asked me to sit to him, and I have twice, I hope politely, refused. The matter is insignificant in itself, but I venture to ask you to give publicity to these facts by way of protest against a method of book-making which seems to me as questionable as it is highly disagreeable to one at least of its victims.'

on his own admission, he has once been inside a church, I fear lest we may soon have another *Book of Beauty* of the Virgin Mary and the more select saints. But to my mind Mr Beaton's position is very much that of a literary pirate in New York. As everybody knows, according to the actual copyright law, American publishers have frequent opportunity of pirating the work of English authors. They would be quite within their legal rights to do so, but the more reputable publishers would never think of filling their lists in this way, and the less reputable suffer from public opinion. Let us hope that Mr Beaton will have the same experience.[1]

> I am, Sir,
> Your obedient servant,
> T. S. Eliot

TO *William Temple*   CC

19 December 1930   [Faber & Faber Ltd]

Your Grace,

I am extremely grateful for Your Grace's two most helpful letters and notes.[2] Some points are already under revision: the Revd J. M. Wilson was

---

1–Harold Wright, editor of *N&A*, returned this letter to TSE with a covering letter (23 Dec. 1930): 'Our printers were nervous about the publication of the enclosed letter, on the ground that it might involve them in an action for libel. I do not myself feel any misgivings on that score, but the letter seems to me to be somewhat deficient in that urbanity which generally characterises correspondence in the "Nation". I therefore venture to send it back for your consideration.' Wright also made two emendations on TSE's text: drawing a line through TSE's phrase 'vermifugitive principle' he wrote in its stead 'principles of fumigation', and he deleted the word 'once' in the next sentence. TSE commented on Wright's letter: 'This is discouraging. I must try again. T.S.E.' He wrote by hand too: '"Is England getting soft?"'

2–Temple replied to TSE's first draft on 17 Dec.: 'You ask for some comments and I therefore offer some, but of course you will pay as much or as little attention as you feel disposed.

'*Page 5.* Of course it is true that Jeans stops short at the point where religious interest would begin, but even Jeans carries us very remarkably further than typical scientists of the Victorian period such as Huxley. I feel inclined to say that if Jeans will give us ground for believing in a Creator who is mathematical I could do the rest: but what fun it is to see a mathematician saying that God is thought and nothing more, and then supposing that he is not being anthropomorphic! "Thou thoughtest wickedly that I am even such an one as thyself" applies to the scientists quite as much as the moralists. Personally I feel that Eddington is in another class, but this may be only because I happen to know that personally he is a Christian. Whitehead seems to me to provide an excellent philosophical introduction to religion without ever getting past the introduction. He only leads one to the threshold, but then he does lead one to that. My own estimate of the situation is something like this. Modern philosophy and science, when it is philosophical, are not hostile to a belief in a spiritual interpretation of the universe. So far there is a new harmony between them and

only a name to me until a few days ago; and when I had some information about him I decided to delete that note. But I thought the Bishop of Durham's letter quite brilliant, and was depressed by the poverty of the replies to it.

I am ready to admit that my observations upon scientists may be excessive;[1] but in view of the danger foreseen, I cannot feel that there is

---

religion, but it is possible that they are more insidiously dangerous to vital religion than the old hostile folk, because they offer what may satisfy mere religious impulse without making any claim on real faith.

'*Page 21.* Your note is hardly fair to the aged J. M. Wilson (N.B. He is ninety-six, and was already a science teacher at Rugby when Darwin brought out the *Origin of Species*) What he means is not that the House of Commons has temporal over spiritual concerns, but that it is in his judgement the chief illustration in the world of power controlled for the most part by religious men in accordance with their religious convictions. I do not share his view, but I know that is what it is.

'*Page 28, line 2.* You say "Who says they are?" The answer is the popular Press says the Bishops say so. This may have made it worthwhile for the Bishops to say that they do not say so.

'*Page 28, lower down.* I suppose the chief author in mind was B. Russell.

'*Page 31.* I am glad you refer to the article by Spens. It is excellent in itself and I think perfectly represents the balance of thought that lies behind the resolution.

'*Page 34.* I, personally, hate this contrast of logic and life, because it involves what I think a false view of logic. Logic not only requires that I should argue correctly from my premises and also that I should secure that the premises give a complete statement of the relevant facts. It is only in life that these can be found, and strict deductions from any propositions which omit any aspect of life will therefore be false, but also logically fallacious. It is not true that the French are markedly logical. What is true is that they are governed by a bad kind of logic.

'*Page 35.* Quotation from Report. In the original the words are "any *one* particular theory". We did not invite people to adopt Episcopacy without *any* meaning, but there are several meanings attached to it in the history of the Church, and we did not insist that any one of these should be adopted by others any more than it is by ourselves.

'*Page 34, line 4 from the bottom.* This is rather obscure. I am not quite sure how the Episcopal minds come in here.

'*Page 36.* Phantom Unity. This phrase suggests that no allowance is made for the effective institutions in creating their own mentality. For myself I am quite sure that any Church which becomes Episcopal will, in course of time, become Episcopalian.

'*Page 37.* My answer would be that we start from the fact of division and are aiming at unity. For this we must not only uphold our traditions, but enable others to enter into some living appreciation of them when it is possible to do this on grounds so plainly exceptional as not to compromise the principle itself. Your last sentence is open to a possible interpretation that Confirmation is a price paid for admission to Communion, instead of being in itself an added blessing.

'*Page 38.* No doubt you mean to recast this if you use it at all; but you will remember that the Lambeth Report, whether you agree or not, draws a very sharp distinction between encouraging a ministry of women during the diaconate, which it wants greatly to develop, and any question of admission to the priesthood, which it bars.

'Again let me thank you for showing me your paper in its early shape.'

1 – 'Let us consider the quantity of nonsense that some of our most eminent scientists, professors and men of letters are able, each for himself, to turn out during every publishing

any harm in my exaggerating at that point. I know that Eddington is a Christian, but I object to his loading his dice so heavily on behalf of the Society of Friends.

I am not clear whether your note on my page 34 indicates approval of what I say there or the reverse. I quite agree, in any case, that the French are not particularly logical. Their philosophical works often have a superficial clarity which only cloaks obscurity or ambiguity.

I do not intend to include the note on the Bradford Diocesan Conference. It struck me as extremely funny, that is all.

On pages 35 and 36 I am not sure how you interpret my remark on the Episcopate. My point is merely that it may not be clear to the uninstructed, and particularly the non-Anglican, that 'any one particular theory' refers to theories already in existence within the Church, or perhaps also to any other possible theories tenable in the same way, and that it gives no advantage to an hypothetical dissenter capable of duplicity or self-deception.

I cannot quite follow Your Grace's conviction that 'any Church which becomes Episcopal will in course of time become Episcopalian.' Might not the significance of 'Episcopalian' become transformed in the process?

My chief point, however, is one which I have been discussing with Kenneth Ingram. I know now, what I did not know when I wrote my note, that the permission and encouragement to Presbyterians and dissenters to communicate under certain conditions, had reference to peculiar conditions in missionary dioceses. I do not object to the principle, having understood the conditions; but it does seem to me to raise a point of doctrine upon which the Church ought to pronounce, if authorising the practice. There is surely implied a doctrine of degrees of reception of the benefits of the Eucharist, and perhaps of degrees of value of the sacrifice offered. I feel that there is a good deal to be said in favour of such a doctrine, which would incidentally overcome my doubt about the communication of the unconfirmed. Am I talking nonsense here? I should be still more grateful if you could find time to let me have a word on this one question.[1]

---

season. Let us imagine (if we can imagine such persons agreeing to that extent) the fatuity of an encyclical letter produced by the joint efforts of Mr H. G. Wells, Mr Bernard Shaw and Mr Russell; or Professors Whitehead, Eddington and Jeans; or Dr Freud, Dr Jung and Dr Adler; or Mr Murry, Mr Fausset, the Huxley Brothers and the Reverend Mr Potter of America' (*Thoughts after Lambeth*, 6–7).

1 – Temple responded to this letter on 20 Dec.: 'I will try at once to answer your points briefly.

(1) As regards p. 34. I agree with your main point, but personally regret the now frequent contrast between Logic & Life. Of course Life is more than Logic, but there is only real divergence or conflict between them when the Logic is bad.

(2) I cordially agree about the absurdity of that Bradford discussion.

(3) Pp. 35, 36. I ntnt [*sic*] about requiring the fact, but not any one theory, of Episcopate. And I agree that the text of the Report is not clear to the un-instructed. If this is read with the repeated emphasis on "continuity of succession and consecration" and the continuous identity of function, I think all pernicious obscurity is removed. This does rule out all such theories as would actually condemn the restriction of these functions to the episcopate; but it does not require that the restriction shall be interpreted or justified only in prescribed ways.

(4) My point that "any Church which becomes Episcopal will in course of time become Episcopalian" is, of course, based on the Platonic argument which pervades Republic VIII & IX that the constitution of any society tends to produce in members of that society a mentality & character corresponding to the principles implied by the constitution, e.g. in a plutocratic state men tend to think economic wealth the chief good. I think you can trace this at work in the steady recovery of hold on essential Catholicism in the C. of E. as compared with the difficulty of any similar movement in German Lutheranism, which was at first no more anti-Catholic in outlook, but lost Catholic order.

(5) The last part of Resolution 42 does not refer only to missionary dioceses, though the first part does. But it does refer to "special and temporary circumstances".

The question of degree of reception is very complicated. The outline of my own answer would be this:

(a) There are no degrees in the self-giving of Christ. That is always complete. And wherever men do what they believe that He commanded in the hope of receiving what He promised, He offers Himself in fullness to their need.

(b) Consequently there are no degrees in the offering of the sacrifice. But there may be no intention to offer the sacrifice at all; and then there is no sacrifice. No outward act, apart from intention, is a sacrifice, any more than a butcher is a (Levitical) priest. If, in the process of doing what Christ commanded in hope of receiving what He promised, there is the intention to offer the sacrifice (based on the belief that this *is* part of what He commanded) then (I cannot doubt) the sacrifice is fully offered.

(c) But there are many degrees of receptivity, based on degrees and varieties of faith. A total lack of charity would make reception impossible. So would a total lack of faith either in God or in the reality of the Sacrament. Now the special characteristic of Sacramental worship is that it draws us away from our feelings. I believe that if I obediently do what Christ commanded I shall receive what He promised, whether or not I have at the time any conscious realisation of this. But the fundamental Sacrament is the Incarnation, which is continued in principle in the Church. The Sacraments belong to the Church, and are only considered rightly in the context of the Church's sacramental life. For the maintenance of that life through the ages the due order of the Church is necessary – so much so that St Thomas [Aquinas] put Order along with Baptism & Penance as the only three sacraments necessary to salvation in the sense that without it the end cannot be obtained (S. T. Pt. III Q. 65 A4) – but his argument is of course quite different from mine. The fundamental question then is not Does A B receive the same grace as X Y? (I see no way in which that could ever be answered.) – but What is the Order of the Church which belongs to & expresses its sacramental character? For to that we must adhere, and through it alone can we look for that reception of grace which is utterly separate from all question of "feeling". And the assurance that is attended by a "valid" ministry is one normal condition of this. It is therefore to be expected that dissenters are in fact less receptive of sacramental grace than Catholics, though this could not be laid down as a universal principle. Is this any use? It can only indicate my approach to the problem – to handle it requires a treatise. / Yours v. sincerely / William Ebor.

Again with many thanks,

> I am, Your Grace,
> Yours very sincerely,
> [T. S. Eliot]

TO *Ezra Pound*   TS Beinecke

20 Dec[ember] 1930   Faber & Faber Ltd

Dear Rabbit:

Dont blame me. The B.B.C. appealed to me asking Who was the best Person to translate two stanzoes of Villon for their new Year's Eve festivities, and I told them to wire you in my name. After a little discussion eight guineas was decided upon: I hope that is satisfactory. Let me know if they dont pay you.[1]

Some parts of this suspicious corporation have spiritual strivings; they have taken on a few aspiring youths from the universities; I am trying to get them to take an interest in the Joyce record and other matters. They have plenty of money.

I have been in touch with Porringer and also with the Eric Gill Press about Guido.

With love to D. and yrself, and goodwill to all men with numerous exceptions, at this season of the year, I am

> Yrs etc.
> T. S. E.

TO *Mario Praz*   CC

30 December 1930   [Faber & Faber Ltd]

My dear Praz,

Many thanks for your letter of the 20th instant, and for the two copies of your beautifully produced book.[2] Thank you particularly for sending

---

1 – R. A. Rendall (Central Council for Broadcast Adult Education, BBC) wrote to TSE, in an undated letter, that the BBC Producer Archie Harding wanted to include in 'a rather special programme for New Year's Eve' two verses of a poem by François Villon: would TSE translate them? The feature on Villon, co-written by Harding and EP, turned out to be a major event in the development of radio – 'the first British example of radio reportage' (*ODNB*).

2 – Praz expressed the wish that F&F might consider the 'first part' of *La carne, la morte e il diavolo nella letteratura romantica* for translation.

me a copy for myself. I shall have pleasure in reading it, though I fear I have not time to make rapid progress at present. The other I shall send out for an opinion as soon as possible.

I hope you will be in London long enough for me to see you about the 10th January. There is also a young American named Warren who would like to see you again. I am trying to think of American critics who might be interested.

With best wishes for the New Year,

Yours ever,
[T. S. Eliot]

FROM *Vivien Eliot* TO *Ottoline Morrell*   MS Texas

30 December 1930   68 Clarence Gate Gardens, Regent's Park

Dearest Ottoline

How *can* I thank you for those 6 lovely handkerchiefs which you have given me for Christmas? They are all delicious, & remind me of you. Thank you for your charming thought & kindness.

Thank you for yr. letter saying that you had received that strange peice [*sic*] of stuff, which by the way, comes *from ROME*. It amuses my Mother so much, that she is never without a peice of it. I too have a peice, & we consider it a kind of symbol. So I am glad you have it.

How are you?

Can you write a line (or card) to tell me what afternoon next week you could give me? I would either come to you or you come here, whichever you like best?

I hope you have had a happy Christmas, and I wish you a *very happy New Year*.

I heard the other day that you had been seen recently by someone we both know, looking splendidly well.

I am very *lame* at present. Thanking you again –

Your loving
Vivienne Haigh Eliot

TO *R. E. Gordon George (Robert Sencourt)*[1]　　　　CC

30 December 1930　　　　　　　*[The Criterion]*

Dear Gordon,

I am sending you back your essay on Mrs Wharton's poetry immediately, as I know your address for this week but am uncertain of your further movements. I am very glad that you speak a good word for *Ethan Frome* which I think a very fine novel indeed, but I am afraid, judging solely by the extracts you give, I cannot concur with your admiration for Mrs Wharton's verse. It may be due to defective understanding or to some weakness of the flesh, but this poetry leaves me feeling as cold as if I had been reading the Sonnets of Mr Santayana or stroking a dead fish. I think it is probably that I put my emphases in different places from yours. At any rate, many thanks for letting me see the essay, and I shall look forward to reading it again in the *Hound and Horn*.[2]

As for the pen, the only thing to do with a useless gift is to pass it on to someone to whom it may be useful.[3]

Ever affectionately yours,

[T. S. Eliot]

TO *Michael Sayers*　　　　CC

30 December 1930　　　　　　　[Faber & Faber Ltd]

Dear Mr Sayers,

I am returning herewith your latest poems, on some of which I have scribbled a few comments. I think that you are doing very well in rhythm and verse-form, and you seem to have a good ear, which is capable of development. But you do use too many words, some of which recur rather monotonously, and some of them do not seem to have much meaning.

---

1 – Robert Esmonde Gordon George – Robert Sencourt (1890–1969) – critic, historian and biographer: see Biographical Register.
2 – 'The Poetry of Edith Wharton', *The Bookman* 72: 5 (July 1931), 478–86.
3 – George had written (undated), 'can I not trust you as a friend enough to say that while appreciating this in the extreme I dare not trust my writing to even the most advanced invention of the age. Alas, I simply cannot use a fountain pen: but as you have given me a present which ninety nine out of a hundred, and indeed *all* properly balanced people, covet, I can either give myself the enormous pleasure of handing it on to one of them, or the equally great pleasure of leaving it again to you to do so. But I feel quite sure that it is better for us to share the additional giving rather than for me to feign to use a good thing which an incorrigible idiosyncrasy prevents me from using, and which sooner or later would get lost.'

I think that you need to pay more attention to the literal sense of what you have to say. I hope that these few hints may be of some use.

I have only just returned after Christmas, and hope to write to you again later, about your affairs.

Yours sincerely,
[T. S. Eliot]

TO *Karl Erdmann*[1]   CC

30 December 1930   [*The Criterion*]

Dear Mr Erdmann,

Very many thanks for sending me your essay on Burke which interested me very much indeed.[2] I think I could use such an essay if you are willing to accept a few suggestions.

First, I think that such phrases as were meant for address to an audience ought to be removed or altered for the essay to be read. For instance, in one place you say 'this century [*sc.* country]' where to the reader of the paper it is not immediately clear whether you mean England or Germany.

Second, I think that the first half of the paper should be reduced to about half the compass. Your opinions of Burke are interesting, but after all they are shared by many people and what is really of importance is the second part which deals with Burke's influence in Germany.

Would it be possible to trace any influence in more modern times by those German political philosophers who were influenced by Burke? It would be interesting if it would be possible to link up any contemporary German thought with that of Burke.

I shall be very glad if you will let me know what you think of these suggestions. Meanwhile, with best wishes for the New Year,

I am,
Yours sincerely,
[T. S. Eliot]

1 – William Stewart had written to TSE on 19 Mar. 1930, of Karl Erdmann: 'Erdmann is 27, has studied Classics and the law, and knew Europe all but Britain, when he came to visit me at St Andrews last Michaelmas before going up to Cambridge; he is there spending the year at Trinity College . . . He is a close friend of Ernst Robert Curtius who has a very high opinion of him.'
2 – Erdmann wrote from Heidelberg on 15 Dec. He had met TSE in London in July 1930, with introductions from Curtius and Stewart.

30 December 1930   [Faber & Faber Ltd]

My dear Selwyn,

Very many thanks for your letter of the 20th instant.[1] By the way,
I do not know either how or where to address you at present, so will

---

1–Selwyn, who had just been appointed Dean of Winchester, wrote that he had read the
draft of TSE's *Thoughts after Lambeth* 'carefully, & with great appreciation: it is the best
thing, if I may say so, on the Conference as a whole that has come my way. And I think this is
not only because I agree with your definite judgments on particular issues so often – indeed
perhaps always. But you also seem to me to have got exactly the right atmosphere for such
a discussion; your introductory pages, for instance, seem to me admirable.

'One or two queries have occurred to me:–

1) *Prudenti dissimulatione uti*. Canon Belton has written to me to urge that *dissimulatio*
means "tactfulness". I replied that I couldn't quite accept that, but that I would grant that
the word was not quite fairly translated by being transliterated. What it really means, I think,
is "pretending not to see, when you do", "turning a blind eye" – as e.g. when the priest in
the confessional asks no questions about birth-control. However, you don't translate the
phrase – & so I don't see why you should alter what you have written.'

(TSE had written, in *Thoughts after Lambeth*: 'the Roman view in general seems to me to
be that a principle must be affirmed without exception; and that thereafter exceptions can be
dealt with, without modifying the principle. The view natural to the English mind, I believe,
is rather that a principle must be framed in such a way as to include all allowable exceptions.
It follows inevitably that the Roman Church must profess to be fixed, while the Anglican
Church must profess to take account of changed conditions. I hope that it is unnecessary
to give the assurance that I do not consider the Roman way of thought dishonest, and that
I would not endorse any cheap and facile gibes about the duplicity and dissimulation of
that Church; it is another conception of human nature and of the means by which, on the
whole, the greatest number of souls can be saved; but the difference goes deep. *Prudenti
dissimulatione uti* is not a precept which appeals to Anglo-Saxon theology' (*SE*, 365–6). In
answer to Selwyn's 'query' on this point, TSE added a footnote to the text of *Thoughts* as
reprinted in *SE*, 365: 'It has been pointed out to me that here dissimulation should perhaps
be translated as "tactfulness" rather than "dissimulation"; but a tactfulness which consists
primarily in not asking awkward questions seems to me to be pretty close to simulation and
dissimulation.')

Selwyn continued his letter with this query: '2) P. 35 – *power . . . authority*: I think you
allude to the medieval dispute between the theologians & the canonists as to whether
Episcopal ordination conferred "Order" or "Jurisdiction". I think your phrase "the *power*
to induce the Presence in the Eucharist" lends itself to misinterpretation. What about
"confers simply the ministerial grace or power of Order, or the authority to exercise that
power in the Church".

'3) P. 40. One has to remember the important Catholic principle, "*Conscientia semper
sequenda*". A Catholic might sincerely believe *in foro conscientiae* that he was justified in
using contraceptives; & in that case he would not, I think, be bound to confess it as sin. Of
course this makes mince-meat of a lot of Roman theory on the subject: but I am not sure
whether it is the particular mince you speak of. Anyhow, it is worth a thought.

'On Resolution 15 generally you seem to me to have a criterion of first-rate importance –
the one really broad & cogent criticism that is needed.'

continue to Havant till further notice. Perhaps you will let me have a card to announce your translation. I did not even know of your preferment – in which I rejoice – until I went to Chichester a fortnight ago. I met there your parents-in-law and had a long talk about French politics with the Archdeacon.

I cannot see that the slight differences in the translation of *dissimulatio* has any significance, and after all the distinction in English between tactfulness and simulation and/or dissimulation is not always evident. In any case, 'turning a blind eye' still corresponds exactly to my distinction between what I suppose the Roman confessional to be, and what I take it the Anglican confessional ought to be.

As for *Power* and *Authority*, I must confess that this distinction is almost too much for my intellect and that I owe it entirely to a note given me by the Archbishop of York. Hence my own Appendix, which should be incorporated in the text. In spite of what the Archbishop wrote, I still think the words of the phrase in the Report liable to misunderstanding by Laity.

I cannot be convinced that individual judgment *in foro conscientiae* is satisfactory except in so far as the penitent may be allowed to omit mention of very trivial faults. At any rate, on really vital matters I should never trust my own conscience unless I had at least put it to the test of spiritual counsel.

I hope to get the thing finished for publication towards the end of January, before the Assembly. Meanwhile, many thanks for your comments. It would be a very great pleasure indeed to visit you at Winchester. I hope very much that you will find the Deanery more favourable for *Theology* and for your own work than in a rural vicarage.

Yours ever,
[T. S. Eliot]

TO *Gerard Hopkins*   CC

30 December 1930   [Faber & Faber Ltd]

Dear Hopkins,

I have another suggestion to make to you, of a book in preparation, which was prepared [*sc.* presented] to us first, and seemed to me definitely a Clarendon Press book. A Miss Margaret Deas – a former pupil of Grierson's and one of whom I believe he thought highly – is interested in preparing a new edition of Lord Dorset's Poems. This seems to me a piece of work well worth doing and worthy indeed of the format of your Jacobean and Caroline Poets. I do not know Miss Deas personally, but if the idea appeals to the Press, as I think it should, it will be quite easy for you to obtain information about her qualifications.[1]

Sincerely yours,

[T. S. Eliot]

TO *G. Wilson Knight*   CC

30 December 1930   [*The Criterion*]

Dear Wilson Knight,

I return your essay on *Coriolanus* with many thanks for letting me see it.[2] It is not at all too long: I only regret that it is much too long to be considered for the *Criterion*.

You had already, so far as I am concerned, put the gist of it into the notes you sent me. That does not mean at all that you have not done quite right to expand it. What the complete essay adds for me is chiefly the detailed and convincing analysis of the type of imagery. That does increase my understanding and appreciation.

You will know already that I am in close agreement. There is one point which has always puzzled me, upon which you do not throw light. Why, at that moment, should *Coriolanus* turn with such magnificent praise of Valeria, apparently merely a friend of the family of uncertain age, and a person of whom we have such a vague impression. Is it to emphasise his attitude towards his wife?

As for *partly proud* I am afraid that I had always read it simply as 'partly, to be proud'; but that won't hold water; I am inclined to think that the second of your two interpretations is the likelier one.

I am almost sorry that you are passing to *The Tempest*, instead of *Antony and Cleopatra*, which I should like to see done soon. I find *A. & C.* much more complicated than *Coriolanus*; I am inclined to agree that it is later. For in *Coriolanus* you have what may be taken merely as a sudden conversion; in *A. & C.* you have what looks to me like a gradual development. The point to me is this: the love of Antony and Cleopatra at the beginning is on both sides an offence against honour and duty; hence

1–Hopkins replied on 15 Jan. 1931: 'I have heard well of Miss Deas, and I am prepared to think well of Lord Dorset. But on enquiry I cannot find enthusiasm about him in these cloisters . . .'
2–GWK submitted his full essay on *Coriolanus* on 23 Dec.

are stressed Cleopatra's levity – her feeling toward Antony is that of a wanton – and the debilitated luxuriousness of Antony compared to his previous austerity as a soldier, drinking muddy water with the horses. But gradually the situation is reversed; the feeling of Antony and Cleopatra becomes more and more the real thing, purified of self; until at the end Love is actually the true value, and the World is typified by Octavius. A. & C. in short become real mates. The asp 'my baby at my breast' is of course exquisite; but I think the finest touch is the words 'Husband! I come'.

I wonder if this is at all the line that you will take.[1]

With best wishes for the New Year,

Sincerely yours,
[T. S. Eliot]

TO *R. H. Hellyar*[2]   CC

30 December 1930   [*The Criterion*]

Dear Sir,

In reply to your letter of the 6th instant, I have read your communication about Mr Belgion's essay with much interest.[3] I should certainly have chosen to publish it except for the fact that Mr Richards himself, I am happy to say, has sent me his reply to Mr Belgion. I shall publish this in the form of an article in the March issue and I think that it is best that Mr Richards should be allowed to speak first. If, after his article appears, you have further observations to make, I shall be happy to entertain them.[4]

Yours faithfully,
[T. S. Eliot]
Editor.

1–See GWK's essay on *Coriolanus* and *Antony and Cleopatra* in *The Imperial Theme* (1931).
2–Richard H. Hellyar, author of *W. N. P. Barbellion* (1926).
3–Hellyar complained that Belgion limited 'form too narrowly'; he was 'rather unsubtle, too, in his treatment of emotion': 'As he talks, a poet looks like a grocer cutting a pound of cheese.'
4–IAR wrote on 30 Nov.: 'Many thanks for sending along the *Criterion*. I won't deny I was incensed by Belgion for you will see evidence enough in the *Notes* with which I am replying. I've watered them down very much, as you will also see, but I hope they still indicate how very incompetent I think he is. I feel rather disappointed, for I should have liked to see a discussion of some of the things I did see.' He wrote again, with a revised version of his reply, on 13 Feb. 1931: 'Herewith my screams at Belgion.' (*Letters*, 60) See IAR, 'Notes on the

TO *Seán Ó'Faoláin*[1]   CC

31 December 1930   [Faber & Faber Ltd]

Dear Mr O'Faolain,

Many thanks for your kind thought of sending me a card. I am writing
to say that I have just heard from the Cambridge University Press who,
I am sorry to say, do not feel like taking up your book. The secretary
suggests the Irish Texts Society. I know nothing about this and very likely
you have already thought of it. I wish that I had more suggestions to
make, but if you can think of any further use that I might be, please let
me know.

With best wishes for the New Year,

Yours sincerely,

[T. S. Eliot]

Practice of Interpretation', C. 10 (Apr. 1931), 412–20; letter by Belgion, C. 10 (Apr. 1931),
507. (In a note sent on 5 Jan. 1932, IAR was to complain that Belgion had, in his *The
Human Parrot, and Other Essays*, 'fudged up another set of absurdities for me to have said
and thanks you for helping him in his Preface. I suppose we should be glad – like ichthy-
ologists – to attract and catch specimens of strange misunderstanding with our writings.
Probably there is nothing else to be caught.')
1 – Seán Ó'Faoláin (1900–91): novelist and short-story writer. Brought up in Ireland (where
he was born John Francis Whelan), he attended University College, Cork – for a while in the
early 1920s he was an ardent nationalist and joined the Irish Volunteers (later the IRA) – and
he was a Commonwealth Fellow at Harvard University, 1926–8. Later founder-editor of the
Irish periodical *The Bell* – see Kelly Matthews, *The Bell Magazine and the Representation
of Irish Identity* (2013) – he also served as Director of the Arts Council of Ireland, 1957–9.
Following his first book, *Midsummer Night Madness and Other Stories* (1932), he wrote a
wealth of short stories. See *Collected Stories of Seán Ó'Faoláin* (1983); Maurice Harmon,
Seán Ó'Faoláin: A Life (1994): M. Arndt, *A Critical Study of Seán Ó'Faoláin's Life and
Work* (2001).

TO *Patrick Braybrooke*¹   CC

1 January 1931   [Faber & Faber Ltd]

Dear Mr Braybrooke,

Thank you for your letter of the 30th ultimo, and for your interesting suggestion. I have discussed it with other directors and given it careful thought, but we do not feel at the present time that it is a suitable enterprise for us to embark upon. As you say, however, there is always an interest in Oscar Wilde, and I have no doubt that some publishing house would be glad to put such a book into their programme.

With many regrets, I am,
Yours sincerely,
[T. S. Eliot]

TO *Ezra Pound*   TS Beinecke

1 January 1931   *The Criterion*

Right Honourable Rabbit,

The B.B.C. are usually prompt payers. The masterly translation was, I suppose, delivered last night, *Sylvester-abend*,² but as my wireless battery has run down, and as it costs 25/- to get a new one, I did not hear the celebration.

I enjoyed your Canto, featuring Mr Jefferson, Dr Franklin, and my uncle John,³ but I am not sure it is the most suitable to impose upon the illiterate public of Britain. Would you permit me to select one out of Nancy's book, if I give due acknowledgement to Nancy and yourself?

1–Patrick Braybrooke (1894–1956): biographer; author of *Gilbert Keith Chesterton* (1922), *The Life and Work of Lord Alfred Douglas* (1931), and *The Amazing Mr Noël Coward* (1933).
2–German: Feast of St Sylvester, New Year's Eve.
3–Canto 31, made up of extracts from the letters of Thomas Jefferson and John Adams (TSE had given EP a 1905 edition of Jefferson's works). Elsewhere, TSE spoke of EP's '*longueurs* . . . about mysteries of American history . . . in which I, like most readers, am not adept'.

I hope to publish Zukofsky's essay – or as much of it as there is room for – in March and am at present trying to find the typescript.[1]

With the compliments of the Season to Dorothy and yourself,

Yours,

T.

TO *Montgomery Belgion*   CC

1 January 1931   [*The Criterion*]

Dear Belgion,

I ought to have told you, and indeed I thought I had mentioned, that I did not want to give more than a brief note to *The Mysterious Universe*, after your long review of Jeans's bigger books; so I have handed it, with instructions to that effect to a promising young man to cut his teeth on.[2] Anyway, you will be filling up a good deal of space in the review part of the next number.

I am hoping to be away from London for a week from the 17th instant, but I should like very much indeed to meet Malraux, either before or after next week.[3]

With best New Year wishes,

Yours ever,

[T. S. Eliot]

TO *Ernest Rhys*   CC

1 January 1931   [Faber & Faber Ltd]

Dear Mr Rhys,

I have just realised that I should have answered your letter of the 7th ultimo, but I hope that you will have taken my silence as agreement.[4] I hope to get to work on *Pascal* (which will mean a great deal of reading as

1–Louis Zukofsky, 'The Cantos of Ezra Pound', *C.* 10 (Apr. 1931), 425–40.
2–Hugh Sykes Davies reviewed *The Mysterious Universe*, by Sir J. Jeans, *C.* 10 (Apr. 1931), 514.
3–Belgion wrote (27 Dec. 1930): 'Malraux expects to be in London almost certainly about Jan. 15. You must come to luncheon and meet him . . .' In the event, André Malraux visited London in Mar. 1931, but TSE did not meet him.
4–Rhys proposed (7 Dec. 1930): '3–4 thousand words & fifteen pounds? (Everyman has to be economical.) For this, we do not expect you to compile the bibliography; & you retain the right to use the essay again, except as introduction to a volume.'

I have not touched him for years) after about a fortnight when I hope to have completed a piece of work which I have on hand.

Yours sincerely,
[T. S. Eliot]

TO *Ottoline Morrell*   MS Texas

5 January 1931   68 Clarence Gate Gardens, NW1

Dear Ottoline

I was very much pleased to have the Diary from you: all the more, because I should have been disappointed if it had not come. I have kept all the 'back numbers'; and the current number always reminds me of you almost every day.

I found, on enquiry, that *Marina* which I sent you on publication, was sent to *Garsington*. So previous years may have gone astray too. When I signed the copies you sent, I was under the impression that you already had one set from me. So I am getting another set to send you properly signed.

I hope we may see you soon,

Affectionately
T. S. Eliot

TO *Francis Underhill*   CC

5 January 1931   [Faber & Faber Ltd]

Dear Father Underhill,

Thank you for your letter of the 3rd.[1] I have not yet heard from the Revd F. E. Balmforth.[2] I should be very pleased indeed to accede to the request but you know how I am placed. Also I have a great many arrears on my hands; I am hoping to get to Kelham on the 17th; and I have got to address The English Association in the middle of February, and have not yet the slightest idea what about.[3] So I am afraid I could not think

1–'A sixth form boy at Repton, who is a friend of mine, was asking me the other day whether anything would induce you to go down there one day next term, and speak to their literary society. This morning I have heard from the master who fathers the society asking whether you would go. He is the Revd F. H. Balmforth.'
2–Balmforth invited TSE (6 Jan.) to address the Repton School Literary Society.
3–'Charles Whibley: a literary memoir': address given at 5.30 on Fri., 20 Feb. 1931.

of going to Repton until the summer term. That is a bad term for the purpose at the universities and I suppose at schools as well. But thank you very much for conveying the invitation.

I wish you could enlighten me about a communication I received yesterday. It is an impersonal invitation from a Lady Eleanor Keane,[1] addressed from Ireland, inviting me to join some of her young friends at her house in St John's Wood on Thursday evenings, for discussions with you. I should of course enjoy any discussions which you conducted, but I wondered whether the lady did not imagine me to be a good deal younger than I am. I should be grateful if you would let me know what is to happen and what sort of young people are to attend.

Yours very sincerely,
[T. S. Eliot]

TO *George Bell*   TS Lambeth

7 January 1931   68, Clarence Gate Gardens

My dear Lord Bishop,

Thank you for your letter of the 2nd.[2] I am writing now briefly in reply to say that the form of Lenten Offices to which I am accustomed (and to which I am strongly attached) is in *The English Holy Week Book* published by the Society of SS. Peter & Paul (2/6). That contains Tenebrae, the Mass of the Pre-Sanctified and the Blessing of the Font, Blessing of the New Fire, and preparation of the Pascal Candle on Holy Saturday, as we had them at St Mary the Virgin's. Of course the regular Mass of Ashes is equally 'essential'. For the Mass of the Pre-Sanctified, I like both the transference of the Host from the Lady Chapel to the High Altar, and the Procession to kiss the Crucifix, after the unveiling.

I shall look up the passage from Andrewes, which I once read, though I fear with imperfect understanding, as I have never read a word of the voluminous Bellarmine. Your last sentence reminds me that the wording of 'The Divine Praises' is 'Blessed be Christ in the Most Holy Sacrament of the Altar'.

I wonder if I am wrong in feeling (as a result of poring over Lambeth) that the Anglican Church is a little too ready to approve practices which

1–Underhill reported on 7 Jan. that Lady Eleanor 'is a friend of mine . . . who is getting some sorry men together to discuss religion . . . But don't take any notice!'
2–Not found.

are worthy of approval and find the theological justifications afterwards? – I mean that the English mind, when it sees that something ought to be done or to be tolerated, immediately does it or tolerates it, on instinct. I am thinking of that difficult matter of mixed communions, which does seem to me to depend upon some clear doctrine about the Sacrament of the Altar which has not yet been formulated.

With many thanks,

Yours very sincerely,
T. S. Eliot

TO *Horace Gregory*[1]

TS Syracuse

Telegram 8 January 1931

PREPARED PUBLISH ROOMINGHOUSE THIS YEAR STRAIGHT ROYALTY TEN PER CENT STOP HAVE HAD NO LETTER FROM YOU PLEASE WRITE CONFIRMATION BEFORE WE SEND CONTRACT[2]

ELIOT

TO *A. D. Sheffield*[3]

CC

12 January 1931   [Faber & Faber Ltd]

Dear Shef,

I was very glad to get your letter of the 27th ultimo, which reached me this morning together with your leaflet, which I have not yet had time to

---

1–Horace Gregory (1898–1982), poet and critic, majored in English at the University of Wisconsin before moving to New York City. His poetry includes *Chelsea Rooming House* (1930), *No Retreat* (1933), *Poems, 1930–40* (1941), and *Medusa in Gramercy Park* (1961); prose writings include *The House on Jefferson Street* (memoir, 1971) and *Spirit of Time and Place: The Collected Essays of Horace Gregory* (1973). He was awarded a Guggenheim Fellowship in 1951, and won the Bollingen Prize in 1965. His Russian-born wife, Marya Zaturenska, won a Pulitzer Prize for her second volume of verse, *Cold Morning Sky* (1937).
2–Gregory had in fact cabled TSE on 3 Jan. that F&F might publish his book of poems. Covici-Friede, who held the copyright of *Chelsea Rooming House*, had placed the responsibility for finding a British publisher in Gregory's hands, and agreed to share UK royalties with him.
3– Alfred Dwight ('Shef') Sheffield (1871–1961), husband of TSE's eldest sister Ada (1869–1943), taught English at University School, Cleveland, Ohio, and was an English instructor, later Professor, of Group Work at Wellesley College. His publications include *Lectures on the*

read.[1] I will write again as soon as I can, but am answering at once to ask you and Ada to be so kind as to write to my friend I. A. Richards and his wife and ask them to come to see you. I have just written to Richards to tell him that you would ask them, and I sure that you will like them both.

Ever affectionately,

[Tom]

P.S. Richards' address is
    Dunster Hall,
    Harvard University,
    Cambridge.

TO *William Empson*   CC

12 January 1931[2]   [*The Criterion*]

Dear Empson,

I am sorry to hear from Tillyard that he is too busy to be able to tackle your book. It occurred to me that possibly Hugh Sykes Davies might be up to it, but as I have only met him once, and I understand that you know him. I should like to know what you think of the suggestion.[3]

Sincerely yours,

[T. S. Eliot]

Harvard Classics: Confucianism (1909) and *Grammar and Thinking: a study of the working conceptions in syntax* (1912).

1 – 'Shef' had thanked TSE for sending an offprint of his essay 'The Place of Pater'; a copy of his *TLS* piece on Cyril Tourneur; and a copy of FRL's pamphlet *Mass Civilization and Minority Culture*; plus 'the amusing diatribe in the vein of the Dunciad'. Shef was President of the New England Association of Teachers of English, and sent by return a paper that he had prepared – on 'the study of conference method' – for the Dec. meeting of the Association.

2 – Misdated '1930'.

3 – Empson replied ('Wednesday') that he hoped James Smith might be able to review *Seven Types of Ambiguity*. 'I have just sent him a copy and he told me he was making up his mind whether it was all nonsense or not, so I expect he would like to do a review . . . I am against Sykes, myself, as a reviewer for my book, not that he wouldn't be very kind and intelligent, because it wouldn't be far enough outside my own Cambridge clique.'

TO *Eleanor Hinkley*   TS Houghton

12 January 1931   Faber & Faber Ltd

Dear Eleanor,

This note is not an answer to your long and interesting letter,[1] which I was very glad to get, and to which I hope to reply soon. It is merely to ask whether you and your mother would be so kind as to ask my friend Ivor Richards and his wife to come to see you. The address is Dunster Hall, Harvard. I imagine you know pretty well who Ivor Richards is, and he will be lecturing at Harvard this term. I used to see a good deal of him at Cambridge (England). His wife is a very nice person also, and incidentally is a very distinguished mountain climber. I believe that she scaled some Alpine peak which no woman had ever reached the top of before.[2]

                              Affectionately yours,
                              Tom.

I should like Emily to meet them if possible.

TO *I. A. Richards*   CC

13 January 1931   [Faber & Faber Ltd]

Dear Richards,

I was very glad to get your letters and also your photograph, although I regret that the pattern of the Chinese background is very much more distinct than your own features.

I have now sent off new copies of the missing books to Dunster Hall; please let me know if you have received them.

I imagine that you and Mrs Richards will be meeting more people than you want to meet, but I should like you both to see the more intelligent of my own relatives in Cambridge. I am therefore writing to my aunt, Mrs Hinkley, and her daughter and to my sister, Mrs Sheffield, and you will hear from them in due course. I should particularly like you to meet the Sheffields. My sister is by the far the most intelligent and able of my family, and is, or was, the greatest authority in America on feeble-minded female delinquents. Her husband is a professor of English at Wellesley, was born in China, and speaks the Pekinese dialect fluently and has always been

---

1 – Not found.

2 – In 1928 Dorothy Richards (1894–1986) made the first ascent of the Dent Blanche, in company with IAR, Joseph Georges and Antoine Georges: see her *Climbing Days* (1935).

interested in semantics and the problems with which you are concerned, and knows your own works.

I will write to you at more length when I hear from you at Cambridge. With best wishes to you both for the New Year,

[T. S. E.]

TO *F. S. Oliver* CC

16 January 1931 [*The Criterion*]

My dear Oliver,

You will think me a scurvy fellow to have left unanswered so long your kind letter, which I appreciated highly.[1] But on Christmas Day I strained an always weak abdomen by lifting a large gramophone in and out of a very small car; and that always means a couple of days on my back (it serves me right for participating in profane feasts on a holyday); when recovered I was visited with another affliction, gastric influenza, which I passed on to my wife, and which has been flourishing amazingly at her expense.

I quite appreciate the situation, and also the kind way in which you put it. I am very glad indeed that you wrote voluntarily about it, as it saves the embarrassment of application. Of course, the same general economic reasons which harass previous guarantors, chief of whom is yourself, prevent the free flow of seven-and-sixpences into our pocket; on the other hand, when people know that a review is subsidised (and one cannot prevent the knowledge from getting about) they are less inclined to feel that it needs their subscriptions. So that, as our firm has done *relatively* very well among publishers this season (which means of course that we can show a small profit) we shall make an effort to carry on the *Criterion*. That is for your private ear only – in case we should later decide to appeal to other benefactors.

I must add that from the beginning we had no expectation that so generous a supplement as yours would be renewed; even had we, the

---

1–Oliver wrote on 26 Dec. 1930: 'About the future of the *Criterion* in so far as my insignificant personality is concerned with it:– My contribution of £250 p.a. was for a specified period – I forget what – but the half yearly payment due next March is the final one.

'I wish (supposing it wd. be useful) that I could offer to continue my subscription (less or more) for a further period; but I *can't*: & that (unfortunately) is that. I won't go into details; but I've been pretty hard hit since May 1929 . . .'

progressive decline of national health would have made it seem unlikely. I wish to thank you therefore with all my heart, for the help you have given and the encouragement. I wish I could feel that the results had been adequate; had I not been distracted during the whole time by private anxieties, I think that they might have been better.

I hope that the new year, which has begun inauspiciously in most respects, including the influenza epidemic, has not stricken you in any way; and it would be a great pleasure to me to come to see you, when I can come and when you can have me – if good fortune should make the two conditions coincide.

Yours ever
[T. S. Eliot]

I thought the portrait of Whibley by Kelly was excellent; Macmillan sent me an engraving of it.

TO *E. M. W. Tillyard*   TS King's

16 January 1931   Faber & Faber Ltd

Dear Mr Tillyard,

It is very kind of you to ask me to be your guest at the Trinity Candlemas Feast;[1] my previous experience of the hospitality of Trinity is a very pleasant memory; and I should much like to have a talk with you. But I am so much in arrears of work at present, owing to various untoward circumstances, that I cannot afford the luxury of the recreation. I hope that I may become more mobile, but I see no prospect of it at the moment.

With many thanks,
Yours sincerely,
T. S. Eliot

TO *Erich Alport*   TS BL

16 January 1931   *The Criterion*

Dear Alport,

This is to thank you for your letter of the 1st January[2] and to convey my cordial wishes for the present year – which certainly has not begun

---

1 – Feast on Mon., 2 Feb.
2 – Not found.

cheerfully in this country, but with influenza and reduced dividends. As for Zweig, we found that some other publisher has a lien on his work, so there is nothing for us to do about it at present.[1] I am sorry. I have also been unsuccessful in getting American support for the Aristotle book, which I had set my heart upon; but if an American university press is at present 'too poor' to collaborate, what can we do? Yet it is a book which every competent scholar extols. Such are the times.

The delay about Curtius is really my fault; I have been on the point of going through the book carefully myself, so as to take (and be able to take) the whole responsibility; but many trivial things, including influenza, have intervened

I like your suggestion for Clauss, and shall write to him. But why do I never hear from him? I think two letters from me in the last year have gone unanswered.[2] I have not yet read Rohan's book; but there is so much too much to read.

I think it is quite true that there is a great interest in German affairs in England now; more than in French, I think; certainly more than in Italian. I am afraid the time is coming when we shall have to be interested in our own affairs too, but at the moment there is a (I believe) quite temporary, apathy, and the politicians must play out their play.

Do you know anything about a philosopher named Turel, in Germany? Auden recommended him to me a few days ago. By the way, I saw the charming Spender lately, who seems anxious to return to Germany.

Yours ever,
T. S. Eliot

TO *Tom Faber*   TS Valerie Eliot

20 January 1931   *The Criterion*

Dear Tom,

Thank you very much for your Letter To-day,[3] which I should have anwsered answered Before but could not Until after you had Written

---

1–Alport related on 1 Dec. that Stefan Zweig's agent was his publisher Viking-Press, New York. Zweig, who sent 'his kind regards' to TSE, would be happy to place an essay in *C*.
2–Alport ventured on 1 Feb. to explain why Clauss had not written to TSE. 'He fully acknowledges his fault, but the reason, he says, was that the *Nouvelle Revue Française*, the *Nuova Antologia* & the *Revista de Occidente* could not be brought to continue the scheme of the Best Short Story competition. Clauss kept on delaying to write to you about it . . .'
3–Not found.

it, as I have been Ill with Influentia and Milk-Toast; so there will be a Smalstonnerproovle soon.

I am glad you have a Case only if you come to see Me we Must be careful not to get them mixed up, because Mine has Tom on it Too. I am glad you have a Cat, but I do not believe it is So remarkable a cat as My cat. My Cat is a Lilliecat Hubvously. What a lilliecat it is. There never was such a Lilliecat.

ITS NAME IS

JELLYLORUM

and its one Idea is to be

USEFUL!!

For Instance
IT STRAIGHTENS THE PICTURES –

IT DOES THE GRATES –

LOOKS INTO THE LARDER TO SEE
WHAT'S NEEDED –

AND INTO THE DUSTBIN TO SEE
THAT NOTHING'S WASTED –

AND YET

IT IS SO LILLIE AND SMALL

THAT

IT CAN SIT ON MY EAR!
   (Of course I had to draw my Ear rather
Bigger than it Is to get the Lilliecat
onto it).

I would tell you about our Cus Cus Praps except that I can't Draw Dogs so well as Cats, Yet; but I mean to.

Yr affectionatuncle
Tom.
P.S. I Know how Busy you are so dont bother to answer this at Present[1]

TO *Charles Smyth*   cc

23 January 1931   [*The Criterion*]

Dear Smyth,

Thank you for your letter.[2] I have just heard from House (I wonder by
the way if he is the son of a former house-master at Malvern) and I am
very favourably disposed to his suggestion for an essay on Horace.

Davey I have heard great things of, and I look forward to reading the
book which he and Hoskyns have promised.[3] I am very glad to know a
little more about him and will certainly keep him in mind for a review.
Meanwhile, many thanks for your kindness in making suggestions. If, by
the way, you should come to know of any able, untried men, interested in
modern history and contemporary politics particularly, I should be very
glad to get in touch with them.

Now about your Purification Feast.[4] Unfortunately I have already
declined an invitation from Tillyard for their Candlemass Feast at Trinity.
I declined, partly for the reason that, having been to one Purification
Feast there which for the matter of that I thoroughly enjoyed, I could
not help feeling a slight absurdity in celebrating such an occasion with
vast quantities of champagne and port. But partly also because I was too
doubtful of my freedom on that date to venture to accept. So I have two

---

1–GCF wrote in his diary for Mon., 16 Feb. 1931: 'Told T.S.E. of Tom's pleasant casual
observation:- "I think Uncle Tom's a very good writer" – apropos of Uncle T's really brilliant
letter to his godson.'
2–Smyth recommended (21 Jan.) two of his friends as contributors to C.: (i) Humphrey
House – 'a classical usher [teacher] at Repton [School] . . . just down from Oxford, where he
narrowly missed a fellowship at All Souls; will be returning to Oxford almost certainly after
he is ordained, to take up a college chaplaincy . . . an extremely intelligent and well-read
person' – who had planned an essay ('a kind of literary commentary') on the *Ars Poetica* of
Horace; (ii) the Revd F. N. Davey, 'a curate in Manchester . . . a don in petto . . . the finest
intellect this College has turned out since the War': 'At present he is busy finishing a book
on the Riddle of the New Testament, in collaboration with Clement Hoskyns, Dean of this
College, whom of course you know; Faber & Faber are publishing it; it will be a popular
presentation of the findings of modern criticism, with immense learning and originality of
thought behind it.'
3–Sir Edwyn Hoskyns and Francis Noel Davey, *The Riddle of the New Testament* (F&F,
1931).
4–Smyth invited TSE to the Purification Feast on 4 Feb.

465

reasons for declining, but with much greater regret, your invitation: first, that it would hardly be proper to accept yours after declining Tillyard's, and second, the same reason, that I am too uncertain of being able to come. I do hope, however, that I may be able to get down to Corpus for a night during the term, and will let you know if I see any chance of it.

Ever yours,
[T. S. Eliot]

TO *Humphrey House*[1]   CC

26 January 1931   [*The Criterion*]

Dear Mr House,

I have your letter of the 22nd and had already heard about you from Charles Smyth.[2] The article you suggest sounds to me both interesting and suitable for the *Criterion*; I can never venture to commit myself absolutely to accepting an unwritten article by a writer whose work is unknown to me, but I think that your essay on Horace has everything in its favour and I very much hope you will complete it and send it to me.

The earliest number for which it would be possible for me to consider your article would be June next.[3]

If you should be in London at any time, I should be very glad if you would call and see me.

Yours very truly,
[T. S. Eliot]

TO *Herrn Weidmannsche Buchhandlung, Berlin*   CC

26 January 1931   [Faber & Faber Ltd]

Dear Sirs,

I must apologise to you for our delay in coming to a decision about Dr Jaeger's ARISTOTÈLES. The reason was, as I believe we explained to

1 – Humphrey House (1908–55) became a literary scholar and critic.
2 – House proposed an article on Horace's *Ars Poetica*. 'The implicit basis of it would be an extension & in places a criticism of the earlier chapters of Babbit's "New Laocoon", where he seems to make the 17th & 18th century commentators too much of one mind, & that too far a wrong one: and on this built protests against simple rejections of Horace Boileau Rapin etc like I. A. Richards'.'
3 – No article by House appeared in *C*.

you in advance, that we were sure we could not undertake the expense of such a work without the collaboration of an American publishing house. We have used our best endeavours to secure such co-operation but unfortunately, under the present economic conditions prevailing in America, which appear to have affected the book trade very seriously, we have been unable to find a publisher to share the burden with us.

We were aware that the public for such a book is necessarily small, and of course includes many persons who would naturally prefer to read the book in German. Furthermore it would be necessary to spare no expense to get a translator of the highest quality. For this reason we cannot undertake it; although it is very regrettable that a book which has received the highest commendation from the most eminent Aristotelian scholars should not be translated. I am returning your copy under separate cover.

I am, dear Sirs,
Yours faithfully
[T. S. Eliot]

TO *C. E. M. Joad*[1]   CC

26 January 1931   [Faber & Faber Ltd]

Dear Sir,

Although we are not acquainted, I hope you will not mind my troubling you on the following matter.

A very young man, named Michael Sayers who is anxious to write poetry and has shewn me some pieces which are quite creditable for his age, has appealed to me to help him to find work. He was, I understand, articled to a solicitor, but his father can no longer afford to support him during his apprenticeship. Incidentally he seems to be of an emotional, not to say slightly hysterical, temperament, and dislikes living at home.

1–C. E. M. Joad (1891–1953), philosopher, writer, journalist, pundit; at the time of this letter, after some years as a civil servant at the Board of Trade, he was Head of Philosophy at Birkbeck College, London. Eccentric, irreverent and idealistic, rationalistic and Fabian, anti-militaristic and for many years anti-capitalistic, he was for five months in 1931 Director of Propaganda for Oswald Mosley's New Party; subsequently he declared himself against Nazism. Infamously and provocatively, in Feb. 1933 he won the motion at the Oxford Union on the subject 'That this house will under no circumstances fight for its King and Country'. From 1941 to 1948 he was the most popular figure on the popular BBC radio series *The Brains Trust*. Publications include *Common Sense Ethics* (1921), *Common Sense Theology* (1922), *Guide to Modern Thought* (1933) and *Guide to Modern Philosophy* (1936); and, upon his conversion to Anglicanism, *The Recovery of Belief* (1952). See Joad, *The Book of Joad* (1935); G. Thomas, *Cyril Joad* (1992).

He tells me that he has done some work in philosophy, I believe in evening classes under you, and that you commended his work. I should very much like to know, in confidence, if you remember the boy, and anything he wrote for you, and whether he struck you as having any abilities. I am afraid he is one of the most difficult cases to help that I have lately come across.[1]

Yours faithfully,
[T. S. Eliot]

TO *G. Wilson Knight* CC

26 January 1931   [Faber & Faber Ltd]

Dear Wilson Knight,

I must apologise for not having answered your long letter of the 3rd of January[2] or for thanking you for letting me see *Antony and Cleopatra*, but the first fortnight of this year has been rather difficult for me, as I had a touch of influenza and my wife has had it ever since. For that reason, I have been unable to write to you to suggest a day for lunch and I suppose that hereafter you will be too busy to come up. If not, however, I am at

1–Joad replied on 28 Jan., 'I remember Michael Sayers quite well; in fact he is still attending Tutorial Classes of mine in Philosophy. I am afraid, however, that there is nothing verydefinite that I can say about him. He writes fluently and well, although his stuff occasionally wants pruning, and he is quite intelligent and quick in the up-take. But so far as his work for me is concerned, there is no more to him than that. I have, that is to say, no reason to suppose that he has any special abilities beyond his ability to write poetry, as to which I am not in a position to offer any opinion.

'My general impression is that he is one of a number of young men who would like to write and are manifestly unfitted for ordinary office work, but will nevertheless almost certainly have to do it merely because society will not give him any other opening.'

2–Knight's letter of 3 Jan. picks up a point about the character of Valeria, in *Coriolanus*. 'There are three kinds of womanhood generally idealized in Shakespeare: (i) Motherhood, (ii) Wifehood, & (iii) Maidenhood. At this moment Valeria becomes a "symbol" of woman from the "purity" aspect, which is a strong ideal in Shakespeare; so that Coriolanus is, as it were, attacked by the feminine ideal in full strength, a trinity of womanly love & beauty. I think this is why S. *at this moment* chooses to stress Valeria's radiant "chastity" . . . It is to be observed that C. does not *neglect* his wife in this scene – though, as always, he gives more attention to his mother.'

He goes on to say that he is sending both of his essays on *Antony and Cleopatra* under separate cover; and he remarks in addition: 'I am so glad you feel too that "husband" is one of the supreme effects. I have mentioned it in the early part of essay I.

'Your general reading of the play is not *quite* mine. I have treated it as a time-succession very much *within* a certain *stillness* & that stillness is, to me, from the first related to a pure & fine love. I view it as a vision enclosing & transcending base essences but not, even at the end, excluding them . . . But, on the other hand, I do trace a succession, from lust to spiritual love . . .'

your disposal and should be very glad to lunch if you would give me two or three days choice.

With many apologies,
Yours sincerely,
[T. S. Eliot]

TO *Christopher Dawson*   CC

26 January 1931   [*The Criterion*]

Dear Dawson,

Many thanks for your essay, which interests me very much and which exposes facts which certainly ought to be more widely known and accepted.[1] I should like very much to use it, though I cannot say how soon. Are you in any hurry to get it published? Also, I was particularly struck by the postscript to your letter, which is a separate matter, very much needing treatment.[2] Possibly Babbitt is not sufficiently at home in the Middle Ages. Anyway, what he means by 'romanticism' is certainly all in Rousseau.

Yours ever,
[T. S. Eliot]

TO *Charles H. Grandgent*[3]   CC

26 January 1931   [Faber & Faber Ltd]

Dear Professor Grandgent,

I do not know whether you will remember me, and I only know by a circular that I have received that you are to lecture at University College,

1–Dawson wrote on 7 Jan., of his essay 'The Origins of the Romantic Tradition', C. 11 (Jan. 1932), 222–48, 'there is no original scholarship in it . . . Anyhow we should have to wait a long time before the Arabic scholars cover the ground . . . If my view is correct then it would seem that romanticism is not a literary abstraction, but a definite historical tradition parallel to the classical tradition, which entered European culture owing to a series of particular historical causes. And so we can trace the development & interaction of the 2 traditions without getting involved in interminable controversies about them considered as aesthetic & moral absolutes . . .'

2–'It would seem to follow from this view that the Romantic Movement of the early 14th century was a Renaissance of the mediaeval romantic tradition, just as the 15th cent. R. was of the classical tradition, & that it has been confused & contaminated with the Naturalism of Rousseau which is quite a distinct phenomenon, in the same way that the other Renaissance has been confused with the Reformation by so many writers.'

3–Charles H. Grandgent (1862–1939): scholar of linguistics and phonetics, and Dante; Professor of Romance Languages, Harvard, 1896–1932; Secretary of the Modern Language

469

toward the end of February.[1] If this letter reaches you, I hope that I may hear from you as it would be a great pleasure to me to see you while you [are] in London.

It may fix me a little more clearly in your mind if I remind you that I am a cousin of Mrs Grandgent.[2]

Yours sincerely,
[T. S. Eliot]

TO F. E. Hutchinson[3]   CC

26 January 1931   [Faber & Faber Ltd]

Dear Mr Hutchinson,

Thank you very much for your kind letter of the 5th instant, which influenza has delayed my answering.[4] But apart from the fact that I should have to pick my way pretty carefully to find an eighteenth century subject on which I am competent to speak, I dare not make any engagement to lecture in August, as I am not able to say, and shall not know very far in advance, what will be my plans for that month. So I am afraid I must again decline, although with the very greatest regret.

I am very pleased to know that you liked my essay on Andrewes.

Yours very truly,
[T. S. Eliot]

Association, 1902–11, President, 1912. Founding President of the American Association of Teachers of Italian, 1923. His works include *An Introduction to Vulgar Latin* (1907).

1 – Grandgent was to give two lectures on 'Imitation', in a series on Comparative Philology, at University College London on 25 and 27 Feb.

2 – Grandgent replied that he and his wife would be landing at Southampton on 15 Feb., and hoped to meet TSE in London. He added: 'We had the privilege of knowing your mother very well; in fact, she showed me her *Savonarola* – an exquisite work – before it was published.'

3 – The Revd F. E. Hutchinson (1871–1947): Secretary to the Delegacy for Extra-Mural Studies, University of Oxford, 1920–34; Chaplain (1928) and Fellow (1934) of All Souls. An authority on Caroline poetry, he was author of *Richard Crashaw* (1928), *The Works of George Herbert* (ed., 1941) and *Milton and the English Mind* (1946). He had first approached TSE in Mar. 1929.

4 – Hutchinson invited TSE to give an extramural 'lecture or two' in the following Aug., on the Eighteenth Century. 'I may add that I hear much of you from Mr Faber when we meet at All Souls. I have read with particular pleasure your book *For Lancelot Andrewes*; I had kept the article on Andrewes in *The Times Literary Supplement* before I knew that it was yours.'

27 January 1931   [*The Criterion*]

My dear Joyce,

I have not heard from you since you went to Zurich. You will remember that you wrote to me at the time about the format you wished for *Haveth Childers Everywhere*. Since then I have heard indirectly that Voigt [*sc.* Vogt] was pleased with your progress, but wished to defer the final operation until the Spring. I am very sorry that it has had to be postponed, particularly if it is holding up your work.

I heard from a man whom I understood to be your solicitor in Paris about the misunderstanding with Babou and Kahane. We are very sorry about it because we had intended to bring out *Haveth Childers* before Christmas; however, I do not believe that the delay will interfere in any way with its success. According to M. Léon's advices, we have fixed publication for the beginning of May; but I asked him to let us know at any time if Babou could be persuaded to allow publication a little earlier. We are in a position to bring it out as soon as it is released.[1]

Anna Livia keeps on selling and the last weekly figures give a total of 5167.[2]

One reason why I am writing to you now is that I read in the *Publisher and Bookseller* for January 2nd that you were undertaking the libretto for an opera founded on Byron's *Cain*.[3] At first sight I am a little sceptical of the rumour, but if there is anything in it, please remember that we should like to have the opportunity of publishing it here.

With best wishes to Mrs Joyce and yourself from both of us,

Yours ever,

[T. S. Eliot]

1 – *Haveth Childers Everywhere: Fragment from Work in Progress* was due to be published by F&F (Criterion Miscellany 26) on 2 Apr. 1931. It had been published first in Paris in 1930 by Henri Babou and Jack Kahane and was ultimately published by F&F on 7 May 1931.

2 – By 27 Apr. 1931 sales of *ALP* ran to 5492; sales of Gilbert's *James Joyce's 'Ulysses'* to 913.

3 – 'Notes and News', *The Publisher & Bookseller*, 2 Jan. 1931, 14: 'We understand that Mr James Joyce's next work is to be a libretto for an opera based on Byron's poem, Cain. Mr Joyce is shortly to undergo another operation on his eyes; it will be remembered that the last one (in March of last year) was fairly successful.'

FROM *Vivien Eliot* TO *Mary Hutchinson*   MS Texas

Tues. 27 January 1931   68 Clarence Gate Gardens, N.W.1
                                 Ambassador 1518

My dear Mary

How are you?

I have been in bed for *nearly 3 weeks*, with gastric influenza &
bronchitis.¹ So all my hardly acquired *fat* has disappeared. Thank God.
Never get fat. It is the most horrible experience. So is influenza as you well
know. The first part was really awful, but I have been glad to rest since.

We have a man staying here.² I only see him for a few minutes late at
night when all the servants & nurses have departed. He sometimes stays
with us. Tom can bear him. Perhaps you could find out why.

I am writing now to ask if *you & Jack* could possibly come here for
coffee as soon after your dinner as possible, for an hour, on *Friday
evening*? You have never been in this strange flat, altho' many others have.
I often think about you, & I know I am very very fond of you, & of Jack
too. Please come on Friday evening.

Yrs. ever,
Vivienne.

TO *Frederic Manning*   CC

29 January 1931   [*The Criterion*]

My dear Manning,

I was very glad to hear from you. Oddly enough, I had been lunching
with Peter Davies³ the day before and had asked him for news of you,
so that I was already aware that you were back at Bourne.⁴ I am very
sorry to hear about your asthma. From what little I know of the subject,
I understand that there is no one climate or locality prescribed for all
sufferers, but that the right climate for each individual varies. I hope that
you have found the right one.

---

1 – VW recorded in a letter to Clive Bell on 25 Jan.: 'There's Tom [Eliot] on the phone – by
no means a trivial event, because as you are aware, the state of Vivienne's bowel is not
a matter to be despatched in a moment – he wants us to meet a New Zealander [Robert
Sencourt] who admires Leonard, was an intimate of the Empress Eugénie, and is hand in
glove with the Pope. Is this Tom's wit. Goodness knows' (*Letters IV*, 281).
2 – Presumably Sencourt.
3 – Peter Llewelyn Davies (1897–1960), publisher.
4 – Manning had been living in Bourne, Lincolnshire.

It was kind of you to write about Dobrée's review. I have sent your letter on to him and am sure that it will give him much pleasure.[1]

Whenever you feel fit to attempt a visit to London, or if business forces you to come up, I hope you will let me know.

Yours ever,
[T. S. Eliot]

TO *John Gould Fletcher*   CC

29 January 1931   [The Criterion]

Dear Fletcher,

I am indeed surprised to hear that you are still in England and sorry for your sake that you are, as well as for the reasons that keep you here.[2] About the next *Criterion*, I am afraid it has already got to the point at which I am wondering what I can safely leave out, and far beyond the point at which I can expect to put something more in; but if we could settle on something for June, I think that I could arrange an advance payment. As for Ezra's *Cantos*, I have agreed to print part of an essay by Louis Zukofsky on the subject, and *Circumjack Cencrastus* has just been done by Edwin Muir.[3] The only objection to Huxley's *Vulgarity in Literature* is that by June it will have been out such a long time. Anyway, will you suggest a day next week – not Monday – when it will suit you to come and lunch and we will decide on something.

Yours ever,
[T. S. Eliot]

P.S. You should have had your cheque for *Delacroix* by now.[4] If not, will [you] ring up Miss Hill[5] and let her know.

---

1 – Letter not found. Dobrée had reviewed *The Wheel of Fire*, by GWK, in the current *C.*, 342–7; but the letter must have related to a copy of BD's forthcoming review of Manning's *Scenes and Portraits* (July 1931). Manning wrote later (15 Nov. 1931): 'Dobrée told me when I spoke to him in the Spring that he accepted and had applied Landor's distinction between dialogue and conversation, and I accepted it also . . . However I don't any longer, as on reflection I see it would class all Plato's dialogues under the head of conversations. Of course none of *Scenes & Portraits* is purely dialogue, which is really why I described them as Scenes.'
2 – Fletcher wrote (27 Jan.) that his 'financial condition seemed too parlous to attempt America at this juncture'; he asked to review books by EP and Hugh MacDiarmid, or else AH's *Vulgarity in Literature* – '*unfavourably* . . . It seems to me pretentious and bad.'
3 – *To Circumjack Cencrastus*, by Hugh MacDiarmid, was reviewed by Edwin Muir in *C.* 10
4 – 'Delacroix' (article), *C.* 10 (Jan. 1931), 264–79
5 – Laura Maude Hill, TSE's secretary.

TO *F. E. Hutchinson*   CC

30 January 1931   [Faber & Faber Ltd]

Dear Mr Hutchinson,

Thank you for your card of the 27th. It is extremely kind of you to make a further suggestion after my discouraging and discouraged reply, and I confess that the idea attracts me.[1] Of course the Michaelmas term, if you contemplate the Michaelmas term of this year, does not give very much time to so slow a worker as myself; on the other hand, I am so lazy and idle that I never do any work except by committing myself to some undertaking from which I cannot extricate myself. Before considering the matter further, however, I should be very glad if you would let me know the terms of the Foundation. I know that Carpenter was a Unitarian and it occurred to me that there might be some strict limitations of the scope of the lecturers. Secondly, have any series of lectures been given already on this Foundation? And thirdly, what is the remuneration?[2]

With many thanks for all your kindness,

Yours sincerely,

[T. S. Eliot]

TO *Herbert Gorman*   TS Southern Illinois

30 January 1931   Faber & Faber Ltd

Dear Mr Gorman,

I am very glad to hear from you after such a long time, and very much interested to hear of your new book about Joyce.[3] I doubt if I could contribute very much for your information myself. Although I have known Joyce for a good many years now, I have never had the opportunity of seeing very much of him; only when I have been in Paris, and not always then, and when he has been passing through London on his way to

1 – '[T]here is an educational trust by the will of Dr Carpenter (the Master of Balliol & I are Trustees): would it be at all possible for you to consider giving a set of 6 evening lectures in the Michaelmas Term, (say) on the religious & mystical poets of xvii century? This is only a tentative proposal . . .' (Estlin Carpenter [1844–1927], a Unitarian, had been Principal of Manchester College.)

2 – Hutchinson replied on 20 Feb. that there was no restriction on the scope of the lectures; no lecture had yet been given; and the trustees could offer perhaps £50 for a course of six lectures.

3 – Herbert Gorman wrote on 28 Jan. to say he had embarked on 'another book about Joyce, this time a personal biography. Mr Joyce has been kind enough to turn over a deal of material to me, letters, documents, etc., and to permit me to question him unceasingly.'

English watering-places. I mean that I cannot think of anything important enough or sufficiently different from what you can easily obtain from many people who have had the opportunity of seeing more of him, to seem worth while putting down on paper. If, however, you should happen to be in London at any time between now and the completion of your book, I should be delighted to talk it over with you.

But what I should particularly like to know is whether you or Farrar and Rinehart have made any arrangements for the publication of your book in England. You know that we have published his *Anna Livia Plurabelle* and Stuart Gilbert's *Ulysses*, and are about to publish *Haveth Childers Everywhere*. So that I think we should be more interested and better qualified to consider your book than any other London publisher. I hope you will let me know about this.

Many thanks for sending me Robinson's poem.[1] I have only got your letter this morning so have not yet had time to read the poem, but I will return it and write to you again when I have done so.

Please give my kind regards to Paddy and Mary Colum.[2]

Yours ever sincerely,
T. S. Eliot

TO *Bonamy Dobrée*   TS Brotherton

30 January 1931   *The Criterion*

My Dear Bonamy,

I am enclosing a letter from Fred Manning which concerns yourself.[3] Answer it or not, just as you like. I will tell him that I have sent it on to you.

I hope that your indignation over my lamentable mismanagement of the Foreign Periodicals has somewhat abated. I want to use the American Periodicals for the March number. Will you let me know of your charity whether you will let it stand as it is, or whether in the light of subsequent literary matter from America, you prefer, with the minimum of trouble to yourself, to retouch it?[4]

1–Gorman enclosed a poem that Edwin Arlington Robinson had recently sent him.
2–Padraic Colum and his wife had taken a flat in Paris for the year.
3–Not found.
4–BD replied on 31 Jan.: 'I felt more sorrow than anger . . . My point is . . . that these notices of magazines are no good unless they are as up to date as we can make them . . . Will you let me have a copy *by return* of the proof of my last excogitation of Americana & I will add somewhat in the light of recent publications, & *try* to cut the first proof a bit. The last will be difficult . . .'

I was talking to Morley today, about the influence, for the most part pernicious, of Macaulay on literary and other opinion in England. What gave rise to the question was the instance of Dr Johnson, but the subject is much more extensive than that. We wondered whether it would interest you to tackle the subject.[1]

Yours ever,

T. S. E.

P.S. By the way, the next *Criterion* Meeting is February 11th.

TO *Darsie Gillie* CC

3 February 1931   [Faber & Faber Ltd]

Dear Gillie,

Just to be quite on the safe side, can you tell me anything or give me any assurances about the Austrian general Legay, the Austrian general Demue, and the German general Kirchbach. I am enclosing in explanation the relevant pages 224–225, and 236, out of Pilsudski's book.[2] It may seem almost fantastic to you to scent in these comments any possibility of libel, but nowadays publishers like to know exactly what they are in for. I should think it more probable that all three of these personages are now dead. But would it be possible for you to get any information?

1–BD replied (31 Jan.): 'The idea of the Macaulay influence is an interesting one – I agree that it is mostly pernicious. But I doubt whether I have the necessary knowledge. I will gladly discuss.' See 'Macaulay', *C.* 12 (July 1933), 593–604.

2–Pilsudski told a tale of having once come upon General Legay – whom he thought 'a likeable man of personal courage, a type of *vieux troupier*' – in a compromising position: 'In describing the ridiculous scene which I saw, I have no intention of in any way injuring his memory. Besides, the comicality of the situation perhaps checked the rudeness and violence with which I, on my side, was ready. They say, rightly I think, that *le rire soulage*. As soon as I entered the little bedroom, I could scarcely restrain myself from laughing. The first thing that struck my eyes in the room was a couple of broad conjugal beds standing side by side . . . Two figures in nightshirts sat on the beds. Nearest to the candle sat an erect figure, in which it was impossible to recognize the general, since he was clean-shaven; he looked rather like a bony dry old woman with stupid indifferent eyes. On the other bed, likewise in a nightshirt, sat the staff officer, a young man with a little moustache. He wore no uniform, so he was simply a young boy who stared at me with shocked eyes. It was so comical, as if I had found a very ill-assorted pair at exactly the wrong moment . . . [A]fter a short explanation, the general quietly ordered the officer to dress, and with a polite apology requested me to wait a moment in the other room. Almost immediately, with profound apologies, he came out to me in a general's unmentionables, the staff officer following, doing up the last buttons on the uniform he had quickly thrown on.'

As for 'Kirchbach, the commander of the First Corps . . . a Chauvinist German' (as he is called in an author's footnote), he is further characterised by Pilsudski as a 'dry malicious' man.

I am extremely sorry to trouble you with these questions, all the more because you have come out of the situation not so profitably as we intended.

Yours ever

[T. S. Eliot]

TO *Henry Crofton*[1]   CC

3 February 1931   [Faber & Faber Ltd]

Personal

Dear Crofton,

I am sorry to turn up again after a long silence with the usual form of persecution. My only excuse is that I have had it in mind to write to you for a long time, to suggest a date for lunch, so my first question shall be, are you well, and have you time to lunch *next* week, any day you like?

The enclosed letter from C. E. M. Joad explains to you the nature of the enquiry. The lad in question is no particular protégé of mine and I cannot even honestly say that I am sure he will make a name for himself as a writer though he certainly has an excited intellectual interest, under considerable difficulties.[2] He is, I fancy, of quite humble origin, tells me he was articled to a solicitor but that his father can no longer afford to see him through the Law, that he must find a job at once, and would do anything that would enable him just to live away from home. He seems to be entirely friendless and has more or less flung himself upon me for help. He certainly ought to go into an office of some sort. I don't want you to take any great trouble over this, as I have bothered you so often before. The boy is, I think, about nineteen. I don't suppose the Bank is taking many recruits at the present time, anyway.

I have relieved my conscience slightly by writing to you, but you yourself need have no conscience at all; only drop me a line or have me rung up to say when we can lunch.[3]

Yours ever,

[T. S. Eliot]

---

1 – 'I always love your companionship,' wrote Crofton (Colonial & Foreign Department, Lloyds Bank) at a later date (18 Dec. 1931).

2 – Michael Sayers.

3 – Crofton replied on 3 Feb.: 'Even should the boy show any promise of being of use in an office the question does not arise since we have, for the last year, not taken a boy into the Bank's service restricting ourselves solely to girls!'

6 February 1931   *The Criterion*

My dear Brother,

I have been very ungrateful in not writing to you for so long; nevertheless all the gifts and things you have sent have been very much appreciated. Many of the photographs, and photographs of portraits, that you have had sent, I have had framed or passe-partout'd and they are now on my walls. I am very happy to have the letters of mother's which you copied so beautifully, and found them very touching and painful. I was touched too, because it was a minor request, at your responding instantly to my appeal for an autopoint pencil! which I find invaluable.

I have not very much news to give of the last few months. Vivienne still has her car, or rather traded it in for this year's model of the same make; and it has helped her to get out and about very much more than she had done for several years. Only she has now been in bed with influenza for nearly a month; she is beginning to get up, but the weather is so inclement that I fear she will not be able to get out for several days yet.

Ada mentioned in a recent letter that you were writing a detective story. If and when it is finished, I hope that Faber & Faber may be allowed to have a look at it with a view to English rights?[1] Our business has done very well this season, I am glad to say, considering the general depression and the expectation of a General Election; that does not of course bring any immediate financial advantage to me, but it gives me, what is perhaps better, a feeling of greater security. I am very fortunate to have such pleasant surroundings and such agreeable associates; and now that I have a room to myself, and don't have to waste time being polite to people who come to see Frank Morley – and American publishers who come over here on business are about the most long-winded time-wasters that I know; Alf. Knopf is one of the worst – I can work there in peace.

1–HWE replied on 18 Sept.: 'this detective story [*The Rumble Murders* by 'Mason Deal'] . . . has been accepted by Houghton Mifflin for publication in the spring, and . . . without changes. My first reaction to the news was utter disbelief, my second a feeling of embarrassment, for the thing still seems to me, though readable, crude and amateurish . . . Not merely that, but they want another to follow! They say it is "fresh and original", "unusually vivid and amusing" . . . You affectionately said something about considering the English rights of this piece of merchandise. Unless it should have a large sale in this country, which I hardly think likely, I do not want you to think of bringing it out in England for sentimental reasons. I don't think it can be said to have any literary merit whatever, and I do not want you to share any criticisms that may be made of it. The locale is a fictitious mid-western suburban community, and the story contains no gunmen nor hard-boiled gentry.'

I have been harried by various importunate small jobs these last months: I suddenly had to take on the writing of a pamphlet on the Lambeth Episcopal Conference at short notice, which I have about finished; did not want to do, and found very difficult, and had to spend a lot of time consulting bishops and others; have just signed on for three radio talks on Dryden – I wish they would get away from such subjects as Donne and Dryden – in May,[1] which is a waste of time except from a financial point of view, they pay well; and I have got to read up Pascal (which I want to do anyway) to write a preface to an 'Everyman' edition. And now I must stop this brief letter to go to the dentist. But there is one point I ought to ask you –

You said in a letter of December 12 that you supposed I had received my share of the estate, i.e. I suppose, some notification from the Old Colony of what my future income would be. I have heard nothing at all, although I have had correspondence from the Old Colony about the previous trust. Can you throw any light on this?

ever affectionately,
Tom

TO *Bonamy Dobrée*   TS Brotherton

9 February 1931   Faber & Faber Ltd

Dear Bonamy,

Yours of the 6th instant to hand, and the contents noted.[2] You place a great strain upon my personal devotion to yourself, and upon my charitable sensibility, but when have I been known to fail a friend in need? I immediately rang up Siepmann and offered myself for April, so now you can settle down quietly to read *Moll Flanders*. I have a certain amount of

---

1 – TSE's talks marking the tercentenary of John Dryden began with 'The Poet who Gave the English Speech', printed in *The Listener*, 15 Apr. 1931, 621–2.

2 – 'Dear Mistreliot, Sir, / Bein pore and hardupp I writes to our mootual pal Siepmann and sez, wot abaht a job o work I sez. Awright sezee, wot abaht a lil Sunday hominy on Dan Defoe – either last three Sundays in April, or first 3 in May. Awright, I sez, but prefer May. Awright e sez, I think vats awright e sez, but in a posssript (cawnt spell that) e sez May n b g as another blokes got it. Do April e sez an buck up and send in syyllabubs. N b g I sez, cawnt do April and cawnt do no syllabaubs cos I downo nuffink abaht Defoe. Why not Vanbrook I sez, es a good chap. Siepmann e writes back and sez nuffen abaht Vanbrook, but you're the chap as wants May. Suggest a swap e sez, with Mistreliot, friendly-like. So I herewith suggets a swap, but 'as no fathe nor ope, nor to say trewth much wish, but does it formal like to say as 'ow ive done it.'

479

sympathy because I have undertaken to write an essay on Pascal for the Everyman Library and am faced with the unpleasant fact that I must read his works.

I am hung up for lunch on Wednesday, with another B.B.C. man who also, I hope, may have some money to spend. At any rate, he has asked me to lunch, so no more for the present. Will see you at 6 p.m. on Wednesday.

Yours ever,

T. S. E.

TO *George Bell*   TS Lambeth

9 February 1931   Faber & Faber Ltd

My dear Lord Bishop,

I am of course highly flattered by the commission you suggest for your diocesan paper and should very much like to undertake it, but the trouble is this.[1] I have racked my brain over the weekend, and have come to the humiliating conclusion that I have not the slightest idea what I should do if I were a dean. I know that if I were a bishop I should go very quickly into a nursing-home for Nervous Disorders, but even that hardly seems worth saying. I feel that I should have to spend several weeks keeping a dean under close observation before I could think of anything to say. Now in this impasse, can anything be done?

I am, My Lord,

Yours very sincerely,

T. S. Eliot

TO *The Appointments Office, Columbia University*   cc

10 February 1931   [Faber & Faber Ltd]

I do not know Mr Louis Zukofsky personally. I have had a little correspondence with him and have seen specimens of his work which have

---

1 – Bell wrote on 5 Feb.: 'I enclose a copy of the Chichester Diocesan Gazette, current number. I am writing to ask whether you would, of your kindness, write an article for the May number, entitled "If I were a Dean". It would be the second of a series of three articles, the first "If I were a Vicar", the third "If I were a Bishop".

'The articles would be about 1500 words each. It would be most stimulating and really useful if you could see your way to write about a Cathedral from your point of view, and the work of a Dean.'

impressed me very favourably. I have published two short poems in the *Criterion*, and am about to publish part of a long essay by him on the work of Ezra Pound. I was very much impressed by his long essay on Henry Adams, which I only declined for the *Criterion* because it assumed a knowledge of Adams and the Adams family which very few of my readers possess, at least at that time. Mr Zukofsky's work strikes me as that of a critical mind of the first order, and a mind of very considerable poetic sensibility also. From such of his work [as] I have seen I should judge also that his standard of learning and scholarship was very high. He seems to me quite one of the most promising of younger American men of letters today.

TO *Paul Elmer More*

CC

10 February 1931   [Faber & Faber Ltd]

My dear More,

An eccentric young man called Austin Warren, who presents himself as a disciple of yours, tells me that you are coming to England in April.[1] Also that you [are] engaged on a vast work on Seventeenth Century Literature. I hope that both these reports are true. As for the second, I hope that it will not conflict with a request I have to make to you, to contribute an article or articles in this field to an encyclopedia of which I am a sub-editor. As for the first, I hope that you will spend some time in London and that we may have a few cocktails, and some long evenings, accusing each other of heresy.

Sincerely yours,
[T. S. Eliot]

1–More replied on 19 Feb., 'I know that Warren is eccentric, though able withal; I am not so sure about his being a disciple of mine. One of his statements is unqualifiedly true. I am sailing for England by the *Britannic*, April fourth, my object being to welcome into this valley of tears a British grandchild which Alice [his daughter] promises me by the middle of that month.'

TO *William Plomer*[1] CC

10 February 1931   [Faber & Faber Ltd]

Dear Plomer,

I am glad to hear from you.[2] I should have written to you before, but whenever I heard report of you, you were always at some distance away from England. I am fully engaged this week, but will you suggest a day, or preferably a choice of two days, for lunch next week, and I shall be very glad. I like your poem.[3]

> Yours sincerely,
> [T. S. Eliot]

TO *F. S. Oliver* CC

14 February 1931   [Faber & Faber Ltd]

My dear Oliver,

Thank you very much for your letter.[4] I am gratified to hear that Mrs Oliver may be able to come – I had not supposed that either of you would care to or would be able to come, but wished to send you the tickets in any case. I shall let you see a copy of what I have to say whether it is printed or not. I have written for tickets for your daughters-in-law and for Lord Brabourne – I had already sent tickets to Barrie and to Baldwin as a matter of courtesy – as well as of course to Mrs Whibley and Lady Raleigh.

I hope I shall do justice to the subject – it is primarily an attempt at literary criticism, not at personal reminiscence or politics.

---

1 – William Plomer (1903–73): South African-born poet, novelist, librettist; co-founder, with Roy Campbell and Laurens van der Post, of the first bilingual South African literary journal, *Voorslag* ('Whiplash'), 1925–6; author of *Turbott Wolfe* (novel, 1926); a biography of Cecil Rhodes (1933); and *Collected Poems* (1960); reader for Jonathan Cape; discoverer and editor of the diaries of the Revd Francis Kilvert (1938–40); collaborator with Benjamin Britten (*Gloriana*; *Curlew River*; *The Burning Fiery Furnace*; *The Prodigal Son*). He was awarded the Queen's Gold Medal for Poetry in 1963, and appointed CBE in 1968. Roy Campbell told TSE of Plomer, in an undated letter (? Sept. 1929): 'He has the same sort of suspicious mind as [Wyndham] Lewis . . . He leads the same sort of existence as Lewis, and he is always on his guard. But when one gets to know him he is a fine fellow.' See further Plomer, *The Autobiography of William Plomer* (1944); Peter F. Alexander, *William Plomer; A Biography* (1989).
2 – Not found.
3 – 'Corfu', *C.* 10 (July 1931), 626.
4 – Not found. The Olivers had resolved to attend TSE's address on Charles Whibley.

I am sorry to hear about your pleurisy. Most people, I suppose, would urge you to spend your winters abroad; but for anyone in poor health, winter abroad seems to me to be a deception and a cheat.

Yours very sincerely,

[T. S. Eliot]

I have been well enough myself; but my wife is just trying to recover from a month in bed with influenza.

TO *Thomas McGreevy*[1]   TS TCD

St Valentine's Day [14 February], 1931   *The Criterion*

My dear Thomas,

I have just read and perpended your monograph (partly) about myself.[2] I was pleased to receive a copy 'with the author's compliments' (hors de Londres?) but should have been better pleased to have heard direct from the author himself. However, I feel impelled to say that you have produced I think an excellent piece of criticism.[3] It is only disfigured (1) by your remarks about the Church of England, a subject of which you know nothing[4] (2) a gross libel on page 20 of which I hope that as a gentleman you will make public retractation. I am not an Irishman, and can prove it.[5] It is true that I am very remotely descended from a family named Browne of Ulster, which also produced John Brown of Ossawatomie; but on the one hand you did not know this; and on the other hand if you had known it the infusion is so slight that no biologist would consider it as justifying your impudent assertion that I came from that part of the world. However, if the racial, national and religious preoccupations which interfere with your otherwise admirable critical acumen, require

1 – Thomas McGreevy (1893–1967), poet, literary and art critic, arts administrator: see Biographical Register.

2 – *Thomas Stearns Eliot* was published by Chatto & Windus on 22 Jan. 1931.

3 – TSE would tell John J. Sweeney on 5 Sept. 1961: 'It is very strange to look again, after so many years, at a book written about me thirty years ago. I think that some of his critical remarks are quite justified, but I hope that Tom now feels more kindly toward America and Americans than he seemed at the time.'

4 – See for example p. 16: 'Mr Eliot's verse has purified itself of merely social elements as he has moved towards Catholicism, even the bastard, schismatic and provincial if genteel kind of Catholicism that, for the time being, at any rate, he has, somewhat New Englishly, stopped at.'

5 – 'I believe that Mr [Wyndham] Lewis, if not a true-born Orangeman like Mr [St John] Ervine, is partly of north of Ireland, "planter", origin – as is also, I think, Mr Eliot.'

satisfaction I have a very considerable proportion of Huguenot ancestry; so make what you will of *that*.

I understand from Wyndham Lewis that he is of Welsh and Italian origin.[1]

Your *explication de texte* of The Waste Land interested me very much. I can say without irony that it is extremely acute; but I must add that the author was not nearly so acute or learned as the critic. You have told me, in fact, much that I did not know; and I feel that I understand the poem much better after reading your explanation of it. Well! I supposed that I was merely working off a grouch against life while passing the time in a Swiss sanatorium; but apparently I meant something by it.

If Mr Mac Greevy ever visits London, will he not come and eat a bit of fish with

his obliged obedient servant
T. S. Eliot

and if not, the latter would still be glad to have news of his affairs.

TO *Charles H. Grandgent* CC

20 February 1931   [Faber & Faber Ltd]

Dear Professor Grandgent,

Your card followed immediately upon your letter and took me by surprise, but I am very glad to learn that you are here. I am not quite sure whether Mrs Grandgent is with you but if so I hope that my wife will be sufficiently recovered from influenza next week for us to be able to ask you to tea if you are not too busy. In any case to make a meeting assured would you be able to lunch with me at my club at 63 St. James's Street at 1.15 on Wednesday next, the 25th. I hope very much that you can.[2]

Yours sincerely
[T. S. Eliot]

1–Wyndham Lewis (1882–1957), painter, novelist, philosopher, critic, was one of the major modernist writers; the leading artist associated with Vorticism, and editor of *BLAST*, the movement's journal, 1914–15. On Lewis's death, TSE wrote: 'Wyndham Lewis was in my opinion one of the few men of letters of my generation whom I should call, without qualification, men of genius . . . the most prominent and versatile prose-writer of my time' (letter to Hugh Kenner, 27 Mar. 1957). See further *The Letters of Wyndham Lewis*, ed. W. K. Rose (1963); Paul O'Keeffe, *Some Sort of Genius: A Life of Wyndham Lewis* (2000).
2–Grandgent wrote by return to agree to the lunch.

TO *Cyril Clemens*[1]   cc

20 February 1931   [Faber & Faber Ltd]

Dear Mr Clemens,

I thank you for your letter of January 20th which gives me much pleasure, and I should be glad if you would communicate to the Society my appreciation, especially as a Missourian, of the honour which you have thought fit to bestow upon me.[2]

Very sincerely yours
[T. S. Eliot]

TO *George Bell*   cc

20 February 1931   [Faber & Faber Ltd]

My dear Lord Bishop,

If, however, you cannot put your hand on anyone else who is bubbling over with ideas about what he would do if he were a Dean, I have thought the matter over, and think that I might be able to make a few suggestions however fatuous. My notions, however, are naturally concerned with the problem of making a cathedral a living centre of the life of the people, rather than merely a national monument for the inspection of American tourists. I do not know whether there is anything in this.

I am, my Lord,
Yours very sincerely
[T. S. Eliot]

1 – Cyril Coniston Clemens (1902–99) was born in St Louis, Missouri, and graduated from Washington University. A distant cousin of Samuel Langhorne Clemens, in 1930 he was founder and president of the International Mark Twain Society; founder-editor of the *Mark Twain Quarterly*, 1936–82. His works include biographies of Twain and President Harry Truman.

2 – TSE had been offered Honorary Membership of the Society 'in recognition of your outstanding contribution to poetry'. Over twenty years later, when planning a return visit to Missouri, TSE wrote to Alice Martin (19 May 1953): 'I imagine that Cyril Clemens is a person to avoid if possible, though I doubt whether it will be possible to avoid him altogether. However, I hope he can be warded off for the first few days at least. He certainly seems to be eccentric, as some years before the war he wrote to tell me that I had been elected a "Knight of Mark Twain". I should have appreciated this honour more highly if the distinguished order had not included Mussolini and a few other undesirable associates!'

TO *Orlo Williams*   CC

20 February 1931   [Faber & Faber Ltd]

Dear Williams,

Thank you for your note. I was also sorry to miss you the other night. I am not quite sure of my appointments next week, but I could lunch any day the week following that was convenient for you. I should have liked to see you sooner and there is one point which I must ask you about now, before we meet. I am just about to read your leader in the *T.L.S.*,[1] but I should very much like to know your candid and confidential opinion as to the suitability of Praz's book for publication in England. He has been asking me about that. If you don't think there is much point in translating it, or if you think that its sale would be insignificant, just say so, but if you think that there is a good deal to be said for an English edition, I should be grateful if you would let me have a full reader's report, on the usual terms, to transmit to my board.[2]

                                    Yours ever.
                                    [T. S. Eliot]

1–'The Morbid' – on Mario Praz, *La Carne, La Morte e il Diavolo nella Letteratura Romantica* (1931) – *TLS*, 19 Feb. 1931, 121–2. 'Signor Mario Praz's new book, with its picturesque title, its exhaustive survey of its subject-matter, its copious and judicious quotations from four literatures, its extremely valuable and scholarly notes, and its illustrations as skilfully adapted to the text as those of his "Unromantic Spain", will stand very high in the scale. Using to the best advantage his great linguistic knowledge and his unusual aptitude for literary research, he has systematically treated, for the first time, the whole current of morbidity (mainly but not wholly erotic in origin) that rose in the newly awakened sensibilities of the eighteenth century and flowed strongly through the literature of the nineteenth. It was not an easy subject to treat, for pathology needs an endurance of the repulsive and a resistant nose on the researcher's part; but here the extraordinary tact of the author has enabled him to produce a thoroughly readable and highly informing book which tells the truth without offence, with detachment and with just that gleam of humour, more of implication than of expression, which makes even the nasty digestible, illuminates the agreeable and gives a grace of movement to the whole.'
2–OW replied (21 Feb.), 'You will see from my leader . . . how highly I think of it as a book. My general view is that it is the kind of book which a University Press, if it were offered, should *certainly* publish, for it is serious & scholarly in execution. How it would sell I can't say. It verges at times on what booksellers call the "curious", but not in the way that appeals to the ignorant. If it is not translated into some other tongue, it will be a pity.' (Praz wrote to TSE on 19 Feb.: 'You may have seen in today's T.L.S. a leading article on the book I submitted to Faber & Faber for publication last December. As I am likely to receive applications for translation into English from the part of other publishers in the near future, I should be obliged to you if you could ask your firm to give me a definite reply.')

TO *A. L. Rowse*   TS Exeter

23 February 1931   Faber & Faber Ltd

Dear Rowse,

Thank you very much for your letter and for letting me see the first part of your *Politics* book.[1] I will send it back under separate cover as I have lent it to Faber, who has expressed an interest in seeing it. I think that probably it will make an admirable introduction to your book but it is so distinctly *prefatory* that it does not seem to me suitable for separate publication. The force of what you say in the preface is entirely dependent on the reader being able to read on. It does not sum up the line of argument which you are about to take. I am not by any means suggesting that a preface should be a summary but only that unless a preface is a summary, or in some way self-contained, it is not so suitable for separate publication.

I have had the impertinence to make a number of pencilled notes on it which I hope will not be merely a nuisance. You may, if you like, take them merely as a symptom of my interest in the book.

I am, perhaps, not quite such a convinced devotee of the word 'order' as you may think. It seems to me that the word 'order' in political and social theorising, is in danger merely of replacing the Nineteenth Century word 'liberty', and both words in a complete vacuum are dangerous. The question is what order and what liberty?

It is very sweet of you to send me Tawney's book, which I shall certainly read and return to you as soon as possible.[2]

1 – Rowse wrote (n.d.): 'Would you care to publish the enclosed first chapter of my "Politics" book – it is a sort of preface to it – in the *Criterion*? . . . I cannot hope that you will agree with it, either in its point of view or its conclusions, except two points which you will, I know, sympathise with: the insistence upon stability and order in society, and the attack on the pretences by which the present order lives . . . (Later in the full book, I have a chapter on "Society and Values", which has a discussion about you & Lawrence: I hope you will forgive it me!)'

The F&F catalogue entry, which may have been composed or revised by TSE, reads: 'This book is a re-statement of Socialistic principles and politics. Mr Rowse believes that the Labour movement in this country is in need of fresh constructive thinking. "Its leaders", he says, "are men who have grown old in the propaganda for socialism; they are living necessarily on the stock of ideas formed some thirty years ago." At the same time, he holds that the social order proper to the twentieth century can only be achieved under the guidance of socialistic ideas. His appeal is therefore to youth: and in this book he develops an outlook on society framed in accord with their convictions and giving direction to their aims.

'*Politics and the Younger Generation* is a book which no one concerned over the political, social and economic questions of our times can afford to ignore.'

2 – 'May I also send herewith [R. H.] Tawney's *Religion & the Rise of Capitalism* . . . ? . . . I believe Tawney has something in his reading of history which will specially interest you.

487

I have not seen the *Nouvelle Revue Française* lately, and it doesn't seem to have been sent to me. I will try to get hold of Fernandez's article.[1]

I wish that I might come down soon for a night, and have a long talk with you. I think that it would be easier for me in the Summer term, but perhaps you are too busy then.

Affectionately yours,

T. S. Eliot

TO *Marguerite Caetani*

CC

23 February 1931   [Faber & Faber Ltd]

Dear Marguerite,

Thank you for your letter of the 5th, or rather of the 13th,[2] enclosing a cheque for three subscriptions for the *Criterion* for which you will receive a formal receipt from the proper quarter. I had not heard anything about Blunden making a new edition of Wilfred Owen's poems, but I will write to him and find out whether any would be available for *Commerce*.[3]

I have been extremely busy this winter, partly with theological matters resulting in a pamphlet of which I will send you a copy as soon as it is ready. Also Vivienne has been laid up for nearly five weeks with influenza. She sends you her love.

Is Camillo being properly prepared to get him into Oxford or Cambridge?[4] I wondered because you remember a couple of years ago you entertained the notion of finding an English tutor for him and then dropped it as no one quite suitable seemed to present himself.

I don't quite see how he can get in unless he is tutored for a time either by a competent Oxford or Cambridge graduate, or else when he is otherwise ready, comes over to live with a coach for some months. You

---

He provides for example, a strong defence of Royalist and Anglican government as against early Puritan capitalism, & there's no better account of Charles I & Laud's benevolent paternalism in economic affairs . . . It . . . provides a strong historical case for your views.'

1 – Rowse wrote, 'did you notice Fernandez article in the *NRF* on "La Pensée et la Révolution'? I thought it very interesting . . .'

2 – Caetani wrote her letter on 5 Feb. but posted it on the 13th.

3 – 'I have just heard that Edmund Blunden is editing a new ed. of Wilfrid Owen's poems with much new matter and I was wondering if it would not be possible to get hold of a few of the new poems and publish them in "Commerce" first or simultaneously. What do you think.' *The Poems of Wilfred Owen*, ed. Blunden (Chatto & Windus, 1931).

4 – 'I am more and more persuaded that Oxford *or* Cambridge is the best place for Camillo. I do not find Rome an atmosphere propitious to study unless one is *very* much thereto inclined . . .'

had not thought, I suppose, of sending him for any time to an English school? The difficulty of course, nowadays is to find a good one.

This is a very hurried letter, but I will write again as soon as I can.

Affectionately yours,

[Tom]

TO *Bonamy Dobrée*

TS Brotherton

23 February 1931[1]   68 Clarence Gate Gardens

Dear Bonamee,[2]

Yours of the 16th received. Dont worry about Isaacs: to hearken to criticism is to invite paralysis.[3]

1–Headed by TSE: '24 February 1931, St Matthias, in fact: but in fact I write the day before'.
2–BD protested about the greeting, 25 Feb.: 'I am rather alarmed by your calling me Bonamee. It reminds me ominously of Little Billee, and that particular business of the snickersee, and we must eat he. That particular situation was eased by the happy appeareance of Admiral Napier K.C.B., but it wouldn't do to rely on him.' 'Little Billee', by William M. Thackeray (1811–63), includes the lines: '"First let me say my catechism, / Which my poor mother taught me." / "Make haste! Make haste!" says guzzling Jimmy, / While Jack pulled on his snicker-snee.'
3–'I sent you off some stuff yesterday; I hope . . . it will do. I did my best not to incur Jack Isaacs' charge of pomposity, but I fear I may in consequence have made the thing too light.' HR had written to TSE on 5 Feb.: 'There is sure to be a good deal of discussion arising out of Jack Isaacs' onslaught . . . The general charge of Dullness does not worry me. I feel inclined to remind people of the first article ["Dulness"] in the first number, in which Saintsbury put the matter very neatly. The related charge of portentousness, pomposity, and so on, is perhaps nearer the mark. Perhaps a blue pencil might have been used more often, but I think the trouble is rather that pompous books inspire pompous reviews . . .
'But these are details. The trouble, if you agree that there is a trouble, seems to me to be at the heart of things. I mean the subsidised basis of the whole undertaking. I think that all subsidised affairs develop inertia, once the energy that was necessary to establish the subsidy is exhausted. I wish we could be free from the dead hand. I am indeed prepared to say, let us be free or we perish. The only practical way, of course, is for the *Criterion* to become a direct charge on Faber & Faber. The purpose of this letter is really to ask you whether you can come on Wednesday prepared to discuss this possibility. With the energy and organisation of the firm behind it, I think there would be a revival of spirits. The thing would begin to buzz, it would be constantly in the minds, not merely of the directors of the firm, but of all the subordinates (travelling, publicity, finance, etc) in a way that is not inevitable with a subsidised and parasitic concern . . . You may loose [*sic*] a good deal. But hard cash apart, I think it should be realised that the *Criterion* is a good cachet to have as part of a publishing firm, that merely as goodwill it is probably worth more to you than you would actually loose [*sic*] if the subsidy were withdrawn. But as part of any such reform I think the price should be brought down to 3/6, or at most 5/-. I would urge also a little economy on bulk and paper, though the possibilities in this direction are probably not great. But at present (Isaacs made this point) there is a precious subsidised air about the very appearance of the *Criterion*, and

I sent you a letter from Pound: not about *Blues*, but some other American periodical. Merely to call it to your attention; not to prejudice you.[1]

Manning, who is now in London (Park Lane Hotel, W.1.) wd. like to meet you. He refuses to come to a *Criterion* gathering (how wisely!) but if you are in town for the next he wd. like to arrange a lunch with you (and possibly myself) quietly.

Thanks for your suggestion about Epstein.[2] The only other notions in my mind are (1) Garvin's clamour for a Coalition (thinly disguised under the more grandiose title of a National Party, than which I should prefer a *coup de force* (with of course ourselves, Mosley and O. Stanley posing on the balcony). Nothing to my mind could be worse for the country than the present shuffling of Old Gangs, than a Union of all the Old Gangs, with L. George, Snowden, Churchill, Ramsay, Stanley and Jix hanging round each other's necks. That would be the last straw.[3] (2) the alarm raised by the *Sunday Times* that the undergraduate enrolment of the Universities (O. & C.) is falling off. Thank God if it is. (3) Regionalism.

What, may I ask as an ignorant foreigner just landed on these shores, *is* middle-class?[4] I have never been able to find out. I suspect that F. S. F[lint]

---

this I think is due to the fact that it is not worked as a strictly commercial concern, but as a precious thing for a few subscribers . . . I have talked a little with Bonamy about the matter, but with no one else, except, of course, Morley.'

1 – Not found.

2 – BD urged TSE to say something in his next 'Commentary' 'about the ridiculous fuss being made about Epstein's "Genesis". The common accusation that it is obscene is the silliest thing I have ever heard. Not to be afraid of a word, I would call it if anything reverent. The figure of this woman brooding over her big belly with an Easter Island face is at least impressive. The charge one might make against it is that it is a little sentimental . . .' Jacob Epstein's 'Genesis', exhibited at the Leicester Galleries, London, is now in the Whitworth Gallery, Manchester.

3 – TSE wrote in his 'Commentary' (C. 10, Apr. 1931), 481–2: 'The social and political situation in England is such that we now hear from the most orthodox editorial pulpits in the country that something must be done – something, that is, better than merely turning the present Government out and putting the last one back again. For example, in *The Observer* of February 22nd, Mr Garvin had come to the opinion that a new National Government should be formed, to deal with the actual emergency . . . [W]e suggest that a National Government, which seems to be a phrase covering a coalition of all three parties, might arouse somewhat less than one third of the mild enthusiasm which any of the three parties is now able to excite by itself . . . For our part, we think that a coalition government, at the present juncture, would be only one kind of deathblow, and that the most reckless, to the party system.' James Garvin (1868–1947) was editor of *The Observer*, 1908–42; see David Ayerst, *Garvin of the Observer* (1985).

4 – BD reported that at the last Criterion Club meeting (which TSE missed), 'Frank F. let go in an attack on Blunden's war book as a middle-class version by a middle-class mind. I didn't quite see the point, since the vast majority of officers in the war were middle-class, and that

as well as Lord Rothermere and Lord Beaverbrook and Lord Plender belongs to it. Have things not about reached the point which they reached in America 100 years ago, at which the middle class includes everyone except the person speaking and the person spoken to?

I note that we are to lunch on the 4th proximo.

Yours etc.

T. S. E.

TO *J. H. Oldham*[1]   cc

24 February 1931   [Faber & Faber Ltd]

Dear Mr Oldham,

I must apologise for not having answered your several communications sooner. First of all, I very much enjoyed and appreciated your paper, which contained a great deal with which I was in thorough agreement.[2] I shall be sending you shortly a small pamphlet of my own.[3]

I return your card, and hope to be able to attend at 32, Russell Square,[4] on Tuesday morning (the 3d) and Wednesday afternoon (the 4th March). I look forward to receiving a copy of Professor Brunner's paper[5] meanwhile.

With many thanks,

Yours sincerely,

[T. S. Eliot]

---

the war was won and lost precisely by the middle-class mind working through middle-class ideas. You cannot judge a war book by whether it expresses your own particular brand of pacificism.'

1 – J. H. Oldham, DD (1874–1969): secretary of the International Missionary Council, 1921–38; editor of the *International Review of Missions*, 1912–27; Administrative Director of the International Institute of African Languages and Cultures, 1931–8; Chairman of the Research Commission of the Universal Christian Council for Life and Work, 1934–8; and from 1939 to 1945 editor of the *Christian News-Letter* (to which TSE was to be a contributor).

2 – Oldham informed TSE on 26 Dec. 1930 that he was circulating 'a paper I have written for a Conference on Christian Education at Home and Overseas to be held next April'.

3 – *Thoughts after Lambeth*.

4 – A two-day meeting at Student Movement House. He was also planning a series of meetings with Prof. Brunner to be held in March. The following had registered an interest in forming a discussion group – The Moot – D. M. Baillie, J. S. Bezzant, The Bishop of Chichester, TSE, H. H. Farmer, L. W. Grensted, Wilfred L. Knox, John Macmurray, B. Malinowski, Basil Mathews, W. R. Matthews, J. H. Maud, W. H. Moberly, Joseph Needham, C. E. Raven, B. H. Streeter and H. G. Wood.

5 – Emil Brunner, 'Christianity and Reality', trans. from the German by Douglas Horton; written for the 'continental group' and confidentially circulated to interested persons.

TO *Michael Sayers*   CC

26 February 1931   [Faber & Faber Ltd]

Dear Sayers,

I must apologise for not having written to you sooner.[1] It is not that
I have been altogether idle, but that I have not yet, I am sorry to say,
succeeded in finding any suggestion worth making to you. My enquiries
in the city have only informed me that this is as difficult a time as there
ever has been for getting a banking position, or anything similar. In short,
I have not yet made any progress at all. I do not give up hope, but if
meantime you think it would be worth your while to have another talk
with me, I should be very glad to see you again if you cared to ring up and
make an appointment.

                                        Yours sincerely,
                                        [T. S. Eliot]

TO *Mario Praz*   CC

26 February 1931   [Faber & Faber Ltd]

My dear Praz,

I must apologise for my delay in writing to you about your book. I
thought [it] over very carefully and although I have not had the time
to read the book, have dipped into it enough, here and there, to be
able to endorse Williams' enthusiasm as exhibited in last week's *Times
Supplement*. I do feel, however, that this is rather a book for a University
Press than for an ordinary publisher, and as on top of this I hear from you
that Milford[2] is interested, I think, in your own interests, that you ought

---

Subheadings: 'I. Why and to what extent is the preaching and teaching of the Church
today unreal?' II. 'What is the meaning of the unchristian character of present-day reality?'
Brunner comments, on p. 2 of his paper: 'It was false sacralism in preaching – orthodoxy –
that brought the autonomism or secularism of modern times into being . . .' TSE comments
in the margin, in pencil: 'I don't agree.' Brunner's paper was circulated after late Feb.
1–Sayers had written ('Jan. 1931'), 'the urgency of my affairs persuades me to bother you
again. I fear that you have forgotten me . . . I am too worried now to set about any laboured
production, I had hoped to be settled down to a new way of life. Please let me know if you
can possibly find some job for me: you cannot conceive its unrelieved wretchedness – you are
ignorant of the circumstances, but do please let me hear from you: favourable news or ill.'
2–Humphrey Milford, Oxford University Press.

to pursue this line of publication first.[1] If, however, your negotiations with Milford should fall through, I hope you will let me know.

I hope I may have the chance of seeing you in London at the end of this term. I was very sorry indeed to miss you while you were staying with Binyon.

Yours ever,

[T. S. Eliot]

TO *Darsie Gillie*

26 February 1931   [Faber & Faber Ltd]

My dear Gillie,

Very many thanks for your wire and for all the trouble you have taken, which I fear may have put you to some expense. As, however, the book is all ready for publication and as we think the chances of either of the Generals mentioned taking exception to the extent of instituting an action are very slight, we are quite prepared to bring the book out as it stands. So please don't worry about the matter any further. If either of these obscure generals did bring an action in the English courts, I do not suppose for a moment that they could get more than nominal damages.

With best wishes, and apologies for having worried you.

Yours ever,

[T. S. Eliot]

1–Praz wrote on 23 Feb. that Oxford University Press had applied to him for a translation of his book; he accordingly requested of TSE, 'will you please ask Faber & Faber to give me their definite answer by the end of the present week? . . . I am sorry to press you, but as you have had the book for two months, I suppose by now you will have reached a conviction about it.

'By the way, in the case Faber & Faber should like to have it, I hope they are not going to suggest any substantial recasting or cutting down of the notes. Please let me know definitely, and, if the book does not suit the press, please return to me the extra copy.'

2 March 1931   Savoy Hill, London W.C.2

Dear Sir,

We shall be pleased to broadcast your talks as suggested,[1] on the understanding that:-

1. You will submit to us a draft syllabus of your talks for inclusion in our programme of Talks and Lectures for the term:

If required you will supply us with material to be used in issuing a suitable 'Aids to Study' pamphlet to accompany your course:

This contract is subject to our acceptance of your manuscript, which should be in our hands 14 days in advance of each talk of the series, such manuscripts to be the property of the Corporation.

> Title   'John Dryden.'
> Dates   Sundays, April 12th, 19th and 26th.
> Time   5.00 – 5.30 p.m.
> Fee   Twelve guineas each talk,

To include the sole right of publication in Great Britain, if required, of either a part or the whole of the series, such right to expire twenty-eight days after the date of the broadcast.

As our programmes are prepared some time in advance, will you kindly return to us within three days the attached reply duly completed and signed.

It would be greatly assist our statistical records if you could let us see any letters, other than those from personal friends, which you receive as a result of these talks.

> Yours faithfully
> The British Broadcasting Corporation
> C. A. Siepmann
> For Director of Programmes
> [Talks Department]

1–Siepmann proposed to TSE on 29 Jan. 1931 that he might agree to broadcast three talks on Dryden in celebration of the centenary, and aimed at 'people who care for literature'. In answer to a (now lost) letter from TSE, Siepmann declared, 'we no longer recognise the difference between broadcasting and publication. The fee is a composite one . . .' He suggested 36 guineas.

2 [March] 1931[1]   Faber & Faber Ltd

Dear John Hayward,

It is always a pleasure to send you anything, even a rather dull pamphlet, because your acknowledgements are always so – accomplished, I would say if I wished to be flippant, but I don't. Thank you very much.[2]

As for suffering, it is very queer indeed. Of course, I admit that I know little, perhaps less than most, of physical suffering, and I am sure that you know much of both. But I have had considerable mental agony at one time or another, and once or twice have felt on the verge of insanity or imbecility (I mean two quite different experiences). And I never found that I could make any conscious deliberate *use* of suffering – for one always feels that one must turn it to account in some way, and can't. If I had died even five years ago, everything that I had suffered up to then would, so far as I can see, have been just waste and muddle. Then a pattern suddenly emerges from it, without one's seeming to have done anything about it oneself. And I don't suppose it is ever the same pattern for any two people.

And I don't want to 'convert' anyone: it's an impertinence, to begin with; and one man's route is of no use to another; and in the end all conversion is self-conversion – unless one is concerned with purely social phenomena, Clovis etc.

Another thing is that faith is not a *substitute* for anything: it does not give the things that life has refused, but something else; and in the ordinary sense, it does not make one 'happier'. Perhaps it makes it more possible to dispense with 'happiness'. I suppose that whatever I have, that

1 – Misdated as 'February'.
2 – *Thoughts after Lambeth* (Criterion Miscellany 30) was to be published in March. JDH wrote (28 Feb.): 'although I have known you for five or six years, and during that time have very, very slowly come to know you better, I still feel, whenever you send me one of your books, the same pleasure & excitement that the arrival, two or three years ago, of an Ariel poem produced . . . I enjoyed every word of the essay; it was written, as usual, with such exquisite clarity. But I knew that it had been written by one who had found happiness and the means of solving some, at any rate, of his difficulties, by a way that was familiar to me as a child, but has since been closed to me. Perhaps I am too young to appreciate the austerity of your attitude, too young perhaps, to understand your interpretation of asceticism. I have had many troubles – more, I think, than those whom I know well have had, so that it is not the experience of suffering that I lack. What is lacking is the ability, from which springs I suppose the desire, to adopt the solution you have found through Faith. One day it may come without the need of seeking. Until then I subscribe myself / your affectionate and very *humble* / friend and pupil / John Hayward.'

I count of positive goods in my life, are what most men would hold to be merely shadows and deceptions.

Affectionately,

T. S. E.

TO *Viscount Halifax*[1]   CC

2 March 1931   [Faber & Faber Ltd]

Dear Lord Halifax,

I am very much obliged to you for your letter and your generous approval of my pamphlet.[2] This not only gives me great gratification but a very welcome reassurance. Although I had consulted better theologians than myself, I was still very doubtful and apprehensive of invisible flaws. You must know that your commendation on such a subject is more welcome and valuable to me than that of anyone else.

It would give me very great pleasure to visit you again at Hickleton and I hope you will allow me that pleasure some time during the Spring, if my wife's health permits me to be absent from London, and if you are still disposed to see me.

With very grateful thanks, I am,

Yours very sincerely,

[T. S. Eliot]

TO *E. M. Forster*   CC

2 March 1931   [Faber & Faber Ltd]

Dear Forster,

I have not yet seen Charlton's manuscript myself. It was given to de la Mare by Squire and has not yet been read by any other director. I will read it myself, with your opinions in mind, and will also bring your letter up for the consideration of the Board.[3]

1–C. L. Wood, 2nd Viscount Halifax (1839–1934): Anglo-Catholic ecumenist: President of the English Church Union, 1868–1919, 1927–34.
2–Lord Halifax wrote on 27 Feb., 'I have read your pamphlet with the greatest interest, &, if I may say so without the great impertinence, or presumption, think it quite admirable . . .'
3–E. M. Forster had urged, in a letter of 28 Feb., that his friend 'Leo' Charlton should not be required 'to alter his narrative from 3rd person to 1st. He is against doing this, and as I am against him doing it I said I'd venture to write on the matter, and try to put my opinion.

With many thanks for your trouble,

Yours sincerely,
[T. S. Eliot]

TO *Kenneth Pickthorn*[1]   cc

2 March 1931   [Faber & Faber Ltd]

Dear Pickthorn,

Many thanks for your letter and for sending me Leavis's pamphlet.[2]
I had, in fact, already read it and bought several copies to give to various
people. It is the sort of pamphleteering which is very much needed
nowadays.

———

'It seems to me that the 3rd person, like the numerous photographs, is an integral part of
the scheme, and that if it was altered the writer's peculiar dryness and detachment would
disappear, and we should just be left with another addition to the With Rod & Gun through
the Empire series. I don't know that Charlton's good on himself – I don't know who is – but
he is certainly out to be impartial, and that a man of action should be so out, and should not
hide his head in the nearest loyalty, struck me as most remarkable; and I did think that he
was well inspired, under these circumstances, not to admit "I", with its implications of zest.
"He" may seem clumsy, and may hold up the rush of action, but it does the work which has
to be done here, in my judgement.

'I hope you, and the firm generally, won't mind me writing like this – not my business, I
know, but I should be so pleased if he managed to get the MS. taken by F. & F. and so sorry
if there happened to be a hitch over this particular point.'

In response to a further letter from TSE (not found), Forster wrote again on 9 Apr.:
'Thank you so much for your letter about Charlton's book, and for the trouble you have
taken – I had meant to write before. He is delighted, as well he may be, with the arrangement
he has come to with Faber & Faber.'

Forster added in a postscript: 'I liked *Ash Wednesday* very much. I reread it every now and
then, as I reread several others of your poems.'

L. E. O. (Leo) Charlton (1879–1958) had been a general in the Great War, and was subsequently an air commodore. P. N. Furbank notes, in *E. M. Forster: A Life* (Oxford, 1979),
II, 136: 'He wrote boys' books (later becoming the *New Statesman*'s air correspondent) and
lived with a young ex-aircraftsman boyfriend named Tom Wichelo – carrying this fact off
among his fellow-officers with great insouciance, though saying "One is always dreading the
sound of parental hooves up the garden path".' Charlton's book was published as *Charlton*
(F&F, 1931).

1–Kenneth Pickthorn (1892–1975): historian and politician; Fellow of Corpus Christi
College, Cambridge: see Biographical Register.

2–Pickthorn (28 Feb.): 'I read a page of this [*Mass Civilization and Minority Culture*]
yesterday in Heffer's and thought it quite sensible and brought it away and still think almost
all of it is quite sensible . . . I thought perhaps it might be of some slight interest to you, if
only as an example of sincerest form of flattery.'

I am very anxious to find time for a weekend in Cambridge and when I do I shall certainly propose myself to you first, in the hope of being your guest at Corpus.

Yours sincerely,
[T. S. Eliot]

TO *Michael Sadler*   CC

2 March 1931   [Faber & Faber Ltd]

Dear Master,

In spite of your final word, I am writing to thank you for your highly gratifying note about my pamphlet, and to say that I do not know Dr Barnes personally, but hope that I did not criticize him in any way unfairly from a public point of view. He is obviously extremely honest and courageous although, as I think, muddle-headed.[1]

Thank you very much for sending me your lectures on Education,[2] which I am about to read with great interest.

With many thanks,
Yours sincerely,
[T. S. Eliot]

1–Sadler wrote on 1 Mar. 1931: 'I have read your paper *Thoughts after Lambeth* with gratitude to you for sending it to me and with thanksgiving that you are here and have written it.

'To every word, and to all the presuppositions which underlie what you have said, I subscribe . . . Only one thing jarred – it is on p. 3. Since I got to know Barnes, I have loved his quakerishness (? he ought now to have been a Bishop, surely) and deeply honour his courage.'

Ernest Barnes (1874–1953): controversial and outspoken Bishop of Birmingham, 1924–53. See John Barnes, *Ahead of His Age: Bishop Barnes of Birmingham* (1979).

2–*The Outlook in Secondary Education?* (1930).

TO *A. L. Rowse*   TS Exeter

2 March 1931   Faber & Faber Ltd

Dear Rowse,

Many thanks for your letter.[1] I think we are fairly closely in agreement about order and liberty. Of course what I had in mind about Liberty was the 'time lag' precisely.

I should be interested to know what you think of the Mosley lot and the last move. I am the more interested because I have put in an approving word in my next Commentary! as I was influenced by the sneering tone of the *Sunday Times*.[2] I dare say Mosley *is* a 'careerist', but the point is are his ideas right or wrong? which does not matter to the *Sunday Times*. If he could attract one or two of the more intelligent younger *conservatives* (there are very few I know) it would be to his advantage.[3]

My own 'toryism' is only intelligible on the understanding that there are no Tories in politics at all, and that I don't much like any government since Charles I, and that Disraeli was a Jew film producer only commendable because so much less intolerable than Gladstone.

Yours ever,
T. S. E.

1 – Rowse (Feb./Mar.): 'About order, I agree; the important thing is to know what sort of order. And as to that . . . we should disagree . . . Not all people still regard it as a conscious end. Nor do I think the nineteenth century was wrong in attaching such importance to the concept of liberty: it had so much more relevance to their conditions . . .'

2 – TSE wrote in *C.* 10, Apr. 1931, 483: 'The Mosley programme . . . though in some respects vague or feeble, contains at least some germs of intelligence; and a pronouncement by men who have had the courage to disassociate themselves from any party must be read with respect. It recognises that the nineteenth century is over, and that a thorough reorganization of industry and of agriculture is essential . . . What is lacking, perhaps, and what is essential for enthusiasm, is the evidence of profound moral conviction . . . *Politique d'abord*, certainly; but *politique* means more than prosperity and comfort . . . it means the social aspect of the Good Life.'

3 – In 1954 Nora Wydenbruck, TSE's German translator, told him that a correspondent had suggested to her that there might have been some sort of connection in the 1930s between TSE and Mosley. TSE replied on 11 May 1954: 'Will you please disclaim any connection between myself and Sir Oswald Mosley. I am sure that at no time did I ever have any correspondence with him, and have never met him personally. I was never in agreement with his views, and I once refered to him <by implication> in print as a kind of "Catiline". As for what I thought of him in the Thirties, there is some evidence in the Pageant Play, *The Rock*, which was produced and published in 1934. This has been long out of print, but there are copies in existence, and it must be in the British Museum and possibly in the London Library. In this Pageant, I had a scene lampooning the British fascists as well as the communists, and indeed, as somebody got hold of a text and mentioned it in a newspaper before the Pageant was produced, we were in some apprehension lest there might be a demonstration on the opening night. I have no sympathy with Sir Oswald Mosley's attitude towards the Jews.'

TO *Winifred Holtby*[1]   CC

3 March 1931   [Faber & Faber Ltd]

Dear Miss Holtby,

It is very kind of you to invite me to the *Time and Tide* party on March 12th.[2] I wish that I could come but unfortunately there are three reasons against it. First, it is Lent; second, I never drink cocktails, and third, I seldom stay out so late in the evening.

Please don't think the reason for the failure of our interview was your incapacity as a canvasser. It was rather the fact that you probably saw the wrong person and that, in short, my opinions on the subject of advertising carry no more weight inside this office than they do outside of it.

Yours very sincerely,
[T. S. Eliot]

TO *Mario Praz*   CC

3 March 1931   [*The Criterion*]

My dear Praz,

Thank you for your card of the 28th.[3] Of course, if your arrangement with Milford should fall through, I should be glad to hear of it.

I have tried to get you a copy of Rothenstein's *Memoirs* but I am afraid you are a little late in the day as I was told that the copies allocated for review had been exhausted and that no more could be spared.[4] As it is an expensive book I could not press the point, but I am sorry.

1–Winifred Holtby (1898–1935: Yorkshire-born writer, feminist, campaigner; ally of Vera Brittain (whom she met at Oxford). Following early success as a journalist, she became a director of the feminist periodical *Time and Tide*; and was active in feminist and anti-racist causes. Her writings include the posthumous and acclaimed novel *South Riding* (1936, winner of the James Tait Black Memorial Prize), other novels, a study of Virginia Woolf, stories, poems, and a feminist treatise. See Vera Brittain, *Testament of Friendship: The Story of Winifred Holtby* (1940); Marion Shaw, *The Clear Stream: A Life of Winifred Holtby* (1999).
2–Holtby wrote (14 Feb.): 'I don't believe that our interview – qua business interview – was a conspicuous success. My fault. I am not good as a canvasser. But will you put business behind you & come and drink a purely non-utilitarian cocktail with Lady Rhondda [Margaret Haig Thomas, Viscountess Rhondda, founder-editor of *Time and Tide*] & the Directors on March 12th? . . . [W]e should be charmed if the Editor of the *Criterion* were with us.'
3–'Yes, I think myself the course you advise me to take [26 Feb.] is the better; only, as I had applied to you first, I did not wish to withdraw my offer. Thanks all the same . . .'
4–Praz hoped for a review copy of William Rothenstein's *Men and Memories* (F&F).

It is unkind of you to suggest that I should be too busy to see you when you pass through London.[1] The trouble is that you appear at such short notice. If you could let me know a few days in advance exactly what time you will have in London, I hope that we might meet.

Yours ever,
[T. S. Eliot]

TO *Paul Léon*   TS National Gallery of Ireland

4 March 1931   Faber & Faber Ltd

Dear Mr Léon,

Thank you very much for your letter of the 4th February.[2] I have not yet heard from Mr Joyce myself and trust that this does not mean that he is in poor health.

We should be very much obliged if you would kindly write to Mr Babou, asking permission for us to publish our shilling edition of *Haveth Childers Everywhere* as soon as possible. I cannot at the moment give you the exact date on which it would be most desirable to publish it but I think we should like to do so towards the end of this month or the beginning of April. Our publication date is Thursday and it is to everyone's advantage to arrange the publication of each book in relation to others, so as to give each one the best chances for immediate reviews.[3]

Yours very sincerely,
T. S. Eliot

TO *John Macmurray*[4]   CC

6 March 1931   [Faber & Faber Ltd]

Dear Mr Macmurray,

I am sorry that I was unable to catch you for a word after the meeting the other day, because I was very much interested in the discussion (with

---

1–Praz wrote (in an echo of 'The Love Song of J. Alfred Prufrock'): 'I am passing through London on March 9th or 10th, but you seem to be so busy that I shall not dare to disturb you.'

2–Not found.

3–*HCE* was ultimately to be published, as Criterion Miscellany 26, on 8 May 1931.

4–John Macmurray (1891–1976): moral philosopher; Grote Professor of the Philosophy of Mind and Logic, University College, London, 1928–44; Professor of Moral Philosophy, Edinburgh University, 1944–58. His works include *Freedom in the Modern World* (1932). See

the exception of Streeter who, I thought, talked like an undergraduate debating society) and particularly in what you said. My reason for writing at the moment is to ask you whether you would be willing to review for the *Criterion The Revolt Against Dualism* of A. O. Lovejoy, of Johns Hopkins. Lovejoy is an old friend of my family and I do not think that his book has had quite the attention it deserves in London. I do not mention these facts in order that it may get a favourable review but merely that I believe it is worth notice of some kind, whether it be favourable or unfavourable.[1]

Yours very sincerely
[T. S. Eliot]

TO *Max Plowman*[2]

CC

6 March 1931   [Faber & Faber Ltd]

Dear Mr Plowman,

Thank you for your note of the 4th.[3] It is true that I did not understand that what you had in mind was an article rather than a review. This rather increases my apprehension of being unable to do justice either to Lawrence or to Mr Murry, but if you care to let me see a copy of the book immediately it is available, I will return it without delay if I find myself incompetent.

Yours sincerely,
[T. S. Eliot]

J. E. Costello, *John Macmurray: A Biography* (2002); *John Macmurray: Critical Perspectives*, ed. D. Fergusson and N. Dower (2002).

1–Untitled review, C. 10 (July 1931), 766–8.

2–Max (Mark) Plowman (1883–1941): British poet, editor, pacifist (he endured terrible active service in WW1 and was treated for neurasthenia at Craiglockhart). Plowman took to poetry and journalism after working for ten years in his father's brick business; worked for JMM at *The Adelphi* from 1930, becoming editor in 1938; and was a friend of George Orwell. Publications include *A Lap Full of Seed* (poems, 1917), *The Right to Live* (anonymous pamphlet, 1917), *A Subaltern on the Somme* (by 'Mark VII', 1927), *The Faith Called Pacifism* (1936). See further *Bridge into the Future: Letters of Max Plowman*, ed. Dorothy Lloyd Plowman (1944).

3–Plowman had written on 2 Mar. that JMM was reviewing *Thoughts After Lambeth*; he hoped TSE might review JMM's book on Lawrence for the same number of *The Adelphi*. He wrote again on 4 Mar.: 'I am sorry I did not express myself more clearly. What I had hoped (& still hope) was that you would make the book the basis of an article we might have for *The Adelphi*.'

TO *C. M. Grieve*   CC

6 March 1931   [*The Criterion*]

Dear Mr Grieve,

Thank you very much for sending me your essay[1] which I read with great interest and with a great deal of agreement. I should like to make one or two suggestions, however, with which I hope you will be able to find yourself in accord. The first is that the essay in its present form is inconveniently long for the *Criterion*; indeed, anything over 5000 words always makes difficulties for the editor. I should not like to mutilate your essay, but it struck me that one way of abbreviating it without detracting from the effect would be to omit discussion on the Gaelic poets you mention, whom very few of our readers will be able to read, anyway, and concentrate yourself on what is really, I think, more important, the development of Modern Scots. But before I return the essay I should like to know your opinion on this.[2]

Yours sincerely,
[T. S. Eliot]

TO *Desmond Fitzgerald*[3]   CC

6 March 1931   [Faber & Faber Ltd]

My dear FitzGerald,

Thank you very much for your letter of the 24th February. I shall certainly let you know when I am coming to Dublin and had I been able

---

1 – Submitted on 26 Feb.: see MacDiarmid, *Letters*, 437–8. 'English Ascendancy and British Literature', C. 10 (July 1931), 593–613.

2 – Grieve agreed on 9 Mar. that the essay was 'on the long side': 'Your suggestion to omit the discussion on the Gaelic poets seems to me the best way to effect this . . .'

3 – Desmond Fitzgerald (1888–1947): Irish nationalist politician; poet. Having been a member of the Imagist school of poetry in London, where he was friends with EP, he returned in 1913 to Ireland, joining the Irish Volunteers in 1914 and fighting in the Easter Rising, 1916, for which he was imprisoned. Released in 1918, he turned to politics, becoming a Sinn Féin MP. A founder of the Irish Free State, he was Minister for Publicity, 1918–22; External Affairs, 1922–7; Defence, 1927–32. EP wrote in Canto 92: 'And honour? Fitzgerald: "I was." / When he freed a man / who had not been at the Post Office (Oireland 1916).' Robert Speaight wrote of him: 'A man of great personal charm and leonine courage, he had fought in the Easter Rising; spent a short time in prison, chained to Mr de Valera; and served as Press Officer with the Irish delegation that eventually signed the Treaty . . . [A]t the time I met him he was still a member of the opposition in the Dail – for de Valera had recently come to power . . . Michael Collins and Kevin O'Higgins were his heroes and de Valera his villain' (*The Property Basket* [1970], 175).

to fix a date you would have heard from me ere now. I think that it is more likely to be April than March as I have certain business at this end to put in order first.

The business is connected with several streets of houses in Dunlaoghaire which are held leasehold from Lord Longford and Lord de Vesci, and for all of which we have tenants.[1] I should think that the bill you mention would certainly affect us and I should be extremely grateful if you would send me a copy as soon as it is available. I am sorry that so far it has proved impossible to find anyone to do the book on Irish affairs which we wanted. It has struck me since that it might be better to divide the whole subject matter and contemplate two or more possible books, one, for instance, which would naturally be more picturesque, on the years of revolution, and another which would be a more constitutional document, on the development of the present government of Ireland, up to date, and information about the present state of the country, its agriculture, industries, etc. I should very much like to know what you think of this suggestion. It seemed to me that to deal in this way with the subject might make it easier to find authors.

With many thanks for your letter, and looking forward to seeing you,

Yours very sincerely,

[T. S. Eliot]

TO *Leslie Bishop* TS copy

6 March 1931 [Faber & Faber Ltd]

Dear Mr Bishop,

I had had it in mind for some time to try to see you again. By all means let me see your novel and will you please have it sent to me personally? Not that I am any judge of fiction but that if it is sent to me I can see that it is given a careful reading.[2]

1–FitzGerald (Roinn Cosanta, Baile Atha Cliath: Department of Defence, Dublin) wrote on 24 Feb., 'I remember that you said your business here had something to do with a place in Dunlaoghaire. I don't know whether the fact that we are introducing a Town Tenants' Bill that will have some relation to matters of leases will have any interest for you.'

2–Leslie Bishop (who had at some point been TSE's guest) asked permission on 1 Mar. to submit a short novel entitled *Mother's Gone Away*. 'It is not a "pleasant" book and the language of necessity is unrestrained in places – since it is based on intimate observation of a woman who goes "mad" but who, as one of my friends said, "goes mad greatly".' He explained further on 26 Mar. that he intended 'to show the psychology of one whom the conventional would call wholly mad and whom the intelligent might call in some ways great

After it has been read I will write to you again and suggest a meeting.

Yours sincerely,

[T. S. Eliot]

TO *Douglas Jerrold*[1]   CC

7 March 1931   [Faber & Faber Ltd]

Dear Jerrold,

Many thanks for your highly interesting letter of the 6th instant.[2] The project naturally appeals to me very strongly, and I am complimented by your suggesting my collaboration. Before writing to you in detail about it, I am sure that you will not object to my discussing the whole matter, confidentially, with Geoffrey Faber, and taking his opinion as to how far it is feasible for me to co-operate. I will write again on Monday or Tuesday.

Yours sincerely,

[T. S. Eliot]

– to hint at the reasons why society produces such people . . . One must excuse anything in the mouth of a lunatic, and I have exploited this fact to the full . . . The iconoclasm, the bestialities and occasional infringements of the Blasphemy Acts may be readily modified. Please do not think they represent my views. They represent what I saw & heard and I thought best to let you see the whole grim picture.'

1–Douglas Jerrold (1893–1964): publisher and author; director of Eyre & Spottiswoode, 1929–59, Chairman from 1945; editor of *The English Review*, 1931–6 – the organ of 'real Toryism' – which was revived after WW2 as the *New English Review Magazine*. A fundamentalist Roman Catholic, convinced of the moral void of contemporary life and arguing for the restitution of a Christian social order, on occasion his ideals and inclinations ran to the right of the Conservative Party: he came to praise Mussolini's methods and to sympathise with the British Union of Fascists. Though by no means a racist, he confused political rigour with moral righteousness. TSE grew increasingly sceptical towards Jerrold's attitudes. Jerrold's works include *Georgian Adventure* (1937), *The Necessity of Freedom* (1938) and *Britain and Europe, 1900–1940* (1941).

2–Eyre & Spottiswoode was to take over in June 1931 the financial liability of *The English Review* (which was running at a loss of £2,000 a year and would never make a profit), and had undertaken to set up a representative Consultative Council 'on the grounds of public policy'. Lord Lloyd, L. S. Amery, Ernest Benn, Lord Winterton, A. P. Herbert and Professor J. H. Morgan had agreed to participate: 'it is an essential part of the scheme that the group should be non-political in the narrow sense of the term and that it should include those who can speak with authority from the Historical, literary and philosophical standpoint as well as from the purely political point of view.' He explained further: 'I remember that you prefaced a recent book of yours with the statement that you wrote (I quote from memory) from the standpoint of the classicist in literature, the royalist in politics and the Catholic in religion. It would be impossible to put more concisely what our group will stand for and I do feel that it is of real importance that all those who share these principles should join us.'

7 March 1931   [Faber & Faber Ltd]

My dear Lord Archbishop,

I am much gratified by Your Grace's letter,[1] and the reassurance which it gives me about my pamphlet. I was not only diffident about my competence and about my opinions, but I expected that on such a subject, my essay would only take people's notice at the points at which they held contrary views to mine, and not at the points at which they were in accord. But so far the only adverse criticism I have received was a criticism on a few passages, from Middleton Murry, who considered, perhaps justly, that I was tempted to score too many purely 'debating points'.

With many thanks for all the help Your Grace most kindly gave me, and which invaluably corrected my ignorance or misunderstanding,

I am,

Your Grace's obedient servant,

[T. S. Eliot]

TO *A. L. Rowse*   TS Exeter

7 March 1931   *The Criterion*

Dear Rowse,

Thank you very much for your helpful letter (I wish however that you would adopt the practice of dating your letters).[2] You are quite right about

---

1 – Not found.
2 – Rowse had written (n.d.): 'I do not support the Mosley group – not because Mosley himself is a careerist, nor mainly because of disagreement with his policy, though a good deal of it is to my mind wrong . . . The one element which is likely to be vital in the programme is protectionism; and I don't believe protection is any remedy for the world depression . . . I've just been reading their manifesto, & though it's an able document it's not convincing . . . [Y]ou cannot raise the standard of life indefinitely inside one "insulated" system, regardless of what is going on in the outside world. We have in some way or other to get down to the world price-level. They are prepared for what it would involve, the sacrifice of London's position as a world financial centre. This seems intolerable, the City contributes £70 millions a year to our national income, and on the whole is the best managed of our industries.

'But what is wrong with the Group is this: they do not see that in order to be effective in politics, what matters most is to be in relation with some strong economic interest in the community, above all a class . . . And they have made the fatal mistake of getting out of touch with their own basis of strength in the community: and I expect to see them [not] long in being snuffed out . . .'

Popery; the real issue is obscured by the purely legal controversies and Petrine Claims etc.; the real issue is philosophical and even temperamental, rather than historical, and on this point one or two intelligent Papists agree with me.

I did not feel very hopeful about the Mosley group myself. But the point is this: Mosley may have struck a bit too soon; but as things are drifting at present, it seems to me only a question of time before there is a popular movement towards *some* form of Hitlerism in England, and I want to think about it before it happens. For *any* strong definite cry may be the 'programme'; it depends merely on circumstances whether the appeal is to revolution or to reaction, to Toryism or to Socialism. The actual Mosley programme seems to me to fall between two stools; it still aims at those who continue to believe that the whole difficulty can be settled by finding an economic dodge better than the dodges of Baldwin, George, Macdonald & Snowden, or than that of Keynes and the pundits, and who are willing to try any purely *economic* heresy so long as all their other beliefs are undisturbed. Now my instinct is that any heresy violent enough to save matters (and I believe matters to be in a much worse way than most people think) – cannot be a mere economic heresy – we are hardened to those – but must be something requiring real self sacrifice of the individual, whoever he be, to the common good; but I will not admit that the Common Good can any longer imply getting the better of some other nation's Common Good.

I feel, myself, that Protection is merely a plaster on a wound. For instance, if we protect the Motor Car Industry, all goes well; but no one asks, is it for the best that motor-cars should be produced infinitely in Britain *and consumed*. In short: would not British brains and British hands be better employed than in producing too many motor cars, and then finding sufficient employment for all of the British public to use at least one British car? It seems to me that at present the whole of England is being mapped out according to the present development of the motor industry. When one observes the By Passes of London: mile after mile of suburban houses each its attendant Private Garage: this is merely planting out clerks and functionaries in places in which they could not possibly live unless each had his Small Car; it seems to me that the whole present settlement of England is being made to encourage the motor car industry.

Now it seems to me that we build up, by accident, great industries employing great numbers of men, for objects which are *morally* indefensible: example, the Morris industry at Cowley. Then we have got all these men busied in turning out products which we ought not to want to turn out, and we become morally responsible for putting the rest of the population in the morally undesirable position of being able to own motor cars because owing to the motor car industry they have to live in places in which they couldn't live unless they had motor cars.

And I don't see how you can ever get down to a 'world price level' unless you can get a world, or at least a very substantial part of a world, agreeing on what is valuable; on what is the Good Life.

I do not see how the City can be sacrificed (with its revenue) unless you can give people, and make them want, something more intrinsically valuable than prosperity: give them something better than prosperity, something for which they will willingly sacrifice prosperity. From the old game point of view, I quite agree that the Mosley crowd will fail through not attaching to themselves some powerful economic interest: but what when people get to the point of exasperation where they give no damn for any economic interest?

I merely raise these questions, as an ignoramus, though I think a representative one. I think you may be interested by an essay by Thomas Mann on German politics in my next number.[1]

Yours affectionately,
T. S. E.

TO *Viscount Halifax* CC

7 March 1931 [Faber & Faber Ltd]

My dear Lord Halifax,

Thank you very much for your letter of the 6th and for sending me your small book.[2] I ought to have read it on its publication; but indeed, I seldom have time to read anything. I have read your pamphlet this morning, with great pleasure and profit: and as I have in my routine to look at so many books and have the time to read so few, I am always particularly appreciative when anyone can put so much into so few words as you have here. It is a book I am very glad to keep in my library.

1 – Thomas Mann, 'An Appeal to Reason' (a speech delivered in Berlin, 17 Oct. 1930), trans. H. T. Lowe-Porter, C. 10 (Apr. 1931), 393–411.
2 – 'I send you the enclosed booklet that you may see what I have been thinking and saying of late and more particularly on account of the letter from Professor Janssens with which it ends. It seems to me an admirable paper and one which ought to go a long way towards bringing people together.' Viscount Halifax, *The Good Estate of the Catholic Church* (2nd impression, 1930).

I have not seen the Abbot of Buckfast's book, which you also mention in the pamphlet, and should very much like to read it.[1]

I have only heard of La Taille's great work on the Eucharist[2] – first, I think, from Spens.[3] If you are engaged upon it now, I wonder if you would care to have me lend you – unless you have already seen it – a small book *The Mass and the Redemption* by my friend Martin D'Arcy, who is at present the head of the Jesuits in Oxford. I mention it because it is, as he says, partly an exposition in English of La Taille's views; D'Arcy has, I think, the most brilliant philosophical mind of at least any of the Jesuits in England, and expresses himself with great lucidity.

I was, I confess, entirely ignorant of 'The King's Book', though it is not only on this, but on many other points, that your essay is, and will be, of great use to me.[4]

Thanking you most cordially for sending it to me,

> I am,
> Always yours gratefully,
> [T. S. Eliot]

If you have not seen D'Arcy's book and would care to read it I will have it sent to you at once.

TO *Kenneth Ingram*   cc

7 March 1931   [Faber & Faber Ltd]

Dear Ingram,

Thank you very much for your letter of the 6th.[5] I am ashamed not to have written to you before, to apologise and express regret for my

1 – Halifax asked if TSE had read *The Key to the Eucharistic Mystery*, by the Abbot of Buckfast – 'an admirable production, which I should like to offer to you'.

2 – Fr Maurice de La Taille, SJ (1872–1933), who taught from 1919 at the Gregorian University in Rome, exerted a profound influence on the Liturgical Movement. See *Mysterium Fidei: Regarding the Most August Sacrament and Sacrifice of the Body and Blood of Christ* (1921).

3 – 'At this moment I am reading the Abbé de Taille on the same subject . . . a very instructive and interesting book . . .'

4 – 'It is only quite recently that I made acquaintance with "The King's Book" . . .' (*The King's Book* [1543], attributed to Henry VIII.)

5 – Ingram wrote that *Thoughts after Lambeth* was 'one of the best things I have ever read . . . I wished you had been able to come to the "Grecian" for my paper on Liberal Catholicism, because I should so much have liked to have had your criticism. Wilfred Knox has just read it & I'm glad to find, agrees with my thesis.

'I'm sure you will like the atmosphere of the "Grecian" . . . It really is a very interesting circle, & the variety of opinion doesn't make for a merely controversial atmosphere.'

absence, and to ask you whether you would be so good as to let me see your paper on Liberal Catholicism? Or, if it is to be published anywhere shortly, I will not bother you with this request, if you will let me know where I shall find it, and how soon.

It has been a disappointment to me not to have been able to attend any of the meetings of the Grecian, but I have not lost hope. In truth, my present circumstances make it difficult for me to get out in the evening, and I have to space my engagements and prepare in advance. I fear I shall not be able to attend the next either, because I have an engagement for the following night which I cannot escape, as it is a kind of official responsibility. In any case, perhaps we might lunch together soon?

I am so very glad you like my pamphlet: I was very diffident about it.

Yours ever,
[T. S. Eliot]

TO *J. L. Donaghy* CC

10 March 1931   [Faber & Faber Ltd]

Dear Mr Donaghy,

I have delayed, I am afraid, a long time before writing to you but it always takes me a long time to make up my mind. I have finally come to the conclusion, with great regret, that it would make matters very difficult for me were I to preface your book of verse.[1] I am frequently asked to do the same thing for others and sometimes by persons with some personal claim; if I wrote a preface for you it would be difficult to refuse other requests, and the value of an introduction diminishes according to the number of his introduction[s]. So I have made a general rule not to write introductions to the work of any living poet. I hope I may be useful to your book in other ways. Perhaps when it is convenient you would ring up one day and arrange to come in and see me again. I hope things are going well with you and your family.

Yours sincerely,
[T. S. Eliot]

1–Donaghy had asked TSE to write a preface to his next volume of poetry.

TO *Francis Underhill*   CC

10 March 1931   [Faber & Faber Ltd]

Dear Father Underhill,

My young American acquaintance, Mr Austin Warren, writes to tell me that he will be in London until the 1st of April, so that if it proves convenient for you to arrange a meeting with your cousin, we should be very grateful. But please do not put yourself out; and I do not want to ask anything excessive of Miss Underhill. Warren will, I understand, be back in London again for a time, during the summer.[1]

Yours very sincerely,

[T. S. Eliot]

TO *Michael Roberts*[2]   TS Janet Adam Smith

10 March 1931   Faber & Faber Ltd

Dear Sir,

THE CRITERION

I must apologise for the delay in answering your letter of 28th August. I have now read your essay on Hulme with great interest and wish to

---

1 – Warren was to recall, in 'A Survivor's Tribute to T. S. Eliot': 'Eliot graciously asked me if there was anyone I would especially like to meet, and I immediately said "Evelyn Underhill", whose *Mysticism* had been one of my favourite spiritual guides. Eliot said he had never met her but would like to, and could easily arrange a meeting . . . The luncheon frankly disappointed me; in my naïveté I had expected the table talk to be mystical or at least theological: it was neither. Evelyn Underhill and Eliot politely talked personalities; asked each other in a gingerly, tactful way I have never forgotten, "Is he a nice person?" – a question to be answered by delicate characterization' (*Essays from the 'Southern Review'*, 288).

2 – Michael Roberts (1902–48), critic, editor, poet, was educated at King's College, London (where he read chemistry), and at Trinity College, Cambridge (mathematics). In the 1930s he worked as a schoolmaster (in London and at the Royal Grammar School, Newcastle upon Tyne). After WW2, during which he worked for the BBC European Service, he became Principal of the Church of England training college of St Mark and St John in Chelsea, London. Roberts edited the watershed anthologies *New Signatures* (1932) and *New Country* (1933); and *The Faber Book of Modern Verse* (1936). Other writings include *The Modern Mind* (1937), *T. E. Hulme* (1938), *The Recovery of the West* (1941). In 1935 he married the critic and biographer Janet Adam Smith. See further *A Portrait of Michael Roberts*, ed. T. W. Eason and R. Hamilton (1949).

TSE wrote soon after Roberts's death: 'His scientific bent and training were supplemented and corrected by a philosophical cast of mind; by critical abilities of a very high order; and by an imaginative gift which expressed itself in poetry of a meditative type. Such a combination of powers is unusual; and among men of letters of his generation it was unique. His first

publish it in the *Criterion*. I hope that my acceptance of this essay has not been too long delayed.[1]

CRITIQUE OF POETRY

Now, about your book.[2] The Cambridge press has informed us that it is not quite the type of book for them. I have read it with pleasure and have found many things in it both interesting and new, and I think it is an undertaking which ought to be completed, and published by someone. When I say completed, I mean that I find it in its present form difficult to read because of an effect of discontinuity. It reads more like a collection of short essays on closely related themes than like one coherent study, or in other words, it seems to proceed by a succession of short sprints. I think that the difficulty is chiefly a matter of structure and not at all of discontinuity of subject matter, and I do think that what you have to say

---

notoriety was due to the volume *New Signatures*, a presentation of the poetry which was beginning to attract attention in the late nineteen-twenties; a book which seemed to promise him the place of expositor and interpreter of the poetry of his generation. This book was followed in 1934 by *Critique of Poetry*, a collection of essays ranging between literary criticism, aesthetics and philosophy; then by *The Modern Mind*, a more coherent and profound examination of the age; by a study of T. E. Hulme, which remains the essential piece of bibliography for a man who occupied for his generation something like the place to which Roberts was entitled for his own; and finally, in 1941, by *The Recovery of the West*, an important essay in moral and sociological criticism . . . A little earlier . . . appeared *Orion Marches*, which contains, I think, some of the best of his poems.'

TSE noted too, of Roberts's 'isolated superiority' (a phrase he had once used of EP): 'He would have made an admirable editor of a review of ideas: indeed, had the *Criterion* continued, he was the only man junior to myself of whom I could think for the editorship' ('Introduction', *A Portrait of Michael Roberts*, x–xii; 'Views and Reviews: Michael Roberts', *The New English Weekly* 34 [13 Jan. 1949], 164).

1 – Roberts' essay attempted 'to dissociate Hulme's central tenet from the results of his own accidental limitations . . . [R]ecent essays show, I think, that these latent contradictions are not generally perceived.' (Roberts wrote to FVM on 27 Nov. 1930: 'a note on T. E. Hulme has lain for some months at the *Criterion*'s offices. (I do not suggest that the fact implies favourable consideration)' – so it is possible that FVM jogged TSE into this belated positive response. See 'The Categories of T. E. Hulme', C. 11 (Apr. 1932), 375–85).

2 – By a different post (27 Nov. 1930), Roberts had submitted 'Critique of Poetry', to which FVM responded on 6 Jan. 1931: 'We have read the manuscript with much interest and, as you may imagine, with much sympathy. We feel that it should certainly be published but we also feel that it might do more good for all concerned if some other publisher would do it. As some of those mentioned are intimately connected with our own firm, if we did the book it might look a little like cracking up our own wares.

'I am not suggesting that if it should be difficult to find another publisher we would not still be interested in the book, but I wondered if I might suggest trying it on the Cambridge University Press? How would you feel about this? If you would authorise me to do so, I would be glad to send it to them.'

Roberts thanked FVM (8 Jan. 1931) for his 'encouraging letter' and authorised him to forward it to CUP. *Critique of Poetry* was eventually to be published by Jonathan Cape in 1934.

could be presented in a way which would seduce many more readers. I. A. Richards' *Principles of Literary Criticism* was to my mind one of the most flagrant examples of a good book badly handicapped by confused arrangement.

I should be very much interested to know whether my criticism strikes you as pertinent or not, and meanwhile retain the manuscript until I have heard from you. If at any time you should visit London I should be delighted to see you.

Yours very truly,
T. S. Eliot

TO *H. J. C. Grierson*   CC

11 March 1931   [*The Criterion*]

Dear Grierson,

Many thanks for your letter of the 8th. I should be very glad indeed to look at your essay on Carlyle, and particularly if it brings in modern German critics.[1] I have had for some time an essay by Gundolf on Mörike, and as both Gundolf and Mörike are completely unknown in England, I should be glad to be able to publish something even mentioning his name. That, however, is a minor issue. I should very much like to see the article in any case.

Yours sincerely,
[T. S. Eliot]

TO *Douglas Jerrold*   CC

11 March 1931   [Faber & Faber Ltd]

Dear Jerrold,

I have discussed the matter of your letter of the 6th with both Faber and Morley and there appears to be no reason why I should not take an active interest in your plans for the *English Review*.[2]

1–Grierson wrote on 8 Mar. that in Dec. 1930 he had given the Robert Adamson lecture in Manchester on 'Carlyle & the Hero', including later developments in Germany – Nietzsche and Gundolf. Would TSE care to consider the lecture? Grierson's essay did not appear in *C.*
2–See TSE's letter to Jerrold, 7 Mar. 1931, above. TSE was to join 'a sort of small editorial committee' helping to run *The English Review*.

I will try to come to your dinner on the 23rd, though I rarely go out in the evening, never stay out late, and always rather dread dinners which are convened for the discussion of any serious business. My usual experience is that the first two hours is passed in formalities and small talk, and that the serious business only begins when I am feeling tired, and ready to go home. So if you would care to have lunch with me one day next week, I should be very glad to have a private talk with you about the project first.[1]

My chief apprehension after reading your letter was that the council might be so big as to be unwieldy and diffuse, rather than comprehensive. But I suppose you will have a more active inner council as well.

Sincerely yours,
[T. S. Eliot]

TO *Charles A. Pearce*

TS Harcourt Brace

12 March 1931   Faber & Faber Ltd

Dear Mr Pearce,

Many thanks for your letter of the 3rd instant.[2] I like your proposal very well and am flattered that you have given so much attention to the matter. I think your suggestions for contents and arrangement are on the whole excellent. I should have a few suggestions of detail to make; for instance, there are two or three long essays which you probably have not seen and which I should like to include, possibly instead of a few of those in your collection. The first question, however, to discuss, is one of copyrights. Frank Morley is sailing for New York tomorrow and will be seeing you. I have already discussed the matter pretty fully with him, and I should be very glad if you would have a talk with him about it, before we go further.[3]

---

1 – TSE did attend the first dinner.
2 – C. A. Pearce (Harcourt, Brace & Co.) wrote: 'We have been hoping for the past year, as you know, to publish a collection of your essays that would be more or less complete and that would fairly illustrate your position as critic . . . We are therefore enclosing two lists that we have made of your essays, either of which might serve as a table of contents for the proposed book. In one of these lists, the essays are arranged in (approximately) chronological order; in the other, we have presumed to group the essays under several headings [A. Essays on Criticism; B. Essays in Criticism of the Poetic Drama; C. Essays on Poetry; D. Essays in Philosophic Criticism] . . . We do hope that you will not consider this effort of ours, to assist in preparing the book and to arrange for its early publication, too presumptuous and misdirected.'
3 – FVM was to write to Alfred Harcourt on 3 July 1931: 'I am gradually getting nearer to straighten out the Eliot material, essays and verses, for you to do, the only reason it is taking so long is that Chamberlain of Methuen [which published *SW*] is a terribly sticky man.'

With many thanks,

Yours very sincerely,
T. S. Eliot

TO *Ada Sheffield*[1]   CC

12 March 1931   [Faber & Faber Ltd]

Dear Ada,

This is a hurried line to let you know that my friend and fellow director
in Faber and Faber, Frank Morley, is sailing tomorrow for a business visit
to New York, and expects to have a few days in Boston, also. I have given
him your address and asked him to let you know when he reaches Boston,
and I hope that you and Shef will be able to see him.

Affectionately, your brother,
[Tom]

TO *William Rothenstein*[2]   TS Houghton

12 March 1931   Faber & Faber Ltd

My dear Rothenstein,

It would give myself and the inner group of friends associated with
the *Criterion* a great deal of pleasure if you could possibly come to our
monthly At Home on Wednesday next, the 18th. It takes place at Harold
Monro's rooms, over the Poetry Bookshop, 38 Great Russell Street,
W.C.1. and the time is from a quarter past eight, indefinitely. This is rather
short notice but I do hope that you will be able to come, or if not, that you
can offer me some hope of securing you for a later occasion.[3]

I cannot close without telling you that I have enjoyed immensely reading
your *Memoirs*. It is not a form of literature to which I am addicted and
I do not suppose that I should have read yours unless the book had been
under my nose; but once having dipped into them, I read the book straight

---

1 – Ada Eliot Sheffield (1869–1943): eldest of the seven Eliot children; author of *The Social
Case History: Its Construction and Content* (1920) and *Social Insight in Case Situations*
(1937). TSE considered her 'a very exceptional woman': the Mycroft to his Holmes.
2 – William Rothenstein (1872–1945), artist and administrator, was Principal of the Royal
College of Art: see Biographical Register.
3 – Rothenstein did not go – he went to a wedding, and felt too tired to go out in the evening.

through with continued interest, and now look forward eagerly to the second volume.[1]

> Yours sincerely,
> T. S. Eliot

TO *William Empson*   cc

13 March 1931   [*The Criterion*]

Dear Empson,

It would give me great pleasure if you would come as my guest to the next *Criterion* Meeting, at Harold Monro's, The Poetry Bookshop, 38 Great Russell Street. Please drop me a line or ring to say that you can come, and if you can turn up, about quarter past eight or soon after, I shall be there.

> Yours ever,
> [T. S. Eliot]

TO *Hugh Macdonald*   MS Williamson

13 March 1931   Faber & Faber Ltd

Dear Macdonald,

I have a suggestion to make to you, of a book in preparation, which was proposed to us first, but seemed to me definitely more of a Haslewood Press book. A Miss Margaret Deas – a former pupil of Grierson's and one of whom I believe he thought highly – is interested in preparing a new edition of Lord Dorset's Poems. This seems to me a piece of work well worth doing, though rather outside our own line of publication. I do not know Miss Deas personally, but if the idea appeals to you, as I think it should, it will be quite easy for you to obtain information about her qualifications.[2]

> Yours ever,
> T. S. Eliot

1–Rothenstein replied (13 Mar.): 'it is pleasant to . . . get so kind a letter. I, like yrself, dislike the idea of the discussion of one's own, & other's, affairs. I began writing, when I was very ill, some notes for my children: that they were continued you must blame Dick de la Mare, his father, & one or 2 other friends.' *Men and Memories: Recollections of William Rothenstein, 1872–1900* (F&F, 1931).
2–Macdonald replied (24 Mar.) that they had 'lost a good deal over the books lately & I don't wish to lose any more, even of other people's money . . . But . . . I should like to see the

13 March 1931   [Faber & Faber Ltd]

My dear More,

This is merely a hasty note of acknowledgement and thanks for your letter of the 19th February, because you will be in England so soon that I am not inspired to write now at length. This is merely to express interest in your 'library' which seems similar to a notion I had myself several years ago and took up with Duncan Jones, the present Dean of Chichester.[1] So will you on your voyage think over the question of an English publisher for the work, as I am confident that I could interest my firm in it. On the other hand, it is only right to say that I think I could interest the S.P.C.K. or the S.P.C.K. and the E.C.U. jointly just as easily and this might seem to you a better organ for distributing the books.

In haste, with best wishes for the success of your family in Cambridge, and hoping to hear from you there as soon as you arrive.

I am, yours ever sincerely,

[T. S. Eliot]

P.S. I want to talk to you about the Encyclopedia too. My secretary is signing this, in order to catch the mail.

---

material if Miss Deas doesn't mind showing it to me. But I don't believe we could sell sufficient copies to pay her anything & this is an unsatisfactory state of affairs for editor and publisher.' Deas gratefully reported to TSE on 21 Apr. 1931 that she had seen Macdonald, who had 'promised to bring out my work . . . provided it was good, and provided trade conditions were favourable'.

1 – More wrote: 'I have long had in mind to edit an anthology, or "library", of Seventeenth-century Anglo-ecclesiastical literature, in four or five volumes, to embrace sermons, tracts, chapters from books, etc., etc., designed to exhibit what may be called in the most general sense the ethos of the Anglican Church at that critical age . . .' (The Revd A. S. Duncan-Jones [1879–1955] held incumbencies including St Paul's, Knightsbridge, before being elevated to the Deanery of Chichester Cathedral in 1929; his works include *Archbishop Laud* [1927].) See *Anglicanism: The Thought and Practice of the Church of England, Illustrated from the Religious Literature of the Seventeenth Century*, ed. Paul Elmer More and Frank L. Cross (SPCK, 1935).

TO *Harold Rosenberg*[1]   CC

13 March 1931   [*The Criterion*]

Dear Sir,

I must apologise for having kept your essay so long.[2] I found it extremely interesting but as I should be unable to use it in the *Criterion* for some time to come, and cannot definitely accept it now, I am returning it to you with the hope that I may see more of your work from time to time.

                                 Yours faithfully,
                                 [T. S. Eliot]
                                 Editor

TO *F. McEachran*   CC

16 March 1931   [*The Criterion*]

Dear McEachran,

I am sending you a book, *The Prospects of Humanism*, by Lawrence Hyde, which I have dipped into but which looks to me very intelligent. You are flatteringly mentioned in it but I want from you a review of it for our June number, up to 1000 words, and I hope that you will agree with me that the book deserves it.[3]

                                 Yours sincerely,
                                 [T. S. Eliot]

1–Harold Rosenberg (1906–78), American writer, philosopher, art critic (an early fan of abstract expressionism, he coined the term 'Action Painting') and political commentator,read law at St Lawrence College, New York; Professor of Social Thought in the Art Department, University of Chicago; art critic for the *New Yorker*; author of *The Tradition of the New* (1959), *Art on the Edge* (1975), and studies of Willem de Kooning, Saul Steinberg and Arshile Gorky.
2–'Character-Change and the Drama', submitted on 3 Nov. 1930: 'This is one of a series of essays in which I am attempting to show some of the limits of the relation of scientific psychology to poetic and dramatic thought, and also to suggest certain affirmative ideas bearing on poetic creation. The enclosed article treats of the construction of dramatic characters.' The essay would be published in *Symposium* in 1932.
3–McEachran replied on 17 Mar., 'I am very pleased to find myself treated so nicely in it, and shall be glad to review it. It seems among other points to be explicit on the subject of Middleton Murry whose ideas I have not really understood hitherto.' Review in *C.* 10 (July 1931), 750–5.

TO *Edmund Blunden*   TS Reading

16 March 1931   Faber & Faber Ltd

Dear Blunden,

Madame de Bassiano, the proprietor of the French review, *Commerce*, has written to me to ask whether it would be possible for her to publish a few of the poems of Wilfred Owen newly included in your edition, in her review. She would publish the English text with a French translation. I know Madame de Bassiano and *Commerce* very well, have frequently contributed to it myself, and am sure that the translation will be as good as possible. Also, the poem would be properly paid for, not at the ordinary French rates. I should be very grateful if you would let me know whether it is possible to make such an arrangement.[1]

Yours sincerely,
T. S. Eliot

TO *Ezra Pound*   TS Beinecke

16 March 1931   Faber & Faber Ltd

Dear Babbit,

Yours, dated the 11th February, presumably a secretarial error for the 11th or some other instant (*corrente*) is received.[2] I should undoubtedly find both pleasure and profit, in what proportions I cannot say, in advance, in reading your criticisms of my theological prose style. Whether the *Criterion* is a suitable medium is difficult to say beforehand, because I have in general tried to avoid using that organ for either boosting or depressing my works. Please regard this as the chief difficulty and give it your serious consideration.

Yours,
T. S. Eliot

1–Blunden replied (19 Mar.) that he would forward the request to Chatto & Windus, 'with my emphatic desire that they (& Mrs Owen) should readily agree with Mme de Bassiano's request'.
2–Not found.

TO *Ursula Roberts*   Copy of TS

17 March 1931   Faber & Faber Ltd

Dear Mrs Roberts,

Thank you for your letter of the 12th and for sending me the *Contemporary Review* with your article, which I read with great interest.[1] Of course I don't agree with it at all, but found it none the less interesting. I could not help wishing, however, that you had included some allusions to the possibilities of monastic orders and sisterhoods, and especially orders of nursing sisters.

I ought not, however, to waste your time with my own views. The point is this. I have discussed the matter with the Chairman and he agrees with me that it would be unwise from our point of view to attempt any more pamphlets about or around the Lambeth Conference. We had in fact originally intended to have only one pamphlet on the subject, and my pamphlet was only called forth as a rejoinder to the other which we published. We think that it would be best to wait for some later occasion – as the majority of our pamphlets are so definitely occasional – before having another one on Church matters.

Yours very sincerely,
T. S. Eliot

TO *M. C. D'Arcy*   cc

17 March 1931   [Faber & Faber Ltd]

My dear D'Arcy,

Thank you for your interesting note.[2] It strikes me that some of your objections illustrate just that difference of temperament or point of view, or whatever one calls it, at which I tried to hint, but that is very difficult

---

1–Roberts's 'Women & Lambeth' (*Contemporary Review*, Mar. 1931) argued for the ordination of women in the Church of England. She asked in her letter, 'Would there be any chance of your considering a fuller paper on the same issue for the Criterion miscellanies?'
2–D'Arcy thanked TSE (10 Mar.) for *Thoughts after Lambeth*. 'I am not directly interested in Lambeth, but I am very much interested in the reactions of a person like yourself to it. I have no right however to criticise your point of view, though I own you at times took me by surprise. May I say this much, though, without offence. What you praise & what you say you hoped it might have done seems to me to rest on a religio-humanistic (if you will forgive the compound) & not on a religious or at any rate supernatural basis. You give me the impression too of writing as one detached from yourself; or shall I say a general in consultation with a staff.'

to establish. You made, however, one very shrewd remark which caused me much amusement. It was quite correct, except for a slight inaccuracy in the metaphor – in this case the general staff was largely more eminent than the commander.

Would there be any chance of your accepting an invitation to a meal with us during the holidays?

Yours ever sincerely,
[T. S. Eliot]

TO *G. Rostrevor Hamilton*[1]   CC

17 March 1931   [*The Criterion*]

Dear Mr Hamilton,

I must apologise for my delay in answering your letter of the 18th January, but you will have understood, I hope, that there was nothing I could do at the moment.[2] I should certainly be willing to consider an article on Conrad Aiken at some point, but essays on poets, especially on living poets, have to be carefully sifted in, and it happens at present that I have three or four articles on modern poets to work off. Obviously, I cannot make up the whole number out of them. So if you get the article done, I should be very glad to see it, but I would not hold it up in such a way as to interfere with its possible publication elsewhere.

Yours sincerely,
[T. S. Eliot]

TO *John Middleton Murry*   TS Northwestern

17 March 1931   Faber & Faber Ltd

My dear John,

Thank you very much for your letter[3] which was more charitable than I had any right to expect. I am quite prepared to believe that I am too

---

1 – George Rostrevor Hamilton (1888–1967), poet and critic, studied classics at Oxford and worked as a civil servant: he was knighted in 1951. *The Tell-Tale Article: A Critical Approach to Modern Poetry* (1949) includes a section on the achievement of TSE.

2 – Hamilton, who had elicited from TSE an undertaking to write the preface for a projected study of Conrad Aiken, wrote to say he had been unable to find a publisher for such a book; for want of that outcome, he wondered if TSE might publish an article on Aiken in the *Criterion*.

3 – Not found.

inclined to score debating points. This, I daresay, is partly due to a strong political heredity, but perhaps you overlook the fact that the pamphlet is primarily a debating pamphlet and that the methods seemed to me those suitable to the genre. They would be illegitimate, certainly, if I had no serious convictions underneath. But I am sure that the flippant word respectability does stand in my own mind for a certain adaptation of your philosophy to the contemporary mind. From your point of view, which I do, I think, perceive a little, such a term is of course grotesque, and from your point of view it might, I daresay, stick much better to myself, but to me it means something of which I am convinced.

By the way, have you seen Lawrence Hyde's new book[1] which contains a good deal of criticism of yourself to which I should largely subscribe?

I should very much like to come down to stay with you if I could come to stay with anybody, but you know more or less how I am situated. Is there any possibility of seeing you, even for a few moments, on one of your occasional days in town?

I hope that your wife's condition is not desperate, but I will not intrude with questions.

Affectionately yours,
Tom

TO *Will Spens*   CC

17 [or] 18 March 1931[2]   [Faber & Faber Ltd]

Dear Spens.

Many thanks for your note.[3] I had been hoping for your (at least qualified) approval; but I am mystified to learn that you had already seen a copy, as I despatched one to you among the first.

I should very much like to come down for a weekend next term (I had already half promised Pickthorn) and my wife too if possible. If it becomes possible, may I let you know later?

1 – *The Prospects of Humanism* (1931).
2 – 18 Mar. must be correct.
3 – Spens belatedly thanked TSE (17 Mar.) 'for sending me your pamphlet. As a matter of fact I had already got it, and I cannot say how glad I was to see the line you took over the whole thing, and in particular Resolution 15. I need not add that I was very grateful for what you said about my article.' (The article praised by TSE in *Thoughts* was 'Lambeth Conference Reviews: II. (a.) and (b.). – The Life and Witness of the Christian Community: Marriage and Sex', *Theology*, 336–50.) Spens wished to talk with TSE about ecclesiastical affairs. 'Would it be possible for you to spend a weekend with me next term? If Mrs Eliot cares to come please bring her.'

What a pragmatical fellow Dark is. But I was sorry to see him descend to innuendo against some of those who disagree with him.

Sincerely yours,

[T. S. Eliot]

TO *Hugh Sykes Davies* CC

18 March 1931 *[The Criterion]*

Dear Sykes Davies,

Did I tell you that I liked very much your note on Jeans[1] and was sorry that I could not give you more space, but as I explained, we had already dealt with Jeans fairly thoroughly, and I am afraid that soon he will be so prolific that we must ignore him completely. I should be very glad, however, if you cared to write a very short note, say 400 words, on his new book, *The Stars in Their Courses*, which appears to be merely popular astronomical lectures, somewhat less elementary than those of the late Sir Robert Ball. But I won't send the book unless I hear from you, because I asked the Cambridge Press to send it, and if it is not worth noticing, I ought to return it to them.

I am not yet sure whether I shall be able to use your LUCRETIUS in June, although it has been set up. The only difficulty is that I have an accumulation of several essays on Poets, and the appearance of a new edition of Wilfred Owen's Poems makes it rather desirable to publish quickly an essay on him which I have in hand. If I do not use the LUCRETIUS in June it will have to be September.[2] Meanwhile, are there any new books which might interest you for a June review?

Yours sincerely,

[T. S. Eliot]

1 – Review of Sir James Jeans, *The Mysterious Universe*, in C. 10 (Apr. 1931), 514–16. Sykes Davies wrote of his submission, on 30 Jan. 1931: 'The criticism of mathematics is developed mainly from Vico, but there are things remarkably like it in the Summa Theologica of Aquinas – do you remember – in Qu. 3, part ii (1st part), fifth article, especially the Reply Obj. 1 – "The asserted likeness of the practical intellect to God is one of proportion; that is to say, by reason of its standing in relation to what it knows, as God does to what he knows". Thomas could really have dealt adequately with Sir James. I am sorry that I fall so far short of him.

'Did you see the Bishop of London's speech to the Upper House of the Convocation of Canterbury? "Books like those written by Sir James Jeans make the Incarnation more credible than it was before". I should love to hear Thomas on that; though perhaps Scotus would have been even better.'

2 – 'Notes on Lucretius', C. 11 (Oct. 1931), 25–43.

TO *Ian Parsons*[1]   TS Source unknown

18 March 1931   *The Criterion*

Dear Parsons,

I have kept your essay on Wilfred Owen a very long time.[2] That is partly due to working off articles previously accepted or commissioned, and partly due to the necessity for varying as much as possible the subject matter of any one number. But now I have just got Edmund Blunden's new edition which I see your firm have published and I am wondering whether you could be so kind as to alter, or add a few sentences to, your essay to mention the book in comparison with the earlier edition. I don't mean to turn your essay into a review but merely to notice the book and make it the occasion for producing your essay in June. As I say, I think it means only adding a few sentences.[3]

                                        Yours sincerely,
                                        T. S. Eliot

TO *R. Ruggles Gates*[4]   CC

18 March 1931   [Faber & Faber Ltd]

Dear Sir,

Mr G. H. Pitt-Rivers has suggested to me that I might be able to obtain your opinion on a long essay on Eugenics which he has written and

1 – Ian Parsons (1906–80), who read English at Trinity College, Cambridge, was editor of *The Cambridge Review*. On graduation he joined Chatto & Windus, initially as a typographer but presently as a junior partner under the chairmanship of Harold Raymond. His successes included Empson's *Seven Types of Ambiguity* (1930) and Leavis's *New Bearings in English Poetry* (1932). In 1954 he became chairman of Chatto & Windus (which had taken over the Hogarth Press in 1946); and he was President of the Publishers' Association, 1957–9. Later years saw Chatto & Windus merge with Jonathan Cape, 1969, and with the Bodley Head, 1973: Parsons became joint chairman. His publications include *The Progress of Poetry: An Anthology of Verse from Hardy to the Present* (ed., 1936), *Men Who March Away* (ed., 1965), and *The Collected Works of Isaac Rosenberg* (1979). He was made a CBE in 1971, and retired in 1975.

2 – Submitted on 3 Apr. 1930.

3 – Parsons completely agreed with the suggestion (19 Mar.), and returned his essay on 18 May: 'The Poems of Wilfred Owen (1893–1918)', C. 10 (July 1931), 658–69.

4 – R. Ruggles Gates (1882–1962), Professor of Biology at King's College, London, specialised in heredity and variation in plant species; but he also undertook research on heredity and evolution in humans. Works include *The Mutation Factor in Evolution* (1915), *Heredity and Eugenics* (1923), and *Heredity in Man* (1929; extended as *Human Genetics*, 2 vols, 1946).

submitted for our Criterion Miscellany, as we are doubtful whether this essay is suitable for our purposes.[1] If you have the time to read it and give me your opinion of its suitability, I shall be extremely grateful to you, and if you are willing to do so, I will make quite clear, in sending the manuscript to you, the particular place which in our view it ought to be qualified to occupy. It is not so much a question of confirming the scientific accuracy of the work as considering its fitness for the public which our pamphlets address.

For such specialised opinions we, of course, like other publishers, always pay a reader's fee.

I am,
Yours faithfully,
[T. S. Eliot]
Director.

TO *E. McKnight Kauffer*   TS Morgan

19 March 1931   *The Criterion*

Dear Ted,

I should have written to you over the weekend, but that I hoped we should see you on Monday evening, though it was very short notice. My thanks at the door were quite inadequate, especially after examining the book, and I feel almost embarrassed by the receipt of so magnificent a gift. But what is more important, I do sincerely congratulate you on your success with what was surely a most difficult task of illustration; all of your illustrations delight me.

I hope we can make some engagement to meet very soon.
Yours ever,
T. S. E.

1–Pitt-Rivers (Eugenics Society) submitted his 'corrected' essay on 10 Mar.: 'The main points are (1) eugenic problems and the increase or decrease of the best or worst elements of the population underlie all political questions and are by far the most important. (2) We must pay attention to causes instead of tinkering with symptoms. (3) Opponents are hostile either for irrelevant reasons or because they don't understand. (4) Public opinion must be increasingly aroused.' (He also sent TSE a copy of the 2nd edn of *Eugenic Sterilization*, published by the Committee for Legalising Eugenic Sterilization.) See too Donald J. Childs, *Modernism and Eugenics: Woolf, Eliot, Yeats, and the Culture of Degeneration* (2001), 75–98.

TO *R. Ruggles Gates*   CC

23 March 1931   [Faber & Faber Ltd]

Dear Sir,

Thank you for your note of the 19th.[1] I am sending Captain Pitt-Rivers' typescript herewith.

What we questioned was not so much the accuracy of the author's knowledge, of which none of us is competent to judge, but rather the suitability of his essay for any one definite public. That is to say, for enlightened readers who are already persuaded or who are inclined to believe that Eugenics is a serious study which has a great deal to do with the amelioration of mankind, this essay does not seem to carry the matter very much further. On the other hand, for the larger public which is either prejudiced against practical Eugenics or else merely seeking information, no very clear conclusions seem to emerge. I feel myself that the author has perhaps attempted to deal with too many ramifications of the problem and has not followed any one of them out to a practical conclusion. The present social and economic situation, which tends to reduce the numbers of the better parts of the community, and to encourage the reproduction of the least desirable, is a very important problem in itself and it does not seem to me adequately solved merely by encouraging the lower and lowest classes to limit their families severely.

I feel that the author should either assume more intelligence and goodwill on the part of his audience, and carry their ideas further, or else that he should, in simple and clear language, lay a practical programme and its advantages before the uninstructed.

I am sending you two able pamphlets on cognate subjects which may serve to give some clue to the mode of treatment required. I am very well aware of the difficulty of giving an opinion for the particular purpose of our requirements, and in view of the particular criticisms which I have indicated but I shall be very grateful for any comments that occur to you.

Yours very truly,
[T. S. Eliot]
Director.

1 – Ruggles Gates agreed to offer an opinion on Pitt-Rivers's essay on Eugenics.

TO *Aldous Huxley*   CC

23 March 1931   [Faber & Faber Ltd]

My dear Aldous,

Very many thanks for your letter of Thursday[1] which I intended to answer on Friday night, but as usually happens with me, I wanted to write at some length and therefore postponed it. I hope that you are still free for lunch tomorrow. The Athenaeum would do for me quite well, or if anywhere else suits you better, will you ring up and let me know?

I hope that your play may keep you here some little time.[2] Is Maria with you? I know that Vivienne would love to see you both.[3]

Yours ever,
[T. S. E.]

TO *William Force Stead*   TS Beinecke

28 March 1931   68 Clarence Gate Gardens

My dear Stead,

I am delighted to hear that you are going to have a holiday, which I am sure you need very badly, in the South with our Robert (yes, I prefer his proper name)[4] and I shall be happy to lunch with you on Tuesday at 12:30 and I will bring the Clock; I don't remember a Dante, but I dare say my wife has put it away with the Clock.

You will I hope have forgiven me for failing to answer two letters[5] – I should have enjoyed very much staying with you and listening to Temple – but I assure you I appreciated your kindness which never fails.

Ever affectionately,
T. S. Eliot

1 – Not found.
2 – AH's play *The World of Light: A Comedy in Three Acts* – a satire on spiritualism – opened at the Royalty Theatre on 30 Mar.; it was not a success, and closed early.
3 – AH recorded at about this time that Vivien's face was 'mottled, like ecchymmotic spots, and the house smelled like a hospital' (cited in Ackroyd, 158).
4 – Robert Sencourt.
5 – Not found.

TO *Conrad Aiken*[1]   TS Huntington

28 March 1931   68 Clarence Gate Gardens

Dear Conrad,
   Yours of the 26th received – with mss.[2] which I haven't had time to
study yet, but it looks interesting – the Highest compliment I can pay to
poetry – why does nearly everybody try to make it as Dull as possible –
influence of Bridges perhaps? – Anyway, Peters must be getting very lazy
– but in considering this, what about seeing the Magnum Opuss – if it is
coming out in U.S.A. in the Fall, can't you let the Opuss out of the Sleeve
for a private view directly?[3] And will you try to save up a few nickels
and come to the next *Criterion*, mid-April (the budding musk-rose, mid
April's eldest child)? I am only temporarily solvent myself because I have
not paid my income tax for three years.
                                        Yours ever,
                                        Tom

TO *Stephen Spender*   TS Northwestern

28 March 1931   68 Clarence Gate Gardens

Dear Spender,
   It is a long time that I have not answered your letter,[4] but that always
happens with me – I have so many letters to write that are concerned
merely with one or two immediate and usually practical matters that the
others are deferred from week to week. I am glad to hear that Germany
wears so well. I hardly know anyone in Berlin, as I told you; and probably
Prinz Rohan[5] and Clauss would only worry you with general intellectual

---

1 – Conrad Aiken (1889–1973), American poet and critic: see Biographical Register.
2 – Aiken sent *The Coming Forth by Day of Osiris Jones*, which Scribners was to publish
in June. His agent, A. D. Peters, had reported that there was no hope of finding a British
publisher for it. 'It's an oddity [but] the American Scribners are quite excited about it.'
3 – 'To this I might add that I have up my sleeve a much heftier book, Preludes for Memnon,
which will come out in America in the fall, and this too I could send along, should Faber
be inclined to take an interest.' He wrote (30 Mar.) in answer to this letter: 'Herewith, as
you suggest, the 63 preludes for Memnon. I'm sorry the typing is so damned dim – faulty
carbon . . .'
4 – Spender's letter not found.
5 – Prince Karl Anton Rohan (1898–1975), Austrian landowner and political writer, resided
at Castle Albrechtsberg; he was proprietor of the *Europäische Revue* (Berlin), 1925–36. His
publications include *Umbruch der Zeit 1923–30* (1930), *Schicksalsstunde Europas* (1937),
and *Heimat Europa: Erinnerungen und Erfahrungen* (1954).

discussion of the condition of Europe, and I don't want to check your delivery, I hope speedy and comparatively painless, of your novel. Have you found anything worth reading? There is a philosopher named Martin Heidegger[1] – a disciple of the great Husserl,[2] who really is good, I think, though far from lucid – whom I have been agonising over. I am delighted to hear that you have been at the late Beethoven – I have the A minor quartet on the gramophone, and find it quite inexhaustible to study. There is a sort of heavenly or at least more than human gaity [*sic*] about some of his later things which one imagines might come to oneself as the fruit of reconciliation and relief after immense suffering; I should like to get something of that into verse once before I die.

I was amused by your opinion of Lewis on Hitler. Have you seen his book by that name, just out?[3] I had thought of asking you to review it; the trouble is that unless a review is wholly laudatory, it does not seem to give Lewis much pleasure; furthermore, as Lewis is so much on the right side, so far as he is on any side, it would be inexpedient and bad for the uneducated public if an unfavourable review of any of his books appeared in the *Criterion*. That is why we have reviewed nothing of his since *Time and Western Man*. However, may I send you the book to look at; and you will let me know whether you can speak well enough of it or not?

English politics seem to me about as depressing as German at present, though not so uproarious. But I understand that three men were bound over and one fined forty shillings during the progress of the Duff Cooper election in St George's.[4]

I like the poems you sent – but as I said, how can you get seriously to work until you have unloaded this novel – then you must try something of greater *envergure*.[5] I should like to publish a few more in the *Criterion* in the autumn, out of a selection – I sympathise with your being in no hurry to publish a volume – but it helps one in self-criticism, I think, to see something one has written objectified into print.

Yours ever sincerely,
T. S. Eliot

1 – Martin Heidegger (1889–1976): existentialist and phenomenologist; Professor of Philosophy, Freiburg, from 1928; acclaimed for *Sein und Zeit* (1927; *Being and Time*, 1962); traduced for supporting Hitler and the Nazi Party.
2 – Edmund Husserl (1859–1938): Jewish-born philosopher and mathematician; founder of the School of Phenomenology; taught at Freiburg, 1916–28.
3 – WL's *Hitler* was published by Chatto & Windus on 26 Mar.
4 – Alfred Duff Cooper (1890–1954), Conservative MP, lost his seat in the General Election of 1929 but regained it by way of a by-election in the St George's Division of Westminster, 1931.
5 – *The Temple* was ultimately to be published by F&F in 1988. *Envergure* = wingspan.

TO *Douglas Jerrold*   CC

30 March 1931   [Faber & Faber Ltd]

Dear Jerrold,

Thank you for your letter of the 27th.¹ Your scheme seems to me to
be perfectly practical. As for times and days, lunch suits me for a regular
appointment better than any other time. Wednesday is a bad day because
I always have a committee here at 2.45. Thursday is all right except that
once a month we have our Board Meeting that afternoon, and it is not
always the same Thursday in the month; so that the best day for me is
Tuesday; though for a meeting next week Thursday would do equally
well. Will you drop me a line or ring up about it next week?²

                                        Sincerely yours,
                                        [T. S. Eliot]

TO *The Editor,* The Dublin Review³

April 1931   [Faber & Faber Ltd]

                    Classicism and Romanticism

Sir,

I have read with much interest the correspondence of Mr Maritain
and Mr Belgion in your January issue.⁴ If I venture to intervene, it is not

1-Jerrold hoped to have lunch once a month with TSE and J. C. Squire – 'to talk over
the critical side of the *English Review*', as Jerrold told Squire in a letter of 26 Mar. He
affirmed to TSE: 'the work which interests us will I am pretty certain be done entirely
between ourselves'.
2-They met for lunch on 9 Apr., and agreed to have regular monthly business meetings.
3-Text taken from *The Dublin Review* 188: 377 (Apr. 1931), 313.
4-'Correspondence', *The Dublin Review* 188: 376 (Jan. 1931), 134–6. Montgomery
Belgion had severely criticised Maritain's *Art et scolastique* in *The Dublin Review* 187:
375 (Oct. 1930), 201–15. Maritain posted his riposte in the *Dublin Review* 188: 376 (Jan.
1931), 134–5; and Belgion replied to it in the same issue, 135–6. Maritain had argued
against Belgion's romanticist views: 'Je pense toutefois que ce qui distingue les beaux-arts
des autres arts, ce n'est pas seulement la situation sociale de l'artiste qui les pratique, c'est
avant tout que dans ces arts l'élément spirituel introduit par le contact avec la beauté deviant
prépondérant.' He went on: 'Si cet approfondissement a été ressenti par le romantisme sous
les espèces d'une déification de l'artiste et des passions, ce n'est pas la première fois que
quelque chose de vrai est véhiculé et déformé par une hérésie. Au surplus je tiens pour
périmée la dispute du classique et du romantique. Avouerai-je que devant certains défenseurs
des éternels principes classiques je trouve au romantisme des charmes enivrants. Que T. S.
Eliot me pardonne, pour qui j'ai tant d'admiration et d'amitié. Il sait bien d'ailleurs que
ce n'est pas à lui que je pense ici' (135). See further Arthur Sherbo, 'Eliotiana', *Studies in
Bibliography* 50 (1997), 401–7.

to correct any misstatement of my own views, as Mr Maritain does not impute any to me. I dare say that I write primarily from the flattery of being mentioned so charmingly by Mr Maritain, who should know very well my very high opinion of *him*; but secondarily to cast doubt on two of his sentences.

Mr Maritain admits that '*devant certain défenseurs des éternels principes classiques je trouve au romantisme des charmes enivrants*'. This admission is robbed of its piquancy when it is perceived to be one which everyone may make. For he is contrasting, not classical theory with romantic theory, nor classical works with romantic works, but certain critics (I suppose) with certain poets. The comparison is not in kind. If he said that after reading La Harpe[1] for half an hour he found inebriating charm in Verlaine no one would be likely to protest. And, on the other hand, I cannot conceive anyone finding such charm either in *romanticism* or in *classicism*; whereas, if one finds it at all, one will probably find it in works of art of both types.

I quite agree that the 'dispute' between classicism and romanticism is *périmée*; but then it always was. The terms do not mean quite the same thing for any two people, or for any two decades; and they even shift their meaning for the same observer considering different ages and material. They are affected by every new work of art. Yet such apparently unsatisfactory terms have a way of being extraordinarily useful.

I am, Sir,
Your obedient servant,
T. S. Eliot.

TSE, who was a friend of Maritain, remarked, in *The Idea of a Christian Society* (1939), 6: 'I am deeply indebted to the works of Jacques Maritain, especially his *Humanisme intégral.*' 1 – Jean François de La Harpe (1739–1830): writer, playwright and critic.

TO *Richard Rees*[1]   CC

2 April 1931   [*The Criterion*]

Dear Sir Richard Rees,

Thank you for your note of the 2nd, and for having *Son of Woman* sent to me.[2] As a matter of fact, I had already received an advance copy from Cape, and had just read it for the first time. Meanwhile I had spoken to some of my colleagues about it and they were of the opinion that I ought to review the book myself for the *Criterion*. After reading it, I am of the same opinion myself, and I think that this would be more suitable for me than writing an article for you, in as much as I do not know Lawrence's work well enough to justify an article. I am therefore having the copy returned direct to the *Adelphi*.

I am immensely interested in the book, and think it one of the most brilliant pieces of writing that Murry has done.

Yours sincerely,

[T. S. Eliot]

1 – Sir Richard Rees, 2nd Baronet (1900–70) – diplomat, writer, artist – the original of Ravelston in George Orwell's *Keep the Aspidistra Flying* – was editor of *The Adelphi*, 1930–6. His works include *Brave Men: A Study of D. H. Lawrence and Simone Weil* (1958), *George Orwell: Fugitive from the Camp of Victory* (1961), *Simone Weil: A Sketch for a Portrait* (1966).

2 – Rees asked TSE to review for *The Adelphi* JMM's *Son of Woman: The Story of D. H. Lawrence*. JMM inscribed a copy on 15 May 1931: 'For T. S. Eliot affectionately John Middleton Murry.' (TSE Library)

See TSE's review, C. 10 (July 1931), 768–74. 'What Mr Murry shows, and demonstrates with a terrible pertinacity throughout Lawrence's work, is the emotional dislocation of a "mother-complex". (It should show also how inappropriate is the common designation of "Œdipus complex".) And he makes clear that Lawrence was pretty well aware of what was wrong; and that Lawrence, throughout the rest of his life, was a strange mixture of sincerity or clairvoyance with self-deception – or rather with the effort towards self-deception . . . It is an appalling narrative of spiritual pride, nourished by ignorance, and possibly also by the consciousness of great powers and humble birth. Now, the "mother-complex" of Lawrence does not seem to me in itself a sign of the times . . . Such family life, with such consequences to a sensitive child, can hardly have taken place only in the latter part of the nineteenth century . . . [Lawrence] would probably have been always an unhappy man in this world; there is nothing unusual about that; many people have to be unhappy in this world . . . and some learn not to make a fuss about it, or at least to strive towards, a kind of peace which Lawrence never knew . . . I was brought up outside the Christian Fold, in Unitarianism; and in the form of Unitarianism in which I was instructed, things were either black or white . . . What a pity that [Lawrence] did not understand the simple truth that of any two human beings each has privacies which the other cannot penetrate, and boundaries which the other must not transgress, and that yet human intimacy can be wonderful and life-giving . . . And that the love of two human beings is only made perfect in the love of God.'

Easter [5 April] 1931   [Faber & Faber Ltd]

My dear Lord Halifax,

I am returning to you immediately De La Taille and the Bourget novel.[1] I should not retain the De La Taille longer, because it would take me a very long time indeed to digest the whole; so if I have time and occasion to study it more carefully, I shall get it by the London Library or purchase. I have read the first essay carefully, and glanced at the others, one particularly which deals with religious symbolism. On some points he confirmed what I already believed – as the unity of the Passion and Sacrifice – and he provides valuable suggestion on one point that had puzzled me, the Agony of Gethsemane after the Last Supper – I incline to feel that sometimes he is over-ingenious; and I feel that the term 'symbolism' in his context needs very careful logical definition, as the 'symbolism' in the Eucharist seems to me *sui generis*, and in danger of confusion with ordinary types of symbolism. But I speak only as a beginner; I look forward to reading Vonier.

I am on much more familiar ground with Bourget – he develops a thesis with all his accustomed skill – no one else has ever handled the *roman à thèse* better. There seem to me two defects – the common French habit of involving the Faith with the *fille ainée de l'Eglise*, and consequently with French Nationalism – we could well bear to be reminded that there were German counterparts to Le Gallic. The other weakness is more personal; his surgeon is the old-fashioned type of scientist of the time of Taine; and the real issue today, I am sure, is between the orthodox and dogmatic Christian and the sentimental physicist – the enemy of the moment is not even such dogmatic atheism as that of Russell, but the doctrine-less religiosity of Eddington and Jeans.

With many thanks,

       Yours very sincerely,
       [T. S. Eliot]

1 – Paul Bourget, *Le Sens de la Mort* (1916).

TO *Tom Faber*   TS Valerie Eliot

Easter [5 April] 1931   Faber & Faber Ltd

Dear Tom

   I believe that you are to have a Birthday soon, and I think that you will
then be Four Years Old (I am not Clever at Arithmetic) but that is a Great
Age, so I thought we might send out this
                         INVITATION
       TO ALL POLLICLE DOGS & JELLICLE CATS[1]
         TO COME TO THE BIRTHDAY OF
                    THOMAS FABER

Pollicle Dogs and Jellicle Cats!
Come from your Kennels & Houses & Flats;
Pollicle Dogs & Cats, draw near;
Jellicle Cats & Dogs, Appear;
Come with your Ears & your Whiskers & Tails
Over the Mountains & Valleys of Wales.
This is your ONLY CHANCE THIS YEAR,
Your ONLY CHANCE to – what do you spose? –
Brush Up your Coats and Turn out your Toes,
And come with a Hop & a Skip & a Dance –
Because, for this year, it's your ONLY CHANCE
To come with your Whiskers & Tails & Hair on
To
        Ty Glyn Aeron
           Ciliau Aeron[2] –   (A musicle
Because you are INVITED to Come   Instrument
With a Flute & a Fife & a Fiddle & Drum,   that makes a
     With a Fiddle, a Fife, & a Drum & a Tabor   Joyful
     To the Birthday Party of   Noise)
        THOMAS ERLE FABER!

1–On 25 June 1959 TSE's secretary would explain to C. S. Kreiter (who asked about
copyright in the word 'jellicle'): '[Mr Eliot] does not wish to copyright the word "jellicle"
and is quite content that it should be used without acknowledgement, so long as its use
conforms to the definition of Jellicle Cats given in his poem about them. And jellicle, by
the way, is not a diminutive of "angelical' [as Kreiter had supposed] but is a diminutive of
"Jellylorum" which was the name of a cat of that description which Mr Eliot once owned.'
TSE told Jennifer Fairman (aged eleven) on 14 Apr. 1961: 'I also had a Jellicle Cat which ran
away, but I think he was frightened being out of doors by a thunder storm and ran in the
wrong direction. Anyway, we never saw him again. His name was Jellylorum.'
2–Ty Glyn Aeron, Ciliau Aeron, Cardiganshire: the Faber family's holiday home.

Oh But P.S. we mustn't send out this Invitation after All, Because, if All the Pollicle Dogs & Jellicle Cats came (and of course they all *would* come) then all the roads would be blocked up, and what's more, they would track muddy feet into the House, and your Mother wouldn't Like that at ALL, and what's More Still, you would have to give them ALL a Piece of your Birthday Cake, and there would be so Many that there wouldn't be any Cake left for *you*, and that would be Dreadful, so we won't send out this invitation,

so no more for the Present from your

Silly Uncle
Tom.[1]

TO *Ernest Rhys*   cc

6 April 1931   [Faber & Faber Ltd]

Dear Mr Rhys,

My sins have come to roost – but I ought certainly to have written to you before now.[2] I did hope to have my essay completed by the end of March – but a small theological pamphlet I had to write cost me very much more labour than I anticipated, and pushed forward all my other undertakings – I have just finished an essay on Donne promised two years ago; and this month am giving, solely from mercenary motives, three B.B.C. talks on Dryden. That is difficult only for the reason that I have already said all I have to say about the subject. Meanwhile I can proceed with my preparation of Pascal – a subject on which I find I knew even less than I thought I did – and hope to let you have it by the end of April. Does this inconvenience you, and Messrs. Dent, very seriously? I feel cordially contrite about it.[3]

Yours sincerely,
[T. S. Eliot]

---

1 – Tom Faber replied (undated): 'It is a funny letter – why do you think you are silly? I think you are MY BEST WRITER and MY BEST DRAWER too . . . Why did you send me a funny letter like that? & I liked the letter very much . . . So love from TOM *Dictated*.'

2 – Rhys asked (16 Mar.) after TSE's progress with the Introduction to Pascal.

3 – Rhys (9 Apr.) requested TSE to submit the preface by the end of April. TSE was sent the proofs of his piece on 9 May, and returned them by 19 May.

TO *Montgomery Belgion*   CC

6 April 1931   [*The Criterion*]

Dear Belgion,

I am reminded by just having read your admirable & persuasive Soviet essay in the *Dublin*[1] that I have been intending to write to you for a long time. I wonder if you found satisfactory lodging, and whether the work on *This Quarter* promises well, and is at all interesting.[2] So I hope I may hear from you again soon.

You should have received your copy of the much delayed April *Criterion* by now. It seemed to me, that as I had to put the Richards retort and your letter into that number,[3] and also as I found myself with a large number of reviews (Robertson always takes up as much room as three ordinary writers) and finally, as your review is still very long, and as a considerable time has elapsed since the books were published, that it will be best to set it up once more, as an article again, and use it thus next time. I hope this will not Annoy you: but with all respect your review obstinately remains an article!

Jeans's new guide to the stars does not seem to add much to anything except Jeans's total sales, so I don't propose to review it at all. Murry's book on Lawrence is an interesting, if rather ghoulish study, and I want to write about it myself – it throws more light on Murry, however, than on Lawrence.

                                        Yours ever,
                                        [T. S. Eliot]

1–Belgion, 'Statecraft in Russia', *The Dublin Review* 188: 377 (Apr. 1931), 183–215. 'The Russian Government, despite the programme which, it claims, makes it superior to all other existing governments, is actually no different from any other government. It consists of a group of men who, being in power, wish to remain there as long as possible, and are simply doing all they can to that end' (215).
2–Belgion had moved to Paris to work for E. W. Titus, editor of the periodical *This Quarter*.
3–IAR, 'Notes on the Practice of Interpretation', *C.* 10 (Apr. 1931), 412–20; letter by Belgion, *C.* 10 (Apr. 1931), 507.

TO *D. L. Murray* CC

7 April 1931   [*The Criterion*]

Dear Mr Murray,

I have your letter of the 30th, together with the volume of poems, and will try to see that it is given a note of some kind.[1] I am not myself a very good judge of modern verse so that I must pass it on to someone else, with the recommendation.

Yours sincerely,
[T. S. Eliot]
Editor.

TO *Muriel St Clare Byrne*[2] CC

7 April 1931   [*The Criterion*]

Dear Miss St Clair [*sic*] Byrne,

I had already attached the correct name to your appearance long ago, so that there was no question of identity.[3] I have read your paper with much interest and sympathy, but I do not feel, candidly, that the issue is sufficiently important at the present time for me to use it. That does not mean in the least that I should not very much like to see it published, but in a quarterly like the *Criterion* I feel that the issues should be chosen with considerable care. I am afraid I by no means succeed in living up to this ideal, but there the ideal is. For one thing, Housman was certainly a great influence twenty or thirty years ago, and I only just escaped his influence myself, but at the present day I feel that so far as the *Criterion* is concerned, he ought to be left to as tranquil an old age as he is capable of enjoying in the cloisters of Trinity. I hope I am not unduly affected by the fact that he has always been very pleasant to me and that I have found him a delightful person in conversation, but I do feel that it would be rather going out of our way to criticize him now.

---

1 – Murray (editor of *The Times*) submitted 'a little volume of poems by a young man, now at New College, who is likely to become my son-in-law'. He sent also four unpublished poems.
2 – Muriel St Clare Byrne (1895–1983): scholar and lecturer; author of *Elizabethan Life in Town and Country* (1925), *The Elizabethan Home* (1925), and an edition of the letters of Henry VIII; but most famous in later years for the fifty-year labour that produced *The Lisle Letters* (1981) – a selection of the correspondence of Arthur Plantagenet, Lord Lisle: Lord Deputy of Calais, 1533–40 – which TSE encouraged in the early years.
3 – St Clare Byrne identified herself (17 Mar.) as 'the other member of the Shakespeare Assn. council who smokes Caporal!'

May I hope that you will have something else to shew me before long?
Yours very sincerely,
[T. S. Eliot]

TO *G. H. Lane Fox Pitt-Rivers*   CC

8 April 1931   [Faber & Faber Ltd]

Dear Pitt-Rivers,

I only got your typescript back from Ruggles Gates two days before Good Friday, then submitted it to one other Director; after which the Easter holiday intervened.

Whilst Professor Ruggles Gates was wholly complimentary to the matter of your essay – I could show you his letter if it was not a strict rule that we must never disclose Readers' Reports – I feel that the main questions put to him were really out of his way, and not such as he could reasonably be expected to answer with confidence. I made it quite clear, I think, that we did not need any report on questions of scientific accuracy – indeed, anything questionable of this sort would be indifferent to us, as we should be shielded behind your reputation! But one thing of which I believe my fellow directors and I are convinced, is that had we known as much about Eugenics as we have come by experience to know about pamphleteering, we should not have supposed the subject to be capable of treatment in our series. There is one sentence in the Report which indirectly has some bearing upon our present opinion:

> 'The ultimate solution must of course be a sociological one, and as such may have to be proposed by one who is primarily a sociologist; but the sociologists must themselves be educated in these subjects before they can be prepared to offer any solution which really meets the case.'

This does inform me, I believe, (though it was obviously not the intention of the writer) that the whole field you have covered in this essay is more suitably traversed in a longer book; or perhaps even by this same essay (possibly a little developed with statistics and details) published either alone, with a more substantial appearance than we give our pamphlets, or in a specialised series of a different type: hence it would be much more suitable for another publisher. And that is my opinion; not in spite of, but as much because of, my own interest in the essay and my profit in reading it. So I very much hope that it will be published, though the consensus of opinion of my Board prevents our publishing it ourselves.

I remain of my first opinion, when I found so many problems, related to Eugenics, touched upon, each of which seemed to me adequate for a pamphlet in itself, if the state of science is such as to make any dogmatic conclusions possible. For instance, there are (1) the propagation of aments, 'moral imbeciles', and borderline cases; (2) the effect of the dole, which raises also the moral question of the 'right' of any couple to have as many children as they choose, or not; (3) inbreeding (a most interesting point) – what practical guidance have we as to who should marry their cousins, and what provision could be made for accumulating genetic information about every family in the country; (4) Eugenics and Anti-Semitism; (5) comparison of our society with primitive and even with mediaeval organisation; (6) maternal versus infant mortality: what is to be done about it?

Then questions are raised in the reader's mind, such as, what qualities are desirable or not to breed for? and as not all good qualities can co-exist in the same individual, how are they to be distributed? is there no danger, in eliminating the unfit, of eliminating the exceptional genius as well, and reducing mankind to uniformity? is it possible at the present stage to discriminate with certainty between true Eugenics and false? I also fear that a much stronger case can be made out for the Church than you suppose – as well as a much stronger case *against* it (I am not a Roman Catholic) and I do not believe that the theological argument can be disposed of just in passing.

All these considerations make the essay very stimulating to a person like myself – and I am much in your debt for what I have learned from it and from you in conversation – but militate against its success for the purpose we had in mind.

Will you let me know when you are next in town and give me the pleasure of lunching with me?

Yours sincerely,
[T. S. Eliot]

TO *Michael Sayers*   CC

9 April 1931   [Faber & Faber Ltd]

Dear Sayers,

It is very difficult to advise without more information. I know very little about South Africa, and know no one there; and on the face of it, it seems to me unwise to go out there without acquaintance, without prospects, and without the money to get back. Could you not, at the least, make enquiries of the High Commissioner's Office, where they could surely at least tell you of the conditions, and in what parts of the Union English immigrants are wanted, and for what types of occupation? Possibly too there are better opportunities in some of the Crown Colonies. But I wish you could hang on in England for another year, to see what happens to this country in that time.

If you would care to come in again and discuss matters, if you think it might be helpful to talk rather than write, simply ring up my secretary and make an appointment. I should like to have a word with you about the fragment of your novel also.[1]

> Yours sincerely,
> [T. S. Eliot]

TO *Susan Hinkley*[2]   TS Houghton

9 April 1931   68 Clarence Gate Gardens

Dear Aunt Susie,

Thank you very much for your letter.[3] I have been meaning to write to you ever since I heard from Henry of Aunt Nellie's death. I understood that it was quiet and painless. I feel very sorry for Uncle Rob, who must be very lonely at Davis Avenue, but I understand his not wanting to live elsewhere. Does he get about at all, and see anyone in Cambridge or Boston?

It is kind of you to take so much trouble about the books. I once had a Bryce (my impression was that I had given it to Marion! but apparently not) – anyway, I have only text book associations with it; and I shall much prefer to have the others you mention, which have longer family associations – I treasure those of mother's which I have, and the one you sent me which was Aunt Cabot's. Is there any kind of portrait or copy of a

---

1 – Sayers had written (undated): 'I send you an extract from my novel, for finding on consideration the subject to be above my years and dissatisfied with the little I had accomplished, I decided to leave it unfinished. It was to have been nothing less than a dramatic allegory of all those forces in the world today that trouble or ennoble our endeavours.

'It would have been a work of supererogation to have rewritten the manuscript, better far to submit to you will [*sc.* with] all its imperfections of immaturity on its head. You can see for yourself how impossible it was to continue after 150 pages of such irrelevant talk and incident.'

2 – Susan Heywood Hinkley, née Stearns (1860–1948): TSE's maternal aunt.

3 – Not found.

portrait in existence of Great grandmother Priscilla? I should like to get a photograph for my gallery; a sort of tintype of Grandfather Stearns stands on my mantelpiece, with all the immediate family that I can get, and all the elder notables, except of course the family black-sheep Lawrence [*sic*],[1] whose works bore me extremely.

I hope to hear from Eleanor soon and will really reply promptly. It is delightful to know that you will both be in England again this *next* autumn: that is something we shall both look forward to.

Affectionately your nephew
Tom

TO *Colin Dunlop*[2]   CC

11 April 1931   [Faber & Faber Ltd]

Dear Father Dunlop,

I enclose a brief note on Deans. Would you please ask the Bishop to let me know if it will do, or if not, to give me hints? There is enough time, and I would willingly amend it.[3]

Yours sincerely,
[T. S. Eliot]

My first thought of 'If I were a Dean' is not of what I should want to do, but of what I should *not* want to do: and I make no apology. I have nothing but admiration and pity for those Deans who have toiled unceasingly, made appeals and collected subscriptions year after year, for – what? Merely to keep their minsters from tumbling about their ears. To me a cathedral is primarily a place of worship, the focus of devotions of its diocese, and not a National Monument: but I think – the State being already so far Socialised, and the position of the Church in the State

1–TSE's mother claimed descent from Laurence Sterne (1713–68), great-grandson of Richard Sterne (*c*.1596–1683), Archbishop of York. In 1954, however, TSE's cousin Eleanor Hinkley sent a family tree which disabused TSE of the idea that the family was (as he put it in a letter of 22 Oct. 1954) 'nearly related to Laurence Sterne. I am sure my mother would not have wanted . . . the rather unsavoury 18th Century parson in her house (she certainly didn't admit Laurence Sterne's works into the library) but she was rather proud of the connexion all the same. But the coat-of-arms that you show is totally different from that in the Sentimental Journey, which we had always supposed to be ours as well . . .'

2–Revd Dunlop of The Palace, Chichester.

3–Published as 'Lay Views of Ecclesiastical Persons: If I were a Dean', *Chichester Diocesan Gazette*, 12: 5 (May 1931), 188–91.

being what it is – that the structural repair of cathedrals, and perhaps also of all those churches which have historic and architectural importance, ought to be at the cost of the State. We hear a good deal, in the Press, about the necessity of attracting American tourists, or of inducing them to spend more time and money in Britain, in proportion to what they spend on the Continent – even the new Park Lane ogles the American tourist. Well, cathedrals are a valuable asset to a country, particularly if a dignified urban and rural amenity is preserved around them; they are an asset, that is, to steamship lines, railways, motorbus services, local tradesman, postcard makers, and tourist agencies. The nation as a whole, I contend, should be made to pay for their mere *preservation*, rather than that part of the nation for which they are primarily places of worship and devotion.

I am quite well aware of all the difficulties involved in carrying out such a drastic proposal; and if I were a Dean under the settlement I suggest, I dare say I might in the end prefer to be buried by the collapse of the roof of my own cathedral, rather than buried under a mass of correspondence, memoranda and instructions from the Office of Works, to say nothing of the visits of committees and inquisitory officials. To my irresponsible vision, however, these difficulties are details to be settled by ingenious compromise; the point is that in my Utopian deanery there will be no anxiety about the framework of the cathedral.

I should thus hope to be free to collect, and to use, funds not for the mere preservation of the bones of my cathedral, but for the interior beautification of its living body. And I should try to avoid the fault of making my interior a period piece, of being overawed by the designs of its remote builders. I have seen old and beautiful churches which modern hands seemed afraid to touch, and which therefore remained mere remains; and I have also seen modern churches in which the decorator seems fearful of departing by a decade, in the least ornament or altar cloth, from the period style in which the church was built. I prefer rather a church which shows the loving attempts of generation after generation, each according to its own notions of beauty, to leave visible testimony of its devotion. I should like to be able to encourage the best contemporary artists in stone, metal, paint and wood, to apply themselves to the decoration of my cathedral; and the best musicians to make music for its offices. As for music, if I were to be the ideal dean for my ideal deanery, I should have to know a great more about it than I do. I have, however, one heretical notion. I admit that the organ of St Cecilia must be considered indispensable everywhere, but I should like at least to supplement it by a small orchestra, of strings and woodwind, assembled from local talent (and I am sure that there is plenty of musical talent in rural England). There would be two advantages. Anyone who has heard instrumental music in certain continental churches knows that the organ is by no means the only medium for church music. And everything that engages more individuals in the responsibility and pride of beautifying the church service, is an encouragement to the communal life.

My cathedral, then, would be richly decorated inside: with tapestries (as, for example, they hang round the bases of columns in the cathedral of Toulouse), with modern religious paintings, with memorial tablets (but only to good churchmen), with chapels and church furniture. Should not the resources of art be devoted to God, instead of merely to the palaces of the rich and finally to museums? I hold also the theory, that it is chiefly in the life of such a centre as a cathedral that art can vitally effect us. Who, except the technical expert, can really enjoy a visit to an art museum or an evening in a concert room? I might enlarge upon this, but I must stick to my points and keep within my space: a cathedral where art – not merely archaeology – is dedicated to God, seems to me the best place in which art can flourish.

All my notions of decoration and of music, however, are ancillary to one main purpose: to make the cathedral the centre of religious and artistic activity in its diocese. In the Anglican Church, parishioners (and I think this is equally true, so far as it is true, of every division within the church) tend to grow an excessive devotion to their own particular parish church, or the particular church of their election (and even to a particular vicar or rector). The best way to offset this particularism, would be to encourage in them the same sort of affection towards the Cathedral of their diocese. I realise that for the immediate future such an ideal is impossible in many dioceses – but my ideal deanery is not for the immediate future either.

I should devise as many cathedral ceremonies as possible beyond those which take place at times when the faithful are usually in attendance at their own churches, and with special relation to the seasons of the church year. I am sure that I should pay particular attention to the performance of religious drama. I do not underrate the beauty of our mediaeval religious drama, and I should try, not I hope, to 'revive' it, but to keep it alive; but at the same time I should still more encourage the composition and the performance of plays by contemporary authors. Some people maintain that a good religious play cannot be written nowadays; I believe, as I believe of religious painting and sculpture, that if the opportunity is given, the work will be done. We must expect that the early attempts will be imperfect; but I am sure that in time poets and dramatists, as well as painters and sculptors and artisans, will not be lacking.

But in no two cathedrals would or should conditions be quite the same; and, wherever my deanery is situated, I should wish to encourage and stimulate first the local spirit. I should not wish my cathedral celebrations to be like getting Moiseivitch[1] or Jelly d'Aranyi[2] to entertain the guests at a country house party. And for such activities as religious drama, I should want to have them performed, as far as possible, *within* the cathedral itself.

But besides all these interests and duties, and besides all the functions of a Dean which I know nothing about, I maintain that a Dean should have sufficient continuous leisure to be able to apply himself to some considerable work of scholarship or of original theological and philosophical writing. If his other duties make this impossible, then his other duties should be reduced; for the importance of this opportunity, and the freedom to employ it as he pleases, seem to be capital.

And lastly, I should want for myself a little more leisure still. There is a book which I have never been able to buy, and which I have never had room to accommodate even could I buy it, and which I have never had the time to read even could I buy it and house it. If I were a Dean, I should hope that I might be able to have it, to have shelves for it, and to read as much of it as one man can reasonably expect to read in a lifetime: it is Migne's *Patrologia Latina et Graeca*.[3]

T. S. Eliot

1 – Benno Moiseiwitsch, CBE (1890–1963): Ukrainian-born British pianist.
2 – Jelly d'Aranyi (1893–1966): Hungarian classical violinist long resident in London.
3 – *The Patrologia Latina* (1844–55), published by Jacques-Paul Migne, is part of a compendium of writings by the Church Fathers and other ecclesiastics; *Patrologia Cursus Completus* includes the *Patrologiae Graeco-Latina* – patristic and medieval Greek works with Latin translations.

TO *Derek Verschoyle*[1]   CC

13 April 1931   [Faber & Faber Ltd]

Dear Sir,

My friend, Mr F. W. Bain, has told me of you, and I am writing to say that I would be very glad if you cared to come to see me one day.[2] If you are now in London and would care to call, would you ring up my secretary here and make an appointment with her?

Yours faithfully,
[T. S. Eliot],

TO *T. O. Beachcroft*   CC

13 April 1931   [*The Criterion*]

Dear Beachcroft,

I owe you an apology which you shall now have in full.[3] I had, in fact, intended to use your 'Emblem' at one time or another from the moment I read it but I was not quite sure even when I saw you last when that would be. I found at the last minute that I had space in the April number, and had the poem set up at once in page. In this way the efforts [*sc.* errors] occurred and I was painfully aware of the dislocation of the Bells.

In similar circumstances, were it yourself or anyone else, I would have the matter set up to be held in galley from the moment I decided to use it so that there would be plenty of time for correction of proof. When one rushes things in at the last minute such errors are almost certain to occur and I submit my humble apologies and promise to reform.

1–Derek Verschoyle (1911–73), writer and editor, was to become literary editor of *The Spectator*, 1932–9. Educated at Arnold House Prep School in Wales (where he was taught by Evelyn Waugh) and Malvern College; he took degrees at Trinity College, Dublin, and Trinity College, Oxford. After distinguished service during WW2 in the RAF (wing commander), he was First Secretary at the British Embassy, Rome, 1947–50; and for four years he ran his own publishing house, Derek Verschoyle Ltd, 1952–6. His publications include poetry and editions.
2–F. W. Bain (1863–1940), author and scholar, had requested TSE (8 Apr. 1931) to interview Verschoyle, who had 'come to London to realise his ambitions – he is not without intelligence – Trinity College, Dublin. His people live in a public house . . . in the West of Ireland . . . He is a great admirer of your work . . .' See also TSE to Bain, 8 July 1931, below.
3–Beachcroft had written on 7 Apr. that he was pleased to see his poem 'Emblem' in C. 10 (Apr. 1931), 480; but he was disappointed not to have seen a proof – especially as there was an important misprint in l. 3.

I have read your paper on 'John Taylor' with much interest and pondered it with hesitation.[1] It certainly convinces me that Taylor was a much more important poet than I had ever supposed him to be, but I am doubtful whether the collaboration with the Sitwells does not do him more harm than good. It seems to me that the matter would be better handled if it were possible merely to imply the existence of the Sitwells or refer to them only in passing rather than giving them so much importance. I have a feeling that the essay will not do for us in its present form, so I am returning it. If, as I think likely, it is not worth your while to recast it completely, I should rather suggest trying it on the *English Review*.

Yours ever,
[T. S. Eliot]

TO *William Empson*   CC

14 April 1931   [*The Criterion*]

Dear Empson,

I have taken a good deal of time over your paper on Dogs, etc.[2] My conclusion is that I think this paper would rather misfire in the *Criterion*. It seems to me to be a small part of some very much more extensive study, the plan of which is by no means obvious, and that the reader would get rather lost in the details without perceiving what you were really after. It would be a help to me, indeed, if you could at least let me know whether I am right in thinking that you have something larger in view, and in this case I suspect that some other part of the essay might be more effective by itself. It certainly aroused my curiosity and I should like to hear from you about it.

Yours sincerely,
[T. S. Eliot]

1 – 'Are you by any chance using the article about John Taylor [1578–1653] and the Sitwells? It is a little slender in body matter perhaps.' (Taylor's poetry reminded Beachcroft of that of the Sitwells.)
2 – An early version of 'The English Dog', which was eventually to be published in 1936–7 and revised for Empson's collection *The Structure of Complex Words* (1951). Empson wrote (n.d.): 'It is rather a mixture of pedantry and journalism, but I think the subject is important in its way.'

TO *F. McEachran*   CC

14 April 1931   [Faber & Faber Ltd]

Dear McEachran,

I have read your Introduction to Aesthetics with interest although I have at the moment only been able to give it enough time for me to form an opinion, so as to write to you. Candidly, I cannot see any possibility of publishing a book of this length on this subject at the present time, whatever its merits. It is a little long for the Criterion Miscellany but its length is not the main difficulty in that connexion: it would be impossible to include in the Miscellany any essay on such an abstract subject which certainly could never have enough readers to justify its inclusion in that series. On the other hand it is really too short for a book. The only possibility I can suggest for it would be that of inclusion in such a series as Chatto and Windus's Dolphin Books, and even there I doubt if philosophical essays are welcome.

So I really don't know what to advise. Personally I feel that the only way at the present time to discuss aesthetic questions and get even a small number of people [to] read what one writes, is to approach general problems through concrete instances, and through more specific problems of contemporary art and society. Will you be in London again before long? I should much like to discuss these questions with you.

Yours sincerely,
[T. S. Eliot]

TO *J. M. Reeves*[1]   CC

14 April 1931   *[The Criterion]*

Dear Sir,

I have your letter of the 21st [*sic*] of March and have read your poem with interest.[2] I am afraid that it is impossible for us and probably for almost any publisher at the present time to consider any increase of staff.[3]

1–John Morris Reeves (1909–1978), who published as James Reeves, was at this time a final-year student of English at Jesus College, Cambridge (where he edited *Granta* and collaborated with Jacob Bronowski in founding the periodical *Experiment*). He was a schoolmaster and lecturer in teachers' training colleges, 1933–52. A prolific poet, author, writer for children and critical anthologist, his publications included *Collected Poems, 1929–74* (1974); *Complete Poems for Children* (1973); *Understanding Poetry* (1965).
2–Reeves asked on 25 Mar. about a poem he called "Lidbetter", 'sent . . . some months ago'.
3–Reeves was looking for a job in publishing.

But you say that you would also like to find reviewing work, and as I expect you will either be in London, or near London, after the end of term, I think that the best thing is to ask you to come and see me as soon as it is convenient. I should not suggest your coming to town especially for the purpose, but if you should be in London meanwhile, would you ring up my secretary and make an appointment with her.

Yours faithfully,
[T. S. Eliot]

TO *Bruce Richmond* CC

14 April 1930   [Faber & Faber Ltd]

My dear Richmond,
    This is to introduce to you Mr J. L. Donaghy about whom I spoke to you the other day at lunch.

Yours sincerely,
[T. S. Eliot]

TO *Ian Parsons* TS Reading

16 April 1931   Faber & Faber Ltd

Dear Parsons,
    I wonder if you would allow me to send you, for consideration by Chatto's, the manuscript of a very short novel by a young friend of mine named Leslie Bishop? He brought it to me in the hope that we might publish it. It strikes me as having a great deal of merit, but one or two directors to whom I have shewed it are strongly of the opinion that it is not the type of fiction which Faber and Faber are best qualified to sell. For one thing, it is, as I said, very short, not much longer than one of David Garnett's short pieces, and for another thing, I really believe that it is for a public which we cannot at the present reach as easily as you. Even if you should not find it acceptable, I should be most interested to know what you think of it, because I should like to place it somewhere. But I hope you will at least be able to read it.[1]

Sincerely yours,
T. S. Eliot

1–TSE had written to Bishop himself, in a now lost letter, conveying his fellow directors' views that it was too short for a novel, and that, if published, it might go unnoticed. Bishop

TO *Lucille Goldthwaite*

16 April 1931   [Faber & Faber Ltd]

Dear Madam,

Messrs. Liveright have forwarded on to me your letter of the 28th of March, as the copyright is in my hands. I shall be very glad to give you the permission for which you ask in your letter, so long as you will see that not only the text itself, but the title, is correctly transcribed, as I note that it is incorrectly given in your letter.[1]

Yours faithfully,
[T. S. Eliot]

TO *Bonamy Dobrée*

16 April 1931   Faber & Faber Ltd

Dear Bonamy,

Many thanks for your kindly note of encouragement.[2] I shall be extremely glad if you will rock the crib as violently as you like, because on Sunday next, 2nd after Easter, I shall make much use of you without acknowledgement – but after all, when it [is] only a matter of twelve guineas, and my Study is being distempered and I havent time to go to the London Library or the Museum, why should I revive my memory of texts and re-form my own opinions, when I have *Restoration Tragedy* at hand? The next talk is more difficult; it is easier to applaud Dryden in general than to make out a popular case for his Tragedy – but my method is to proceed from the simple to the complex, which was the method laid down

---

questioned F&F's decision in a letter of 12 Apr.: 'I should be delighted if Chatto could be induced to take it, but even more delighted if you could . . . Certainly it is short. But then the modern movement, of which you have been the protagonist, holds that "the terrible, eager business of personal experience" can only properly be conveyed by vivid, clear cut language . . . The feeling of uncertainty, which the reader should have at the end is deliberate. I defy anyone to make a representation of madness emotionally satisfying, but I claim to have made it dramatically satisfying.' Parsons agreed on 17 Apr. to read the novel.

1–Lucille Goldthwaite, Librarian for the Blind, The New York Public Library, requested permission of Boni & Liveright (28 Mar. 1931) to put into braille by hand 'one copy of "Wasteland [*sic*] from Prize Poems, 1913 to 1926"'.

2–BD asked on 13 Apr., 'you will be kind enough to receive by typescript and not viva voce the expression of my admiration of your first Dryden talk. I shall crib wholesale for my *T.L.S.* article due in August. My own talks on Defoe will seem lamentable popular chatter after your Drydens.' See 'The Poet who Gave the English Speech', *The Listener*, 15 Apr. 1931, 621–2.

by Johannes Procopius in his great work *De Flatu*, which begins 'All farts are in three dimensions' before proceeding to his elaborate theory of the time-space reality in flatulence, anticipating modern physics.

As for Elliott,[1] that provokes me to a discursion on my theory that the higher a race is in culture, the greater number and variety of surnames – I am not ready to give that theory to the world, because, although it annihilates the Welsh, and to a less degree the Scotch and Irish, I am not quite sure yet how good a case I can make out against the Russians and the Bengalis.

I look to see you on the 29th. The 'portrait' by the way was evidently made from a very bad photograph taken by a Jew for *Vogue* some years ago:[2] it is not a study from the Life: you will find, if you have any photographs in circulation, that the Americans will do that sort of thing.

> Your obliged
> T.

TO *Maurice Haigh-Wood* CC

17 April 1931   [68 Clarence Gate Gardens]

Dear Maurice,

Thank you for your letter of the 13th inst. I will have the enclosures completed and forwarded; I should add, I think, to my covering letter to Birks, that they are to use their discretion as to the moment for disposing of one or another.

Meanwhile I have written to Birks to say that the reinvestment of the proceeds might well be considered in connexion with the reinvestment of the £700 redemption (Liverpool and London Electric) which is now lying to the Trustees' Account in the District Bank. I have their reply hereunder:

> 14/4/31: 'In reply to your letter of yesterday, and having looked down the list of investments comprised in this Estate, we do not think there is anything in the Trustee line that can be added to at the present moment with advantage.
>
> The Irish Free State Loan 4½% 1956–2004 is an excellent security and is guaranteed as regards principal and interest by the British Government. It is redeemed by drawings at par and its estimated

---

1 – The *Radio Times* had billed TSE as 'Elliott', as BD pointed out.
2 – 'I enclose a portrait of you, enhaloed like a saint. It just does to send you; because if it was any better I should keep it.' Maurice Beck (1886–1960): chief photographer for *Vogue* (London).

life is 65 years. The stock can at this moment be bought at 100. We can safely recommend this for the reinvestment of the £700 to which you refer.

   PS. There are two non Trustee items which might be added to with advantage, viz: Westminster Bank £1 fully paid shares and P.&O. Steam 5% Debenture.'

I have replied pointing out that this appears to me not quite consistent with their previous recommendation of New Zealand 5s. and asking for their explanation. The remarks on Irish F. State were in response to my suggestion, from a note in the 'Financial Times'. I am inclined myself to invest part in Westminster Bank, if the price is satisfactory. I think you are right in witholding [*sic*] Johannesburg for the moment; and I certainly prefer N. Z. to CPR debs. I may be wholly justified, but I believe N.Z. Stock, certainly far in preference to any Australia. I agree in seeing no advantage in dealing through James. Will you let me have your comments very soon?

Yours affectionately
[Tom]

TO *W. J. Lawrence*   CC

18 April 1931   [*The Criterion*]

Dear Mr Lawrence,

   I owe you an apology for not having acknowledged your Massinger article (that should have been done automatically from the office). You may be sure that almost anything you write can be published in the *Criterion* – sooner or later; if you sent me a contribution and meanwhile published it elsewhere I should depend upon you to let me know; but of course in such a review the Elizabethan matter, like that on any other subject, has to be well sifted in. May we leave it then on the usual terms? It may be six months, or even more; and it will depend partly on whether, in the meantime, you have something else which you feel ought to take precedence.[1]

   If you are now so near London, might we not lunch together one day?

Yours sincerely,
[T. S. Eliot]

---

1 – 'Massinger's Punctuation', C. 11 (Jan. 1932), 214–21.

TO *A. L. Rowse*   CC

18 April 1931   [Faber & Faber Ltd]

Dear Rowse,

Thank you very much indeed for your useful letter. I might perhaps
have delayed my answer, in order to perpend your admonitions, but that
two points call for an immediate reply.

As for a Miscellany Pamphlet,[1] both Faber and Morley (who has the
most to do with that department) are away, but I know that they would
say what I say: that unless a political or economic pamphlet is signed by
an author whose name will sell it, or unless its views are so original and
striking that we should feel compelled to publish it whether it was likely
to sell or not – otherwise, this sort of thing is now a drug on the market.
You will observe that we have already had pamphlets on similar subjects
by some of the most respectable people, and unless this one was to be
really startling I don't think he shd. be encouraged to write it.[2]

Bowra,[3] I know, Blok[4] I do not. I have a stubborn belief that no
good art can come out of Russia (at least as much qua Russian as qua
bolshevist) but I hope my mind is not entirely closed – at any rate, I should
be interested in any article by Bowra, on its own merits: that's as far as
I can go. Irving (or Isaiah) Berlin I have heard of as clever; I am not sure
I have not seen poems by him; I thought from his name he must be an
American possibly a Rhodes scholar; with him, still more positively, I
couldn't commission anything; but should be interested to see whatever
he cares to do. All this is no doubt just what you expected me to say.[5]

1–ALR had written on 14 Apr.: 'I enclose a note from a young Fellow of Queen's, Fraser
by name, who has a pamphlet on Free Trade & Protection that he wd like Faber to look
at for the Criterion Miscellany. He is a quite clever, energetic & pushing young man,
whose pamphlet will be quite good, and, I confess, probably thoroughly orthodox and
commonplace.' *Protection and Free Trade* by Lindley Macnaghten Fraser (1904–63) was to
be published in 1932.
2–FVM was to write to J. F. Davidson on 28 Nov. 1932: 'We have not done anything
lately in this series because in excessive zeal we somewhat overloaded it with pamphlets on
economics, and we are waiting for booksellers to recover. The law of sales in pamphlets is in
inverse proportion to the seriousness of any crisis with which they may deal.'
3–Maurice Bowra, classical scholar: see TSE to Bowra, 24 June 1931.
4–Alexander Blok (1880–1921): accomplished and influential Russian lyric poet.
5–'Do you know C. M. Bowra, of Wadham Coll., who has recently published a first-class
book, *Tradition and Design in the Iliad*? He is, I gather, an extremely good scholar. He
knows Russian, & would like to write an article on Blok for the next *Criterion*: it's just ten
years from his death or some such thing.
   'Then a very brilliant Oxford Jew called I. Berlin, who also knows Russian, would like to
translate some Blok for the *Criterion* sometime. Might they try?'

I will get you v. Doren's *Swift*;[1] I don't think Carl is as able as his brother Mark, who wrote an excellent study of Dryden;[2] but it ought to be worth a review. I am holding up Siegfried on the chance that I may feel inspired to use it in my commentary; after that we shall see; in any case, there is plenty of time, as the June reviews are complete.[3]

I quite agree about Thos. Mann. I understand that there was a riot when he delivered it. I like his courage.[4]

I don't at all mind your disagreeing with my attitude about politics;[5] but I should much like to know what you think my attitude about politics is: I mean, it would help me to know what I think, if I knew what someone like yourself thinks I think. Let us divide the subject into

---

1 – Carl van Doren, *Swift* (1930). Carl van Doren (1885–1950), critic and writer, was author of *The American Novel* (1921) and the Pulitzer prize-winning *Benjamin Franklin* (1938).

2 – Mark Van Doren, *The Poetry of John Dryden* (1920).

3 – 'May I review next one or other of these books: [André] Siegfried's *England's Crisis* (Cape 10/6.) and Carl Van Doren's *Swift*; the latter because I have put in a good deal of work on Swift & wd like to see what sort of a job has been made of him.'

4 – 'You asked me what I should think of Thomas Mann's Address ['An Appeal to Reason', *C*. 10 (Apr. 1931), 393–411]. I read it with great appreciation . . . It showed such a really political judgment of political affairs. It's clearly no use having a literary judgment of politics; any more than it is having a political judgment of literature. One needs the sort of judgment that is appropriate to the activity in question: it's good Aristotelianism, & it's only good sense.'

5 – 'I hope you won't mind my disagreeing with the attitude you take about politics . . . This has some bearing on your comments on my first chapter. I was amused rather when I first read them, & determined to preserve them as a literary curiosity. But on reflection, I know that there's more in it than that . . .

'Now I regret this all the more, since you have it open to you to be what Arnold was on the intellectual side of politics, fifty years ago. (Now don't go & say, Heaven forbid! for one ought to have the highest respect for Arnold's political writings; & there is something in common between his attitude and yours.) Only, he had a much more real, a righter judgment about politics, tho' God knows sufficiently detached, than you.

'It was this right judgment that made what Mann said remarkable; for there was, to be candid, nothing intellectually remarkable about it. I suppose its courage was the most admirable quality; the same courage which had enabled him to transcend the barriers of the middle-class, and to see that socialism was the best foundation for future political development, even though anybody can see its many inadequacies & shortcomings & futilities.

'Now when you query, I can hardly think seriously, a remark of mine about the greatness of the English political tradition, you are making just this mistake of judgment. For politics is the activity by which we have lived, and become a great nation . . . Or again, when I suggest that people of my age are not disillusioned with politics, and you say, "They will be, give 'em time", – it's really very silly, for I can see just as well as you that they may become disillusioned, – but it would be a disastrous thing for us if they were to be . . . I know that you will not mind my saying exactly what I think, – a thing impossible in politics, though they are not the less clever for that. But in a correspondence like this, (and I like to think of it as a Jacques Rivière–Alain Fournier correspondence! – though I wish we were nearer together) it isn't much use suppressing genuine divergences of opinion.'

two parts: first and more important, can we make precise the 'intellectual issue'? and second (also very interesting) can we settle from time to time our agreements about practical measures?

It is more than likely that I have not the 'feel of English politics'; but as everybody else has that particular tactile sense, I imagine that if my comments have any value at all, which is doubtful to myself, they can only be valuable just for that reason, as from someone who has *not* the feel. I don't even think that my French friends have the 'feel' of French politics; certainly no Frenchman outside of their own party would admit that they had. But I should like you to make a little clearer how Arnold (I puzzled for some moments whether 'Arndt' was some great German socialist whose name at least I ought to know) how Arnold comes into it. I have the greatest respect for *Culture and Anarchy* – at one time I could almost repeat passages by heart; but the weakness of his political or rather social views, I have come to believe, is due to the flimsiness of his religious views; and if he had had any religious convictions that one could stick a pin into his politics also would have been stronger. At times Arnold doesn't seem to me to believe in anything except good breeding; he is certainly the most thoroughly Philistine writer of his age. And his literary essays don't impress me as they once did; he seems to be inspired more often by his passion for reading the English a Lesson, rather than by ecstatic enjoyment of any work of art.

Your remark about the English political tradition, as it stood, read to me rather like a patriotic effusion. All I mean was that one is conscious nowadays of how large an element of just good luck entered into the political (and even the military) success of the English; and I thought of the disgrace of the 18th century Church, and the disgrace of India in the 18th century, and the improvident recklessness of nineteenth century industrial expansion. And how many great statesmen have been great men? I think of my friend Whibley's remark (at the beginning of an admirable essay on Halifax): 'politics is the profession of the second-rate'.

You probably, however, exaggerate my pretensions: I don't know anything about politics, except ecclesiastical politics; all I do is to ask questions, and try to stick pins into people who I know write bad prose, like Winston Churchill and Macdonald (the former adopts, no doubt from his mother, the *New York Journal* style, the latter the kailyard [*typing runs off the page*] I thought I was writing on a plain sheet of paper, not on the back of a stamped sheet.

About disillusion: a truer statement of my opinion would be this. Disillusion is balls – the only people who are really disillusioned are good catholics, and very few of them. The great illusion of young people – or rather of the people who in the press express what they think young people think – is the illusion of being 'disillusioned'. I mean, more seriously, that you cannot be disillusioned unless you have a criterion; to be really disillusioned about anything one must believe in something. I should call myself 'disillusioned' in the only sense possible to me, that is, that I have ceased to care about some things, and ceased to respect some things, and ceased to accept some things, and ceased to believe some, and ceased to expect many, merely in the process of acquiring certain of what most people would call 'illusions' – and I don't mean narrowly theological illusions either.

But after all, my jottings are not to be taken as political criticism; it matters very little whether I think you are right or wrong; my objections were really on the ground of writing: I wanted to get my teeth into your ideas quickly, instead of being fed, as I felt I was, out of a very small teaspoon page after page.

So I will stop here, as there seems to be no strong reason for stopping at all.

Ever yours,
[T. S. E.]

TO *Bonamy Dobrée* TS Brotherton

18 April 1931 Faber & Faber Ltd

Dear Bonamy,

Yours of the 15th with enclosure (which shall be read over the weekend) received. I hope, if you do me the honour to listen to my 2 following talks, you will note that I do not, I believe, exaggerate Dryden's influence on prose by his *prose* (which of course does fall in with what other people were doing) but that I hold an undemonstrable theory that he influenced prose as well as verse by his *verse*. His prose is of capital importance in the history of criticism, but not, I think, in the history of prose.[1]

1–BD wrote, 'I am a little in doubt as to the question of Dryden's influence on the language. Granted, as you say, that he did more than anybody to approach written English to spoken, would not the process have taken place anyhow, though perhaps a few years later? How different is his prose from Dorothy Osborne's, or Temple's, or Mrs Hutchinson's? Poetry, yes, No Dryden, no Pope. But prose again. Take Clarendon. There is a difference, of course, but is it not rather difference of personality rather than the instrument to hand?'

No, I haven't, and don't mean to; but perhaps you will read some of them aloud of a Sunday.[1] I am having some pourparlers with Siepmann about next year in general, and hope that we may find more pickings.

> yours etc.
> T. S. E.

TO *Rosemary Freeman*   CC

18 April 1931   [*The Criterion*]

Dear Madam,

I have your letter of April 10th.[2] The *Criterion* is conducted with a very small staff, and the prospects of expansion are spectral. But from your letter I am inclined to doubt whether the *Criterion* work, even if it existed, would be the sort of opening you are looking for, or would provide you with the sort of experience which you seek. It could hardly give anyone the experience which would be of any use towards real journalism; and I should say that you probably want a position on a monthly, or preferably a weekly periodical.

If, however, the kind of reviewing which the *Criterion* publishes, interests you, I should be very glad to see anything that you have written, that you care to show me.

> Yours very truly,
> [T. S. Eliot]

TO *Ruth Harrison*   CC

23 April 1931   [*The Criterion*]

Dear Miss Harrison,

In reply to your letter of the 14th, I don't feel that a review of the book on Péguy[3] – which I have seen – would be quite suitable for the *Criterion* as we have never really discussed Péguy anywhere in the past. But if you are working on the subject, I should be interested to see any

---

1 – 'By the way, since you spoke of the poems dealing with religious thought, and claimed them as the only ones in the language, have you read Defoe's? I haven't.'
2 – Freeman, who was about to come down from Cambridge, requested work on the *Criterion*.
3 – *La Pensée de Charles Péguy*, recently published by Roseau d'Or, vol. 43 (1931). Harrison was pursuing research at Westfield College, London.

part of your writing that might possibly be suitable for publication. I put the suggestion in this way as I never like to commission articles or to encourage people to write articles which after all I might not publish; but it struck me that Péguy's work might not be a bad subject.

Yours very truly,
[T. S. Eliot]

TO *Geoffrey Tandy*[1]   CC

23 April 1931   [Faber & Faber Ltd]

Dear Tandy,

I have not, as you may charitably have supposed, left London with the Royal Commission for Malta; nor have I been wholly neglectful, though in various directions distracted during the last few weeks. The fact is that I am now, more than ever, totally incapable of judging Poetry: I can still sometimes spot what is really Bad, but after seven or eight years at this Game my Palate is quite Dead; so I have been Waiting until I could consult some close and trustworthy Critic about this and a few others. Can you be Patient with me?[2]

Yrs. in the Faith
[T. S. E.]

1–Geoffrey Tandy (1900–69), Assistant Keeper in the Department of Botany at the Natural History Museum, London, 1926–47, did broadcast readings for the BBC (including the first reading of TSE's *Practical Cats* on Christmas Day, 1937). During WW2 he served as a commander in the Royal Navy, working at Bletchley Park. He and his wife Doris ('Polly') were to become intimate friends of TSE. FVM would tell W. W. Norton on 1 May 1931 that Tandy was 'a very promising scientist . . . He has the possibilities of a Jennings or even of a Bateson.' Tandy was to write to Martin Ware (who had invited him to talk about TSE to a small literary society) on 20 Nov. 1935: 'I believe that anything I may be able to do to help anybody to a better understanding of Eliot's work will be a good work. Against that I have to set the fact that he is a pretty close personal friend (whatever that locution may mean) and my judgement may be vitiated in consequence. The text of "this side idolatry" may be used against me. However, having asked the man himself if he have any serious objection, I say yes and hope that you will not regret having asked me.' See further Miles Geoffrey Thomas Tandy, *A Life in Translation: Biography and the Life of Geoffrey Tandy* (thesis for the degree of MA in Arts Education and Cultural Studies, Institute of Education, University of Warwick, Sept. 1995).
2–Tandy replied on 21 May: 'I sail for Florida tomorrow so I take the opportunity of sending you another vapour [poetry] knowing that I shall be out of reach of your wrath . . . You need not to think that there is any limit to my patience. / yours also in the Faith, Geoffrey Tandy.'

TO *William Rothenstein*   TS Houghton

24 April 1931   Faber & Faber Ltd

Dear Rothenstein,

When I wrote to you last you held out some hope that you might be able to come to a subsequent *Criterion* meeting. We are having one at the same time and place, at Harold Monro's, 38 Great Russell Street, (the private door is round the corner in Willoughby Street), at 8.15, on Wednesday next, the 29th. I am afraid this is very short notice, but if you are free even for part of the evening we shall be delighted to see you.

Yours sincerely,
T. S. Eliot

TO *Frederick Heath*[1]   CC

27 April 1931   [Faber & Faber Ltd]

Dear Heath,

I am having a copy of *An Adventure*[2] sent to you personally though I believe that a review copy has already gone to the *English Review*. I found the book absolutely fascinating myself; I think it is well worth a notice.

The book by Lawrence Hyde is called *The Prospects of Humanism* and is published by Gerald How.[3] I am afraid I know nothing whatever about the author except that he published a book a year or two ago called *The Learned Knife*, which I did not read, but which, I believe, is on the same lines, but he strikes me as a highly intelligent man who deserves notice.[4]

Yours sincerely,
[T. S. Eliot]

1 – Frederick Heath was editor of *The English Review*.
2 – C. A. E. Moberly and E. F. Jourdain, *An Adventure*, 4th edn, with Intro. by Edith Olivier and Note by J. W. Dunne (F&F, 1931).
3 – Frederick Heath asked TSE by return (1 May) to review the Hyde volume for him.
4 – TSE, in his review of *The Prospects of Humanism* (*The English Review*, June 1931), praised Hyde as 'a brilliant and thoroughgoing critic of critics'. Among the aspects of Hyde's study that he admired was that, to his mind, 'the author makes a very good job of demonstrating the inconsistency and inadequacy of both doctrines, the purely human, and the more ambitious "naturalism" of Mr [John Middleton] Murry: their inconsistency with themselves, and their inadequacy to the religious instincts of humanity. Mr Hyde's double success is all the more remarkable for his genuine sympathy with both of two writers so opposite in sensibility, and for his admirable temperateness and indifference to mere debating points. He is the first critic, so far as I know, to point out the affinity of Mr Murry with Mr Santayana.' For all his respect for the criticism of Hyde the humanist, however, TSE

TO *Bruce Richmond*   CC

4 May 1931   [*The Criterion*]

Dear Richmond,

I saw, the other day, the young man Donaghy, who has done some reviewing for you, and told him that I would try to put in a word with you on his behalf. It appears that he has had to give up his teaching temporarily; he has sent his wife and children back to Ireland for a time, to stay with relatives; and I gather that he is financially worried. He would very much like to do any reviewing that he can get and says that he is now in a position to deliver any reviews punctually. I believe that if you had any work to give him, he would do it to time, as he seems to me a conscientious fellow.[1]

By the way, I have just completed the last of my outstanding engagements, the Pascal essay, and should be very glad if the Heywood were forthcoming.[2] Meanwhile I shall get to work on Ford.[3]

                                    Yours ever,
                                    [T. S. Eliot]

TO *Will Spens*   CC

4 May 1931   [Faber & Faber Ltd]

My dear Spens,

I must apologise for not answering your kind invitation immediately. The fact is that I at once mislaid your letter – I am a person who destroys nothing and loses everything – and I wanted to find it rather than bother you by writing to ask which dates you had suggested. So now, if it is not too late, may I accept for the weekend of the 30th? My wife would be very happy to accompany me, but her health is so variable that she cannot make binding engagements too far ahead. So will you let me know if it

---

drew the line at Hyde's ultimate claim that 'the religion of the Churches is a dead religion; on that point we must remain firm'. TSE was equally firm in his categorical rebuttal: 'Many people have had that thought; what is Mr Hyde's "life"? I have yet to hear of anything more living than the word of Christ in His Church.'

1 – BLR responded on 5 May: 'We have done a little with Donaghy, and I will do more.'

2 – 'Thomas Heywood' – on Arthur Melville Clark, *Thomas Heywood: Playwright and Miscellanist* – *TLS*, 30 July 1931, 589–90.

3 – 'John Ford' – on *Materials for the Study of the Old English Drama, New Series, First Volume: John Ford's Dramatic Works*, vol. ii, ed. H. de Vocht – *TLS*, 5 May 1932, 317–18.

would be possible for her to leave the invitation open until a few days before?

Much looking forward to seeing you,

I am,
Yours sincerely,
[T. S. Eliot]

TO *F. S. Flint*[1]   CC

4 May 1931   [Faber & Faber Ltd]

Dear Frank,

Many thanks for your letter of the 30th.[2] I like the idea and am trying to meet Williams in a week or so and talk it over with him.

As for your parallel suggestion, it naturally occurs to me that it would be admirable if the regular review of verse might be signed by F. S. Flint. I cannot think of anyone else who could be trusted to do it, and I think that in any case we ought not to have a young man, but someone of mature enough years not to be poisoned by the stuff he would have to review.

Awaiting a reply to this,

I am,
Yours ever,
[T. S. Eliot]

P.S. From what you say about Richard's novel, don't you think that it would be only decent for the *Criterion* to ignore it completely?[3]

1–Frank Stuart ('F. S.') Flint (1885–1960), English poet, translator and civil servant: see Biographical Register.

2–'After you left last night, I had a word with Orlo Williams about novel reviewing. He said he would love to do a quarterly article for the C., on the following conditions:-

'(1) He to have a free hand in deciding what novels to review.

'(2) You to send him all novels received.

'(3) You to obtain for him any novel which he thinks ought to be reviewed, but which has not been sent to the C.

'(4) Length of the article 2/2500 words . . .

'I would suggest that a quarterly review of novels would be an interesting feature; and perhaps a half-yearly review of verse, the latter in one hand and pursued with a general principle of some kind: an attitude; as too the novel review.'

3–'R[ichard Aldington]'s novel [*At All Costs*] is about recognisable people in the village. I know *all* the chief characters, so far as I have read; and I don't think the girl it's about has anything to be pleased with (as far as I have read). In fact, there is a semi-seduction, and I am certain an action for libel would *lie*; if not several!'

TO *Orlo Williams*   CC

4 May 1931   [*The Criterion*]

Dear Williams,

I have had a letter from F. S. Flint reporting to me the heads of an interesting conversation he had with you after I left. If the scheme is one that you like and is, as I understand, your own invention I am cordially in favour of it. The only point that I have to raise is this: I still think that the *Criterion* ought to have from time to time retrospective reviews of the work of contemporary novelists, and I would have suggested to you the other evening, had I been able to stay longer and have any private talk with you, cleaning up in one long review, the work of J. B. Priestley, unless that sort of scavenging is repellent. Can we think of a way of fitting in these occasional articles with a regular chronicle of novels? I should think that they might alternate. Would you be able to lunch with me *next* week, any day except Tuesday the 12th, and talk these matters over.[1]

                              Yours ever,
                              [T. S. Eliot]

TO *Ernest Rhys*   CC

4 May 1931   [Faber & Faber Ltd]

Dear Mr Rhys,

I enclose a preface on Pascal. I am very doubtful about it as this is the first time that I have attempted an introduction to a popular edition of anything; so I do not know whether it is too elementary or not elementary enough. If you have any suggestions, I shall be glad to amend it. In any case I want to add a note or two after I have looked up a few bits of bibliography.

                              Yours sincerely,
                              [T. S. Eliot]

---

1 – Williams replied on 5 May: 'The scheme you speak of was Flint's suggestion entirely, but I am quite ready to fall in with anything that is considered advantageous to the *Criterion* . . .'

TO *J. Gordon Macleod*   CC

7 May 1931   [Faber & Faber Ltd]

Dear Mr Macleod,

Thank you for your note of the 29th.[1] I should like to see you in Cambridge if possible. I expect to be going down for a weekend at the end of May but I am afraid that my hosts at Corpus will dispose of all the time that I have. So in any case, will you let me know when you are next in London and come and lunch with me?

I should like to know how the theatre business is getting on, and especially whether it seems likely to prove of any use to you for your own writing. I should very much like to know also what you think of Auden's *Paid On Both Sides*. We brought out his book in a similar format to yours and it should have been sent to you. He is particularly interested in verse drama and I should like him to meet you. Do you know of anywhere where this sort of thing might be tried out on a stage?

                                    Yours sincerely,
                                    [T. S. Eliot]

TO *Caresse Crosby*   CC

7 May 1931   [Faber & Faber Ltd]

Dear Mrs Crosby,

Thank you for your letter of May the 5th.[2] A letter which I wrote to you, or rather which my secretary wrote to you for me, after I had heard from you last, when you said you were just leaving for New York seems to have gone astray. Furthermore, as no reply came, my secretary wrote to you again and asked whether you had received the first letter.

The point was, I think, that the book to which you suggested that I should contribute a preface did not appear to have reached me and I asked, I think, that you would kindly send me another copy, before I answered. I think I have had all the other books, but not this one. If you

---

1 – Macleod thanked TSE for printing 'Mount Pindus' (from *Foray of Centaurs*) in *C.* 10 (July 1931), 654–7.

2 – Caresse Crosby (Black Sun Press, Paris) invited TSE to write a preface to Harry Crosby's posthumous volume of poetry entitled *Transit of Venus*. She hoped also to publish a book of dreams, and a volume of Harry Crosby's diary entitled *Shadows of the Sun*.

get this note in time, could you let me have a copy of the book, and then I shall look forward to seeing you if you come to London.

Yours sincerely,
[T. S. Eliot]

TO *John Hayward*

MS King's

7 May 1931   68 Clarence Gate Gardens

Dear John

As my wife has not been very well this week, it is quite likely that she might have to fail at the last moment: so, rather than that, we wondered whether you would on this occasion concede the point, & come to lunch here this Saturday? Which, after all, was always our intention – to get you here *first*. I hope you won't mind – if it is for any reason impossible, can you ring me up?

Yours ever
T. S. Eliot

<Please do come here. *V. H. Eliot*>[1]

---

1 – Added by hand by VHE.

7 May 1931   Faber & Faber Ltd

Dear Spencer,

Thank you for your letter of April the 20th and for your cheque for one hundred dollars which I acknowledge herewith.[2] I hope that I have not contributed seriously to the delay in bringing out the book. Anyway, I will make no further delay in returning the proofs and answering your queries.

I have heard of you indirectly from one of my sisters who, I believe, is a friend of an aunt of yours.

I am delighted to hear that Richards has had such success. I was sure that he would give new life to the English Department.[3]

Yours sincerely,
T. S. Eliot

1–Theodore Spencer (1902–49), poet and critic, taught at Harvard, 1927–49; as Boylston Professor of Rhetoric and Oratory from 1946. Co-editor of *A Garland for John Donne 1631–1931* (1931), for which TSE wrote 'Donne in Our Time'; author of *Shakespeare and the Nature of Man* (Lowell Lectures on Shakespeare, pub. 1951).

TSE wrote on 30 May 1939 to T. R. Henn – Spencer had applied for a Cambridge University Lectureship – 'I imagine that Theodore Spencer is so well-known to most of the English lecturers in Cambridge that any testimonial from me should be superfluous. Also, it is only fair to say that Spencer is a close personal friend of mine, and that I may be biased in his favour . . . I have a very high opinion indeed of Spencer's abilities. I did not meet everyone even in the English department at Harvard, but I have no reason to believe that there was anyone there of greater ability or greater gifts for teaching. I saw enough of his relations with the students whom he tutored (that was before he had been made an assistant professor) to say that no one could have devoted more zeal than he to work with individuals, or with better effect. He was very popular with the undergraduates, and it was by his initiative and under his direction that the members of Eliot House started their productions of Elizabethan plays, which became a rather important college event.

'I have a high opinion, also, of Spencer's appreciation of literature, both new and old.'

The Master of Eliot House, Harvard, writing to TSE on 24 Apr. 1950, spoke of 'Ted's grace and wisdom'.

2–*A Garland for John Donne* was published on 1 Dec. 1931.

3–IAR had been 'lecturing with enormous success, and putting some color into the watery liquid of our English department'.

7 May 1931   Faber & Faber Ltd

Dear Tom,

Thank you for your Letters. I hope you like the Book, because it is a Poetry Book and I like it. I was very much Interested to hear about Ty Glyn Aeron, and the Island, and the Trout, and the Bees. I told the Practical Cat all about it, and the Practical Cat was so Excited that we finally said we would

Go in for COUNTRY LIFE.

Forinstance, there's

TENNIS    GOLF

FISHING   ROUGH
                        SHOOTING

PICKING FLOWERS   AND   WATCHING BIRDS

Your uncle
Tom

TO *Arthur Wheen*   TS Gretchen Wheen/Tanya Crothers

7 May 1931   Faber & Faber Ltd

Dear Wheen,

   I very much appreciate your inscribing a copy of the Remarque book for me.[1] I have now read it. The translation seems to me brilliant – you get just the right line between being too literal and too colloquial. And the book seems to me almost as good – and in a way more interesting at this moment – than *All Quiet*. It has similar literary defects – for instance the introduction of the scene of the School Cadet Corps or whatever it was, seems to me a blemish in the way of propaganda – but some of the scenes and many of the small touches are very fine. I don't think he is as destructive as Grosz, but still, it is a good book. Is there room for a good book of English post-war, I wonder?

                         With grateful thanks,
                         yours ever,
                         T. S. Eliot

TO *W. H. Auden*   CC

8 May 1931   [Faber & Faber Ltd]

Dear Auden,

   I am afraid that I see very little hope for Turel[2] in practical publishing. I have found it extraordinarily difficult myself, where I have dipped into it and in places practically unintelligible, particularly as the English equivalents of so many of the words are equally beyond my understanding. So I think we had better leave it to someone else. I don't know quite whom to suggest. Possibly Allen and Unwin. But I don't see why you should be bothered with this. Would it not be better for your friend to put it into the hands of a literary agent? I am more than doubtful, however, whether anyone would venture to publish at this time, a book which is certain to have only a small public.

   I have got into touch with Macleod again, and have written to ask him what he knows about the possibilities of the contemporary stage of the extreme left.

                         Yours ever,
                         [T. S. Eliot]

1 – *The Road Back* – Wheen's translation of *Der Weg zurück*, by Erich Maria Remarque – was published in June 1931.
2 – Adrien Turel (1890–1957): Swiss-German writer and philosopher.

11 May 1931   Faber & Faber Ltd

Dear Mr Gregory,

I must apologise for the long delay in writing to you again.[1] I am afraid that it is due to my having been very busy, and to the fact that as we were unable to publish your book during this Spring, in any case, I was not pressed for time. It was, however, rude of me to keep you waiting so long.

We have had the book paged out in the form which we shall use. I believe that Dahlberg has shewn you two books I sent him which will give you an idea of its appearance. On going through *Rooming-House* carefully there seemed to me to be very little to cut out, and I have been guided partly by the fact that we wanted a reduction of about four pages for our format. My suggestion, therefore, is to leave out the following poems:

Jesse James, The Preacher's Son.

Colombo Dominico.

Hellbabies.

Flora.

I propose to have the remainder galleyed at once and of course in the same order in which your New York publishers have printed them.

You said that you wanted to know what I wished to omit before you signed the contract. I enclose the contract herewith and hope that you will not object to the omissions. As I said, they are for the purpose of making the book the right number of pages; but I do feel, if I may say so without impertinence, that the two first of these seem to me below the level of the rest of the book. There is just a suggestion of the old Vachel Lindsay swing here and there, and I think they might distract the attention of the publikum from the essential merit of the rest.

Sincerely yours,

T. S. Eliot

1–Gregory had written on 9 Jan.: 'Since I have the utmost confidence in your integrity as an editor and your ability as a poet, I believe whatever suggestions you may offer regarding the publication of the book to be helpful and sound . . . Before signing a contract, however, I would like to know the specific changes you have in mind.' *Chelsea Rooming House* was published by Covici, Friede (1930), and as *Rooming House* (F&F, 1932). The F&F blurb, probably by TSE, reads: 'This is the first book of poems by a young New York poet, who is as yet little known either here or in America. The poems are characterized by a bitter realism in treating the lives of the poor and oppressed in New York, but exalted by a rare lyric quality. They constitute a document upon our time which is as interesting and significant here as it is for America.'

TO *John Hayward*   TS King's

11 May 1931   68 Clarence Gate Gardens

Dear John,

I asked my secretary to send you the number of *Theology* with Sparrow's article on Donne (and another by the Chaplain of All Souls);[1] I don't want it back.

I feel I did not succeed in expressing my pleasure at your gift of the Pickering *Preces Privatae*;[2] I never do appear very appreciative, I fear. I shall truly treasure it; but the next time you come I want you to write my name in it, please.

                              Yours ever,
                              T. S. E.

If you ever reconsidered the subject of reading a paper to the Shakespeare Association I should be glad.

TO *W. H. Auden*   CC

11 May 1931   [Faber & Faber Ltd]

Dear Auden,

I have read *The Orators* with great interest. The first section seems to me to come off the best as it stands and I shall be very glad to use this part in the *Criterion* if you think fit to separate it from the rest.[3] The second part seems to me very brilliant, though I do not quite get its connexion with the first. My chief objection to it is that it seems to me to have lumps of undigested St Jean Perse embedded in it. I admire your success with the Perse method, which I should not have believed possible, but I think it still needs a further process of purification.

And the third part is apparently perfectly lucid, but I must confess that so far I cannot make head or tail of it.

                              Yours ever,
                              [T. S. Eliot]

1–John Sparrow, 'Donne's Religious Development', *Theology: A Monthly Journal of Historic Christianity* 22: 129 (Mar. 1931), 144–54; F. E. Hutchinson, 'Donne the Preacher', ibid., 155–63.
2–*Preces Privatae Quotidianæ, Graece et Latine, Editio Tertia et Emendator* (London: Guilielmi Pickering, 1848), inscribed by JDH to TSE, 1931, is in TSE's Library.
3–'Speech for a Prize Day', C. 11 (Oct. 1931), 60–4.

TO *John Crow*[1]   CC

13 May 1931   [*The Criterion*]

Dear Crow,

I am sorry that you have had to put yourself into such a depressing situation and hope that it will not be too long.[2] I am also sorry that you feel capable of nothing but Detective Fiction at the moment because I think that the time for the *Criterion* to devote space to that form of literature has passed. I am sending you however a complimentary copy of our latest which I hope will help to pass your time in hospital.[3]

Yours sincerely,
[T. S. Eliot]

TO *Paul Elmer More*   CC

13 May 1931   [Faber & Faber Ltd]

My dear More,

This is very good news;[4] but as my wife is very anxious to renew your acquaintance, and as she almost never goes out in the evening, I very much hope that you will consent to dine with us instead. Our present address is 68 Clarence Gate Gardens, N.W.1., which is near Regent's Park and Baker Street Station. Would you please let me have a line when you get this as I feel uncertain that it will reach you. I am very much looking forward to seeing you.

Yours ever sincerely,
[T. S. Eliot]

1–John Crow (1904–69) studied medicine before taking a BA in English from Worcester College, Oxford (where he edited *Isis* with Peter Fleming). For twelve years he was a journalist, working as boxing correspondent for the journal *Boxing* and for various US boxing journals. Declared unfit for war service, he taught during WW2 at Wellington College; and thereafter he taught English for several years at King's College, London, being promoted to Reader in 1962. He was Professor of English at the University of Pittsburgh, 1968–9. Though not a productive scholar, he was held in very high esteem for his erudition in Elizabethan and Jacobean drama.
2–Crow wrote from Guy's Hospital, London, 12 May: 'I have had to come into this wretched place for a slight operation. Could I have a detective story or two to review for the *Criterion*?'
3–TSE sent a copy of . . . *And Then Silence*. Crow wrote on 2 June: 'I am no longer unemployed as when we last met. I have contrived to become the junior reporter on the staff of a Bristol evening paper, *The Evening Times and Echo*. I find the work pleasing.'
4–Letter not found.

P.S. Tuesday would be a little better than Monday, if it is all the same to you, but if not, I shall hope that you can come on Monday.

P.P.S. I almost forgot the following: have you seen Canon Mozley's *The Beginning of Christian Theology*? It is a small popular book, but it seems to me quite good. I had intended to give it only a brief notice but as I have a real authority near at hand, would he consent to review it for the *Criterion* at whatever length he pleases? I should be glad to send you also T. R. Glover's *World of the New Testament*, which might possibly fit into it.[1]

TO *Arthur Quiller-Couch*[2]   CC

14 May 1931   [*The Criterion*]

Dear Sir Arthur,

Your young friend, Mr Gittings, has sent me a few poems, together with your letter.[3] They do indeed strike me also as having more than usual merit, and I think that he ought to have a little encouragement to allow his gifts to develope [*sic*] normally, and not be distorted by the influence of the young *literati* at Cambridge or elsewhere. I have written him a line to say that I should like to see more of his work from time to time, and would be glad to meet him if he ever comes up to London.

1 – More replied (16 July) that the works by Mozley and Glover were 'scarcely worth noticing'.
2 – Sir Arthur Quiller-Couch (1863–1944) – 'Q' – critic, poet, novelist, editor and anthologist; King Edward VII Professor of English Literature, Cambridge; Fellow of Jesus College. His publications include the *Oxford Book of English Verse 1250–1900* (1900), *On the Art of Writing* (lectures, 1916), and, with John Dover Wilson, volumes in the New Shakespeare series. See A. L. Rowse, *Quiller-Couch: A Portrait of 'Q'* (1988).
3 – 'Q' wrote (10 May): 'Will you do me a favour, & (this is more important) a young poet a great favour by looking over a little selection of his verses that he is sending with this to cover his approach to you?

'Do not let it count against him that he won the Chancellor's Medal up here with a poem on Roman Road, for it happened to meet with a discriminating brace of examiners, and is full of good lines. But I particularly like some of the thoughtful lyrics he is sending to you: & because of this – and also as a sort of pious offering to the shade of Charles Whibley (who never missed a chance to give young merit a chance, good man that he was) I pass these verses on to you. You will forgive anyhow & believe me / Yours sincerely / Arthur Quiller-Couch

' – Or Q., if you don't mind connecting any charitable thought with that initial.

'P.S. My young friend's name is R. W. V. Gittings, of this College.'

I am very doubtful, however, about publishing poems by anyone so young, and although I like to encourage anyone who seems to me to have merit, I am always inclined to urge such young writers to preserve their solitude as long as they can. The great danger, it seems to me nowadays, is that a young undergraduate who likes writing verse comes in contact with so many others with the same interest, and they tend to fall into groups of individuals who admire each other's work and come to write more and more alike. But perhaps I am unduly depressed. Anyway, I thank you for letting me see some rather promising verse which is out of the ordinary.

Yours sincerely,
[T. S. Eliot]

TO *Robert Gittings*[1]   CC

14 May 1931   [Faber & Faber Ltd]

Dear Sir,

I have your letter of the 10th together with Sir Arthur Quiller-Couch's, and have read the poems you sent.[2] They interested me very much and I should like to see more of them. I feel, if I may say so, that it is rather premature for you to consider collecting them into a volume yet, but I should like to see more of your work from time to time and watch its development. And I will add that if you are in London at any time I shall be very pleased if you can come and see me. Will you let me know whether you wish the poems returned as otherwise I should keep them in the hope of comparing them with your later work.[3]

Yours sincerely,
[T. S. Eliot]

1 – Robert Gittings (1911–92): poet, biographer, BBC writer and radio producer. Educated at Jesus College, Cambridge – where he was cultivated by Sir Arthur Quiller-Couch, and where he gained a first in 1933 – he was to work for the BBC 1940–64. His prose writings include *John Keats: The Living Year* (1954); *John Keats* (1969; winner of the W. H. Smith Literary Award); *The Young Thomas Hardy* (1975); *The Older Hardy* (1978; winner of the James Tait Black Memorial Prize); *The Second Mrs Hardy* (co-authored with his wife Jo Manton, 1979); *Dorothy Wordsworth* (with Jo Manton, 1985); *The Nature of Biography* (1978).

2 – 'I am in my first year . . . I have been awarded the Chancellor's Medal for English Verse. I am sending you a dozen or more of my shorter lyrics, and would be most grateful if you will regard them, for better or for worse, as fairly representative specimens of my work.'

3 – Gittings replied (15 May) that he should be able to send a further selection in June. Later (1 Oct.) he sent 'a few' more poems, 'written since I returned from Germany': TSE interviewed him on 7 Oct. 1931.

TO *Charles Smyth*   CC

14 May 1931   [*The Criterion*]

Dear Smyth,

Thank you for your letter of the 8th.[1] I am not at all sure whether
Osbert Sitwell and his book are worth the amount of high explosives
which you propose to direct at him. In any case a review would have to
be for September and then it is rather too long after the appearance of the
book. I think it might be better if you cared to meditate a more general
article; what do you think? Only if you are going in for invective, don't
confuse the Sitwells with Bloomsbury. These birds do not fly together and
can hardly be hit by the same shot.[2]

                                    Yours ever,
                                    [T. S. Eliot]

TO *H. J. B. Gray*   CC

14 May 1930   [Faber & Faber Ltd]

Dear Sir,

My secretary tells me that she answered your kind letter during my
absence,[3] but I am adding a note to express my appreciation of the
invitation and my regrets at my inability to accept it. The inability is
primarily one of time; but also of competence, for I am not by any means
an Italian scholar; and had I been able to accept, I should no doubt have
disappointed the Club more severely than by not accepting at all.

1–Smyth wrote on 8 May: 'I should like to deliver an onslaught on Osbert Sitwell's
Victoriana (pub. Duckworth). It is meant to hold up the "great & good" Victorians to
ridicule. I admit that 5% of the extracts do make the Victorians look silly: but the remaining
95% do as much for Mr Sitwell . . . Never have the Bright Young People so completely given
themselves away. I feel like Cromwell at Dunbar when he saw Leslie marching down the hill:
"the Lord hath delivered them into our hands" . . . I have a blood-lust on me, and should
be more than grateful if you could help me glut it. Fat bulls of Bloomsbury close me in on
every side.'
2–Smyth replied on the 'Sunday after Ascension Day', 1931: 'Geography was never my
strong point: and to me "Bloomsbury" is a vast and undefined region inhabited by all the
pseudo-literary people I dislike; in fact, a moral rather than a geographical expression. Nor
did I realise how much the Sitwells are out of touch.'
3–The Revd H. J. B. Gray, OP (Blackfriars), President of the Oxford University Italian Club,
wrote on 1 May to invite TSE to 'read us a paper, or to talk to us on any subject concerned
with Italy or things Italian'.

But with many thanks for the invitation,

I am,

Yours very truly,

[T. S. Eliot]

TO *W. K. Lowther Clarke*   CC

20 May 1931   [Faber & Faber Ltd]

Dear Dr Lowther Clarke,

My friend Dr Paul Elmer More, of Princeton University, is in London for about ten days, and has been discussing with me a project of a kind of anthology of seventeenth century theological and devotional literature. The scheme is a rather ambitious one and the work will be largely subsidised in America; Bishop Rhinelander has interested himself in the collection of the funds. The question of an English publisher arises; and it seemed to me that the S.P.C.K. could probably do better with such a work than either my own firm or the Clarendon. More has already had a conversation with Milford.

Would you let me bring More to see you one day next week, or preferably, could you lunch with More and myself on either Tuesday, Wednesday or Thursday next?[1]

Yours sincerely,

[T. S. Eliot]

TO *Montgomery Belgion*   CC

27 May 1931   [*The Criterion*]

Dear Belgion,

I am very much in arrears and owe you a long letter, but this is merely to say that of course Faber and Faber have no objection to the proposals in your letter of May 15th.[2]

1–Lowther Clarke replied on 21 May, 'It is an honour to be thought of in connection with so important a book and to be asked to meet Dr More', and agreed to meet him at TSE's office. Clarke wrote further on 28 May that he had written a memo on More's proposal, for circulation to the S.P.C.K. Committee; he would also have it put up to the E.C.U. Committee. The book appeared as *Anglicanism: The Thought and Practice of the Church of England, Illustrated from the Religious Literature of the Seventeenth Century*, ed. Paul Elmer More and Frank L. Cross (1935).

2–Belgion asked permission to use his article 'The Human Parrot' as the title-piece of his next book (*The Human Parrot, and Other Essays*, 1931); and also to re-use three or four

My paper on Pascal is not for the *English Review* but for the Everyman edition of the *Pensées*. I will send you a copy as soon as it is out. That reminds me, however, to suggest that the *English Review* is worth your keeping in mind for placing essays. They pay better than the *Criterion* although as a monthly they may not be able to take such long articles. I am on a sort of small editorial committee of it and should like to see something of yours published there, and so if you send anything, tell them that it is at my suggestion.

Yours ever,
[T. S. Eliot]

TO *J. Gordon Macleod*

27 May 1931   [Faber & Faber Ltd]

Dear Macleod,

Very many thanks for your letter of the 18th[1] and for the trouble you have taken over Auden.[2] I am very much interested in all that you say about verse production and the modern actor, and I am doubtful whether the contemporary actor is not prohibited by his whole social and economic condition, as well as by his training, from the kind of work in which we are interested. For one thing, it simply does not give the opportunity for star parts or for 'interpretations'.

Of course we have no objection whatever to your re-printing 'Sagittarius'. The *Criterion* only expects first periodical rights. The copy of *Poetry* does not seem to have arrived. I don't think it will do any harm for you to re-publish there. Harriet Monroe is a worthy person who has been just behind the times for as long as I can remember, except for a few occasions when someone has given her a smart push. Perhaps she is trying to catch up.

I am afraid I shan't see you this weekend as I may not be coming to Cambridge after all, so if there is any chance of you coming up to London I hope you will let me know, as I should very much like to have a talk with you.

Yours sincerely,
[T. S. Eliot]

---

paragraphs from his essay 'The Irresponsible Propagandist' (from *Our Present Philosophy of Life*).

1 – Not found.

2 – See letter to W. H. Auden, below.

P.S. I find that Miss Harriet Monroe has asked me for permission to reprint *Prufrock* and *Marina* in the same anthology. I shall allow her to use *Prufrock* for nothing for the reason that it first appeared in *Poetry* but I shall charge her two guineas for *Marina*. I think that you ought not to ask less than three guineas for 'Sagittarius'.

TO *Harriet Monroe*   CC

27 May 1931   [Faber & Faber Ltd]

My dear Miss Monroe,

I am so sorry that I overlooked your previous letter. The copyright of both *Prufrock* and *Marina* is in my own hands and I will gladly give you permission to use them.[1] As *Prufrock* first appeared in *Poetry*[2] and was the first of my verses to be published I should not think of asking any fee from you for the present anthology, but I will ask two guineas or ten dollars if you will, for reprinting *Marina*.

Yours very sincerely,
[T. S. Eliot]

TO *W. H. Auden*   CC

27 May 1931   [*The Criterion*]

Dear Auden,

Thank you for your letter of the 14th.[3] I think I understand much better after your explanation, but in any case the first section seems to me quite possible by itself, and is the only [one] of suitable length for the *Criterion*. So may I have it back to use in the September number?

I have a letter from Gordon Macleod, who knows and admires *Paid on Both Sides*. He thinks that the Festival Theatre in Cambridge is the only theatre in England where such a thing might be attempted, but he adds that the director always turns down direct suggestions and apparently

---

1–Monroe wished (15 May 1931) to reprint both 'Prufrock' and *Marina* in a revised edition of her anthology *The New Poetry*. She had first written on the subject on 31 Mar. 1931. When the first edition of her anthology was published in 1917, she said, TSE had not wished 'Prufrock' to be included 'because that was to be the title-poem of your forthcoming book' (31 Mar.).

2–June 1915.

3–Not found.

the only way by which he might come to take up anything new would be to hear about it from various sources and then to imagine that he had discovered it himself. There are a good many people like that. Meanwhile we must hope that some group of amateurs may appear, but I think it would be very risky for you to allow anybody to do it except under your own supervision. You will practically have to teach the people the A.B.C. of speaking poetry. From this point of view I am not sure that the theatre in Cambridge is not already spoilt. I am sure we shall find a way sooner or later, however.

Yours sincerely,
[T. S. Eliot]

TO *Arthur J. Penty*[1]   CC

28 May 1931   [Faber & Faber Ltd]

Dear Sir,

I and another director[2] have read with great interest and sympathy your essay, 'Means and Ends'. After considerable deliberation we came to the conclusion that it was not quite suitable material for the Criterion Miscellany. It is in a way much too good for that purpose. We feel, I mean, that it is a wedge which should be directed toward a more exclusive public to begin with. The Miscellany public is really a public of people who want

---

1–Arthur J. Penty (1875–1937), architect (he was early involved in the development of Hampstead Garden Suburb) and social critic influenced variously by Ruskin, Carlyle, Matthew Arnold and Edward Carpenter, as well as in part by G. K. Chesterton and Hilaire Belloc, was an advocate of guild socialism, anti-modernism and anti-industrialism, agrarian reconstructionism, and Anglican socialism. A regular contributor to periodicals including *The Guildsman*, *G. K.'s Weekly*, *The Crusader* and *C.*, his works include *Old Worlds for New* (1917), *A Guildsman's Interpretation of History* (1920) and *Towards a Christian Sociology* (1923).

TSE wrote in *The Idea of a Christian Society* (1939) that 'modern material organization . . . has produced a world for which Christian social forms are imperfectly adapted'; but there are simplifications of the problem that are 'suspect': 'One is to insist that the only salvation for society is to return to a simpler mode of life, scrapping all the constructions of the modern world that we can bring ourselves to dispense with. This is an extreme statement of the neo-Ruskinian view, which was put forward with much vigour by the late A. J. Penty. When one considers the large amount of determination in social structure, this policy appears Utopian: if such a way of life ever comes to pass, it will be – as may well happen in the long run – from natural causes, and not from the moral will of men' (New edn with Intro. by David L. Edwards [1982], 60).

2–FVM wrote to Penty on 15 May 1931: '[Eliot] and I have both read *Means and Ends*, and are both interested in it. I think he wants to make a suggestion to you regarding it . . .'

to read a more or less controversial pamphlet about some already pretty clearly defined subject of the day, not too philosophical in scope.

I wish therefore to ask you whether you would not consider reducing the size of this essay so as to make it possible to include it in the *Criterion* itself. It is just the sort of writing that I want, and I am very much in sympathy with your point of view. If you cannot do this, would you be willing at least to prepare some statement of your ideas in the form of an essay from five to ten thousand words that I could publish?[1]

Sincerely yours,

[T. S. Eliot]

P.S. Should you be in London at any time, I should be very happy to talk the matter over with you.

TO *F. S. Oliver*   CC

29 May 1931   [*The Criterion*]

Dear Oliver,

I am glad to hear from you again.[2] I can re-assure you about Bonamy Dobrée, who is now a small squire in Norfolk and is, I believe, in the best of health though I have not seen him for about six weeks. For some months past he has been engaged chiefly upon an edition of Chesterfield's Letters which Eyre and Spottiswood are to publish. He has however given three broadcast talks on Defoe and has written a review for the number of the *Criterion* which is about to appear.[3]

My wife and I are both in moderately good health. I hope that your plans for going to Scotland mean that you have completely recovered from the effects of your pleurisy. If you had time and inclination and did not find it too fatiguing to see visitors, I should like to make one more attempt to come out to see you before you leave.

Yours ever sincerely,

[T. S. Eliot]

1–Arthur J. Penty, 'Means and Ends', C. 11 (Oct. 1931), 1–24.
2–Letter not found.
3–BD, review of Frederick Manning, *Scenes and Portraits*, and G. Lowes Dickinson, *After 2000 Years*, in C. 10 (July 1931), 733–6.

30 May 1931   *The Criterion*

My dear Spender,

Many thanks for your summer address.[1] I do not know that coast, but it sounds most satisfactory – I think you are wise to avoid mountains – I recall a summer, long ago, in the Salzkammergut – intense heat, innumerable flies, and the village brass band two evenings a week. Mountains are only tolerable if one is not too near, and if there is a bit of water to break the monotony of the imprisonment – Lake Geneva possibly.

I do not think that I have written since you explained in full your reasons for not wanting to review Lewis.[2] They are in fact remarkably like every one's else [*sic*] reasons for declining to review Lewis, so they need no further elucidation. I have accordingly presented the Hitler book to Alport, to pass on to Clauss, in the hope of collecting privately a few German opinions. Alport is in England at the moment and has set me some reading – an essay by Scheler on *Krieg und Frieden*, which is quite good,[3] Kurt Singer on Plato,[4] and Auden's friend Adrien Turel, who is almost undecipherable.[5]

I fear that you exaggerate the precision and detail of my knowledge of Beethoven: I am quite unconscious of any of the parallels you mention, and one or two of the works I do not know, or at least do not remember. I can claim nothing but a profound impression, mostly from the better known symphonies, sonatas and overtures, but dating certainly from an early time – and my eldest sister was playing Beethoven incessantly before I was out of the cradle. But my theory of writing verse is that one gets a rhythm, and a movement first, and fills it in with some approximation to sense later.

---

1 – Spender wrote on 20 May from the Insel Rügen, Sellin, where he was staying for two months. 'I tried to get rooms in the mountains near Munich, but they were all too expensive, and, besides that, I don't like mountains very much. The country here is really lovely. Our house is divided from the Baltic by a little wood, and immediately behind them is a lake . . . I have got a large room with a big table and with a balcony . . .'
2 – The letter from Spender to which these paragraphs respond has not been found.
3 – Not published in C.
4 – Alport lauded, on 1 Feb., Singer's 'remarkable paper [on] Plato and the Modern World in which he discusses Valéry's conception of European culture & arrives at a different conclusion'.
5 – Alport brought with him to London (as he told TSE in an advance letter of 8 May) a gathering of Adrien Turel's writings including 'Die Eroberung des Jennets' and a book entitled *Selbsterlösung* (1919) – 'containing essays, a paper & tales, all rather fascinating & beautiful'.

I hope the novel will soon be finished, since it must be, and separated from you.[1] I expect to have the June *Criterion* quite off my hands in a couple of days, and will then go through the poems of yours that I have with a view to choosing some for September.[2]

Yours sincerely,

T. S. Eliot

TO *Selden Rodman*[3]   TS Wyoming

30 May 1931   *The Criterion*

Dear Mr Rodman,[4]

Thank you very much for sending me a copy of *The Harkness Hoot*.[5] Of course I have no direct acquaintance with conditions at Yale, but this seems to me a bold and needed attempt – not a moment too soon, either. I suspect that Harvard is in just as bad a way or worse, and I know that the shadow of the Harkness beneficence is now over Oxford as well. I dare say there is still some higher education in France and Germany, but the English-speaking countries will soon have forgotten completely the meaning of the word. So I wish you success, and hope that you will let me see future numbers of the periodical.

1–*The Temple*. Spender wrote again on 18 Sept. that he was 'rather alarmed' to have received an acknowledgement from F&F.: 'I thought you had understood that *The Temple* was with the Hogarth Press now, and that my sending it to you was a private arrangement: I am so sorry if I did not make this clear. Curtis Brown are managing the Manuscript which is for publication. However, I believe the Hogarth Press are going to reject it as they were very annoyed because I said I couldn't let them have my poems: if they do reject it, shall I ask Higham (Curtis Brown's manager) to send the book to Faber?'
2–'Three Poems ('Moving through the silent crowd', 'Your body is stars whose million glitter here', 'The Prisoners')', C. 9 (Oct. 1931), 47–9.
3–Selden Rodman (1909–2002): poet, cultural critic, advocate of folk art (especially Haitian); he co-founded the Yale satirical magazine *Harkness Hoot*; funded by family money, he travelled in Europe and introduced himself to celebrated figures including EP and JJ. In the 1930s he co-edited the left-wing journal *Common Sense* (publishing pieces by the likes of W. H. Auden, Stephen Spender, Theodore Dreiser and Edmund Wilson). His own works include *Mortal Triumph and Other Poems* (1932) and *Challenge to the New Deal* (with Alfred Bingham, 1935).
4–Rodman told EVE on 17 Oct. 1988 that a fire in 1972 had 'consumed' his correspondence; surviving letters, including damaged ones, had been taken over by the University of Wyoming.
5–'My personal reason for sending it to you arises out of my interest in your work and a desire to have your reaction to my long poem "Departure" printed in this number.'

I was interested by your poem, and should like to see more of your work.
Yours sincerely,
T. S. Eliot

TO *C. S. Lewis*[1]   CC

1 June 1931   [*The Criterion*]

Dear Sir,

I must apologise humbly for having kept your essay such a very long
time.[2] It did not, however, lie unread but has been under consideration
almost ever since I received it. It is an essay which I should like very much
to use at some time but I have been rather overloaded with essays in the
Theory of Criticism, some of them quite excellent, and have really had
more of this type of writing than even the *Criterion* can well bear. So I
think I had better return it to you with apologies, but with the suggestion
that I would gladly see it again in nine months time if you have not meanwhile published it, and that I should also very much like to hear from you
if you have any other essays or suggestions for essays which you would
like to submit to the *Criterion*.[3]

Yours very truly,
[T. S. Eliot]

---

1 – C. S. ('Jack') Lewis (1898–1963): Northern Irish novelist, scholar-critic, medievalist, lay
theologian, Christian apologist (a convert to Anglicanism in 1931), broadcaster; member of
the 'Inklings' (with J. R. R. Tolkien, Nevill Coghill, Charles Williams and Owen Barfield);
Fellow and Tutor in English Literature, Magdalen College, Oxford, 1925–54; Chair of
Mediaeval and Renaissance Literature, Magdalene College, Cambridge, 1954–63. His works
include *The Chronicles of Narnia* (1949–54); *The Allegory of Love* (1936); *The Discarded
Image: An Introduction to Medieval and Renaissance Literature* (1964); *Surprised by Joy*
(1955); *A Grief Observed* (1961). See also Humphrey Carpenter, *The Inklings: C. S. Lewis,
J. R. R. Tolkien, Charles Williams and Their Friends* (1978); and Barry Spurr, *'Anglo-Catholic
in Religion': T. S. Eliot and Christianity* (2010), App. 3: 'T. S. Eliot and C. S. Lewis', 254–6.
2 – Lewis had submitted 'The Personal Heresy in Criticism' *c.* Oct. 1930; six months later
(19 Apr. 1931), he was politely impatient: 'I contended that poetry never was nor could be
the "expression of a personality" save *per accidens*, and I advanced a formal proof of this
position. As I believe that you had some sympathy with the contention, and that, though
often asserted, it had not before been proved, I had anticipated a fairly early reply.' Owen
Barfield had approached TSE twice (2 Nov. 1930, 28 May 1931) on behalf of Lewis (who
favoured the pen name 'Clive Hamilton'). On the second occasion, Barfield had importuned
TSE: 'I dare not say that so helpless and unjustifiable a creature as a freelance contributor
is "entitled" to anything but in the circumstances it certainly seems to me that equity looks
to you for an act of grace.'
3 – Lewis replied to this rejection on 2 June that he would 'have no objection to waiting nine
months: what I should like to be more assured of is the prospect I have at the end of the nine

2 June 1931   68 Clarence Gate Gardens

My dear Mary

I am dreadfully sorry and shocked at what happened last night and this morning. I had so much looked forward to you all 3 coming. Something seemed to upset Tom very much indeed yesterday. It may be that the message from Jack had *something* to do with it. At any rate he was quite beside himself for most of the night. And we have had so much trouble with the dog – it fell ? off the roof (the sloping roof of the coal cellar) a week ago: & has had to be taken to the Vet. every day since. To be bandaged, etc. A sickening job. The incident was sent from God, as a birthday present for me, last week.[1] But it did not quite come off.

I feel dreadfully ill tonight, so must go to bed. I do like sometimes to think how near you are.

We are now quite 'calm' and so *please* can you telephone tomorrow morning & *suggest* any meal for you & Jim to come here, and Jack OF COURSE. I really shd. like a few words with yr brother before he goes back. If you prefer it, I can be at home any afternoon this week, and *any* evening *after* dinner.

You probably understand all this *better than I do*. But do ring me up even if you have nothing immediately to suggest.

With love,

Vivienne Haigh Eliot

---

months . . . I am quite prepared for the risk of your "corrected impressions". What I am less ready to lie at the mercy of is the mere richness or poverty of suitable contributions – the fullness or emptiness of your drawer – nine months hence, which nobody can predict . . .

'The essay does, as you have divined, form the first of a series of which I have all the materials to hand. <It is merely a question of giving me a less technically philosophical turn.> The others would be

   2. Objective standards of literary merit.
   3. Literature and Virtue (This is not a stylistic variant of "Art & Morality:" that is my whole point).
   4. Literature and Knowledge.
   5. Metaphor and Truth.

'The whole, when completed, would form a frontal attack on Crocean aesthetics and state a neo-Aristotelian theory of literature (not of Art, about which I say nothing) which *inter alia* will re-affirm the romantic doctrine of imagination as a truth-bearing faculty, though not quite as the romantics understood it.'

1 – VHE's birthday was on 28 May.

TO *Conrad Aiken* CC

3 June 1931 [Faber & Faber Ltd]

My dear Conrad,

I apologise feebly for the long delay[1] – but matters were by no means in my own exclusive hands – though when they are, candour says that the delays are often much longer. But the question had to come up as one of general policy at this juncture: whether we were sufficiently prosperous or times promising enough for the next season or two to allow us to consider publishing reputable poets, or even One: and the conclusion is that in the present unsettled conditions we are compelled to stick to rubbish. – What about the Hogarth, in conjunction with Scribner's?

I am more than sorry myself, but perhaps personal remarks would be impertinent while in my rôle of publisher.

Can you come up for Harold's on the 9th? I wish you could: no one has seen you for years.

Yours ever
[Tom]

TO *James Joyce* MS Buffalo

4 June 1931 Faber & Faber Ltd

I could not change this here and did not have time to send to the Bank.

If you want this changed into £1's will you please send them back to me in the morning? I'm very sorry I did not manage to get them changed.

T. S. E.

FROM *Vivien Eliot* TO *Mary Hutchinson* TS Texas

Sunday, 8 June 1931 68 Clarence Gate Gardens

My dear Mary,

I tried three times on the telephone today to make an arrangement with your brother, (Tom tried once himself) and nothing whatever came of it. No-one seemed to know anything, so we at last gave up.

---

1 – On 19 May, Aiken had sent this telegram: 'HURRY UP PLEASE ITS TIME = CONRAD.' He was hoping against hope for a good word from F&F about the two works he had submitted to TSE late in March: *The Coming Forth by Day of Osiris Jones* and *Preludes for Memnon*.

I am really sorry, because I had reasons for wanting to see him before he went back to Dalmatia (is it?)

At any rate I *expect you here* tomorrow afternoon at 3 o'clock, and we will go for a drive, as we arranged on the telephone, and discuss everything.[1] If however your brother decides to stay on longer, do just *bring him with you.*

With love,
Vivienne Haigh Eliot

TO *Eleanor Hinkley*   TS Houghton

8 June 1931   Faber & Faber Ltd

Dear Eleanor,

Thank you very much for your delightful May 23d letter, which I hardly deserve. I am glad you like Richards – I wonder what on earth Mrs R. is doing, and when she will join him – the sunstroke, I gather, was not inflicted in Cambridge Mass. I should not have thought of him as effeminate – rather sexless perhaps, just an intellect and a body, but the body is a very muscular and intrepid one: at any rate, I, who dislike looking out of a third storey window should not call effeminate such a daring mountain climber as he. Not that Mrs R. is not just as great a climber – I believe quite a celebrity in the Alps – when and if you meet her, inspect the muscular development of her calves – unless she has conceded so far to recent fashions in dress as to make that impossible. I can hardly believe that he meant to be nasty about Virginia, whom he can hardly know very well. For that matter, it is no secret that she was once raving insane – I have it not only on her husband's authority but her own, and know more about it than most people outside of the family. On the other hand, when a woman can refer calmly to the period 'when I was mad' it is a very good sign that she is perfectly sane; and if Richards does think that her sanity is any judgment against her writings, he is quite mistaken. There is unfortunately hereditary insanity in the family – her cousin Fitz

1–Edith Sitwell gossiped to Siegfried Sassoon on 16 Mar. 1932: 'The Eliots are coming to tea with me today, and I am terrified. Vivienne gets more and more possibilities into her conversation. Did you hear the story about the bees? – Smutch [Mary] Hutchinson was having tea with her, in June, and Vivienne enquired if she was enjoying the honey, – (there being no honey). On Smutch replying, nervously, that she was enjoying it very much, Vivienne asked if she kept bees. Smutch said no. Whereupon V. replied, very dreamily: "Neither do I. I keep *hornets. In my bed*!" Sensation. Curtain' (Holland Library, WSU; cited in Richard Greene, *Edith Sitwell: Avant-Garde Poet, English Genius* [2011], 222).

James Stephen was a tragically brilliant person;[1] but those who are sane are perfectly sane.

I don't know much about Elton,[2] and have never read anything of his. I feel greatly flattered however if I could be useful to you in his course – and what did he think about it, I wonder? I have written only a few scraps of papers lately – my theological pamphlet which I sent you took a terrible length of time, and involved a great deal of correspondence too – I could hardly have done it without the help of the Archbishop of York, but that is not for publication, as my views are not supposed to have any official sanction, and as a whole, they are solely my own. And I have just finished a long essay on Pascal for a preface to the Everyman edition, and have just got the June *Criterion* off my hands – I took on Murry's book on D. H. Lawrence to review myself, and that took up a good deal of time.

Vita (Victoria) Sackville-West (i.e. the Hon. Mrs Nicolson) is a very charming person, with almost the most beautiful voice I have ever heard; she is a great friend, of course, of Virginia Woolf.[3] She was somewhat handicapped in life by being an only child and not being a boy to inherit the peerage which goes to her cousin; she is married to Harold Nicolson, a hearty fellow who was doing well in the diplomatic service, and who unaccountably chucked it up merely to engage in London journalism, in which his literary merits have steadily deteriorated.[4]

I imagine that the Spencer (Spenser (sic)) [*sic*] you saw was probably the elegant Theodore, who is now a Fellow or whatever Lowell calls it of one of the new Halls or Colleges, but I understand that his Hall or College has not yet been built. We have just had here his Aunt, Miss Katharine Spencer who was a neighbour of mother's in Concord Avenue, a most jolly and cultivated woman whom we liked immensely.

I enjoyed your account of your social activities immensely. I should love to drop in on one of your Sunday evenings, unexpectedly! Perhaps

1 – Sir James Fitzjames Stephen, 1st Baronet (1829–94), lawyer, judge and writer, was VW's uncle; his final years were marked by physical and more conspicuous mental decline.
2 – Oliver Elton (Emeritus Prof., University of Liverpool): Eleanor was taking his course on 'Poetics and Criticism', 1930–1.
3 – Clive Bell wrote to Mary Hutchinson, 2 Aug. 1931: 'at lunch the other day Tom Eliot (poet) Kauffer (engraver-printer) Frankie Birrell (book-seller) and Clive (brother-in-law) had a thorough good talk about the Hogarth Press: it would have done the proprietor good to have heard every word of it. It does seem to me odd that they should grow rich on the sale of Vita's books.'
4 – Harold Nicolson (1886–1968) relinquished in 1930 a thriving career in the Diplomatic Service to work as a journalist for the *Evening Standard*. In Mar. 1931 he left the *Standard* to join Sir Oswald Mosley's New Party and soon became editor of the New Party's journal *Action*.

one day I will. Now WHAT are you going to do this summer, and are you coming over in the autumn as Aunt Susie promised?

Ever affectionately,
Tom

TO *Sonia Hambourg*[1]

8 June 1931   [Faber & Faber Ltd]

Dear Miss Hambourg,

I am now able to make tentative suggestions for your approval about the poems.[2] I understand from you that you have a duplicate copy of them, exactly as you sent them to me, and therefore I will merely refer to the ones I want to use.

I am leaving out, for this volume, all of the early work. Of the sheaf headed *Unpublished Poems* I should take everything except 'Leaving the Hook of Holland'. From that headed *Published in Oxford Poetry, 1929*, I should use all three. Also 'Sudden Death', 'The Winter Sunlight' and possibly 'Restaurant' though I am not so sure about this last.

That is the omission of all the poems marked up to the age of eighteen, and those *Published in Oxford Poetry, 1917 and 1928*. If, however, these should turn out to make not quite enough pages, I should add a few from 1927 and 1928.

I shall be glad to hear before you go away whether you approve of this choice and whether you have any suggestions to make. I should also be very glad if you would let me know any preference you may have about the arrangement of those selected.[3]

Yours sincerely,
[T. S. Eliot]

1–Sonia Hambourg (b. 1898) studied History at Somerville College, Oxford (where she was a friend of the poet Clere Parsons), and later worked as editorial director of Albatross Publications in Paris. Her works included two successful anthologies (both edited with R. H. Boothroyd), *The Albatross Book of Living Prose* (1937) and *The Albatross Book of English Humour* (1938).
2–HR had been asked earlier in the year to 'help and advise on the question of Clere Parson's [*sic*] relicts,' as he put it in a letter to TSE of 26 Mar.
3–Hambourg responded on 11 June: 'I am in entire agreement with your choice of poems and am most grateful to be able to leave the judging of what is best to you.'

TO *Alistair Cooke*[1]   CC

10 June 1931   [Faber & Faber Ltd]

Dear Mr Cooke,

I am so sorry to have been a nuisance by my neglect to reply to your first very full letter which, as a matter of fact, I thought I had answered.[2] I have not the slightest objection to your making any use of whatever ideas *The Hollow Men* has suggested to you or to your using in the performance the lines which you quote. I should only have serious objections to the use of the whole text or of the title, either of which might suggest that this was an authoritative interpretation and not a separate invention suggested by my own. My objection of that kind would be exactly the same as my objection to having certain of my poems illustrated, that it would tend to interpose the interpretation of one reader between myself and the general reader. I did, as a matter of fact, once decline an invitation to allow *The Hollow Men* to be produced on stage, as a sort of small ballet.

But to what you intend, as I understand it, I have no objection, and I should be very interested to hear from you later about the success of your venture.

Yours sincerely,
[T. S. Eliot]

1 – Alistair (Alfred) Cooke (1908–2004), broadcaster and writer, was brought up in Salford, Lancashire, and read English at Jesus College, Cambridge – where he founded the Mummers, the university's first dramatic group to admit women as well as men, and contributed to *Granta*, which in due course he also edited. From Cambridge he proceeded in 1932 to visit the USA on a Commonwealth Fund fellowship which enabled him to study theatre at Yale and linguistics at Harvard. (He had long nurtured a passion for all things American including jazz music.) During his extensive travels round America, he interviewed *inter alia* Charlie Chaplin, who hired him as a scriptwriter for a film about Napoleon that was never in fact completed. From the mid-1930s, back in London, he made shift to begin a career with the BBC, while also working for the American network NBC on a London letter that was broadcast to New York every Sunday. In later years he wrote a great deal for the *Manchester Guardian*; and in 1946 he essayed a short series of radio talks entitled *Letter from America* which eventuated in a record run of fifty-eight years. In the 1970s he became ever more famous with a TV series entitled *Alistair Cooke's America* – the accompanying book sold two million copies – and a series on American music. Having taken US citizenship in 1941, he was made an honorary KBE in 1973. See further Nick Clarke, *Alistair Cooke: The Biography* (1999).
2 – Cooke wrote first on 15 May, then on 1 June, with the request that he might set to music the first stanza of 'The Hollow Men' as an item in a sentimental fantasy to be produced in The Mummers 1931 Revue (which was due to tour in Devon from 20 June). The script had to be submitted for approval by the Lord Chamberlain's office by the second week of June.

TO *Lincoln Kirstein*[1]   TS Beinecke

12 June 1931   Faber & Faber Ltd

Dear Mr Kirstein,

Many thanks for your note of the 5th June.[2] Had I had any verse to offer you, you would have received it, but I am not likely to have anything this year except a piece which I am working on for the Ariel Poems.[3] I am afraid it would be impossible to give you that as it is a condition of this series that the poem should not have been previously published. So I am afraid we must wait.

I wish that I could see the *Hound and Horn* more regularly, but as you know, the exchange copies go direct to Bonamy Dobrée.

Yours sincerely,
T. S. Eliot

TO *Max Rychner*[4]   CC

12 June 1931   [*The Criterion*]

My dear Dr Rychner,

It is now some time since we have had a German Chronicle from you for the *Criterion*, and I should be more than grateful if you could let us have one for the September number. I should like to have the copy by August 1st; if this is inconvenient would you be so kind as to let me know, so that I can make other arrangements.

1–Lincoln Kirstein (1907–96), writer, impresario, connoisseur of art, was born into a wealthy and cultivated Jewish family (his father was chief executive of the Boston department store Filene's). At Harvard he set up, with a contemporary, Varian Fry, the periodical *Hound & Horn: A Harvard Miscellany* – specifically modelling it on C. – which ran from 1927 until 1934. Smitten by what he styled 'balletptomaine', he launched in 1933, with his friend M. M. Warburg, the School of American Ballet, and then the American Ballet, which became the resident company of the Metropolitan Opera in New York. In 1946, he founded, with George Balanchine, the Ballet Society, later the New York City Ballet, of which he was General Director, 1946–89. In the 1960s he commissioned and helped to fund the New York State Theater building at the Lincoln Center. In 1935 he published *Dance: A Short History of Classic Theatrical Dancing*. See Martin Duberman, *The Worlds of Lincoln Kirstein* (2007).
2–Kirstein offered (5 June) to publish in *The Hound & Horn* any poetry 'you might care to send': 'I have no idea at all as to your attitude towards the possibility of printing, for example, such verses as MARINA or ANIMULA, before they come out in the Criterion Miscellany.'
3–*Triumphal March* was to be published as Ariel Poem no. 35 on 8 Oct. 1931.
4–Max Rychner (1897–1965): writer and critic; editor of *Neue Schweizer Rundschau* (Zurich).

As *Die Neue Schweizer Rundschau* goes to Randall in Bucarest for review, I never see a copy except when you send it to me personally. Would it be possible to arrange to have another copy sent to me direct, as I should like to keep in closer touch with your review. I should be very glad to send another copy of the *Criterion* in exchange if that would be of any use to you. I should particularly like to have a back number in which you published a part of Scheler's Essay on Pacifism.[1] I have seen the part which was published in the *Europaische Revue*[2] and I have the whole essay which has just appeared, and I am thinking of using a part in the *Criterion* if permission can be obtained.[3]

With all best wishes,

Yours sincerely,
[T. S. Eliot]

TO *John Cournos*   CC

12 June 1931   [*The Criterion*]

Dear Cournos,

I am writing in the hope of catching you before you leave for America. I am very sorry to hear that you have to migrate once more and I hope that the result will justify it, and that your and your family's health will be good.[4] The supply of Russian Periodicals has been very meagre of late, otherwise I should have liked to have had a review of them at once. Miss Malnick[5] has written again to Moscow and I hope that more will be forthcoming. You do not say where you are sailing from but I take it that you will not be passing through London, otherwise I should certainly have hoped to see you both.

Yours ever sincerely,
[T. S. Eliot]

1 – *Die Idee des Friedens und der Pazifismus.*
2 – *Europäische Revue* 7.
3 – Rychner replied (15 June) that henceforth TSE would receive *Neue Schweizer Rundschau* on a regular basis – he had instructed the publisher to that effect – and he would send a German chronicle for *C*. He said too that he would be grateful to receive TSE's books; he had seen *Dante* while visiting E. R. Curtius in Bonn, and found it 'very enticing'.
4 – Cournos wrote (9 June) that he was leaving for the USA on the 19th. 'Health of the family good, but economics, like health, can play the very devil with one. The present depression has hit me very hard, and I've always managed to pick up a little money on the other side.

'It is one of my regrets that fifteen minutes was all we've seen of one another since my last flight . . .'
5 – Bertha Malnick.

TO *Michael Sayers*   CC

15 June 1931   [Faber & Faber Ltd]

Dear Sayers,

I am glad to hear from you after such a long time and to know that at
least there has been no acute crisis meanwhile.[1] I am inclined to think that
you are obeying the right instinct in keeping out of political occupation
although, of course, that depends partly on the inducements, the nature of
the job and your own necessities. I shall look forward to seeing your new
series of poems as soon as you are ready to show them to me.

Yours sincerely,
[T. S. Eliot]

TO *George Williamson*   CC

15 June 1931   [Faber & Faber Ltd]

Dear Mr Williamson,

I shall not attempt to answer adequately your charming letter of the 12th
of May.[2] This is merely to say that I shall look forward with particular
pleasure to seeing you whilst you are in London, and I shall count upon
you to let me know as soon as you arrive.

1–Sayers wrote on 12 June: 'Mr Joad suggested some position for me in the New Party,
but I am temperamentally and intellectually averse to politics. I believe the solution to our
disintegration lies, not in any economic redistribution of money and production, or in a
political upheaval, but rather in that sphere of human activity circumscribed by, to speak
loosely, Religion.' He was writing more poems and 'endeavouring to have published a
selection'; but he wished 'to be allowed to beg' TSE's advice on 'the chances of success'.

2–Williamson was due to spend a year in England, researching seventeenth-century
literature, and hoped to meet TSE. 'I have been reading your "Thoughts after Lambeth"
with the greatest pleasure. It seems to me that you have allowed your various qualities fuller
play in this essay than in almost anything you have written. Since I fall under your stigma
of American academic respectability, I may at least plead a respectability that appreciates its
predicament, though it is not the same as Mr Foerster's. In the Harvard tercentenary volume
on Donne I have an essay which, I hope, will not be found to have drawn too much nonsense
out of your latest poetry; but I was asked to write on the precarious topic of "Donne and
the Poetry of Today". Ever since your last letter I have regretted becoming the cause of your
recasting "The School of Donne", for I, for one, would hate to miss anything that you had
planned to say on the subject. My one consolation is that so far my own work on the subject
has not been held to reflect discredit upon you, and may have brought your thought to some
in the deepest academic slumber. It would be a small (perhaps ambiguous) return for an
increasing debt of stimulation and pleasure.'

With many thanks,

Yours sincerely,
[T. S. Eliot]

TO *Hugh Ross Williamson*[1]   CC

15 June 1931   [Faber & Faber Ltd]

Dear Mr Williamson,

Thank you for your letter of June 9th.[2] I have thought over very carefully your suggestion for your anthology and I very much regret that I cannot allow either of the poems you suggest to be included. *The Journey of the Magi* still has a small sale in its shilling form and I prefer not to allow it to appear in any anthology in England until it has been included in a book of my own verse. The section 'Because I do not hope to turn again' is part of a poem which is, at least, intended to have a certain unity and I should not care to have any parts of this appear separately. I am very sorry indeed that I cannot give you my consent.

With all best wishes,

Yours very truly,
[T. S. Eliot]

TO *Sonia Hambourg*   CC

15 June 1931   [Faber & Faber Ltd]

Dear Miss Hambourg,

Thank you for your letter of the 11th. Of the two arrangements you suggest, I think that the first is preferable as arranging short poems

1–Hugh Ross Williamson (1901–78), author, historian, dramatist, journalist and broadcaster, worked as a journalist on the *Yorkshire Post* (leader-writer, drama critic) before becoming editor of *The Bookman*, 1930–4. Geoffrey Grigson would recall that Williamson 'worked hard to drag that tame old-fashioned literary journal from allegiance to the Squirearchy to support of Eliotry and Audenism [and] to conduct what we thought was the necessary game of harassing the Sitwells as pretenders to modernism' (*The Times*, 21 Jan. 1978). Robert Waller wrote of him, in *Pilgrimage of Eros*: 'He was exuberant, witty and a bit of a dandy.' In 1943 he was ordained in the Church of England and was for twelve years an Anglo-Catholic curate before converting to Roman Catholicism in 1955. A prolific author, he wrote over thirty-five books, including *The Poetry of T. S. Eliot* (1932), biographies and histories. See too *The Walled Garden* (autobiography, 1956).

2–Williamson was revising *The Bookman Treasury of Living Poets* (1925), ed. St John Adcock, and asked to include *Journey of the Magi* and 'Because I do hope to turn again' (*Ash-Wednesday* I) – 'I think the latter would not necessarily lose by being printed separately . . .'

according to subject matter seems to me to defeat its own object. I am writing at once to ask for information on one small point. In your list you put 'Winter Sunlight' third, and again in the fourth line; which is the proper place for it?

I agree with you about the desirability of some indication that the publication is posthumous, and am discussing the matter and will write to you again.

Yours sincerely,
[T. S. Eliot]

TO *Horace Gregory*

TS Syracuse

17 June 1931   Faber & Faber Ltd

Dear Mr Gregory,

Thank you for your letter of the 25th returning the contract.[1] Your instructions about the dedication have been noted and the book is now well under way. I look forward to reading your Catullus with curiosity.[2]

I have received and read the manuscripts from White and Grudin;[3] both interested me but especially the latter. I *was* very sorry to have to say to them both, however, that we could not contemplate taking on any more books of verse at the present time. I am very glad to have seen them, however, and as I hope that our series may have a long life, even though the volumes appear but rarely, I shall always be interested to see such manuscripts from time to time.

With many thanks,

Sincerely yours,
T. S. Eliot

1 – The contract for *Rooming-House*.
2 – 'My Catullus is completed . . .' Gregory, *The Poems of Catullus* (New York, 1931).
3 – Gregory had sent manuscripts by Hal Sanders White and Louis Grudin. 'You may have noted Grudin's "Definition of Poetry" which appeared in the April 1930 issue of THE SYMPOSIUM and which received favorable mention in THE CRITERION.' Hal Saunders White (New York City), an instructor in English at Harvard – husband of Margaret Marshall (1900–74) – submitted 'The Rock' on 25 May.

TO *Louis Grudin*[1]   CC

17 June 1931   [Faber & Faber Ltd]

Dear Mr Grudin,

Thank you for your letter of the 4th of June and for *Equations*, and for
A Primer of Aesthetics.[2] The last I look forward to reading, the second
I have read with real pleasure, and wish that we could see our way to
publishing it. But in the present condition of publishing in England, we
can only expect to produce a bare minimum of verse. I doubt if we shall
bring out any more volumes for another year or two.

Meanwhile, I shall hope to see your poems again when they are
published by Harcourt Brace.

> With many thanks,
> Yours sincerely,
> [T. S. Eliot]

TO *Stuart Gilbert*   CC

17 June 1931   [*The Criterion*]

Dear Mr Gilbert,

I have read your sketch[3] with much enjoyment, but as the *Criterion* has
a good deal of accepted matter on hand, and as this does not seem to us
quite suitable for our purposes, I am returning it with thanks.

> Yours sincerely,
> [T. S. Eliot]

1–Louis Grudin (1899–1993): Ukrainian-born American poet, artist, critic and editor,
denizen of Greenwich Village, who published poems and reviews in *N.*, *The Saturday
Review of Literature*, *The Little Review*, *Broom* and *The Dial*. Works include *A Primer
of Aesthetics: Logical Approaches to a Philosophy of Art* (1930), *Mister Eliot Among the
Nightingales* (1932).
2–Grudin, who was formerly an editor for Covici, Friede, sent *A Primer of Aesthetics*
together with a new book of his poems, *Equations*, which was due to be published by
Harcourt, Brace.
3–Gilbert submitted on 10 May 'a brief story, or, rather sketch . . . I fear there is little in the
"plot" (which, however, is based on an actual experience I had in Switzerland last summer),
but venture to hope that the technique may be of some interest – and the means justify
the end.'

TO *Monk Gibbon*[1] CC

17 June 1931   [Faber & Faber Ltd]

Dear Mr Gibbon,

I regret that we have been unable to use your poem for the Ariel Series, which is designed, as a matter of fact, for authors whose names are already well-known to the public.[2]

I shall always be glad to see more of your work.

Yours sincerely,
[T. S. Eliot]

TO *John W. Nance* CC

17 June 1931   [Faber & Faber Ltd]

Dear Mr Nance,

You may remember that we had a little correspondence a considerable time ago. I have read your *Notes on the Qualitative Analysis of Emotional Sensibility* with great interest, and have been puzzling my head over the question of what can be done about them.[3] Things being as they are, I cannot consider the book a possible publishing venture for us and I am not sure that I can think of any publisher at the moment who would care to undertake it. Yet I should be very sorry if such investigations had to remain completely obscure and unknown to the possible two or three hundred individuals who are interested in Poetic Theory. Having at the moment no suggestions to offer, I must merely return you the manuscript,

1–(William) Monk Gibbon (1896–1987): Irish poet and author; cousin of WBY – see *The Masterpiece and the Man: Yeats as I Knew Him* (1959). See further Norman MacKenzie, 'The Monk Gibbon Papers', *The Canadian Journal of Irish Studies* 9: 2 (Dec. 1983), 5–24.
2–Gibbon asked on 16 Dec. 1930, 'Are the Ariel Poets reserved for writers of established reputation or are you open to consider anyone's work?', and then submitted on 17 June 1931 a poem entitled 'The Babe' – possibly because he had not received a reply to his initial letter.
3–Nance wrote to TSE on 4 May 1931, 'I enclose a typescript with a terrifying title which may nevertheless interest you ... I have been disgustingly interested in poetry ever since I was a very small boy: and the mechanics of the art interested me hugely. Later, reading the poems of Pound primarily, and then of Lawrence and of Aldington, I found a singular progression from the purely emotional to the largely intellectual which I thought demanded some explanation. I studied the question separately in its motives, and in its results. The study of the results, which was of course a study of the development of the modern technique, was sent some time ago to Mr Eliot, who expressed interest in it. But I very soon found that the two things were inextricably mingled. There was only one solution – a combination, and naturally a most unsatisfactory one.'

but if you should offer it to anyone else I should be glad if you cared to use my name, and should be glad also to put in a personal word if I happen to know the publisher in question.

> Yours sincerely,
> [T. S. Eliot]
> Director.

TO *Marguerite Caetani*

23 June 1931   Faber & Faber Ltd

Dear Marguerite,

I suppose it is impertinent to ask for news of you, because I think that I ought to have written long ago – but I have had no poem to offer in justification. I have done a part of a projected long poem, but this part must be used for our 'Ariel' series in the autumn, so I cannot give you use of the English text; but when I have done another section, I can offer you that if it proves suitable.

When you are next in Rome, may I give my brother-in-law (Vivienne's brother) an introduction to you? He is a very nice fellow, was a regular-army officer, retired after the war, and is now Rome representative of some American Bankers, G. H. Burr & Co., and is married to an American girl from New York. I suppose that you are probably at Versailles, and will be going to the seaside. I hope that your family are now all in good health.

> Affectionately yours,
> Tom

Did you see a book we published, of spook experience at Versailles, called *An Adventure*?[1] I thought it extremely interesting. The brother of Miss Jourdain was a friend of mine.

1–C. A. E. Moberly and E. F. Jourdain, *An Adventure* (1931).

TO *Allen Tate*   TS Princeton

23 June 1931   *The Criterion*

Dear Tate,

I like your essay but I am very doubtful whether it is suitable for the *Criterion*.[1] I don't mind in the least extreme views, but it seems to me, merely as a matter of strategy, that satire of this sort, being directed primarily at local abuses or local manifestations of general abuses, has to [be] applied locally, like the old Indian's painkiller. Being mainly applicable to America it would hardly be sufficiently irritating to the British Public. Will you not have something more for me before long, and perhaps a few poems?

Yours sincerely,
T. S. Eliot

TO *Ruth Harrison*   CC

23 June 1931   [*The Criterion*]

Dear Miss Harrison,

I have read your essay on Péguy with sympathetic interest.[2] I hope I have not deluded you but I feel on reading it that there is not much more in our publishing an essay on Péguy at the moment unless we can shew some particular pertinence to the present time. I hope that you will, as you suggest, submit an article on somewhat different lines.[3]

Yours sincerely,
[T. S. Eliot]

---

1 – Tate wrote on 9 May: 'Even if you like this essay, I have little idea that you, or for that matter anyone else, will be able to print it. I have tried it everywhere here, and I am beginning with you in England. Possibly it follows Swift too closely, so perhaps for that reason no less than because of its extreme views, it has been rejected in this country?' The essay is unidentified, but was possibly 'Religion and the Old South' (1930): *Collected Essays* (1959), 303–22.

2 – Ruth Harrison had submitted her article on 8 June 1931.

3 – In a later year, TSE wrote on the page next to a reprint of his article 'The Idealism of Julien Benda' (12 Dec 1928): 'I am surprised, & somewhat shocked, by my abuse of Péguy' (*The New Republic Anthology 1915:1935*, ed. Groff Conklin [1936], 293). TSE's Library.

TO *E. A. Harding*[1]   CC

23 June 1931   [Faber & Faber Ltd]

Dear Mr Harding,

I have kept the scripts of your two programmes for an unconscionable time, and I hope that I haven't been a nuisance, and that you are not annoyed with me.[2] They both interested me very much and I think there is considerable possibility for further development. If you should happen to be in town during part of July, will you allow me to return your hospitality by your lunching with me one day?

                              Yours sincerely
                              [T. S. Eliot]

TO *Sylvia Beach*   CC

23 June 1931   [*The Criterion*]

Dear Miss Beach,

Thank you very much for sending me Miss Monnier's lecture, which I found very interesting, but I do not think quite suitable for the *Criterion* at the present time.[3] I really want to wait until Joyce's new book is ready, or nearly ready, before publishing anything more about him, and then I should want to publish something which brings in the new work, which, it is to be hoped, will be more accessible than *Ulysses*. Please give my kindest regards to Miss Monnier, and believe me,

---

1–E. A. 'Archie' Harding (1903–53), educated at Keble College, Oxford, joined the BBC as announcer in 1927 and rapidly became one of the great movers and shapers of radio drama and reportage, based at Savoy Hill, London. In 1936 he joined the BBC's staff training department, of which he became director. From 1948 he was recruited to the drama department as deputy to Val Gielgud, nurturing radio techniques and talents (including the dramas of Louis MacNeice).

2–Harding had lent TSE, on 23 Feb., the scripts of two (unidentified) programmes he had mentioned when they met. 'They are only rough notations of works which do not properly exist except in terms of sound, and unless one is familiar with the technical devices we use here in productions it is difficult to get an idea of what they sound like . . . The lines allocated to the speakers are delivered with varying degrees of emphasis and in the different sound perspectives which the sense demands. The underlined directions indicate the addition to, or the superimposition upon, the sound picture of music or sound effects. That, I think, is about all the explanation I can give, but these scripts may suggest the extreme flexibility of wireless as a means of dramatic expression.'

3–Beach sent TSE (2 May) Adrienne Monnier's lecture 'Joyce et le Public Français', delivered at La Maison des Amis des Livres on 26 Mar. 1931.

With many thanks,

Sincerely yours,
[T. S. Eliot]

P.S. I wonder if you would be so kind as to transmit to Miss Monnier an apparently frivolous request? Would you mind asking her to send me the complete set of Arsène Lupin books, with an invoice; perhaps you could do it yourself but I imagined that this would be more convenient for her than for you? I do not want the other Leblanc books but only the ones dealing with Lupin.[1]

TO *John Gould Fletcher*   CC

23 June 1931   [*The Criterion*]

Dear Fletcher,

Thank you for the two reviews. I have sent them both to be set up although I am not quite sure that I shall be able to use them both. I should like, however, to do Ransom a good turn.[2]

I am glad to hear that you are getting on well and that your doctor has discharged you for the time being, but sorry to hear, as is my wife also, that we shall not see you again for some time.[3] I hope the weather in America will not be too hot for you. I should like to be going myself at this time, but if I went I should want to get Down East for the summer and not attempt the Mississippi Valley at this season.

Best of luck to you.
Yours ever,
[T. S. Eliot]

1–Maurice Leblanc (1864–1941): French novelist and short-story writer; creator of the gentleman-thief and detective Arsène Lupin (a character who featured in twenty-one volumes).

2–'I am afraid', wrote Fletcher (18 June), 'that the review of [John Crowe] Ransom's book is rather long – but I saw no way to shorten it, as the book is highly controversial.' See review of *God Without Thunder: An Unorthodox Defence of Orthodoxy*, in C. 11 (Oct. 1931), 127–31.

3–'My doctor tells me that the spot on my nose (treated finally out of hospital) is going on nicely. So I am taking the opportunity of slipping over to America for a brief visit.'

TO *E. E. Phare*[1]   CC

23 June 1931   [*The Criterion*]

Dear Madam,

I have read your essay on Father Hopkins with much interest, but have decided that we cannot give any more space to criticism of his work at the moment. I should much like to see more of your work.

Yours faithfully,
[T. S. Eliot]

TO *C. M. Bowra*[2]   CC

24 June 1931   [*The Criterion*]

Dear Mr Bowra,

Thank you for sending me your interesting paper on *Blok*. I think that I can use it if you will give me time. My September number has just been

---

1 – Elsie Phare (1908–2003) is better known by the surname Duncan-Jones: in 1933 she was to marry Austin Duncan-Jones (1908–67), who became Professor of Philosophy at Birmingham. She read English at Newnham College, Cambridge, where she was taught by IAR, FRL and Enid Welsford; she took a starred First with Special Distinction in both parts of the Tripos. As President of the Newnham College Arts Society, she invited VW (whom she found 'haughty') to give the talk that would become *A Room of One's Own* (1929). She went on to teach at Southampton University, 1931–4; Birmingham University, 1936–75. Her works include *The Poetry of Gerard Manley Hopkins: A Survey and Commentary* (1933); articles on subjects including TSE (1946); a British Academy Warton Lecture, 'A Great Master of Words: some aspects of Marvell's poems of praise and blame' (1976); and the third edition (with Pierre Legouis) of H. M. Margoliouth's *The Poems and Letters of Andrew Marvell* (2 vols, 1971).

2 – C. M. Bowra (1898–1971), educated at New College, Oxford (DLitt, 1937), was a Fellow and Tutor of Wadham College, Oxford, 1922–38; Warden of Wadham College, 1938–70; Oxford Professor of Poetry, 1946–51; Vice-Chancellor, 1951–4. President of the British Academy, 1958–62, he was knighted in 1951; appointed CH in 1971. Works include *Tradition and Design in the Iliad* (1930), *The Romantic Imagination* (1950) and *The Greek Experience* (1957).

TSE exclaimed to JDH on 23 June 1944: 'was there ever a more vulgar little fat Head of a House than he?' For Hope Mirrlees ('Christmas 1944') he turned to verse: 'Mr Maurice Bowra / Gets sourer and sourer, / Having been in a hurry / To succeed Gilbert Murray / And is now (poor soul) at the bottom: / I.e. Warden of Wadham' (Bodleian). He advised Theodore Spencer, 5 June 1948 (when Bowra had been appointed Eliot Norton Professor): '*If* you don't know him, I may mention that he is extremely social, a very amusing talker, with a trained palate (it is well known that he has at Wadham the best chef in Oxford) and a keen interest in people and their humours . . . He likes wealth and fashion as well as intelligence and wit.'

See further Leslie Mitchell, *Maurice Bowra: A Life* (2009); and Henry Hardy and Jennifer Holmes, '"Old Croaker": A new T. S. Eliot poem – by Maurice Bowra', *TLS*, 16 Sept. 2005, 14–15.

collected and I cannot be quite certain yet what I shall have to publish in December. So if meanwhile you wish to publish elsewhere will you merely notify me so that I may avoid duplication?[1]

By the way, is Bérard's book on *The Odyssey* important enough for us to review? And if so would you be inclined to review it for me yourself? There is also a new book on Greek Literary Criticism by the President of St John's which I dare say you know about.[2]

Yours sincerely,
[T. S. Eliot]

TO *William McC. Stewart*[3] CC

24 June 1931 *[The Criterion]*

Dear Mr Stewart,

Thank you for your letter of the 8th and for taking so much trouble over Erdmann's paper.[4] It puts me, however, in rather a quandary. I do not

1 – Bowra, 'The Position of Alexander Blok', C. 11 (Apr. 1932), 422–38.

2 – Bowra replied on 25 June, 'Bérard seems thin stuff to me, but Sykes [*sic*] deserves more attention, if only because he deals with a subject of first-rate importance. I would gladly review him . . .' See review of *The Greek View of Poetry*, by E. E. Sikes (1867–1940) – President of St John's College, Cambridge, 1925–37 – C. 11 (Oct. 1931), 116–18: 'He has no explicit standards of value, and he is completely free of any philosophical or historical outlook. He is, in the best sense of the word, an amateur; and his work has an amateur's value, but no more.' Victor Bérard's study *L'Odyssée d'Homère: étude et analyse* (1931) was not reviewed in C.

3 – William McCausland Stewart (1900–89) was educated at Trinity College, Dublin. Resident Lecteur d'Anglais, École Normale Supérieure, Paris, 1923–6 (while studying at the Sorbonne), he taught too at the École des Hautes Études. He was Lecturer in French, University of Sheffield, 1927–8, and taught at St Andrews and Dundee before becoming Professor of French at Bristol, 1945–68. He was elected Chevalier de la Légion d'Honneur, 1950; Officier des Palmes Académiques, 1950; Commandeur, 1966. Works include translations of Paul Valéry's *Eupalinos, or, The Architect* (1932) and *Dialogues* (1956).

Stewart wrote on 15 Dec. 1929 from St Andrews, Fife, Scotland, where he was joint Head of the French Department: 'I am sending you a small book in French on French Studies in Great Britain of which I am part-author – and sending it you, not because I hope that you will read it all, but mainly because in the concluding chapter . . . some points are raised which bear on the interests – or causes – you defend and attack in your *Criterion* commentaries.' Of his colleagues, he said: 'A. E. Taylor is no longer here but in Edinburgh; but recently Jonathan Tate, the clearest headed scholastic I know, came here as Lecturer in Greek.' He ended with this wish: 'So when you come to Scotland please do not neglect St Andrews . . .'

4 – Stewart had been correcting Karl Erdmann's paper on Edmund Burke (see TSE to Erdmann, 30 Dec. 1930, above), and writing an introduction to it. 'I confess that in composing this Introduction . . . I had in view the possibility of it and the paper appearing together in a collection like the *Criterion Miscellany* – with a general covering title such as:-

think that such an essay, even with your introduction would be practicable as a Miscellany pamphlet; it is essentially a periodical article in treatment. On the other hand, I still feel, as I think I told Erdmann at first, that the article falls into two parts and that the part which would be interesting to our readers is the second, dealing with Burke's influence in Germany. And I do not feel that Erdmann's general appreciation of Burke, however interesting, quite justifies itself as a preface to the subject of Burke in Germany. Do you think it would be possible to re-vamp the second part to make it independent, and do you think that Erdmann would object? Also, I think that there are still a few minor changes to be made to attenuate the tone of a paper read before a college society. Your suggestion that Mueller influenced Hofmannsthal and Becker is very interesting and I wish that it could have been made in Erdmann's essay itself.

Thank you very much for the copy of the *Modern Scot*, with your review, which is certainly very satisfying to the author.[1] I had, as a matter of fact, seen it when it came out but am very glad to have your corrected copy as one or two of the typographical errors did rather puzzle me.

I do not remember ever having seen your essay on 'Great Britain and Europe'.[2]

Yours sincerely,
[T. S. Eliot]

"Burke, Conservatism and Europe – A German View".' He added, *inter alia*: 'As regards Adam Mueller, Curtius attributes great importance to him, he inspired to a considerable extent Hofmannsthal's later conservatism, and [Carl Heinrich] Becker, the Prussian Culture-Minister, is I understand an admirer of his.'

1 – Stewart sent his review of *Ash-Wednesday*, written 'last summer' for *The Modern Scot*: 'I was somewhat annoyed at the time of its appearance by the misprints. However I have decided to send it to you – corrected. J. H. Whyte, the editor, was sorry, he read the proofs in great haste.'

2 – 'I do not know if I ever sent you a paper I read in Heidelberg and later in Paris and which was published in the *Europaïsche Review* on "Great Britain and Europe" . . .'

TO *C. A. Siepmann*   TS BBC

29 June 1931   Faber & Faber Ltd

Dear Mr Siepmann,

I shall look forward to coming to the Union Club at 1:30 on Thursday. I am afraid I have no general suggestions to make until I have discussed matters with you and Dawson and Macmurray.[1] My only suggestion at the moment is that perhaps the categories ought to be carefully subdivided, so that no two persons should appear as representative of quite the same point of view. As for individuals: I don't know who is the Revd F. R. Barry;[2] Mrs Woolf is a friend of mine and Mrs Mitcheson[3] I do not know at all; but I do not at first sight see the reason for having *both* – I should have thought their generation and in some respects their outlook too similar. And if there is to be but *one* representative of the Church, then I do not think Raven is representative enough:[4] he could only represent a Modernist-Evangelical outlook, and I think there would be complaints – and you would have to have two or three others. If there is to be only one for the Church, then it seems to me that it should be someone in a middle position who could not be accused of belonging to a party – e.g. the Bishop of Chichester. I think the Dean of Winchester one of the most brilliant younger men in the Church. A very able layman is the Master of Corpus.

Yours in haste,
T. S. Eliot

1 – Plans were in hand for a series of radio programmes under the title 'Our Changing World'.
2 – Frank Russell Barry, DSO (1890–1976), was Principal of the Ordination Test School, Knutsford; Archdeacon of Egypt; Professor of New Testament Interpretation at King's College, London; Fellow and Tutor of Balliol College, Oxford; Canon of Westminster Abbey; and Rector of St John's, Smith Square, London, before being elevated as Bishop of Southwell, 1941–64. His works include *The Relevance of Christianity* (1931) and *The Relevance of the Church* (1935).
3 – Naomi Mitchison.
4 – Charles Earle Raven (1885–1964), theologian; Dean of Emmanuel College, Cambridge, and residentiary canon of Liverpool Cathedral, 1924–31. From 1932, Regius Professor of Divinity at Cambridge; Master of Christ's College, Cambridge, 1939–50. His publications include *Christian Socialism, 1848–1854* (1920) and *Apollinarianism* (1923).

TO *James Joyce*   TS Buffalo

30 June 1931   *The Criterion*

Dear Joyce,

I have had an appeal couched in exactly the same terms as yours. I consulted a knowing Scot of my acquaintance in Fleet Street today, and he tells me that the applicant is a respectable but indigent young man of that quarter, the son of a journalist who died in poor circumstances; and he doubts whether the person in question, to judge from his youth and small means, would be canvassing for a hospital solely out of philanthropic zeal. It was his opinion that any appeal of this kind ought to come from the Chairman of the institution, or at least bear evident signs of authority. In which I concur. I shall therefore ignore the appeal.

The record is magnificent – your voice to perfection. It ought to have more publicity, as it should be a great help to people who find A.L.P. difficult – as well as for the sake of its own beauty.[1] As I told you, when I played the record you lent last year it was on a very inferior instrument, and I did not grasp at all how very fine it is. My wife is overjoyed.

Yours ever,

T. S. Eliot

1 – In an introductory note to *Introducing James Joyce: a selection of Joyce's prose* (1942), TSE remarked of *Finnegans Wake*: 'I think . . . that most readers of that massive work would agree to the choice of the passage which was published separately, before the completion of the whole work, as *Anna Livia Plurabelle*. This fantasy of the course of the river Liffey is the best-known part of *Finnegans Wake*, and is the best introduction to it. It was recorded by the author: I have found that the gramophone record of the author's voice reciting it revealed at once a beauty which is disclosed only gradually by the printed page' (6–7). Later, in 'The Approach to James Joyce', he noted too: 'Joyce's last book has to be read aloud, preferably by an Irish voice; and, as the one gramophone record which he made attests, no other voice could read it, not even another Irish voice, as well as Joyce could read it himself' (*The Listener*, 14 Oct. 1943, 446–7).

TO *Evelyn Underhill*[1]

1 July 1931   [*The Criterion*]

Dear Mrs Stuart Moore,

Please excuse my delay in replying to your letter of the 25th[2] – a rush of business coincided with a fit of slothfulness. I rather took for granted before writing that you would have done v. Hügel for the *Spectator*, so that does not matter – but I really should be more pleased if you would write an article on v. Hügel for me, using the last book as a peg, for the *December* number (I say December instead of September solely to give you more time). So, as you say that you leave the matter in my hands, may I expect an article from you by November 1st (the number appears Dec. 15 and is called 'January')?[3]

I wonder what you will think of the article on S. John of the Cross by Robert Sencourt which I have published in the last number.[4]

1–Evelyn Underhill (1875–1941): esteemed spiritual director and writer on mysticism and the spiritual life. Compelled by deep study and the counsel of Baron Friedrich von Hügel, she became an Anglican in 1919 and dedicated her kindly life to religious writing and guidance, notably as a retreat director. She wrote or edited 39 books and over 350 articles and reviews; among her other activities, she was theological editor for *The Spectator* and wrote too for *Time and Tide*. Her works include *Mysticism: A Study of the Nature and Development of Man's Spiritual Consciousness* (1911) and *Worship* (1936). In 1907 she married Hubert Stuart Moore (1869–1951), a barrister. TSE wrote to Sister Mary Xavier, SSJ, on 1 Aug. 1962: 'I . . . wish that I could tell you more about the late Mrs Moore, otherwise Evelyn Underhill. I did not know her intimately and knew [her] I think in the first place through her cousin, Francis Underhill, who was my spiritual director and later Bishop of Bath and Wells. I remember her, however, with affection and regret. I do not know whether you would call her a mystic though she was certainly an authority on mysticism. She was a very cosy person to meet and have tea with in her home in [no. 50] Campden Hill Square and was also very fond of her cats. I should not call her a mystic whether qualified by the adjective Anglican or not, but I should call her an authority on mysticism and indeed would accept your phrase for her "deep spirituality". She was, I am sure, an admirable spiritual director herself and I am pretty sure was a great help to many young women . . . I think that any correspondence we had would have been merely to do with social engagements and I never remember having had any long correspondence with her on spiritual or other matters. I remember her not at all as an intimate friend, but as a very highly valued and regretted acquaintance.'

In an unpublished note to *The Times*, 1941, he wrote too: 'She gave (with frail health and constant illness) herself to many, in retreats, which she conducted and in the intercourse of daily life – she was always at the disposal of all who called upon her. With a lively and humorous interest in human beings, especially the young. She was at the same time withdrawn and sociable. With shrewdness and simplicity she helped to support the spiritual life of many more than she could in her humility have been aware of aiding.'

See further Donald J. Childs, 'T. S. Eliot and Evelyn Underhill: An Early Mystical Influence', *Durham University Journal* 80 (Dec. 1987), 83–98.

2–Underhill's letter was in response to a (now lost) letter from TSE.

3–Underhill, 'Finite and Infinite: A Study of Friedrich von Hügel', C. 11 (Jan. 1932), 183–97.

4–Sencourt, 'St John of the Cross', C. 10 (July 1931), 637–53.

It is kind of you to ask me to lunch on the 14th, and I should like to see D'Arcy again. Does the invitation include my wife – perhaps you did not know that I was married?

Sincerely yours,
[T. S. Eliot]

TO *James Joyce*   cc/handwritten copy in the
                                      Sylvia Beach Archive, Princeton

6 July 1931   [Faber & Faber Ltd]

Dear Joyce,

First of all, there is no question about our wanting to publish the book; or about our wanting to do it a year hence just as much as today. We have had this in view not only whilst publishing the pamphlets, but also in accepting both Stuart Gilbert and Herbert Gorman.

So far as we can see from the data available, we could certainly offer an advance of £300 on the book of from 190,000 to 200,000 words to be published at a guinea: there is no need to stipulate the number of words – the only point is that if you particularly wished it to be published at a lower price we should have to reconsider the advance. We could pay the advance in either of two ways (1) £100 on signing contract, £100 on delivery of manuscript, and £100 on publication; or (2) £150 on signing contract and £150 on publication. This is on a royalty of 15% up to 5000 copies and 20% after that. Furthermore, if you agreed to the publication of a limited signed edition, we should suggest a further 100 signed copies to be sold at £5:5:– each. (We think that a small number of signed copies at a high price would be better than a larger number at a lower price). On this we could offer a straight 20% royalty. Our Sales Manager thinks that 100 copies at five guineas could surely be subscribed before publication, which means that on publication of the limited edition (which, as well as being signed, would be rather more elaborately produced than the ordinary edition), you would be entitled to a further £100 besides the £300 on the ordinary edition.

These terms are of course for British rights only. You will consider whether you would wish us to take up the matter on your behalf with an American publisher: I think that an American Publisher should offer from 50% better terms than an English publisher can do.

Here is a basis for negotiation. I should like to come in on *Thursday* morning next and have a talk; so you need not answer this unless that morning is inconvenient for you.

I am writing to Ogden to ask him to lunch with me one day soon. I need not mention to him that I have discussed the matter with you.

Yours ever,
[T. S. Eliot]

TO *Bruce Richmond*

6 July 1931   [Faber & Faber Ltd]

Dear Richmond,

Many thanks for sending me the letter which I return herewith.[1] I know the name of this young man in Upsala, and dare say I have had some communication with him; but I should have been exceeding annoyed if you had given him this information! As a matter of principle, it seems to me that such persons ought to apply first to the author for permission to apply to the Editor. As for myself, my 'column' reviewing for you has always been deliberately impersonal; I cannot say, without going through it carefully, how much I might not have written differently had I been writing over my signature. It seems to me perfectly legitimate and proper that a man should write differently when he signs and when he writes anonymously; and I cannot help thinking that most of my reviews would have been only the worse, if I had written them with an eye to their future inclusion in a 'bibliography'. Nay, I should be deterred from ever reviewing another book for you, if I thought it was sure to be unearthed later by some industrious bibliographer.

As for Leaders, for myself I don't want these included in bibliographies until I have included them in books. They can wait till then. When an

---

1–BLR enclosed (3 July) a letter (not found) from a scholar asking for a list of the articles and reviews that TSE had published in the *TLS*. BLR wrote: 'My own inclination would be to say "no" very firmly. Our contributions are anonymous; and, unless they are re-published by the author over his name, I think they should remain anonymous. I imagine that you yourself would object to having short notices (which may or may not have been curtailed here) publicly identified as yours; and my own idea is that in saying no I am protecting the author. I think this is really inquisitiveness; and if you are going to write a book about an author you should confine yourself to what the author has acknowledged . . . I ought to get some idea of what writers feel about this; as I suppose this kind of thing will grow. I have already had one request from a persevering American to supply him with a list of everything that Virginia Woolf had ever written for us. This, considering that she began about 1906 with small things in the Book List, was rather a tall order!'

author signs or initials anything, he is surely legitimate prey for the bibliographer. But not in anonymity.

That is merely one writer's opinion – but I do feel strongly – and I should be surprised to find that any large number of reputable writers thought otherwise. I feel sure that Virginia would agree.

Yours ever,
[T. S. E.]

FROM *Vivien Eliot* TO *Mary Hutchinson* MS Texas

6 July 1931 68 Clarence Gate Gardens, N.W.1

My dear Mary

I was so sorry not to be able to go to the telephone when you rang up this morning. Do forgive me. I am dreadfully sorry.

The message was that you invited me to tea tomorrow and I said I could not come. And then I *think Thursday* was arranged for me to come to tea with you. I could come to tea with you that day, & I have been wanting to see you *so much* ever since you and Jack could not come to dinner here.

I am writing now to ask you if you *could* possibly let me come to tea on *Saturday instead*. Or *Sunday or Monday* next.

Thursday is an *almost impossible day*. I did not think enough before I spoke.

BUT, if neither Saturday, Sunday, Monday, *or Tuesday* are possible, then *rather than not see you will* you let me just come for half an hour on *Thursday* at 4. o'clock.

Now about dinner – *I made a mistake about Friday*. It is not possible for Tom, so again I am very sorry indeed.

He *sends* the message – *will you & Jack* come come [*sic*] to dinner *any night next week*. We should both be delighted indeed. If possible please make it Monday or Tuesday, and *do do come*.

Can you ring me up early tomorrow morning, and as I say, if no other day will do I *will* come on Thursday because I MUST see you. SOON.

Yrs. as ever,
Vivienne Haigh Eliot

TO *Leonora Eyles*[1]   CC

8 July 1931   [Faber & Faber Ltd]

Dear Mrs Murray,

I am sorry to have been so long in reporting to you on the subject of
your manuscript which you sent me on the 12th of May; but it has taken
several of us to come to a conclusion, and that only with considerable
deliberation. Personally I liked the story very much indeed except for
the transfiguration at the end, which I confess, especially in the case of
Robin, I found improbable. There is only one other detail which I should
question – the priest's theory of the Sacrifice on Calvary does not seem to
me to be in harmony with any of the views between which one is allowed
to choose – but the main difficulty for me is the ending. We felt, however,
that in any case we were not quite the right people to do the best for this
type of book. If, however, I can be of any help in enabling you to place it
elsewhere I should be very glad, and in any case I am grateful for having
had the opportunity of reading it.[2]

                                        Yours sincerely
                                        [T. S. Eliot]

1 – Leonora Eyles (1889–1960), author, was the wife of D. L. Murray, editor of the *TLS* from
1938. Works include *Women's Problems of To-day* (1926) and *Shepherd of Israel* (1929).
2 – Eyles sent her 'little book' (untitled) with a covering letter: 'It is an attempt to shew
through the eyes of a peasant girl, what the teaching of Jesus, as expressed by Anglo
Catholicism, can mean in simple lives . . . This book is not propaganda, of course, except in
so far as it shews the impact of religion on Jeannie and those about her.'
  TSE wrote in his reader's report (13 June 1931): 'This is a tale of humble people in some
small fishing village in the north, perhaps the northeast coast. The style, by my guess, is
rather that of one of the people themselves, who has arrived at considerable self-education,
than of a "writer" of another class who has made a local study – I mean it has the kind
of fidelity and also the kind of artificiality that one would expect from such a person. It
is a very simple tale. Jennie, the daughter of a respectable ploughman and his wife, a girl
intellectually above the average, loves Jimmy. Jimmy is the grandson of an old fisherman
in almost destitute circumstances, and probably of Norwegian origin. Jimmy's mother had
fallen to the attractions of a foreign sailor shipwrecked nearby *en passage*, who was probably
a Breton; anyway, Jimmy has now no father or mother, but is a stout Anglo-Catholic, and
serves at Mass. This is where Father Carswell, the regular saintly vicar of pietistic fiction,
comes in; he is the presiding angel of the story. Jimmy joins an Antarctic expedition to make
his fortune and come back to marry Jenny. He is reported dead in an Antarctic blizzard;
and finally Jenny, in order to keep her parents from the workhouse, consents to marry
Robin Grey, the proprietor of the General Store and local usurer. Robin is the most devilish
personage I have met with in all the mss. I have been privileged to read for Faber & Faber.
He leads her a hell of a life; poisons the cat, breaks the canary's neck, and manages to get
an injunction against good Father Carswell for illegal vestments and ornaments (that could
only have happened in Birmingham, but this is fictional licence).

8 July 1931   [Faber & Faber Ltd]

Dear Marguerite,

This is merely a hurried note in answer to your letter of the 4th July. I am very sorry indeed to hear of all your troubles, particularly following the family anxieties which you have had during the winter.[1]

I wish that I could be more helpful about the possibilities of a lucrative advertising in *Commerce,* but our experience with the *Criterion* and indeed the experience, I think, of most of the better class of English reviews is not encouraging.[2] We do get a little out of advertisements, but beyond a few insurance companies and cigarette manufacturers the English advertiser is very wary of spending money in a highbrow periodical. We get a few publishers as well, but they are not very dependable, and one is always obliged to include a few mere exchange advertisements with other periodicals. Also it is much more difficult for a quarterly to get

---

'Eventually, as we all expected, Jimmy turns up again; there is a stormy scene of passion; but Father Carswell persuades Jimmy and Jenny not to elope, so Jimmy goes away again and Jenny continues to put up with the fiendish Robin, who to perfect his criminality has joined the local Chapel. Jimmy's grandfather dies; Jenny's parents die in great misery; Jimmy eventually, in obedience to his heredity, marries a Breton girl, a "little brown woman" with gold ear-rings, and a Roman Catholic at that, and has a large family. Jenny ends with a mystical vision, a sort of transformation scene which to me is completely hysterical and unconvincing. She now sees everybody as a glass figure through which, or inside of which, she perceives the person of Our Lord. That is well enough for Father Carswell, but when the same phenomenon is exhibited in the fiendish Robin, it almost arouses scepticism. Moved by this transfiguration she is able to kiss Robin on the top of his head. I am very doubtful of the orthodoxy of this vision, and I am quite certain that the Doctrine of the Eucharist attributed to Father Carswell is flagrantly different from any of the tenable theories.

'I dislike religious fiction by hysterical women; but I must say that the story held my attention throughout; and I think it needs a third opinion. Perhaps Paterson can tell us whether it would sell.'

Eyles replied on 9 July: 'it is very difficult to "get across" to anybody any mystic experience like the end of the book and I know I have failed to do it . . . It seems to me that once you have seen the Incarnate God in a human being you see Him in every human being and it must alter all your attitude to them. I used to be rather intolerant until the meaning of the incarnation dawned on me one day, and altered everything.'

1 – 'I have been having all sorts of worries – financial – Ruffredo principally but I also more than is comfortable. Everyone is so much in the same case that it is foolish complaining.' Her husband Ruffredo (1871–1961) was Prince of Bassiano and Duke of Sermoneta: composer, art collector and patron.

2 – 'I feared being obliged to give up *Commerce* but instead I am making all the economy possible in the printing and starting in the Autumn I want to have a few (12 to 20) pages of publicity and I was wondering if you could help me a bit there or put me in relation with a person who does that sort of thing. I would like two or three English and American Reviews or even more if possible or publishers whatever one can get that pays well.'

advertisements than for even a monthly. Perhaps we could talk this over if [you], as I hope you will, stop for a few days in London on your way back to Scotland.[1] I shall probably be here throughout August. I will have a poem to give you in the autumn if you want it.

Every affectionately
[Tom]

TO *John Middleton Murry*   TS Northwestern

8 July 1931   *The Criterion*

My dear John,

Thank you very much for your kindly and tolerant appreciation of my review.[2] There is only one point in your letter on which I do not feel quite sure that we can be in accord. You speak of having been just as much shocked by the passage from *Lady Chatterley's Lover* as I am, but having come to see the whole matter from a further point of view beyond good and evil. I still cannot see how the point of view beyond good and evil can affect one's opinion of the rightness or wrongness of a specific instance of human behaviour of this sort.[3] But I wish that we might meet instead of writing.

In haste,
Affectionately yours
Tom

1 – 'The children and I go to Scotland on a visit to the Crawfords in August . . .'
2 – Not found.
3 – TSE noted, in his review of JMM's *Son of Woman: The Story of D. H. Lawrence*, 'a fault' which corrupted DHL's 'whole philosophy of human relations . . . his hopeless attempt to find some mode in which two persons – of the opposite sex, and then as a venture of despair, of the same sex – may be spiritually united. As Mr Murry spares no pains to show, the whole history of Lawrence's life and of Lawrence's writings (Mr Murry tell us that it is the same history) is the history of his craving for greater intimacy than is possible between human beings . . . There is a passage from *Lady Chatterley's Lover* . . . which Mr Murry quotes very much to the point.

"I held forth with rapture to her, positively with rapture. I simply went up in smoke. And she adored me. The serpent in the grass was sex. She somehow didn't have any; at least, not where it's supposed to be. I got thinner and thinner. Then I said we'd got to be lovers. I talked her into it. So she let me. I was excited, and she never wanted it. She adored me, she loved me to talk to her and kiss her: in that way she had a passion for me. But the other she just didn't want. And there are lots of women like her. And it was just the other that I *did* want. So there we split. I was cruel and left her."

'Mr Murry has analysed this passage so shrewdly that it is an impertinence to say much more; but I should like to be sure that it shocked Mr Murry, as a confession, as deeply as it shocked me. Such complacent egotism can come only from a very sick soul, and, I should say, from a man who was totally incapable of intimacy' (C. 10 [July 1931], 772).

TO *Algar Thorold*   CC

8 July 1931   [*The Criterion*]

My dear Thorold,
    In reply to your card of the 6th Belgion's article called 'God is Mammon'
did not appear in the *Criterion* but, if I remember correctly, in the *Hound
and Horn*.[1] I can't lay my hand on it at present, so perhaps if you want
the article you had best write to Belgion. No doubt you know his address,
4 rue Delambre.
    Thank you also for replying to the question I asked in my pamphlet.[2] It
may interest you to know, however, that I asked it at the suggestion of an
R. C. friend of mine who wanted to know the answer himself. Of course
the answer removes the difficulty one step because it is very difficult to
determine what are reasonable motives of economic pressure. I quite
agree, of course, with your further remarks.
    Brémond is under way, but may take a considerable time. Later on I
may want to borrow the volumes on the History of Religious Sentiment in
France, but I dare say I could get them from the London Library.
                                        Yours ever
                                        [T. S. Eliot]

TO *F. W. Bain*[3]   CC

8 July 1931   [*The Criterion*]

My dear Bain,
    I am very sorry indeed to hear your bad news, and I hope that I may
hear from you later that matters have improved. Of course in such a

---

1 – 'God is Mammon', *Hound & Horn* (Spr. 1930); *The Human Parrot and other essays*
(1931).
2 – Thorold wrote (6 July): 'Re pages 18 & 19 of your *Thoughts after Lambeth*, Rome does
not teach that the family must not be limited, but that the only legitimate method is by
continence [illegible] from a free agreement between the *conjuncti*. If their motives were pure
& reasonable – motives of health, or economic pressure – they would receive the necessary
grace. This seems quite consistent. No motives whether of ill-health or poverty wd justify
frustrated commerce or contraceptives. The *primary* object of marriage is not pleasure. I
do not see how on Christian principles, one can say anything else. It is a hard saying, but
Xtianity is a hard religion.'
3 – F. W. Bain (1863–1940): author and scholar; Fellow of All Souls College, 1889–97;
Professor of History and Political Economy at the Deccan College, Poona, where he was
esteemed 'not only as a professor but also as a prophet and a philosopher', 1892–1919. An
old-style High Tory, enthused by the writings of Bolingbroke and Disraeli, his works include

state of anxiety it is quite impossible for you to attempt a full article, and although I very much regret not having it I shall be very grateful for the short review.[1] I hope that we may meet again as soon as you have less anxiety on your mind.

Yours ever
[T. S. Eliot]

TO *William Empson* CC

9 July 1931   [*The Criterion*]

My dear Empson,

I am sorry to bother you again with something which may turn out to be rubbish, but I am sending you a book herewith in the confidence that if it is not worth a review you will let me know at once.[2]

Yours sincerely,
[T. S. Eliot]

TO *William Rothenstein* TS Houghton

9 July 1931   Faber & Faber Ltd

Dear Rothenstein,

In the absence of de la Mare who is away on holiday it has been suggested that I should write to you and tell you our conclusions – which in this case I fear are merely my conclusions – about Jacques Blanche's *Les Arts Plastiques*[3] which I believe you recommended to de la Mare. I have read the book, or the greater part of it, with much interest and enjoyment, but I am very sceptical about it as a book to be translated for

---

The English Monarchy and its Revolutions (1894), *On the Realisation of the Possible and the Spirit of Aristotle* (1897), and a series of 'Hindu love stories' purportedly translated from Sanskrit originals. See K. Mutalik, *Francis William Bain* (1963).

1–Bain (5 July 1931): 'I will send you in a few days about 2 pages Review. I am sorry I haven't had time to answer before, but my wife is very ill, and I am sending her to Devon in a day or two. Her position is very precarious – that is why I dare not undertake an article – as, should things go ill – I should have to chuck it – in other circumstances I should have had much pleasure in compiling something on the legend of Napoleon – which I know a good deal about.'

2–The book was Arthur Sewell's *The Physiology of Beauty*. Empson replied (n.d): 'My word, it is bad. I don't think reviewing it would do any good.'

3–*Les Arts plastiques de 1870 à nos jours, collection 'La Troisième république'* (1931), by the artist Jacques-Émile Blanche (1861–1942).

a new public. It seems to me that the only justification from a publisher's point of view for translating such a French work into English would be its appeal to a large uninformed public. I thought that this book went into so much detail about minor men, early salons, etcetera that it would merely be discouraging for such readers; and that sort of person who would be interested would probably better read it in French and would prefer to do so. It has all of Blanche's charm and informal style which would be very difficult to preserve in a translation, so I am really opposed to the attempt.

I don't know, however, what you said to de la Mare about it, or whether you had any reasons in your mind which might influence us, so it seemed to me best to write to you about it while the impression was fresh in my mind and before we rejected it definitively. But of course you need not bother to answer this letter unless you feel particularly disposed to do so.[1]

Sincerely yours
T. S. Eliot

TO *John Middleton Murry* CC

9 July 1931   [*The Criterion*]

My dear John,

I suppose you know Quiller-Couch's *Shakespeare's Workmanship* from the 1918 edition. I have never read it. A new edition has just appeared in his uniform edition, and I wonder if you think it of sufficient importance to write a note at whatever length you please for the *Criterion*? I will not send you the book until I hear from you about it, but I should very much like to have a long review by you of some book whenever you have time to write one for me.[2]

Affectionately yours,
[Tom]

1–Rothenstein responded (10 July): 'Blanche seems anxious to have his book published in England, and knowing that De La Mare is on the look out for interesting books on art I told him about Blanche's novel and his last book on artists. I did not think, of course, of bringing any pressure to bear upon De La Mare, and I can see your point of view regarding the book itself.'

2–JMM said (10 July) he would be 'glad of the opportunity': see C. 11 (Oct. 1931), 120–6.

TO *Hamish Miles*   CC

9 July 1931   [Faber & Faber Ltd]

My dear Miles,

When Charles Whibley died he was the owner of the original manuscript of unpublished notes and aphorisms of Sir Thomas Urquhart which he had been intending to prepare himself for publication. Mrs Whibley is very anxious that her husband's intentions should be carried out, and some time ago she engaged John Sparrow of All Souls to edit the text. I have not seen the manuscript myself but I understand from Mrs Whibley that some of it is more or less indecent. She is particularly anxious, however, that the text should not be expurgated even though there may be a good deal of matter in it which could well be omitted. It appears that the preparation of a wholly unexpurgated edition did not suit Sparrow's taste or possibly his interests, and he has retired from the work. Mrs Whibley has now asked me to suggest someone else who might be willing to edit it, so I am writing to you first to ask whether you would consider taking on such a job before I put you in touch with her. I do not know whether you have either the time or the inclination for it, but naturally your name occurred to my mind before anyone else's and I hope you are willing to consider it. I don't know what Mrs Whibley could pay for this work and I think in any case it would better be a question of negotiation between you, if you are interested, after you have looked at the material and estimated the difficulties of the task. I am sorry to say that Faber & Faber have no interest in the book, as Whibley promised it to Peter Davies who now has the manuscript in his safe. My only direct interest in the matter is to try to help Mrs Whibley.

                                    Sincerely yours
                                    [T. S. Eliot]

FROM *Vivien Eliot* TO *Mary Hutchinson*   MS Texas

9 July 1931   68 Clarence Gate Gardens

My dear Mary

I tried to get you on the telephone at 6.45 p.m. with the frequent result. '*No reply*'.

So I am *writing* to say that Tom and I will be delighted to come to tea tomorrow at 3.45, as we arranged on the telephone this morning. This is also to confirm that we are expecting you & Jack here to dinner on Tuesday the 14th at 7.30.

I *think* Tom has invited Mr & Mrs James Joyce also, but if you will *be so kind* as to *ring me up early* tomorrow morning (between 8 & 9) I tell you for certain.[1]

Well good night, Mary Hutchinson.

Yours affectionately *& always*
Vivienne Haigh Eliot

I am too tired now to write or telephone any more.

V. H. E.

FROM *Vivien Eliot* TO *Mary Hutchinson*   MS Texas

Friday 10 July 1931   68 Clarence Gate Gardens

My dear Mary

Just a line to say I was sorry to be so hot & flustered today.

I was not feeling very well & had to hurry back as Tom's neices [*sic*] were coming to dinner and are leaving London tomorrow morning.

I have had *ever* so much on my hands all this summer, and now my Mother has gone off on a visit to Anglesey and has seemed to be so unwell lately that I shall be miserably uneasy until she returns.

Maurice being tied in Italy does make everything quite awful.

I am looking forward *immensely* to seeing you & Jack here to dinner on Tuesday at 7.30. & dont let *anything* interfere with that, please.

I loved the scarf you brought me, it was *sweet* of you. Do please bring it on Tuesday. I just felt stupid today, but I think you are so good to me *always*.

I so enjoyed seeing Barbara,[2] & think she is charming.

We should so much like it if you could bring her here & meet Tom's neices *at lunch* on *Thursday* 23rd at 1.30. Could you? They are going to

---

1–Joyce came alone. On 20 July OM was entertained to tea with JJ at the Eliots', as Seymour-Jones writes in *Painted Shadow*, 470: 'Nor was the Eliots' tea-party for James and Nora Joyce in July 1931 any more successful. Tom and Vivienne greeted Joyce like a king . . . and this time it was Ottoline who felt left out as the two writers fell into deep conversation . . . The company listened to a gramophone recording of Joyce reading "Anna Livia Plurabelle", followed by Tom reading "Ash Wednesday"; it was, thought Ottoline, greatly inferior to Joyce's work.' (Seymour-Jones's source here is the Journal of OM, 23 July 1931: Goodman Papers.)

2–Barbara Hutchinson (1911–1989); later wife of Victor Rothschild, third Baron Rothschild; subsequently wife of Rex Warner.

Cornwall tomorrow and are returning to London for that one day before going to Cambridge to take a course of lectures. If that is *not* possible will you not please bring her here to tea with me on either Friday or Monday next?

With love, yours ever
Vivienne Haigh Eliot

TO *Henry Eliot*

TS Houghton

11 July 1931   *The Criterion*

My dear brother,

This is a hurried line only to mention two matters. I took the liberty of explaining to Frank Morley as much as was necessary of your affairs.[1] He knows more about New York publishers than anyone else in our firm, as he goes there every year, and knows most of them personally, and is particularly responsible for this end of our business. He concurs with me in recommending Harcourt Brace as one of the most substantial and serious of the more enterprising firms, and as one which is likely to last and to expand; so he has written personally to Harcourt.[2] If there is the

1–HWE, who was out of a job, wrote on 10 June: 'I should rather like to get a job in Boston for which I am angling, though on the whole I think I should prefer staying here in New York. The general tone of everyone just now is quite depressing, though there is some belief that things have hit bottom and are bound to improve. Everyone's morale is low, including my own. I do not know which way to turn or what to do with the rest of my life. There are things which I should like to do but doubt my capacity, or my ability to convince others of it.'

2–FVM wrote to Alfred Harcourt on 3 July 1931: 'T. S. Eliot has shown me a letter from his brother . . . Henry is older than our Eliot; I think he is 50 and I think he is somewhat deaf. He has had considerable experience in both publishing and advertising – I think he ran an advertising business in which he still retains an interest and which is still successful, but he wants something to do. What he is thinking about is something in a publisher's advertising department or possibly in the book manufacture department. I gather it is not so much the money that he is interested in as the activity, and knowing the Eliot family (although I have never met Henry) I felt I could mention him without any of the usual qualifications that one would make for anyone looking for work in this kind of way. As he is a man of standing and probably of sensibility I wonder, if you happen to be able to think of anything, if you would drop him a line at the address above. If you can see your way to fitting him in I don't imagine you would regret doing so. I have not sent him any introduction to you, nor have I suggested that he should call on you but if you can spare the time to ask him in for an interview, both Eliot and I would be extremely grateful.' Harcourt replied on 22 July: 'I hardly see a chance for his fitting into our picture now, but I want to talk to Brace about it. So all I can do is to thank you and T. S. Eliot for the suggestion.'

slightest chance of an opening there you should hear from Harcourt direct; if you do not hear within a fortnight please let me know.

Would it be impossible for you to sell a large part of your holding in Buchen's to one or more of the active members on the spot? The situation seems to me unsatisfactory.

About your other question.[1] I think it would be possible to live in England on the sum you quote. But I do not think the climate would suit you in the winter, and I am going to enquire, in a general way, of a friend who has very little money and who lives in the South of France.

Affectionately,
Tom.

TO *C. A. Siepmann* TS BBC

12 July 1931 *The Criterion*

Dear Siepmann,

I enclose a rough draft of four talks. It is rough because I have made no attempt to keep the abstracts of all four the same length; finding it useful to detail the first in order to get steam up. And I also expect that in any case I shall have to introduce modifications when I know what the others have to say. I think that when we have finally settled upon three outlines, it might be useful to each to have copies of the two others.

Yours sincerely
[T. S. Eliot]

TO *C. A. Siepmann* TS BBC

12 July 1931 *The Criterion*

Dear Mr Siepmann,

Enclosed is the best I can do in the time, as I have been very busy with committees this week, and wanted to look in at the library before writing. Even now I have forgotten who edited the two volume edition of Dryden's prose, I think W. P. Ker.

1–HWE had asked: 'Are there places in England, France, or Switzerland, where two persons can live on $3000 a year? I have given some, though not much, thought to a year abroad as a temporary measure of economy . . . if the depression continues.'

It is unfortunate that one has to write a syllabus before one has had time to think out the form and content properly, but if this will do for your pamphlet, that is all that matters, and I may depart from the scheme wherever desirable.[1]

I am not quite sure that I understand the second paragraph of your letter. Does it mean that now the *Listener* does not pay for the talks it uses? I hope not! In any case, it is quite welcome to the 28 days option.

Yours sincerely,
[T. S. Eliot]

TO *Paul Elmer More*   TS Princeton

12 July 1931   [Faber & Faber Ltd]

My dear Moore,

Thank you for your letter of the 10th.[2] I am grateful for the suggestion of the name of Fraser Mitchell.[3] I don't quite think that the volume of lives of six divines is quite in our line, and should have thought that it was much more in the way of the S.P.C.K.; but I will bring it up to my committee. He might very well be of use in the Encyclopaedia, however, and I shall at any time be grateful for the names of any other possible contributors, British or American.

I hope that your relations with the S.P.C.K. will progress to a satisfactory fruition.

If you are sailing on the 18th, I do not suppose that you will have time to see me again. I had indeed hoped that we might meet oftener; a few more long evening talks would have been of great pleasure and profit to me, as always in the past. May I entertain the hope that when you return to visit your family next year, you may be able to give us more time in London? I am no very good correspondent, yet I hope to keep in touch with you during the winter.

I am looking forward to reading your brother's MS.; it is now in the hands of Frank Morley, who, as the first mover in the Newton project, is entitled to the first reading.[4]

---

1 – The proofs of TSE's syllabus were sent out to him on 23 July.
2 – Not found.
3 – William Fraser Mitchell (1900–88): a student of English pulpit oratory in the seventeenth century; writer and academic.
4 – Louis T. More, *Isaac Newton: A Biography* (1934).

My wife is very disappointed not to see you again; but she also looks forward to next year.

Thank you for your kindnesses of word as well as deed! So I am an enigma? Well, I suppose no man seems an enigma to himself, however little he may know himself; and the people who find themselves interesting are usually the most deluded. I cannot assert that I am wholly disillusioned, however; though I am a tired little journalist, I still fancy that I might have made a brilliant corporation-lawyer, and of course I wish I had been. And whatever one does, I imagine that we all like to think of ourselves as connoisseurs of Dead Sea Fruit, even though one's experience be only of some small gnurly varieties.

I am always, with devotion and respect,

Your humble servant,
[T. S. Eliot]

TO *Bonamy Dobrée*   TS Brotherton

16 July 1931   Faber & Faber Ltd

DAMB you Bombaby We shall have yr. Name Struck off the Rolls before long. Wed. 22d I am Lunching Prebendary Harris and on Thursday my Nieces are having a farewell Lunch before going to Cambridge, and so you Ought to ask me to lunch on Tuesday, and I will have cold Lobster please and a bottle of Hock.[1]

Yrs spitefully
Tom

1–BD had invited TSE (15 July) to lunch at his club on 22 July.

TO *Margaret Woods*[1]   CC

16 July 1931   [Faber & Faber Ltd]

Dear Mrs Woods,

Thank you very much for your letter of the 9th July.[2] I am of course much honoured by being asked to join your Academic Committee, and I should like to ask just two questions before accepting. The first is, do the meetings take place in the daytime or in the evening? As in the latter case I may not be able to attend regularly and should hesitate in accepting. Secondly, I must confess that I am not familiar with the Benson Medal Awards. Are they given for general accomplishment or on the strength of particular books? In the latter case I suppose that the members of the Committee might have the task of considerable reading? I should be very grateful if you would enlighten me on these two points.

Yours sincerely
[T. S. Eliot]

TO *Orlo Williams*   CC

16 July 1931   [*The Criterion*]

Dear Williams,

I have read your fiction chronicle and, although rather startled by your slighting reference to George Eliot,[3] I think that your general plan of this sort of thing is exactly what it should be, and I am particularly pleased because I like it much better than anything of the sort that I have seen in any other periodical.

Perhaps you would suggest a day to lunch with me before you leave. I have no engagements the week of the 26th.

1 – Margaret Louisa Woods, née Bradley (1855–1945) – her late husband, the Revd H. G. Woods, was President of Trinity College, Oxford, 1887–97; Master of the Temple, 1904–15 – was a poet and novelist: works include *Sons of the Sword* (1901) and *Collected Poems* (1913). She was active as Hon. Secretary and Member of the Council of the Royal Society of Literature.
2 – Woods invited TSE to become a member of the Committee. 'The duties of Members are not heavy. They consist in attending not more than four Meetings in a year for the purpose of awarding the Benson Medals.'
3 – OW responded on 17 July, 'I agree about G. Eliot & I'll alter that to express more nearly what I mean: but am glad you like the chronicle.' (TSE was to declare in 1948, 'I was brought up in an environment of that intellectual and puritanical rationalism which is found in the novels of George Eliot – an author greatly admired in my family' – *A Sermon preached in Magdalene College Chapel* [1948], 5.)

With many thanks,

Yours sincerely,
[T. S. Eliot]

TO *F. W. Bain*   CC

16 July 1931   [*The Criterion*]

My dear Bain,

I am very sorry to hear your news and offer you my sincere sympathy.[1]
I expect to be in London most of the summer and should be very glad if
I might believe that you would drop me a line at any time when you are
ready to see me.

I like the review very much and only wish that it might have been an
article.

Yours sincerely
[T. S. Eliot]

TO *William Plomer*   CC

16 July 1931   [Faber & Faber Ltd]

Dear Plomer,

Forgive my delay in replying to your letter of the 8th, but I have been
very busy last week outside of the office.[2] I should be delighted to see your
poems, and hope that you will send them to me directly. If you are to be in
town will you come and lunch with me a week or two afterwards?

Yours
[T. S. Eliot]

TO *James Joyce*   TS Buffalo

17 July 1931   Faber & Faber Ltd

Dear Joyce,

I enclose draft of a letter to Miss Beach.[3] It strikes me as longwinded,
and I think it could be reduced. I am not satisfied with it and shall be

1–Bain's wife had died (13 July 1931).
2–Plomer had decided to publish a small collection of poems, which the Hogarth Press
wished to issue; all the same, he would be obliged if TSE would look at them for F&F.
3–See TSE's letter to Sylvia Beach, 31 Aug. 1931, below.

glad to have any suggestions that occur to you. The difficulty is that Miss Beach herself could get nothing out of it, unless you forewent your own 10%; and you know already how little profit a pamphlet brings. The appeal to her has to be to her public spirit and devotion to your work etc., and I don't know her well enough to know how to make that appeal.

Please let me have this draft back with your observations – or I will come in one morning and discuss it. I have at last heard from Ogden and hope to catch him for lunch on Tuesday.[1]

Yours,
T. S. Eliot

TO *Sonia Hambourg*   CC

17 July 1931   [Faber & Faber Ltd]

Dear Miss Hambourg,

I enclose a contract for Mrs Parsons and hope that it will reach you before you leave for Paris. My delay in sending it has been entirely due to the fact that I was going to write to you at the same time about the introductory note once more, and I have been in several minds on this question. The more I have thought about the matter and looked at the little paragraph which I drew up after your letter of the 27th of June[2] the more strongly I feel that even this information about Clere Parson's achievements is not merely irrelevant to the value of the poetry, but being irrelevant still suggests the apologetic note, which, as I think I said to you when I saw you, I particularly want to avoid. It seems to me now that it would really be enough to show clearly and conspicuously the dates of his birth and death. It seems to me that it is much better to leave readers to ask questions about a poet than to provide answers before the questions are asked. But I should very much like to know how you feel about the [*word omitted*] before settling the matter.

Yours sincerely
[T. S. Eliot]

1 – C. K. Ogden wrote (16 July) to arrange the lunch: 'let us meet at 58 Frith St & lunch thereabouts . . . Call there first for a drink & hear the Joyce under favourable circumstances.'
2 – TSE's draft paragraph, drawing on a letter by Hambourg of 27 June, read: 'Clere Parsons was born February 13th 1908 and died February 22nd 1931. He was Douglas Jerrold Scholar in English Literature at Christ Church College, Oxford, 1926. He edited *Oxford Outlook* and *Oxford Poetry: 1929*. He took First Class Honours in Modern History in 1929 and was Dixon Research Scholar, 1930. At the time of his death he had just been nominated to the post of Senior Assistant in the Department of Western MSS. at the Bodleian Library.'

TO *J. H. Oldham*

21 July 1931   [Faber & Faber Ltd]

My dear Mr Oldham,

Many thanks for your letter of the 9th enclosing the list of your continental group which promises a very interesting session.[1] I wish that I could hope to attend your meeting at Marburg in October which would interest me very much as I have the pleasantest memories of the town, and there is a friend of mine, an old lady whom I should like to see again. I should very much like to give myself the pleasure, but it is more than doubtful if I shall be able to get away. In any case I hope you will let me know, and lunch with me when you return in the autumn.

                              Yours very sincerely,
                              [T. S. Eliot]

TO *D. S. Mirsky*

21 July 1931   [Faber & Faber Ltd]

My dear Mirsky,

I must apologise for having kept your syllabus for several weeks without acknowledgment, particularly as I understand you would like the book to be published in the autumn.[2] After a good deal of reflection we decided that the book was probably not in our line, and it was suggested that Williams and Norgate might be the most suitable people.

Thank you very much for letting me see the syllabus. I am very sorry not to have seen anything of you during the past year, and shall make an attempt when you return in the autumn.

                              Yours very sincerely,
                              [T. S. Eliot]

1–Oldham sent a list of figures who were due to meet for a five-day discussion at Marburg in Oct., 'to consider the problem of Christianity in the modern world . . . While the group is a continental one, and the language of discussion will be German, I promised that I would try to bring two people from Great Britain, in order to maintain a link between continental and British thinking. Is there any possibility of your being able to come?' The 'Continental Group' included Emil Brunner, Professor of Theology at Zurich, and Karl Heim, Professor of Theology at Tübingen.

2–Mirsky wished (27 June) to publish a series of lectures he had recently given as a University extension course at the City Literary Institute.

to *G. R. Elliott*[1]   cc

21 July 1931   [*The Criterion*]

Dear Mr Elliott,

I am ashamed to be returning so tardily your essay on Donne,[2] and for giving you also the trouble of cabling for a reply at the time. I found the essay extremely interesting and of course it would be perfectly suitable for the *Criterion*. My only reason for not using it was that so much about Donne has been published in other periodicals at the time, and I have a very strong aversion to recognising centenaries. I should be very glad if you could be a contributor to the *Criterion* and hope that you will soon have something else to offer us. I imagine that you must be tired of writing about Humanism, and unfortunately that has never been such a lively issue in England as in America. But I do wish you would suggest something.

Yours very truly
[T. S. Eliot]

to *Lilian Donaghy*[3]   cc

21 July 1931   [Faber & Faber Ltd]

Dear Mrs Donaghy,

I was very sorry indeed to learn the news contained in your letter of the 15th July.[4] I had thought on the last occasion of seeing your husband that he was looking much more than ordinarily tired, and I had got the impression more recently that he was in an overwrought state. I had a short letter from him, however, two days ago which seemed to me very

---

1 – G. R. Elliott taught at Amherst College, Mass.; author of *The Cycle of Modern Poetry: A Series of Essays toward Clearing our Present Poetic Dilemma* (1929).
2 – Submitted on 21 Mar. 1931; published as 'John Donne: The Middle Phase', *The Bookman* 73: 4 (June 1931), 337–46.
3 – Lilian Donaghy, née Roberts: wife of the Irish poet John Lyle Donaghy.
4 – 'While staying over here [Bray, Co. Wicklow, Ireland] with the children I had a wire to say that my husband, Lyle Donaghy, was very ill. When I arrived in London I found he had had a serious nervous break-down. He is in a nursing-home now, & seems better, but the doctors think it may be some time before he is well . . . I must get work until my husband is better and able to take care of us again. I wonder do you know of any job I could do here or in London? I think I could teach French or English fairly well. I have done a good deal of acting in Dublin. I would like to do some book-reviewing & have done some before.'

much more normal, and so I hope that he will not have to remain in a nursing home very long.[1]

Meanwhile, however, I have thought of your affairs, and have taken the liberty of discussing the matter with Mr Richmond. We both felt that there seemed to be nothing that we could do to assist you at this distance. I should not encourage you to come to London simply in the hope of finding work here but, of course, if you should be coming at any time I should be very glad to have a talk with you.

I wish to say, however, and I can say it on Mr Richmond's behalf, that if there is anything I can do to be of use or comfort to your husband during his illness I hope you will let me know at once. I should be very glad to go out to see him whenever the doctors think it suitable. So will you be so kind as to let me know from time to time how he is getting on, or put me in touch with the head of the sanatorium?

> With all sympathy,
> Yours sincerely
> [T. S. Eliot]

TO *Algar Thorold*   CC

21 July 1931   [*The Criterion*]

My dear Thorold,

I have just seen D'Arcy's book this morning, and I don't blame you for withdrawing, though I had every reason to believe that it would be a very tough book.[2] I saw D'Arcy the other day, by the way, and he tells me that he is going to Salzburg at the end of the month. Thank you for suggesting Collingwood.[3] I have written to him today, but I don't suppose that either you or I could get the book reviewed in time for the autumn number.

1–Lyle Donaghy wrote to TSE on 17 July, from Northumberland House, Green Lanes, Finsbury Park, enclosing a poem: 'my hope is . . . that you may like it. The poem does not, of course imply, necessarily, a giving up of free verse.' Earlier, at 5 o'clock in the afternoon of Fri. 2 July, he had rung up TSE in an incoherent frame of mind; he wrote on 13 July that he 'would hasten to offer [an explanation for the incident] but that my inalienable self-centredness still leaves me in the certainty that the ever-ready harbingers of the Lord have been before me'. He was presently to be transferred to the Down County Mental Hospital, Downpatrick, Co. Down.
2–Thorold cried off (19 July) from reviewing D'Arcy's *The Nature of Belief* (1931). 'I admire it very much, but I have not the time, or perhaps the learning, to do it as it should be done in the *Criterion*.'
3–R. G. Collingwood. TSE's letter to him not found.

Now is there any other book about which you would like to have news?

Yours ever,

[T. S. Eliot]

TO *Charles Smyth* CC

24 July 1931   *[The Criterion]*

My dear Smyth,

Many thanks for sending me your offprint with which I was delighted. I am going to ask you if you could manage to let me have a few more copies, as I should like to send them about to a few people I have in mind. Possibly some of them will have seen it already, or will have received it from you. But that won't matter. I hope that you can arrange to let me have half a dozen or so.[1]

In great haste
Yours ever sincerely,
[T. S. Eliot]

TO *William Temple* CC

24 July 1931   [Faber & Faber Ltd]

My dear Lord Archbishop,

I had meant from the time of its announcement to obtain and read your Grace's Charge, and I shall now do so with particular pleasure in consequence of your Grace's kindness in sending me the book.[2]

With very many thanks,

I am your Grace's obedient Servant
[T. S. Eliot]

1–Smyth had advised TSE on 28 Apr.: 'I have just done a paper on The State and Freedom ... It is very Burkian, and might amuse you.' He replied to this letter on the '8th Sunday after Trinity', enclosing as many offprints as he could manage: 'I am very glad that you liked the apologia: its Toryism is too High for most tastes. I go to Oxford tomorrow to defend it (it is really a paper for the Anglo-Catholic Summer School of Sociology, & came out in their organ, *Christendom*, last month). Moriturus te saluto. They won't like it a bit.' See Smyth, 'The State and Freedom', *Christendom: A Journal of Christian Sociology* 1: 2 (June 1931), 109–20.

2–Temple had written on 20 July: 'I have meant from the time of its publication to send you a copy of my recent Charge, because it mainly deals with questions arising out of the Lambeth Conference Report on which we corresponded when you were preparing your admirable pamphlet. I enclose a copy with this.' *Thoughts on Some Problems of the Day: A Charge delivered at his primary visitation* (1931).

27 July 1931   *The Criterion*

Dear Spender

Thank you for your letter of July 24.[1] I had given up all expectation, after what you had said about the subject from time to time, of getting your poems in time for this autumn. We had put them down pretty definitely for the beginning of next year, between seasons, and as this seemed to us probably the best time to publish, my mind was easy. I am afraid, too, that September 1 is too late for autumn publication, too late at least to get the book out before the time when the market is inundated.

In short, if you let us have the manuscript about the beginning of September that will be very convenient and will allow the book plenty of time to go through the press without being hustled. I should propose to bring it out in late January or early February, about the beginning of the term, and I still think that this is the best time. When Mr C. W. Stewart returns next week I will ask him to draw up a contract for you.

I have had a word with Faber about your novel, and I gather that it is very much changed since I read it.[2] I shall therefore read it again myself, and will let you hear within a week or ten days.

I am surprised that you did not receive a copy of the July *Criterion* as one was sent to you. I will have another sent. As for the proofs the trouble was that we received your manuscript too late for proofs to be possible. I hope that you will not find anything that you would have preferred to change.[3]

This is only a business letter so as I probably shall not have time to write in the next few days I shall be glad to have your Berlin address, and shall look forward to seeing you early in September.

Yours sincerely

T. S. Eliot

1 – 'I now have only one more poem to write in order to complete my book of poems, so I can quite easily let you have the typescript on Sept 1st . . . I will have 35 poems, and I could let you have them easily by August 17th . . .' Still, he preferred the later date because it would allow him 'a little more time for reflexion on the book, and also that I may be able to enlarge the book . . .'

2 – 'I believe Faber have read the MS of my novel [*The Temple*]. If they should wish to take this, but to publish it after my poems, as you suggested they might do, I would be very willing to wait, and also to discuss with you and to make any changes in the novel which you may like.'

3 – Spender had not received a copy of the July C., nor seen proofs of his review of Rilke's *The Notebook of Malte Laurids Brigge*: C. 10 (July 1931), 744–5.

TO *Henry Eliot*   TS Houghton

28 July 1931   Faber & Faber Ltd

My dear Brother,

I am very sorry to bother you once more about my legal difficulties with
New York publishers, but I have received another cheque from Horace
Liveright for 61 dollars and 67 cents with a statement that this represents
royalties on *The Waste Land* for the six months ending December 31
1930.[1] Now as you know Liveright's copyright expired on December 31
1927 and I do not admit his right to continue publishing it. Therefore I
have not collected the cheque lest that should imply permission to him to
publish. On the royalty statement is printed the following sentence: 'It is
assumed that all accounts between the author and publisher previous to
this period are in perfect balance.'

I do not know whether you have sufficient confidence in Stern to refer
the matter to him or whether you know of some other more dependable
lawyer. And by the way you have never told me what charges Stern made
for the ineffectual business he did for me before. You will remember that
I told you that Faber & Faber would divide the costs with me.

> Affectionately
> Tom

TO *James F. Courage*[2]   CC

28 July 1931   [Faber & Faber Ltd]

Dear Mr Courage,

I and two other directors have read with much interest and sympathy
your manuscript 'The Promising Years',[3] and while we are more than
doubtful whether it would be possible to publish this in its present form
we are interested in your work and would like to discuss it with you. I
should be very glad if you could come and have a talk with me. Would it

---

1 – *TWL*, published by Horace Liveright Inc., sold 2,458 copies to the end of June 1930.
In the six-month period ending on 31 Dec. 1930, it had sold 116 copies in the USA, 5 in
Canada.
2 – James F. Courage (1903–63), expatriate New Zealand author: short-story writer, poet,
bookseller; a graduate of St John's College, Oxford, where he was a contributor to *Oxford
Outlook* and *Oxford Poetry*.
3 – Submitted on 24 June 1931.

be convenient for you to ring up my secretary, and ask her to make an appointment for one morning in the near future?

Yours very truly
[T. S. Eliot]

TO *Lincoln Kirstein*   TS Beinecke

28 July 1931   Faber & Faber Ltd

Dear Mr Kirstein,

Thank you very much for your letter of the 17th and for your suggestion.[1] On thinking it over I feel that I had rather not at the present time attempt any critical writing about Joyce's work. For one thing I have been concerned with the publication of some of his later work, and also at the moment I feel rather too close to the object. I am thinking of asking Stuart Gilbert to write something about the later work for the *Criterion*, and if he does I should have no objection at all to its simultaneous publication in the *Hound and Horn*.[2] Of course, in another year or two I might feel differently about it, but I feel something ought to be published about the later work within the next six months.

Yours sincerely
T. S. Eliot

TO *Margaret L. Woods*   cc

28 July 1931   [Faber & Faber Ltd]

Dear Mrs Woods,

Please excuse me for my delay in replying to your letter of the 19th July.[3] I have thought the matter over very carefully, and I have come to the

---

1 – Kirstein wondered whether TSE 'would be interested in writing about Joyce'.
2 – Kirstein thought (18 Aug.) that it would be 'inadvisable for us to attempt simultaneous publication of any work however interesting, in this case, Mr Gilbert's remarks about the *Work in Progress* would be. We feel the limitations of space very acutely . . .'
3 – 'The late Arthur C Benson left money to provide the Medals. They are given as a rule for special books but the writers' general work is frequently mentioned together with the particular book, for instance, when Mr Siegfried Sassoon received the Medal it was for his "Memoirs of a Fox-hunting Man" *and* his Poems . . . There are now five books before us and Mr Lowes-Dickinson had proposed Miss Stella Benson's work in general. Two medals are to be awarded. The list of the books shall be forwarded to you when or if we receive your formal acceptance of Membership of the Committee.'

conclusion that I am not really a suitable person to share the responsibility for awarding literary prizes. I am not really interested in contemporary literature to begin with, and it frequently happens that what I do like is, by a natural coincidence, published by my own firm. This is, indeed, the chief reason for declining the proposal: I do not feel that a director of any publishing firm, or indeed anyone connected in any capacity with one publishing firm should take part in any such committee of selection.

With many thanks for your invitation, and [I] regret that I cannot accept it.

I am,
Yours sincerely
[T. S. Eliot]

TO *Max Planck*[1]   CC

29 July 1931   [Faber & Faber Ltd]

Sir,

I understand from my friend Dr Erich Alport of Hamburg that he has already approached you at my suggestion about the possibility of publishing an English translation in the *Criterion* of your essay on *Positivismus und reale Aussenwelt*.[2] I am writing to confirm Dr Alport's approaches and to say that I should be greatly honoured if you would allow me to see a copy of this paper, which I should have much interest in reading, and which I hope might prove suitable for our readers. In any case I hope that the *Criterion* may have the distinction of publishing something by yourself.

I am, Sir,
Your obedient Servant
[T. S. Eliot]

1 – Max Planck (1858–1947): German theoretical physicist who originated quantum theory; winner of Nobel Prize for Physics, 1918; Professor of Physics, University of Berlin, from 1892.
2 – Planck had told Alport he would 'gladly' send a copy of his paper 'Positivism and Realism' – which Alport considered 'very interesting & important' – if TSE himself requested it (Alport letter to TSE, 3 July 1931).

TO *Lascelles Abercrombie*[1]   CC

29 July 1931   [Faber & Faber Ltd]

Dear Professor Abercrombie,

Thank you for your letter of the 18th July.[2] I am honoured by your invitation to contribute to what will surely be a most interesting miscellany. I regret that there are two objections. The first is that I like to preserve all my work, with the exception of course [of] contributions to periodicals and occasional introductions and prefaces, for my own firm. The second objection is, however, final, because it is that I have absolutely nothing on hand which I should care to publish. I have only a small part of an unfinished poem with which I am not yet satisfied, and which I do not want to publish at all until the whole poem is finished. So that I am afraid that I must decline your kind invitation.

Yours sincerely
[T. S. Eliot]

TO *Charles K. Colhoun*   CC

5 August 1931   [*The Criterion*]

Dear Mr Colhoun,

I must acknowledge your two letters of the 3rd August, and thank you for the foreign periodicals. I am glad to hear that you have already met Mr Joyce.[3] I suppose that you have already left town, or are on the point of doing so; but I should be very glad if you could on your return come and see me at your convenience.[4]

Yours sincerely
[T. S. Eliot]

1 – Lascelles Abercrombie (1881–1938): poet and critic; Hildred Carlile Professor of English Literature in London University, 1929–35; later Goldsmiths' Reader in English at Oxford, and Fellow of Merton College. *Collected Poems* appeared from Oxford University Press in 1930.
2 – Abercrombie was assembling an anthology of 'new (i.e. hitherto unprinted) poems' for publication by Victor Gollancz, and invited TSE to contribute a work.
3 – Colhoun asked (31 July), 'I hope that you will excuse my writing to ask you if you could possibly give me an introduction to Mr James Joyce? He has taken the flat below mine, and I feel that it would be a little difficult to break in upon him, and introduce myself, just at present . . .' His letter of 3 Aug. revealed, 'I have managed to meet Mr James Joyce. I cannot help thinking that he may be able to help me with translation work, or be able to put me in the way of any such work of this kind of which he may know.'
4 – Colhoun said he was passing through London on Tues. 11 Aug., on his way to Scotland.

TO *Lilian Donaghy*   CC

5 August 1931   [Faber & Faber Ltd]

Dear Mrs Donaghy,

Thank you for your letter of the 30th.[1] I shall ring up the nursing home,
and arrange to go and see your husband as soon as I can, and after I have
seen him I will let you know how I found him.

Yours very sincerely
[T. S. Eliot]

TO *Algar Thorold*   CC

5 August 1931   [*The Criterion*]

My dear Thorold,

I have a book which is just what I should like you to review, if you are
familiar with the subject. It is *André Gide* by Ramon Fernandez. I found
it very interesting myself, and I think that Fernandez's case for Corydon
is very plausible. If you would care to make an article about it and
include Charles du Bos's book on Gide, that would please me still better.
Unfortunately I should have to ask to have the books back eventually, as
they are both inscribed to me, but you could keep them as long as you
wanted.[2]

Yours ever sincerely,
[T. S. Eliot]

1–'I feel sure he would be very very glad to see you. His address is – Northumberland
House, Green Lanes, Finsbury Park. He is allowed to see visitors any time between 11
o'clock & six in the evening as far as I can remember . . . [T]he only news I have had from
the doctor . . . is that his physical health has improved & that it would be difficult to give
any definite opinion about him for at least a month. It is extremely hard waiting for news.
I wonder, when you go to see him, could you write & tell me [how] you think he seems to
be? I would be very grateful.'
2–Thorold responded on 12 Aug.: 'I fear I cannot do Gide. I know him and feel a profound
repulsion, not only on the grounds of his morals. I admire his art as much as that of any
living writer, but that makes him worse & more dangerous. To my intuitional apparatus
there is something demoniac about him. A *mauvais pasteur*!'

TO *Louis T. More*[1]   CC

5 August 1931   [Faber & Faber Ltd]

My dear Mr More,

I also was sorry not to see you last week, but when you were in London
I had not yet had time to read your manuscript, which I have done since.
I am glad to hear that you will be in London after the 26th, and I am
anxious to see you then. Would you kindly drop me a line or have me
rung up as soon as you return to London?

                              Very sincerely yours
                              [T. S. Eliot]

TO *C. A. Siepmann*   TS BBC

6 August 1931   Faber & Faber Ltd

Dear Siepmann,

I enclose a new outline, which I hope is nearer the mark than the first
one. What does not emerge from it, but what I think will issue in the talks,
is that my position seems to be naturally in a *via media* between Dawson
and Macmurray. Do you think furthermore that I ought to make the talks
more concrete by dwelling on what is possible for each individual to do,
with himself and in the world, here and now?

                              Sincerely yours,
                              T. S. Eliot

TO *J. M. Reeves*   CC

7 August 1931   [*The Criterion*]

Dear Mr Reeves,

I have been very slow in acknowledging your conscientious report on
McDowall's book on Hardy.[2] It confirms my impression that the book

1–Louis T. More (1870–1944) – physicist, humanist, critic of the Darwinian theory of
evolution; Dean of the Graduate School, University of Cincinnati – was brother of Paul
Elmer More. His works include *Isaac Newton: A Biography* (1934), *The Dogma of
Evolution* (1925).
2–Reeves wrote (1 July) about Arthur MacDowall's *Thomas Hardy* that 'its chief value is in
the accurate and sensitive commentaries on individual novels; but these commentaries have
an air of casualness because they do not stand against an adequate theoretical background
or imply any coherent critical attitude. The author [is] more an intelligent reader of Hardy

although very good of its kind is not of sufficient curiosity to be worth reviewing in the *Criterion*, being neither good enough to praise highly or bad enough to condemn. Your report, however, makes me hope that you will be able to suggest to me, either immediately or when the autumn lists appear, some other book which you would like to review.

Do come in and see me whenever you happen to be in London.

Yours sincerely
[T. S. Eliot]

TO *Henry Hazlitt*[1]   CC

7 August 1931   [Faber & Faber Ltd]

Dear Mr Hazlitt,

Many thanks for your letter of July 28th.[2] I should be very glad indeed to write something for the *Nation*, and particularly happy to earn a hundred dollars. With respect to this occasion I must say that I have no desire to emulate such eminent people as Lord Russell, J. B. S. Haldane, Beatrice Webb, or Morris R. Cohen.[3] If some other subject should occur to you more suitable to my capacities I should be very glad indeed.

---

than a critic.'

1 – Henry Hazlitt (1894–1993) – influential free-market economist, author, critic, philosopher – worked for newspapers including the *New York Sun*, *Wall Street Journal*, *The New York Times* (as finance and economics editor), *American Mercury* (where he was chosen successor to H. L. Mencken – 'one of the few economists in human history who could really write'), *Century*, *Freeman*, *National Review*, *Newsweek*; and he was the founding vice-president of the Foundation for Economic Education. A prolific author, he wrote twenty-five books including *Thinking as a Science* (1915), *The Anatomy of Criticism* (1933), *Economics in One Lesson* (1946) and *Will Dollars Save the World?* (1947). At this time he was Acting Managing Editor of *N*.

2 – 'The *Nation* is running a series of articles by men and women of high standing in the field of abstract thought, literature, scientific or practical achievement, under the general title of "What I Believe". We have already printed contributions to this series from Bertrand Russell, J. B. S. Haldane, Beatrice Webb, and Morris R. Cohen, and we should be delighted if we could have the same type of confession of faith – or confession of doubt – from yourself. This "philosophy of life" might take any of a number of forms – a discussion of beliefs on religion, on the larger social questions (democracy, education, moral codes, one's Utopia, etc.), on the value, place, promise or menace of science, one's beliefs regarding probable future trends, or a brief intellectual autobiography ... We naturally desire ... that each contributor will accordingly emphasize those problems or aspects of life which seem to him most important.' For an article of 2,400–3,500 words, the honorarium would be $100.

3 – Morris R. Cohen (1880–1947): American philosopher, lawyer and legal scholar.

With many thanks,

Yours sincerely
[T. S. Eliot]

TO *E. R. Curtius*   CC

7 August 1931   [Faber & Faber Ltd]

My dear Curtius,

It is a long time since I have written to you, and I have never answered a very kind letter from you some months ago.[1] About the little book by McGreevy, I wonder if you have seen a most thoroughgoing denunciation of it by Mr Titus, the Editor of *This Quarter*? There were many things in the book which irritated me, but none more so than his childish reference to yourself, on which point all of my collaborators here were in strong agreement.[2]

I have not for a long time suggested that the *Criterion* would like another contribution from you because you had told me that you were too busy to undertake anything. But is it unreasonable for me to hope that you may now have a little more leisure and may consider writing something for us? There is certainly enough to think and talk about in the present situation of Europe. I only wish that it were otherwise.[3]

Yours ever sincerely
[T. S. Eliot]

---

1 – Not found.

2 – Thomas McGreevy wrote, in *Thomas Stearns Eliot* (1931), 62: 'Mr Eliot has . . . turned his magazine into a kind of exchange for ideas between the second-raters of all Europe. I remember one truly ridiculous and impudent article by a German professor in the *Criterion*. It began, in apparently unconscious romantic fashion, apropos of the pleasantness of the nocturnal atmosphere that surrounded the writer. And then it transpired that what it all amounted to was that romanticism was over, and therefore that *Der Tag* had arrived for professors. In the future professors would keep the artist in his place. As if most of the professors had not tried their best to keep the romantics in their place, and failed, and made their living out of writing and talking about them ever since. Great fleas have little fleas . . .'

3 – Curtius replied on 21 Aug.: 'I see in your journal one of the few ideal places today where intellectual values are measured according to absolute criteria, that is, in complete independence from parties, interests and institutions . . . If there is such a thing as the Platonic idea of a journal, then it is certainly an organ like yours . . . "There is certainly enough to think and talk about in the present situation of Europe," you tell me. I will not contradict you. But is not too much being written already about our European troubles, about the problems of our time?'

TO *Lilian Donaghy*

12 August 1931   [Faber & Faber Ltd]

Dear Mrs Donaghy,

Thank you for your letter of the 7th August.[1] I am very sorry indeed to hear your news. Your husband's friend was certainly ill-advised, but his statement of facts is correct.

Meanwhile I have heard from C. M. Grieve, whom you may or may not know, to say that he called at Northumberland House and was informed that your husband left with his father.

You will, I hope, excuse me for writing about the matter as if I knew you, but it is only because I happen to have more knowledge of this type of nervous illness than most people. Such cases are very difficult to handle, because they rarely want to stay in a sanatorium voluntarily, and no one wants to go so far as certification. In your case, I think that it is merely a question of how difficult it becomes, especially in view of the children. All the symptoms you describe are known to me. I am quite certain that people in such a state ought not, as much for their own sakes as for that of others, be with their family and friends. The manifestations of mania are always more pronounced with the persons they know best than with others. Furthermore, those near can do no good but only harm; and it is a heartrending business to wear oneself to shreds for anyone when one knows all the time that he or she only becomes the worst for it. I hope that his parents will see the matter in this light. Professional outsiders are the only people to deal with such cases, and the only people whose nerves can stand the strain of dealing with them. It need be only a temporary cure – two months might do it – but so long as he stays with near relatives the cure is only being postponed.

> With much sympathy,
> Yours sincerely,
> [T. S. Eliot]

---

1 – Lilian Donaghy wrote from Bray, Co. Wicklow, that a 'very foolish friend' of her husband had 'told him that – a thing I did not know – he could leave on giving three days notice. He did so, & arrived here on Sunday morning. Yesterday he went to Co. Antrim to see his own people . . . He tells me that every one, including me, are in league against him in what he calls a "plant". He believes that some books Mr Richmond sent him to review were written & published specially to this end . . . Sometimes for even a whole day he will bathe & play tennis in an apparently normal way & seem happy, but we never know when he will take exception to something one of us may say or do . . . I feel very certain he should not be with his relations . . .'

TO *J. M. Robertson*

14 August 1931   [*The Criterion*]

My dear Robertson,

Thank you for your letter of the 8th enclosing Part 1 of your essay on *Shakespeare's Workmanship*.[1] I am rather in a dilemma what to do about it. Quiller-Couch's book came in for review some weeks ago. I have not read it, and I really did not attach much importance to it; so I sent it to Middleton Murry to do what he liked with for the September number. I shall therefore have to use Murry's review, and it would be giving too much space to use yours at the same time. I do not know what Murry has said about the book, but to judge from your essay it must be a very foolish one. Had it occurred to me that the book was one likely to attract your notice in this way I should certainly have sent it to you. Perhaps you can think of some other way in which you could tackle the subject in a later number of the *Criterion*.

Yours sincerely
[T. S. Eliot]

TO *Colin Dunlop*

14 August 1931   [Faber & Faber Ltd]

Dear Mr Dunlop,

Thank you very much for returning the typescript. I have not, of course, any further use for it, but I know how one feels about other people's manuscripts, and I should have done the same thing myself.

I wonder if I may bother you on another point? I have been trying to find out if there is any English translation of Heiler's *Das Gebet*.[2] I have discovered that Hodder & Stoughton published a book called *The Spirit of Worship* by Heiler in 1928 with a preface by the Dean of Canterbury.[3]

1–Robertson had written for the *Literary Guide* a review of the new edition of Sir Arthur Quiller-Couch's *Shakespeare's Workmanship* – which included, said Robertson, 'a gratuitously defiant preface' – but he now thought it more suitable for C. 'In recent years I had only incidentally, & lightly, dealt with Q, because I had heard that the poor man was going blind. But he insists on trailing his coat with a book that is essentially & critically bad.'

2–Friedrich Heiler, *Das Gebet: Eine religionsgeschichtliche und religionspsychologische Untersuchung* (1919); translated by Samuel McComb as *Prayer* (1932). Heiler (1892–1967), German theologian and historian of religion, taught at Marburg University.

3–*The Spirit of Worship*, trans. W. Montgomery, with a foreword by the Very Revd G. K. A. Bell, Dean of Canterbury (1926).

It had occurred to me in any case that the Bishop was as likely to know about Heiler's work and the translations as anybody; but as he appears to have written the preface to *The Spirit of Worship* I should like to ask him whether the book published under this title is actually *Das Gebet*. I had not wanted to bother him on such a small matter, but I should be more than grateful if you could ask him from me, and let me know, whether the two books are the same, and if not whether he knows of any English translation of *Das Gebet* having been published, and if there is no English translation of *Das Gebet* does he think that it would be a commendable undertaking for my publishing firm?[1]

Yours sincerely
[T. S. Eliot]

TO *Ian Parsons*   TS Bertram Rota

14 August 1931   Faber & Faber Ltd

My dear Parsons,

Thank you very much for taking so much trouble over Leslie Bishop's book.[2] I am quite of the opinion that it is a book worth publishing, but I am afraid that it may be difficult to find a publisher. I think, however, that your suggestion of Peter Davies is a good one, and I will take that up.

I now want to send you another book of quite a different kind. Please don't think that I am trying to work off on Chatto's the books by my acquaintances which Faber's don't want. My reason for thinking of Chatto's for this book, which is entitled *Critique of Poetry* by Michael Roberts, is that you published Empson's book.[3] Roberts, by the way, is a friend of Empson, and I think was a little after your time at Cambridge. I don't particularly want Faber's to publish the book for the following reasons. First that we are too obviously the people to do it. I do not want Faber's to be the only publishers of books written by people acquainted

1–Dunlop replied on 15 Aug.: 'The *Spirit of Worship* is not a translation of *Das Gebet*, but of some other book. Somebody has in fact translated *Das Gebet* & the Oxford Press is considering its publication. The matter is however being hung up at the moment because the man who is reading the rough & reporting on the translation (he is no other than the Dean of Chichester!) is not being very quick about it.' He reported too that Bishop Bell suggested that TSE should get in touch with Heiler, who was in the UK just then.
2–Parsons reported on 7 Aug. that the vote at Chatto & Windus had gone against Bishop's book, *Mother's Gone Away*, though he himself had been in favour of publishing it – 'principally because I think the man can write . . .'
3–Empson, *Seven Types of Ambiguity* (1930).

with the work of T. E. Hulme, I. A. Richards etcetera. It would be far better for everyone if critical writings of this sort could be dispersed through various channels. Secondly it is a type of book of which we have already produced two or three, and I do not see why Faber's should publish all the admirable books critical of modern literature and society inasmuch as there cannot be any profit in them! At any rate I think that you would find Roberts's essay interesting, and I should like to send it round to you if I have your permission.[1]

Yours sincerely,
T. S. Eliot

Are you in town through this month? We might lunch together at last.

TO *Bruce Richmond* cc

14 August 1931   [Faber & Faber Ltd]

Dear Richmond,

I wonder if you could make any use of a Scot named C. M. Grieve, who under the name of Hugh MacDiarmid has written a good deal of Scottish verse published by Blackwood?[2] His verse is highly praised by some of his contemporaries and seems to me to have a good deal of vigour although I have not the patience myself to take much trouble over dialect poetry. He is a man of about 36, with a young family, quite reckless and improvident, who has succeeded in antagonising some people in Scotland by his Nationalistic views and his outspoken contempt of people he dislikes. Some years ago he used to write, sometimes quite brilliantly, in the *New Age*. He is extremely erratic and his prose work is usually either quite brilliant or quite wrong-headed. He seems to be well educated, and has certainly a touch of genius. This all seems very discouraging, and as if it would be more trouble to you than it is worth; but I was thinking that a little discipline such as you could give would be very good for him; and I wish that he might have some opportunity to do a few shortish notes on appro. He is out of a job, and apparently not likely to get one.[3]

1–Michael Roberts, *Critique of Poetry*, was published in 1934 by Jonathan Cape. See Samuel Hynes, 'Michael Roberts' Tragic View', *Contemporary Literature* 12: 4 (Aut. 1971), 437–50.
2–Grieve asked TSE on 11 Aug.: 'I wonder if you have found an opportunity to speak to the editor of the "Times Literary Supplement" on my behalf. I am anxious to get something to do . . .'
3–'I am afraid I cannot manage Mr Grieve,' replied BLR (17 Aug.). 'We have frequently praised his ~~efforts~~ poems – much to his annoyance. I have no doubt, as you say, that he

My last news of Donaghy is from his wife who has written to me to tell me that he has got out of his Finsbury nursing-home and returned to Ireland, evidently bursting with persecution mania and likely to be a great nuisance to his family. I have written to impress upon her the importance in such cases of separating the patient from his friends and family, not only for their sake, but primarily for his own. He will never get over this without two or three months separation, and I don't see that there is anything more that anyone on this side can do.

Yours ever,

[T. S. E.]

TO *Edouard Roditi*[1]

TS UCLA

17 August 1931   Faber & Faber Ltd

Dear Roditi,[2]

So far as Clere Parsons' poems go we have no intention of exercising translation rights, and whatever Miss Hambourg approves is agreeable to us. At the same time I think to be quite in order it would be best if you wrote to Mrs Parsons saying that both we and Miss Hambourg are in accord, and asking her permission. In case you do not know it, Mrs Parsons' address is 33 Trebovir Road, S.W.5.

I hope to see you again soon, but will wait till I hear from you about Auden. There again it would be quite sufficient if you let me know what poems are chosen, and to save time you might as well write to Auden simultaneously. I believe that he is off in the Orkneys or Shetlands at present, but I daresay you are as likely to know as I am.

Yours sincerely

T. S. Eliot

P.S. I have not seen this new book by Bernanos and should like to see it.[3]

---

is erratic and brilliant; but I am too busy and too old to try, now, to tame the probably untameable.'

1–Edouard Roditi (1910–92), poet, critic, biographer, translator: see Biographical Register.

2–Roditi had notified TSE (n.d.): 'Some friends of mine in Brussels, "Le Journal des Poetes", have decided to devote a page of their newspaper to English poetry – and for the first number have chosen: Stephen Spender, Auden, Clere Parsons, and myself. I have been asked, as translator of Spender, to collect the other necessary translations ... Miss Hambourg seems pleased at the idea and told me to ask you for the necessary permissions ... About the Auden stuff I will write to you later when I know what piece the syndicate have chosen.'

3–Roditi was reading a work by Georges Bernanos, *La grande Peur des Biens-Pensants* – 'a rather long "pamphlet" of slightly Action Française tendencies – I thought it might interest

But at present I have the responsibility of two books of yours which I have not had time to read.[1]

TO *Charles Duff*[2]

CC

17 August 1931   [*The Criterion*]

Dear Mr Duff,

Thank you for letting me see your article or pamphlet about James Joyce.[3] After thinking it over carefully I have come to the conclusion that it would serve a better purpose if published by someone else rather than by ourselves. I should suggest that you try the *Listener* or *Everyman*, although of course neither of these papers would be able to publish it entire. It might be better if some other publisher undertook the whole thing as a booklet. If I can be of any use in adding a word of recommendation I shall be glad to do so.

Yours sincerely
[T. S. Eliot]

TO *Erich Alport*

TS BL

17 August 1931   Faber & Faber Ltd

Dear Alport,

Some interest has lately been expressed in the work of Leo Frobenius.[4] I am obliged to say that I know nothing about his work except that Ezra Pound has spoken to me of it in terms of the highest praise. I should be

---

you ... It is about Édouard Drumont.' Édouard Drumont (1844–1917): journalist and writer; founder-editor of *La Libre Parole*; anti-Semite; prominent accuser of Alfred Dreyfus.

1–TSE had perhaps undertaken earlier in the year to recommend to the Hogarth Press a book of poems by Roditi – 'now merely Poems 1927–1930', as Roditi had designated it in a letter of 30 May. Roditi said his 'French book', entitled *La Vie Nouvelle*, was to be published 'shortly'.

2–Charles Duff (1894–1966): British author of books on language learning and other subjects.

3–Duff wrote on 27 July: 'I enclose an article of about 11,000 words on James Joyce's work. My idea in writing it was to provide in pamphlet form a statement which would give the ordinary person a general notion of what Joyce means.' Duff, *James Joyce and the Plain Reader: An Essay* (Desmond Harmsworth, 1932).

4–Leo Frobenius (1873–1938): German ethnologist and archaeologist; much promoted by EP.

very grateful if you would let me know anything you know of him and his work, and of his standing in Germany.[1]

Yours sincerely
T. S. Eliot

TO *Charles Smyth*   CC

17 August 1931   [Faber & Faber Ltd]

My dear Smyth,

Your essay on the State and Freedom has made such an impression that I am writing to suggest to you that if you are thinking now or at a later time of writing a book I hope that Faber & Faber may have the first opportunity. I have thought for a long time that there was need for a book on Church and State, going into the whole matter thoroughly. It is a subject on which most people's notions are very confused, and I doubt whether even the Bishop of Durham has thought out all the implications of his attitude. But of course you may not want to do this, and may have some other project in hand. In any case I should be very glad to know what you are interested in doing.[2]

Yours ever
[T. S. Eliot]

TO *Nika Standen*[3]   CC

18 August 1931   [Faber & Faber Ltd]

Dear Madam,

I have to thank you for your kind letter which gave me very much pleasure, and I am very happy to know that my verses have given you some satisfaction.

1–Alport replied (20 Aug.): 'Thank you . . . for sending me "*De Luther à Wagner*". This book is quite interesting, I shall send you a note about it soon – together with an account of Frobenius & his work which certainly is very important.'

2–Smyth replied on 19 Aug., 'Your letter is absurdly kind. But I fear that I cannot commit myself to anything at the moment. I am struggling with a rather dull and academic work on Political Theory in the Bible (hardly in your line) . . . Of course, what I should most like to write would be a defence of the Establishment . . . And my days as a scholar are numbered, as you know, since I hope to be burying myself in some London curacy about this time next year.'

3–Nika Standen (1908–92), journalist and food writer, daughter of a German diplomat, was born in Rome; after schooling in Switzerland, she went on to study under Harold Laski

As for your request, I am afraid that I am not well enough informed to give you any exact references. A year or so ago the *Hound and Horn*, 1430 Massachusetts Avenue, Cambridge, Mass. published two essays on my work by Mr R. C. Blackmur, and also a bibliography up to that date, and I have no doubt that if you enquire of the editor of that periodical, and say I have referred you to him, he would be happy to supply you with the numbers. I cannot think of any other essay which merits your attention except an article by E. R. Curtius two or three years ago in the *Neue Schweizer Rundschau*. There again I am unable to give you the reference, but if you cared to write to Dr Max Rychner, the editor of the *Neue Schweizer Rundschau* in Zurich, he also would probably be glad to provide you with the number in question. There is a very intelligent article by an Egyptian lady, Amy Nimr,[1] in a recent number of a French review called *Echange*. My friend Mr G. B. Angioletti of Milan would probably tell you more than I can about anything else in French or Italian.

> With many thanks, I am
> Yours very truly
> [T. S. Eliot]

TO *G. Wilson Knight*   CC

18 August 1931   [Faber & Faber Ltd]

My dear Knight,

I have two letters of yours to which to reply. One of the 23rd July enclosing your essay 'The Eternal Triangle', and one of the 11th August enclosing poems by one of your scholars. As for the latter I have not had time to consider them very carefully. In any case a boy of sixteen is far too young to have his poetry published anywhere but in a school magazine,

---

at the London School of Economics. In the early 1930s she was a journalist, covering the League of Nations for the German Press Association; and in 1935 she removed to the USA (where in 1956 she married Harold Hazelton). She wrote for the *New Yorker*, *Family Circle*, *Vogue*, *The New York Times* and *Harper's Bazaar*, and was editor of *Woman's Day Encyclopedia of Food*. Her publications include *The Art of Cheese Cookery* (1949) and *American Home Cooking* (1967).

1 – Amy Nimr, 'Introduction to the Poety [*sic*] of Mr T. S. Eliot', *Échanges* no. 4 (Mar. 1931), 35–57. Nimr (b. 1898), a Syrian artist who had studied at the Slade School of Fine Art and visited Paris and Rome, held her first exhibition in 1925. In 1932 she married Walter Smart (later Sir Walter), Oriental Secretary at the British Embassy, Tehran, who was to be the model for Mountolive, Ambassador to Egypt, in vol. 3 of Lawrence Durrell's *The Alexandria Quartet*.

but from glancing at his verses I should certainly say his people ought to send him to Oxford or Cambridge if it is at all possible.[1]

I found your essay very interesting, but I am very doubtful about its effect if published as it stands.[2] It seems to me that it is, or ought to be, part of a very considerable book in which each of its sections would be very fully developed. The whole question of Symbolism is extraordinarily difficult and subtle, and I think ought to be dealt with at considerable length and detail if at all. That you *can* write the book if you wish to I have no doubt. Whether you want to do so I have yet to learn from you.

I look forward with keen interest to the appearance of your second volume, and I hope very much that you will give me the opportunity of seeing you again before you leave for Canada.

Yours sincerely,
[T. S. Eliot]

TO *Hamish Miles*   CC

19 August 1931   [*The Criterion*]

My dear Miles,

I should be very glad if you are willing to review for the December *Criterion* Ramon Fernandez's *André Gide*. I have read it myself, and like almost everything of Fernandez's it is well worth the trouble. Have you read *Si le Grain ne meurt* and *Corydon*? About the last quarter of the book is concerned with these.[3]

I hope that you will be in town and able to come to the *Criterion* meeting on the 26th.

Yours ever
[T. S. Eliot]

1–Knight had submitted four poems – 'Kataga Kifna', 'Duae Voces', 'The Lampost' [*sic*], 'Gold' – by Francis Berry (a pupil at Dean Close School, Cheltenham) – 'a boy I have taken some interest in. I have no aim in view beyond that I should like you to see them. Later it might be good for him that you had. I think them quite exceptional myself & in some ways characteristic especially of the rising generation. My knowing him may have influenced me. He is 16 & I have urged that he go to Oxford if possible. He lives here & I know his people.' See Francis Berry, 'G. Wilson Knight: Stage and Study', in *The Morality of Art: Essays Presented to G. Wilson Knight by his Colleagues and Friends*, ed. D. W. Jefferson 1969), 135–43.

2–Knight wrote on 23 July: 'It is a considered & careful statement about religion etc. I believe I have some valuable things to say thereon, & this essay holds the essence of my outlook.'

3–See Miles's review in C. 11 (Jan. 1932), 336–9.

TO M. C. D'Arcy

19 August 1931   [*The Criterion*]

My dear D'Arcy,

I am very anxious to persuade you to review Husserl's *Ideas* for the December number. The book is a translation of his essay entitled 'Ideen zu einer reinen Phänomenologie und phänomenologischen Philosophie'. I don't know whether you are familiar with Husserl's work. In 1914 his 'Logische Untersuchungen' provided me with distraction during some anxious weeks when I was immured in Marburg. I must say that it proved to be about the most difficult German that I have ever read, with occasional flashes of clarity. But I do think that he is a really important man. I know that I could get to review it a young Englishman of whom I have heard, who was a pupil of Husserl's for some years, but I do not want the criticism of the disciple but of someone with an outside and positive point of view. So I should be very grateful if you would undertake this.[1]

I am trusting that this letter will be preserved to await your return from Salzburg.

Yours ever sincerely
[T. S. Eliot]

TO C. M. Bowra

19 August 1931   [*The Criterion*]

Dear Mr Bowra,

I have a small book by a well-known American critic John Jay Chapman called *Lucian, Plato and Greek Morals*. There is not a great deal about Lucian of any importance, and there is a good deal of rather superfluous translation from the *Dialogues*, but towards the end of the book there is a rather interesting point of view about Plato and the Greek attitude in general which I think is original enough to give the opportunity for some interesting remarks. I should be very glad to send you the book if you are willing to consider reviewing it for our December number.[2]

Yours sincerely
[T. S. Eliot]

1 – See D'Arcy's review of Edmund Husserl's *Ideas – Ideen zu einer Phänomenologie und phänomenologischen Philosophie*, trans. W. R. Boyce Gibson – C. 11 (Jan. 1932), 339–44.
2 – Review of John Jay Chapman, *Lucian, Plato and Greek Morals*, C. 11 (Jan. 1932), 319–22.

20 August 1931   [Faber & Faber Ltd]

Dear Joyce,

Many thanks for your letter of the 11th, together with the enclosures, and particularly for your trouble in calling McCarthy's[1] attention to that anthology. I will return the *Frankfurter Zeitung* as soon as I know where you are. I wanted to read the story to see what kind of feuilleton the *Frankfurter* had chosen to father upon you.[2] On Saturday we went to tea with Harriet Weaver, and she gave me some explanation which I was not able to follow very well at the time, from which I understood that the author was a certain Michael Joyce, and that the *Frankfurter* had published some statement to this effect since, but I may have got this all wrong. Anyway I am doubtful whether such publicity as one could get in any English papers would have very much effect. It is of course a monstrous thing, and apparently the *Frankfurter* are not very penitent about it. I have been told that one of the best lawyers in London on copyright and such subjects is a Mr Medley[3] of Field Roscoe & Co. Solicitors. Field Roscoe are the solicitors to the Society of Authors, and if you saw Medley he could probably tell you whether the Authors' Society could itself do anything about the matter. Incidentally I think that Medley would be a good man to consult if you consider taking up my suggestion about a supplementary contract with Sylvia Beach over *Ulysses*.

I have not written again to Miss Beach because I wondered whether it would be better to leave that question until it was decided whether we or Cape or someone else was to publish the book of essays. I thought that she might merely be annoyed by my going into the matter and then finding that we had passed it on to some other publisher. But if you think that it would be better for me to find out definitely from her at once on what terms she could turn the book over to any publisher, I will do so. I trust you will let [me] know as soon as you return to town.

Yours sincerely

[T. S. Eliot]

1–Desmond MacCarthy had written on 8 Aug. to thank JJ for drawing his attention to 'Schücking's shocking anthology'.
2–See JJ, *Letters* III, 228, for a letter from Irene Kafka, who translated and published short stories by Michael Joyce. A story by Michael Joyce had been sent by Kafka's new secretary for publication in the *Frankfurter Zeitung* as being written by JJ: the secretary knew only of James Joyce. JJ thought the text 'an impudent forgery' (as he told TSE in a letter dated 11 Sept. 1931).
3–C. D. Medley, solicitor.

P.S. Owing probably to my not having explained your wishes fully enough to de la Mare he has not had the whole of those pages of *transition* set up yet. What he has done is to have two pages set up in eleven different types. These specimens we have ready. I suggest that you should look over these eleven different specimens and pick out the most likely ones so that we may have more pages set up.

TO *Frederick Heath*

20 August 1931   [Faber & Faber Ltd]

Dear Heath,

I have no doubt that General Charlton's book[1] has already gone to the *English Review*, but I am sending you a personal copy, because it struck me as one of our autumn books which might be particularly suitable for you to have reviewed. I think myself that it is very interesting, and quite out of the ordinary.

Yours sincerely
[T. S. Eliot]

TO *Willard Thorp*[2]

TS Princeton

25 August 1931   Faber & Faber Ltd

Dear Mr Thorp,

I understand from Emily Hale that you and Mrs Thorp are arriving in London for the winter, so I hope that I may see something of you.[3] And if

---

1–[L. E. O. Charlton], *Charlton* (F&F, 1931).
2–Willard Thorp (1899–1990), scholar, author and lecturer, taught in the English Department at Princeton for forty-one years until retirement in 1967; becoming a full professor in 1944; chair of the Department, 1958–63; and Holmes Professor of Belles Lettres, 1952–67. He co-founded and chaired the American Civilization Program. His publications include the *Oxford Anthology of English Poetry* (with Howard Lowry, 1935), *A Southern Reader* (1955), *American Writing in the Twentieth Century* (1960), *American Humorists* (1964); a pioneering annotated edition of Herman Melville's *Moby-Dick* (1947); *The Princeton Graduate School: A History* (with Minor Myers Jr. and Jeremiah Finch, 1978); and he co-edited, and contributed to, the *Literary History of the United States* (first published in 1948). See further the special Willard Thorp issue of *Princeton University Library Chronicle* 54: 2 & 3 (Winter–Spring 1993).
3–Thorp had befriended Susan Hinkley and her daughter Eleanor when he was their neighbour on Berkeley Place, Harvard, in 1920–1; he knew too that they were friends with Emily Hale.

I can be of any use in helping you to get settled, or find proper lodgings, I shall be delighted.

Yours sincerely,
T. S. Eliot

TO *Eleanor Hinkley*   TS Houghton

26 August 1931   Faber & Faber Ltd

Dear Eleanor,

This is primarily to introduce you to Mr Austin Warren, address 17 Garrison Street, Boston. Under 30, I am sure; claims to be a kinsman of the rich Warrens of Milton etc & Mrs Fiske Warren; poor relation? as went to a High School and then to Princeton. Was pupil of Paul More;[1] Anglo-Catholic; has been in England investigating records of Crashaw, at Peterhouse etc. and intends to write a book about him. I took him to Father Underhill's to have him meet Evelyn, who apparently was kind to him afterwards. Now lecturer or something at Boston University. That is all I know about him, but he seems an agreeable fellow, and I thought might do for one of your Sunday evenings. So if you cared to write and invite him once, I should appreciate it. English literature his lifework.

I enjoyed *Dear Jane* immensely.[2] I confess I am not enough of a Janeite to know how much was arrangement and how much your own creation; but I thought the dialogue moved most easily and brilliantly, and the whole thing genuinely moving. For production, I wondered whether the Johnson scene might not be played better as a curtain-raiser – otherwise I should think the audience might get bewildered, and feel held up – because the connexion is only apparent later. I should think this difficulty would be got over by letting them think at first that scene had nothing to do with Jane – and then being pleased with their own percipience in finding out that it did.

As to the general moral of the piece I should like more time, and these comments are quite provisional. The difficulty seems to me inherent in any period piece: the danger that the audience should not generalise enough – also the uncertainty as to how much you generalised yourself. (1) The situation is not to be thought of as the sort of thing that could happen a

1 – 'At Princeton, where I did my graduate work, I once called on Paul Elmer More, Babbitt's closest friend and ally, whom, some years later, I came to know well and with whom I carried on a considerable correspondence' (Warren, 'A Survivor's Tribute to T. S. Eliot', 287).
2 – Hinkley's *Dear Jane* was to be performed at the Civic Repertory Theatre, 13 Nov. 1932.

hundred years ago, but we have outgrown all those narrow notions etc. We haven't outgrown them at all. (2) Nor is it (and here I am less sure of your agreement) confined to one sex; the most general formula is I think the eternal conflict between the needs of life and the needs of the artist – and the question whether the artist can ever live satisfactorily. At any rate, he needs to be a very astute fellow to succeed in both – astuter than poor Jane.

Forgive the random first comments. We enjoyed having you and Aunt Susie immensely, more than I can express; and I wish we could hope to see you next year. If Britain survives the coming winter.

ever affectionately,
Tom.

The Nuts were widely appreciated.

TO *Hugh Ross Williamson* CC

31 August 1931   [*The Criterion*]

Dear Mr Williamson,

Thank you very much for sending me the *Bookman* so promptly.[1] I have found the whole number very interesting and am sorry that I missed it at the time. I enjoyed your essay very much, although I found the spectacle of the two photographs depressing;[2] but, as I warned you, I am entirely at sea in attempting to criticise my own critics. I am too pleased by any attention that I receive to be able to preserve any discrimination. Only one point occurred to me at the moment; why should the mention of 'sitting still' suggest a static conception of life, and is the distinction between the static and the dynamic so easily transferable from physics to ethics as everybody seems to think?[3]

Trusting that I may meet you again,

I am yours gratefully,
[T. S. Eliot]

1 – Williamson met TSE on 26 Aug., and the next day sent him a copy of The Bookman – 'with my slight essay on you in it. You may also be interested in two at least of the Donne articles – one by Leavis . . . and one by [Christopher] Saltmarshe, Empson's friend.' See Williamson, 'T. S. Eliot and His Conception of Poetry', The Bookman 79 (Mar. 1931), 347–50.

2 – The piece was illustrated by two photos of TSE: one by E. O. Hoppé, the other by Vandyk.

3 – Williamson adjudged that in Ash-Wednesday, TSE 'has made complete renunciation; all the things outside himself, which have so baffled and beaten him, have fallen away . . . Here

TO *Sylvia Beach*   TS Princeton

31 August 1931   Faber & Faber Ltd

Dear Miss Beach,

At Mr Joyce's request, I am sending you the enclosed correspondence from the Japanese, who propose translating *Ulysses* into their language. From the only enquiry that I have made, I understand that he would be advised to ask the same terms from Japan as from Germany, or, at least, 25% less.

I was under the impression that I had written to you some time ago about the *Exagmination* but I cannot find any copy of the letter I thought I wrote. It is very likely that I only thought I had written it. I understood from Joyce that you had a reasonable number of copies on hand, and we thought that we might be able to reach a new public for this book of essays through an English publisher. For sale in England the book would, of course, have to be rebound in cloth. If the suggestion appeals to you, I should be much interested to know on what terms you would consider supplying copies as sheets for an English publisher, and how many copies would be available.[1]

Yours very sincerely,
T. S. Eliot

TO *Marguerite Caetani*   CC

31 August 1931   [Faber & Faber Ltd]

Dear Marguerite,

I have not the slightest idea where you are, but I think that there may be some chance of catching you with this letter before you leave for Scotland

---

at last is the joy of creativeness; the acceptance of the Birth and all its implications . . . It is too early yet to predict the outcome of the new experience. Some of us indeed are fearful that it may lead to a conception of religion which is static – or even reactionary – instead of dynamic, and some of the notes in *Ash Wednesday* confirm our fears . . . We have not wrestled with doubt in order to betray our courage at the end by relinquishing the struggle and throwing ourselves into the arms of infallibility. We do not want to have to turn a mood into a creed' (350).

1–Beach ('Shakepeare and Company', Paris) replied on 3 Sept. 1931: 'Mr Joyce did send me this summer a fragment of a proposed letter from you, but I have not heard anything further. I think, indeed, that as you are going to have his "Work in Progress", "Our exagmination" [*Our Exagmination Round His Factification for Incamination of Work in Progress* (1929)] would be more in its place with you and would certainly have a much wider sale.

'There were three thousand copies printed plus 96 de Luxe. Two thousand are left . . .

'Thank you for sending me the Japanese correspondence, and for your advice . . .'

– unless you are there already. I have a section of a much longer poem which I should be glad to let you see for *Commerce*, though I do not know whether it is translatable or whether you will like it. But as there is some remote possibility that I may finish the poem some day, I should like to know, in the event of your accepting it, when you would be likely to use it.[1]

At the same time, I am writing on behalf of a young friend of mine, Edouard Roditi, who tells me that he sent you about six weeks ago c/o *Commerce* the translations which he made of some poems by another young friend of mine named Stephen Spender.[2] I hope that you have had them, and that you will be able to use them, because I have a very high opinion of Spender's work, and am publishing some more of his verse in the *Criterion*. The translations also seem to me very competent, but of that I am [by] no means the best judge.

I hope that you will not disappoint us, and that you will definitely stop over in London on your return from Crawfords.

Affectionately yours,

[Tom]

---

1 – 'Difficulties of a Statesman': English text with facing-page translation by Georges Limbour, *'Difficultés d'un homme d'état'*, *Commerce* 29 (Winter 1931/1932), 79–87.

2 – Roditi had translated into French three poems by Spender: 'Never being'; 'How strangely this sun'; 'Your body are stars'. Spender would write to Erich Alport on 10 Dec. 1931: 'Having read your nauseating "medaillon" of W. H. Auden in the *Journal des Poètes*, I am writing at once to Roditi in order to recover the poems I gave him for translation in that paper. In future I wish it to be understood that I dissociate myself entirely from you and your colleagues of the hybrid "Comité Anglais". If you publish anything of the sort about me, I shall have much pleasure in retaliating.

'Christopher [Isherwood] wishes me to say that he is equally disgusted.'

Spender told Alport on 23 Dec. (?1931), apropos *The Temple*: 'You will know, perhaps before a year is out, that my book, although not directly concerned with you, contains a great deal of adverse criticism of your character. I am very grateful to you for many things: most notably, that I have met many good friends through you: yet I am never at ease with you.' In another, undated letter to Alport: 'Thanks for what you say. I am sure you are right about my novel. The point is though that I am not attempting a portrait of you: certain things about you, which struck me, suggested the idea of an entirely new character. Anyhow, I believe that whatever I say about you is fully revenged on me by W. Lewis who has, apparently, made me the moron hero of the *Apes of God*.'

3 September 1931   Faber & Faber Ltd

My dear Brother,

Thank you very much indeed for your further letter of the 21st August[1] and for all the trouble you have taken. I am, however, afraid that we have been somewhat at cross purposes. The Boni compilation is certainly a serious matter to me; and if he is going on to reprint the volume I should certainly like to take every reasonable step to prevent or dissuade him from including *The Waste Land*. But the offence of Liveright about which I wrote you is quite different. I did not suppose that he was offering me royalties, beyond the flat $75.00 originally paid, on his concession to Boni. I take it that the royalties he is now offering are on sales of the original edition of *The Waste Land* which he published; and which he has *no right to publish after Dec. 31st 1927*.

The question is therefore whether I should take out an injunction against Liveright for continuing to sell the book after expiry of copyright, and against Knopf (against whom, however, I have no ill feeling) for continuing to sell *Poems*.[2]

Alternatively, I might settle the matter more simply by bringing out in New York a new edition of 'collected poems', so as merely to kill the sale of Knopf's and Liveright's books. This would be the only economical way to act. I had not wanted to bring out another collected edition for some time. I can't include *Ash Wednesday* because Putnam's are publishing that; I could only include as extras four 'Ariel' poems. But in any case I should not bring out another 'collected edition' *here*: it would be an American edition only.

The American rights of *The Waste Land* and of *all* my poems are *mine*, not Faber & Faber's.

---

1 – Not found.
2 – Alfred A. Knopf had written to FVM on 6 Feb. 1931: 'I am particularly concerned about Eliot's attitude towards his poems . . . Eliot is the kind of writer who belongs to our list . . . At the same time, there is obviously no chance of a large sale for any of them, and so from a strictly commercial point of view I ought not to be writing you at all . . . We have, however, established a definite if small market for his poems, and I wish we could arrange a new contract so that we could issue them in their collected form. I don't think this would materially affect the sale of your edition in the States and it would produce a steady, if small additional revenue for Eliot . . .'

I should at the same time, as I said, like to proceed with the Boni question; but as so far as there is any evidence Boni is innocent in the matter, to proceed as amicably as possible.

Ever affectionately,
Tom

TO *Arthur J. Penty* CC

3 September 1931 [Faber & Faber Ltd]

Dear Mr Penty,

I am sorry that we have taken so long in considering the ms. of your book *Means and Ends*; but you will understand that during the holiday season it is not easy to obtain quickly the opinions of a sufficient number of directors. Now, enough of us have read it to come to a decision. We can hardly hope that such a book could be an immediate popular success; and indeed, it is entirely because we are very sympathetic to your point of view and general ideas that we are anxious to back it. But you will understand that we can only offer a 10% royalty, particularly as we could not price the book at more than five or six shillings.

I hope that this will be acceptable to you. If so, the book should be put in hand as soon as possible. If it is not impossible, would you suggest one or two days and come up to lunch to talk things over with myself and my colleague Mr Morley in the immediate future?[1]

Sincerely yours,
[T. S. Eliot]

TO *Harriet Weaver* CC

4 September 1931 [*The Criterion*]

Dear Miss Weaver,

At Joyce's request, I am sending herewith a copy of the solicitor's draft letter to the *Frankfurter Zeitung*. I have also at his request sent the two copies of the *Frankfurter Zeitung* in question to Mr Robert Lynd. You will be hearing from Joyce himself about the matter.

---

1 – *Means and Ends* was to be published by F&F in 1932.

We enjoyed very much having tea with you the other day, and I hope that we will see you again before you go North.

Yours sincerely,
[T. S. Eliot]

TO *Robert Lynd*[1]   CC

4 September 1931   [Faber & Faber Ltd]

Dear Mr Lynd,

At the request of James Joyce, I am sending you herewith the two copies of the *Frankfurter Zeitung* of the 19th July and the 9th August last, the one containing the piece of fiction attributed to him, and the second the editorial note 'Michael and James'. I have just spoken to Joyce on the telephone, and he asked me to tell you that he will be writing to you to give you the other information necessary.

Yours sincerely,
[T. S. Eliot]

TO *George Boas*[2]   CC

4 September 1931   [Faber & Faber Ltd]

My dear Boas,

It is always pleasant to hear from you, even though it be only every few years. You seem to spend your summers in France from time to time – and now you write from a particularly pleasant department, as I know very well – but do you never pass through London on your way to and fro?

I am flattered by the invitation of your Society.[3] If I had any real prospect of coming to America next year, I should certainly accept, because the terms are satisfactory, supposing that I was anywhere in the vicinity,

1–Robert Lynd (1879–1949), journalist and essayist, worked from 1908 for the *Daily News* (from 1930, *News Chronicle*), and contributed to periodicals including *N.* and *NS*. Born in Belfast, his love of Ireland and commitment to Irish nationalism and socialism informed his writing. Works include *Rambles in Ireland* (illus. Jack B. Yeats, 1912), *If the Germans Conquered England* (1917), *Essays on Life and Literature* (intro. by Desmond MacCarthy, 1951), and *Galway of the Races: Selected Essays*, ed. Sean McMahon (1990).
2–George Boas (1891–1980), who had known TSE in 1914, taught philosophy at Johns Hopkins University, 1921–56; he was author of *A Primer for Critics* (1937).
3–Boas (La Roch Beaucourt, Dordogne, France) invited TSE (31 Aug.) to lecture to the Poetry Society of Baltimore 'next year': 'they could probably raise $150'.

and I have never been to Baltimore, and one of my nieces is going to be teaching in a girls school there. So I should very much like to come, but what can I say? As it is so unlikely that I shall get to America this year, I can only say that if I do I will let you know in the hope that the invitation may be renewed.

Yours ever sincerely,
[T. S. Eliot]

TO *J. B. Trend*[1]   CC

4 September 1931   [*The Criterion*]

My dear Trend,

Many thanks for your letter of the 31st.[2] I should very much like to see the rest of [the] d'Ors essay, which I assume, of course, is not too long for the *Criterion*; perhaps if it is, it could be cut down. I should be very glad to have him in the *Criterion*.

I am sorry that you were unable to come to the Monro's [*sic*] last Wednesday, but if you are in town now for a short time, is it possible that we might lunch together one day? We are temporarily at the United Universities,[3] you know.

Yours ever sincerely,
[T. S. Eliot]

TO *Edouard Roditi*   TS UCLA

7 September 1931   Faber & Faber Ltd

Dear Roditi,[4]

I have written to Madame de Bassiano about the translations of Spender. I do not know, however, where she is at the moment and it is possible that

---

1–J. B. Trend (1887–1958), journalist, musicologist, literary critic – he wrote the music chronicles for *C.* – was to become Professor of Spanish at Cambridge, 1933–52. Works include *Alfonso the Sage & Other Spanish Essays* (1926), *Manuel de Falla and Spanish Music* (1928), *The Origins of Modern Spain* (1934). See Margaret Joan Anstee, *JB: An Unlikely Spanish Don: The Life & Times of Professor John Brande Trend* (2013).

2–Trend sent, by way of his 'good offices', an article on Baroque music by Eugenio d'Ors (1881–1954, Catalan writer): he enclosed a rough translation of the first few pages.

3–United Universities Club, London.

4–Roditi wrote (undated) that he had written to Marguerite Caetani, 'about 6 weeks ago', to offer her, for *Commerce*, his translations of certain poems by Stephen Spender. He was to

she is visiting in Scotland, so that I may not have any news for you much before your return. If you will let me know as soon as you get back, I shall look forward to seeing you. I am glad to hear that you are to be in London for the coming winter.

I look forward also to seeing your article on Rosenberg.

Yours sincerely,
T. S. Eliot

TO *William Plomer*   TS Texas

7 September 1931   Faber & Faber Ltd

Dear Plomer,

I am sorry for the delay in returning your MS., but in the midst of other occupations I have had some difficulty in making up my mind what to ask for and what to neglect. But if it would not be too much to ask, I should like to have copies of all of the poems in the section called *The Sprig of Basil,* because I think that a small selection of these might be made which would go very well together. If I could have them all, I should be very glad, but of course I should submit any selection of three or four to you before publishing.[1]

I am sorry I did not see more of you the other afternoon.

Yours sincerely,
T. S. Eliot

---

be away on holiday for a month from 12 Sept., but would be returning to London for the winter. He was working on an article on Isaac Rosenberg which he would send 'as soon as it is printed, as I have made a few sweeping statements there of which I would rather like to hear your opinion'. He wrote again on 17 Oct. to say he had nearly finished his 4,000-word essay on Rosenberg, for publication in the Dec. issue of *Illustration Juive*. 'Unfortunately the public of this paper needs a certain type of rhetoric and sweeping statements which I have done my best to tone down.'

1 – The last of Plomer's poems to be published in C. was 'Corfu': C. 10 (July 1931), 626.

TO *A. L. Morton*[1]   CC

8 September 1931   [*The Criterion*]

Dear Morton,

I have read your essay on Forster[2] with much interest but I do not think
that the *Criterion* is quite the place for it. Your contention is quite worth
making, and I daresay Forster would be in partial agreement, but I think
that in the *Criterion* such a study of a novelist ought to be primarily from
the angle of literary criticism, rather than of sociology.

> Yours sincerely,
> [T. S. Eliot]

TO *R. S. Wilson*[3]   CC

8 September 1931   [Faber & Faber Ltd]

Dear Sir,

We have carefully considered your MS. 'Marcion'[4] and, though we were
considerably interested by it, we felt that the sale would be too limited to
justify our undertaking its publication. Mr T. S. Eliot, who read the MS.,
suggests that you might do well to submit it to the Oxford University
Press, and is quite willing for you to mention his name if you do so.

> Yours truly,
> For Faber & Faber Ltd.
> Manager.

---

1 – A. L. Morton (1903–87), Marxist historian; in the 1930s he worked for the *Daily Worker*
and contributed to other magazines. See also TSE to LW, 4 Feb. 1930, above.
2 – Morton wrote (31 Aug.), of his essay: 'I don't know how far you will agree with the
theory I have been working on, but I feel that I have said some things about Forster that
needed saying rather badly. He never seems to have been taken up as seriously in this country
as he deserves to be.' See Morton, 'E. M. Forster and the Classless Society', in *Language of
Men* (1945).
3 – Of the Manse, Ecclefechan, Lockerbie. See TSE to Wilson, 14 Sept. 1931, below.
4 – Submitted on 31 Aug.

TO *J. M. Reeves*

9 September 1931   [*The Criterion*]

Dear Mr Reeves,

I have your letter of the 6th.[1] By all means come and see me, either next Monday, the 14th, or Wednesday the 16th, at one o'clock, but please let me know which day it shall be.

I will keep you in mind for a Skelton and/or Dunbar. If you are to be in London, would you care to come to a *Criterion* evening at the Poetry Bookshop on Wednesday, Oct. 14? If you think you are likely to be able to come, I will send you a notification later.

Yours truly,
[T. S. Eliot]

TO *J. B. Trend*

10 September 1931   [*The Criterion*]

My dear Trend,

Thank you for your letter of the 7th.[2] I am rather overwhelmed by receiving so many closely typed pages of a language in which, to tell the truth, I am anything but proficient. However, I will make what I can of it, although I really trust entirely to your own judgment and the specimen which you sent me. I am sorry to hear that the whole thing may have to be divided over two issues, but perhaps when you have it all in your hands, you might consider whether it could possibly be sufficiently abbreviated to appear all at once. Unless the essay falls definitely into two parts, each one self-contained, I am very much averse to serialisation. You do not give any indication of when you expect to recover from your mysterious ailment,[3] so if I do not hear from you again for a few days, you may be prepared for my dropping in unexpectedly to make enquiries.

Yours ever,
[T. S. Eliot]

1–Reeves wrote on 6 Sept., 'I did not think you would consider that the book on Hardy needed reviewing . . . Dents' are publishing an edition of Skelton and a book on Dunbar in your "Poets on the Poets" is announced, either of which would interest me very much.'
2–Trend had sent the first part of a very long essay by Eugenio d'Ors: not published in C.
3–Trend had 'been been stung by some more than usually venomous insect'.

10 September 1931   Faber & Faber Ltd

My dear Harold,

In reply to yours of the 8th,[1] I should like it as late as possible, but if October is what you really need, may we make it the 29th of that month, and as you are leaving this week, will you let me know as soon as you get back so that we may arrange a lunch, as I should like to have a private talk with you before the 29th?

You will remember also that [we] have fixed upon the 14th October for a *Criterion* meeting.

Yours ever,
Tom

TO *Caresse Crosby*   CC

10 September 1931   [Faber & Faber Ltd]

Dear Mrs Crosby,

I know that I am very much behindhand, and I am quite aware that I must have inconvenienced you considerably.[2] I have to put it down to indifferent health and fatigue, which has evinced itself more in a form of mental impotence than in physical illness. I am more than dissatisfied with what I have done and enclose, not so much on account of its brevity (I am always shortwinded) but on account of its poverty of ideas; and I am afraid that it will sound rather listless. I have been trying to revamp it for a week; but this morning your wire arrives and I have no alternative but to send it as it is. But if it does not seem to you good enough I shall not be offended![3]

Apologetically,
[T. S. Eliot]

---

1 – 'I am rather loth to approach you again because I know you are not very keen on making appointments of the kind, but the moment has arrived at which another visit from you becomes due and when I approached you last Spring you certainly did say that in the Autumn you would be willing to give a Reading or a Talk [at the Poetry Bookshop, Great Russell Street, London].'

2 – Crosby had asked TSE to send his preface to Harry Crosby's *Transit of Venus* by 15 July; but that was put back to 25 Aug. TSE telegraphed on 4 Aug.: 'Very sorry indeed delayed Promise definitely within fortnight.' On 10 Sept. Crosby cabled: 'May we have introduction as promised urgent.'

3 – On 14 Sept. Crosby thanked TSE for his preface: 'the brevity I approve of. I could not expect Harry to be one of your great enthusiasms but I find what you have written wise and

11 September 1931   [Faber & Faber Ltd]

Dear Miss Weaver,

Thank you for your letter of the 9th.[1] I am afraid I cannot let you have your sets of pages back just yet. We do [*sc.* did] two pages only[,] set up in eleven different types. Of these types, Mr Joyce chose one which, however, he wished to have set with greater spacing. The new pages are in the process of setting; but when Mr Joyce is finally satisfied with their appearance, he will want to have set up in the same way *all* of the pages which you sent then, so I hope you will forgive me for not letting you have these pages just yet.

We certainly hope to see you before the end of the month.

Yours sincerely,
[T. S. Eliot]

---

illuminative.' On 20 Sept.: 'On re-reading what you have written I like it more and more. At first it seemed so very impersonal to me but I believe now that that is the best kind of criticism you could have made. It says a great deal of truth in a few words.'

TSE's Preface included these candid, if equivocal, remarks: 'I am far from asserting . . . that I understand in the least what Crosby was up to, or that I am sure I should like it if I did. I doubt whether anyone himself engaged in the pursuit of poetry can "like", any more than he can "understand", the work of his contemporaries . . . What I do like, in a serious sense, is the fact that Crosby was definitely going his own way, whether I like the way or not. And in spite of occasional conventional phrases – so conventional as perhaps to be deliberate – I am more interested in his work because of its imperfections, its particular way of being imperfect. What interests me most, I find, is his search for a personal symbolism of imagery. Not that the scheme of imagery which he was using was necessarily exact, or corresponded finally to what his mind was reaching for; he might, I dare say, have scrapped it all in favour of some other. But here, I am sure, is a right and difficult method. A final intelligibility is necessary; but that is only the fruit of much experiment and of mature synthesis; but Crosby was right, very right, in looking for a set of symbols which should relate each of his poems to the others, to himself' (vi–vii).

1 – Weaver, after thanking TSE for 'the copy of the solicitors' draft letter to the *Frankfurter Zeitung* which is to go on to Mr Lynd when some further information has been obtained about Mr Michael Joyce', went on: 'Mr Joyce tells me that the specimen pages from *Work in Progress* has been set up in type. Could you therefore kindly let me have back the two sets of pages I lent?'

TO *Marguerite Caetani*   cc

14 September 1931   [*The Criterion*]

Dear Marguerite,

I have spoken to the Advertising Manager and we shall be very glad
to exchange a page with you.¹ I am afraid, however, that it is quite out
of the question to advertise *Commerce* in our October number as the
advertisements have already gone to press and the number itself should be
ready almost any day now. So shall we begin with our December number,
in which I suggest you would advertise your autumn number? We should
like the copy for your advertisement at the beginning of November, and I
should be glad if you would let me know by what date you would want
our copy, as I am only just beginning to compose our December issue.

I have been reading Miss Lion's MS. and hope to write to her in a day
or two.²

As for my poem, you shall have it as soon as I have time to type out a
copy.

Ever affectionately,
[Tom]

TO *B. C. Windeler*³   cc

14 September 1931   [Faber & Faber Ltd]

Dear Windeler,

In reply to yours of the 11th,⁴ I do not know where Ezra Pound is at
the moment but his permanent address is Rapallo, Via Marsala, 12 int. 5,

---

1 – Caetani wrote on 10 Sept.: 'I am going to take advertisements in *Commerce* as I told
you and I am wondering if you would like to "exchange" a page of advertisement. In your
October No. you could announce our Summer No. which will appear in October and we
could announce your October No. What do you say?'
2 – 'Aline Lion lunched here [Villa Romaine, Versailles] yesterday and I told her I would
speak to you about her manuscript. She begs you exceptionally to send back her manuscript
if you are not taking it as she has no other copy. She fell ill just as she was finishing it . . .'
See TSE to Lion, 29 Sept. 1931, below.
3 – Bernard Windeler worked in the City, on Basinghall Street, EC2; wrote poems, songs and
stories. His story *Elimus* (1923) had been illustrated by Dorothy Shakespear Pound.
4 – 'I am writing to ask if you by any chance know Ezra Pound's address . . . I have been
doing some more writing recently and want to see him about some of this work.

'I have also nearly finished a small collection of verse that I have done. Would you care
to give me an introduction to the firm that brought out your book of verse, Faber & Gwyer
I think they were called?'

where I expect you will be able to reach him. About the second paragraph of your letter, there is no need to give you an introduction, for, as you will see from this letter, I am myself connected with the firm of Faber and Gwyer, which is now Faber and Faber, so you have only to send the collection here and address it to me. Not, I confess, that the publishing business can at present bear very much poetry; so I cannot hold out much hope to anybody; at the same time, I do think that you might as well send the book to me as to anyone else.

Yours cordially,
[T. S. Eliot]

TO *R. S. Wilson* CC

14 September 1931   [Faber & Faber Ltd]

Dear Mr Wilson,

Although I remember quite well our acquaintance on shipboard and also your previous book which was reviewed in the *Criterion*,[1] I had quite failed to connect you with the MS. which I had just read, and my message was sent to one whom I believed to be a complete stranger.[2] *Marcion* was given to me to read because I am supposed to have a particular interest in such matters, although I cannot profess any great knowledge. Certainly, I was very much interested by your book and liked it. It immediately struck me as a University Press book and I can take the fact of its having been returned by both the Oxford and Cambridge presses merely as a sign of the way in which all publishing business is affected by the economic conditions of today. A thoroughly good book on a very special subject, like this, is one on which the publisher must expect a loss or, at least, must not expect to recoup his outlay for some years. Our situation, which is that of most general publishers, is that we cannot afford to publish any books of such dimensions on which we cannot expect some immediate return. I hope that things may improve but, as you may imagine, the publishing business is one of those which particularly has to trim its sails to the prevailing winds in order to survive at all.

1–See K. de B. Codrington's review of *The Indirect Effects of Christian Missions in India*, C. 8 (July 1929), 720.
2–The Revd Wilson had met TSE in the autumn of 1925, when he was en route as a missionary to South India; they travelled on the 'Billy Oxfordshire' as far as Marseilles – 'a very slight personal acquaintance . . . A slender connection – but I have always been proud of it.' Wilson, who wrote on 10 Sept. that his MS had already been read by both OUP and CUP, asked of TSE: 'I suppose it is not likely that they [F&F] might be persuaded to alter their decision?'

I should think of Allen and Unwin as a possibility but, candidly, I am very doubtful whether any publishers will undertake such a specialised work in the conditions of the moment. There is also the S.P.C.K., and, if you care to write to them, I should be quite glad if you mentioned my name as I know the secretary of that firm, Dr Lowther Clark.

Hoping that you will remember to look me up if you are ever in London.

I am,
Yours sincerely,
[T. S. Eliot]

TO *Stephen Spender*

TS Northwestern

15 September 1931   Faber & Faber Ltd

Dear Spender,

Thank you for your note of the 14th. I shall look out for your MS. tomorrow.[1] Meanwhile, I send you the page proof of your poems which never reached you. If there are any serious errors, I can only ask your pardon.

I should be very glad if you cared to do some reviewing, particularly for the December number, as the October number is already finished. At this time of the year it is rather difficult to know what there will be for review. It makes the December number a particularly difficult one to manage, as, by the time the important books come out, there is very little time to review them. So I should be very glad of your help and will ask you to keep an eye open for any books that you want. I will keep in mind the series you mention, of which so far I know nothing.[2]

When I saw you I forgot to mention that there would be a *Criterion* after-dinner meeting at Harold Monro's on the evening of October 14, and I hope that you can come. Any time after 8.15.

I hope too that you will decide to stay in London longer for me to see more of you.

Yours very sincerely,
T. S. Eliot

1 – 'The Manuscript of my novel [*The Temple*] will be sent to you on Tuesday. I shall be very interested to hear what you think of it, as I hope to be able to see how to rewrite it entirely, so I am looking forward to the help I may get from your criticism. If it interests you at all, I am afraid it will interest you as a document rather than as a work of art.'
2 – Spender expressed interest in reviewing 'the new series of Letters which the Hogarth Press are bringing out in October'.

TO *W. H. Auden*   CC

15 September 1931   [*The Criterion*]

Dear Auden,

I liked your Pindaric Ode immensely,[1] and had it not been for the Prize Day,[2] I should have annexed it for the *Criterion* at once. As it is, I have taken the liberty of handing it to Montgomery Belgion with a recommendation that he should ask your permission to print it in *This Quarter*. I hope you do not object to this. Of course, you may not like it as much as I do, and alternatively you may not want to publish it in that way, but there is no need for you to give permission unless you choose. I do not know how much *This Quarter* pays, but I imagine about the same rates as the *Criterion*.[3]

Are you sufficiently interested in northern verse to care to review either the new edition of Skelton which is coming out or a small book on Dunbar which we shall be publishing in the Poets on the Poets Series?[4]

Yours ever
[T. S. Eliot]

TO *Charles Smyth*   CC

15 September 1931   [Faber & Faber Ltd]

Dear Smyth,

I do not appear to have answered your letter of the 19th August, for which I apologise as my letter could have been written immediately.[5]

1 – Auden wrote on 2 Aug.: 'Here is an attempt at Pindar's kind of verse in English. I shall be interested to know if you think it comes off.' The poem proffered was probably Ode II ('To Gabriel Carritt, Captain of Sedbergh School XV, Spring, 1927'), *The Orators*, 89–92; repr. in *The English Auden*, ed. Edward Mendelson (1977), 96–8.
2 – WHA's 'Speech for a prize-day' was forthcoming in C. 11 (Oct. 1931), 60–4.
3 – WHA replied on 17 Sept.: 'I shall be very pleased to let Mr Belgion have the Ode if he wants it.' He wrote again on 28 Oct.: 'I heard from Mr Belgion the other day: *This Quarter* would have nothing to do with the Pindaric Ode, so I have given it to the *Twentieth Century*, one of those dreadful little papers with a priggish title and no money.'
4 – 'I should like either of the books . . . very much,' replied WHA (17 Sept.), ' – unless the Skelton is a critical edition and I am expected to criticise the Editor's punctuation etc.' Review of *The Complete Works of John Skelton*, ed. Philip Henderson, C. 11 (Jan. 1932), 316–19.
5 – 'There is a faint possibility of my doing a little essay in defence of Property with Kitson Clark of Trinity, which might be something in your line: it would be a sort of Tory apologia . . .
'Of course, what I should most like to write would be a defence of the Establishment.'

I only wanted to say that it struck us that your projected essay with Kitson Clark, 'In Defence of Property', sounds very suitable for the Criterion Miscellany, although even if it proved to be too long to appear in that form, we should still be equally interested. Also or alternatively, we suggest your treating the defence of the Establishment in the same way. So do please consider either of these suggestions, which are, of course, urged upon you on the assumption that you will not have the time to give us a longer book.

If your London curacy is going to interfere with study and writing, as I suppose it will, I yet hope that it will give me the compensation of enjoying something of your company, although you speak as if you expected to become wholly invisible.[1]

Yours ever,
[T. S. Eliot]

TO *Montgomery Belgion*   CC

18 September 1931   [Faber & Faber Ltd]

Dear Belgion,

We are interested in your project[2] and in the preliminary draft which you have left with me, and would like very much to go further into the matter. As I think I told you on my own responsibility, we should want to do the book as early as possible in the new year, so that it would have to be completed at the end of November and, indeed, if you could manage it, the middle of October would be much better. The best terms that we could offer on a book of this type would be an advance of £25 on a royalty of 10%, say up to 3000, and 15% thereafter. I am assuming that it would be a book of about 30,000 words, and that it could be priced at not more than 5/-, and at 3/6 if possible, so please let me know as soon as you can what you think of this; and I suppose you will want the provisional draft manuscript returned to you. Incidentally we think it might be possible to

---

1 – Smyth was due to give up Corpus Christi by 1932: 'The change from Academe will have its compensations, but I can scarcely hope to keep up my reading.' He was to become Curate of St Clement's, Barnsbury, Islington, 1933–4.
2 – Belgion proposed (22 May) a pamphlet for the Criterion Miscellany series – *The Refutation of Marxism* – on 'what socialism and liberalism really are today, the first Bolshevism and the second Americanism; and the drawbacks of both'.

find a better title for selling the book, although I confess that at the moment none of us has any suggestion to offer.

Yours ever
[T. S. Eliot]

TO *César Saerchinger*[1]   CC

18 September 1931   [Faber & Faber Ltd]

Dear Mr Saerchinger,
    Thank you for your letter of the 15th instant.[2] I am interested in your suggestion and would be glad to discuss it further. I should be pleased if you could call to see me here on any morning next week at about twelve o'clock, if you would kindly let me know which morning is convenient for you.

Yours sincerely
[T. S. Eliot]

TO *Charles Smyth*   CC

18 September 1931   [*The Criterion*]

My dear Smyth,
    If you have the time and are not disinclined to the task I should be very glad if you would review for the December number A. L. Rowse's book *Politics and the Younger Generation* which my firm is just publishing. I think you would find it interesting and probably extremely irritating, and I should much prefer to have it reviewed by you rather than anyone else.[3]

Yours ever,
[T. S. Eliot]

---

1 – César Saerchinger was Director of European Service, Columbia Broadcasting System Inc.; author of *Hello, America! Radio Adventures in Europe* and *Artur Schnabel: A Biography*.
2 – 'As this is John Dryden's tercentenary year, I wonder whether you would care to make a short radio address for American listeners, some time early in November, on a subject which you have made peculiarly your own . . . This talk would be one of a series of transatlantic broadcasts, which started here at the time of the Naval Conference, and in which not only statesman and scientists but a few of your colleagues, including John Masefield, have been heard.'
3 – Smyth said he would be 'delighted to review' Rowse's book: 'I am the Younger Generation', C. 11 (Jan. 1932), 304–13.

TO *Ian Parsons*   CC

18 September 1931   [*The Criterion*]

Dear Parsons,

I was very stupid when I spoke to you on the telephone yesterday about Powys's book.[1] I was really thinking at the moment that I should like to have a review by Leavis[2] and I forgot that I have undertaken to turn over all fiction to Orlo Williams, who is starting to do a regular fiction chronicle twice a year. It would obviously detract from the interest of this chronicle if I also had separate reviews of novels by other hands; though we shall, of course, occasionally review the whole work of a novelist. Furthermore I think that Williams would have a legitimate grievance were I to give single novels to other critics to review.

I am anxious to think of something else to offer to Leavis, and meanwhile shall I pass this book to Williams, and having received the second copy under false pretences return it to you?

I am afraid neither Wednesday nor Thursday next is possible for me. Could you make it Friday or one day early the week after?

Yours apologetically
[T. S. Eliot]

TO *W. H. Auden*   CC

23 September 1931   [Faber & Faber Ltd]

Dear Auden,

I have just sent you the Skelton book. You needn't bother about punctuation and critical apparatus, but I daresay you may find a few sharp words which I should be glad to hear about modernisation of such poetry. Poor Dryden has been so abused for bringing Chaucer up to date that it is time someone else had a turn.[3]

About *The Fronny*, I should be very much obliged if you could let me have a copy of it again for a few days, to show the other Directors. When you showed it me before I do not think I gave it to anyone else to read. We

1 – T. F. Powys, *Unclay*.
2 – Parsons had written on 17 Sept., 'I am sure Leavis would be very glad of a chance to write about Powys, and I think he would be certain to do something interesting.' See FRL, 'T. F. Powys' – on *Kindness in a Corner* – *Cambridge Review*, 9 May 1930, 388–9.
3 – Review of *The Complete Poems of John Skelton*, ed. Philip Henderson, C. 11 (Jan. 1932), 316–19.

should not think of standing in the way of its publication, but it has never yet been discussed for that purpose by this firm, and I should like to have another chance. If for any reason they do not want to do it at present, you could of course go ahead with the Hogarth.[1]

> Yours sincerely
> [T. S. Eliot]

TO *Herbert Gorman*   TS Southern Illinois

23 September 1931   Faber & Faber Ltd

Dear Gorman,

I have heard a rumour, and I cannot remember from what source, that you had put aside your biography of James Joyce in order to complete first the book on Mary Queen of Scots which as I know you have been working on for some time.[2] Joyce himself knows no more about the matter than I do. We had understood that the manuscript would be forthcoming this autumn, and as we should very much like to know for what publishing session it will be available, I should be glad to hear from you as to the probabilities. I am relying upon Miss Beach to know where you are at the moment.

> Yours sincerely,
> T. S. Eliot

TO *Willard Thorp*   TS Princeton

23 September 1931   *The Criterion*

Dear Mr Thorp,

I am glad to have got into touch with you at last.[3] I am pretty busy every afternoon this week, and in any case I should like to arrange for you and Mrs Thorp to come to tea with us first. Meanwhile, however, I have asked Professor George Williamson of the University of Washington, whose name you may know, to lunch with me on Friday. I have never

---

1 – WHA had written on 17 Sept.: 'I have heard that the Hogarth Press want to see *The Fronny* with a view to publication. While I should be glad to get it off my hands, I can't help feeling it is rather shabby to go to another publisher, particularly when Faber and Faber have been so very good to me. Could you let me have your opinion on this?'

2 – *The Scottish Queen* (1932).

3 – Thorp and his wife were staying at the Hotel Alexandria, Bedford Place, London.

met him before. If you care to join us I shall be very glad. It will be at the United Universities Club, Suffolk Street, at 1.15. But if you would rather wait till the beginning of next week and lunch with me on Monday or Tuesday, please choose either day.

Yours sincerely
T. S. Eliot

TO *John Maynard Keynes* CC

24 September 1931   [Faber & Faber Ltd]

My dear Keynes,

I believe that I have approached you once before with some publishing suggestion, and entirely without success. Even repeated failures, however, are hardly likely to prevent me from writing from time to time with similar proposals.

It has been suggested that the present time would be a particularly desirable one for the *Criterion Miscellany* to have a pamphlet from you. The particular issue which caused your name to be discussed among the Board was the case for or against the Banks (or for or against the Bank of England), but that was merely the particular occasion; and if the present circumstances should stimulate you to expressing your views on any aspect of the political situation I hope you might give a thought to the *Criterion Miscellany*. If I put the question in such a vague and tentative way it is only because I know that it is no use making it unless it happens to coincide with your own intentions.[1]

Yours sincerely
[T. S. Eliot]

1 – Keynes replied (28 Sept. 1931): 'I do not want to take on anything which is not forced on me by the course of events. Please excuse me. But I always have more on hand for which there is an inner impulse than I can manage, so I am not often free enough to yield to outside suggestion.'

TO *Aline Lion*[1]   CC

29 September 1931   [*The Criterion*]

Dear Miss Lion,

I must apologize for not having written to you before about your manuscript.[2] I have sent it to the printers to be set up, to be used in our December number. I found it very interesting reading, but you will understand that in the form in which you sent the manuscript it is difficult to offer detailed criticism. I am not quite sure what length it will reach, and if it should prove to be longer than is possible for the *Criterion* I hope you will not mind reducing it a little. I may have a few minor comments of detail to make as soon as I am able to read the essay in galley proofs. In any case you may count upon it appearing, with your consent, in our December number.

                              Yours sincerely
                              [T. S. Eliot]

TO *Marguerite Caetani*   CC

29 September 1931   [Faber & Faber Ltd]

Dear Marguerite,

I have your letter this morning enclosing the frantic appeal from Miss Aline Lion.[3] I know her only to the extent of having read her book on Fascism and an article in the *Dublin Review*, and I had no idea that her

1 – Aline Lion (1891–1964), philosopher, had been a scholar at Lady Margaret Hall, Oxford (BLitt. and PhD), 1926–30. Author of *The Pedigree of Fascism: A Popular Essay on the Western Philosophy of Politics* (1927) – evaluated by TSE in 'The Literature of Fascism', C. 8 (Dec. 1928), 280–90 – she was teaching at Roedean at the time of this exchange.
2 – Lion, who was friends with Marguerite Caetani and M. C. D'Arcy, had written a long essay on 'Property and Poetry', which was published, at her request, under the pseudonym 'Gallox' – 'it is better people should not know I am a woman, a foreigner, a student of philosophy of doubtful orthodoxy' – in C. 11 (Jan. 1932) 253–67; (Apr. 1932) 443–66. She wrote in an undated letter: 'When I shall have the pleasure of meeting you, it may amuse you to hear how my idea of a parallel with poetry was born out of a visit at Villa Romaine [the Caetani residence in Paris], where Paul Valéry & Marguerite, in their opposition to my "pompier" tendencies, teased me so much that the conclusions of previous reading crystallized itself in a paradox. What was the difference between property & poetry? For once my heavy limited "pompier" mind got the better of these brilliant people.' She later wrote a letter on the subject to C. 12 (Jan. 1933), 271.
3 – Caetani wrote (26 Sept.): 'Please excuse me for bothering you again about the manuscript of Aline Lion. On second thoughts I am sending you her letter just received as you will see her state of mind and perhaps if you are refusing it for the *Criterion* you could send me a *very* short piece of advice which I could pass on to her! . . . Please tear up the enclosed letter

temperament or state of mind was such. I have written at once to calm her and assure her that the article will appear in our December number, so I hope that she will be restored to a state of equilibrium.

About a translator for myself.[1] Menasce, as you may now know, has now passed his novitiate in a Dominican monastery in Belgium, and is presumably no longer available for such frivolities. I very much regret this as I could not have had a better translator, and I hoped that he would continue to translate my verse. So now I have no suggestion to offer. I suppose that Léger, of whom I have no news since he was last in London, is far too busy to entertain such a thought, so I will leave the matter to you in full confidence. The only point that I should like to make to any possible translator is that the refrain at the beginning, which is from Isaiah 1.40 should be translated into the usual French version.[2]

I am delighted to hear that we may hope to see you in November. Will your whole family be coming or will it only be yourself and Lélia?[3] The enclosed cutting is from today's *Evening Standard*.[4]

I was very sorry indeed to hear that you had to have an operation,[5] and I hope that your intention to come to London in November means that your recovery will be very rapid.

Yours affectionately,
[Tom]

---

when you have read it.' In a separate letter (n.d.), Lion told TSE: 'I do not mind confessing that outside my actual work I seem often perfectly irrational.'

1 – 'Of course,' wrote Caetani (n.d.), 'you know very well that I will be too delighted to have anything of yours – Especially a poem and the longer the better. Please say who you wish to translate it. Is Ménasce available?'

2 – The opening of 'Difficulties of a Statesman' – 'Cry what shall I cry? / All flesh is grass . . .' – alludes to Isaiah 40: 6: 'A voice says, "Cry!" / And I said, "What shall I cry?" / All flesh is grass . . .'

3 – 'I will see you in November! – Lélia is going to be a bridesmaid to Anne Lindsay Nov. 12th so I suppose we will be in London 5 or 6 days.'

4 – Corisande, 'Woman's World', *Evening Standard*, 29 Sept. 1931, 17: 'The Primate and Diplomat's Wedding: Lady Anne Lindsay, whose engagement to Mr P. E. Folke Arnander, First Secretary to the Swedish Legation in Rome, was announced earlier in the month, has already started making plans for her wedding.

'The date is fixed, November 12, and the church, St Margaret's, Westminster, is the same as that chosen for their respective weddings by the bride's sisters, Lady Mary Manningham-Buller and Lady Margaret Illingworth.

'Further, the Archbishop of Canterbury will be at the head of the clergy officiating at the ceremony.

'The bridesmaids selected so far are Lady Barbara Lindsay, the youngest sister of the bride, and a cousin, Dona Lelia Caetani, daughter of Prince and Princess Bassiano of Rome and Paris.'

5 – 'I forget if I told you I had had a very small operation last week . . .'

FROM *TSE's Secretary* TO *Jean Duvoisin*   CC

30 September 1931   [Faber & Faber Ltd]

Dear Madam,

Mr Eliot asks me to say that he very much regrets that he has never read any of the novels of Marcel Proust, and that he can therefore be of no use to you in your interesting undertaking.[1]

Yours faithfully
[Laura Maude Hill]

TO *Robert E. Brittain*   CC

30 September 1931   [Faber & Faber Ltd]

Dear Mr Brittain,

I am glad to have your letter of September 9th, with news of yourself, though I could wish that your news was altogether happier than it is.[2] You are certainly starting a career, as indeed are many of your generation, under the most difficult circumstances, which are wholly beyond your control. It is hard enough for those who like myself are merely trying to keep on under these conditions, but still harder for those like yourself. I hope that something will come of the job which you have in mind, and that you will keep me posted about your movements. Also that you will continue to let me see specimens of your verse.

---

1 – Jean Duvoisin wrote on 21 Sept.: 'I am collecting information on the manner in which Marcel Proust was introduced to the English public and would feel very grateful if you could supply me with a brief statement of when and how you got interested in Proust and began to read his novels.' On 30 June 1954 TSE wrote to Elliott Coleman, 'Your Proust book looks to me extremely interesting, and I shall look forward to reading it myself. I shall submit it to my Board, but I must confess that I am not by any means a Proust authority myself, having read so far only about the first thirty pages of the first volume.' *Cf.* Ronald Schuchard, 'Editor's Introduction', *VMP*, 14.

2 – Brittain wrote from Princeton, New Jersey: '[M]y hopes and plans for marriage ended tragically three days after my arrival in Oklahoma City, and the shock and mental strain have been almost too much for me.

'But my life must be lived, and for your great assistance in planning my future I thank you again. Your letters were of great help to me in New York . . . Mr Ballou, a very charming and sympathetic man, told me of one job he had heard of – the editorship of a small magazine of men's fashions in London . . . I should really prefer the kind of work you suggested, but . . . I shall make every effort to get this place if it is offered. Conditions in America are almost as bad as they are abroad, and the existence of six million unemployed makes entrance into the business world by a beginner a very difficult undertaking. My father's business is in a state of chaos . . .' He would be returning to Graduate College at Princeton in the Autumn, he went on, but the length of time he would stay there would be determined by developments in London.

I hope that you will go to see Paul More whom you will find to be an extremely kind man and loveable personality.[1]

Yours sincerely
[T. S. Eliot]

TO Seán Ó'Faoláin

CC

30 September 1931   [*The Criterion*]

Dear Mr O'Faoláin,

I have your letter of the 26th, and am interested to hear your new plans.[2] As for introductions, I feel that I could be of more use to you by writing individual letters to any editors whom I happen to know than by giving a form of blanket recommendation, which upon me at least never makes much impression. I suggest that you should let me know what periodicals you have in mind. To the editors I know I will write personally. In the case of any I do not know I think the best method would be for you to say when you write yourself that you are authorised to use my name, and that they can communicate with me about you if they think it necessary.

With all best wishes
Yours sincerely
[T. S. Eliot]

1–Brittain wrote again on 3 Nov. to say that, thanks to TSE's introduction, he had been 'received . . . very kindly' by Paul Elmer More. 'I was charmed by his conversation.'
2–Jonathan Cape and Viking were publishing a volume of stories by Ó'Faoláin. He was working too on a novel. 'I have managed to get some advance royalties from both and after long debate, vacillation and planning am decided to throw up London next summer for ever and "go native" in the Irish hinterland for ever to write more novels, ad lib. Between this and then I want to develop in a small way a connection with some periodicals, or newspapers – for reviews or articles – so that I shall not starve in Ireland when my cash begins to ebb, but keep making a little all the time.' Might TSE feel able 'to make the way smooth' for him with a letter of introduction which he could copy and send on to editors 'before going to the lions' himself?

TO *Montgomery Belgion* CC

30 September 1931 [Faber & Faber Ltd]

Dear Belgion,

I have your letter of September 24th.[1] In the circumstance and to save your conscience we are prepared to go up to £30 for a book of the description and length mentioned, to be delivered not later than the end of October. I needn't repeat that every day sooner that we could have it would facilitate its early production which I think is highly desirable. I hope to hear again from you soon about the other matters you mentioned.

Yours ever,
[T. S. Eliot]

TO *Sonia Hambourg* CC

30 September 1931 [Faber & Faber Ltd]

Dear Miss Hambourg,

I must apologize for the delay in sending you the proofs. I delayed writing because you told me to write to Cumberland Terrace after a certain date, and as a result of waiting for that date I forgot the matter for several days. I do not remember whether I mentioned in writing to you last that I am still dissatisfied with the title page. We agreed, you remember, that it was undesirable to publish a note about the author, but I think that they have now gone to the opposite extreme. 1904 (?) – 1931 might almost suggest that the poems were written between those dates. I should propose at least expanding it to 'Born . . . . . Died . . . . .,' but I should prefer that the final form should be settled by yourself.[2]

When this point is settled and you have read and approved the proofs I do not think that I shall have to bother you again.

Yours sincerely
[T. S. Eliot]

1 – Belgion requested an advance of £30 rather than £25.
2 – *Poems* by Clere Parsons noted, below the author's name, simply 'born 1908 – died 1931'. The volume, published in 1932, bore no blurb.

TO *Evelyn Underhill*   CC

30 September 1931   [Faber & Faber Ltd]

Dear Mrs Stuart Moore,
   Thank you for your letter of the 26th.[1] I did not realize that your
connection with the *Spectator* was so very official. I shall be very glad to
contribute an article to your series if we can settle on a subject. I hardly
feel that I know enough about Lancelot Andrewes to write any more
about him. Indeed I fear that the one essay which I have written appears
to lay claim to a much more profound knowledge than I possess – and I
feel that I should probably be considered to speak with more authority
if I wrote about somebody like George Herbert. Will you let me know
whether this would be suitable, and if not make some other suggestion?[2]
   I took the liberty of sending you a copy of the Everyman Pascal to
which I wrote an introduction. You are not called upon, please, to make
comments on my effort which was meant for a popular audience, but I
should like to know that you received the book.

                                        Yours very sincerely
                                        [T. S. Eliot]

TO *David Garnett*[3]   CC

2 October 1931   [*The Criterion*]

Dear Garnett,
   I have your letter of the 28th together with the copy of Hotson's book
which arrived last night.[4] I know all about Hotson and his previous work,

---

1–Evelyn Underhill (Mrs Stuart Moore) wrote, 'I am arranging a series of short articles on
Saints and great spiritual personalities, to begin in the *Spectator* in the New Year; and should
feel so *deeply* grateful if you could possibly find time to do one for us. I would particularly
like a study from you on Lancelot Andrewes, or one of the saintly figures of the 16th or
17th century Anglican church, but shall most gratefully accept anything that you are kind
enough to suggest.'
2–Underhill was pleased (7 Oct.) for TSE 'to write on George Herbert in our Saints series'.
3–David Garnett (1892–1981): author, publisher; founder with Francis Meynell of the
Nonesuch Press; author of *Lady into Fox* (1922; James Tait Black Memorial Prize), *The
Sailor's Return* (1925), *Aspects of Love* (1955) – the source for Andrew Lloyd Webber's
musical (1989).
4–Garnett, writing from The Nonesuch Press, praised Leslie Hotson as 'a fine sleuth-hound
. . . [H]ere is the last batch of his discoveries which eclipse all that have come before.' If
Hotson was not sufficiently noticed in the UK, wrote Garnett, 'I am really afraid one of the
results will be to get Hotson a permanent job in Washington – far from the Record Office.'

but knew nothing about the subject of the present book until I saw the *Times Literary Supplement* yesterday.[1] I wish that you had sent me a copy earlier to Russell Square because it is always a rush to get the autumn books reviewed for the December *Criterion*. But I will certainly try to get a review in though I may have to approach two or three people before I can find a suitable reviewer to do it within the time.

I thought by the way that Hotson had already accepted a permanent job at Haverford College near Philadelphia.

Yours sincerely
[T. S. Eliot]

TO *John Dover Wilson* CC

2 October 1931   [*The Criterion*]

Dear Dover Wilson,

I have only just received a review copy of Leslie Hotson's *Shakespeare versus Shallow*, and am writing at once to ask if it would be possible for you to let me have a review of it for my December number, if the book interests you. I should want the copy by November 18th at the latest. If you can't or don't want to do it, I should be very grateful if you could let me know at once so that I can find someone else.[2]

Yours ever sincerely,
[T. S. Eliot]

1–'Shakespeare and Shallow' – on Hotson's *Shakespeare versus Shallow* (1931) – *TLS*, 1 Oct. 1931, 749.
2–Dover Wilson replied (4 Oct.) that it was 'an important book', but that he was 'so frightfully full up with all sorts of things' that he had to decline. In the event, *Shakespeare versus Swallow* was reviewed by Frederick S. Boas, C. 11 (Jan. 1932), 347–51.

TO *Elizabeth Wiskemann*[1]   CC

2 October 1931   [Faber & Faber Ltd]

Dear Mrs Wiskemann,

Thank you for your letter of the 1st.[2] Mr Gillie mentioned the project to me when I saw him last week, and I told him that it seemed to me personally to be worth consideration. He suggested that you might be sending a brief outline of the book you contemplate writing. As, however, you are now in London and for only such a short time I should be very glad to discuss the matter with you personally on Monday morning if you could call here at about 12.

> Yours very truly
> [T. S. Eliot]

TO *Charles Harris*   CC

3 October 1931   [Faber & Faber Ltd]

My dear Harris,

I enclose for your consideration a provisional list of the literary articles for the Encyclopaedia. I have also made a brief outline of art articles, but if I may have the time, I should prefer to wait until I have heard from Chandler Post, to whom I should defer in such subjects, before submission. I am writing to Duncan Jones also, and hope that he can come up and talk over several questions of both art and literature, particularly mediaeval literature. I have not included mediaeval hymns, as I expect that e.g. Prudentius and Adam of St Victor will receive some treatment in his department. I want to make a few comments upon the list which I do enclose.

At first sight it will look, and indeed still looks to me, very haphazard. It is largely however a question of how to get the most into the space; so that, allowing much more space to English writers than to others, I have tried to select rather typical representatives of the religious (or non- or anti-religious) sentiment of a language and a time. I should propose to

---

1–Elizabeth Wiskemann (1899–1971): English journalist and historian; Montague Burton Professor of International Relations, Edinburgh University, 1958–61; author of *Czechs and Germans* (1938), *Undeclared War* (1939), *The Rome–Berlin Axis* (1949), *The Europe I Saw* (1968). See L. K. Duff, 'Elizabeth Meta Wiskemann, 1899–1971', *Newnham College Roll*, Jan. 1972, 70–4; and *Selected Letters of William Empson*, ed. John Haffenden (2006), 11.
2–Wiskemann wished 'to attempt a History of Germany-for-the-fairly-young'.

ask the authors of comprehensive articles to deal as fully as possible in the space with individuals; and to ask the authors of articles on individuals to include as much of an epoch as possible. E.G. the article on 17th century verse should discuss such poets as Donne, Crashaw and George Herbert severally; and the article on Dante should discuss the Provençal and the Islamic background.

In the art section: (1) should such a modern subject as *films* be mentioned? That might possibly be covered in the article on Modern Religious Drama. Personally, I am rather horrified by the notion of modern religious films. (2) Are the articles to be illustrated or not? This question is rather important.

[*Line(s) missing*]

[Ency]clopaedia and printed in a separate book together, the book would have an independent interest as a kind of history of religious thought and sentiment in literature. I am not recommending this as a publishing venture; I merely think that it is a useful ideal in the actual selection of subject matter and treatment.

Yours sincerely,
[T. S. Eliot]

ALPHABETICAL:

Arnold
Blake
Bridges
Browning
Bunyan
Carlyle
Chateaubriand
Chaucer
Christianity in Later Latin
  Literature
Cowper
Corneille
Dante
Dryden
Elizabethan & Restoration Drama
Emerson
English Carols
Ethics in the 19th Century Novel
Goethe

Greek Tragedy
Ibsen
Johnson
Lucretius
Lucian
Mediaeval Drama
Mediaeval Latin Literature
Middle English Literature
Milton
Modern Religious Drama
Modern Production of Religious
Drama
Moralities & Interludes
Pater
Pope
Rousseau
Racine
Religious Verse of the 16th &
  17th Centuries

Religious Verse of the 19th
Century (English)
Romantic Movement
Shakespeare
Shelley
Spenser
Seneca

Spanish Tragedy (Lope &
Calderon)
Tennyson
Virgil
Voltaire
Wordsworth

COMPREHENSIVE ARTICLES:

Greek Tragedy
Christianity in Later Latin
Literature
Mediaeval Latin Literature
Middle English Literature
Mediaeval Drama
Moralities & Interludes
English Carols
Spanish Tragedy
Elizabethan and Restoration
Drama

Religious Verse of the 16th & 17th
Century
The Romantic Movement
Modern Religious Drama
Modern Production of Religious
Drama
Religious Verse of the 19th
Century (English)
Ethics in the 19th Century Novel
(e.g. George Eliot, Meredith,
Hardy).

INDIVIDUAL AUTHORS:

Lucretius
Virgil
Seneca
Lucian
Dante
Chaucer
Spenser
Shakespeare
Corneille
Racine
Milton
Bunyan
Dryden
Pope
Cowper
Johnson

Blake
Rousseau
Voltaire
Goethe
Wordsworth
Shelley
Chateaubriand
Tennyson
Browning
Carlyle
Emerson
Arnold
Pater
Ibsen
Bridges

TO *Evelyn Underhill*   CC

4 October 1931   [Faber & Faber Ltd]

Dear Mrs Stuart Moore,

Thank you for your letter of the 1st. I am very pleased and proud to
have a copy of *Malaval* inscribed by you. A review copy came in, but it
was bespoke by Algar Thorold, who is writing about it in our December
number;[1] so I had to let it go with hardly a glance; and I am very happy
to have a copy of my own from you.

February 1st will suit me well for the *Spectator*;[2] but may I ask for a
reminder from someone in the *Spectator* office during December? I shall
be busy with several odds and ends until the middle of that month, and
am afraid of forgetting.

At the same time may I remind you of your promise to write about
v. Hügel for the December *Criterion*? I don't want to worry you – March
will *do* if December is impossible – but I should just like to know whether
to count upon it or not.[3]

                                    Sincerely yours,
                                    [T. S. Eliot]

TO *Bonamy Dobrée*   MS Brotherton

5 October 1931   Faber & Faber Ltd

Dear Bumbaby,[4]

To remind you we are lunching on the 13th (Tues.) Will you fetch me
here or meet me at the Oxford & Cambridge?

We also meet at Harold's on the 14th. Don't fail. I have invited an American Professor from Princeton named Thorp (not Willie) who is working
on Restoration Drama & admires you & your works intemperately.[5]

                                    Yours ever,
                                    T. S. E.

1–François Malaval, *A Simple Method of Raising the Soul to Contemplation*, trans. Lucy
Menzies: reviewed by Thorold in C. 11 (Jan. 1932), 358–60.
2–'George Herbert' ('Studies in Sanctity VIII'), *Spectator* 7 (12 Mar. 1932), 360–1.
3–Evelyn Underhill, 'Finite and Infinite: A Study of Friedrich von Hügel', C. 11 (Jan. 1932),
183–97.
4–BD replied on 6 Oct.: 'Dear Tomarse, / Since you've repeated your bad joke, I head this
letter (marked *personal* on the outside) with your pet aversion. And who shall say that you
are not rightly served?'
5–'Why do these American Professors want to write about Restoration Drama?' protested
BD by return. 'Haven't Allardyce [Nicoll] & I said all the last words?'

TO *Leonard Woolf*   CC

6 October 1931   [Faber & Faber Ltd]

Dear Leonard,

This is to introduce to you Mr W. H. C. Bishop who is acting on behalf of his cousin, Mr Leslie Bishop in the matter of the manuscript of a novel which Mr Leslie Bishop has written. I read the novel some time ago, and found it extremely interesting, but was unable to persuade my fellow directors that it was a book which we should publish. One difficulty is that the novel is very short. I am sure, however, that it is worth serious consideration, and I should be personally grateful if you would have the book read with a view to publication.

Yours ever,
[T. S. Eliot]

TO *Seán Ó'Faoláin*   CC

6 October 1931   [Faber & Faber Ltd]

Dear Mr Ó'Faoláin,

I have your letter of the 1st October, but I don't want you to be grateful to me until something has come of my efforts.[1] I am writing about you to Mr Richmond of the *Times*. Unfortunately I do not know either the *Observer* or the *Sunday Times* people, so in these two places you will use my name as I suggested. I believe the person to write to on the *Observer* is Miss Viola Garvin whom I do not know but who will know my name.

In the question of a regular engagement to contribute to an American periodical I cannot at the moment think of any way of being of help. As a matter of fact, so far as I am concerned it was a mirage which I pursued for some years without the slightest success. Other people may have better luck than I, and I quite agree that the prospect of small regular remittances is very desirable. But if you have any particular American periodical in mind let me know, and I will write if I happen to know anyone connected with them.

---

1 – Ó'Faoláin hoped the following newspapers might be hospitable to him: *TLS*; *The Sunday Times*; *The Observer*. He hoped too that he might secure a monthly retainer from an American periodical, such as *The Atlantic Monthly*, for a 'London literary letter kind of thing'. Might TSE write 'what in Ireland they call "a bit of a note"' to some such American periodical?

I will let you know if Richmond thinks there is any possibility of work.

Yours sincerely

[T. S. Eliot]

TO *Bruce Richmond*   CC

6 October 1931   [Faber & Faber Ltd]

Dear Richmond,

Once more I am applying to you on behalf of an Irishman. The present from the peat-bogs is named Sean O'Faolain, and he is, I believe, a product of Trinity Dublin, further academised by sojourn at Harvard. He is, I believe, a very good Celtic scholar; Harvard is rather particularly good in the study of Celtic languages and literature, and it was in that department that he was working there. He has written a few reviews for me, and I have also tried in vain to help him find a publisher for a volume of selections of early Irish poetry, text and verse translation. I have also seen one or two very sensible essays of his on Irish literature. He says that he thinks he is equipped to review English literature, history, criticism and fiction, but I think it is safest to present him primarily as a specialist in Irish and Anglo-Irish literature. He lays claim to a considerable acquaintance among Irish politicians.

I shall not give him a note of introduction to you unless I hear from you that there [is] any possibility of your giving him work.[1]

Yours ever

[T. S. Eliot]

P.S. When are we to have that lunch which was talked of?

TO *Max Rychner*   CC

8 October 1931   [*The Criterion*]

My dear Rychner,

I am writing to ask whether the *Criterion* might have permission to reprint 'Heroischer Pazifismus' of Scheler from your May number.[2]

1–BLR replied on 9 Oct.: 'I am afraid I cannot encourage your Irishman, at any rate at present. I am always glad to know of this sort of specialist; but for this particular kind of stuff there is Robin Flower, at the British Museum, whom I have no reason to throw over.'

2–'Die Idee des Friedens und der Pazifismus' ('The Idea of Peace and Pacifism'), *Neue Schweizer Rundschau* 24 (1931), 3.

I have read the whole of Scheler's essay with much interest and wanted to publish a part in the *Criterion* if permission is available; and the section which you have published is about the right length to be possible for our December number.

If the *Neue Schweizer Rundschau* has no objection may I ask you to let me know also whether your consent is sufficient, or whether I should speak to Frau Scheler or to the publishers of the pamphlet. I should be very grateful if you could let me know quickly as time is rather short. I wish that the whole essay might be translated into English; it is very pertinent at the present time although I fear that in England as elsewhere the Disarmament Conference is likely to be overshadowed by other difficulties.[1]

Yours cordially
[T. S. Eliot]

TO *Noel Carrington*[2] CC

8 October 1931 [Faber & Faber Ltd]

Dear Sir,

I thank you for your letter of the 1st instant, and appreciate the honour which the Committee of the Double Crown Club have done me in asking me to read a paper at their next dinner.[3] I should very much like to respond affirmatively to this flattering invitation, but I am afraid that the date of the next dinner falls out very ill for other engagements which I have. I should be very happy indeed if I might receive a similar invitation at some time in the New Year when I hope I might be freer to give my time to prepare a paper worthy of the Society.

Yours very truly
[T. S. Eliot]

1 – Scheler's essay did not appear in C.
2 – Noel Carrington (1895–1989) – brother of the artist Dora Carrington – book designer, editor and publisher, worked for Oxford University Press; creator of Puffin picture books.
3 – Carrington invited TSE to be the guest at a dinner of the Double Crown Club, and to address them or read a paper 'on some subject connected with printing'. The next dinner was to take place on Thurs., 29 Oct., or 5 Nov. – 'according to which date suits you best'. The Double Crown Club, founded in London in the early 1920s, is a dining club and society of printers, publishers, book designers and illustrators; the first president was Holbrook Jackson.

TO *Charles Smyth*   CC

8 October 1931   [*The Criterion*]

My dear Smyth,

Thank you for your letter of the 6th instant.[1] It was because I thought
Rowse's book would exasperate you to the last degree that I sent it to
you, and I still am anxious that you should review it. But while I wholly
agree with you that the book is second-rate, and that Rowse is merely a
belated Liberal I hope that you will be able to tear it to pieces in a spirit of
cold irony rather than of violence. Rowse is rather a friend of mine and of
Faber's; I have often found him extremely intelligent in conversation and
correspondence whenever he was not occupied in cramming everything
into his own narrow theories. We encouraged him to finish the book, and
although I expected to dislike extremely the views expressed, I hoped for
a much better book of its kind, and thought that it would be a good thing
that Rowse's views should be published, if only to have something definite
from a younger man for someone else to attack. The ideas are not new,
and the spirit is hardly even young, though it might be called immature.

Nevertheless with the history back of the volume you will see that
Rowse might justly be hurt if I published a denunciation of it under the
title which you suggest – 'Confessions of a Prig'. But I shall be very grateful
if you accept the task with this limitation. It seems to me that you could
destroy his arguments, if such they may be called, all the more effectively
for such moderation of manner.

                              Yours ever
                              [T. S. Eliot]

1 – 'Many thanks for Rowse's book [*Politics and the Younger Generation*]. With all due
respect, I think it is utterly second rate. May I be allowed a short article in which to say so
(and may I use for it the obvious title – The Confessions of a Prig): or would you rather have
somebody else do it? I am in your hands.

'Some of the anti-clerical bits aren't bad, but that's about all. The man is simply an old-
fashioned Radical who has read Karl Marx and wants us all to do the same. And we must
give up pub-crawling and huntin' and all that, and settle down to Improve Our Minds under
perfectly hygienic conditions. And that is the New Utopia! (or Eutopia, as you will). – His
old *Criterion* stuff was so much better.

'Well, may I please do it all the same? I do feel rather a cad. That you may forgive. I hope
so: because I gather that you aren't really very deeply implicated in this belated contribution
to the thought of the day before yesterday.'

P.S. I am glad you liked Penty.[1] We are publishing a little book of his early in the new year, which I will send you.[2]

TO *Herbert Gorman*   TS Southern Illinois

8 October 1931   Faber & Faber Ltd

My dear Gorman,

I am very glad to hear from you, and to know that the Joyce biography is going forward.[3] I hope that you will let me know later on as soon as you are in a position to give a fixed date for delivery of the manuscript, as until then we must leave the publication date unsettled.

I understand that your American publishers have all English-speaking rights and that they put the British and Colonial rights into the hands of Curtis Brown as agents, who naturally came to us. With regard to the business dealings we must do business through Curtis Brown; but for the delivery of the manuscript I suggest that it would be to everyone's advantage if you would have two copies prepared – one for your New York publishers, and one to send direct to us. This will be quite in order.

As for the question of libel in connexion with naming the originals of characters in *Ulysses*.[4] It seems to me impossible to generalize. I cannot think at the moment of any possibility of libel, and of course everybody in Dublin, and a good many people outside of Dublin know who some of the originals are. In some cases I expect that the originals would be flattered rather than otherwise by the notoriety. So I suggest that you let us have the manuscript without concealing personalities, and if in any particular case we thought that the name should be concealed, we would then discuss the matter with you.

As for the book which Louis Golding, whom I know only by name [*sic*] I have heard of the book from Joyce himself. Apparently it was to be

1 – 'I enjoyed Penty's article in the current number . . . He isn't a great man, but he is often stimulating, and always a dear.'
2 – *Means and Ends* (F&F, 1932).
3 – Gorman wrote (n.d.): 'I laid this by during the summer because I found it impossible to get Stanislaus Joyce, in Trieste, to copy the long diaristic letters his brother had sent him during the years and which were absolutely indispensable to my venture. However, this material is all coming in now and I am actively engaged on the Joyce biography. If luck is with me I ought to have it finished by January. Do I send copy direct to you or through the agent?'
4 – 'Is it libel in England to announce the names of the real personages who unconsciously sat for characters in *Ulysses*?'

one of a cheap and not very distinguished series of biographies of living authors. Joyce was extremely incensed about the matter because he had not been consulted, and did not know either Golding or the publishers. I daresay the book will never appear, and if it does we can ignore it.

Nothing further has happened in the gramophone world except that Joyce succeeded in persuading Ogden to reduce the retail price of his record from two guineas to one, and it is now on sale at the lower price at Imhof's in Oxford Street.

Yours ever sincerely,
T. S. Eliot

TO *William Force Stead*   MS Beinecke

12 October 1931   Faber & Faber Ltd

My dear Stead,

I am delighted to know that we can expect you on Wednesday evening. That is good news. I have notified Morley. As for poor Harold Monro, he will not be present, as he has just undergone an operation in a nursing home.[1] (You need not be so disturbed by him. In 1912, when I was wholly unknown, a mutual friend[2] tried 'Prufrock' on him, in MS, and he rejected it without hesitation. But I have never reminded him of this, so don't mention it to anybody.)

May we have a word about your tempting invitation on Wednesday?[3]

Affectionately
T. S. E.

8.15 the Poetry Bookshop.
Ring the Monro bell, side door on Willoughby Street.

1–Stead wrote on 10 Oct., 'that benevolent soul Morley has asked me to go with him to Harold Munro next Wed evening . . . I have lost Morley's letter and forgotten the address: but I expect it is at the Poetry Book shop; is that right? . . . And will you be there to support me? I have always been terrified of Monro, the few times I've seen him . . . I shall be stricken dumb and shall need some friendly support – will you and Morley stay up my drooping form?'

Monro had written to TSE on 7 Oct. 1931: 'I had in Germany an uncanny improvement for eyes, but now I come back to a London Dr. who tells me I must have an operation for another part of my body this week – or possibly die.

'Have the *Criterion* here on the 15th, or postpone. I should love to think of you all chatting here while I am in possible agonies. That is really true.'

2–Conrad Aiken.

3–Presumably an invitation to visit and dine with him at Worcester College, Oxford.

TO *Raymond Gram Swing*[1]   CC

14 October 1931   [Faber & Faber Ltd]

Dear Sir,

I have been in communication with Mr César Saerchinger about a broadcast talk which he has fixed up for me on the 13 December. I understand from his letter to me of the 7th instant that he may have already left for his visit to America, and as he tells me that you are representing him in his absence I am replying direct to you.

The point is that the arrangement was only discussed by Mr Saerchinger and myself in conversation here, and so far I have nothing in writing to confirm the fee offered and the time at my disposal. Before proceeding any further with the matter I should like to have a full and formal proposal from the Columbia System which would have the validity of a contract.[2]

Yours very truly
[T. S. Eliot]

TO *Lincoln Kirstein*   TS Beinecke

14 October 1931   Faber & Faber Ltd

Dear Mr Kirstein,

I find that I have never answered your letter of the 18th August. Please accept my apologies.

In any case I have not asked Stuart Gilbert to write about Joyce because I find that he has already done an article which has been accepted by another periodical in London.[3]

I am afraid that I still feel that I have nothing to say about Henry James, but I will keep the matter in mind and will write to you again if I should be inspired.[4]

1 – Raymond Gram Swing (1887–1968): American print and radio broadcast journalist who was to be celebrated for his influential broadcasts from London during WW2. At the time of this exchange he was London correspondent of the *New York Evening Post*, 88 Fleet Street.
2 – Gram Swing wrote on 15 Oct. formally to confirm the arrangements for TSE's fifteen-minute 'address' on John Dryden, for a fee of fifteen guineas. The broadcast was to take place in the studios of the BBC at Savoy Hill on Sun., 13 Dec. at 5.30; introduced by César Saerchinger.
3 – Kirstein thought it 'inadvisable for us to attempt simultaneous publication of any work however interesting, in this case, Mr Gilbert's remarks about the *Work in Progress* would be. We feel the limitations of space very acutely and generally speaking, I think we have a common audience.'
4 – Kirstein asked TSE to write on Henry James for the forthcoming memorial number on him.

I should have let you know long ago that the Six Reviews Prize has been abandoned.[1] I am not quite clear what the trouble was but I gather that Max Clauss and Jean Paulhan failed to agree about some detail of [the] arrangement. I am very sorry myself, and should be glad if the scheme could be revived and carried through. My idea had been, in fact, that English short stories and American short stories should be dealt with separately, in which case the American selection would of course have fallen to you.

Sincerely yours,

T. S. Eliot

TO *Maud Fortescue Pickard*   CC

14 October 1931   [Faber & Faber Ltd]

Dear Madam,

Mr T. S. Eliot has asked me to say that he has no objection to your including the short extracts from his poems mentioned in your letter of the 18th ultimo, in an anthology, on the understanding that the profits from that anthology are entirely for the benefit of St Bartholomew's Hospital.[2] But he wishes me to say that he can give you no authority for publishing the first of the four extracts, for the reason that it is not by him; he is not at the moment certain of the author, but he believes it to be Mr Charles Williams.

Yours truly

[Secretary]

1–'In January 1930 you spoke to us about including us in the Six Reviews Prize, and mentioned that the Wiechert story might be printed as soon as possible. Since then we have heard nothing about it. Is the prize still in existence . . .? Would it be possible to have an American Short Story submitted for this prize, to be selected by us? This would be an enormous help to us . . .'

2–Mrs Pickard asked permission (20 Sept.) to include brief extracts from some of TSE's poems in a 'day by day Anthology' – 'only a sort of glorified Calendar, composed of snippets (or "unset jewels" I prefer to call them), with a few beautiful thoughts clothed in poetry' – that she was compiling for the benefit of St Bartholomew's Hospital. She asked leave to use extracts opening (i) 'Put out the light and then put out the light . . . after the last tired shout'; (ii) "sound of water over a rock / Where a hermit-thrush sings in the pine trees'; (iii) 'Then at dawn we came down to a temperate valley . . .'; (iv) 'The river's tent is broken, the last fingers of leaf . . .' Charles Williams's sonnet opening 'Put out the light, and then put out the light . . .' is in *Poetry at Present* (1930), 174.

TO *Aline Lion*   CC

14 October 1931   [*The Criterion*]

Dear Miss Lion,

I enclose herewith two copies of the proof of your essay 'Property and Poetry', one of which I have marked with a few corrections. Some of the corrections are doubtless due to the fact that the printers have made mistakes owing to the essay not being typed. The only serious difficulty, however, is that I now find the essay runs to about 37 pages, which I am sorry to say is far beyond the capacity of the *Criterion*. I wonder if it would be asking too much of you to see if you can reduce it for our present purposes to 25 pages. I even think, if I may venture to say so, that for periodical readers your extremely interesting point may be made more effective in the shorter space.

I hope that you will be able to effect this reduction, as I am very desirous of publishing the essay in the December number.[1]

Yours sincerely,
[T. S. Eliot]

TO *E. E. Kellett*[2]   CC

14 October 1931   [Faber & Faber Ltd]

Dear Mr Kellett,

Thank you very much for your very kind note of the 8th instant.[3] If, as you say, I have created an example among reviewers it is still more certain that you have created an example of courtesy for authors with books reviewed.[4]

I am rather appalled to hear of the advice which was given you in Cambridge, which I can hardly believe was meant seriously. I must say,

1 – The essay was ultimately published in two parts, under the pseudonym 'Gallox': 'Property and Poetry: I', C. 11 (Jan. 1932), 253–67; 'Property and Poetry: II', C. 11 (Apr. 1932), 443–66.
2 – Ernest Edward Kellett (1864–1950), a graduate of Wadham College, Oxford, was English master, 1899–1924, at The Leys School, Cambridge (his pupils included Malcolm Lowry); author or editor of books including *Carmina Ephemera; or, Trivial Numbers* (1903); *The Story of Myths* (1927); *A Short History of the Jews* (1929).
3 – Letter not found.
4 – TSE reviewed Kellett's *Fashion in Literature: A Study of Changing Taste*, in the *English Review* 53: 5 (Oct. 1931), 634–6.

however, that you have succeeded in obliterating the traces of the lecture room. That is a task at which I have never had any success myself.

Yours sincerely
[T. S. Eliot]

TO *L. C. Knights*[1]

14 October 1931   [*The Criterion*]

Dear Sir,

I have read with much interest your essay on 'Education and the Drama in the Age of Shakespeare', and I shall be glad to use it although I fear that it must wait for six months or so.[2] The amount of work on Elizabethan subjects which the *Criterion* can publish must necessarily be restricted in proportion to the other matter; and as I have a paper on Massinger[3] which must appear shortly, it will delay publication of your article. But if you should wish to publish it elsewhere in the meantime I should be obliged if you would let me know.

Yours very truly,
[T. S. Eliot]

1–L. C. Knights (1906–97), literary scholar and critic, held a Research Fellowship at Christ's College, Cambridge, 1930–1, and became founder-editor of *Scrutiny: A Quarterly Review*, 1932–53. He taught at Manchester University, 1933–47, and was Professor of English at Sheffield, 1947–53; Winterstroke Professor of English at Bristol; and King Edward VII Chair of English at Cambridge, 1965–73. Works include *How Many Children had Lady Macbeth?* (a lecture published by Gordon Fraser's Minority Press, 1933); *Drama and Society in the Age of Jonson* (1937); *Explorations* (1946); *Some Shakespearean Themes* (1959). TSE would tell Helen Gardner on 29 Oct. 1956 that he considered Knights 'very intelligent'.

2–'Education and the Drama in the Age of Shakespeare', C. 11 (July 1932), 599–625. Knights was at this time a research student at Cambridge, supervised by L. J. Potts, studying the background of early seventeenth-century drama. Potts had written to TSE on 23 Aug. 1931, urging: 'He is most deserving, and I think the work he is doing is useful and I should be very glad to see some of it published as soon as possible. But of course it may be of no use to you.'

3–W. J. Lawrence, 'Massinger's Punctuation', C. 11 (Jan. 1932), 214–21.

TO *Harriet Weaver*   CC

14 October 1931   [Faber & Faber Ltd]

Dear Miss Weaver,

Thank you very much for your note of the 4th.[1] It would of course
be a great pleasure to me to sign anything of mine for you, and indeed
you should have had everything there is immediately upon publication.
Whenever you let me have the books I shall be very happy to sign them.

Yours sincerely

[T. S. Eliot]

TO *Kay Boyle*[2]   CC

16 October 1931   [*The Criterion*]

Dear Madam,

I have had for a long time a piece of prose of yours which I intended
to use. I did not write to you at first because of having a good deal of
material that had to be published, and later I failed to write out of pure
laziness, merely because I did not know your address and was afraid that
it would take some time to find it. Having recently seen something of
yours in the *Adelphi* I have obtained from their office what I hope is your
actual address, and I am now writing.

I daresay that by this time 'Three Little Men' may have appeared in
some other periodical, but if it has only appeared in America or Paris that
will not matter, and I should like to use it quite soon. I hope, therefore,
that I may soon hear from you to the effect that it has not appeared in
England and that I may have the permission to use it.[3]

1–'It was very nice of you to send and sign for me your poem *Triumphal March*. Thank
you very much. I think I now have all your poems and perhaps some day I shall summon up
courage to ask whether you would honour me by signing one or two of the others.'

2–Kay Boyle (1902–92): American author, editor, teacher and political activist, whose early
novels, including *Plagued by the Nightingale* (1931), *Year Before Last* (1932), and *My Next
Bride* (1934), were published by F&F. From 1923 to 1941 she lived primarily in France,
marrying in 1932 Laurence Vail (ex-husband of Peggy Guggenheim) and enjoying friendships with numerous artists and writers including Harry and Caresse Crosby (who published
in 1929 her first fictions, entitled *Short Stories*, at their Black Sun Press), and Eugene and
Maria Jolas; she also contributed to *transition*. See further Robert McAlmon and Kay Boyle,
Being Geniuses Together, 1920–1930 (1968), and Jean Mellen, *Kay Boyle: Author of Herself*
(1994).

3–The story was to be included in *Three Little Men* (F&F, 1932).

With many apologies for the delay,

I am

Yours very truly

[T. S. Eliot]

TO *Willard Thorp*   TS Princeton

19 October 1931   68 Clarence Gate Gardens

Dear Mr Thorp,

My wife and I would be very much pleased if you and Mrs Thorp could come to tea with us on Friday next at 4:15.[1] If that is inconvenient I hope you will suggest a day next week: but Monday and Thursday are never possible for me.

I hope you have settled on an abode by now; if not, we shall be glad to help if we can.

Yours sincerely,

T. S. Eliot

P.S. This is just round the corner from Baker Street Station.

TO *Maurice Haigh-Wood*   CC

19 October 1931   [68 Clarence Gate Gardens]

Dear Maurice,

I have had to let some days elapse before answering yours of the 7th. It was merely because I feared my letter might have gone astray that I wired to you.[2]

---

1 – In 1985 Thorp was to tell Lyndall Gordon that TSE had treated VHE 'like a patient father with a fractious child' (*T. S. Eliot*, 293). Gordon adds: 'Evie Townsend, Faber's secretary, also noticed Eliot's patience when his wife would ring him soon after his arrival at the office, and demand his return. He would apologise for interrupting his dictation, and leave' (ibid.).

2 – Maurice wrote on 7 Oct.: 'I am very sorry indeed that your letter has not been answered & that you had to telegraph.

'In mitigation I plead an accumulation of worries, personal and professional, plus a few days of ill health . . . The last few days have in fact been rather filthy . . . Yes I agreed with Coall that half yearly payments should be made. I don't think we definitely said that this should come into effect this year . . . However, if it is particularly desired, I suppose there is no reason why it should not come into effect this year, & a payment be made in respect of the first half . . .

'The position as regards Duffy's lease appears to be now in order . . . Incidentally Coall told me that Duffy's visit to James & James cost us £30 (the amount which it was agreed to

The situation is that Vivienne is extremely hard up at present, owing to the fall in the dividends of securities and not having yet reduced her expenditure to fit. (Her chief expenses are of a kind difficult to reduce). It is also in general that the autumn is a lean time for her: most of her dividends come in January and July, which is why I hope that her Irish rents can be spread over March and September. It is at present necessary either to get a proportion of Irish rent or borrow, which is highly undesirable.

I cannot see any reason why it should be more inconvenient for Coall to pay a half year's rent now (i.e. rents Jan.–June inclusive) than it will be next year. If he pays regularly in future say on March 25 and September 29, he will always have three months leeway; and he will now have had the Jan.–June rents for four months. So I should be very glad if you could write to Coall at once to make this arrangement.

I have spoken to James & James about the Duffy lease, and they have had no news at all. They feel quite sure that if the Duffy lease had been completed they would have heard from Hayes to that effect. So I think you might remind Coall also that we want official notification of the lease having gone through.

I do not understand Coall's remark about the £30. I understand that Duffy told Shapcott (or Mr James, I forget which) that he was in London on official business; his visit to James was unexpected and not by appointment. The notion of asking for repair allowance may not have occurred to him till then; but so far as I can see it is perfectly reasonable and the repairs are such as he is justly entitled to.

I am extremely sorry for your bad news. Of course I anticipated that exchange business would be almost dead; but it is distressing to hear that your anxieties are increased by personal worries. I hope the latter are smoothing out; as for the former, we shall see whether the election will mend matters.[1] I do not worry over the result of the election itself; but I am very depressed about the coming winter, at the very best.[2]

---

allow him towards repairs). According to Coall Duffy had no intention previously of asking for anything. This, however, might be taken with a grain of salt . . .

'The situation has become very difficult here, as no purchases of foreign currency or securities are now permitted. The exchange position is also unfortunate.'

1–Labour Prime Minister Ramsay MacDonald had resigned on 24 Aug. and set up an all-party 'National' Government in order to seek to combat the financial crisis. Britain abandoned the gold standard on 21 Sept., and the 'National' Government won the popular mandate on 24 Oct. GCF wrote in his diary on 27 Oct. 1931: 'Frank Morley & Tom Eliot both rather gloomy at the absence of any opposition in the new H[ouse] of C[ommons]. That is a real danger . . .'

2–Maurice replied on 23 Oct. with the news that his job as representative of George H. Burr

Affectionately
[Tom]

TO *James Joyce*   cc

20 October 1931   [Faber & Faber Ltd]

Dear Joyce,

Thank you for your letter. As you say you have lost the two last specimens of type, I enclose two more copies.[1] Of the larger of these two, De la Mare is having another page set, the same type with more leads and spacing. We hope very much that this will be satisfactory: it will increase the size of the book from 488 to about 525 pages, which is still a possible bulk. The next larger size type is considerably larger, and would therefore increase materially the cost of production, so that we should be unable to sell the book at a guinea. We should be extremely sorry to have to price the book higher than that.

I will send you the new setting as soon as it is ready. I enclose also a carbon copy of a letter from you to Pinker of October 14th, which I received from Miss Weaver. I confess that Miss Beach's price seems to me prohibitive, unless at best she made considerable concessions in the way of instalments, and in the event [*one line of carbon copy missing at the foot of the page*] thing like that sum at the start would have to price the book pretty high; and then people like Roth could easily carry on by underselling him. So I don't know what to advise.[2]

I am very sorry for all the rest of your bad news: I feared that it would be impossible to obtain satisfaction in Germany, but the difficulty over

---

& Co., bankers, was 'over': he had been advised by his superior that 'in view of the bad times & the necessity to curtail expenses he considered it necessary to close the Italian office.

'He has offered to take me on in London, but this will necessitate my working up an English connection of my own . . .'

1 – JJ wrote from Paris (*c.*15 Oct.): 'I have mislaid in moving here the proof [a specimen page of *Finnegans Wake*] you sent me. The opinion here is that it is good but that the slightly larger and heavier one you spoke of sending would be better. Can I have a page?' (*Letters* III, 232).

2 – JJ wrote: 'I saw Miss Beach. She says Roth has brought out a new American edition of *Ulysses* (10,000 copies!?) and she stands by her terms . . . The people to whom I ceded my flat in London let me down very badly. They cried off the contract they had agreed to thereby worsting me out of £100. There is no redress, according to my solicitors. Also according to the same and this Frankfurt colleague there is none in that Michael & James case except that I have to pay fees and expenses in London Vienna and Frankfurt amounting to £48' (ibid). Sylvia Beach had determined that any American publisher of *Ulysses* must needs pay her $25,000 for the rights.

the flat is a disaster not to have been anticipated. I hope nevertheless that you are finding work more possible in Paris than it was in London this summer.

My wife wishes me to send her love to Mrs Joyce and yourself. Are you going to Zurich in the near future?

Yours cordially,
[T. S. Eliot]

TO *Max Planck* CC

20 October 1931   [Faber & Faber Ltd]

My dear Sir,

I must apologise for not having acknowledged immediately your courtesy in sending me 'Positivismus und Reale Aussenwelt'.[1] I must explain that both I and my colleagues have admired this essay, and we feel that it ought to be circulated in some form in this country. It is of course very much too long to publish in the *Criterion*, except in instalments, and I feel strongly that such an essay would lose much of its effect were it published in two or three parts at an interval of three months (the *Criterion* is published quarterly.) We should like to suggest, therefore, as the best vehicle for circulating this essay, the form of a series of pamphlets which we publish from time to time and of which I send you a few specimens. You will understand that I send you these specimens merely to find out whether you approve of the form, and not because of any relevance of subject matter. The majority of these pamphlets, as you will see from the list on the cover, have been by distinguished politicians and men of letters. We have not yet published a pamphlet by a man of science, and all the more for that reason we should like to be able to introduce this department with a name so eminent as yours.

The margin of profit on pamphlets published at one shilling is small, and we cannot in fact hope to make any profit at all except on those pamphlets which we can sell in very large numbers. We have not, so far, published any pamphlet translated from another language, and this introduces another consideration. After receiving your pamphlet I noticed that it was the same as two articles contributed by you to the *International Forum*. Before going into the arrangements more fully I should like to

1–Planck had despatched a copy of his paper on 31 July. It was published in Leipzig by the Akademische Verlagsgesellschaft (1931).

ask you first whether you are satisfied yourself with this translation, and secondly whether you think Dr Murphy, the editor of the *International Forum* would allow us to use it? Furthermore, are the translation rights vested in the *International Forum*, or should we negotiate exclusively with yourself?

I should be very happy to hear from you that we may be able to come to an agreement for the publication of this essay, which would very much distinguish our series.

I am, my dear Sir
Yours very truly
[T. S. Eliot]

TO *Henry Eliot*

MS Houghton

20 October 1931   68, Clarence Gate Gardens

My dear Henry,

Many thanks for your letter.[1] I don't want you to trouble yourself any further about Liveright & Boni.[2] I will write in a few days.

Affectionately
Tom

---

1 – HWE offered (18 Sept.) to ask Liveright 'whether he has destroyed the plates yet or not'; he asked Ober (the agent for his detective story) 'what steps are customarily taken in such cases'?

2 – T. R. Smith, for Horace Liveright Inc., had written to TSE on 13 Oct. with apologies for the firm's 'inexcusable business carelessness concerning THE WASTELAND [*sic*]': the fault lay with their accounting department, which had overlooked the fact that the contract in question was for five years rather than the usual term of 28 years for copyright – 'and because of this disturbances have been created which certainly seem to have annoyed you, and perhaps rightly'.

Liveright had permitted the *Anthology of Prize Poems* to reprint *TWL* – 'for we felt we had the privilege of doing that according to our agreement with you' – and had been paid $74 for the privilege, with half of that sum having been remitted to TSE. The publishers of the *Anthology* had about 2,000 sets of sheets and could now either remainder them or carry on selling them at a slow rate of demand. Likewise, Liveright still held about 40 bound copies, and 250 unbound copies, of their edition of *TWL*: they too could remainder the stock or continue to sell them until the edition was exhausted. As for the plates of *TWL*, they could destroy them or else sell them to TSE at a nominal price of $57.47 (half the original cost).

Finally, having learned from HWE that TSE wished to publish his collected poems in the American market, Smith remarked that they would be 'very happy, indeed' if 'this company' could undertake to put out such an edition.

TO *Wynyard Browne*[1]   CC

20 October 1931   [*The Criterion*]

Dear Mr Brown,

I am answering your letter of last Saturday, and at the same time apologising for having failed to answer a previous letter from you.[2] First, so far as the previous letter is concerned, I am not sure whether it is possible to discuss the drama regularly in the *Criterion*; I have attempted it twice in former years, and without any great success; but I should be very glad to discuss this and other subjects with you whenever you are in London, and could come to see me; so I hope you will keep this in mind and let me know when you are in town.

As for the Gundolf article, I want to make clear to Clemen that when he suggested it I had no suspicion that Gundolf would die so suddenly, and also I had no intimation that Dr Rychner was going to devote his chronicle to an obituary notice until I received the notice.[3] It was, of course, quite natural and proper that Rychner should do this, but I am rather afraid that it makes another essay on Gundolf at present superfluous. I should, however, like very much to see Clemen's article so that I may form an impression of his writing, but I do not want you to go to any great trouble in the matter yourself. I infer that Clemen has written the article in English. In either case I suggest that you send it to me as it is.

Yours sincerely
[T. S. Eliot)

TO *John Middleton Murry*   TS Berg

20 October 1931   *The Criterion*

My dear John,

Thank you very much for your letter, which gave me genuine pleasure.[4] On the point of your objection, you may be perfectly right: consciously, I had in mind the ordinary chatter of a crowd, and also the general state

1 – Wynyard Browne (1911–64), English playwright.
2 – Browne had written on 12 July to propose undertaking a regular theatre chronicle for the *Criterion*. In an undated note ('Saturday') from Christ's College, Cambridge, he reported: 'Wolfgang Clemen had sent me an artice on Gundolf to correct and forward to you.' Clemen (1909–90) was to be an eminent literary scholar; Professor of English at Munich, 1946–74; author of *Shakespeare's Imagery* (1951) – a revision of his 1936 doctoral dissertation.
3 – Rychner, 'German Chronicle' (obituary essay on Gundolf), C. 11 (Oct. 1931), 96–104.
4 – JMM's letter about 'Coriolan' has not been found.

of paganism in this country; but in any such phrase, there are undertones only audible to the writer, and other undertones ignored by the writer but audible to readers like yourself. Anyway, I can't do anything about it; except to mention that this is a part of a much longer piece, of which the second part is already written, of which the third part is I think writable, and of which I doubt whether I am able to write the fourth part – which must be largely derivative from S. John of the Cross – at all.[1]

I should like to meet Rees:[2] for several reasons – because he is a kind of substitute for you, and I can't see you; because I think he runs the *Adelphi* very well; and because I feel that the *Adelphi* and the *Criterion* must draw closer together because of the political economic social situation (a small witness: the coincidence of our having both mentioned, and nobody else having mentioned, Canon Quick (whom I know nothing about) in connexion with G. B. Shaw).

It is also odd that I have just re-read *Prometheus Unbound*, with, I think, more sympathy than since the age of fifteen, when I read it first with secretive delight.[3]

Affectionately,
Tom

Shall I just write to Rees and ask him to lunch with me? I should like to, but wait to hear from you.

T. S. E.

TO *V. A. Demant*[4]   CC

20 October 1931   [Faber & Faber Ltd]

Dear Sir,

Your letter of the 13th instant with the accompanying papers has been

---

1–See Lyndall Gordon, *T. S. Eliot*, 246 footnote: 'Eliot told Middleton Murry on 20 October 1931 that he doubted that he could write the fourth part on the life of the saint, and on 17 February 1932 he wrote to [Elmer] More that he wished to discuss St John of the Cross when next they met. Of the third part he says no more than that it was writable. My guess is that it would have been about the recovery of spiritual power, still "hidden" from the would-be prophet of part two.'

2–Sir Richard Rees.

3–P. B. Shelley, *Prometheus Unbound* (1820).

4–The Revd Vigo Auguste Demant (1893–1983) trained as an engineer but embraced a wholly different career when he converted to Christianity and became a deacon in 1919, priest in 1920. Following various curacies, he became, while working at St Silas, Kentish Town, London, Director of Research for the Christian Social Council, 1929–33; as noted in the *Oxford Dictionary of National Biography*, he was 'the major theoretician in the

given to me for consideration.[1] It is difficult to judge of the publishing possibilities from such small material, but I am very much interested in your work, and should like to explore the matter further. As I suppose that you are in this neighbourhood much of the time, may I suggest that it would be a pleasure to me if you would look in and see me one morning. My secretary would make an appointment for me.

I was also much interested by some recent contributions of your own to the *Church Times*.

Yours very truly
[T. S. Eliot]

Christendom Group of Anglican Catholic thinkers, whose concern was to establish the centrality of what they termed "Christian sociology", an analysis of society fundamentally rooted in a Catholic and incarnational theology'. The Group's quarterly, *Christendom*, ran from 1931 to 1950. He was vicar of St. John-the-Divine, Richmond, Surrey, 1933–42; Canon Residentiary, 1942–9, at St Paul's Cathedral. He was Canon of Christ Church and Regius Professor of Moral and Pastoral Theology, Oxford, 1949–71. His works include *This Unemployment: Disaster or Opportunity?* (1931), *God, Man and Society* (1933), *Christian Polity* (1936), *The Religious Prospect* (1939) and *Theology of Society* (1947).

On 8 Aug. 1940 TSE was to write this unsolicited recommendation to Sir Stephen Gaselee (Foreign Office): 'My friend the Reverend V. A. Demant, whom I have been associated with intellectually for some years, has been recommended by the Bishop of Bath and Wells for a vacant canonry at Westminster. Demant is, in my opinion, one of the most brilliant, or perhaps the most brilliant, of the younger theologians in England, and I also consider him thoroughly sound both in theology and politics. His book, *The Religious Prospect*, was one of the very few important books of last year. He is a very conscientious parish priest, with a large straggling parish in Richmond, and if he is to make the most of his gifts and do what he should do for Anglican theology in the future, he ought to be freed from this routine.'

Demant remarked at the Requiem Mass for TSE at St Stephen's Church, 17 Feb. 1965: 'The Revd Frank Hillier, to whom Eliot used to go for confession and spiritual direction after the death of Father Philip Bacon, writes to me: "Eliot had, along with that full grown stature of mind, a truly child-like heart – the result of his sense of dependence on GOD. And along with it he had the sense of responsibility to GOD for the use of his talents. To his refinedness of character is due the fact that like his poetry he himself was not easily understood – but unbelievers always recognized his faith"' (*St Stephen's Church Magazine*, Apr. 1965, 9).

1 – 'At a recent meeting of our Research Committee it was felt that the kind of literature we are responsible for encouraging might appeal to your publishing house. A work that we have now in hand is the outcome of a conference on "Christianity and Politics" and we are contemplating a booklet containing the papers already contributed together with supplementary ones. At this stage I submit to you three of the original papers and a summary, and would ask your opinion as to the possibility of your publishing such a booklet, and suggestions for further essays to make the work more complete.'

TO *Vachel Lindsay*[1]   CC

22 October 1931   [Faber & Faber Ltd]

My dear Lindsay,

I was very glad to have your letter of October 3rd, and shall be delighted to see Robert Fitzgerald, and do anything for him I can.[2] I do not get to Cambridge very often, but I have written to him to ask him to let me know whenever he is in London.

With all best wishes,

Yours sincerely,
[T. S. Eliot]

TO *Robert Fitzgerald*[3]   TS Beinecke

22 October 1931   Faber & Faber Ltd

Dear Sir,

I hear from Mr Vachel Lindsay that you are to be at Trinity this year, and I am therefore dropping you a line to say that I hope you will let me know when you are in London at any time and come to see me.

1–Vachel Linsday (1879–1931), writer, militant Christian, peripatetic performance poet, was author of the hugely popular *General Booth Enters into Heaven and Other Poems* (1913) – to which TSE alludes in *Murder in the Cathedral*. It was at TSE's prompting that Michael Roberts included 'General William Booth Enters into Heaven' in *The Faber Book of Modern Verse* (1936). See *Letters of Vachel Lindsay*, ed. Marc Chénetier (1979).

2–Lindsay introduced Robert Fitzgerald – 'a very young poet' – who was to become a student at Trinity College, Cambridge, this year. 'Please let him sit in when there is good talk going, if that is agreeable to you. He is a shy, but very able youth. Critical writing is one of his destinies.' (Lindsay died within weeks of writing this kind letter.)

3–Robert Fitzgerald (1910–85), American poet, critic, and translator of Greek and Latin classics including Euripides, Sophocles and Homer, studied at Harvard, 1929–33, and worked in the 1930s for the *New York Herald Tribune* and *TIME* magazine. He was Boylston Professor of Rhetoric and Oratory at Harvard, 1965–81; Consultant in Poetry to the Library of Congress, 1984–5.

TSE was to write to the Bollingen Foundation on 29 Nov. 1951 (when Fitzgerald was beginning his work on the *Odyssey*): 'I have known Mr Robert Fitzgerald ever since he was a Senior in Harvard College. He is a poet of original merit, who has hitherto produced all too little work of his own. He is a very good Greek scholar – of his scholarship there will no doubt be testimony on better authority than mine; but I speak with some confidence when I say that as a translator of Greek verse into English verse he is quite in the front rank. The publishing firm of which I am a Director (Faber & Faber Ltd) have published in England two of his translations of Greek tragedy – his *Oedipus* and the *Alcestic* [*sic*] which he translated in collaboration with Mr Dudley Fitts. For the project which he has submitted I have not the slightest hesitation in recommending him, and shall look forwards with keen interest to the fruits of his labours.'

Meanwhile I hope that you are enjoying Cambridge and surviving the climate.

> Yours sincerely,
> T. S. Eliot

TO *H. M. Tomlinson*   TS Texas

22 October 1931   [*The Criterion*]

My dear Tomlinson,

I should be very grateful if you were willing to contemplate reviewing for the *Criterion* Leonard Woolf's *After the Deluge: a study of communal psychology* Vol 1. I should like to get it reviewed for the December number, but on the other hand, if that were pressing you too much, and you were still willing to tackle it for the following number, I would much rather leave it to you than find someone else to do it. At any rate may I send you the book? I do not know whether you have seen it already. In any case I am quite incapable of describing it. I cannot help feeling, however, that the title is, if anything, too optimistic.[1]

> Yours ever
> T. S. Eliot

TO *W. H. Auden*   CC

22 October 1931   [Faber & Faber Ltd]

Dear Auden,

Thank you for your letter of the 13th.[2] I look forward to receiving the manuscripts you promise me, and particularly for the following reason. It seems to me on reflection that it would be a good thing to bring out another book of yours rather larger than the first, and in a different form, within a year or so, and I think it would be better to keep 'The Fronny' as a part of this book than to publish it at once. I merely put this suggestion

---

1 – Tomlinson replied (26 Oct.), 'I hope I like it – I'm getting into the soft headed state when I'd rather say nothing than sweat, if I don't like a book: unless, of course, it's a blooming enemy of ours. Then a little exercise does one no harm.' Untitled review, C. 11 (Apr. 1932), 512–14.

2 – 'I will send the reviews of the Skelton and the Saga book soon, also the second half of *the Orators* and *A Birthday Ode* as soon as they come from the typists. Is there any news of the *Fronny*?'

forward for your consideration. You know what you have in hand that you would care to include in a book and also what you intend to write in the immediate future.

Of course if the Hogarth Press or anybody else would like to publish 'The Fronny' separately in the immediate future we should not think of standing in your way. I am merely saying what I think would be the best from everybody's point of view. If you have or will have the material and are interested in the notion of publishing a larger book of collected verse in a year's time I should certainly urge it here very strongly.[1]

As for the election I suppose that the best thing you can do is to mark an X opposite the names of all the candidates in your constituency.[2] This is the only way I can see of fulfilling your obligations towards the lady canvassers who have engaged your attention. But seriously I feel that between two schools of humbug and quackery it is better to support the one which has some expectation of having to carry out a few of its promises than the one which is making promises because it is sure it will not have to fulfil them. After all this election is merely a beginning and not an end.

I enclose a cutting which will give you some inkling of the future of misrepresentation and calumny which you must expect. I discovered it in *Action*, but it is only fair to say that it comes from the correspondence column, for which the editor takes no responsibility.[3]

Yours sincerely
[T. S. Eliot]

1 – WHA replied on 23 Oct.: 'I am relieved at what you say about *The Fronny*. I personally would much rather publish a larger book later but was afraid that you wouldn't risk the expense.'

2 – 'What line is the *Criterion* taking about the Election? I have promised my vote to three very serious and alarming young lady-canvassers, all equally convincing, so I shall have to hide I suppose next Tuesday.'

3 – The only possible source of TSE's remark is a column headed 'A Novelist's Answer', *Action* I: 3 (22 Oct. 1931), 18: 'Mr Harold Nicolson has received the following letter from Mr William Plomer, whose book *Sado* he reviewed in the last issue of *Action*:–

'While thanking you for the compliment you have paid me in reviewing *Sado* at such length in your last issue, may I draw your attention to one or two doubtful points in the review? I am not, as you state, a South African. Even if I were, white South Africans are not necessarily detached from European prejudices. On the contrary, they usually cherish them.

'If my book is, as you say, "pretty feeble" as a novel, I can only hope to do better in the future but is it altogether fair to accuse me of a want of courage, and of having failed to "grasp the nettles"? What nettles? You admit that I have made the homosexual theme "abundantly plain", and at the same time reprove me for reticence. But am I to blame

TO *William Plomer*   TS Texas

22 October 1931   Faber & Faber Ltd

My dear Plomer,

I have been very slow in thanking you for the inscribed copy of *Sado*[1] which you so kindly sent me. When people do send me the books they have written I usually write to thank them at once as a matter of prudence. So you may take it as a testimony of confidence that I waited to write until I had read it. I had no intention of reading the book at all, but I did so. So I can say that I enjoyed it very much. It seemed to me really to throw light on Japan and on a situation which had not been dealt with before. A remark of this sort sounds rather impertinent, but you may perhaps consider that I speak with more authority if I say that I found it thoroughly interesting, very mature and well written.

With many thanks,

Yours sincerely
T. S. Eliot

TO *C. A. Siepmann*   TS BBC/CC dated 16 Oct.

22 October 1931   Faber & Faber Ltd

Dear Siepmann,

Looking over your letter of the 8th October I felt that you might want something more from me than the vague assurances of our conversation at lunch.[2] To put it in writing I have no objection to Allen & Unwin having my four talks in the programme for publication in an inclusive volume of that series. I should want to have control of my own text. That is to say I should want to settle the final text myself. I should not want the publisher

---

because it is not possible to be so frank in this country as in France or Germany or China?

'Finally, calling one of the characters a "type of modern futility" you approvingly quote a "picture of his state of mind" as an indication of what *Action* stands for. You are thus rather unfortunately implying the "modern futility" of *Action* as well, an idea which is naturally far from acceptable to your numerous well-wishers.'

1–*Sado* (Hogarth Press, 1931), a novel.

2–'The B.B.C. has been approached by Messrs. Allen & Unwin, who are anxious to secure rights of publication for all talks in our programme "The Changing World" . . . It is an ambitious scheme and one which should enhance the value of this educational programme . . . We do not, of course, want to interfere with your normal arrangements for publication of your writings, but we think you will agree that there is some advantage in a uniform publication of all talks in a programme which has already created widespread interest.'

merely to take the text as delivered on the microphone or as published in the *Listener*. I mean that in any case of disagreement I might make minor concessions to the B.B.C. but am not prepared to make any concessions for a published text. If, owing to differences of opinion, any or all of the talks are not delivered, then I take it that the agreement would fall through. Secondly the question of terms has not yet been raised. Thirdly, I assume that the authors would be at liberty to use their contributions in the same, or in any other form that they choose at any time.

I cannot, however, help putting on record my strong objection to the principle of re-publishing broadcast talks in book form. If I agree to this publication it is only on the assumption that all the other speakers quite approve of such publication, so that I do not wish to be a solitary obstructionist.

Yours sincerely,
T. S. Eliot

TO *C. M. Grieve*   TS Edinburgh

22 October 1931   Faber & Faber Ltd

Dear Mr Grieve,

I must apologise for my delay in answering your letter of the 8th.[1] I have been trying for some days to compose a letter to Donaghy, but I find it rather difficult, particularly because I am under the impression that he imagines that I have injured him in some way.

I should be very glad to have lunch with you and Major Douglas at your convenience.[2] There are several points which I should like to discuss with him. As a matter of fact I have met him some ten or twelve years ago, but there is no reason why he should remember the meeting.

I am rather busy for the next ten days, but should be very glad to lunch almost any day in the week of the 2nd November if that suited you.[3]

---

1 – Grieve had received a letter from Donaghy. 'He is in the Down County Mental Hospital, Down Patrick, and he says that he is now very much better.' See MacDiarmid, *Letters*, 439–40.

2 – 'I was talking to Major C. H. Douglas last night and discussing the relation of his economic ideas to Nationalism and the idea of atomisation as against the acceptance of any convention. Your name cropped up and Douglas said that he had never met you and would very much like to do so. I wonder if you would care to . . . arrange to meet together for lunch somewhere soon.' C. H. Douglas (1879–1952) was the theorist of Social Credit.

3 – TSE lunched with Douglas and Grieve at the Royal Societies Club on 11 Nov. 1931.

With all best wishes,

Yours sincerely,
T. S. Eliot

TO *F. R. Leavis*   TS L. R. Leavis

22 October 1931   *The Criterion*

Dear Mr Leavis,

I must apologise for keeping your essay on T. F. Powys for so long, and I only hope that this has not interfered with your publishing the essay elsewhere.[1] But as I have not heard from you meanwhile I trust that no harm has been done. After mature consideration I cannot feel that there is any special reason why the *Criterion* should publish an essay on Powys. That is not any criticism of his work, but merely a suggestion that it does not seem particularly to fit in with any of the things which the *Criterion* stands for, and which no one else will defend.

I have quite a different subject on which I wish to approach you. I enjoyed so much your pamphlet in Gordon Fraser's series that I have been dreaming ever since of the hope of getting you into the *Criterion Miscellany*. It seems to me that there is a great deal which might be done in England on the lines of that pamphlet and in the same spirit. I am sending you as a suggestion or merely as a stimulant a short notice which I discovered in a current issue of the American periodical *Poetry*. What is particularly interesting here in connection with the enclosed article is the discovery that just as great absurdities of this kind are committed in England as in America. Of course for the British public one conceives of something of this sort with the proportions reversed. The kind of British folly with only such references to America as will serve to make clear the universality of nonsense. For instance there are institutions in England like the Royal Society of Literature which I believe would not, in the ordinary sense of the phrase, bear exposure to the light of day. Being myself a Fellow of this society, and having no particular reason for retiring from it I can only offer it as a morsel to someone else to bark over.

These are merely random suggestions. I merely want to direct your attention to the possibilities of an examination of the study of literature

1–FRL, who had submitted a piece on T. F. Powys's novel *Unclay* (1931), wrote on 14 July: 'It is more for his sake than mine (if I may say so in all modesty) that I hope it can be published in the *Criterion*. He seems to me a great writer who has been shamefully neglected.'

in Britain today which should be conducted with concrete illustrations such as these.

Yours very sincerely
T. S. Eliot

TO *Bernard Bandler*   TS Beinecke

22 October 1931   *The Criterion*

Dear Mr Bandler,

I find I have not yet acknowledged your letter of August 19th enclosing your essay on Charles du Bos.[1] I shall be very glad indeed to publish it if there is no immediate haste. I am afraid that du Bos is almost as unknown in England as he is in America. Nevertheless it is up to the *Criterion* to do something for him if anyone can. I may have to hold the essay up, however, for six months or so. Let me know if that does not suit you.[2]

Sincerely yours,
T. S. Eliot

TO *Kay Boyle*   CC

23 October 1931   [*The Criterion*]

Dear Madam,

Thank you for your letter of the 19th.[3] I am sorry to hear that you have twice written to me to ask me about this story. As for the terms, it is of course far beyond the means of the *Criterion* or, I believe, of any other English periodical to offer you anything like the payment which you got from America. So I think that the only thing I can do in the circumstances is to return you the story herewith, as you say it is your only copy, and to ask you to let me see it again after publication in America has been arranged.

1–Not found.
2–Not published in *C*.
3–Boyle had 'twice sent letters' asking after 'Three Little Men', of which TSE had the only copy. 'I would be very glad if you would use it, but I should like to know your terms. The lowest price they pay me in America is $200 for a short piece, and as I am far from rich at the moment, and as publication in England *first* rather spoils the story for the American market, I have to think of such tedious matters.' 'Three Little Men', *C*. 12 (Oct. 1932), 17–23.

I should be very glad to consider the other story which you mention.

Yours very truly,

[T. S. Eliot]

то *A. L. Rowse*

23 October 1931   Faber & Faber Ltd

Dear Rowse,

What an exasperating fellow you are to write in this way, and to come to London apparently for the first time in five years and not let me know until you have arrived and are on the point of leaving.[1]

But as to the content of your letter I hope that you are not really so silly as to imagine that there is any connection between my not having written to you for some time and the possibility of my having been annoyed by any of your remarks about politics in your last letter. I was, at the time, slightly annoyed by your remarks about Charles Whibley, which I know to be unjust, because he was a close friend of mine; but as you did not know him very well, and as you had no reason for knowing that I did know him well, I should have been more than silly myself to have cherished irritation. As for the general political observations, I am glad to believe that there was more agreement than difference between us.

I have heard that Mirsky's *Lenin* is very good.[2] I had a review copy, but seem to have given it out to somebody without having taken any record of who it was, and no review has ever been sent. The only difficulty about reviewing it now is that so much time has elapsed. If you could think of some more recent book to review in connection with which *Lenin* could be mentioned I should be very content.

I mean to write you a long letter as soon as I have time about *Politics and the Younger Generation.*

Ever yours

T. S. Eliot

---

1 – ALR wrote in an undated letter from 1 Brunswick Square, London – '(for a day, or possibly two)' – 'I hope you are not annoyed with me for having been so cantankerous about politics earlier in the summer . . . I'm frightened to ask for you when I go to Fabers now!'
2 – ALR asked, 'may I send a review of Mirsky's *Lenin*, which is a very good little book.' No review of D. S. Mirsky's *Lenin* (1931) appeared in *C.*

28 October 1931   Faber & Faber Ltd

My dear Mary,

Thank you very much for your sweet letter.[1] It is a great satisfaction to me if you do like the poem – or part of a poem, for it is merely the first of four sections of which only one other is written. I have found it an interesting problem to try to work out how to write a poem which should be in *one* aspect, and that the most obvious, a political satire. So far, I do not seem to have succeeded, because one reader – quite an intelligent German – wrote to me of this fragment as being 'militarist' – I should have thought that if anything it was distinctly the contrary.[2]

No, Vivienne is not more ill.[3] Except for lack of fresh air and external stimulus, on which she is always dependent, I think she is much as you saw her this summer. I mean there is no particular acute problem at the moment, only the permanent one. There are always many things which I could explain much more easily and naturally if I could normally see you from time to time alone: but it would take a long talk merely to explain why that, from my side I mean, is never proposed. But, as for your being able to be of use to her, I am always sure of that. I should very much like to come and dine with you soon, and I think surely she would love to come – especially at this moment, it would be a help. But also, I should be grateful if you could occasionally see her without me: the more people she can see without me the more people I might be able to see without her! but that is not the point – which is that if she can be persuaded to believe that people she likes want to see *her*, the more self-confidence and independence she might acquire. And also, I wish that you might some time induce her to go out of doors with you. She can't *drive* without me or a driver; but I see no physical reason why she should not walk a little,

---

1 – Mary Hutchinson wrote ('October') that *Triumphal March* 'remains to excite me – for your words never [fail] to have that beautiful moving and I must say exciting quality. Thank you.'

2 – In response to a student essay, sent in Sept. 1957 by Mary C. Petrella (Rhode Island, USA), TSE was to write: 'I am much interested by what you say and struck by certain incidental remarks. Your emphasis on compassion and your comment which I think is quite true, that satire is not in my make-up at all.'

3 – Of VHE, Hutchinson asked: 'Is she very much more ill than she was? Can I really be of any use to her? I am so often puzzled about her – I also feel powerless – I wish you would tell me about her though perhaps you would prefer me just to come and see her quite simply – Would you both come and dine one night next week or the week after?'

or go out in somebody's else conveyance; and also the present situation considerably limits my activity.

Perhaps you will ring her up or drop a note to her suggesting a night for dinner soon. I should so like to see you; and Jack, if he remembers me.

Ever affectionately,

Tom

P.S. I am terribly depressed by the election![1]

TO *Roger Hinks*[2]

CC

28 October 1931   [*The Criterion*]

My dear Hinks,

Thank you for your note of the 26th. I shall be very glad to have your chronicle by the 9th November.[3] I understand that you have seen a copy of Herbert Read's *Meaning of Art*.[4] I want to have some notice of this book in the *Criterion*, and therefore am asking you whether you propose to do a review of it yourself, because if you do not want to review it I shall try to find someone else. I thought his selections of illustrations for the book extremely good.

Yours ever,

[T. S. Eliot]

1–In the General Election on 27 Oct., the Conservatives won 472 seats, Labour only 52.
2–Roger Hinks (1903–63) – son of Arthur Hinks (Secretary of the Royal Astronomical Society and Gresham Lecturer in Astronomy) – was educated at Trinity College, Cambridge, and at the British School in Rome. From 1926 to 1939 he was Assistant Keeper in the Department of Greek and Roman Antiquities, British Museum, from which he resigned in consequence of a scandal caused by his arrangements for deep-cleaning the Elgin Marbles. He later worked at the Warburg Institute, at the British Legation in Stockholm, and for the British Council (Rome, The Netherlands, Greece, Paris). His writings include *Carolingian Art* (1935), *Myth and Allegory in Ancient Art* (1939) and *Caravaggio: His Life – His Legend – His Works* (1953). See also 'Roger Hinks', *Burlington Magazine* 105: 4738 (Sept. 1964), 423–34; and *The Gymnasium of the Mind: The Journals of Roger Hinks, 1933–1963*, ed. John Goldsmith (1984).
3–Chronicle based on 'the Ozenfant book'.
4–HR's *Meaning of Art* was published by F&F on 29 Oct. 1931.

TO *D. S. Mirsky*   CC

28 October 1931   [Faber & Faber Ltd]

Dear Mirsky,

Thank you for your letter of the 26th.[1] I am very glad to hear that you might be willing to do translating work. At the moment there is nothing on hand unarranged for to offer you, but we will keep a note about the matter in the hope and likelihood of something turning up which would suit you.

I should be very glad if we could meet before long. Would Tuesday or Wednesday the 3rd or 4th November suit you for lunch?

Yours sincerely,
[T. S. Eliot]

TO *F. R. Leavis*   TS Texas

28 October 1931   *The Criterion*

Dear Mr Leavis,

I am glad to get your letter of the 23rd. I hope you will go ahead with preparing to do such a pamphlet in what spare time you have. I quite understand the difficulty, and the necessity for producing serious work.[2] Meanwhile I trust that the *Criterion* may receive a review copy of your forthcoming book.

I find it a little difficult to understand why Cambridge worries so much about Montgomery Belgion. Is it supposed that everything published in the *Criterion* represents an official policy or a party point of view? After all, Belgion is at least interested in some of the things which deserve interest and for which few periodicals except the *Criterion* find any space at all. If

1–Mirsky, who needed money, asked whether he could do some translating for F&F: he had four languages (Russian, French, German, Italian), and preferred anything to fiction and drama.
2–FRL had replied to TSE's letter of 22 Oct.: 'Yes, there is plenty of material for such a pamphlet as you suggest: it needs doing . . . The difficulty is to find time. I live by teaching, & that means doing a great deal; & at present I am trying to put into a shape that I could bear to publish some work with a scholarly enough appearance to offset the damage my very precarious academic status will suffer when my book on modern poetry [*New Bearings in English Poetry* (1932)] comes out (i.e. after Christmas). The proposed pamphlet won't raise my "stock" here, which (I have been told) is "very low". But I should like to write it, & will see what I can do in the Christmas vacation. And so I yield to my weakness, which (I gather from Richards) is that I'm a "moral hero". But I'd better keep off the teaching of English in Universities.'

he irritates people, is it not to some extent at least a valuable stimulant?[1] But perhaps my failure to see why you take the matter so seriously is due to my misfortune in having been unable to visit Cambridge for a long time, and therefore, no doubt, being out of touch with its intellectual pulse. I hope I may be able to come down for a weekend this winter, but I am not sure.

Meanwhile can you give me two pieces of information? Where is Richards at the moment, as I have not heard from him for about ten months. Second, do you ever come up to London?[2]

Yours sincerely
T. S. Eliot

TO F. B. Folsom

cc

29 October 1931   [Faber & Faber Ltd]

Dear Mr Folsom,

I have your letter of the 27th. A certain amount of work has already been done on the subject in which you are interested.[3] There is for instance a fairly recent book by Matthew Josephson called *Portrait of the Artist as an American*.[4] This is, of course, not to say that there is no need for anything more to be written. It is very difficult for me to say very much about the subject myself as I am perhaps too closely involved to be able to generalize about *causes*, and I should be anxious not to attribute my own motives indiscriminately to others. Pound is perhaps the most significant of my own generation. But it would be much easier to talk to

---

1–Leavis had protested (23 Oct.), 'Can't something be done about Montgomery ("Mummery" they call him here) Belgion? You would hardly believe how he's used here to discredit those of us who have insisted on treating the "Criterion" as something important. One hoped after his chastisement by Richards to have a rest from him. Not that a critique of Ricardianism (especially of the Ogdenian side of Richards) isn't wanted. But surely M.B.'s irresponsible & stupid exhibitionism merely queers the pitch?'

2–FRL replied that IAR had returned to Magdalene College; and that he himself might at some time face the 'ant-heap' of London – perhaps by way of escorting his wife to the British Museum 'where she will probably be wanting to look up something (my best material in "Mass Civilization" came from her stores: she has just finished "Fiction & the Reading Public" – social-anthropological, with the bent suggested by my pamphlet).'

3–Folsom was proposing to read a paper at Merton College, Oxford, on the subject of 'the more important expatriate Americans' – including Whistler, Henry James, EP and TSE – with the aim of 'analyzing if possible the effect which transplantation has had on the art of each.'

4–Matthew Josephson, *Portrait of the Artist as an American* (1930).

710 TSE at forty-three

you about the matter than try to put anything on paper. So as you make the suggestion I should be very glad if you would let me know, if possible in advance, when you are coming to London.

Please give my kind regards to Mr Blunden and to the Bodley Society.[1]

I imagine from your name that you may possibly be of New England origin.

Yours sincerely,
[T. S. Eliot]

TO *Max Planck*   CC

29 October 1931   [Faber & Faber Ltd]

My dear Sir,

I thank you for your letter of the 24th instant and am gratified to learn that you approve of the form of publication which we propose.[2] As for the translation I am writing to Dr Murphy, and you shall hear from me further.

I am, my dear Sir,
Yours very truly
[T. S. Eliot]

TO *James Murphy*[3]   CC

29 October 1931   [Faber & Faber Ltd]

Dear Dr Murphy,

I owe you a letter of apology for having failed to provide you with the article on Contemporary English Literature which I more or less promised and fully intended.[4] But a number of irritating small jobs have turned up

---

1–Folsom reported that his tutor, Edmund Blunden, had encouraged him to contact TSE.
2–Planck approved of the format proposed for *Positivismus und reale Aussenwelt*. 'But I ask you . . . to come to terms with Dr [James] Murphy, because, as you know, I have given the essay to *The International Forum*. The translation is, so far as I have checked, satisfactory. Incidentally, I have not handed over the translation rights exclusively to *The International Forum*.'
3–Editor, *The International Forum*.
4–Murphy approached TSE on 16 May 1931 for 'an article on the tendency of the very latest literature in England, including the poetic literature. You need have no hesitancy whatsoever about slam-banging, because when one writes for an international audience I think that a little severe selection in the presentation of British authors that are representative ought to be made.'

this year which have proved more than my indifferent energy can cope with. I should still like to consider writing the article, but as I am now situated I cannot even think of what I should say until the beginning of the New Year. Will you let me know if you would still be interested or not?

Another matter has arisen which I should like to discuss with you. Some time ago a German friend of mine recommended very strongly to me Dr Max Planck's pamphlet *Positivismus und Reale Aussenwelt* for possible publication in the *Criterion* or in some other form. I procured a copy of the pamphlet from Dr Planck myself and only after I had begun to read it realised that it was identical with the English translation published in two numbers of the *International Forum*.

Now we should very much like to publish a translation of this pamphlet in our series called the Criterion Miscellany, which are sold at one shilling each. Dr Planck has given me his authority and approval, but as you have already published the pamphlet in the *Forum* I thought it only right to discuss the matter with you as well. The publication which we project is not, of course, even second serial rights. It is a separate publication of the pamphlet. This would be, however, our first attempt to publish in such a form and at such a price anything translated from another language, and that raises the question of Ways and Means. These pamphlets are not, and are not intended to be a very profitable venture. So far as self-interest is concerned, they may be considered rather as a form of advertisement, and as a way of showing the enterprise of our firm. On all of the 35 pamphlets which [we] have so far published, most of them by quite undistinguished people, we have given the same terms – that is, a straight 10% royalty. Even a sale of several thousand copies brings us in only a few pounds, and on some items we lose, and are prepared to lose money. We do not think that Dr Planck's pamphlet, by the nature of the subject and treatment, could possibly have a large circulation. We wish to publish it as an addition to a distinguished list of names, and because it is an essay which ought to be available to those people in England who are capable of appreciating it.

You will understand, therefore, that we cannot afford to publish if we have to pay a fee to a translator as well as 10% royalty to the author. There are only two possibilities – one is that I or one of my friends should translate it out of good-will without taking any fee, and the other is that you might give your permission to use the translation in the *International Forum*. As I say, it would be economically unreasonable to consider paying anybody a fee, but we should be prepared, if of course we had Dr. Planck's agreement, to split the royalty between the author and the translator. The profits for both author and publisher are trifling at best, but we do feel that it would be a good thing if such a valuable essay as this, by one of the most distinguished physicists of the world, could be circulated in this form.

I hope I may hear from you soon about this matter.[1]

> With all best wishes, I am
> Yours sincerely
> [T. S. Eliot]

TO *Marguerite Caetani*   CC

30 October 1931   [Faber & Faber Ltd]

Dear Marguerite,

Thank you for your letter of the 20th, enclosing your cheque for £30, which I return herewith. Perhaps I ought to apologise for not having explained the *Criterion* position to you before, and so having saved you the trouble. You will remember that the guarantees of annual subsidy of which there were nine or ten were for three years, expiring in 1930. During that time one of the guarantors died, and at the end of the time another found himself unable to continue the subscription. We reviewed the whole matter and came to the conclusion that for the present we would not ask for any of the guarantees to be renewed, and would not approach any other possible guarantors, but would carry on the *Criterion* wholly at the expense of the firm. Accordingly I return your cheque cancelled.

I should, however, be glad to have a cheque for £15 for the poem.[2] I have not heard a word from Ungaretti,[3] but curiously enough I have had exactly the same application from an Italian journalist in London, a Dr Govoni, who I believe represents the *Gazzetta del Popolo*. As I had already some acquaintance with Dr Govoni I have promised him some sort of reply for his paper.[4] I did not know that Ungaretti was associated with the

---

1 – See further TSE's next letter to Planck, 5 Nov.
2 – 'Triumphal March'.
3 – 'I can't make out from Ungaretti's letters if he has already sent you this [?]. He at any rate has asked me to beg you to reply and if possible to ask an answer from any other representative American or English poet if you could possibly do so.' Giuseppe Ungaretti (1888–1970), Italian poet.
4 – Dr G. C. Govoni, London correspondent of the Italian newspaper *Gazzetta del Popolo*, had asked TSE on 20 Oct. 1931 to complete a questionnaire that he was sending to 'the greatest writers and poets of all nations'; his questions included 'What are today the new sensibilities that are seeking a new material on inspiration and new original forms?' and

same journal. Incidentally I discussed the matter of other contributions with Govoni, and have offered him introductions to other people.

I look forward keenly to seeing you during the week of the 9th.[1]

Affectionately

[Tom]

TO *J. S. Barnes*   CC

[30 October 1931][2]   [Faber & Faber Ltd]

Dear Jim,

This is just to thank you for your note, and to say how very sorry I was not to see you during your brief visit.[3] I rang up Higham, but only succeeded in getting, after two attempts, his secretary, who told me that your book[4] had already been sent to some other publisher. All I could do, therefore, was to leave word that I should like to see it if it came back to him. Do let me know how things go with you, and whether or when you will be returning to London. I believe that my brother-in-law also will probably be obliged to give up his business in Rome, owing to the economic depression there.

I am hoping to see Mary next week.

Yours ever

[T. S. Eliot]

TO *Aline Lion*   CC

3 November 1931   [*The Criterion*]

Dear Miss Lion,

I have given a good deal of thought to the matter, and I must confess that I do not see any more clearly than you do how your essay could possibly be cut without thorough revision. It is quite impossible on account of

---

'Which are the new technical possibilities of poetry and what value do you attribute to its evolution, which from the old rhythms has led to the blank verses and from this to the freedom of words?'

1 – 'Lélia and I are certainly spending from Nov. 9 to 14th in London.'

2 – Misdated 10 Oct. 1931.

3 – Barnes, who had been visiting London – 'Very likely I shall be going a few days to Rome & I shall certainly look up Haighey [MHW]' – had authorised David Higham to offer his book to F&F.

4 – Unidentified.

the matter which I [have] promised to publish to include the whole essay in the December number, or even in the following number, as the body of the *Criterion* can vary only between about 65 and 80 pages; and you will understand that 37 pages would be quite disproportionate. The best suggestion which I can make, and I hope you will find it acceptable, is to divide the essay into two at a point at which there is a natural break, that is to say toward the middle of the fifth galley page. It is in itself more than 15 pages, but I could just do that in this number, and publish the suite in the March number. I do not think that this break is unnatural, as it is in the second part chiefly that you are concerned with the Papal Encyclical.[1]

If this suggestion is not acceptable to you I must confess that I am at a loss for any other, but if you think that some other review might publish the essay I should not of course wish to stand in your way. In any case I hope you will be so kind as to let me know by return of post, as time has become rather pressing.

I saw Mrs Fremantle yesterday, but as Marguerite is to be in London next week and as in fact I do not know very much more than Mrs Fremantle herself what is required, I suggest that the best thing would be for me to arrange a direct interview.[2]

Yours very sincerely
[T. S. Eliot]

TO *Eric Blair*[3]   CC

3 November 1931   [Faber & Faber Ltd]

Dear Mr Blair,

It is true that Rees spoke to me about you, and I am glad to hear from you. In general the prospects of publishing translations of French novels

1 – The condemnation of socialism by the Pope in his last Encyclical.
2 – Anne Fremantle (1909–2002) – author; friend of W. H. Auden, Evelyn Waugh and other intellectuals and writers; prominent Catholic convert – who was working at this time for the *London Mercury*, wrote (29 Oct.) that Aline Lion had suggested she contact TSE because she wished her to become the British agent for *Commerce*.
3 – Eric Blair – George Orwell (1903–50) – novelist and essayist, was educated at Eton College and worked for the Burma police, 1921–7, before resolving to endure periods of slumming in London and Paris. From Feb. 1941 to Nov. 1943 he worked for the Far Eastern Section of the BBC, based at Oxford Street, London, where he became a friend of William Empson. His publications include *Down and Out in Paris and London* (1933), *The Clergyman's Daughter* (1935), *Keep the Aspidistra Flying* (1936), *The Road to Wigan Pier* (1937), *Homage to Catalonia* (1938), *Coming Up for Air* (1939), *Animal Farm* (1945), *Nineteen Eighty-Four* (1949). See *The Complete Works of George Orwell*, ed. Peter Davison (20 vols, 1986–98).

is [*sic*] never bright, but this might be an exception, and I should be very glad if you could lend us the French book to read.[1] I would let you know our decision within a reasonable length of time, and if that decision was favourable I should then have to ask you for a few specimen pages. The subject of the story rather suggests that of *Bubu de Montparnasse* which I thought a very fine novel. It has never been translated into English so far as I know.

> Yours every truly,
> [T. S. Eliot]

TO *F. S. Oliver*   cc

3 November 1931   [*The Criterion*]

Dear Oliver,

I was very glad to get your letter of the 21st, though sorry for your news about yourself which, however, is of a sort which is never unexpected at the present time.[2] I do hope, however, that you will not find the winter in Scotland too inclement to be safe for you.

I hope that you found the election satisfactory. All that I feel about it myself is that had it been otherwise it would have been far worse; but I confess I do not look forward to this winter with much hopefulness.

TSE was to write to Ian Angus on 25 July 1963: 'I regret that I did not know George Orwell well enough to have had any correspondence with him. He was a man whose integrity I highly respected and I liked him personally . . . I am sorry for my own sake that I did not know him well enough to have correspondence to offer' (TS University College London). To Howard R. Fink (a PhD student at London University), 2 Aug. 1963: 'I remember him and his wife lunching with me once, but I am afraid I have no correspondence which could be anything more than merely making an appointment and I do not remember in what year that meeting took place.'

1–Blair, whom Richard Rees had mentioned to TSE, wrote on 30 Oct. to recommend 'a rather interesting French novel called *À la Belle de Nuit*, by Jacques Roberti. It is the story of a prostitute, quite true to life so far as one can judge, & most ruthlessly told, but not a mere exploitation of a dirty subject. It seems to me worth translating, and if Messrs. Faber & Faber would like to try a translation I think I could do the job as well as most people. I don't pretend to have a scholarly knowledge of French, but I am used to mixing in the kind of French society described in the novel, & I know French slang, if not well, better than the majority of Englishmen. I don't know whether such a book would sell, but I believe Zola's novels sell in England, & this author seems to have some resemblance to Zola.'

2–Oliver had installed himself at Edgerston, Jedburgh, 'for the rest of [his] life': 'like many other people I am oppressed by "a financial stringency" & the future is very doubtful'.

I am very much gratified by your approval of the *Criterion*.[1] As for your comment on Scottish Nationalism[2] I was much struck by it and raised the point recently with a Scottish Nationalist friend. It struck him as of such importance that the Nationalists ought to provide themselves with an answer, even if they had none ready. However, here is verbatim the report which I received, the name of the author only being omitted. So that is that. I am myself only an uneducated though interested onlooker, but I still hope that I may some day, like Dr Johnson, pay a visit to your country.

'It disturbs me to learn that a Scot so influential as Mr F. S. Oliver should apprehend the dominance of Glasgow in the Scottish Nationalist movement. Actually, this implies a complete misunderstanding of the situation. The movement is, if anything, Highland, Tory, and a swing away from industrialism and its effects.'

'The headquarters of the Party are in Glasgow – largely because it started effectively among Highland Students at the University. It argues just now largely in economic terms – because the electorate will listen to nothing else at the moment. It is stealing votes from Labour – because it can, in the issue, talk of something more than wages.'

'The essential strength of the movement is in Inverness and the fine branch there, made up of solicitors, parsons, chartered accountants, and some landed gentry, over and above the rank and file.'

'Take it as a simple quotation of arithmetic. The population of Scotland is about 4,000,000. Allow Glasgow and district 1,500,000. Can't the balance of 2,500,000 look after themselves and outvote Glasgow?'

'I do wish that Mr Oliver could find time to have a talk with a Nationalist of the best type – somebody like Neil Gunn or young Oliver Brown.[3] Would he like to see the literature?'

With best wishes to Mrs Oliver and yourself, in which my wife joins me.

Yours very sincerely,

[T. S. Eliot]

---

1 – 'I thought your Oct. number was very good. The C seems to gain in strength each number.'
2 – 'Politically speaking my greatest objection to Scottish nationalism is that it wd. put Scotland under the heel of Glasgow & its environs, i.e. under a largely alien population whose God is the machine. I'd rather bear the gentler, if occasionally stupid, control of Whitehall.'
3 – Oliver Brown (1902–76), celebrated Scottish nationalist, academic, intellectual and teacher.

3 November 1931   [*The Criterion*]

Dear Smyth,

Many thanks for your undated letter enclosing the review.[1] Except for the difference of religious outlook I should be inclined to exclaim 'Whibley redivivus'! It seems to me a good onslaught though the book might also be attacked directly from another angle; that is, the defect of any constructive economic programme. The only phrase that I query is the reference to Cornwall mining origin and All Souls. It is of course legitimate inasmuch as it was made on the wrapper of the book, but I felt that the reference on the wrapper was itself in doubtful taste. Of course the combination of Cornish non-conformity, seriousness and tin-mines with All Souls does account for Rowse, but I still hold with Coleridge, I think it was, that only the inside of the book matters.

I hold out to myself vague hopes of coming down to Cambridge during the term. All I can say, however, is that if I come I will come to Corpus, and if I come to Corpus I hope it may be as your guest.[2] I saw Penty two or three days ago, and he spoke very warmly of you. I agree with you about the election, and of course whenever the Bishop of London finds an opportunity to make a fool of himself he is sure to do it. The only marvel is that he doesn't find more opportunities.[3]

                                        Yours ever
                                        [T. S. Eliot]

---

1 – 'I have spent a good deal of trouble on it,' said Smyth of his review of ALR's *Politics and the Younger Generation*, C. 11 (Jan. 1931), 304–13, 'but it is the concluding paragraph for which I most desire your approbation'. He replied to this letter on 8 Nov. ('Feast of the Martyrs, Confessors, and Doctors of the Church of England'): 'I am relieved that you have accepted the article: I had my doubts whether the Extreme Right of the *Criterion* group ought to be allowed to go for the Extreme Left of the same group with such fratricidal violence. As to your criticism: the Cornish village (it is true that mining is not mentioned) is referred to in the book (p. 222) and "Fellow of All Souls College, Oxford" stands on the title page – wld not Coleridge have allowed that to be a part of the inside of the book? I think I am within my rights.'

2 – Smyth hoped TSE might come to Corpus Christi College for a weekend during the term.

3 – 'The Election seems to me to be the General Strike over again – the victory of political democracy over economic democracy. We have registered our protest against the control of Parliament by the T.U.C. [Trades Union Congress] ... As the unknown "clergyman" said at the London Diocesan Conference apropos of the winged words of the Bishop of London, "This isn't politics, it is spiritual guidance." Seriously, I hope that during the next 5 years the Church will hold a watching brief for social justice.' Smyth responded (8 Nov.) to TSE's comment here: 'The Bp. of London did apologize – at least, he thanked the unknown layman, & said that he was perfectly within his rights: *vide* the *Church Times* account.'

TO *Hugh Ross Williamson*   CC

3 November 1931   [Faber & Faber Ltd]

Dear Mr Williamson,

I have now read Mary Butts's 'Alexander of Macedon'[1] and it has been read also by two of my colleagues.[2] I agree that it is a very good book of its kind, and it certainly deserves to be published. It shows both knowledge and a special enthusiasm for the subject as well as the literary ability which I expected from the author of *Asshe of* [   ].[3] We all felt, however, that it was not a type of book which could have a very wide public at the best, and in the present state of things we do not feel that it would be wise to offer to publish it.

I am therefore returning it direct to you with many thanks and regrets. In your letter of the 15 September you said that you were sending the illustrations with it. It has just occurred to me that I ought to have let you know immediately that no illustrations came, only the text.

Looking forward to seeing you,

Yours sincerely
[T. S. Eliot]

TO *Eleanor Hinkley*   TS Houghton

3 November 1931   Faber & Faber Ltd

Dear Eleanor,

This note is merely to inform you (for if I wait till I can write a proper letter I shall certainly leave it till too late) that after negotiation with Mr César Saerchinger, a slightly Jewish gentleman, subsequently conducted with his substitute Mr Raymond Gram Swing, I am going to broadcast a fifteen-minute comprehensive biographical and critical study of John Dryden and all his works, by the courtesy of the Columbia Broadcast[ing] Corpn. Inc. (I think it is called) on the SUNDAY *13th December* next at 5.30 Greenwich time, that is 12.30 N.Y. time. *Retenez bien le date*:

1–Williamson had submitted Mary Butts's historical narrative 'Episodes in the Life of Alexander of Macedon' on 10 Sept. The work was to be published as *The Macedonian* (1933).
2–Mary Butts had been Mrs John Rodker (married in 1918, they separated in 1920, divorced in 1926). Rodker's Ovid Press had published early work by TSE, whom Butts had met at the time. See Nathalie Blondel, *Mary Butts: Scenes from the Life* (1998).
3–Space for remainder of title left blank on carbon ts. *Ashe of Rings* was reviewed by TSE in C. 3 (1925), 209.

will you be so kind as to advise any near relatives who may possess sets? The date has only just been fixed. The negotiations were prolonged and difficult and nice, as all important political negotiations are; and I feel very strongly that I got the worst of them. But how could I expect to get the better of a N.Y. radio man? Mr Saerchinger maintained that as the British Broadcasting pay twelve guineas for half an hour, I ought to be satisfied with fifteen guineas for 14 minutes; he was not affected by my argument that it is more difficult to say anything – at least twice as difficult – in 15 minutes than in 30, and that therefore I ought to have 30 guineas; nor was he touched by my request to be paid in dollars instead of pounds. I finally said I would give way just for this once, because it would be a pleasure to me to be able to address my American friends; but that I would not do it again for the money. It did not seem to have occurred to him that they might ever want me to speak again, so the matter was settled amicably.

I trust that the atmospherics or statics will not be too bad. Mr Saerchinger says that what it costs the company to do this is simply cruel, because they have to pay the transatlantic telephone company for the use of their lines.

I must thank Aunt Susie for letting me know about young Barbara, and sending the cutting. I hear from other sources that Mr Dane is highly thought of, and everything seems to be perfect. And I suppose they will be married in the spring or summer? It all makes me feel very aged! We should like to have been present for Chardy's wedding;[1] but that was too sudden for us to come: perhaps young Barbara will give us more warning. I did not approve of Chardy's being married so late in the day, it suggests heresy; 10 a.m. is the proper time, and have *breakfast* afterwards.

I wonder if you have any interesting or amusing English lecturers this year. Do let me know what you are doing, and how the Brontës are progressing.

With much love to both of you from Vivienne and myself,

Tom

P.S. Did you ever get a copy of *Triumphal March* that I sent?[2] If so, can Miss Wise explain it?

1 – Charlotte Stearns Smith (b. 1911), daughter of George Laurence and Charlotte Eliot Smith, married Agnew Allen Talcott on 30 Oct. 1931. HWE would tell TSE on 14 Dec. 1931: 'Chardy and Agnew are a charming couple; he is a fine young chap, in my opinion, and they seem admirably suited.'
2 – *Triumphal March* (Ariel Poem 35), with two illustrations by E. McKnight Kauffer, was published on 8 Oct. 1931, in a run of 2,000 copies.

TO *Willa Muir*[1]   CC

Dear Mrs Muir,

Thank you for your letter of the 1st.[2] Your suggestion sounds very interesting, and I should be delighted to look at the chapter you suggest sending. The only difficulty that I foresee – one to which I am accustomed, and which is the most troublesome of all – that is to say the difficulty of length. 15,000 words is impossible; even 10,000 words is extremely

---

1 – Willa Muir, née Anderson (1890–1970), novelist and translator, married the writer Edwin Muir (1887–1959) in 1919. Her works include *Women: An Enquiry* (1925) and the novels *Imagined Corners* (1931) and *Mrs Ritchie* (1933). The Muirs' joint translations included works by Gerhart Hauptmann, Lion Feuchtwanger and Heinrich Mann ('I am a better translator than he is,' she reflected in 1953; 'Most of this translation, especially Kafka, has been done by ME. Edwin only helped'). See further Willa Muir, *Belonging: A Memoir* (1968), Edwin Muir, *An Autobiography* (1953); Aileen Christianson, *Moving in Circles: Willa Muir's Writings* (2007).

2 – 'Edwin and I are translating the third volume of an extraordinary trilogy [*The Sleepwalkers*] written by a new Austrian writer, Hermann Broch, a trilogy which is more than a simple survey of three generations (1883, 1903, 1918), (although at its lowest it might be called that) because it works out a profound and fascinating analysis of the tendency of our whole age. Herr Broch is a mathematician by profession, obviously a logician and a philosopher, and in these books a literary artist on a very high level. It may sound absurd to one who has not read him, but this work seems to us a very important book both as literature and as philosophical analysis. The philosophical excursus (which explains the aim of the whole three books) occurs in the last volume, which is in itself a daring experiment in technique (I mean, it runs in parallel strands) and the excursus comes in at intervals, a chapter at a time. Now, this being the kind of country it is, such a philosophical essay may not be recognised by the novel-reviewers as it deserves, and we both think it should be printed by itself, so that intelligent people may have access to it. Herr Broch is willing and eager to have it so printed: and I write to you now to ask if you would care to see it as a possible contribution to the *Criterion*? It is called "Disintegration of Values": it is in nine chapters, and comes in all to between 10,000 and 15,000 words. The difficulty is that it would have to appear before the trilogy, which is due to come out sometime in the spring: so that if you could not find room for it before that, there is no use in bothering you with it.

'The general thesis, starting from the significant absence of ornament in modern style, architectural & otherwise, is that the "point of plausibility", i.e., the probable focus of convergence for all lines of enquiry in a certain age, has been pushed further and further out into the infinite, so that now instead of a relatively near point of plausibility (such as the mediaeval God) we have now an infinitely receding point of plausibility, thus making all lines of enquiry, all lines of development, run in parallel strands which have no chance of meeting, as far as we can see at present. This straining out into space too great for us, he would say, leaves us incapable of ornament, for we are committed to the severity of an abstract world. But the whole argument is so fascinatingly worked out that it is stimulating to read. He has a notion of saving us all from utter & final disintegration: which is some comfort! The trilogy, I may say, is called *The Sleepwalkers*. The sleepwalkers – that is all of us.'

awkward, and can only be managed when the other contributions which I want to use in a number happen to be very short. The proper length of a *Criterion* article is 5000 words – 7000 can just be managed, even 8000 distorts the shape of a number. So before we go any further I should like to ask you whether any part can be separated from the part you have in mind, preferably of 5000 words, but possibly of 7000.

In any case I should be very interested to read the manuscript, and look forward to the book.[1]

With best wishes to your husband and yourself.

Yours sincerely,
[T. S. Eliot]

TO *G. W. S. Curtis*

TS Houghton

3 November 1931   Faber & Faber Ltd

My dear Curtis,

It was good to hear from you, and to hope that I may be again in touch with you. I have had it in my mind for many months to write to you about your poetry, about yourself, and in general, and so long a time had elapsed that I was glad to have a scrap of printed verse to send you to prepare the way for correspondence.[2]

I wish you would write again and tell me more of what you are doing, and what you intend to do. I am afraid that my notions of the Christa Seva Sangha are very vague, and I should like to know more.[3] Has it anything to do with Canon Streeter's Sadhu?

I hope that the lovely country of Huntingdonshire is proving more beneficial to your health than were the close streets of Southwark.

Affectionately yours,
T. S. Eliot

---

1 – Broch, 'Disintegration of Values', trans. Edwin and Willa Muir, C. 11 (July 1932), 664–75.
2 – Curtis thanked TSE (27 Oct.) for *Triumphal March* – TSE's 'scrap' – 'It gave me joy.'
3 – 'I am living now at the English headquarters of the Christa Seva Sangha at Cromwell's one-time home, S. Ives in Huntingdonshire. Fr Algy Robertson invalided home from India has turned the vicarage into an English headquarters for the order.'

Curtis explained on 12 Nov.: 'Christa Seva Sangha . . . is a very real attempt to let the gospel come alive in India released from its European grave clothes. The brotherhood has a Franciscan spirit but no scrupulosity about ransacking all the niches of Eastern metaphysic and devotion . . . William Temple has said of the society that it is the most manifest movement of the Holy Spirit at the time . . .'

TO L. C. Knights

CC

3 November 1931   [*The Criterion*]

Dear Mr Knights,

I have your letter of the 16th.[1] It is quite likely that I shall be unable to use your essay until the June number, and for that reason I am writing to ask whether you would care to review for the March number Mr G. Wilson Knight's second book of Shakespeare essays, *The Imperial Theme*. If you have not seen his first book *The Wheel of Fire* I hope that you will look at it, and from that you will know whether you are sufficiently interested to care to review the second. I have only read parts of this in manuscript, but thought the first volume extremely good.[2]

Yours sincerely
[T. S. Eliot]

TO *Scott Buchanan*[3]

TS Houghton

3 November 1931   Faber & Faber Ltd

Dear Mr Buchanan,

Thank you for your letter of the 22nd.[4] I was very sorry to miss you during your flying visit to London, but I hope that you will be up again before very long, or at least during the vacation. Meanwhile I have McKeon's novel which another director is reading at the moment, and which I shall read afterward.[5]

1–Knights was happy for his essay to be printed at TSE's convenience; and he asked for some reviewing work, particularly relating to Elizabethan drama.

2–Knights reviewed GWK's *The Imperial Theme*: C. 11 (Apr. 1932), 540–3.

3–Scott Buchanan (1895–1968), scholar and educator, was educated at Amherst College, as a Rhodes Scholar at Balliol College, Oxford, and at Harvard. At the time of this letter he was a professor of philosophy at the University of Virginia, 1929–36; thereafter Chairman of the Liberal Arts Committee at Chicago – where he worked to establish the enormously influential 'Great Books' programme – and from 1937 as Dean of St John's College, Annapolis. His writings include *Poetry and Mathematics* (1929), *Symbolic Distance in Relation to Analogy and Fiction* (1932) and *Tragedy and the New Politics* (1960). See further *Scott Buchanan: A Centennial Appreciation of His Life and Work, 1895–1968*, ed. Charles A. Nelson (1995).

4–Buchanan said he was briefly visiting London: he would bring McKeon's novel to F&F. Thomas Dawes Eliot, Dept. of Sociology and Anthropology, College of Liberal Arts, Northwestern University, Evanston, Illinois, had written to TSE on 20 Aug.: 'This will serve to introduce Professor Scott Buchanan of the University of Virginia, of whom I wrote you at length recently. Any courtesies you may find it possible to extend to him will be greatly appreciated.'

5–Richard McKeon (1900–85), philosopher and educator, studied at Columbia University, where he wrote a doctoral thesis published as *The Philosophy of Spinoza: The Unity of His*

I hope that Cambridge is proving satisfactory. Don't forget to let me know if there is anyone I can help you to meet. D'Arcy is at present in Oxford for the term, but if you do not go to Oxford you can almost certainly meet him in London during one of the vacations. Meanwhile I envy you your pleasant surroundings.

Yours sincerely

T. S. Eliot

TO *John Gould Fletcher* CC

3 November 1931   [The Criterion]

Dear Fletcher,

Thanks for your letter of the 23rd.[1] I was very sorry that you could not come to the meeting, and much more so because of the reasons. I hope that Mrs Fletcher is now better. If so will you let me know of a day soon when we could lunch together.

I should like to use one of your manuscripts in March, preferably the poem. Of course what I should prefer would be to leave the choice open until a little later because although I like the poem my great difficulty is usually to find suitable short sketches or stories. But if you want to know definitely at once, then I will keep the poem for March and return the story. In either case I can promise to use one or the other in March.[2]

Yours ever

[T. S. Eliot]

Thought (1928). After further study in Paris (where his teachers included Etienne Gilson), he taught philosophy at Columbia from 1925 before becoming Professor of History at the University of Chicago; from 1935, Professor of Greek Philosophy; Dean of the Division of Humanities, 1940; later Charles F. Grey Distinguished Service Professor of Philosophy and Greek. He was instrumental in establishing at Chicago the interdisciplinary Committee on Ideas and Methods. During WW2 he became a foremost intellectual advisory figure to the United Nations Educational, Scientific and Cultural Organization (UNESCO). Author of eleven books including *Freedom and History: The Semantics of Philosophical Controversies and Ideological Conflicts* (1952) and *Thought, Action and Passion* (1954), as well as over 150 articles, he was also a legendary and award-winning teacher and mentor: his students included Robert Pirsig, Robert Coover, Susan Sontag, Paul Goodman, Richard Rorty, Wayne Booth. He was President of the American Philosophical Association, 1952; Vice-President, the International Federation of Philosophical Societies, 1953–4; President, International Institute for Philosophy, 1953–7.

1 – 'I hope you received my note explaining my unavoidable absence from the last *Criterion* meeting.' JGF's note has not been found, but he must have explained that his wife had been ill.

2 – 'Elegy on an Empty Skyscraper' (poem), C. 11 (Apr. 1932), 439–42.

TO *Hugh Gordon Porteus*[1]   CC

5 November 1931   [*The Criterion*]

Dear Mr Porteus,

Thank you for your kind letter of the 30th, and the copy of the *Twentieth Century*.[2] It is a periodical of which I have recently heard, but which I have never before seen. It is distinctly interesting, although in parts very irritating. I thought that Fenner Brockway was offensively patronising toward Gandhi, a man so much bigger than himself that he cannot come anywhere near understanding him. With regard to asceticism, for instance, it is just possible that Gandhi may be right and Brockway wrong, but one does not expect anything but insularity from such a member of the Labour Party.[3]

As for myself, as I told you, it is quite impossible for me to criticize criticisms, particularly when they appear at all flattering, and I always imagine that they are flattering, if there [is] the slightest possibility for that interpretation. At any rate I was very much pleased, particularly because you mentioned one piece of mine which I very much like, and which everybody ignores, that is the two fragments which I now call *Sween[e]y Agonistes*. You perhaps remember the quotation 'at the mill with slaves'?[4]

1 – Hugh Gordon Porteus (1906–1993): literary and art critic (trained as an artist); literary editor of *The Twentieth Century*, magazine of the Promethean Society, Mar. 1931–May 1933; author of *Wyndham Lewis: A Discursive Exposition* (1932); *Background to Chinese Art* (1935).
2 – Porteus, who had met TSE at the Poetry Bookshop, sent the first of two 'expository articles' on TSE's work. 'I fear you will not be flattered by the company you keep in these pages. But I have tried not to vulgarize your ideas, only to expound them . . . If my prose style is intolerably bad, please put it down to the fact that I have never been trained to do anything but paint.'
3 – A. Fenner Brockway, 'Mahatma Gandhi: An Appreciation and a Criticism', *The Twentieth Century* 2: 8 (Oct. 1931), 5–7, remarked: 'Many of us cannot follow Mr Gandhi in the conflict which he holds exists between material and spiritual things. He would do without material things in order that the spirit might grow. The opposing philosophy would utilise material things in order that human personality might develop. Mr Gandhi's view of sex is characteristic of this. He believes that sexual life must be foregone by the sincere seeker for truth and spiritual expansion. He rejects birth control, and regards sexual experience, except for the deliberate purpose of procreation, as carnal and wrong. The opposing view is that sexual experience may mean the expansion of human personality and the enriching of the best in human life' (7).
4 – 'T. S. Eliot', *The Twentieth Century* 2: 8 (Oct. 1931), 7–11. Porteus replied to this letter on 10 Nov.: 'The "Fragment of an Agon" especially excites me. The tension of the atmosphere is created with marvellous economy; the nightmare chorus is astonishingly effective. Merely from a technical point of view it seems to me something of immense significance – read, of course, in conjunction with your essay on The Poetic Drama. The abrupt clipped rhythm

I hope to read your poems within the next few days, and if possible I shall try to get to Zwemmer's to see your drawings.[1]

> Yours sincerely
> [T. S. Eliot]

TO *M. C. D'Arcy*   CC

5 November 1931   [*The Criterion*]

My dear D'Arcy,

I am terribly sorry about my misunderstanding of your invitation.[2] I had got it fixed in my mind that it was the following Tuesday, the 10th, which was very stupid of me; but in any case I should, of course, have written to you several days since. I am particularly disappointed because I would rather have come when you were reading a paper than on any other occasion. It would be a small crumb of comfort, however, if I might still come as your guest on the 1st December at 5.p.m., although I have no notion of who Principal Robinson may be, and I would far rather have heard you.

For the moment I assume that you are in Oxford, and so am writing there. I should feel far more apologetic except for my awareness that the loss is entirely mine.

> Yours very sincerely
> [T. S. Eliot]

---

is an admirable (and probably necessary) substitute for the blank verse of the Elizabethans. It has always seemed to me that a subordinate musical background, such as Antheil might compose, would throw the lines into relief and at the same time preserve the "feeling" which runs through both fragments. I have in mind something like Ezra Pound's "Broadcast Melodrama": *Francois Villon*; but instead of lutes;- the hissing of pistons, a death-jazz, the monochrome music of a misfiring gashouse-engine.' In 'T. S. Eliot (II)', *The Twentieth Century* 2: 9 (Nov. 1931), 10–13, Porteus wrote that TSE's 'poems, since *The Hollow Men*, have been a series of Preces Privatae – not addressed to the reader at all, it seems – yet not inaccessible to him that hath eyes to see, ears to hear.'

1 – Porteus wrote further (10 Nov.): 'My miniature decoration (or Illumination) for your poem "The Hollow Men" was serving a commercial purpose in Zwemmer's shop last month: it will probably remain there until the end of this week.' Porteus had sent TSE two poems of his own.

2 – D'Arcy had written on 24 Oct. to invite TSE to two meetings of the London Society for the Study of Religion, on the subject of 'Revelation'. He himself was to give the talk on 3 Nov.; and on 1 Dec., 'Principal Robinson'.

TO *I. A. Richards*   TS Magdalene

5 November 1931   *The Criterion*

My dear Richards,

I do think it is rather shabby of you not to let me know that you are
back. I had heard vague rumours of you being in Cambridge, but it was
only by asking Leavis for news of you that I heard definitely of your
return. Did you receive a copy of an Ariel poem which I sent you,[1] and
is there any hope of seeing you in London within measurable time? My
wife wishes me to send her kindest regards to you and Mrs Richards. I am
looking forward most inquisitively to hearing your opinion of Harvard
and the people there.

Yours ever
T. S. E.

TO *Max Planck*   CC

5 November 1931   [Faber & Faber Ltd]

My dear Dr Planck,

After receiving your last letter I was very gratified to think that the
essentials of the matter were settled, and that it merely remained to
arrange a few details with you and Dr Murphy. As I informed you I wrote
to Dr Murphy about our project, and had a reply from him this morning
which plunges me into the deepest dejection. Dr. Murphy informs me that
the *International Forum* is itself about to bring out a series of pamphlets,
of which this essay by yourself, with an introduction by Dr Einstein is to
be the first. He tells me that this publication is already in proof, and that
the British rights have been arranged with Messrs. Elkin Matthews and
Marrot Ltd. Dr Murphy adds that you gave him full English rights, and
he thinks that perhaps in writing to me you had some other essay of yours
in mind. In any case it would appear that Dr Murphy has the publication
rights, and that your pamphlet is to be published shortly in English.[2]

I very much regret, and my colleagues share my regret that we cannot
have the honour of publishing this essay in our series. I can only add that
we should be very glad to consider any similar essay of yours, that [is] to

---

1 – *Triumphal March* (1931), the first section; reprinted in full in *Complete Poems* (1969), 127.
2 – James Murphy wrote from Berlin on 1 Nov., to tell TSE about his series of 'International
Forum Brochures': the first of the brochures (already in print) was the Planck essay in
question.

say, an essay directed toward the general intellectual public rather than toward technical experts, and that also the *Criterion*, a quarterly review which I edit, would be very much honoured to publish some shorter essay, say from 5000 to 6000 words.

With many regrets; but still hoping to be able to publish something by you.

I remain
Yours very truly
[T. S. Eliot]

TO *John Middleton Murry*

TS Berg

6 November 1931   *The Criterion*

My dear John,

Thank you for your letter of the 21st.[1] Meanwhile I have met Richard Rees, and liked him. He struck me as a young man whose mind was still open and who was seriously desirous of being useful in whatever way he could. I shall try to see something of him from time to time, and I am glad you effected an introduction.

I have perpended, as you would say, your letter very carefully, but am still waiting for more light. I wish that we might have enough time together to arrive at a closer understanding of terms. I am a little puzzled because I believe that you are rather severe on Hulme's notion of discontinuity, and it seems to me that you have arrived at another kind of discontinuity, which to me is rather alarming.[2] I am not yet quite in a position to reply because my actual knowledge of Marxism is indirect and inaccurate, and I suppose I ought to read *Das Kapital*. As for Spinozism, you can conceive my opinion of it without my telling you. It seems to me merely a particularly brilliant and pernicious heresy. It seems to me that if you make such a sharp distinction between the spiritual and what you call the ethical–political, you must end by corrupting the spiritual, and making it a mere luxury for a few *illuminati*. It is difficult for me to conceive of what you call ethical passion as being what you call wholly human, and of course the perfection of a Lord who is merely human doesn't seem to

---

1–Not found.

2–On 30 Dec. 1959 TSE would write to Victor Gollancz, who sent him an advance proof copy of *The Life and Opinions of T. E. Hulme* (1960), by A. R. Jones: 'I never met Hulme or had any communication with him . . . I certainly owe him two ideas, one on original sin and the other on discontinuity, as well as the enjoyment of two or three lovely poems.'

me to be perfection at all. It seems to me that you are merely on the way to a kind of spiritual materialism, but these are only immediate comments intended to provoke a fuller explication.

Yours ever affectionately
Tom

TO *Maud Fortescue Pickard*   CC

6 November 1931   [Faber & Faber Ltd]

Dear Madam,

I thank you for your letter of the 27th October.[1] Mr Eliot is glad that St Bartholomew's will benefit from the anthology, and wishes it the best of luck. He has no objection himself to your including the passage beginning 'Put out the light', but once more he would like to say that he hopes you will put the name of Mr Charles Williams to this extract, as he fears that he can lay no claim to its authorship. (It was this passage that was put first by you in your original letter).

Yours truly
[Pamela Wilberforce][2]

1 – Mrs Maud Fortescue Pickard wrote first on 20 Sept. to ask if she could use some extracts from TSE's poetry in an anthology she was compiling in aid of St Bartholomew's Hospital: all the proceeds were to go there. Her proposed extracts included 'Put out the light and then put out the light . . .'; 'After the last tired shout' (4 lines); ' . . .Sound of water over a rock / Where the hermit-thrush sings in the pine trees' (2 lines); 'Then at dawn we came down to a temperate valley' (8 lines); and 'The river's tent is broken, the last fingers of leaf' to 'departed . . .' (8 lines) She remarked too: 'This last one is very beautiful! – I hope you will go on with this type, & forget those housemaids & areas & beefsteaks & things, that one is eternally trying to escape!'

2 – Pamela Wilberforce, a graduate of Somerville College, Oxford, had been appointed 'secretary-typist' to the Chairman's office on 1 July 1930, at a salary of £2. 10. 0. a week: she was expected to learn typing and shorthand, and she asked also for time to improve her German.

TO G. W. Rylands[1]

CC

11 November 1931   [*The Criterion*]

Dear Rylands,

Many thanks for your note of the 8th, enclosing A. F. Blunt's essay on Sacheverell Sitwell.[2] My feeling about the matter is that had I known of him and his interests at the time of the appearance of one of these books I should have been very glad to have him review it; but as it is he seems to me to have made an article out of what is merely review material. The subject, that is Sacheverell's knowledge and views on baroque art, does not seem to me important enough to warrant an article at the present moment.[3] But I am very glad to know about Blunt, and I wish you would encourage him to send me something else or perhaps he would care to have some book to review?

Yours,

[T. S. Eliot]

1 – George ('Dadie') Rylands (1902–99), Fellow of King's College Cambridge since 1927. An associate of the Bloomsbury circle, he worked for a while as assistant to LW and VW – 'a very charming spoilt boy . . . pink as a daisy and as proud as a wood-lion,' said VW of him – at the Hogarth Press, which published his early verse, *Russet and Taffeta* (1925) and *Poems* (1931). But he earned a major reputation through his passion for nurturing plays and speaking verse (he acted and produced at the Amateur Dramatic Club and Arts theatres, and succeeded John Maynard Keynes as chairman of the Arts). Actors and directors including Michael Redgrave, Peter Hall, John Barton and Ian McKellen learned their craft under his direction at Cambridge.

2 – Rylands wrote: 'Anthony Blunt is a B.A. of Trinity, a very strong candidate for a Fellowship there next year. I like him very much & believe in him, & I thought that this searching examination of Sitwell & the Baroque might find a place in the *Criterion*.'

Anthony Blunt (1907–83), art historian and spy, was a Fellow of Trinity College, Cambridge, 1932–6, before joining the Warburg Institute, 1937–9. From 1939 he was Reader in the History of Art, London University, and Deputy Director of the Courtauld Institute of Art. He was Professor of the History of Art, and Director of the Courtauld, 1947–74; Surveyor of the Queen's Pictures, 1952–72; Advisor for the Queen's Pictures and Drawings, 1972–8. He was Slade Professor of Fine Art, Oxford, 1962–3; Cambridge, 1965–6. He was awarded the KCVO in 1956 (but the award was cancelled and annulled in 1979 following his exposure as a Soviet spy during WW2); Commander of the Order of Orange Nassau (Holland), 1948; Commandeur de la Légion d'Honneur, 1958. His publications include *The Drawings of Nicolas Poussin* (1939), *Artistic Theory in Italy* (1940), *The Nation's Pictures* (1951), *Nicolas Poussin: Catalogue Raisonné* (1966), *Nicolas Poussin* (2 vols, 1967), *Picasso's Guernica* (1969) and *The Drawings of Nicolas Poussin* (1979).

3 – Sacheverell Sitwell, *Southern Baroque Art* (1924).

TO *Denys Saurat*[1]   CC

11 November 1931   [Faber & Faber Ltd]

Dear Monsieur Saurat,

Thank you very much for your invitation for myself and my wife to
come to meet Julien Benda on Friday. Unfortunately on Friday night we
have a dinner engagement which will make it impossible. I only heard
of M. Benda's visit to London a few days ago. Had I known further in
advance I should certainly have written to him about it, and tried to
make an appointment to see him. I suppose that he is returning to Paris
immediately. But if he should be over here at the beginning of next week
I should be very glad if you and he could lunch with me. But if he is
returning to Paris at the end of this week, you need not bother to reply. In
that event will you please tell him how sorry I am not to have seen him.

                                With many thanks
                                Yours sincerely
                                [T. S. Eliot]

TO *I. A. Richards*   TS Magdalene

11 November 1931   *The Criterion*

Dear Richards,

I did not get your letter of the 6th until Monday morning, and as I
had the whole day filled and you said you were returning to Cambridge
the same evening, it did not seem worth while to ring up.[2] Is there any
likelihood of your being up again soon? And what are your ultimate
plans? Do you propose to settle in Cambridge again, or will you, as you
once purposed, take a flat in London?

Many thanks for your comment. I shall be interested to know what
further impression you will get from the second part of this poem, which
I have finished, and from the third and fourth parts which are not yet
written. But I should like to show you the second part when I see you.
As for the allusions you mention, that is perfectly deliberate, and it was

---

1–Denys Saurat (1890–1958): Anglo-French scholar, writer, broadcaster; Professor of
French Language and Literature, King's College, London, 1926–50; Director of the Institut
français du Royaume Uni, 1924–45; author of *La pensée de Milton* (1920: *Milton: Man and
Thinker*, 1925).
2–IAR had come up to London for a day.

my intention that the reader should recognize them.[1] As for the question why I made the allusions at all, that seems to me definitely a matter which should not concern the reader. That, as you know, is a theory of mine, that very often it is possible to increase the effect for the reader by letting him know a reference or a meaning; but that if the reader knew more, the poetic effect would actually be diminished; that if the reader knows too much about the crude material in the author's mind, his own reaction may tend to become at best merely a kind of feeble image of the author's feelings, whereas a good poem should have a potentiality of evoking feelings and associations in the reader of which the author is wholly ignorant. I am rather inclined to believe, for myself, that my best poems are possibly those which evoke the greatest number and variety of interpretations surprising to myself. What do you think about this?[2]

Are you ever going to write anything for the *Criterion*? I look forward to seeing you.

Yours ever
T. S. E.

If Mrs Richards is more or less in London at present, would she come & see me?

---

1 – 'Yes I did get *Triumphal March* just a week ago,' wrote IAR (6 Nov.), 'and have been really meaning to tell you that it comes off for me perfectly – but seems an easy thing, for *you*, to be writing. Still the pounding of the hoofs and the central swoon of significance so soon forgotten and the sacred trivial winding it off all come so easily into the reader's mind that he doesn't measure the poet's problem with them. But do you consciously dovetail into your other poems – or is that just the pathetic critic's whim?' (*Letters of I. A. Richards*, CH, 61). The example of self-allusion he had in mind, he pointed out, occurred in these lines from 'Triumphal March' –
> That is all we could see. But how many eagles! and how many trumpets!
> (And Easter Day, we didn't get to the country,
> So we took young Cyril to church. And they rang a bell
> And he said right out loud, *crumpets*.)
– wherein 'crumpets' and 'eagles' seemed to him to hark back to 'A Cooking Egg':
> Where are the eagles and the trumpets?
>   Buried beneath some snow-deep Alps.
> Over buttered scones and crumpets
>   Weeping, weeping multitudes
> Droop in a hundred A.B.C.'s.
2 – IAR was to write to Robert Winter (a friend long resident in Peking) on 23 Nov. 1931: 'The only news I have is that Eliot is writing a new cycle of poems of which Triumphal March is no. 1. V. topical & lucid, what I have seen of them. He is inclined to take the view that the best of his poems are those in which readers have been able to find the greatest number & variety of interpretations surprising to the poet! So you see its up to us to send the value of odd portions up by our disagreements' (Richards Diary, Old Library, Magdalene College, Camb.).

Our present address is
    68, Clarence Gate Gardens
    Regent's Park
    N.W.1.

FROM *Geoffrey Faber* TO *Harold Raymond*[1]   MS

11 November 1931   Faber & Faber Ltd

My dear Raymond,

I am writing on a matter that I would have preferred to speak to you about, but I couldn't get you on the telephone.[2] It is not a very easy matter to open. I can best do so by saying that I am not writing officially as Eliot's publisher, but as a very intimate friend, who is perhaps as well acquainted as any man with his private circumstances. That I am also his publisher enables me to approach you, so to speak, behind the scenes. Let me add that I have not been asked by him to write; that he has indeed said nothing to me upon the matter; and that he does not know that I am writing.

A copy of Aldington's *Stepping Heavenward*, which is, I understand, to appear tomorrow, was put into my hands this evening, as I was on the point of leaving the office. That it is a bitter and indeed a malevolent attack on Eliot will, of course, be immediately obvious to everybody with any knowledge of contemporary letters. I am not suggesting that there is anything in *that* to which exception should be taken, however ill-natured

1 – Harold Raymond (1887–1975) was a partner in Chatto & Windus, 1919–53, Chairman, 1953–4. He is celebrated for inventing the Book Tokens scheme adopted by the British Book Trade in 1932.

2 – GCF set down in his diary that on Wed., 11 Nov., he had been 'about to leave [his office] when Frank [Morley] came in with Aldington's "Stepping Heavenward" – a bitter attack on Eliot, & – what is worse – on his relations with his wife. An *incredible* thing. I wrote to Raymond of Chatto's about it, & then home to dinner.' He noted too, on 12 Nov.: 'Charles Prentice of Chatto rang up to say that *Stepping Heavenward* had already been published in Florence. So that's that.' (Giuseppe Orioli [1884–1942] had published 808 numbered and signed copies of *Stepping Heavenward: A Record* as no. 7 in his Lugarno series, Florence, 1931.) Chatto & Windus was to reissue *Stepping Heavenward* in RA's collection of short fiction, *Soft Answers* (1932), which Penguin Books would republish in paperback in 1949. (For Prentice, see Richard Aldington, *Pinorman: Personal Recollections of Norman Douglas, Pino Orioli and Charles Prentice* [1954]. RA wrote of Prentice in a letter to HD of 16 Dec. 1930: 'Under a very shy, almost hold-you-off exterior, he has one of the sweetest natures I have ever known, and quite a flaming enthusiasm for literature' [*Richard Aldington: An Autobiography in Letters*, ed. Norman T. Gates (1992), 118].)

some of it may seem. If any reputation suffers from *Stepping Heavenward* it will not be Eliot's.[1]

But, knowing you, I cannot believe that you can be aware of the extent to which, in one particular direction, Aldington's satire oversteps the

1–Richard Aldington, who had worked for a while as TSE's assistant on *C.* and who came to know TSE and his wife on fairly close but critical terms, had decided ultimately to turn against both of them with the publication of his satirical burlesque, *Stepping Heavenward: A Record* (1931), in which TSE is figured as 'Jeremy Pratt Sybba' – a name which is otherwise spelt, for obvious Popeian reasons, as 'Cibber' – and Vivien Eliot as 'Adèle Paleologue'.

The focus of Aldington's piece is to poke fun at Eliot's supposed efforts to transcend human bondage, to overleap the limits of human love and to come straight to the love of God, eschewing Eros for Agape.

'Like the wives of many great men, Adèle has been severely blamed . . . Enthusiastic admirers . . . forget that Adèle was one of the earliest to proclaim Cibber's peculiar genius and to push him on in the world . . . Could she help it if his presence – owing to the will of God, no doubt – drove her into wild neurasthenia? After all, it must be rather a shock to think you are marrying a nice young American and then to discover that you have bedded with an angel unawares . . .

'Adèle became more and more unhappy. It is always rather unpleasant to live with a genius, but quite awful when he is a Cibber. Few persons now take the view that marriage is or should be a merry bacchanal, accompanied by flutes and the capering of panisks to the tune of "Hymen Hymenaee!" But Cibber considered it as an inviolable legal contract, implying none but social obligations . . . So, many a time poor Adèle gazed into the mirror, clutching her hair distractedly, and whispering: "I'm going mad, I'm going mad, I'm going mad." Cibber invariably stood up when she came into the room, and their quarrels were conducted on coldly intellectual grounds' (46–7, 57).

TSE was later to write: 'Richard was very sensitive, not to say touchy, in some ways and I am afraid that with good intentions, but clumsy lack of imagination, I hurt his feelings once or twice very deeply indeed. After that, I saw nothing in him and he wrote a cruel and unkind lampoon of me and of my wife who died some years later, and of friends of mine such as Lady Ottoline Morrell and Virginia Woolf . . . We were on the same side for a long time and I was the first to give offence, although unintentionally, which made a breach between us' (*Richard Aldington: An Intimate Portrait*, ed. Alister Kershaw and Frédéric-Jacques Temple [1965], 24–5).

TSE's use of the apparent pleonasm 'cruel and unkind' may seem odd – though it must allude, consciously or unconsciously, to the English Bill of Rights 1689 and the Eighth Amendment to the Constitution of the United States (Bill of Rights, 1791): 'Excessive bail shall not be required, nor excessive fines imposed, nor cruel and unusual punishments inflicted' – but still more curious is the phrasing 'my wife who died some years later', which might be taken to include a redundant relative clause – except that such a construction may imply a causal relation between the burlesque and VHE's death. It is as if to say that Aldington's satire was all the more brutal because VHE had to suffer from it for so long: it might have had something to do with her death.

(TSE wrote to Richard Church on 2 Aug. 1963 [TS Texas]: 'I have the letter from this man Temple which I have never answered. I will try to write something about Richard Aldington for him. Please tell him so. It is only one of several requests which I have not had time to gratify. But I cannot say very much. I was sorry for Richard, but, of course, I broke off relations with him after he published a very obvious lampoon which was certainly a blow beneath the belt. After that he seemed to show his dislike of everybody and, I believe, wrote disparaging books about T. E. Lawrence, D. H. Lawrence and Norman Douglas.')

limits of permissible criticism. The principal passage in which this occurs is on pages 46 to 49, though there are some other references of a similarly distressing nature – for example on page 53. It cannot be suggested that, while Cibber is clearly Eliot, Adele is to be regarded as a wholly imaginary character. The accidental trappings are of no importance. The fact remains that Aldington permits himself – and you permit him – to air in public his own opinions on the relationship between Eliot and his wife. I do not recollect such a license being taken by any writer, since the 18th century. Nor is it merely a question of taste, or of a man's right to keep his private life to himself, or of the pain which such comments must cause. It is an unpardonable interference with the lives of two people.

I can well understand that a publisher may easily find himself in the position of having taken & being about to publish a work of this kind,

---

Also in a later year, after going over the typescript of Lawrence Durrell's correspondence with Henry Miller, TSE wrote to Durrell on 3 Aug. 1962 to request a specific deletion: 'You speak of having read a brilliant satire on me by Richard Aldington. Now whether a story that Aldington wrote and published introducing myself and my first wife, Ezra Pound, Virginia Woolf and Lady Ottoline Morrell under different names but in very thin disguise – whether that is a "brilliant satire" is a matter of opinion, but what is quite certain is that it was a most scurrilous and offensive lampoon. In the last few days Aldington has died – God rest his soul – but after that publication it was for me or my closer friends to have nothing to do with Aldington. It was a kind of travesty which one could do nothing about because to take him to court or take any other such step would have been merely to give more publicity to a painful situation. Your commendation of this so-called satire might attract readers who, since your letters will be published by Faber & Faber, might think that I had no objection so I must ask you to delete this one on page 72 of your ms.'

Durrell was happy to make the cut that TSE suggested (5 Aug. 1962), and he explained: 'By the way, I beg you to believe that while I knew that "Stepping Heavenward" was aimed mildly in your direction, I regarded it as a good satire; but owing to my ignorance of your personal life, and indeed that of all the other people you mention, I had not the faintest notion of its scurrility until three years ago when Aldington himself told me of the matter – to do him justice most ruefully. Indeed so naieve [*sic*] was I that I remember praising R. A. to you once and being puzzled and surprised when you looked peeved and said "I wouldn't receive him if he called now"; I thought it unusual and put it down to pique, but was quite unaware how far below the belt the piece was; I then read it as one read Lewis' trepanning of Pound, as a good piece of gasconading. And while I frequently heard people say it was aimed your way I was also told that it could have been Henry James. My ignorance was total.' (EVE)

FVM wrote to HWE on 8 Jan. 1940, apropos the Bel Esprit scheme: 'Aldington was once one of his best friends, and took against him in a way which hurt Tom . . . So to mention it to Tom would be what I would not want.' HWE replied to FVM on 3 Feb. 1940, 'I can't see why it should pain Tom so greatly to be reminded of Aldington.' (Berg)

In the early 1940s HWE made this note on the copy of *Stepping Heavenward* deposited in the TSE collection at Eliot House, now Houghton: 'A fictional account of the early life and later career of (presumably) T. S. Eliot, of incredible vindictiveness. In it T. S. Eliot's father is represented as saying "hell" and "goddam" and spitting tobacco juice into the stove.'

See also Michael B. Thompson, 'Richard Aldington and T. S. Eliot', *Yeats Eliot Review* 6: 1 (1979), 3–9.

from an author in whom he has confidence, without having fully realised some of its implications. If I were in that position, I should prefer to learn what I had let myself in for, even at the eleventh hour. I am sure you must feel the same. Unhappily, it is so long past the eleventh hour already that it may prove very difficult to prevent the harm from being done.

Yours very sincerely
Geoffrey Faber.

TO *Michael Roberts*   TS Janet Adam Smith

12 November 1931   *The Criterion*

Dear Mr Roberts,

I have your letter of the 6th. I have discussed with other directors your suggestion for a book on the Jura.[1] But although I agree that it would be interesting and desirable to have a travel book on that district in English, I feel that it is not a suggestion which we can take up. At the moment we have undertaken one or two other such books, and in the present state of affairs, it remains to be discovered what market can be found for them before undertaking anything else. Of course it may be possible that when people are too poor to travel abroad they will have all the more recourse to travel books as a kind of dream substitute. But that remains to be discovered. Meanwhile I will keep your suggestion in mind. I wish that I could be more helpful.

I should have been writing to you in any case, because I have just discovered that for the December number I have more material than I can use, and I am afraid it will be necessary for me to postpone your essay on Hulme until the March number.[2] Your review, of course, will appear in the December number.[3] I am very sorry about this, and apologise for my lack of foresight. I have not yet heard anything from Chatto about your book. I suggest that it might be a good thing if you wrote to them yourself to stir them up.

I hope to see you again before long, and will drop you a line.

Yours sincerely,
T. S. Eliot

1 – 'I do not know any description of the district in English, but having spent some time there it seems to me quite as attractive to the walker as is the Black Forest.'
2 – 'The Categories of T. E. Hulme', C. 11 (Apr. 1932), 375–85.
3 – Review of Bertrand Russell, *The Scientific Outlook*, C. 11 (Jan. 1932), 313–16.

TO *Max Planck*

12 November 1931   [Faber & Faber Ltd]

My dear sir,

I thank you for your kind letter of the 8th instant.[1] While I am still very regretful over the loss of your essay which we wished to publish, I look forward hopefully next year to receiving something else from you which, if short, shall be suitable for the *Criterion* Review, and if longer, suitable for the Criterion Miscellany. If I do not hear from you early in the spring I shall write to you again.

With very grateful thanks,

I am
Yours very truly
[T. S. Eliot]

TO *John Hayward*

13 November 1931   *The Criterion*

Dear John,

I daresay that the personal anxieties on your mind at the moment have made you more apprehensive about the Browne than you would other-wise have been.[2] Anyway do not worry about that. Is there anything I can

---

1 – 'I see with regret from your letter of 5 inst. that there are obstacles to your plan to publish an English edition of my essay on Positivism etc.

'I also admit willingly that Dr Murphy is right when he claims exclusive rights to the English translation. This point had slipped my mind.'

2 – Review of *The Works of Sir Thomas Browne*, vols V & VI, ed. Geoffrey Keynes, C. 11 (Jan. 1932), 328–31. JDH wrote on 11 Sept.: 'I am very dissatisfied with it: it seems to have no point of contact with its subject, but to wander aimlessly around it: Destroy it, if you will: I would myself, if I did not need every penny I can earn. I have just received notice to quit, and I have'nt [*sic*] the slightest idea what to do or where to go, and feeling so depressed, I find it hard to begin to think of a solution. Please send me a book occasionally . . .'

TSE promptly sent JDH an early copy of *Triumphal March* (published 8 Oct. 1931), to which JDH responded from 125 Queen's Gate on 7 Oct.: 'Dear Eliot: this must be, I think, the third or fourth anniversary of the sending of the first Ariel poem. In return for the latest I can send you only fuller thanks and renew with them a friendship wch I value very deeply. I wish I could give you something of my own, but, alas, no clumsy tome of mine, full of petty learning, is worth two loosely sewn pages of your poetry. I think this "Triumphal March" is magnificent. I read it in Ted [McKauffer]'s flat in the early summer; perhaps he should not have allowed me to see it . . . – but I thought it superb then; I still do. And I am glad that the interval of three months has not altered my opinion, I have just read it aloud again: I enjoy it best then and catch more fully the rumble & clutter of the procession and the sudden stillness when the rider passes. I call out the numbers of the *impedimenta*, although I enjoy

do to help to find what you want in the way of a habitation? If I knew exactly what you will be looking for, and in what part of London, I might possibly be of a little use. I hope to see you again before long, and will write.[1]

Affectionately,

T. S. Eliot

---

as much reading at that point and speaking again at, "What a time that took". I think that is legitimate because one sometimes counts & at others merely watches a succession of things.

'How glad I am when I remember that I know the author of this astonishing event! I'm Pacific-deep in your debt!

'Thank you very much. / Your affectionate friend / John.

'P.S. Will you have an opportunity soon of paying me a visit.'

1 – JDH replied to this letter on 15 Nov.: 'it was very kind of you to write – to trouble to write, because I did not expect an answer to my complaining! Now, after hours of discussion – I felt as if I was pleading for my life – my affairs are settled. I have not got to leave, but I have to find another 80£ a year for the privilege of staying; and I am going to try to find them. I am glad that I shall not have to [find] a place where I should probably not find some of the advantages I have here; in any case it is a relief not to have to pull oneself up by the roots. And it is easier, I think, for *me* to concentrate on the single task of finding more money, than to be compelled to re-adjust my way of life to a different set of circumstances. My one fear, of course, is that the present time may not bring me the opportunity I need of getting more work. Perhaps I shall have to give up the car, but I could bear that so long as my friends came here to see me instead of my going to see them; I'm sure they would. If you happen to meet anyone who needs the services of a "home-worker" for proof-reading or some such sordid task, remember me! The Oxford & Cambridge Examination Board have enlisted me as an examiner, but they have no work for me at present. Please do not write to me again! I have, already, made a great nuisance of myself and my affairs and, I dare say, taken too much advantage of the privilege I have assumed in subscribing myself: / Yours, most gratefully & affectionately / John H.'

He wrote again on 11 Dec. 1931: 'My dear Eliot: will you forgive me if I refuse your invitation to the "Criterion" on Thursday? I should not have accepted in the first place, but I always feel so well in myself & eager to do things that I sometimes refuse to admit to myself the difficulty I have in getting about. It *is* boring to have to admit it; never the less the fact remains that I cannot do quite as much as I used to, and I have had to deny myself all extra-ordinary pleasures. I only go, now, to houses which I know very well and to people who understand how to deal with my disabilities; more and more I am inclined to welcome people here, rather than go to them. Alas! I see you so seldom that you cannot take my refusals for granted as they can who meet me every week or so, and so I have had to explain how much I regret these refusals: I should have loved to have heard your lecture on Marston, and I shall miss, I know, great pleasure on Thursday evening. One day, perhaps, you might organize a "Criterion" evening in Queen's gate, but I shall have to work hard before I deserve such an honour! . . . Your affectionate and contented / John.'

16 November 1931   Faber & Faber Ltd

Dear Siepmann,

I have not yet acknowledged or thanked you for sending me the copies of Dawson's talks. I hesitated for some time whether to write to Dawson, but finally decided not to do so. There were certain comments which I felt I might have made in conversation, but which I felt might seem rather impertinent in a letter, particularly as he himself did not invite me to criticize his talks.

I do feel that, excellent as they are, they are much too continuously abstract to make a very strong impression on any large public. If he could occasionally descend abruptly to concrete and striking illustrations I think his talks would seem very much more living. But I came to the conclusion probably that it was better not to bother him with such comments, even if he asked for them, because when a man tries in that way to do something not congenial to him he is so apt to make matters worse.

I have only been able to hear one of his talks. What I thought more serious than the comment I have made above was the manner of his delivery. He seemed to me to make his pauses too long and too regularly between sentences; but on a point like this I am perhaps no person to judge, and you can certainly judge better than I.[1]

There is one other matter about which I wanted to talk to you. I have had a letter from Curtis Brown Ltd. saying that they are in a position to arrange for the publication of this series and want to deal with me about the terms.[2] Am I to understand that Allen & Unwin have put the whole matter into Curtis Brown's hands, or is it merely that Curtis Brown are offering themselves as agents to the various contributors? I do not ordinarily deal with agents, and have no particular advantage in doing so.[3]

Yours

T. S. Eliot

1–Siepmann replied on 17 Nov. that he was 'in absolute agreement' about Dawson's talks. 'They are much too abstract, and he simply hasn't come to the point as I hoped he would do in relation to our modern dilemma. His voice, as you say, has been his worst enemy. We have tried desperately to improve this but with little success . . .'

2–David Higham told TSE on 5 Nov. that he had 'the full approval of the B.B.C' to 'arrange for the publication in volume form of the series of talks entitled "The Changing World"'.

3–Siepmann said on 17 Nov.: 'I am sorry that you should have been confused by Curtis Brown. They are acting for Allen & Unwin. I hope you will repeat to them the reservation as regards publication that you communicated to me. I have some sympathy with your point of view.'

TO *Douglas Jerrold*   CC

16 November 1931   [Faber & Faber Ltd]

My dear Jerrold,
    We have considered very carefully your new suggestion, which of
course is an entirely different matter from the pamphlet which I am sorry
you were unable to do. I certainly think that your essays ought to be
published after you have made the revisions indicated in your letter of the
22nd October; but you no doubt know with what difficulties a volume of
essays must contend in establishing itself with the contemporary public.[1]
Furthermore I very much doubt if we are the most suitable publishers
for the book you have in mind. In different times we should probably
be more adventurous in attempting books rather outside our ordinary
scope. But at the present moment it seems to me that Sheed & Ward, for
instance, would have a better chance of reaching an interested public than
we should ever have.
    I hope I may see you again before long.
    I enjoyed the essays very much myself, and wish them every success.
                                        Yours sincerely
                                        [T. S. Eliot]

TO *John Rodgers*[2]   CC

16 November 1931   [*The Criterion*]

Dear Mr Rodgers,
    Thank you for your letter of the 4th. Your suggestion is interesting,[3]
and although I do not see how any more than a fragment from such a
book could be published in the *Criterion*, I should still like to look at it

---

1 – Jerrold had sent sample essays: three pieces from *The English Review*, four articles
in uncorrected ts, and a copy of *Soldier's Testament* (of which he thought to use the
introduction).
2 – John Rodgers (1906–1993) was at this time teaching at University College, Hull (he had
been an Oxford contemporary of Harold Acton: both belonged to the Ordinary, a literary
club). Later in his career he became Deputy Chairman of the advertising agency J. Walter
Thompson; Member of Parliament for Sevenoaks, 1950–79. He was appointed Baronet in
1964.
3 – Rodgers urged F&F to publish an English translation of Jean-Richard Bloch's *Le Destin
du Théâtre* (1930); he believed that the avant-garde director Jacques Copeau (1879–
1949), who built and directed the Théâtre de Vieux Colombier, 'would willingly write an
introduction to it'.

with a view to possible publication entire. If you will send me your copy
I will read it and hope to return it to you without undue delay.

Yours very truly

[T. S. Eliot]

TO *W. L. Gorell Barnes*[1]   cc

16 November 1931   [*The Criterion*]

Dear Sir,

Mr Morley has given me your translation of Rilke's letters, and I have
been considering them with a view to using perhaps two or three of
them in the *Criterion*. I confess that I can see little chance of success for
the whole series as a book or pamphlet, but if you wish to pursue this
endeavour I should recommend you to the Hogarth Press. Meanwhile
I am writing to ask if you would be averse to the publication of two or
three letters in the *Criterion*. I would of course submit the selection to you
before sending them to press.

I am ignorant of the position with regard to translation rights, and
whether we should have to pay any fee direct to the German publishers
or heirs of Rilke; but if you are inclined yourself to publish two or three
letters in the *Criterion* you will acquaint me with the position.[2]

Yours very truly

[T. S. Eliot]

TO *Willa Muir*   cc

16 November 1931   [*The Criterion*]

Dear Mrs Muir,

Thank you for your letter of the 12th, and for sending me the sections
of the essay which I shall read, and if possible, digest within a week.[3]

---

1 – W. L. Gorell Barnes, later Sir William (1909–87), civil servant and company director – he
was at the time of this letter a student at Pembroke College, Cambridge – was to become
Assistant Under Secretary at the Foreign Office; knighted in 1961.
2 – No letters by Rilke appeared in C.
3 – Willa Muir had sent 'a part, at least', of Broch's novel. 'Sections one to four are omitted:
they are not so fully developed, being a tentative approach to the main line of thought
which is to be found in its most severe & unmitigated form in sections 5 and 9. But even
the omitted sections are provocative and stimulating.' 'Disintegration of Values', C. 11 (July
1932), 664–75.

I should be very glad to lunch with you and your husband on Friday, 20th, wherever you suggest.

Yours sincerely,
[T. S. Eliot]

TO *Kenneth B. Murdock*[1]

17 November 1931   [Faber & Faber Ltd]

Dear Dr. Murdock,

Thank you for your letter of the 27th ultimo.[2] As I meditated the matter for several days, and as you had asked me to write at once, I wired you my acceptance on Friday last.

There are only a few points of detail, if the nomination is approved. I hope that some instalment of the salary is paid *early*; because my cash resources are always meagre, and what with the expense of the voyage, and the necessary provision of money that I must leave for expenses here in my absence, and the foregoing of my salary here during my absence, I should otherwise arrive in Boston in a destitute condition!

And while I think that far too many lectures are delivered and listened to, I should feel very shabby to deliver only six lectures during seven

1–Kenneth B. Murdock (1895–1975): Associate Professor of English, Harvard University, 1930–2, Professor, 1932–64; Dean of the Faculty of Arts and Sciences, 1931–6; Master of Leverett House, 1931–41. Works include *Increase Mather* (1924), *Literature and Theology in Colonial New England* (1949), *The Notebooks of Henry James* (with F. O. Matthiessen, 1947).

2–TSE had been offered the visiting position of Charles Eliot Norton Professor at Harvard for the academic session 1932–3. Murdock sent a copy of the 'Essential Terms', subscribed by a committee including Professor Paul J. Sachs (Chairman), Henry James and Professor John L. Lowes, which included these ambiguous provisions:

'It is the wish and intention of the giver, (the late C. Chauncey Stillman) that in the administration of this gift, the term Poetry shall be interpreted in the broadest sense, including, together with Verse, all poetic expression in Language, Music or the Fine Arts, under which term Architecture may be included.

'The lectures shall not have been previously printed or delivered in public. Within six months after their delivery, the manuscript of these lectures shall be delivered to Harvard University, whose property this manuscript shall then become. These lectures shall be published by either the Harvard University Press or otherwise, as the Corporation of the University shall determine.

'Should any profits accrue from the publication and sale of these Charles Eliot Norton Lectures, then these profits may, in the discretion of the Corporation, be shared by the author of the lectures and Harvard University, or not, as the Corporation may determine; but all profits so received by the University shall be added to the principal of the gift, or otherwise used in promoting the objects of this gift.'

months. Perhaps twelve would be enough, but I should hope that the lecturer might find other and better ways as well, of filling his time and being of some use to the students.[1]

Yours very sincerely,
[T. S. Eliot]

TO *Lilian Donaghy*   CC

18 November 1931   [Faber & Faber Ltd]

Dear Mrs Donaghy,

Thank you for your letter.[2] I am very glad to hear that your husband has agreed to go into a nursing-home for a time as it is obvious that if left to himself he will merely continue to overwork and precipitate repeated collapses. While I am very sorry that he connects me in any way with his supposed persecution I know enough about these matters not to be in the least surprised. As I said before his behaviour seems to be wholly true to type, and if he can be made to rest for a long enough time I do not think you need to take these manifestations very seriously. It is true that there was a passage about a woman named Lil in the poem you mention, but apart from that slight coincidence it has not the slightest bearing whatever, and there is not any mention of epilepsy anywhere in the poem. Your husband is of course mistaken in thinking that the text

1 – Murdock responded on 27 Nov.: 'I feel sure that an instalment of the salary can be paid at any time you request after July 1, and . . . we shall, of course, be delighted to have you give as many lectures as you will; and we even have a fond hope that you might be willing to take a small group of students in a regular "course" for the year or for one of the half-years.'

2 – Mrs Donaghy wrote that her husband Lyle had been admitted to a home in the North of Ireland. 'One morning the testimonials which he had sent to the head-master of a school where he hoped to get a post were returned, & it upset him very much & he has been ill ever since.

'His people felt that the strain on them was too great & realized that he would have a much better chance of getting better under proper care, so his Father arranged about his going into the home. Lyle went like a child, though he did not want to. He believes it is another move in the plot against him. We are all "plasticine" in the hands of experimentalists! You and a nerve-specialist called Dr Gillespie . . . are the instigators of the plot & move me & his parents & most other people with whom he comes in contact about like pawns. I do not know why Lyle considers you as one of the chief instigators. He told me that, when he was in Northumberland House, he was lent a copy of "The Waste Land" & that in it he read a new portion, which he told me was not in it when he read it before, about a woman called Lil who had epileptic fits. This part of your book he insisted was mimicking him & me. I do not know if such a part is even in the book, but at any rate my name is Lilian & I have been having epileptic fits for the last few years, though they are ever so much better. Is it just a strange coincidence or did my husband imagine he read it?'

743

he saw recently is in any way altered from the original, and it could easily be shown that the whole thing was composed long before I knew him or anything about him; but reasoning is merely a waste of time. I shall try to write him a letter before long, but of course will make no allusion to any of these troubles or to having heard from you. The authorities of the nursing-home will no doubt decide whether it is suitable for him to receive letters from persons outside his family.

With all sympathy, I am,

Yours sincerely
[T. S. Eliot]

TO *Frances Gregg*[1]   CC

19 November 1931   [*The Criterion*]

Dear Madam,

I remember your story[2] very well although it is a long time since I have heard from you again. I am very sorry to hear of all the unfortunate circumstances of which you tell me, and wish that I might be of some help by using 'Waterside Bungalow'.[3] But I have found it quite impracticable to serialize long stories in the *Criterion* and for book publication my firm is not anxious to undertake at the moment another novel, as we have

---

1 – Frances Gregg (1884–1941), American writer, was brought up in Philadelphia. Friend of EP and intimate of H.D. (Gregg wrote in her diary: 'Two girls in love with each other, and each in love with the same man. Hilda, Ezra, Frances'), she married in 1912 the writer Louis Wilkinson ('Louis Marlow') after breaking with H.D. (and she divorced Wilkinson in 1923). She had contributed poems to *The Egoist* and *Others*. See Gregg, *The Mystic Leeway*, ed. Ben Jones (1995), which includes an account of Gregg by her son Oliver Wilkinson. Her career is reviewed by Helen Carr in *The Verse Revolutionaries: Ezra Pound, H.D. and The Imagists* (2009).
2 – 'Locust Street', *MC* 6 (Sept. 1927), 206–9.
3 – Gregg wrote (n. d.) that she had lost her job on the 'Woman's Page' of the *News Chronicle*. 'My son has been a semi-invalid for nearly two years and I can't take another post even if I could get it. So I wrote a play, and with my usual near-success, got a fifty pound option on it. It may – or may not – be produced in February next . . . But what I need at the moment are some shillings to feed us with.' In a further letter, dated 6 Nov., she related that she had 'come such a financial cropper that I "haven't a roof over my head" except an antique bus roof. I am starting off for Cornwall with my children and a five pound note . . . I do not anticipate taking up tramping for life. I have a perfectly good house up here into which I shall go as soon as I can get fifty pounds together to send my furniture from London . . .' See 'Little Goat', *C.* 12 (Apr. 1933), 438–40.

already numerous commitments. I shall look forward however to seeing more of your shorter stories from time to time.

> With best wishes
> Yours very truly
> [T. S. Eliot]

TO G. C. Catlin[1]   CC

19 November 1931   [*The Criterion*]

Dear Catlin,

I am sending you herewith the Gerald Heard book for which you asked.[2] I have only just glanced at it, and in spite of having had good report of the author from various sources, I must say that a few minutes browsing gave me the impression that it is a very silly book. But I may be quite wrong, and I should like to hear from you when you have read it whether you think it is really worth reviewing, and if it is how much space it is worth.

> Yours sincerely,
> [T. S. Eliot]

TO A. L. Rowse   TS Exeter

19 November 1931   *The Criterion*

Dear Rowse,

Thanks for your note of yesterday.[3] I did not know that you were now permanently in London for half the time, but I am very glad to hear it. I wish that you would come and lunch with me soon. My time is pretty well filled up for the next ten days, but would you care to fix a day during the week of Monday 30?

---

1 – George Catlin (1896–1979): Professor of Political Science, author of numerous books on political philosophy – including *Thomas Hobbes* (1922) – and later on Anglo-American relations; friend and associate of Harold Laski, Ramsay MacDonald, Herbert Morrison and Nehru; and husband of Vera Brittain (author of *Testament of Youth*). See John Catlin, *Family Quartet: Vera Brittain and her family* (1987). HR wrote to TSE on 3 Jan. 1930, 'Avoid Catlin: he is a dreadful windbag. Morley had lunch with him recently & will concur.'
2 – *Social Substance of Religion: An Essay on the Evolution of Religion* (1931).
3 – Rowse wrote ('Tuesday'): 'I was very touched by your sending me your poem & by your letter . . . You know I am living in London most of the week now & wd love to come round & see you sometime soon.'

Most of the books you mention have already been allocated, but I am sending you today Woodward's book, and should like to know how much space you think it requires.[1] It would be of course for the March number, so that you will not be pressed for time. As for your essays I will wait in patience.[2]

> Yours ever,
> T. S. Eliot

Chas Smyth is after scalp.[3]

TO *Ramon Fernandez*   TS Dominique Fernandez

19 November 1931   *The Criterion*

Dear Fernandez,

I enclose a letter from the National Library of Mexico which may amuse you. They wrote to me a long time ago for a photograph, and seemed disposed to invite my nomination of other immortals worthy of a position in their portrait gallery. So naturally I told them that the first person they should ask was yourself. Why they should have thought [it] necessary to appeal through the Mexican Legation in Paris I cannot understand. They did not approach me through the American Embassy.

I have lately seen Gordon George, who told me that he had seen you in Paris and had some good conversation. Are you still too busy ever to have any contribution to offer to the *Criterion*?

> Yours ever
> T. S. Eliot

1 – The books that ALR requested included E. L. Woodward, *War and Peace in Europe 1815–1870*; Herbert Butterfield, *The Whig Interpretation of History*; Nikolai Berdyaev, *The Russian Revolution*; and Jeremy Bentham, *The Theory of Legislation*. See his review of Woodward, *War and Peace in Europe, 1815–1870*: C. 11 (July 1932), 735.
2 – 'I have a very painful feeling about not having written for many months for the *Criterion*. Not that it's any loss to it! But my head is so full of the various subjects I have been dying to write on: there are those essays on Newman (and I've read a good deal more of him lately); and the one on "The Social Criticism of M. Arnold"; & "The Defence of Politics" etc. etc. But in time I shall, I hope.'
3 – Rowse replied ('Sunday'): 'How can Chas Smyth be after my scalp? I hope he's not reviewing my book; by all I can gather he's such an ass.'

TO *I. A. Richards*   TS Magdalene

19 November 1931   *The Criterion*

Dear Richards,

I have read your paper which I enclose,[1] as I imagine you want the copy back, with great interest, and not a few chuckles, considering the audience to which it was addressed, and the sort of thing on which they will probably have been fed before reading yours, which seems to me exactly the kind of disturbance which is most required for the present time. Would you care or have time to put it into shape for the *Criterion*? I say put it into shape because in its present form it obviously implies the series for which it was designed, and starts off rather abruptly for separate publication.

I also enclose a rough copy of the draft which I mentioned to you, and hope to hear from you on Friday evening.[2]

Yours ever
T. S. E.

TO *The Warden, House of the Sacred Mission*   CC

19 November 1931   [Faber & Faber Ltd]

Dear Father Bedale,

Thank you very much for your letter of the 13th.[3] As you know I have been hoping for an opportunity to visit Kelham for the last eighteen months, and it would be very pleasant for me to be able to accept your invitation. It is possible that I might be able to come in February next for a weekend, and to give some sort of address, but it is impossible for me to fix any engagement at present. If it is a question of filling up a programme

---

1–Unidentified; possibly an early version of IAR's paper 'Science Value and Poetry'.
2–TSE sent a draft of 'The Difficulties of a Statesman' (which follows 'Triumphal March' in the unfinished 'Coriolan'), *CPP*, 129. IAR commented, in an undated letter (24/25 Nov. 1931): 'The Second Lap seems to me to go even better than the first and they go a long way together. I very much like the echoes of *Anabasis* . . . My only complaint is that I want more. Possibly II stops a shade too suddenly' (*Letters of I. A. Richards*, 62).
3–Fr Bedale, Warden of the House of the Sacred Mission, Nottinghamshire, invited TSE to give a lecture at Kelham Theological College 'on some literary topic'. 'As a friend of Father Tribe, our Director, you know you are most welcome to come to Kelham when you have the opportunity, but so far you have been hindered . . . Some Saturday evening in February next year would be the convenient time for us for the lecture . . .' Fr Reginald Tribe was Director, 1925–43.

I had better decline, but if it [is] possible that you might still at a later date have one or two such evenings unfilled I should be very glad to reconsider the question at about Christmas time. If you feel that it is worth further consideration I should be interested to know what kind of lecture would be appropriate.

Yours sincerely
[T. S. Eliot]

TO *Elizabeth Wiskemann* CC

19 November 1931   [Faber & Faber Ltd]

Dear Miss Wiskemann,

I must apologise for the delay in replying definitely to your letter of the 21st ultimo, with its enclosure, but the matter had to be gone into very thoroughly from every point of view.[1] While we found that the scheme which you set forth is extremely interesting and attractive, our enquiries unfortunately led to the opinion that there would be very little prospect of success for such a book on Germany at the present time. We should certainly not feel justified in commissioning it, and I should personally feel that it would be wrong to encourage you to undertake such a very considerable piece of work without being commissioned. It is possible, of course, that some other publisher might view the prospect more hopefully than we do, but much as I should like to see such a book, and much as I regret that my own firm cannot undertake to produce it, I am obliged to agree that at the present time it would be for us an unjustifiable risk.

With many thanks and regrets

Yours sincerely
[T. S. Eliot]

TO *James Joyce* CC

19 November 1931   [Faber & Faber Ltd]

Dear Joyce,

I have not heard from you for nearly a month, but I find that I promised to continue my letter of the 20th October, which I have not done. Herewith

---

1–Wiskemann had submitted a handwritten outline of her proposed 'History of Germany for the fairly young'. She added: 'The title can be whichever you prefer . . . I suppose one always modifies the original plan a good deal in writing – I am sure I shall want to be inconstant.'

is the revised specimen which I mentioned and which I ought to have sent you some days ago. You will see that this setting appears to bring the book up not to 526 pages, but to 598. I therefore very much hope that you will be satisfied with this expansion, for as I said, any further increase must substantially increase both the bulk and the space, and decidedly throws out our estimates.

I should be very glad to have news of you, and to know whether and when you are going back to Zurich.

Yours ever sincerely
[T. S. Eliot]

FROM *Harold Raymond* TO *Geoffrey Faber*   TS

20 November 1931   Chatto & Windus, 97 & 99
                                    St Martin's Lane, London W.C.2

My dear Faber.

I have not replied to you before concerning *Stepping Heavenward* partly because I expected that I should be running across you some day in the Club or elsewhere, and partly because I gather that your letter was answered to some extent by my partner reminding you that the book had already been published before we issued it ourselves.

I am sorry that you regard it as so bitter an attack. I fear that I personally am not in a position to gauge its bitterness, as I do not know Aldington well enough, and Eliot not at all. But with regard to the passages which you mention as particularly distressing, I can hardly think that Aldington intended them to apply in the manner you suggest.

I quite appreciate the difficulty of your position, and should indeed be sorry if the distress which the book has caused proved any upset to our own friendly relations. At the same time I feel sure you in turn will appreciate the delicacy of the relationship between a publisher and his author if any question of censoring a book is involved. I cannot quite agree with your phrase 'and you permit', and I can hardly think that any author would accept such a phrase as expressive of what is or should be the relation between author and publisher. In other words, I feel that this issue really lies between Aldington and Eliot, and not between you and me.

Yours very sincerely,
Harold Raymond

TO *Seán Ó'Faoláin*   CC

20 November 1931   [*The Criterion*]

Dear Mr O'Faolain,

I seem to have forgotten that I promised to let you know in any case the results of my approach to Richmond.[1] I am afraid that he has no vacancies at all at the moment. I imagine that classical Irish literature is dealt with for the *Times* by Robin Flower, and of reviewers in contemporary literature and history he seems to have more than he can use.

I am very sorry indeed about this, but of course I know that the *Times* always has more applicants for review work than it can employ.

Is there anything else that I can do?

Yours sincerely
[T. S. Eliot]

TO *Caresse Crosby*   CC

20 November 1931   [Faber & Faber Ltd]

Dear Mrs Crosby,

Thank you very much for your letter of the 12th and for the cheque for my introduction, which seems to me more than munificent for a short preface which was written amongst the distractions of many other affairs, and which falls far short of what I should like it to be. Your new project sounds extremely interesting, and I should like to hear more details of it.[2] I suppose that you would try to distribute the translations into English in England as well as on the continent. I cannot think of any two French novels that I know better worth translating than the *Diable au Corps* and *Bubu de Montparnasse*. In some respects the *Bal du Comte d'Orgel* seemed to me when I read it a more brilliant performance than Radiguet's first book, but I doubt if it is really suitable for translation. For one thing it

1 – O'Faolain wrote on 18 Nov. to ask if TSE had yet heard back from Richmond of the *TLS*. 'I thought of calling on him on Friday when I should be in the city.'
2 – Crosby's project was to bring out 'a continental collection in the same manner as Tauchnitz but including translations from European languages. The first translation to appear is Raymond Radiguet's *Diable au Corps*, translated by Kay Boyle, with an introduction by Aldous Huxley. I am also doing *Bubu de Montparnasse*, and a story of Kafka from the German. I am including also Scandinavian and Italian literature, etc . . . I should be awfully interested and pleased to have any suggestions that you might offer as to what you consider most worth while, either to re-print from English or to translate into English. I give rather better terms than Tauchnitz . . .'

is unfinished, and for another a good deal of the comedy would be lost on people who did not know the originals of the personages. I should think that *Bubu* would be extremely difficult to translate. It really ought to be done by someone who knows something of the underworld of London as well as that of Paris. A young man was recently recommended to me as a translator because of his peculiar knowledge of the French underworld vocabulary, but I have seen no specimen of his translation and cannot vouch for him myself.

I have never read any of the books of André Malraux, but from what I have heard of him I should imagine that some of them might be interesting in translation. I will try to think of any English novels suitable for re-printing, and let you know.

I have read five of the detective stories by Simenon, and really enjoyed two or three of them.[1] Whether they would take on with English readers I do not know because I think that all, or nearly all, French thrillers are slightly unsuitable to the English mind. The only two I know of which did fairly well are the first two of Gaston Leroux, *The Yellow Room* and *The Lady in Black*. I have myself a particular admiration for Maurice le Blanc and should like to see a complete Arsène Lupin translated, but there again I am rather doubtful of the market.[2] I hope to hear from you on your return from America.

With very many thanks,

I am yours sincerely
[T. S. Eliot]

1–'I may also do a series of detective stories by a Dutch-Frenchman who calls himself Simenon. As I know that good detective stories appeal to you perhaps you would be willing to write an introduction for me but this is only an idea as I have not yet the contract for them.'

2–In his Twenty-Fifth Anniversary Report (1935) to the Harvard Class of 1910, TSE was to declare that he admired Arsène Lupin more than Simenon; in his Fiftieth Anniversary Report, written in June 1960, he was to reveal: 'I now prefer . . . Inspector Maigret to Arsène Lupin.' To the journalist Richard Jennings he expostulated in 1952 (undated note): 'What a great writer!' To Anthony Cronin c. 1960 ('Ulysses and The Waste Land', *The Irish Times*, 16 June 1972, 10): 'Oh dear no . . . I read nothing nowadays . . . nothing at all . . . except perhaps a little Simenon.'

TO *Mary Hutchinson*   TS Texas

20 November 1931   Faber & Faber Ltd

My dear Mary,

That is very kind of you.[1] But as I am engaged for lunch the four first days of the week, and as I know Vivienne would like very much indeed to come to dinner, and as she is as likely to be fit for it on Tuesday next as at any time that can be foreseen, may we keep to that programme?

The following week I am not so busy, but Friday the 4th would be the best day for me, if convenient.

I enjoyed immensely coming in for the tail end of the afternoon, and look forward.

                                        Affectionately,
                                        Tom

FROM *Geoffrey Faber* TO *Harold Raymond*   CC

23 November 1931   [Faber & Faber Ltd]

My dear Raymond,

Many thanks for your friendly rejoinder. May I say, first, that I wouldn't have written if I hadn't felt that I knew you well enough to speak my mind without any fear of upsetting our own relations. Nor would I have written, if it hadn't been that I knew, better than most, just what harm Aldington's book will do to one of my closest friends.

I agree of course that the earlier publication in Florence – of which I, and others, had never heard – alters the basis of my protest.

But, as to the character and intention of the allusions which made me protest, there can really be no reasonable doubt at all – no doubt whatever, that is, in the minds of those who know the circumstances. Aldington is, or was, a friend of Eliot's and knows those circumstances as well as anybody; it is simply not conceivable that he was not intentionally using them to edge his satire. It is something to know that the point won't be taken by many who, like yourself and your partner, haven't any knowledge of the facts. But by those who have the knowledge and read the book, and particularly by the two people most concerned (which is where the real rub comes), it can't be mistaken.

1 – Hutchinson wrote on 18 Nov.: 'If you would rather come to lunch with me [at 3 Albert Road, Regent's Park] next week and have our dinner à quatre the following week – let me know.'

Eliot, of course, has his legal remedy; though, equally of course, it is unthinkable that he should use it. So perhaps there was some justification for my suggesting that the publishers might have had something to say. Don't you sometimes warn an author that he's on dangerous ground?

Anyhow, it was nice of you to write as you did.

Yours ever
[Geoffrey C. Faber]

TO *John Middleton Murry*   MS Northwestern

Monday night, 23 November 1931   Faber & Faber Ltd

My dear John,

I am sorry I did not write at once, but I was waiting to see whether any time was possible. I have had no time at all: I have had lunch engagements on both Monday and Tuesday, a committee this afternoon (as usual) and a board meeting tomorrow afternoon: which means that I must try to do in the morning the work I should have done in the afternoon.

Even two hours would not be enough; and with every week, even, that passes, there is more to discuss. You must not think of my position as in every way settled: there are the fixed points of Royalism & Catholicism; but for *me* the latter is revolutionary – and the former expresses the movement from conservatism toward revolution – I was quite aware beforehand to how much ridicule I shd expose myself – that is a small matter: but I would not like you to think that I am definitely fixed in existing group modes of thought.

But at present, in a perfectly healthy body, I have a mind so tired as to be of little use to anybody.

Ever affectionately
Tom

TO *Eric Blair*   cc

24 November 1931   [Faber & Faber Ltd]

Dear Sir,

I and another director have read *À la Belle de Nuit*, and while we agree that the book has great power, and appearance of authenticity, and is certainly very interesting, we do not feel that its literary merit is quite sufficient to justify our publishing a book on such a subject.[1] If it could be considered as a work of humanitarian propaganda of advantage for this country, alternatively to being a work of great literary merit, we should look at the matter differently.

I hope, however, that you will bring before us any other suggestion that occurs to you.

Yours sincerely,
[T. S. Eliot]

TO *James Joyce*   CC

24 November 1931   [Faber & Faber Ltd]

Dear Joyce,

Thank you for your letter of the 22nd; but you are not quite right about the identity of the two specimens.[2] I thought I explained that although the type is the same, the second specimen has more leads than the first, that is to say it is more widely spaced. If you will look again, and I return the pages, you will see that the specimen of October 16th has estimated for 598 pages, whereas that of September 21st has only 488, a difference of 110 pages. We found that the next largest size would mean a book of probably 800 pages, and I explained that such a size would be very unwieldy, and furthermore could not be published at one guinea. It merely happens that the first of these two specimen pages is more heavily inked than the second. We are quite ready to start setting up, and should be glad to have Part 1 as soon as you can send it.

I shall have to let you know further about the volume of essays.[3] The matter has not been neglected, but I have not been handling it myself, and do not know at the moment just what stage has been reached. I was very sorry that I had to dine out last night with some people who had no wireless set, and was unable to hear what Harold Nicholson said about you.[4] I shall read it next week in the *Listener*.

1 – Blair had submitted *À la Belle de Nuit* on 4 Nov. He added that if ever F&F had need of a translator of any other French book, he would be grateful for 'a trial': 'I am anxious to get hold of some work of this kind, & I think I could do it as well as the average translator.'
2 – JJ wrote that he had just received a proof, 'apparently pulled' on 16 Oct., but that it was 'identical' with the one pulled on 21 Sept., which he considered 'not clear enough' (*Letters* III [1966], ed. Richard Ellmann, 235).
3 – 'Has anything been arranged about the volume of essays [*Our Exagmination*]?'
4 – Siepmann wrote to TSE on 25 Nov. 1931: 'In the last but one of his talks on Modern Literature Harold Nicolson is to make reference to James Joyce and his work. He is

Have you got the London flat off your hands yet, and if not can I be of any use?[1] I hope you will let me know when you have decided definitely about Zurich.[2] My wife wishes to be remembered to you and to Mrs Joyce.

Yours very sincerely
[T. S. Eliot]

TO Messrs. C. Vandyk

cc

24 November 1931   [Faber & Faber Ltd]

Dear Sirs,

I have received from you a copy of one of your portraits of myself, and I must refer you to the letter in which I ordered a print, and from which it should be quite clear to you that you have sent the wrong portrait. The portrait you have sent is a portrait in profile, and I think that my letter made it abundantly clear that it was not another copy of the profile, but a three-quarter face.[3] In the circumstances I must ask you to send and take away this portrait for which I have no occasion, and if you cannot identify the pose for which I ask you, I suggest that it would be best to send me one proof of all three, so that I may return to you the one which is wanted. Would it not be better when you make several studies of the

---

particularly anxious to include in this talk the record made by James Joyce himself of which you once spoke to me. I think at the time you yourself were anxious that this should be broadcast on some appropriate occasion, and this seems to be a useful opportunity for introducing it to listeners.'

1–TSE was to recall in a much later year: 'In the early thirties Joyce discovered that for reasons connected with the legality of his testamentary disposition he needed to spend a period of two or three consecutive months in England. Being the man he was, he rented, for this brief sojourn, an unfurnished flat: a dreary little flat, for which he then proceeded to buy some still drearier necessary pieces of furniture. (How he eventually disposed of flat and furniture I do not remember.)' ('Miss Sylvia Beach', *Mercure de France*, Août–Septembre 1963, 10).

2–'I cannot make up my mind about Zurich yet.'

3–The confusion may have arisen because TSE's secretary had written to C. Vandyk (court photographer) on 6 Feb. 1931, 'I am desired by Mr T. S. Eliot to inform you that the London Electrotype Company are authorised to reproduce on behalf of the *Bookman* a copy of the photograph you took of him recently. He would prefer it if you would supply them with that of the half-face.' Vandyk advised TSE on 26 Feb. – in response to another letter (not found) – 'I beg to acknowledge receipt of your letter with thanks, also order for four camera studies in Cabinet size. I note the positions required and am placing the copies in hand accordingly.' TSE was billed £2–2–0 on 26 Mar. for the four camera studies.

same person to sign or number or letter each one in order to avoid this sort of difficulty and loss of time in future?[1]

Yours faithfully

[T. S. Eliot]

TO *Dougal Malcolm*[2]   CC

25 November 1931   [*The Criterion*]

Dear Mr Malcolm,

I am wondering whether you would find the time, and would do me the kindness of reviewing for the *Criterion* the Warden of All Souls' book of translations into Greek and Latin called *Musa Feriata*.[3] It is a form of composition the persistence of which should I think be encouraged in every way, and the Warden's translations, so far as I am competent to judge, seem to me very accomplished. Unfortunately there are very few people living who can either write good Greek or Latin verse or judge of its merit when written, and you are the obvious person to review this book if you will.

Sincerely yours

[T. S. Eliot]

1–Vandyk replied on 27 Nov. that TSE in his previous correspondence had ordered 'half face shoulders square to the front'; they would send by messenger 'the position you have described'.

2–Dougal Orme Malcolm (1877–1955), a Fellow of All Souls, worked for the Colonial Office before joining in 1913 the board of the British South Africa Company – he was to be Director and President – which enjoyed remarkable profits from Rhodesian mineral rights and railways. See Malcolm, *The British South Africa Company, 1889–1939* (1939). He had been on the losing side in lending support to TSE's candidature for a research fellowship at All Souls in May 1926. He gave generous financial support to C. ALR recalled, in *All Souls in My Time* (1993): 'Sir Dougal Malcolm, Dougie to us, was eminently clubbable . . . and sat long over the port . . . Cousin to half the Scottish aristocracy, he was . . . a gifted linguist as well as Latin versifier . . . Rich and kindly, he invited me to dine at his London house' (85).

3–*Musa Feriata* (1931), by Francis Pember, Warden of All Souls, 1914–32, was reviewed by Malcolm in C. 11 (Apr. 1932), 523–5.

TO *Caresse Crosby*   cc

26 November 1931   [Faber & Faber Ltd]

Dear Mrs Crosby,

Thank you for your letter of the 23rd.[1] If you want to use my sentence I think I had better re-form it in the following way.

'I cannot think of any two modern French novels that I have read, which I should be more interested to see in translation, than the *Diable au Corps* and *Bubu de Montparnasse*'.

Yours sincerely,
[T. S. Eliot]

TO *David Higham*   cc

26 November 1931   [Faber & Faber Ltd]

Dear Higham,

In reply to your letter of the 5th November which I am sorry you were obliged to repeat on the 20th.[2] I understand that you are acting for Allen & Unwin on this matter, and I will repeat to you briefly what I have already said to Siepmann of the B.B.C. I do not feel the slightest enthusiasm for reprinted collections of broadcast talks, and so far as I personally am concerned I do not want to have anything to do with it. But if my colleagues in this series all wish to have their lectures published I should not like to interfere with the project by withholding my own. This refers particularly to Christopher Dawson and John MacMurray.

If the series are to be published in book form I shall give my consent subject to arrangement of terms to be the same to all contributors, on the understanding that I am at liberty to make whatever other use of the material I choose, and that in the event of any censorship being exercised by the B.B.C. my own contribution is to be published in such form as I choose, and not in such form as the B.B.C. chooses.

Yours sincerely
[T. S. Eliot]

1–Crosby asked to quote, as a blurb, this sentence from TSE's previous letter: 'I cannot think of any two French novels that I know better worth translating than the *Diable au Corps* and *Bubu de Montparnasse*.'
2–Higham reported that he was in a position, 'with the full approval of the BBC', to arrange for the publication in volume form of the series of talks entitled "The Changing World"'. Would TSE consent to the general principle of publication, and authorise Curtis Brown to proceed?

P.S. I have already discussed this proposal with Dawson, and find that he is not very interested, but I must take the matter up with MacMurray also.[1]

TO *Bruce Richmond*   CC

26 November 1931   [Faber & Faber Ltd]

Dear Richmond,

I might have explained to you the position about Ford when I last saw you but forgot to do so.[2] It is merely that in the meantime I have got involved with the Elizabethan Society[3] of King's College here owing to the intervention of Boas, and as he begged me to read to that Society a paper during this season, and as he was very kind to me some years ago I finally consented, and am to read them on next Wednesday a paper on John Marston which I have not yet written. I should of course never dream of reading to a Society as a lecture a paper written as a leader for the *T.L.S.* so I had to find another subject. But for this misfortune I should have been working on the Ford, and should have been able to let you have it before the end of the year. So may we say February, and I will try to finish the essay by the beginning of January?

I am not clear whether you want a whole leader or a couple of columns on Lodge, but I do not think I am quite the man for it. Had I sufficient leisure during the next month I would take it on anyway, but in the circumstances I think that someone else had better have it.

With many thanks

Yours ever
[T. S. E.]

1–Curtis Brown wrote again on 16 Dec. 1931 that it had not proved possible to arrange for the publication of the talks entitled "Modern Dilemma" in "The Changing World" series, 'since a sufficient number of contributors were not willing to allow their contributions to be published'.

Macmurray's talks were to be published as *Freedom in the Modern World* (F&F, 1932).

2–BLR had written (on same date) that if TSE still 'cared to do' his postponed essay on Ford, the *TLS* 'would be glad to have it' for Jan. or Feb. 1932. 'John Ford', *TLS*, 5 May 1932, 317–18.

3–Elizabethan Literary Society.

TO *Charles Harris*   CC

26 November 1931   [Faber & Faber Ltd]

Dear Harris,

I have had a talk with Poncin[s], and expect to hear more from him later.[1] I should be very glad to lunch one day, but my lunch times are rather full up at present. Any week-day of the week of the 14th December would suit me quite well, and I hope that one of these days may be convenient to you.

Yours sincerely
[T. S. Eliot]

FROM *Harold Raymond* TO *Geoffrey Faber*   TS Faber

1 December 1931   Chatto & Windus, 97 & 99
                                   St Martin's Lane, London W.C.2

My dear Faber,

I am sorry to have to revert to the question of *Stepping Heavenward*. The reason I do so is this.

The story was written by Aldington nearly a year ago and designed to form one of a book of stories by him, which we were to publish in the spring of 1932. At the date of your first letter we had in the house the complete proofs of this volume, for inclusion in which *Stepping Heavenward* was reset from our Dolphin edition. We accordingly felt it necessary to inform Aldington of the gist of what has passed between you and me, and though I realise that you expressed a wish that we should not raise the question with him, I trust that you will see that in the circumstances what we did had to be done.

Aldington in reply asks us to inform you of his original plans regarding the story, in order that you may apprise Eliot. Would it be too much to

---

1 – Harris (*The Nineteenth Century & After*) wrote on 13 Nov. to introduce Vicomte Léon de Poncins. 'He is a frequent contributor to the "Mercure de France" & I think would be interested to become a contributor also to the more serious English Reviews. His chief subjects in this line are modern social questions, especially Revolutionary movements, & I think you will find him interesting.' Léon de Poncins (1897–1976), French Catholic journalist and author, was increasingly obsessed with a Masonic–Jewish conspiracy working to undermine Catholic doctrines and institutions. His several publications include *Les Forces secrètes de la Révolution* (1928): *Freemasory and Judaism: The Secret Powers behind Revolution* (1929) and *Judaism and the Vatican* (1967). He met TSE in London in the week beginning 18 Nov. 1931.

request you to let me know that you have done this? When you have told Eliot, he then may, if he so desires, communicate with Aldington. I still feel strongly that it is a matter between Eliot and Aldington rather than between you and me, and I hope you will put this further matter so to Eliot.

Yours very sincerely,
Harold Raymond.

FROM *Geoffrey Faber* TO *Harold Raymond*   CC

2 December 1931   Faber & Faber Ltd

Dear Raymond,

I am very reluctant to say anything to Eliot, who at present does not even know that there has been any correspondence between you and me about *Stepping Heavenwards* [*sic*], and has not discussed the book with me at all.

For, in the first place, what action could he take? He could only write to Aldington a letter of protest, or a letter appealing to him to withdraw the story. The latter course is one that nobody could take, in the circumstances, and retain his self-respect. And the former course would seem to me both unwise, and unprofitable. Since you have told Aldington the gist of our correspondence, he must know that Eliot's friends regard certain passages in the story as libellous. Would it help matters for the libelled to start a correspondence with the libeller?

And, in the second place, since you raise the matter again, I must say that I don't really agree with you that it is not a matter for Chatto's to feel concerned about. I must, of course, agree that it isn't any obvious business of mine. This just happens to be one of those uncomfortable occasions when one is obliged to become an unlicensed nuisance. I didn't press the point in my last letter, because the book was published and it was no use going on about it. But, after all, a libel is a libel, and the publisher can't say it's nothing to do with him. It is true that I cannot imagine Eliot founding a libel action upon *Stepping Heavenward* – nobody with the instincts of a gentleman could! But that doesn't alter the facts, or – in my view – the publishers' responsibility.

I understand how very difficult and uncomfortable a situation you feel yourselves to be in; but I do really feel it's your problem. If you are inclined to think that I have jumped to unwarrantable conclusions about *Stepping Heavenward*, why not ask one of your own people what he makes of it? Aldous Huxley, for instance – I imagine he knows all about both the parties.

Yours ever
[Geoffrey C. Faber]

TO *Elizabeth Wiskemann* CC

2 December 1931 [Faber & Faber Ltd]

Dear Miss Wiskemann,

Thank you for your note of the 27th.[1] As for the question of Catherine the Great. What you suggest is such a completely unknown subject to me that it would be impossible to commission a book, though I should be immensely interested to see it when done. If you think that some of the material could be cast in the form of an article for the *Criterion* I should be interested in that, and would be in a better position to speak about the book. If this notion appeals to you, and is possible, I should like to hear a little more about Catherine's financial views before definitely commissioning the article.

Yours sincerely
[T. S. Eliot]

TO *Sylvia Beach* TS Princeton

2 December 1931 Faber & Faber Ltd

Dear Miss Beach,

I have your letter of the 28th.[2] I understand that Mr Nicolson is to give his talk about Joyce after all on Tuesday evening next. The difficulty at the B.B.C. was a rule that they have that no book under censorship

---

1 – 'I suppose no alteration of scope or treatment would make a book that you would take on?' asked Wiskemann. She proceeded in a postscript to remark that she had been 'reading a good deal about Catherine the Great lately which makes me contemplate a quite different piece of writing, viz. about her currency & credit notions as compared with her & our contemporaries. She was quite remarkable. But that would not be at all your kind of book, would it?'

2 – 'I wonder if you have heard that Mr Harold Nicholson was to have talked about Joyce last Tuesday evening in the lectures on Modern English Literature that he is broadcasting for the BBC, and that he was not permitted to, at the last minute, for some reason. I am sending you a copy of the [newspaper] *Intransigeant* with a little notice that appeared in it the next day. The French writers were amazed and amused.'

should be mentioned in any of their talks, so I expect that Nicholson has recast his talk in such a way as to be able to talk about *Ulysses* without mentioning the name of the book. If he has succeeded in doing this, the talk should certainly be a remarkable tour de force. Thank you for the copy of *l'Intransigeant*. I hope to listen to the talk if it does take place, and perhaps comment on the matter later.

Yours sincerely,
T. S. Eliot

FROM *TSE's Secretary* TO *H. N. Hurst*[1]   cc

2 December 1931   [Faber & Faber Ltd]

Dear Sir,

Mr T. S. Eliot has asked me to thank you for your letter of November 12. He was born on September 26th (The Feast of St Cyprian and St Justina) in 1888. Further details, including time are not available. Mr Eliot will be interested in the result of your investigations, if you think it proper that he should be acquainted with them.[2]

Yours very truly
[Pamela Wilberforce]

FROM *Harold Raymond* TO *Geoffrey Faber*   TS Faber

3 December 1931   Chatto & Windus, 97 & 99
                                   St Martin's Lane, London W.C.2

Dear Faber,

Many thanks for your letter. I wish I could see eye to eye with you in this matter, but I fear I cannot. We must agree to differ on the question what is a publisher's job, and what isn't. We still do not feel it is our problem; we still feel that the issue lies between Aldington and Eliot; and we do not think it is reasonable to land the problem on to any other party, Aldous Huxley or anyone else.

If you do not want to put the question to Eliot and suggest that he write to Aldington, why not write to Aldington yourself, not in the position of Eliot's publisher but simply as his friend? Alternatively, we could send him copies of your letters, but I think it would be better if you re-stated the

1–H. N. Hurst, Stellenbosch, Cape Province.
2–Sadly, nothing further is known.

case, setting out more definitely than in your previous letters in what ways you think the story might cause unhappiness and what you suggest should be done. The decision must rest with Aldington; we do not consider it our business to influence his decision even if we could; that is why I should like him to have set before him as clear-cut an issue as possible.[1]

Yours ever,

Harold Raymond

FROM *Geoffrey Faber* TO *Harold Raymond*   CC

4 December 1931   Faber & Faber Ltd

My dear Raymond,

I'm afraid I can't do that, and I hope you won't send my letters to you on to Aldington. I put the matter to you, knowing you. But I don't know Aldington. I never met him in my life. And nothing would induce me to start a correspondence like this with anyone I didn't know. As for putting the thing more definitely, I couldn't do that without the permission of Eliot himself. And apart from the fact that he would be most unlikely to give me such permission, the mere fact of my asking it would bring the whole matter back into the front of his mind – the one thing I most want to avoid.

No, I could do no more than point out to you, as Aldington's publisher, that his story contains at least one passage which I and others think to be not only a libel, but a peculiarly unpleasant libel. To which you reply, in effect, that it's no business of yours – a view of a publisher's responsibilities from which I, most respectfully, dissent. And there, so far as I am concerned, the matter ends.

I didn't, by the way, in the least intend to suggest that you should land the problem on to Aldous Huxley. What I meant to suggest was merely that, if you wanted independent confirmation or refutation of my reading of the story, you could probably get it from Aldous Huxley.

I am sorry to have been such a gad-fly.

Yours ever

[Geoffrey C. Faber]

1–Seymour-Jones notes, 473: 'Aldington told Sidney Schiff that if Eliot were to send him a straightforward request, that is, one that was not too "Christian-slimy" he might feel obliged to cancel publication but, since none was forthcoming, and the story had already been previously published twice, he went ahead' (9 Dec. 1931: BL Add MS 52916). See also Charles Doyle, *Richard Aldington: A Biography* (1989), 149.

6 December 1931   68 Clarence Gate Gardens

Dear Mrs Thorpe [*sic*],

We are having a small party on Dec. 12th (next Saturday) at 8 p.m. & we think it might possibly amuse you & your husband to come & – as my husband says – see some of the natives or aborigines together. Altho' there will, as a matter of fact, be a few cosmopolitans also.

Do come, both of you, & let me know as soon as possible,
Yours sincerely
V. H. Eliot

Do come if you can – but it is a very humble party. TSE²

TO *Mary Hutchinson*   MS Texas

7 December 1931   Faber & Faber Ltd

My dear Mary,

I am very much ashamed of myself for not ordering matters better, as well as disappointed. I had been trying to ring you up for two days before, and could not find the opportunity; nor, after failing to get you on Friday, did I have the opportunity to write!

The difficulty was a very simple and even silly one – but my life is largely regulated by trifling considerations. I took it that Friday was fixed, but having failed to mention it when I saw you at tea, I had several extremely busy and tired days, and forgot to mention it to Vivienne: and she is apt to be rather hurt if I do not tell her of my engagements well in advance. This is what I should have told you by telephone on Wednesday. I hope you will comprehend the situation: and may we fix another day when you come to dinner on Thursday? If you plead you are too busy so near to Christmas, I shall be disturbed.

Affectionately
Tom

---

1 – Margaret Thorp, née Farrand (1891–1970), educated at Smith College (AB, AM) and Yale (PhD, 1934), was a distinguished author and biographer; works include *Charles Kingsley, 1819–1875* (1937), *America at the Movies* (1939), *Female Persuasion: Six Strong-Minded Women* (1949), *Neilson of Smith* (1956), *Sara Orne Jewett* (1966). She and Willard Thorp were married in 1930 and forthwith spent a year in England on a travelling fellowship.
2 – The postscript sentence by TSE is written by hand.

TO *Geoffrey Faber*   TS Valerie Eliot

9 December 1931   [Faber & Faber Ltd]

CONFIDENTIAL

I have been for some time increasingly dissatisfied with our *style* of
advertising, and increasingly doubtful of the *system*. As my dissatisfaction
with the first led to my questioning the second, I will take the two in order.

Our advertisements seem to hesitate between the methods of the
younger houses which *advertise* and those of the older houses which
merely publish *booklists*, for the most part, in the newspapers. While I
should be very sorry to see F.&F. adopt the extreme style of one or two
publishers, I still think that it is much too young a firm to adopt such
conventional advertisement as we do. Our advertisements seem to have
an apologetic tone and a lack of confidence in the value of what we have
to sell. Mere lists of books impress no one; and commendatory quotations
in small type, even from the best papers, carry very little weight. I should
like to see advertisements which would give the impression that we have
at any moment at least one book to advertise, in the potential popularity
of which we have ourselves entire confidence.

I must make it clear that I do not pretend to possess the slightest ability
for advertising, which is a special study for special talents. But I think
that the ordinary educated reader's impression of our advertisements may
be very similar to my own. I am however sure that whatever *schemes*
of advertising may be preferable, we need a new *method of producing*
advertisements. At present our advertisements seem to be the product of
one man – and that is too few – and in a sense also the product of the
whole committee – and that is too many. The committee thinks from hand
to mouth; and the subject with which it chiefly deals – what books to
include and what to leave out of the week's advertisements – is really,
from the point of view of general programme, a mere detail. This general
programme does not exist. What I wish to emphasise is that advertising is
a study demanding special capacities; it does not fit in with the other work
of C.W.S., who already has quite enough to do in his own departments
without it;[1] and that it requires a certain *continuous* study of the situation,
and a continuous creative or inventive exercise.

I suggest that a small sub-committee should have full powers; within
the sum allotted they should have control, and of course subject to
retrospective criticism from the whole book-committee. They should be

---

1 – C. W. Stewart, a director of F&F, was in charge of advertising.

responsible for the whole programme for each season, including circulars and catalogues.

. . . .

A subject which intersects that of advertisement is that of our volume of production. I think that we tend to publish too many books. This is related to advertising in this way, that we cannot afford more space at present than we do take, and this space is almost invariably overcrowded. I do not object to taking risks on those types of book which may be either great successes or great failures; but we seem to have too many books which may make a little money, and (especially in the present times) will probably lose just a little money. I do not think that the principle of publishing *any* book which is good of its kind, and which seems likely just to "get home", is the right one; though I think every publisher ought to publish a few books, if they are *very* good, on which he *knows* that he will lose money. And in general, we do not seem to be quick enough in following changes of the market: if we had, we might have saved money dropped on limited editions.

In fine, I feel that the committee system has been a little overdone, in that it tends to relax individual responsibility. In such an atmosphere, and especially in a committee which has to deal rapidly with a great variety of business and of books in an afternoon, any one person may now and then wake up to find that something has been done against which he would have protested had he been alert. I do not know whether it is possible to give the committee more organic unity by a clearer division of functions between individual members, but just as the man who *produces* books naturally has a slightly different point of view from the man who has to *sell* them, so if each member were expected to have devoted more attention to certain aspects of the integral problem of publishing, the result might be less haphazard. It is not enough to publish a good and marketable book, or even a number of them; I feel that one of the best advertisements for a publishing firm is for that firm to develop a distinct character which shall become recognised by the trade and the public.

T. S. E.[1]

---

1 – GCF recorded in his diary on the following day, 10 Dec.: 'dined with the Eliots'.

TO *Sonia Hambourg*

10 December 1931   [Faber & Faber Ltd]

Dear Miss Hambourg,

I am sorry to find that your letter of October 22nd has remained so long unanswered. There will be plenty of time to send you another proof of the inscription, and we shall be able to bring the book out on February 4th next.[1] As for the cover it would be similar to those of the Auden and McLeod poems which I think I gave you. If you have not got these volumes with you I can send you others. It will be a coloured cover of similar paper, but presumably in some different colour. I should be glad if you could let me know if you have any preference in the matter of colour, and we will get the nearest to what you want that the paper manufacturers can provide.

Yours sincerely
[T. S. Eliot]

TO *Marianne Moore*[2]

10 December 1931   [*The Criterion*]

Dear Miss Moore,

I have just had your address from Ezra Pound. I have been wondering if you have anything which you have written or which you would like to write that you would care to offer to the *Criterion*, or whether there might be from time to time some book which you would be interested to review.

Yours sincerely,
[T. S. Eliot]

1–'I agree with you about the dates. Of course they are wrong as it is. They should be 1908–1931 not 1904–1930. I have corrected this on the proof but have not inserted Born and Died as I thought it best to leave that to you . . . However I think it would be better to insert these words as without them the dates are ambiguous . . . Clere would have been delighted with the way in which the poems are being published and I am most grateful to you for the trouble you have taken . . .'
2–Marianne Moore (1887–1972), American poet and critic: see Biographical Register.

TO *T. O. Beachcroft*   CC

10 December 1931   [*The Criterion*]

Dear Beachcroft,

Thank you for your letter of the 29th ultimo together with the essay on Ferrars which I like very much, and accept for publication at the earliest opportunity. I am wholly in agreement about Wordsworth, though I know that many others will object violently.[1]

When your domestic anxieties are relieved I should like to see you again.[2] If you can make the time do come to the *Criterion* meeting at Monro's on Wednesday, 16th next.

Yours sincerely,
[T. S. Eliot]

TO *John Rodgers*   CC

10 December 1931   [Faber & Faber Ltd]

Dear Mr Rogers,

I have finally read the copy of *Destin du Théatre* which you sent me with your letter of the 17th ultimo. I am grateful to you for having introduced me to the book, because I very much enjoyed reading it, and found myself largely in agreement with it. But I am afraid that for purposes of translation it is quite hopeless. The public in England for such a book would be very small especially as, like most French books it draws the majority of its illustrations from the Paris theatre, and even the names of some of the dramatists would be unknown here. So I return the book with this.

1 – 'Nicholas Ferrar and George Herbert', *C.* 12 (Oct. 1932), 24–42. 'I found it better to write less about Ferrar himself than to say briefly who he was, and what he did; and then to treat him as an influence on the most characteristic religious poetry of the 17th century – an influence exercised especially on Herbert.

'To make more plain the result of such an influence on poetry and also to discuss possible meanings for the terms religious and mystical poetry I have then examined the so-called religious element in Wordsworth – returning to some more detailed remarks about Herbert at the end.'

2 – 'I have been particularly busy at my office, and my wife has just had a baby: all rather distracting.'

I hope you will continue to let me know of any new books that you would like to review. We do not seem to have had any luck so far, but it frequently happens that several people ask for the same book.

Yours sincerely

[T. S. Eliot]

FROM *Vivien Eliot* TO *Ottoline Morrell*   MS Texas

11 December 1931   68 Clarence Gate Gardens

Dearest Ottoline,

Please excuse the old notepaper, we have to use it up.[1] I am so afraid that I did not *explain* to you properly this afternoon, at your most *glorious* tea party, the reason why I have had to postpone the party I was going to have here tomorrow evening. I found, after I had invited you, that *Tom* has got to Broadcast a Speech on the Wireless at Savoy Hill, on Sunday afternoon at 5.o'clock. And it was decided that the preparations for the party, & the party itself would interfere with the Broadcasting. So we have decided to have the *same* party, on *December 31st, New Year's Eve.* And you will remember that date, & be ready for it, *won't you, dear Ottoline*??

I was so happy at your house today. I feel so 'family' with you, & among *yr. friends, always*, & always did.[2] Particularly today did it strike me, for I had just been through such a fearful time, with T. All of a sudden. We had 4 people to dinner last night, & they did not seem to have at all a good effect, anyhow, not in *combination*. I was really horrified, for it is now so long that anything like it had happened.

---

1 – The letter is written on paper headed '177 Clarence Gate Gardens'.

2 – Carole Seymour-Jones writes of an earlier encounter: 'July 1931 found Vivienne sitting next to Ottoline at a Gower Street tea-party with Virginia Woolf, David Cecil, Elizabeth Bowen, Alida Monro, Leslie Hartley, Juliette Huxley and Dorothy and Simon Bussy among others. Diplomatically, Ottoline decided to look after Vivienne, whom she feared might make a scene, and left Virginia and Elizabeth Bowen to talk to each other, while L. P. Hartley discussed with Vivienne a detective story she was planning to write. It was, decided an exhausted Ottoline afterwards, rather like conducting an orchestra, trying to induce harmony among her disparate guests' (*Painted Shadow*, 464; citing the Journal of OM, 16 July 1931: Goodman Papers). Seymour-Jones remarks further: 'But Vivienne did not forget Ottoline's kindness: in her 1934 diary she recalled how, "ill, late, flustered", she used to motor to fetch Tom to take him to 10 Gower Street. "Inconspicuous [and] as inoffensive as possible", she would sit in the shadows of the garden: "Ottoline used to keep me by her which was kind of her," while the literary ladies and gentlemen talked' (ibid., 464–5, citing VHE's diary entry for 12 Nov. 1934: Bodleian).

I find now, more & more, that Tom is *happier*, & his best self with you, & with the people you have about you. Now please dont speak of this to anyone – but I *know you won't*. That man Gordon George is very good in that way – especially as a visitor in the house. He wanted me to tell you how much he had enjoyed meeting you, & how he looked forward to coming back to London – he is now in *Basingstoke* – so that he could come to tea at yr. house. I told you that he is in great difficulties.

Do please realise how enchanted I was to meet 'Kot' again – & to meet Ralph Hodgson. The latter is truly delightful, *but so is 'Kot'*.[1]

1–TSE and Ralph Hodgson met at a gathering at OM's house at 10 Gower Street on 11 Dec. OM also invited S. S. Koteliansky, Lord David Cecil and L. P. Hartley.

Ralph Hodgson (1871–1962), Yorkshire-born poet; author of *The Last Blackbird* (1907); winner of the 1914 Edmond de Polignac Prize of the Royal Society of Literature; lectured in English at Sendai University, Japan, 1924–38. He was awarded the Order of the Rising Sun, 1938; Annual Award of the Institute of Arts and Letters (USA), 1946; the Queen's Gold Medal, 1954. Other publications include *A Song of Honour* and *The Skylark*. Robert Sencourt said of Hodgson, 'his accent was homely, his figure portly and his manners hearty'. See further Vinni Marie D'Ambrosio, 'Meeting Eliot and Hodgson in Five-finger Exercises', *Yeats Eliot Review* (2005); John Harding, *Dreaming of Babylon: The Life and Times of Ralph Hodgson* (2008). TSE was to write to Colin Fenton on 22 Oct. 1963: 'I took great delight in his company and saw a great deal of him during that one year . . . Hodgson well deserves a biographical record.'

Samuel S. Koteliansky (1881–1955), Ukrainian émigré, translated works by Tolstoy and Dostoyevsky, some in collaboration with VW and LW; see Galya Diment, *A Russian Jew of Bloomsbury: The Life and Times of Samuel Koteliansky* (2012).

Robert Sencourt relates: 'Lord David Cecil has told me that once at a party of Lady Ottoline's, Tom turned sharply on Koteliansky when he suggested that Christian faith was merely escapism. Never had Cecil heard anyone speak with such intensity as came into Tom's voice while he explained that Christian faith, far from softening the edges of life, made each of them more cutting, because it gave a fuller and therefore more intense life; it also made life more poignant because it brought every issue of the soul into direct relation to Infinity; it made every obligation more pressing; at every turn, it demanded greater sacrifice and commitment' (*T. S. Eliot: A Memoir*, 110).

John Harding writes, in *Dreaming of Babylon*: '"Kot" . . . berated Eliot loudly for not joining in the struggle for a Lawrentian "new world order", Hodgson's quiet aside that "the future is a mystery and man's only obligation is to find the courage to face it" appeared to strike a chord with Eliot. At the end of the evening, as the coats were being handed out, Eliot said to Hodgson, "Must I wait another 43 years before we meet again?"' (148).

According to Seymour-Jones (*Painted Shadow*, 469–70), 'Ottoline balefully observed Vivienne flirting excitedly with Hodgson who was, apparently, a patient listener; but his hostess, grotesque in flowered chiffon, her little face with its grey-green make-up reminding Ottoline of an overdressed monkey, presented a bizarre yet pitiful spectacle.'

See Harding's chapter 18 ('The Man in White Spats', *Dreaming of Babylon*, 147–58) for a detailed account of the Eliots' friendship with Hodgson and his partner Aurelia Bolliger – a young American missionary teacher whom Hodgson had befriended in Japan in 1926; later his wife. Sencourt related (118): 'Hodgson had just come over from Tokyo with a very young and unsophisticated blonde girl. "He calls her," said Vivienne in her caustic way, "his secretary".'

<I hope Lord David Cecil will remember his promise to *let me know*
when you will bring him here to hear *the Joyce records.*>

Yr. very affect. Friend.

Vivienne Haigh Eliot

TO *Susan Hinkley*   TS Houghton

15 December 1931   Faber & Faber Ltd

Dear Aunt Susie and Eleanor,

Thank you very much for your letter of the 2nd and especially for your
cable which arrived simultaneously.[1] It was difficult to believe, while I
was talking, that I really was talking to No. 1 Berkeley Place; and still
more difficult to believe that it would be audible. And I was so fidgety,
from abstinence from tobacco and indulgence in throat lozenges, having
had a heavy cold for days past; and the small studio was full of the Cesar
Saerchinger family; that it was the most difficult broadcasting I have ever
had to do. So you may be sure that your cable was a most welcome relief
to my anxieties; and I am very grateful to you. And I hope I may hear in
detail what everyone thought of it, however critical!

And so, with most fervent Christmas wishes,

I remain,

Your nephew & cousin,

Affectionately,

Tom

Hodgson would write to TSE on 13 July 1952: 'Numberless moments of those months 20
years ago come back repeatedly as fresh as ever. One I dwell on with profoundest pleasure:
driving through a Surrey lane one evening, you stopped the car to listen for a nightingale,
and suddenly stood up, murmuring half to yourself, "It is a beautiful world".

'We did not hear a nightingale; by now you must have heard hundreds and know how
they compare with the hermit thrush. That bird I have never heard: they don't visit Ohio, I
understand.'

1 – Not found.

TO *William Plomer*

15 December 1931   [Faber & Faber Ltd]

My dear Plomer,

I have just discovered that your kind invitation is for to-night and apologise for not having answered sooner.[1] I should very much have liked to join you but I very seldom go out in the evening and as I have to be out, an engagement of a month's standing, I should have been unable to come in any case. I hope to see you again early in the New Year.

With all best wishes,

Yours sincerely,
[T. S. Eliot]

TO *Arthur J. Penty*

CC

16 December 1931   [*The Criterion*]

Dear Mr Penty

I have read with much interest 'Tradition and Modernism in Architecture'. I should very much like to use it in the *Criterion* though I cannot yet tell you whether it is likely to appear in the April or the July number. I will let you know as soon as possible.[2]

Meanwhile I am wondering whether you would care to review for the next number Maynard Keynes's *Essays in Persuasion*. He seems to me almost the most interesting of the more academic economists, and he does for the most part write good English. I seem to remember also that you once spoke rather appreciatively of him. I have only glanced at this book and it seems to me in general that Keynes is absorbed in financial technique rather to the exclusion of industrial. But it would be interesting to have a kind of summary view of Keynes's place and importance.[3]

Yours sincerely
[T. S. Eliot]

1–Plomer had invited TSE (2 Dec.) to a small house-warming party on 15 Dec.; he was sharing a house with a friend named Anthony Butts at 2 Canning Place, Palace Gate, W.8.
2–'Tradition and Modernism in Architecture' (a lecture delivered to the Art Workers' Guild, 29 May 1931), C. 12 (Apr. 1933), 421–37.
3–Arthur J. Penty, 'The Philosophy of J. M. Keynes', C. 11 (Apr. 1932), 386–98

TO *Marguerite Caetani*   Photocopy of TS

16 December 1931   The Criterion

Dear Marguerite,

I have two letters from you[1] unacknowledged, but during the last fortnight I have had two lecture engagements and a bad cold so that I have missed you in Versailles, and must send this to Rome. As for your first note, there is really nothing to say in reply except that I very much appreciate and am fortified by your understanding. For the second, I acknowledge with thanks the cheque for three subscriptions to the *Criterion* for which you will receive an official receipt. Our Sales Manager tells me he wrote to *Commerce* about the exchange advertisement, but had no reply. He will, however, send at once a page advertisement of the current issue. This issue, i.e. January, is now out, and no doubt you will receive a copy forwarded from Paris. We cannot therefore put in any advertisement of *Commerce* until the March number but shall be glad to have the copy for that issue.

I hope that you are now quite recovered enough to be able to travel safely. I do not think that we, and I daresay no one else in London, appreciated the fact that when you came over you were at best in a state of convalescence. I hope that the visit did not tire you too much, and that you will persist in your intention of taking a house in the summer season.

I do not think that we should have come over now in any case.[2] Things are too uncertain, and the expense of a prolonged stay really beyond our means, and furthermore it is impossible for anyone to make plans for a long stay abroad because of the possibility of a further depreciation of the pound.

Yours ever affectionately

Tom

P.S. Have you come across an extraordinary woman from Buenos Ayres named Victoria Ocampo, who runs a review there which seems to be modelled on *Commerce*?[3] She came to see me the other day. I believe she is a friend of the Huxleys.

1–Not found.

2–Caetani said ('Tuesday', n.d.) that her doctor had ordered her to stay put for a while 'to see that all was well during a certain time after that little operation I had in Sept. If I had only known sooner you might have come now perhaps? What a pity.'

3–Sylvia Beach wrote on 5 Dec. to introduce a 'friend of ours' – the 'editress' of *Sur* – 'the most influential woman in Buenos Aires and the most charming one'. Victoria Ocampo (1890–1979), a wealthy Argentinian publisher who visited Europe from time to time, was to become in 1934 a friend of VW: see *Review* 23 (Center for Inter-American Relations, New

TO *Edouard Roditi*   TS UCLA

16 December 1931   *The Criterion*

Dear Roditi,

Thank you for your letter of the 10th and for your essay on Rosenberg which I will return as soon as I have read it.[1] I have not had time to think much about Siemsen.[2] I am very doubtful about volumes of short stories although I am always interested in stories for the *Criterion*. I shall have my time pretty full until after Christmas and then hope to see you again.

Yours sincerely,
T. S. Eliot

TO *William S. Paley*[3]   CC

16 December 1931   [Faber & Faber Ltd]

Dear Sir,

This is to express my gratitude for your kind cable of yesterday following my broadcast talk to American audiences.

Yours very truly
[T. S. Eliot]

York, 1978); and Doris Meyer, *Victoria Ocampo* (1979) On 28 June 1962 TSE told The Secretary of 'Comision de Homenaje a Victoria Ocampo' (Buenos Aires): 'I would be glad to be recorded as one who recognized the place occupied by Senora Victoria Ocampo in the literary world . . .'

1 – Roditi wrote of his essay: 'The style is probably bad, too involved and too abstract; but it is difficult to grasp certain facts except by attacking them from all sides, which produces a certain Proust effect . . . I would like to know whether you think it worth translating, adapting and enlarging, into English.'

2 – Earlier in the year, Roditi had translated into French, 'as a grammatical exercise', some stories by the German author Hans Siemsen (1891–1969).

3 – William S. Paley (1901–90): broadcasting executive. Born in Chicago, and educated at the University of Pennsylvania, he went into the family's prosperous cigar business, which in 1928 bought up the ailing Columbia Phonographic Broadcasting System: renamed the Columbia Broadcasting System (CBS), with Paley as President, it rapidly grew into a major network, rivalling NBC. Edward R. Murrow was recruited in 1935, and 'CBS World News Roundup' became a predominant news resource for millions. In time, CBS became a major player too in the entertainment industry, attracting stars such as Jack Benny, George Burns and Gracie Allen, and programmes such as *I Love Lucy* and *The Ed Sullivan Show*. Paley himself (who also built up a large art collection and served on the board of the Museum of Modern Art) remained the driving force of CBS for decades, ever expanding the business to engross magazines, the publishing house of Holt, Rinehart and Winston, and even for a while the New York Yankees.

TO *Orlo Williams*   CC

16 December 1931   [*The Criterion*]

Dear Williams,

I like very much 'Fiction and Life' and think that it would do very well
as a chronicle in spite of its length, though I wish that it might be a little
bit shorter. I think, however, that I can manage it by slightly reducing the
rest of the body.

I shall be very glad, however, if you could manage somewhat to reduce
or attenuate the references to myself. You will understand that the
Criterion is always exposed to outside criticism as being merely a small
group of backscratchers and log-rollers. I once had to write to one of the
weeklies to point out that Read, Richards, Fernandez and myself do not
hold identical views about everything. In any case it seems to me proper
that the name of the editor should appear as seldom as possible.

Assuming that you have another copy yourself I will keep the one you
have sent until I hear from you.[1]

                              Yours ever
                              [T. S. Eliot]

TO *James Joyce*   CC

16 December 1931   [Faber & Faber Ltd]

Dear Joyce,

Many thanks for your long letter.[2] About the Gorman book we have
signed the contract, but not with Gorman himself. The English rights
of the book recite that [*sc.* reside with] Gorman's New York publishers,
Farrar & Rinehart. We have sent them our half of the contract, but have
not yet, I believe, received the counterpart. Meanwhile it is so far as we
know uncertain when Gorman will finish his book. I am looking up the
figures of royalties on *A.L.P.* and *H.C.E.* and will include them at the end
of this letter. Up to date we have sold 6100 copies of the former and 3532
copies of the latter. I take it that you are resigned, if not satisfied, to the
last proof page sent you. De la Mare tells that the printers will really be
glad to tackle *Work in Progress* as soon as the manuscript is available.
Apparently printing work is rather slack at present and printers are glad

---

1 – 'Fiction Chronicle: Fiction and Life', *C.* 11 (Apr. 1932), 474–89.
2 – Not found.

to have work to keep their men employed. Although I daresay they will not congratulate themselves over this. But if lack of work reconciles them to the labour of *Work in Progress* then I think we have happened upon a fortunate period for the composition of that book.

I thought that Nicolson put up a very good fight and handled the subject very ably last Tuesday.[1] He seems to have precipitated a crisis in the affairs of the B.B.C. and I daresay there will be a good many wigs on the green before it is finished. Alfred Noyes, whose poetical works I believe have never been mentioned by broadcasters, has started the trouble with a letter to the *Times*, and I think there will be a good many letters on both sides before the affair is concluded.[2]

Huebsch's offer seems to me only reasonable on the likelihood that he would have a public prosecution to meet, and in any case the rate of royalty is ludicrous. However, I suppose the conclusion was foregone and Miss Beach's action would have been the same even if Huebsch's offer had been better.[3]

You don't say what is the present situation about the flat. Will you at least tell me what agents have charge of it, so that if I hear of anyone wanting a furnished flat I can send them in that direction.

Please let us have as much of your manuscript as possible directly after Christmas, and the printers will go ahead with it at once.

With best wishes to Mrs Joyce and yourself from both of us.

Ever sincerely yours
[T. S. Eliot]

1 – Harold Nicolson's scheduled talk on JJ was called off by the BBC; but after lodging a formal protest he was allowed to go ahead with the broadcast on 6 Dec. 1931.

2 – Alfred Noyes (1880–1958): English poet and man of letters. JJ wrote to Harriet Shaw Weaver on 18 Dec. 1931: 'There is a crisis in the B.B.C. precipitated by H.N. [Harold Nicolson] and Mr Alfred Noyes has started a polemic about me in the *Times*, T.S.E. says.' (*Letters of James Joyce* III, ed. Richard Ellmann, 234) (Nicolson had delivered a series of nineteen talks on the BBC, beginning on 29 Sept., on 'The New Spirit in Modern Literature': his definition of 'modernism' included TSE and JJ, but relegated Galsworthy, Barrie, Priestley, Walpole as 'old-fashioned'.) Noyes, in a letter to *The Times*, 14 Dec. 1931, 8 – 'B.B.C and Modern Literature: Talks about Books' – took pride in the BBC's new policy of eschewing talks on contemporary novels, in the interest of inoffensiveness – most especially with a view to avoiding the mention of 'very modern' and 'objectionable' works – though Noyes did not specifically mention JJ.

TSE, along with GCF, LW and VW, and other luminaries from the world of publishing and bookselling, were to sign a letter printed in *The Times* on Tues, 22 Dec. 1931, 6 – 'B.B.C. Talks on Fiction: The Change of Policy' – protesting against such 'a seriously retrograde step'.

3 – TSE's judgement here was referred by JJ to Shaw Weaver on 18 Dec. 1931: *Letters* III, 236.

P.S.   *Anna L. P.*   Royalty to Dec 31 1930
                      Paid to J. B. Pinker Feb 3 1931 £7. 3s. 3d.
                      to June 30th 1931
                      Paid to J. B. Pinker July 27 '31 £2. 18s. 2d.
       Haveth C.E.   Royalty to June 30 1931
                      Paid to J. B. Pinker July 27 '31 £18. 7s. 5d.

TO *Virginia Woolf*   CC

16 December 1931   [Faber & Faber Ltd]

Dear Virginia,

I suppose that you will be going to Rodmell for Christmas, and as the last fortnight of December is a very trying time to everybody, and especially to anybody so irritable as myself, I should not have made any attempt to see you until the New Year. But it happens that I am being urged, coaxed and coerced to approach you on a small business matter as soon as possible. That being the pretext, could you spare me a few moments for a business interview before you leave?[1]

                      Yours respectfully,
                      [Tom]

TO *John Middleton Murry*   CC

16 December 1931   [Faber & Faber Ltd]

Dear John,

I hope that my reply to your letter of a week ago is not unduly delayed. I ought to have written to you on Thursday or Friday last after discussing the matter with my committee, but was bothered by a severe cold and a broadcast talk which had to be finished at short notice.

We should be very glad to have you do your pamphlet.[2] Evidently, as I enclose a memorandum of agreement which is identical with all the rest of the Miscellany. I can say definitely that we have given exactly the same

---

1–F&F was hoping to be able to bring out a 'cheap edition' of the novels of VW.

2–JMM proposed (7 Dec.) a Criterion Miscellany pamphlet called *The Fallacy of Economics*, which he was 'fermenting'. 'It will show (a) the intellectual and (b) the moral viciousness of the assumptions of modern economic argument. Negatively, on its destructive side, it will please you; constructively, not so much, but even there I suspect you will be largely in agreement.'

terms to all of the authors, and that the margin of profit, when there is any, is so small on such publications that we cannot do better.

As for the length, it should be between 10 and 15,000 words. 20,000 is really too long, and indeed anything over 15,000 reduces that margin of profit to something below zero. Do you think that you could manage it between 12 and 15,000?[1]

Yours affectionately
[Tom]

TO *Erik Mesterton*   TS Erik Mesterton

16 December 1931   Faber & Faber Ltd

Dear Mr Mesterton,

I remember quite well being in communication with you a year or more ago, and even if I had not remembered I should have been reminded of it as I have lately seen Mr Osbert Sitwell who spoke appreciatively of meeting you in Sweden this summer. Thank you very much for your letter of the 2nd.[2] I am quite willing and interested to have a Swedish translation of the *Waste Land* published in *Spektrum*. I should of course be curious to know beforehand, if you do not purpose to translate it entire, what parts you choose for this purpose. I thought that both Curtius and Menasce's translations were good, and I think that the fact that some parts translated better than others was largely due to the difficulties of the language. The Spanish translation of Flores also seemed to me good although there were a few definite mistranslations; but I was not in such close contact with Flores as with Curtius and Menasce.

1–JMM replied on 17 Dec. to say the lapse of time made it impossible for him to complete the book by 31 Dec.: 'with small children Christmas is hard labour'. He hoped for a harmless delay.

2–Mesterton, who was a co-editor of *Spektrum* (Stockholm), requested permission to publish in his periodical part of *TWL*, in a Swedish translation by the poet Karin Boye in association with the poet Erik Blomberg ('the author of the best verse translation in the language'). Mesterton himself would supply a commentary explaining the context of passages chosen for translation – elucidating rather than interpreting. 'One essay of yours which appears to have some importance for the understanding of the *Waste Land*, I haven't been able to look up: your contribution to the first number of *The Enemy*, where, if I am not mistaken, you were concerned with the question of Belief and its bearings on *The Waste Land*. Judging from your comments, in *Dante*, on Mr Richards's view and on his pronouncement on *The Waste Land*, I think the essay must be of particular interest to the student of your poem.' Mesterton wished too to be able to reproduce a line drawing of TSE by WL that was in TSE's possession.

As for the slight contribution to the *Enemy*, I am afraid that I am not in any better position than you are to obtain a copy.[1] I do not think that this really matters inasmuch as the gist of that short paper is embodied in my much more carefully considered note on Dante. I will try to find a copy of the drawing by Louis [*sc.* Lewis] but I believe that there was some question of reproduction in a periodical at the time, and that it appeared to be too fine a line drawing to reproduce well.[2] As for the photograph by Vandyk I enclose a letter to that photographer so that you can obtain a copy.

Yours sincerely
T. S. Eliot

TO *Sonia Hambourg* CC

16 December 1931 [Faber & Faber Ltd]

Dear Miss Hambourg,

Thank you for your letter of the 13th. I have shown it to Mr de la Mare, who is going to have specimens set in blue and yellow, and if there is time it is just possible that we may be able to send you these for your approval.[3]

I am surprised that you have been unable to find the *Criterion* in Paris. Sylvia Beach always used to take a certain number of copies and it used to be on sale I think at Smith's and Galliani's, though I have not looked into the situation for some time. Meanwhile I am having the current number sent to you.

Yours sincerely
[T. S. Eliot]

1–'A Note on Poetry and Belief', *The Enemy* 1 (Jan. 1927), 15–17.
2–EVE was to write to Charles Monteith, Chairman of Faber & Faber Ltd., on 5 Sept. 1973: 'I have just bought from the estate of Professor Jack Isaacs a Wyndham Lewis drawing of Tom done in 1922. It is faintly drawn, and unfinished, and gives Tom a rather prim look. However, it is unusual and has not been reproduced.' The drawing is reproduced in *L* 2.
3–'Clere liked blue or yellow but as Auden's poems are bound in blue paper perhaps blue would not be a good choice.'

TO *Marguerite Caetani*   Photocopy of TS

17 December 1931   Faber & Faber Ltd

Dear Marguerite,

I should very much like my brother-in-law, about whom I have spoken to you, to meet you if possible before he leaves Rome for good.[1] His wife has just had a child and is still in a nursing home in Rome;[2] and he is merely waiting in Rome until she and the child are strong enough to make the journey to London, which will be, I suppose, about the middle of January. It would be a great kindness, which I know he would appreciate, if you could ask him to call on you before he leaves – his address is

>   Maurice Haigh-Wood,
>   Hotel Ludovici (or is it Ludovisi?)
>   Rome

And I, of course, should be very grateful to you, too.

Affectionately,

Tom

TO *Herbert Read*   CC

17 December 1931   [Faber & Faber Ltd]

Dear Herbert,

Thank you for your letter of the 16th.[3] But this is beginning to be very irritating. For one thing I have had no official confirmation myself. Secondly it is in fact the Norton Chair. Thirdly my life has been made miserable for the last three days. Various newspapers and press bureaux have been ringing up. Yesterday I saw Mary Hutchinson, who said their man-servant had heard the news on the wireless, and was very excited, and the last blow was an invitation this morning over the telephone to

---

1 – Caetani responded on 25 Dec.: 'The moment I arrive in Rome I will write to Vivienne's brother and please explain to him why I have not done so before.'

2 – Charles Warren Haigh-Wood was born on 15 Dec. 1931. See further Ken Craven, *The Victorian Painter and the Poet's Wife: a biography of the Haigh-Wood family* (Kindle, 2012).

3 – HR posted from Edinburgh (where he was Professor of Fine Art) 'a cry for an explanation of the news in this morning's *Scotsman*. As given there it implies that you are going to Harvard for good, but I find it hard to believe this, in fact, refuse to believe it; and can only imagine that the appointment must be the Norton chair which [Eric] Maclagan occupied with 7 months.'

lunch with Lady Astor to meet Mr Bernard Shaw.[1] This is only a hurried note as I am looking forward to seeing you on Tuesday. In the meantime will you correct any impression in anybody's mind that I am going to Harvard permanently?

Yours ever

[T. S. E.]

TO *The Editor,* The Times CC

17 December 1931   [Faber & Faber Ltd]

Sir,

In your issue of today, the information which you give about the terms of tenure of the Norton Professorship at Harvard, (to which you inform me that I have been appointed), is correct; but I fear that your heading of the paragraph may tend to confirm a misapprehension caused by the form of announcement in other newspapers less accurately informed.[2] I should therefore be grateful for an opportunity to state that the appointment is only for seven months, and that I am not returning permanently to America, and that I am not giving up any of the work in which I am regularly engaged in London.

I am, Sir,

Your obedient servant,

[T. S. Eliot]

1 – Sencourt notes (*T. S. Eliot*, 119): 'One morning . . . I heard Tom speaking on the telephone. In his smooth, courteous voice he was saying: "will you tell her Ladyship that I am unable to come to lunch with her because I don't accept invitations from ladies I have not met, nor from one who invites me without my wife, nor from one who is divorced". "Her Ladyship" was none other than Lady Astor, another American who had taken out British nationality, who was much better known than he was in 1930, and who was considered one of the most brilliant of hostesses both in her London home and in the country – her weekend parties at Clivedon [*sic*] were celebrated for their gatherings of men of power. On this occasion she had invited Eliot to meet Bernard Shaw and H. G. Wells, neither of whom he even wished to come into contact with.' There is no independent corroboration of Sencourt's account – nor whether TSE went to the lunch.

2 – 'Professorship for Mr T. S. Eliot', *The Times*, 17 Dec. 1931, 11: 'Mr T. S. Eliot has accepted the invitation of Harvard University to become Charles Eliot Norton Professor of Poetry for the year 1932–33 in succession to Sigurthur Nordal, Professor of Icelandic Literature in the University of Iceland. Mr Eliot, who is a graduate of Harvard and a relative of the late Mr Charles W. Eliot, President of the University, is the first American to hold the professorship since it was endowed in 1925 by Mr C. C. Stillman, of New York, as a memorial to the great Dante scholar. The terms of the endowment call for the selection as lecturers of men "of high distinction within the field of literature."'

TO *Conrad Aiken*

TS Huntington

19 December 1931   Faber & Faber Ltd

Dear Conrad,

Many thanks for your letter.[1] It's a blessed relief to find one man who knows what the Norton Professorship is, and to whom I do not have to explain that I am not giving up my job here or the *Criterion* or going to Harvard permanently. The joke is, and a very poor joke too, that I have had no official notification from Harvard, and have no better reason for believing it than that I read it in *The Times*. If true, however, it is good news that you may be at Harvard too, as we never seem to meet in England.

Please let me know about the story as soon as possible.[2]

Yours ever,
Tom

TO *J. S. Barnes*   cc

22 December 1931   [Faber & Faber Ltd]

Dear Jim,

I am very sorry to have to tell you that the balance of opinion is finally against our publishing the Odyssey. Of course our decisions, like those of any other publisher, are at the present time governed by the general economic and trade position, and we are now particularly disinclined to expand our list. I am very sorry about this as I should very much like to see the book published, and if I can be of any use elsewhere I shall be very glad. I look forward to your return to London at the end of the year, and I hope meanwhile that the investigations you were pursuing have led to a successful issue.

Yours ever
[T. S. Eliot]

1–Aiken congratulated TSE (18 Dec.) on his appointment to the Norton Chair: 'I may myself spend next winter in Cambridge (my son John will probably be at Harvard); we can again have a glass of arak at the Greek restaurant, and short circuit these eighteen years.'
2–Aiken had been informed by his former agent A. D. Peters that C. had agreed to publish one of his stories as long as there was 'no serious conflict' with a limited edition to be brought out by the Ulysses Bookshop. See 'Mr Articularis', C. 11 (Apr. 1932), 399–419.

TO *Bruce Richmond*

22 December 1931   [Faber & Faber Ltd]

Dear Richmond,

Thank you for your note of the 19th,[1] but may I take this opportunity of expressing my opinion of the methods of the abominable newspaper with which you are associated. It is true that every other newspaper notice gave people the impression that I was going to America permanently, whereas the *Times* merely gave the impression that I was going for two years. I wrote a brief note to the *Times* to explain the situation, which they boiled down still further, and printed in the very smallest type in a column which is headed 'Telegrams in Brief'.[2] Who on earth would even see the sentence published in that column? Meanwhile I am still receiving letters of condolence. I must also add that the nearest approach to an official notification I have had is the notice in the *Times*, as I have heard nothing from Harvard University; but I suppose that the *Times* never tells a lie even though it may sometimes suppress the truth.

I do not feel safe in sending this to the incredible address at the head of your note, so direct it to Sumner Place,[3] with best wishes of the season to Mrs Richmond and yourself.

Yours ever,
[T. S. E.]

TO *Susan Hinkley* MS Houghton

28 December 1931   68 Clarence Gate Gardens

Dear Aunt Susie,

I am delighted with the old brass crucifix. I wish I knew where it comes from and what its history is. I have long been inclined to believe that objects pick up qualities from their owners – ever since the elderly member of the Lycaeum Club who explained the Tarot cards to me experimented on my great grandfather's seal ring – and devotional objects should have the best associations. (After all, that is the whole point of 'blessing' articles). Also,

---

1 – Not found.
2 – 'Telegrams in Brief', *The Times*, 19 Dec. 1931, 9: 'Mr T. S. Eliot asks us to say that his appointment as Charles Eliot Norton Professor of Poetry in the University of Harvard, which was announced in *The Times* on Thursday, is for seven months only. Mr Eliot will not relinquish any of the work on which he is regularly engaged in London.'
3 – The Richmonds lived at 3 Sumner Place, London SW7.

I don't ever remember seeing a crucifix with a Virgin & Child on the back. I can't decipher the inscription, alas.

Vivienne is worn out by Christmas and other things & is in bed with a bronchial cough & bad headache: but she will be writing as soon as she can.

I shan't try to write a *letter*; this [is] only a *thanking* letter. I suppose you are all engrossed with Barbara junior's wedding. Barbara & Chardy bring home to me the 'flight of time'. As the Fleet Gate Keeper in *Pickwick* said:–

'What a rum thing time is, ain't it, Neddy?'[1]

And there can't be more than half a dozen people in London who know where Fox-under-the-Hill was. Uncle Rob may know, if you don't.

Very affectionately to both,

Your nephew

Tom

Vivienne thanks you for the lovely bag & will be writing as soon as ever she can.

TO *Ottoline Morrell* MS Texas

28 December 1931   68 Clarence Gate Gardens

Dear Ottoline

Your diary, which is now in my pocket with entries, differs from other presents in giving me a cumulative pleasure: renewing past years and forerunning, I hope, years to come. So if you give me a diary next year you may be sure I shall be still *more* pleased!

We look forward to Friday the 8th (and to seeing you also on the 12th). I should like to see Hodgson again. We are both very tired from Christmas week – a festival, which as observed in Anglo-Saxon countries, seems to me to fall between two stools. It has neither the exaltation of a Christian memorial feast, nor the abandon of Saturnalia.

Vivienne is really in very poor health, and I want to get her to bed – She is in bed, but I mean, to settle down.

Affectionately

Tom

1 – Mr Roker in *Pickwick Papers*, ch. 42. EVE wrote to Barbara Hardy, 30 June 1977: 'My husband would often quote passages of Dickens to me from memory, especially when he was happy. You may be interested to know that his original epigraph for *Four Quartets* was "What a rum thing Time is, ain't it, Neddy", but he was afraid it might be misunderstood.'

Monday 28 December 1931   68 Clarence Gate Gardens

Dearest Ottoline

First of all thank you for your Christmas presents. They are very beautiful, & also they have some strange connections in my mind, which I could not possibly put in writing to you but which I am sure have some meaning which certainly if I tried to explain to anyone, they would either not hear me, or else say what ridiculous & childish nonsense & please do not say anything more about it as I refuse to listen to you. But it is difficult to communicate with you privately – as you do not hear me when I speak in a low voice & writing is always a risk.[1] And if there is anything I do hate & fear it is communicating by *signs*. I think it is *low* & *brutal* & *degrading*, & rather than that, I think it would be better to go & 'live' alone on the top of a high mountain.

Next. Thank you for your letter about the funny little Christmas token I left at yr. door on Christmas Eve. You feel it to be a Wand, but although it might be I do not take it, or give it, as that. To me it is a Sword, & one has to be careful to whom one gives swords. In the right hands it might prove that the sword is mightier than the pen – or even the loud speaker. But please see it as a Sword.

Next. The party I invited you for on Dec. 12th & then postponed until Dec. 31st, is chiefly for the purpose of having Alida Monro[2] read aloud Tom's poems, to a picked audience. She read them, as you know, at the Poetry Bookshop some weeks ago, & did it so marvellously that I then decided it must be done again here.

I now find that many of the people will be away all this week, so I am trying to change the party to Tuesday Jan. ~~7th~~ 12th. And Alida Monro wants that too. So can you & *will you* come on *Tuesday Jan. ~~7th~~ 12th at 8.30?*[3]

Next. Thank you for yr. letter of Dec. 25th inviting us for tea on Jan. 8th. Thank you very much. We shall be delighted *to come at 4.15*. If still living.

Do not fail me on Tuesday night Jan ~~7th~~ 12th. It seems to me very

---

1 – OM suffered from increasing deafness.
2 – Alida Klemantaski (1892–1969) had married Harold Monro on 27 Mar. 1920.
3 – Dominic Hibberd notes that Alida Monro read some of TSE's poems at the Poetry Bookshop 'so well that Vivien Eliot ... had arranged a repeat performance in January 1932: a ghastly evening, according to Ottoline, with chairs arranged in the Eliots' flat like a dentist's waiting room, and Vivien talking wildly in the street outside' (*Harold Monro*, 260).

important to have this reading. It should have happened years ago.

I am glad your Christmas Day was nice & calm.

Ours was rather terrible.

Your ever loving friend
Vivienne Haigh Eliot.

A *post card* in reply about Jan ~~7th~~ 12th will do & is better.

A very happy New Year to you, & to all of yours.

V.H.E.

Please excuse all the rubbings out. I *thought* it was to be the 7th, and only now find that the date fixed is the 12th.

TO *Margaret Thorp* MS Princeton

28 December 1931   68 Clarence Gate Gardens

Dear Mrs Thorp,

I have to write to tell you that we have had to put off our small party once more! Two of the guests [are] suddenly away for a week, another in bed with a cold. My wife has herself been in bed for two days, partly with a bronchial chill & partly from Christmas fatigue; and everyone rather jaded. So we have re-set the assembly for *Tuesday evening Jan 12th.* That is a fortnight ahead, so I pray that you are free then; and that you and your husband will be very patient people and say that you will come then instead.

I am writing for my wife because she is in bed with a splitting headache.

With all good wishes for the New Year from us both, and for your comfortable winter in Lincoln's Inn,

Yours sincerely
T. S. Eliot

TO *Tom Faber* TS Valerie Eliot

28 December 1931   Faber & Faber Ltd

Dear Tom,

FIRST OF ALL Thank you very much for the beautiful Napkin Ring you sent me. I like it Very Much and am very Proud of it, and I think it must have taken a Great While to make it and even Now I don't see how you made it, but perhaps you will tell me some time; and I shall use it on Sundays as my Best Napkin Ring.

NEXT I must thank you for your lovely letter, and I think you Print very well and such pretty colours too. I can't answer you in the same way because I have no Coloured Crayons.

NOW I must tell you about my Cat. You Remember that we had a black & white Jellicle Cat[1] that lived with us? Well, it got to staying out Nights and trying to be a Big Bravo Cat[2] and it took to visiting Neighbours and then it began to complain of the Food and saying it didn't like Dried Haddock & Kippers and why wasn't there more Game even when there was no Game in Season, so finally it went to live somewhere else. So then I advertised for Another Cat to come and Board with us, and now we have a Beautiful Cat which is going to be a Good Old Gumbie Cat[3] in Time. It is a very Grand Cat too because it is a Persian Prince and it is Blue because it has Blue Blood, and its name was MIRZA MURAD ALI BEG[4] but I said that was too Big a Name for such a Small Cat, so its name is *WISKUSCAT*. But it is sometimes called The MUSICAL BOX because it makes a noise like singing and sometimes COCKALORUM because it Looks like one. (Have you ever seen a Cockalorum? Neither have I). Well when it sits still it looks like this

and when it Runs about it looks like This

and it Gets on Beautifully with the Pollice Dog,[5] like This

and it is very Happy and almost Good, only we think it will be Quite Good in Time.

1 – See 'Song of the Jellicles'.
2 – For Bravo Cat, see 'Growltiger's Last Stand'.
3 – See 'The Old Gumbie Cat'.
4 – See 'Lines for Cuscuscaraway and Mirza Murad Ali Beg': first published in C. 12 (Jan. 1933), 220–2; *CPP*, 136.
5 – See 'Of the Awefull Battle of the Pekes and the Pollicles'.

And Now I hope you are Glad in Wales, because it is raining and fogging and cold in London, and that you have had a nice Christmas and please give my Love to Dick and Ann; and No More for the Present from

Your
Wopsical[1]
Uncle
Tom

TO *Sonia Hambourg*   CC

30 December 1931   [Faber & Faber Ltd]

Dear Miss Hambourg,

I received your letter of the 21st just before Christmas, but did not have time to answer it until after the holiday.[2] We will have the yellow wrapper which you chose. I agree that the suggestion for the title page is a good one, and I understand that the alteration is easily made. There will probably be time to send you still another proof before we go finally to press. I shall be very much surprised if Sylvia Beach keeps no copies of the *Criterion* in stock any longer. If you have not tried 12 rue de l'Odeon yet you would be doing me a favour if you could go and beard Miss Beach, and complain at what on her part is almost criminal negligence.

With best wishes for the New Year.

Yours sincerely
[T. S. Eliot]

TO *F. R. Leavis*   CC

30 December 1931   [*The Criterion*]

Dear Mr Leavis,

This is just to say that your letter of Christmas day will go directly to the printers.[3] I am rather glad that you have written because I felt myself

1 – See 'Lines for Cuscuscaraway and Mirza Murad Ali Beg': 'How unpleasant to meet Mr Eliot! . . . With a bobtail cur / In a coat of fur / And a porpentine cat / And a wopsical hat . . .'
2 – Hambourg wrote among other things, 'Do you think that the suggestions I have made for the new frontispiece would be either possible or desirable? I do not quite like "Born" and 'Died" as they are and feel that it would perhaps look better if the line in question were an "even" line . . .'
3 – FRL had written to protest against F. S. Flint's 'Verse Chronicle', C. 11 (Jan. 1932), 276–81 – Flint had dismissed the overwhelming majority of the twenty volumes of poetry

that Flint had been too summary in his executions and that we do not want to mete out treatment which will discourage young poets about the *Criterion*.

Yours sincerely,

[T. S. Eliot]

TO *Bonamy Dobrée*   TS Brotherton

30 December 1931   *The Criterion*

My dear Bonamy,

The visit to Harvard, a subject which I have not yet raised myself with anybody for the reason that I have no official confirmation, is to take place next September, and to last until next May.[1] As soon as I know that the appointment is official I propose to discuss at the *Criterion* meeting the ways and means of carrying on the *Criterion*.

As for the next meeting, Harold has been ordered out of London for convalescence, and it is by no means certain that he would be back for either date in January.[2] Even if he is, I don't want to have the meeting if there is any doubt of his fitness, as he seemed to me still very ill at the last meeting on the 16th of this month. So I am writing to ask whether the first Wednesday in February would suit you equally well. You could take in the French Exhibition just as well in February as in January. If I hear from you that you can come I shall propose to Harold that we hold our next meeting on the 3rd of February, the 10th unfortunately being Ash Wednesday. For that matter there is no longer any strong reason why meetings should be on Wednesdays.

Don't worry about John Hayward.[3] I don't suppose he meant any harm by it. I am sorry that he wrote the review, because it is entirely in the second-rate *Times* style.

---

reviewed, including *The Loosening* by Ronald Bottrall. See FRL, 'Correspondence', C. 11 (Apr. 1932), 509–10: 'I think highly of Mr Bottrall's work . . . Mr Bottrall's work appears to me to be the first serious instance of fecundation by that great modern poem, *Hugh Selwyn Mauberley*.

'You will in any case believe that I am moved only by disinterested concern for Mr Bottrall's poetry in particular and English poetry in general . . .'

1 – BD had asked on 25 Dec., 'Now what's all this about your going to Harvard for a year?'

2 – 'Important. Is the next *Criterion* meeting on the 13th or the 20th?'

3 – 'It has been revealed to me that John Hayward wrote that rather spiteful review of the Anthology for the *T.L.S.*' See 'The Art of Prose' – on *The London Book of English Prose*, ed. HR and BD – *TLS*, 26 Nov. 1931, 943. Dobrée had already sent a letter to the Editor,

Best wishes to your family for the New Year
                              From
                              TSE

TO *Erik Mesterton*   TS Erik Mesterton

30 December 1931   *The Criterion*

Dear Mr Mesterton,
    Thank you for your letter of the 21st.[1] I hope that by this time you
have quite recovered from your illness. For the translation to appear in
Spektrum I have no objections to your making what suggestions and
cuts you see fit, so long as the breaks are clearly indicated, and a note
explains why these particular parts were selected. If it were a question
of a translation in book form I should not wish any mutilated version to
appear, but I have no objection for periodical publication. The same thing
was done, as a matter of fact, in Italy.
    I will try to find a copy of the plate from the Lewis drawing, but as I
said, I fear it is much too fine for reproduction. Kauffer has never had the
opportunity to make a drawing of me or else you would have seen it.[2]
                              Yours sincerely
                              T. S. Eliot

TO *Marguerite Caetani*   Photocopy of TS

31 December 1931   *The Criterion*

Dear Marguerite,
    Thank you very much for your letter of Christmas Day. You speak as if
you were enclosing corrected proofs, but perhaps you mean that you want

---

published as 'The London Book of English Prose', accusing the reviewer of 'Defamation of
Character': 'Your reviewer accuses Professor Read and myself of being veritable kill-joys,
dour fellows repelled by the idea of enjoyment, especially that of other people' (*TLS*, 3 Dec.
1931, 982).
1 – Mesterton, who was unwell, sent details of the parts of *TWL* he aimed to publish,
including Part I down to Sosostris; the Tiresias section of Part III; and the whole of Part V.
See 'Det Öde Landet', trans. Karin Boye and Erik Mesterton, *Spektrum* (Stockholm) 2: 2
(Feb. 1932), 25–44.
2 – 'Mr McKnight Kauffer once promised me a drawing of you, but I haven't heard from him
for a long time – I am told he is ill.'

me to return them as soon as I get them.[1] I am sorry about the page of publicity.[2] I find that after all there was an oversight, and the page was not sent, but it shall go off today. I am having the matter of the subscriptions looked into.

I am so sorry to hear that you have not yet picked up enough to have the strength to travel, because I should think that Rome might be pleasanter in the way of climate, if none other, at this time of year, than Paris, and be a better place to recuperate in.[3] I hope that you really will pay a visit to America next year. I expect to be there from some time in September to the beginning of May, so I should like to see you there either in the autumn or the spring.[4]

With best wishes for the New Year,

Ever affectionately
Tom

trans. just come. Will return in 2 days.

1 – 'I was so sorry to bother you about your poem but Limbour in sending the translation forgot the original and I thought it quicker to get it from you and I beg you to send back to corrected proofs as quickly as possible.' See '*Difficultés d'un homme d'état*', trans. Georges Limbour, *Commerce* 29 (Winter 1931/32), 79–87.

2 – '*Are* you sending a page of publicity for *Commerce*[?]'

3 – 'I have been obliged to stay on and am forbidden to travel by my doctor until Dec. 30th. I am so cross about it because you and Vivienne might have come after all! It is sickening.'

4 – 'I am *so* happy about your appointment at Harvard. I didn't know they were so clever over there. I think the change will be fine for you . . . Lélia and I will go and pay you a visit at Harvard.'

BIOGRAPHICAL REGISTER

Conrad Aiken (1889–1973), American poet and critic. Though he and Eliot were a year apart at Harvard, they became close friends, and fellow editors of *The Harvard Advocate*. Aiken wrote a witty memoir of their times together, 'King Bolo and Others', in *T. S. Eliot: A Symposium,* ed. Richard Marsh and Tambimuttu (1948), describing how they revelled in the comic strips of 'Krazy Kat, and Mutt and Jeff' and in 'American slang'. In the 1920s he settled for some years in Rye, Sussex. His writings include volumes of poetry, among them *Earth Triumphant* (1914); the Eliot-influenced *House of Dust* (1921); *Selected Poems* (1929), which won the Pulitzer Prize; editions of *Modern American Poets* (1922) and *Selected Poems of Emily Dickinson* (1924); and *Collected Criticism* (1968). His eccentric autobiographical novel *Ushant: An Essay* (1952) satirises TSE as 'Tsetse'. On 7 Nov. 1952 TSE thanked Aiken for sending him an inscribed copy: 'It is certainly a very remarkable book. After the first few pages, I said to myself, this is all very well for a short distance, but can he keep it up through 365 pages without the style becoming oppressive? Anyway, you have done it, and I have read the book through with unflagging interest and I hope that it will have a great success.' Asked in Feb. 1953, by the editor of *The Carolina Quarterly*, if he would contribute to a symposium on *Ushant*, TSE replied on 17 Feb. that he had no time to prepare a critical piece but that '*Ushant* fully deserves such extended and varied critical treatment'. However, TSE was to write to Cyril Connolly on 17 Apr. 1963: 'Aiken is an old & loyal friend – I don't think he is a booby, though *Ushant* is a curiously callow work.' Stephen Spender noted in 1966 that Eliot 'once told me that he always felt disturbed and unhappy that . . . Aiken had had so little success as a poet. "I've always thought that he and I were equally gifted, but I've received a large amount of appreciation, and he has been rather neglected. I can't understand it. It seems unjust. It always worries me"' ('Remembering Eliot', *The Thirties and After* [1978], 251). See too *Selected Letters of Conrad Aiken*, ed. Joseph Killorin (1978); Edward Butscher, *Conrad Aiken: Poet of White Horse Vale* (1988).

Richard Aldington (1892–1962), poet, critic, translator, biographer, novelist. A friend of Ezra Pound, he was one of the founders of the Imagist movement; a contributor to *Des Imagistes* (1914) and assistant editor of *The Egoist*. In 1913 he married the American poet H.D., though they became estranged and in due course separated (albeit they did not divorce until 1938). In 1914 he volunteered for WW1, but his enlistment was deferred for medical reasons: he went on active service in June 1916 and was sent to France in December. (TSE replaced him as Literary Editor of *The Egoist*.) During the war, he rose from the ranks to be an acting captain in the Royal Sussex Regiment. He drew on his experiences in the poems of *Images of War* (1919) and the novel *Death of a Hero* (1929). After WW1, he became friends with TSE, working as his assistant on *The Criterion* and introducing him to Bruce Richmond, editor of the *TLS* (for which TSE wrote some of his finest essays). From 1919 Aldington himself was a regular reviewer of French literature for the *TLS*. In 1928 he went to live in France, where, except for a period in the USA (1935–47), he spent the rest of his life. He is best known for his early Imagist poetry and translations (see for example his edition of *Selections from Rémy de Gourmont*, 1928), for his WW1 novel *Death of a Hero* (1929), and for the controversial *Lawrence of Arabia: A Biographical Inquiry* (1955), which is widely held to have damaged his own reputation. In 1931, he published *Stepping Heavenward*, a lampoon of TSE – who is portrayed as 'Blessed Jeremy Cibber': 'Father Cibber, O.S.B.' – and Vivien ('Adele Palaeologue'). This ended their friendship. His estrangement from Eliot was further publicised in an essay written in the 1930s but published only in 1954, *Ezra Pound and T. S Eliot: A Lecture*, which takes both poets to task for their putatively plagiaristic poetry. He published further biographies, including a controversial study of his friend D. H. Lawrence, *Portrait of a Genius, But . . .* (1950); *Complete Poems* (1948); and *Life for Life's Sake* (memoirs, 1941). See also *Richard Aldington: An Intimate Portrait*, ed. by Alister Kershaw and Frédéric-Jacques Temple (1965), which includes a brief tribute by Eliot (with a comment on the 'cruel' *Stepping Heavenward*); 'Richard Aldington's Letters to Herbert Read', ed. by David S. Thatcher, *The Malahat Review* 15 (July 1970), 5–44; Charles Doyle, *Richard Aldington: A Biography* (1989); *Richard Aldington: An Autobiography in Letters*, ed. Norman T. Gates (1992); and *Richard Aldington & H. D.: Their lives in letters 1918–61*, ed. Caroline Zilboorg (2003).

W. H. Auden (1907–73), prolific poet, playwright, librettist, translator, essayist and editor. He was educated at Gresham's School, Holt, Norfolk, and at Christ Church, Oxford, where he co-edited *Oxford Poetry* (1926, 1927), and where his friend Stephen Spender hand-set about thirty copies of his first book, a pamphlet entitled *Poems* (1928). After going down from Oxford with a third-class degree in English in 1928, he visited Belgium and then lived for a year in Berlin. He worked as a tutor in London, 1929–30; then as a schoolmaster at Larchfield Academy, Helensburgh, Dunbartonshire, 1930–2; followed by the Downs School, Colwall, Herefordshire, 1932–5. Although Eliot turned down his initial submission of a book of poems in 1927, he would presently accept 'Paid on Both Sides: A Charade' for *The Criterion*; and Eliot went on for the rest of his life to publish all of Auden's books at Faber & Faber: *Poems* (featuring 'Paid on Both Sides' and thirty short poems, 1930); *The Orators* (1932); *Look, Stranger!* (1937); *Spain* (1936); *Another Time* (1940); *New Year Letter* (1941; published in the USA as *The Double Man*); *The Age of Anxiety* (1947); *For the Time Being* (1945); *The Age of Anxiety: A Baroque Eclogue* (1948); *Nones* (1952); *The Shield of Achilles* (1955); *Homage to Clio* (1960); and *About the House* (1966). Eliot was happy too to publish Auden's play *The Dance of Death* (1933), which was to be performed by the Group Theatre in London in 1934 and 1935; and three further plays written with Christopher Isherwood: *The Dog Beneath the Skin* (1935), which would be performed by the Group Theatre in 1936; *The Ascent of F6* (1936); and *On the Frontier* (1937). In 1935–6 Auden went to work for the General Post Office film unit, writing commentaries for two celebrated documentary films, *Coal Face* and *Night Mail*. He collaborated with Louis MacNeice on *Letters from Iceland* (1937); and with Isherwood again on *Journey to a War* (1939). His first libretto was *Paul Bunyan* (performed with music by Benjamin Britten, 1941); and in 1947 he began collaborating with Igor Stravinsky on *The Rake's Progress* (performed in Venice, 1951); and he later co-wrote two librettos for Hans Werner Henze. Other works include *The Oxford Book of Light Verse* (1938); *The Enchafèd Flood: The Romantic Iconography of the Sea* (1951); *The Dyer's Hand* (1963); and *Secondary Worlds* (1968). See further Humphrey Carpenter, *W. H. Auden: A Biography* (1981); Richard Davenport-Hines, *Auden* (1995); and Edward Mendelson, *Early Auden* (1981) and *Later Auden* (1999).

Montgomery ('Monty') Belgion (1892–1973), author, was born in Paris of British parents and grew up with a deep feeling for the language and culture of France. In 1915–16 he was editor-in-charge of the European edition of the *New York Herald*; and for the remainder of WW1 he joined up as a private in the Honourable Artillery Company, 1916–18, and was commissioned in the Dorsetshire Regiment. Between the wars he worked briefly for the Paris review *This Quarter* and then for newspapers including the *Daily Mail, Westminster Gazette* and *Daily Mirror*, and for a while he was an editor for Harcourt, Brace & Co., New York. In WW2 he became a captain in the Royal Engineers, and he spent two years in prison camps in Germany. In 1929 Faber & Faber brought out (on TSE's recommendation) his first book, *Our Present Philosophy of Life*. Later writings include *Reading for Profit* (1945) and booklets on H. G. Wells and David Hume.

Marguerite Caetani, née Chapin (1880–1963) – born in New London, Connecticut, she was half-sister to Mrs Katherine Biddle, and a cousin of TSE – was married in 1911 to the composer Roffredo Caetani, 17th Duke of Sermoneta and Prince di Bassiano (a godson of Liszt), whose ancestors included two popes (one of whom had the distinction of being put in Hell by Dante). A patron of the arts, she founded in Paris the review *Commerce* – the title being taken from a line in St-John Perse's *Anabase* ('*ce pur commerce de mon âme*') – which ran from 1924 to 1932 (see Sophie Levie, *La rivista Commerce e il ruolo di Marguerite Caetani nella letteratura europea 1924–1932* [Rome: Fondazione Camillo Caetani, 1985]); and then, in Rome, *Botteghe oscure*, 1949–60, a biannual review featuring poetry and fiction from many nations – Britain, Germany, Italy, France, Spain, USA – with contributions published in their original languages. Contributors included André Malraux, Albert Camus, Paul Valéry, Ignazio Silone, Robert Graves, Archibald MacLeish, E. E. Cummings, Marianne Moore.

John Cournos (1881–1966) – Johann Gregorievich Korshune – naturalised American writer of Russian birth (his Jewish parents fled Russia when he was ten), worked as a journalist on the *Philadelphia Record* and was first noted in England as an Imagist poet; he became better known as novelist, essayist and translator. After living in England in the 1910s and 1920s, he emigrated to the USA. An unhappy love affair in 1922–3 with Dorothy L. Sayers was fictionalised by her in *Strong Poison* (1930), and by him in *The Devil is an English Gentleman* (1932). His other publications include *London Under the Bolsheviks* (1919), *In Exile* (1923), *Miranda Masters* (a *roman à clef* about the imbroglio between himself, the poet H.D. and Richard Aldington, 1926), and *Autobiography* (1935).

Ernst Robert Curtius (1886–1956), German scholar of philology and Romance literature. Scion of a family of scholars, he studied philology and philosophy at Strasbourg, Berlin and Heidelberg, and taught in turn at Marburg, Heidelberg and Bonn. Author of *Die Französische Kultur* (1931; *The Civilization of France*, trans. Olive Wyon, 1932); his most substantial work was *Europäische Literatur und Lateinisches Mittelalter* (1948; trans. by Willard R. Trask as *European Literature and the Latin Middle Ages*, 1953), a study of Medieval Latin literature and its fructifying influence upon the literatures of modern Europe. In a letter to Max Rychner (24 Oct. 1955) Eliot saluted Curtius on his seventieth birthday by saying that even though he had met him perhaps no more than twice in thirty-five years, he yet counted him 'among my old friends', and owed him 'a great debt': 'I have . . . my own personal debt of gratitude to acknowledge to Curtius, for translating, and introducing, *The Waste Land*. Curtius was also, I think, the first critic in Germany to recognise the importance of James Joyce. And when it is a question of other writers than myself, and especially when we consider his essays on French contemporaries, and his *Balzac*, and his *Proust*, I am at liberty to praise Curtius as a critic . . . [O]nly a critic of scholarship, discrimination and intellect could perform the services that Curtius has performed. For his critical studies are contributions to the study of the authors criticised, which must be reckoned with by those authors' compatriots. *We cannot determine the true status and significance of the significant writers in our own language, without the aid of foreign critics with a European point of view.* For it is only such critics who can tell us, whether an author is of European importance. And of such critics in our own time, Curtius is one of the most illustrious.' Eliot praised too 'that masterly work, *Europäische Literatur und Lateinisches Mittelalter*, on which he had been at work during the years when freedom of speech and freedom of travel were suspended. It bears testimony to his integrity and indomitable spirit . . . Curtius deserves, in his life and in his work, the gratitude and admiration of his fellow writers of every European nation' (Eliot's letter is printed in full in 'Brief über Ernst Robert Curtius', in *Freundesgabe für Ernst Robert Curtius zum 14. April 1956* [1956], 25–7.) See too Peter Godman, 'T. S. Eliot and E. R. Curtius: A European dialogue', *Liber: A European Review of Books*, 1: 1 (Oct. 1989), 5, 7; and J. H. Copley, '"The Politics of Friendship": T. S. Eliot in Germany Through E. R. Curtius's Looking Glass', in *The International Reception of T. S. Eliot*, ed. Elisabeth Däumer and Shyamal Bagchee (2007), 243–67.

Martin D'Arcy (1888–1976), Jesuit priest and theologian, entered the Novitiate in 1906, took a first in Literae Humaniores at Pope's Hall – the Jesuit private hall of Oxford University – and was ordained a Catholic priest in 1921. After teaching at Stonyhurst College, in 1925 he undertook doctoral research, first at the Gregorian University in Rome, then at the Jesuit House at Farm Street, London. In 1927 he returned to Campion Hall (successor to Pope's Hall), where he lectured and tutored in philosophy at the university. He was Rector and Master of Campion Hall, 1933–45; and Provincial of the British Province of the Jesuits in London, 1945–50. Charismatic and highly influential as a lecturer, and as an apologist for Roman Catholicism (his prominent converts included Evelyn Waugh), he also wrote studies including *The Nature of Belief* (1931) and *The Mind and Heart of Love* (1945). Louis MacNeice, in *The Strings Are False: An Unfinished Autobiography* (1965), wrote of Fr D'Arcy: 'he alone among Oxford dons seemed to me to have the glamour that medieval students looked for in their masters. Intellect incarnate in a beautiful head, wavy grey hair and delicate features; a hawk's eyes.' Lesley Higgins notes: 'Five of his books were reviewed in *The Criterion*, some by Eliot himself; his twenty-two reviews and articles in the latter certainly qualify him as part of what Eliot termed the journal's "definite . . . [and] comprehensive constellation of contributors".' See further H. J. A. Sire, *Father Martin D'Arcy: Philosopher of Christian Love* (1997); Richard Harp, 'A conjuror at the Xmas party', *TLS*, 11 Dec. 2009, 13–15.

Christopher Dawson (1889–1970), cultural historian. An independent and erudite scholar of some private means (he would inherit estates in Yorkshire on the death of his father in 1933), he taught for a while, part-time, at the University College of Exeter, 1925–33; and, though not a professional academic, was ultimately appointed at the good age of sixty-eight to the Chair of Roman Catholic Studies at Harvard, 1958–62. A convert to Roman Catholicism, he devoted much of his research and published output to the idea of religion as the driver of social culture. His works include *Progress and Religion* (1929), *The Making of Europe* (1932), *Religion and Culture* (1948), and *Religion and the Rise of Western Culture* (1950); as well as a substantial series of books entitled *Essays in Order*, which he edited from the 1930s for the Catholic publishers Sheed and Ward: his own contributions to the series were *Enquiries into Religion and Culture* (1934), *Medieval Religion* (1934), *The Judgement of Nations* (1943). For TSE he would write Criterion Miscellany pamphlet 13, *Christianity and Sex* (1930). See Christina Scott – Dawson's daughter

– An Historian and His World: A Life of Christopher Dawson 1889–1970 (1984); Bradley H. Birzer, *Sanctifying the World: The Augustinian Life and Mind of Christopher Dawson* (2007); James R. Lothian, *The Making and Unmaking of the English Catholic Intellectual Community, 1910–1950* (2009). See too Dawson, 'Mr T. S. Eliot and the Meaning of Culture', *The Month* ns 1: 3 (Mar. 1949), 151–7.

Bonamy Dobrée (1891–1974), scholar, editor and critic, was to be Professor of English Literature at Leeds University, 1936–55. After service in the army during WW1 (he was twice mentioned in despatches and attained the rank of major), he read English at Christ's College, Cambridge, and taught in London and as a professor of English at the Egyptian University, Cairo, 1925–9. His works include *Restoration Comedy* (1924), *Essays in Biography* (1925), *Restoration Tragedy, 1660–1720* (1929), *Alexander Pope* (1951), and critical editions and anthologies. From 1921 to 1925 Dobrée and his wife Valentine resided at Larrau, a village in the Pyrenees, where he worked as an independent scholar. He was one of TSE's most constant correspondents. On 8 Sept. 1938, TSE would write to George Every, SSM, on the subject of the projected 'Moot': 'I think [Dobrée] would be worth having . . . He has his nose to the grindstone of the provincial university machine . . . but he is not without perception of the futilities of contemporary education. His mental formation is Liberal, but he has the rare advantage of being a man of breeding, so that his instincts with regard, for instance, to society, the community and the land, are likely to be right. He is also a person of strong, and I imagine hereditary, public spirit.' On 23 Feb. 1963, TSE urged his merits as future editor of Kipling's stories: 'He is far and away the best authority on Kipling . . . I have often discussed Kipling with him, and know that we see eye to eye about the stories. As for Dobrée's general literary achievements, they are very high indeed: his published work is not only very scholarly, but of the highest critical standing, and he writes well . . . If this job is ever done – and I should like to see it done during my lifetime – Dobrée is the man to do it.' See also Jason Harding, *The 'Criterion': Cultural Politics and Periodical Networks in Inter-War Britain* (2002).

Henry Ware Eliot, Jr (1879–1947), TSE's elder brother, went to school at Smith Academy, and then passed two years at Washington University, St Louis, before progressing to Harvard. At Harvard, he displayed a gift for light verse in *Harvard Celebrities* (1901), illustrated with 'Caricatures and Decorative Drawings' by two fellow undergraduates. After graduating, he spent a year at law school, but subsequently followed a career in printing, publishing and advertising. He attained a partnership in Husband & Thomas (later the Buchen Company), a Chicago advertising agency, from 1917 to 1929, during which time he gave financial assistance to TSE and regularly advised him on investments. He accompanied their mother on her visit to London in the summer of 1921, his first trip away from the USA. In February 1926, he married Theresa Anne Garrett (1884–1981), and later the same year the couple went on holiday to Italy along with TSE and Vivien. He was one of TSE's most regular and trusted correspondents. It was not until late in life that he found his true calling, as a Research Fellow in Near Eastern Archaeology at the Peabody Museum, Harvard, where his principal publication was a discussion of the prehistoric chronology of Northern Mesopotama, together with a description of the pottery from Kudish Saghir (1939): see too his posthumous publication *Excavations in Mesopotamia and Western Iran: Sites of 4000 – 500 B.C.: Graphic Analyses* (Harvard University: Peabody Museum of American Archaeology and Ethnology, 1950), prefaced by Lauriston Ward: 'It was a labor of love, of such magnitude as to be practically unique in the annals of archaeology . . . a monument to his scholarship and devotion . . . Eliot had all the qualities of the true scholar, which include modesty as well as ability.' In 1932 he published a detective novel, *The Rumble Murders*, under the pseudonym Mason Deal. He was instrumental in building up the T. S. Eliot collection at Eliot House (Houghton Library). Of slighter build than his brother – who remarked upon his 'Fred Astaire figure' – Henry suffered from deafness owing to scarlet fever as a child, and this may have contributed to his diffidence. Unselfishly devoted to TSE, whose growing up he movingly recorded with his camera, Henry took him to his first Broadway musical, *The Merry Widow*, which remained a favourite. It was with his brother in mind that TSE wrote: 'The notion of some infinitely gentle / Infinitely suffering thing' ('Preludes' IV).

Vivien Eliot, née Haigh-Wood (1888–1947). Born in Bury, Lancashire, on 28 May 1888, 'Vivy' was brought up in Hampstead from the age of three. After meeting TSE in company with Scofield Thayer in Oxford early in 1915, she and TSE hastened to be married just a few weeks later, on 26 June 1915. (TSE, who was lodging at 35 Greek Street, Soho, London, was recorded in the marriage certificate as 'of no occupation'.) The marriage was not a happy one for either of them. She developed close friendships with Mary Hutchinson, Ottoline Morrell, and others in TSE's circle. Despite chronic personal and medical difficulties, they remained together until 1933, when TSE resolved to separate from her during his visit to America. She was never to be reconciled to the separation, became increasingly ill, and in 1938 was confined to a psychiatric hospital, where she died (of 'syncope' and 'cardiovascular degeneration') on 22 January 1947. She is the dedicatee of *Ash-Wednesday* (1930). She published sketches in *The Criterion* (under various pseudonyms with the initials 'F. M.'), and collaborated on *The Criterion* and other works. See Michael Karwoski, 'The Bride from Bury', *Lancashire Life*, Mar. 1984, 52–3; Carole Seymour-Jones, *Painted Shadow: The Life of Vivienne Eliot* (2001); Ken Craven, *The Victorian Painter and the Poet's Wife: a biography of the Haigh-Wood family* (2012).

Geoffrey Faber (1889–1961), publisher and poet, was educated at Malvern College and Christ Church, Oxford, where he took a double first in Classical Moderations and Literae Humaniores (1912). He was called to the Bar by the Inner Temple (1921), though he was never to practise law. In 1919 he was elected a prize fellow of All Souls College, Oxford, which he went on to serve in the capacity of estates bursar, 1923–51. Before WW1 – in which he served with the London Regiment (Post Office Rifles), seeing action in France and Belgium – he spent eighteen months as assistant to Humphrey Milford, publisher of Oxford University Press. After the war he spent three years working for Strong & Co., brewers (there was a family connection), before going in for publishing on a full-time basis by joining forces with his All Souls colleague Maurice Gwyer and his wife, Lady Alsina Gwyer, who were trying to run a specialised imprint called the Scientific Press that Lady Gwyer had inherited from her father, Sir Henry Burdett: its weekly journal, the *Nursing Mirror*, was their most successful output. Following protractedly difficult negotiations, in 1925 Faber became chair of their restructured general publishing house which was provisionally styled Faber & Gwyer. After being introduced by Charles Whibley to T. S. Eliot, Faber was so impressed by the personality and aptitude of the 37-year-old American that he chose both to take on the running of *The Criterion* and to appoint Eliot to the board of his company (Eliot's *Poems 1909–1925* was one of the first books to be put out by the new imprint, and its first best-seller), which was relocated from Southampton Row to 24 Russell Square. By 1929 both the Gwyers and the *Nursing Mirror* were disposed of to advantage, and the firm took final shape as Faber & Faber, with Richard de la Mare and two additional Americans, Frank Morley and Morley Kennerley, joining the board. Faber chaired the Publishers' Association, 1939–41 – campaigning successfully for the repeal of a wartime tax on books – and helping to set up the National Book League. He was knighted in 1954, and gave up the chairmanship of Faber & Faber in 1960. His publications as poet included *The Buried Stream* (1941), and his works of non-fiction were *Oxford Apostles* (1933) and *Jowett* (1957), as well as an edition of the works of John Gay (1926). In 1920 he married Enid Richards, with whom he had two sons and a daughter. He died at his home in 1961.

John Gould Fletcher (1886–1950), American poet and critic, scion of a wealthy Southern family, dropped out of Harvard in 1907 (his father's death having secured him temporarily independent means) and lived for many years in Europe, principally in London; a friend of Ezra Pound, he became one of the mainstays of Imagism and published much original poetry. In later years he returned to his native Arkansas and espoused Agrarian values. His *Selected Poems* won the Pulitzer Prize in 1939. Fletcher wrote of TSE in *Life Is My Song: The Autobiography of John Gould Fletcher* (1937): 'As an editor, I found him to be practically ideal, willing for opinions to be mooted that ran contrary to his own avowed toryism, so long as those opinions were not merely emotional prejudices, but were backed up by something resembling intellectual judgment' (308). See also Fletcher, *Life for Life's Sake* (1941); *Selected Letters of John Gould Fletcher*, ed. Leighton Rudolph, Lucas Carpenter, Ethel C. Simpson (1996) – 'One of my difficulties with Eliot, whom I knew fairly well for nearly 15 years, was his intellectual snobbery'; Lucas Carpenter, *John Gould Fletcher and Southern Modernism* (1990); and Ben F. Johnson III, *Fierce Solitude: A Life of John Gould Fletcher* (1994).

Frank Stuart ('F. S.') Flint (1885–1960), English poet and translator, and civil servant, grew up in terrible poverty – 'gutter-born and gutter-bred', he would say – and left school at thirteen. But he set about to educate himself in European languages and literature (he had a deep appreciation of the French Symbolists and of Rimbaud), as well as in history and philosophy. In 1908 he started writing articles and reviews for the *New Age*, then for the *Egoist* and for *Poetry* (ed. Harriet Monroe). Quickly gaining in reputation and authority (especially on French literature – his influential piece on 'Contemporary French Poetry' appeared in Harold Monro's *Poetry Review* in 1912) – he soon became associated with T. E. Hulme, Ezra Pound, Richard Aldington and Hilda Doolittle; and he contributed poems to the *English Review* (ed. Ford Madox Hueffer) and to Pound's anthology *Des Imagistes* (1914). In 1920 he published

Otherworld Cadences (The Poetry Bookshop); and with TSE and Aldous Huxley he was one of the contributors to *Three Critical Essays on Modern English Poetry*, in *Chapbook* II: 9 (March 1920). Between 1909 and 1920 he published three volumes of poetry, though his work as essayist, reviewer and translator was the more appreciated: he became a regular translator and reviewer for *The Criterion* from the 1920s – and a member of the inner circle gathered round TSE – even while continuing to work in the statistics division of the Ministry of Labour (where he was Chief of the Overseas Section) until retiring in 1951. See also *The Fourth Imagist: Selected Poems of F. S. Flint*, ed. Michael Copp (2007).

E. M. Forster (1879–1970), novelist and essayist, was educated at King's College, Cambridge, where he gained a second in the classics tripos (and where he was elected to the exclusive Conversazione Society, the inner circle of the Apostles). Though intimately associated with the Bloomsbury group in London, where his circle of friends and acquaintances came to include Edward Marsh, Edward Garnett, Duncan Grant, Roger Fry, Lytton Strachey, and Leonard and Virginia Woolf, he derived much from visits to Italy, Greece, Egypt and India – where he worked for a while as private secretary to the Maharaja of Dewas: that experience brought about one of his most acclaimed novels, *A Passage to India* (1924), which sold around one million copies during his lifetime. His other celebrated novels include *Where Angels Fear to Tread* (1905), *A Room with a View* (1908), *Howards End* (1910), and the posthumous *Maurice* (1971, written 1910–13), a work that addressed his homosexuality. He gave the Clark Lectures at Cambridge in 1927 – in succession to TSE – which were published as *Aspects of the Novel* (1927). He turned down a knighthood, but in 1953 he was appointed a Companion of Honour; and he received the OM in 1969. See also Forster, 'Mr Eliot and His Difficulties', *Life and Letters*, 2: 13 (June 1929), 417–25; P. N. Furbank, *E. M. Forster* (2 vols, 1977, 1978); *Selected Letters of E. M. Forster*, ed. Mary Lago and P. N. Furbank (2 vols, 1983–5); and Nicola Beauman, *Morgan: A Biography of E. M. Forster* (1993).

H. J. C. Grierson (1866–1960), Regius Professor of Rhetoric and English Literature, University of Edinburgh, 1915–35; knighted in 1936; celebrated for his edition of *The Poems of John Donne* (2 vols, 1912) and *Metaphysical Lyrics and Poems of the Seventeenth Century* (1921) – which TSE reviewed in the *TLS*, 21 Oct. 1921. Cairns Craig, in 'The last Romantics: How the scholarship of Herbert Grierson influenced

Modernist poetry' (*TLS*, 15 Jan. 2010, 14–15), argues that '*The Waste Land* is saturated with echoes of Grierson's *Metaphysical Lyrics and Poems*. When Eliot sent a copy of his *Collected Poems* to Grierson, it was inscribed "to whom all English men of letters are indebted".' (Letty Grierson remembers a slightly different wording, 'to whom all poets of today are indebted': noted in the Grierson catalogue issued by James Fergusson Books & Manuscripts (2010.) TSE contributed to *Seventeenth Century Studies Presented to Sir Herbert Grierson* (1938).

Maurice Haigh-Wood (1896–1980), TSE's brother-in-law. He was six years younger than his sister Vivien, and after attending Ovingdean prep school and Malvern School, trained at Sandhurst Military Academy, before receiving his commission on 11 May 1915 as a second lieutenant in the 2nd Battalion, the Manchester Regiment. He served in the infantry for the rest of the war, and on regular visits home gave TSE his closest contact with the nightmare of life and death in the trenches. After the war, he found it difficult to get himself established, but became a stockbroker, and he remained friendly with, and respectful towards, TSE even after his separation from Vivien in 1933. In September 1968 he told Robert Sencourt – as he related in a letter to Valerie Eliot (2 Sept. 1968) – 'I had the greatest admiration & love for Tom whom I regarded as my elder brother for fifty years, & I would never think of acting against his wishes.' In 1930 he married a 25-year-old American dancer, Emily Cleveland Hoagland – known as 'Ahmé' (she was one of the Hoagland Sisters, who had danced at Monte Carlo) – and they were to have two children.

John Hayward (1905–65), editor, critic and anthologist, read modern languages at King's College, Cambridge. Despite the early onset of muscular dystrophy, he became a prolific and eminent critic and editor, bringing out in quick succession editions of the works of Rochester, Saint-Évremond, Jonathan Swift, Robert Herrick and Samuel Johnson. Other publications included *Complete Poems and Selected Prose of John Donne* (1929), *Donne* (1950), *T. S. Eliot: Selected Prose* (1953), *The Penguin Book of English Verse* (1958), and *The Oxford Book of Nineteenth Century English Verse* (1964). Celebrated as the learned and acerbic editor of *The Book Collector*, he was made a chevalier of the Légion d'honneur in 1952, a CBE in 1953. Writers including Graham Greene and Stevie Smith valued his editorial counsel; and Paul Valéry invited him to translate his comedy *Mon Faust*. Hayward advised TSE on various essays, poems, and plays including *The Cocktail Party* and *The*

Confidential Clerk, and most helpfully of all on *Four Quartets*. See also Helen Gardner, *The Composition of 'Four Quartets'* (1978).

When it was proposed during WW2 by Robert Nichols that Hayward might be nominated for the Oxford Chair of Poetry, TSE wrote to Nichols on 27 July 1944: 'I would certainly back up any testimony for John to the best of my command of the resources of the language; but I am wondering whether, at this stage, it would not be best for you to have a talk to John and sound him. I believe that such a suggestion would come as a surprise to him; he might need winning over to it; or he might have positive objections and difficulties beyond any of which you or I are aware . . . I suppose John's best official credentials are his "Nonesuch" editions of Donne and Swift, and the work he has been engaged upon, off and on, for some years, on Dryden, for the Oxford Press. I don't think he has done much formal lecturing; but I believe he has sometimes addressed undergraduate societies, as well as talked regularly to Mrs Whatshername's young ladies, during these last years in Cambridge. I think he stands well as an editor of texts, and therefore as an English scholar . . . [M]y own preference had fallen upon Dobrée, among the possibles, as John had not occurred to my mind . . .'

Mary Hutchinson, née Barnes (1889–1977), a half-cousin of Lytton Strachey, married St John ('Jack') Hutchinson in 1910. A prominent Bloomsbury hostess, she was for several years the acknowledged mistress of the art critic, Clive Bell, and became a close, supportive friend of TSE and VHE. TSE published one of her stories ('War') in *The Egoist*, and she later brought out a book of sketches, *Fugitive Pieces* (1927), under the imprint of the Hogarth Press. She wrote a short unpublished memoir of TSE (Harry Ransom Humanities Research Center, Austin, Texas). See David Bradshaw, '"Those Extraordinary Parakeets": Clive Bell and Mary Hutchinson', *The Charleston Magazine*, in two parts: 16 (Autumn/Winter 1997), 5–12; 17 (Spring/Summer 1998), 5–11.

Aldous Huxley (1894–1963), novelist, poet and essayist, whose early novels *Crome Yellow* (1921) and *Antic Hay* (1923) were successful satires of post-war English culture. While teaching at Eton, Aldous told his brother Julian in December 1916 that he 'ought to read' Eliot's 'things', which are 'all the more remarkable when one knows the man, ordinarily just an Europeanized American, overwhelmingly cultured, talking about French literature in the most uninspired fashion imaginable'. For his part, Eliot thought Huxley's early poems fell too much under the spell of Laforgue (and of his own poetry), but Huxley went on to become, not only a popular novelist, but, as the author of *Brave New World* and *The Doors of Perception*, an influential intellectual figure. See Nicholas Murray, *Aldous Huxley: An English Intellectual* (2002); Aldous Huxley, *Selected Letters*, ed. James Sexton (2007).

Alexis St Léger Léger (1887–1975) – pen name **St-John Perse** – poet and diplomat. Scion of a Bourgignon family, he passed his early years on an island near Guadeloupe in the West Indies, but the family returned to France in 1899. After studying law at the University of Bordeaux, he joined the Foreign Office as an attaché and worked for six years as Secretary at the French Legation in Peking: his poem *Anabase* is inspired in part by aspects of his life and observations in China, which included a journey to Outer Mongolia. In 1921, at a conference in Washington, DC, he was recruited by Aristide Briand, Prime Minister of France, as his *chef de cabinet*; and after Briand's death in 1932 he retained high office, serving as Sécretaire Générale of the Foreign Office, 1933–40. Dishonoured by the Vichy regime (he was a Grand Officier of the Legion of Honour), he spent the years of WW2 in the USA (serving for a time as a 'consultant' to the Library of Congress); and he went back to France only in 1957 (he had formally closed his diplomatic career in 1950, with the title of Ambassadeur de France). His publications include *Éloges* (published with help from André Gide, 1911), *Anabase* (1924; trans. TSE as *Anabasis*, 1930), *Exil* (1942), *Pluies* (1943), *Vents* (1946), *Amers* (1957) and *Oiseaux* (1962). In 1924 he had published in *Commerce* a translation of the opening section of 'The Hollow Men'. He was made Nobel Laureate in Literature in 1960.

In a copy of *Anabase* (Paris: Librairie Gallimard/Éditions de La Nouvelle Revue Française, 1925: limited edition copy no. 160), St-John Perse wrote: 'À T. S. Eliot / dont j'aime et j'admire l'œuvre / fraternellement / St. J. Perse.' (TSE Library)

In 1960 TSE was to recommend St-John Perse for the Nobel Prize. When requested on 10 Mar. 1960 by Uno Willers, secretary of the Svenska Akadamiens Nobelkommitté, to 'write down a more detailed motivation for your suggestion', TSE responded on 23 Mar. 1960: 'My interest in the work of St-John Perse began many years ago when I translated his *Anabase* into English. This task gave me an intimacy with his style and idiom which I could not have acquired in any other way. It seemed to me then, and it seems to me still, that he had done something highly original – and in a language, the French language, in which such originality is not easily attained. He had invented a form which was different from "free verse" as practised in France to-day, and different from the "prose-poem" in which some French writers, anxious to escape the limitations of the conventional metrics of their language, take refuge.

'He is the only French poet among my contemporaries, with the solitary exception of Supervielle, whose work has continued to interest me. With some of my contemporaries writing in other languages I feel a certain affinity – with Montale, for example, and with Seferis so far as I can judge from translations – with Perse, I have felt rather an influence which is visible in some of my poems written after I had translated *Anabase*.' He added: 'My remarks are, of course, to be taken as confidential, as I am always careful never to express in public my opinions of the relative value of the works of poets who are my contemporaries or my juniors.'

See also Richard Abel, 'The Influence of St.-John Perse on T. S. Eliot', *Contemporary Literature*, XIV: 2 (Spring 1973), 213–39.

Thomas McGreevy (1893–1967) – the family name was 'McGreevy', but by the 1930s he would assume the more Irish spelling 'MacGreevy' – Kerry-born poet, literary and art critic, and arts administrator, worked for the Irish Land Commission before serving in WW1 as a second lieutenant in the British Royal Field Artillery: he fought at Ypres and the Somme, and was twice wounded. After reading History and Political Science at Trinity College, Dublin, he moved in 1925 to London, where he met TSE and started to write for *The Criterion*, *TLS* (with an introduction from TSE) and *Nation & Athenaeum*. His poem 'Dysert' appeared in *NC* 4 (Jan. 1926) under the pseudonym 'L. St. Senan' (the title was later changed to 'Homage to Jack Yeats'). In 1927 he took up teaching English at the École Normale Supérieur in Paris, where he became friends with Beckett and Joyce (to whom he had been introduced in 1924) and with Richard Aldington. (His promotional essay on Joyce's incipient *Finnegans Wake* – 'The Catholic Element in Work in Progress' – appeared in *Our Exagmination Round his Factification for Incamination of Work in Progress* in 1929.) In addition, he journeyed through Italy with W. B. Yeats. Back in London in 1933, he lectured at the National Gallery and wrote for *The Studio*. Ultimately he was appointed Director of the National Gallery of Ireland, 1950–63. He was made Chevalier de la Légion d'Honneur, 1948; Cavaliere Ufficiale al merito della Repubblica Italiana, 1955; and Officier de la Légion d'Honneur, 1962. In 1929 he published a translation of Paul Valéry's *Introduction à la méthode de Léonard de Vinci* (*Introduction to the Method of Leonardo da Vinci*); and in 1931, two short monographs, *T. S. Eliot: A Study* and *Richard Aldington: An Englishman*; and his *Poems* would appear in 1934. His publications on art include *Jack B. Yeats: An Appreciation and an Interpretation* (1945) and *Nicolas Poussin* (1960). See also *The Collected Poems of Thomas MacGreevy: An Annotated Edition*, ed. Susan Schreibman (1991).

Frederic Manning (1882–1935), Australian writer who settled in 1903 in England, where he came to know artists and writers including Max Beerbohm, William Rothenstein, Richard Aldington and Ezra Pound (the latter would compliment him as 'the first licherary ComPanionship in Eng/ of Ez'); author of *Scenes and Portraits* (1909; 2nd edn, revised and enlarged, 1930). Despite being an asthmatic, he served in the ranks (Shropshire Light Infantry) in WW1, being involved for four months in heavy fighting on the Somme: this experience brought about his greatest achievement, a novel about the Western Front, *The Middle Parts of Fortune* (privately printed, 1929; standard text, 1977; expurgated as *Her Privates We*, credited pseudonymously to 'Private 19022', 1930; republished in full, with intro. by William Boyd, 1999) – 'the best book to come out of the First World War', Eliot is said to have said of it. In a letter to Aldington (6 July 1921), Eliot described Manning as 'undoubtedly one of the very best prose writers we have'; and he wrote of him in a later year: 'I did not know him well myself, though I have met him – I think directly after the first World War – and I have a precious copy which he gave me of *Her Privates We* and later I went to his funeral in Kensal Green . . . I remember him as a very careful and meticulous letter writer – one of few people I knew who put the first word of the next page at the bottom of every page of their letter' (letter to L. T. Hergenhan, 26 Oct. 1962). See Verna Coleman, *The Last Exquisite: A Portrait of Frederic Manning* (1990).

Harold Monro (1879–1932), poet, editor, publisher and bookseller. In 1913 he founded the Poetry Bookshop at 35 Devonshire Street, London, where poets would meet and give readings and lectures. In 1912 he briefly edited *The Poetry Review* for the Poetry Society; then his own periodicals, *Poetry and Drama*, 1913–15, and *The Chapbook* (originally *The Monthly Chapbook*), 1919–25. From the Poetry Bookshop, Monro would put out a remarkable mix of publications including the five volumes of *Georgian Poetry*, ed. Edward Marsh (1872–1953), between 1912 and 1922 (popular anthologies which sold in the region of 15,000 copies), the English edition of *Des Imagistes*, and the first volumes by writers including Richard Aldington, F. S. Flint and Robert Graves, along with some of his own collections including *Children of Love* (1915) and *Strange Meetings* (1917). TSE was to accept *The Winter Solstice* for publication by Faber & Gwyer as no. 13 of the Ariel Poems. Though a homosexual, Monro was to marry the sister of a friend, 1903–16; and in 1920 he wed Alida Klemantaski (daughter of a Polish-Jewish trader), with whom he never cohabited but who was ever loving and supportive to him: both of them endeared themselves to Eliot, who would occasionally use the premises of the Poetry Bookshop for meetings of contributors to *The Criterion*. After Monro's death, TSE wrote a critical note for *The Collected Poems of Harold Monro*, ed. Alida Monro (1933), xiii–xvi. See further Joy Grant, *Harold Monro and the Poetry Bookshop* (1967); and Dominic Hibberd, *Harold Monro: Poet of the New Age* (2001).

Marianne Moore (1887–1972), American poet and critic, contributed to *The Egoist* from 1915. Her first book, *Poems*, was published in London in 1921. She went on to become in 1925 acting editor of *The Dial*, editor, 1927–9, and an important and influential modern poet. Eliot found her 'an extremely intelligent person, very shy . . . One of the most observant people I have ever met'. Writing to her on 3 April 1921, he said her verse interested him 'more than that of anyone now writing in America'. And in Eliot's introduction to her *Selected Poems* (F&F, 1935) he stated that her 'poems form part of the small body of durable poetry written in our time'. See *The Selected Letters of Marianne Moore*, ed. Bonnie Costello (1998); Linda Leavell, *Holding On Upside Down: The Life and Work of Marianne Moore* (2013).

Paul Elmer More (1864–1937), critic, scholar and prolific writer, had grown up in St Louis, Missouri, and attended Washington University before going on to Harvard; at one time he had taught French to TSE's brother Henry. Initially a humanist, by the 1930s he assumed an Anglo-Catholic position not unlike that of TSE (who appreciated the parallels between their spiritual development). See also 'An Anglican Platonist: the Conversion of Paul Elmer More', *TLS*, 30 Oct. 1937, 792. At the outset of his career, More taught classics at Harvard and Bryn Mawr; thereafter he became a journalist, serving as literary editor of *The Independent* (1901–3) and the New York *Evening Post* (1903–9), and as editor of *The Nation* (1909–14), before finally turning to freelance writing and teaching. TSE keenly admired More's many works, in particular *Shelburne Essays* (11 vols, 1904–21), *The Greek Tradition* (5 vols, 1924–31) and *The Demon of the Absolute* (1928); and he went to great trouble in the 1930s in his efforts to secure a publisher for *Pages from an Oxford Diary* (1937), which More stipulated he would only ever publish in anonymity.

In 1937, TSE wrote in tribute: 'The place of Paul More's writings in my own life has been of such a kind that I find [it] easiest, and perhaps most effective, to treat it in a kind of autobiographical way. What is significant to me . . . is not simply the conclusions at which he has arrived, but the fact that he *arrived* there from somewhere else; and not simply that he came from somewhere else, but that he took a particular route . . . If I find an analogy with my own journey, that is perhaps of interest to no one but myself, except in so far as it explains my retrospective appreciation of the *Shelburne Essays*; ~~but~~ for my appreciation of the whole work cannot be disengaged from the way in which I arrived at it.

'When I was an undergraduate at Harvard, More was editor of the *Nation*, and to occupy that position in those days was to be a public figure. I sometimes read the *Nation* and I sometimes read a Shelburne Essay, but I cannot remember that I liked or disliked More's writing . . . I certainly did not have the background for appreciating the kind of critical intelligence at work in the *Shelburne Essays* – to say nothing of Ste. Beuve. It was not until my senior year, as a pupil of [Irving] Babbitt's, that More's work was forced on my attention: for one of the obligations of any pupil of Babbitt was to learn a proper respect for "my friend More". But while one was directly exposed to so powerful an influence as Babbitt's, everything that one read was merely a supplement to Babbitt.

'It was not until one or two of the volumes of *The Greek Tradition* had appeared, that More began to have any importance for me. It was possibly Irving Babbitt himself, <in 1927 or 1928>, in a conversation in London~~, in 1927 or '28,~~ during which I had occasion to indicate the steps I had recently taken, who first made me clearly cognizant of the situation. In the later volumes of *The Greek Tradition*, and in the acquaintance and friendship subsequently formed, I came to find an auxiliary to my own progress of thought, which no English theologian <at the time> could have given me. The English theologians, born and brought up in surroundings of private belief and public form, and often themselves descended from ecclesiastics, at any rate living mostly in an environment of religious practice, did not seem to me to know enough of the new world of barbarism and infidelity that was forming all about them. The English Church was familiar with the backslider, but it knew nothing of the convert – certainly not of the convert who ~~came~~ had come such a long journey. I might almost say that I never met any Christians until after I had made up my mind to become one. It was of the greatest importance, then, to ~~meet~~ have at hand the work of a man who had come by somewhat the same route, to <almost> the same conclusions, at almost the same time: with a maturity, a weight of scholarship, a discipline of thinking, which I did not, and never shall, possess.

'I had met More only once in earlier years – at a reception given by the Babbitts to which some of Babbitt's pupils had the honor of invitation and that remained only a visual memory. My first meeting with him in London, however, seemed more like the renewal of an old acquaintance than the formation of a new one: More was a St. Louisan, and had known my family; and if he had remained a few years longer, ~~I also~~ he would have ~~learned my~~ <taught me> Greek ~~from him~~, as ~~did~~ he had taught my brother' (*Princeton Alumni Magazine* 37 [5 Feb. 1937], 373–4); TS at Princeton C0896, Box 1, folder 3).

See further Arthur Hazard Dakin, *Paul Elmer More* (1960) – of which TSE wrote on 29 Mar. 1960: 'What the author says about Paul More and myself seems to me very accurate . . . [W]e did see very nearly eye to eye in theological matters.'

Lady Ottoline Morrell (1873–1938), daughter of Lieutenant-General Arthur Bentinck and half-sister to the Duke of Portland. In 1902 she married Philip Morrell (1870–1941), Liberal MP for South Oxfordshire 1902–18. A patron of the arts, she entertained a notable literary and artistic circle, first at 44 Bedford Square, then at Garsington Manor, nr. Oxford, where she moved in 1915. She was a lover of Bertrand Russell, who introduced her to TSE, and her many friends included Lytton Strachey, D. H. Lawrence, Aldous Huxley, Siegfried Sassoon, the Woolfs and the Eliots. Her memoirs (ed. by Robert Gathorne-Hardy) appeared as *Ottoline* (1963) and *Ottoline at Garsington* (1974). See Miranda Seymour, *Life on the Grand Scale: Lady Ottoline Morrell* (1992, 1998).

Edwin Muir (1887–1959), Scottish poet, novelist, critic; translator (with his wife Willa) of Franz Kafka. TSE was to write to LW on 22 Aug. 1946: 'I am anxious to do anything I can for Muir because I think highly of his best poetry and I think he has not had enough recognition.' To his cousin Eleanor Hinkley, 25 Dec. 1955: 'I have always found Willa rather oppressive. Edwin is a sweet creature, who never says anything when his wife is present, and only an occasional word when she isn't. An evening alone with him is very fatiguing. But he is a good poet, and I believe, what is even rarer, a literary man of complete integrity. He is not really Scottish, but Orcadian – in other words, pure Scandinavian.' On 1 Jan. 1959, when pressing the claims of Muir upon the Royal Literary Fund, TSE wrote to Alan Pryce-Jones: 'I have a very high opinion indeed of Edwin Muir as a poet, and admire him particularly because his poetry has gone on gaining in strength in later years. And I think that both he and Willa deserve recognition because of their work in translation. It is through them, you remember, that Kafka became known in this country, as they translated, I think, all his novels . . . P.S. Robert Sencourt surprised me by telling me that the Royal Literary Fund had granted him £300, and Sencourt's contributions to English literature are negligible in comparison with those of Edwin Muir.' In a tribute: 'Muir's literary criticism had always seemed to me of the best of our time: after I came to know him, I realised that it owed its excellence not only to his power of intellect and acuteness of sensibility, but to those moral qualities which make us remember him, as you say justly, as "in some ways almost a saintly man". It was more recently that I came to regard his poetry as ranking with the best poetry of our time. As a poet he began late; as a poet he was recognised late; but some of his finest work – perhaps his very finest work – was written when he was already over sixty . . . For this late development we are reminded of the later poetry of Yeats; and Muir had to struggle with bad health also: but in the one case as in the other (and Muir is by no means unworthy to be mentioned together with Yeats) we recognise a triumph of the human spirit' (*The Times*, 7 Jan. 1959). Willa Muir commented on TSE's plaudits: 'Eliot, in his desire to present Edwin as an orthodox Christian, overdid, I think, the desolations and the saintliness. Edwin's wine could never be contained in any orthodox creed' (letter to Kathleen Raine, 7 Apr. 1960). TSE would later say of Muir: 'He was a reserved, reticent man . . . Yet his personality made a deep impression upon me, and especially the impression of one very rare and precious quality . . . unmistakable integrity'; and of his poems: 'under the pressure of emotional intensity, and possessed by his vision, he found almost unconsciously the right, the inevitable, way of saying what he wanted to say' ('Edwin Muir: 1887–1959: An Appreciation', *The Listener*, 28 May 1964, 872). Muir's publications include *First Poems* (Hogarth Press, 1925); *Transition: Essays on Contemporary Literature* (1926); *An Autobiography* (1954); *Selected Poems of Edwin Muir*, preface by TSE (1966); *Selected Letters of Edwin Muir*, ed. P. H. Butter (1974).

John Middleton Murry (1889–1957), English writer, critic and editor, founded the magazine *Rhythm*, 1911–13, and worked as a reviewer for the *Westminster Gazette*, 1912–14, and the *Times Literary Supplement*,

1914–18, before becoming editor from 1919 to 1921 of the *Athenaeum*, which he turned into a lively cultural forum – in a letter of 2 July 1919, TSE called it 'the best literary weekly in the Anglo-Saxon world'. Richard Church thought him 'a dark, slippery character, who looked over my shoulder (probably into an invisible mirror) when talking to me, and referred to himself always in the third person . . . In spite of these characteristics . . . he was possessed by a strong literary sensibility.' In a 'London Letter' in *Dial* 72 (May 1921), Eliot considered Murry 'genuinely studious to maintain a serious criticism', but he disagreed with his 'particular tastes, as well as his general statements'. After the demise of the *Athenaeum*, Murry went on to edit *The Adelphi*, 1923–48. In 1918, he married Katherine Mansfield, who died in 1923. He was friend and biographer of D. H. Lawrence; and as an editor he provided a platform for writers as various as George Santayana, Paul Valéry, D. H. Lawrence, Aldous Huxley, Virginia Woolf, and Eliot. His first notable critical work was *Dostoevsky* (1916); his most influential study, *The Problem of Style* (1922). Though as a Romanticist he was an intellectual opponent of the avowedly 'Classicist' Eliot, Murry offered Eliot in 1919 the post of assistant editor on the *Athenaeum* (which Eliot had to decline); in addition, he recommended him to be Clark lecturer at Cambridge in 1926, and was a steadfast friend to both TSE and his wife Vivien. Eliot wrote in a reference on 9 Sept. 1945 that Murry was 'one of the most distinguished men of letters of this time, and testimony from a contemporary seems superfluous. Several volumes of literary essays of the highest quality are evidence of his eminence as a critic; and even if one took no account of his original contribution, his conduct of *The Athenaeum*, which he edited from 1919 until its absorption into *The Nation*, should be enough to entitle him to the gratitude of his contemporaries and juniors. His direction of *The Adelphi* should also be recognised. Since he has devoted his attention chiefly to social and religious problems, he has written a number of books which no one who is concerned with the same problems, whether in agreement with him or not, can afford to neglect. I am quite sure that no future student of these matters who wishes to understand this age will be able to ignore them, and that no future student of the literary spirit of this age will be able to ignore Mr Murry's criticism.' He wrote to Murry's widow (his fourth wife, the author Mary Gamble) on 29 May 1957: 'The friendship between John and myself was of a singular quality, such that it was rather different from any other of my friendships. We did not often meet. We disagreed throughout many years on one point after another. But on the other hand, a very warm affection existed between us in spite of differences of view and infrequency of meetings. This affection was not merely, on my part, a feeling of gratitude for the opportunities he had given me early in my career during his editorship of *The Athenaeum*, but was something solid and permanent. He was one of the strangest and most remarkable men I have known, and no less strange and remarkable was the tie of affection between us.' See F. A. Lea, *The Life of John Middleton Murry* (1959); and David Goldie, *A Critical Difference: T. S. Eliot and John Middleton Murry in English Literary Criticism, 1919–1928* (1998).

F. S. Oliver (1864–1934), businessman and polemicist, was educated at Edinburgh and Trinity College, Cambridge, before joining forces in 1892 with Ernest Debenham in the firm of Debenham and Freebody (drapers, wholesalers, manufacturers), which they caused to flourish and expand (buying up Marshall and Snelgrove and Harvey Nichols); Oliver, who had become a wealthy man, retired as managing director in 1920. A radical Tory, he engaged himself in many public issues. His publications included *Alexander Hamilton* (1906), *Ordeal by Battle* (1915) and *The Endless Adventure* (3 vols, 1930–5).

Kenneth Pickthorn (1892–1975), historian and politician; Fellow of Corpus Christi College, Cambridge, from 1914; Dean, 1919–29; Tutor, 1927–35; President, 1937–44. From 1950 to 1966 he was to be the Conservative MP for a Midlands constituency; an independent-minded and outspoken parliamentarian, critical of cant, he was made a baronet in 1959, Privy Councillor in 1964. His publications included *Some Historical Principles of the Constitution* (1925) and *Early Tudor Government* (2 vols, 1934).

Ezra Pound (1885–1972), American poet and critic, was one of the prime impresarios of the modernist movement in London and Paris, and played a major part in launching Eliot as poet and critic – as well as Joyce, Lewis and many other modernists. Eliot called on him at 5 Holland Place Chambers, Kensington, on 22 Sept. 1914, with an introduction from Conrad Aiken. On 30 Sept. 1914, Pound hailed 'Prufrock' as 'the best poem I have yet had or seen from an American'; and on 3 October called Eliot 'the last intelligent man I've found – a young American T. S. Eliot . . . worth watching – mind "not primitive"' (*Selected Letters of Ezra Pound*, 40–1). Pound was instrumental in arranging for 'Prufrock' to be published in *Poetry* in 1915, and helped to shape *The Waste Land* (1922), which Eliot dedicated to him as 'il miglior fabbro'. The poets remained in loyal correspondence for the rest of their lives. Having initially dismissed Pound's poetry (to Conrad Aiken, 30 Sept. 1914) as 'well-meaning but touchingly incompetent', Eliot went on to champion his work, writing to Gilbert Seldes (27 Dec. 1922): 'I sincerely consider Ezra Pound the most important living poet in the English language.' He wrote an early critical study, *Ezra Pound: His Metric and Poetry* (1917), and went on, as editor of *The Criterion* and publisher at Faber & Faber, to publish most of Pound's work in the UK, including *Selected Shorter Poems*, *The Cantos* and *Selected Literary Essays*. After his move to Italy in the 1920s, Pound became increasingly sceptical about the direction of TSE's convictions and poetry, but they continued to correspond. TSE wrote to James Laughlin, on the occasion of Pound's seventieth birthday: 'I believe that I have in the past made clear enough my personal debt to Ezra Pound during the years 1915–22. I have also expressed in several ways my opinion of his rank as a poet, as a critic, as impresario of other writers, and as pioneer of metric and poetic language. His 70th birthday is not a moment for qualifying one's praise, but merely for recognition of those services to literature for which he will deserve the gratitude of posterity, and for appreciation of those achievements which even his severest critics must acknowledge' (3 Nov. 1955). TSE told Eaghor G. Kostetsky on 6 Jan. 1960 that the *Cantos* 'is unquestionably the most remarkable long contemporary poem in the English language'. After TSE's death, Pound said of him: 'His was the true Dantescan voice – not honoured enough, and deserving more than I ever gave him.' See A. David Moody, *Ezra Pound: Poet: A Portrait of the Man and his Work* I: *The Young Genius 1885–1920* (2007), Humphrey Carpenter, *A Serious Character* (1988), *The Selected Letters of Ezra Pound 1907–1941*, ed. D. D. Paige (1950).

Mario Praz (1896–1982), scholar and critic of English life and literature; author of *La Carne, la Morte e Il Diavolo nella Letteratura Romantica* (1930; *The Romantic Agony*, 1933). Educated in Bologna, Rome and Florence, he came to England in 1923 to study for the title of *libero docente*. He was Senior Lecturer in Italian, Liverpool University, 1924–32; Professor of Italian Studies, Victoria University of Manchester, 1932–4; and Professor of English Language and Literature at the University of Rome, 1934–66. His many other publications include *Il giardino dei sensi* (1975). In 1952 he was conferred the title of Knight Commander of the British Empire (KBE) by Queen Elizabeth II. In 'An Italian Critic on Donne and Crashaw' (*TLS*, 17 Dec. 1925, 878), TSE hailed Praz's study *Secentismo e Marinismo in Inghilterra: John Donne – Richard Crashaw*

(1925) as 'indispensable for any student of this period and these authors'. In 'A Tribute to Mario Praz', written 15 Apr. 1964, he noted: 'My first acquaintance with the work of Mario Praz came when, many years ago, the *Times Literary Supplement* sent me for review his *Secentismo e Marinismo in Inghilterra*. I immediately recognized these essays – and especially his masterly study of Crashaw – as among the best that I had ever read in that field. His knowledge of the poetry of that period in four languages – English, Italian, Spanish and Latin – was encyclopaedic, and, fortified by his own judgment and good taste, makes that book essential reading for any student of the English "metaphysical poets".

'Had I any suitable unpublished essay to offer, I would gladly give it now in tribute to a great scholar. I tender these few words in testimony to my gratitude and admiration, not wishing my name to be absent from the roster of men of letters who, as well as more learned scholars of the period, owe him homage' (*Friendship's Garland: Essays presented to Mario Praz on His Seventieth Birthday*, ed. Vittorio Gabrieli [1966]).

See Praz, 'Dante in Inghilterra', *La Cultura*, Jan. 1930, 65–6; 'T. S. Eliot e Dante', *Letteratura* 15 (July 1937), 12–28; 'T. S. Eliot and Dante', *Southern Review* 3 (Winter 1937), 525–48; and *The Flaming Heart* (1958).

Herbert Read (1893–1968), English poet and literary critic, and one of the most influential art critics of the century. Son of a tenant farmer, Read spent his first years in rural Yorkshire; at sixteen, he went to work as a bank clerk, then studied law and economics at Leeds University; later still, he joined the Civil Service, working first in the Ministry of Labour and then at the Treasury. During his years of service in WW1, he rose to be a captain in a Yorkshire regiment, the Green Howards (his war poems were published in *Naked Warriors*, 1919); and when on leave to receive the Military Cross in 1917, he arranged to dine with TSE at the Monico Restaurant in Piccadilly Circus. This launched a lifelong friendship which he was to recall in 'T.S.E. – A Memoir', in *T. S. Eliot: The Man and his Work*, ed. Allen Tate (1966). Within the year, he had also become acquainted with the Sitwells, Ezra Pound, Wyndham Lewis, Richard Aldington and Ford Madox Ford. He co-founded the journal *Art & Letters*, 1917–20, and wrote essays too for A. R. Orage, editor of the *New Age*. In 1922 he was appointed a curator in the department of ceramics and glass at the Victoria and Albert Museum; and in later years he was to work for the publishers Routledge & Kegan Paul, and as editor of the *Burlington Magazine*, 1933–9. By 1923 he was writing for *The*

Criterion: he was to be one of Eliot's regular leading contributors and a reliable ally and adviser. In 1924 he edited T. E. Hulme's posthumous *Speculations*. His later works include *Art Now* (1933); the introduction to the catalogue of the International Surrealist Exhibition held at the New Burlington Galleries, London, 1936; *Art and Society* (1937); *Education through Art* (1943); and *A Concise History of Modern Painting* (1959). In 1947 he founded (with Roland Penrose) the Institute of Contemporary Art; and in 1953 he was knighted for services to literature. Eliot, he was to recall (perhaps only half in jest), was 'rather like a gloomy priest presiding over my affections and spontaneity'. According to Stephen Spender in 1966, Eliot said 'of the anarchism of his friend Herbert Read, whom he loved and esteemed very highly: "Sometimes when I read Herbert's inflammatory pamphlets I have the impression that I am reading the pronouncements of an old-fashioned nineteenth-century liberal"' ('Remembering Eliot', *The Thirties and After* [1978], 251). Joseph Chiari recalled TSE saying of Read: 'Ah, there is old Herbie, again; he can't resist anything new!' See Herbert Read, *Annals of Innocence and Experience* (1940); James King, *The Last Modern: A Life of Herbert Read* (1990); and *Herbert Read Reassessed*, ed. D. Goodway (1998). Jason Harding (*The 'Criterion'*: see citation under Dobrée) calculates that Read wrote 68 book reviews, 4 articles and 5 poems for *The Criterion*.

I. A. Richards (1893–1979), theorist of literature, education, and communication studies. At Cambridge University he studied history but switched to moral sciences, graduating from Magdalene College, where in 1922 he was appointed College Lecturer in English and Moral Sciences. A vigorous, spellbinding lecturer, he was to the fore in the advancement of the English Tripos. His early writings – *The Foundations of Aesthetics* (with C. K. Ogden and James Wood, 1922), *The Meaning of Meaning* (also with Ogden, 1923), *Principles of Literary Criticism* (1924), *Science and Poetry* (1926), *Practical Criticism: A Study of Literary Judgment* (1929) – are foundational texts in modern English literary studies. After teaching at National Tsing Hua University in Peking, 1929–30, he repaired for the remainder of his career to Harvard University, where he was made a university professor in 1944. His other works include *Basic Rules of Reason* (1933), *Basic in Teaching: East and West* (1935), *Mencius on the Mind* (1932), *Coleridge on Imagination* (1934), *The Philosophy of Rhetoric* (1936), *Interpretation in Teaching* (1938), *Speculative Instruments* (1955), and translations from Plato and Homer. He was appointed Companion of Honour in 1963, and awarded the Emerson-

Thoreau medal of the American Academy of Arts and Sciences, 1970. Out of the teaching term, he enjoyed with his wife Dorothea (1894–1986) an adventurous life of travel and mountain-climbing. See *Selected Letters of I. A. Richards, CH*, ed. John Constable (1990); John Constable, 'I. A. Richards, T. S. Eliot, and the Poetry of Belief', *Essays in Criticism* (July 1990), 222–43; *I. A. Richards and his Critics*, ed. John Constable (vol. 10 of *I. A. Richards: Selected Works 1919–1938* (2001); John Paul Russo, *I. A. Richards: His Life and Work* (1989).

Bruce Richmond (1871–1964), literary editor, was educated at Winchester and New College, Oxford, and called to the Bar in 1897. However, he never practised as a barrister; instead, George Buckle, editor of *The Times*, appointed him an assistant editor in 1899, and in 1902 he assumed the editorship of the fledgling *Times Literary Supplement*, which he commanded for thirty-five years. During this period, the *TLS* established itself as the premier academic and critical periodical in Britain. He was knighted in 1935. TSE, who was introduced to Richmond by Richard Aldington in 1919, enthused to his mother that year that writing the leading article for the *TLS* was the highest honour 'in the critical world of literature'. In a tribute, he recalled Richmond as possessing 'a bird-like alertness of eye, body and mind . . . It was from Bruce Richmond that I learnt editorial standards . . . I learnt from him that it is the business of an editor to know his contributors personally, to keep in touch with them and to make suggestions to them. I tried [at *The Criterion*] to form a nucleus of writers (some of them, indeed, recruited from *The Times Literary Supplement*, and introduced to me by Richmond) on whom I could depend, differing from each other in many things, but not in love of literature and seriousness of purpose. And I learnt from Richmond that I must read every word of what was to appear in print . . . It is a final tribute to Richmond's genius as an editor that some of his troupe of regular contributors (I am thinking of myself as well as of others) produced some of their most distinguished critical essays as leaders for the *Literary Supplement* . . . Good literary criticism requires good editors as well as good critics. And Bruce Richmond was a great editor' ('Bruce Lyttelton Richmond', *TLS*, 13 Jan. 1961, 17).

J. M. Robertson (1856–1933), author, journalist, politician, began his career as a clerk; then worked on newspapers including the *Edinburgh Evening News* and *National Reformer*. He was Liberal MP for Tyneside, 1908–18. Though self-taught, he was a prolific writer, publishing over

100 books and pamphlets including *The Problem of Hamlet* (1919), *Hamlet Once More* (1923), *Mr Shaw and the Maid* (1926) – a study of *St Joan* which TSE reviewed in *The Criterion* (Apr. 1926) – and *The Problems of Shakespeare's Sonnets* (1927), which TSE reviewed in *The Nation* (12 Feb. 1927). A fervent disintegrationist, Robertson sought to isolate the pure Shakespeare. TSE wrote to Duff Cooper on 30 Nov. 1949, in response to his book *Sergeant Shakespeare*: 'I must let you know that I am no longer under the influence of Robertson, and no longer quite agree with what I said about *Hamlet*.' See also Leo Storm, 'J. M. Robertson and T. S. Eliot: A Note on the Genesis of Modern Critical Theory', *Journal of Modern Literature* 5: 2 (Apr. 1976), 315–21; Martin Page, *Britain's Unknown Genius: The Life-Work of J. M. Robertson* (1984); *J. M. Robertson, 1856–1933: Liberal, Rationalist and Scholar*, ed. G. A. Wells (1985); Odin Dekkers, *J. M. Robertson: Rationalist and Literary Critic* (1998).

Edouard Roditi (1910–92), American-Jewish poet, critic, biographer, translator and essayist. With a background that was partly Spanish-Portuguese and partly Greek, he attended schools in England, and went up (for a single year, 1927–8) to Balliol College, Oxford. Precocious as both poet and translator, by the age of twelve he had translated into Latin and Greek a good deal of the poetry of Byron; and at fourteen he put Gerard Manley Hopkins into French. His adult works included *Prison Within Prison: Three Elegies on Jewish Themes* (1941); the prose poems of *New and Old Testaments* (1983); collections of essays including *The Disorderly Poet* (1975) and a treatise, *De L'Homosexualité* (1962); as well as translations into English, German and French. The *Times* obituary remarked (18 May 1992): 'In 1926 he was sent to a Swiss clinic, where he set himself the task of translating the French poet Saint-John Perse's *Anabase* into English. A little later he discovered that T. S. Eliot was engaged in the same project, and so sent him his version, from which, he claimed, Eliot took up more than a few interpretations. But Eliot also made encouraging comments about some of the boy's original verse.'

On 11 Nov. 1936 TSE wrote on Roditi's behalf to the Undersecretary of State: 'I am glad to offer myself as a sponsor for Mr Edward Roditi in his application to be allowed to reside in this country. I have known Mr Roditi for some years as a poet and man of letters, and neither in my personal acquaintance nor in his literary work – he has been a contributor to *The Criterion* – have I regarded him as a foreigner in any way. He writes English as his native tongue, and his poetry has distinction and beauty. I believe his abilities, experience and education to be such that I should consider it for the good of English letters that he should be allowed to reside here. And so far as I know him personally, my opinion of him supports my opinion of his literary work' (UCLA).

Roditi later wrote to *The Jewish Quarterly*, no. 142 (38: 2, Summer 1991), 72: 'I was barely eighteen when I first met Eliot in 1928 because I too had undertaken a translation of Saint-John Perse's *Anabase* without knowing that its French author had already granted Eliot the right to translate and publish it in English.

'Eliot then proved to be very cordial and almost paternal in his typically reserved manner. After discussing our different interpretations of some of the more cryptic passages in *Anabase*, Eliot invited me to submit to him some of my own poems. From some of these he was soon able to conclude that I was of Jewish origin and attempting somehow to discover my Jewish identity in a few of my poems. Very kindly, he suggested corrections to these somewhat immature poems and encouraged me to continue submitting my poetry to him for guidance. After a while, he even suggested publishing in *The Criterion* one of my most overtly Jewish poems – in fact one of the sections of my long elegy entitled "The Complaint of Jehuda Abravanel"; but this particular section of my poem had already been accepted for publication either in *The Spectator* or *The Jewish Review*. I then submitted a group of shorter poems and Eliot published three of these in *The Criterion*.

'I continued to see Eliot fairly regularly in London between 1928 and 1937 and can testify to the fact that he expressed to me on several occasions after 1933 his horror of the anti-Semitic outrages which were already occurring in Nazi Germany. My personal impression is that, after writing *The Waste Land*, Eliot had become a much more devout Christian, before writing the so-called "Ariel Poems" and *Ash Wednesday*. As a Christian he no longer felt or expressed the kind of somewhat immature and snobbish anti-Semitism that can be detected in the earlier poems and letters . . .'

See also Roditi, 'T. S. Eliot: Persönlichkeit und Werk', *Der Monat* 3 (1948), 86–9; 'Corresponding with Eliot', *London Magazine* 28: 5/6 (Aug./Sept. 1988), 33–44. Roditi wrote two articles about St-John Perse, in *Contemporary Poetry*, 6: 3 (1944) and *La République libre*, 26 Jan. 1951.

William Rothenstein (1872–1945), Bradford-born son of Jewish immigrants, painter and administrator, was Principal of the Royal College of Art from 1919; knighted in 1931. See *Twelve Portraits* (F&F, 1928); *Men and Memories: Recollections of William Rothenstein* (2 vols, 1931–2); *Since Fifty: Men and Memories, 1922–1938* (1939); and Robert Speaight, *William Rothenstein: The Portrait of an Artist in His Time* (1962).

A. L. Rowse (1903–97), Cornish historian, was educated at Christ Church, Oxford, and elected a Prize Fellow of All Souls in 1925. He was a lecturer at Merton College, 1927–30, and taught also at the London School of Economics. His numerous books include *Sir Richard Grenville of the Revenge* (1937), *The England of Elizabeth* (1950), *William Shakespeare: A Biography* (1963), *Shakespeare the Man* (1973), *Simon Forman: Sex and Society in Shakespeare's Age* (1974), *All Souls in My Time* (1993), and volumes of poetry gathered up in *A Life* (1981). Though he failed in 1952 to be elected Warden of All Souls, he was elected a Fellow of the British Academy in 1958 and made a Companion of Honour in 1997. See Richard Ollard, *A Man of Contradictions: A Life of A. L. Rowse* (1999), and *The Diaries of A. L. Rowse* (ed. Ollard, 2003). TSE was to write to Geoffrey Curtis on 1 May 1944: 'Rowse is an old friend of mine, and a very touching person: the suppressed Catholic and the rather less suppressed Tory (with a real respect for Good Families), the miner's son and the All Souls Fellow, the minor poet and the would-be politician, the proletarian myth and the will-to-power, are always at odds in a scholarly retiring mind and a frail body. He is also very patronising, and one likes it.' Rowse was to hail Eliot as 'nursing father to us all'.

Robert Esmonde Gordon George – Robert Sencourt (1890–1969) – critic, historian and biographer. Born in New Zealand, he was educated in Tamaki and at St John's College, Oxford. By 1929 – perhaps to avoid confusion with Professor George Gordon (President of Magdalen College, Oxford) – he was to take the name of Robert Sencourt. He taught in India and Portugal before serving as Vice-Dean of the Faculty of Arts and Professor of English Literature, University of Egypt, 1933–6. *The Times* obituarist noted that he was 'born an Anglican [but] was converted to Roman Catholicism which alone could inspire him with the spiritual dimension of the life of grace . . . [He] was the most fervent and devout of religious men, with the same personal mysticism which makes his life of St John of the Cross a joy to read. Never fearing to speak his mind in religious matters, even when (as often) his view ran counter to the church's, he was intolerant of any form of ecclesiastical cant or humbug.' His books include *The Genius of the Vatican* (1935), *Carmelite and Poet:*

St John of the Cross (1943), *St Paul: Envoy of Grace* (1948), biographies of George Meredith, the Empress Eugénie, Napoleon III, King Alfonso and Edward VIII, and *T. S. Eliot: A Memoir*, ed. Donald Adamson (1971). EVE wrote to Russell Kirk, 15 May 1973: 'Sencourt's memoir is, to put it mildly, unfortunate, and leaves a nasty taste. As you say, the whole background is both strange and malicious. He had nothing whatsoever to do with Tom's conversion – this long, slow process had come to fruition before they met.' See too Sencourt, 'T. S. Eliot: His Religion', *PAX: A Benedictine Review*, no. 312 (Spring 1965), 15–19.

On 17 July 1936 TSE was to write to the Master of Corpus Christi College, Cambridge, in support of Sencourt's application for the Chair of English at Bucharest: 'I should think Sencourt would do admirably for it. He is a New Zealander, and has lived abroad a great deal, largely in Italy and France, and has what would be called a cosmopolitan mind. He gets on well with foreigners – he had three years as Professor of English in Cairo, and is very tolerant of inferior races, and gets on well with them. He is an R.C. convert. He knows everybody or nearly everybody. George Gordon will probably speak for his work as an undergraduate at Oxford (some years ago). He is very much more than competent in English literature (you will learn his official qualifications from other sources), is I believe a first-rate horseman, and of physical courage to the point of recklessness. He is regarded as an odd creature, and a snob: but I know that his kindness and generosity are boundless. I will also say what one could not very well say in a formal testimonial, that I think he is absolutely good enough, and *not too good*, for such a position. It wouldn't be a question of blocks being chopped (rather badly) with a razor; he is just the right sharpness and weight; he wouldn't despise the job and he would do it thoroughly; and he would do his best to like and to understand his pupils. I think the Roumanians would be lucky to get him.' Similarly, two years later, when Sencourt applied to be Professor of English at Raffles College, Singapore, TSE urged the Universities Bureau on 11 Feb. 1938: 'I am eager to add my recommendation, as I am sure that no more suitable incumbent could be found: Mr. Sencourt is qualified for such a position to an unusual degree, both by his academic and literary attainments, by his experience of teaching, and in particular by his experience in teaching Orientals. He has furthermore all the social and personal qualifications – such as patience, tactfulness, and a cosmopolitan experience which gives him a sympathy with foreign minds.'

Sencourt wrote to TSE in Oct. 1930, after staying for a few days with him and VHE: 'I could hardly imagine a spirit more congenial and refreshing than yours . . . I know I can count on you both to give me more of what means so much to me.'

Charles Arthur Siepmann (1899–1985), radio producer and educator, was awarded the Military Cross in WWI. He joined the BBC in 1927, and was Director of Talks, 1932–5; Regional Relations, 1935–6; Programme Planning, 1936–9. He was University Lecturer, Harvard, 1939–42; worked for the Office of War Information, 1942–5; and was Professor of Education, New York University, 1946–67. His works include *Radio's Second Chance* (1946), *Radio, Television and Society* (1950), *TV and Our School Crisis* (1959). See Richard J. Meyer, 'Charles A. Siepmann and Educational Broadcasting', *Educational Technology Research and Development* 12: 4 (Winter 1964), 413–30. TSE told HWE on 9 Mar. 1937: 'In spite of his name he is in all appearance a perfectly English person, and was educated at Rugby and Oxford. I think his father or grandfather was German. Siepmann is an extremely serious, not to say solemn, young man, of about 36, who has been in the British Broadcasting Corporation longer than anyone I have ever heard of except Sir John Reith himself . . . [H]is political sympathies are rather liberal and left. He is a very nice fellow, although somewhat humourless.'

Stephen Spender (1909–95), poet and critic, won a rapid reputation with his first collection *Poems* (F&F, 1933), following an appearance in Michael Roberts's anthology *New Signatures* (1932). He cultivated friendships with some of the foremost younger writers of the period, including W. H. Auden, Christopher Isherwood, John Lehmann and J. R. Ackerley. For a brief while in the 1930s he joined the Communist Party and went to Spain to serve the Republican cause. With Cyril Connolly he set up the magazine *Horizon* in 1940. In the post-war years he was to be a visiting professor at a number of American universities, and he undertook trips on behalf of the British Society for Cultural Freedom, the Congress for Cultural Freedom and PEN. He served too as poetry consultant to the Library of Congress, 1965–6. For fourteen years from 1953 he was co-editor of the magazine *Encounter*, which – as it was ultimately proven – was from the start the beneficiary of funding from the CIA (just as writers including William Empson had suspected). Spender's other works include *The Destructive Element* (1935), *Vienna* (1934), *Forward from Liberalism* (1937), *The Still Centre* (1939), *World within World* (autobiography, 1951), *The Creative Element* (1953), *Collected Poems* (1955), *The Struggle of the Modern* (1963), *Love–Hate Relations* (1974),

The Thirties and After (1978), *Journals, 1939–83* (1985), *New Selected Journals 1939–1995*, ed. Lara Feigel and John Sutherland with Natasha Spender (2012), and *The Temple* (novel, 1989). He was instrumental in setting up *Index on Censorship* in 1971, and worked as Professor of English at University College, London, 1970–5. He was awarded the CBE (1962), elected a Companion of Literature by the Royal Society of Literature (1977), and knighted in 1983.

Willliam Force Stead (1884–1967), poet, critic, diplomat, clergyman, was educated at the University of Virginia and served in WW1 as Vice-Consul at the American Foreign Service in Liverpool. After working for a while in Florence, he was appointed in 1927 Chaplain of Worcester College, Oxford, where he became a Fellow. While in England, he befriended literary figures including W. B. Yeats, John Masefield and Robert Bridges, as well as TSE – whom he was to baptise into the Anglican Church in 1927. In later years, after living through WW2 in Baltimore, he taught at Trinity College, Washington, DC. His published poetry included *Moonflowers* (1909), *The Holy Innocents* (1917), *Uriel: A Hymn in Praise of Divine Immanence* (1933), and an edition of Christopher Smart's *Rejoice in the Lamb: A Song from Bedlam* (1939) – a work which he discovered.

TSE wrote a testimonial on 4 Dec. 1938 (sent to the Dept. of English, University of Cairo, on 9 Dec.): 'I have known Mr. William Force Stead for over eleven years and count him as a valued friend. He is, first, a poet of established position and an individual inspiration. What is not so well known, except to a small number of the more fastidious readers, is that he is also a prose writer of great distinction: his book [*The Shadow of*] *Mt. Carmel* is recognised as a classic of prose style in its kind. And while the bulk of his published writing on English literature is small, those who know his conversation can testify that he is a man of wide reading and a fine critical sense.

'Mr. Stead is, moreover, a man of the world in the best sense, who has lived in several countries and is saturated in European culture. By both natural social gifts and cultivation, accordingly, he has a remarkable ability of sympathy with all sorts and conditions and races of men.

'I would say finally that I know from several sources, that Mr. Stead was most successful as a teacher of young men at Oxford; that he gained both the affection and the respect of his students; and that he exercised upon them a most beneficial influence. He has the scholarship necessary to teach English literature accurately, and the personal qualities necessary to make the subject interesting to his pupils; and I could not recommend anyone for the purpose with more confidence.' (Beinecke)

See 'Mr Stead Presents An Old Friend', *Trinity College Alumni Journal* 38: 2 (Winter 1965), 59–66; George Mills Harper, 'William Force Stead's Friendship with Yeats and Eliot', *The Massachusetts Review* 21: 1 (Spring 1980), 9–38.

Allen Tate (1899–1979), poet, critic and editor, grew up in Kentucky and attended Vanderbilt University (where he was taught by John Crowe Ransom and became associated with the group of writers known as the Fugitives). He taught at various universities before becoming Poet-in-Residence at Princeton, 1939–42; Poetry Consultant to the Library of Congress, 1944–5; and editor of *The Sewanee Review*, 1944–6; and he was Professor of Humanities at the University of Minnesota (where colleagues included Saul Bellow and John Berryman), 1951–68. Eliot wrote of him in 1959: 'Allen Tate is a good poet and a good literary critic who is distinguished for the sagacity of his social judgment and the consistency with which he has maintained the least popular of political attitudes – that of the sage. He believes in reason rather than enthusiasm, in wisdom rather than system; and he knows that many problems are insoluble and that in politics no solution is final. By avoiding the lethargy of the conservative, the flaccidity of the liberal, and the violence of the zealot, he succeeds in being a representative of the smallest of minorities, that of the intelligent who refuse to be described as "intellectuals". And what he has written, as a critic of society, is of much greater significance because of being said by a man who is also a good poet and a good critic of literature' (*The Sewanee Review*, 67: 4 [Oct.–Dec. 1959], 576). Tate's publications include *Ode to the Confederate Dead* (1930), *Poems: 1928–1931* (1932), *The Mediterranean and Other Poems* (1936), *Reactionary Essays on Poetry and Ideas* (1936) and *The Fathers* (novel, 1938).

Harriet Shaw Weaver (1876–1961), English editor and publisher, whom Virginia Woolf described as 'modest judicious & decorous' (*Diary*, 13 April 1918). In 1912, Weaver began by giving financial support to *The Freewoman*, a radical periodical founded and edited by Dora Marsden, which was renamed in 1913 (at the suggestion of Ezra Pound) *The Egoist*. Weaver became editor in 1914, turning it into a 'little magazine' with a big influence in the history of literary Modernism. TSE followed in the footsteps of Richard Aldington and H.D. to became assistant editor in 1917 (having been nominated by Pound), and remained so until it closed in 1919. When Joyce could not secure a publisher for *A Portrait of the Artist as a Young Man*, Weaver in 1917 converted *The Egoist* into a press in order to publish it. She went on to publish TSE's first book, *Prufrock and Other Observations* (1917), Pound's *Dialogues of Fontenelle* and *Quia Pauper Amavi*, Wyndham Lewis's novel *Tarr*, and Marianne Moore's *Poems*, and other notable books. (She played a major role as Joyce's patron and confidante, and went on to be his literary executor and to help put together *The Letters of James Joyce*.) TSE wrote to Patricia Lloyd, 4 Oct. 1951: 'She was a generous and enlightened patron of letters, and I believe was of very material assistance to James Joyce.' And he paid tribute in 1962: 'Miss Harriet Shaw Weaver . . . was so modest and self-effacing a woman that her generous patronage of men of letters was hardly known beyond the circle of those who benefited by it . . . Miss Weaver's support, once given, remained steadfast. Her great disappointment was her failure to persuade any printer in this country to take the risk of printing *Ulysses*; her subsequent generosity to James Joyce, and her solicitude for his welfare and that of his family, knew no bounds . . . [Working for her at *The Egoist*] was all great fun, my first experience of editorship. In 1932 I dedicated my *Selected Essays* to this good, kind, unassuming, courageous and lovable woman, to whom I owe so much. What other publisher in 1917 (the Hogarth Press was not yet in existence) would, I wonder, have taken *Prufrock*?' See also Jane Lidderdale and Mary Nicholson, *Dear Miss Weaver: Harriet Shaw Weaver, 1876–1961* (1970).

Orlando (Orlo) Williams (1883–1967), Clerk to the House of Commons, scholar and critic; contributor to *TLS*. Chevalier, Légion d'honneur. His publications include *The Clerical Organisation of the House of Commons 1661–1850* (1954); *Vie de Bohème: A Patch of Romantic Paris* (1913); *Some Great English Novels: The Art of Fiction* (1926).

Leonard Woolf (1880–1969), writer and publisher; husband of Virginia Woolf, whom he married in 1912. A friend of Lytton Strachey and J. M. Keynes at Cambridge, he played a central part in the Bloomsbury Group. He wrote a number of novels, including *The Village and the Jungle* (1913), as well as political studies including *Socialism and Co-operation* (1919) and *Imperialism and Civilization* (1928). As founder-editor, with Virginia Woolf, of the Hogarth Press, he was responsible for publishing TSE's *Poems* (1919) and *The Waste Land* (1923). In 1923 he became literary editor of *The Nation & Athenaeum* (after TSE had turned it down), commissioning many reviews from him, and he remained a firm friend. See *An Autobiography* (2 vols, 1980); *Letters of Leonard Woolf*, ed. Frederic Spotts (1990); Victoria Glendinning, *Leonard Woolf: A Life* (2006).

Virginia Woolf (1882–1941), novelist, essayist and critic, was author of *Jacob's Room* (1922), *Mrs Dalloway* (1925), and *To the Lighthouse* (1927), *A Room of One's Own* (1928), a classic of modern feminist criticism, and *The Common Reader* (1925). Daughter of the biographer and editor Leslie Stephen (1832–1904), she married Leonard Woolf in 1912, published her first novel *The Voyage Out* in 1915, and founded the Hogarth Press with her husband in 1917. The Hogarth Press published TSE's *Poems* (1919), *The Waste Land* (1923) and *Homage to John Dryden* (1923). TSE published in *The Criterion* Woolf's essays and talks including 'Kew Gardens', 'Character in Fiction' and 'On Being Ill'. Woolf became a friend and correspondent; her diaries and letters give first-hand accounts of him. Woolf wrote to her sister Vanessa Bell on 22 July 1936: 'I had a visit, long ago, from Tom Eliot, whom I love, or could have loved, had we both been in the prime and not in the sere; how necessary do you think copulation is to friendship? At what point does "love" become sexual?' (*Letters*, vol. 6). Eliot wrote in 1941 that Woolf 'was the centre, not merely of an esoteric group, but of the literary life of London. Her position was due to a concurrence of qualities and circumstances which never happened before, and which I do not think will ever happen again. It maintained the dignified and admirable tradition of Victorian upper middle-class culture – a situation in which the artist was neither the servant of the exalted patron, the parasite of the plutocrat, nor the entertainer of the mob – a situation in which the producer and the consumer of art were on an equal footing, and that neither the highest nor the lowest.' To Enid Faber on 27 Apr. 1941: 'she was a personal friend who seemed to me (mutatis considerably mutandis) like a member of my own family; and I miss her dreadfully, but I don't see her exactly as her relatives see her, and my admiration for the ideas of her milieu – now rather old-fashioned – is decidedly qualified.' See further Hermione Lee, *Virginia Woolf* (1996).

INDEX OF CORRESPONDENTS
AND RECIPIENTS

GENERAL INDEX

Page references in **bold** indicate a
biographical note

Aaronson, L.: *Christ in the Synagogue*, 53
Abercrombie, Lascelles, 406n, **603n**
Ackerley, Joe Randolph, 304n
Action (journal), 584n, 701, 702n
Action Française, L' (newspaper), 67n, 207,
  271n, 356
Action Française (movement), 376
Active Anthology, 304n
Acton, Harold, 740n
Adams family, 360, 410
Adams, Elbridge L., 296n, 300–1, 309
Adams, Henry, 213, 481
Adams, John, 454
Adelphi (journal) *see New Adelphi*
Adler, Alfred, 443n
Aiken, Conrad, **817**; on Bolovians, 45n;
  returns to Rye, 311; Rostrevor Hamilton
  on, 521; offers TSE's 'Prufrock' to
  Monro, 685n; at Harvard, 782; *The
  Coming Forth by Day of Osiris Jones*,
  528, 582n; *Preludes for Memnon*, 582n
Alasdair, Alasdair MacMhaighstir, 423n
Albigensians, 248
Aldington, Richard, **794**; on Whibley,
  122n; attack on TSE, 733–5, 749, 752,
  762–3; *At All Costs*, 560; *Stepping
  Heavenward*, 733–5, 749, 752, 759–60
Alfred A. Knopf, Inc., 215, 651
All Souls College, Oxford, 756n
Allen and Unwin (publishers), 662, 702,
  739, 757
Alliance Insurance Company: shares,
  322–3, 333
Allport, G. J. B.: TSE recommends Roy
  Campbell to, 113n
Alport, Erich, **8n**; letter from Geoffrey
  Faber on Singer's Plato, 29n; on Jaeger's
  Aristotèles, 101n; TSE sends *Ash
  Wednesday* to, 204; and Gundolf, 223; in
  England, 578; and translation of Planck's

Positivismus und reale Aussenwelt, 629;
  letter from Spender, 650n
American Ballet, 587n
American Civil War, 376
'American Critics', 145n
Amery, L. S., 329, 505n
Anderson, Margaret, 186
Andrade, Edward, 289
Andrewes, Lancelot, Bishop of Winchester,
  212, 319, 457, 470, 674
Angioletti, G. B., 642
Anglo-Catholic Congress: Fourth (London,
  1930), 137, 221; TSE declines to join
  Executive Committee, 237
Anglo-Catholic Summer School of
  Sociology, 410n
Angus, Ian, 716n
Animula, 402n, 587n
Antheil, George ('Stacey Bishop'), 54–5,
  726n; *Death in the Dark*, 164n, 726n
Anthology of Prize Poems, 695n
Apollinaire, Guillaume, 35
Approximations, 207
Aquinas, Thomas *see* Thomas Aquinas, St
Aragon, Louis, 253n
Aranyi, Jelly d', 544
'Ariel Poems', 38n, 495n, 587, 593, 594
Aristotle, 30, 37, 48, 101, 124, 138, 292n,
  463
Arlen, Michael, 253n
Arnander, P. E. Folke, 670n
Arnold, Matthew, 60; *Culture and
  Anarchy*, 554
Art and Letters (journal), 186
Arts League of Service, 200
Ash Wednesday: publication, 38, 162n;
  Selwyn requests copy, 136n, 137; TSE
  sends to Curtius, 150n; TSE sends MS
  to Sadler, 166; as modern *Vita Nuova*,
  171, 183; copy sent to Monro, 178;
  Rowse on, 179; Leonard Woolf on, 184n;
  Parker enquires about metaphor in,
  187n; Wilson Knight on, 192n; Charles

Bedale, Father, Warden of the House of the Sacred Mission, 747n

Bee, The (Goldsmith's journal), 306

Beethoven, Ludwig van, 529, 578; *Coriolan*, 368

Belgion, Montgomery ('Monty'), 795–6; TSE mocks, 44; skin complaint, 116; TSE introduces to Rowse, 176; and D'Arcy, 201; gives Scanlan's address to TSE, 244; and Dobrée, 294; seeks introduction to Bruce Richmond, 382; on I. A. Richards, 408; Hellyar on, 452; Richards criticises, 452; criticises Maritain, 530; works on *This Quarter* in Paris, 536n; TSE sends Auden's 'Pindaric Ode' to, 663; proposes *The Refutation of Marxism*, 664n; requests advance, 673; effect in Cambridge, 709; 'God is Mammon', 202n, 610; *The Human Parrot, and Other Essays*, 453n, 573n; *Our Present Philosophy of Life*, 41, 72, 116n, 150, 167, 176, 574n; 'Statecraft in Russia', 536n

Bell, The (journal), 453n

Bell, Clive, 256n; letters from Virginia Woolf, 83n, 472n; blindness, 426; on Hogarth Press, 584n

Bell, George Kennedy Allen, Bishop of Chichester (earlier Dean of Canterbury), 105n; invites Eliots to Chichester, 257n, 413; reads TSE's draft of Lambeth Conference pamphlet, 404, 406n, 413, 419, 435; on Thomson's *Will the Scottish Church Survive?*, 405n; and *Encyclopaedia of the Christian Religion*, 406; and *Devotions*, 437–8; TSE discusses doctrine with, 457–8; invites TSE to write article on being a Dean, 480; TSE proposes for radio broadcast, 601; writes preface to Heiler's *Spirit of Worship*, 636–7

Bell, Julian, 7n, 272n

Bell, Vanessa (née Stephen), 256n, 371n

Belloc, Hilaire, 30n, 78, 365n

Benda, Julien, 244n, 595n, 731; 'Of the Idea of Order and the Idea of God', 244, 267

Benn, Sir Ernest, 329, 505n

Bennett, Alan, 234n

Bennett, Arnold, **364n**

Bennett, Joan, **407n**

Benson, Arthur C., 628n

Benson, Stella, 628n

Bérard, Victor: *L'Odyssée de Homère*, 599

Berdyaev, Nikolai Aleksandrovich, 42

Bergson, Henri, 92

Bergsträsser, Arnold: *Frankreich* (with Curtius), 302–3, 397

Berlin, Isaiah, **261n**

Bernanos, Georges: *La grande Peur des Biens-Pensants*, 639

Berry, Francis, 643n

Berryman, John, 169n

Bertram, Ernst: *Nietzsche*, 4

Bifur (French journal), 226

Binyon, Laurence, **181n**

Birks, H. W. & Co., 214, 216, 322, 333, 408, 550

Birrell, Francis: 'Mr T. S. Eliot', 207n, 584n

Bishop, Leslie: *Mother's Gone Away*, 504, 548, 637, 680

Bishop, Stacey *see* Antheil, George

Bishop, W. H. C., 680

Black Sun Press, 383n

Blackmur, R. C., 642

Blackwood, George, 235n

Blackwood's Magazine, 235, 268

Blair, Eric (George Orwell), **715n**; offers to translate, 754n

Blake, George, 206

Blanche, Jacques-Émile: *Les Arts plastiques de 1870 à nos jours*, 611

BLAST (journal), 382n

Blavatsky, Helena Petrovna, 351n

Bloch, Jean-Richard: *Le Destin du Théâtre*, 740n, 768

Blok, Alexander, 552n, 598

Blomberg, Erik, 778n

Blood, Thomas H., 306n

Bloomsbury Group, 256n

Blunden, Edmund, 83n, **97n**, 305n, 357n, 490n, 519, 711; (ed.) *The Poems of Wilfred Owen*, 488, 519, 523–4

Blunt, Anthony F., 730, **730n**

Boas, Frederick S., 675n

Boas, George: invites TSE to lecture to Poetry Society in Baltimore, 653; and TSE's talk to King's College London Elizabethan Society, 758

Bodley Head (publishers), 524n

Bodley, John Edward Courtenay, 243

Boillot, Félix, **129n**

Bolgan, Louise, 264n

Bolingbroke, Henry St John, Viscount, 56

Bolliger, Aurelia (later Hodgson), 770n
Bollingen Foundation, 699n
Bolo, King (and Bolovians), 45, 294
Bone (writer on architecture), 298
Boni & Liveright (publishers), 169n, 549n, 695
Boni, Albert, 169n
Boni, Charles, 169, 174, 175n, 651–2
Bookman (journal): controversy over humanism, 65–6, 132–5, 146, 159, 280; and TSE's Pater essay, 160; TSE contributes to, 169; Gordon George submits essay to, 438; Hugh Ross Williamson edits, 590n, 648
Boothby, Robert, 78, 94n
Boswell, James, 306n
Bottrall, Ronald, **262n**, 789n
Bourget, Paul: *Le Sens de la Mort*, 533
Bourne, Lincolnshire, 472
Bowen, Elizabeth, 769n
Bowra, C. Maurice, 552, **598n**
Boye, Karin, 186n
Boyle, George (ed.): *'Twixt Lombard Street and Cornhill*, 321
Boyle, Kay (later Vail), **690n**, 750n; 'Three Little Men', 705n
Boys-Smith, Revd J. S., 68n
Brabourne, Cecil Marcus Knatchbull, 4th Baron, 482
Brace, Donald, 615n
Bradford Diocesan Conference, 443, 444n
Bradley, F. H., 292, 370
Braun, Gustav (Heidelberg bookseller), 259
Breit, Harvey, 50n
Brémond, Henri, 610
Brentford, William Joynson-Hicks, Viscount, **39n**, 86n, 236, 239n; *Do We Need a Censor?*, 104
Brewer and Warren (NY publishers), 230
Bridges, Robert, 287, 418n, 528
British Broadcasting Corporation (BBC): TSE broadcasts for, 6, 11, 32, 38, 60, 65, 90, 109, 121, 127, 479–80, 494, 535, 616–17, 702–3, 771; broadcasts TSE poems, 333; TSE proposes Joyce recording to, 426; and Villon translation, 445; and publication of TSE's broadcast talks, 703, 739, 757; Nicolson broadcasts on Joyce, 761–2, 776; policy on talks about fiction, 776n
British Union of Fascists, 505n
Brittain, Robert E., 671n

Brittain, Vera, 500n
Britten, Benjamin, 482n
Broch, Hermann: *The Sleepwalkers*, 721n, 741n
Brock, Lynn, 335
Brockway, Fenner, 725
Bronowski, Jacob, 7, **229n**, 319, 547n
Brooks, Benjamin Gilbert, 389 & n
Brooks, E. St John, 6n
Brown, Oliver, 717
Browne, E. Martin, 406n
Browne, Sir Thomas, 737
Brunner, Emil, 622n
Bruno de Jesus Marie, Père, 33
B. S.: 'Calculated Refinements', 276n
Buchan, John, 94n
Buchanan, Scott, **723n**
Buckfast Abbey *see* Vonier, Anscar
Buddhism, 209
Bunting, Basil, **304–5n**
'Burbank with a Baedeker; Bleistein with a Cigar', 272n
Burdett, Francis, 195n, 198
Burdett, Osbert: *The Two Carlyles*, 400
Burke, Edmund, 448, 599n
Burlingame, Eugene Watson, 153
Burns, Tom F., **221n**, 290, 325n, 359
Burr, George H. & Co. (bankers), 592n
Burritt, Elijah: chart of heavens, 307
Burtt, E. A.: *The Metaphysical Foundations of Modern Science*, 116n
Bussy, Dorothy and Simon, 769n
Butts, Anthony, 772n
Butts, Mary (earlier Rodker): 'Alexander of Macedon' (published as *The Macedonian*), 719; *Ashe of Rings*, 719
Byrne, Muriel St Clare, **537n**
Byron, George Gordon, 6th Baron: *Cain*, 471

Caetani, Camillo, 162n, 335, 488
Caetani, Lélia, 162, 372, 670
Caetano, Marguerite (née Chapin; Princess Bassiano), **796**; and Kassner, 254, 355; TSE recommends English writers to, 372–3; and Roditi's translations of Spender, 654; and Aline Lion manuscript, 669; operation and convalescence, 670, 773, 791; visits London, 715; *see also Commerce* (journal)
Caetano, Ruffredo (Pince of Bassiano and Duke of Sermoneta), 162, 608n

Cambridge Mediaeval History, vol. VI, 68
Cambridge Poems (series), 230, 407n
Campbell, James: 'Out of darkness', 232n
Campbell, Roy, 113n, 139n, 140n, 252,
  372, 389n, 482n; Adamastor, 177;
  The Flaming Terrapin, 389n; Taurine
  Provence, 114n; 'Tristan da Cunha'
  (poem), 139n
Canby, Henry S., 206n
Cape, Jonathan (publishers), 48, 52n, 672n
Carlyle, Thomas, 513
Carpenter, Joseph Estlin, 474
Carpenter, S. C., 350n
Carrefour Press, 23n
Carrington, Noel, 682
Carritt, Gabriel, 190n
Cary, Henry Francis, 183n
Cassirer, Ernest, 227
cathedrals: TSE's views on, 542–4
Catherine II (the Great), Empress of Russia,
  761
Catholic Poetry Society, 188
Catlin, George C., 745n
Cavafy, Constantine P., 9
Cavalcanti, Guido, 325
Cecil, Lord David, 25n; TSE wishes to
  write for Criterion, 25, 51; in Inklings,
  100n; fails to deliver review, 179; at
  Ottoline Morrell tea party with Vivien,
  769–70n, 771; The Stricken Deer, 238
Cervantes Saavedra, Miguel de: Don
  Quixote de la Mancha, 330
Chamberlain (of Methuen), 514n
Chambers, Sir Edmund K., 395, 428n, 429;
  William Shakespeare: A Study of Facts
  and Problems, 377, 400n
Chamson, André: L'Homme contre
  l'histoire, 431
Channa the Elder, 209
Chaplin, Charlie, 586n
Chapman, Frank M., 390
Chapman, George, 12
Chapman, John Jay: Lucian, Plato and
  Greek Morals, 644
Charles Eliot Norton Lectures, 181n, 183n
Charles I, King, 488n
'Charles Whibley: a literary memoir', 456n
Charlton, L. E. O. (Leo), 496
Chatto & Windus (publishers), 519n,
  524n, 548, 733n, 760; see also Raymond,
  Harold
Chaucer, Geoffrey, 188n

Chekhov, Anton, 347
Chesterfield, Philip Dormer Stanhope, 4th
  Earl of, 45, 577
Chesterton, Gilbert Keith, 29n, 106n, 262,
  365
Chiari, Joseph, 9n, 423n
Chichester: TSE visits, 407n
China, 167n
Chisholm, A., 243n
Christa Seva Sangha (brotherhood), 722
Church of England: TSE on doctrines,
  378–80
Church, Richard, 304, 422n, 734n
Church Times, 379, 407, 412, 421
Churchill, Winston S., 242n, 243n, 294,
  554
Citizens of the World (peace movement),
  383n
Clark, Arthur Melville: Thomas Heywood,
  559n
Clark, David R., 183n
Clark, G. N., 277; The Seventeenth
  Century, 24
Clark lectures, Cambridge (1930), 70, 301n
classic, classicism: as terms, 27, 210, 285
Clauss, Max: and German nationalism, 8;
  and Five Reviews Award, 41; leaves TSE's
  letters unanswered, 463; Spender and,
  528, 578
Clemen, Wolfgang, 696
Clemens, Cyril, 106n, 485n
Clemens, Samuel Langhorne ('Mark
  Twain'), 485n
Coall, Talbot & Sons, 214, 216, 691–2
Cobden-Sanderson, Gwladys (Sally), 401n
Cobden-Sanderson, Richard, 401n
cocktails, 401
Codrington, Kennneth de Burgh, 93n
Coffey, Brian, 312n
Coghill, Nevill, 188n, 409
Cohen, Israel, 295n
Cohen, Morris R., 633
Cole, G. D. H., 78, 298
Coleman, Elliott, 671n
Coleridge, Samuel Taylor, 353, 362n, 718;
  Biographia Literaria, 391; Lectures on
  Shakespeare, 391n
Colhoun, Charles K.: asks to join F&F,
  211, 326n; TSE recommends to Blunden,
  357; TSE invites to Criterion Club, 381;
  meets James Joyce, 630
Collingwood, R. G., 24, 25n, 624

Collins, Harold Poulton, **150n**
Collins, Michael, 503n
Collins, Seward, 132n, **159n**, 280, 360
Colonial Society of Massachusetts: TSE elected Corresponding Member, 63
Colum, Mary, 475
Colum, Padraic, **170n**, 174, 320, 475
Columbia Broadcasting System Inc., 665n, 686, 719
Commerce (journal), 70n, 238, 266, 519, 608, 650, 654n, 660, 773
Committee for Legalising Eugenic Sterilization, 525n
Comstock, Will, 43
Comyns Carr, A. S., 329
Connington, J. J., 335
Conrad, Joseph, 345
contraception, 404n, 411n
Cooke, Alistair, **586n**
'Cooking Egg, A', 249n
Cooper, Alfred Duff, 529
Copeau, Jacques, 740n
Cornford, Francis M.: *Myth-Historicus*, 234; *The Origin of Attic Comedy*, 171
Courage, James F.: 'The Promising Years', 627
Cournos, John, **796**; in Switzerland, 63n; financial difficulties, 84n; proposed for grant from Royal Literary Fund, 114; family misfortunes, 115n; payments to TSE, 311; leaves for USA, 588
Cournos, Mrs John, 63, 84n, 115n
Covici-Friede (publishers), 458n
Cowper, William: 'On Receipt of My Mother's Picture Out of Norfolk', 275
Cran, Ralph, 153
Cranch, Abigail Adams, 360n
Cranch, Richard, 360n
Crane, Ronald, 153n
Crashaw, Richard, 58, 199n, 201, 396–7n, 647, 677
Craster, Herbert, 355n
Crawley, W. J., 315n
Cretan Liar, 210
Criterion Club, 218n, 375n, 476, 515–16, 558, 643, 657–8, 662, 685, 768, 789
Criterion (later *New Criterion*): TSE sends to Bertha Malnick, 3; Donaghy published in, 7; reviewers, 26, 33, 158, 167, 180n, 211, 418; under threat of closure, 48; contributors meet for drinks, 63n; fiction publishing, 69; payments,

197–8, 223, 356; Henry Eliot keeps copies, 306; Gertrude Page refuses to subscribe, 338n; financed by Faber, 489n; reviews of contemporary novelists, 561; advertisements, 608; and election (1931), 701n; financing, 713; Dougal Malcolm supports financially, 756n; criticised for cliquishness, 775; availability in Paris, 779, 788
Criterion MIscellany (series), 28, 56, 93n, 104n, 111, 140, 142n, 192, 198, 247–8, 256, 272, 274, 291, 299n, 501n, 525, 552, 599n, 600, 664n, 667, 704, 712
Croft, Freeman Wills, 335
Crofton, Henry, **118n**, 263, 334
Cronin, Anthony, 751n
Crosby, Caresse (née Jacob), 383n, 690n
Crosby Gallery of Modern Art, Washington, DC, 383n
Crosby, Harry, 383n, 690n; *Shadows of the Sun*, 562n; *Transit of Venus*, 562n, 658n
Crow, John, **569n**
Cunard, Sir Bache and Maud Alice ('Emerald'), Lady, 253n
Cunard, Nancy, **253n**
Curtis Brown Ltd (literary agents), 231, 579n, 684, 739, 757n
Curtis, Revd Geoffrey W. S., **220n**, 226n, 722n
Curtis, Sir George, 339, 341
Curtius, E. R., **797**; as literary judge, 10n; TSE requests Hogarth Press send Virginia Woolf's works to, 82; and Belgion, 116; moves to Bonn, 150n; influence on TSE, 186; praises Spender poems, 190; recommends Hofmannsthal works to TSE, 228n; on Gundulf, 238; praises *Ash Wednesday*, 254n; marriage, 303n; on Balzac, 397; translates TSE poem, 420; recommends Erdmann to TSE, 448n; Rychner visits, 588n; writes on TSE, 642; and translation of *The Waste Land*, 778; *Die französische Kultur* (*Frankreich*, with Bergsträsser), 302, 397n, 463
Curwen Press, 296n
Cyprian, St, 412n
'Cyril Tourneur', 121n, 382, 399n, 439

Dahlberg, Edward, **52n**, 567; applies to Guggenheim Foundation, 63n; recommends Horace Gregory to TSE, 346–7n; *Bottom Dogs*, 52, 54, 62

Dakin, Arthur Hazard: *Paul Elmer More*, 67n

Daniels (writer on politics), 51, 77

Dante, 57, 58n, 141, 208, 588n

Dante Alighieri: on beauty of universe, 17–18; TSE writes on, 57, 141, 208, 374n, 588n; Binyon translations, 181–3; philosophy, 203–4; *Divina Commedia*, 172n, 374n; *La Vita Nuova*, 183, 187, 197, 209, 258

D'Arcy, Father Martin, 80n, 798; reviews Harris's *Pro Fide*, 161n; and Catholic Poetry Society, 189; plans volume of essays on Authority, 328n, 367, 376, 382; praises 'Marina', 366n; edits Roman book of Essays, 378n; on *Thoughts after Lambeth*, 520n; TSE meets, 604; reviews Husserl's *Ideas*, 644; in Oxford, 724; invites TSE to meetings of London Society for the Study of Religion, 726n; *The Mass and the Redemption*, 509; *The Nature of Belief*, 624; *Thomas Aquinas*, 249

Dark Horse, The (Lloyds Bank house magazine), 321, 329–30

Dark, Sidney, 98n, 523

Daudet, Léon, 271

Davenport, John (J. D.): 'Eagle's Wings', 201n

Davey, Revd Francis Noel, 465

Davidson, J. F., 552n

Davies, Hugh Sykes, 310n, 459; 'Notes on Lucretius', 523

Davies, Peter, 236n, 613, 637

Davies, Peter Llewellyn, 472

Dawson, Christopher, 798–9; contributions to *Criterion*, 42; article sent to *Tablet*, 193; and religious attachment, 194; Eric Gill reviews, 198n; and Unicorn club, 290; and TSE's broadcasts, 601, 632; broadcast talks, 739, 757–8; *Christianity and Sex*, 92n, 291; 'The Origins of the Romantic Tradition', 469n

Day Lewis, Cecil: influenced by Hopkins, 417n

Deans (ecclesiastical): TSE's views on, 480, 541–4

Deas, Margaret, 450–1, 516

'Death by Water', 341

Defoe, Daniel, 549, 556n, 577

de la Bedoyère, Michael, 350

de la Mare, Amy Catherine (née Donaldson), 270n

de la Mare, Richard: and Barfield, 101n; and Knopf's lack of interest in TSE's *Anabase* translation, 215n; and illustrations for TSE's *Marina*, 270, 283, 330; marriage, 270n; and publication of *Ash Wednesday*, 296n, 301n; and publication of Joyce's *Haveth Childers Everywhere*, 299; on Elbridge Adams, 300; signs books for Ottoline Morrell, 369n; reads Charlton's manuscript, 496; and Rothenstein's *Men and Memoirs*, 516n; absence on holiday, 611; sets up type for James Joyce, 646, 693; and Joyce's *Work in Progress*, 775

de la Mare, Walter, 15n; contributions to *Criterion*, 42; TSE contributes essay on Pater for RSL, 121, 128n, 145, 145n, 154, 160, 208; on TSE's dilatoriness in answering letters, 127n; and TSE's paper, 128n; thanks TSE for *Ash Wednesday*, 165n; *Desert Islands and Robinson Crusoe*, 154, 165; (ed.) *The Eighteen Eighties*, 11; *On the Edge*, 367; 'The Picnic', 16n

Demant, Revd Vigo Auguste, 697n

Demue, General (Austrian), 476

Derek Verschoyle Ltd (publishers), 545n

Deussen, Paul, 284

de Valera, Eamon, 503n

Dewey, John, 153, 225n

Dial, The (journal), 174, 222

Dickens, Charles: TSE quotes, 784; *Great Expectations*, 345

'Difficulties of a Statesman, The', 650n, 670n, 747n, 791n

Disraeli, Benjamin, 499

Distributist League, Glasgow University Branch, 262n, 365n

Dobb, Maurice, 77n

Dobrée, Bonamy, 799; edits Chesterfield's Letters, 57; broadcasts, 109; TSE sends *Ash Wednesday* to, 202; and Criterion Club, 218; TSE recommends to Gordon Fraser, 245; proof reads Read's *William Wordsworth*, 314; and Van Doren's *Dryden*, 365; on prospective revolution, 375n; reviewing, 416, 473; on foreign periodicals, 475; Isaacs criticises, 489; on Dryden's prose, 549n, 555; talks on Defoe, 549n; reviews Manning, 577n; invites TSE to lunch, 618n; 'American Periodicals', 275n; *The London Book of*

English Prose (ed., with Herbert Read), 789n; 'Thrillers and "Teccers"', 416n
Dolphin Books (Chatto & Windus), 547
Donaghy, John Lyle, 5n; reviews Aaronson, 53n; TSE recommends to Blunden, 97; TSE declines to write preface for, 510; TSE recommends to Bruce Richmond, 548, 559; nervous breakdown, 623–4n, 631, 635; persecution mania, 639, 743; Grieve (MacDiarmid) on, 703n; returns to nursing home, 743
Donaghy, Lilian (née Roberts): seeks work during husband's breakdown, 623; on husband's return to nursing home, 743n
Donaldson, Revd S. A., 270n
Donne, John: TSE invites Beachcroft to review book on, 14; devotional verse, 109; punning, 204; TSE writes on, 535; Sparrow on, 568; George Williamson on, 589n; G. R. Elliott on, 623; The Bookman publishes articles on, 648; in Encyclopaedia of the Chrtistian Religion, 677; 'Devotions upon Emergent Occasions', 239n; 'The Ecstasie', 123, 124n
'Donne in Our Time', 564n
Doolitle, Hilda (H. D.), 744n
Doré, Gustav, 330
Dorn, Marion, 19n, 283
Dorset, Charles Sackville, 6th Earl of: Poems, 414, 450, 516
Double Crown Club, 682
Doughty, Charles, 423n
Douglas, Major C. H., 51, 77, 180n, 703
Douglas, Norman, 253n, 734n; Three of Them, 297
Dreyfus, Alfred, 640n
Drumont, Édouard, 640n
Dryden, John: Van Doren on, 245, 365, 553; TSE broadcasts on, 479, 494, 535, 549; Dobrée on, 549n, 555; Ker edits prose works, 616; TSE invites to make US broadcast on, 665n, 686n, 719; revises Chaucer, 666; 'Ode to the Memory of Anne Killigrew', 157; Of Dramatick Poesie, 195n
Dublin: TSE visits, 503–4
Dublin Review: Dawson published in, 40; reviews, 108, 147–8; TSE sends Criterion Miscellany to, 198; and attack on Charles Oman, 248; publishes Maritain-Belgion

correspondence, 530; Belgion's 'Statecraft in Russia' in, 536n
du Bos, Charles, 207n, 714; proposes to publish La Vigile, 50; champions Stefan George, 64, 224; praises Ash Wednesday, 207n, 254; and Gundolf, 238; essay on Stefan George, 254–5; writes to TSE, 266; book on Gide, 631; Bandler's essay on, 705
Duff, Charles: James Joyce and the Plain Reader, 640n
Duffy (tenant), 691n, 692
Dunbar, William, 423, 657, 663
Duncan-Jones, Revd Arthur Stuart, Dean of Chichester, 517, 676
Duncan-Jones, Austin, 598n
Duncan-Jones, Elsie see Phare, Elsie E.
Dunlaoghaire, Ireland, 504
Dunlop, Colin, 637n
Dunne, Annie, 281
Durrell, Lawrence, 735n; The Alexandria Quartet, 642n
Duvoisin, Jean: on Proust in England, 671n
Dyhrenfurth, Günther, 168

Eagle Oil Transport Company Ltd, 214, 216, 296, 322–3, 333
'East Coker', 288n
Échanges (French review), 217
Eckermann, Johann Peter: Conversations with Goethe, 209
Eddington, Arthur, 373, 413, 441n, 443 & n, 533
Editions Narcisse (publishing house), 383n
Egoist Press, 175, 219
Egoist, The, 186
Eikhenbaum, Boris Mikhailovich, 252, 269n
Einstein, Albert, 727
Eliot, Abigail Adams (née Smith), 308
Eliot, Andrew, 44
Eliot, Charlotte (TSE's sister) see Smith, Charlotte
Eliot, Charlotte Champe (TSE's mother): reminiscences, 99–100; friendship with Grandgent, 470n; Savonarola, 470n; William Greenleaf Eliot, 43
Eliot, George, 619
Eliot, Henry Ware (TSE's father), 99, 306, 331, 721
Eliot, Henry Ware, Jr (TSE's brother), 799–800; letter from TSE on Jim Barnes,

842

172n; sends father's books to TSE, 331; writes detective story (*The Rumble Murders*, by 'Mason Deal'), 478, 695n; out of work in depression, 615–16; on Chardy and Agnew Talcott, 720n; and Aldington's attack on TSE, 735n

Eliot, Marion Cushing (TSE's sister), 306

Eliot, Rose Greenleaf (TSE's aunt), 43–4, 100

Eliot, Theresa (née Garrett; TSE's sister-in-law), 282n, 308

Eliot, Thomas Dawes, 723n

Eliot, (Esmé) Valerie, xix–xxxvii, 330n, 344n

Eliot, Vivien (TSE's first wife; née Haigh-Wood), 800–1; TSE separates from (1933), 87n; health, 203, 229, 241, 295, 468, 472, 478, 483, 488, 559, 563, 707, 784, 786; investments, 214, 333; motoring, 216–17, 308–9, 478; on TSE's *Uncle Remus* talk with Pound, 219n; adultery with Bertrand Russell, 288n; makes tray cloth, 306; anxiety over mother's health, 307; lunches with Aiken and TSE, 311n; hostility to TSE, 337n, 363n; and Mary Hutchinson, 353, 606, 613–14, 707, 752; and Ottoline Morell, 363, 369n, 446, 769–70; Virginia Woolf on paranoia, 371n; proposed separation, 414n; Spens invites to stay, 522; Aldous Huxley describes, 527n; and More's proposed visit to dine, 569; irrationality, 583n; misses seeing P. E. More, 618; TSE's forbearance with, 691n; financial difficulties, 692; Aldington lampoons in *Stepping Heavenward*, 733–4n, 735; invites Margaret Thorp to party, 764; postpones party, 769; on Wyndham Lewis drawing of TSE, 779n

Elkin Matthews and Marrot Ltd (publishers), 727

Elliott, G. R., 136, 146

Elliott, Walter, 77–8, 94n, 95

Ellmann, Richard, 300n, 315n

Elton, Oliver, 584

Empson, William: Julian Bell recommends to TSE, 7; TSE offers Burtt book to review, 116; co-edits *Experiment*, 310n; reviews Katherine M. Wilson, 424n; TSE invites to *Criterion* At Home, 516; 'The English Dog', 546; *Seven Types of Ambiguity*, 436, 459n, 637; *The Structure of Complex Words*, 546n

Encyclopaedia of the Christian Religion, 113n, 161n, 318, 356, 394–5, 406, 517, 617, 676–8

Enemy, The (journal), 778n, 779

English Association, The, 456

English Church Union (ECU), 80, 155n, 161n, 318n

English Holy Week Book, The, 457

English Review, The (later *New English Review Magazine*), 505n, 513, 530n, 574, 646

Epimenides, 210n

Epstein, Jacob, 490

Erdmann, Karl: essay on Burke, 448, 599–600

Eric Gill Press, 445

Ervine, St John, 483n

Etchells, Frederick, 348n

Eugenics, 524, 526, 538–9

Eugenics Society, 525n

Euripides, 369

Evans, Caradoc, 226n

Everyman's Library, 351, 352n, 415, 455n

Exile, The (review), 225n

Experiment (journal), 310n, 547n

Eyles, Vivyan Leonora (Mrs D. L. Murray), 22n, 607n

Eyre & Spottiswoode (publishers), 505n

Eyre, Edward, 328n

Faber & Faber (publishers): succeeds Faber & Gwyer, 140n; acquires Porpoise Press, 206; TSE's position at, 206; proposes publishing Jaeger's *Aristotle*, 332; and James Joyce recordings, 343, 362; Orlo Williams and, 486; and Rowse's *Politics*, 487; finances *Criterion*, 489n; and Mario Praz's *La carne, la morte e il diavolo*, 493n; Poets on the Poets Series, 663; advertising style, 765–6; proposes cheap edition of Virginia Woolf novels, 777n

Faber, Geoffrey, 801–2; raises TSE's salary, 85; on Morley, 88n; on Feiling's *Conservatism*, 180n; translates Hesse's *Partenau*, 200n; writes to Nicolls on Colhoun, 211n; biography of Jowett, 235n; on Philip Graves's *The Pursuit*, 238n; on US publication of *Ash Wednesday*, 296n, 301n; and *The English Review*, 505; correspondence with Raymond on Aldington's attack on TSE in *Stepping Heavenward*, 733, 749, 752, 759–60, 762–3; and TSE's concern over F&F advertising style, 765; dines with Eliots, 766n; criticises BBC's fiction policy, 776n

Faber, Tom (Thomas Erle Faber), **433n**; replies to TSE's letter, 535n; makes napkin ring for TSE, 786

Fairman, Jennifer, 534n

Family Reunion, The (play), 288n, 309n

Farrar & Rinehart, Messrs (NY publishers), 74n, 775

Farrar, John, 74n

Fassett, Irene Pearl, 120n

Fausset, Hugh l'Anson, 443n

Feiling, Keith, 94n, 95; *Conservatism*, 180

Feldman, R. V., 295

Fernandez, Ramon, **40n**; reviews for *Criterion*, 26, 33, 167; and Hulme, 35; and humanism, 135; and I. A. Richards, 168; friendship with Belgion, 176; TSE requests photograph of, 399; sees Sencourt in Paris, 746; *André Gide*, 631, 643; *A Humanist Theory of Value*, 168n; 'La Pensée et la Révolution', 488; *La Vie de Molière*, 72

Ferrar, Nicholas, 768

Field Roscoe and Co. (solicitors), 645

Fink, Howard R., 716n

Fitts, Dudley, 304, 699n

Fitzgerald, Desmond, **503n**

Fitzgerald, Edward, 412n

Fitzgerald, Robert, 699

Five Reviews Award, The, 10, 41; *see also* Six Reviews Prize, The

Flaxman, John, 307

Fleming, Peter, 569n

Fletcher, John Gould, 802; reviews Maritain, 149n; reviews I. A. Richards, 168n; proposed for Criterion Club committee, 218n; proposes writing on modern poetry, 252n; and Munguía, 334; contributes to *I'll Take My Stand*, 409n; financial difficulties, 473; wife's illness, 724; 'Elegy on an Empty Skyscraper' (poem), 724n; *Europe's Two Frontiers*, 348, 415

Flint, Frank Stuart ('F. S.'), 218n, 231, 490, 561, 802–3; 'Verse Chronicle', 788n

Flores, Angel, 334, **420n**, 778

Flower, Robin ('Bláithin'), 144, 681n, 750

Foerster, Norman, **145n**, 396n, 589n; (ed.) *Humanism and America: Essays on the Outlook of Modern Civilisation*, 74n, 108, 132n, 136, 146n, 149

For Lancelot Andrewes, 470n

Forbes, Mansfield Duval, 263n

Ford, Ford Madox (Ford Madox Hueffer), 304n

Ford, John, 122, 758

Forster, Edward Morgan, 803; books sent to Curtius, 82; praises D. H. Lawrence, 130, 337; supports Charlton's book, 496–7n; A. L. Morton on, 656; 'Mr D. H. Lawrence and Lord Brentford', 39

Forum (journal), 39

Fountain Press, 296–7, 300, 309n

Four Quartets: epigraph, 784n

Foy, Peter, 184n

'Fragment of an Agon', 10n, 725n

'Fragment of a Prologue', 20n

France, Anatole (Jacques Anatole Thibault), 416

Frankfurter Zeitung, 645, 652–3, 659n

Franklin, Benjamin, 454

Fraser, Gordon, **195n**

Fraser, Lindley Macnaghten: *Protection and Free Trade*, 552n

Freeman, Austin, 335

Freeman, Rosemary, 556

Freidegger, Franz Hammond, 116–17

Fremantle, Anne, 715

Freud, Sigmund, 397n, 443n

Friede, Donald: owns first edition of TSE's *Poems*, 326

Frost, Robert, 287n

Fry, Roger, 256n, 398, 417n

Fry, Varian, 326

Gabain, M. (translator), 355n

Gandhi, Mohandas Karamchand, 725

Gardner, Helen, 191n, 689n

Gardner, Isabella, 347n

Garnett, David, 548, **674n**

Garrett, Mrs (Henry Eliot's mother-in-law), 307

Garrigou-Lagrange, Réginald Marie, 30

Garvin, James, 490

Garvin, Viola, 119, 680

Gaselee, Sir Stephen, 698n

Gate Theatre, London, 20

Gates, R. Ruggles: and Pitt-Rivers's essay on Eugenics, **524n**, 526, 538

Murry's book on, 502, 532, 536, 584; TSE on mother-complex, 532n; Aldington disparages, 734n; *The Escaped Cock*, 158; *Lady Chatterley's Lover*, 609; *Obscenity and Pornography*, 95n
Lawrence, T. E. (Shaw), 238n, 734n
Lawrence, W. J., 224, **259n**; 'Massinger's Punctuation', 551, 689n
'Lay Views of Ecclesiastical Persons: If I were a Dean', 541
Leahy, Maurice, **188n**
Leavis, F. R., **233n**, 262–3n, 427n, 648n, 666, 727; *Mass Civilization and Minority Culture*, 364, 459n, 497; *New Bearings in English Poetry*, 709n
Leavis, Queenie, 263n; *Fiction and the Reading Public*, 710n
Leblanc, Maurice: Arsène Lupin stories, 597, 751
Le Gallienne, Eva, 344n
Legay, General (Austrian), 476
Léger, Marie René Auguste Alexis Saint-Léger (pseud. Saint-John Perse), **806–7**; TSE seeks address, 71; TSE writes to, 96; TSE meets, 148; Wheen praises, 352; Auden cites, 568; TSE hopes for as translator, 670; *Anabase*, 25, 147, 162, 167, 193, 208, 215, 228–9, 252, 254, 265, 275, 283–4, 402; *Eloges*, 49
Leigh, Gertrude: *New Light on the Youth of Dante*, 18, 28n
Léon, Paul, **426n**, 471
Leroux, Gaston: *The Lady in Black*, 751; *The Yellow Room*, 751
Leslie, Sir Shane, **243n**, 375
Leverson, Ada, **20n**
Lévi, Sylvain, 153
Levin, Harry, 206n
Lewis, Clive Staples ('Jack'), 100n, 196n, **580n**
Lewis, Wyndham, **484n**; Spender reserves poems for, 190n; Plomer compared to, 482n; background, 483n, 484; on Pound, 735n; line drawing of TSE, 778n, 779, 790; *The Apes of God*, 650n; *Hitler*, 529; *Time and Western Man*, 529
Libre Parole, La (journal), 640n
Life and Letters (journal), 336
Limbour, Georges: translates 'Difficulties of a Statesman', 650n, 791n
Lindbergh, Charles, 308

Lindsay, A. D.: *The Essentials of Democracy*, 179
Lindsay, Lady Anne, 670n
Lindsay, Lady Barbara, 670n
Lindsay, Vachel, 567, **699n**
Lion, Aline, 660, **669n**; 'Property and Poetry', 669n, 688, 714–15
Lipton, Sir Thomas, 329n
Listener (journal), 90, 157n, 199n, 211n, 617
Little, Clarence C., **332n**
Little Review, 186
Liveright, Horace, 169, 174, 175n, 202, 307, 627, 651, 695n
Liverpool and London Electric: stock, 550
'Lives of Jesus, The', 38
Lloyd, George, 1st Baron Lloyd of Dolobran, 339, 341, 505n
Lloyds Bank: house magazine, 321n
Lockwood, Mrs (schoolteacher), 281
Loisy, Alfred, 416
London: Burleigh Mansions, 61; Chester Terrace, Eaton Square, 163; Clarence Gate Gardens, 20, 61, 203, 217, 229, 241, 309, 335, 569, 691, 733; Schoolbred's Warehouses, 61
London Electrotype Company, 755n
London Library, The, 32, 533, 549, 610
London Society for the Study of Religion, 726n
London Surrealist Exhibition (1936), 310n
Longfellow, Henry Wadsworth, **183n**
Looming (journal), 385
Lopokova, Lydia (Lady Keynes), 274n
'Love-Song of J. Alfred Prufrock, The': French translation, 403n, 575
Lovejoy, Arthur O., **266n**; *The Revolt Against Dualism*, 502
Lowe, T. D., 29n
Lowell family, 410
Lowenfels, Walter, **23n**
Lowes, John Livingston, 206n, **366n**, 742n
Lowes-Dickinson, Goldsworthy, 628n
Lowther Clarke, William Kemp, **356n**, 662
Lucas, F. L. ('Peter'), 168, 573n; *Cécile*, 180n
Lucian, 644
Lucretius, 310
Ludington, G. Franklin: on TSE's *Ash Wednesday*, 428n
Ludwig, Emil, 324; *Lincoln*, 149
Lynd, Robert, 652, **653n**, 659n

Macaulay, Thomas Babington, Baron, 476
MacCarthy, Desmond, **336n**, 363n, 645
MacDiarmid, Hugh *see* Grieve, Christopher
 Murray
MacDonald, Aeneas *see* Thomson, George
 Malcolm
Macdonald, Hugh, **11n**, 31n, 110n, 122,
 156n, 157n, 348, 360; *Circumjack
 Cencrastus*, 473
MacDonald, James Ramsay, 554, 692n
MacDowall, Arthur: *Thomas Hardy*, 632
McEachran, Frank, **234n**, 518, 547;
 The Civilized Man, 358; 'Tragedy and
 History', 358n
McGreevy, Thomas, 361n, 807–8; *Thomas
 Stearns Eliot*, 483n, 634
Machiavelli, Niccolò, 317
Mackay, H. F. B.: *Adventure of Paul of
 Tarsus*, 399n
McKeown, Richard, **723–4n**
Mackie, Albert, 422n
McKnight, Joseph, 19n
Maclagan, Eric, 780n
McLaren, Christabel, 440
Macleish, Archibald, 304
Macleod, Joseph Todd Gordon, 54, **89n**,
 372, 428, 562, 566, 574; *The Ecliptic*,
 238; 'Mount Pindus', 562n
Macmillan, Sir Frederick, 236, 462
Macmillan (publishers), 55, 301
Macmurray, John, **501n**, 601, 632, 757–8
MacNeice, Louis, 263n
MacVeagh, Lincoln, 169, 174
Madariaga, Salvador de, 185
Major, Revd H. D. A., **68n**, 76
Malaval, François: *A Simple Method of
 Raising the Soul to Contemplation*, 679
Malcolm, Sir Dougal Orme, **756n**
Malinowski, Bronislaw, 272
Malnick, Bertha, **3n**, 252, 269n, 311, 588
Malraux, André, 455, 751
Mann, Thomas, 10n, 553; 'An Appeal to
 Reason', 508, 553n
Manning, Frederic, 199n, **808**; at Bourne,
 Lincolnshire, 472; and Dobrée, 475, 490;
 Her Privates We (by Private 19022), 199;
 Scenes and Portraits, 416, 473n, 577n
Manningham-Buller, Lady Mary, 670n
Marchant, Sir James: 'The Spiritual
 Pilgrim', 147
Marichalar, Antonio, **241n**

'Marina', 270, 283n, 330, 366, 367n–8,
 385n, 456, 575, 587n
Maritain, Jacques: and classicism, 185; TSE
 wishes to discuss 'opportunity' with, 194;
 Scanlan translates, 244n; TSE likes and
 admires, 255; Belgion criticises, 530–1;
 TSE pays tribute to, 531n; *Le Docteur
 Angélique*, 248; *Scholarship and Art*, 149,
 186, 194, 244n, 255
Marivaux, Pierre Carlet de Chamblain de,
 186
Mark Twain Society, 485n
Marlow, Buckinghamshire, 287–8
Marshall, H. J. C., 114n, 115
Marshall, H. P. J., 189n
Marshall, Margaret, 591n
Marston, John, 758
Martin, Alice, 485n
Martin, Revd Dr E. J., 68n
Martin, Kingsley, 77n, 78
Martindale, Cyril Charlie, **15n**; Morley
 criticises, 88n; broadcasts, 117; lecture
 on Newman and Manning, 161; 'The
 Censorship of Books and the Roman
 "Index"', 86n, 98
Mary Magdalen, St, 5
Mary Queen of Scots, 667
Masefield, John, 395, 665n
Massinger, Philip, 689
Massis, Henri, **267n**
Matthews, T. S.: *Great Tom*, 346n
Mauron, Charles, 9; 'En lisant Bergson',
 225n
Maurras, Charles, **67n**, 132n, 133–4, 186,
 243, 271n, 431; *L'Avenir d'Intelligence*,
 243
Maxton, James, 77n, 78–9
Mayo, Elton, 332
Meacham, Harry M., 219n
Medley, C. D., 645
Melchett, Henry Mond, 2nd Baron, 59
Menai, Huw (pseud., i.e. Hugh Owen
 Williams), **129n**
Menasce, Jean de (Father Pierre de
 Menasce), **255n**, 266, 670, 778
Mencius, 284n
Mendelson, Edward, 264n, 386n
Merry del Val, Cardinal Rafael, 29n
Merton College, Oxford, 413
Mesmer, Anton, 397n
Mesterton, Erik, 163n, **186n**, 778
Metaphysical Poets, 391

Methuen (publishers), 514n
Middleton, Thomas: and authorship of *The Revenger's Tragedy*, 439–40; *A Game at Chesse*, 12
Migne, Jacques-Paul: *The Patrologia Latina et Graeca*, 544
Miles, Hamish, **226n**, 232, 235–6, 239–40
Milford, Humphrey Sumner, 122, 191, 196, 492
Miller, Francis P., 140n
Miller, Henry, 735n
Milton Academy, Mass, 282
Milton, John: Bunting on, 305; *Samson Agonistes*, 188
Minority Pamphlets, 364
Minority Press, 195n
Mirsky, Dmitri S., **251n**; recommends Hayward for Traherne, 96n; reviewing, 119, 415; collected essays, 347; wishes to publish lectures, 622n; translating, 709; *Lenin*, 706
'Miss Sylvia Beach', 755n
Mistral, Frédéric, 431
Mitchell, William Fraser, 617
Mitchison, Naomi, 198, 291, 601; *Comments on Birth Control*, 291
Moberly, C. A. E. and E. E. Jourdain: *An Adventure*, 558, 594
Modern Scot, The (journal), 600
Modernist: as word, 313
Moe, Henry Allen, 31, **52n**, 313n
Moiseiwitsch, Benno, 544
Monnier, Adrienne, 403n; 'Joyce et le Public Français', 596
Monro, Alida, 769n, 785
Monro, Harold, 808–9; surgical operation, 177, 685; and Criterion Club meetings, 218, 314, 428, 516, 662, 668, 679, 768; TSE recommends to Bronowski for anthology, 231; review of Campbell, 252; health, 294, 789; lends trousers to TSE, 316; marriage, 785n
Monroe, Harriet, 574–5
Montague, A. J., 365n
Montale, Eugenio, 57
Monteith, Charles, 779n
Montfort, Simon de, 248
Moore, George, 253n
Moore, Hubert Stuart, 603n
Moore, Marianne, **809**; TSE invites to contribute to *Criterion*, 767; *Poems*, 176

Moravia, Alberto, 396; *L'Indifferente*, 395n
More, Louis T., **632n**; *Isaac Newton*, 617n
More, Paul Elmer, **809–11**; and Austin Warren, 67n, 396n; on Carroll Romer, 70; TSE on, 132n, 134, 298; and controversy over humanism, 135, 159, 280n; TSE recommends to Charles Harris, 153; and Thorold, 195; religious doctrines, 292; on *Ash Wednesday*, 361n; visit to England, 481; proposes library of 17th-century Anglican ecclesiastical literature, 517n; in London, 573; and proposed anthology of 17th-century religious literature, 573; teaches Austin Warren, 647; TSE recommends to Brittain, 672; 'An Absolute and an Authoritative Church', 80n; *Christ the Word*, 94; 'A Revival of Humanism', 134n, 135n
Morgan, J. H., 505n
Möricke, Eduard Friedrich, 228n, 425, 513
Morison, Frank (pseud., i.e. A. H. Ross), 47; *Who Moved the Stone?*, 38n, 98, 102, 105–8, 136n, 147
Morison, Samuel Eliot, **36n**, 44, 153, 308
Morley, Frank Vigor (FVM), **87n**; meets Martindale, 87, 117, 121; on George Blake, 206n; Colhoun impresses, 211; proposed for Criterion Club committee, 218n; and Burns on Malta, 222; on Joyce's *Anna Livia Plurabelle*, 226n, 299; on Macleod's *Ecliptic*, 238n; and Auden's poems, 264n; and US publication of *Ash Wednesday*, 301n; on Arthur Wheen, 352n; invites J. G. MacLeod to Criterion Club, 381; on Macaulay's influence, 476; and Michael Roberts, 512n; and Harcourt publication of TSE essays, 514n; visit to New York and Boston, 515; on Criterion Miscellany, 552; on Tandy, 557n; letter to Penty on 'Means and Ends', 576n; and Henry Eliot's hopes for job in publishing, 615; on National Government, 692n; and Aldington's *Stepping Heavenward* attack on TSE, 733n, 735n
Morning Post, 16
Morrell, Julian, 396
Morrell, Lady Ottoline, **811**; antipathy to TSE, 363n; and Vivien Eliot, 363, 369n, 446, 769, 785; TSE declines to sign books

852

for, 369n; TSE signs books for, 396; TSE entertains to tea with James Joyce, 614n; Aldington lampoons, 734–5n; Christmas gifts to Eliots, 784–5
Morris industry, Oxford, 507
Morris, Sir William Richard (later Viscount Nuffield), 202
Morrison, William S., 423n
Morse-Boycott, Revd Desmond, **74n**, 213
Morton, A. L., 83, **83n**, 97
Mosley, Sir Oswald, 467n, 499, 506n, 507–8, 584n
Mozley, Canon J. K.: *The Beginning of Christian Theology*, 570
'Mr Eliot's Sunday Morning Service', 249n
Mueller, Adam, 600
Muggeridge, Malcolm, 252n
Muir, Edwin, 811–12; reviews MacDiarmid, 423, 425, 473; essay on Kafka, 425; translates Hermann Broch, 721n; 'After the Fall', 314
Muir, Willa (née Anderson), 425n, **721n**; 'Disintegration of Values', 741n
Mummers (Cambridge University dramatic group), 586n
Munguía, Enrique, Jr, **334n**
Murder in the Cathedral, 105n
Murdock, Kenneth B., **742n**
Muret, battle of (1213), 146n, 248
Murphy, James, 695, 711, 727, 737n
Murray, D. L., **102n**, 607n
Murry, John Middleton, 812–14; on Vivyan Eyles story, 23; and Fernandez, 41; gives up *New Adelphi*, 48n; declines Shafer article for *Adelphi*, 66; and decline of *Adelphi*, 107n; reviews for *Criterion*, 158; Geoffrey West on, 168; edits *Athenaeum*, 298n; on G. Wilson Knight, 399; Temple on, 443n; Plowman works for, 502n; reviews *Thoughts after Lambeth*, 502n, 506; McEachran on, 518n; Hyde on, 558n; reviews Quiller-Couch's *Shakespeare's Workmanship*, 636; on 'Coriolan', 696n; 'The Detachment of Naturalism', 32n, 168n; *The Fallacy of Economics* (proposed), 777n; 'A Humanist Theory of Values', 72n; *Son of Woman: The Story of D. H. Lawrence*, 502, 532, 536, 584, 609
Mussolini, Benito, 79, 172n, 485n, 505n

Namier, Louis B., 354

Nation, The (journal), 97, 207, 633
National Government: formed (September 1931), 692n
National Library of Mexico, 388, 746
Needham, Joseph, **112n**; 'Religion and the Scientific Mind', 112n
Neue Rundschau, Die, 227, 260
Neue Schweizer Rundschau, Die, 587n, 588, 682
New Adelphi, The (journal, formerly *Adelphi*), 48, 66, 107n, 502n, 697
New Age, The (journal), 77, 180, 638
New Party (Mosley's), 467n, 584n, 589n
New Signatures (ed. Michael Roberts), 511n, 512n
New Statesman (journal), 59n, 392, 399
New York City Ballet (earlier Ballet Society), 587n
New York Sun, 428, 434
Newbridge, Henry, 15n
Newman, John Henry, Cardinal, 60; 'Essay on the Development of Christian Doctrine', 24n
Newton, Sir Isaac, 273, 289
Nickerson, Hoffman, 246n; 'Oman's Muret', 279
Nicoll, Allardyce, 121n, 679n
Nicolls, B. E., 211n
Nicolson, Harold, 701n, 754, 761, 776
Nietzsche, Friedrich, 513n
Nimr, Amy (later Lady Smart), 642
Nixon, James, 166n
Nordal, Sigurthur, 781n
Norton, Charles Eliot, **183n**; *Cotton Mather*, 210n
Norton, W. W., 557n
Nouvelle Revue Française (NRF), 298, 488
Noyes, Alfred, 147, 776
Noyes, Penelope, 345
Nursing Mirror, 194–5n

Oakeshott, Michael, 68n
Obelisk Press, 426n
Ober, Harold, 695n
Obermer, Dr Edgar, 232
O'Brien, Edward (ed.): *Best British Short Stories*, 250n
Observer (newspaper), 265, 348
Ocampo, Victoria, 773
O'Casey, Sean, 320n
Ockham, David: 'Celluloid', 104n

Ó'Faoláin, Seán (né John Francis Whelan), 453n; translations of old Irish verse, 144, 432; Cambridge University Press declines publication of Irish texts, 453; TSE helps with introductions to editors, 672, 680–1, 750

Ogden, C. K., 142n, 343, 362, 605, 621, 685

Ogden, J. A. H.: 'The Camp' (poem), 247

O'Higgins, Kevin, 503n

Oldenbourg, R. (publishers), 324n

Oldham, J. H., 41n, 407n, 438

Oliphant, E. H. C., 439; financial contribution to *Criterion*, 461n

Oliver, F. S., 122n, 716n, 717; *The Endless Adventure*, 55–6, 60, 242n

Oman, Sir Charles, 246n, 248, 279

Oppfer (Danish portrait painter), 201

Orage, A. R., 180n

O'Rahaille, Aodhagan, 423n

Oras, Ants, 385n

Order (journal), 40

Ors, Eugenio d', 654, 657n

Orwell, George (Eric Blair), 250n; *Keep the Aspidistra Fying*, 532n

Osborne, Dorothy, 555n

O'Sullivan (Sullivan), John Francis, 300

Owen, Wilfred, 372; Ian Parsons' essay on, 524; *The Poems*, ed. Edmund Blunden, 488, 519, 523, 524

Oxford Outloook, 261

Oxford University Italian Club, 178

Oxford University Press, 414, 493n

Paley, William S., 774n

Pares, Sir Bernard, 252n

Parker, Philip, 187n

Parsons, Clere, 354n, 585n, 621n, 639; *Poems*, 673n, 767n, 779, 788

Parsons, Mrs Clere, 621, 639

Parsons, Ian, 524n, 549n

Partridge, Eric, 44

Pascal, Blaise, 351, 414–15, 455, 479, 535, 559, 561, 674

Pater, Walter, 60, 121, 154n, 208, 254, 349n, 416

Paterson, A. J. B., 299

Paul, St, 352n

Paulhan, Jean, 50, 687

Pearce, Charles A., 514n

Péguy, Charles, 556, 595

Pember, Francis: *Musa Feriata*, 756

Penty, Arthur J., 718; 'Means and Ends', 576, 652, 684; 'The Philosophy of J. M. Keynes', 772n; 'Tradition and Modernism in Architecture', 772

Pericles, 270, 305n, 368

Périgueux, France, 287, 288n

'Perversity of D. H. Lawrence, The', 132n

Peters, A. D. (literary agent), 528, 782n

Petrella, Mary C., 707n

Phare, Elsie E. (later Duncan-Jones), 598n

Philip, André: *L'Inde Moderne*, 339

Philippe, Charles-Louis: *Bubu de Montparnasse*, 716, 750–1, 757

Picasso, Pablo, 256n

Piccoli, Raffaello, 99n

Pickard, Maud Fortescue: asks permission to include TSE poems in anthology, 687n, 729n

Pickering, William: *Preces Privatae Quotidianae*, 568

Pickthorn, Kenneth, 814; reads Leavis's *Mass Civilization and Minority Culture*, 497n; TSE proposes visit to, 522

Pigotts Press, 195n, 325n

Pilsudski, Jósef, 103n, 476; *The Memoirs of a Polish Revolutionary and Soldier*, 103

Pinchard, Revd Arnold, 155n

Pinker, James B. & Sons (agents), 315–16, 693

Pitt-Rivers, George Henry Lane-Fox, 272n, 524, 526

'Place of Pater, The' (in USA as 'Arnold and Pater'), 11n, 160n, 349n, 459n

Planck, Max: *Positivismus und Reale Aussenwelt*, 629, 694, 711n, 712

Plato, 4, 8, 29n, 473n, 578, 644

Platonoff, C., 119

Pleiad Press, 235

Plender, William, Baron, 491

Plomer, William, 482n, 620n, 701n; 'Corfu' (poem), 655; *Sado*, 701

Plowman, Max (Mark), 502n

Poe, Edgar Allan, 250n

'Poet who Gave the English Speech, The', 549n

Poetry (US journal), 704

Poetry Bookshop, 218n, 294, 515–16, 685, 785

'Poetry and Propaganda', 169n

Poets' Translation Series (Egoist Press), 175–6

854

Remarque, Erich Maria: *All Quite on the Western Front*, 352n, 728; *The Road Back* (transl. of *Der Weg zurück*), 566

Rendall, Richard A., **109n**, 445n

Repton School Literary Society, 456n

Revue Universelle, La, 267n

Rhinelander, Philip Mercer, Bishop of Pennsylvania, 573

Rhodes, Cecil, 482n

Rhondda, Margaret Haig Thomas, Viscountess, 500n

Rhys, Ernest, **351n**; *Letters from Limbo*, 352n

Richards, Dorothy, 460n, 583, 732

Richards, I. A., **817–18**; reviews for *Criterion*, 26; Barfield on, 101; dogmatism, 136; TSE sends *Humanism and America* to, 149; in Peking, 167; supports Ronald Bottrall, 262n; on *Ash Wednesday*, 283n; denies aesthetic emotion, 407n; praises Empson to TSE, 424n; on Belgion, 452; at Harvard, 459–60, 564, 583, 727; TSE recommends to A. D. Sheffield, 459; and Donaghy, 548, 559; Faber publish, 638; TSE recommends Ó'Faoláin to, 680–1, 750; on Leavis, 709n; TSE loses contact with, 710, 727; TSE misses in London, 731; comments on *Triumphal March*, 732n; *Mencius on the Mind*, 402n; 'Mencius through the Looking-Glass', 284n; 'Notes on the Practice of Interpretation', 536n; *Practical Criticism*, 17; *Principles of Criticism*, 408n, 513; 'Science Value and Poetry', 747n; 'Thomas Heywood', 559n

Richards, Philip S., 146, 359

Richmond, Bruce, **12n, 818**; on Nicholl's edition of Tourneur, 121n; introduces Colhoun to TSE, 357; on TSE's anonymous contributions to *Times Literary Supplement*, 605n; and Mrs Donaghy's request for work, 624; TSE recommends C. M. Grieve (Hugh MacDiarmid) to, 638; and TSE's essay on Ford for *Times Literary Supplement*, 758

Rilke, Rainer Maria, 64, 224, 254, 741; *The Notebook of Malte Laurids Brigge*, 626n

Rimbaud, Arthur, 383

Rimington, Critchell, 258n

Robbins, Lionel (later Baron), 77n, 78

Robert Adamson lecture, Manchester (1930), 513n

Roberti, Jacques: *À la Belle de Nuit*, 716n, 753

Roberts, Michael, **511n**; reviews Bertrand Russell's *The Scientific Outlook*, 736n; 'The Categories of T. E. Hulme, 736; *Critique of Poetry*, 512, 637

Roberts, Richard Ellis, **399n**

Roberts, (Sir) Sydney Castle, **432n**

Roberts, Ursula ('Susan Miles'), **192n**; 'Women & Lambeth', 520

Roberts, William, 382n

Roberts, Revd William Corbett, 192

Robertson, Fr Algy, 722n

Robertson, J. M., 224, 536, 636, **818–19**; 'Shakespearean Idolatry', 73, 377n

Robinson, Edward Arnold, 475

Rock, The (church pageant), 407, 499n

Rodgers, John, **740n**

Roditi, Edouard, **819–20**; translates Léger, 49; afterword to Clere Parsons's *The Air Between*, 354n; translates Spender, 639n, 650, 654; *La Vie Nouvelle*, 640n

Rodker, John, 719n; *Adolphe*, 354

Rodman, Selden, **579n**

Rohan, Prince Karl Anton, 528

Roman Catholics: and censorship, 85–6

romantic, romanticism: as terms, 27, 210, 285, 569

Romer, Carroll, **69n**

Romer, Mrs Carroll, 69

Rootham, Helen, 383n

Rosenberg, Harold, **518n**; 'Character-Change and the Drama', 518

Rosenberg, Isaac, 53–4, 655, 774

Ross, A. H. *see* Morison, Frank

Ross, W. D., 47

Rossetti, Christina, 52

Roth, Samuel, 693

Rothenstein, William, **820–1**; TSE invites to *Criterion* meetings, 515, 558; on Blanche's *Les Arts plastiques*, 612n; *Men and Memories*, 500, 515, 516n

Rothermere, Harold Sidney Harmsworth, 1st Viscount, 491

Rothschild, Victor (later 3rd Baron), 614n

Rousseau, Jean-Jacques, 469

Rowse, A. L., **821**; contributions to *Criterion*, 42; on Daniels, 77; recommends Tawney to TSE, 95n; TSE introduces Belgion to, 176; on

Ash Wednesday, 179n; on order and liberty, 499n; on Mosley, 506n; on *Criterion Miscellany*, 552; disparages Whibley, 706; stays in London, 745; on Dougal Malcolm, 756n; 'G. N. Clark's Conception of History', 179; 'Historical Materialism and G. N. Clark', 277; *A Man of the Thirties*, 156n; *Politics and the Younger Generation*, 155n, 156, 180, 487, 665, 683, 706, 718; 'Society and Values', 277n; 'The Theory and Practice of Communism', 51

Royal Literary Fund, 114

Royal Societies Club, London ('Low Society Club'), 5, 38, 69, 80, 116–77, 231n, 328–9, 350, 484

Royal Society of Literature: TSE elected to Fellowship, 16, 145, 154n; book of essays, 65, 160, 703n; TSE reads paper to, 349n; TSE invited to serve on committee, 619, 628n; TSE on, 704

Russell, Bertrand: Christopher Dawson on, 40; TSE disparages, 78; on paradox, 210n; adultery with Vivien, 288n; TSE recommends to Marguerite Caetani, 373; on sexual promiscuity, 411n; Temple on, 442n, 443n; atheism, 533; writes for *Nation*, 633; *The Scientific Outlook*, 736n

Russell, George (Æ), **6n**

Rychner, Max, 241, 420, 642, 696; 'German Chronicle', 205n

Rylands, George W. ('Dadie'), 730n

Sachs, Paul J., 742n

Sackville, Edward Sackville-West, 5th Baron ('Eddy'), **64n**, 254, 387

Sackville-West, Vita, 360n, 371n, 584

Sacred Wood, The, 215n, 374n, 514n

Sadler, Michael, 166n; *The Outlook in Secondary Education*, 498n

Saerchinger, César, 686, 719–20, 771

St Bartholomew's Hospital, London, 687, 729

St Louis, Missouri, 281–2

Saint-John Perse *see* Léger, Marie René Auguste Alexis Saint-Léger

Saint-Tropez: Hostellerie de l'Ayoli, 398

Salmon, André, 35

Saltmarshe, Christopher, 648n

Santayana, George, 298

Sassoon, Siegfried: awarded Benson Medal, 628n

Sayers, Michael, **250n**, 467–8, 477, 492n; sends extract of novel to TSE, 540n

Scanlan, J. F., **244n**

Scheler, Märit (earlier Furtwängler), 46, 205, 227n, 578, 588

Scheler, Max, 4, 46; 'The Idea of Peace and Pacifism', 681

Schiff, Sydney ('Stephen Hudson'), **384n**, 763n

Schulman, Grace: 'Notes on the Theme of "Marina" by T. S. Eliot', 270n, 283n

Schwartz, Jacob, 33, 82, 177

Scientific Press, 194n

Scott, Richard, 306

Scott, Sir Walter, 32

Scott Moncrieff, C. K., **58n**; cancer and death, 93n; mother writes memoir, 429n; lives in Italy, 430n; 'Cousin Fanny and Cousin Annie', 59

Scott Moncrieff, Jessie Margaret: 'Mr C. K. Scott Moncrieff', 429n

Scribners (US publishers), 528n

Scripps College, Claremont, California, 371n

Scudder, Vida, 153

Sedgwick, R. R.: 'Eighteenth-Century Politics', 242n

Selwyn, Revd Edward Gordon, **37n**; TSE lunches with, 76; TSE gives *Who Moved the Stone?* to, 102; and Revd Thomas J. Hardy, 286; TSE shows Lambeth Conference pamphlet to, 406; comments on TSE's *Thoughts after Lambeth*, 421, 449n; appointed Dean of Winchester, 449n; TSE recommends to Siepmann, 601

Sencourt, Robert *see* George, R. E. Gordon

Seneca: *Hercules Furens*, 368–9

Sewell, Arthur: *The Physiology of Beauty*, 611n

Seymour-Jones, Carole, 769–70n; *Painted Shadow*, 222n, 614n

Shafer, Robert, **65n**, 133n, 211, 280, 358

Shakespear, Olivia, **238n**

Shakespeare & Company, Paris (bookshop), 403n

Shakespeare Association, 368, 400, 568

Shakespeare, William, 164n, 170–2, 196n, 203–4, 223–4, 377n; *Antony and Cleopatra*, 388n, 451–2, 468; *Coriolanus*, 368, 388n, 451, 468n; *Cymbeline*, 399n;

Julius Caesar, 316n, 376n; *King Lear*,
191; *A Midsummer Night's Dream*, 192n;
The Phoenix and the Turtle, 388, 400;
'Sonnet 29', 428; *Two Gentlemen of
Verona*, 207n; *The Tempest*, 171, 172n,
176n, 451
Shamrock X (yacht), 329
Shapcott (lawyer), 692
Sharp, Clifford, 59
Shaw, George Bernard, 133, 443n, 697,
781
Sheed & Ward (publishers), 198, 325n, 740
Sheen, Revd Fulton, Bishop of Rochester,
NY, 268n
Sheffield, Ada (née Eliot; TSE's sister),
459–60, 478
Sheffield, Alfred Dwight ('Shef'), 458n
Shelley, Percy Bysshe, 19, 58; *Prometheus
Unbound*, 697
Sheridan, General Philip Henry, 376
Sherman, General William Tecumseh, 376
Shield, The (journal), 192
Shklovsky, Viktor, 54
Shopenhauer, Arthur, 284–5
Shufelt, R. W., 390
Siemsen, Hans, 774
Siepmann, Charles Arthur, 479, 494n, 556,
739n, 757, 823
Sies, E. E., 599n
Simenon, Georges, 751
Simon, Sir John, 227
Simpson, Celia, 275n, 278n
Singer, Kurt, 578; *Platon der Gründer*, 4,
8, 29
Sitwell family, 113n, 546
Sitwell, Edith, 18n; *Ash Wednesday*
compared to, 184; TSE recommends for
inclusion in Bronowski anthology, 231;
Charles Smyth attacks, 572; on Vivien
Eliot, 583n; *Alexander Pope*, 19, 179n
Sitwell, Osbert, 294n; Ada Leverson
parodies, 20
Sitwell, Sacheverell, 18, 231, 730
Six Reviews Prize, The, 687; *see also* Five
Reviews Award, The
Skelton, John, 657, 663, 666, 700n
Skemp Memorial Lecture, 129
Slater, Frank, 13n
Smart, (Sir) Walter, 642n
Smith Academy, St Louis, 281
Smith, Charlotte (née Eliot; TSE's sister),
308n

Smith, Revd Christopher Rhodes, 308
Smith, George Lawrence (TSE's brother-in-
law), 308
Smith, James, 427n, 459n
Smith, Janet Adam, 60n, 511n
Smith, Mary Smoot (Mrs Robert Parkman
Blake), 308n
Smith, Theodora Eliot (TSE's niece), 202n,
237
Smith, T. R., 695n
Smyth, Charles, 60n, 466; reviews Rowse's
Politics and the Younger Generation,
665, 683, 718, 746n; takes up London
curacy, 665n; 'In Defence of Property'
(with Kitson Clark), 664; 'The State and
Freedom', 625n, 641
Smythe, Frank: *The Kangchenjunga
Adventure*, 169n
Snowden, Philip, 242
Society for Promoting Christian Knowledge
(SPCK), 617, 662
'Song for Simeon, A', 229
Southwell, Robert, 12
Sparrow, John, 239, 239n, 613; 'Donne's
Religious Development', 567
Speaight, Robert, 503n
Spectator, The (ed. Addison and Steele),
306
Spectator, The (journal): special number,
278; Evelyn Underhill and, 674, 679
Spektrum (Swedish journal), 778, 790
Spencer, Katherine, 584
Spencer, Theodore, 311n, 564n, 584, 598n
Spender, Stephen, 823–4; Rowse
recommends to TSE, 25n, 51; sends
poems to TSE, 190; in Germany, 357,
528, 578; TSE recommends to Marguerite
Caetani, 372; influenced by Hopkins,
417n; TSE meets, 463; prepares poems
for *Criterion*, 626; Roditi translates,
639n, 650, 654; 'The Haymaking' (story),
56; *The Temple* (novel), 357n, 529n, 579,
625, 650n, 662; *World Within World*, 5
Spens, Will, 98, 273n, 405n, 406, 522
Spinoza, Benedict de (Baruch), 17
Squire, Sir John Collings, 496, 530n
Stachiewicz, General Julian, 104
Stalin, Josef V., 79
Standen, Nika (later Hazelton), 641n
Stanley, Oliver, 78, 94n, 95
Stationers' Register, 439

Stead, William Force, **824–5**; and Eyles's story, 23; letter from TSE on Maurras, 67n; recommends Charles Harris to TSE, 69; sends poem to TSE, 75n; absence in USA, 178, 222n, 223; Sencourt on, 439; holiday with Sencourt, 527; invited to Criterion Club meeting, 685; *The House on the Wold and other Poems*, 287

Stearns, Susan Heywood (TSE's maternal aunt), 344n

Stephen, Sir James Fitzjames (VWs cousin), 584

Stephens, James, 369n

Stern (US lawyer), 308, 627

Sterne, Laurence, 254, 541n

Steuart, Father R. H. J., SJ: *The Inward Vision*, 121

Stewart, C. W., 626, 765

Stewart, William McCausland, 448n, **599n**; 'Great Britain and Europe', 600

Still, Colin, **164n**, 191; *Shakespeare's Mystery Play: A Study of 'The Tempest'*, 164n, 170n

Stillman, C. C., 781n

Stokes, Adrian, 42

Stone, Allan K., 47n

Strachey, Sir John, 77n, 78, 94n, 95, 172n

Strachey, Lady, 172n

Summers, Montague, **44n**

Sunday Referee, 213, 221n

Sunday Times, 499

Sutherland, John, 190n

Sutherland, T. W., 354n

Sweeney Agonistes, 192n, 199, 217–18, 725

Sweeney, John J., 483n

Swinburne, Algernon Charles, 12

Swing, Raymond Gram, 719

Symbolism, 643

Symonds, John Addington: *The Renaissance in Italy*, 307

Taggard, Genevieve (ed.): *Circumference: Varieties of Metaphysical Verse*, 249

Taine, Hippolyte, 533

Talcott, Agnew Allen, 720n

Talcott, Charlotte Stearns (née Smith; 'Chardy'), 720, 784

Tandy, Doris ('Polly'), 557n

Tandy, Geoffrey, 272n, 381, **557n**

Tate, Allen, **825**; and Howard Baker, 22n; threatens TSE, 66n; and Shafer, 135n,

211; first marriage, 157n; essay for *I'll Take My Stand*, 360n, 409, 411n; 'The Fallacy of Humanism', 65n; 'Religion and the Old South', 595n; 'The Same Fallacy of Humanism', 66n

Tate, Jonathan, 599n

Taupin, René, **34n**

Tawney, R. H., 77–8n, 95; *Religion and the Rise of Capitalism*, 48n, 94n

Taylor, Alfred Edward, **4n**, 29n, 30n, 75, 124, 138, 332, 599n

Taylor, Jeremy: *Holy Living*, 269n

Taylor, John, 546

Tchernichovsky, Shaul, 295

Temple Bar Club, 290

Temple, William, Archbishop of York (later of Canterbury), **393n**; edits *Social and Political Science*, 405; comments on TSE's pamphlet on Lambeth Conference, 411–13n, 421, 441–4n, 450, 506, 584; prose, 555n; on Christa Seva Sangha, 722n; *Thoughts on Some Problems of the Day*, 625n

Terrell, Carroll F., 304n

Thackeray, William Makepeace: 'Little Billee', 489n

Thales of Miletus, 284

Theology (journal), 38, 421, 568

This Quarter (journal), 344, 536, 663

Thomas Aquinas, St, 4, 30, 248, 444n; *Summa Theologica*, 523n

Thomas, John Heywood, **131n**

Thompson, Edward, **339n**

Thompson, F. Gilchrist, 87n

Thompson, Francis, 199n

Thomson, George Malcolm ('Aeneas MacDonald'), 404, 411n; *The Lambeth Conference*, 340, 378n, 379, 393–4, 405n, 419, 421; *Whisky*, 378, 400; *Will the Scottish Church Survive?*, 405n, 410n, 412n

Thorold, Algar, **108n**; recommends Steuart's *Inward Vision*, 121; and René Hague's review of *Dante*, 147; on faith, 184n; offers to review French periodicals, 197n; on Unicorn Club, 290; TSE recommends to edit Pascal, 351; TSE meets, 359; declines to review D'Arcy's *Nature of Belief*, 624n; declines to review book of Gide, 631n; reviews Malaval, 679

Thorp, Margaret (née Farrand), 764, 786

778, 790n; Bunting on, 305n; Spanish
translation, 334, 420n, 778; TSE opposes
fragmentation, 341–2; proposed edition
with David Jones engravings, 359n; Brian
Howard on, 389n; McGreevy on, 484;
braille version, 549n; US rights, 651;
Donaghy misreads, 743n
Watkins, Vernon, 67n
Watson, E. L. Grant, **381n**
Watson, George, 310n
Waugh, Evelyn, 545n
Weaver, Harriet Shaw, 175, 186, 645, 693,
776n, 825–6
Webb, Beatrice, 633
Weber, Max: *Protestant Ethics and the
Spirit of Capitalism*, 277n
Week-end Review, The, 201
Wells, Herbert George, 133, 443n, 781n;
The Autocracy of Mr Parham, 278
Wells, James R., 296n, 300
Welsford, Enid, 395, 598n
West, Geoffrey, 168: *Deucalion*, 168n
West, Rebecca, 360n
Westphal, Otto: *Feinde Bismarcks* (*Enemies
of Bismarck*), 227n, 228, 324
Wharton, Edith, 16n, 447
Wheen, Arthur, 158n, **352n**, 566n
Whibley, Charles, **122n**; death and
tributes, 122, 125, 131; wife contributes
information on, 143; and classicism, 186;
owns original MS of Urquhart aphorisms,
236n, 239n, 613; and life of Henley,
268n; Kelly portrait of, 387, 462; TSE
gives talk on, 456n, 482; and R. W. V.
Gittings's poems, 570n; Rowse criticises,
706
Whibley, Philippa, 143, 236n, 268n, 482,
613
'Whispers of Immortality', 392n
Whistler, Rex, 154n
Whitby, Father, 155
White, Hal Sanders, 591
White, T. H., 7, **89n**
Whitehead, Alfred North, 373, 441n,
443n; *Process and Reality*, 27
Whitworth, Geoffrey, 406n
Whyte, J. H., 600n
Wichelo, Tom, 497n
Wilberforce, Pamela, 729n, 762
Wilde, Oscar, 20n, 454
Wilkinson, Louis ('Louis Marlow'), 744
Wilkinson, Oliver, 744n

Willey, Basil: 'Cosmic Toryism and the
Religious Attitude', 247
Williams, Charles, 100n, 144n, **196n**,
417n, 418n, 421, 435, 687, 729
Williams, Hugh Owen *see* Menai, Huw
Williams, Iolo, 395
Williams, Orlo (Orlando), **826**; reviews
for *Criterion*, 180n, 560n, 666; as Italian
translator, 395; on George Eliot, 619;
'Fiction and Life', 775
Williamson, George, 169, **391n**, 589, 667;
The Donne Tradition, 391n; 'T. S. Eliot
and His Conception of Poetry', 648n
Williamson, Hugh Ross, **590n**
Wilson, Colin: *The Outsider*, 101n
Wilson, Edmund, **34n**, 252n, 434
Wilson, Edward Meryon, **21n**, 185, 327–8,
342, 432
Wilson, Revd J. M., 441, 442n
Wilson, John Dover, 12, **73n**, 143, 224,
377, 570n, 675n
Wilson, Katherine M.: *Sound and Meaning
in English Poetry*, 424n
Wilson, R. N. D., 304
Wilson, R. S.: *Marcion* (manuscript), 656,
661
Windeler, Bernard: *Elimus*, 660n
Winnington-Ingram, Arthur, Bishop of
London, 718
Winter, Robert, 732n
Winterton, Edward Turnour, Baron, 505n
Winthrop family, 36
Wishart Books Ltd, 305n
Wiskemann, Elizabeth, **676n**
Women Against War (peace movement),
383n
Wood, John G.: *The Illustrated Natural
History*, 66, **73n**
Woodfall, Henry Sampson, 293n
Woods, Revd H. G., 619n
Woods, James Houghton, **137n**
Woods, Margaret Louisa, **619n**
Woodward, E. L.: *War and Peace in Europe
1815–1870*, 746
Woolf, Leonard, **826–7**; TSE introduces
Donaghy to, 5–6; on Chesterton and
Belloc, 29n; at Hogarth Press, 61; on
papal censorship, 86; Blunden succeeds
on *Nation*, 97; as reviewer, 98; praises
TSE's poetry, 184n; and Clive Bell, 256n;
prejudices, 298n; and first edition of
TSE's *Poems*, 326; and Wilson's Góngora

translations, 327, 342n; proposes anthology of poems, 541; criticises BBC's fiction policy, 776n; *After the Deluge*, 700; 'A Censorship at Work', 86n

Woolf, Virginia, 827; TSE arranges for works to be sent to Curtius, 71, 82; letter to Clive Bell on TSE's moving house, 83n; health problem, 228–9; Curtius on, 303n; friendship with TSE, 327n, 370n, 601; and Leavis's *Mass Civilization*, 364n; thanks TSE for books, 370n; on Vivien's paranoia, 371n; Marguerite Caetani hopes to publish, 372; objects to drawings in Beaton's *Book of Beauty*, 440; letter to Clive Bell on Vivien, 472n; Richards disparages, 583; friendship with Vita Sackville-West, 584; contributions to *Times Literary Supplement*, 605n; describes Dadie Rylands, 730n; Aldington lampoons, 734n; at tea party with Vivien, 769n; criticises BBC's fiction policy, 776n; F&F propose cheap edition of novels, 777n; *A Room of One's Own*, 598n

Worcester College, Oxford, 413

Wordsworth, William, 302, 406, 768

Worringer, Wilhelm, 4, 205

Worthen, John: *T. S. Eliot: A Short Biography*, 288n

Wright, Cuthbert: 'Pater', 160

Wright, Harold, 441n

Wu Mi, 25

Wydenbruck, Nora, 499n

Wynne, Veronica, 200n

Wyss, Johann David: *The Swiss Family Robinson*, 165

Yeats, William Butler: affair with Olivia Shakespear, 238n; and Rhys, 351n; signs books for Ottoline Morrell, 369n; Virginia Woolf on, 371n

Yoxall, H. W., 39n

Zaturenska, Marya, 458n

Zola, Émile, 716n

Zukofsky, Louis, 225n; TSE writes references for, 212–13, 240, 304, 480–1; essay on Pound, 240, 253, 290, 455, 473

Zweig, Stefan, 397, 463